LIFELONG EDUCATION FOR ADULTS

AN INTERNATIONAL HANDBOOK

Advances in Education

This is a new series of Pergamon education reference works. Each volume in the series is thematically organized and aims to provide comprehensive and up-to-date coverage of its own specialist subject area. The series is being developed primarily from the highly acclaimed *International Encyclopedia of Education* using the latest electronic publishing technology for data capture, manipulation and storage of text in a form which allows fast and easy modification and updating of copy. Where appropriate a number of other volumes have been specially commissioned for the series. Volumes that are not derived from *The International Encyclopedia of Education* are indicated by an asterisk.

DUNKIN (ed.)
The International Encyclopedia of Teaching and Teacher Education

ERAUT (ed.)
The International Encyclopedia of Educational Technology

KEEVES (ed.)
Educational Research, Methodology, and Measurement: An International Handbook

LEWY (ed.)
The International Encyclopedia of Curriculum

POSTLETHWAITE (ed.)
The Encyclopedia of Comparative Education and National Systems of Education

PSACHAROPOULOS (ed.)
Economics of Education: Research and Studies

REYNOLDS (ed.)*
Knowledge Base for the Beginning Teacher

THOMAS (ed.)
The Encyclopedia of Human Development and Education: Theory, Research, and Studies

WALBERG & HAERTEL (eds.)
The International Encyclopedia of Educational Evaluation

WANG, REYNOLDS & WALBERG (eds.)* (3 volumes)
Handbook of Special Education: Research and Practice

A Related Pergamon Journal†

International Journal of Educational Research

Editor: Herbert J Walberg, University of Illinois, Chicago, Illinois, USA

†Free Specimen copy available on request.

LIFELONG EDUCATION FOR ADULTS

AN INTERNATIONAL HANDBOOK

Edited by

COLIN J TITMUS

University of Leeds, UK

PERGAMON PRESS

OXFORD · NEW YORK · BEIJING · FRANKFURT

SÃO PAULO · SYDNEY · TOKYO · TORONTO

U.K.	Pergamon Press plc, Headington Hill Hall, Oxford OX3 0BW, England
U.S.A.	Pergamon Press, Inc., Maxwell House, Fairview Park, Elmsford, New York 10523, U.S.A.
PEOPLE'S REPUBLIC OF CHINA	Pergamon Press, Room 4037, Qianmen Hotel, Beijing, People's Republic of China
FEDERAL REPUBLIC OF GERMANY	Pergamon Press GmbH, Hammerweg 6, D-6242 Kronberg, Federal Republic of Germany
BRAZIL	Pergamon Editora Ltda, Rua Eça de Queiros, 346, CEP 04011, Paraiso, São Paulo, Brazil
AUSTRALIA	Pergamon Press Australia Pty Ltd., P.O. Box 544, Potts Point, N.S.W. 2011, Australia
JAPAN	Pergamon Press, 5th Floor, Matsuoka Central Building, 1-7-1 Nishishinjuku, Shinjuku-ku, Tokyo 160, Japan
CANADA	Pergamon Press Canada Ltd., Suite No 271, 253 College Street, Toronto, Ontario, Canada M5T 1R5

Based on material from *The International Encyclopedia of Education*, first published 1985, with revisions and updated material.

First edition 1989

Library of Congress Cataloging-in-Publication Data

Lifelong education for adults:
an international handbook/edited by Colin J. Titmus.—1st ed.
p. cm.—(Advances in education)

1. Adult education—Handbooks, manuals, etc.
2. Continuing education—Handbooks, manuals, etc.
I. Titmus, Colin J. II. International encyclopedia of education.
III. Series.
LC5215.L495 1989
374'.0202—dc19 88-36623

British Library Cataloguing in Publication Data

Titmus, Colin
Lifelong education for adults.—(Advances in education)
1. Adult education
I. Title II. Series
374

ISBN 0-08-030851-1

Database design and computer composition by Maxwell Data Management Ltd., Derby

Printed in Great Britain by BPCC Wheatons Ltd., Exeter

Contents

† deceased

† deceased

(b) Subjects and Approaches to Research

Preface

In March 1985 UNESCO held its Fourth International Conference on Adult Education in Paris, at which 122 member states and a host of other organizations were represented. In all 841 participants attended. In November 1985, in Buenos Aires, the International Council for Adult Education, a non-governmental organization, held a World Assembly, which also attracted adult educators from all over the world.

Anybody present at either or both of these gatherings must have been convinced, if they were not already, of the importance of the education of adults nowadays to the total educational experience of human beings, no matter where they live, particularly in the context of lifelong education. They would have been aware that there was a strong sense of common interest, of confronting similar problems. The participants were conscious that they had much to learn from each other and were keen to do so. Publications describing particular initiatives or overall provision in individual countries were widely available and eagerly snapped up. People felt guilty about their ignorance of the work done by colleagues in other places and of the knowledge that might be derived from it. There was, however, a considerable lack of publications which set out to present adult education, as a whole and in its various aspects, from a worldwide perspective.

Coincidentally, in the Spring of 1985, Pergamon Press published *The International Encyclopedia of Education*, under Torsten Husén and T Neville Postlethwaite as Editors-in-Chief, and with an Editorial Board of distinguished scholars from many countries. A publication of some 6,000,000 words, in ten volumes, it was the first major attempt to present an up-to-date overview of scholarship brought to bear on educational problems, practices, and institutions all over the world. It was also the first such encyclopedia to accord to Adult, Recurrent, and Lifelong Education coverage on equal terms with other sectors of education. Indeed under that heading were listed 128 articles.

The *Encyclopedia* has been a great success and has been awarded the prestigious Dartmouth Medal in the United States. It has rapidly proved a widely used mine of material for practitioners and scholars in all fields of education. However, not all have access to the full *Encyclopedia*, some have not the means to obtain a copy or have not the interest to buy the whole. Their interest lies in a particular part of the field it covers. To meet the needs of such people, it has been decided to publish a series of subsets of the *Encyclopedia*, each of which will bring together articles on a specific aspect of educational provision or research.

1. The Planning of the Handbook

In view of the rapidly growing commitment throughout the world to adult education and the dearth of literature taking a global view, it is wholly appropriate that among those subsets should be the present volume on *Lifelong Education for Adults*. Although the *Encyclopedia* articles on the subject would of themselves have constituted a valuable collection, it was felt that a volume of them detached from those written on other aspects of education would be strengthened by the addition of some newly commissioned material. Some of the latter would fill gaps created by detachment from the larger whole, some would deal with topics which, as was inevitable with so vast a field, have proved to have been inadequately covered in the *Encyclopedia*. Contributors would also be given the opportunity to update their *Encyclopedia* articles.

In order to make room for the new pieces within the confines of a single volume a small number of articles on adult, recurrent, and lifelong education which appeared in the *Encyclopedia* have been omitted from this *Handbook*. The order of articles has also been changed. Instead of appearing in alphabetical order, they are grouped according to themes, so that the reader wishing to pursue a subject will not have to jump from one part of the volume to another in order to do so. This has been facilitated by cross-referencing.

A proposed outline of the form and contents of the *Handbook* was drawn up by the editor and referred to experts in a number of countries. They were unanimous in approving the publication of the planned *Handbook* and made several suggestions for its improvement. The work as it now appears owes much to them. In particular the order of sections was revised, so that they now run from principle to practice, and a glossary of adult education terms has been added. For reasons of space there are no articles on the teaching of specific curriculum areas, such as the plastic arts and mathematics. For the same reason, with the exception of China and Japan, there are no single-nation studies of adult education provision, as originally proposed; countries are grouped instead into regions. Some changes of terminology have also been introduced. For example, it was pointed out that, as in North America the term *vocational education* denotes school-age education preparatory to entering working life, use of the term *adult vocational education*, commonly used in Great Britain to denote occupational education during working life, might cause some confusion. Where appropriate therefore it has been replaced in the *Handbook* by the expression, *adult education for employment*.

2. *Purpose and Public of the Handbook*

In its published form the aim of the *Handbook* remains, as was originally intended, to offer as wide-ranging, balanced, and authoritative a coverage as is possible within the confines of one volume, of the concepts, principles, purposes, practices, people, organization, and scholarship of adult education throughout the world, seen from the point of view of lifelong education. To this end 117 contributors have been drawn from 23 countries. There have, of course, been certain human limitations to the comprehensiveness of the coverage. Although he has called upon the help of many colleagues and of agencies in a number of countries, the range of content and of contributors has been restricted by the editor's perspective. It has also been a handicap that the *Handbook* has been limited to one language, English, although that probably opened it to more writers than would any other language. Thirdly it may be seen as having a marked Anglo-Saxon bias, from the fact that most of the systematic study of adult education has been undertaken in North America.

The *Handbook* is designed to be of interest and value to all those worldwide who, in any capacity, are engaged in educational activities for adults—not only those who are employed fulltime in planning or administering educational programmes, but also those who, paid or unpaid, play only an occasional part to advance learning activities of people who have completed their initial education at whatever level, or may never have had any childhood schooling at all.

Those who may find assistance in this *Handbook* include workers in adult schools, community centres, or institutions of higher education, literacy tutors, trainers in skilled crafts, those undertaking continuing education for the professions, leaders of women's groups, those engaged in family education, political or religious education, teachers in penal establishments, and those promoting leisure or recreational activities. As adult education becomes increasingly an instrument of national policy, politicians and other decision makers, together with their advisers, require to know about it, not only in their own but in other countries. Doctors, nurses, lawyers, ministers of religion, librarians, social and development workers, trade unionists, people who would not call themselves adult educators, nevertheless have major educational roles to play and need help in understanding them. This volume has material which will be of help to them all and to those who train them.

3. Structure and Content

The term *adult education* is used to denote both a process and structures and organization which have been created to promote it. This *Handbook* examines both. It consists of 10 sections, some of which have been divided into subsections according to the topics treated in the articles of which it is composed. To some extent this classification is arbitrary, as a number of articles might have been placed more or less appropriately in any one of several sections. Such cases are cross-referred to other sections to which they are relevant. Each section and subsection is preceded by an introduction, which includes a summary of the articles in it.

The first two sections address themselves to the broad area of concepts. Section 1, Theory and Principles of Adult Education, has three subsections: Lifelong Education considers the development of lifelong education and its relationship to adult education; The Field of Adult Education is concerned with its terms, curriculum, and policies; and Thematic Variations in Adult Education examines recurrent education, sociocultural animation, community education, nonformal, and other ideas. In Section 2, Purposes of Adult Education, attention is focused on four specific areas. Two of these, Adult Literacy and Adult Education for Employment, review two of the principal objectives of learning activity; in the third, Role Education, examples are discussed of major nonvocational functions that individuals are called upon to fulfil; finally, Education for Change considers that traditional function of adult education, which was to bring about beneficial changes in society.

The next two sections address the problems of how adults can be drawn to take part in education, and how they can be helped to learn. Section 3, Participation and Recruitment, considers motivation, the level of participation, and methods used to encourage people to study. Section 4, Teaching and Learning, is not only the core of the *Handbook*, but the longest part, divided into four subsections. The first of these, Learning and Life, presents what is known about adult development and the factors affecting learning. This is followed by a group of articles under the heading, Teaching and Evaluation, which treat how people may be helped to learn and the assessment of educational activities. The third subsection, Learning: Organization and Support, presents examples of methods used to improve teaching and learning. Finally, Self-directed and Distance Learning examines the related themes of self-directed and distance learning.

Then follow two sections which present major examples of organizations engaged in the offer of education to adults and specific groups of people at whom such offers are directed. The field of Section 5, Providers, is so diverse and ever-changing that only a few instances can be given. Those chosen are both important and long-enduring. The same is the case for Section 6, Target Groups. It has three subsections: Age and Sex Groups, Socially Isolated Groups, and Occupational Groups.

In Section 7, National Programs and Organization, it has not been possible, as has already been explained, to devote an article to the adult provision of each country. The introduction to the section has therefore been used to provide an in-depth cross-national perspective on educational systems and organization, with individual systems being grouped into broad geographical regions and presented in the two subsections — Developed Countries and Developing Countries — to give broad, if not quite comprehensive, coverage. The passage of adult education organization beyond national frontiers has been one of the most interesting features of recent decades. Section 8, Regional and International Organizations, charts this phenomenon, again on a regional basis.

Adult educators have not in the past given the function of laws and processes of funding much thought, as long as the first were benign and the second adequate. The articles in Section 9, Legislation and Finance, tend therefore to describe the present situation and identify issues rather than solutions. Only a beginning has been made to the serious study of either. This is true, indeed, of adult education research as a whole. The last part of the text, Section 10, Research, is subdivided into Regional Overviews, surveying the range of scholarly work done in different areas of the world, and Subjects and Approaches, presenting major topics and methods of inquiry. A reading of these will show that progress has recently been made, but also how much more needs to be done.

Adult education has developed a vocabulary all its own, some of it international in use, some of it specific to one particular region or country. Many of these terms are employed in the *Handbook*. Although the meanings are for the most part explained at some point in the text, it has been considered helpful to make these expressions conveniently available in an alphabetical glossary, in which the meaning of each is briefly outlined. This appears at the end of the volume. The meaning given for the majority of the terms included is based on that given in the UNESCO *Terminology of Adult Education* (first edition 1979, Paris; second edition in press at the time of writing), of which the Editor of this *Handbook* is the Chief Editor.

4. Acknowledgements

The International Encyclopedia of Education and ultimately, therefore, this volume owe their birth to the imagination of Robert Maxwell. To the Editors-in-Chief of the parent work, Torsten Husén and T Neville Postlethwaite, I am indebted for suggesting that there should be a volume on *Lifelong Education for Adults* and that I should edit it. I personally owe much to J R Kidd, whose compilation of articles on adult, recurrent, and lifelong education for the *Encyclopedia* was interrupted by his untimely death. My work on the *Encyclopedia* and the *Handbook* has been built on his foundations.

My sincere thanks are extended to Elizabeth Burge, Chris Duke, Joachim Knoll, Jack Mezirow, and Michael Stephens for their careful and constructive advice on the original proposal for this *Handbook*, and to Mike Toye for his help in suggesting topics which would strengthen the coverage of adult learning. I also acknowledge the kind cooperation of UNESCO in permitting definitions culled from the *Terminology of Adult Education* to be reproduced in this book. I am grateful to all the contributors, more so to those whose articles were submitted on time than to those who were late.

At Pergamon Press, Barbara Barrett, Priscilla Chambers, Clare Watkins, and Joan Burks have supported, harassed, and stimulated both the Editors and the contributors throughout, with skill, zeal, and warm friendship. To them and to all the others at Pergamon Press without whom this book would not have been completed, I offer my gratitude.

Finally I am grateful to my wife, for her copy-reading, her correction of spelling, punctuation, and grammatical mistakes, tactfully referred to as typing errors, and for her patience and encouragement.

April 1989

C. TITMUS
Leeds, UK

Introduction

This article is intended both as a review of and introduction to a field of education that is commonly given the generic term "adult education". Sections will deal with its history and evolution, major concepts, educational principles and practices, and some of the current issues. Additional articles from all parts of the world examine aspects of the field with greater penetration.

Although it is a common belief that adult education has developed only since the 1930s, measures of organized instruction for adults have been known since early in the history of humankind. The first book in the English language to speak directly of a special field called adult education was *The History of Adult Education* by J. H. Hudson, published in London in 1851, but Dr. Thomas Pole had published *A History of the Origin and Progress of Adult Schools* in 1816. During the latter half of the nineteenth century, organized learning activities increased in many countries and references continued to appear, and indeed, to increase, in languages other than English. However, most of the important developments and the significant writings have occurred only since the First World War, with the most noteworthy occuring only during the second half of the twentieth century, and the pace seems still to be quickening. Perhaps the most informing comment about the status and recognition of adult education is that it has never before been the subject of major attention in a national or international encyclopedia.

Adult education, then, as a field of study, has advanced in most parts of the world from comparative obscurity to a recognized component of educational programmes, although it may still be overshadowed by a common phenomenon of equating education with schooling of the young. Its transformation has had many dimensions. From a vague concept not fully translatable from language to language or country to country, a group of terms has emerged, still evolving but having established meanings and content in most of the world's languages. From seemingly random activities reported primarily from a few countries, there are movements and emerging systems to be discerned in all countries. Programmes that were local, often invented as a response to specific needs, have become linked with national endeavours sometimes internationally planned, often based on legislation and directed to broad political, economic, social, and cultural goals, with consistent and sustained international communications. The programmes in adult literacy are perhaps the foremost example of what can be achieved through this kind of international cooperation. Where formerly individual or group improvization was typical, there are now national support systems of finance, training, research, and development. Statistics show that in some countries where there were scattered groups of students or clients, participants now exceed the numbers enrolled in schools and universities. By the 1960s, while the field showed much evidence of immaturity and latent development, and was still growing and evolving, there were uniform, consistent characteristics, and directions of development could everywhere be anticipated, if not predicted with statistical accuracy.

1. A Lengthy History

The title of Hudson's book, *The History of Adult Education*, reveals that there had been previous activities to review, at least in England. Adult education has a very lengthy history worldwide, and evidence is beginning to accumulate to substantiate the fact that organized and systematized instruction for mature people long preceded the formal organization of schools for children and youth. One of the earliest published books on education, Xenophon's *Cyropaedia* is about formalized instruction of adults in what is now Iran. These adults were then given responsibility for the nonformal education of the young. Some of the systematized training provided for adults in Egypt, China, and India was national and even international in scope, enrolled hundreds of thousands of students, and was well-planned and well-evaluated. It is only now that the records of some of these earlier civilizations are beginning to be rediscovered that assertions are being made that some of the extraordinary early achievements were partly the result of well-organized systems of advanced education; the training of people to design and build edifices and monuments, training for water engineering, agricultural technology, religion, and war, as well as for management and statecraft.

Similar practices, sustained and thorough, and later recorded, were characteristic of the Islamic World during the centuries in which Islamic scholars and teachers (generally teachers of other adults) were the creative forces for the whole world in mathematics, sciences, medicines, the arts, literature, engineering, and architecture. A combination of Mosque universities, Koranic schools, organized study circles, book publishers, and book shops served as cultural centres and all fostered the culture of the time and created a condition and environment that can properly be assigned the title of "a learning society". Educational activities were pursued over thousands of miles, traversing three continents, not just in such centres as Baghdad and Cairo, but stretching from Persia to Spain and southwards to Africa. Hartley Gratton (1955) has reviewed equivalent, planned educational efforts in Athens and Rome, and in many places during the Middle Ages, even during the so-called "dark ages", where these efforts were particularly associated with monasteries and later with the guilds. Remarkable achievements of these times are now being studied for contemporary relevance. However, since they did not result in permanent institutional forms, they rarely outlasted a particular philosophical or political epoch. Probably the most critical factor in their demise was the fact that these programmes were so significant as modes of cultural and political expression that they were targets for destruction by any military invader. Consequently, few permanent examples of such activities were ever left.

During the eighteenth, nineteenth, and early twentieth centuries in Europe and North America, educational programmes for adults increased in number, penetration, and scope, but most people, including those who organized and those who participated, did not view them as part of a coherent field of education. The factors that shaped educational response to change and growth had some common characteristics, but that the events constituted a field of education was rarely anticipated or perceived. Some of the compelling pressures of change which evoked a response were religion; social or political revolution; new economic needs arising from changes in technology, both in agriculture and in industry; the need for training and education associated with changing military technologies and strategies; pressures and opportunities arising from transformations in class, occupation, and place of residence; as well as the vast numbers of migrant peoples beginning to move to cities or to countries far from their birthplaces. The organization of adult education has been fuelled by faiths, by revolutions, by migration, by inventions and renaissances, by nationalist ardour, by internationalist organizations, and now by the demands of high technology.

During the twentieth century, religious orders and institutions have rarely carried "faith with the sword" but there have been many examples of attempts to indoctrinate. In some countries and over two centuries, the desire to prepare adults to read for themselves a sacred book led to mass literacy classes. For this purpose and by this means thousands of adult people of Wales became literate in the middle of the eighteenth century. Between 1737 and 1760 at least 150,000 people, participants of the "circulating schools" organized by Reverend Griffith Jones, had learned to write and to read the Bible.

Following successful revolutions, an initial upheaval would be followed by a considerable, sometimes almost total shift of personnel for the governments, for the bureaucracy, and for the management of the economy. Often to the surprise of the former rulers, the men, and women too, who had been caught up in a great social or military adventure, found it possible to learn new skills and roles and to train themselves for new tasks. The American, the French, and the Russian Revolutions were all events that grew from and fostered extraordinary measures of adult education. During the second phase of the Russian Revolution the first great national campaign for literacy occurred, advocated by Lenin as essential to prepare people for a new social order and carried out under the ministerial direction of his widow, Nadiezhda K. Krupskaya. Much later, after events in countries like Cuba, China, and Vietnam, it is almost anticipated as part of revolutionary dogma that literacy work should predate and accompany revolutionary struggles.

The Industrial Revolution, occurring first in England then throughout Western Europe and North America, was an upheaval that produced the need for writing and computation skills, particularly for armies of clerks, secretaries, and sales persons, and provided the opportunity for people to be educated considerably beyond their previous expectations. In some European countries, notably in northern Europe and Russia, changes in farming technology and rural living also required and stimulated further education. In the United States, the truly formidable effort in agricultural extension, involving the collaboration of government, universities, and the farm organizations, with a peak strength of at least 10,000 well-trained, full-time workers, was made by an education–training–research force that resulted in a vast increase in agricultural production by a farm population that was simultaneously shrinking in numbers. There were, as well, prodigious side effects on science, higher education, and social life. Education and training were provided for the military forces of many countries, respecting changing technologies and social organization as much as armed combat. Thousands of men and later women benefited and in many cases also won the entitlement to further education in civilian life. In the eighteenth century, only the British Navy and Prussian Army had regular schools and schoolmasters. Now the armed forces of all countries do and have provided a reservoir for future teachers of both children and adults.

The imposition of new social roles and opportunities forced adults worldwide to adapt to changing conditions. Born two centuries ago, Bishop N. F. S. Gruntvig of Denmark was a theologian–educationist who advocated and planned a new kind of institution, the famed Danish "folk high school" which was an organized school for young adults to help farm people cope with their radically altered circumstances. This is one adult education institution that has had a wide effect and continues to be influential. The folk high school as an institution has been adopted chiefly in Nordic countries and Western Europe, and usually after considerable modification, but the idea or notion of education provided in a folk high school has affected many countries. Education for upward mobility, for "getting on" and "getting ahead" was characteristic alike of England and North America during the late nineteenth century. Migration, from rural to urban centres and across frontiers, in Canada and the United States and later in many other countries, has demanded, if the newcomer was to be successful, an education for coping with new economic problems, new languages, new communities, and new political and social arrangements. Some of the most effective educational programmes and methods devised for mature people have been worked out first in classes and programmes for migrants. For several decades in the United States these were called classes for "Americanization".

Some distinctive institutions for adult education had been created primarily during the nineteenth century, for example, the Mechanics' Institutes and Workers' Educational Associations in England, folk high schools, study circles and people's universities in Nordic countries, SOKOL in Czechoslovakia, Women's Institutes in Canada and Chatauqua, and distinctive new forms of agricultural and university extension in the United States. Public libraries were flourishing in most of these countries, museums and art galleries were being created, and correspondence education was not uncommon. In several countries what had been a "mechanics' institute" became a public library. However, programmes offered by these institutions were still seen as singular or specific responses to institutional or local needs. While the organizers of adult education would occasionally meet together in church, union, or regional conferences to talk about their common interest and about how to improve methods and materials, no national organization for adult education appeared until the 1920s.

National nongovernmental associations appeared almost simultaneously in England and the United States, around the late 1920s. Some international contacts already existed before the Second World War, within the Workers' Educational Association and movements such as the churches and Young Men's Christian Association (YMCA). An international organization, the World Organization for Adult Education, did function well from 1925 until the beginning of the Second World War, with Albert Mansbridge of England serving as Secretary General and Thomas Masaryk, President of Czechoslovakia, serving as Honorary President. This organization held international seminars and symposia, encouraged people to observe programmes in other countries, published a journal, and arranged an international conference in Cambridge in 1929 that attracted 300 representatives from 24 countries. Most of the countries that could respond at this date did so. However, because of the upheaval that occurred in Europe during the Second World War, the Association was not able to survive and ceased to operate or publish.

2. *Consciousness of a Movement*

Between the World Wars, a number of adult educationists from several countries, engaged in national and international activities, discovered a sense of movement and began to believe and assert that they served in a substantive field of education with common goals and unique methods, serving large numbers of learners, deserving its own organization and establishment which might appear under several names but was usually classified as adult education. Through international meetings, a growing foundation of experience and of literature, including books in several languages, (some of them still considered exemplary) and also several journals, there was a beginning of effective communication. The Second World War and postwar events increased some contacts just as others were limited. It was true, however, that only a comparatively few countries were represented within this exchange. By 1945, the world map of adult education included many but not all of the countries of Europe, North America, Australia, and New Zealand, and a few persons or societies from some of the territories colonized by England and France.

Beyond these parameters, while it was assumed that some forms of adult education might exist, little was known about them.

The transition from such a situation to one of almost universal acceptance of adult education has taken place in a relatively short time—since the 1950s. However, many steps were necessary, each of them proceeding in linear fashion, but all of them interconnected. Changes were necessary in concept, in governmental recognition and public support, in organization, methods, learning theory, research, training, all the technical means by which isolated activities take on the colour and dimension of a coherent field of study. No such transformations could have occurred unless there had been increasing international interaction, aided by the organizations of the United Nations, much of it both the cause and result of four world conferences, organized by UNESCO in 1949, 1960, 1972 and 1985 at Elsinore, Montreal, Tokyo and Paris respectively.

3. An Accepted Definition

For several years debate has continued about the meaning and use of the term "adult education". Since it emerged independently in different places at different times it is not surprising that there has been debate concerning a number of issues:

(a) the definition and scope of the term adult education;

(b) use of equivalent or rival concepts instead of adult education;

(c) translation from language to language.

Some of the consequent confusion was settled in 1976 when representatives of 142 countries at a General Conference of UNESCO endorsed a General Recommendation on the Development of Adult Education, which included the following definition:

> The term "adult education" denotes the entire body of organized educational processes, whatever the content, level, and method, whether formal or otherwise, whether they prolong or replace initial education in schools, colleges, and universities, as well as in apprenticeship, whereby persons regarded as adult by the society to which they belong develop their abilities, enrich their knowledge, improve their technical or professional qualifications, or turn them in a new direction and bring about changes in their attitudes or behaviour in the two-fold perspective of full personal development and participation in balanced and independent social, economic, and cultural development.

The definition has been widely accepted, but although it is consistent there are some difficulties, both educational and administrative, in applying it in practice. It would, for example, cover any activities of planned learning, including those requiring full-time attendance in university or professional school, and including vocational, political, military, or religious training. So far, however, its use to cover adults enrolled in higher education for credit is not commonly adopted. This contradiction may become more important because of the increasing number of older people in higher education. Moreover, the definition covers adult education as process, but ignores the use of the term, as in Australian adult education or Yugoslav adult education, to denote the apparatus and activities of promotion and provision which make it possible for the adult public to undergo the process.

While efforts have been made to arrive at an agreed definition of adult education, other terms replacing it, or covering a wider field including some part or all of that of adult education, have been devised. Some terms reflect an effort to find a more exact term for the concept; others seek to repair the processes of distortion, diffusion, and erosion of meaning through which the term adult education has gone, by replacing it with another expression; others reflect changing ideas of what adult education is, or of its emphases or its place in the total educational process and system.

That adult education may still appear "a semantic quagmire" is not necessarily to be taken as a criticism either of it or its practitioners. It may be that it has inspired ideas and attitudes which do more credit to the holders' hearts than their heads, or that as a subject of study it is still young enough for research and thinking to be tentative. On the other hand, its shifting terminology may be a product of its richness and changing nature. The price of precision and fixation of terms could be stagnation and would therefore be unacceptable.

In any circumstances, definitions will tend to abstraction and generalization. A more living picture of adult education may be arrived at by delineating its various features as one would fill in an outline map. To some extent the UNESCO definition does this, by its prescription of content, target, public, objectives, function in individual life and society, and its implications of the philosophy behind the process. It is, however, incomplete in that it attempts to comprehend anything that adult education might be and it shows an ideal rather than what is true in reality.

That is true also of most consideration of the philosophy or animating principles of adult education if indeed there exist any generally applicable to this diverse field. It is possible to treat adult education almost as having no philosophy, as a purely technical device to provide repair and maintenance, remedying the deficiencies of initial schooling, inculcating new knowledge and skills needed to meet economic and social change. Much vocational education does operate in this way. Some people, while not going as far as that, may doubt whether there is any value in arrogating to adult education distinctive principles of its own. They may claim that the ones it follows are those of any form of good education, coloured no doubt by the ideology of the society which it serves. Insofar as these ideas are those of lifelong or recurrent education, they may have a case, but it should be remembered that these two concepts developed to a major extent from the ideas and needs of adult education.

Adult education, while drawing upon the religious, political, and social movements of which it has been an instrument, has evolved a body of principles and of issues of philosophic debate peculiar to itself. Fundamental to it is the idea that any adult is a free agent, responsible for his or her own actions, who is therefore at liberty to participate or not in any educational experience as he or she chooses and who should determine the content and nature of that experience. On the other hand, both the individual and society need education to be continued during adult life. All adults need education, but those who received least in childhood need it most and should be the priority targets of provision, although it should serve the needs of society as a whole. With the growing acceptance of the principle of lifelong education has gone the idea of adult education as a right of every individual.

These principles have received widespread if not universal assent in theory. In practice there are problems of interpretation, of conflict between principles, of reconciling these principles with political and philosophical ideas prevalent in society, and of adapting them to concrete situations. To maintain that participation should be voluntary, while requiring, as some societies do, members of certain professions to undergo continuing professional education, or seeking to engage undereducated adults in learning activities presents intractable problems. How can the needs of society always be reconciled with those of the individual? What limits to the right to education and to free choice of what and how to study should be accepted, given the practical constraints of resources and organization?

These contradictions do not, however, neutralize the effect of the principles. Indeed, it can be argued that the tensions they generate may be fruitful. Very little can be taken for granted, there is a continuing process of questioning and debate.

4. Participation in Adult Education

The question of who participates and who does not is a recurring preoccupation of adult educators. Adult education may in principle be aimed at every adult; in practice it is a long way from reaching that goal. Even the most advanced countries, which approach 100 percent attendance for initial education of children, get nowhere near the figure for adult continuing education. Statistics are imperfect, but it seems clear that in no country does more than a minority participate in any given year. This may not be important: it is not seriously maintained that all adults need to undertake formal study continuously throughout life. Indeed, the principle of recurrent education argues that the alternation of periods of study with periods of other activity is beneficial. Nor is the desired frequency of educational experiences laid down, since this will vary with individual need. What is unsatisfactory is that in all societies a substantial proportion of adults never take part in any purposive educational experience at all.

More particularly, the categories of people which adult educators claim as their priority targets contain the largest proportion of nonparticipants. The nineteenth-century movements, out of which modern adult education developed, were directed, with few exceptions, at the socially, economically, and therefore educationally disadvantaged. The concept that every adult needed continuing education only became a significant principle of provision in the twentieth century (Ministry of Reconstruction 1919). Even when it did, adult education has continued largely to be seen and to operate as a remedial activity, offering to adults what for one reason or another they had not received in childhood.

Nevertheless, in practice the people who have most readily responded to the offer of learning opportunities, while they have not been the highest educated, have been those who have reached a higher than average level of attainment in childhood education, whatever that level may have been in a particular country at a particular time. The more a person's initial education falls below the norm, the less likely he or she seems to be to continue to study in adult life (Johnstone and Rivera 1965, NIAE 1970, OECD 1979). A serious consequence has been that adult education tends to increase educational differences rather than to reduce them, as it set out to do.

Advanced countries, from which the most reliable statistics derive, also show a different pattern of participation between the sexes and between age groups. Women outnumber men in leisure-time general and cultural courses, but there are many more men in vocationally related study. The age of peak participation runs from the mid-20s to the early 40s, but the figures for under 25 years are affected by the fact that many are still in full-time initial education and are not counted as adult students. After the age of 45 there is a continuing decline in participation rates. Statistics for developing countries are sketchy, but the pattern seems broadly to be that women and the elderly participate less than men and younger adults.

The reason for the discrepancy between the ideal and actual publics of adult education is not merely that there is not enough education provided for adults, although that is true. If every adult wanted to follow an organized course of study the system could not cope. It is argued, however, that much of the responsibility for nonparticipation lies with the providers of study opportunities. Everyone could be attracted to take part, if the content, the methods, the conditions, and the time of study were right, it is said. If middle-aged, middle-class women predominate in evening classes, it is because the curriculum is designed for that clientele. If postexperience vocational courses are attended mainly by supervisors and executives, that is the fault of employers, who commission the courses and release the personnel to follow them.

Adult education, in claiming to meet the needs of adults, has largely provided what educators themselves of above average schooling have believed they ought to need. In some types of provision, notably in vocational education, the goal is less to offer what individual learners want than to meet the requirements of society or employers, and that may best be done, in the eyes of sponsors and providers, by recruiting persons who have shown some capacity to profit from education and are in positions to apply what they learn to best effect. In this situation the educationally disadvantaged are likely to miss out.

Against these cases must, however, be set efforts which have been continually made to reach those thought to be in special need. Education for workers goes back to the nineteenth century, and study opportunities tailored for other specific groups (including women, the elderly, ethnic minorities, the physically and mentally handicapped, the unemployed) have increased. Above all, campaigns to provide for the illiterate have been conducted in both developing and developed countries. In addition to content and method intended to appeal to particular groups, financial and organizational measures to facilitate attendance or give incentives demonstrate both private and public concern for the undereducated.

Adult educators have had some, but only partial, success for the evidence suggests that many nonparticipants are held back by factors that adult education alone is unable to change. People have been led by school experience to believe that they are incapable of further learning, that they would not enjoy it, or that it has nothing of value to offer them. The attitude of family, neighbours, friends, or workmates is against their participation. There are competing claims on their time (OECD 1979). There is evidence also that many adults know that education means change, which is to some extent unpredictable, and that they are not sufficiently dissatisfied with their lot to undergo the effort of study for a doubtful outcome (David 1974). The growing acceptance of lifelong education may remove the other disincentives, but not the last one, which, like truancy from school, seems likely always to be a factor.

5. Purposes of Providers of Adult Education

It seems probable that conditions can be created to attract most people to study at some time in adult life. The implications of the discussion of participation are, though, that provision of learning opportunities is not for the most part a response to demand by potential students, but an initiative of persons who believe other people ought to study. Some people do, it is clear, make their own opportunities, but most participants in organized learning experiences, although they have their own motives, would not be stimulated to study if the occasion to do so had not been organized for them. The purposes or motives of the providers are therefore of major interest.

The avowed ones have been diverse, inspired by altruism and self-interest, concern for the individual and for the collective. From this variety derive adult education's contradictions of principle. Nineteenth-century mutual instruction groups and modern self-directed learners have worked to open education to themselves and their fellows for the many advantages it could bring. Education has been offered to save souls, to divert from alcoholism and from fornication, to encourage clean and respectable habits. Its providers have sought to preserve the social and economic status quo or to overthrow it, to stimulate national feeling, to preserve national culture against foreign threat. They have offered study in order to get a trained workforce and an informed citizenry capable of fulfilling effectively its social and political role. They have tried to offer to all adults the fullest possibility of individual self-development through education.

As adult education has grown, the providers' purposes have become more specific. Not only are there courses for different disadvantaged groups, including language programmes for migrants and English as a foreign or second language, but in the Third World all provision is education for development.

6. Curriculum

Such diverse purposes have bred varied curricula and some of the liveliest debate about adult education. Since the nineteenth century, particularly in the United Kingdom and countries impregnated with the British tradition, there has been argument about the nature and purpose of adult education and thus about its content. It has been presented in a number of forms, in terms of education versus training, education for living as opposed to education for earning a living, education as an end in itself versus education as a means to other ends. For many years in the literature of the field, education for its own sake enjoyed the higher status and the most suitable curriculum for that purpose was considered to be rooted in the humanities and social sciences. Technical studies, natural sciences, the acquisition of psychomotor skills, being linked to job training, were to some degree suspect.

In fact the controversy has been largely a false one. If the highest aim was to produce an educated adult (Paterson 1979), it was because such a person was a more complete individual, a better citizen, therefore education to that end was, and is, just as instrumental as political education, vocational education, or education for peace. Not that education cannot provide knowledge and understanding which are enriching and enjoyable in themselves, independently of any other purpose they may serve, but they are not tied to a particular content, nor does the enjoyment of them for their own sake prevent them being also a means to an end.

In practice, most adult study opportunities have probably been offered and accepted as instruments, but the instrumentality does not necessarily reside, either primarily or at all, in the outcomes, namely the body of knowledge and skills acquired; it may lie in the process of learning. Studies of student motivation show that adults frequently participate for the social interaction in the learning experience, and for pleasure in the action of learning, but educators too find the process of major importance. Many believe that any adult course should above all help people learn how to learn, so that ideally educators will work themselves out of a job. Subject matter is therefore of value not in itself, but for its suitability for that purpose.

From what is known about the purposes of providers and learners, however, it is clear that adult education is viewed above all as an opportunity to master a body of knowledge and to acquire competence which may subsequently be used outside the study environment. It may be used in widely different situations, in the home, in leisure and recreation, in social and community roles, and most frequently in job-related contexts. The content will be equally diverse. Since it is mostly agreed that an adult should be allowed to study what he or she wishes, every discipline, every knowledge field and skill is likely to be included in the curriculum somewhere at some time.

Nevertheless, human and financial resources are limited, so there are finite practical boundaries to purpose and curriculum, even if there are no theoretical ones. The self-directed learner is more free, but even he or she is for the most part restricted by the availability of library and other learning resources. The participant in organized educational experiences can only study what the providers offer. This is a compromise between what the providers wish and what the learners will accept and is largely determined by the priorities of the former, which in turn are set by social, cultural, political, and economic factors in society as a whole.

It is possible to list from empirical observation major categories of study currently to be found in adult education. It is more difficult to say how relevant that content is to the purposes of students or providers. There has indeed been little study of curriculum to back up animated discussion founded purely on value judgments. The principle that each person should be free to choose what he or she studies has obscured to some degree the possibility that free choice may not result in what the individual or society most needs. In some fields, work has been done in curriculum studies, but the question of the content of adult education requires further research.

7. Learning and Teaching

Much more attention has been devoted to how adults learn, to methods of teaching, and to modes of delivering instruction. It may not be for the adult educator to prescribe what shall be learnt, but it is his or her task to present knowledge in the best ways to facilitate learning. It is accepted by most people that not only is the adult different from the child in being a voluntary participant in study, but he or she is physically, psychologically, and socially different enough to require distinctive approaches to instruction. Whether these differences are of kind or merely of degree is a moot point, although most adult educators would maintain that some at least are of the former type. In some countries, indeed, particularly in Europe, the term "andragogy" has been coined to denote the science of educating adults as distinct from "pedagogy", that of educating children. Its use has been strongly resisted in some parts of the world, but in most countries where adult education is established as a field of practice, the area covered by andragogy is nevertheless recognized as a distinctive field of study.

How far adults continue to be capable of learning, usually on the assumption that this ability is affected by the physiological process of ageing, has been a major topic of research. Experimental evidence is conflicting and while it does suggest an age-related decline in certain skills significant for learning, others seem to be maintained and others even to increase during adult life (Bromley 1974). Overall, growing old, at least until late middle age, does not in itself appear significantly to reduce learning ability; lack of practice seems to be a more important factor. It is more fruitful, it has been argued, to view adulthood as a period of change rather than decline, to be divided into stages of development during which the most influential factors in learning are motivation, self-concept, and social role.

The need for adult education to adapt to times and situations suitable to learners, to recognize that learners are persons accustomed to taking responsibility for their actions and with a body of prior experience which may be of value to themselves and others has had an effect on methods and techniques which has been felt in other sectors of education. Distance education, in the form of correspondence teaching, was originally and still is primarily directed at adults. Self-directed learning is a principally adult phenomenon. Computerized learning, small group work, case study, and role play were all tried and tested in adult education. Nevertheless, in the majority of teaching situations the methods used are traditional. Lowe (1982) wrote, "Orthodox teaching methods still prevail. In the realm of theory a great deal is written about what ought to be done and in the realm of action original methods are constantly being tried out on a small scale. . . . The method of instruction which still dominates adult education is oral teaching in the classroom . . .".

8. Structures, Organization, and Finance

There must be some organization in order to make studying opportunities available and known to adults. Whereas school systems throughout the world conform to or are working towards a broadly similar, comparatively simple structure, based on the primary, secondary, tertiary model, education for adults varies widely from country to country and, indeed, many countries lack a nationwide organization. To a large extent this is due to the recent development of postinitial, continuing education, or whatever name may be attributed to it. There are, however, other factors which have obstructed the growth of coherent, integrated structures on a national scale, a number of which have already been referred to.

In the first place there have been a number of nongovernmental providing or sponsoring agencies, even in socialist countries. Many of these have either been in competition with each other, or at least pursuing diverse aims. In some countries organizations sponsoring adult education include labour groups, corporations, farm and cooperative movements, churches, women's associations, citizen groups, political parties, groups fostering the arts, culture, and recreation, ethnic societies, and many more. Only governments have been capable of bringing these together, and they have been slow to do so for a number of reasons, not the least of which in many cases has been failure until the second half of the twentieth century to recognize that the adult sector was essential to national education.

Whereas for the child the aim of all states is to make education the obligatory prime preoccupation of life and whereas to that extent the clientele can be made to fit the system, provision for adults must adapt itself to their status as voluntary participants and their quite other preoccupations, notably work, family life, and leisure. Given the variety of their situations and concerns, it has been widely argued that a comparatively simple structure such as that of the school system would be inappropriate. Against that, however, it must be recognized that many attempts are being made to extend school and higher education systems to cover adult education and thus build a system of lifelong education.

In many parts of the world, belief that adults should have a direct say in the how, when, where, and what of their own learning has helped to keep decision making and organization at the local level. This tendency has been particularly strong in such countries as the United States, France, and Scandinavia, where for one reason or another distrust of the centralizing power of the state or of any other national body is firmly rooted.

The proponents of adult autonomy have had increasingly to reconcile this principle with the need to ensure for all persons adequate and equal opportunities to learn. They therefore have to accept national mechanisms to provide resources which self-help and mutual help cannot offer. For example, high technology, such as multimedia and computer learning programmes, requires large capital expenditure and incurs high running costs which only become economical if there are many users and would be beyond reach of most purely local organizations. Larger scale ones, at national or regional levels, are needed. Those who believe adult education's first goal is to promote individual self-development look for mechanisms which encourage cooperation and facilitate provision in response to local needs and without central direction. There are others, however, who see adult education primarily as an instrument of social engineering. They believe some form of central planning and authority is required. For the most part, public authority intervention has been inspired by the second view, although in many countries it attempts to take into account the first.

This may help to explain why the state, having become the major agency both as sponsor and provider in many countries, does not control adult education as tightly as it does schools. Another factor may be that government departments engaged may be labour, agriculture, immigration, health, economic development, communication, justice, or national defence as often as ministries of education, and governments do not necessarily speak with one voice. This diversity is a reflection of adult education's range of functions. The power of the state is exerted through its role as a direct provider of study opportunities and through overt commands based on legislation and regulation. A substantial body of adult education law has been passed since the Second World War. Much, if not most, of government influence is exerted, indirectly, however, through its ability to grant or withhold financial assistance.

Typically, the provision of financial resources to adult education is more complex than for schooling or higher education, which are usually supported directly from taxation through well-established administrative channels. Much of the money for adult study is provided by students themselves in the form of tuition fees. A significant contribution to vocational education is made by employers, either voluntarily or through training taxes. Other kinds of adult education are supported by private associations such as labour unions, churches, and political parties.

In almost every country, however, the maintenance of adult education is increasingly dependent on national, regional, or local government subsidy, raised by taxation. Considerable freedom under the law permits public authorities to influence policy by the ways in which they channel these funds, to whom, and for what. The desire to influence government policy and largesse has been a potent factor, together with the economics of training and the creation of educational materials, in encouraging private adult education associations to set up regional and national organizations within and between associations.

9. Adult Educators

Throughout the history of adult education the majority of persons engaged in administering provision or teaching adults have either been unpaid volunteers, or have not depended for their living on the payment they have received. Some organizations have avoided full-time paid staff as a matter of principle—it was considered very important to rely on the commitment of conviction rather than on cash motivation (Titmus 1967). With the growth of adult provision throughout the world though, organizations have discovered that part-time staff are inadequate to their needs. Not only that, the skills required to run large-scale operations, the importance attached by society to adult education, the expectations of participants, and the awareness that a distinctive body of expertise has been evolved specific to adult education have contributed to a sense that there is a need for staff, not only full-time and therefore paid, but as professionally trained as those in schools.

To meet the need, training programmes and institutions have been established. There is no uniform pattern of training, but in the preparation of full-time workers universities have acquired a major role in most countries and adult education is increasingly becoming a graduate profession. In spite of the continuing scepticism of many adult educators about the value of training, on the grounds that expertise will separate teacher from taught and may become a substitute for commitment, more and more opportunities for training are being offered to part-time adult educators. These are mostly short courses conducted by employer organizations. Persons who have undergone such training still form only a minority of adult educators. However, it is not a condition of employment and to become an adult educator all that is needed is knowledge or skill of value to adults and the desire to pass it on to others.

10. International Influences on Adult Education

Partly because it was the latest educational field to grow, and because it began to develop worldwide just as major bodies such as UNESCO that foster international interaction had been recently created, the field of adult education has responded to, and has encouraged international contacts, meetings, programmes, and publications, perhaps more than any other field of education. Paramount among international influences have been the intergovernmental agencies of the United Nations, particularly UNESCO, the International Labour Organization (ILO), The Food and Agricultural Organization (FAO), the World Health Organization (WHO) and Unicef, some regional organizations such as the Council of Europe, some more specialized agencies such as the Organisation for Economic Co-operation and Development, and at least a hundred international nongovernmental organizations. Several of the United Nations agencies, notably UNESCO, have both offices for special purposes and strong regional offices such as the one in Bangkok. All of these offices have periodically arranged meetings and published proceedings and studies about literacy and adult education.

The positive impact of these international contacts in education has never been assessed in any comprehensive way, nor has there been any comparative scrutiny of the productive tendencies that have been thus stimulated, although countries are now receiving more financial aid. On the whole their influence seems to be favourable, even though more rigorous assessment is needed. The results that have been noted include reaching consensus on social and economic goals, agreement on a range of methods and processes, the setting of standards, making available able practitioners to developing countries, and assistance in developing both innovative and indigenous forms of culture and adult education.

Some of the special offices of UNESCO have made significant contributions. The International Institute for Educational Planning (IIEP) (Paris) has provided studies and arranged international meetings on distance learning, nonformal adult education, and literacy, to which subjects it is now devoting greater attention. The IIEP has also been a continuing advocate of the notion that any plan or any evaluation by educational authorities should be concerned with the whole system of education, including the informal and nonformal elements, as well as the school system. The International Bureau of Education (Geneva) has been responsible for publishing abstracts on research in adult education, and has collaborated in the publication of a glossary of terms in several languages, extracts from which have been included as an Appendix to this *Handbook*. The UNESCO Institute of Education (Hamburg) has for many years continued a project on lifelong learning and fostered other elements of social research bearing on adults. The European Centre for Leisure and Education (Prague) has, despite its title, constituted a regional office for adult education and has developed a programme of comparative studies including publishing monographs on national adult education systems of European countries.

Some other intergovernmental agencies of the United Nations have also assumed responsibilities for the education of men and women. With expenditures on adult education considerably in excess of what UNESCO could provide, the International Labour

Organization, as part of its service to its constituency of trade unions, has offered since the early 1960s an extensive programme of workers' education, directed by an experienced staff at headquarters and in regional centres.

Much of the work of the Food and Agricultural Organization is directed to food production and food management, and has been in the form of training and agricultural extension that is a significant part of adult education. So is the basic programme of the World Health Organization, directed to primary health care, a specialized programme of adult education reaching into every country and to millions of people. UNICEF directs many of its programmes for youth and adults to rural education and literacy and is now employing a secretariat experienced in adult education. Increasingly, since 1964, the World Bank has made funds available for adult and nonformal education, as has the United Nations Development Fund, which agency, for example, furnished most of the funds for the World Experimental Literacy Programme. The efforts of these agencies are not always consistent and sometimes cooperation and mutual support is lacking, but the total impact is growing and their potential value, when full measures of planning and cooperation are achieved, internationally, regionally, and nationally, is very great.

Another form of international interaction has arisen from the national assistance programmes of a number of industrial countries. The provision of aid varies in nature and extent, and much of it has been in the form of food, or economic assistance. However, some countries, notably Sweden, have placed a major emphasis on support to adult education as a form of development assistance. Sweden's support of Tanzanian adult education has been noteworthy but countries like the Federal Republic of Germany, the Soviet Union, and Czechoslovakia have also given substantial aid in the form of technical education and vocational training. Other countries that have fostered assistance programmes in adult education include the United States, the United Kingdom, the Netherlands, Norway, and Denmark, as well as Australia and Canada. Another recent trend has been for some of these countries to employ in their assistance programmes citizens from some of the developing countries who have the necessary experience appropriate to other developing countries. The result has been some further strengthening of the international network of adult education.

11. International Nongovernmental Organizations

The activities reported above have all been initiated through governmental or intergovernmental action. However, there are nongovernmental agencies working on behalf of international development. The number of these organizations, referred to as NGOs, depends somewhat on the definition employed, but the total figure would exceed 100. Some of them, like the World Alliance of the Young Men's Christian Association (YMCA), have experience in international development that goes back at least to the earliest years of the twentieth century. A great many of the principles and practices of literacy, adult education, community organizations, health, and agricultural extension were first worked out by such agencies, who also were able to win some public support for such efforts. For example, the International Federation of Library Associations has helped stimulate growth and the planning of libraries in all parts of the world and has been a strong advocate of the role of libraries in development. Four international labour organizations have all supported workers' education, particularly the International Workers' Educational Association, and the International Cooperative Alliance has been active in promoting forms of adult education that have featured economic education and the growth of credit unions and cooperatives, The International Congress of University Adult Education has organized international seminars and conferences, supported comparative studies in adult education, and published a journal. The International Council for Adult Education has since 1973 included in its membership most countries possessing national agencies of adult education, it has helped strengthen regional cooperation and national movements, it has fostered training and research, and it has arranged national case studies of women's studies, literacy, and basic education.

12. Regional Organizations

In addition to worldwide associations, like UNESCO and the ICAE, there are numerous regional organizations which often operate with or through the world ones. Adult education is one of the concerns of such intergovernmental associations as the Council of Europe and the Organization of American States. In some regions, governments have combined to form associations specifically for the promotion of adult education, such as the Arab Literacy and Adult Education Organization and CREFAL, the Regional Centre for Adult Education and Functional Literacy in Latin America. Influential nongovernmental associations include the Asian–South Pacific Bureau of Adult Education (ASPBAE), the African Adult Education Association (AAEA), and the European Bureau of Adult Education. All these bodies exist to encourage cooperation in the practice and study of adult education.

13. Research and Issues

For the most part, advances in adult education have taken place as pragmatic responses by practitioners to perceived needs. They have not been derived from a body of theory built on or confirmed by research. What research there has been, has been closely linked to the needs of practice. Academic study has been slow to develop and has been distrusted by workers in the field. Nevertheless, as adult education has grown, it has become more and more apparent that it requires substantial and systematic inquiry.

Since 1960 the amount of research has increased dramatically, carried out by governmental and nongovernmental organizations, universities, and specialized research institutes. International organizations have played a particularly valuable role. However, work has on the whole been piecemeal, without the national or regional planning that might lead to significant progress, and all of the major issues which have been discussed in this article need a great deal more research to back up the arguments of faith and pragmatism on which the case for adult education still rests to a large degree.

If research remains as closely related to the immediate needs of practice as it has done in the past, then it is necessary to look to the trends in the latter for those in the former. Unfortunately, in so diverse a field as adult education it is difficult to point with confidence to worldwide trends. Adult educators have generally agreed that primary efforts should be directed to what are termed the undereducated—the poor, the illiterate, the handicapped, and specific publics such as rural people, women, the elderly, the unemployed, and ethnic minorities. Government interest in adult education appears increasingly to be directed to its use as an instrument of economic and social policy. In advanced countries, the prospect of greatly increased leisure time for adults, as a result of early retirement, technological advance, and high unemployment rates, seems to open up a new area of opportunity and responsibility for adult education. In many developing countries, on the other hand, the principal function of adult education for some time to come will certainly be to offer opportunities for basic education to the millions who have had none or very little in childhood. One other trend also seems to be apparent throughout the world. Although it may change its form and its emphasis, the education of adults will continue to grow and to occupy an increasingly important place in the process of lifelong education.

Bibliography

Bordin A, Kidd J R, Draper J A 1973 *Adult Education in India: A Book of Readings*. Nachiketa, Bombay

Botkin J W, Elmandjra M, Malitza M 1979 *No Limits to Learning: Bridging the Human Gap: A Report to the Club of Rome*. Pergamon, Oxford

Bromley D B 1974 *The Psychology of Human Ageing*, 2nd edn. Penguin, Harmondsworth

Brunner E de S 1959 *An Overview of Adult Education Research*. Adult Education Association, Chicago, Illinois

Centre for Educational Research and Innovation (CERI) 1975 *Recurrent Education: Trends and Issues*. Organisation for Economic Co-operation and Development (OECD), Paris

Coombs P 1978 *New Paths to Learning*. UNICEF, New York

Dave R H (ed.) 1976 *Foundations of Lifelong Education*. Pergamon, Oxford

David M 1974 *L'Individuel et le collectif dans la formation professionelle et générale des travailleurs*, Vol. 2. Université de Paris I, Institut des Sciences Sociales du Travail, Paris

Elias J L, Merriam S 1980 *Philosophical Foundations of Adult Education*. Krieger, Huntington, New York

Faure E, Herrera F, Kaddoura A-R, Lopes H, Petrovsky A V, Rahnema M, Ward F C 1972 *Learning To Be: The World of Education Today and Tomorrow*. UNESCO, Paris

Grattan C H 1955 *In Quest of Knowledge: A Historical Perspective on Adult Education*. Association Press, New York

Hall B L, Kidd J R 1978 *Adult Learning: A Design For Action: A Comprehensive International Survey*. Pergamon, Oxford

Hudson J W 1851 *The History of Adult Education*. Longman, Brown, Green, London

Huston P 1979 *Third World Women Speak Out: Interviews in Six Countries on Change, Development, and Basic Needs*. Praeger, New York

International Council for Adult Education (ICAE) 1979 *The World of Literacy*. International Development Research Centre (IDRC), Ottawa

Jessup F (ed.) 1969 *Lifelong Learning: A Symposium on Continuing Education*. Pergamon, Oxford

Johnstone J W C, Rivera R J 1965 *Volunteers for Learning: A Study of the Educational Pursuits of American Adults*. Aldine, Chicago, Illinois

Jourdan M (ed.) 1981 *Recurrent Education in Western Europe: Progress, Projections and Trends in Recurrent, Lifelong and Continuing Education*. National Foundation for Educational Research (NFER)–Nelson, Slough

Kidd J R 1962 *Financing Continuing Education*. Scarecrow Press, New York

Kidd J R 1975 *A Tale of Three Cities: Elsinore–Montreal–Tokyo. The Influence of Three UNESCO World Conferences Upon the Development of Adult Education*. Syracuse University Press, Syracuse, New York

Knox A B 1980 *Developing, Administering and Evaluating Adult Education*. Jossey-Bass, San Francisco, California

Lengrand P 1970 *Introduction to Lifelong Education*. UNESCO, Paris

Lowe J 1982 *The Education of Adults: A World Perspective*, 2nd edn. UNESCO, Paris

MacBride S et al. 1980 *Many Voices One World: Communication and Society Today and Tomorrow: Towards a New More Just and More Efficient World Information and Communication Order*. UNESCO, Kogan Page, London

Megarry J, Schuller T 1979 *Recurrent Education and Lifelong Learning*. Kogan Page, London

National Institute of Adult Education (NIAE) 1970 *Adult Education: Adequacy of Provision*. NIAE, London

Ministry of Reconstruction 1919 *Adult Education Committee, Final Report.* His Majesty's Stationery Office, London

Organisation for Economic Co-operation and Development (OECD) 1977 *Learning Opportunities for Adults*, Vol. 4: *Participation in Adult Education.* OECD, Paris

Organisation for Economic Co-operation and Development (OECD) 1979 *Learning Opportunities for Adults*, Vol. 3: *The Non-participation Issue.* OECD, Paris

Paterson R W K 1979 *Values, Education, and the Adult.* Routledge and Kegan Paul, London

Paulston R G 1972 *Non-formal Education: An Annotated International Bibliography.* Praeger, New York

Simmons J (ed.) 1979 *The Education Dilemma: Policy Issues for Developing Countries in the 1980s.* Pergamon, Oxford

Suchodolski B 1972 *Lifelong Education: Problems, Tasks, Conditions.* UNESCO, Paris

Titmus C J 1967 *Adult Education in France.* Pergamon, Oxford

Titmus C J (ed.) et al. 1979 *Terminology of Adult Education.* UNESCO, Paris

UNESCO 1979 *Directory of Adult Education Periodicals.* UNESCO, Paris

UNESCO 1980 *Directory of Adult Education Documentary and Information Services*, 2nd edn. UNESCO, Paris

Xenophon 1914 *Cyropaedia.* (With an English translation by Walter Miller.) Heinemann, London

J. R. KIDD
C. J. TITMUS

Section 1

Theory and Principles of Adult Education

Section 1

Theory and Principles of Adult Education

Introduction

Most adult education began as a response to a perceived practical need. It did not begin as ideas looking for application. For a large part of its history it has been slow to develop a body of coherent theory and principles relative to itself. For the most part practitioners have been busier doing than reflecting, though there have been justly notable exceptions, such as Bishop Grundtvig in nineteenth-century Denmark. Not that they lacked thought, but it was sharply focused to action. They were, almost without exception, persons of strong principle.

Their principles and their theories, such as they had, derived less, however, from their perception of adult education as a distinctive field of action, with its own specific characteristics and worthy of commitment in its own right, than from goals of work and belief, for the achievement of which adult education promised to be a useful instrument. Adult education was therefore marked and continued to be so by the motivating ideas, religious, political, economic, cultural or social, of those who offered it and, to a lesser degree, of those who sought it.

For the most part adult educators have derived their ideas of what education is about from the formal provision of school and higher education. The majority of them had no other model. Their function has largely been seen as compensating for and supplementing initial education, adult education being seen as a marginal activity. Some people might always have need of it to meet special circumstances, but the implication of education as a once-for-all preparation for life, a concept which still predominantly shapes practice, was that, if initial schooling could be got right, the generality of persons would need no educational provision to be made for them in adult life.

Even when it was recognized that there would always be such a need, adult educators have continued to be marked by practices and theories of school and university, either to the extent of following them (as in the United Kingdom), or of reacting against them (as in France). They have not been able to ignore them, nor have they wished to do so, since what they have had to deal with is the consequence of initial education, or of the lack of it.

In addition to the educators' motives, their considered or unconsidered ideas on education, they have been subject to external pressures, economic, social, cultural, and spiritual, in the societies in which they worked, of which they have been to a greater or lesser extent aware. To this has been added, in the twentieth century, a growing consciousness of important elements, from an educational point of view, in the circumstances and, perhaps, the nature of adults, which are not shared by children.

The multifariousness of adult needs has strongly militated against attempts to impose the kind of uniform pattern that obtains in initial education. Educators have repeatedly stressed the national and even local particularities of their activities. In many countries provision for adults has not been treated as a separate, coherent sector of education, but has been divided into smaller entities, such as workers' education, or vocational training, or has been subsumed, in whole or in part, within other educational activities such as out-of-school education, popular education or, more recently, nonformal education. A consequence of this has been that theories of, or relating to, the education of adults have tended to be fragmented.

Attempts to develop a coherent foundation of theory in which to ground practice have been pursued largely since the Second World War alongside the rapid growth of educational activities for adults throughout the world. The main aim has been to provide arguments for expansion, to justify the large resources which have been put into the work, to attract participants, and to provide necessary guidance to policy makers, planners, and practitioners who are being drawn into this field. About adult education there now exists a body of ideas notable for its diversity and richness, rather less for its clarity and precision, unstable and changing, sometimes eroded as it rubs against the realities of practice. No theory commands universal acceptance, some are more widely approved than others. As for their application, that is always restricted by the pressures of circumstance.

This section of the *Handbook* concentrates on those aspects of theory and practice which appear to have the widest application. The articles within it are particularly concerned with theories which seek to provide broad, general frameworks and directions, and with fundamental questions of principle which arise in any educational activity in which adults are engaged. The section is divided into three subsections. The first sets the education of adults in a wider context which seeks to encompass the whole of education at all ages and of all kinds throughout life. The second treats adult education by itself, conceptualized as a distinctive sector of education, with a clearly definable clientele and range of action. The third concentrates on major variations of the concept, showing different conceptualizations of out-of-school education, of which adult education, or a part of it, forms a constituent element.

Such considerations are not, however, confined to this section. They inform all the articles in the book to a greater or lesser degree and in other sections matters of theory and principle particularly relevant to those sections are also treated.

Lifelong Education

Introduction

The belief that education can and should be a process that continues throughout the duration of life is not new. What is new about the contemporary development of the concept is its elaboration as the guiding principle of universal education; as a product of dissatisfaction with the now conventional once-for-all system of initial education; as a response to knowledge growth and technological change, which make any education limited to childhood and youth incapable of meeting the lifetime needs of individuals and society, however effective it may be made; and as a means of achieving equality of opportunity in education.

The first article in this subsection, *Lifelong Education: Growth of the Concept*, outlines the role played by all these factors in the development of the idea. It also presents lifelong education as a wider view of education than that enshrined in the term "schooling", one giving more scope to individual self-development, without the threat of the stigma of failure that is strong in formal education. It recounts how the concept has achieved wide acceptance in theory, largely assisted by UNESCO advocacy, but points out that practice still falls far short of theory.

In any scheme of education throughout life, learning in adulthood must play an essential role. It has not been unusual, indeed, for lifelong education to be treated as a synonym of adult education. The article *Lifelong Education: Interaction with Adult Education* makes it clear that the addition of adult education as it now exists to initial education would not constitute lifelong education as currently conceived. It then examines changes in the scope and purpose of adult learning, changes in teaching, and changes in the organization and finance of adult education which will be necessary if it is to form an adequate element of the larger process. This is dealt with further in Section 10b.

Lifelong Education: Growth of the Concept

P. Lengrand

Lifelong education can be considered an alternative to the shortcomings and insufficiencies of traditional education. In the past, the success of the introduction of compulsory education can be attributed to the fact that it met the interests of both the ruling class and the general public.

In the view of the various existing authorities, school was the tool needed to meet the aims of the state which represented the ruling class of the bourgeoisie. Among these aims were the development of the work force required by an expanding economy, the recruitment and training of managerial staff for the various levels, the strengthening of the military capacities for defensive and offensive purposes, and the maintenance of public order through the moulding of minds in accordance with the values prevailing in society.

As far as the masses were concerned, school instruction was considered as a means of securing access to knowledge while at the same time providing the working classes with an opportunity to climb the rungs of the social ladder.

In reality, a good number of the objectives aimed at by the promoters of the educational structures have been attained. Mass instruction has contributed enormously to the establishment of modern states. It has favoured the development of the industrial society and has been instrumental in the absorption by the various social strata of the nationalistic ideology which served as a support to the more or less commendable undertakings of the state. In this regard it cannot be forgotten that in France and Germany, for instance, the instruction dispensed by teachers was directed towards preparing the minds and hearts of their pupils for the forthcoming conflict between the two countries.

At the same time and in a contradictory manner, schooling has served the development of a political awareness among the masses. It has favoured the emergence of strong personalities in the ranks of the working class, who have become the builders of growing opposition to the ruling class.

In opposition to these elements which have secured wide support in favour of the role of the school, the objectives and functioning of the system have been subject to strong criticism from the very start. The main reproach was of a political nature. Many progressive people found it difficult to accept that, under the cover of humanism and universal values, ethnocentric preoccupations were predominant as exemplified by the teaching of the human disciplines such as history, literature, and even philosophy.

As to the didactic aspect, the inconveniences and shortcomings of the system were rapidly identified. It became patently evident that the scholastic structures were not adapted to meet the general needs of human nature and the peculiarities of the various pupils.

In the curricula, essential elements of the human being were neglected or nearly forgotten, such as the body, the development of feelings, the ability to express oneself through art, familiarization with technology, and initiation into the economical and political aspects of life. Emphasis was and still is placed on the reproduction of models but not on creativity. This situation, detrimental to any human being, becomes a force of aggression and can be taxed as cruelty where young people, who are not in accordance with the imposed model, because of their particular kind of perception and feelings, are involved.

Other aspects have been questioned, such as the role of school in the process of social selection (which engenders new forms of inequalities) and, least justifiable of all, the institutionalization of failure for which the pupil is held responsible while the process of instruction is not.

These defects, which have been manifest for a long time in the eyes of many specialists in human disciplines, have been accepted docilely by the general public for as long as they were felt to be something inherent to any training process. This favourable situation no longer exists. Public opinion has changed. Many factors have arisen which have given rise to dissatisfaction. Among them, the development of a democratic spirit, the claim for greater equality in opportunities, and the general feeling that education is no longer adequate to face the main challenges of modern life must be taken into account. In this respect, many observers have identified an "education crisis" which can only be solved if the objectives, structures, curricula, and methods are substantially modified within a global context of lifelong education.

1. What Lifelong Education Means

The term "lifelong education" covers a very wide field. In some cases it is applied to strictly vocational education, that is, training and refresher courses in a particular technical skill. It may also cover much the same ground as adult education, taken in a broader sense than training for a specific job, though not embracing the development of all facets of an individual's personality. But more and more frequently it is being applied to new activities and fields of research which are not included in the traditional notion of adult education, much less vocational training, and which express a desire for evolving a new style of education.

At the present stage of thinking and practice, lifelong education is a very complex notion which cannot as yet be clearly defined. An attempt should perhaps be made to systematize its various elements and show their interrelationship with one another.

1.1 A Radical Transformation of the Concept of Education

If people can and should continue learning, training, and improving their professional qualifications, developing their intellectual, emotional, and moral potentialities, contributing more to their personal relationships as well as to the community at large, and if adult education is to provide adequate facilities to help them achieve these aims, then educational thinking and processes must undergo a radical transformation. Up until now, the basic aim of primary, secondary, and university education was dictated by the traditional view that life was divided into distinct parts: a period of preparation and training, followed by a period of action.

Within this context the aim of education was to provide the future adults with the attributes they would need to fill the various roles they might be called upon to play in life. As a result, the whole education system was designed to cram the pupils' heads with all kinds of facts, and they were supposed to draw on this accumulated capital as best they could to lead a satisfactory life. But if, on the contrary, people can and should continue to learn and educate themselves throughout their life, there is no reason to overburden their brains as children.

The role of the school, in this perspective, changes completely. Instead of being essentially a process of acquiring knowledge, basic education becomes a kind of prelude. Rather than offer courses in different subjects, it should provide future adults with the means of expressing themselves and communicating with others. The main emphasis should be on mastery of language, on the development of faculties of concentration and observation, on knowing how and where to obtain information, and on the ability to work with others. The very existence of a broad and vigorous system of adult education will have an impact on all educational thinking and practice, firstly in the university, then in secondary and primary schools, and beyond that in the family and community in which it is applied.

According to a second interpretation of lifelong education, which is closer to the true nature of this concept, all educators, and particularly those engaged in adult education, must undertake a complete overhaul of all the different forms of education and training required by modern human beings in all the different stages of their existence. Each period of a person's life in fact represents at the same time a unique and valuable experience and a preparation for future stages. This duality is true not only of childhood and adolescence, but also of the early years of adult life, maturity, as well as the periods later in life. Each phase of a person's existence should be lived to the full and should contribute experiences, pleasures, and satisfactions to the long process by which he or she gradually comes to know himself or herself through a series of revelations. The extent to which each individual benefits fully from each period of their life depends on their preparation for subsequent periods. To live as if one had been granted some kind of reprieve is merely a form of escapism. Yet this is very often the case with children and adolescents. Schooling acts as a brake on their development and prevents them from leading the kind of life they should at that age, with the result that they develop a negative attitude towards education which seems to restrict their freedom instead of being a source of joy and personal fulfilment. A truer understanding of life and its different phases leads to a much more comprehensive view of lifelong education, embracing far more varied activities than adult education, which however will have a very important role to play. Since all aspects of education are interwoven in an organic whole, it would be illogical to introduce vital reforms in the first phase unless there was an active and well-organized system of adult education.

1.2 Other Aspects of Lifelong Education

Consideration must also be given to other less fundamental aspects of lifelong education, conceived as a process of learning which must meet the needs of each successive phase of life. Firstly, there can be no question of an age limit for education: education is a way of life, or rather a way of being aware of what is happening in the world.

Secondly, and this is very important, the notions of failure and of success lose their significance. It goes without saying that in a system of education which finishes at a certain age and is marked by "initiation rites" consisting of examinations, diplomas, or other forms of selection, those who succeed are cut off from those who do not. Society is thus divided into two groups: the fortunate on the one hand, and the unlucky or unacademic on the other, who thus find themselves labelled for life by often entirely fortuitous circumstances. But if, with the appropriate structures, individuals are engaged in a continuous process of education and are constantly learning something new, then a failure is only relative. If they do not succeed in one particular venture, many other opportunities are open to them in which they can test their abilities. They do not *become* failures, they merely *have had* a failure among others in their lives; in the same way, a success is also relative and only applies to one in a series of undertakings which may or may not prove successful.

The aim is to increase each individual's possibilities of expressing himself or herself on the intellectual, emotional, social, and professional planes, as well as in relationships between the sexes, between parents and children, and so forth. There are countless situations in which people may succeed or fail, but the important thing is that they should have a positive approach to these situations, that they should be vigilant and enquiring, not passive observers. Certainly, selection cannot be entirely ruled out: industrial and commercial firms or administrative enterprises, for example, are not prepared to recruit staff on trust but demand certificates and diplomas. In actual fact, therefore, there is a contradiction which cannot be ignored between the development of lifelong education and the practical necessity for selection. But in the main this is not a problem for educators, but one which must be solved by employers who will have to find their own means of recruiting the men and women they need, on condition that this necessity for selection at a given moment does not have a backlash on general education, which is governed by other imperatives.

1.3 Education for the Development of Personality

Another important consequence of lifelong education is that it will, to a far greater extent than traditional education, reveal the originality of each individual. Human nature is the same the world over, but every human being is unique. People are to a certain extent aware of the need to develop their potentialities and live their life as fully as they can. Consciously or perhaps subconsciously, they strive to free themselves from anonymity and to leave their own imprint on the contributions they make to their environment, to their times, and to the type of civilization of which they are a product. Their contributions only partially reflect and express their personality and cannot represent the rich and varied amalgam of elements which make them unique.

Education at the present time takes no account of this basic factor of human individuality. Under the present system, there is no time for it. Schooling is spread over a fixed span of years and ends at a given age, without taking account, for example, of the fact that individuals of equal intelligence and ability progress at varying rhythms: some may arrive at full maturity by the age of 20 while others may not reach this stage until they are 30 or even later.

An important role is played in this process of depersonalization by examinations and diplomas. The criteria—very often arbitrary—on which they are based were established many years ago to meet the demands of a type of society, of categories of employment, and temperaments and casts of mind that are by no means universal. In school, the criterion is not the individual, with his/her biological, psychological, sociological, historical, and geographical characteristics, but whether he/she is a good or bad pupil. These evaluations are very superficial and neglect the day-to-day realities and laws of individual development.

In each succesive stage of life, through various trials, in relationships with others and private reflections, human beings reveal their true originality, unless they are subjected to the tyranny of more forceful patterns such as those imposed in school. Only a small minority can adapt to the accepted—and very restrictive—intellectual patterns which do not take full account of the real resources of the mind.

When lifelong education becomes a reality, it will be possible to offer greater scope to each individual human being, to be less ruthless and tyrannical, and to provide for the needs of a greater diversity of people.

1.4 Lifelong Education and Modern Thought

Through the process of lifelong education, each individual will be able to benefit from some of the outstanding advances in modern thought that have occurred since the early nineteenth century, including such concepts as historicity, scientific thought, and relativity.

Historicity implies an awareness that the elements of knowledge are not revelations, nor can philosophic reasoning be taken as fact; that knowledge is a series of conquests but that all advances in knowledge are subject to revision.

Secondly, there is the scientific approach, the spirit of discovery, of constant questioning. The scientist who undertakes an investigation does not know at the start what he or she will find. For him or her the main interest lies not in gaining knowledge but, once he or she has discovered a fragment of truth, in recognizing it as provisional and in proceeding on the basis of that discovery. In contrast to the dogmatic attitude, the scientific approach consists of never formulating a judgment without verifying the facts. It is diametrically opposed to the search for security, which refuses to study problems afresh, seeks to avoid risk, demands ready-made answers, and evades fundamental questions. Countless men and women are educated to go through life accumulating answers and basing their attitude on accepted opinions. This is the antithesis of the scientific spirit, which readily admits the possibility of risk, including that of being mistaken.

Thirdly, the process of lifelong education must include the notion of relativity which is the natural consequence of the development of historicity and of scientific approach. Since truth and reasoning are the products of an historical process and all knowledge is provisional and subject to constant revision and verification, the notion of the "absolute" becomes singularly restricted. Education should systematically inculcate in each individual the idea that beliefs, convictions, ideologies, habits, and customs are not universal patterns or rules applicable for all time and in any civilization or way of life.

Lifelong education therefore can and must assimilate these essential conquests of modern thought and introduce them into the thinking and actions of each individual.

Due to the lack of training, many people are unprepared to rise to their full stature and devote all their energies to seeking new solutions. They do not seem to realize that the main interest of life lies in this search. Through lifelong education, it will eventually be possible for everyone to acquire this mental faculty, this attitude towards life and truth. Compared with present adult education programmes, particularly in their more limited interpretation, this is obviously a far richer and broader concept. It is an entirely new view and interpretation of the educational process and even—on a higher plane—of human destiny, which projects the notion of a continuous struggle for self-conquest as a substitute for that of allowing oneself to be lulled into a sense of false security. It is also a guide for future action, because the principles of lifelong education offer clear orientations for the educational reforms which must be made if such action is to be vigorous, intelligent, and constructive. Lastly, it is the concept of education which will enable people effectively to fulfill their destiny in the true spirit of modern thinking.

2. How the Concept was Accepted

The set of proposals for reshaping the educational system was developed and defined during the 1960s. The International Conference on Adult Education held in Montreal in 1960 shed light on the necessity to situate adult education within the global context of education continued throughout life. However, the meeting of the International Consultative Committee on Adult Education in 1965 can be considered as a key event. On the basis of a document prepared by UNESCO secretariat, the Committee formulated a series of proposals referring to lifelong education, which were well-received, extended to, and specified in, many educational spheres.

During the ensuing period, reference to the concept met with many reservations, if not hostile attitudes. Some educators expressed the view that lifelong education was nothing more than a new term to designate adult education and that its use led to confusion. Others, while recognizing the rationality underlying the concept, looked upon it as Utopian, reaching far beyond the possibilities of implementation of a great number of countries.

In spite of these negative reactions, the constructive aspects of this new approach to education were extensively recognized in an astonishingly rapid way. Much resistance lost ground and general acceptance of the idea became evident. Already in 1970 the General Assembly of UNESCO proposed the adoption of lifelong education as an interpretation of the process of education as a whole and recommended it to member states as a general guideline for the implementation of necessary reforms. Since that time, lifelong education is constantly referred to in all areas of the educational programme of the organization. In 1973, the International Commission on Development of Education, after analyzing the world situation, issued a series of recommendations on activities to be undertaken. In the chapter of the final report entitled "Elements for Contemporary Strategies", it is noteworthy that the first principle was formulated in these terms: "Every individual must be in a position to keep learning throughout his life. The idea of lifelong education is the keystone of the learning society." Then followed principles concerning the strategies to be adopted, which constitute an elaboration of this initial statement.

Since that time, the concept of lifelong education has spread to all educational spheres and it is, nowadays, a normal practice for educators, administrators, and official bodies dealing in educational matters to refer readily to this notion. Already the written material on lifelong education occupies numerous shelves in specialized libraries. It is evident that from the theoretical point of view the principle has progressed considerably, but in practice the situation is less impressive. Undoubtedly numerous activities can be quoted, along with projects and experiences which are more or less in conformity with the spirit of lifelong education. However, in most cases, the interest manifested by the authorities of many countries has gone no further than lip-service. Nevertheless it is too early to draw up an inventory of the concrete results in this field, but it does not appear that the set of traditional structures has in fact been substantially modified. It is obvious that the necessary reforms in structures and changes in methods cannot be achieved without constant battle against vested interests, attachment to tradition, and fear of innovation.

See also: Lifelong Education: Research Strategies; Recurrent Education

Bibliography

Council of Europe 1970 *Permanent Education: A Compendium of Studies Commissioned by the Council for Cultural Cooperation.* Council of Europe, Strasbourg

Faure E, Herrera F, Kaddoura A-R, Lopes H, Petrovsky A V, Rahnema M, Ward F C 1972 *Learning to Be: The World of Education Today and Tomorrow.* UNESCO, Paris

Husén T 1974 *The Learning Society.* Methuen, London

Lengrand P 1970 *An Introduction to Lifelong Education.* UNESCO, Paris

Lifelong Education: Interaction with Adult Education

A. J. Cropley

Acceptance of the principle that education should be available during the entire life cycle (i.e., to adults and not merely to children), and that this access should be practicable (i.e., it should be genuinely possible for adults to engage in systematic learning experiences from time to time during their postschool lives), raises the question of how this state of affairs is to be achieved—what structural, organizational, administrative, and procedural characteristics of organized education would be necessary for the facilitation of lifelong learning?

1. New Educational Demands

The idea that education should last the life of each individual is by no means new. Extended modern discussions appeared in English in about 1920, while writings in both the Middle Ages and also in ancient times often stressed the importance of continuing to learn throughout the adult years. Lifelong education is thus in principle an old idea. Nonetheless, it seems that there are special conditions of modern life which give it a new urgency. These arise out of what Coombs (1982 p. 145) called the "crisis" of modern education: the dimensions of this crisis include emergence of new learning needs as a result of changed patterns of work and recreation or of changes in the nature of job qualifications, increased emphasis on the contribution of education to self-fulfilment and self-realization, and a recognition that democratization of education and equality of opportunity cannot be achieved if systematic support of learning is confined to childhood. It is also apparent that the traditional "front end" model, according to which people are loaded with all they will ever need to know during an intensive preparation in childhood, is financially impossible in poorer nations and is, in any case, inappropriate in settings where large segments of the already adult population, who provide the work force for modernization of the nation's way of life, do not possess an adequate level of basic education (as for instance in many less developed states). The reasons why learning in the adult years is receiving increased emphasis are thus partly practical and concrete (vocational, financial, and so on), and partly idealistic or "moral" (democratization, equality, and the like).

2. Learning in Adulthood

Of course, adult education already exists. Indeed since most lifelong learning is carried out by adults, for the simple reason that most people spend much more of their lives as adults than as children, it is obvious that adult education would be a major element in a system of lifelong education. At one time, it was even assumed that the two terms were virtually synonyms (e.g., Cross 1981). However, it is now apparent that the implementation of lifelong education would require considerably more than simply the extension of conventional adult education to a wider audience: participation rates in existing adult education are relatively low, while it also suffers both from a tendency to be dominated by the values and methods of school as well as from stigmatization as being either recreational or remedial in nature.

Key principles in lifelong education, by contrast, are that procedures for fostering lifelong learning are an integral part of any education system, with status equal to that of other elements such as schools and universities, and that such learning should be naturally and normally engaged in by all adults—universal education for adults is seen as just as important as universal education for children. The relevant definitive characteristics of lifelong education have been summarized by Dave (1973). They include (a) totality and universality in settings covered and clientele served; (b) dynamism and diversity in teaching and learning methods and materials; (c) focus on promotion in learners of the personal characteristics necessary for lifelong learning (motivation, self-image, values, attitudes, and the like). The central theme of the present article can thus be restated as being that of how to implement forms of adult education having these properties.

3. *Role of School*

It is important to make clear at once that the promotion of lifelong learning would not be a matter of extension of the values, goals, methods, materials, and organizational forms of traditional schools to the entire lifespan. Such "educational imperialism" (Karpen 1980) would lead to the prospect of school "for the term of one's natural life". While it is, in any case, absurd to imagine all adults returning to school, and also financially impossible (especially in less highly developed societies), there are grounds for believing that traditional school learning procedures do not match the special characteristics of adults as learners. This means that the implementation of lifelong education would necessitate changes in traditional institutions.

Although it has already been pointed out that lifelong education cannot be equated with schooling, while most lifelong learning will be done by adults, schools would nonetheless be expected to have a special role in any system of lifelong education (see Cropley 1977 for a detailed discussion). Psychologically speaking, this role would consist of helping pupils develop the knowledge, skills, attitudes, values, and self-image necessary for lifelong learning (personal prerequisites)—implicit in this point of view is the belief that most schools do not already do this.

4. *"Integration" of Learning Settings*

From the organizational point of view, what is needed are "vertical" and "horizontal integration". Essentially, these two principles mean that learning experiences should be presented as (a) part of a chain of learning, which commenced in the past and stretches ahead unbroken into the future (vertical integration or articulation); and (b) as part of a network of learning which stretches out laterally into other settings (horizontal integration). These embrace not only obviously "educational" settings such as libraries, museums, zoos, and the like, but also the home, work, recreation and hobbies, clubs, societies, churches, union halls, meeting rooms of political parties, even possibly such unlikely places as sports fields or bars. In other words, the relationship between formal learning and both "nonformal" and "informal" learning (Coombs and Ahmed 1974) is stressed.

Although it is apparent that the contribution of school-level education to lifelong learning would not be insignificant, the present article concentrates on learning in the adult years. It could be conceptualized as concerned with the question of how adult education could be incorporated into a system devoted to lifelong learning. In particular, the emphasis here is on how to link up all learning experiences available to adults—how to achieve vertical and horizontal integration. It is important to remember that this integration is not simply an end in itself, but is a necessary step in the achievement of a system of lifelong education. The importance of vertical integration is obvious, since without it lifelong education would not be lifelong. Emphasis on links among learning experiences in many settings, what might be called "lifewide" learning, is not simply an association with the word "life" in the expression "lifelong education". On the contrary, horizontal linkage is an essential precondition for lifelong learning, since, as has already been pointed out, learning in the postschool years could not be exclusively based on traditional institutions, despite the undoubted importance of their role.

5. *Role of Adult Education*

Emphasis on the importance of learning in ages beyond the traditional school years implies an important role for adult education: this encompasses clientele, settings, teaching and learning methods, evaluation procedures, and many more. The role would be partly remedial—helping to overcome the inability or unwillingness of many adults to engage in systematic, purposeful learning. Previous paragraphs have already indicated what this would mean for the learners: not only development of appropriate skills and knowledge, but also of attitudes, values, self-image, motives, and the like. The task confronting adult education is that of changing itself so that it provides experiences for learners which lead naturally to increased interest, positive motivation, self-confidence, and similar properties. In other words, it should set in motion an "avalanche effect" (Suchodolski 1979).

6. *Making Adult Education "Lifewide"*

One major task is that of linking adult education with people's day-to-day lives. Not only is such a linkage important in overcoming unwillingness or lack of interest on the part of learners, but it is also a practical necessity—a prerequisite for lifelong learning. This is seen here as having several aspects.

6.1 Institutional Issues

A great deal of learning by adults takes place outside traditional "educational" settings, not only at the place of work, but also in the bosom of the family, in clubs or societies, during leisure activities, and many more. As Tough (1971) pointed out, adults engage in large numbers of "learning projects". Adult education would make an enormous contribution to the fostering of lifelong learning if it succeeded in finding ways of acknowledging, legitimizing, and strengthening learning in such settings (always bearing in mind the rejection of imposition of school-like values and norms, which has repeatedly been emphasized). At the organizational level, this would present great challenges, requiring coordination of the work of different kinds of institutions, often with well-established traditions of independence, and cooperation among teachers, not only professionals (conventional teachers) and semiprofessionals (librarians, museum staff), but even "amateurs" (people who possess and pass on valuable knowledge or skills, usually without seeing themselves as teaching). At the moment, both institutions and individuals often view each other with suspicion or condescension.

6.2 Teaching and Learning Activities

Linking learning in many settings could not be achieved, short of enschooling all learning, through exclusive reliance on conventional teaching and learning activities. On the other hand, the call for new approaches in this area should not be trivialized to mean the conducting of classes in adult education under unconventional conditions, such as by arranging chairs in a circle. Similarly, although democratization of decision making, joint planning of content, the holding of "post mortems" on courses, and the like, are all worthwhile changes, they do not go far enough. The danger also exists that they will simply allow a few confident individuals to dominate, especially those with strong opinions or fixed ideologies, and will actually leave most would-be learners feeling frustrated or dissatisfied. Needed are approaches which permit the learners to identify problems or needs, to pace themselves, to evaluate their own efforts, and the like.

This suggests that special procedures such as distance education, self-directed learning or self-evaluation would be of particular importance. Such activities have the advantage that they would permit learners to move at their own pace, work when and where they wanted to, choose materials more closely attuned to their own special needs, and so on, while also tending to discourage enschooling. In the present context such procedures can also be seen as ways of coping with organizational problems involved in achieving totality and universality, and pedagogical/psychological problems involving promotion of the personal prerequisites for lifelong learning.

6.3 Content

Links with learning in different settings, especially day-to-day life, also have implications for the choice of subject matter. Once again, this should not be trivialized as meaning simply that people should be asked what they are interested in, or what they want to learn. What it does mean is that even conventional subject matter should be taught with an emphasis on relevance to work, family, leisure, and similar activities. This would not only make a contribution to developing attitudes according to which learning and subject matter are regarded as part of a lifewide network, but would also help the growth of positive feelings about learning itself, and about oneself as a learner, by linking classroom learning to settings in which adults feel competent and knowledgeable.

6.4 Credentialing

Despite the tendency to regard any kind of evaluation procedure as inimical to effective teaching and learning, it is clear that a large number of adult learners see some form of evaluation as the hallmark of a worthwhile learning experience. For those who wish to acquire some saleable knowledge or skill, some kind of credential may be absolutely necessary. Thus, evaluation and the issuing of credentials may be vital elements of adult education in the perspective of lifelong education—indeed, it is difficult to see how coordination among learning settings could be achieved without some system of credentialing, so that it may be a prerequisite for horizontal integration. It is crucial, nonetheless, that credentials do not derive their legitimacy from the setting in which they were obtained, but from the knowledge or skills which have been acquired, while it is also essential that they be portable or transferable in the sense that they are recognized in many settings. Otherwise, they would not facilitate linkages between learning settings, but would impede them.

7. Some Existing Practices and Trends

Although the principle of lifelong education has not been unreservedly accepted by all adult educators, or has been misunderstood by some as simply a grander name for what already exists, a number of practices and trends of kinds which would be favourable to the emergence of an integrated system of adult education in the framework of lifelong education already exist. Nonetheless, it must be admitted that many of these were developed without reference to lifelong education.

7.1 Development of "Open Learning"

The British Open University is probably the best known example of open learning, and one which now has parallels in many parts of the world. Openness also takes somewhat different forms, for example a school in Oslo where subject matter is decided by teachers and pupils, parents and other adults attend lessons, classes may be held at unorthodox times, and so on. It may also refer to open entry requirements, where entry to formal programmes is decided on the basis of existing knowledge and skills, not on the possession of formal certificates.

7.2 Contribution of "Noneducational" Agencies

In many countries agencies and institutions with either no obvious educational function or only a marginal such function are beginning to play an increasing role in adult education. These include corporations, government ministries, state-owned industries, professional associations, foundations, and similar bodies, which offer courses, issue credentials, publish learning materials, engage in public education programmes, and the like.

7.3 Expansion of Noncredit Courses

Formal institutions of higher education are making an increasing contribution to lifelong adult education by offering learning opportunities outside their traditional degree structures. In some countries traditional institutions are becoming centres of learning for a much wider range of learners than is usually the case—to take an example, a teachers' college which has students from the age of 12 or 14 up to the 90s, who may be secondary school pupils, trainee teachers, civil servants taking a retraining course, or old people keeping their minds alert, all attending some common classes, some for credit, some out of general interest, some in order to obtain a promotion at work.

7.4 Localization of Decision Making

Adult education activities are more frequently coming to be linked directly with existing community decision-making processes and procedures. What courses are offered may be decided on the basis of concrete community needs, while many of the teaching staff may be enlisted on an ad hoc basis as special expertise becomes necessary. An example is an adult education programme in which a well was built for a village by students and teachers.

7.5 Provision of Information to Learners

One possible problem for potential learners in adult education is their lack of information about the array of learning opportunities which are available, or about the possibilities of linking their past learning with present or future further opportunities—in other words, their need for information and counselling. Various ways of meeting this need are emerging, including information networks, newsletters and forums, and brokering services.

7.6 Provision of Financial Aid

The best-known form of such aid is probably paid educational leave, although other forms such as repayment of course fees, accommodation costs, and the like to learners by employers or government, or even direct rewards to successful participants in learning activities are becoming more common.

Although these are merely examples of appropriate activities, while their emergence owed, in some cases, nothing to the literature on lifelong education, they show that adult education is developing in directions capable of giving it a genuine place in systems of lifelong education.

Bibliography

Coombs P H 1982 Critical world educational issues of the next two decades. *Int. Rev. Educ.* 28: 143–57

Coombs P H, Ahmed M 1974 *Attacking Rural Poverty: How Nonformal Education can Help.* Johns Hopkins University Press, Baltimore, Maryland

Cropley A J 1977 *Lifelong Education: A Psychological Analysis.* Pergamon, Oxford

Cross K P 1981 *Adults as Learners: Increasing Participation and Facilitating Learning.* Jossey Bass, San Francisco, California

Dave R H 1973 *Lifelong Education and School Curriculum: Interim Findings of an Exploratory Study on School Curriculum Structures and Teacher Education in the Perspective of Lifelong Education.* UNESCO Institute for Education, Hamburg

Karpen U 1980 Implementing lifelong education and the law. In: Cropley A J (ed.) 1980 *Towards a System of Lifelong Education: Some Practical Considerations.* Pergamon, Oxford, pp. 31–66

Suchodolski B 1979 Lifelong education at the cross-roads. In: Cropley A J (ed.) 1979 *Lifelong Education: A Stock-taking.* UNESCO Institute for Education, Hamburg, pp. 36–49

Tough A 1971 *The Adult's Learning Projects: A Fresh Approach to Theory and Practice in Adult Learning.* Ontario Institute for Studies in Education, Toronto, Ontario

The Field of Adult Education

Introduction

This subsection is concerned with the informing principles and expressions of those activities and processes called adult education, rather than other names.

One of the principal difficulties in reconciling theories of, and relating to, adult education has lain in the variety and looseness of definition of the terms used to denote it and other linked activities. Problems of communication, significant enough because of differences of thought, have been compounded by terminology, which has often created misunderstandings, not only between persons speaking different languages, but between people whose language is the same. The article *Concepts and Definitions* examines the scope and nature of this problem and considers the lexigraphical work, sponsored by several organizations, to facilitate international understanding and communication, and what may be learned from it.

To fit the specific circumstances of adults, different approaches to teaching and learning from those appropriate to children and adolescents have been and are being continually devised. These are discussed in the article *Andragogy*, the term which is used to denote the art of educating adults and the study of theory, processes, and technology to that end. Widely used in some, particularly European, countries, it has been strongly resisted in others. In the United States it has been adopted to signify a specific philosophy of adult education.

The topic of curriculum is one that has been neglected in adult education until recently. It is here considered from two different points of view. *Content, Purpose, and Practice* explores the relationship between those three elements of an educational experience, to bring out the complex interrelationships of institutions in society which lie behind adult teaching and learning processes, while *Curriculum* draws attention to opposition that has traditionally existed within adult education to developing curricular strategies and examines both the contemporary pressures to submit to more formal curricula and the conflicts with deep-rooted adult education principles that have to be resolved. Discussion in *Ideologies in Adult Education* focuses on the shaping of provision by social and political ideas, particularly in terms of the conflict between liberal and instrumental education.

Since 1945 the most effective single agency for the encouragement of adult education throughout the world has probably been UNESCO. It has not only sponsored projects, particularly in developing nations, but the UNESCO World Conferences in Adult Education have been potent occasions for urging policy makers to action and suggesting guidelines for it. It has always been difficult to obtain a generally agreed definition of adult education. The most widely accepted is the one to be found in the UNESCO Recommendations on Adult Education, which was adopted at the 1976 session of the General Conference.

Concepts and Definitions

D. J. Ironside

This article discusses the emergence and growth of the professional language of adult education. The multidisciplinary nature of the field and its practitioners creates many problems in international communication. It is only recently that the concept of adult education as a discrete sector of education has been recognized in many countries; even today some societies view the education and training of their citizens from the perspective of the function such training performs or the class to which participants belong; for example, trade union education or working class education.

With the emergence of mass communication and computer technology, information sharing among professionals engaged in the education of adults has multiplied rapidly, forcing some rationalization in the technical language of the field. UNESCO's World Conferences on Adult Education and the UNESCO/International Bureau of Education's International Consultations on Adult Education Documentation have made major contributions to the international acceptance of many definitions of key concepts in the study and practice of adult education. As in all other fields, the language will continue to evolve and develop as the profession matures.

1. The Language of Adult Education

All professions develop languages which facilitate communication among their members. To people outside the profession, such languages may appear highly technical, specialized, even incomprehensible; sometimes the language is denigrated as "jargon". Yet the professional terms and the concepts they represent are the tools of a profession's trade, used to transmit information and to develop new knowledge. The languages become shared by all new entrants to the profession, mainly through the medium of professional education, and professional schools in many cultures will teach common concepts and use common technical terms to express those concepts.

Adult education is different in some respects from the more traditional professions in the development of its language. The profession has been growing most rapidly in the years since the Second World War and so has its language, although such important concepts as "cooperative extension" have been part of the language for much longer. The practitioners of adult education during this period of rapid growth did not have a homogeneous background; unlike lawyers, doctors, and engineers, the professional education of these practitioners of the 1940s and 1950s was extremely varied. They gained entrance to the profession more through their practice than through a background in educational theory. No certification or examinations were required to become a member, nor are any required today to be an adult educator. These workers brought into their practice the concepts and terminology of their own academic background and their previous work experience; as they began to communicate with one another, they traded concepts and ideas. So the professional language grew from diverse origins and took on meanings common in daily use.

2. The Problem of Communication

When the universities began to teach adult education as a field of graduate study, as early as 1930 in North America (Jenson et al. 1964) but later in other parts of the world, the process of absorbing the ideas and concepts used by practitioners into the study of adult education became more systematic. The multidisciplinary roots and the applied nature of adult education practice forced its practitioners and researchers to borrow theories and ideas from such fields as psychology even more than from pedagogy: this borrowing further expanded the terminology of adult education. As the field and the language developed and grew, they absorbed a flood of new concepts from business administration, organization development, operations research, and psychotherapy, thereby heightening the polyglot nature of this applied field of practice.

When communicating with practitioners even within one country, problems arose in explaining the nature of the adult educator's task to the public, to legislators and policy makers, to government officials, and to other professions and groups. These problems became compounded when adult educators attempted to share experiences and ideas with practitioners in other countries and cultures. In the 1950s and 1960s, adult education in developing countries grew rapidly and technical assistance programmes at the national and international level were an important means of sharing adult education experience. Yet so often the lack of an internationally accepted or understood language of practice impeded the fullest sharing of that experience. The need to overcome some of these barriers to communication became critical as computer technology matured and made high-speed international information sharing a distinct possibility, even in fields with such imprecise and multilayered languages as the behavioural and social sciences, including adult education.

3. The Nature of the Language

3.1 The Concept of Adult Education

For many decades, educators have argued about the concept, the meaning, and the use of the term "adult education" and terms related to it. Many countries have had no concept of adult education as a distinctive sector of education, if it were to be conceived as a sector whose public, adults, is defined in terms of age, maturity, or whether persons have terminated their initial education. Countries or languages lacking such a concept described educational provision for adults from many different perspectives. For example, from the perspective of class, such terms as *éducation populaire, Volksbildung*, "people's or popular education", "*scuola popolare*, people's school" were used. Such terms as "vocational education", "trade union education", "social education", "citizenship education", described the concept in terms of function. Other terms were seen from the perspective of initial education, for example, "*Weiterbildung*", "further education", "continuing education", and "*formation continue*".

The use of age as the determining factor of whether one is an adult is a contentious issue. When adulthood is reached depends on a person's particular culture, social or economic responsibilities, and the legal system in place. To educators, however, what matters is to be able to assist individuals to mature, to engage in and enjoy adult behaviour, to be autonomous and self-directing persons. Such a process has little to do with chronological age. In some societies with a requirement for a compulsory school attendance, once individuals reach a particular age, they attend school on a voluntary basis and thereby could be considered adults. In other societies, adult education is seen as outside the elementary, secondary, and tertiary systems entirely, whatever the age of attenders. Many writers have attempted to define adult education as a process unrelated to age, whereby persons who have terminated their initial cycle of continuous education may undertake any "sequential and organized activities with the conscious intention of bringing about changes in information, knowledge, understanding, or skills, appreciation, and attitudes" (Liveright and Haygood 1968 p. 8).

> In everyday life, however, the expression, "adult education", is often used in another sense, as a collective term covering the institutions and procedures by which adults are enabled and encouraged to experience the process. For many people, this mechanism is adult education. (Titmus 1980 p. 135)

That is what is meant when one refers to Hungarian adult education, or public adult education.

The General Conference of UNESCO in 1976 may have settled much of the confusion through having a General Recommendation on the Development of Adult Education accepted unanimously by representatives from 142 countries. It included the following definition:

> The term, "adult education", denotes the entire body of organized educational processes, whatever the content, level, and method, whether formal or otherwise, or whether they prolong or replace initial education in schools, colleges, and universities, as well as an apprenticeship, whereby persons regarded as adult by the society to which they belong develop their abilities, enrich their knowledge, improve their technical or professional qualifications, or turn them in a new direction and bring about changes in their attitudes or behaviour in the two-fold perspective of full personal development and participation in balanced and independent social, economic, and cultural development. (UNESCO 1976)

3.2 Broader/Wider Concepts

Many concepts closely related to adult education, used in the literature since the early 1960s, continue to be subject to controversy. These include "formal", "nonformal", "informal", "lifelong learning", "lifelong education", "continuing education", and "recurrent education".

In some countries the term "nonformal education" has been used, as "social education" formerly was used, as a synonym for adult education, but this is not a fully acceptable practice since the term can and should be applied equally to children and youth. In an earlier period in North America the term "informal education" was applied almost as an equivalent of adult education but that usage has almost disappeared. Instead, now that a considerable part of adult education is formal, there is increasing pressure for more precise use of three terms: formal, nonformal, and informal education as they apply to children, youth, and adults so that all of them can describe the components of a total and integrated system of education. The term "formal education" is used to describe the hierarchically structured, chronologically graded system, from primary school through university and including, in addition to general academic studies, a variety of specialized programmes and institutions for full-time teaching and professional training. Informal education is the lifelong process whereby all individuals acquire attitudes, values, skills, and knowledge from daily experience and from the educative influences and resources in their environment—from family and neighbours, from work and play, from the marketplace, the library, and the mass media. Nonformal education could be defined as any organized educational activity outside of the established formal system—whether operating separately or as an important feature of some broader activity—that is intended to serve identifiable learning clienteles and learning objectives.

The term "lifelong learning" is used internationally, but still lacks a commonly accepted definition. Cross describes the term as, "slippery, strikingly inconsistent, and subject to varying interpretations" (1981 p. 253). Another more narrowly conceived definition appears in the reports prepared by the Lifelong Learning Project (1978). "Lifelong learning refers to the process by which individuals continue to develop their knowledge, skills, and attitudes over their lifetimes" (1978 p. 1). Other writers describe the concept variously, from meaning "anything you want it to mean" (Richardson 1979 p. 48), to being "a banner for a movement around which various educational and social interests have rallied" (Green et al. 1977 p. 3).

Gross says that:

> Lifelong learning means self-directed growth. It means understanding yourself and the world. It means acquiring new skills and powers—the only true wealth which you can never lose. It means investment in yourself. Lifelong learning means the joy of discovering how something really works, the delight of becoming aware of some new beauty in the world, the fun of creating something, alone or with other people. (1977 p. 16)

"Lifelong education", although used often as a synonym for "lifelong learning", should more properly refer to the organized provision of opportunities for persons to learn throughout their lives. Delker makes the distinction between adult learning "as a major continuing mode of behaviour", and adult education as the "organized and sequential learning experiences designed to meet the needs of adults" (1974 p. 24). Likewise, lifelong learning is the habit of continuously learning throughout life, a mode of behaviour, whereas lifelong education is "the principle on which the overall organization of a system is founded" (Faure et al. 1972 p. 182). Dave integrates the characteristics of the concept into what may be the most satisfactory description:

> Lifelong education seeks to view education in its totality. It covers formal, nonformal, and informal patterns of education, and attempts to integrate and articulate all structures and stages of education along the vertical (temporal) and horizontal (spatial) dimensions. It is also characterized by flexibility in time, place, content, and techniques of learning and hence calls for self-directed learning, sharing of one's enlightenment with others, and adopting varied learning styles and strategies. (1976 pp. 35–36)

"Continuing education" is another broad term about whose meaning there is little agreement. Thomas provides a very broad definition:

> It is a system(s) of education which includes formal and nonformal education, that is defined with respect to its various parts and agencies (elementary schools, secondary schools, colleges, and universities, for example) in terms of specific educational objectives to be fostered, rather than in terms of the ages or circumstances of learners. The system is available to persons of any age, part-time or full-time, voluntary or compulsory, and is financed by a mixture of private and public resources. It is distinguished from other educational activities in the society by the possession of the exclusive right to provide public recognition or certification for those completing its programs, though not all of its programs need lead to such certification. (1981 p. 8)

It would not be agreed in all countries, however, that the system possesses the exclusive right to provide certification. A much more restricted definition of this concept has been posed in terms of its function:

> The envisaged function of continuing education is that of rounding off the individual's education, of providing further education or of retraining, so that, for example, the individual can always meet increased or new professional demands. (Houghton and Richardson 1974 p. 9).

In the early 1970s, yet another general term came into use, first in Europe: "recurrent education" was coined to lend a more precise meaning to the concept of *éducation permanente*. It was conceived as a "comprehensive educational strategy for all post-compulsory or post-basic education over the total lifespan of the individual in a recurring way, i.e., in alternation with other activities, principally with work, but also with leisure and retirement" (OECD/CERI 1973 p. 24). Another definition has been offered by Houghton and Richardson:

> Recurrent education is a lifelong process consisting of a discontinuous, periodic participation in educational programmes aimed at gradually dissolving the blocks of compulsory education and working life (front-end model). (1974 p. 7)

These definitions with their overlapping tendencies and their lack of precision illustrate the phenomena of erosion of meaning and geographic specificity. Some writers use "continuing education" to mean "continuing higher (university level) education", others use "recurrent education" as a synonym for "continuing education", or "lifelong education" to signify "adult education". These habits, which function to impede communication internationally, may be modified in the near future.

4. Efforts to Enhance Communication

In the early 1960s, it became increasingly obvious to many national and international agencies that this evidence of increased controversy around the terminology of the field, as well as the growth in the research literature, demanded effective mechanisms for communicating research and field experience internationally. A first step in developing a standard terminology was taken in 1964 when a United States Office of Education research grant was awarded to Syracuse University to design a computer information system for adult education (DeCrow et al. 1968). In 1967, this project became part of the Education Resources Information Center (ERIC) network just then being established. The project staff contributed its work on a standard adult education terminology to the ERIC thesaurus. ERIC set up the first Clearinghouse on Adult Education at Syracuse University (now at Ohio State University) and the field has benefited greatly from its services and publications.

In 1972, the third UNESCO Conference on Adult Education in Tokyo recommended that UNESCO should "establish, in order to promote information and knowledge about adult education, national institutes of adult education to act as national documentation centres and clearinghouses for information on adult education at both national and international levels" (UNESCO 1972). The following year, UNESCO's Division of Adult Education and the International Bureau of Education convened a consultation:

> to discuss means of improving international collaboration among documentation centres serving adult education, and through development of mutual exchange of services to lead to the eventual formation of an international network of documentation centres in the field of adult education. (UNESCO/IBE 1973)

This consultation was the first of four meetings devoted to studying methods for strengthening exchange of information. These discussions included the formation of national and regional documentation centres/libraries; the publishing of national and international directories of centres, associations, and journals; the preparation of an international abstracting service, and the standards for an international computerized information system including such elements as an adult education thesaurus for use in indexing the literature.

At the 1976 meeting, consultation members agreed that it was very important to develop a dictionary or glossary of terms currently used in adult education; its purpose was "to give, in international languages, the principal terms used specifically in adult education and more general terms given some particular meaning in adult education.... The aim of the work is to provide adult educators in all countries with the basic list of terms so as to facilitate communication" (UNESCO/IBE 1976). For several years prior to 1976, two organizations had been attempting to compile comparative lists of terms: the International Congress of University Adult Education (ICUAE) and the European Bureau of Adult Education. The Bureau's glossary, first published in a provisional edition in 1976, contains a trilingual list of nearly 500 terms used in European adult education, in English, French, and German. Its success has been such that a second, enlarged, edition appeared in 1980. The work of ICUAE, begun in 1973, was brought into the UNESCO/IBE project in 1976 and a panel of four editors was set up to continue developing a glossary with definitions in three of UNESCO's official languages—English, French, and Spanish. In 1979, the *Terminology of Adult Education* (Titmus et al. 1979) was published, extracts from which have been reproduced in the appendix to this *Handbook*; work is underway to add Russian, Arabic, and Chinese terms to the glossary.

This glossary represents the first attempt on an international level to provide a dictionary of the field of adult education; UNESCO plans to update it periodically. In its present form, it is designed for use by readers of any of the languages covered; parity of treatment is accorded to all three languages. Descriptions of the terms rather than strict definitions are given, with the emphasis being on the way the terms are used in practice. If concepts were considered somewhat abstract, concrete examples of their use are given. Throughout the glossary, the intention was to record existing use rather than to indicate preferred terms or meanings.

5. *Problems of Definition and Translation*

Some idea of the problems which arise in translating concepts and terminology may be gained from that part of the UNESCO *Terminology of Adult Education* in which the editors examine the variations in meaning of certain basic terms and the difficulties of finding equivalents in other languages, even when, as in that volume, they are comparatively closely related languages, belonging to European cultures.

The UNESCO editors begin by noting the distinction between "education" and "training" in English. Most commonly nowadays "training" is subsumed within the broader concept of "education", but in the United Kingdom and some English-speaking countries whose educational tradition derives from the United Kingdom, "training" is considered to be separate from education. "Adult education", therefore, will mean in most contexts, ". . . a process whereby persons who have terminated their initial cycle of continuous education undertake any sequential and organized activities with the conscious intention of bringing about changes in information, knowledge, understanding, or skills, appreciation, and attitudes". In the United Kingdom, however, it sometimes, although by no means always, signifies only that process undertaken for nonvocational purposes.

In French "*éducation*" and "*formation*" would appear from a standard dictionary to have the same meanings as "education" and "training". This is misleading, because in current usage the two terms are interchangeable, for the same thing sometimes "*éducation des adultes*" is used, sometimes "*formation des adultes*", sometimes even "*éducation permanente*" or "*éducation populaire*".

In Spanish "*educación de adultos*" and "*educación continua*" exclude training, for which there are three terms: "*formación*" is employed for "the acquisition of knowledge and attitudes, skills, and behaviour usually associated with a professional field, such as those required by lawyers, medical doctors, educators"; "*capacitación*" denotes "education and training for skilled labour and technical employment", as in "*capacitación vocacional*"; "*entrenamiento*" is usually only used for military training, sports training, and training for unskilled jobs".

In the case of "lifelong education", the editors found that not only is its distinction from "lifelong learning" unclear, but the position is complicated by the existence of other terms, "lifelong integrated learning", "continuous learning", and "permanent education", which may be used as synonyms of either or both. In French the existence of "*éducation permanente*" and "*formation permanente*", and in Spanish of "*educación permanente*" would render translation between the languages comparatively easy, were it not that in all three languages the concept they denote has been eroded. Frequently the terms are used, for example, as synonyms of "adult education".

The two terms "community development" and "community education", although not specific to adult education, are in close relationship to it. In both "community" has the sense of "the inhabitants of a limited urban or rural locality, sharing a sense of group identity and a body of common interests, or having an unrealized potential for group identity and common interests". In Spanish "*desarrollo communitario*" and "*educación communitaria*" derive from and have the meanings of the English, but French has no term enshrining the same concept of community. Either, as in the case of "*animation globale*", the stimulation of all aspects of a community or region to encourage its general development (a more than local dimension) may be covered, or the concept of a geographical group is replaced altogether by one of a socioeconomic group or class. The term "*promotion collective*", for example, is normally employed to denote the process of "improving the conditions of work and advancing the situation and status of the urban or rural working-class".

For "community education", used to mean "the body of social, recreational, cultural, and educational activities organized outside the formal school system for people of all ages, intended to improve the quality of life of the community", the nearest in French are "*animation socio-culturelle*" or "*animation socio-éducative*", which have rather different overtones, emphasizing the method, "animation", which is the favoured one to achieve the process they denote.

"Adulthood" and "ageing" present problems of translation. Unlike "adulthood" and the Spanish, "*edad adulta*" which denotes either the period following adolescence and extending to the end of life, or the state of physiological, psychological, and social maturity which characterizes the period, the French "*âge adulte*" only extends from the end of adolescence to the beginning of old age, and for the second meaning French has no current expression, the nearest being "*état de maturité*".

The English "ageing" means the continuous process of change to which an individual is subject throughout life as a consequence of advancing chronological age, with emphasis in adult education literature usually being placed on the process of decline after the attainment of peak physical and psychological development. Neither French nor Spanish has an equivalent expression. They use "*développement à l'âge adulte*" and "*desarrollo en edad adulta*", which also express as the English "adult development" does, the idea that adult life is a continuous process of change and "growth".

As the editors of the UNESCO terminology remark, the uncertainty reflects reality. "Adult education is a field of activity characterized by diversity and instability. New goals, new forms of action continually appear and modify the content covered by these... terms". It is also true that adult education is more remarkable for its richness than its precision, either of thought or action. Not only is the sense of existing terms eroded, but new terms and concepts proliferate. A list of generally accepted meanings attributed to the vocabulary of adult education might encourage greater exactness of thinking.

A continually updated glossary of terms may therefore be desirable not only for international communication but also for use within countries. The task of compiling the UNESCO terminology was made harder by the absence of a dictionary of adult education terms in any of the languages, English, French, or Spanish, which it contained and by the omission of most adult education terms from standard dictionaries of those languages. Although the lesson has not yet been acted upon in those tongues, there has been some activity in other linguistic areas, for example in Austria and in the socialist countries of Eastern Europe, notably Czechoslovakia. The project, Comparative Research on Organization and Structure of Adult Education in Europe has given considerable attention to terminological questions, both international and within the countries covered by the study.

Not all students of adult education are convinced, however, that such lexicographical activities are either practical or desirable. Dictionaries, it is said, will always lag behind practice and therefore be misleading. Alternatively, it is feared that to pin down terms to a limited number of specific meanings, as dictionaries must do, will in some way restrict the range and suppleness of thought on adult education. In order to achieve necessary clarity in communication it may be necessary to sacrifice equally essential richness. Perhaps linguistics may have something to offer in this dilemma.

Bibliography

Cross K P 1981 *Adults as Learners: Increasing Participation and Facilitating Learning.* Jossey-Bass, San Francisco, California

Dave R H (ed.) 1976 *Foundations of Lifelong Education.* Pergamon Press, New York

DeCrow R, Ironside D J, Miller R 1968 *Adult Education Information Services: Establishment of a Prototype System for a National Adult Education Library: Final Report.* United States Department of Health, Education and Welfare, Washington, DC. ERIC Document No. ED 020 489

Delker P V 1974 Governmental roles in lifelong learning. *J. Res. Dev. Educ.* 7(4): 24–33

European Bureau of Adult Education (EBAE) 1980 *The Terminology of Adult Education/Continuing Education.* EBAE, and the German Adult Education Association, Amersfoort

Faure E, Herrera F, Kaddoura A-R, Lopes H, Petrovsky A V, Rahnema M, Ward F C 1972 *Learning to Be: The World of Education Today and Tomorrow.* UNESCO, Paris

Green T F et al. 1977 *Lifelong Learning and the Educational System: Expansion or Reform?* United States Department of Education, Health and Welfare, Washington, DC

Gross R 1977 *The Lifelong Learner.* Simon and Schuster, New York

Houghton V P, Richardson K (eds.) 1974 *Recurrent Education.* Ward Lock, London

Jensen G E, Liveright A A, Hallenbeck W (eds.) 1964 *Adult Education: Outlines of an Emerging Field of University Study.* Adult Education Association of the United States, Washington, DC

Lifelong Learning Project 1978 *Lifelong Learning and Public Policy.* Report prepared by the Lifelong Learning Project, United States Government Printing Office, Washington, DC

Liveright A A, Haygood N (eds.) 1968 *The Exeter Papers.* Report of the First International Conference on the Comparative Study of Adult Education, Exeter, 1966. Center for the Study of Liberal Education for Adults, Boston University, Boston, Massachusetts

Organisation for Economic Co-operation and Development/Centre for Educational Research and Innovation (OECD/CERI) 1973 *Recurrent Education: A Strategy for Lifelong Learning.* Organisation for Economic Co-operation and Development, Paris

Richardson P L 1979 Lifelong education and politics. In: Gilder J (ed.) 1979 *Policies for Lifelong Education.* Report of the 1979 Assembly, Washington, DC, Jan. 8–10, 1979. American Association of Community and Junior Colleges, Washington, DC

Thomas A M 1981 *New Reflections on a Learning Society.* A Response to the Report "Continuing Education: The Third System." Ontario Institute for Studies in Education, Toronto, Ontario

Titmus C J 1980 Local decision making, private provision and the role of the state in adult education. *Internationales Jahrbuch der Erwachsenenbildung* 8: 133–58

Titmus C J et al. 1979 *Terminology of Adult Education.* UNESCO, Paris

UNESCO 1972 *Third International Conference on Adult Education, 25 July–7 August: Report.* UNESCO, Tokyo

UNESCO 1976 *General Conference, 19th Session Report.* UNESCO, Nairobi

UNESCO/International Bureau of Education 1973 *Meeting of Experts on Documentation and Information Services for Adult Education, Geneva 29 May–1 June: Final Report.* UNESCO, Paris

Andragogy

A. Krajnc

Andragogy has been defined as "...the art and science of helping adults to learn and the study of adult education theory, processes, and technology to that end" (Titmus et al. 1979). It is a neologism formed, by analogy with pedagogy, from the Greek words *andros* (man) and *agein* (to lead), and it means to lead or educate adults. The term was first used by E. Rosenstock in Berlin in 1924 and then in Switzerland in 1951, when it appeared as the title of a book (Hanselmann 1951).

Up to the late 1980s, the term has only achieved general acceptance in a few European countries—Poland, the Federal Republic of Germany, the German Democratic Republic, the Netherlands, Czechoslovakia, and Yugoslavia. It also appears sometimes in other professional literature, for example in UNESCO documents. In English-speaking countries the adoption of the term has on the whole been resisted. Such penetration as it has achieved in the United States has been greatly assisted by Malcolm Knowles's advocacy (Knowles 1980).

The need for a separate term to denote the practice and study of helping adults to learn became apparent when it was widely perceived that the principles and practices of pedagogy, belonging as they did to child and youth education, were not entirely appropriate to the education of adults. Although some knowledge derived from the education of children was equally applicable to adults, there was much that was not. Having passed through childhood development, people followed a further series of physical and psychological developments in adult life. They had status, responsibilities to others, and functions different from those of children; a larger and usually richer body of experience, different motives and learning needs, and a time scale different from that of childhood. It was necessary for the organization of learning experiences to be adapted to adult life, since adult learning was different in degree and, many held, sometimes in kind from the learning of children. Study was required to build up theories and practices adapted to the adult situation. In fact, a new discipline was required, hence the concept of andragogy. If English-speaking countries have resisted the term, it is not that they reject the specificity of adult education, but that they doubt whether education, or any part of its study, such as pedagogy or andragogy, qualifies as a distinct science or discipline.

1. *Andragogical Subdisciplines*

In those countries where usage of the term andragogy is accepted, the diversity of adult education has led to the development of a number of subdisciplines. Basic andragogy, for example, treats the structure of fundamental concepts, principles, and definitions concerning adult education. It usually forms a part of introductory training courses for adult educators. Comparative andragogy, or comparative adult education, is the study of macrosocial variables, across and between countries, which contribute to regional and national differences in adult education processes.

The concept of lifelong learning has given to adult education new perspectives on the methods and means by which people may achieve the knowledge, skills, attitudes, and values necessary to total personal development. The integration of learning with other activities and obligations typical of adult life; the differences of the adult socioeconomic situation from that of children; adults' experience, self-image, readiness to learn, and their attitudes to learning require specific methods of teaching and learning which are the field of andragogical didactics.

In addition to these subdisciplines which cover adult education activity of any kind there are some which relate to specific situations, such as industrial andragogy, military andragogy, social andragogy, penological andragogy, family andragogy, and gerontological andragogy.

Andragogy has not yet evolved its own research methods. For the most part it uses the standard ones of the social sciences. The classical experimental method is, however, more rare than in school research, no doubt because adults, as free agents, are less easily manipulated and have less time to give to researchers than children at school. It is also true that whereas cognitive learning may be adequately measured, it has not been possible to observe and evaluate accurately the affective learning outcomes of adult education by methods now in use. Since adult education is largely directed at achieving changes in feelings, values, and attitudes, this is a serious weakness.

2. *Andragogical Definition of an Adult*

There is little agreement in adult education literature on what constitutes an adult. Some authors bring in other disciplines to help solve the problem. Some hold that one becomes an adult at a certain age, usually 18 or 21, according to country. Others use psychological criteria, defining an adult as one who is emotionally, socially, and intellectually mature. This approach is sometimes complicated by linking maturity to social and economic status, so that young people still pursuing their initial education, at whatever age, are not considered adults.

For andragogy all these approaches are inadequate. In some countries persons under 18 years of age enrol in adult education programmes because they have finished school. Personal maturity is not an absolute state, reached once and for all, but more a lifelong process conditioned by personal and social needs. In any case, an immature person may have more need of adult education than a mature one. It makes more sense, for the purposes of andragogy, to define adulthood in terms of a person's relation to the educational process, since it also permits a clear definition in relation to pedagogy. Pedagogy is concerned with those for whom education is the primary or central activity or social role (children and adolescents); andragogy is concerned with the education of those who have completed or interrupted their initial education, in order to take part in other major activities or take on other social roles. These are then, by definition, adults (Ogrizović 1966).

3. The Andragogical Cycle

The rigid centralized planning of the formal educational system in some European countries, and the uniformity of timetables and curricula in schools have been much criticized, notably by John Holt and Ivan Illich. They have also been generally seen as quite inappropriate to adults. Indeed, in the early years of its evolution during the 1950s and 1960s, andragogy developed to some degree as a direct reaction against the then dominant practices in pedagogy. In those years, before the emergence of lifelong education to prominence, a basic scheme was devised for the adult educational process, which has been called the andragogical cycle.

It consists of five different stages: the identification and analysis of educational needs; the identification and selection of programme contents required to achieve the proposed educational goals; the planning of methods, rhythm, and pace; the implementation of the programme; and the evaluation of the programme process and outcomes.

A single adult educator, or andragogue, may carry out all the stages, fulfilling different functions. He or she may appear as the analyst of the educational needs and status of potential participants; as the programmer selecting content, hierarchy, and sequence of learning; as the course planner designing the whole series of educational experiences; as the teacher who realizes the programme; or as the evaluator of the educational outcomes (Pöggeler 1974).

In large educational institutions each function may be carried out by different specialists, but this is not possible in small ones, which have only two or three full-time staff. Most commonly the implementation and evaluation of the programme is undertaken by part-time educators (Titmus 1981)—needs analysis, programming, and planning being carried out by full-timers.

(a) *Identification of educational needs*. The andragogue has to discover the real educational needs of the learners. Even in formal, second chance education, where the standards and the course content are fixed to meet external requirements, there is a difference between the demands of the course and the learners' educational needs which ought to be resolved. The andragogical approach is both inductive and deductive. It analyses the situation of the learner both as an individual and as a member of society, with its own development goals and ideology at local and national levels. Goals and objectives are then set to meet individual and social needs.

(b) *Curriculum planning*. Education can only be effective if its starting point is related to the prior experience and education level of the learner. Therefore the curriculum should be prepared by an adult educator who has a good knowledge of the participants. Their formal education is only one indication of their actual knowledge, their informal education should also be taken into account. The curriculum should remain flexible and open to change throughout the cycle as continuing interaction between educator and participants reveals new educational needs.

(c) *Planning programme formats*. If the second stage of the andragogical cycle establishes the content of learning, the third serves to establish the forms the learning experiences are to take. These are determined by the aims and objectives of the programme, the situation of the participants, and the circumstances in which the programme will be carried out. The frequency of the learning experiences and whether they are to be continuous or discontinuous must be considered, as their distribution affects the intensity of the education that is planned (Turos 1980). The variety of social roles that participants play, in their families, their work place, and their public life, may complicate planning. Often a mixture of individual and group work formats is required. The methods and techniques to be employed should be appropriate to learning styles and habits of students.

(d) *Programme implementation*. If the first three stages, the preparatory phase, of the andragogical cycle are properly conducted, then the implementation of the programme will be greatly simplified. If adequate attention has been paid to the needs and situation of the participants, then there will be much independent learning, with the use of appropriate educational resources. The adult educator's responsibility will be mainly for group work; in independent study the individual should take major responsibility for his or her own learning.

In adult education practice the most typical forms of learning experience are single lectures, lecture series, sandwich courses, discussion groups, study circles, group and individual consultations, and tutorials. Some countries, such as Poland, the Federal Republic of Germany, Switzerland, and the Netherlands, have adopted forms adapted to their individual circumstances. Besides face-to-face forms of education, distance learning modes are becoming more popular, although they remain largely based on correspondence education, because of the high cost of multimedia education (Titmus 1981).

(e) *Evaluation*. The last stage of the andragogical cycle is evaluation. This does not take place exclusively at the end of the cycle but in part it goes on simultaneously with the implementation of the programme. Adult education may be seen as a spiral of andragogical cycles proceeding to a final educational aim, which in reality is never achieved, and in this context evaluation serves both adult educators and participants. It provides feedback to the educator which helps him or her to improve the organization, content, and conduct of future programmes. For the student, it not only allows decisions to be made on the award of certificates or diplomas, but also provides data on learning performance, which may assist him or her to determine further educational needs and approaches. The difficulties of assessing changes in personality, attitudes, and values brought about by education, which have already been noted, mean that present evaluation methods do not meet all the needs of andragogy.

4. Andragogy in the United States

The term *andragogy* has become quite widely used in the United States under the influence of Malcolm Knowles. He took the name, but little else, from Europe, applied it to ideas of the art and science of teaching adults which were already current in North America, and developed them. Knowles's concept of andragogy is based on four assumptions:

> "...as a person matures, (a) his self-concept moves from one of being a dependent personality toward one of being a self-directing human being; (b) he accumulates a growing reservoir of experience that becomes an increasing resource for learning; (c) his readiness to learn becomes oriented increasingly to the development tasks of his social roles; and (d) his time perspective changes from one of postponed application of knowledge to immediacy of application, and accordingly his orientation toward learning shifts from one of subject-centredness to one of problem-centredness." (Knowles 1980)

The consequences for the educator are numerous. It follows that adults should play a part, with the educator, in diagnosing their needs, and in planning, conducting, and evaluating the educational experience on which they embark. Since they have greater experience than do children, adults have more to contribute to the learning process, and they have a richer foundation to which to relate new experiences. They have, however, fixed habits and patterns of thought, which leave them less open-minded to new ideas than children. The educational process frequently needs to free them from these preconceptions.

It is argued that because adults go through a number of developmental stages, with which certain social roles are associated, and because they look for immediate rather than deferred applications of knowledge, the timing and content of educational experiences should be planned to fit in with these developmental and role needs, as the learner perceives them.

Andragogy, as proposed by Knowles, has taken on the tone of a doctrine rather than a field of study. It is based as much on ideological premises as on experience and research. In its ideas it differs from European, and particularly Eastern European, approaches principally in the overriding emphasis it attributes to the development of the adult as an individual. Self-direction and responsibility for one's own educational choices are perceived as essential to self-realization; learning for social roles is perceived as important for self-fulfilment. While not denying that these principles are important, European thinking on andragogy stresses the necessity of meeting society's needs rather more than American thinking does (see *Adult Education Research: General*). It takes adult education as having a function of socialization as well as one of self-satisfaction to fulfill.

5. New Fields of Andragogy

Andragogy has grown past the stage when its development was mainly determined by the search for its own specific characteristics and the need to emphasize its differences from pedagogy. The elaboration of the concept of lifelong education and its effect on theory and practice require that education be treated as a single, integrated process. Therefore andragogy must seek for its similarities and links with other parts of education.

The attention of researchers is increasingly devoted to adults' motivation for learning rather than their abilities. Social and personal value systems and attitudes are seen to play major roles in effective adult education (Krajnc 1973). In Europe, nonformal education is becoming a major field of andragogical development. Hitherto, it has been primarily occupied with formal and professional education; now the special problems of education for leisure are attracting more attention.

Bibliography

Hanselmann H 1951 *Andragogik: Wesen, Möglichkeiten, Grenzen der Erwachsenenbildung*. Rotapfel, Zurich

Husén T 1974 *The Learning Society*. Methuen, London

Kidd J R 1973 *How Adults Learn*. Association Press, New York

Knowles M S 1980 *The Modern Practice of Adult Education: From Pedagogy to Andragogy*. Association Press, New York

Krajnc A 1973 *The Identification of Educational Values as a Factor in Adult Education: A Cross-national Approach*. Ontario Institute for Studies in Education, Department of Adult Education, Toronto, Ontario

Ogrizović M 1966 *The Problems of Andragogy*. Problemi andragogije, Savez narodnih sveučilišta Hrvatske, Zagreb

Pöggeler F 1974 *Erwachsenenbildung: Einführung in die Andragogik*. Kohlhammer, Stuttgart

Titmus C J 1981 *Strategies for Adult Education: Practices in Western Europe*. Open University Press, Milton Keynes

Titmus C J et al. 1971 *Terminology of Adult Education*. UNESCO, Paris

Turos L 1980 *Andragogika: Zarys Teorii Oswiaty i Wychowania Dorostych*. Panstwowe Wydawnistwo Naukowe, Warsaw

Content, Purpose, and Practice

P. Jarvis

This article endeavours to explore the interrelationship of content, purpose, and practice in adult education from a wider perspective than that normally undertaken by curriculum theorists. It demonstrates the problematic nature of the concept of content which may be defined as that which is taught and/or learned within an educational setting: that which is taught also embodies an element of social control while that which is learned may result in either conformity to or freedom from the social structures within which the education occurs. Purpose may refer to either philosophy or policy, and practice may relate to either methods or organization. The article has three main sections: content, content and purpose, and content and practice.

1. Content

The traditional approach to education, stemming from the Greeks, has assumed that education is about the transmission of knowledge from one generation to its successors, but, with the growth of continuing education, the intergenerational aspect is assuming decreasing significance. Neither the idea of "transmission" nor the concept of "knowledge" are free from anomaly; the former is discussed in the final section of this article and the latter constitutes the focus of this section. Because education has been equated with knowledge, it has almost been taken for granted that curriculum content is synonymous with knowledge. However, such an equation cannot be maintained any longer as this article will argue. Even so, it is necessary to explore the nature of knowledge before this argument can be constructed and, thereafter, it will be shown that curriculum content is always wider than the cognitive dimension alone.

1.1 The Nature of Knowledge

The concept of knowledge has occupied the minds of philosophers throughout the history of the discipline although no attempt is made here to chronicle this debate. More significantly, it is recognized that this philosophical discussion has omitted elements that are crucial to a wider comprehension of the nature of the content of the curriculum, elements that stem from a sociological perspective. In order to illustrate this point the following paragraphs contain both a philosophical and a sociological discussion.

The English philosopher Hirst (1974 p. 33) has suggested that "knowledge is achieved when the mind attains its own satisfaction or good by corresponding to objective reality" and later in the same paper (pp. 40–41) he states that man has objectified conceptual schema over millenia so that forms of human knowledge have been achieved. It is significant that Hirst utilizes the idea of objectification whereas Paterson (1979 p. 69) regards knowledge as objective and that all adult education is about the expansion of individual knowledge, that is the acquisition of that objective knowledge. While Hirst uses the term objectification, he actually appears to treat knowledge as if it is objective when he suggests that there are seven forms of knowledge: mathematics, physical sciences, human sciences, history, religion, literature and the fine arts and philosophy. This is not the place to debate the validity of his claim, so it is merely pointed out here that liberal adult education theorists, such as Paterson (1979) and Lawson (1975) have tended to follow this position.

The assumption that knowledge corresponds to objective reality is, however, open to severe doubts. Mannheim (1936 p. 44) reversed Hirst's position in maintaining that reality "is discovered in the way that it appears to the subject in the course of his self-extension". In other words, individuals construct their own realities within the context of their social existence. This is not to deny that there is an objective reality, only to claim that any perception of it is socially constructed, so that knowledge equating to such a perception is itself socially constructed. Herein lies one of the major debates within curriculum studies, and consequently in adult and lifelong education, in recent years: if knowledge is objective then education can be about the transmission of worthwhile knowledge, but if it is socially constructed, whose construction is presented in education? It will be seen in the following discussion that this debate has a central part in the theory of content and, thereby, in both planning and practice.

Knowledge is not a static entity, it is constantly growing and changing. As early as 1926, Scheler (1980 p. 76) also suggested that there are seven categories of knowledge: myth and legend, knowledge implicit in natural language, religious knowledge, mystical knowledge, philosophical–metaphysical knowledge, positive knowledge of mathematics and the natural sciences and technological knowledge. The latter types of knowledge he regarded as artificial since they change "from hour to hour". Indeed, it is these forms of knowledge that change but they also subdivide, so that Berger and Luckmann (1967 p. 95) claim:

> . . . we can assume that, because of the division of labour, role-specific knowledge will grow at a faster rate than generally relevant and assessible knowledge. The multiplication of specific tasks brought about by the division of labour requires standardized solutions that can be readily learned and transmitted. These in turn require specialized knowledge of certain situations. . .

Hence, they claim that knowledge will subdivide as the division of labour proceeds and to a certain extent they are correct. However, this fission of knowledge is also accompanied by a fusion of subdivisions of knowledge forming new "bodies of knowledge" for new professional groups. Rapidly changing knowledge has a profound effect upon curriculum content especially in relation to the expansion of professional continuing education.

1.2 The Nature of Curriculum Knowledge

The question of the nature of curriculum knowledge was posed by Paterson (1979 p. 85) as follows:

> ...in constructing a curriculum for adult education, designed to enlarge the student's awareness and put him in more meaningful touch with reality by building up in him rich and coherent bodies of worthwhile knowledge, on what principles can we decide which items of knowledge ought to be included and which kinds of knowledge ought to be assigned priority?

Paterson does not really answer the question he posed, except by claiming that worthwhile knowledge is of those "fundamental and architectonic features of reality which are determining or constitutive of the whole of our experience" (p. 95). What is worthwhile, then, appears to be a rather nebulous value judgment about certain aspects of knowledge. In contrast, sociologists have been much more incisive in their discussion about why knowledge is included in the curriculum.

Following the claim of Marx and Engels in *The German Ideology* that:

> The ideas of the ruling class are, in every age, the ruling ideas: i.e. the class which is the dominant material force in society is at the same time its dominant intellectual force. (cited from Bottomore and Rubel 1963 p. 93)

Sociologists have recognized that in most forms of teaching and learning the knowledge included in the curriculum reflects, at least, a middle-class construction of reality, if not an upper-class one. Westwood (1980 p. 43), for instance, claims that adult education, especially that offered by universities, contains a middle-class bias. However, much of this knowledge content is presented as if it were objective reality and this is the manner in which cultural hegemony operates.

Knowledge that is included in the curriculum achieves high status within relevant social groups while that which is omitted is automatically relegated to low status. Young (1971 p. 38) suggests that the former tends to be abstract, literate and individualistic, while the latter reflects daily experience. This distinction is important in adult and lifelong experience as will be shown in the following sections.

1.3 Subject-based versus Experience-based Knowledge

Perhaps the most well known discussion of this distinction in adult education is that made by Knowles (1980 p. 44) where he suggests that pedagogy is subject based and andragogy is based upon performance or competency in life. Elsewhere he suggests that children are subject centred in their learning whereas adults tend to be problem centred. His crude distinction between andragogy and pedagogy has been challenged by many scholars in the West, whilst in Poland, and some other countries in Eastern Europe, the concept of andragogy has been rejected in favour of adult pedagogy (Skalka and Livečka 1977 pp. 79–85). Nevertheless, it is valid to note that the content of some curricula, in both primary schools and adult education, is based upon problem solving and life experience, since this reflects the progressive perspective in education, while secondary school, higher education and much initial vocational education tend to have subject-based content. The status of the latter in most societies in the world is higher than that of the former. Even so, developments in continuing education suggest that content is often problem based in these instances.

1.4 Classification of Content

In more formal education of adults the content of the curriculum usually relates to its purpose, so that many institutions within which adults are educated might be described as "monotechnic". A number of occupations and professions, however, are beginning to argue for broader curricula and a wider hidden curriculum by ensuring that trainees are prepared for their occupation in conjunction with recruits to other occupations. This move reflects the fission and fusion of knowledge discussed earlier. Broader curricula also suggest that there is an underlying belief that a person who is "educated" should have a knowledge of many of the disciplines of knowledge rather than merely be an expert in one of them.

In contrast to this, Mee and Wiltshire (1978 pp. 28ff) analysed the prospectuses of liberal adult education institutes and discovered that their content could be classified as follows: personal care and household economy (34 percent); leisure-time craft courses (19 percent); maintenance of health and physical fitness (10 percent); other leisure physical skills (14 percent); languages (12 percent); other intellectual courses (6 percent); work with the disadvantaged (5 percent). They noted that the proportion of courses having cognitive, intellectual content increased when university extension courses were included. This analysis was of prospectuses only, in other words, the intended content of the curriculum rather than the actual taught content.

1.5 Curriculum Content and Social Change

For a variety of reasons the actual content of curricula changes in response to changing demands, needs and social policy. It is, perhaps, significant to note that while some professions are seeking broader curricula, the speed of change of technological knowledge and the increasing demands of the market economy of the world has resulted in greater emphasis being placed upon technological and scientific knowledge which is included in curricula in compulsory initial and in higher education. This is in accord with the claims made by Kerr et al. (1973 p. 47) that as education is the handmaiden of industrialism, there is a need for a technologically trained workforce, so that the humanities and arts should be appreciated in leisure-time pursuits. Hence, curriculum content may be seen as a derivative of social change with the humanities and arts relegated to the periphery of the school curriculum as a leisure time pursuit for the middle-classes during their adulthood.

1.6 Curriculum Knowledge, Skills, and Attitudes

While much of the philosophical debate about content has referred specifically to the cognitive dimension, the content of a variety of professional education curricula is specified as being much wider. For instance, the Registered Mental Nurse in the United Kingdom is expected to follow a course of preparation that specifies both skills and knowledge. Once skills are included in the curriculum content it needs to be asked whether the professional preparation is educational or merely training? This distinction is similar to the one referred to above (Young 1971) in which academic, high-status knowledge is distinguished from everyday, low-status knowledge. Whilst recognizing that training and education are not completely incompatible, Paterson (1979 pp. 182–83) suggests that training turns its back upon the cognitive. This distinction may be far too simple, since the application or acquisition of skills may not be a mindless procedure in many instances. This does not deny that there are some forms of training that may deny the cognitive. Even so, in profesional practice the combination of knowledge and skill in unique situations may be the source of new knowledge. Hence, some professions recognize that "knowledge that" and "knowledge how" are complemented by "knowledge why" (Jarvis and Gibson 1985). In addition to professional preparation, some of the youth training schemes are including skills, both practical and social, within the content of their curricula.

Until very recently, professional preparation used to include a practical component such as teaching practice, in which it was expected that the knowledge taught in the theory part of the course could be applied in practice and the skills of practice acquired. This approach to technical rationality has more recently been called into question. In many parts of the world (see Chisnall 1983, inter alia) it has been recognized that cognitive learning follows practical experience and that new knowledge is "created" in practice. Thus the relationship between theory and practice is now being completely reconceptualized and in many instances this different approach is proving to be a very effective basis for learning.

Other professional curricula such as the District Nurse curriculum in the United Kingdom include specific attitudes that should be acquired during professional preparation. Once attitudes are included, the possibility that the professional preparation is indoctrinational needs to be raised. At the same time it must be recognized that certain types of attitude are required for various types of occupation and it may be more open to specify the type of person considered suitable to practise that profession than to have such criteria but not to publish them.

1.7 Affective Education

Professional education has recognized that cognitive education is not sufficient for professional practice so that considerable emphasis has been placed upon affective education (Heron 1982), the feelings of participants being the predominant focus. Heron, in the United Kingdom, has worked especially with doctors and others whose work involves interpersonal skills. The work of Carl Rogers is perhaps the best known in this field. While his work stems from psychotherapy it nonetheless is important for many forms of adult education, especially in preparation for management, business and the professions.

1.8 Curriculum Content as Taught or Learned

Lawton (1973 p. 11) has noted that "in the past definitions of the curriculum tended to emphasize the *content* [his emphasis] of a teaching programme, now writers on the curriculum are more likely to define it in terms of the whole learning situation". There has been a move away from regarding curricula as instructional content to recognizing that it might include all that is learned during the teaching and learning transaction, or, in the words of Griffin (1978 p. 5), "the entire range of educational practices or learning experiences". This change is reflected in the preceding discussion on the concept of content. Yet that discussion has only itemized some features of content rather than producing a conceptual framework within which content might be discussed, so the following discussion takes tentative steps in this direction. Teaching might be both overt and covert: the knowledge content is the former and the creation of a climate conducive to learning is of the latter type. The learning outcomes may be both intended and unintended, and when these four are put together the model shown in Fig. 1 may be constructed.

The syllabus is clearly the content, be it cognitive, emotive, psychomotor or attitudinal, which is specified as that which should be taught within the teaching and learning transaction. There is a sense in which the other three boxes constitute the "hidden curriculum", some of which is not hidden from the teachers, for example the creation of a group dynamic that will enable weaker students to be supported by those who appear more able and socialization into the class or profession. These are examples of a hidden syllabus. However, learning is not merely a process of acquiring the knowledge presented by the teacher in the syllabus, for the learner may reflect upon the syllabus and reject or modify it in a variety of ways. This constitutes independent learning. Finally, there is reactive learning, in which the learner responds to a specific teaching situation, including to cues that the teacher may not even be aware of "giving off". Such cues may also be considered to be an element in curriculum content.

		Learning outcomes: Intended	Learning outcomes: Unintended
Teaching	Overt	syllabus	independent learning
	Covert	hidden syllabus	reactive learning

Figure 1
Content—taught and learned

From the above analysis it may be seen that the concept of content in the curriculum is a problematic one, and this discussion only raises some of the issues that require further consideration. However, content does not appear in isolation; content and purpose and content and practice are explored in the following two sections.

2. Content and Purpose

Whatever the content, it does not just appear. As Lawton (1973 p. 21) suggested, curriculum content may be regarded as a "selection from culture", so it must be assumed that those who make the selection have a reason for their choice and this may be stated as the aims of the course. Traditionally, it has been assumed that it is either the teacher or the learner who chooses, since the curriculum has been viewed as the teaching and learning transacted in the classroom. Such a view of curriculum is clearly very limited and Jarvis (1983b pp. 211–50) produced curricular models which suggested that purpose is much broader than this. For instance, it is possible to see purpose at a number of different levels, namely: the learner; the teacher; the teacher–learner transaction; the educational institution; the prescribing agency; the government. Influence over the selection of content can be exercised at each of these levels and they will each be discussed in turn.

2.1 Learner-centred Education

In discussing learner-centred education it is important to draw a distinction between the individual and the group. Tough's research, and that emanating from it, into adults' self-directed learning projects demonstrates that adults undertake a wide variety of learning projects relating to their occupation, interest, domestic necessities, leisure pursuits, etc. Similarly, Gross' (1977) narratives of lifelong learners indicate the breadth of interests that individuals have. Groups may also be learner centred and the Swedish study group has traditionally operated on this principle. In practice it appears that since study circles are using material which has been prepared for them by central agencies, the control over the selection of the content no longer resides entirely with the group, but with whoever prepares the material.

It must be pointed out that as content can be selected by the learners and because the learning is not usually externally examined nor accreditation sought, the very nature of this process results in the status of the content being regarded as low. It also raises the question about whether it is actually curriculum content that is being discussed because the whole process might not actually be considered as education, which raises a further question about the nature of education itself. It is maintained here that among the essential features of education are planning and continuity of learning but not teaching (Jarvis 1983a p. 5), so it is possible to regard self-directed learning as educational. This would enable learner-controlled selection of content to be treated as one manifestation of curriculum.

2.2 Teacher-orientated Education

Teacher-orientated education has always been regarded as the opposite of learner-centred education, but this is a false dichotomy since teachers often have little actual control over content. Frequently, the syllabus is prescribed from above. Even so, teachers may exercise some control over the content to be taught and this is more absolute where the teachers are the acknowledged "experts" in their discipline. Hence, in many forms of higher education teachers both devise their own syllabus and examine it. In other instances teachers may only have secondary control, for example, they may select from a prescribed syllabus the content of a specific session. The degree of control that either the teacher or the prescribing body wishes to exercise over the session or course may be reflected in the use of objectives: behavioural objectives specify what content will be learned and, therefore, the learning outcomes of a specific session; both the morality and the practicality of this have been discussed elsewhere (Jarvis 1985). Teachers seeking less control may utilize expressive objectives. Clearly the use of different forms of objectives signifies the different levels of control exercised over teaching and the different ideological orientation towards education itself.

2.3 The Teacher–Learner Transaction

In the two subsections above it is clear that totally different philosophies operate. The first enables learners to develop in whatever direction their interests take them, while in the second the learner is initiated into a body of knowledge which is prescribed by some other agency. Often, in such cases, the term "need" is used to convey a deficiency in the learner's knowledge and it is perhaps significant that "need" is often a symbol of control, since the term is frequently used by prescribers or educators. However, there have been some significant attempts to draw together these two apparently contradictory positions, since it has been recognized that some, but by no means all, adults appear to learn better through self-direction. Hence, the concept of the negotiated curriculum is appearing. It is one in which the teacher and learners negotiate the content of the learning together. It is a very useful approach in continuing education in which professional practitioners return for inservice courses, since as practitioners they are aware of those aspects of their professional practice which they wish to develop, so that they frequently welcome the opportunity to negotiate the content of such courses. The Open University, in the United Kingdom, has tried to introduce an element of negotiation in its course on education for adults in which the learners are expected to negotiate the topic of their project with their tutor and then negotiate the criteria by which it is assessed. For this reason, aspects of the content of the course are open to negotiation while, significantly, the method whereby the learning occurs, namely, the project, is non-negotiable.

Another approach to this synthesis is one in which the method is more open to negotiation—the learning contract. This approach recognizes that the content of the curriculum, especially in vocational education, may be prescribed, but, as individual adults bring to their learning different experiences and knowledge, they may not feel the need to study every element, nor may they wish to follow a prescribed course. Thus, they enter a learning contract with their tutor. Knowles (1975) describes how he enters into such contracts with his learners. A significant factor in his approach is that while the learners are free to pursue their own learning, they have to produce supportive evidence to demonstrate that they have fulfilled their contract and Knowles indicates that he assesses both the contract and the evidence.

2.4 The Educational Institution

Institutional purpose is another factor which needs to be considered in relation to content. Entrepreneurial organizations can, and often do, offer a limited number of popular topics which attract a large number of students. By contrast, those institutions offering a general education to adults, for example, folk high schools and adult education institutes, usually offer a wide variety of courses which will run if there is sufficient demand. Similarly, the Open University and many US universities that cater for adult and part-time students also organize their programmes in a modular manner, with modules often being of relatively short duration. This structure seems to be best suited to the demands of the market, considering the domestic and vocational commitments of potential adult students. In complete contrast to this are those institutions that seek to provide a vocational education and often a higher education for adults. They cater for full-time students who are able to follow courses through a longer duration, which enables them to pursue the demands of the discipline more easily than can the former type.

2.5 The Prescribing Agency

Frequently the prescribing agency is a professional association concerned to ensure that new entrants to the profession are adequately prepared to enter professional practice, to which end the association lists the content it considers the recruit should learn. There is a significant element of control in this situation since it is claimed that the learner does not have the experience to reach a decision about what is required. Usually the prescription is restricted to the content of what is to be taught, although this, it is claimed, is related to professional practice. Often professional associations delegate the actual teaching of the curriculum to educational institutions but only license them to teach the material for a specified period before revalidation.

2.6 Government

Adult education is rarely analysed in terms of government policy but it is possible to examine it in social policy terms. Finch (1984) suggests three approaches to analysing social policy in education: welfare, beneficiary, and social engineering.

There are a number of variations of the welfare model proposed by Titmuss (1974) and others. These include a residual welfare model in which government makes temporary provision to meet temporary needs, for example, pump-priming educational activities to overcome a temporary problem such as adult basic education; an institutional achievement model by which needs are treated on the basis of merit, such as work performance and paid educational leave; and an institutional redistribution model in which resources are redistributed to pursue social equality, so that considerable adult education may be funded in order to ensure greater equality of opportunity and resources.

The beneficiary approach suggests that a commodity should be offered to everyone because it is so valuable, for example, liberal adult education. The third approach is social engineering and once more there are three variations: change in education designed to change educational outcomes such as the establishment of open learning systems designed to enable adults to pursue education at a higher level without first acquiring passes in school examinations; change in other areas of social policy designed to change educational outcomes, for example, the use of media for institutionalized education; and changes in education designed to produce other social change such as the use of education in community development projects that result in changes in the community itself. For a number of examples of how this occurred in India see Stone (1983 pp. 297–304).

It may be seen from the above discussion that purpose may be seen initially in terms of both philosophy and policy. However, there is another set of relationships that emerges on further analysis of the above: some forms of education, such as learner-centred education, are designed for personal development while others, such as vocational education and teacher-oriented education, are designed for professional development. It has been argued that these may be synonymous, but whilst this may be so in some instances, there are fundamentally different purposes behind the two. In the former, the learner is involved in the choice of both content and direction whilst in the latter the choice remains entirely with the teacher. Thus the former is more likely to respond to the learner's needs whereas the needs of the organization or the social group, as determined by persons other than the learner, predominate in the latter.

Education may also be used in community development, that is in the process of preparing people to play their part in deciding how to make their community a better place in which to live and then working to achieve that end. But it has also been used as an agent in community action (Freire 1972, Lovett et al. 1983, inter alia) in which it prepares people to be activists within their community in both a political and social manner. In the former education is involved in examining issues and advising and equipping people to play an informed part but the educator is marginal to the process, whilst in the latter the educator is committed to the community and involved in the political and social action within the community.

It must be noted that whilst education is generally regarded as having beneficial purposes, it may also be used to control and to inhibit egalitarian changes in society.

3. Content and Practice

"Practice", as a term, has normally been employed to refer to teaching methods; this is probably because curriculum has traditionally referred to classroom activity. Once the concept of curriculum is expanded then that of practice is automatically broadened, so that while it is used here to refer to classroom practice, it is also used to relate to a wider range of activities. Therefore, this section has two main subsections, the first referring to teaching methods and the other to the organization of adult education.

3.1 Teaching Methods

In the first section of this article it was pointed out that education used to be defined in terms of the transmission of worthwhile knowledge, but the concept of "transmission" was itself problematic in education generally. It is especially problematic in the education of adults, where it might be claimed that the emphasis is placed more upon the learner than it is in initial education. There is less concentration upon the nature of the content to be learned by the adult, although this is not entirely so if role-specific knowledge, skill or attitude are taken into consideration. In addition, if knowledge were regarded as objective, correct and unchanging then there might be a greater emphasis upon the idea of transmission than there would be if it were seen as socially constructed and relative. A variety of factors must be taken into consideration when seeking a relationship between content and practice at this level. Theorists of teaching methods (Jarvis 1983b pp. 112–57, Elsdon 1984 inter alia) have examined a wide variety of methods that may be employed with adults which may be classified into didactic, socratic and facilitative. Didactic methods are usually teacher centred and the content is most frequently teacher chosen and presented; socratic methods are teacher centred in as far as it is the teacher who poses the questions for the learner to answer but the direction that the questioning process takes may be guided by either the students' answers or the teacher's intent that the students should achieve a correct understanding; facilitative methods enable the students to direct their own learning as a result of the learning experience that the teacher provides. The style of the teacher is also important: a nonauthoritarian teacher may use a didactic method, such as a lecture, to provoke thought rather than to transmit knowledge. While the content and the practice are interrelated, they cannot be divorced from the purpose. The interrelationship of these three factors at the level of the classroom forms the basis of any model of curriculum in education and this is especially true in adult education.

3.2 The Organization of Adult Education

The planning and provision of adult education is the implementation of policy in practice. The model of curriculum in adult education is much broader than the traditional understanding and this is because adult education is such a complex and often uncoordinated phenomenon. The Ministry of Education in Ontario (p. 42 1980) expressed the following view:

> The variety of education agencies, the informality of courses, and the voluntary aspect of attendance, among other factors, require not control and regulation, but coordination, cooperation and advocacy.

This Canadian statement suggests that in Canada adult and continuing education is being institutionalized. Implicit in the above claim is the fact that there are two models of provision: a free-market model and a centrally planned model.

The free-market model has two variants: one based upon demand and the other on supply. The free-market demand model assumes a classical liberalism, namely, that people are free, rational, and able to follow their own interests. Hence, the consumers of adult education are able to select the content, i.e. the courses of study that suit their interests, and less popular courses will not run. This is the manner in which liberal adult education is supplied in the United Kingdom. The free-market model is one that makes an offering to the potential consumer based upon the idea of deficiency in knowledge, skill, or attitude rather than on consumer interest. Potential students, however, are still free to choose from the offerings made, so that the free market still operates but the ideology of provision is different. Adult basic education, some continuing professional education and some community development approaches to adult education all fall within this conceptual framework.

By contrast to this the centrally planned model of adult education assumes that the free market does not operate. While it espouses cooperation and coordination in order to ensure that duplication in content and other inefficient practices do not occur, it frequently becomes a model of control. In the countries in which adult education has become institutionalized and is implemented by legal statute, central planning occurs. For instance, Livečka writes about Czechoslovakia:

> In the course of its evolution and development, adult education gradually formed a unified, relatively compact, system which has increasingly become an inseparable part of the managing process in ensuring the main objective of the national economy. (Skalka and Livečka 1977 p. 18)

Similar sentiments are expressed by Pachociński and Półturzycki (1979 p. 33) about Poland and by Micheva et al. (1982 pp. 64-67) about Bulgaria. It is significant to note that in these societies the content of adult education is largely vocational, so that education is regarded as a handmaiden to industrialization and the content of the courses reflect the needs of the society, as seen by those who control the service.

This article has endeavoured to draw links between content, purpose and practice at at least two levels, that of the classroom and that of society. It can be seen that the teaching and learning transaction occurs as the result of a complex interrelationship of a variety of institutions in society, and that no classroom is an isolated island and no element of content occurs that does not reflect that social process. Curriculum, therefore, is seen as a much more complex phenomenon than many of the earlier models suggested.

Bibliography

Berger P L, Luckmann T 1967 *The Social Construction of Reality*. Allen Lane, Penguin, London

Bottomore T B, Rubel M (eds.) 1963 *Karl Marx: Selected Writings in Sociology and Social Philosophy*. Penguin, Harmondsworth

Chisnall H (ed.) 1983 *Learning from Work and Community Experience: Six International Models*. NFER-Nelson, Windsor

Elsdon K T 1984 *Adult Education*, Education Documentation and Information, Bulletin of International Bureau of Education No. 233. UNESCO/IBE, Paris–Geneva

Finch J 1984 *Education as Social Policy*. Longman, London

Griffin C M 1978 *Recurrent and Continuing Education: A Curriculum Model Approach*. Association for Recurrent Education, University of Nottingham, Nottingham

Gross R 1977 *The Lifelong Learner*. Simon and Schuster, New York

Heron J 1982 *Education of the Affect*. Human Potential Research Project, University of Surrey, Guildford

Hirst P H 1974 *Knowledge and the Curriculum*. Routledge and Kegan Paul, London

Hoyle E, Megarry J (eds.) 1980 *Professional Development of Teachers*. Kogan Page, London

Jarvis P 1983a *Professional Education*. Croom Helm, London

Jarvis P 1983b *Adult and Continuing Education: Theory and Practice*. Croom Helm, London

Jarvis P 1985 *The Sociology of Adult and Continuing Education*. Croom Helm, London

Jarvis P, Gibson S 1985 *The Teacher Practitioner in Nursing, Midwifery and Health Visiting*. Croom Helm, London

Kerr C, Dunlop J T, Hobison F, Myers C A 1973 *Industrialism and Industrial Man*, 2nd edn. Pelican, Harmondsworth

Knowles M S 1975 *Self-directed Learning: A Guide for Learners and Teachers*. Follett, Chicago, Illinois

Knowles M S 1980 *The Modern Practice of Adult Education*, 2nd edn. Association Press, Chicago, Illinois

Lawson K H 1975 *Philosophical Concepts and Values in Adult Education*. Department of Adult Education, University of Nottingham, Nottingham

Lawton D 1973 *Social Change, Educational Theory and Curriculum Planning*. University of London Press, London

Mannheim K 1936 *Ideology and Utopia*. Kegan Paul, London

Mee G, Wiltshire H 1978 *Structure and Performance in Adult Education*. Longman, London

Micheva P, Bizhkov G, Petkov I 1982 *Adult Education in the People's Republic of Bulgaria*. European Centre for Leisure and Education, Prague

Ontario Ministry of Education 1980 *Continuing Education: The Third System*, A Discussion Paper. Ontario Ministry of Education, Ontario

Pachociński R, Półturzycki J 1979 *Adult Education in People's Poland*. European Centre for Leisure and Education, Prague

Paterson R W K 1979 *Values, Education and the Adult*. Routledge and Kegan Paul, London

Scheler M 1980 *Problems of a Sociology of Knowledge*. Routledge and Kegan Paul, London

Skalka J, Livečka E 1977 *Adult Education in the Czechoslovak Socialist Republic* (CSSR). European Centre for Leisure and Education, Prague

Stone H S 1983 Nonformal adult education: Case studies from India. *Int. J. Lifelong Educ.* 2(3): 297–304

Thompson J L (ed.) 1980 *Adult Education for a Change*. Hutchinson, London

Titmuss R M 1974 *Social Policy: An Introduction*. Allen and Unwin, London

Westwood S 1980 Adult education and the sociology of education: An Exploration. In Thompson J L (ed.) 1980 *Adult Education for a Change*. Hutchinson, London pp. 31–44

Young M F D (ed.) 1971 *Knowledge and Control*. Collier-Macmillan, London

Curriculum

J. H. Knoll

This article deals with an area of adult education which until recently has received no more than marginal attention in some countries, and has barely been researched or has got bogged down in theoretical discussions in others. Although the concept of curriculum can be traced back a long way in the history of general education, it was not until the early 1970s, and in connection with the so-called educational reform, that it was reactivated in politicoeducational discussions in the Federal Republic of Germany. At first, curriculum, curriculum revision, and curriculum development were only discussed in the context of school-based education, but since the mid-1970s there have been various attempts, models, and projects which aim at applying the concept and content of curriculum to adult education too. Adult education has shunned the idea of curricular strategies for a long time because it always has been and still is based on such principles as topicality, openness, flexibility, and—with the exception of selective corrections—has always been opposed to rigid determination of content. However, the host of new demands made on adult education has called into question the validity of these principles.

1. *Introduction*

The essential impetus for the discussion of the theory and practice of curricula in adult education in the Federal Republic of Germany and elsewhere came from Saul Robinsohn's situation-analytical approach to the question, which was intended as a contribution to the educational reform of the 1970s (Robinsohn 1972). The theory of adult education has approached this concept only relatively recently, but in so doing has always stressed that the dividing principle between the school curriculum and the curriculum in adult education is that of determination by external agencies and self-determination. This is why adult educators prefer to talk about "open curricula", which are codetermined by the participation of the students, rather than "closed curricula" which are subject to stronger external standardization. The German Education Council defines curriculum as follows:

> The historical concept of curriculum which modern educational science has taken up refers to the learning processes: Which knowledge, aptitudes, skills, attitudes, and behaviour patterns is the learner to acquire? With which subject matter and content is he to be confronted? What is he to learn? When and where is he to learn? By which learning steps, in which manner, with the aid of which materials is he to learn? How is the attainment of the aims and objectives to be determined? The whole of this extremely complex field of questions is subsumed under the term curriculum. In essence, curriculum means the organised arrangement of learning processes and content with regard to certain aims and objectives. These can be defined either as behaviour or as type and degree of certain skills and aptitudes, or of knowledge.

This raises a complex of questions which also apply to the curriculum discussion in adult education. A curriculum discussion in adult education needs to consider the aspects of fixity, participation, needs, and the establishment of different areas of competence (personal competence, social competence, and subject competence), and is confronted with the problem of which needs exist and what demands are made on establishments of adult education by the participants, and with which content, procedures, and teaching methods the establishments react to these needs and demands.

In the past, supply and demand, and the relationship between suppliers and consumers were regulated on the basis of a view of education that was rooted in the neohumanistic tradition of defining the learning content as free from serving a specific purpose, yet individualistic and contributing to personal growth. This concept is closely linked with the concept of *Volksbildung*—popular education. Today, a further factor enters into the relationship between establishments and participants in adult education: the adult is expected to have certain qualifications which are derived from his or her roles as wage earner, as parent, as citizen, and so on. The previous individualistic educational need has been replaced by the objective educational needs, in which the aims are defined by a set of different roles.

Once the needs arising from the individual's roles as worker, citizen, and parent have been determined, the content of the programme to be offered by the establishments of adult education can be specified.

Of course, those concerned with the theory and practice of adult education are perfectly aware that curriculum discussions threaten the characteristics of openness, topicality, and flexibility, and that this could open adult education to that rigid form of external control which is considered quite legitimate in the case of schools (Arabin 1980).

Unlike curriculum discussions for various subjects in different types and levels of schools, the discussions concerning adult education moved very soon from theoretical considerations to concrete curricula. With the aid of the Council of Europe's projects on the needs of adults it was possible to develop models of open curricula for a whole range of different adult education subjects and purposes. These discipline-centred curricula were drawn up on the basis of the participation theory of the 1970s, with the intention of producing situational and subject competence (Schlutz 1976). Work on these concrete curricula soon led to the realization that the distinction between school and adult education through the antinomic distinction between "didactic external determination" and "didactic self-determination" could no longer be reliably upheld. Schlutz was probably the first West German educationalist to apply the insights gained from curriculum discussion to a specific discipline and model. He is of the opinion that as far as the establishment of situational and subject competence is concerned, the participant in adult education is a competent expert of his own educational needs only in so far as this competence relates to "his own specific situation" in his various roles.

Curriculum discussion in adult education has concentrated above all on two phenomena. Leaving aside the discipline-centred need for structuring the courses on offer in accordance with situation analysis, the interest in curricular strategies grew above all as a result of the growing demand for examination courses and programmes, and because of increasing professionalization. In the Federal Republic of Germany, as well as in other systems of differentiated and career-orientated adult education, examination-orientated education (in schools as well as in occupational training) has played a dominant role since the 1960s. The certificate courses in the Federal Republic are an almost classical example of closed curricula in adult education (Tietgens et al. 1974). The system of closed curricula, which is by no means a universal feature of all adult education offered by the public sector, seems to collide with the ideals of "free adult education", such as flexibility, openness, and equal opportunity without regard to formal qualifications. The Open University (UK), University without Walls, University of the Air—to name but a few examples from the tertiary sector of education—all represent a concept of adult education in which an attempt is made to free education from the requirements of formal qualifications, thus giving everybody a chance to regulate their own educational needs and correct the deficit as perceived by them. The fact that most countries operate differentiated adult education systems seems to indicate that the view and the concept have gained acceptance that open curricula must retain their adult-appropriate status in scientific, political, leisure-, family-, and growth-orientated education, side by side with the closed curricula of school-based education and occupational training. Even with open curricula though, the starting point for determining their content will have to be situation-analytical considerations as defined by Robinsohn (Kaiser 1977).

The second reason for the intensified curriculum discussion in adult education is the increase in professionalization. On the whole, there is a tendency to employ a proportion of the teaching staff on a full-time basis, or to professionalize them. This increased professionalization of tutors also results in greater professionalism of programme planning.

2. Authorities Determining Curriculum Construction

In his situation-analytical approach to the question, Robinsohn argues that the construction of the curriculum has to anticipate future life situations in order to design teaching content and learning methods based on these projected needs, enabling the learner to cope with future life situations. This prognosis of future life situations is to be assigned to a group of experts consisting not only of subject specialists, but also of persons who can forecast future social, political, and employment and economic conditions and tendencies. This means that, taking into account the school curriculum which preceded it, adult education has to examine the learners' needs and expectations and the possibilities adult education establishments can offer, and on this basis design a programme which orientates itself on the objective educational needs of adults. As far as curricular strategies are concerned, Siebert (1975) assigns to them four dimensions. He writes the following comments on the individual aspects:

> (a) *Deductive strategies:* Concrete aims and objectives are derived in linear fashion from general norms, aims, social theories, etc. . . .
>
> (b) *Inductive strategies:* Empirically acquired data regarding necessary qualifications, educational needs, and areas of application form the elements of this curriculum . . .
>
> (c) *Analytical strategies:* Existing curricula and curricular theories are analysed, criticized, and evaluated, i.e. they are examined for their presuppositions, congruence, concreteness, and effectiveness; existing curricula are then revised on the basis of this critical analysis . . .
>
> (d) *Educative strategies:* Curricular decisions are not made before but during lessons and are discussed and justified together with experts, teachers, pupils, and parents. . . .

A number of points have to be raised with regard to the strategies adopted to decide curricular content.

Firstly, in conceiving and realizing lifelong education, the curriculum of adult education must be based on the school curriculum—where it exists—and the school curriculum must lay the foundations for the curricula of adult education, in other words: school curricula and adult education curricula must be seen as a unit (Skager and Dave 1977).

Secondly, curricula in schools and adult education must take national requirements into consideration. In the context of adult education this is of particular relevance in connection with the literacy programmes in developing countries. While formalized school curricula impart a repertoire of general knowledge which transcends the national context—although the supranational principle may be limited by that of cultural coherence—it is the task of adult education to make a contribution towards cultural and national identity. From this claim "various aspects of the national curricula" can be derived which would make a supranational curriculum impossible in more ways than one (Skager and Dave 1977).

Thirdly, curricula in adult education must attempt to combine traditional and new knowledge in flexible ways, that is the internal constitution of adult education establishments must allow for both standardization as well as for more unconventional new approaches which have not yet been worked out in detail. The majority of experts concerned with the theory or the policies of adult education fear though that adult education will succumb to the trend towards systematization. Writing about this danger, Janne points out that a heightened sensitivity is needed in order to recognize "the dangers of sclerosis inherent in any standardization, dangers which can only be circumscribed by a 'constant revision'" (Janne 1977). The author is further of the opinion that curricular decisions can only be legitimized when there is an ongoing dialogue between the institutions, the participants, and the tutors.

International discussion is particularly concerned with the question of what the participants in adult education expect, and how the interaction between establishments, participants, and objective educational needs can be made to function. In this connection, a distinction has to be made between the educational needs of certain target groups and a need for education and information in general which applies to all adults. Initially, it can be seen as an advantage that adult education programmes cater for the needs of particular target groups (Brundage 1980, Cross 1981). However, this gives rise to the danger that adult education becomes fragmented or segmented and that too much concern for the particular aspects may lead to neglect of general aspects. In UNESCO conferences (e.g., Preparatory Meeting to a European UNESCO Conference on Adult Education, Hamburg 1982) particular attention is paid to target group orientation and problems of marginal groups, which arise within the context of adult education strategies. This could create the impression that more comprehensive programmes, which are addressed to adults in general, play only a minor part in adult education. This is a danger if the predictions are considered of future social change described under the heading "postindustrial society", and investigated for their possible educative and innovative–creative consequences by the Club of Rome. In concrete terms this means that, although a curriculum in adult education can and must on the one hand limit itself to specific national, social, and situational questions, it must on the other hand not forget that it has the task of helping all adult education to face contemporary problems.

The following is a definition of curriculum on a world scale:

> Moving the "curriculum" (aims, content, methods, modes of evaluation) into a world perspective and reconsidering it, implies that it should serve the basic interests of every country, every national community. There is no contradiction between the more courageous opening up of the education system to the problems of our world, and the specific aims every society attributes to education, and which are inevitably and more and more concerned with the improvement of the environment, the use of the achievements of modern technology, world peace, and human relations, etc.... (Vaideanu 1979)

Summing up, it can be said that curricula in adult education should cater for specific occupational, national, and social conditions, but at the same time adult education needs to consider changes affecting the whole of society and devise strategies for dealing with them, which put general needs before specific and specialized ones.

3. Factors Determining a Curriculum

The content of a curriculum is subject to a variety of external influences; it depends on the objective educational needs which prevail within a given educational system, and which are composed of the correlation between individual demands and those made by society. While the objective educational needs arise from the prevailing technical and technological conditions—certain occupational qualifications are required because of each country's need to be competitive within the system of international economic competition—the respective weight given to individual and objective educational needs is determined by the "philosophy" behind adult education. In popular education (*Volksbildung*)—to quote a central European example—adult education was based on the theory of personal growth. According to this theory it is the prime aim of education to aid personal development, that is, personal growth, which is sought for its own sake and not for any specific purpose. Growth-centred education thus overlooked the career aspect of self-realization. In socialist countries the implementation of continuing occupational education within the system of adult education has given expression to the school of thought which holds that adult education has to fulfil a comprehensive task.

According to some politicoeducational statements (e.g., *Comprehensive Educational Plan of the Federal/Provincial Commission for Educational Planning,* FGR 1973), adult education should establish a union of political, occupational, and general education. During the mid-1970s the emphasis in numerous national education "philosophies" was on "continuing education", combined with rigid qualifications of a scholastic and occupational nature, and it was not until the end of the 1970s that a new balance was achieved between occupational and general, that is, sociocultural education; from then on, renewed weight was given to "open curricula" for cultural education in the widest sense, while "closed curricula" for examination-based programmes have retained their importance. Apart from the compensatory effect of a change of paradigm, this is also due to a new understanding of the concept of culture, which has freed itself from its narrow definition of a "national high culture", and is now understood in the sense of socioculture, everyday culture, and so on. This movement for an expansion of the concept of culture has found its strongest supporters in France (sociocultural animation (see *Sociocultural Animation*), in England (community development)), and in Scandinavia (adult education by self-government), although the theory of socioculture has in the meantime also spread beyond the borders of Europe. Based on his knowledge and experience of the North American educational system, J. R. Kidd for example has pointed out that curriculum discussion and design are governed by the educational theories prevailing in any one country and are at the same time dependent on mainly political and economic conditions (Kidd 1975). Also owed to J. R. Kidd is the general agreement that differentiation must be made between curricula which are national, those based on educational theory, those specific to adults, and those directed at special target groups.

Current politicoeducational discussions show a growing equilibrium between closed and open programmes in adult education. Internationally too, general and sociocultural programmes have increased their rating in comparison with those that are examination orientated. The first sign of this was the UNESCO Recommendation on the Development of Adult Education which was unanimously adopted by its general assembly in Nairobi in 1976, after the UNESCO world conference in Tokyo had done valuable groundwork for it. In adult education in the Federal Republic of Germany, the imbalance in favour of systematic further education leading to occupational or academic qualifications has gradually been redressed since 1976. At almost the same time socialist countries too experienced a rejection of the one-sided orientation of adult education towards providing occupational qualifications (Knoll 1983b). In the case of the German Democratic Republic, attention could be drawn to the "Joint Resolution of the Council of Ministers of the GDR and the executive of the Federal Trades Union Council" of 21. 7. 1979 "for a further raising of the standards in adult education", which advocates an equilibrium between occupational training and cultural education, thus following the example of other socialist countries, such as Hungary, which have a long tradition of open adult education.

While quite a lot has been written about the advantages, content, and formal qualifications of closed curricula, similar information on open curricula is still rather hard to find (Siebert 1974).

In conclusion, it can be said that the content of adult education curricula is determined by a number of factors. In the first instance, economic pressures and objective educational needs as a whole play a decisive role. Secondly, the composition of curricular content also depends on the "philosophy" behind a national educational system—sociocultural education versus professional qualifications— although integrated models placing varying degrees of emphasis on one aspect or the other probably predominate in the majority of cases. Curricular strategies are also influenced by the way the various partners in a pluralistic system of adult education see themselves, pluralistic here meaning divergence in the participants' outlook on life, as well as in organizational terms. Finally, the expectations participants have of the adult education functions in which they take part will also influence the composition of curricula. In more concrete terms this means that participation is founded on the learners' insight into their own situation and the needs derived from this insight. It follows that monocausal arguments for curricular strategies are ruled out.

4. Legitimization and Justification of Curricula

In the Federal Republic of Germany, politicoeducational discussions resulted above all in two documents dealing with the subject of adult-specific curricula as their central theme: the *Structural Plan of the Education Commission of the German Education Council* (1970), and the *Comprehensive Educational Plan of the Federal/Provincial Commission for Educational Planning* (1973).

Both documents discuss the need to establish various forms of competence with the aid of curricula (personal–social–subject competence), and with regard to the concept of lifelong education, stress the special character of adult-specific curricula. The Comprehensive Educational Plan contains the following considerations under the heading "Curricula for further education":

> Aims: The introduction of adult-specific curricula in the area of further education.
>
> Measures:
>
> (a) The development of curricula which can be used in a "modular construction system" (Baukastensystem). It should be possible to relate the various courses to each other and combine them with each other. This applies particularly to those areas of further education which prepare students for formal examinations, such as university or college entrance or occupational qualifications. This system is also suitable for programmes offered to students on educational leave.
>
> (b) Offering equivalent modular units for full- and part-time study, including media tuition. The exchangeability of learning units is to be guaranteed through minimum standards and validation procedures. The mutual recognition of leaving certificates by the various establishments, including state institutions of further education (e.g. technical colleges, night schools preparing students for the "Abitur"), is to be guaranteed. Increased counselling facilities are to make the modular construction system comprehensible to individual students. The introduction of an "education passport" is to be investigated.

In view of the increased demands made on adult education (objective educational needs), and the opening up of new areas of activity (educational leave, work with target groups, literacy programmes, community work), as well as increasing professionalization, the development of curricula will make the work of adult education more efficient and more intensive. On the whole, curricula will be most useful in those areas which deal with systematic and sequential acquisition of knowledge. Such curricula have more than regional validity and can be applied to a whole country. It is also conceivable that certain curriculum elements are used in several countries simultaneously.

As a rule, curricula in adult education use recognized needs as their starting point and devise teaching content and methods on their basis (Benseman 1980). While the legitimization and justification of curricula in adult education is widely uncontested in the areas of occupational and political education and in programmes offered to students on educational leave, the development of open curricula in other areas is still largely in its infancy. Curricula for continuing adult education will probably be designed on the basis of the situation-analytical approach, although the apparatus for anticipating employment and occupational conditions of the future is largely lacking. Consequently, curricula for continuing adult education are modelled largely on traditional patterns of occupation, or try to meet technological change through additional qualifications. [Russia is one example (Tonkonogaja 1978), and the GDR with the so-called "B-Qualifizierungs-Sondermassnahmen" another.] Benseman has characterized the situation with these words: "While much has been written on 'needs' in other circles, comparatively little has been written about this approach within the particular context of continuing education—although the same is also true of the whole issue of curriculum in continuing education." The same author links "needs" with a curriculum design and lists the main areas in which curricula need to be developed, referring largely to Knowles:

(a) the self-perceived needs and interests of the learners themselves (e.g., hobby classes);

(b) the requirements (or "needs") of society (e.g., training of tradespeople for the labour market);

(c) the requirements (or "needs") of the local community (e.g., Programme for Youth Leaders);

(d) the goals of a particular institution (e.g., Country Women's Institutes);

(e) some recognized body of knowledge, "subjects" or "disciplines" (e.g., history, sociology).

According to Benseman and other authors, the curriculum should play a dominant role in adult education (Mackie 1981). Systematization and standardization extend beyond the narrow field of professional and political knowledge.

Other authors, on the other hand, do not pay particular attention to the concept of "curriculum". Lowe 1982, for example, and no doubt many other experts in adult education, give the concept of "curriculum" only marginal consideration and identify it with "subject matter". Viewed against the background of international developments, they think that there is very little chance that the hitherto largely open system of adult education could be exposed to rigid systematization. They plead almost exclusively for open curricula which provide the necessary scope for national, regional, and structural requirements and have little use for "closed curricula".

5. *Areas of Application of Curricula*

Even allowing for the fact that the need to establish curricula is insufficiently recognized even in areas where the acquisition of knowledge can be standardized, there are nevertheless numerous fields where application is already practised and has produced convincing effects. Naturally, this applies above all to assessable units and sequential learning in the area of occupational and work-orientated education (qualifications for the purpose of promotion and adaptation to new technological conditions).

If tertiary education is included in adult education—this happens in the Soviet Union, the German Democratic Republic, Canada, the United States, and in part in the United Kingdom—a number of seemingly conflicting tendencies can be observed. On the one hand authors plead for greater flexibility and openness (Clement and Edding 1979), for example for access to education without formal qualifications (Open University, UK, the Netherlands; Correspondence University Pretoria; and—though only partly—*Fernuniversität Hagen*). On the other they plead for greater fixity and systematization (shorter courses). In many cases such extreme positions are dictated by the author's philosophy of life or politicoeducational persuasion. Here, as in many other cases, the principle of balancing out extremes will have to be called upon. Today, first degree courses in nearly all disciplines and almost all countries exhibit curricular fixedness, they are standardized, and are internationally exchangeable. Segments of adult education studies in England, France, and Germany can be related to each other; possibilities of curricular agreements which would enable the exchange of lecturers and students are under discussion.

No-one challenges the fact that basic degree courses can be followed by research studies which allow students greater options, while postgraduate studies are based almost entirely on the participants' interest and initiative. It cannot be discussed here whether the move from fixed curricula to an openness which is limited only by the discipline imposed by the subject studied should also involve moving between different educational institutions. The American system of college, university, institutes for advanced studies, and postgraduate schools seems to be favoured by other countries too. For some countries, however, (e.g., the Federal Republic of Germany) the institutional division of the tertiary sector according to the degree to which curricula are fixed would touch the very foundations of the concept of a university as such. A problem which is probably more urgent than that of university reform is that of continuing professional education (see *Continuing Education of the Professional*). This type of education needs to be defined by a curriculum which tries to strike a balance between new professional skills and bringing participants up to date with the newest state of research in their own discipline. The terms used vary from country to country: "*weiterbildendes Studium*" (FRG), "recertification" (US), "mandatory continuing professional education" (MCPE, USA/New Mexico), "continuing learning in the professions", and so on. Houle (1980) has made a special and comprehensive study of this field of education. Despite his fundamental vote for an open university system (external degrees), he approves of continuing professional education, although he does not want to see it subjected to rigid curricular reglementation. In his view, the emphasis should be on practical professional requirements and the idea of brushing up on knowledge. He writes: "Purists sometimes argue that continuing professional education should always be based solely on established supporting disciplines or systems of practice related to the occupations. But if a course which does not conform to this dictate attracts a group of professionals who would not otherwise participate in education and helps them to practice their learning skills and build the informal bonds of association and affiliation that hold a profession together, it is hard to argue that diversity of curriculum should be frowned upon." Other advocates of continuing professional education go one step further and make continued practice of a profession dependent on "recertification". In the Federal Republic of Germany for example the licensing regulations for doctors make continuing education mandatory. Similar regulations apply to areas of the civil service—although they are not yet strictly adhered to in all cases. In the United States this idea of recertification became established in the early 1970s (Rockhill 1983), and the present situation is outlined in a report which is based on a survey of all 50 states of the United States:

> In 1979, Louis Phillips of Furman University conducted a national survey of state statutory mandates of continuing education for 16 professions. All 50 states reported regulations requiring continuing education for at least one profession; they range from Virginia and Missouri, which have requirements only for optometrists, to Iowa which reports continuing education regulations for all but social workers.

Mandatory continuing education has become established above all in the health field, but in adult education too continuing education based on curricula which become increasingly more structured is recommended (e.g., California) (see *Mandatory Continuing Education*).

Other areas where curricular structures can be found are those of health education in developing countries and consumer education in industrial states (Lowe 1982), although the experts in both cases advise against excessive standardization, which would make it impossible to allow for regional differences and also different educational levels.

Two further fields must be mentioned which have recently seen the development of curricular structures. One of these is the area of educational leave, for example in European Economic Community (EEC) countries (Degen and Nuissl 1983). Programmes aimed at promoting literacy in the sense of basic adult education also come into this category, as such literacy curricula include social as well as literacy and numeracy skills. Examples of these can be found in the United Kingdom and in West Africa (Bown and Tomori 1979). Some rather conceptual strategies, such as "recurrent education", and "self-management", and "self-government" cannot be discussed here. Another area that has not been included is the no doubt interesting relation between life cycles and interests (Huberman 1974, Lasker et al. 1980) in the sense of curricular ministructures, as there are as yet no recognizable instances where they have been implemented in adult education.

Many of the works listed in the bibliography contain reflections on the theory of curriculum development for adult education, but in contrast to curriculum construction for schools, scientific investigation of the subject with regard to adult education is still rudimentary and marginal (Skager and Dave 1977, Schlutz 1976, Dieckmann 1979). An international compendium bringing together all current findings is still lacking.

See also: Lifespan Learning: Implications for Educators

Bibliography

Arabin L 1980 Curriculum. In: Beinke L, Arabin L, Weinberg J (eds.) 1980 *Zukunftsaufgabe Weiterbildung*. Luxika, Weil der Stadt, Forchenrain

Benseman J 1980 *The Assessment and Meeting of Needs in Continuing Education*. Department of Education Research, Institute of Education, Stockholm

Bown L, Tomori S H O (eds.) 1979 *A Handbook of Adult Education for West Africa*. Hutchinson University Library for Africa, London

Brundage D H 1980 *Adult Learning Principles and their Application to Program Planning*. Ontario Ministry of Education, Toronto, Ontario

Clement W, Edding F 1979 *Recurrent Education und Berufliche Flexibilitätsforschung*. Duncker und Humblot, Berlin

Cross P K 1981 *Adult as Learners: Increasing Participation and Facilitating Learning*. Jossey-Bass, San Francisco, California

Degen G, Nuissl E 1983 *Studie über den (möglichen) Einfluß von Bildungsurlaub auf den Stand und die Entwicklung des Arbeitsmarktes in den Ländern der Europäischen Gemeinschaft*. Amt für amtliche Veröffentlichungen der Europäischen Gemeinschaften, Luxembourg

Dieckmann B 1976 Professionalisierung und einige Folgen für die Curriculumplanung in der Erwachsenenbildung. *Hessische Blätter für Volksbildung*. Max Hueber, Ismaning

Dieckmann B 1979 Legitimation von Curricula der Erwachsenenbildung auf der Grundlage empirischer Analysen. In: Siebert H (ed.) 1979 *Taschenbuch der Weiterbildungsforschung*. Burgbücherei W. Schneider, Baltmannsweiler

Houle C O 1980 *Continuing Learning in the Professions*. Jossey-Bass, San Francisco, California

Huberman A M 1974 *Some Models of Adult Learning and Adult Change*. Council of Europe, Strasbourg
Janne H 1977 *Organisation, Content and Methods of Adult Education*. Council of Europe, Strasbourg
Kaiser A 1977 Gesellschaftliche Bedingungen der Curriculumentwicklung im Weiterbildungsbereich. *Soziologie der Erwachsenenbildung*. Kohlhammer, Stuttgart
Kidd J R 1975 *How Adults Learn*. Association Press, New York
Knoll J H 1981 Findings and trends in adult education in a European perspective. In: Knoll J H (ed.) 1985 *Motivation for Adult Education*. German Commission for UNESCO, Saur, Munich
Knoll J H 1983a Alphabetisierung und Nachsorge-Maßnahmen. Beschreibung eines UNESCO-Projektes. *Bildung und Erziehung*. Böhlau, Cologne
Knoll J H 1983b Tendenzen beruflicher Erwachsenenbildung in der Bundesrepublik und in der DDR. *Volkshochschule im Westen* 4: 204
Knoll J H (ed.) 1986 *Internationales Jahrbuch der Erwachsenenbildung* Vols. 12, 13 Böhlau, Cologne
Kolfhaus S 1986 Von der musischen zur soziokulturellen bildung. *Studien zur Internationalen Erwachsenenbildung*, Vol. 6. Böhlau, Cologne
Lasker H, Moore J, Simpson E L 1980 *Adult Development and Approaches to Learning*. United States Department of Education, National Institute of Education, Washington, DC
Lowe J 1982 *The Education of Adults: A World Perspective*, 2nd edn. UNESCO, Paris
Mackie K 1981 *The Application of Learning Theory to Adult Teaching*. Department of Adult Education, University of Nottingham, Nottingham
Müller J, Biebrach I n.d. *Training and Orientation in Non-formal Basic Education*. UNESCO DOK 1168 A/a SE 21–6982, Berlin
Robinsohn S B 1972 *Bildungsreform als Revision des Curriculum und ein Strukturkonzept für Curriculumentwicklung*. Luchterhand, Neuwied-Berlin
Rockhill K 1983 Mandatory continuing education for professionals. *Trends and Issues in Adult Education* 33(2): 106
Schlutz E 1976 *Deutschunterricht in der Erwachsenenbildung*. Lexika, Grafenau
Siebert H 1974 *Curricula für die Erwachsenenbildung*. Westermann, Braunschweig
Siebert H 1975 Die Relevanz der Curriculumforschung für die Erwachsenenbildung. In: Knoll J H (ed.) 1975 *Internationales Jahrbuch der Erwachsenenbildung 1975*. Bertelsmann Universitätsverlag, Düsseldorf
Skager R, Dave R H (eds.) 1977 *Curriculum Evaluation for Lifelong Education: Developing Criteria and Procedures for the Evaluation of School Curricula in the Perspective of Lifelong Education: A Multinational Study*. Pergamon, Oxford
Tietgens H, Hirschmann G, Bianchi M 1974 *Ansätze zu einem Baukastensystem. Werkstattbericht über die Entwicklung des Zertifikatsprogramms der Volkshochschulen*. Westermann, Braunschweig
Tonkonogaja E P (ed.) 1978 *Unterricht mit Erwachsenen*. Wissenschaftliches Forschungsinstitut für Allgemeine Erwachsenenbildung der Akademie der Pädagogischen Wissenschaften der UdSSR, Volk und Wissen, Volkseigener, Berlin
Vaideanu G 1979 Die Problematik der modernen Welt, das Curriculum und die ständige Weiterbildung: methodologische Betrachtungen. *Bildung und Erziehung*. Böhlau, Cologne

Ideologies in Adult Education

H. Entwistle

Adult education has become, with great rapidity, a worldwide movement. Its advance and support has come as the result of economic, social, and religious forces, mobilized to achieve goals as widespread as to read a religious book, to advance political revolution, or to get a better job or social position. Ideologies abound. In Moslem or socialist countries there are orthodoxies which are expounded and expressed throughout most forms of adult education. In many developing countries, the main debate is about basic skills and knowledge that will lead to an improved economic position and some people claim that ideological enquiries are luxuries that can be engaged in later. However, for many adult educationists, Freire, Nyerere, and Gelpi for example, ideological considerations come first and affect all other decisions. Debate about these various positions is beginning to appear at national and international seminars.

Despite this ferment of ideas, many people view adult education typically as a technical process while for others in Moslem, socialist, or some Western countries, there is little debate because the answers are already accepted. Criticism is beginning to be heard about this refusal to engage, primarily in Western Europe and North America. While it is often charged that many adult educationalists in these Western countries are oblivious to political realities, it is in these countries where the main debate about ideologies occurs, often about the notion of liberal education and more recently of recurrent education.

1. Dispute in Western Countries

The classical conception of adult education in Europe and North America was of a network of institutions, developed over more than a century, transmitting the great tradition of Western culture to voluntary, interested adults from all walks of life. However, particularly since the Second World War, there has been recurrent questioning of this notion that, at its best, adult education consists of liberal education pursued for its own sake. Critics contend that this conception is ideological in the sense of being an inaccurate explanation of the nature of adult education, and one which serves only the interests of a particular social group, the middle class. This ideology has been continually challenged throughout the present century by those who believe that the education of adults should serve the different interests of the underprivileged.

These critics have argued, first, that the more traditional view ignores the origins of adult education within the Labor Movements of Europe and North America. Further, they argue, the development of adult education has always been politically motivated as a means towards amelioration of social and economic deprivation, even towards political revolution. To see adult education merely as a mode of continuing liberal education of individuals is to ignore the historical, radical imperative towards the creation of institutions for the education of adults. Hence, it is argued, the view that adult education is for the liberal education of individuals is not only deficient but reduces it to the status of a leisure activity and, therefore, a luxury which inevitably becomes an early casualty of economic recession in societies where economic instrumentalities define educational priorities.

Secondly, it is argued, the conventional liberal educational ideology with reference to adult education provides a rationale for takeover by the middle class of institutions created by or for the underprivileged. It has been a recurrent phenomenon within the history of adult education, that institutions intended for the education of workers have been exploited by high-school and college graduates for their own continuing education; a particular example of the sociological "law" that the middle class will appropriate for its own benefit any social institution intended to benefit the disadvantaged. Most adult classes, from university extension courses to those offered by local school boards, are now overwhelmingly attended by the already well-educated. Modern critics also argue that a major impetus towards this middle-class takeover of adult education has been its pursuit of control over other social classes. That is, when members of other social groups do occasionally attend adult classes, they experience not a radical questioning of the status quo, but a "high culture" curriculum embodying "high status knowledge." Consequently, the argument goes, working-class participants in adult classes acquire a taste for "bourgeois" knowledge and, far from learning to question the existing state of the social universe, they develop and come to defend middle-class tastes and values. Advocacy of the traditional liberal curriculum becomes an attempt to draw "the radical teeth" from adult education by prescribing a safe, disinterested curriculum which neglects those studies which are essential to radical social criticism. Thus, if adult education is inescapably political education, the historical outcome of this liberal dilution has been to sustain the political hegemony by stressing responsible citizenship and the pursuit of individual improvement, rather than to develop class consciousness aimed at the overthrow of the status quo. However, there lies a paradox in this twofold criticism that adult education has become a middle-class preserve; the more that middle-class acquisitiveness leads it to appropriate adult educational institutions for its own "consumption," the less these are available as instruments for the social control of other classes.

To the extent that adult education has become a luxury commodity for middle-class consumption and a means for disarming working-class radicals, it has prompted discussion of how to "restore" it to the educationally underprivileged. Given the revisionist view that, even in its heyday, workers' adult education never appealed to more than a small elite of the working class, how might it be brought for the first time to those for whom it was originally intended? This discussion focuses on two related problems. First, how can adult education be made to appeal more widely to the educationally underprivileged through radical change of curriculum and teaching method? This is the question of relevance. Secondly, there is the problem of whether such relevance can only be secured when the underprivileged themselves control adult education, defining its objectives, perhaps themselves providing the teaching, administration, and finance. This is the question of control and of adult education—independent of the state authority.

The argument for independence is that, whatever the proper objectives of adult education, these can only be secured when institutions are freed from control by the socially and educationally privileged. The classic confrontations on this issue occurred towards the end of the nineteenth century on both sides of the Atlantic, but it is a persistent issue. Recently, the kind of criticism which the "deschoolers" made of schools has been applied to adult education (Illich 1970). Adult education also needs to be "deschooled," according to its critics, especially in order to dissociate it in the perceptions of underprivileged adults from that institution where, as children, they experienced repeated failure, prompting the conclusion that education is irrelevant to their needs. According to critics, independence is also required because "bourgeois" values and cultural norms dominate the adult curriculum such that the underprivileged become "permanent prisoners of someone else's conception of their happiness."

However, there are several problems in the notion of independent adult education. The first is economic. With reference to the financing of adult education, insistence upon independence implies private provision. Indeed, in the past, adult education has often been provided by private institutions: political parties, cooperative societies, labor unions, societies for ad hoc political reform, churches, as well as by industrial enterprises. But, especially when adult education is advocated as radical political education, one difficulty has been that even when it is funded privately by associations of the underprivileged for the betterment of their own members, it has appealed to only a minority—a minority, even, amongst their own members—thus leaving untouched the mass of underprivileged citizens without institutional affiliation. Hence, from the point of view that everyone, *qua* citizen, requires adult education, private provision must remain grossly inadequate. Yet the view that public funding should be made available for the pursuit of radically new initiatives to make adult education relevant and widen its appeal, obviously places the advocates of independence on the horns of a dilemma. On the one hand, independence implies the rejection of state aid (as Jonothan Kozol 1975 has eloquently argued of schooling): public financing (even if this were not subject to retrenchment in times of economic recession) inevitably carries strings which are unacceptable to advocates of independence. On the other hand, those private institutions founded by the underprivileged which have traditionally provided adult education, lack the economic means to fund this on a scale which would make it universally available.

One way out of this predicament is to conclude that, as an instrument of social change, the provision of adult education need not reach all adults within a country. (Leaders in socialist or Moslem states would not relinquish ideas of universality.) Arguably, vast social gains over a century and a half have been achieved in Europe by the underprivileged through the leadership of what Gramsci called "organic intellectuals": those from the working class who have availed themselves of adult education in order to provide leadership for their fellow workers. Hoggart characterized these relatively few who, historically, have been students in adult classes as "a saving remnant" (Hoggart 1958). The implication is that although those who seek their own further education are few—an "earnest minority," in another of Hoggart's phrases—they also have a mission with reference to their fellows which succeeds out of all proportion to their numbers. Hence, the conception that the success of an educational enterprise is to be measured by external criteria having to do with social and economic change does not require the counting of heads, such that adult education is judged a failure if it lacks widespread appeal. However, those who believe that adult education should appeal to more than "an earnest minority" cannot be satisfied with a criterion of success which leaves the majority untouched by any kind of continuing education as adults. For one thing, it can be argued that social change would be more comprehensive and radical if everyone were politically educated; even that the only satisfactory state of affairs would be one in which every individual's consciousness were so raised by education that none would accept exploitation and each would actively labor for his or her own and his or her neighbor's good. On this view, there would be no question of some few providing leadership and nurture for a majority. Moreover, as well as the macro social and economic problems to which associations of the underprivileged have to address themselves, there are the micro individual and domestic problems which loom large in personal life as well as the problems of local communities whose solutions seem to require local initiatives. This conviction has inspired an approach to adult education as, essentially, community education which focuses not upon the disinterested pursuit of knowledge from the traditional disciplines of the arts and natural sciences, but which concentrates, pragmatically and relevantly, upon the problems of local communities and the groups and individuals within them. Those favoring a community-organized approach have long been arguing that the education of these is ill-served by public and voluntary institutions which seek to impose an irrelevant "liberal" curriculum. From this point of view, the majority declines to participate in adult education, not because of apathy or hostility towards education, but because it deems existing provision to be indifferent to its dilemmas: asking for bread it is offered a stone.

Thus, a second major emphasis upon the need for independent adult education (for which economic independence is, indeed, a condition) relates to questions of curriculum and the organization of teaching. The curricular emphasis in institutions which have provided education for the underprivileged (for example, universities in England) either directly through university extension programs or through graduates working as tutors in independent agencies like the Workers' Educational Association (WEA) has been upon conventional academic subjects, especially from the arts and sciences (but often deliberately excluding the social sciences) and upon the disinterested pursuit of these. Radical critics who have stressed the need for independence from this "liberal" provision have campaigned either for a curriculum rooted in the social sciences, especially economics and sociology, or for one focused pragmatically upon insistent, immediate social problems. As long as a century ago in England, when criticizing the Mechanics Institutes, one artisan complained at being made to study the behavior of "the winds" when more pressing problems claimed his attention than those of meteorologists. Some revisionist accounts of the Mechanics Institutes have faulted them for failing to provide a radical political education for the working class and (probably a consequence of this) for their takeover by the middle class in pursuit of its own further education. Earlier this century, the defectors from Ruskin College, Oxford, explained their action, in part, as resulting from its preoccupation with "disinterested" literary and historical studies, its neglect of sociology and, especially, of an alternative Marxist economic theory.

The response of the defenders of the "liberal" tradition of adult education against this radical, instrumentalist criticism amounts to the claim that social change is only possible through the agency of men and women who are educated in the traditional disinterested sense. If the "high culture" of the traditional curriculum has served to confer status, privilege, wealth, and power upon the ruling class, why should the underprivileged and exploited believe that they can replace the existing hegemony without such knowledge. Gramsci, the late Italian Marxist, mocked instrumentalist critics of his own advocacy of traditional humanistic schooling by asking them to explain how, if the education of the ruling class were dismissed as "bourgeois" (in the sense of decadent or effete), it had succeeded in keeping other classes in its hegemonic thrall. For Gramsci, the superiority of traditional "high culture" (though he did not use the term) over utilitarian alternatives lay precisely in its political utility. Traditional academic knowledge can be politically powerful precisely because it offers more logical, coherent, systematic, and complete accounts of the sociopolitical universe than does knowledge acquired piecemeal and pragmatically for the solution of immediate local problems. Gramsci believed that, for want of adequate cultural and educational provision, the Italian working class had been driven to improvise hurried, careless, emergency solutions to its problems; with proper education it would learn to approach its problems "in a disinterested manner without waiting for the stimulus of actual events." Hence his claim was that the educational problem was that of the underprivileged gaining access to exactly the kind of education which had so well served the socially privileged.

The conviction that a person learns to solve particular ad hoc problems by first turning his or her back on them in the disinterested pursuit of a liberal education which widens his or her horizons (and, hence, helps to deepen their perception of the nature of problems) led Gramsci to a positive evaluation of the tradition of liberal adult education which he found elsewhere in Europe, especially in Germany and England and Wales. He believed these countries to be served by "some very powerful organizations of working class socialist culture." In England and Wales, the strength of adult education lay in its having put "into the service of [the] work of cultivation and spiritual liberation, a great part of the English intellectual and university world." This refers to the well-known English tradition of workers' adult education whose best-known practitioner was R. H. Tawney.

The success of the Danish Folk High Schools for Young Adults provides another example of the way in which practical consequences can follow from a curriculum providing a liberal education. Although the curriculum of these schools contained no technical or management training, it is generally assumed that their graduates revolutionized the techniques and organization of Danish agriculture.

A further problem in much of the instrumentalist advocacy of adult education which focuses pragmatically upon education for social change is that it intimates little of what might constitute the good life if all our social dilemmas were solved; or, indeed, of what education might contribute to the quality of individual lives whilst society struggles towards the millenium. Tawney's mature conclusion was that adult education must contribute towards radical social change, but he did not renounce an earlier conviction that liberal education could also nourish the cultural life of the economically exploited. The first British Labour MP, Thomas Burt, reinforced this belief in the liberal cultural potential of adult education: "We say educate a man not simply because he has got political powers... but educate him because he is a man." A more recent conclusion that underprivileged adult learners look for something more from education than knowledge having simply instrumental political and social value was derived by Lovett from his experience in an adult educational enterprise related to community development in Liverpool. Convinced of the importance of bringing educational resources to bear on community problems, but open-minded about the experiment, Lovett discovered a demand for courses related to personal development or recreation. But it was also as a by-product of these individually oriented activities that "most local residents became actively involved in community affairs."

A modern resolution of the clash between "liberal" and "instrumental" ideologies with reference to adult education might be approached through the dialectic of a pedagogy which incorporates both approaches. Indeed, a modern practitioner of adult education within the university extension system (the Marxist historian E. P. Thompson) has pointed to the inevitable dialectic which is implicit in the "abrasion of different worlds of experience, in which ideas are brought to the test of life," when the academic viewpoint of the adult teacher has to justify itself against the commonsense everyday experience of the working student. Incidentally, Thompson believes that one outcome of this abrasion (at least in his own discipline) has been the exploration of areas of social history long neglected in the university. And, arguably, the correlate of this fact that academic life is enriched by juxtaposition with commonsense experience is that adult students' everyday perceptions of social reality are probably similarly transformed.

The notion of teachers and underprivileged adult students bringing their different insights to bear upon problems facing local communities has led recently to advocacy of "participatory research." Similarly, it is crucial to Freire's "pedagogy of the oppressed" that adult education should be a dialogue, requiring a reciprocal relationship between teacher and learner. The educator, as well as the educatee, also requires to be educated. Only when every teacher becomes a student and every student a teacher can schooling avoid degenerating into tyranny.

2. Conclusion

This discussion of the ideologies of adult education has focused upon a century-long debate about the aims, methods, and clientele of institutionalized learning, a debate conducted largely in terms of social class. If the modern version of this debate is not always posed in conventional terms of class conflict, it *is* often concerned with the failure of adult education to engage the interests of groups of the underprivileged—disaffected (often unemployed) youth, racial minorities, ghetto and slum dwellers—those who have been characterized as living in the "culture of poverty." On the other hand, if there exists a modern ideological threat to the interests of such groups, it probably lies in the advocacy of recurrent education as a universal requirement in a period of dramatic technological and social change. For example, the notion that everyone needs recurrent vocational or professional retraining to avoid skill obsolescence is more applicable to those already trained in skilled and professional occupations than to the unskilled and semi-skilled whose initial training and education was minimal. The conclusion that recurrent education is required by everyone in a modern society must not be allowed to obscure adult education's historic mission to bring the benefits of schooling to those who remain underprivileged despite the universalization of primary and secondary schooling in advanced industrial societies.

This concern about the possible consequences of one concept such as recurrent education upon other forms of adult education, or renewed support for and criticism of programs for literacy, are reminders that adult education will continue to be an activity suffused with political attributes and effects, and that the candid debate of ideas and ideologies are at its very center.

Bibliography

Elias J L, Merriam S (eds.) 1980 *Philosophical Foundations of Adult Education.* Krieger, Huntington, New York

Entwistle H 1979 *Antonio Gramsci: Conservative Education for Radical Politics.* Routledge and Kegan Paul, London

Freire P 1970 *Pedagogy of the Oppressed.* Herder and Herder, New York

Freire P 1973 *Education for Critical Consciousness.* Seabury, New York

Hoggart R 1958 *The Use of Literacy.* Hebian Books, Harmondsworth

Illich I D 1970 *Deschooling Society.* Harper and Row, New York

Kozol J 1975 *The Night is Dark and I am Far from Home.* Bantam, New York

Lovett T 1975 *Adult Education, Community Development and the Working Class.* Ward Lock, London

Simon B 1974 *Education and the Labour Movement.* Lawrence and Wishart, London

Thompson E P 1968 *Education and Experience.* Leeds University Press, Leeds

Thompson J L (ed.) 1980 *Adult Education for a Change.* Hutchinson, London

UNESCO Recommendations

H. Körner

Because the greatest growth in recognition and acceptance of adult education as a field of education has occurred since the late 1950s, it has been more influenced by international documents and actions than any other field. The most impressive example of the impact of international action upon the field is the *Recommendation* passed at the 1976 session of the General Conference of UNESCO. In fact, action had begun several years earlier, at the Second World Conference on Adult Education (Montreal 1960), and at a similar conference held in Tokyo in 1972. In between these years, there had been several enquiries about the most appropriate form of international action that might be taken and a degree of consensus had been achieved about concepts and definitions on which, previously, there had been considerable disagreement.

The Third International Conference on Adult Education, convened in Tokyo, 1972, invited UNESCO to investigate the desirability of elaborating an international normative instrument setting out the principles and fundamental problems of adult education (Recommendation no. 7).

Pursuing this initiative, the General Conference of UNESCO decided later the same year, at its 17th session, that a preliminary study would be carried out on the technical and legal aspects of the preparation of such a normative instrument. Produced with the assistance of Marcel Hicter, Director-General at the Ministry of French Culture of Belgium, the study was presented to the Governing Bodies of UNESCO in 1974. After concluding that an international regulation on adult education was both desirable and feasible, it listed the fields suited for the application of normative measures. They included questions of general policy, structures, institutions, organization, financing, condition of adult students, profile and professional status of personnel, means to be used, and international cooperation.

After examining this preliminary study, the General Conference considered it desirable that an international normative instrument should be elaborated and that it should take the form of a recommendation which would invite member states to take legislative or administrative measures in order to put into effect the principles and norms set forth in the recommendation.

A preliminary draft of the Recommendation on the Development of Adult Education was subsequently prepared and sent to all UNESCO member states for comment in 1975. It undertook to define the theory and practice of adult education in the context of lifelong learning, to mobilize political support for its development, and to pave the way for action at the national level. Thirty-six member states, 12 of which were developing countries, responded with comments bearing on matters of both the form and substance of the preliminary draft. A revised draft was then prepared taking these comments into account and submitted to a Special Committee of Technical and Legal Experts, which met in Paris in June 1976 and was attended by specialists from 69 countries and some 20 international organizations. The work of the Committee focused primarily on the treatment of a substantial number of proposed amendments to the draft Recommendation. At the final meeting, a text was approved which consisted of a preamble and 67 articles divided into 10 chapters. After a slight modification, this test was unanimously adopted on 26 November 1976 by the UNESCO General Conference at its 19th session, held in Nairobi, Kenya.

Chapter One of the Recommendation defines adult education as follows:

> the term "adult education" denotes the entire body of organized educational processes, whatever the content, level and method, whether formal or otherwise, whether they prolong or replace initial education in schools, colleges and universities as well as in apprenticeship, whereby persons regarded as adult by the society in which they belong develop their abilities, enrich their knowledge, improve their technical or professional qualifications or turn them in a new direction and bring about changes in their attitudes or behaviour in the twofold perspective of full personal development and participation in balanced and independent social, economic, and cultural development. (Para 1, Chap. 1)

Chapter Two of the Recommendation sets forth the general objectives of adult education, indicating, in particular, that it should foster the development of a critical understanding of contemporary world problems and of the necessary aptitudes for the acquisition of new knowledge and qualifications, as well as encourage adults to participate in the development of their society in an active and creative manner. In addition it advocates including provision for adult education in national development plans and defining the goals of this education in relation to those of other components of the educational system and to those of social, cultural, and economic development policies.

Regarding the content of adult education activities, the Recommendation states that they should be adapted to the needs and aspirations of social groups or local communities to which they are addressed, with priority accorded to the specific needs of educationally underprivileged groups. The salient features of the content, organized by type or by target group, are then described.

After defining the circumstances which should be taken into account in the choice of methods and listing several that favour high rates of participation, the chapter dealing with methods, means, research, and evaluation specifies that "participation in an adult education programme should be subject only to the ability to follow the course of training provided and not to any (upper) age limit or any condition concerning the possession of a diploma or qualification" (Para 30, Chap. 4).

Questions relating to structure, on the one hand, and to management, administration, and coordination in adult education, on the other, are treated in two distinct chapters in the Recommendation. Mention is made of the necessity of establishing flexible networks of bodies capable of responding, in a complementary manner, to the educational needs of individuals and collectives. Particularly emphasized is the need to maximize the utilization of organizations and institutions which do not necessarily have adult education as their primary concern. Examples include schools, universities, mass media, trade union and cooperative organizations, and industrial and commercial firms. Another issue addressed is the need to set up, at various levels, structures or procedures for consultation and coordination between public authorities competent in the field of adult education and the numerous bodies conducting programmes in this area. Finally, several articles concern the financing of adult education, particularly through public funding. Points which are particularly emphasized include: the need to allocate to adult education resources corresponding to its importance in the promotion of social, cultural, and economic development; the importance of safeguarding the autonomy of nongovernmental organizations that receive state subsidies; and the necessity of ensuring that the lack of financial resources should not constitute an obstacle to participating in educational activities for those who so desire.

Persons working in adult education should, according to the Recommendation, have special skills, knowledge, understanding, and attitudes. They should have working conditions and salaries comparable to those of their counterparts in other branches of the educational system.

Two chapters of the Recommendation are devoted respectively to the relationships between adult and youth education, on the one hand, and between adult education and work, on the other. The first places special emphasis, in a perspective of lifelong learning, on the necessity of preparing youth for continuing education in adulthood. The second refers to the facilities which should be accorded to workers to enable them to participate in educational activities for the purpose of improving their professional qualifications to meet constantly evolving economic and technological demands.

The Recommendation concludes with a series of provisions on bilateral and multilateral international cooperation and, in particular, on technical assistance and on exchanges of persons, ideas, information, and documentation.

The Recommendation on the Development of Adult Education is a document which is broad in scope to the extent that it seeks to cover all those aspects of adult education which lend themselves to regulation. At all stages of the preparation of this instrument, great effort was made to incorporate the views of specialists from many countries and to elaborate a draft which would be not only acceptable to a maximum number of member states, but also sufficiently diverse in its appeal to elicit action in the form of concrete decisions in a wide variety of socioeconomic contexts. The Recommendation thus is more a set of possible approaches than a manual of technical advice.

The adoption of the Recommendation has led a certain number of countries to hold special meetings, to publish reports, and to prepare studies comparing the state of adult education under specific conditions, to the principles enunciated in the normative instrument. The authentic text of the Recommendation, adopted in the five working languages used by the UNESCO General Conference (Arabic, English, French, Russian, and Spanish), has been translated into many other languages. Two years after the adoption, the governments of 22 countries presented to UNESCO special reports on the action taken to follow up the Recommendation.

In 1982–1984, within the framework of the preparation of the Fourth International Conference on Adult Education (Paris, March 1985), information was collected among UNESCO member states on the follow-up, from 1977 onwards, to the Recommendation. Seventy-six replies amounting to approximately 2000 pages were received. Their detailed analysis formed the basis of a synoptic report which was made available to participants in the above mentioned Conference (UNESCO 1985).

See also: International Adult Education

Bibliography

Kidd J R 1974 *A Tale of Three Cities, Elsinore–Montreal–Tokyo: The Influence of Three UNESCO World Conferences upon the Development of Adult Education.* Syracuse University, Syracuse, New York

Lowe J 1982 *The Education of Adults: A World Perspective*, 2nd edn. UNESCO, Paris, OISE, Toronto

UNESCO 1974 Possible adoption of an international instrument on the development of adult education: A preliminary study of the technical and legal aspects of an international instrument on the development of adult education, 94 EX/12. UNESCO, Paris

UNESCO 1975 Development of adult education: A preliminary report of the Director-General concerning the position with regard to the problem to be regulated and the possible scope of the regulating action proposed, ED/MD/37. UNESCO, Paris

UNESCO 1976a Development of adult education: A final report of the Director-General on the same, ED/MD/40. UNESCO, Paris

UNESCO 1976b Draft recommendation on the development of adult education, 19 C/24. UNESCO, Paris

UNESCO 1977 *Records of the General Conference, Nineteenth Session, Nairobi 1976*, Vol. 1. UNESCO, Paris

UNESCO 1985 Adult education since the third international conference on adult education (Tokyo 1972): Round-up of replies to the survey carried out by UNESCO among national commissions with a view to gathering information on the development of adult education, ED-85/CONF 210/4. UNESCO, Paris

Thematic Variations in Adult Education

Introduction

In the eyes of a number of theorists and educators neither lifelong education as usually defined, nor adult education as it has been traditionally practised meet completely the requirements of modern individuals and society. A number of ideas, all including both concepts to some degree, have been elaborated to formulate an approach to educational activities which will spell out more adequately what needs to be done.

One criticism of lifelong education has been that the concept is too vague and unrealistic, that one cannot be a permanent student, and that therefore something more precise and closer to the possible should be formulated. One concept is outlined in *Recurrent Education*, which argues for alternation between education and other activities throughout life and presents some of the factors which have influenced the development of this idea and the arguments which are affecting its realization in practice.

Recurrent education has been widely welcomed in occupationally related education. The articles *Community Education and Community Development*, and *Sociocultural Animation* treat a number of ideas, between which there are close similarities, whose impact is intended to be felt outside job-oriented study. Both articles make it clear that the concepts they discuss are founded on the idea that communities should have power and responsibility in their own educational and cultural life and that the activities associated with it should cover all ages. Community education attempts to integrate formal schooling with the out-of-school education which it is the function of sociocultural animation to stimulate. Community development, which has been tried in both advanced and developing countries, includes educational initiatives as part of a wider process designed to improve the overall standard of life of a society.

"Nonformal education" is a term more commonly used in many developing countries than "adult education". It denotes any education outside the formal system of school and higher education. The article *Formal and Nonformal Education: Future Strategies* considers the interrelation of the two, their integration with projects for development, and their possible lines of growth. That on *Nonformal Education* presents the characteristics—methodological, economic, political and sociocultural—which make nonformal education so attractive. Although it is widely practised in advanced countries (where it usually goes under other names, such as "out-of-school education" or "sociocultural animation"), the term itself is most current among the developing nations, where nonformal education is particularly attractive to countries which cannot afford expensive formal provision, or which have become somewhat disillusioned with the latter's performance. *Nonformal Education Policy: Developing Countries* examines the goals nonformal education is intended to achieve, its apparent advantages and the achievements and shortcomings it has revealed in practice.

Fundamental to all the concepts of, and relating to, adult education and lifelong education has been the principle that participation in adult learning activities should be voluntary, although in practice there have been exceptions. The rapid changes in knowledge and skills associated with certain professions, particularly since the early 1980s, have put the principle under severe threat. It is widely believed that, for the protection of their clientele, practitioners of these professions should be obliged, as in many cases they already are, to undergo training to update their competence. *Mandatory Continuing Education* discusses how the pressure for enforcement arose, the arguments for and against it, and future trends in this matter.

Recurrent Education

J. Bengtsson

This article is divided into three sections: the first presents an overview of recent developments in recurrent education as they relate to educational policy making, changes in the educational system, and supporting socioeconomic policies; the second section presents a set of new emerging socioeconomic trends and factors that are likely to have an impact on the future development of recurrent education; and the final section presents some ideas and arguments concerning the possibility today of expanding recurrent education opportunities for both youth and adults.

1. An Overview of the Present Situation

In the development of recurrent education as a policy strategy there is hardly a single point at which one can firmly state that "this system is now a system of recurrent education". Although many educational developments in recent years possess specific recurrent education characteristics, they have nevertheless to be seen as a number of sequential developments. Therefore, even if the adoption of recurrent education as a planning principle can be made at a single determinable moment, the actual implementation consists of a series of measures whose cumulative effect will, only over a certain period of time, give the appearance of a more fully fledged recurrent education system.

It is therefore no surprise that for most people the dominant life pattern is still education, then work, and then retirement. The basic aim of the recurrent education proposition, as it was presented in the early 1970s, was the modification of the existing educational system so that access to it was not confined to the individual's early years but was available at intervals over the whole life-cycle in alternation with work and other activities.

To be more specific, the basic principles of recurrent education as originally outlined by the Organisation for Economic Co-operation and Development (OECD) are:

(a) The last years of compulsory education should provide a curriculum that gives each pupil a real choice between further study and work.

(b) After leaving compulsory school, access to postcompulsory education should be guaranteed to the individual at appropriate times over his or her total life cycle.

(c) Distribution of facilities should be such as to make education available to all individuals, so far as possible wherever and whenever they need it.

(d) Work and other social experience should be regarded as a basic element in admission requirements and design.

(e) It should be possible to pursue any career in an intermittent way, alternating between study and work.

(f) Curricular design and content and teaching methodology should be designed in cooperation with the different groups involved (students, teachers, administrators, etc.) and adapted to the interests and motivations of different age and social groups.

(g) Degrees and certificates should not be looked upon as an "end result" of an educational career but rather as steps in a process of lifelong education, a lifelong career, and personality development.

(h) On completion of compulsory school, each individual should be given a right to periods of educational leave of absence with necessary provisions for maintaining job and social security.

Since the idea first became prominent, progress has been somewhat uneven in the above areas. For the purpose of this overview it is possible to distinguish developments at the policy level; at the level of educational institutions and practice; and at the level of supporting policies outside the educational sphere.

1.1 Educational Policy Sphere

It can be safely stated that recurrent education, like similar concepts such as lifelong learning or permanent education, has been accepted in principle as a policy objective. On numerous occasions educational policy makers in a number of countries have paid tribute to the basic idea that educational opportunities should not be confined to the individual's early years but should be available over the whole life span.

It is true that there is still certain confusion as to the exact meaning of concepts like recurrent education, lifelong learning, permanent education, and so on, but they all have a fundamental common denominator, namely the belief that given rapidly changing cultural and socioeconomic conditions, education cannot be limited to the front-end model but also has to be available to individuals at intervals throughout their lives. This acceptance of the overall recurrent education objective was clearly manifested in the ministerial declaration at the first OECD ministerial meeting in 1978 of the OECD Education Committee: "To stimulate the development of more recurrent education opportunities for young people and adults to continue education at all levels after periods of work".

However, as the recurrent education strategy, distinct from the lifelong learning and permanent education concepts, has given strong emphasis to the notion of coordination with other policy areas like human resources and social policies, it is also important to stress that progress in this respect has been less clear. One might conclude that this reflects a certain gap between verbal adherence to the overall concept and actual policy practice. The existence of such a gap can of course be seen as a consequence of the long-term character of a recurrent education strategy, but it leads also to the interpretation that the diversity of national conceptions and situations has resulted in a more piecemeal and ad hoc approach than the unified and demanding approach suggested by the initial formulation of the strategy.

1.2 The Educational System

Actual changes in the structure and content of the existing system towards recurrent education, have been less marked. There has certainly been a considerable increase in individual demand for education later on in life and different kinds of postsecondary and adult education institutions have responded in innovative ways through short courses and modular systems as well as by changing rigid admission requirements, including in some cases the recognition of work experience as a qualification in its own right. Similarly, the physical availability of educational facilities has increased with important innovations in the establishment of new institutions and in the development of nontraditional kinds of education, so that geographical and temporal constraints have been less severe. The growth of distance teaching through the mass media and other technical developments, and pressure from community educators to allow round-the-clock use of facilities, have also contributed to the expansion of access to learning opportunities. But on the whole, and in most countries, this expansion has taken place at the "periphery" of the postsecondary system leaving for instance the traditional institutions more-or-less unaffected.

As to the crucial level of upper-secondary education, however, the recurrent education proposition has had a very limited effect, even if today one can observe an increasing interest for the extension of recurrent education to these levels, due basically to the persistent and burning problem of youth unemployment. But in most countries upper-secondary education still continues to be the big sorting mechanism despite recent efforts to provide more vocationally oriented education to certain categories of pupils considered as risk groups in terms of unemployment. It can be argued that the credibility of a recurrent education strategy to a large extent depends on what changes can be made to incorporate this part of the educational system within such a strategy, and this will be returned to later on in this article.

1.3 Supporting Policies

When the strategy of recurrent education was originally formulated, it was recognized that its realization would depend on certain supporting policies outside the traditional educational policy field. One of the most far reaching of the suggestions which would coordinate policies from the different sectors was that of an integrated insurance system, or drawing right, which could be used for recurrent education as well as other activities, but in no country has there been significant progress in this direction. Paid educational leave (PEL) was one policy strategy, dependent upon supporting policies, and perhaps one of the most important and interesting developments over this period has been precisely the spread of educational leave schemes, drawing attention to the notion of alternation between education and work.

In recent developments of recurrent education there is clearly both progress and stagnation. There has been definite progress at the level of education policy making in acceptance of the concept of recurrent education as an area for further educational development. On the other hand, actual implementation of the concept within the existing system has been either of a piecemeal character or else completely lacking. It is perhaps premature to seek an explanation of this, but the fact that there is a certain scepticism about the values of education today, coupled with budgetary constraint, gives, certainly, a part of the explanation behind the inadequate implementation of the concept.

Finally, it is therefore not unduly cynical to pose the question whether recurrent education, originally conceived during the period of educational expansion, will become one of those educational ideas that are verbally and policywise accepted and supported but have very little impact on educational practice. Such a scenario can certainly not be excluded in the 1980s with serious uncertainties concerning the economy, employment, and public expenditures. However, it might also be that this new and emerging socioeconomic situation will accelerate the development of recurrent education.

2. New Socioeconomic Factors Impinging on the Future of Recurrent Education

The development of recurrent education has always been closely tied to the social and economic trends and changes within countries. This has hardly been very surprising for a number of reasons:

(a) recurrent education, as a policy strategy of redistributing educational opportunities and resources over the whole life span of individuals through alternation of education with the other major life activities, is thereby immediately located in people's worklives and the labour market, their family, domestic and leisure lives, and with the social and economic forces which shape all these domains;

(b) it has never been viewed as a purely educational policy, but extends into the area of social and economic policy more generally and its main purposes and rationales have mirrored this breadth; and

(c) a great deal of recurrent education is organized outside the formal education system, or at the blurred boundary between this system and other agencies and institutions.

As a long-term strategy and one still in its formative stage, it is therefore important to look at major macroeconomic and social trends to see how they might influence its evolution, to examine how the arguments and rationales for such a strategy can be related to these patterns and changes, and to look for ways in which recurrent education can contribute to the solution of some of the major societal problems and issues facing it now and in the future.

In looking particularly at the developed countries in the mid-1980s and comparing the situation with the one when recurrent education was first formulated as a major policy strategy in the late 1960s one is struck by both stability and change. For instance, the education–work–retirement life pattern is still dominant—arguably even more so as more and more women enter the labour market and follow a similar course and as people live longer, thus prolonging a normal period of retirement at the end of their life spans. The distribution of income and life chances is still strikingly unequal and income inequalities have got little better and, if anything, have been exacerbated in the 1970s and 1980s. Moreover, the climate which existed in the 1960s—that social change was desirable and feasible and possible through social policies—has often given way to one of retrenchment and much greater caution as to either the necessity or possibility of social policies bringing about desired large-scale change. With economic recession and high levels of unemployment and inflation, there seems to be a trend towards less state activity and expenditure and less active involvement in redistributing social welfare than there was in the 1960s. Individuals have frequently become more concerned about the value of the money in their pockets and their survival in the labour market than about the less tangible social, distributive concerns which hitherto seemed so important.

Amidst this imposing array of structural changes can be added another at least as important—the speed and direction of technical change. The conventional view of technological development and its impact on growth and employment, was that technological development created at least as many jobs as it displaced. Moreover, the reduction of menial and unskilled jobs was claimed as a welcome spin-off. While it is impossible to assert with any degree of certainty what the precise contribution of technological change has been to unemployment, still less to predict its future impact, it is becoming widely alleged that such change, and particularly the development and use of microtechnology, is having a significant adverse impact on the number of available jobs. Moreover, its effect is right across the board—public and private sector, manual and nonmanual occupations. This adds a critical new dimension and tension to an already serious disequilibrium between the demand for and supply of labour. It has also been asserted in some quarters, partly due to the timing of what is being labelled the "technological revolution" during a period of severe economic difficulties, that the extensive use to which this technology is already being put is much more to rationalize than to innovate. Since such obviously labour-saving technologies cannot create new jobs without innovation and the establishment of new markets, without such a change of its use its impact is likely to be significant and negative upon the demand for labour.

Whatever their disagreements on other matters, economists are generally agreed that the present economic situation and levels of unemployment have to be accounted for by the demand rather than the supply side of labour. Nonetheless, it is clear that changes in the supply of labour have come at a time when the labour market has been least ready to meet them. Two of the main changes are familiar enough—the increased, and still rising, numbers of women who work or seek paid work, and the ageing of the "baby boom generation", who no longer fill school classrooms but often jobs or unemployment registers. Also people often wish to remain in the labour market in some way rather than be suddenly forced into retirement at a given age, since they are now more healthy and live longer. These developments in the labour supply are not just economic phenomena. They are, of course, rooted in demographic and social changes which cannot be reversed. The problem remains, nonetheless, of how to meet the demands and wishes of different groups in the present situation, especially as these supply-side changes affect not only overall job prospects but may be seen to lead to fiercer competition between social groups for jobs.

The issues raised above relate also to one of the most important emerging questions for the 1980s, namely, the distribution and changes in work and nonwork time for the individual over his or her whole life cycle. Most developed countries have experienced a gradual decline in the working week, marked increases in holidays and vacations, and perhaps most significantly, changes in length of working lives and the balance of work to other activities during the life cycle. People enter the labour force later, retirement policies are changing, and life expectancy has increased significantly during this century—with the possibility of still greater life expectancy in the future. Moreover, the time spent in work activities has been increasingly concentrated into the middle years while nonwork has been concentrated in the early and late years of life. Another major component in nonwork time is now unemployment, which raises strongly the question of how work and nonwork should be distributed for different groups in society, as high unemployment becomes a permanent feature for a number of countries. Certainly, education is only one amongst several institutions that will have to respond in a creative way to these emerging new social and economic forces, but making educational opportunities available over the individual's whole life cycle and during his or her increased nonwork time could be of vital importance.

Relating these trends to recurrent education is now more pertinent than ever, as a highly trained work force, which can rapidly adjust to the changing demands of production, seems now even more essential. It may be countered that countries suffer from a surplus, not a shortage, of trained labour. Yet the indications are that in certain highly skilled, both manual and nonmanual occupations, there is frequently a lack of trained personnel, resulting to some extent both from the sluggishness of training and education to adjust to new needs and from the economic difficulties of firms which have led to a heavy reliance on existing personnel and to increasingly firm-specific training. Now that the need is pressing for a labour force which is both skilled and flexible, greater recurrent education opportunities seem needed indeed.

Nor is this argued only from the point of view of fitting people into available slots in the job market. It is increasingly said that Western societies will have to readjust the nature of their economies in recognition of the situation which faces them in the 1980s. To say that they will be knowledge based and innovative is to be unhelpfully general. Nonetheless, if and when the restructuring of economies of countries takes place, it is hardly imaginable that it can happen without a highly developed education and training system, to which individuals will have access not just once in their lives but on a recurrent basis, and in which there will be much greater coherence and coordination between the various education and training sectors—in other words, a recurrent education system.

It is also possible that countries are moving into an epoch where standards of living can be maintained, or increased, while demanding less work from individuals over their life cycles. Thus in such a changing mixture of work and nonwork time, it may be argued that, even with a much more extensive recurrent education system, full employment in the traditional sense will not be restored to former levels. Hence, while due emphasis should be placed on the development of a highly skilled and flexible work force, it will be equally important that people can use their education for their own interests or as a meaningful activity in its own right during periods when they are not working. Whilst the notion of a "leisure society" is still only a cliché, it is perhaps no longer a far-away dream but part of an image of the "post-industrial" society which is within reach and of which recurrent education would be an integral part.

3. Education for Young People and Adults: The Recurrent Education Alternative

The principal idea of recurrent education is that individuals will have systematic and genuine opportunities and access to education throughout their lifetime, both as an objective in its own right and closely related to the realities and objectives of the economic and social worlds in which they live. Whilst this will surely involve careful organization and planning, the widening of access to existing institutions and agencies, a certain redistribution of educational and financial resources, and innovatory approaches to new clientele, it is not a call for the creation of large new administrative machinery and institutions.

Given the experience from many countries that the development of such coordination needs both time and serious efforts, one must not expect any changes to arrive overnight. However, this should not mean that educational authorities see recurrent education as something always to be realized in the future. There are many things which could be done today by educational authorities if they decided to materialize their concern for recurrent education. At least two fairly well-defined educational policy areas could be seen as potential fields for experiments with recurrent education; namely upper-secondary education and adult education.

3.1 Recurrent Education and Youth

As was mentioned earlier, recurrent education has so far had a very limited impact on the age group 16–19 years old, despite the stress that originally was put on necessary changes at this level of the system in order to lay the platform for a recurrent education system. A large proportion of the pupils who leave the system at this age still enter the labour market inadequately prepared and increasingly the jobs they get, if they are lucky enough to find employment, are relatively unlikely to form part of a proper career structure. The tendency of the education system at this stage to close more options than it opens for many young people is further aggravated by the persistent and burning problem of increasing youth unemployment.

It is in this context that the recent interest in recurrent education for the 16–19 age group has to be seen, coupled with a certain scepticism vis-à-vis the measures against youth unemployment that have been tried out over the last few years, both on the education and work force side. It can be said that the bridge between education and work is not functioning very well for a large number of this age group, although existing policies aim at patching it up. At the education end, policies and programmes are directed towards a better guidance and counselling service and more and better vocational preparation for the pupil. At the work end, different job creation and job subsidies schemes are being tried out to facilitate the insertion of young people into working life.

It is certainly necessary, at least in the short term, to patch up the old bridge, but the basic question is whether this old route from education to work is becoming a cul-de-sac for a growing number of young people. Without wishing to stretch the analogy of bridges too far, the real problem may lie in the lack of several small bridges allowing a flexible transition from education to work and back again. For the majority of young people in the foreseeable future the old bridge will certainly continue to function, but for an increasing number of young people there is an urgent need for new links in both directions between education and work. It is here that a particular role can be envisaged for recurrent education.

Broadly speaking, the present educational responses and proposals for this category of young people who face problems in finding jobs, and who have rejected the option of staying on in school, have been rather insufficient and unclear. They have been mainly of three kinds. First, an increased concern has been observed for more efficient guidance and counselling services directed to all pupils and not, as before, to only a minority of problematic individual cases—the underlying assumption being that information for everybody will facilitate realistic occupational and educational choices and thereby make the transition smoother. No doubt this is very important, but no guidance and counselling service, however efficient, can fully compete with the benefits of a concrete and real experience gained by a young person from some kind of work experience.

A second kind of educational response has been the different attempts to strengthen the vocational component in the last years of schooling in the hope that this will make the insertion into working life easier. Judging from the situation that the unemployed youngster faces today, such an educational response may certainly be extremely important since for many of the unemployed the difference between having a job or not is often due to a lack of some basic vocational education or training. However, for many young people these measures will not suffice as they are tired of anything at present being offered in school, or simply uncertain or reluctant to choose vocation-oriented courses because of the risk of being "closed-in" too early in life in a particular occupation. Moreover vocationally oriented courses in themselves will do little unless employers believe them to be genuinely useful.

A third type of educational response being discussed is simply to force young people to stay on in school. In other words, in periods of prolonged recession, education could operate as a holding mechanism for keeping young workers out of a tight labour market. But, given the consequences if delayed gratification from postponing entry into the job market through prolonged schooling is not rewarded, and the pressures on the education system of a great number of young people who would rather not be at school, the social and individual risks in the long run make such an educational response hard to defend.

To these inadequate patchwork measures the possible recurrent education response comes as an important complement. The main thrust of the recurrent education proposal for this age group as well as for adults is the principle of alternation and/or combination of education and work, which would complement the old bridge through the creation of a number of new ones, where the transition would go in both directions, that is, from education to work and back again.

Therefore it seems possible to identify two particular target groups of youth for which a recurrent education alternative might be an important option.

The first group consists of those 16–19 years old who have opted for some form of upper-secondary education but who for different personal, motivational, and social reasons would prefer a less rigid and traditional form of education at this level; in other words, a study process that would include periods of work experience in alternation with school. The second group consists basically of those who left school at the end of compulsory education and who after some years of varied labour market experience, including in most cases spells of unemployment, recognize the importance of some kind of education and/or training in order to get a firm foot into the labour market.

3.2 The 16–19-year-olds in Upper-secondary Education

For the first group, 16–19-year-olds in upper-secondary education, the possibility of more universal options to experience work during their study seems essential. For instance, about 5–10 percent of the places on every educational line in upper-secondary education could be reserved for pupils who would prefer to go through this educational level in a different way while ending up with the same qualifications and diplomas as those who go through it in the normal way. Such a model would give each pupil at the end of compulsory schooling a study-form choice between going through upper-secondary education in the traditional way or through a recurrent education alternative.

For such an experiment to be realistic and successful, it would certainly also be necessary to rely heavily on the resources at the local level in terms of developing the curricula and finding places for work experience. In many cases, the role of the central authorities could be limited to initiating, supporting, and evaluating such experiments, as well as lifting and changing certain legal and financial restrictions to allow for a different and recurrent-education inspired "study-form" at upper-secondary education level.

Such experiments would be a first step towards the introduction of a different form of transition from school to work that would be made available as an option for all pupils leaving compulsory schooling. It could, of course, be argued that in a period of increased concern for standards, these experiments would adversely affect them. However, and without elaborating on the difficult issue of standards at school, it is well-known that the pupil's motivation plays a fundamental role in relation to his/her school performance. It is also well-known in many countries that a great number of pupils in upper-secondary education would prefer some form of alternation between school and work.

The arguments in favour of experiments along the lines above are basically of three kinds. First, upper-secondary school is still in many countries being criticized because it has insufficient contact with the world outside school and because watertight walls exist between the world of theory and that of practice. Therefore, these experiments would better bridge these two worlds and they would have a positive effect on many pupils' motivation. Secondly, it is argued that those young people who have had some kind of work experience do get a better and more realistic idea of the labour market and their own possibilities—a fact that is of great importance when they leave upper-secondary education for either work or further study. Thirdly, it can be argued that such experiments would give us a better understanding of how many and what kinds of pupils would prefer a different study form at this level, a study form that might better correspond with their personal development and social situation.

3.3 *The School Leaver*

The second target group, those who left school at the end of compulsory education, today constitutes in most countries the majority of the unemployed youth. Although in many OECD countries those who have left school at 15 or 16 rather than stay on in education constitute the majority, the heterogeneous collection of services being offered to them rarely adds up to a coherent policy, and no department seems consistently willing to assume the responsibility. For those who leave school at the earliest opportunity, prospects are at present meagre for finding a job, for further education, or for any kind of career. Many countries have some form of legislation for an apprenticeship system of day or block release schemes, but often these measures are not sufficiently effective, even when there is a statutory right. To place a compulsory obligation on employers may look appealing, but it entails numerous complications, in particular a probable deterioration in the employment prospects of young people who carry with them such a "negative right". Their prospects are further diminished as far as the males are concerned, by the combination in some countries of compulsory military service with the imposition of job security spanning the period of service, thereby discouraging employers from taking on those who will soon be drafted for military service.

Furthermore, those who leave school at the earliest possible moment often rule themselves out as future beneficiaries of education expenditures both indirectly, since they do not use the education provisions, and directly, since in most cases, and in the absence of a financing system of deferred right to education, they receive no financial assistance.

Three main conclusions can be drawn from this. First, that the major responsibility for assuring members of this age group (i.e., up to the age when pupils leave upper-secondary education) access to learning opportunities should rest entirely with the public education authorities. This is not to propose that ministries of education should be directly responsible for all relevant programmes but that they should accept the legal and administrative responsibility, based to a large degree on local administration, of ensuring and stimulating these youngsters to return to education for shorter or longer intervals.

Secondly, in most countries there exists a variety of different and often uncoordinated educational and training programmes for this group of young people. In too many cases the financial assistance given to the youngsters varies considerably, thereby creating a situation where real job perspectives, which could be opened up by taking a certain educational course, become blurred because of insufficient financial support in comparison with some other programmes. For this reason a certain modification of the rather regressive character of expenditures for the whole 16–19 years age group could be envisaged. For instance, a certain percentage of the budget for this age group could be earmarked to enable educational authorities to fulfil their responsibility to those who leave school at the minimum age.

The third conclusion concerns the kind of course that could be offered. It is clear that for many of these youngsters, going back to school is not really an alternative, since they have in many cases left school with a rather negative attitude towards it. However, it is equally true that, after a couple of years in the labour market, often in boring and unqualified jobs, many of them start to recognize that some kind of further education seems to be needed in order to get a better job. The content of the educational courses and the manner of providing them would have to take this aspect of motivation into consideration if they were to be successful. It would also be important that the courses at upper-secondary level for these young people should be arranged in a flexible way allowing for part-time work and modular courses, and that the young people themselves should have an influence on the actual content of the courses.

As a minor example of the kind of courses that might be of significant importance to many of these youngsters is the theoretical preparation for a driving licence. It is well-known that in many countries the lack of driving licence excludes many of them from a variety of jobs where one is necessary. Through appropriate consultation with other national authorities, the educational authorities could take an interesting initiative in preparing and helping many of these youngsters to get a better start than when they left compulsory school. No doubt for many of them, their attitudes towards the educational system would change if they could see that something concrete and useful for active life could be provided for them.

In summing up this section on recurrent education and youth it has to be stressed again that recurrent education so far has had a very limited effect on young people. The reasons for this are manifold, ranging from a traditional social demand for education which reinforces, rightly or wrongly, the view that the best guarantee of later status and success in the world of work is to stay in education as long as possible; to the very concrete problem of how to organize alternation, in particular how to find a job which enables its alternation with education.

Yet it can be strongly argued, given a serious job situation for a growing number of young people, that the educational authorities should now assume a particular responsibility for launching recurrent education experiments at the upper-secondary level, both for those young people who cannot find a job and for those who would like to try out some new ways of mixing education and work within the overall framework of upper-secondary education.

3.4 *Recurrent Education and Adults*

The need to bring the 16–19-year-olds into the recurrent education orbit has been emphasized. But obviously this goes beyond limiting the recurrent education option of today and tomorrow only within those early years. Recurrent education is concerned with the whole life cycle, and alternation for older workers can have an impact on youth as well, not least by the possibility that extended educational leave of absence may vacate jobs which younger people can fill.

But in more concrete terms and within the general sector of adult education, it should be possible for educational authorities to take a more active role, particularly in the context of some of the emerging socioeconomic forces already discussed. A strategy for recurrent education requires that the adult education sector play a fundamental role in the process of distributing education opportunities over the total life span of an individual in a recurring way and in alternation with other activities.

The growth of adult education, both in quantitative and functional terms, has been very substantial. The result is that today, despite the relative lack of support from public authorities, adult education is no longer serving a very small minority of national populations but a significant part of it.

However, although its importance as an educational activity is today taken for granted, it remains structurally and financially weak. One important reason for this is the mixture of public authority, voluntary organization, and private provision, which is involved in this sector, as well as the heterogeneous learning needs to which this sector is responding. For instance, in an OECD publication, four possible futures for adult education are envisaged:

(a) to let it evolve, as in the past, in a spontaneous sporadic fashion without reference to any explicit public intervention;

(b) to strengthen and coordinate the existing range of activities, but not to perceive it as an active instrument of public policy in the social and economic arena;

(c) to strengthen and coordinate the existing range of activities while simultaneously pursuing a positive policy of support for specific activities judged to be national priorities, for example, secondary education equivalency programmes designed to promote equality;

(d) to create a comprehensive service of adult education as an integral element of broadly conceived educational systems and to relate its functions to the social, economic, and cultural objectives of the nations.

It is also observed in the report that most OECD countries find themselves pursuing (c), with some countries moving in the direction of (d). The main policy conclusions therefore to be drawn are that governments should attempt to adapt a long-term strategy based on a mixture of (c) and (d). But today and in the years to come, budgetary constraints are most likely to become even more severe for adult education, not least because it does not share statutory status with youth education and because it is still considered by many as a luxury commodity. However, and this reflects the general conflict between short- and long-term policy concerns in the education sector, if the trends discussed earlier are taken seriously as indicating a development towards a new mixture of work and nonwork time for individuals, as well as increased concern for new skills at work, then it is difficult to deny that a great challenge lies in front of recurrent education for adults. It is one that should give an important role to both publicly and privately supported and coordinated recurrent education opportunities for adults, particularly as it is probable that national policies and priorities will be required to meet and respond to significant changes in work and nonwork time for individuals.

It is also obvious, as has already been pointed out, that these changes in work and nonwork time have different effects and meanings for different social groups. Consequently, the educational response to a general increase in nonwork time and/or changes in the way work is being scheduled, if it is to be effective, will have to be based on a deeper understanding of the specific work/nonwork mixture and work organization that different groups of people are experiencing or experimenting with.

This is not, however, to postulate that more nonwork time would automatically increase the demand for education although that certainly remains a strong possibility. But apart from the fact that people will choose all sorts of activities during increased nonwork time, the big question for education will be whether it can and wants to respond to these changes. Moreover, such changes in work and leisure would affect a number of other policy sectors in society and it would be unrealistic to expect that only the educational sectors would have to respond. Even so, and with gloomy prospects concerning financial resources for adult education, there is certainly the possibility for some new initiatives in order to create more recurrent education policies for adults.

See also: Lifelong Education: Research Strategies

Bibliography

Organisation for Economic Co-operation and Development (OECD) 1973 *Recurrent Education: A Strategy for Lifelong Learning*. OECD, Paris

Organisation for Economic Co-operation and Development (OECD) 1976 *Developments in Educational Leave of Absence*. OECD, Paris

Organisation for Economic Co-operation and Development (OECD) 1978a *Alternation Between Work and Education: A Study of Educational Leave of Absence at Enterprise Level*. OECD, Paris

Organisation for Economic Co-operation and Development

(OECD) 1978b *Technical Change and Economic Policy: Science and Technology in the New Economic and Social Context.* OECD, Paris
Organisation for Economic Co-operation and Development (OECD) 1978c Education committee meeting at ministerial level. *Communiqué.* OECD, Paris
Organisation for Economic Co-operation and Development (OECD) 1979 *Interfutures: Facing the Future, Mastering the Probable, and Managing the Unpredictable.* OECD, Paris
Rehn G 1973 Towards flexibility in working life. In: Mushkin S (ed.) 1973 *Recurrent Education in the National Institute of Education.* National Institute of Education, Washington, DC
Roberti P 1978 Income inequalities in some Western countries: Patterns and trends. *Int. J. Soc. Econ.* 5(1)

Community Education and Community Development

C. Fletcher

There are many sociological and anthropological definitions of community (Bell and Newby 1972). The common elements of these definitions are that community means a local environment of people who have interests in common as well as differences of interests. A community has an identity, a sense of place, of "us" and "them". A community is all of "us" who are not "them" and this is the collective significance of a distinctive name.

Educators work within and with their host communities. Education is a stimulus for, and response to, community whether the relationship be conscious or unconscious, positive or negative. Community education and community development are twentieth-century innovations designed to make explicit the connection with the problems of communities.

The problems vary according to the local environment. There are rural villages faced with a subsistence economy, inadequate services, and depopulation; old towns faced with physical decay. Inner-city neighbourhoods are often poverty traps. In new towns and cities, migrant workers feel dislocated and face problems of mental health. The perspective of community education and community development is that there are potentials as well as problems, and that specific connecting activities also resolve some of the problems within education itself.

Community education is the participation of communities within education. Community development involves the committing of educational activities to the welfare of host communities. The distinction is more than one of emphasis as community education means working out from schools and colleges, whilst community development means working out beyond educational buildings altogether. Community education means bringing educational centres into active service for social life. Community development means a process of self-help which begins with identifying and expressing needs and is directed towards taking more responsibility and control. The aims of both therefore include major changes in what is taught and in the role of teacher. They both take a critical stance in relation to mainstream education, whether it be in schools or adult education centres. Questions concerning what "is" education are challenged by asking what "ought to be" the prospects for communities. For beyond matters of education's content and relationships, there are the issues of self-reliant communities and decentralized education systems (Maliyamkono 1980).

There is a contrast between the strategies being pursued in Westernized nations and in newly independent nations. The former emphasize community education whilst the latter usually give priority to community development. Whilst there are, then, community schools and community development programmes throughout the world, and they can be regarded as one of the common factors of democratic nations, there is a First World model and a Third World model to guide the understanding of contrasting practices. It is also important that activities take place outside the state sector and that the middle ground between the two models is often occupied by voluntary organizations.

There are comparatively few studies and even fewer first-hand accounts of either community education or community development. Given national and international variations and the dearth of documentation, the following sketchmap will be inevitably flawed.

1. Community Education

Community education is normally understood as the process of transforming schools and colleges into educational and recreational centres for all ages. It began with determined initiatives by individuals. Many nations still draw upon the inspirations of their earliest achievements: for example, Grundtvig's Folk High Schools (Denmark), C. S. Mott's community primary schools (Michigan, US), and Henry Morris's village colleges (Cambridgeshire, England).

It is the combination of compulsory education with other welfare functions, the coordination of many "extra" activities, and the gradual evolution of local control which characterize community education. Each successive stage in the process has provoked redefinitions and realignments of the common elements. In a 1976 booklet on the "Federal Role" (US) the following elements are listed:

(a) use of a public facility such as the school;

(b) involvement of people of all ages, income levels, and ethnic groups;

(c) identification by the people of their needs and problems;

(d) development of a variety of programmes to meet these needs;

(e) coordination among diverse agencies and institutions in the community;

(f) multiple funding sources, both public and private, at the local, state, and federal levels.

The diversity of these elements indicates the different views of the school or college being taken by politicians, administrators, and professional teachers. All three are brought into an explicit alliance. For politicians, there is the desire for an active constituency. For administrators, there are the cost benefits of capital sharing and time-sharing agreements. For professional teachers pastoral care (home–school links) becomes a factor in both curriculum development and school management.

Community education centres are either newly built or old schools so designated. Each period of new educational building has offered the prospect of multifunctional centres which can be readily designated: The Vennen (Holland); Maison Pour Tous (Yerres, France); The Parks (Adelaide, South Australia); Westerhailes (Scotland), and Britannia (Vancouver) are all 1970s' developments from which an education authority can learn and establish the implications of designating existing schools. Each period of new building has coincided with an increase in size and a more comprehensive approach to education. Community education in each nation has often been taken to refer only to large schools within very large community centres. The huge purpose-built centres have often attracted most attention because of the innovations which their fabric allowed for and the fresh approach of the hand-picked staff. Designation has had a much more humble point of departure: the head or principal's job description and salary are enhanced, some space is given over to community use, and the office of a coordinator (or tutor or manager) is created. This is how the long process of efficient school usage and experimental formal and informal adult education begins.

Understanding the concept can depend upon the light cast by examples of "good practice". Hagley High School (New Zealand) has published its findings on adults coming back to school and joining classes. Burra Community School (South Australia) has published the reasoning for, and results of, its needs assessment survey. Sydney Stringer School and Community College (Coventry, England) has prepared a booklet on its residential unit, Fairfax House. Sutton Centre (Nottinghamshire, England) has published material on its block timetable, profiles, and voluntary learning sessions in the evening. Deans Community High School (Livingston, Scotland) prepared a booklet entitled *Community Across the Curriculum: The Beginnings*. A consortium of village college "wardens" (the name of head having been changed to refer to a wider custody and care) made a film to show their distinctive daily life. Most of the *Countersthorpe Experience* (Watts 1977) has been expressed in books and articles. All the community education centres just referred to have a secondary school at their heart. The international picture, though, is that there are as many, or more, community primary schools. This is easily understood as primary schools have more compact catchment areas and parental involvement is more widespread with the lower age group (Rennie 1985). Community colleges (tertiary) have also developed, particularly in Canada and the United States (Campbell 1971).

Community education leads to the possibilities and pursuit of local control. Schools or colleges form associations which can raise and retain revenue, debate, and decide upon priorities. New constitutions and articles of government are adopted in states and nations which have adopted a community education policy. Minneapolis (US) has draft resolutions for school boards who are considering extending their responsibilities into community education.

2. Community Development

Third World community education is set almost always in the context of community development. In 1982 the President of the Indian Adult Education Association said "one of the functions of the school-cum-community centre should . . . be the propagation of the various government schemes for self-employment and rural development". From the perspective of nonformal education in Africa, Sine (1979) wrote: "For our purposes community education has a precise meaning; it means educational activities that are organised for the people and answer their needs with a view to raising their scientific standards and inducing them to realise that they must take responsibility for their own future." There are two models for community development; planning (from the "top down") and participation (from the "bottom up"). Both relate to long-term processes, the key aspects of which become clear in specific projects. In the planning model, projects are proposed to the community and the method involves having community members realize that the project is consonant with their interests. Planning, in Tanzania, is called "education for self-reliance". Its aim is to "instill among students new attitudes and values about the functions of education, about the importance of social service in relation to personal benefit and . . . duty to the nation and the community" (Maliyamkono 1980 p. 341).

In one example—the participatory model, in Damfa, Ghana—cooperation "is secured by meetings of farmers, at which they express their needs, discuss the new agricultural techniques envisaged and the problems of the pilot farm, which serves as a real agricultural school, where new seed varieties . . . are tried out. . . . Sessions of three to seven days duration are organised for farmers delegated by their villages. . . . The trainee farmers are expected to transmit what they have learned, to act as advisers and to encourage activities foreseen by the plan. . . the most essential condition for cooperation is respect, especially respect for the values of the community" (Sine 1979 pp. 15–17).

There have been community development projects in Westernized nations too. Amongst the earliest, in the 1930s, were those of Moses Coady's Antigonish Movement (Canada) and Myles Horton's Highlander Folk School (US)—neither of which made distinctions between adult education and social action and both of which were soon in conflict with authority. The two pioneers adopted different strategies. Coady initiated social reform and used methods which included "mass meetings, study clubs, radio listening groups, short courses, kitchen meetings, conferences, leadership schools, and training courses" (Lovett 1980 p. 158). Horton "concentrated on identifying and working with emerging social movements,. . . providing them with practical advice and assistance. . . as well as workshops at Highlander". Their respective communities—the eastern seaboard and Tennessee—were equally and severely deprived.

Community development projects mushroomed throughout North America and Europe in the late 1960s. Communities under stress were selected for informal adult education campaigns, which would put resources at their disposal, encourage the emergence of indigenous groups, and then discreetly withdraw, leaving responsibility in the hands of the groups. There is some doubt about the effectiveness of this approach. An alliance of English workers engaged in this kind of work described their mandate as that of "guilding the ghetto". A key issue became the use of national funds to fuel local conflicts. All projects tended towards the same set of problems: poor houses, poor prospects, harsh treatment, and plans which would tear community fabric yet further.

Those projects which had an educational base, and typically that of a university, reached positions similar to those of Coady and Horton. The Community Action and Research Project at Londonderry (Northern Ireland) first became involved in existing local initiatives, then undertook specific ones of its own, before establishing a residential centre (The People's College) which, in the words of Lovett (1980 p. 172), "would link local resource centres to provide research and educational facilities concentrating upon weekend and week long workshops with staff employed in the centre and in the field."

Both community education and community development encourage the creative as well as the critical—celebratory events; festivals; participatory music and drama; and play. Summer schools have become the special contribution of community arts to community development. There are many bands of artists supported by state aid, charities, and community contributions who have community development as their explicit purpose. It has proved difficult to maintain the momentum of community development, particularly where it has taken the form of a limited term project, fed by outside money and human resources. When the project ends, there is a tendency for a local voluntary organization to take over the work. This may help to explain why church and charitable funds have been so important.

3. The Prospects

Community education is less of a marginal movement than it was. Where primary schools were first designated there are now secondary schools and vice versa. Designation is slow and irreversible. National and international modelling is likely. In England, for example, the American community college concept could be widely adopted. The new factor is extending the designation of schools from neighbourhoods of greatest need to the more average towns and suburbs. Designation is moving closer to the norm. The initiative is now also being taken by alliances of teachers and parents. The pace could quicken should designation be recognized as an affirmative response to falling school rolls and high unemployment.

Whilst the community education process draws closer to community development, the latter concept is inherently larger. This difference in scope is apparent in Western nations' projects like the Dunbar Center (Baltimore, US), Rosny College (Tasmania, Australia), and Scottish Community Education. Such projects combine community criteria of education with those of the wider society.

Scotland is unique in having a national training scheme for community education. The scarcity of initial, postgraduate, and inservice training dampens the prospects considerably. The prospects, though, do not depend upon policy, resources, and training alone. There are also the obstacles of differences of interests within communities and the devotion to hostilities between those interests.

Community development could become more widespread too. On the one hand it makes practical connections between literacy, numeracy, individual training, and collective determination. On the other hand there are the reconstruction necessities which come in the aftermath of war and enforced migration. In both rural and urban policies the prospect is for extensive use of telecommunications, be it by radio, by teleconferencing, or by television broadcast. The Open University's continuing education commitment is a good example of the role of media in a Western national policy.

The prospect is for continued stress upon communities to be the acid soil in which the seeds of self-help and local control struggle to grow. The timescale is that of generations rather than decades. The longest term prospect which can be envisioned to date is for a fusion of community education and community development. There would then be a new term which would refer to the following features in its process: indigenous leadership, lifelong learning, and community realizations.

Bibliography

Bell C, Newby H 1972 *Community Studies: An Introduction to the Sociology of the Local Community*. Allen and Unwin, London

Campbell G 1971 *Community Colleges in Canada*. Ryerson, Toronto, Ontario

Carnegy E (ed.) 1977 *Professional Education and Training for Community Education*. Her Majesty's Stationery Office, Edinburgh

Lovett T 1980 Adult education and community action. In: Thompson J L (ed.) 1980 *Adult Education for a Change*. Hutchinson, London, pp. 153–73

Maliyamkono T L 1980 The school as a force for community change in Tanzania. *Int. Rev. Educ.* 26(1): 335–47

Minzey J D, LeTarte C E 1979 *Community Education: From Program to Process to Practice: The School's Role in a New Educational Society*, 2nd edn. Pendell, Midland, Michigan

Reé H 1972 *Educator Extraordinary: The Life and Achievements of Henry Morris, 1889–1961*. Longman, London

Rennie J (ed.) 1985 *British Community Primary Schools*. Falmer Press, Brighton

Sine B 1979 *Non-formal Education and Education Policy in Ghana and Senegal*. UNESCO Educational Studies and Documents No. 35. UNESCO, Paris

Watts J (ed.) 1977 *The Countersthorpe Experience: The First Five Years*. Allen and Unwin, London

Sociocultural Animation

J. A. Simpson

Sociocultural animation may better be described as a movement than as a theory or body of doctrine. It involves a broad range of loosely associated and sometimes inconsistent ideas, but only a few are essential to it, and its practitioners vary as to which parts of its ideology and techniques they emphasize. It cannot be traced to any one thinker or institution or book. It originated in North America and the gallicism of its title suggests Canadian influence, although it clearly owes much to the "higher horizons" type of community development adopted in the mid-1960s in several areas of the United States. It differs from this in two respects. They, like most community development projects, were concerned not merely with the sociocultural milieu but with the physical and economic conditions and the societal status of their target populations; and their target populations were those beset by the multiple deprivation occurring in inner urban areas, among certain ethnic minorities, and in grossly underdeveloped or decayed rural communities.

By contrast, sociocultural animation has looked for its work where there is average material well-being but "cultural poverty", for example, in the common types of municipal housing estates. Again, to whatever economic or quasipolitical initiatives animation may conduce, and no matter what local issues of these kinds it may exploit in making an impact on an area, the expressed aim of its programmes is cultural—concerned with the quality of social life and expressive behaviour. It must be said, however, that many animateurs have ignored this artificial distinction, finding more response among the populace when they have also concerned themselves with physical and economic conditions.

Sociocultural animation is known in the United Kingdom as something belonging to continental Europe. It emerged in France, Belgium, parts of Switzerland, and also in Holland and was soon taken up elsewhere. By 1965 the terms *animation socioculturelle* and *animateur* were coming into common use in francophone discussions of cultural affairs. "Sociocultural animation", however, has never become part of the educational vocabulary in the United Kingdom, and attempts to establish the equivalent term "sociocultural community development" have failed. Still, while regarding the movement as exotic, the British have drawn lessons and imitated some techniques from it. Knowledge of it in the United Kingdom has been mostly confined to people in touch with the proceedings of the Council of Europe, to which the Department of Education and Science has given a certain amount of publicity. In 1976 the Department of Education and Science financed a Council of Europe Symposium on "'Animation' in New Towns"—the inverted commas around "Animation" are significant—and sponsored a substantial preparatory document on animation projects in the United Kingdom.

A French definition says: "Animation is everything which facilitates access to a more active and creative life for individuals and groups, and which increases capacities for communication and participation in community life" (Théry and Garrigou-Lagrange 1966). A more comprehensive definition is given in a 1973 Report of the European Cultural Foundation: "Animation is that stimulus to the mental, physical, and emotional life of people in a given area which moves them to undertake a wider range of experiences through which they find a higher degree of self-realisation, self-expression, and awareness of belonging to a community which they can influence. In urban societies today this stimulus seldom arises spontaneously from the circumstances of everyday life. It has to be contrived as something additional to the environment."

Animation is an egalitarian movement. It seeks to reduce a so-called "culture-gap" between the culturally affluent and other broad sections of society which suffer from "cultural poverty". Cultural poverty exists when there is a needlessly restricted range of experiences from which the individual may choose. Even though the restriction seems to be self-imposed and a matter of inclination, it is in fact the outcome of centuries of underprivilege, exclusion, and ignorance together with low self-expectation. Poverty of this kind is not merely quantitative. Creative and expressive group experience are of especial value, and an habitual repertoire deficient in these is poverty stricken. Unawareness of the deficiency is a symptom of it.

A marked feature of animation is acceptance of the principle of cultural democracy. This avers that cultural policy must not conceive of culture as an optional adornment of life composed of the arts and fine arts but as the framework of behaviour and communication patterns specific to any community; and that it must take account of the coexisting plurality of such cultures in our national societies, recognizing that all have equal validity as media for expression and creativity, whether they be the cultures of a factory floor or an opera house foyer. Cultural policy should not privilege any one of them although, in view of past injustice, some positive discrimination in favour of the cultures of the "uncultivated" may be desirable.

Cultural democrats react explicitly against "the democratization of culture"—the hallowed processes of popularizing "bourgeois", or "elite", or "heritage" culture. Thus, they would regard making professional performances of opera or ballet cheaper and more accessible to the populace, as less worthy of support than stimulating the emergence of an autochthonous steel band or mimegroup. (Many animateurs, in fact, combine both procedures.) The apparently limitless range of creativity propounded by cultural democracy is restricted, with doubtful logic, by the assertion of certain standards to be applied over the whole cross-cultural spectrum. According to these, active experience is better than passive; critical participation in community affairs is better than preoccupation with family life and private pursuits; and in the arts and entertainment, whatever evokes the involvement of physique, heart, and mind is better than anything which merely lulls or diverts.

With these principles, then, the spokespersons and practitioners of animation set high value on promoting independence of commercially produced goods and mass entertainment, and on reducing the amount of time spent by the target population in multicellular isolation devoted to television. In more concrete terms, the aims of animateurs coming into an area are to multiply occasions for group life, particularly that which centres about creative and expressive experiences and which will combat the underusage of personal resources; to foster community consciousness and participation; and to promote as many community and neighbourhood events and happenings as possible so that the public life of the area is enriched. This concern to bring "life on the streets" is a strong element in the work of animateurs, who profess regret for the vigorous social manifestations of Victorian working-class neighbourhood thoroughfares and concourses as compared with the lifeless deserts of housing estates today, broken only by small rows of quiet shops.

The practice of animation often ignores the principles outlined above (Berrigan 1976, Council of Europe 1978). There are many examples which should more properly be called "community development" as they are merely aspects of programmes aimed, as at Bari in Italy, at the total rehabilitation of an area including its housing, employment, and formal education. Other projects stray far from cultural democracy and are frank efforts to take the heritage arts to the masses.

In each project much depends upon whether the animateurs are working as an independent team or as part of local government-sponsored programmes. In any case, the initial impact on an indifferent population is usually made in two ways. Firstly, there is a programme of what have come to be called "the community arts"—peripatetic demonstrations on the streets with portable equipment of minitheatre, mime, role playing, music-making, dance, games, pavement and mural artistry—and every attempt is made to enlist the active participation of the spectators. Secondly, the animateurs seek to identify points of popular dissatisfaction and to create action groups around them. Sometimes a house-to-house survey is held for this purpose—an "*enquête participation*". From these action groups have emerged schemes for group credit and group purchase, protests against defective public transport and, by picketing, the price policy of a local supermarket.

At a very early stage, the animateurs find a sufficiently large centre to which people can come to deepen their involvement and enjoy sociable relaxation. Care is taken to see that the premises and furnishings reflect popular taste and habits and do not have the daunting atmosphere, middle class and school-like, of established cultural centres. A residents' council is set up to further the animation process and act as a pressure and publicity agency. A news sheet is commonly issued, backed up by loudspeaker vans and, where possible, local radio. The cooperation of pre-existing interest groups is sought—parent–teacher, allotment, and angling associations, and so forth. The help of the schools is enlisted and some have not only taken their events and displays onto the streets but have opened their practical classes to adults who wish to learn, say, cookery alongside the children. Support is looked for from established cultural facilities in the city centre, and libraries, galleries, repertory theatres, and orchestras are asked to come and do missionary work. Specially designed street displays by public utilities—gas, electricity, transport—are welcomed as life-giving elements. Every opportunity is taken to hold festivals, processions, street parties, sports, and carnivals.

Much costlier governmental projects as at Grenoble or Yerres in France involve major construction. The Agora at Dronten in Holland provides a vast roofed-in area for market, leisure and refreshment, and arts facilities. Some local authorities have appointed full-time animateurs or "resident artists" to stimulate creativity.

Extraordinary inventiveness has been shown by animateurs who have pioneered the use of modern materials, polystyrene units, inflatables, and others, to create portable proscenium arches and games and display facilities.

The animation movement continued to gain ground in Europe in the early 1970s and it fortified those in the United Kingdom who wished for the development of community arts. It was explicitly made a part of the cultural policy of the Council of Europe and many local governments began to give it a place in their budgets. In 1972 the French Minister of Culture assembled a much publicized colloquy at Arc et Senans where a score of the world's leading publicists on cultural affairs strongly endorsed the ideology of animation. In 1976 the Conference of European Ministers for Culture met at Oslo and resolved that cultural policy must aim at cultural democracy. "It cannot limit itself to the popularisation of the heritage arts. It must assist people to overcome the pressures and seductions which confine their leisure to the passivity of the mass media and the escapism of commercially produced mass culture." The conference recommended that local governments should work "through the rich variety of techniques found effective by Socio-cultural Animation". Probably this was the high-water mark of the animation movement. Since then it seems to have receded somewhat.

Reasons for this are not hard to find. The energy crisis and ensuing economic recession have restricted cultural budgets. This has sharpened the choice for policy makers between expenditure on traditional major civic facilities and on experimental projects of the animation type. The numerical response of the populace to animation had nowhere constituted a massive breakthrough, and usually seemed marginal.

A number of particularly vocal animateurs blamed this on the niggardliness of the authorities and turned increasingly to the exploitation of points of dissatisfaction among the population, also with strident criticism of the establishment. This clamorous minority gave the impression that animation was a form of left-wing militancy, although it should be said that Marxists had from the outset condemned animation as a tool of the capitalists to soften the contours of a hierarchical consumer society. With the same motivation, the malcontent animateurs often pushed their hostility to the prescriptive claims of heritage culture to offensive lengths. All this raised dubiety about the animation movement.

It called into question, also, the status and function of the animateur. This has always been hotly debated among animateurs themselves, a heterogeneous collection of people with widely differing backgrounds and motivations. Some are young freelance enthusiasts, often students or postgraduates, not seeking a career in animation, but undertaking a period of socially committed work as unpaid or low-paid assistants. Others have been appointed by authorities or officially sponsored agencies. Across this distinction there is the further difference between those whose background and interest is in the arts and those with sociological leanings. For all of them a question is likely to arise as to how far they are free to assail the public authorities and the ethics of contemporary society. Indeed, there are some who contend that the ideal profile is that of the "emergent animateurs", members themselves of the target community, gaining their bread from the support of the converted, like the Christian missionaries of St. Paul's day.

Over the same period, and no doubt, in reaction against the claims of extremist animateurs, powerful voices, such as that of Richard Hoggart at UNESCO, were raised on behalf of the heritage arts. Were they, it was asked, to be discounted because their appeal was not immediate for thoughtless people but demanded a preparatory input of patient effort? Their sheer volume and their long durability were contrasted with the miniscule and ephemeral contribution of spontaneous creativity in other cultures, much of which, in any case, was an uncouth imitation of mass-media presentations. The difficulty of maintaining any distinction in the arts between active and passive was exposed. Where was the passivity in watching critically a Beckett play or a Truffaut film? There was ridicule for much of the pretension to "audience participation" which consisted of little more than punctuation with cries or gestures as in the old music hall.

The chairman of the British Arts Council said, "Inevitably and rightly most of our money goes to the traditional arts" and he condemned as demagogic nonsense "the creed calling itself 'Cultural Democracy' which rejects discrimination between good and bad and proposed the romantic notion that there is a cultural dynamism in the mass of the people which will emerge if they can be liberated from elite culture". Other critics began to ask whether, if all coexisting cultures were of equal validity, there could be any objection to the culture of the mass media which was incontrovertibly rooted in popular taste. Possibly mindful of this type of comment, the Council of Europe terminated its separate concern with sociocultural animation and entrusted its furtherance to a general project in urban cultural development of all kinds, where, naturally, care for the major civic cultural facilities and the heritage arts predominated.

Perhaps above all responsible for any slowing-up there has been in the animation movement has been its indifferent record in making an impact upon any substantial number of people. The vast majority of the populace has remained impervious to attempts to animate it. The small processions or demonstrations underline this as they contrast with the overwhelming mass of uninterested citizenry through which they pace. It has become increasingly clear that at present, at any rate, large-scale success cannot be expected of a movement which goes against the grain of some of the most powerful trends in European social life today—trends which make for leisure fragmented almost entirely into isolated family groups around the television, in the car, in shopping in which the husband and children take part—

trends which are maintained and enforced by a vast complex of industries for family touring, family holidays, do-it-yourself, home embellishment, and by the unrelenting emphasis by the mass media upon sex relationships as the main ingredient of a satisfactory life. Only where sociocultural animation has formed a subordinate part of wider conceived projects can it lay claim to any notable numerical success, and this applies to the usage figures quoted for multipurpose facilities like those at Yerres and Grenoble in France or the Billingham Forum or the Abraham Moss Centre in the United Kingdom.

It would be wrong, however, to infer from this that the animation movement, which is by no means moribund, has been ineffective. It has had what promises to be long-term effects. In the United Kingdom, which has been only on the periphery of the movement, one can note the extent to which it has created a climate of responsible opinion in favour of the community arts. It has too, brought about a benign tolerance on the part of the populace at large for manifestations of these arts on the streets, and there can be no doubt that because of it many a high street is a livelier place than it was in the past. The housing estates, however, the original targets, have experienced no such lasting effects. The aims and techniques of British youth centres and organizations of community centres and settlements have been noticeably influenced by reports from and visits to examples of sociocultural animation on the continent. Perhaps, however, it is the work of adult educationists and of adult education institutes which has been most markedly affected, animation being seen by them as a promising means for removing the reproach that their work caters mainly for the already educated and for the middle classes.

If one regards Europe as a whole it seems safe to say that one of the most striking achievements of sociocultural animation as a movement is that it has placed an indelible question mark against any cultural policy and cultural expenditure which serves only a minority of the population. Its terms "culture gap" and "cultural poverty" embody incontrovertible facts. Whether anything can be done about them by purely sociocultural methods is still conjectural. Some might say that the movement has been only one more of those foredoomed attempts to change society through education instead of vice versa. It is too early to say. If widespread unemployment persists, and leisure hangs heavy for many millions for whom the factory and the office have hitherto provided a life metronome and for whom the pay packet has hitherto provided the expressive satisfactions of consumership, and if there also continues the trend in a rising proportion of the old and retired—people from whom family interests and adventurous personal relationships have largely fallen away—then sociocultural animation may find a readier and wider audience.

Bibliography

Berrigan F J 1976 *"Animation" Projects in the UK: Aspects of Socio-cultural Community Development*. National Youth Bureau, Leicester

Council of Europe 1978 *Socio-cultural Animation*. Council for Cultural Cooperation, Strasbourg

Haworth J T, Veal A J (eds.) 1976 *Leisure and the Community*. Conf., Birmingham University, 10–11 Dec., 1976. Centre for Urban Studies, University of Birmingham, Birmingham

Jor F 1975 *The Demystification of Culture: Animation and Creativity*. Council of Europe, Council for Cultural Cooperation, Strasbourg

Mennell S 1979 Theoretical considerations on the study of cultural 'needs'. *Sociology* 13: 235–57

Simpson J A 1976 *Towards Cultural Democracy*. Council of Europe, Strasbourg

Théry H, Garrigou-Lagrange M 1966 *Equiper et animer la vie sociale*. Editions du Centurion, Paris

Formal and Nonformal Education: Future Strategies

P. H. Coombs

This article examines some critical issues of future educational strategies that grew out of the world educational crisis of the late 1960s and the great broadening of educational and development concepts and goals in the early 1970s. It addresses in particular some perplexing questions about forging stronger linkages between formal and nonformal education and between both of them and various other development activities.

1. Basic Concepts and Misconceptions

An educational development strategy, as the term is used here, is a framework for specific educational policies and actions, intended to keep these policies and actions reasonably balanced and integrated, well-timed, properly weighted, and headed in the right direction.

There is a broad consensus today that future educational strategies in all nations must be much more comprehensive, innovative, and integrated than the narrow and inflexible strategy of rapid linear expansion of inherited formal education systems that dominated the 1950s and 1960s and culminated in the worldwide educational crisis (Coombs 1985a). In principle, it is generally agreed, these future strategies should view education not simply as schooling but as a lifelong process of learning for all people of every age, which might involve a complex mixture of informal, formal and nonformal education (UNESCO 1972, Coombs et al. 1973, Coombs and Ahmed 1974). They would also emphasize continuous change and innovation in all educational provisions to keep them in harmony with the rapidly changing world around them, fostering stronger linkages not only among various educational activities but between these and related development activities.

The practical application of these basic principles has been seriously hampered, however, by three persistent and widely held misconceptions: first, that education is a separate development sector (comparable to industry, agriculture, transportation, etc.) and as such can be organized, planned, and managed as a unified and integrated whole without reference to other sectors; second, that nonformal education is simply an alternative to formal schooling and constitutes a parallel system, which should be brought within the fold of ministries of education and national education plans "to keep it from getting out of control"; and third, that nonformal education is essentially a poor person's education—an inferior ersatz substitute for the real thing.

A close look at the real world of education and development, however, might challenge both the validity and feasibility of these three notions. Clearly, education is not a separate sector; it is instead an essential component, taking many different forms, of all sectors and all types of development. To isolate it as a separate sector seriously inhibits education's contribution to development. Similarly, nonformal education (unlike formal education) is not a system in the true sense. It is simply a convenient generic name for the motley family of organized educational activities outside the formal system, intended to serve particular learning needs of particular subgroups in the population. Finally, nonformal education is not just for the poor and unschooled; it serves people of all ages and in different stations in life, including the most highly trained experts (e.g., doctors, scientists, engineers, or top executives) who must keep up with developments in their respective fields of knowledge and technology.

2. Guides to Developing Strategies

When properly clarified and interpreted, these basic concepts and principles may provide useful guidance for developing future educational strategies and for dealing with the much discussed question of linkages. They emphasize at the outset that a national educational strategy cannot exist in a vacuum; it can be seen as a necessary and integral part of a nation's overall development strategy, in the broadest sense. It must encompass all important forms and modes of education, whether operating separately or as a part of a larger activity.

A central objective of strategy might be to encourage the steady development of a highly diversified and flexible network (not a fully integrated, self-contained system) of educational provisions that can increasingly serve the evolving and changing lifelong learning needs of all groups in the population, from earliest childhood to mature adulthood. Formal education would obviously play important roles in this network, but would not dominate it. It will play these roles most effectively when it carries out its own mandate and leaves to other modes of education what they can more effectively achieve in specific situations.

As to the question of linkages, formal education need not, and indeed cannot and should not, be tightly tied—by explicit design and bureaucratic connections—to all types of nonformal education. There is evident advantage in fostering close and fruitful collaboration, though not necessarily iron-clad linkages, between formal and nonformal education wherever the two have similar learning objectives. Cases in point would be nonformal school-equivalency programs for out-of-school youth, or literacy programs for adults. Even here, however, it is important not to stifle the flexibility, innovativeness, and unconventionality of nonformal education by superimposing on it formal education conventions or constraining standardized regulations. There can also be great advantage in encouraging hybrids of formal and nonformal education, especially with a view to making formal schooling more affordable, flexible, and adaptable to different groups of learners, and more relevant to differing local conditions.

Conversely, it may make good sense to link many other kinds of nonformal education to particular sectors or multipurpose development programs and community activities with which they have a natural relationship, rather than to the formal education system. Programs and activities of this sort are sponsored and managed by a vast variety of governmental agencies and voluntary organizations and by individual communities themselves, which must take prime responsibility for their educational as well as other key components. Any serious attempt to link all these diverse nonformal education components primarily to the formal system would only lead to bureaucratic chaos.

It is inevitable that in any country, whatever its particular ideology or type of government, building and executing a comprehensive educational strategy and a workable lifelong learning network must inevitably involve the joint effort of many different organizations, both public and private, that are playing significant educational roles in relation to different clienteles and different socioeconomic objectives. Achieving such a joint effort is, of course, not easy, and it cannot happen overnight.

The first requirement is to develop a genuine sense of community and common purpose, based on a widely shared concept of the nature and importance of the lifelong educational network and a clear understanding by each organization of where its particular activity fits into the whole. It also needs the development of a broad process of consultation and sharing of information, ideas, and future plans that will reveal opportunities for mutually beneficial collaboration, and the forging of new linkages among various network members whose interests and activities coincide.

Developing such a process and climate of cooperation must be, by its very nature, a step-by-step process. It cannot spring full-blown from the brow of some imaginative technocrats, skilled at redesigning organization charts, for it is fundamentally a very human and political process requiring creative leadership and a pervasive atmosphere of mutual trust and good will.

3. A Few Examples of New Initiatives and Innovations

Although few if any countries have yet formulated and articulated overall educational strategies of the sort described above, many have initiated significant steps in that direction. A few examples are cited below.

3.1 New Hybrids of Formal and Nonformal Education

Many developing countries have become convinced that traditional primary schools are not the only or even the best way to provide their children and youth with the basic skills and knowledge they will need in life. Thus they have embarked on a variety of new approaches, combining elements of both traditional schooling and nonformal education, designed in many instances to provide not only the usual academic basics such as the "3Rs" (reading, writing, and arithmetic), but also other types of locally useful basic skills and knowledge not usually provided by schools. Some also serve youth and adult learners as well as children. Almost all draw upon previously untapped local talent and other resources, which not only makes them more affordable than traditional schools but more relevant to local needs and circumstances.

Examples of such homegrown hybrids include: the second-chance program for out-of-school youth in Thailand; distance learning in Lesotho; MOBRAL in Brazil; community schools in Tanzania; the Centers of Integrated Popular Education in Guinea–Bissau; and versions of "production schools" and community learning centers in a number of other countries. Not surprisingly, such radical innovations often have to fight an uphill battle against the deep-rooted popular prestige of conventional schooling, and the fear of accepting any substitute. Only time and proof by performance can overcome such prejudices on the part of both parents and more conventional school educationalists.

A quite different type of hybrid, involving higher education, is multiplying rapidly in industrialized countries. Many colleges and universities have opened their doors and adopted unconventional methods to serve over-age students desiring to initiate or continue their higher education, usually on a part-time basis, either to earn a degree or simply to pursue selected studies that interest them or can help advance their career. The most innovative of these programs have broken clean from the old classroom and lecture hall syndrome and are making extensive use of distance learning, involving combinations of new self-study texts, broadcasts, and correspondence. The Open University in the United Kingdom is an outstanding example, but there are many others. The proportion of such unconventional studies in total higher education enrolments has increased dramatically in recent years in Europe and the United States and is expected to keep rising in the future.

3.2 Integration of Nonformal Education with Specific Development Efforts

The radical broadening and humanization of development goals in the 1970s and the greatly increased emphasis on meeting the basic needs of disadvantaged people, especially in rural areas, has led to an explosive increase in requirements for many kinds of nonformal education, particularly in relation to programs aimed at improving family health, nutrition, sanitation, housing, local employment opportunities, income, and the status of young children and women. Simultaneously there has also been a greatly increased emphasis on adopting a more integrated and community-based approach to these objectives, which also has far-reaching implications for education.

Numerous extensive case studies of such integrated, community-based programs have confirmed the diverse and crucial roles played by their educational components (e.g. Coombs and Ahmed 1974, Coombs 1980). Most such programs are supported in one way or another by formal education, for example, by training doctors, nurses, managers, technical specialists, and other high-level personnel involved in them. However, the training and education of their much more numerous front line workers and of the people themselves to do their own essential part is largely handled, and must be, by well-tailored nonformal education components.

3.3 New Directions in Adult Education

Adult education, especially as formerly perceived in most developing countries (largely in terms of adult literacy classes), has been expanding and branching out into new territory where it can serve a much wider range of adult learning needs, including becoming an important part of integrated multipurpose community-based development efforts in which the people themselves participate and take initiatives. As a general rule, experienced adult educators tend to be more pragmatic and versatile than most formal educators—and less inhibited by the orthodoxies of formal education—in improvising relevant and workable educational provisions to fit particular needs and circumstances and in collaborating smoothly with specialists from various sectors.

Ironically, one clear piece of evidence of the progress being made by adult education is that it is now encountering an identity crisis over just what adult education includes and does not include, and who is and who is not an adult educator. It has also encountered a semantic dilemma, for often the most numerous and enthusiastic participants in local adult education programs turn out to be teenagers.

Perhaps the most important general conclusion to be drawn from the above examples is that a broad movement toward more comprehensive educational strategies and more effective linkages between all sorts of education and development goals is already well underway in many countries. But it still has a long way to go to catch up and keep up with the rapidly growing and changing learning needs of people of all ages in all countries.

See also: Lifespan Learning Development; Organizational Change and Adult Education

Bibliography

Ahmed M, Coombs P H (eds.) 1975 *Education for Rural Development: Case Studies for Planners*. Praeger, New York and International Council for Educational Development (ICED), Essex, Connecticut

Botkin J W, Elmandjra M, Malitza M 1979 *No Limits to Learning: Bridging the Human Gap: A Report to the Club of Rome*. Pergamon, New York

Coombs P H 1985a *The World Crisis in Education: A View from the Eighties*. Oxford University Press, Oxford

Coombs P H 1985b Suggestions for a realistic adult education policy. *Prospects* 15(1) UNESCO, Paris

Coombs P H (ed.) 1980 *Meeting the Basic Needs of the Rural Poor: The Integrated, Community-based Approach*. Pergamon, New York/International Council for Educational Development (ICED), Essex, Connecticut

Coombs P H, Ahmed M 1974 *Attacking Rural Poverty: How Nonformal Education can Help*. Johns Hopkins University Press, Baltimore, Maryland

Coombs P H, Prosser R C, Ahmed M 1973 *New Paths to Learning for Rural Children and Youth*. International Council for Educational Development (ICED), Essex, Connecticut

Faure E, Herrera F, Kaddoura A-R, Lopes H, Petrovsky A V, Rahnema M, Ward F C 1972 *Learning to Be: The World of Education Today and Tomorrow*. UNESCO, Paris

Kidd J R 1974 *Whilst Time is Burning: A Report on Education for Development*. International Development Research Centre, Ottawa, Ontario

Nonformal Education

D. J. Radcliffe and N. J. Colletta

The classic definition of nonformal education devised by Coombs et al. (1973 p. 10) is "any organized educational activity outside the established formal system—whether operating separately or as an important feature of some broader activity—that is intended to serve identifiable learning clienteles and learning objectives". To clarify this definition further, the same authors distinguished between informal and formal education. Informal education is "the truly lifelong process whereby every individual acquires attitudes, values, skills and knowledge from daily experience and the educative influences and resources in his or her environment—from family and neighbours, from work and play, from the marketplace, the library, and the mass media". Formal education refers to "the hierarchically structured, chronologically graded 'education system', running from primary school through the university and including, in addition to general academic studies, a variety of specialized programmes and institutions for full-time professional and technical training". However, in practice no hard lines of demarcation exist between formal, nonformal, and informal education: while many activities may be perceived as falling exclusively into one category alone, many share aspects of two or all of them. In discussing nonformal education this article is therefore not concerned simply with structure or format, but with educational purpose and function.

1. Recent Development of the Concept

Nonformal education is a term which gained currency very rapidly in the 1970s but is not an entirely new concept. UNESCO reports dealt with the same issues in terms of "community development and community education" in the 1950s, and of "literacy and functional literacy" in the 1970s. Historically there has been a progression from informal to nonformal education, with formal education as the latest arrival. What is new is the recent rediscovery of nonformal education by development planners and the fresh values placed upon its contribution to human resource development.

The publication by Philip Coombs in 1968 of *The World Educational Crisis: A Systems Analysis*, was a landmark in this rediscovery. In 1985 Coombs returned to the broader topic with his book *The World Crisis in Education: A View from the Eighties*, which contains some pertinent observations on the debate for which his earlier work had sounded the keynote. By the late 1960s it had become clear not only in education but also in other areas of development planning, such as agriculture, health, and personnel training, that many prevailing assumptions about progress and growth were out of touch with both the realities of available resources and the dynamics of human motivation. Coombs pointed out that universal compulsory formal education, with its high costs and labour-intensive technology, was not necessarily the most effective means for meeting the diverse learning needs of a developing society. Furthermore, it became evident that the cost-per-student of nonformal programmes generally could be less than for formal schooling.

Even if universal primary education, to be followed later by universal secondary education, is the ideal, many countries appear to be approaching a ceiling on the percentage of gross national product available for education. For them such an ideal would be unattainable. On the other hand, once it is recognized that much valuable educational activity can occur outside the formal school system, ways of re-allocating resources so as to extend educational opportunity further by alternative means can be considered. It is from this perception of "new strategies for education" (Brembeck and Thompson 1973) that interest in nonformal education grew.

During the 1970s, nonformal education gave rise to many expanded definitions, bibliographies, case studies, and manuals (Paulston 1972, Ahmed and Coombs 1975, Colletta and Radcliffe 1980). There has been renewed interest in earlier work on "indigenous" or "native" education (Furnivall 1948), on parallel discussions of "out-of-school education" (Faure et al. 1972), on "the shadow school system" (Paulston 1971), and on "learning-networks" (Illich 1970), as well as in emerging concepts of "basic human needs", "lifelong learning", and "human resource development". In principle, nonformal education theory has questioned the adequacy of learning rigidly organized within a limited time span and circumscribed space. It criticizes both the traditional content of education and the built-in inequality of educational systems which, neglecting the needs of the poor, the illiterate, and the unemployed, reinforce existing social mobility patterns. Formal education is reproached for its promotion of inequities and for the alienation and wastage of youth, as reflected in high dropout rates and unfulfilled expectations.

From these beginnings, the debate has led to a consideration of nonformal education as complementary to, additional to, or even alternative to formal education. Initially, interest lay in its possible use to spread educational opportunity beyond the capacity of the resources available for building up the formal schools and therefore as an extension of schooling. This leads on, however, to an evaluation of nonformal education per se and discussion of whether it may not be peculiarly appropriate to certain kinds of learning. If such types of learning prove valid in specific sociopolitical contexts, nonformal education is advocated as the preferred mode of education for certain economic and political systems. The following section looks at the ways in which nonformal education relates to or contrasts with the formal school system?

2. Methodological Considerations

Nonformal education can be viewed as lying on the continuum from formal to informal education. In comparison with formal education it is generally less structured, more task- and skill-oriented, more flexible in timing, and more immediate in its goals. It is also more decentralized in organization and locally specific in application. Visible costs are lower, although this is achieved by the sharing of resources, facilities, and time. Thus, definitive assessments of the economics of nonformal education present problems of allocation. Likewise rewards tend to be tangible and immediate—though often short term—but clearly apparent. In teaching method, nonformal education is often relatively flexible, learner centred as contrasted with teacher centred (Knowles 1970); it is also concrete and experiential rather than abstract and theoretical. Participation by learners is not defined by age but by interest and opportunity. Similarly, teachers' qualifications vary considerably but are frequently governed more by opportunity, inclination, and experience than by formal certification and training.

Considerations of practicality and immediate application, locally specific content and programming, and integration with other programmes, for example in agriculture, personnel development, health services, or nutrition, mean that nonformal education arises, so to speak, from the "grass roots" rather than being centrally planned. The political aspects of this situation and the way in which nonformal education can become contentious in a political analysis of development objectives are dealt with later.

Besides the operational distinctions already referred to, attempts have also been made to differentiate between formal, nonformal, and informal education, in terms of pedagogy and learning domains (Colletta and Radcliffe 1980). Thus, formal education is generally seen to be more effective for meeting the cognitive needs of literacy and numeracy, while nonformal education applies more appropriately to technical and motor skills. This allows the construction of a tentative structural–functional paradigm for human resource development (Table 1). Such a model, although primarily analytical and academic rather than practical and prescriptive, may provide a convenient framework for

Table 1
Education and human resource development

Learning needs: ecologically based	Delivery system: learning environment	Behavioural objectives: development orientation
Cognitive	Formal (school)	Knowledge
Affective	Informal (family, community)	Attitude
Psychomotor	Nonformal (workplace)	Skill

Note: An elaborated version of this "ideal typology" may be found in Colletta and Radcliffe 1980 the comparision of differing educational methods, processes, and styles, but requires further development in order to be of use.

3. Case Studies and Examples

The identification of nonformal education as a process which could profitably be supported by development agencies led to a search for models and examples and the publication of many case studies. Sheffield and Diejomaoh (1971) reported on nonformal education in Africa and Van Rensberg (1972) on his pioneering work in Botswana. Coombs and Ahmed followed up their original report for UNICEF (1973) with two World Bank publications: *Attacking Rural Poverty: How Nonformal Education Can Help* (1974), and an edited collection, *Education for Rural Development: Case Studies for Planners* (1975). La Belle (1976) edited a study of programmes in Latin America, and also put together a symposium for the *Comparative Education Review* (1976 Vol. 20, No. 3). Other important studies are by Bock and Papagiannis (1976) and Simkins (1977).

Perhaps the most ambitious programme was that at Michigan State University, developed with the backing of the United States Agency for International Development (USAID) which adopted nonformal education as a major programme of its Technical Assistance Bureau in 1970. A Nonformal Education Information Center (NFEIC) was established in 1974. As a clearing house for information, NFEIC has published a newsletter, *The NFE Exchange*, which regularly summarizes information in the form of "project highlights", and prepares selected annotated bibliographies. The Michigan/USAID programme has concentrated on the development of innovative instructional materials, for example, gaming and simulations, and methodologies, for example, group dynamics. A number of technical notes and monographs have been published by the University of Massachusetts on these aspects (Evans 1981a, 1981b).

Paulston's bibliography (1972) and works by Paulston (1980), La Belle (1981), and others have explored the role of nonformal education in more developed societies.

4. Economic Considerations

A problem in discussing case studies of nonformal education arises from the fact that nonformal education is more directly integrated into other development programmes than the formal school system. It must inevitably be examined in conjunction with agricultural and industrial development programmes, with health, nutrition, and family planning, with literacy for community development, and with social action. Since nonformal education cannot be discussed in isolation, this leads to difficulties in economic analysis. It can be argued that nonformal education will generally prove its economic value for the individual learner, but it is less easy to measure the costs and returns for those institutions and facilities on which nonformal programmers draw for resources and time. For example, a complex formula of shadow pricing and opportunity cost analysis would have to be used to asses the voluntary and self-help contributions of such nonformal programmes as the Botswana Youth Brigades (Van Rensberg 1972) or the Sarvodaya Shramadana Movement of Sri Lanka (Colletta et al. 1982) in order to calculate adequately the economic returns to outlay in such programmes.

Much recent interest in nonformal education has arisen because it was believed that such education would permit a significant extension of educational opportunity and human resource development beyond the constraints of the formal school system, coupled with an equally significant reduction of direct educational costs. This estimation overlooks the shift of expenditure in resources and time to indirect, shared and buried costs in other areas, and the parasitical aspect of having education "ride piggy-back" on other programmes. Indeed, a more conservative argument would point to historical trends toward formal schooling as showing increasing cost–benefit efficiency, notwithstanding Coombs' systems analysis of crisis referred to above. The role of nonformal education then becomes an expedient in the process of adjustment to a changing situation. While the measurement of nonformal costs is thus problematic, certainly effective programmes should be calculated as accurately as possible (Ahmed 1975, Hunter et al. 1974).

5. Political Considerations

The politically naive sometimes argue that formal education can and should be discussed as though it were politically sterile, the aseptic transmission of language and computational skills, without any ideological preconceptions or direction. While it is true that formal education deals more in abstractions, this idea is plainly simplistic. Political implications are certainly embedded in nonformal education.

Despite the specific context of each nonformal programme, there is no doubt that, because it relates more directly to learner interest and relies on intrinsic learner motivation, nonformal education is an inherently political process, explicitly dealing in "conscientization" (Freire 1971). Since, by definition, it is more learner directed, it would also seem to be by implication more decentralized, community inspired, and democratic. On the other hand, those who perceive any educational programming as inducing coercive socialization will find this tendency to coercion in nonformal education, particularly when it becomes part of state planning policy. There is legitimate concern about the possible uses of nonformal programmes as pacifiers to cushion elite-mass separation. Such nonformal education may direct the energy of the masses toward lower status occupations, as a second-class expedient with dubious recognition for employment purposes, as compared with formally acquired qualifications. It may also become a surrogate welfare programme concealing unemployment in second-chance expectations, a cooling-out mechanism to counter the aspirations of formal schooling, or, quite bluntly, a device for overt political indoctrination and control in national youth service movements and similar institutions. Bock and Papagiannis (1976) argue that nonformal education generally lacks the "credentialling" powers of formal education and that this gives it second-class status in the employment market. Thus it does not affect the larger socioeconomic structures and is therefore relegated to the role of another shifting mechanism for the allocation of class status.

While the debate over the promotion of nonformal education therefore ranges from measures for the establishment of effective nonformal programmes as a sort of vague system, to ones for the creation of an open social, political, and economic environment within which nonformal educational networks can flourish, there is also an undercurrent of political interest which sees it either as a prop for an overextended but nevertheless desirable formal system, or as a fundamental challenge to the political–social systems which formal schooling has come to represent. In either case it is necessary to consider the particular political content and political role of nonformal education, for broad generalizations can have little justification. It is important to recognize, however, that nonformal education has excited heightened interest during a period in which there has also been a sharper discussion of the hidden political influence at work in formal school systems (Carnoy 1974). Therefore, the political aspect of nonformal education inevitably becomes an issue. Ultimately, however, as Evans (1981b) notes, nonformal education is trapped in the same web of societal constraints as formal education. While he confirms its power to produce something of value in limited local situations, he suggests that in a larger social context nonformal education has little prospect of accomplishing substantial reform of either the educational system or of the social and political structure of which it forms a part.

6. The Sociocultural Dimension

Consideration of education in relation to economic and political structures must include reference to the cultural environment. Recent studies (Colletta and Kidd 1980, Colletta 1977) have paid increasing attention to how traditional values contribute to the development process. It has been argued that the crux of the culture-development dilemma is to discover the most efficient means of introducing knowledge, skills, and attitudes within existing cultural patterns so that economic development is optimized and sociocultural change occurs in a harmonious fashion. The entire theme of "institution building" in development theory, perhaps especially with reference to formal education, often implicitly assumes that there are no viable institutions existing within the client or "target" population. Development agents should not assume that natural networks of leadership, organization, and the transmission and assimilation of skills, knowledge, and attitudes are lacking, nor that alleged needs for change imposed from outside will have greater legitimacy within a community than the logic of real needs as established by traditional indigenous processes.

The contribution to development from external agencies can be made more effective by taking better account of the processes of indigenous decision making. Between formal schooling as the agent of a wider universe of knowledge which is, however, often perceived as an alien imposition, and informal indigenous education as the bearer of cultural identity and community values, nonformal education can play a harmonizing role. Nonformal education is often therefore seen as a peculiarly appropriate means of mediating across a cultural divide and matching indigenous or local resources with extraneous assistance or technical solutions (Foster and Sheffield 1974, Colletta 1977).

See also: Economics of Nonformal Education

Bibliography

Ahmed M 1975 *The Economics of Nonformal Education: Resources, Costs, and Benefits*. Praeger, New York

Ahmed M, Coombs P H (eds.) 1975 *Education for Rural Development: Case Studies for Planners*. Praeger, New York

Bock J, Papagiannis G 1976 *The Demystification of Nonformal Education*. Center for International Education, Amherst, Massachusetts

Brembeck C S, Thompson T J (eds.) 1973 *New Strategies for Educational Development: The Cross-cultural Search for Nonformal Alternatives*. Heath, Lexington, Massachusetts

Carnoy M 1974 *Education as Cultural Imperialism*. McKay, New York

Colletta N J 1977 The use of indigenous culture as a medium for development. *PRISMA, The Indonesian Journal of Social and Economic Development*, Jakarta

Colletta N J, Kidd R 1980 *Indigenous Structures, Folk Media, and Nonformal Education for Development*. German Foundation for International Development (DSE), Berlin

Colletta N J, Radcliffe D J 1980 Non-formal education: An educological approach. *Can. Int. Educ.* 9(2): 1–27

Colletta N J, Ewing R T, Todd T 1982 Cultural revitalization, participatory nonformal education, and village development in Sri Lanka: The Sarvodaya Shramadana Movement. *Comp. Educ. Rev.* 26: 271–85

Coombs P H 1968 *The World Educational Crisis: A Systems Analysis*. Oxford University Press, London

Coombs P H 1985 *The World Crisis in Education: A View from the Eighties*. Oxford University Press, London

Coombs P H, Ahmed M 1974 *Attacking Rural Poverty: How Nonformal Education Can Help*. Johns Hopkins University Press, Baltimore, Maryland

Coombs P H, Prosser R C, Ahmed M 1973 *New Paths to Learning for Rural Children and Youth*. International Council for Educational Development (ICED), New York

Evans D R 1981a Ghana and Indonesia: Reforms in non-formal education at the community level. *Prospects* 11: 225–41

Evans D R 1981b *The Planning of Non-formal Education*. UNESCO/IIEP, Paris
Faure E, Herrera F, Kaddoura A-R, Lopes H, Petrovsky A V, Rahnema M, Ward F C 1972 *Learning to Be: The World of Education Today and Tomorrow*. UNESCO, Paris
Foster P J, Sheffield J R (eds.) 1974 *Education and Rural Development*. Evans, London
Freire P 1971 *Pedagogy of the Oppressed*. Herder and Herder, New York
Furnivall J S 1948 *Colonial Policy and Practice: A Comparative Study of Burma and Netherlands India*. Cambridge University Press, Cambridge
Hunter J M, Borus M E, Mannan A 1974 *Economics of Non-formal Education*. Institute for International Studies in Education, Michigan State University, East Lansing, Michigan
Illich I D 1970 *Deschooling Society*. Harper and Row, New York
Knowles M S 1970 *The Modern Practice of Adult Education: Andragogy Versus Pedagogy*. Association Press, New York
La Belle T J 1976 *Non-formal Education and Social Change in Latin America*. University of California Latin American Education Center, University of California, Los Angeles, California
La Belle T J 1981 Introduction to the non-formal education of children and youth. *Comp. Educ. Rev.* 25: 313–29
Paulston R G 1971 *Society Schools and Progress in Peru*. Pergamon, New York
Paulston R G (ed.) 1972 *Non-formal Education: An Annotated International Bibliography*. Praeger, New York
Paulston R G 1980 Education as anti-structure: Non-formal education in social and ethnic movements. *Comp. Educ.* 16: 55–66
Sheffield J R, Diejomaoh V P 1971 *Non-formal Education in African Development*. Report of a Survey conducted by the African–American Institute. African–American Institute, New York
Simkins T J 1977 *Non-formal Education and Development: Some Critical Issues*. Department of Adult and Higher Education, Monograph 8, Manchester University, Manchester
Van Rensberg P 1972 *Swaneng Hill: The Botswana Youth Brigades*. The Hammarskjold Foundation, Uppsala

Nonformal Education Policy: Developing Countries

J. C. Bock and C. M. Bock

Nonformal education has been defined as "any organized, systematic educational activity outside the framework of the formal school system designed to provide selective types of learning to particular subgroups in the population, adults as well as children" (Coombs and Ahmed 1974). Many of the activities which comprise nonformal education, such as on-the-job training, literacy programs, political re-education, community development programs, and religious training, have a long history. However, the concept has gained in popularity particularly since the Second World War and the creation of many newly independent nations. The decision makers of these less developed nations have increasingly come to view various alternatives to formal schooling as a means to help solve their social and economic development problems.

This article focuses primarily on those nonformal education programs which are sponsored by the governments of less developed nations, often with financing from external sources. However, there are many other nonformal education programs in the Third World which are sponsored by nongovernment agencies such as religious groups, industries, and other private organizations. In fact, Paulston and Le Roy (1982) contend that there is a great potential for social reform through nongovernment-sponsored grass-roots efforts. This is not to say that all nonformal education takes place in less developed countries. The industrialized Western countries also have extensive nonformal education programs particularly aimed at the middle class for self-improvement, professional updating, and renewal.

The principal areas of discussion in this article are: (a) the reasons for the relatively recent attractions of nonformal education to the decision makers and educational planners of the less developed countries as a promising new strategy for solving problems of national development; (b) the goals and problems of this educational development strategy; and (c) the implications which nonformal education may have for national development policy.

1. Problems of New Nations

In their quest for national development, new nations have had to confront and attempt to find solutions for similar sets of problems. As a consequence of historical factors resulting from their colonial pasts, these nations often include widely heterogeneous populations—ethnically and linguistically diverse, sharing little in the way of common history, culture, or political allegiances. In addition, these nations are often characterized by a cleavage between the modernized, frequently Western-educated elites and the traditional, uneducated, or vernacular-educated mass population. This mass–elite gap in turn tends to be coterminous with urban/rural residence patterns and sharp divisions between socio-economic classes. These pluralistic factors of the less developed countries are almost universally exacerbated by conditions of rising inflation, largely uncontrolled population growth, health and nutrition needs, serious unemployment, underemployment (especially of the rural population), and the consequent condition of disruptive rural-to-urban population shift.

Moreover, these new states must attempt to respond to these domestic crises within a world context which has become, since the Second World War, increasingly characterized by an intensely competitive world economic market, the widespread penetration and acceptance of scientific rationalism, and the ideology of equality. Thus, the less developed countries must attempt to consolidate and extend the state's authority in order to compete more effectively in the world economic market, while, at the same time, they must respond to frequently competing demands by their diverse and mobilizing citizenry for expanded opportunities for political participation and the redistribution of the nation's resources.

2. The Attractions of Nonformal Education

Education has had enormous appeal as a potentially powerful institutional remedy for underdevelopment by both the governments and the citizenry of the less developed countries. This is evidenced by the governments' substantial allocation of scarce resources for the expansion of education at all levels and by the ever-increasing demand for education by the mass population. To the citizen, schooling seems to provide the only legitimate access to the modernizing political and economic sectors, and thus to an improved quality of life. To the governments, education is seen as the primary vehicle for providing their citizens with the competencies and values believed to be necessary for participation in the drive for national development.

However, in recent years there has been increasing disenchantment with formal education as the principal institutional vehicle for national development. Sharply rising costs of education together with population growth have resulted in far less access to schooling—especially for the disadvantaged—than had been anticipated. Moreover, there has tended to be considerable discrepancy between the planned labor force needs of the economy and what the schools have actually produced. The school systems, usually inherited from a colonial past, have tended to continue to serve a primary function of elite recruitment and, thus, have been geared to an academic structure which prepares students for the next level in the academic hierarchy rather than for specific jobs in the modernizing labor force. Everywhere, schooling has served to escalate aspirations and expectations for white-collar and professional occupations while the economic structure has not been able to keep pace with this educationally generated demand. Entrenched in tradition, and protected by elites who owe their own position to formal school credentials, the school system has proved to be highly resistant to change.

Largely as a response to these frustrations at the failure of schooling to raise the socioeconomic level of the poor and to train people for the modernizing work force, decision makers began to explore alternative methods of education as a means of solving their development problems. Philip Coombs, one of the earliest advocates of nonformal education, proposed that the solution to many of the inadequacies of formal schooling was the promotion of the rapid expansion of nonformal education. It was his contention that nonformal education "when well-aimed has a high potential for contributing quickly and substantially to individual and national development" (Coombs 1968).

Among the many virtues claimed for nonformal education by its advocates is that it is far less expensive than formal schooling in that it can call upon the services of volunteers, borrowed facilities, and even radio broadcasts to reach large numbers of people at low cost. Since it is not as highly regulated as formal schooling, nor bound by an entrenched bureaucracy, it can be more rapidly deployed to meet immediately pressing problems. Theoretically, at least, nonformal education is seen as flexible and, therefore, more easily modified to meet the needs of specific clients and more responsive to the problems of individual communities. Since nonformal education is not age graded, it can provide for the needs of both adults and young school leavers.

The advocates of nonformal education claim a number of additional benefits, including a greater potential for cooperation and integration with other development-related agencies and a more immediate linkage to the requirements of the job market. It is also believed to be better able than formal schools to provide learning methods and settings which are better suited to elicit learning and participation from the uneducated rural poor.

3. Goals of Nonformal Education

The characteristics of nonformal education described above raised new hopes that this alternative to schooling might contribute to the accomplishment of a variety of goals related to national development. Particularly in the early 1970s, there was an "electric excitement about its possibilities" (Coombs 1976). In response to the frustration with schooling, nonformal education was thought to have the potential to achieve some of the goals that formal education had failed to accomplish. In addition, nonformal education was seen as having the unique capacity to fulfill specialized functions that schooling was never designed to serve.

3.1 Alternative Route to Upward Mobility

This broad goal of nonformal education has probably been the most widely proclaimed by the development planners. Since formal schooling failed to increase the status of the poor, nonformal education was viewed as an alternative mobility route. It was believed that through this alternative channel education could be provided for those for whom schooling was not a realistic alternative and as a means to circumvent the cultural obstacles that prevent some people from utilizing school effectively. Through nonformal education people could learn specific occupational skills, become more productive, and thus raise their status in society.

3.2 Training for the Modernizing Work Force

As a consequence of foreign aid the new nations found that they had more capital with which to develop their industrial capacity than they could put to good use, on account of their lack of trained people with the necessary capabilities. This shortfall of a trained work force led to the "human capital" approach to development which focused upon investment in the improvement of human beings (Sobel 1982). Thus, the demand for labor was linked to the supply of schooling. Since the formal school system was clearly not effective in preparing workers for the jobs required by modern industry, development planners increasingly looked toward nonformal education as the means of providing for these work force needs in both rural and urban industry.

Nonformal education was seen, therefore, as serving two diverse objectives: by aiding the increase in both industrial and agricultural production, the nation would be better able to compete in the world market; and, as a consequence, the "trickle down" from this affluence at the top would improve the standard of living of all of its clients.

3.3 Rural Development

The emphasis on economic development with its concern for gross domestic product (GDP), gross national product (GNP), and balance of trade did not have the "trickle down" effect that was predicted. It did not demonstrably benefit the masses, particularly those in rural areas. As a result, social planners began to promote a nonformal education strategy more specifically directed at alleviating the conditions of the rural poor.

The United Nations Second Development Decade for the 1970s conceived of the goals of rural development not simply in terms of agricultural and economic growth but as balanced social and economic development. This was to include improvements in health, nutrition, and housing; opportunities for individuals to realize their potential more fully; and a stronger voice for rural people in the decisions and actions that affect their lives. In response, many nonformal education programs have been implemented which are designed to achieve the goal of a more balanced rural development. There has been some attempt to coordinate training components with other critical factors such as financial assistance and marketing advice.

3.4 Political Incorporation

Among the new nations, with widely heterogeneous populations often lacking a common culture and language, there has been a concerted effort to use the educational system as the principal means for extending the influence of the state. Like formal schooling, nonformal education is expected to serve as a vehicle for resocializing its recipients to those values and competencies believed to be consistent with the state's goals for modernization. In the case of nonformal education, however, the target population is a different, more marginal clientele—adults and youthful school leavers from economic and ethnic subgroups which have had little or no access to formal schools. Thus, one of the important goals of nonformal education is the political incorporation of these largely unschooled subgroups as allegiant citizens of the state.

4. The Impact of Nonformal Education

Given such high expectations for nonformal education, the results to date have been disappointing. Nonformal education has been no more successful in achieving a more equal distribution of resources and power than has formal schooling. In fact, in common with formal schooling, nonformal education may serve to maintain, or even to increase the differences between the poor and the more advantaged.

Nonformal education has realized some success in training people for the lower levels of the modernizing labor market, but it appears that even vocational training courses are best utilized by those who already possess some formal schooling. Further, this vocational training has generally been very narrow in scope and has not been shown to enhance mobility chances outside of the "secondary labor market"—the lower segments of the work force. This is in contrast to formal education where there is, at least, the chance for lower-class youth who do manage to advance in the formal school system to attain jobs in more prestigious occupations.

Similarly, there is some evidence that nonformal education has had a positive effect on agricultural productivity. However, results are contradictory: the research of Lockheed et al. (1980) shows both some small effects and no effect at all. By and large, nonformal education has not been found to be a substitute for formal schooling with respect to rural or urban populations. In fact, nonformal education programs aimed at increasing agricultural production have had the greatest impact on farmers who already have some economic resources and several years of schooling, since they are better able to understand the information and are more financially able to experiment with new techniques. At best, by increasing the yield of the marginal farmers, some nonformal education programs may alleviate their poverty to some small degree, but it is doubtful that such programs can remove their condition of marginality in society.

Development projects which are aimed primarily at the rural poor have often attracted a large number of villagers. However, these programs have not been successful in reaching a large proportion of the very poor and uneducated people of the village—the very ones for whom the programs were designed. Instead, they tend to be consumed and most effectively utilized by those villagers who already have some years of schooling, as well as more resources available to invest in the new skills learned. For example, nonformal education programs have attracted a great many women of all socioeconomic groups to the classes teaching domestic and family-related skills: child care, nutrition, hygiene, and other homemaking skills. However, very poor women lack the funds to utilize this knowledge, and there is little being offered that would help these women supplement their income.

Attempts to help peasants gain greater decision-making power over their lives or to introduce some structural changes in agricultural practices have been largely unsuccessful (Colletta and Todd 1982, Moulton 1982). Nonformal education programs have not been able to bring about major institutional changes in the power and control of village affairs. Nevertheless, such programs may in some cases have served to raise the consciousness of the rural participants, making them more aware of new options. In the process they may become more discriminating consumers of the variety of government and privately sponsored nonformal education programs. For example, one unexpected consequence of the *animation rurale* program in Senegal was that the participants became resistant to passively accepting directives from the central planners when the peasants did not perceive them to be in their best interests (Moulton 1982).

Government-sponsored nonformal education programs have served as effective vehicles for transmitting the state's nation-building messages and for helping to incorporate previously marginal groups into allegiance to the nation. Moreover, such programs have in some cases been an effective means for transmitting a unifying national ideology to a wide diversity of cultural, linguistic, and socioeconomic groups.

At the same time, there is evidence that exposure to nonformal education may tend to lower the occupational aspirations of its graduates, since it does not carry the social power to bestow a legitimate claim to white-collar and professional jobs in the primary sector of the labor market (Bock 1976, Papagiannis 1977). It is important to note that, from the standpoint of the state, nonformal education appears to produce low-level subject citizens who, because of their modest occupational aspirations, are not as likely to participate in political turbulence as are secondary-school graduates who have had their high expectations frustrated by the harsh realities of the world of work (Bock 1981).

5. *Problems in Attaining the Goals of Nonformal Education*

Few of the broad goals of nonformal education have been achieved. There are many reasons for this, some unique to particular programs and their contexts. There are some problems, however, which appear to be common to nonformal education programs in a variety of countries and methods of approach.

One problem which appears to be universal is that of reaching the very poor uneducated people—the ones for whom the programs were particularly designed. One reason is that the very poor often cannot afford the time to participate since they are involved in more immediately pressing economic needs. There is also the problem of social distance felt by the target population relative to those participants who have more education and status, as well as to program organizers and tutors. The programs themselves are frequently not conducive to attracting the very poor in that they often require fees or equipment which the poor cannot afford, and are conducted in a national language which many of them cannot understand. As a result, even when enrolled, the very poor experience the highest dropout rate. This is particularly true of literacy classes, partly due to lack of motivation when the participants fail to see an immediate application in their daily lives (Jiyono et al. 1981).

Even in those cases where the poor have been successfully recruited, nonformal education has proven to be inadequate as an alternative means of upward social and economic mobility. Recipients of nonformal education programs have a much narrower and more limited social definition of what kinds of occupations they are believed to be competent to perform. The formal school certificate continues to be the essential "gate pass" without which access to high-status jobs is nearly impossible.

At the national level, elites have been supportive of nonformal education in that it is seen as limiting competition for elite access. However, at the village level, the entrenched hierarchy are seldom enthusiastic about the introduction of a new resource base which they perceive as having the potential to alter the local power base. To these village elites, nonformal education threatens old social and economic institutions by introducing new economic organizations and options.

Rural development projects often depend too heavily upon the leadership of field workers or facilitators who have the major responsibility for the attainment of the goals of the nonformal education program in their designated villages. Their success often depends upon their charismatic ability to engage the support of village elites and attract participants to the program (Coombs 1976, Moulton 1982). These people are often not well-trained or experienced in this type of work, nor do they receive much support or feedback from the central administration. Consequently, the results vary greatly from village to village.

The lack of success of nonformal education programs is also a result of underfinancing for the area they are intended to cover. The impact of the program is diluted because resources are spread too thinly. On the other hand, it is not always financially possible to replicate, on a national basis, intensive pilot projects which have been successful because of a concentrated infusion of resources.

There is also the common problem of the unsuitability of output of nonformal education: for example, participants are taught skills which are not marketable in their region. This is partly due to the lack of adequate needs assessment of the area. A more critical reason, however, is the lack of available jobs for landless rural people and the shortage of opportunities for marginal farmers to supplement their incomes even when they have learned new skills.

6. Policy Implications for Nonformal Education

The ideological hopes for nonformal education have not been supported by the empirical evidence. Thus, it has been necessary to temper expectations of the impact of this education innovation. Nonformal education alone cannot be viewed as a panacea for those development problems that formal schooling has failed to solve. At best, this alternative form of education is but one additional tool in an array of tools for national development.

6.1 Greater Integration with Other Institutions

Past experience indicates the need for greater cooperation and integration with other institutions at the national level. For example, more planning with both private and public sectors regarding the possible investment of more capital in rural areas is needed in order to create the potential for new jobs. More coordination of training efforts with industry may be indicated since industry-sponsored training has been found to be more productive than preemployment government training (Fuller 1976, La Belle 1975).

The unsuitability of output of nonformal education indicates a need for coordination of effort with other government agencies to determine both the work force needs at the local level and the marketability of local products. This national-level needs assessment can then be negotiated with the self-perceived needs of the village poor in order to plan for more effective nonformal education programs.

There is a great deal of duplication of effort by various government agencies which are providing nonformal education programs in the same geographical areas. Greater coordination at the national administration level, and at the village level, will reduce the competition for participants and teachers as well as maximize the use of available resources.

6.2 Greater Integration with the Formal School System

Research indicates that there will be an increasing demand for formal schooling as people realize that nonformal education does not provide the credentials necessary for upward social and economic mobility. Nonformal education itself also helps create this demand among the poor by imparting attitudes which proclaim the value of education for their children and themselves. In addition, evaluation research indicates that those who benefit the most from nonformal education are those who have had some years of formal schooling. As a result, in most cases nonformal education appears to be more effective as a complement or supplement to formal schooling than as a substitute.

These findings imply a strategy of even greater investment in formal primary schooling, perhaps adapting some of the methods devised by nonformal education for reducing costs. The PAMONG project in Indonesia, for example, is already experimenting with methods originally introduced by nonformal education to reduce costs (Non-Formal Education Exchange 1980). More integration with the formal school system, which implies some restructuring of formal education, will probably be necessary. Schooling conducted at times more convenient for the poor is also being tried by the CRAT program in Venezuela (La Belle 1975). Further restructuring of primary education to assist those students who will continue learning through nonformal education programs, rather than continuing on to secondary school, may help bridge the gap between formal and nonformal education.

6.3 The Need for Greater Support at the National Level

Many nonformal education theorists argue that, by definition, nonformal education must be decentralized and initiated from below by the needs of the village poor. However, there is some evidence to suggest that in the less developed countries these grass-roots programs are often small in size, affecting few clients; are difficult to generalize; and rarely succeed in achieving their planned outcomes (La Belle 1976, Moulton 1982). If nonformal education is going to be employed broadly as an instrument of national development, it requires a well-organized central administration and funding base.

It has been found that nonformal education organizers working at the village level need a great deal of training, monitoring, feedback, and other types of support from a committed central administration. It often requires national-level authority to obtain cooperation or acquiescence from local leadership, and to assure effective cooperation with other parallel development agencies.

The dangers of top-down organization are over-institutionalization and becoming captive to a rigid, inflexible bureaucracy. To reduce the consequences of overbureaucratization, a significant participatory element at the grass-roots level is required. As field workers gain more experience and programs are initiated, more and more decisions can be transferred to the local level.

This combination of top-down and bottom-up organization may be better able to accommodate unique geographical and cultural differences. It may also empower the poor clients of nonformal education to participate in those decisions which are critical to their well-being. Institutionalization may be necessary to achieve maximum planned effect, but to take nonformal education out of the hands of the consumers is to strip it of its potential for responding quickly to grass-roots needs.

6.4 *Providing Access to the Poor*

One of the most persistent problems in nonformal education programs is that of attracting and retaining the poor, particularly uneducated adults. They often do not perceive the need for education at this point in their lives. In order to attract the poor to nonformal education programs they must see an immediate economic gain or some tangible outcome. Literacy programs, for example, need to be part of an integrated strategy where some other knowledge or skill is learned which can demonstrate the value of literacy. In fact, there is evidence that literacy courses are most effective when preceded by skills courses which have short-run payoff.

Most important, these training programs are of limited use to the poor unless it is possible to help them utilize the skills or knowledge learned in a profitable capacity. Responsibility should not end when the class terminates. Follow-up activities should include help in locating relevant jobs and finding markets for their products as well as, perhaps, providing some "seed money" assistance.

There is a potential paradox concerning the expectations for, and the outcomes of, nonformal education. By its observed role in creating low-level subject citizens with lowered occupational aspirations, it may serve, in the short run, to limit excessive claims upon the state for resources and for primary-sector jobs. In the long run, however, nonformal education may have the unanticipated effect of introducing new meanings and options, thus serving to awaken the consciousness of the poor to a new set of choices, thereby creating the conditions for future organized, assertive political and economic action by formerly passive and isolated subjects.

See also: Economics of Nonformal Education

Bibliography

Bock J C 1970 Education and nation building in Malaysia: A study of institutional effect in thirty-four schools (Doctoral dissertation, Stanford University) *Dissertation Abstracts International* 1971 32: 1101A. (University Microfilms No. 71-19, 653)

Bock J C 1976 The institutionalization of nonformal education: A response to conflicting needs. *Comp. Educ. Rev.* 20: 346–67

Bock J C 1981 Educational correlates of violence. Paper presented at the Comparative and International Education Society annual meeting, Tallahassee, Florida

Bock J C 1982 Education and development: A conflict of meaning. In: Altbach P G, Arnove R F, Kelly G P (eds.) 1982 *Comparative Education.* Macmillan, New York, pp. 78–101

Colletta N J, Todd T A 1982 The limits of nonformal education and village development: Lessons from the Sarvodaya Shramadana movement. In: Bock J C, Papagiannis G J (eds.) 1982 *Nonformal Education and National Development.* Praeger, New York

Coombs P H 1968 *The World Education Crisis: A Systems Analysis.* Oxford University Press, London

Coombs P H 1976 Nonformal education: Myths, realities, and opportunities. *Comp. Educ. Rev.* 20: 281–93

Coombs P H, Ahmed M 1974 *Attacking Rural Poverty: How Nonformal Education Can Help.* Johns Hopkins University Press, Baltimore, Maryland

Easton P A 1982 Functional literacy in the West Africa Sakel: The Operation Arachide project in Mali. In: Bock J C, Papagiannis G J (eds.) 1982 *Nonformal Education and National Development.* Praeger, New York

Evans D R 1981 Ghana and Indonesia: Reforms in non-formal education at the community level. *Prospects* 11: 225–41

Fuller W P 1976 More evidence supporting the demise of pre-employment vocational trade training: A case study in India. *Comp. Educ. Rev.* 20: 30–41

Harbison F H 1973a *A Human Resource Approach to the Development of African Nations.* Overseas Liaison Committee of the American Council on Education, Washington, DC

Harbison F H 1973b *Education Sector Planning for Development of Nationwide Learning Systems.* Overseas Liaison Committee of the American Council on Education, Washington, DC

Jiyono, Pakpahan E, Sinaga T, Hartone H, Bock J, Bock C, Shaeffer S 1981 *Final Evaluation on the Mid-Term Evaluation of the PENMAS Nonformal Education Project.* Office of Educational and Cultural Research and Development, Jakarta

La Belle T J 1975 The impact of nonformal education on income in industry: Ciudad Guayana, Venezuela. In: La Belle T J (ed.) 1975 *Educational Alternatives in Latin America: Social Change and Social Stratification.* UCLA Latin American Center, Los Angeles, California, pp. 257–92

La Belle T J 1976 *Nonformal Education and Social Change in Latin America.* UCLA Latin American Center, Los Angeles, California

Lockheed M E, Jamison D T, Laurence L J 1980 Farmer education and farm efficiency: A survey. *Econ. Dev. and Cult. Change* 29: 37–76

Moulton J 1982 *Animation rurale*: Education for rural development. In: Bock J C, Papagiannis G J (eds.) 1982 *Nonformal Education and National Development.* Praeger, New York

Non-Formal Education (NFE) Exchange 1980 *Nonformal Approaches to Primary Education in Asia.* Institute for International Studies in Education, Michigan State University, East Lansing, Michigan

Papagiannis G J 1977 Nonformal education and national development: A study of the Thai mobile trade training schools and their institutional effects on adult participants (Doctoral dissertation, Stanford University) *Dissertations Abstracts International* 1978 38: 5191A–5192A. (University Microfilms No. 7802213)

Paulston R G, LeRoy G 1982 Nonformal education and change from below. In: Altbach P G, Arnove R F, Kelly G P (eds.) 1982 *Comparative Education.* Macmillan, New York, pp. 336–62

Sobel I 1982 The human capital revolution in economic development. In: Altbach P G, Arnove R F, Kelly G P (eds.) 1982 *Comparative Education.* Macmillan, New York, pp. 54–77

Mandatory Continuing Education

J. W. Apps

Most of the research and writing about mandatory continuing education has been produced in the United States and it usually concerns such persons as doctors or engineers. However, there have been forms of educational compulsion affecting adults throughout history, and such legally sanctioned education or training appears in many parts of the world. Examples are found in almost any military organization, in many forms of education and training for adults in socialist countries, in classes for illiterates in many countries, such as Ethiopia, and in many penitentiaries. There are also cases where people convicted of drunken driving or child abuse are sentenced to a form of compulsory education rather than fines or penal servitude.

The phenomenon is widespread but careful research about its consequences is limited primarily to North America and most of it has been published since the early 1960s (Houle 1980). Despite a growing amount of research evidence, considerable disagreement still exists about the value of such procedures.

Mandatory continuing education is usually associated with the continuing education of professionals. Either through rules passed by a professional organization or through laws passed by state or federal governments, certain professionals are required to participate in educational activities to keep their membership in their professional organization or maintain their certification or license.

1. Background

Such education for professionals is not a new idea. As far back as 1889, physicians in some states in the United States were required to update their knowledge as a prerequisite for licensing (Edwards and Green 1981 p. 6). Public-school teachers in some countries have been required to participate in further training for many years. In 1980, every state in the United States had some form of compulsory continuing education for some of its professionals. Most frequently included are the personnel in health services, including optometrists, nursing-home administrators, physicians, nurses, pharmacists, dentists, osteopaths, dental hygienists, and physical therapists.

Beyond government mandated continuing education, many professional organizations, such as law and engineering, require further education as a condition for renewal of certification.

2. Reasons for Growth of Mandatory Continuing Education

A fundamental question behind such educational provisions is: how can society be assured that professional and skilled workers, once they have been initially deemed competent to practice, continue to be competent? With the so-called knowledge explosion in most professional and technological areas in recent years, this question has become important for both professionals and the public. For the public, forcing personnel to participate in continuing education is one way to insure that they will be exposed to the new knowledge in their fields. And for the professionals, supporting mandatory continuing education demonstrates to the public their concern for their competencies.

Because it is relatively difficult to assess the professional performances of practitioners, mandatory advanced education is often viewed as a valid substitute for assessment of performance. The reasoning goes that if people have participated in continuing education, then their chances of competent performance are much greater than if they had not. Some professional groups advocate further education for their members as a way of avoiding more threatening and restrictive laws and government control. The profession would rather make the rules itself than have a legislative body make them.

As an additional motive, some college decision makers have tacitly encouraged such education because increased numbers of adult students on campus may help overcome the problems associated with declining enrollments. University administrators believe that they are more capable than politicians, or even professional associations, of designing and offering such programs effectively.

The chief advantages of mandatory study are usually summarized as those of:

(a) providing a stimulus to present low rates of voluntary advanced study;

(b) improving the "public image" of the occupation;

(c) easier funding for such study programs than for other services of the university—a support for higher education;

(d) raising the performance of the least able members of the occupational group to a minimum standard;

(e) reducing costs of professional service by improvements in performance;

(f) decreasing the number of costly malpractice suits.

The strongest argument that is generally heard also suggests the need for continuing critical enquiry: namely that mandatory education is an appropriate transition phase in the direction of achieving greater professional accountability.

The amount of research in Europe and North America respecting these claims has been on the increase but has been limited chiefly to issues of participation rates, attitudes toward mandatory versus voluntary controls, and amounts of content or skills learned for immediate recall or use. However, few if any studies have been about the improvement of professional performance which, though it is difficult to measure, is the central question at issue.

Mandatory continuing education is usually placed within the context of professionals concerned with certification, recertification, licensure, and credentialing. When recertification and relicensure are involved, participation in continuing education is often viewed as the basis for making such decisions.

Another argument offered to support continuing education is that if education is good for the preparation of professionals, then it should also be good for those who are practicing. As Barbara Shore points out:

> Assumptions have been made for many years that professional education is the best available measurement of one's ability to practice. It is, indeed, by most standards, an entry-level requirement. It is interesting to note, moreover, that no challenges to this approach have been raised in disagreement about mandatory continuing education. If education has relevance at one point in the continuum, however, why would it not have relevance throughout the continuum of one's professional life? (Edwards and Green 1981)

3. Problems with Mandatory Continuing Education

One of the most serious problems with mandatory continuing education is the lack of evidence showing a strong direct relationship between continuing education and more effective professional practice. By depending on such education as a basis for making decisions about whether or not a professional should be relicensed or recertified, the real question about the competency of that professional is often overlooked. Because of the lack of evidence linking educational participation with improved performance, reliance on mandatory continuing education as a measure of competence is a disservice both to the profession and to the public.

A second problem is that some professionals consider mandatory education degrading, insulting, and superfluous for people who should be viewed as responsible for their own skill development.

Furthermore, critics of mandatory education say that it often places a premium on attendance rather than learning. They note that professional competence is gained through a wide spectrum of other sources including practical experience, reading professional journals and other literature, and communicating with fellow practitioners, as well as attending classes, workshops, and conferences. These additional kinds of learning experiences have been emphasized in recent years as more effective than lectures.

Finally, enforcing the continuing education laws is often as great a problem as contending with substandard performances. The time, costs, and energy devoted to enforcement of mandates may consume resources that could better be used contending with those professionals who do not meet minimum standards.

4. Trends

It would appear that the growth of mandatory continuing education is beginning to wane as many groups have taken a firm position in opposition to it. This is reflected in a decision at the 1976 UNESCO General Conference in Nairobi, Kenya, where delegates passed unanimously the following recommendation:

> Participation in an adult education program should be a voluntary matter. The State and other bodies should strive to promote the desire of individuals and groups for education in the spirit of life-long education and learning. (UNESCO 1976)

A report from the US Adult Education Association Task Force on Voluntary Learning made this point:

> Mandatory continuing education lulls the unexpecting public into unwarranted assumptions about the competence of professionals. Mandated education is an inappropriate response to those who demand recertification or relicensure. (Heaney 1980)

On the other hand, Cyril Houle's decade-long review of the research turned up evidence that, at least in certain professional groups, a majority of the members accept mandatory continuing education. Houle reports, for example, on an inquiry made of certain groups of physicians, nurses, and accountants who experienced continuing education as a requirement for relicensure. A majority of the professionals in each of these groups favored mandatory advanced study (Houle 1980).

In many professions, though, there is an increasing interest in relicensure and recertifying professionals based on some measure of competency rather than solely on participation in educational activities so that research about what constitutes competency is becoming more common. However, this trend will not diminish the importance of continuing education for professionals because that process will continue to be an important way by which professionals acquire new knowledge and enhance their skills. But rather than forcing professionals to participate, the trend will rely more on them selecting educational offerings that relate directly to the proficiencies they need to enhance.

Bibliography

Apps J W 1979 *Problems in Continuing Education.* McGraw-Hill, New York

Baskett H K 1981 *Continuing Professional Education: Moving into the 80s.* Proc. of Conf. on Continuing Professional Education, Oct. 22–24, 1980. University of Calgary, Calgary, Alberta

Edwards R, Green R 1981 Should continuing education be mandatory? Counterpoint. *National Association of Social Workers' News.* National Association of Social Workers, Washington, DC

Heaney T 1980 *Task Force Report*. Adult Education Association, Washington, DC

Houle C O 1980 *Continuing Learning in the Professions*. Jossey-Bass, San Francisco, California

Knox A 1980 *University Continuing Professional Education*. University of Illinois, Urbana, Illinois

Le Breton P P (ed.) 1979 *The Evaluation of Continuing Education for Professionals: A Systems View*. University of Washington, Seattle, Washington

Schein E H 1978 *Career Dynamics: Matching Individual and Organizational Needs*. Addison-Wesley, Reading, Massachusetts

Shore B 1981 Mandatory continuing education: Point. *National Association of Social Workers' News*, Vol. 26. National Association of Social Workers, Washington, DC, pp. 6–7

Slayton P, Trebilcock M J (eds.) 1978 *The Professions and Public Policy*. University of Toronto Press, Toronto, Ontario

Section 2

Purposes of Adult Education

Section 2

Purposes of Adult Education

Introduction

The issue of purpose in education is multifaceted. It embraces considerations of the kind of knowledge which should be its concern, for example, that which is of value in itself, or that which is useful because it enables the possessor to perform certain actions. Should education exclude some kinds of knowledge from its agenda, or admit all in its concerns? If the latter, is it necessary to strike a balance between different kinds? Should the purpose of education be socialization or the development of the individual? Is the full achievement of either possible without some element of the other? Who is to decide what the answers to these issues shall be in practice?

In adult education the question of purposes may be treated on three levels. The most general level concerns consideration of what the purpose of education is and of the questions raised above; the second, more specific level, relates to the purposes specific to adult as distinct from other sectors of education; the third level, then, is concerned with the purposes of particular manifestations of adult education.

In so far as adult education is considered to be an integral part of education as a whole, and this is now more or less universally the case, then it shares the purpose of education as a whole. It may, because it touches age groups not reached by other forms of education, make it possible to extend the purpose of education; it may also provoke some rethinking on the subject.

Since education has traditionally been concerned with the teaching of children and young people, its purposes have been marked by a view which essentially saw the learner in a position of subordination to the educational agency, whether person, books, or other media. It has been generally seen as predominantly a process of socialization. Hence, for example, the idea that education consists of the *transmission* of worthwhile knowledge, whose value is determined by the teacher.

The inclusion of adult education as an integral element, without which the purposes of lifelong education and recurrent education cannot be achieved, calls into question many of the basic assumptions on which ideas of the purpose of education have been based. It is generally accepted that the adult, not the educator, has the ultimate responsibility for what and whether he or she shall study. In principle, at least, the adult learner is *not* subordinate. So far the educational implications of reconciling this with the status of children within a single concept of education have only been marginally considered. Emphasis has been laid, for the most part, on the social, economic, and political implications, as the articles in Section 1 indicate.

Whatever the accepted concept of education as a whole may be, adult education has purposes specific to itself within the larger process. It provides adults with a second chance to obtain the kind of education available in the initial education system. At whatever level initial education may be completed, the purpose of adult education is also to carry it on. Thereby adults have the opportunity to supplement their initial education by continuing the studies they have begun and undertaking ones which, for one reason or another, were not available to them in school or higher education. It is argued that it is the purpose of adult education and the right and duty of the adult to continue throughout life his or her individual educational development.

Almost all societies have recognized that for some people new needs may arise in adult life, which either could not have been foreseen in youth, or for which educational provision could not be made during childhood. One of the novel features of concepts of lifelong education in the 1980s lies in maintaining that this applies to all people. There are needs which may be foreseen, but must be met in adulthood, if at all, because children's experience, maturity, or motivation is, or is believed to be, inadequate, or because it is considered that there are more immediately or generally important things for children to study during the process of initial education. There enters the concept of the teachable moment, at the core of which lies the argument that for each person certain times are particularly favourable for the acquisition of specific knowledge and skills. It is maintained that educational needs should not be met in anticipation of some possible future contingency, but as and when they are felt by the learner: then will come the motivation essential to effective learning. It is a peculiarly appropriate purpose of adult education to provide for this. For example, childcare is sometimes taught in school, but probably with less effect than to people who have or are about to have children.

In practice, although policy makers and educators may harbour strongly held beliefs about the purpose of education in general, and adult education in particular, most provision is not made with such beliefs in mind, but is planned and operated to achieve specific, discrete, largely limited, and short-term objectives. Insofar as there is evidence, it would suggest that most teachers of adults do not primarily, if at all, set out to educate, and most adult participants do not seek consciously to be educated; both have more particular, less theoretical ends in view, such as teaching/learning effective childcare.

It would in fact be difficult to enrol for a course of education as such; one is constrained to undertake the study of a discipline, the mastery of a skill, the solution of a problem. The school curriculum may be planned, however misguidedly in the light of modern thinking, to constitute a whole; that of adult education shows little sign of such planning. What is offered to adults is a multifarious collection of learning opportunities, whose purpose is to meet specific requirements both of individual learners, and also of various kinds of collective, such as society as a whole, employers, or social interest groups. It would be impossible to cover all the opportunities which are offered at some time in some place, but the following articles treat the ways in which, and the extent to which, some of the purposes are achieved.

Adult Literacy

Introduction

One of the longest running purposes for which education has been offered to adults has been to teach them to read and write. There were active campaigns to this end in eighteenth-century Europe, throughout the nineteenth and into the twentieth centuries, and now advanced countries are becoming aware that a new effort is required for their own native-born citizens. In many developing countries the drive for literacy *is* adult education. Until that is successful, the scope for other educational activities among adults is seen to be severely limited.

The value of being able to read and write lies not in itself, but in other skills and knowledge to which it opens the way. Where the latter are not perceived to be of utility or interest, there is no incentive to become literate, or if one has a certain level of literacy, no incentive to maintain it. This, as well as the economic and organizational difficulties of mounting mass educational campaigns, is a major reason why illiteracy remains a significant problem throughout the world.

The term adult literacy goes beyond activities designed to teach adults to read and write simple sentences. It has been observed that such restricted skills are of little utility and so subject to the decay already mentioned. The aim of literacy campaigns now is functional literacy, the achievement of a level of reading, writing, *and* numeracy adequate for effective participation in the life of one's community. The lack of such technical competence is not, however, seen merely as a cause, but, perhaps more fundamentally in advanced countries, as a consequence of exclusion from effective participation. This exclusion is seen as a product of social, cultural, economic, and political conditions rather than educational ones, but some improvement may be achieved, it is believed, by including training in life skills under the umbrella of literacy and numeracy. Such programmes are generally designated "adult basic education".

In this subsection, the article *Literacy and Numeracy Policies*, offers a general overview of the subject. It covers the history of the struggle against illiteracy in Europe, and the birth of literacy campaigns. With particular attention to the developing countries it discusses conditions which favour literacy and the issues to be confronted in the formulation of literacy policies, including problems of language, ideology, and organizational structures. It briefly touches on the use and maintenance of literacy and the work of international agencies. *Adult Literacy in Developed Countries* examines not only the efforts made to wipe out illiteracy in the Soviet Union, Italy, and other European countries, but the problem, only recently recognized, of continuing illiteracy in those countries and others in which universal schooling was thought to have almost eradicated it among the native born. The following article, *Adult Literacy: Size of the Problem*, looks at the results of these efforts. It indicates how variable has been the success of literacy campaigns in different parts of the world and points out that although the number of literate adults is increasing, so, for demographic reasons, is the number of illiterates.

One of the problems that has emerged from studies of the long-term successes and failures of literacy campaigns, particularly in the context of developing countries, is that literacy skills, once mastered, can often deteriorate or even disappear, through disuse. The final article, *Second Stage Adult Literacy*, looks at the measures that need to be taken to avoid this.

Literacy and Numeracy Policies[1]

J. W. Ryan

A literacy policy consists of the purposes, principles, priorities, and plans which guide government action in the promotion of literacy. A successful policy must include three main aspects: (a) the generalization of

1 The author, a UNESCO staff member, is responsible for the choice and presentation of the facts in this article and for the opinions expressed therein, which are not necessarily those of UNESCO, and do not commit the organization.

primary schooling; (b) programmes of instruction for out-of-school youths and adults; and (c) the fostering of economic and social conditions favourable to the promotion and maintenance of literacy. Following a cursory review of the historic conditions out of which widespread literacy arose in the West, this article examines the emergence of the state as the main force in education and the development of policies to confront situations of mass illiteracy in the Soviet Union, in the aftermath of revolution, and in the Third World today. A number of key issues in the formulation and implementation of literacy policies are discussed and the role of UNESCO in supporting national literacy efforts is reviewed.

1. Definitions

UNESCO's Revised Recommendation concerning the international standardization of educational statistics distinguishes between literacy and functional literacy. A person is literate "who can with understanding both read and write a short simple statement on his everyday life", whereas an individual who is functionally literate is able to "engage in all those activities in which literacy is required for effective functioning of his group and community and also for enabling him to continue to use reading, writing and calculation for his own and the community's development" (UNESCO 1978a p. 18). It will be observed that calculation (or numeracy) is included in the definition of functional literacy, but not of literacy. Since most literacy programmes provide instruction in numeracy, literacy will be considered here to subsume numeracy.

2. Diffusion of Literacy in Europe

With the emergence of the nation–state, in the eighteenth and nineteenth centuries in Europe and areas of European settlement, and in the twentieth century elsewhere, it became meaningful to speak of literacy policies. However, the diffusion of literacy did not await the creation of the state. Literacy apparently advanced rapidly in Europe from the fifteenth century onward; by the middle of the nineteenth century it is estimated that more than half of the adult population could read (Cipolla 1969 p. 71). This progress was the consequence of cultural, social, economic, and technological forces. The emergence of vernacular languages in written form, which gradually displaced Latin, provided the media for popular literacy. With the replacement of parchment by paper, introduced into Europe by the Arabs, and the invention of moveable-type presses during the fifteenth century, a wide selection of printed texts became available for the first time. The Reformation provided a powerful motive for literacy by linking the reading of the Bible to religious virtue, and ultimately to eternal salvation. It was not by accident that literacy advanced most rapidly in Protestant Europe. In those parts of the continent which did not experience the Reformation, the Industrial Revolution provided an impetus for literacy. As the city replaced the village and the factory replaced the farm, life and work were transformed in myriad ways which, if painful for humanity, were favourable to the spread of reading and writing.

The manner in which these forces of change reinforced one another is demonstrated by the interrelationships among literacy, science and technology. It is convincingly argued that the spread of literacy in the fifteenth and sixteenth centuries rescued science from the sterility of the universities and brought it into the workplace, where applied and experimental sciences, the precursors of modern sciences, came into being. Conversely, in the nineteenth and twentieth centuries, science was harnessed to technology and provided the motivation for literacy: the nature of work and the manner of life were so altered that the abilities to read, write, and calculate became essential economic skills and not merely scholarly attributes.

In retrospect, it can be seen that literacy progressed rapidly in what is now referred to as the "developed world" because intellectual, cultural, political, and economic forces associated with a profound transformation of society had created the need, demand, and means for literacy. Fishman has noted that the introduction of writing systems and, by extension, the promotion of literacy are "revolutionary rather than narrowly technical acts. They succeed or fail on the basis of the success of the larger revolutions with which they are associated: revolutions in the production and consumption of economic goods . . . and revolutions in the distribution of power and influence" (quoted in Gorman 1977 pp. 277–78). By these measures and others, the eighteenth and nineteenth centuries were auspicious for literacy.

The role of the state in the advancement of literacy appears to have been incidental and indirect until the second half of the nineteenth century. Although measures providing for compulsory schooling were introduced in Prussia as early as 1717, the major states of Europe did not have well-defined educational policies until more than a century later. Opposition to compulsory schooling in France was finally overcome by the conviction that defeat in the Franco–Prussian war was due to Prussia's superior education system. In England, it was not until 1880 that attendance was mandated nationwide. By the end of the nineteenth century, however, the state had emerged as the dominant force in education, and the school as the main instrument of educational policy.

By this time, economic and social conditions favoured and supported the diffusion of literacy. A popular press and publishing industry existed. Bank and postal services were widespread and widely used. Reading, writing, and calculation were necessary for the more rewarding forms of employment; without these skills possibilities in life were narrowly circumscribed. The school, thus, took its place in a social environment which facilitated and supported its educational mission. Much discussion of education in developing countries tends to concentrate upon the school and to neglect the importance of a sustaining community environment. It is, hence, worth emphasizing the observation of a French historian: "*L'alphabétisation n'est pas l'école et l'histoire de l'école ne suffit pas à épuiser celle de l'alphabétisation*"(Limage 1980 p. 142). [Literacy is not schooling and the history of the school does not suffice to explain the history of literacy.]

3. *Birth of the Literacy Campaign*

The Soviet Literacy Campaign, inaugurated in 1919, was perhaps the first example of a state policy directed to the eradication of illiteracy among both adults and school-age children. Lenin hoped that this ambitious goal might be achieved before the tenth anniversary of the Bolshevik Revolution. The task was colossal: an illiteracy rate of 70 percent, a widely scattered population of 100 million speaking 122 different languages, and a situation of economic and social chaos occasioned by a lost war and a victorious revolution (Bhola 1984 Chap. 4). The motivation behind the campaign was both ideological and pragmatic. "An illiterate person", Lenin asserted, "is outside politics and has to be taught his ABCs. Without this there can be no politics." The political revolution had to be completed by a cultural revolution. At the same time, a new government had to prepare the masses for the rapid modernization which both ideology and the survival of the state required.

The Soviet literacy campaign is a fascinating and instructive chapter in the history of education. There is space here to emphasize only certain points:

(a) The ultimate success of the campaign was a victory for persistence and steadfastness of purpose in what proved to be a difficult struggle. The campaign, in several phases, lasted until 1939, by which time the estimated literacy rate was 87 percent (Bhola 1984 Chap. 4).

(b) Although in the initial phases the campaign depended upon improvization and inspiration, this progressively gave way to a carefully planned strategy of action, a fuller appreciation of the difficulties inherent in such an enterprise, and more realistic estimates of the time and resources required for success. Enormous efforts, for example, were invested in the systematic study of languages and the development of instructional materials.

(c) The launching of the literacy campaign was coordinated with energetic efforts to provide schooling for all children, thereby eliminating illiteracy at its source.

(d) Revolutionary ferment and the anticipation of a fundamental socioeconomic transformation created an environment of expectancy and optimism in which the efforts of linguists and educationists could have an effective outcome.

Following the Second World War, literacy programmes and campaigns became commonplace. Whereas the developed countries had relied upon school systems to diffuse literacy (see *Adult Literacy in Developed Countries*), many newly independent nations sought to confront and overcome the problem of mass illiteracy and undereducation in a shorter time through an approach which combined expansion of schooling with adult literacy. As President Nyerere of Tanzania explained:

> First we must educate adults. Our children will not have an impact on our economic development for five, ten, or even twenty years. The attitudes of adults. . . on the other hand, have an impact now. The people must understand the plans for development of this country; they must be able to participate in changes which are necessary. . . (quoted in Bhola 1984 Chap. 10).

4. *Conditions Favouring Literacy*

Literacy policies, like all social policies, are implemented in a socioeconomic environment, the favourability or adversity of which is itself the principal determinant of the success or failure of such policies. This is particularly the case for literacy, which ultimately depends upon the individual's motivation to learn, an inclination strongly conditioned by social, political, cultural, and economic circumstances, perceptions, and aspirations. The landless peasant or impoverished urban dweller will not be made literate until the basic conditions of their lives are transformed. Literacy has meaning and is actively sought only when it is perceived as leading to a fuller participation in culture and society and to a more equitable sharing of social, economic, and political rights and privileges.

The Declaration of Persepolis, a statement issuing from an international conference held in Iran in 1975, cites the structures most favourable to literacy:

> Those that, from the economic point of view, aim at an endogenous and harmonious development of society, and not at blind and dependent growth.
>
> Those that, from the social point of view, do not result in making education a class privilege and a means of reproducing established hierarchies and orders.
>
> Those that, from the professional point of view, provide communities with genuine control over the technologies they wish to use.
>
> Those that, from the institutional point of view, favour a concerted approach and permanent cooperation among the authorities responsible for basic services (agriculture, welfare, health, family planning, etc.). (Bataille 1976 p. 274)

This list may be challenged or amplified. Adequate economic incentives, for example, may be more important in fostering literacy than the "harmonious development of society". There can be little doubt, however, that the need and motivation for literacy normally arises from fundamental transformations in society. Efforts to promote literacy which are not associated with these broader currents of change are unlikely to be successful.

In the economic sphere, the relationship between literacy and development is convincingly supported by empirical evidence. Bowman and Anderson (1963), for example, found that all countries with 1955 per capita incomes of US$500 or more had literacy rates exceeding 90 percent whereas all countries with per capita incomes below US$200 had literacy rates below 30 percent. It would be perilous to cite these correlations as evidence that literacy results in economic growth, but they are testimony that literacy and development go hand-in-hand. It would appear hazardous either to formulate a literacy policy which is not articulated with wider national development goals or, conversely, to propose a national development policy which makes inadequate provision for education and literacy.

The existence of a widely shared written language, a press, and a publishing industry are among the more evident factors which foster literacy. Where these are present, the task at hand can be accurately defined as diffusion of literacy. Where they are absent, the initial challenge is to establish them; without them, the rewards of literacy will be meagre and the motivation for it feeble.

5. *Issues in the Formulation of Literacy Policies*

In formulating a literacy policy, policy makers and planners confront a series of intricately interrelated issues. In multilingual societies—which are the rule in the Third World—there is, first, the choice of language or languages in which literacy is to be attained and the chain of consequences which ensue from this decision. Then, there is the question of programme goals and strategies. Next, a series of organizational issues have to be addressed and the proposed solutions measured against available resources. Lastly, there is the issue of ultimate importance: how a literate and literacy-sustaining society can be created to replace an illiterate one. This list is representative and not exhaustive. The challenge in formulating a policy is not only to address these issues but to do so in a coherent and consistent manner. In the subsections which follow, a number of key issues will be examined.

5.1 Language Issues

Among the first and most emotive matters to be settled in formulating a literacy policy is the choice of language, or languages, which is to be the medium of literacy. This choice has a direct bearing upon the probable success of literacy instruction. Many political, social, and economic factors influence that choice. In many cases there has been a desire to assimilate small groups into larger communities and to integrate cultural and political entities within the state into a larger whole. There have been financial and technical considerations, including budget allocation for education, availability of trained staff, and physical resources. Countries have wished to ensure access to Western culture and technology and have had to confront changes in traditional customs relating to the distribution of population, the division of labour, and social and religious taboos. Such considerations, as well as obviously linguistic ones, as, for example, the translation of new and technical vocabulary into traditional written or nonwritten languages, have to be taken into account.

In countries with the highest illiteracy rate a large proportion of those who can neither read nor write speak only their own dialect. This hampers their participation in area development activities. Their inability to speak the language of administration or power is one reason why they do not get their due economic and social benefits. They need also to be able to read and write the official language, if they are to be able to change their situation. They have therefore not only to acquire literacy skills, but in many cases a second language.

On the other hand a literacy student can be expected to achieve more rapid success and greater fluency in his mother tongue than in a second language. This is why international meetings have recommended that initial literacy should be achieved, wherever possible, in the learner's mother tongue. There has been some practical experience to support this approach. The Mali literacy project, using the mother tongue, made a big contribution to functional literacy and gave the peasantry fresh opportunities for gaining access to the values of its own civilization (Dumont 1973). In Nigeria use of the mother tongue seemed to enhance the interest and learning in classes (Kahler 1974).

There is some evidence to suggest that learners who begin in their mother tongue move easily to a second language. In Togo they were able to master a second language in about four months of additional instruction. In Peru and Papua New Guinea it was noted that when the mother tongue was used pedagogically, the participants' progress was found to be significantly better in the acquisition of literacy skills. The literacy programmes were regarded as sound from the viewpoint of national interests because the participants had then been able to transfer easily to a national or to a trade language (Harris 1974 p. 2).

There are, however, enormous obstacles to the teaching of literacy in the mother tongue. They are of three kinds: the multiplicity of languages spoken in developing nations; the limited scale and restricted uses of most such languages; and the paucity of resources, both financial and human, for rendering purely spoken languages into effective media for literacy (Gorman 1977). India gives some idea of the scale of the problem which exists. In the subcontinent there are 15 regional languages, which have the same status as the national language, Hindi. Each has its own grammar and literature. Some east and south India languages also have different scripts. In addition the 1961 census recorded the existence of 1,652 mother-tongue dialects.

In many countries, a serious beginning cannot be

made in literacy work until the issue of language choice is confronted and resolved. The progress of literacy in Tanzania is due, in part, to favourable historical circumstances and wise political leadership which enabled the selection of a single language, Swahili, to be developed as the national language and medium of instruction in schools and literacy classes. In the 20 years since this policy was implemented, Swahili has become the national language, and is used and understood in all parts of the country. On the other hand, an effort under the Imperial Government of Ethiopia to make Amharic the national language failed. Literacy courses are now offered in 15 languages.

The choice of language in Somalia was evident, but the progress of literacy was halted by the need to decide whether Somali would be written in Arabic, Roman, or an indigenously developed script. To religious leaders, Arabic script was the only choice, whereas those bent upon modernization argued that the Roman script provided privileged access to Western science and technology. The indigenous script had a tribal constituency. In 1973, the national leadership opted for romanization, thus clearing the way for the launching of a massive literacy campaign.

Even where the choice of orthography has been made, its standardization or simplification may become an issue. Arabic presents a case in point. Although the alphabet has only 28 letters, most have a variety of forms depending upon the position in which they are used or the letters which follow or precede them. Thus, in most printing houses, 119 letter forms are in use, although some religious publishers still employ up to 470 forms. Experiments have demonstrated that learning results are improved when the number of letter forms is reduced (Ryan 1980 p. 116). Policy decisions on matters such as orthography can have a direct bearing upon the feasibility and success of literacy campaigns. Where the decision is in favour of standardization the learning task is significantly reduced, as are the cost and complexity of producing reading materials, without which literacy has little meaning or relevance.

As the People's Republic of China includes one-quarter of humanity, a brief note on the special problem of becoming literate in Chinese may be justified. In this ideographic language, characters are based upon the lexical and grammatical aspects of the language and only slightly reflect its pronunciation. This has enabled the language to serve as a medium of communication among all literate Chinese (Han), even though they speak a variety of dialects and languages. Its major drawback in terms of literacy is that it is not possible to read after having mastered thirty or so letters; a command of 2,000 or more characters is necessary depending upon the nature of the text to be interpreted. Although the experience of Japan demonstrates that ideographic writing is not a bar to universal literacy, in China it imposes a heavy educational burden upon a populous and poor country.

As the examples cited indicate, language issues loom large in planning literacy activities. There are no ready-made solutions to these problems. Policy must be based upon careful analysis of the costs and benefits of possible courses of action. Gains in instructional efficiency from the use of mother tongues may, for example, have to be measured against the reduction in scale of communication which is inherent in a multilingual policy. Political considerations or cultural values often may preclude otherwise acceptable approaches. These issues are not easily resolved, but literacy work presupposes a language and an alphabet which can serve as the media of literacy.

5.2 Objectives and Strategies

The past decades have witnessed an intense debate over the objectives and design of literacy programmes. This disagreement is expressed in methodological terms, for example, comprehensive versus selective approaches, education versus training, but is rooted in sharply divergent philosophies of development and the differing missions they assign to literacy. Three of the more influential approaches are discussed briefly below: the campaign strategy, functional literacy, and the method of Paulo Freire—literacy as cultural action.

(a) *The campaign strategy*. A campaign is "an organized large-scale series of activities, intensely focused on a set of objectives to be achieved within some pre-determined period of time" (Bhola 1984). According to its advocates, the mass literacy campaign is the only approach commensurate with the scale of the problem to be confronted. The campaign is for literacy but its essence is social mobilization. It is a means for calling up national energies for the pursuit of a comprehensive set of goals: economic, sociostructural, and political. Indeed, Bhola insists that a successful campaign has to be simultaneously an educational and a political event. There must be a propelling and guiding ideology: a vision of the just society, the restored nation, or the vindicated faith. Bhola observes, however, that social technology is as important as ideological fervour. A successful campaign will involve millions of participants, perhaps tens of millions. At this scale of operation, there is no substitute for organizational and technical skills of a high order.

A recent study prepared for UNESCO examines successful literacy campaigns conducted in the Soviet Union, Vietnam, the People's Republic of China, Cuba, Burma, Brazil, Tanzania, and Somalia. Although these countries differ considerably from one another, the campaign strategy reportedly achieved a substantial degree of success in all of them. The essential aspect of the campaign is that it focuses national attention on illiteracy and, by setting explicit and unequivocal goals, commits national authorities to energetic action to overcome it. Doubtless, the ultimate usefulness of such efforts will depend upon the extent to which the economic, social, political, and cultural conditions in which illiteracy is rooted are transformed. This is recognized by advocates of the campaign, who insist that literacy in and of itself is not the goal. Literacy is, however, considered essential to the emergence of new individual and collective identities and to the development of a society in which participation and concerted national action for development are possible.

(b) *Functional literacy.* This concept is usually associated with the experimental World Literacy Programme carried out in 11 countries between 1967 and 1973 under the auspices of UNESCO and the United Nations Developmental Programme (UNDP). It was formulated as a reaction to the campaign strategy, which was considered by its critics to be too general, too diffuse, and too weakly structured to be effective. The original notion was that literacy training should not be restricted to the three Rs, but should constitute a preparation for social, civic, and economic roles. Subsequently, as the projects were challenged to demonstrate their cost–effectiveness, the concept came to be defined in the narrower sense of "work-oriented literacy". Special courses were offered for particular occupational groups which integrated literacy with elements of vocational training. Courses for farmers, for example, were related to particular crops, for example, sugar beets in Iran and groundnuts in Mali. This was termed the "selective and intensive" approach. The aim of the training was not only to raise the general educational level of the population, but to achieve specified economic or employment outcomes.

It was not accidental that functional literacy came to the fore at the same moment that interest in manpower planning was nearing its zenith. The illiterate masses were seen to represent a vast pool of underutilized manpower which had to be upgraded and integrated into the modern sector of the economy. This underestimated the social, political, cultural, and economic requirements for mobilizing the masses for development. A particular difficulty was the relatively high cost per course completer in relationship to the per capita income of the poorer countries (UNESCO/UNDP 1976).

In retrospect, the Experimental World Literacy Programme appears to have made an important qualitative contribution to literacy work. It introduced a concept—functional literacy—which correctly stressed the need to relate literacy to individual motivations and to community needs. The programme and, more particularly, the publication of the evaluation report, subtitled "a critical assessment", kindled a fruitful debate on the strategy and design of literacy programmes. With appropriate adaptations, functional literacy has continued to be applied in many developing nations, including most of those which participated in the Experimental Programme. Interestingly, the selective and intensive approach developed in the Programme has also found application in the industrialized countries where the illiterate and functionally illiterate are a "select group" and available resources permit a higher cost per trainee.

The major shortcoming of the programme was the narrow view of the development process and the role of literacy therein which characterized certain of the projects. This orientation seems to have been a response to the impossible demand that functional literacy justify itself as a short-term economic investment. It cannot. Literacy is the yeast and not the dough of development. Its role cannot be measured directly, but only through its facilitation of the socioeconomic processes which constitute development.

(c) *Literacy as cultural action.* To Paulo Freire (1970), illiteracy is an imposed condition, the consequence and evidence of oppression. The goal of "cultural action", the term Freire prefers to education or literacy work, is to overcome oppression through thought and action based upon a critical awareness of reality. Learning to read and write are not ends in themselves, but ways through which the oppressed come to understand their environment and learn "to hold history in their hands". The pedagogy of the cultural circle does not have as its objective the teaching of fluent reading, but the rediscovery and reinterpretation of reality through the critical analysis of a limited lexicon of "generative words" chosen for their sociopsychological connotations as much as their suitability as linguistic building blocks.

The rich and subtle work of Paulo Freire offers a pedagogy for the oppressed, an instrument for identifying and defining injustice. His goal is fundamental change in social relationships, one which does not normally have great appeal to established governments. Hence, Freire's methods have been used primarily by voluntary organizations working with disadvantaged populations and by governments of revolutionary persuasion. His influence has perhaps been greater upon scholars than upon practitioners. Like functional literacy, cultural action is difficult to apply on a large scale. Where Freire differs fundamentally from others is in his definition of the problem: illiteracy is the symptom, and oppression the disease. To act as if illiteracy itself were the problem is to Freirians, at best, self-delusion and, at worst, wilful deception.

5.3 Organization and Professional Support

The choice of organizational structures is constrained both by circumstances and ideology. In many Third World countries, literacy work was introduced by missionaries and carried out by voluntary organizations until independence, following which governments have assumed a growing role and responsibility. In most cases, the scale of activities has simply expanded beyond what voluntary organizations could manage. In other instances, the views and goals of government and voluntary organizations have proven incompatible. New forms of cooperation have also emerged. Voluntary organizations of diverse kinds were, for example, invited to participate in the Indian National Adult Education Programme and were provided with financial support to enable them to do so. The programme that was implemented, however, had to conform to government-established standards as a condition for payment. Moreover, the government did not surrender the field to voluntary organizations; it directly conducted literacy activities on an enormous scale. In brief, the general trend in the

Third World is unmistakably toward an expanded government role in literacy work, but opportunities are normally still provided for the participation of voluntary organizations.

As the scale of literacy work and the role of the government therein have expanded, the need has arisen for organizational arrangements that facilitate interministerial cooperation and delineate the division of duties and responsibilities among levels of government. The practice which has emerged is the establishment of coordinating committees representing the principal agencies concerned. In Ethiopia, for example, the Minister of Education is the chairman of the National Literacy Campaign Coordinating Committee, which has 28 members drawn from government agencies, mass organizations, professional associations, and religious institutions. The Committee's purpose is to formulate policy and provide coordinated action in support of literacy. Its decisions are implemented by an executive committee which has task forces dealing with educational materials, staff training, propaganda and support, and data collection and monitoring. These coordinating structures are reproduced at regional, provincial, and district levels. The vertical linkages ensure that the programme conforms to the national policy, whereas the horizontal networks facilitate implementation at each level.

Another issue which organizers must address is the provision of professional support for literacy work: programme formulation, materials development, staff training, monitoring, evaluation, and the like. The approach employed in India is to establish "resource centres" at national, state, and, in many cases, district levels. In addition to having their own professional staffs, these centres are authorized to contract with research institutes, universities, and other agencies for specialized services. This flexible arrangement has enabled programme development to take place closer to the level of operations than a more centralized structure would have permitted, with the result that the programmes probably have been better adapted to local needs and interests.

5.4 The Use and Maintenance of Literacy

If an overall evaluation of literacy efforts since the early 1960s were possible, it might well reveal that relatively too much effort has been expended on teaching people to read and write, and relatively too little on making literacy a rewarding and useful skill to possess. In recognition of this difficulty, a good deal of attention has recently been focused upon *postalphabétisation* or literacy follow-up. This has involved the organization of follow-up classes for literacy-course graduates, development of rural presses, encouragement to various development ministries to issue printed material, workshops on techniques of writing easy-to-read materials, and the like. These are all necessary and desirable measures, but by themselves they are unlikely to prove sufficient.

The solution to the problem of postliteracy is the development of a literate and literacy-sustaining society. This is not a narrow technical task; it involves a profound cultural change in the information needs people have and the manner in which they seek to satisfy them. Thus, a follow-up programme which, as the name implies, is designed with the needs of the literacy-course completer in mind, may be too narrowly conceived. Primary-school completers and dropouts are likely to be far more numerous than literacy-course graduates. The literate and semiliterate have to be considered collectively as a social group whose need and desire to read are to be fostered. Action is required on a national scale. The development of the press and publishing industries—and in many countries the paper industries upon which these depend—as well as banking and postal services have to be encouraged as means for modernization of society as much as for literacy. All the institutions of society have to change a basic behavioural assumption and begin to act as if they are dealing with a literate society, even if this assumption is, at the time, premature.

In general, literacy has more to do with urban than with traditional rural life. But rural life need not remain traditional. If it does, literacy is without purpose. The peasantry have little need for literacy and neither will their children if they remain peasants. But if they become progressive farmers for whom agriculture is a science as well as a craft, who are engaged in the market place as well as the field, literacy will become a valuable and increasingly indispensable skill. Postliteracy should not be considered as a specialized aspect of literacy work. Rather, it is a phase in education which naturally follows when development meets with success and literacy is thereby imbued with value and meaning. At the collective level, it is the passage from the illiterate to the literate society; at the individual level, it is the progression from learning to read to reading to learn.

6. International Support for Literacy

UNESCO is the organization of the United Nations system most immediately concerned with the problem of illiteracy. This concern traces to the very origins of the organization. In 1946, Julian Huxley, who was to become UNESCO's first Director General, called the attention of the Preparatory Commission of UNESCO to the "existence of immense numbers of people who lack the most elementary means of participating in the life of the modern world" and proposed that their education receive priority in the programmes of the organization they were then in the process of creating. In 1978, the present Director General, Amadou-Mahtar M'Bow, presented a detailed analysis of the literacy situation in the world and the organization's action in respect of it (UNESCO 1978b). He emphasized two points: (a) progress in overcoming illiteracy depends primarily upon effective action at the national level, and (b) the international community has a responsibility to demonstrate its solidarity and support for countries vigorously engaged in the struggle against illiteracy. The role of UNESCO in an international strategy for literacy is to rally the support of the international community and to assist the national literacy efforts.

In his introduction to the *Draft Programme and Budget for 1981–83*, the Director General of UNESCO made the following observation regarding the extent, nature, and urgency of illiteracy and the action at national and international levels needed to overcome it:

> In point of fact, the persistence of illiteracy, which is a consequence of underdevelopment but also a major impediment to development, makes it impossible for millions of men and women to play an effective part in the shaping of their own destinies: it condemns to failure the battle against poverty, the elimination of inequalities, and the attempts that have been made to establish relations of equity between both individuals and nations. (UNESCO 1980 p. 16)

See also: Literacy Research

Bibliography

Abyan I B et al. 1981 *Somalie, l'alphabétisation, composante de la campagne nationale de développement rural.* In: UNESCO 1981 *Alphabétisation des adultes: Quatre campagnes characteristiques.* UNESCO, Paris

Bataille L (ed.) 1976 *A Turning Point for Literacy: Adult Education for Development: The Spirit and Declaration of Persepolis.* Proc. of the Int. Symp. for Literacy. Persepolis, Iran, 3–8 Sept. 1975.

Bhola H S 1984 *Campaigning for Literacy.* UNESCO, Paris

Bowman M J, Anderson A C 1963 Concerning the role of education in development. In: Geertz C (ed.) 1963 *Old Societies and New States: The Quest for Modernity in Africa and Asia.* Free Press, Glencoe, Illinois

Cipolla C M 1969 *Literacy and Development in the West.* Penguin, Harmondsworth

Dumont B 1973 Functional Literacy in Mali: Training for Development. *Educational Studies and Documents.* New Series No. 10 UNESCO, Paris

Freire P 1970 *Pedagogy of the Oppressed.* Herder and Herder, New York

Gorman T P (ed.) 1977 *Language and Literacy: Current Issues and Research.* International Institute for Adult Literacy Methods, Tehran

Harris S G 1974 From Kanite to English: A transfer project in Papua New Guinea. *Papua New Guinea J. Educ.* 9(1): 58–66

Johansson E 1977 *The History of Literacy in Sweden in Comparison with some other Countries,* Educational Report No. 12. Umeå University, Umeå

Kahler D 1974 Literacy and the mother tongue. *Literacy Work* 4(2): 11–37

Limage L J 1980 Illiteracy in industrialized countries: A sociological commentary. *Prospects* 10(2): 141–55

National Literacy Campaign Coordinating Committee 1981 *Every Ethiopian will be Literate and will Remain Literate.* National Campaign Coordinating Committee, Addis Ababa

Ryan J W 1980 Linguistic factors in adult literacy. In: Kavanagh J F, Venezky R L (eds.) 1980 *Orthography, Reading and Dyslexia.* University Park Press, Baltimore, Maryland

Street B V 1984 *Literacy in Theory and Practice.* Cambridge University Press, Cambridge

UNESCO 1978a *Records of the General Conference, Resolutions,* Vol. 1. UNESCO, Paris

UNESCO 1978b *The Organization's Literacy Programme.* Document 20 C/71, 20th Session of the General Conference. UNESCO, Paris

UNESCO 1980 *Draft Programme and Budget for 1981–83.* UNESCO, Paris

UNESCO United Nations Development Programme (UNDP) 1976 *The Experimental World Literacy Programme: A Critical Assessment.* UNESCO, Paris

Adult Literacy in Developed Countries

C. St. J. Hunter

In many developed countries universal childhood education has been established for at least 100 years. In others it is hardly yet established. A number of these latter countries recognize that a significant proportion of their adult citizens have not achieved an adequate level of literacy. Some of the larger developed states have been reluctant to do so, but there is growing awareness that there probably exists a considerable amount of functional illiteracy among adults in all developed states. Some of them have taken important steps to tackle this problem.

1. Definitions and Statistics: A Basic Contradiction

The currently accepted definitions of literacy are all variations on the 1962 UNESCO statement:

> A person is literate when he has acquired the essential knowledge and skills which enable him to engage in all those activities in which literacy is required for effective functioning in his group and community and whose attainment in reading, writing, and arithmetic make it possible for him to continue to use those skills toward his own and the community's development.

This definition assumes that the person so described can function effectively within his or her own society. The United States of America is generally said to have a 99 percent literacy rate. Recent studies show very clearly that there is no basis for a claim that so high a proportion of the adult population in the United States is able to "engage in all those activities for which literacy is required." What, then, does the 99 percent mean? The definition used by census-takers and respondents is based on traditional understandings of literacy, that is, the ability to write one's name and to read simple passages or complete elementary mathematical tasks. It is a definition out of phase with the realities of a modern, advanced technological society.

The achievement of functional literacy, or functional competence, is something quite different from what is being reported in statistics from the industrialized nations. If an assessment was made of the ability of citizens within these societies to use their skills toward their own and their community's development, the comparative rating of technologically developed nations would be lower and, certainly, more honestly comparable on a world scale.

The attempt to describe literacy as a fixed inventory of skills that can be assessed outside their context of application is, in reality, an impossible task. Definitions of what it means to be literate must vary according to place and time. What it means to be fully functional in one society at any given point in time is quite different to what it means in another society. What should be compared is the degree to which individuals and groups are able to function effectively within their own societies. The number of Americans who have sufficient literacy skills to function in rural Indonesia is meaningless. What needs to be compared is the percentage of Americans who can function in the contemporary United States as compared with the percentage of Indonesians, or any other national group, who can function in their society. In addition, functional literacy is more than a set of skills. It includes, also, the ability to use those skills to solve problems in daily life. That is even harder to measure.

Given these reservations, contemporary comparative statistics have limited value. It would, however, be possible to achieve more meaningful comparative figures once there was general acknowledgment of the fact that literacy was not static in time and place. The general requirements for participation in any given society could be determined and overall assessments made of the percentage of the population who were competent to function at the baseline levels.

2. Problems of Basic Literacy

Whatever the requirements for participation may be, it cannot be assumed that all citizens, even of the most advanced countries, meet them. Moreover citizens vary in the degree to which they are developed. Some countries have had until recently (and some still have) a substantial number of basic illiterates among adults. Italy is one example. After the Second World War the Italian Government launched a major campaign to eradicate illiteracy, setting up popular schools, which offered both day and evening classes and subsidizing a large private initiative. The effort was considered to be a success in that the proportion of illiterates in the population fell to 5 percent by 1974 (De Sanctis 1978). There still remained, however, a big task of basic education, because in 1971, 33 percent of the people aged 16 and over had not successfully completed five years of primary schooling and 77 percent did not hold a lower secondary-school certificate (Von Moltke and Schneevoigt 1977).

The eradication of illiteracy was a major task confronting several of the European socialist countries after the Second World War. Poland had 3 million illiterates, 12 percent of the population, but by a large-scale campaign the government had largely overcome the lack of basic reading and writing skills by the early 1950s (Pachocinski and Polturzycki 1979). Bulgaria and Hungary too had similar experiences.

3. Levels of Functional Literacy

In Italy and the socialist countries illiteracy among adults may be principally attributed to a failure by the state to provide universal childhood education of adequate duration. As schooling has extended, so the level of adult literacy is rising. The problem that now confronts these states is not basic, but functional illiteracy. For example, in Hungary 9 percent of the school population do not complete the primary stage (Fukasz 1978). Given the recent history of these countries, this is not surprising. What is, is the scale of functional illiteracy in countries which have long had virtually universal childhood education of long duration. This has become particularly apparent in the United States of America and the United Kingdom.

Two different sets of data have been used to define the extent of literacy-related problems in the United States: school completion statistics and the results from a major study of competency levels.

For many in the United States, the completion of secondary school has become a benchmark definition of functional literacy. The majority of persons who have difficulty functioning are assumed to be found in that portion of the population that did not complete high school. About 38 percent of the adults 16 years of age and older, not currently enrolled in school, do not have high-school diplomas. The United States Bureau of Labor Statistics estimates their number to be about 57,654,000 (US Bureau of Labor Statistics 1976). Large numbers of persons who have not completed secondary school are, in fact, functioning very well. An alarming number who *do* have their diplomas have been found to lack skills associated with their level of schooling. However, it is roughly true that the bulk of persons with literacy-related difficulties are among the 57 million.

The University of Texas at Austin published the results of a major study of competency among American adults (University of Texas 1975). Using nationwide sampling techniques, they looked at the adult population from the point of view of individuals' ability to function regardless of their level of academic achievement. An official of the United States Office of Education, relying on the criteria and findings of this study, inferred that almost 23 million Americans lacked the basic competencies required to function in this society.

He also stated that an additional 34 million were able to function but at very low levels of proficiency.

It is interesting to note that whichever data are used, the number of adult Americans expected to experience some literacy-related problems is the same, roughly 57 million. It is therefore abundantly clear that a literacy problem of sizable proportions does exist in the United States.

Similar statistics for the United Kingdom are not available, but in the early 1970s, the figure of 2 million adult illiterates out of a population of 55 million began to be bandied about. It was a guess based on very limited research, but a not insignificant amount of literacy teaching. Action inspired by this guess confirmed that the number of adult functional illiterates was substantial, although an accurate estimate is still impossible.

4. *Who are the Functionally Illiterate?*

It is still not possible to identify with certainty who the functionally illiterates are, since many conceal their disability in order to avoid social stigma. However, some groups can be identified where functional illiteracy is rife.

There is a relatively small group who never learned to read at all. Some suffer from physical or mental handicap, are dyslexic for instance; others have slipped through the school net in childhood for family, health, or economic reasons.

A larger group went to school but gave up trying or dropped out because both the teaching and the atmosphere to which they were exposed seemed irrelevant to their lives. They failed or were failed in their first encounter with the educational system. They are the same persons who are included in statistics on every other major social or economic disadvantage—poverty, unemployment, racial or ethnic discrimination, inadequate housing, deteriorating communities, lack of access to health services. Among the poor, racial and ethnic minorities are found in disproportionate numbers. Female heads of households and the elderly account for large numbers of those living in poverty. The lack of ability to perform literacy-related tasks or the failure to possess credentials are of far less concern on their list of priorities than resolving immediate problems.

There are people who are even more marginal than the group described above. They are the hard-core stationary poor. Some are from families whose members have been on welfare for two or three generations. The difference between them and those in the previous group is the level of hope they are able to maintain. These persons have ceased to believe that anything they can do will make a difference to their overall situation. Their interactions with the bureaucracies set up to serve them often contribute to their alienation and sense of powerlessness.

These persons are surrounded by family members, friends, and neighbors who manage to get along without the skills so prized in the dominant culture. Information passed on by word of mouth is more common than written or even media-transmitted messages. In the United States they are largely isolated and unresponsive to initiatives of help, observing, quite legitimately in the majority of cases, the lack of respect that characterizes their treatment by those who offer help. Yet strong patterns of mutual support, loyalty to friends and family, and commitment to their local community and its improvement also exist.

Evidence from the United Kingdom indicates, however, that functional illiteracy is not restricted to these groups. Nearly one-half of those seeking help with literacy problems hold relatively skilled or demanding jobs and are not socially marginal.

5. *Educational Programs*

In the United States, private agencies have perhaps made their greatest contribution to those who have never learned to read. Basic literacy tutoring and small-group work have enabled those who must start at the very beginning to gain skills and self-confidence to get jobs and enroll in more advanced studies.

Legislation during the 1960s established adult basic education (ABE) as a means of providing instruction for adults 16 years of age and older who are out of school and who have not completed high school. It runs on federal, state, and local funding. While state education agencies are ultimately responsible for the administration and supervision of all ABE programs within the state—including teacher training, curriculum selection and development, evaluation, and fiscal accountability—decentralization and local autonomy are the rule rather than the exception. Local programs are diverse but the majority use local school facilities and tend to reproduce with adults the atmosphere and practices of traditional schools. There are many innovative exceptions, but, on the whole, the students come from adults who already know that education will help them to achieve their goals. The school dropouts and the hard-core stationary poor are hardly touched.

When the size of the problem became apparent in the United Kingdom, the British Government was persuaded to subsidize a national Adult Literacy Campaign, which ran from 1975 to 1978. Most of the organization and administration fell on local education authorities, but the British Broadcasting Corporation backed it with a large publicity campaign, and some teaching by television and radio. To overcome their anticipated reluctance to expose themselves, those with literacy problems were encouraged to telephone a confidential referral service, which put them in touch with help. This was mainly given on a one-to-one basis by unpaid volunteer workers, who underwent short courses of training. During the campaign 79,000 people offered their services as tutors and 137,000 adults began to study. The campaign was therefore a success, but it could only begin to tackle the problem. As a consequence, adult literacy and basic education is now an important integral element in the national adult education provision, and continues to receive special state subsidy.

6. Research Experience and Needs

The British Adult Literacy Campaign highlighted the lack of accurate data on adult literacy in advanced societies. Not only could one merely guess how many illiterates there were, in what sections of society they were to be found, why they were illiterate, and what was the degree of illiteracy, but there was also little concrete information about how they might be reached or how they might be helped. Much was learned from the campaign, which was carefully monitored (Jones and Charnley 1978), but there is still a need for more systematic research and development work. The Adult Literacy and Basic Skills Unit, which was set up with government funding in England, and its sister unit in Scotland have been concentrating on identifying learning needs and developing ways to meet them.

Response to the campaign made it clear that these learning needs go beyond basic reading and writing skills. Only 30 percent of those who asked for assistance were absolutely illiterate; 40 percent had some basic reading ability; and 30 percent could read with ease. Apart from these groups easily identified as having special problems, the ethnic minorities, prison inmates, the physically and mentally handicapped, there were others who, for a number of reasons felt themselves, or were felt by others, to lack the competence to function adequately in society. Their needs are still imperfectly diagnosed.

It has been argued by some workers in the field that illiteracy among the poorest sectors of the population, in advanced societies as in the developing world, is only a symptom of more basic social, economic, political, and cultural contradictions. The satisfaction of their needs, it is said, depends more on basic social and economic changes and on political will than remedial programs. It is certain that such programs aimed at those with minimal schooling have had only limited success, whether in capitalist or socialist states (Fukasz 1978 p.22), and that they require more study and experiment.

Certain conditions for success, however, have been suggested by the International Council for Adult Education (ICAE 1982):

(a) Learning programs must emerge from the needs and problems of the participants themselves. Active, conscious, organized participation of the population in all levels and stages of the program is fundamental.

(b) Programs must have credibility with, and inspire trust in, the illiterate population in order to motivate and mobilize them for the learning process.

(c) Programs must include both the study of theory and opportunity for practice.

(d) Programs should make use of animateurs who are integrated in the life of the local communities where the programs are to take place.

(e) Learners must have opportunity to participate in the construction of materials to be used in the program.

One reason why research into adult illiteracy in advanced countries has been sparse may be a limited awareness of the problem. Most European countries, for example, the Scandinavian countries, France, the Federal Republic of Germany, the Netherlands, and Belgium, have been slow to admit to a problem of adult basic literacy on the scale of the United Kingdom or the United States, except among migrant workers and resident ethnic minorities. Only in the 1980s have countries such as Sweden, France, and the Federal Republic of Germany shown their awareness by beginning to develop literacy provision for native born adults on a significant scale. It seems a need of all developed countries.

Bibliography

De Sanctis F M 1978 *L'Educazione degli Adulti in Italia, 1848–1976*. Editori Riuniti, Rome

Fukasz G 1978 *Adult Education in the Hungarian People's Republic (HPR)*. European Centre for Leisure and Education, Prague

Hunter C St J, Harman D 1979 *Adult Illiteracy in the United States: A Report to the Ford Foundation*. McGraw-Hill, New York

International Council for Adult Education (ICAE) 1982 *Towards Total Literacy*. Report from Policy Working Group no. 5. International Council for Adult Education Conference, Paris

Jones H A, Charnley A H 1978 *Adult Literacy: A Study of its Impact*. National Institute of Adult Education, Leicester

Pachocinski R, Polturzycki J 1979 *Adult Education in People's Poland*. European Centre for Leisure and Education, Prague

UNESCO 1962 *Statement of the International Committee of Experts on Literacy*. UNESCO Paris

United States Bureau of Labor Statistics 1976 *Special Labor Force Report No. 186*. US Bureau of Labor Statistics, Washington, DC

University of Texas 1975 *Adult Functional Competency: A Report to the Office of Education Dissemination Review Panel*. Division of Extension, University of Texas, Austin, Texas

Von Moltke K, Schneevoigt N 1977 *Educational Leaves for Employees: European Experience for American Consideration*. Jossey-Bass, San Francisco, California

Adult Literacy: Size of the Problem

R. Lazarus

World illiteracy is still one of the great social problems of our time. Although much progress has been made in the recent past, both through increased primary-school enrolments and mass campaigns for adults in many developing countries, the absolute number of adult illiterates keeps increasing, due mainly to the population explosion. Illiteracy has a close correlation with poverty and although the vast majority of adult illiterates are found in the least developed countries, there is still an illiterate population in many of the Western industrial countries. The solution to the problem depends mainly on the political will of the governments concerned, but also calls for international solidarity and support.

1. The Quantitative Problem

Adult illiteracy is not easy to quantify. Exact statistics are not always available, census returns often do not exist, and illiteracy figures are not always presented in the same way. UNESCO has, however, developed a system of presenting statistics, which gives estimates based on previous census returns or surveys in its member states, observed and projected school enrolment ratios, and the demographic estimates and projections of the United Nations demographic office.

These estimates are usually accepted as universal guidelines. According to UNESCO statistics published in 1978, it was estimated that 814 million adults would still be illiterate in 1980 (UNESCO 1978a). That is, of every 10 people in the world over 15 years of age, three cannot read, write, or do simple arithmetic.

Asia has by far the largest number of illiterates, over 70 percent, followed by Africa 20 percent, and Latin America, 5 percent. More than 400 million illiterates, the majority of the world's illiterate population, are to be found in only 11 countries, seven of which are Asian. Twenty-three countries have an illiteracy rate of more than 70 percent, including 18 African and four Asian ones. Of these illiterates, the majority, over 60 percent, are women, and this percentage is rising. In some isolated communities, virtually all women are still illiterate. One person in four is said to enter employment without reading or writing skills.

In addition to the illiterates who have never received formal education, there are a growing number of early school leavers who have not acquired sufficient education to play an active part in their societies. They often revert to illiteracy, or play a peripheral role in political, social, or economic life.

This phenomenon also exists in many Western countries, and it is estimated that the "functional" illiteracy rate in these countries varies from between 2 and 10 percent.

Yet, on the positive side, since the early 1950s, there has been a steady fall in the percentage of illiteracy: from 44.3 percent in 1950 to 34.2 percent in 1970, to 28 percent in 1980, and an expected 25 percent in 1990. These improvements are due to considerable efforts by many Third World countries to extend and improve primary school facilities, and in some countries, as the result of the introduction of compulsory primary schooling. This has been complemented by major efforts to eradicate adult illiteracy through mass national campaigns, with target dates for complete eradication. Countries including Afghanistan, Brazil, Cuba, Ethiopia, India, Jamaica, Nicaragua, North Korea, Somalia, Tanzania, and Vietnam opted for such campaigns, some with complete success, others with remarkably good results, considering social, economic, and language difficulties. Many other countries, where national campaigns have not been feasible, have chosen "selective" programmes concentrating on specially chosen sections of the population.

Notwithstanding these considerable efforts, the absolute number of illiterates is still increasing, and before the end of the century it is expected to reach 850 million, if present trends are maintained. This increase in absolute numbers is largely due to demographic factors, that is the rapid population growth. But inadequate and misdirected educational provision is also a cause. It was estimated in 1980 that six out of ten children did not complete their primary education in developing countries. This is also a growing problem in many Western countries, despite compulsory primary education.

2. Economic and Social Factors

Needless to say if children were to receive more and better schooling, there would be fewer illiterates. The problem however has deeper roots. Illiteracy is largely a result of political and social inequalities. Centuries of colonial rule held back the rights of people to their own self-determination. In many countries, land reform and attempts at more equitable income distribution have not yet been tackled. The proportion of illiterates living in rural areas is also much higher than those living in urban ones.

The mass eradication of illiteracy is thus primarily a political problem, with economic and social implications which must be tackled in conjunction with educational efforts. The problem of literacy thus posed, that is in the context of development, calls for solutions of a global nature: of integration into overall national social and economic plans, with strategies that mobilize all possible resources.

3. The Ethical Aspect: Literacy as an Individual Right

The above facts point to the worldwide dimensions of the problem and bring into question the individual and ethical aspects of illiteracy. The right to literacy is inalienable. It is an essential element in the "right to education" proclaimed in the *Universal Declaration of Human Rights* of the United Nations (1948). Every child, man, or woman learning to read and write does so for individual as well as social and economic reasons. That is for personal enlightenment and pleasure. Being literate also means that adults can assume their full responsibilities as citizens, and play a more decisive role in the exercise of political power in their local communities as well as at the national level. It is therefore a basic human right as well as a tool for modern living. It is not an end in itself, but an entry point to formal education, as well as the acquisition of further knowledge and skills outside the formal school system.

Although the solution to the problem of illiteracy depends firstly on a genuine political will on the part of the governments of individual nations, it also calls for a determined and coordinated effort on the international level.

UNESCO is the United Nations specialized agency most concerned, and has over the years given a high priority to the struggle against illiteracy. Its efforts are concentrated on cooperation, both technical and financial, between its member states in their literacy endeavours, promoting an awareness at the international level of the complexities of the problem and of finding solutions by mobilizing world opinion and finding international financial resources. Bilateral projects between countries also exist. Many international nongovernmental organizations also have programmes of cooperation and assistance. In recent years, exchanges between developing countries themselves have developed, passing on technical knowledge and exchanging specialists and technicians.

The United Nations International Children's Emergency Fund (UNICEF), the World Health Organization (WHO), the Food and Agriculture Organization (FAO), and the International Labour Organization (ILO) also contribute to literacy programmes in their fields of competence.

There is, however, still a great disparity between resources available and those needed to overcome what the Director General of UNESCO has termed "the minimum of education and human dignity necessary to survive" (speech on occasion of the 14th International Literacy Day, UNESCO, 8 Sept 1980).

As the end of the twentieth century approaches, one-third of humankind is still illiterate and the numbers are growing. Technically it is considered possible to totally eradicate illiteracy before the year 2000. If this does not happen, then the right to education will still be violated and a serious obstacle to the overall development of societies will remain. It will be a major challenge to all humankind.

Since this article was written, UNESCO has published updated statistics giving the world total of adult illiterates (over 15 years) as 889 million i.e. 27.7 percent of the world population. The percentages of illiterates for regions are given as 75 percent for Asia, 18 percent for Africa, 5 percent for Latin American and the Caribbean. Although the majority of the world's illiterates are to be found in Asia, the illiteracy rate for the continent is lower than that for Africa, Africa having the highest rate of illiteracy at 54 percent or more, Asia 36 percent and Latin America and the Caribbean, 17.3 percent. Thirty two countries have an illiteracy rate of between 50 and 75 percent, while 8 have over 75 percent.

Bibliography

UNESCO 1978a *Estimates and Projections of Illiteracy*. UNESCO Division of Statistics, Paris

UNESCO 1978b *Approved Programme and Budget, 20th Session, General Conference, 1978*. UNESCO, Paris

UNESCO 1982 *Medium Term Plan, 1984–89. Approved by 22 session, General Conference, 1982*. UNESCO, Paris

UNESCO 1985 *The Current Literacy Situation in the World*. UNESCO, Paris

Second Stage Adult Literacy

R. Lazarus

The second stage of literacy programmes (postliteracy), is not only related to adults who have become literate, but also to a growing number of young people who have left the formal school system before completing primary school. Although the problem is largely one which concerns developing countries, many Western industrial ones are faced with an increasing number of early "dropouts", who are reverting to illiteracy and semiliteracy.

Ideally, postliteracy programmes should be conceived within a wide structural framework, or "literate environment", the objectives being (a) the retention of reading, writing, and calculating skills, enabling the learners to function effectively in their everyday lives, and (b) the provision of further educational programmes, both formal and informal, for youths and adults, to enable those, who so wish, to continue their education.

1. Implications of the Second Stage

The modern view of literacy is that it is no longer equated with reading, writing, and arithmetic alone, but is also an element of socioeconomic progress and should aid in the creating of responsible citizens, as well as the safeguarding of cultural identity and national interests. The retention of literacy, especially among adult groups, is thus an essential element in the planning of the initial literacy programmes, as clearly, unless efforts to make people literate are sustained, literacy campaigns are self-defeating.

Generally speaking, adults learn more slowly than children, their time for study and attending classes is usually much more restricted, and opportunities for using new academic skills, or their continuation, are often not possible, as the necessary motivation and facilities are lacking. For these reasons many adults who successfully attain a reasonable level of reading and writing, subsequently lose their new skills for lack of use, reverting to semiliteracy or illiteracy.

Younger people who leave the formal school before mastering reading and writing, or "dropouts", as they are called, form a sizable number of the school-age population in developing countries. According to UNESCO statistics published in 1980, estimates on the number of people who drop out before the completion of the final grade of primary school, ranged from 0 to 75 percent in Africa, 72 percent in Latin America, and 89 percent in the region of Asia and Oceania. These statistics show that 17 percent of students in Africa leave school between the first and second year of tuition. In south Asia, this figure is 30 percent and in Latin America it is 36 percent. Only three out of five reach the fifth grade in Africa, and two out of three in Latin America. Statistics published by UNESCO in 1984 show that the general trend of survival rates at primary levels in developing countries, between 1970–1980, is in fact one of improvement. Drop-out rates before the fourth grade, however, still remain very high. There is, of course, also the problem of absenteeism, which also increases the number of semiliterates. In industrially developed countries, dropouts are also becoming a serious and growing problem, and an illiterate or semiliterate population has been detected in a number of Western countries.

The planning and provision of the "second stage" concerns, therefore, not only the newly literate adults, but also many premature school leavers. It implies much more than simple "follow up" courses, which in the past were often offered as the "postliteracy phase" in many literacy programmes. The dimensions of modern postliteracy programmes are thus much wider in scope and design. They involve cultural, social, and economic inputs, as well as educational ones. No adult literacy programme can thus be considered viable, unless planned in conjunction with further educational programmes, and/or integrated into an environment in which the written word is required and regularly used. Unfortunately this further dimension to literacy programmes has been neglected in many national campaigns, resulting in a wastage of educational effort and resources.

2. Motivation

Unless a newly literate person has a use for the written word, further education is pointless. In many traditional societies people have lived for centuries in an oral culture, which has enabled them to survive. History, traditional skills, folklore, health practices, and so on have been transmitted by word of mouth. But political advancement and modernization have brought with them economic patterns, new technologies, modern communications, social and economic institutions, which require the mastery of the written word, as well as new skills and formal education. The transfer from old ways to new is not always self-evident, or easy to implement. The role of the written word in personal, economic, and social situations must be meaningful to the learner, and therefore a basic motivation for literacy. Similarly, unless the newly acquired knowledge is systematically introduced into work and everyday living situations it will be lost. The learners need to be made aware of ways in which formal education, ability to read and write, will improve their conditions of life and enhance their knowledge. Further, unless they themselves are actively involved and responsible for changing their environments, programmes devised for them will not have the same impact.

3. Creating a "Literate Environment"

The need to provide such opportunities, in an organized and systematic way at a national level, goes well-beyond formal education provision. It involves a commitment at the highest level which ensures economic, cultural, as well as educational structures. In other words, the creation of a "literate environment." A literate environment implies the development of an infrastructure to ensure, firstly, the easy availability of written material, newspapers, books, pamphlets, leaflets, and so on for newly literates at the level of their comprehension; secondly, the possibilities for further educational provision through evening schools, correspondence education, and so on; thirdly, the possibility of the new literates becoming their own "agents of change", by using their new skills in their work as well as in their social and personal lives. That is, by the integration of the written word into productive activities, health and hygiene measures, community activities, personal communications, and so on.

This process involves commitments not only for the ministries of education, but also for ministries of labour, health, communications, culture, or their equivalents. It entails support by voluntary organizations, such as trade unions, cooperatives, women's organizations, religious groups.

The strategy involves a combination of specially designed structures and support services, as well as the conditions which would enable learners to use their new knowledge creatively and productively in everyday life and work situations. A relationship is thus developed between education and training on the one hand and development on the other. In view of the diversity of situations, approaches need to be flexible, diverse, and meaningful to meet different conditions. The complexity of providing these elements cannot be underestimated. Problems abound. The rural areas, where the vast majority of illiterates and semiliterates are found, are invariably poorer in that they lack the structures, services, and communications required. The needs of different geographical areas are not alike. The multiple language situation, which exists in most parts of Africa and in some parts of Asia, further complicates the problem. (In fact, the existence of many different languages within national boundaries causes considerable difficulties in the provision of further education for adult groups in many countries, and seriously hampers the production of written materials.) Poor communications, lack of roads, transport, trained personnel, as well as the availability of paper and printing facilities, can all contribute to the complexities of the task.

4. *Objectives of Postliteracy*

As has been mentioned, the objectives of postliteracy are basically the retention of literacy for those who do not continue with formal classes and the provision of continuing education for those who can continue their studies. The retention of literacy involves a number of elements. Perhaps the most important is the production of written materials at a level easily understandable to the new literate. These written materials take many forms; wall newspapers (a most dynamic educational tool when properly used—involving the active participation of the learners), rural newspapers, distributed at the local level, appropriate books for reading clubs, rural libraries, and the creative writings of the learners themselves (often products of organized writers' workshops). Retention also requires that efforts be made to rewrite selected official documents which have essential information for citizens concerning their rights, obligations, and so on. Safety precautions, health information, pharmaceutical products, consumer items and so on, should all be re-examined to be sure that they are comprehensible to new readers. National and regional newspapers can also carry special sections which present news and information at the level of the new literates, essay competitions, recording of oral traditions, songs, history, and so on, and their reproduction in written form. With imagination and the availability of the required resources, much has been and can be done.

A good example of the production of reading materials at the postliteracy level is the Jamaican FULFIL (Follow-up literature for individual learners) programme. It was launched in late 1975 by the Jamaican Movement for the Advancement of Literacy (JAMAL), the agency for public information, the University of the West Indies, and the Institute of Jamaica library services. The aim was to encourage people from all over the country to contribute short stories, essays, poems, plays, and even comic strips. The categories included "unsung heroes" (little known people who had made a useful contribution to Jamaican life), stories with elements of excitement, adventure, romance. A publication called *Let's Read* was produced to help people express themselves by telling their own life experiences. The FULFIL programme was also engaged in simplifying existing materials that would be of particular interest to younger age groups.

Radio and, in a few cases, television (although the latter remains expensive and technically unrealistic for most situations), are used successfully to promote postliteracy and sustain ongoing programmes. The Tanzanian experience is a good example. The radio component started as an integral part of the national literacy campaign (1973–75) to produce promotional materials to encourage people to join classes and radio listening groups. The programme for the listening groups included supportive written materials, readers, recipes, songs, and so on. These radio programmes also helped to reinforce the literate environment by stimulating interest in rural library services, rural newspapers, and so on. Audiences soon identified themselves with these programmes, and an evaluation gave evidence of improved reading habits and better knowledge of Swahili. Cheaply available radio transistors allowed these programmes to reach a wide national audience; thus radio became an essential element in the promotion and sustaining of literacy.

However, retention does not only depend on the availability or promotion of reading materials, but also on the learners' use of the written word. New literates must have opportunities of using writing and calculating in their jobs, community activities, cooperatives, and in their social and political lives. The most successful application of the use of this "new dimension" is when learners themselves develop structures and activities which enable them to take new responsibilities involving the use of their new knowledge. A good example of how literacy skills have been introduced into work situations is from Mali.

Following the experimental functional literacy project of 1967–73, the government, through its national literacy agency *Direction Nationale de l'Alphabétisation Fonctionelle et de la linguistique appliquée* (DNAFLA), progressively introduced a series of innovative practices at the village level. In the area of Kita, for example, new literates were given the responsibility of registering local births and deaths, as well as aiding with health measures involving malarial control, prophylactic, and hygiene practices. In agriculture, the weighing, counting, and preparation for marketing of the peanut crop was entrusted to new literates. This in turn, led to other responsibilities both social and economic. To support these activities, the production of written pedagogical material was undertaken in cooperation with relevant technical services—the ministry of health, cooperatives, marketing boards, and so on. Training in the field was instituted under the guidance of the technical services involved. The local press and national radio services produced supportive information and promotional programmes. A follow-up and evaluation system was devised to provide regular checks and corrections on progress, a good example of action research. Some positive results in the health field alone included the creation of teams of community health workers who were able to provide primary health care, run a village pharmacy, improve water purification practices, to mention a few.

5. *Continuing Education*

The provision of continuing education, formal and nonformal, or technical, takes a variety of forms in different countries. In countries with socialist structures, such as Cuba, Vietnam, North Korea, the concentration has been on the establishment of workers' and peasant schools. Under the direction of the ministries of education, these schools provide special tuition for adult and young workers, with special syllabi, which enable them to follow the equivalent of formal education: the completion of primary, elementary, and secondary education up to university level. The secondary schools include both technical and academic options. Classes are held at times convenient to workers, usually after working hours.

Tanzania exhibits an example of another kind of continuing education for new literates. In addition to courses provided by the Institute of Adult Education and the Extra Mural Department of the University of Dar es Salaam, a new and innovative type of institution called "*People's Colleges*"—modelled partly on Scandinavian folk high schools—has been established. These colleges (already 20 in number), situated in rural areas, offer further education in a vocational context related to development needs.

Still other countries concentrate on nonformal aspects of continuing education, offering short- or long-term courses not directed to terminal examinations or certificates. Many of the universities in Africa, Asia, and the Caribbean area have contributed to nonformal education programmes designed for new literates. In all cases, the need for an articulation between the formal school system and adult learning needs is evident.

6. *Conclusion*

The success of all these approaches depends on the active support of governments, the articulation, planning, and support of relevant structures and services at the national, regional, and local level, as well as the involvement of the people themselves. Adaptations and components might differ from country to country, depending on the level of development, existing administrative and communication structures, social services, and the availability of personnel.

In other words, the active collaboration of a vast network of structures and activities all contribute to providing the "literate environment" which ensures that literacy skills are not lost, and which fosters new learning situations. Planning on these lines is a relatively new concept. Much thinking, research, and experimentation still needs to be done.

Bibliography

Adult Literacy Board 1976 *Publications on Post Literacy* (*FULFIL*). Prime Ministers Office, Kingston, Jamaica

Lazarus R 1982 Reflections on creating a "literate environment". *Convergence* 15: 67–72

Mbakile E P R 1975 *Radio Education Programmes, as a Support for Literacy*. Ministry of Education, Dar es Salaam

Ministry of Education 1981 *Report of Sub-regional Seminar on Post Literacy: Kita*. Bamako, Mali

UNESCO 1980 *Wastage in Primary and Secondary Education*. UNESCO, Paris

UNESCO 1984 *Evolution of Wastage in Primary Education in the World between 1970-1980*. UNESCO, Paris

Adult Education for Employment

Introduction

The central concern of most adults in the world is to keep body and soul together. To earn the means to do this they either need to work themselves, whether it be for cash payment or for a return in kind, or they must depend on the labour of others. It is not therefore surprising that education for employment, that is, education as a preparation for, or for improved competence in, paid work is, if not the most important kind of adult education, the kind that attracts the most support both from sponsors and learners.

So strong is the demand for education for employment that its purposes and procedures threaten to affect all adult education thinking and practice, to the extent that some educators fear they will take over the whole field. It has been common since the mid-nineteenth century to divide adult education into two parts, vocational and nonvocational, in recognition of the distinctive purposes, ethos, policies, organization, and forms of provision of the former. In a number of Western European countries agencies existing to achieve other purposes have, as a matter of survival, tended to distance themselves from the provision of education for employment. It is tempting to see the widespread tendency in the United Kingdom to label education for employment as "training" and to deny that it is education at all, as a defensive reaction to the inroads that education for employment is perceived to be making into liberal adult education.

Not that this view is universally held, in the United Kingdom or elsewhere. Most countries subscribe to the UNESCO definition of adult education. In socialist countries preparation for work is a central purpose of all education, including adult education. The distinction between study for work and study directed to other ends is recognized, but not seen as an issue; no conflict or competition is perceived. The two kinds constitute equally essential elements of the integrated educational experience all citizens should have.

In developing countries any learning that may be perceived as helping the participants to confront more successfully the struggle for living is valuable, and that which does not runs a great risk of being rejected. But in societies where there are few paid jobs and many adults lack the basic education to master them, the simplest acquisition of job skills, whether called education or training, may have little relevance. A different approach is needed, as the concept of integrated development recognizes.

Articles concerning adult education for employment are to be found in a number of parts of this book. This subsection is largely taken up with a broad overview of the subject. *Purposes and Principles* examines at length the question of the purposes of work-related study, for the students, employers, and society as a whole. It also discusses the major principles, mostly economic, but some social or even moral, which animate provision. *Policies, Participation, and Structure* develops this discussion, highlighting the factors that influence individual participation, who provides work-oriented education, and how.

Questions of recruitment, status, and training of those who teach adults in this field are treated in *The Educators*, while the article *Employment Policy and Adult Education* gives special attention to the past, present, and future use of the education of adults as an instrument of socioeconomic engineering. The subsection closes with a case study, *Adult Education for Employment: United States.*

Purposes and Principles

C. J. Titmus

The fundamental reasons for providing or participating in occupational education are the same throughout the world, whatever the level of development of the society or the ideology of its government. The principles on which occupational education operates are varied, however, influenced as they are by political and social factors.

The great growth of state support of adult education for employment and, consequently, of provision in this field, has taken place since the Second World War, as has the development of adult education as a whole. This expansion of adult education for employment has taken place as the purposes of occupational education, for both providers and participants, have developed.

1. Purposes

There are simple and obvious reasons for the existence of adult vocational education. On the one hand employers engage in it or support it, when they perceive that the efficient operation of their enterprise, whether measured in terms of profit or product, requires that their employees acquire knowledge and/or skills, which they do not possess on appointment. On the other hand individuals, either as employees or self-employed, engage in it because they have insufficient knowledge and/or skills to obtain gainful employment at all, or to achieve advancement in their employment or because for reasons of personal satisfaction they wish to become more competent in their work.

The state provides or supports adult vocational education in part to enable the employer and the individual worker to achieve the purposes already listed, but principally—and this is not necessarily the same thing—to meet the country's need for an appropriately trained labour force. A trained labour force is perceived as necessary for the economic performance and thus the material prosperity of the state, the level of which exerts, in every sphere, a determining influence on the government's capacity to act.

These purposes have been valid since the beginning of the Industrial Revolution, but have acquired added urgency in the last half century through the greatly increased rate of technological and economic change throughout almost the whole world. There has been a shift of emphasis from manufacturing to services; old products and processes have been, and continue to be, replaced by new ones, which require new, more sophisticated knowledge and skills and new forms of organization. All this is taking place in many fields of activity at such a speed that skills acquired in several years of apprenticeship may become obsolete almost as soon as the training is completed (Shepherd 1985). Consequently, employers have to have their existing employees retrained or given further training, or else they have to appoint new ones with the skills they require. Employees run the risk that the occupational competences they learned on entry to working life may in a very few years prove not only inadequate to gain them job promotion, but no longer of value to ensure them employment at all. They need new or further training. The state feels itself less able than ever to leave the economy to the employers and the employed, as competition with other countries becomes more intense, and mastery of new technological developments requires planning and investment on a national scale. All countries, not only socialist states, are involved in workforce planning to a greater or lesser extent, which entails ensuring that adequate opportunities are available for adults to obtain up-to-date work skills at a level the economy needs.

The purposes of many advanced countries in supporting occupational education for adults have been complicated by the growing problem of unemployment. This has in part been caused by technological advances which reduce the demand for labour, but also in part by a world economic crisis which built up in the second half of the 1970s. The young and the unskilled have been particularly affected. For many years now governments have offered courses to the unemployed and those threatened with unemployment (Nordic Council 1976 p. 122, Titmus 1981 pp. 151–52). This work has continued, and even expanded, but in the more difficult circumstances of the 1980s, there has been much rethinking. Emphasis has continued to be laid on making the unskilled more employable by equipping them with skills, and on replacing old skills for which there is no longer a market, with skills that are in demand.

But there have also been shifts of purpose. Much training has been offered, not to meet the needs of an existing market, but in anticipation of requirements when economic activity recovers. To some degree training has recently been promoted by the state as an activity valuable in itself, whatever the outcome in future jobs, in that it helps to keep the unemployed out of socially dangerous idleness and off the job market, which cannot, for the present at least, absorb them. In socialist countries, where in principle unemployment does not exist, but appears to be replaced by the problem of overstaffing, training fulfils the function of reducing or disguising this problem.

Thus, for the state, work-related education has become an instrument of social planning as well as one of economic policy. It is now the practice of a number of countries, in an attempt to further social justice, to try to secure equality of employment opportunity for disadvantaged groups through legislation. Laws to combat sex discrimination or to oblige firms to employ handicapped or disabled persons exist, for example, in the United Kingdom. Since women, the handicapped, and migrant workers are widely disadvantaged by their lack of occupational education, parallel measures have been brought into operation to ensure that equitable opportunities of education for employment are available to them. Employers' involvement in the implementation of this policy is essential, if frequently reluctant, on the grounds that social welfare is no part of the employer's function.

This account of the purposes which animate adult occupational education is commonly accepted, and correct as far as it goes. It is limited, however, to avowed and perhaps superficial purposes and ignores questions of what purposes ought to animate it. An examination of the principles which lie, or might lie, behind adult education for work, will reveal the possible influence of other purposes.

2. Principles

The increasing preference in the English language for the term "education" rather than "training" to describe work-oriented study indicates a tendency to attribute to it purposes and values going beyond the mere acquisition of job skills. Some educators would not include learning directed to work performance as education, on the grounds that the latter is a process undergone for the acquisition of knowledge which is of value in itself, and not as a means by which the possessor is enabled to undertake a further purpose. That is to say, it is not instrumental learning. Since work-oriented study is intended to equip the student to perform better in his or her occupation, it should not be called education (Paterson 1979).

Against this it is argued that any knowledge has value in itself, whatever instrumental role it plays, and it is increasingly believed that work-related study designed only to achieve competence in a specific task is inadequate for contemporary needs. Tasks change rapidly, so that such skills become obsolete. It makes more sense, it is argued, to extend skill training to include a basis of theory and principle, which will enable it to be adapted to varying requirements. In that way it will contain, as in principle it should, knowledge that is of value in itself, or valuable in contexts outside work. Examples of two contrasting attitudes are to be found in the United Kingdom and France. In the former an explicit distinction between education and training was made in the Industrial Training Act 1964; in the latter, as in the Law of 1971 (Organizing Continuing Vocational Education within the Framework of Permanent Education) *éducation* and *formation* (training) are treated as synonymous terms.

The work/nonwork distinction is a live issue only in certain advanced capitalist countries. Because of the Marxist view of the centrality of economic considerations to the behaviour of society and the individual, the question does not arise in socialist states. In the Soviet Union, for example,

> the social role of adult education consists in its being one of the conditions of further economic progress of the society and at the same time creating equal opportunities of intellectual development for all socio-demographic groups of the population. (Onushkin and Tonkonogaya 1984)

In Hungary "...the systematic completion and renewal of the culture of work and professional qualifications..." is one of the seven general tasks of public education (Hungarian Ministry of Culture 1977).

3. Principle of Self-interest

The most powerful principle behind adult education for work is that of economic self-interest. An individual studies to improve his or her own competence for the rewards it reaps in money or status. The employer, whether individual or organization, looks for increased profit or production. Educational institutions, private or public, seek higher income. The state expects higher national prosperity, in order that it may pursue the policies it has in mind. It has been customary to see occupational education as an investment, which is only justifiable if it brings in an adequate return (Besnard and Liétard 1982).

The principle is rarely challenged by sponsors, providers, or recipients. Controversy, usually expressed in terms of who should bear the cost, centres for the most part on the interpretation of self-interest. How wide or narrow a view should be taken? Should an employer have a duty to offer employees education only in skills specifically related to creating or improving the output of the firm? Or is it in the enterprise's interest to offer more general education, as, if it is large enough, a firm provides facilities for recreation outside working hours? Is the employee's advantage limited to learning how to do the job better, or would he or she benefit from knowing how it fits into the overall pattern of the enterprise or society, or from having the knowledge to understand why, or if, he or she should do the job at all? Is it in the interest of society to have an educated or merely a trained workforce?

Even the issue of whether occupational education for adults should be used as an instrument of social as well as economic engineering can be argued in terms of self-interest. Some politicians and employers would accept that it is a matter of moral duty to assist the disadvantaged. Some see it as a matter of self-interest, in the long, if not the short, term. Those employers who resist pressure to contribute resources for their occupational education, perceive no advantage, and reject moral responsibility for them.

Because providers are more conscious of the investment status of adult education for work, it tends to be subjected to more stringent evaluation than other kinds of adult education. Measurable outcomes are sought, which, given the time scale of most managerial and political thinking and the adult student's observed tendency to look for immediate gratification, are expected to be achieved in the short term. Activities concentrate on achieving results that are susceptible to reliable measurement, and which are expressed in behaviour.

The argument that it makes economic sense not only to educate employees in immediately applicable job skills, but also to develop the understanding of general principles and learning skills, which will pay off when they are required to retrain in order to respond to future technological advances, is one that receives only limited acceptance. It is quite widely followed for managerial grades, but such long-term goals are less often thought justifiable for manual or routine clerical grades. It is commonly advanced as a reason that the turnover in lower-grade workers is such that no benefit will accrue to a firm by long-term investment in them.

It is also a longstanding contention that one should only educate people up to the level of the jobs available to them. To do more than that is to create frustration and to foster discontent both in the workplace and in society at large. A different approach, apparently increasingly practised in industrial relations in the United States, is that the employer should offer a level of work-related education and other measures which enrich the whole personality of the employee, so that he or she will find self-realization within the company and so feel bound to it.

4. *Who Should Pay?*

It is fairly generally accepted that those who benefit from education for work should pay for it. Disagreements arise when employers, the participant workers, and society are all beneficiaries. In socialist countries the problem does not arise as employers are state agencies and the state pays for all education. In some developing countries the inability of the state and the learner to finance adequate programmes of education for work makes the argument academic. It is, however, a live issue in many advanced nonsocialist countries, as was demonstrated in the discussion on paid educational leave at the 1974 conference of the International Labour Organization (von Moltke and Schneevoigt 1977).

One argument suggests that if society as a whole benefits, then the state should pay the whole cost. There is another argument, however, that if specific enterprises or workers derive advantage, then they should meet the cost of that advantage. At one extreme it is held that the state should have no role at all in adult education for work, and that it ought to be left to the free play of market forces. This would leave it all in the hands of firms and employees. A middle position would limit state intervention to the correction of imbalances in national provision and responsibility for those such as the unemployed who are unfairly disadvantaged by the play of the market. At the other extreme it is believed that the state should both pay for all education for work and ensure that it is provided. The issue is largely unresolved, and national policies on the matter are essentially provisional, depending on the political superiority for the moment of employer or organized labour interests.

5. *The Principle of Lifelong Education*

It is generally accepted that an individual has a right to free education and a moral, if not a legal, obligation to participate in it. It is also obvious that a once-for-all education in childhood and adolescence is insufficient to meet a person's educational needs throughout life. As a corollary to this, states accept in principle, if not always in practice, that adults should have opportunities to continue their education through adulthood. For reasons of self-interest they are particularly inclined to accept the continuation of work-related education. There is disagreement, however, over the kind of education, and the amount, to which an individual is entitled, and over whether adult education, as a necessary supplement to initial education, should be offered free of charge.

Adult education for employment attracts support above that of other sectors of adult education because it is specifically directed to improving the material standards of all those engaged in it. It is seen on the whole, however, to lack the element of altruism which has run as a continuing thread through other sectors. It is largely for this reason that in some circles it is viewed as a lower form of educational activity. Nevertheless its utility is generally accepted, its position unassailable. For the good of education as a whole, research and education on the subject for parties on both sides of the fence is needed in order to discover the means, and to cultivate the will, to reconcile it with other sectors of education for adults.

Bibliography

Besnard P, Liétard B 1982 *La Formation continue*, 2nd edn. [Continuing Education]. Presses Universitaires de France, Paris

Hungarian Ministry of Culture 1977 *Act on Public Education*. Corvina Press, Budapest

Nordic Council 1976 *Adult Education in the Nordic Countries*. Nordic Council, Stockholm

Onushkin V G, Tonkonogaya E P 1984 Adult education in the USSR. *Adult Education in Europe, Studies and Documents*, No. 20. European Centre for Leisure and Education, Prague

Paterson R W K 1979 *Values, Education and the Adult*. Routledge and Kegan Paul, London

Shepherd R A 1985 A case in the motor industry. In: Titmus C (ed.) 1985 *Widening the Field: Continuing Education in Higher Education*. SRHE and NFER–Nelson, Guildford, pp. 83–89

Titmus C 1981 *Strategies for Adult Education. Practices in Western Europe*. Open University Press, Milton Keynes

von Moltke K, Schneevoigt N 1977 *Educational Leave for Employees: European Experience for American Consideration*. Jossey-Bass, San Francisco

Policies, Participation, and Structure

C. J. Titmus

As in any area of adult education, education for employment varies from country to country. Some variations are due to political or ideological factors, others, of degree, depend upon the level of economic development. Countries throughout the world are, however, increasingly subject to the same macroeconomic pressures, while cultural differences count less, perhaps, in job education than in other educational spheres. It is therefore easier to suggest some trends which are frequent, if not universal, in all but the least developed areas.

Except in a very few countries it would be true to say that "work-related training is the single most important facet of adult education" (Peterson et al. 1982). Studies in a number of countries over many years have shown that most adults who participate in adult education are motivated by "vocational-pragmatic factors" (Knoll 1985). How far this demand has helped to create the supply of job-related programmes, or is a response to it, is not clear. But it does mean that the policies of employers and states have largely been in tune with the wishes of applicants, in that where employers have provided or sponsored adult education, they have been most willing to do so for occupational purposes.

In socialist states the vocational aim of education has always been central. For example the guiding principles in the People's Republic of China for the period 1978–85 have been to revolutionize education to contribute to the modernization of the economy (Hunter and Keehn 1985). Since the mid-1960s the educational preoccupation of more advanced countries generally and of some developing countries has increasingly been to achieve a national workforce competent to meet the demands made upon it by modern technology.

The importance attributed to adult education for work may be judged from the fact that, whereas authority over planning and provision of other kinds of adult education is widely devolved to regional or local level, central government retains a closer control over occupational education. In the federal states of Austria and Germany, for example, other adult education is subject to provincial laws, but federal laws govern work education. It is a sign of its peculiar characteristics, if not of its importance, that even in unitary states, preparation for work is frequently the subject of laws separate from those dealing with the rest of adult education (EBAE 1985).

State intervention in adult occupational education takes the form both of economic planning and social engineering. Its form and extent depend largely on ideology, but also on the resources of the state. Marxist governments, as in the Soviet Union and the People's Republic of China, take complete responsibility as a matter of principle. Capitalist governments, whether democratic or authoritarian, intervene as a matter of convenience or necessity. They tend to leave action to other agencies where possible. They have stepped in only when the failure of employers, labour unions or professional and trade associations has appeared to threaten perceived national well-being to a significant degree. Between the extremes, however, there are gradations of policy, depending on the mixture of state planning and market forces in the society and on specifically national conditions.

Outside the socialist states, government has been reluctant to exert its authority over other agencies in adult occupational education. It has preferred persuasion and the offer of inducements, or sometimes coercion, rather than direct compulsion. Most governments make it clear that they believe employers ought to make a contribution to the education for work of their own employees, but they do not force them to do so. Instead other measures are used. For example, employers are taxed to help fund programmes, as in Sweden, but are also offered remission of tax to the extent that they provide training for their own workers, as in France and the United Kingdom.

Education policy for the unemployed contains, as has been pointed out, a strong element of social engineering. Certain categories of the adult population, which are particularly susceptible to unemployment, such as young adults, immigrants and ethnic minorities, and women wishing to return to paid employment after raising a family, attract special educational measures in a number of countries. In the United States voluntary organizations are active in this work, but in many countries it is an area considered to require state support. Employers are on the whole unwilling to accept responsibility, because the goals sought are less economic than social, including the achievement of more equal opportunities and the greater integration of the target groups into society.

It is, however, the practice of most governments to involve representatives of employers and organized labour in the planning and supervision of occupational education policy, either in a decision-making or in an advisory role.

1. Policies of Employers

Outside the socialist countries few employers are required, as they are in Hungary, for example, to provide both general and cultural education (Hungarian Ministry of Culture 1977). Their reluctance to do so is perhaps the main reason why in France the stated national obligation to include general and cultural education in occupational education remains a dead letter (Titmus 1981). Western European and North American employers on the whole share the view of the Danish Employers' Confederation that they are willing to contribute towards the financing only of those educational and training schemes that will benefit production (Hurup 1985).

So although there are exceptions, employers have for the most part taken a fairly narrow view of such involvement. Outside large enterprises, which need a wide range of workers, employers have tended to restrict the education they provide or sponsor to the acquisition of skills specific to the tasks carried out in the firm. In return for this training, which, because it has been non-transferable to other enterprises, has reduced job mobility and labour turnover, workers so trained have, on the whole, had a high degree of job security. This is the case in Japan.

Even in times of economic prosperity this practice has been open to criticism. While on the one hand workers felt more secure in their employment, on the other hand they were ill-prepared to take advantage of opportunities for job mobility. From the point of view of employers, the rising rate of technological change and skill obsolescence created the need for repeated retraining of workers if they were not to become redundant. In time of recession and any other situation in which a company's labour needs declined, not only could job security not be assured, but workers who were made redundant experienced greater difficulty in finding new employment, because they lacked transferable skills (CEDEFOP 1979).

Despite this, many firms remain unwilling to undertake training, since its benefits may be reaped by competitors. Their policies are therefore at odds with those of society as a whole, which requires a labour force with the knowledge and skills to adapt to changing demands and encourages job mobility.

This may be the case even in companies where a wider and longer view is taken. In the United States educators and enterprises are working on a strategy called human resource development, which seeks through various activities to integrate the development needs, both personal and occupational, of individuals working in an organization, with the missions and goals of that organization. Such activities go beyond mere job skills to embrace both personal enrichment and social education. But the policy does not increase the mobility of workers outside the firm; on the contrary it seeks to bind them to it.

2. *Policy and the Workers*

Adults studying to obtain occupational qualifications or to improve existing skills are under pressure to develop the knowledge and competence desired by the state or their employer. To a degree it is inevitable that this should be so, since all three will benefit from education for occupations in which there is employment. This simple pressure of the market is, however, complicated and reinforced by other factors. Most of the opportunities for work-related study are sponsored or provided by government, or by companies for their employees. Leave from work to undertake study is largely at the discretion of employers, or, if a legal right, it is largely couched in terms that favour participation in approved courses. Financial support for study, the source of which is almost exclusively the state or the employer, is more readily available to workers who follow designated or approved courses. In socialist states, of course, participation is possible, in fact and in law, only with government approval.

Even in countries such as France, the Federal Republic of Germany, and Sweden, which have passed laws to protect workers' freedom of choice to study what they wish, there is evidence to show that employees are reluctant to exercise their rights lest, among other reasons, their job security or chances of promotion should be threatened. If adults seek a course of study not in fields given priority by government or business enterprises, then it becomes more difficult to find an appropriate course and the chances that they will have to pay for it themselves and study in their leisure time are increased.

Studies show that most adult students accept this without resentment. In the United States, at least, they do not appear to be put off by it, judging by the rich and varied occupational programmes offered by both public and private educational institutions to meet the demand from individual adults, in addition to those mounted at the instigation of government corporations or professional bodies. For the most part too, adults take as limited a view of the preferred goals and content of occupational education as do most employers. They wish to acquire skills that may be used immediately on the job and many do not perceive the relevance of broader or more theoretical studies, whose application is conditional upon the occurrence of hypothetical situations at some unspecified time in the future. This attitude, very strong among the unskilled, declines as the level of job status rises.

3. *The Recipients of Occupational Education*

Since the Second World War there has been a considerable and continuing growth in the number of adults undergoing work-related education. In Latin America, for example, enrolment in vocational training institutions increased sixfold between 1960 and 1973 (Corvalan 1977). In the Federal Republic of Germany the proportion of the age group between 19 and 65 years of age engaged in vocational further training rose from 12 to 16 percent from 1979 to 1982 (Federal Republic of Germany 1985). It would be fair to say that this has been a product, for the most part, of initiatives on the part of both state and employer. The larger demand from workers which does exist, appears to be rather a response to the growth in opportunities. If a worker undertakes a programme of education or training in working hours, as a high proportion do, it will, with comparatively few exceptions, be under the employer's direction, or with his permission. Even those who study in their own time, for example in evening classes, frequently enrol at the suggestion, or with the encouragement, of their employers. A not insignificant number of adults do undertake occupational education on their own initiative, but for most the stimulus of the firm appears to play a major role. They study not only what is prescribed by the employer, but also at his request. Although it is a generally accepted principle that participation in adult education should be voluntary, many adults find it difficult to resist if pressure is applied to take part in job-related education, by companies, professional licensing bodies or the state. There is coercion, if not obligation.

4. Equality of Opportunity

It is argued and, indeed, it is public policy in many countries, that occupational education should contribute to the equalization of opportunity in society. In fact, as in other kinds of adult education, opportunities remain very unequal because of a number of factors. One is the field of economic activity in which an adult is employed. In those occupations that are strongly knowledge based and in which technological change is rapid, in the petroleum and electronics industries, for instance, updating and retraining are repeatedly required. Those that are more labour- than knowledge-intensive offer comparatively little training. Size of unit is also a factor. Reports from governments repeatedly show that the smaller the firm the smaller the proportion of its employees who undergo occupational training (Imprimerie Nationale 1982). Thus workers in shops and hotels, agricultural workers and those in the construction industry are less likely to be offered job-related education than those in other industries, both because they require a comparatively low knowledge base and because they are largely employed in small firms.

Job status, age, and sex also seem to affect an adult's chances of undertaking education for employment. Statistics show that although in absolute terms a larger number of manual workers obtain such education than those in other categories, if their numbers in the labour force are taken into account they are underrepresented compared with technicians and managerial grades. Roughly, the amount of occupational education on offer to an individual correlates positively with the employer's investment in that person's salary.

The level of participation is at its peak between the ages of 20 and 35–40. After that it declines sharply and continues to do so until normal age of retirement. This phenomenon too may be explained in terms of investment. As age increases, so the value of the return, in working years, on the time and money devoted to work-oriented study falls, both for the student and for the employer. Similar investment considerations appear to have been applied to the disadvantage of women, who generally receive proportionately less occupational education, both at school and in working life, than men. The strong possibility that family responsibilities will lessen their occupational commitment reduces their willingness to seek job training and that of employers to offer it.

The pattern of participation is a product of economic forces, as they are interpreted by employers and, to a lesser extent, by employees. Efforts to achieve a more equitable distribution of opportunities derive, as has already been said, from the state. Where the state is authoritarian and directive, its pressure has had some results. In the People's Republic of China, for example, (Hunter and Keehn 1985), the proportion of women engaged in study has greatly increased, as it has in the Soviet Union and other socialist states. But in some countries where pressure has been more persuasive than directive, as in France, the percentage of working women undertaking study for employment has also risen in comparison with the percentage of men (INNFO 1980). Through specific measures to that end there has been an increase in the participation of other groups with special needs. Emphasis has been laid on ethnic minorities/migrant workers, mentally and physically handicapped adults and on other undereducated, unskilled persons, particularly among the unemployed.

5. The Attitude of Trade Unions

It has been observed that an adult who undertakes study to prepare for work in an enterprise, trade or a profession is making an investment in society. He or she is adapting to that society, is undergoing a process of socialization (Besnard and Liétard 1982). This has contributed to the suspicion with which job-related education has been viewed in certain parts of the labour movement, where a fundamental goal of some unions continues to be to change the existing economic system. This has been the case in France, where some unions have also viewed occupational education as a device for weakening the working class by encouraging its brightest members to rise out of it. In the Federal Republic of Germany, on the contrary, unions have embraced with enthusiasm the existing economic system and they actively promote and provide occupational courses for their members.

Even when organized labour has reservations, it is committed to a greater or lesser extent to participating in national policy making, in cooperation with the advisory and supervisory machinery of government or employers. Indeed French occupational education legislation is based on a collective agreement between unions and management. Whatever their views, unions appreciate that they can best protect the interests of their members from within the system.

6. Structures of Adult Education for Employment

The tendency, already noted, to keep adult education for employment more closely under the control of central government than other kinds of adult education is principally due to the increasing utility attributed to it, through its concrete objectives and the support it attracts from enterprises and workers, as an instrument of labour planning and social engineering. To a greater degree and in more precise terms than for other kinds of adult education, legislation for adult education for employment tends to fix control in central government hands and to lay down effective structures of consultation and decision-making at national rather than at regional or local level (EBAE 1985). The extent to which this is so reflects a country's ideological attitude towards state planning, but it also appears to correlate with the degree of economic development, on which the level of progress in occupational education in a country appears highly dependent. Central authority is complete in socialist countries. It is much less complete in the United States where there is, however, a significant degree of federal intervention. In Italy, where adult education for work is comparatively underdeveloped, authority lies very largely with the regions. In many developing countries there is little national structure at all.

In those countries that have a well-developed system of occupational education for adults it is standard to have a tripartite structure of consultation, and sometimes of decision making, involving representatives from the state, the employers, and organized labour, for the planning and implementation of national policy and its realization at regional level.

Because of the role of adult education for employment in labour-force planning, ministries responsible for labour and economics have usually a major, if not a controlling, voice in determining policy, although the participation of the education ministry remains important. Other ministries, too (e.g. those of agriculture, justice, and defence) have an interest. They frequently function as direct providers of occupational education in the fields of national life for which they are responsible. In the Federal Republic of Germany, for instance, the armed forces are the largest providers at federal level (Knoll 1980).

Providers of occupational education for adults fall into five categories, not all of which are to be found in any single country. They are public authorities, employers, professional and trade associations, labour unions, and private educational organizations operating for profit.

Much of public provision is given as a supplementary function of technical and other institutions of formal, further, and higher education, including universities, under direction, or encouraged by financial inducements. If space allows, some of this occurs in the daytime, but much takes place out of working hours. In socialist countries, where job-related education for adults is more structured and bureaucratic than in capitalist societies, there are separate vocational schools for adults (Fukasz et al. 1978). In Latin America too, vocational training institutions, some for young people and adults, others specifically for adults in the labour market, are operated by the state (Corvalan Vasquez 1977).

A number of countries have for a long time maintained public institutions that offer training, largely in manual trades, to persons unemployed, threatened by unemployment, unskilled, or faced by the obsolescence of their job skills. They come under the National Labour Market Board in Sweden, under the Association for the Vocational Training of Adults (AFPA) in France, and are called Skill Centres in the United Kingdom.

Large enterprises frequently run their own permanent inhouse educational establishments, offering to their own personnel training for work in the enterprise, often to a very high standard. Smaller firms are unable to afford this and rely on public institutions, or on private training companies, which are also patronized by large firms for training which they themselves consider it uneconomic to provide.

Professional and trade associations provide courses in their own spheres of activity both to member organizations and to individuals. Where political conditions permit their operation, private training companies flourish, attracting both corporate and individual clients. They are frequently favoured by employers over other providers, because, as they operate for profit, they are more sensitive to the clients' wishes. On the other hand, in many parts of the world they are inadequately supervised and criticized for the quality of their performance.

The educational work of labour unions is principally devoted to the education of employees in their rights and duties as members of the union. However, in addition to Marxist countries, where unions have a duty to cooperate in job training, there are examples of countries, at the highest and the lowest levels of economic development, in which unions sponsor or directly provide work education for their members. In the United States, for example, the promotion of training and retraining forms part of a collective agreement between the United Automobile Workers and the Ford Motor Company. At the other extreme, in Singapore, Malaysia, India, and some African states, trade unions organize vocational courses for their members, to fill a gap that national governments are unable or unwilling to fill (Hopkins 1985).

The financial issues related to adult education for employment are treated in depth in Section 9. Expenditure in this sector, particularly in industrialized countries, already surpasses that contributed to other sectors of adult education and is increasing continually. More effort has also been devoted to the national structuring of occupational education than of any other sector, but still often in a piecemeal fashion. Even large corporations, with training budgets running into millions, frequently have no training strategy, but only react to circumstances (Titmus 1985). There is widespread opinion that occupational education for adults is worth the effort, yet it is unclear how effective current provision is in achieving its goals, or whether they are the correct goals. There is a dearth of research on policies and structures. Work undertaken by such organizations as the European Centre for the Development of Vocational Training (CEDEFOP) has barely begun to fill the gap. This is true of advanced countries, but the problems of developing countries are much greater and perhaps of a different kind. However, less is known about them. Much more needs to be done.

See also: Financing Adult Education; Paid Educational Leave; Workers' Education

Bibliography

Besnard P, Liétard B 1982 *La Formation Continue*, 2nd edn. Presses Universitaires de France, Paris

CEDEFOP 1979 *Relationships Between Education and Employment and their Impact on Education and Labour Market Policies: A Franco–German Study*. European Centre for the Development of Vocational Training, Berlin
Corvalan Vasquez O 1977 *Vocational Training in Latin America: A Comparative Perspective*. University of British Columbia, Vancouver
European Bureau of Adult Education (EBAE) 1985 *Survey of Adult Education Legislation*. EBAE, Amersfoort
Federal Republic of Germany 1985 *Adult Education in the Federal Republic of Germany*. Secretariat of the Standing Conference of the Ministers of Education and Cultural Affairs of the Laender in the Federal Republic of Germany, Bonn
Fukász G et al. 1978 Adult education in the Hungarian People's Republic (HPR). *Adult Education in Europe, Studies and Documents*, No. 3. European Centre for Leisure and Education, Prague
Hopkins P G H 1985 *Workers' Education: An International Perspective*. Open University Press, Milton Keynes
Hunter C St J, Keehn M M (eds.) 1985 *Adult Education in China*. Croom Helm, London
Hurup M 1985 Lifelong education, paid educational Leave—the Danish Employers' Confederation's view of education. In: Himmelstrup P (ed.) 1985 *Adult Education in Denmark*. The Danish Institute, Copenhagen, pp. 42–44
Imprimerie Nationale 1982 *Projet de Loi de Finances pour 1983*, Document Annexe: *Formation Professionnelle* [Finance Bill for 1983. Appendices. Vocational Training]. Imprimerie Nationale, Paris
INNFO 1980 *La Formation professionnelle continue en France* [Continuing Vocational Training in France]. Centre INFFO, Courbevoie
Knoll J H 1980 Adult education in the Federal Republic of Germany. *Adult Education in Europe, Studies and Documents*, No. 8. European Centre for Leisure and Education, Prague
Knoll J H (ed.) 1985 *Motivation for Adult Education*. German Commission for UNESCO–Saur, Bonn
Hungarian Ministry of Culture 1977 *Act on Public Education*. Corvina Press, Budapest
Peterson R E, Gaff S S, Helmick J S, Feldmesser R A, Valley J R, Nielsen H D et al. 1982 *Adult Education and Training in Industrialized Countries*. Praeger, New York
Titmus C 1981 *Strategies for Adult Education: Practices in Western Europe*. Open University Press, Milton Keynes
Titmus C (ed.) 1985 *Widening the Field: Continuing Education in Higher Education*. Society for Research into Higher Education and NFER/Nelson, Guildford

The Educators

E. Frank

As a consequence of the increasing importance attached to all forms of adult education in our societies, and of the steady increase in the number of people who, in one capacity or another, are part-time students in adult life, there has been a corresponding increase in the number of men and women who are professionally engaged, full-time, in adult education, including directors, administrators, organizers, supervisors and, of course, teachers. The number of those who are so engaged part-time has increased even more markedly. These increasing numbers have involved both the highly qualified and amateurs with only limited experience and qualifications. It has taken place in employment in statutory authorities, voluntary organizations, and combined systems involving radio and correspondence, in areas of both vocational retraining schemes and "cultural" programmes.

1. Types of Educators for Employment

The area of adult education which has experienced the largest growth and attracts the largest expenditure and the highest number of students is job-related education. Consequently more people are engaged as adult educators in this field than in any other. They may be classified in several ways: according to the agency in which they work, according to the function they fulfill, or according to whether they are engaged full- or part-time in adult education for employment.

There are many bodies offering occupational training to adults and therefore employing educators for that purpose. In the United States most blue-collar workers are trained at their work stations and their supervisors get on-the-job training and attend company-sponsored courses. Middle managers tend to take part in programmes provided by outside consultants and professional associations. Top executives are more likely to attend university-based courses (Craig 1979). Most advanced countries offer occupational courses for adults in public education institutions, such as technical colleges, further education colleges, universities and polytechnics, whose main function lies in other areas. There are specialized adult training institutions, publicly maintained and administered, for example, those providing skilled operator training, such as state Skill Centres in the United Kingdom, or institutions run by the Association for the Vocational Education of Adults (AFPA) in France and the Labour Market Board in Sweden. There are private training agencies and those operated by trade and professional associations, already mentioned and there are the training schemes run by individual employers, or groups of employers.

The American Society for Training and Development (ASTD), the principal national association of adult educators for employment in the United States, identified, through a literature search, 15 roles for persons so employed including that of programme designer, strategist, media specialist, instructional writer, group facilitator, counsellor, instructor, transfer agent, evaluator, needs analyst, task analyst, theoretician, manager of training and development and, marketer (McLagan and

Bedrick 1983). To these may be added, for senior staff at least, the reponsibility for recruiting, training, and supervising part-time staff.

In relation to the total number of educators involved in adult education for employment the number of full-time workers is small. In public education institutions they may constitute a small cadre of administrators and organizers, with specialist subject teachers in some well-staffed institutions. In such centres as those AFPA, the instructors, as well as the managers of the programmes, are full-time workers. Private training organizations providing high-level courses have full-time teaching staff. Employers may have full-time training officers, as well as instructional staff at skilled worker level.

Part-time staff are much more common. In all kinds of educational agencies, part-time faculty members help maintain flexibility in programme planning, play a significant role in establishing and maintaining links with the environment, and provide access to special expertise unavailable in any other way. Some institutions have found that part-time staff are the best source from which to recruit full-time faculty members.

In institutions of tertiary and higher education, some full-time staff, primarily engaged in other work, devote a part of their time to occupational education for adults. For example professional continuing education courses in universities of the Federal Republic of Germany are, as a matter of principle, taught by internal staff from undergraduate teaching departments. Most part-time teachers are recruited, however, from outside the institution. Educational institutions use two such kinds of part-timer workers: those employed in other educational institutions who help to keep the organization in touch with developments in basic disciplines and who handle specific teaching or other tasks that do not justify a full-time appointment, and those from industry and commerce, and business and government administration, whose contribution lies mainly in enhancing the practical bias of training programmes by enlivening their teaching with illustrations from current practice. In-company training is frequently both organized and conducted by personnel who have other responsibilities within the company.

2. *Organizers, Managers, and Administrators*

There is a great variety of levels at which management takes place in adult education for employment and a wide variety of appointments involve management functions. Some examples would include principals or directors of schools and colleges of vocational training and education, directors of continuing education in higher education, administrative officers, training managers and staff of government departments, ministries of education and/or manpower and/or industry.

The director of a vocational training school and his or her deputies, as befits the responsibilities they have, are usually appointed from among the most experienced staff of the education for employment sector. It would seem reasonable to expect that they should have high pedagogical qualifications appropriate to their particular type of establishment and a broad and thorough knowledge of the principles and practices of adult education and education for employment.

Yet in many countries, administrators and organizers are often treated as though they only need apply a little common sense and follow the lead of their predecessors and stick to established precedents. With a view to raising management standards in institutions for occupational education, however, there are now regular seminars for the various levels of managerial staff and for the senior officials of local administrative bodies responsible for vocational training. The subject matter of these seminars is both theoretical and practical, the former including the exchange of experience, new teaching requirements and the organization and supervision of the training process, the latter comprising activities such as visits to actual training classes, their analysis by seminar members, and the subsequent discussion of these analyses. The Department of Education and Science in Britain maintains a Further Education Staff College for the training of senior staff in further education and higher education institutions throughout the United Kingdom. In some other countries, notably socialist ones, courses in pedagogy, andragogy, and management subjects have become compulsory for newly appointed senior staff.

3. *Training Officers*

The term "training officer" is usually applied to persons of managerial status who fulfill a variety of educational roles in commerce and industry. They include training advisors for a whole industry or for a variety of large companies; training administrators who are responsible for large organizations and who may operate in a number of locations; officers responsible for organizing training in a single company or unit; those responsible for training in a particular area within a company training programme, such as marketing or computer training; and those working exclusively or primarily with one level of the organizational hierarchy such as trainers of supervisors and managers.

Although groups of training staff may have very similar needs, the variety of roles, organizations, and people means that there is no one set of abilities required by everyone. A 1982 study carried out in the Republic of Ireland revealed that most training managers in the study came from production or personnel management backgrounds. For the majority, their training work was part-time, combined, for the most part, with personnel management. It was also found that those with professional qualifications were qualified mainly in this field (McGennis and Leigh Doyle 1982). Previous studies in the United Kingdom and United States showed that in these countries too, training roles were largely part-time and combined frequently with personnel work. In Ireland, the majority of training managers in the study said their main training duties were to plan, implement, and manage the training programme and only secondly to identify needs and design programmes. In the United States, designing programmes came first and establishing and maintaining good relationships with managers came second, while in the United Kingdom the first task was to sell training to senior management, with identifying needs coming second.

The Irish study indicated that few training managers had undergone specific education for training work. Nevertheless, many countries have programmes to train trainers. Courses vary in length, but they usually deal with the analysis of present performance of personnel, the skills needed for the enterprise, methods of planning vocational training, teaching methods, behavioural science, the organization, administration and costs of training, and the evaluation of its effectiveness. The need for training officers to update their technical and pedagogic skills from time to time is increasingly recognized. The principal means of achieving this are regular or ad hoc refresher courses, correspondence courses, participation in seminars and meetings dealing with topics relevant to their work, self-tuition, and voluntary study groups formed by training staff.

In selecting a training officer, the employer will look for many of the characteristics which are found in effective managers, for if a training officer is to be accepted by managers as a colleague whose counsel is respected, he or she should be of management status and of a calibre and competence which will warrant that status. Many training officers are not, however, considered part of management and have difficulty in carrying out their function.

4. Teachers and Instructors

It is clear that teachers in adult education for employment are chosen less for their teaching ability than for their competence in and knowledge of the subject or skill they are to teach. In educational institutions, other than those maintained in companies and skilled worker training centres, teachers are increasingly "subject teachers", specializing in a limited field. They may be specialists in one subject or teach a variety of related ones, being classified as monovalent or polyvalent accordingly. A distinction is sometimes made between teachers of general and technical subjects and teachers of practical ones.

Many teachers are appointed on the basis of some recognized subject qualification, for example a degree, a craft certificate, or a technical award. In many countries, the principal selection criterion is proven skill in the occupation concerned. General education background and formal education qualifications are taken into account, but to a lesser extent. Because of this selection criterion, vocational teachers are often recruited at a comparatively advanced age.

Those persons teaching and lecturing in colleges of further and higher education, and particularly in institutions of university status, are, however, increasingly recruited on the basis of high academic standing, as exemplified by diplomas or degrees, their contributions to workshops, seminars and conferences, and their research activities and publications.

A substantial proportion of vocational teachers (mainly of practical subjects) have not received any special teacher education. It is unfortunate that in most cases there has been an assumption that knowledge of a subject is equivalent to an ability to teach it, that "experience is the best kind of training", and that the addition to subject knowledge of a few hints and tips on teaching can be adequate training. In the United Kingdom it is significant that long after teachers in secondary schools have, by regulation, needed to have a professional teaching qualification, those in further education, which is mainly vocationally oriented, have not.

There are two further categories of personnel who perform a major teaching function in adult education for employment: instructors and on-the-job trainers. Instructors are usually craftspersons with a specific part-time or full-time responsibility for the instruction of students, predominantly off-the-job, mainly in schools run by companies or in adult training centres, of the kind already mentioned, whose function is to produce skilled craftspersons. Their job is to teach practical skills, with a little theoretical backing, and they operate largely in workshop settings. They may occasionally have to undertake some of the simple duties of the teacher or training officer, but they do not normally play any major part in the formulation of policy.

Instructors in adult training centres usually have full-time, permanent appointments and they have generally undergone a substantial period of instructor training. In company schools, however, the work is often part-time and temporary and little training is given. The qualities needed for a good instructor are much the same as for a good supervisor, indeed many full-time instructors have previously held supervisory positions, or alternatively, take up such posts after a period of instructing.

Where formal preparation for instructors is available, it may range from induction courses of two or three weeks for newly appointed instructors to longer courses lasting up to four years. In order to qualify for entry, candidates require a sound general education, including or in addition to vocational training. On longer courses the curriculum is usually designed to provide a balanced mixture of general and technical studies, including teaching theory and practice.

An on-the-job trainer is usually a supervisor or manager, whose responsibilities include giving short pieces of instruction, coaching, and correcting performance in the work situation. The training responsibility is an integral part of his or her job.

5. Training of Educators

It is now generally accepted that vocational teaching and training personnel should have a broad educational background. The range of professional competence required to meet the varied demands made upon such personnel and the personal qualities fundamental to a good teacher, as well as pedagogical (or andragogical) competence, are all considered important. Specialized knowledge and unique skills are obviously required for particular kinds of programmes, such as, for instance, industrial training, but anyone professionally engaged in the education of adults should acquire a good deal of core knowledge and skills. Generic training should be supplemented by specialized training on the job or by means of an induction course.

Only a few of the full-time staff and virtually none of the part-time staff currently employed in adult education for employment have, however, been formally trained for that work, though many have completed school teacher training courses. Until recently, indeed, it was commonly assumed that adult educators had a natural flair for organizing or teaching and they did not, therefore, require any training, or at least not the sort that necessitated attending regular courses. Today there is pressure for them to become as professionally competent as possible and establish a professional identity. The growing sophistication of administrative and organizational procedures have combined to produce a demand for the professional training of adult educators, including those in education for employment, a demand that comes not only from the profession itself but from outside. In France, for example, working parties set up by the Minister of Vocational Training, recommended that all those engaged in adult education should be trained and that all teachers in the public school system should be trained to teach adults (Actualité de la Formation Permanente 1982). The People's Republic of China, where adult education concentrates heavily on improving the country's economic performance, has expressed a need to improve teaching skills (Hunter and Keehn 1985).

In the United States in 1982, a large project was conducted to determine the competencies required for effective performance in each of the roles that an adult vocational educator might have to play. Organizational leaders, managers, trainers, and academicians were surveyed and participated in meetings to identify and refine the respective competencies list. A final report (McLagan and Bedrick 1983) listed a total of 102 inputs (products, services, and information) which the vocational educator of adults should ideally be able to produce in performing at a level of excellence. Additionally, it gave a measure of direction to trainers, their supervisors, and academicians for the design and implementation of curriculum and instruction intended to improve the knowledge and performance of these practitioners.

The preparation of adult vocational educators in countries outside the United States tends to emanate more from the liberal arts tradition in its emphasis on both the curriculum and methods of schooling. In those countries which have a strong centralized state economy, the function of adult education for employment is frequently part of a total educational and economic plan, which includes the preparation of those selected to be vocational educators. Finland approaches adult education for employment as part of a lifelong education perspective, which is concerned with developing the knowledge and skills needed by adults to remain up-to-date in the face of changing demands in the workplace. Equally important, however, is the development of knowledge, skills, and attitudes in general cultural and educational areas, with an emphasis on civic and social responsibility (Absetz 1979).

6. Numbers, Status, and Careers of Educators

For most countries it is no more possible to give an accurate estimate of the number of educators engaged in education for employment than in any other part of adult education. The United States has probably the most highly developed provision and a projection from a national survey there estimated the number of trainers employed full-time in business and industry at 212,877, with additional 33,000 associated with government agencies. To these must be added the unknown number employed in public and private educational institutions. Nearly 60 percent of the organizations responding to the survey reported employing at least one full-time trainer but, of these, only 16 percent of companies with fewer than 100 employees were so staffed. Among all industry groups, health care institutions had the highest percentage of full-time professionally staffed training units, with over 84 percent so reported.

In spite of these impressive numbers, the five major associations serving the field list memberships totalling approximately 60,000, far less than the potential number and, in part, a testimony to the lack of professional identity which still characterizes adult training (Editorial 1982). This evidence is supported by figures from Ireland and United Kingdom, which show that only 20 percent of training officers belong to their national associations (McGennis and Leigh Doyle 1982).

The marginality of the occupation of training contributes to the lack of identity on the part of adult educators for employment. Teachers in public educational institutions identify themselves primarily with their subject or as teachers of late adolescents, with whom they are mostly concerned. A high proportion of training officers, as we have seen, belong to the more established field of personnel management and are largely part-time, or employed temporarily in training, as are many in-company instuctors.

Adult educators for employment also lack status. In a number of countries, notably France, they have expressed anxiety about the insecurity of their position (Actualité de la Formation Permanente 1982). It is still common for those in educational institutions to feel disadvantaged by the traditionally higher value placed on pure academic studies than vocationally applied ones, with the notable exceptions of teachers in such fields as medicine and the law. Training officers may officially have management status, but in practice they frequently have no part in management decisions and are not treated as equals by other managers.

Yet, given the public stress on the importance of adult education for employment, the career prospects ought to be good. Every institution is likely to require a core group which shares the burden of building, managing, and carrying out major institutional tasks. Many of these are full-time permanent professionals who have chosen to make their career in vocational education. They are likely to be interested in movement up the professional ladder, rather than in administration, management or outside the field of education for employment. It is desirable that each institution should provide opportunities for promotion to its professional staff and that such professional advancement should receive the appropriate pecuniary rewards, so that key professionals do not have to look elsewhere in order to improve their economic condition. The same is true of training officers in companies.

Nevertheless, if there is a certain lack of quality in some of the personnel currently employed in adult education for employment, it is mainly because of the absence of attractive career prospects. Well-qualified people are either ignorant of the professional opportunities in adult education for employment, or regard them as insufficiently secure and prestigious. It is commonly claimed that people do not stay in the field because (a) they do not identify themselves with it and (b) the salary structure is inadequate. The acute scarcity of properly trained, full-time personnel capable of assuming a broad range of responsibilities has become a major concern.

There are currently conflicting tendencies. On the one hand there is a growing trend towards professionalism which is due to two mutually reinforcing factors. The first is that governmental and nongovernmental institutions have perceived the need for specialists and, even if on a small scale, they have accordingly established specialist posts. This is true of universities in several European countries. The second is that men and women appointed as specialists, or who eventually come to regard themselves as specialists, have become aware of the community of interest between them and others similarly placed.

One must, however, set against this the fact that, in the economic recession of the late 1970s and 1980s almost the first activity that companies cut was training. There was a sharp fall in the number of training officers employed or attending courses of professional education. Although individual workers may derive benefit from occupational education and governments desire it for a variety of reasons, it seems that although some companies may say, "If you think training is expensive, try ignorance" (Shepherd 1985), many employers are less convinced of its essential contribution to profits.

There is indeed a lack of hard evidence on this point and the future of adult education for employment as a profession is unlikely to be secure until more is obtained. At the moment, questions as to whether such educators are needed at all, whether they should be educators or simply skill trainers, are answered on the basis of value judgments. When it is known what adult education for employment can achieve, then it will be possible to address, with more confidence, issues such as the recruitment, education, and methods of educators, their status and careers.

See also: Training of Adult Educators

Bibliography

Absetz B 1979 The government decision of principles concerning planning and development of adult education in Finland. *Adult Education in Finland.* 16(2): 6

Actualité de la Formation Permanente 1982 *Réforme de la formation continue. Le rapport de synthèse des groupes de travail* [Reform of continuing Education. Consolidated Report of Working Groups], No. 57, March–April

Craig R 1979 *National Report for Training and Development.* American Society for Training and Development, Washington, DC

Editorial 1982 Who gets trained and how. *Training Magazine* 19(10): 30–31

Hunter C St J, Keehn M M 1985 *Adult Education in China.* Croom Helm, London

McGennis B, Leigh Doyle S 1982 *The Training Manager in Irish Industry. A Summary Report.* AnCO—The Industrial Training Authority, Dublin

McLagan P, Bedrick D 1983 Models of excellence: The results of the ASTD competency study. *Training and Development Journal* 37(2)

Shepherd R A 1985 A case in the motor industry. In: Titmus C (ed.) 1985 *Widening the Field: Continuing Education in Higher Education.* SRHE and NFER–Nelson, Guildford, pp. 83–89

Employment Policy and Adult Education

T. Schuller

In this article, adult education is understood in a broad sense, to include all organized learning activities intended to increase the skills of the adult population, technical, social, or political. Its relation to employment policy is reviewed in terms of its objectives, the sources of its provision, and its organization and finance. Finally, some specific issues are selected as significant for future developments. Illustrations are drawn largely, but not exclusively, from Europe and the United States.

Adult education has always had an implicit connection with employment policy in the very broad sense that it influences the overall skill level of the population. However, it is only relatively recently that explicit links have been developed between the two. Certainly adult education figured prominently in the British plans for rebuilding the country at the end of the First World War, but it was regarded then as a social policy separate from the task of reconstructing the economy and creating full employment. Even between the two World Wars, the potential of adult education for combating the problems of massive unemployment was left largely unexplored throughout the countries affected by the depression.

After the Second World War came massive growth in the world economy, full employment, and an explosion in postcompulsory education. This was perhaps most evident in the formal institutions of tertiary education, notably universities, catering for younger students coming straight from secondary school. But economic growth had two major consequences for adult education. First, it meant that resources were available for substantial expansion, even if in relative terms adult education benefited less than other sectors. Second, the surge of economic activity came up against bottlenecks caused by skill shortages, and this drew attention to the need for new education and training policies. The 1950s and 1960s thus witnessed the expansive phase of adult education. Its links with employment policy were evident, in different ways, in the active manpower policy pursued by Sweden; in the 1969 German Labour Promotion Act; and in the establishment of the Industrial Training Boards in the United Kingdom in 1964; all were intended to develop adult learning opportunities in order to smooth the path of sustained economic growth.

The 1970s and, more acutely, the 1980s, have seen the same links interpreted in a very different and essentially defensive fashion. Researchers and policy makers had already been interested in educational policies which encouraged alternation between work and education in a recurrent pattern (OECD/CERI 1973). A version of this pattern was now forced on many people by the massive surge in unemployment, the disappearance of the demand for many traditional skills, and the imposition of periods of involuntary leisure. Budgets for adult education as a consumption good dried up, to be replaced in part by expenditure on support for the unemployed, sometimes including an educational component. Adult education came to be seen as a buffer against unemployment as much as an instrument of positive employment policy (Stonier 1979).

1. Purposes

The goals of adult education seen in relation to employment policy are broadly threefold:

(a) To help supply the overall skills needed to sustain economic growth. The extent to which this is upheld as an objective depends on how clearly adult education is distinguished from vocational training, but in any case general skills are needed which are unrelated to a particular industry. At a basic level, for example, many adults lack literacy and numeracy; they may be motivated more by a desire to participate socially than by the demands of a specific job, but a wider spread of these skills will help the functioning of the labour market and their own employment prospects (ACACE 1979).

(b) To counteract inequities in employment. This may take the form of helping groups with low economic participation rates to enter the labour market, or of countering the process of segmentation which locks workers into low-paying unskilled jobs and cumulates inequalities (Edwards et al. 1973). Immigrant workers are one such target group, helped in Sweden by the establishment of a right to 240 hours of language training. Educational assistance to rural workers, especially in less developed countries, aims to redress the inequality between town and country, as well as to help balanced economic development (Coombs and Ahmed 1974). Nurturing confidence in women to enable them to enter the labour market even in male-dominated occupations is another such objective.

(c) Thirdly, adult education is a means whereby individuals can directly or indirectly further their own career development. In many instances this takes place informally, through seminars and conferences which may last only one day. In all countries, day and evening classes exist which provide opportunities for adults to acquire the skills and qualifications needed to progress occupationally.

Specific mention should be made of two broad groups within the general adult population.

(a) Young adults seeking an entry into the labour market. For these, adult education (as distinct both from initial education and from specifically designated vocational training) varies enormously in the closeness of its association with employment. Local Initiative Programs (LIPs) in Canada and the Youth Opportunity Schemes (YOPs) in the United Kingdom are examples of proliferating attempts to mix education with work experience.

(b) Adults approaching retirement, that is, preparing to leave the labour market. Demographic trends have made the elderly an increasingly significant group, and educational provision for those in retirement is growing (e.g., *Université de Troisième Age* in France). By definition the retired are marginal to a discussion of employment policy, but national policies of promoting earlier retirement, mainly as a way of reducing overall unemployment, clearly have major implications for adult education. Moreover, preretirement courses are becoming an integral part of company personnel practice.

2. Providers

All countries rely on a combination of providers, but vary in the extent to which they draw on different sources (Lowe 1975).

2.1 The Formal Education System

Many institutions within the formal education system put on courses for adults which have a more or less close connection with employment. Universities and other institutions of higher education tend to concentrate on professional categories such as teachers or medical personnel. The demand for certification and recertification has prompted a substantial growth in this area, notably in the United States—in some states, for example, doctors are required by law to undertake regular periods of refresher training. At other levels, technical colleges and community colleges obviously play a large role in supplying courses which meet employment needs. Typical of this is the Technical and Further Education (TAFE) sector in Australia. France and the Federal Republic of Germany are prominent examples of countries which rely heavily on the institutions of the formal education system.

2.2 Other Public Institutions

Establishments exist which provide education similar to that of the formal education system but which are separately administered. Most obviously, ministries of labour or employment run training centres as part of their industrial policy. In other instances the institutions are not directly under one ministry, or they function semi-independently of the state.

2.3 "In-house" Courses

Companies and public administrators put on many courses themselves for their employees. Naturally these tend to be tightly related to their own specific needs and therefore stand at one end of the education–training spectrum, but should not be ignored as a source of skills relevant to employment policy. Countries with a trade of strongly developed internal labour markets, such as Japan, are prominent in this respect.

2.4 Private Institutions

Partly as a consequence of the public sector's indifference to the needs of adults, there are many private establishments at various levels. Some are straight commercial operations, such as the agencies which proliferated in France following the 1971 law on educational leave. Others are non-profit-making organizations, particularly strongly represented in the United States.

2.5 Trade Unions

Trade Unions are an important source of adult education related to employment issues, and provide training for their representatives at all levels. In some countries this is carried out in public institutions (e.g., United States); in others (e.g., Federal Republic of Germany, Norway) the unions run an independent system.

3. Organization and Finance

As indicated above, there is a massive variety of provision and the organization and finance are correspondingly complex. Different ministries (education, labour, industry, health) are involved and different levels of government (national, regional, local). Perhaps the most that can be said is that there is everywhere a problem of coordinating the provision, whilst at the same time permitting diversity. In the United Kingdom, for example, education is for the most part the responsibility of local government whilst employment and workforce policies are operated centrally.

In many countries, formal rights to educational leave have been established, linked in varying degrees to employment considerations (von Moltke and Schneevoight 1979, OECD/CERI 1978). In France, a legal right to such leave has existed since 1971, but financial assistance for it is conditional upon approval by a joint labour/management committee of the enterprise. Laws also exist in several of the states in the Federal Republic of Germany, usually to the benefit of public employees. Australia provides an example of a different right: workers accumulate entitlement to long service leave (3 months after 10 years), which can be used for educational purposes at the individual's own discretion. In Italy, trade unions have been responsible for negotiating leave of 150 or more hours for workers in certain industries. The distribution of this leave is concentrated on groups lacking in basic educational qualifications. Several companies in the United States provide financial assistance for their employees to pay their way through college under so-called "tuition aid refund" schemes.

The link with employment policy is central to the consideration of the financing of adult education (Peston 1979). The costs are always difficult to quantify exactly, but cannot be properly estimated unless they are set against alternative uses of the resources. At times of high unemployment, the costs of adult education are low in that there is little output forgone. Financing people to participate in education may seem in any case to be a more positive use of resources than paying them the same amounts as unemployment benefit. The actual mechanisms for financing cover a combination of private fees and public subsidy. They may be oriented to the individual, the educational institution, the company, the industry, or the region. Specific forms which deserve mention are the payroll tax used in France and Sweden to finance their educational leave schemes, and the levy-grant system previously used in the United Kingdom to encourage industrial training by raising a levy from firms and paying it back in the form of assistance for training.

4. Some Topical Issues

Of many that exist, three crucial issues may be singled out:

(a) The implications of new patterns of education, work, and leisure—even should the world regain its economic momentum, it is unlikely that the old model of education–work–retirement will dominate to the same extent. Not only can a much more varied pattern of alternation between education and work be expected, but also greater leisure time (more or less voluntary) and far less rigid retirement ages can be expected. The relationship between the organization and financing of education, work, and leisure will therefore become far more complex.

(b) The content of adult education in its relation to employment—the analysis of learning needs and the extent to which they are determined by employees, companies, or public bodies will pose new problems. In particular, the impact of technological developments on skills in manufacturing and service industries is not a simple technical issue; the scope and character of jobs, and the extent to which they make use of human resources, are matters of social as well as economic choice, and this will be reflected in the content of education.

(c) Education and democracy—shifts in authority patterns at home and in the workplace will present new challenges. Moves towards greater economic and industrial democracy, and towards greater equality between the sexes have major learning implications; for the groups that currently hold power; for those that aspire to a greater share; and for those involved in teaching. Increased attention to the quality of paid and domestic labour can generate radically different learning requirements.

See also: Paid Educational Leave

Bibliography

Advisory Council for Adult and Continuing Education (ACACE) 1979 *A Strategy for the Basic Education of Adults*. A report commissioned by the Secretary of State for Education and Science. ACACE, Leicester

Coombs P H, Ahmed M 1974 *Attacking Rural Poverty: How Non-formal Education Can Help*. Johns Hopkins Press, Baltimore, Maryland

Edwards R, Reich M, Gordon C 1973 *Labor Market Segmentation*. Conf. Harvard University, 1973. Heath, Lexington, Massachusetts

Lowe J 1975 *The Education of Adults: A World Perspective*. UNESCO, Paris

Organisation for Economic Co-operation and Development/Centre for Educational Research and Innovation (OECD/CERI) 1973 *Recurrent Education: A Strategy for Lifelong Learning*. OECD, Paris

Organisation for Economic Co-operation and Development/Centre for Educational Research and Innovation (OECD/CERI) 1976 *Developments in Educational Leave of Absence*. OECD, Paris

Organisation for Economic Co-operation and Development/Centre for Educational Research and Innovation (OECD/CERI) 1978 *Alternation Between Work and Education*. OECD, Paris

Peston M 1979 Recurrent education: Tackling the financial implications. In: Schuller T, Megarry J (eds.) 1979 *Recurrent Education and Lifelong Learning*. Kogan Page, London

Stonier T 1979 The third industrial revolution. *Effects of Modern Technology on Workers*. International Metalworkers Federation, Geneva

von Moltke K, Schneevoight J 1979 *Educational Leave of Absence*. Jossey-Bass, San Francisco, California

Adult Education for Employment: United States

G. G. McMahon

The purpose of adult education for employment in the United States is to prepare those who receive it to earn a living wage in specific occupational areas. A particular class may be designed to provide a portion of the skills and supportive technical knowledge for initial employment or, indeed, to extend what the individual already knows or is able to demonstrate.

1. The Local Public System

The system of adult education for employment in the United States could probably be viewed as an excellent example of what can happen under a liberal democratic system. The director of vocational education, an official employed by a local Board of Education, has the administrative responsibility for both the in-school and adult programs of vocational education. The director's office seeks approval for all courses—whether they be a part of the secondary program or for the postsecondary adult programs. Once programs receive approval and are completed, the director then applies to the state office for the state and/or federal funds available to those school systems which conduct programs in accordance with the guidelines of the State Plan. This is a contractual arrangement between each state and the United States Office of Education outlining the standards for operation.

An individual or a very small group of individuals can petition the local director of vocational eduction to initiate a special class in a small and select area of a single occupation. The director will often depend upon those who desire this special instruction to assist in the identification of an instructor. However, the directors have the responsibility of determining whether the special instruction requested is reasonable for those making the request and whether a qualified instructor is available.

Although the overall policies of adult education for employment in the United States are determined through legislation on a national level by the federal government, each State Department of Education has considerable liberty in the interpretation of the laws and regulations. The local directors of adult education for employment receive frequent updating of the guidelines from the appropriate personnel of their respective State Departments of Vocational Education and are encouraged to request assistance at any time. Since local school systems receive reimbursements, by way of their state Departments of Education, from both the state and federal governments for each approved class, the lines of communication between the state and the local offices remain open.

It should not be construed from the above that adult education for employment in the United States is dominated by the state and federal governments. Local programs are very much a reflection of the occupations represented in the businesses and industries within a particular community. It is the duty of the local director to select a local advisory committee to assist in charting directions to be followed to best accommodate the adult vocational needs of their community. Even the selection of the committee members is critical to the smooth operation of a local program. Care must be taken not to permit a single industry or business to dominate committee decisions. A carefully selected committee can prove resourceful to the benefit of the local director and the adult vocational program if a wide variety of local political problems arise.

2. Community Colleges

Since the mid-1950s, many new community colleges have been established in the United States. For the most part, they are two-year county educational units with the cost of operation divided equally between the state, county, and student. Most of the programs offered reflect the employment opportunities of the local community and, therefore, fall within vocational categories. It is common for the community college student to be employed in a full-time position at a local business or industry and, at the same time, attend the two-year school on a part-time basis. An individual following this pattern may require three to five years to complete a two-year associate degree. This movement has provided many new laboratories representing a much wider range of occupations, and quite naturally new technical personnel have been recruited to serve as instructors. This development has required new approaches to coordinating the local adult education for employment programs and has, in most cases, changed the perspective of the advisory group.

3. Credit and Noncredit Courses

Whether a specific course should or should not be offered for college credit is now an item for consideration. If a particular course is offered for college credit, then college admission standards have to be considered. If credit is not to be granted, then it may be questioned whether the college instructor is the best qualified person available. Adults usually want specific kinds of instruction and often within a fairly remote part of a very skilled area. If the program director is not totally aware of the special needs of a particular adult class and if sufficient care is not exercised in the selection of an instructor, those enrolled may simply cease to attend. Usually the director of adult vocational education will conduct classes within the classrooms and laboratories of the local vocational facilities or in appropriate quarters of a nearby business or industry during the evening hours. In some cases, classes may be held during the day for those who may have night-time employment. The community college classes are most often conducted in the classrooms and laboratories of the college campus.

At present there are no tight guidelines for determining whether there should be one program of adult education for employment in a given community under the direction of the local school system or the community college, or two programs under separate administrations. In spite of what may appear to be an area offering the potential for considerable conflict, a very limited number of problems have developed. In the vast majority of cases, the administrators of both the local school and community college have agreed to concentrate their efforts in only those areas where they have the best equipped laboratories and the best instructional staff. In many cases, a joint advisory committee is also utilized. This in itself is a very effective tool for avoiding conflict in programs offered. It is also recognized that the particular demands of the students to be served provide a partial answer to this problem. Most of the people who attend the adult vocational programs in the United States desire specific instruction which can usually be categorized as an extension of their present skill area or job title. Therefore, they have limited interest in taking a series of courses already established as the requirements for an associate degree .

4. Company Training Programs

The training director of a local industry will often initiate a request for a very specific class for company employees. The director will not be particularly concerned about location of the class but will be concerned about whether it meets the needs as expressed by company employees. The company training director may work with the vocational director of the local schools to set up the class, or he/she may set up the class independently within company working hours, on site, and utilize someone within the company as the instructor. In such cases, the company would bear all costs and the employees would not be charged a fee.

Quite apart from local public adult vocational programs, those in business and industry may conduct a variety of preservice and inservice programs for their employees without contacting the local director of vocational education. Only when the business or industry involved is conducting some sort of educational program subsidized by state or federal funds are they under legal obligation to file reports to either state or federal government, and thus one of the largest sources of adult training hours for that state is lost. Since those within the business and industrial complex in the United States do not employ a common method of recordkeeping with regard to training, it is virtually impossible to determine what each individual company spends on training and upgrading its employees. It is the general opinion, however, that the total figure greatly exceeds that spent on public adult education for employment.

There are some good reasons for those in the business and industrial sector to keep their training programs separate from the public system. It is natural that they wish to maintain the privilege of selecting those who will attend their own training programs and, although the appropriate advanced technology is presented in most cases, one of the best reasons for the program is that it also serves as an ideal way of identifying potential supervisory personnel.

Although business and industry may categorize their training under such titles as "engineering," "sales," or "production," they are not restricted to specific titles, class size, or to the kind of employee who may attend unless such items happen to be part of a union agreement between the company and its employees.

5. *Official Categories of Training*

The vocational and adult educational section of the United States Office of Education provides guidelines to the State Education Departments which indicate how classes and programs will be categorized for administration and reporting purposes. These categories are a direct reflection of the job titles under which individuals are employed in the workforce of the United States. There are seven categories or areas of vocational education: agriculture, business education, distributive education, health occupations, home economics, trade and industrial education, and technical education. These will be detailed below.

5.1 Agriculture

When reporting to the state vocational office the information relative to adult classes held in agriculture, a local director of vocational education would report them as either "young farmer" classes or as "adult farmer" classes. The "young farmer" title denotes that the participants of that particular class have been in farming less than five years regardless of their age, and those in the "adult farmer" group would include those who have had more than five years' experience in full-time farming.

The classes offered under agriculture may be in particular areas, for example, animal care and feeding, planting, care, and harvesting of a specific crop, or identification and treatment of animal diseases. The instructor could be a local veterinary, a professor from a nearby college of agriculture, or the local secondary teacher of vocational agriculture.

As the percentage of those employed in full-time agriculture decreases, the types of classes offered in the adult vocational classes also changes. There are many part-time farmers now in the United States who hold down full-time positions in areas unrelated to the farm. A large number of part-time farmers are also involved in occupations closely related to plant and animal life. Thus, the kind of classes offered in adult vocational agriculture is a definite reflection of the everyday activity of those enrolled and is indeed a reflection of what those enrolled have requested.

5.2 Business Education

It is logical that those undertaking business education should consist largely of individuals working in the business and industrial offices of the community. The class titles of these courses cover a wide range of categories. With growth in all areas where computers may be utilized, business education has become one of the most popular areas in adult education for employment and one of the most difficult with which to stay up to date. It should also be noted that the computer has drawn all occupations, including the professional ones, closer to business education because of the countless new applications for the computer now taught in adult business classes.

5.3 Distributive Education

Distributive education includes all of the occupations where people who are in any way involved with wholesale or retail sales work. Approximately 18 percent of the workforce in the United States is presently involved in some way in this area. The titles of adult classes offered in distributive education may cover any phase of the operation from a very small store with one or two employees to the very large retail or wholesale operation. This is another area where the appearance of the computer is changing the complexion of most operating procedures. Advertising is a very important aspect of the sales field and one that is given considerable attention in the education of employees. Here, again, it is not unusual for many of the larger companies to hold classes for their own employees.

5.4 Health Occupations

Health occupations are somewhat new to the adult vocational scene in the United States. Local directors of adult vocational education attempt to offer several basic preparatory programs in the health fields and many special courses as well. The special courses are most often designed to upgrade both professional and semiprofessional personnel in their areas of speciality. Hospital staff and directors of nursing education are cooperative in this effort and in nearly every community, classes can be found for training practical nurses, nursing aides, emergency medical technicians, respiratory therapy technicians, x-ray technicians, and personnel in many other allied health areas.

5.5 Home Economics

There was a time when home economics was considered to be a program conducted exclusively for females who were prospective homemakers. This is no longer true. Both sexes are now accommodated at both the secondary and postsecondary levels. Since 1968, the programs of home economics have been categorized under two titles: occupational home economics, and consumer and homemaking. The occupational title was added because some of the areas now offered refer specifically to occupations outside the home, that is, quantity foods, food services, and child care appropriate to the child-care center. The programs offered to adults in the occupational areas of a particular school depend greatly upon the employment situation in the community. Local administrators make every effort to offer programs which will upgrade the individual employees in their specific occupational areas.

The consumer and homemaking title refers to those courses which are specifically designed to create a more intelligent consumer and a more efficient homemaker. In the United States, it is said that the wife in a family situation usually makes more than 80 percent of the decisions regarding when and where to spend the family income. It is important, therefore, that whoever is doing the marketing develops a keen understanding of the values involved.

5.6 Trade and Industrial Education

The largest area of vocational education, in terms of numbers enrolled, is trade and industrial (T & I) education. Nearly 100 percent of those who work in the "trades" and a great many of those employed in heavy industry fall under the "T&I" nomenclature. At the last count, there were some 132 job titles included and the list grows each year. Nearly all of the occupations for which formal apprenticeships are conducted fall under trade and industrial education. It is worth noting that this area of education in the United States is more affected by the political climate than other vocational areas. When the national congress chooses to assist in some sort of emergency situation such as a depression or a war, it will legislate that special classes be conducted to prepare large numbers of personnel in specific areas and those areas usually fall under trade and industrial education. An example of this occurred just prior to the involvement of the United States in the Second World War. Congress passed legislation to initiate the "war production" classes. Nearly every available public school shop or laboratory was suddenly utilized full-time—except when needed by local secondary classes. Factory workers of every description were trained as quickly as possible.

A more recent example of congressional reaction to a national problem was the Comprehensive Employment and Training Act (CETA). Large sums of money were appropriated and expended by the federal government in an effort to train those who were out of work and assist them in finding appropriate employment. The latest legislation in this field, the Job Training Partnership Act (which replaced CETA), is yet another effort on the part of the federal government to alleviate unemployment.

This latest legislation requires that a private industry council be established—usually within the mayor's office of a given city. This council is then required to contract with either private or public schools to conduct specific types of training programs that are designed to meet the training needs of those unemployed in that particular community.

5.7 Technical Education

Technical Education is a title very much in use at the postsecondary level—particularly within the community colleges of the United States. When this title was originated by the US Office of Education, it was designed to be used only by those programs having high levels of mathematics and science regardless of whether the program was secondary or postsecondary.

Although there are at present many high schools designated as "technical" in the larger cities of the United States where standards are very high and the related mathematics and science are indeed a part of the curriculum, the title "technical" is now most commonly used by the postsecondary institutions and often is applied to their entire curriculum. Thus, the adult vocational classes which are reported to the United States Office of Education by the postsecondary institutions are most often reported as "technical."

6. Quality and Qualification of Instructors

There is much concern in the United States about the quality of instruction in adult education for employment. The United States Office of Education requires each State Department to submit periodically a plan outlining how it will conduct vocational education at the local level in its state. This plan must be approved before the state can receive federal funds. These plans present the certification procedures to be followed by the local administrative and instructional staff and detail the involvement of the various state universities who provide the teacher education programs.

Although the requirements established for becoming an instructor in adult education for employment differ somewhat from one state to another, there are at least three characteristics which most local directors and the deans of community colleges look for in potential instructors.

First, they want individuals who have a good work-experience record in the occupational area in which they will be teaching. Second, they want persons who have practised good interpersonal relations with their fellow workers, and they usually request evidence of this from past employers. Third, they desire persons who have either completed or are near completion of an academic course required for certification. If such individuals are not available, then they require evidence that those applying are both willing and capable of completing the required college work for certification.

It should be noted that administrators utilize a multitude of different criteria during the process of staff selection. Some administrators strongly emphasize that only those having a specified number of years' experience in the particular occupational area shall even be considered as potential instructors in the area to be served. Other administrators will indicate that a baccalaureate degree represents the minimum requirement to qualify, but that the occupational experience is most desirable. The specific certification requirements of the particular state must be adhered to closely if the state and federal reimbursements are to be received.

Role Education

Introduction

The person who undertakes learning to get a job, or to obtain a better one, is studying for a role; he or she is seeking to improve his or her performance as a breadwinner. This is only one of the many roles adults fulfil. Some they choose, as, for example, that of trade union activist; others, such as that of citizen, are an inevitable part of the adult condition. Many roles are given to few to fill, but others, such as those of parent or spouse, come to most adults.

The number of roles now open to adults seems to be considerably greater than in previous generations. Whether this is indeed the case and is a reflection of the greater complexity and wider opportunities of contemporary life, whether living is more compartmentalized and fragmented than it used to be or whether the roles have always been there, but have only recently been identified, it is not possible to say for sure. Possibly the truth contains something of all these alternatives.

Education has always had an element of role preparation in it. In the nineteenth century, when universal primary education was introduced, one of its explicit functions was to prepare children to "live in the station to which God had called them". The education of adults had as an early purpose to make people better members of the Christian Church. For many roles, however, there was no systematic training; one learned, as one learned child rearing, from practice, from one's own experience as a child, and from observation of what one's elders did. Or one learned incidentally, as one learned one's civic duty or one's duty as a spouse, from the sermons of one's priest. The belief that it is worthwhile, if not necessary, to acquire role skills and knowledge through participation in systematic study is, for the most part, a product of the twentieth century. Moreover, as the perception of roles has become more specialized, so has the education associated with them.

The employment role of adults has been covered in Section 2b; others can be classified into two broad types: those associated with one's duty as a citizen, with social and cultural life, such as a membership of a club or association; and those related to family life. Some roles may fall under more than one of these headings.

The article *Adult Education for Social Action* looks at the kind of education that is directed towards, or devoted to, improving participation by individuals in the public life of the societies to which they belong, considering different approaches and the problems that arise from particular ideological standpoints. *Political Education* looks at what is meant by political education and reviews major controversies about its working and its objectives. It examines trends in pluralistic societies, the developing countries, and Marxist states.

While it is possible for an individual to ignore the issues raised in the preceding articles, to dodge participation in the political process or any form of public life, few people are able or would wish to avoid the responsibility of fulfilling family roles. In the twentieth century the functions of the family and relationships within it have come under considerable stress, with the lessons of older relatives and of religion, from which adults have traditionally learned to perform their family functions, being decreasingly seen as relevant or adequate. It is to fill this gap that educational opportunities for systematic acquisition of skills related to adults' functions in their family have started to be developed. *Family-life Education* sets out the range of programmes that are classified under that heading, and the methods used, both informal and formal, to achieve its goals, and attempts some evaluation of its achievements.

Adult Education for Social Action

A. M. Thomas

This article looks at the kind of education that is directed towards or devoted to increasing and improving participation by individuals in the public life of their communities, societies, or nations. One endemic difficulty in defining participation is the confusion of ends and means reflected by the fact that "we need education for participants and we get education through participation" (Groombridge 1981). Argument abounds about where to begin.

A second problem that pervades discussion of this form of adult education is whether it must be considered to be part of all adult education, in Mhaiki's sense that "political education gives meaning to all other subjects" (Mhaiki 1973) or whether it is simply "part of adult education in the same way as agricultural extension education, cooperation education, or workers' education" (Kassam 1974). However, despite the relatively lengthy spectrum of individual and organizational attitudes and responses to this form of adult education, any examination of the literature of adult education as a whole that has appeared since the early 1930s will provide support for Groombridge's claim for "the classic connection between adult education, democratic politics, and social progress" (Groombridge 1981).

In all societies, it is clear that some version or vision of citizenship lies behind programs of political education, or any forms of education for participation. Therefore, any consideration of this topic must concentrate on the period since the early 1930s, or at least on the period that "has been marked by an ever accelerated increase of citizens, and a corresponding decrease in subjects, chiefly through the extension of the franchise to ever larger groups" (Brinkmann 1959a). In addition, this increase in numbers of citizens has been accompanied by:

> . . . the continuous development not only of the press, but of the increase in radio and many other vehicles of public education and propaganda into self-sufficient services [which] seems to open an ever widening competitive market where all types of old and new creeds, political and non-political, can hope to win public attention and government support and thus become fairly important factors in the molding of national types. (Brinkmann 1959b)

While this may appear to apply mainly to the wealthier Western democratic states, the fact is that other developments primarily of an economic and technical character make the condition nearly universal. The rapidly increasing dependence of all societies on the learning capacities of more and more of their citizens, over longer and longer periods of their lives, an inescapable consequence of technical and industrial development, means the "mobilization" (Deutsch 1953) of all societies that pursue such objectives. In turn, this means increased demands for participation in public life, on citizens and by citizens. To survive, every nation has had to examine the degree to which those demands contribute to the maintenance or development of the sense of nationality, cultural identity, or national purpose among the citizenry. If these are perceived to be in danger, then some self-conscious intervention in the form of political or citizenship education, directed towards increased participation, ensues. The creation of the folk high schools in Denmark (Rørdam 1965) in the last century, and the use of radio and discussion in such programs as the "Farm Radio Forum" (Schwass 1972) in Canada in this century, are both examples of such interventions.

One factor that has influenced the prominence and form of such intervention has been and remains the state of "development," usually economic, at which a country perceives itself to be. Therefore, there can be found a high preoccupation with this form of adult education in those newly formed countries that achieved independence following the Second World War. In these cases, whole new visions of citizenship had emerged from the struggles for independence, which themselves involved a high level of participation on the part of whole new groups in the society. In many cases, particularly in African countries, these programs represented an attempt to sustain the energy release and commitment that the struggle for independence had provoked, and to turn these resources to the more long-term and tedious tasks of economic growth and national evolution. The radio discussion program of Tanzania is one example of such programming (Hall 1978).

A rather different setting was to be found in the Federal Republic of Germany immediately after the Second World War. There,

> German adult educators were convinced that education for democracy must be the prime purpose in their activities in these post-war years, that all education for adults, whatever the subject matter or other purpose it might have, should, like liberal education, be animated by democratic ideals and contribute to education for democracy. . . that all adult education should be citizenship education. (Titmus 1981)

As a result of this commitment, a wide variety of organizations engaged in the provision of an equally wide variety of courses and other opportunities directed towards the improvement of democratic citizenship. As the new Republic became stronger and more confident, interest in this type of adult education declined, though even now activities devoted to citizenship education remain considerable.

A variation on these activities can be found in those societies with normative codes of behavior embedded in their legal structure and prevailing official codes of conduct. In these countries, which include all of the socialist states, and theocracies such as Iran, all of which have distinct visions of ideal citizenship, "political education" is carried out by means of a web of political organizations, the chief of which is the political party.

> Participation in decision-making is routinely possible for the Chinese adult. Small discussion groups, apparently political in nature, exist everywhere and every adult is expected to participate. (Batdorf and MacNeil 1974)

Implicit in both of these examples is the notion of an "ideal citizen," and presumably an ideal society composed of such citizens. While the hope of achieving such a state may be and may have always been fragile, nevertheless the notion of a knowable ideal of citizenship, delineated in considerable if not total detail, that is, of a single goal to be aimed at, remains, and influences the type of education for participation that occurs.

In contrast to this are the "common law" societies, where citizenship is defined by means of a few positive relationships, such as freedom of speech, freedom of associations, freedom from violations of human rights, and a few negative ones, forbidding behavior of an outright seditious, treasonable, or antisocial nature. No clearly revealed ideal of citizenship is involved beyond these basic rules, and indeed the constant evolution of new forms of behaviors is actively encouraged. The fact that a number of these countries, principally the United States, Canada, and Australia, have also been recipients of large and continuous numbers of immigrants, has not only supported the necessity of evolving notions of citizenship, but shaped the nature of adult education for participation (citizenship education) dramatically. While sporadic efforts are made to include the entire citizenry in self-conscious programs of citizenship education, such as those associated with carefully planned anniversaries like the Australian Bicentennial celebrations, for most citizens of these countries citizenship education is confined to the teaching of customs, rules, and languages to new arrivals.

The issues that surround education for participation continue to be related to objectives and methods. For example, in liberal–democratic theory, it is never quite clear whether the overriding objective is the development of the "liberal" individual who arrives at his or her full maturity by means of participating, responsibly, in the liberal state, or whether it is the development and maintenance of a humane state which can only be created and maintained by means of the participation of free, thoughtful, responsible individuals (Locke 1973, Mill 1921). Presumably the two are inextricable, and the dilemma could be dismissed as an intellectual one if it were not for an endemic conflict between two traditions of programs that bear powerful resemblances, namely adult education and community development. In most countries, these two activities often exist together. Nevertheless, there is a point at which the collective objectives of the community developer come into direct conflict with the individual objectives of the adult educator. Since both involve participation as goals and as methods, their conjunction is frequent, as is the confusion and conflict that often result. Neither Coady in his development of the St. Francis Xavier Cooperative Movement in Canada in the 1930s (Coady 1939), nor Freire in his practical and theoretical development of "consciousness raising," particularly in Africa and Latin America (Freire 1970), have been able to resolve the difficulties involved between the two approaches.

Nevertheless, supporters of each of these schools frequently share views with respect to appropriate methods for improving participation. In most cases they are extremely skeptical of the value of formal classes, and even of the usefulness of the participation of formal agencies in this kind of adult education:

> There are three sets of problems associated with education for participation .... First the administrative regulations and requirements established for other purposes are irrelevant for much of the provision .... Second there is a need for more tutors who are able to undertake adult education for participation with a full understanding of the possibilities and constraints .... Third there are perennial problems of politics and balance. (Groombridge 1981)

These misgivings seem to be widely shared, and there is repeated evidence of strong preference for education arising out of some form of participation. There has been increased understanding that such participation does not have to be on an extremely large scale, such as that represented by the Canadian television discussion program called "People Talking Back" (Thomas 1979), but that "there is much evidence to suggest that people learn to participate, and that this learning can begin in local, functional, and voluntary settings before reaching out to encompass the policy itself" (Groombridge 1981). However, much of the discussion reveals a preference for reaching out to encompass the policy itself on the large scale, and it is important to acknowledge some of the real difficulties and dangers involved in such projects. The difficulties lie with the fact that learning is doing, and learning to participate effectively in public must take place in public, and must involve as many members of the public as possible. Not only is this expensive, involving access to substantial resources, financial and other kinds, such as broadcasting networks, but such activities are usually distrusted by the political establishment, no matter how democratic in character. It is properly distrusted by that group, because in itself the activity represents interference with the normal or current patterns of communication upon which political power depends. Kassam, speaking of Tanzanian activities, commented that:

> It is interesting to note that one of the problems faced by about seventeen percent of the professional adult educators as revealed by the study ... was paradoxically the lack of cooperation from some local teachers and politicians. One of the main reasons advanced was that very often the local teachers and politicians felt overshadowed by the political impact on and the general popularity of the adult educator with the people. (Kassam 1974)

In addition, there is no way to "experiment" in this form. Once the public means by which this kind of adult education is accomplished are brought into play, the program itself becomes a public event, and both the world and the consequences become real. For that reason, research in this area is difficult to accomplish. Most of what exists consists of descriptive studies of programs, some of which are reported here.

In this light, it might seem that such educational activities are virtually impossible, but they are undertaken sporadically, despite the attendant risks. It would appear that timing is critical, and successful undertakings are often associated with unexpected events, in the form of some national disaster, or as the result of the introduction of a new technology, the true importance of which is not fully understood.

> While the general course of . . . development has exhibited an increase in the active collaboration of the mass of citizens, in public affairs, it must not be inferred that such a tendency is necessarily indicative of a rise in political standards. On the contrary, it may often lead to new forms of corruption and oppression. (Brinkmann 1959a)

The originators of liberal–democratic theory placed the ultimate political power in the hands of the individual, who alone can learn. At the same time, they wrote a treatise on education, indicating their beliefs that participation alone would not lead to ideal politics or an ideal society. Perhaps that is the reason why adult education for participation, despite the mixed feelings it generates, and despite the ever-present danger of merely being a brand of propaganda, remains for many educators and politicians at the zenith of all adult education. Clearly, whatever particular strategy is involved, it can no longer be the difference between learning and not learning about public matters, or of participating or not participating in them. Any intervention by adult educators is an intervention in learning and participation already taking place, often with very specific objectives involved. To ignore that fact is to misinterpret contemporary society and to underestimate the importance of such interventions.

Bibliography

Batdorf L, MacNeil T 1974 The making of a responsible person. *Convergence* 7(3): 14–17

Brinkmann C 1959a Citizenship. *Encyclopedia of the Social Services*, Vol. 3. Macmillan, New York

Brinkmann C 1959b Civil education. *Encyclopedia of the Social Services*, Vol. 3. Macmillan, New York

Coady M M 1939 *Masters of Their Own Destiny: The Story of the Antigonish Movement of Adult Education through Economic Cooperation.* Harper, New York

Deutsch K W 1953 *Nationalism and Social Communication: An Enquiry into the Foundations of Nationality.* MIT Press, Cambridge, Massachusetts

Freire P 1970 *Pedagogy of the Oppressed.* Herder and Herder, New York

Groombridge B 1981 Adult education and political participation: Self-critical notes from Britain. *Convergence* 14(1): 44–55

Hall B L 1978 Continuity in adult education and the political struggle. *Convergence* 11(1): 8–16

Kassam Y O 1974 Political education vis-à-vis adult education in Tanzania: The dynamics of interaction. *Convergence* 7(4): 40–49

Locke J 1973 *The Educational Writing of John Locke.* Cambridge University Press, London

Mhaiki P J 1973 Political education and adult education. *Convergence* 6(1): 15–21

Mill J S 1921 *John Stuart Mill on Education.* Teachers College Press, Columbia University, New York

Rørdam T 1965 *The Danish Folk High Schools.* Det Danske Selskab, Copenhagen

Schwass R 1972 National Farm Radio Forum. Unpublished doctoral dissertation. University of Toronto, Ontario Institute for Studies in Education, Toronto, Ontario

Thomas A M 1979 *Report on People Talking Back.* Canadian Association for Adult Education, Toronto, Ontario

Titmus C J 1981 *Strategies for Adult Education: Practices in Western Europe.* Open University Press, Milton Keynes

Political Education

H. Entwistle

This article looks at the problem of defining what counts as political education for adults and focuses on some of the controversies about its aims and functions. It notes the trends and tendencies in affluent pluralistic societies, in developing countries, and in Marxist states, and concludes that a major problem in this area is the almost total absence of any empirical research.

1. Liberal Education as Political Education

Little systematic evidence has emerged from empirical research on what constitutes effective political education, either in terms of the degree of a person's commitment to political activity and understanding or its ideological bias. However, from the evidence of voting behaviour and participation in pressure groups, it seems clear that the greater the length of one's formal schooling, the more likely one is to be a participant and the better one's understanding of political issues. Historically, a consequence of this has been that educational provision for adults has often been "remedial" or "compensatory", concerned either with adults who have had no formal schooling, or those whose schooling terminated at the elementary level. A second consequence has been that groups and associations promoting the education of their members, as part of their pursuit of political aims, have been as likely to offer a curriculum consisting of the study of literature, philosophy, history, and science, as one explicitly focused upon the political culture itself. For example, teachers of young adults in Chartist schools reported that "unless there were some stirring local and political topics", they spent their time lecturing on English history, poetry, and drama.

The idea of the pursuit of political education through nonpolitical studies is as old as Plato. The protracted political education of the guardians of Plato's *Republic* consisted of the study of mathematics and mathematically oriented subjects like astronomy and harmonics, not of political theory and institutions. In modern democratic states where all citizens are, in some sense, guardians, this tradition of seeking the political good through general, liberal studies has persisted. And, at a more fundamental educational level, from John Stuart Mill to Freire there has been the insistence that the achievement of literacy itself is the cardinal means towards political understanding. Hence, the first problem in trying to give an account of current provision for the political education of adults is that of deciding what it is that best constitutes a political education: a good general education or one which focuses explicitly upon political content.

With reference to advanced, industrial, pluralist societies, many different agencies provide for the education of adults: political parties and groups, consumer, environmental, and community groups, churches, cooperatives, labour unions, leisure and recreational clubs, philanthropic societies, local school boards, and universities, but rarely the state itself (except for indirect financial provision). Generally speaking, it would be true to say that the more specific and restricted the end for which an association exists, the more likely it is to provide political education explicitly, with its teaching biased towards an understanding of the particular issue which is its raison d'être. Some would question whether this kind of biased provision properly constitutes an educational experience or ought, properly, to be characterized as indoctrination: one person's "understanding" is another person's prejudice or bigotry. This is a problem not only with the teaching supplied by political parties and groups having ideologically slanted aims, but also with the political education which is often explicitly promoted by churches. The "moral majority", for instance, claims that political conservatism is implicit in fundamentalist Christianity in general, not only in its particular crusades against abortion and pornography, which are aims shared, more or less, by other Christian denominations. Others however would subscribe to more radical political and social aims. The point to be underlined here is that, in pluralist societies, membership of almost any voluntary association—even the local tennis club—can constitute an education or training in politics.

2. Education for Citizenship

The more disinterested view, that the best possible general education also constitutes the best possible political education, is tied to the conception of education for citizenship. Citizenship implies a satisfaction with the political and social status quo. Classically, the citizen is a free and autonomous member of the polity—a cause of both satisfaction and pride. To the extent that there is discontent, the change necessary to restore the citizen's confidence will be through peaceful and, probably, piecemeal reform within the existing political status quo. "Empowerment", a keyword for adult educationalists, will come from learning how to harness one's intellectual resources in order to maximize one's rights and privileges as a citizen. Political education will aim at producing patriotic, but also rational, critical, and active individuals.

Perhaps the most serious and growing problem for the citizen comes from the modern bureaucracy, and it is far from clear what kind of skill and knowledge would constitute the best possible education for coping with this, not merely for resisting, defensively, the threat from bureaucracy (Shakespeare's "insolence of office") but also for exploiting the benefits (welfare and other public services) which make for the burgeoning of bureaucracies. Again, there appears some evidence that a good general education is the best "empowerment" to cope with bureaucracy. However, in Sweden special consideration is being given to this problem. Abrahamsson has identified the bureaucratic threat to citizens as resulting from "knowledge gaps" between authorities and citizens, resulting in "missing" or "frozen" dialogue (Abrahamsson 1982). Implicitly, this requires encouragement of the kind of dialogue which Freire has insisted is fundamental to political education, and it is interesting that a continuing research project in Sweden has been concerned with "the study circle as a pedagogical situation".

At first glance, the model of the patriotic, autonomous, and free, but rational and critical, participant citizen best fits modern, advanced, industrial, social democracies, where free enterprise capitalism, its "unacceptable face" softened by the institutions of the welfare state, appears to have afforded most people a life-style of such quality that they feel a stake in the status quo and eschew "extremist" solutions to remaining social problems. But, apart from the threat to this view posed by growing and persistent unemployment and civil disorder, there remain not only the injustices and inequities suffered by marginal groups and individuals, and those in the decaying city cores of affluent societies, but also those which afflict the vast majority of people in developing countries. For this overwhelming majority of the human race, the classical citizen model of political education is inadequate. A much more radical account of political education seems required to address their dilemma.

3. Radical Solutions

Advocates of radical social solutions have tended to criticize historical provision for adult education on two counts. First, however well-intentioned it may be, it has been dismissed as provision for the disadvantaged, as an instrument of social control, often hampering radical political activity and leaving poverty and deprivation much as it found it (Lovett 1980). As an imposition by educators, it has signally failed to identify the predicaments and dilemmas facing disadvantaged adults. And, by using the methods and content of formal educational institutions (university *extension*, for example), it has merely offered adults more of the kind of experience which failed them and with which they suffered disenchantment when in elementary and secondary school.

Further, it is argued, those who do acquire a taste for the traditional fare of adult classes experience not a radical questioning of the status quo, but a "high culture" curriculum embodying "high status" knowledge. Consequently, working class participants in adult classes acquire a taste for "bourgeois" knowledge, and far from learning to question the existing state of the social universe, they develop and come to defend middle-class tastes and values. On this view, imposition of the traditional "liberal" curriculum is an attempt to draw the radical teeth from adult education through a safe, disinterested curriculum which neglects skills and knowledge essential to fuel radical social criticism.

This leads to a second criticism of conventional provision. It has failed to touch those for whom it was contrived, appealing only to what Hoggart has called "an earnest minority", utterly untypical of the underprivileged as a whole (Hoggart 1958). However, Hoggart also considers this minority "a saving remnant", implying to them a leadership role as Gramsci's "organic intellectuals".

Given the history of adult political education in failing to touch large numbers of citizens, major questions concerning its function remain: how far is it most effectively aimed at the cultivation of an elite from amongst the underprivileged themselves and how far should alternatives be sought which engage the majority?

As to the organization of radical, political education, its advocates claim that this should be independent of those public and private institutions which have traditionally provided schooling for adults. It is to be controlled by its clientele and is intended not to stimulate political activity in the apathetic and indifferent, but to serve as an educational resource available to adults already having political purposes of their own. Favoured alternatives combine two notions, in particular "community development" and "participatory research".

4. Community Education

The idea of community education has a number of differing implications as Roberts, Jarvis, and Fletcher demonstrate (Roberts 1979, Jarvis 1983, Fletcher 1980). For instance when tied to the concept of community development, its political implications lie in the objective of deriving the education of adults in disadvantaged communities from attempts to enrich community life through the resolution of economic and social problems within the community itself.

Community education does not encourage the disinterested pursuit of knowledge of the arts and sciences, nor does it attempt to raise the quality of life through leisure or recreational studies. On the contrary, it concentrates pragmatically and, hence, "relevantly" upon the problems of local communities and the groups and individuals within them. It is argued that the education of these is ill-served by educational provision from outside by public and voluntary institutions which seek to impose an irrelevant "liberal" curriculum. On this view, the vast majority of adults decline to participate in adult education, not because of apathy or hostility towards education, but because they deem existing provision to be indifferent to their dilemmas: asking for bread, they are offered a stone.

There is a growing literature on community education, but some of its limitations and possibilities, as exemplified by an experiment in the city of Liverpool in England, are described by Lovett (1975), who sought to bring educational resources to bear on community problems. In fact, Lovett found a demand for courses related to personal development and recreation, rather than to skills and knowledge directly pertinent to community problems. To the extent that local residents became active in community affairs, it tended to be a by-product of their participation in personally oriented educational activities, again lending some support to the view that political sophistication is associated with the improved self-image that comes from participating successfully in a more general educational experience. From his own experiences in Northern Ireland and a review of North American examples of community oriented, adult political education, Lovett (1980) underlines that what underprivileged adults need is not so much courses which cause them to form associations for political activity, but access to agencies which function as educational resources for groups already committed to political activity aimed at community development.

5. Participatory Research

Participatory research is based on the assumption that the research which is necessary for resolving practical problems facing communities is likely to be most productive when the experience of the proposed beneficiaries is canvassed by experts. It is argued that imposed solutions, the outcome of research exclusively by experts, are flawed and provide no educational experience, political or otherwise, for the beneficiaries. With participatory research, ordinary people become creative participants in reform, not just objects of it. Moreover, critics of existing provision for adult education see this kind of participation as essential to removing the widespread apathy towards adult education of those who need it most. On this view, it is not innate stupidity or moral turpitude which blinds the disadvantaged to the benefits of what is clearly in their own best interest, so much as the irrelevance to their perceived problems of what is designed for them by experts.

The notions of community education and participatory research have seemed peculiarly appropriate options for the political education of disadvantaged adults with little or with unsuccessful formal schooling, especially in minority groups like the native people of North America, as well as in communities in decaying urban centres. But as Roberts (1979) observes, the techniques of community development have also seemed attractive to relatively "liberated" people—more or less prosperous suburban and urban groups. In particular, it has been a recurrent phenomenon within the history of adult education that institutions intended for the education of manual workers have been exploited by high school and college graduates for their own continuing education; an example of the sociological "law" that the middle class will appropriate for its own benefit any social institution intended to benefit the underprivileged.

However, participatory research has found its strongest advocates amongst educationalists interested in problems of developing countries, where political and educational models devised in Western democracies have seemed inadequate, if not completely inapplicable. In this context, "empowerment" requires a political education which is, at one and the same time, more radical and more fundamental than is appropriate in advanced industrial societies: Western notions of citizenship have little relevance in the political contexts of developing countries. The best known recipe for political education in this context is Freire's "pedagogy of the oppressed".

6. *Pedagogy of the Oppressed*

Freire conceives political education as an outcome of education for literacy. Although he does not make the point explicitly, it follows from his ideological stance that political education which consists of teaching and learning about existing "mainstream" political institutions would merely be an example of what he calls "extensionism", serving only further to alienate the oppressed. On this view, what the oppressed need is not knowledge of how to engage with traditional political institutions, for this would only signal their acceptance of the existing social hegemony. What they need is knowledge and skill appropriate to the creation of novel, liberating political institutions, which uniquely address their own peculiar predicaments. However, since developing countries not only lack traditional Western democratic institutions, but also have very high rates of adult illiteracy, Freire conceives political education as, primarily, the conquest of illiteracy (Freire 1974).

Historically, widespread illiteracy has been seen as a major instrument of oppression and social control, a gross impediment to the attainment of citizenship and mass participation in democratic political institutions. Where illiteracy is still rife, political radicals have seen no hope of mass liberation in the absence of a literate population. Perhaps the most energetic campaigns to promote literacy have been pursued in Latin America, notably in Cuba and Nicaragua, where teams of high-school students have been sent into villages to subject illiterate peasants to intensive instruction in reading and writing, evidently with some success.

But Freire's pedagogy of the oppressed is less didactic than this. For him, literacy is but an avenue towards "conscientization" and, hence, liberation of the person. The pursuit of this essentially political objective through the education of adults required the transformation of both content and method. Because adults were to be the target of the literacy programme, the unrealistic vocabularies of traditional reading primers had to be rejected. These vocabularies were "disconnected from life, centred on words emptied of the reality they are meant to represent, [and were] lacking in concrete activity". Instead, the approach to literacy would be based upon identification of a culturally realistic vocabularly aimed at "the problem of teaching adults how to read in relation to the awakening of their consciousness". The words which would be the basis of their literacy would be *their* words, already familiar in the daily articulation of dilemmas and predicaments.

The teacher who would liberate the oppressed must first learn the vocabulary of the oppressed, not attempt to impose the language of an alien political culture, however democratic that might be. A liberating pedagogy would be a dialogue, implying a reciprocal relationship between teacher and learner; not a matter of an authority teaching the "correct" vocabulary of politics, but of teachers and learners together generating the relevant language for understanding and grappling with their own peculiar oppressions and opportunities. Learning political participation requires rejection of the authoritarian pedagogy of "banking" and the participation of learners in their own education.

In turn, this insistence on focussing upon a vocabulary which addresses the peasants' own felt dilemmas implies that their political learning should be concerned with institutions at the micro level. One learns political responsibility only through experiencing political activity in those cultural, economic, and other institutions which are the fabric of daily social life. Freire's conception is also consistent with the notion of political and educational activity through participatory research.

Freire's pedagogy was developed, originally, with the support of the government of Brazil where, however, its radical potential has made him persona non grata. In practical terms its impact has perhaps been greatest in Africa; in Guinea Bissau, for example, where Freire has himself worked and in Tanzania where others have applied his pedagogy to the peculiar circumstances of that attempt to establish a uniquely African socialism based on the principles of *ujaama* (Hall 1975). There especially, Freire's insistence upon the political education of adults has resonated with Nyerere's own educational priority—the primacy of adult education—and his political philosophy, involving the belief that "socialism cannot function from above": it must be understood and accepted by "enlightened masses". There has been discussion of how far Freire's pedagogy is relevant to different social and political circumstances, especially in advanced industrial societies, where his work has been more inspirational philosophically than influential in provoking practical initiatives. However, as I have argued elsewhere, Freire's pedagogy echoes strategies for learning and teaching which, historically, have characterized adult political education at its best in those once "developing" countries which are now affluent, industrial societies (Entwistle 1981).

That there should be similarities between classical conceptions of adult political education and its modern manifestation in developing countries is understandable, not only because both have been attempts to bring political awakening to oppressed, educationally deprived masses, but also because their principles would constitute a creative approach to education in any time and place and with any kind of clientele: the attempt, through a reciprocal relationship between learner and teacher to bring the different worlds of daily experience and of "scientific" discourse into fruitful juxtaposition.

7. Political Education in Marxist States

In their different ways, adult political education in both the industrial West and in developing countries is rooted in assumptions about democracy. However, it is the received view in all but Marxist states that Marxist states have no interest in encouraging democratic values and institutions. In that context, it is assumed, whatever serves as political learning and teaching must be dismissed as propaganda or indoctrination: implicitly, it cannot be dignified as education. Certainly, in the Soviet Union, for example, adult political education is entirely in the hands of the Communist Party, whether in Party schools and universities or through mass media controlled by the Party (Grant 1979, Matthews 1982, Zajda 1980). However, a distinction has to be drawn between the political education of the communist elite (Party functionaries at all levels in the system) and the rank and file citizen. Only some 5 percent of Soviet citizens are members of the Communist Party, not necessarily from disinclination to join, but because membership is highly selective, vouchsafed only to those with appropriate credentials. One of the principal means of securing these is through membership of the *Komsomol*, the tier of the Party Youth Organization catering for adolescents and young adults up to the age of 27. Branches of the *Komsomol* are to be found in workplaces, colleges, and universities. More political in character than the lower level Pioneers organizations, these strongly emphasize the study of Marxist–Leninist ideology. Successful students will become candidates for recruitment to *politschkola* (political schools) which exist at three levels from elementary evening schools to full-time political universities, each offering courses in Marxist–Leninist theory and in administration and propaganda techniques, aimed at preparing candidates for posts at the various levels of the Party *apparat*.

Though the work in these Party schools is ideologically biased, it is probably no exaggeration to claim that it provides a genuine political education; that is the study of principles (economic, political, administrative) fitting the student to solve problems inherent in managing a modern industrial state. On the other hand, it is probable that what is offered to the vast majority of Soviet citizens is socialization through indoctrination, with the emphasis on "loyalty, obedience, and conformity" (Zajda 1980). Or, as Morison puts it, "The task of the political educator is to ensure that the creative energies of the population are willingly directed towards collectivist rather than individual goals" (Morison 1983). Within the Marxist states, of course, this political socialization process is characterized positively as concerned with the education of the "new socialist man", exhibiting the virtues of love (of country, humankind and fellow workers), honesty, courage, and discipline, especially in one's devotion to work. Rather than in formal classes, this political socialization of the masses is most likely to occur through the press (especially the wall-newspaper), radio, television, literature, cinema, theatre and museums.

8. Mass Media

It is impossible to consider adult political education in any kind of modern society without reference to the mass media. But in the West, with the notable exception of a writer like Raymond Williams, little attention has been paid to the political "miseducation" inherent in the mass media, and to the kind of reforms necessary to democratize the press and broadcasting. The assumption in democratic societies is that the survival of a free (however biased and irresponsible) press is sufficient to guarantee political well-being. One of the few research papers addressed to the problem of adult political education has shown the need for, and possibilities of, cultivating media literacy (Brookfield 1985).

9. Need for Research

This article began by noting the paucity of research in the area of adult political education. An example of this can be seen in the proceedings of the American Adult Education Research conferences of 1984 and 1985. In the former, amongst a total of 50 papers reporting research, only 3 can even remotely be construed as being in the area of political education. In the latter, the comparative figures are 40 and 2. At the 1985 conference of the Canadian Association for the Study of Adult Education, none of 32 papers was concerned with political education. It is true that a growing body of research in the areas of adult literacy, education for the workplace, and the position of women in society will have political overtones and, hence, implications for political education. But it is evident that there is a need for the development of research outside the discipline of politics itself, focusing on the needs and problems of adults confronting the political system, and evaluating initiatives for adult education whose aim is the enrichment of the political culture of individual citizens and the political activities of groups.

See also: Community Education and Community Development; Ideologies in Adult Education

Bibliography

Abrahamsson K 1982 Knowledge gaps, bureaucracy and citizen communication. *Commun. Res.* 7

Brookfield S 1985 Adult education as political detoxification: Towards political literacy for adults. *Proc. Adult Educ. Res. Conf.* Arizona State University, Tempe, Arizona

Entwistle H 1981 The political education of adults. In: Heater D, Gillespie J A (eds.) 1981 *Political Education in Flux.* Sage, London, pp. 233–55

Fletcher C 1980 The theory of community education and its relation to adult education. In: Thompson J L (ed.) 1980 *Adult Education for a Change.* Hutchinson, London, pp. 65–82

Freire P 1974 *Education for Critical Consciousness.* Seabury Press, New York

Grant N 1979 *Soviet Education*, 4th edn. Penguin Books, Harmondsworth

Hall B 1975 *Adult Education and the Development of Socialism in Tanzania.* East African Literature Bureau, Kampala

Hoggart R 1958 *The Uses of Literacy.* Penguin Books, Harmondsworth

Jarvis P 1983 *Adult and Continuing Education.* Croom Helm, London

Lovett T 1975 *Adult Education: Community Development and the Working Class.* Ward Lock Educational, London

Lovett T 1980 Adult education and community action. In: Thompson J L (ed.) 1980 *Adult Education for a Change.* Hutchinson, London, pp. 155–73

Matthews M 1982 *Education in the Soviet Union.* Allen and Unwin, London

Morison J 1983 The political content of education in the USSR. In: Tomiak J J (ed.) 1983 *Soviet Education in the 1980s.* Croom Helm, London, pp. 143–71

Price R F 1977 *Marx and Education in Russia and China.* Croom Helm, London

Roberts H 1979 *Community Development: Learning and Action.* University of Toronto Press, Toronto

Thompson J L (ed.) 1980 *Adult Education for a Change.* Hutchinson, London

Zajda J I 1980 *Education in the USSR.* Pergamon Press, Oxford

Family-life Education

M. E. Brillinger and D. H. Brundage

Family-life education is a broad and amorphous field. Anything which contributes to the total growth and well-being of the family—physical, mental, emotional, economic, spiritual—can be included under the rubric of education for family living. Literacy programmes, population planning, health care, agricultural development, disease control, nutrition, improved housing, can all be considered aspects of family-life education. Without denying the importance of such programmes, especially for Third World countries, the concept of family-life education will here be restricted to a narrower definition as viewed in industrial countries. In addition to reviewing current definitions of family-life education, this entry will deal with goals, topics for learning, a history of the development of the discipline, emerging trends, reasons for increasing interest in the field, major settings providing education for family living, national and international organizations, structures and models, research, and future needs.

Family-life education includes "any activity by any group or medium aimed at imparting information concerning family relationships and providing the opportunity for people to approach their present and future family relationships with greater understanding" (Vanier Institute of the Family 1971). The definition includes those deliberate learning experiences which help to develop the personalities of individuals to their fullest as present and future family members. It excludes any learning that is unintentional or that is directly interpersonal and clinical without specific reference to the family.

In a statement issued by the National Council on Family Relations declaring an official position, family-life education was defined as a programme

> to guide individuals and families in improving their interpersonal relationships and furthering their maximum development. It seeks to improve their quality of life throughout the entire range of human development. This includes physical and emotional growth, individual sexual development, dating and courtship, marriage and parenthood, while continually emphasizing the importance of personal integrity and family responsibility. (1970 p. 186)

The family is the main mental-health unit in today's society. Its main functions are to stabilize and enhance the growth of the adult members and provide a context for the growth and development of the children. There is a close interrelationship among parent, family, and mental-health education. Family-life education is designed to assist the family in being more effective in sustaining the mental health of all its members. Its goal is to help individuals develop interpersonal skills and more enriching human relationships through learning how to relate effectively within their families. Brown (1964) stated that "programmes which strengthen family life are those designed to help families realize, as fully as possible, their own potentialities for creative living in the cultures to which they belong" (p. 823).

Topics for learning can include husband–wife relationships, parent–child relationships, child care and development, sex education, dating, family planning, marriage breakdown and rehabilitation, and personal development and mental health (when directly associated with family relationships). Concerns such as religious or moral doctrines, sociopolitical issues such as poverty, purely theoretical aspects of psychology and sociology, physical health and nutrition, or etiquette are not included.

Informal teaching of parents about child rearing has been practised for centuries but only in the twentieth century has parental education for effective family life become a recognized discipline. In industrialized nations in the nineteenth and twentieth centuries, some of the beliefs and skills formerly learned in the family and community were no longer taught there. As social organizations began to assume more of the functions previously performed by families, there came an awareness of inadequacies in family life. "Radical changes in the roles of women in occupational and economic behaviour, and in the whole industrialization–urbanization movement let everyone know that the world was not what it had been a few years earlier" (Kerckhoff 1964 p. 881). As people turned to external structures for help with alleviating strains experienced in homes, the beginnings of a more formal family-life education movement stirred. The rise of the fields of home economics and child psychology and development, the flourishing of the social and behavioural sciences, and the increased respectability of psychoanalysis contributed to the emerging discipline of family-life education.

Family-life education is truly a folk movement. It has sprung up as a response to needs voiced by people themselves. Even today when a need in a particular area is felt, someone or some agency moves in to begin to address it. Programmes and projects spring up overnight and as quickly cease. The amorphous nature of the field may be demonstrated by an examination of the variety of disciplines and institutions which have an interest in and contribute to it: sociology, psychology, education, medicine, genetics, home economics, nursing, social work, the church, law, anthropology, and marriage and family therapy. There are considerable difficulties in developing definitions, organization, research, and theory that will help practice. The scope is vast and the pieces constantly shifting.

While it is difficult to establish a definition of the field, it is possible to note trends and an emerging consensus. One is the emphasis on the improvement of mental health and the development of human relationships. These two interdependent goals play a strong role in family-life programmes in industrial societies. A second trend has been a move to a more personal approach. Family-life educators and leaders are less interested in the family as a social institution, and more concerned with actual preparation for personal participation in various stages of family living. A third trend has been a move toward increased professionalization and formalization of the field. Although family-life education was originally a response to the people by the people themselves, and is still largely carried out by voluntary associations, there is additionally an increased involvement in family-life education by government, education, social service agencies, and the media of mass communications. Leaders and teachers of family-life programmes, whether volunteers or paid persons, are now expected to have considerable training.

Ironically, family-life education, a field which came into being as a result of public demand, still has to fight for public acceptance as a field of study. In times of economic constraint, family-life programmes and research are viewed by authorities as luxuries, vulnerable to reduced funding. Some people still hold the idea that families are private and should not be intruded upon, while others maintain an independent stance, arguing that they do not need to learn how to be better parents, partners, or family members. Such myths die hard in certain segments of society.

Recent increased interest in the 1970s in the family and education of its adult members to improve family functioning can be attributed to a number of factors. Chief among them is the growing awareness of the family unit as a central educative agent in which social relationships are developed, values and attitudes shaped, and predispositions for lifelong learning established. The social context which most directly affects human beings is their family. A second factor is the rate of social change in most societies which dictates a need to redefine the roles of adult family members. Where tradition once established the norms for family behaviour, parents are now being challenged to examine their roles and to accommodate to the demands of changing family structures and functions. The state, also, has shown an increasing tendency to intervene in family life for reasons of economic and social necessity. National programmes of planned parenthood, for example, have been established in a number of countries to curtail population growth and to promote improved standards of living. The belief, too, that parenting skills, knowledge, and attitudes can be learned through programmes of education as opposed to learning through generational ties has given rise to a host of such programmes around the world (Croake and Glover 1977, Fine 1980).

The impetus for family-life education programmes is based on the pervasive nature of the family life cycle in which each new phase of the cycle gives rise to new learning needs. In the past these learning needs were met through informal learning activities such as reading, seeking advice from peers and professionals (doctors, priests), and reflecting on personal experience. Some of these activities are now being offered as formal learning programmes.

Contemporary education for family living takes many forms. Most of them relate more to learning *about* families rather than to learning *in* families. Most programmes and services are directed primarily to individuals who either are currently, or are preparing to be, family members. Three major settings currently offer family-life education for adults: religious, social, and professional organizations; mass media; and schools and universities.

The most comprehensive programmes in educating for family living have been developed and implemented by religious and secular organizations. Hundreds of diverse organizations and agencies are involved in offering a wide array of courses, workshops, and services covering areas such as parent education, marriage preparation, marriage enrichment, child development, family health and nutrition, sexuality, single parenting, separation and divorce, blended families, family developmental stages, child and spouse abuse, and family budgeting. Traditionally invested with a belief in marriage and the family, the church is one institution in Western society which encompasses complete families and whose clientele spans the entire life cycle from birth to death. Many religious groups are involved in educative matters relevant to the well-being of families. Besides religious denominations, there are community organizations such as the Young Men's and Young Women's Christian Associations (YMCA and YWCA) and the Family Service Association of America as well as volunteer organizations that include a focus on family education in the form of courses and workshops offered to adults on issues related to marriage and family living.

There continues to be great public influence exerted by television, the movie industry, newspapers, magazines, radio, and popular books on molding the values, ideas, attitudes, and beliefs about marital and family living. While the quality of the input may at times be questioned, they nonetheless offer alternative structures, role models, information, and advice on a wide range of family-related issues.

Schools have for some time been introducing more and more learning opportunities for students in marriage and family issues. Many universities and colleges offer credit and noncredit continuing education courses in marriage and family for adults. Adult learning under the auspices of elementary and secondary schools may take the form of evening classes on parenting and family topics, programmes sponsored by parent–teacher associations, and counselling offered to parents by individual teachers and education consultants.

Most countries have developed organizations to deal with their particular concerns in family-life education for adults. These often grow out of professional associations having a special interest in the family, or government agencies giving leadership to educational, social, and health concerns of the family. Some examples include the International Union of Family Organizations (France), the National Council on Family Relations (US), the Research Institute of Adult Education, the USSR Academy of Pedagogical Sciences (USSR), the Study Commission on the Family (the United Kingdom), and the Vanier Institute of the Family (Canada). Further information about agencies of this nature may also be found in various government departments in most countries, or through international agencies such as UNESCO, International Red Cross, Organisation for Economic Co-operation and Development (OECD), and Cooperative for American Relief Everywhere (CARE).

One effective method of education for family living is the use of programmes that involve the total family, in which parents and children participate in activities that stress skill development and attitudinal change in order to enhance family functioning. This particular expression of family education is a significant development of the field because it recognizes the essential strength of the family to support and influence its members. Not only is such programming used in crisis intervention and for prevention of disorders in children, but it may also be used for developing the skills of all members of a family in fulfilling their obligations, and for facilitating the development of the potential of each member. Examples of models using total family involvement in intergenerational learning experiences have been described by Otto (1976) and Sawin (1979, 1982). Another popular format for full family interaction is the family council (Dreikurs and Soltz 1964) or family problem solving (Gordon 1970). This has been found effective in training the young to assume responsibilities and to share in the decision-making processes of the family.

As marriage and family patterns undergo major restructuring, there is a need to develop a new awareness of human affiliative needs and the special opportunities inherent in family bondings. With increasing incidence of step-parenting, adoption, and foster parenting, the concept of "family" is being reinterpreted in the 1980s to include bonds other than those of blood or law. Consequently, skills of group building and group process, long a special interest of the adult educator, are being recognized as relevant to family maintenance. This expanded view of family life increases the importance of the socialization functions of the family of origin in preparing and helping all members to fulfill their affiliative needs and contribute to harmonious life patterns with their intimates and acquaintances. The development thus far of the educative role of the family presages the increasing importance of learning for family living as an essential preparation for personal relationships throughout life, in addition to its more focused parent education role.

Research and writing in family-life education relate to virtually every facet of family functioning: from procreation and the socialization of children through to the concerns of parenting a parent in the later stages of the family life cycle. Five dominant categories are evident. The first relates to family planning, birth control, and prenatal care. In developing countries, family planning is often combined with literacy programmes. A second category focuses on teaching adults the skills of parenting, including a considerable amount of writing aimed at helping parents of children with special needs or disabilities. A third theme pertains to help for parents in improving their economic position. A fourth category concerns researching changes in parenting styles because of shifting social conditions, such as the increased participation of fathers in child care, or the impact of media on children, or new forms of support for changing family structures. Finally, a fifth category focuses on teaching parents about nutrition and the health care of children, as well as about their education and development.

There are several issues that must be confronted if family-life education is to continue to develop as a field. The folk movement beginnings, the interdisciplinary leadership, and the diverse short-lived programmes have the potential for both strengthening and limiting the effectiveness of the field. The movement now needs an integration of its many subcategorizations, of its theoretical contributions from a variety of other disciplines, and of theory, research, and practice. It requires a conceptual framework which can support family-life education as a discrete discipline.

Basic to this theory development and integration, is the importance of continuing to follow an educational model. Guerney and Guerney (1981) emphasized this point:

> Family life educators have a great advantage in going about the business of people changing that practicing social workers, counsellors, and psychologists do not: their self-concept as *educators*. The other helping professions mentioned immediately above often see their role as that of a *healer* . . . . The model which family life educators should avoid is that of clinical medicine. The model which they should adhere to is that of mass education. (pp. 592–93)

Viewing adults as learners rather than as clients has a profound effect on theory and practice for this field. An understanding of adult learning principles is basic to the work of an effective family-life educator. In practice, experiential learning modes are critical in helping adults change attitudes and behaviour. Because the goal of education for family living is to help people acquire the attitudes, skills, and behaviour necessary for effective functioning in families, the dispensing of information through didactic approaches is not sufficient in itself. Learning relational skills and heightening attitude awareness require an experiential, learner-centred approach which involves participants in practising new skills and examining their own perspectives and assumptions.

With increasingly rapid social transformations and cultural interchanges there must be education for choice. No one life-style is "right"; there is no one family structure. Adults must be helped to examine the assets and liabilities of various family and relational patterns as well as to explore alternatives to the serious problems of overpopulation, poverty, environmental resources, and other social concerns which must be addressed in order to allow humankind to exist in peace. Family-life education must be education for choice. This field must ultimately be concerned with the "family of humankind" in which the growth and development of each individual is linked to the growth and development of others beyond the self.

See also: Lifespan Learning Development; Lifespan Learning: Implications for Educators; Population Education

Bibliography

Brown M W 1964 Organizational programs to strengthen the family. In: Christensen H T (ed.) 1964 *Handbook of Marriage and the Family*. Rand McNally, Chicago, Illinois

Croake J W, Glover K E 1977 A history and evaluation of parent education. *Fam. Coord.* 26: 151–58

Dreikurs R, Soltz V 1964 *Children: The Challenge*. Hawthorn, New York

Fine M J (ed.) 1980 *Handbook on Parent Education*. Academic Press, New York

Gordon T 1970 *Parent Effectiveness Training: The No-lose Program for Raising Responsible Children*. Wyden, New York

Guerney B, Guerney L F 1981 Family life education as intervention. *Fam. Relations* 30: 591–98

Kerckhoff R K 1964 Family life education in America. In: Christensen H T(ed.) 1964 *Handbook of Marriage and the Family*. Rand McNally, Chicago, Illinois

National Council on Family Relations 1970 Position paper on family life education. *Fam. Coord.* 19: 186

Otto H A (ed.) 1976 *Marriage and Family Enrichment: New Perspectives and Programs*. Abingdon, Nashville, Tennessee

Sawin M M 1979 *Family Enrichment with Family Clusters*. Judson, Valley Forge, Pennsylvania

Sawin M M (ed.) 1982 *Hope for Families: Stories of Family Clusters in Diverse Settings*. Sadlier, New York

Vanier Institute of the Family 1971 *Report of Family Life Education Survey*, Part 2: *Family Life Education in the Schools*. Ottawa, Ontario

Education for Change

Introduction

All learning is change and all education aims at producing it, within the learner as a person and in his or her behaviour. Education, since it aims at producing more competent, better informed, more understanding people, has implied within its goals the possibility that its activities will indirectly cause change in the society inhabited by those who undergo it.

Much of adult education has, however, gone beyond that. Many of its initiatives have had the explicit goal, not merely of producing people capable of achieving change, but people who will achieve it, and, moreover, in a particular direction, approved or even decided by the educator. One may cite examples such as the temperance movement, nationalist movements, trade union organizations, all of which have undertaken substantial educational programmes for adults with the primary intention of changing society in ways desired by the sponsors.

Activities of this kind, although they are given an honoured place in adult education history, may be considered to approach, or even to cross, the line that divides education from training or indoctrination. It is argued that it is appropriate for an adult educator to present the knowledge about temperance, nationalism, or trade union activities, which is necessary for an adult to make an informed decision whether or not to act, even to teach the skills required for action to be effective, if it is decided upon. The learner must, however, be left in a position to make a free choice. The educator may believe that the logic of the facts will turn the learner in the way desired; he or she may not seek to influence the decision by other means.

This nondirective interpretation of the adult educator's role is widely canvassed as a fundamental principle, particularly in Western Europe, North America, and those parts of the world influenced by Western ideas of democracy and individual responsibility. However, it is not universally accepted even there and has no place in socialist societies, or in developing countries, where the need for education to serve as an effective change agent is too urgent to permit of so dispassionate a view. Nor is it much valued in education for employment, which is a major reason why some educators would question the educational validity of activities to this end. Even when the principle is considered desirable, there are doubts about the feasibility of such an approach to education as a change agent.

Whether it is called education, training, instruction or indoctrination, the potential of systematic teaching or directed learning as an agent for furthering change in society is too great to be renounced. Not all adult education takes place in areas as controversial as religion, politics, or even labour relations—much of it is situated in areas about which there is a general consensus.

The articles in this subsection do raise contentious issues, although less about ends than about means. Education in primary health care has largely to overcome ignorance or inertia and inculcate appropriate skills to bring about change. *Adult Education and Development: The Urban Experience*, while recognizing that the developed world has parallel problems, concentrates on the situation of the urban poor in developing countries. It analyses their condition, what needs to be done to bring them to a more equal standard of living with more prosperous citizens, and what adult education can do to help.

The term "primary health care" designates actions to maintain and enhance the health of individuals and communities, intended to pre-empt the need for curative action, and undertaken outside the medical profession and with the participation of the clientele itself. The article *Primary Health Care* explains the goals of such care worldwide, its emphasis being on those who, for one reason or another, cannot help themselves, and examines adult education's contribution to it.

There are three examples of the kind of specialized education which deals with topical problems and the contribution that individual adults may make as individuals and as citizens to their solution. *Population Education* reviews provision that has been made to help adults understand phenomena such as slow and rapid growth, migration, and urbanization, and their effects on the quality of life. *Environmental Education* considers what is and ought to be done to create a society aware of the environmental problems caused by industrialization, technical change, and underdevelopment. *Peace Education* seeks to define the parameters of its subject, its purposes, its present status, and its need for expansion.

Adult Education and Development: The Urban Experience

M. S. Adiseshiah

At the international conference on adult education in Dar es Salaam in 1976 the delegates affirmed:

> mass poverty, mass ignorance, and illiteracy are recognized by most governments and their citizens as among the major problems of the present day...and that education and in particular that part of education involving adults is an essential factor (though not the only one) in promoting development processes; adult education can moreover contribute decisively to the full participation of the masses of the people in their own development and to their active control of social, economic, political, and cultural change...

Concerns about the education of adults demand attention to the problem of poverty, both rural and urban. Urban poverty deepened during the 1960s: some 50 percent of the world population were living in poverty in 1960; by 1970 this figure had risen to some 60 percent.

1. Urban Poor

Unresolved conceptual and computational problems in measuring poverty relate to varying income definitions and analyses and the absolute and relative cutting points of living levels on the one hand, and data collection uncertainties on the other. Allowing for these constraints, it may be estimated that, of the world population of over 4 billion in the 1970s, around 900 million persons live in urban areas, and about 400 million of them are poor (United Nations 1979). These are rather crude estimates of poverty, as they include among the urban poor 18 million in the United States, 3 million in Canada, 8 million in the United Kingdom, as well as 57 million in India, 20 million in Indonesia, 16 million in Brazil, and 12 million in the Philippines.

This article concentrates on the urban poor in developing countries, who number around 320 million. Just over one-third of them live in the slums and urban shanty towns: 15 to 20 percent of the population of small cities and 20 to 30 percent of the population of large metropolises such as Rio de Janeiro, Karachi, Calcutta, Lagos, Manila, live in slums.

The indices of urban poverty are shown in low employment patterns, even lower income levels, widespread malnutrition and mortality rates, and the underurbanized nature of housing, transport, water supply, roads, health, and education facilities.

The characteristic conditions of the urban poor point to an important consideration for the adult educator. Poverty is not a one-dimensional state of existence which the terms "deprived sections", "weaker sections", "backward sections" seem to suggest. It is not simply a state of deprivation or a series of inadequate conditions—for example, lack of adequate food, proper housing, or curative health care, and so on; rather it is an interrelated social phenomenon in which an urban majority are poor, lacking everything, and a minority are wealthy, with access to all they desire.

These two situations are related. Urban poverty is a social condition resulting from the use of the community's assets in such a way that the basic wants of the majority are not met, whilst the relatively unlimited needs of the minority are increasingly fulfilled. Adult educators working with the urban poor cannot treat this cause of urban poverty directly; they will usually be dealing with some of its symptoms, such as lack of education, gainful employment, and housing.

Turning from causes of urban poverty to some of its manifestations, it may first be noted that there will be an increasing concentration in the urban population in the developing countries until the end of the century. The projected increase of one billion people, will be two-and-a-half times the increase which took place between 1950 and 1975 (World Bank 1979). Within this expansionist trend, a disquieting feature is that the mass of the urban population is being concentrated in large metropolitan cities; small and medium towns are decaying both relatively and absolutely. The problems of the big cities will continue to dominate the future and will challenge adult educators in unforeseen ways.

There is general agreement, in theory and from empirical studies, that this growth of cities is caused by rural–urban migration. In fact, most official documents make migration the sole cause for the growth of our megacities, without allowing for the other major cause of growth, namely the high rate of population increase. There is need for differential studies on the urban population growth due to migration from rural areas, and that due to population increase among the urban poor.

Studies in all developing countries show that the drift from villages to towns is the result of the unemployed (and the poor) of the villages coming to cities to look for employment although not necessarily for better employment and some means of subsistence. In this sense urban unemployment is a transfer of the location of rural unemployment, and urban poverty an extension of rural poverty.

2. The Adult Education Role

The contribution of educational policies and the educational system to the political, social, and economic inequality in society must be noted, because it adds to the burden which adult education has to carry in promoting equality. There are two basic phenomena of inequality: the differing rewards of different jobs and the blocking of access to the better paid positions for the talented poor. The link between the two is the education system. It promotes inequality spatially, between urban and rural areas; sexually, between boys and girls; generationally, between the young and old; socially, between the rich minority and the poor majority; fiscally, acting as a transfer channel of subsidies from the poor to the rich.

Increased education and increased educational expenditure—in the name of equality of opportunity and the even more dubious objective of equality of educational outcomes—have been another hidden way of the poor subsidizing the education of the rich. This takes place in Third World countries as well as in the industrially advanced countries. A study in the United States, for example, points out that schools are an almost perfectly regressive form of taxation. It notes that the cost of schooling the poorest one-tenth of the population is US$2,500 per pupil over his or her lifetime, while the children of the richest one-tenth cost about US$35,000 per pupil (Adiseshiah 1979). In India the highest social group benefits four times as much as does the poverty group, given the fact that 80 percent of those who complete school and college are from the top 20 percent of society (Reimer 1971). Another study shows that up to 70 percent of the expenditure of private schools and colleges is financed through public subsidies and tax avoidance.

An even more serious concern is that the main outcome of school and university is the conditioning of the student to fit into the unequal and unjust society. Thus the major function of the education system in Third World countries is that of legitimizing an unequal social system.

3. Consciousness Raising of the People

Adult education in Third World countries starts with a relatively clean slate in that, with a few exceptions like Cuba and Tanzania, most countries spend between 95 percent and 99 percent of educational finance on school and university education, with little or nothing on adult education.

Three interrelated components of adult education—literacy learning, professional skills formation, and social awareness wakening—are addressed to the three freedoms that the poor majority are looking to: freedom from ignorance, freedom from low-wage employment, and freedom from inequality and injustice. The three are varying facets of single learning experiences—consciousness-raising—whether it be through literacy skills, higher income earning, or organization to fight for rights.

It is both possible and easy for an adult education programme to slide into becoming a literacy effort or an employment training package, both of which are good and beneficial in themselves but have little to do with equality and redistribution objectives. How adult education programmes may become straight literacy programmes is being demonstrated in some parts of India's National Adult Education Programme. The rural power structures and the urban elites are aware of the potential dangers to their dominant position if literacy programmes made the poor aware of their own unequal, weak, and diminished status. Thus power elites aim at either obstructing and terminating consciousness-raising programmes in rural or urban areas, or at diverting them into harmless literacy programmes or irrelevant craft training, such as basket-making for men or sewing classes for women.

It is part of the adult educator's mandate to help create laws that benefit the poor, whether it be through land ceiling surpluses, housing sites, drinking water, cooperative credit, fertilizer, or bank loans. Adult education associations should help in the forming of rural and urban trade unions, and in promoting a working alliance among the small and marginal farmers, cropsharers, the landless, the marginal, and the urban poor. Only then will the participation of the people in political decision making be assured and the scenario set for adult education to be able to discharge its role in the fight for equality.

4. The Tasks of Adult Education

The first task of adult education is the organization of the urban poor, in particular the poor community in each locality. This task is suggested by India's Draft Sixth Plan in the section headed "Distributive Justice", which concludes with the following directive: "and finally, the rural and urban poor have to be organised. Their vigilance alone can ensure that the benefit of various laws, policies and schemes designed to benefit them do produce their intended effect".

Second, the adult education programme should aim at the organization of the poor to undertake studies and surveys on their own behalf, because, contrary to the popular illusion, rural migrants to urban areas are not illiterate and unskilled. Such studies could help open up new lines of gainful occupation for the urban poor, including entrepreneurial avenues, and point to the creation of needed facilities of credit, materials, and markets.

Third, adult educators should address themselves to working along with the organization of the poor to identify the social, political, and environmental infrastructures needed in the locality—lights, roads and pathways, ownership of plots, house construction, safe drinking water, sanitation and latrines, education, training and health facilities—and to take action to see that existing urban facilities in these areas are made available to the members of the organization.

A programme of continuing education would include political and cultural education of various kinds. The general elections in India in 1977 and 1980 demonstrated fertile ground for political education as part of adult education. Cultural education could involve creative writing, participation in drama, music, and various other traditional and new art forms, as well as sports and games for younger members of the community.

In practically all urban areas in Third World countries radio and television are available in abundance. However the networks are controlled by elite groups. The urban poor, like the rural poor, are not participants in the formulation and dissemination of radio and television programmes. The potential the mass media has for transforming unjust societies is being neglected. Programmes are, for the most part, developed to meet the needs of the minority elite urban groups, and in a few cases comprise what these groups think the urban poor should have. Another task for adult education therefore is to organize the urban poor to enter radio and television programmes as producers, formulators, and participants, and not simply as clients.

Before adult education can begin to discharge these functions vis-à-vis the urban poor, a prior condition must be the political commitment of governments to revise their educational priorities. Typically secondary and university education together consume the major part of educational funds at annually increasing rates. Primary and adult education, cost on a per pupil basis, one-third to one-eighth of secondary and university education and are being starved for funds and support. This discrepancy may be the result of the lack of knowledge and understanding of the explosive possibilities of adult education for helping in the attainment of the goals of a democratic and just society. Adult education for the urban poor will have to begin with educating the governing and political network of the country, so that there can be a real and clear political commitment for adult education as a whole.

Bibliography

Adiseshiah M S 1970 *Let my Country Awake: The Human Role in Development: Thoughts on the Next Ten Years.* UNESCO, Paris

Adiseshiah M S 1976 *Financing of School Education.* Government of Tamil Nadu, Madras

Adiseshiah M S 1979 *The Contribution of Higher Education to the New International Economic Order.* International Institute for Educational Planning (IIEP), Paris

Adiseshiah M S 1981 *Adult Education Faces Inequalities.* Sangam Publishers for UNESCO, Madras

Reimer E W 1971 *School is Dead: An Essay on Alternatives in Education.* Penguin, Harmondsworth

The Report of the President's Commission on Income Maintenance Programmes. 1969 Washington, DC

United Nations 1979 *Demographic Estimates and Projection for the World, Regions and Countries as Assessed in 1978, Provisional Report.* United Nations, New York

World Bank 1979 *World Development Report.* World Bank, Washington, DC

Primary Health Care

P. G. Stensland

Adult education builds on principles and theories derived from scientific study of mature learners. While adult educators have regarded methodology as their main area of expertise, their broader concern has been that this professional resource should contribute to the fulfilling of vital human needs. In this spirit, professionals with insights and skills in adult learning seek collaboration with those competent in medical and health sciences.

The following article gives current examples of primary health care programs and explores the role that adult education may play, with particular attention to present emphases toward a global strategy for health for all by the year 2000. Wherever relevant, references to research will be given.

1. Definitions

Two recent international conferences have contributed definitions of primary health care and of adult education, with special reference to their roles in development of society.

The International Conference on Primary Health Care was organized by the World Health Organization (WHO) and the United Nations Children's Fund (UNICEF), at Alma-Ata, Soviet Union, in 1978. Delegates from 134 governments and representatives of 67 United Nations organizations, specialized agencies, and nongovernmental organizations in official relations to WHO and UNICEF accepted a declaration that widened the previous scope of primary health care.

The main target is "the attainment of all peoples of the world by the year 2000 of a level of health that will permit them to lead a socially and economically productive life." "Primary health care is essential health care based on practical, scientifically sound and acceptable methods and technology made universally acceptable to individuals and families in the community through their full participation. . . . It forms an integral part of both the country's health system, of which it is the central function and main focus, and of all social and economic development of the community. It is the first level of contact of individuals, the family and community with the national health system, bringing health care as close as possible to where people live and work, and constitutes the first element of a continuing health care process."

"Primary health care," the declaration further states, "requires and promotes maximum community and individual self-reliance and participation in planning, organization, operation, and control of primary health care, making the fullest use of local, national, and other available resources, and to this end develops through appropriate education the ability of communities to participate."

Two years earlier, an International Conference on Adult Education and Development, organized by the International Council for Adult Education, at Dar es Salaam, had already indicated concern for such "appropriate education." In the words of Julius K. Nyerere, then Council President, the declaration of Dar es Salaam stated that "adult education incorporates anything which enlarges men's understanding, activates them, helps them to make their own decisions, and to implement those decisions for themselves. It includes training, but it is much more than training. It includes what is generally called 'agitation,' but it is much more than that. It includes organization and mobilization, but it goes beyond them to make them purposeful."

2. *Primary Health Care Aims Relevant to Adult Education*

Inherent in the Alma-Ata declaration are three aims particularly relevant to adult education. First, primary health care professes to be holistic, serving total human beings, their families, their communities, and not just physical or biological needs. It involves social as well as medical actions, and aims at prevention as well as cure and care.

Second, primary health care strives to integrate health with other vital concerns, including education. The integration aim assumes collaboration among institutions and agencies, public and private, as well as among agents and professionals working in their separate disciplines and specialities. Consequently, primary health care programs include adult education as an integral part, health care workers collaborate with educators, and research and development are joint efforts.

Third, primary health care builds on participation from the community. People must be partners in choosing priorities, deciding on plans and implementing them. This participatory approach utilizes adult education as voluntary and self-directed learning.

Both declarations are targeted on current human needs and sharpened by differences in available resources and a widening gap between served and underserved, developed and developing countries. Whenever targets for programs of primary health care and adult education are similar, cooperation replaces unnecessary duplication with mutual support.

3. *The Holistic Aim*

Holistic primary health care has been practiced since ancient times, and has been preserved in many developing countries by indigenous practitioners, for example, the Indian Ayurveda and Unani, traditional birth-attendants in Asian and African villages, and herbalists and curanderos in Caribbean and Latin-American countries. In Brazil's literacy program MOBRAL, participants learn to read and write and to practice community health in programs featuring study and reflection on problems of the whole human being. Water and sanitation projects in Ghana and Northern Canada Indian villages build on a combination of action and group education.

Holistic approaches tended to seem obsolete when industrialization entered the picture. Health care in the Western world soon became dominated by scientific medicine. High technology, excessive specialization, and the primacy of hospitals were the hallmarks of "Western medicine" even when it was exported to developing countries.

On the positive side, advanced organization and scientific orientation of professional personnel have made it possible for imaginative planners to develop a sophisticated holism in primary health care. Experiments in multidisciplinary health teams (Sweden), community centers for health care (Scotland and United States), and regional cooperatives for health care (Yugoslavia), indicate this new trend.

4. *Integration as an Organizational Aim*

The step from holistic programs to integrated ones is short—one is the result of a philosophical point of view, the other the response to a need for organizational rearrangements. Factional and fragmented programs in human services are being replaced by overall schemes where multiministerial and interprofessional collaboration are promoted and, later, taken for granted. The Brong-Ahafo Rural Integrated Development Program (BARIDEP) in Ghana may be cited as an example. It was recently reported at a regional African conference in Kintampo, and is intended as a model for a national Ghana health plan, as well as possibly for other African national plans. BARIDEP includes community clinics, nutrition education, school health self-help projects, family planning education, traditional birth attendant services, and community farms in a development scheme where education and information campaigns are intrinsic elements. The basis for this action program was an examination of traditional structures and social organization and their effects on health practices.

Recent case studies from 12 Asian countries and a field survey in Thailand reported to the United Nations Asian and Pacific Development Institute illustrate the continuous application of adult education methods and participatory research to integrated health programming. Such is also the case in current reports from three subregional WHO conferences in Kuwait, Damascus, and Mogadishu, as well as in studies and experiments in member nations to the Pan American Health Organization (PAHO), rendered as contributions to the 75th Anniversary of PAHO.

In contrast, industrialized countries have faced formidable organizational, administrative, and attitudinal obstacles to better integration of health and social services. Firmly entrenched bureaucracies and long-established fractionalized education of professionals have raised barriers against moving interests and action across boundaries of special territories.

There have, however, appeared opportunities for loosening the rigidity: management development programs in many countries have presented welcome incentives for integrating health action with professional continuing education. The search for alternatives to existing patterns of health care delivery to the elderly and the handicapped has led to other experiments with integration. Plans are encouraged for interlocking primary, secondary, and tertiary health care with supportive education. The very existence of networks of local, district, and regional health services, particularly in socialist countries, furthers both vertical and social integration. Extension of central health services to surrounding communities, as in the district nurse programs in Sweden, results in integration of health action with education of clients, patients, and consumers.

5. *Participation as an Aim*

The basic importance of participation in development programs has been brought out in numerous conferences since the early 1960s, including meetings of health planners and professionals. If change is called for, such change must be generated from within, and primary health care depends for its success on acceptance and continuous involvement of all concerned.

Participation of citizens and their leaders to be meaningful has to be supported by education for new roles, for skills in using new tools, and for understanding new goals. The function of adult education has been recognized in such meetings as the Regional Community Health and Information seminar in Maputo, 1979; joint WHO/UNICEF orientation sessions in New Delhi and Bangkok, 1979; the regional workshop in Tacloban City in 1979 for health terms in rural projects; and the Dag Hammarskjöld Foundation seminar on "Another Development for Health" in Uppsala, 1978.

There are obstacles to effective participation in primary health care. In many developing countries there are ingrained hostilities towards change, and vested interests among those in power which build constraints against any cooperative efforts. There is discrimination against landless people, the poor, refugees, new settlers, women, excluding all these from action and from education for action. There is also suspicion and prejudice against Western ideas and patterns of programming. These and other sociopolitical constraints on community change have been the object of research, for example, in the Javanese village of Sukodono and the Bhoomi Sena tribal movement in Maharashtra, India.

In industrialized countries, similar constraints are often created by existing systems and rigid machineries. Participatory primary health care projects are held back by the preoccupation with hospitals and institutional medicine. Legislation and financial arrangements are geared to existing medical machineries.

In post Alma-Ata studies and reports, new trends are visible toward better integration and increased community participation. Recent experiments with regional centers in Sweden (Tierp and Skaraborg), with prepaid health care and family memberships in United States and Argentina (Kaiser Permanente), and with citizen participation in health service administration in United States (Health Systems Agencies) are the beginnings of participatory health care. In other programs, adults are active through study and discussion (Sao Tome), through shared evaluation of health needs in the community (Samoa women's organizations), and through development and experimentation with educational materials and media (Jamaica).

The new approaches to program development have lessened the dependence on outside expertise in research. In the Tanzania literacy campaign, primary health care programs were advanced through extensive involvement of the villagers in necessary research as well as action. Country programs supported by UNICEF (Sri Lanka, Colombia, Burma) include participatory monitoring and case studies. Household surveys in Kenya and Sudan rely on citizen participation to assure greater accuracy and realism. The Philippine Nurses Association has designed an education program to develop people's ability to analyze their common health needs.

6. *Priorities*

Adult education, to be effective, has to have a clear focus on people and communities and on their specific needs. Therefore, adult education for primary health care has to be targeted not on "health" as a general good, but on the health care required by specific groups in specific communities. This focus has unveiled groups and communities with serious, and at times desperate, health needs: the malnourished, the illiterates, the hungry, the disenfranchised, the nomads, the landless, refugees, the resettled; groups exposed to environmental dangers; the underserved in developed as well as developing countries, especially the women and the children. Acknowledgement of a worldwide health crisis of grave proportions has led to the present Global Strategy for Health for All by the Year 2000, the implementation of Alma-Ata decisions. The strategy was adopted by the World Health Assembly in 1981 and has been strengthened by regional and national plans and by commitments made in several recent international conferences by public and private agencies and organizations.

The major thrust of the strategy is health promotion, disease prevention, diagnosis, therapy and rehabilitation, and the development of health systems with primary health care as a central function. These systems will have "interrelated components in homes, educational institutions, workplaces, communities," furthering the holistic aim suggested earlier. They will integrate health sectors with other sectors of society. For their acceptance and effective use, they will require participation by all concerned, providers and consumers, professionals and ordinary citizens.

The need for comprehensive scope and interprofessional collaboration in health care at the community level has been illustrated in the recent broad research study of "Health Services in Shanghai County." In response to an acknowledged poverty of research into nonmedical forces influencing health behavior, what seem needed for the future are longitudinal studies of the effect of education of professionals and citizens alike on health in the community. Toward this end models for studies have been suggested: continuity of health care, primary health care in industrialized countries, continuing education for health professionals, health technology and primary health care, participatory evaluation in adult and nonformal education.

Bibliography

Acuña H R 1980 New directions for health care in the Americas. *Bulletin of the Pan American Health Organization* 14: 1–5

Another Development in Health 1978 *Development Dialogues*. Dag Hammarskjöld Foundation, Uppsala

Barrow N 1981 Knowledge belongs to everyone: The challenge for adult education and primary health care. *Convergence* 14(2): 45–52

Christian Medical Commission 1979 The principles and practice of primary health care. *Contact*. Special Series no. 1. World Council of Churches, Geneva

Darkenwald G G, Merriam S B 1982 *Adult Education, Foundations of Practice*. Harper and Row, New York

Hinman A R, Parker R L, Xue-qi G, Xing-yuan G, Xi-fu Y, De-yu H (eds.) 1982 Health services in Shanghai County. *Am. J. Public Health* 72(9)

International Council of Education 1982 Special report: Adult education and primary health care. *Convergence* 15:2

Long H B 1983 *Adult Learning, Research and Development*. Cambridge, The Adult Education Company, New York

Nyerere J K 1978 The declaration of Dar es Salaam. In: *Adult Learning: A Design for Action: A Comprehensive International Survey*. Int. Conf. on Adult Education and Development, Dar es Salaam, June, 1976. Pergamon, London, pp. 27–36

Participatory research: Development and issues. 1981 *Convergence* 14(3): 5–80

Sepulveda C, Mehta N 1980 *Community and Health: An Inquiry into Primary Health Care in Asia*. United Nations Asian and Pacific Development Institute and United Nations Children's Fund (UNICEF) East Asia and Pakistan Regional Office, Bangkok

Tandon R 1984 *Your Own Health, The Role of Adult Education in Community Involvement in Primary Health Care*. ICAE, New Delhi

United Nations Children's Fund 1978 Governments and the people's health. *Assignment Children* 42

United Nations Children's Fund 1986 *The State of the World's Children 1986*. UNICEF, New York

United Nations Development Programme 1983a *Human Resource Development for Primary Health Care*. Evaluation Study No. 9, December 1983, UNDP, New York

United Nations Development Programme 1983b *UNDP Programme Advisory Note, Primary Health Care with Special Reference to Human Resource Development*. October 1983, UNDP, New York

World Health Organization (WHO) 1978 *Primary Health Care: A Joint Report*. Report of the International Conference on Primary Health Care, Alma-Ata, Soviet Union, 6–12 September 1978. WHO, Geneva

World Health Organization (WHO) 1981 *Global Strategy for Health for All by the Year 2000. WHO, Geneva*

World Health Organization Eastern Mediterranean Region 1980 *Health for All by the Year 2000*. Report on subregional meeting on health for all by the year 2000, Damascus, 2–5 March 1980; Kuwait, 14–17 April 1980; Mogadishu, 17–20 February 1980, Alexandria

World Health Organization Regional Office for the Western Pacific 1980 *Final Report Interregional Workshop on the Development of Health Teams in Rural Work*. Tacloban City, 22–27 October 1979, Manila

Population Education

C. T. Davies

Population education aims to allow learners to acquire the knowledge, abilities, attitudes, and values necessary for the understanding and evaluation of population situations, the dynamic forces that have shaped them, and the effects they will have on the present and future quality of life. Additionally, learners should be able to make informed and responsible decisions, based on their own assessments, and to participate in collective decisions which will help to promote social and economic development. Population education requires the most objective possible teaching–learning situation in which the teacher offers the learner a set of facts and values that will allow him or her to evaluate the whole range of options with respect to a given problem.

Population education emerged from a growing awareness of the importance of population phenomena in the world such as slow and rapid population growth rates, migration, and urbanization. Essentially it is an educational response to demographic problems. For example, a rapidly growing population may outstrip certain resources or make it difficult to meet basic needs such as jobs, education, and health care, resulting in a threat to the quality of life of people. A declining population or an aging population may be seen in some cases as a threat to a country's economy or vitality. Migration from rural to urban areas may deplete rural areas of human resources while placing a strain on urban social services.

Historically, the development of population education goes back to the 1940s, particularly in the United States and Sweden, when there was concern about population decline. However, in the 1950s and 1960s the main concern was that of high birth rates and growing populations. As a result, many family planning programmes were established. These programmes, especially in the developing world, were not highly successful. It appeared that they concentrated on adults who had to overcome deeply entrenched traditional learning. Through the late 1960s and early 1970s, educational programmes were developed for children and youth whose reproductive years were still ahead of them and during this period the term population education was almost synonymous with school population education programmes. During the 1970s, however, the educational settings of population education began to include a whole range of educational institutions both formal and nonformal. Furthermore, the content of population education was broadened, beyond the topics of fertility and growth, to include a much wider range of population processes and characteristics.

It is said, though, that population education is not an attempt to develop a new discipline but that facts, theories, and concepts are borrowed from a broad spectrum of academic disciplines and professional fields in order to assist individuals and societies to understand fully population interactions and the effect of population factors on the quality of their individual and collective lives. Demography and folk demography do, however, form the core of the knowledge base of population education. The sum of all these knowledge bases is referred to as population studies. Thus, population education embraces the field of population studies which comprises the body of knowledge, concepts, and theories that describe and attempt to explain the dynamics of human populations and their relationships with the social, cultural, economic, political, and biological environments. It involves looking into a wide range of population issues and is, therefore, much broader than family planning or demography.

Because of the nature of population education, a number of other educational activities inevitably share some of the content associated with population education. The greatest confusion that arises concerns population education's relation to family-life education, sex education, environmental education, and development education. Family-life education and sex education do indeed share certain concerns with population education, such as human reproduction and life-cycle decision making, but they concentrate on interpersonal relations and in general have not concerned themselves so far with the consequences of population decision making on the wider society.

In rather different ways, environmental education and development education also make use of content drawn from population studies, especially that which describes and analyses how population processes operate in order to understand better the nature of social and economic development or the interaction of humans and the biosphere. However, differences in goals and objectives give population education a separate identity at the present stage of its development.

Nevertheless, there is no systematically organized body of knowledge and no one textbook which can be referred to on population education. The problem stems from the fact that population phenomena affect so many aspects of life at so many different levels—political relations, resources, the environment, health, social services, education, employment, human rights—that nations, regions, and individuals have differing viewpoints about population questions. These range along a continuum from those who see population growth as a crisis, as *the* primary cause of all other social problems, to those who seek to encourage population growth to help solve social problems.

There is no lack in the diversity of positions. Some contend that population is a false issue, fostered by wealthy industrialized nations to divert attention from problems faced by developing nations. The real problem, they say, is not population growth, but the maldistribution of wealth and resources, the lack of integrated economic development, overconsumption, and the affluent life-style of many industrialized nations which pose a more direct threat to the preservation of environment and resources than the higher population growth rates of the developing nations.

The various viewpoints will, of course, be given different emphases in the different population education programmes which are carried out in various parts of the world today. Population education in schools takes a number of forms, moving from the introduction of population concepts at the elementary- and secondary-school levels to universities and specialized training colleges. For example, large-scale projects are being carried out in the Republic of Korea, Tunisia, El Salvador, the Philippines, Indonesia, Malaysia, Thailand, Sri Lanka, Bangladesh, and Togo. Outside the formal education system there is also a great diversity of population education programmes which are of increasing importance since most population learning occurs in this millieu. Examples of population education in the nonformal sector can be found in Kenya as an integral component of the Programme for Better Family Living, in Sri Lanka as part of a workers' population and family planning education project, in Indonesia through the country's Pen Mas (community education) centres, and in Upper Volta in the form of seminars for high-level officials from a number of ministries.

Bibliography

Burleson N 1974 Population education: Problems and perspectives. *Bull. Bur. Int. Educ.* 193(4)

Udo R K, Viederman S 1979 Introduction. In: Udo R K (ed.) 1979 *Population Education Source Book for Sub-Saharan Africa*. Heinemann, Nairobi, pp. 2–10

UNESCO 1978 *Population Education: A Contemporary Concern* (*Educational Studies and Documents*, No. 28) UNESCO, Paris

UNESCO 1980 *Study of the Contribution of Population Education to Educational Renewal and Innovation in El Salvador, the Republic of Korea, Philippines and Tunisia*. UNESCO, Paris

UNESCO 1981 *Socio-cultural Case Studies for Population Education in Morocco, Peru, Rwanda and the United Republic of Tanzania*. UNESCO, Paris

United Nations Fund for Popular Activities (UNFPA) 1978 *Population Education*. (*Population Profiles*, No. 11) UNFPA, New York

Environmental Education

L. Emmelin

A basic premise of most environmental education is that problems caused by industrialization and technological development and underdevelopment are pressing and need urgent solutions. If this is correct, then it is critical that adults understand how the environment functions—at a sophisticated level for effective decision making, and at a general level for informed citizen participation in the discussion of issues. This article outlines some outcomes required from environmental education, and refers to nonformal and formal educational activities which need further development if environmental issues are to be dealt with effectively.

Environmental issues have a twofold place in adult education. First they can present problems which need solutions developed by educated people. Second, they can be used as relevant and immediate examples in the teaching of much basic adult education such as literacy, health, welfare, and competence in civic, political, and community competence.

The demand for solutions can be best met when environmental education produces one or more of the following outcomes:

(a) The integration of environmental concern, knowledge, and skill into all relevant areas of learning, that is many formal adult education programmes; considered on a worldwide basis this has probably progressed only in relation to health and hygiene to any significant extent.

(b) The development of environmentally literate and participative citizens; this is, possibly, the area in which the main thrust of adult environmental education should be made.

(c) The preparation of experts qualified to deal with specific environmental problems.

(d) The deepening of understanding for environmental matters by a large number of politicians, planners, civic leaders, and teachers at all school levels (Emmelin 1977).

The role of adult education in achieving the last two goals depends largely on the limits set to the term "adult education". The education of experts is normally considered the task of postsecondary institutions. It is, however, increasingly clear that this type of education will have to move into the adult education sector, in order to cope with environmental problems.

The United Nations Environment Programme distinguishes between the concept of "education" and "training" (UNEP 1978). Education serves to establish sensitivity to environmental problems, to raise the level of awareness, and to generate commitment. Training is for the development and mastering of skills, for the solution of practical problems, and for specialized action.

Although there is strong evidence that the media help to establish behaviour patterns and the acquisition of values directly detrimental to sound, environmental development, there are few systematic studies of the role of the media in relation to environmental education. Their effectiveness in environmental education is greatly diminished by their inattention to environmental skills training, their lack of educational goals for entertainment, and their delivery of persuasive content into the hands of the environmental exploiters (Sandman 1974).

They may be more effective in motivating people to become aware of issues than in actual teaching. Surveys of attitudes towards pollution control and specific environmental problems show a reasonable correlation between awareness of a given problem and the news coverage given to that problem. When, however, surveys are followed by any form of testing of factual knowledge about a problem, it is evident that the educational role of the media has been rather limited. Their contribution to environmental education has been confined mainly to health and conservation issues.

As educators recognize that participation in concrete action directed towards a defined goal greatly enhances learning, much emphasis in environmental education has been placed on participation in the planning of an urban environment. In a number of major planning controversies, public participation and direct action have evolved from the education of citizens. In less spectacular cases, the educational importance of participation is possibly greater than actual input to the planning process.

The most sustained educational effort is supported by voluntary organizations and citizen groups with a high degree of permanence. Such organizations exist at a national level in many countries and deal with traditional wildlife conservation problems and, more recently, with pollution, environmental quality, and resource depletion.

To date, no systematic study seems to have been made of the educational importance of environmental action and citizen participation. It would seem an urgent priority in developing adult education programmes. A brief summary of such case studies that do exist is found in Holdgate et al. (1982).

Another target group for further environmental education is that of the decision makers. A United Nations review (1978) concludes that there is very little systematic knowledge in relation to the environmental education of decision makers (UNEP 1978). Certain experiments involving university institutes, responsible agencies, and voluntary organizations have been made with formal and informal education for these people, but much more is needed.

Formal adult education dealing with environmental problems is dominated by courses connected with a university or a college. One reason for this may be the pressure on these institutions to provide environmental education, especially when they have available appropriate subject experts. Other factors, such as declining student enrolment, have stimulated them to enter the area. If the argument is accepted that a research base is a prerequisite for sound environmental education, this would strengthen/consolidate the role of universities in environmental education. In several European institutions of higher education, the mixing of undergraduate teaching and adult education is also promoting community ties, which these institutions traditionally have lacked.

In developing nations, environmental education converges significantly with remedial adult education. It is an accepted pedagogic principle that literacy education, in order to be effective, must relate directly to people's daily lives, so the use of environmental education may serve as a vehicle for literacy education goals provided that the relevance of the environmental issues used is apparent to the people. Environmental education for adults has another important role to play in bringing about a cultural identity for many minority groups, and in cultural efforts at the postcolonial stage (UNESCO 1978).

There is a serious lack of organizations interested in environmental education. Those that do exist in many countries are either too limited by finance or competence or have specialized in marketing vocationally oriented education. Institutions of higher education tend to have a distinct advantage because of their funding procedures.

The responsibility of government agencies to provide environmental education for adults has been largely neglected. Existing adult education organizations very often lack contact with competent environmental authorities. The establishment of liaison between various sectors of environmental protection, both official and voluntary, seems to be an urgent task. A related problem is the lack of leadership training and material development for adult education.

There is very little systematic research in the field of environmental education for adults outside the formal university system. An overview of the development during the period 1975 to 1980 is given by UNESCO (1980).

Bibliography

Emmelin L 1977 Environmental education programmes for adults. In: UNESCO 1978 *Trends in Environmental Education*. UNESCO, Paris, pp. 177–90

Holdgate M W, Kassas M, White G F (eds.) 1982 *The World Environment 1972–1982: A Report*. Tycooly, Dublin

Sandman P 1974 Mass environmental education: Can the media do the job? In: Swan J A, Stapp W B (eds.) 1974 *Environmental Education: Strategies Toward a More Liveable Future*. Wiley, New York, pp. 207–47

United Nations Environment Programme, Kenya (UNEP) 1978 *Review of the Area Environmental Education and Training*. Report of the Executive Director, UNEP, Nairobi

UNESCO 1978 *Intergovernmental Conference on Environmental Education, Tbilisi, 14–26 October 1977, Final Report*. UNESCO, Paris

UNESCO 1980 *Environmental Education in the Light of the Tbilisi Conference*. Education on the Move No 3. UNESCO, Paris

Peace Education

H. Kekkonen

Different orientations concerning the principles, contents, and methods of peace education can be found in different countries. There are some countries in which a strain of pessimism operates as an inhibition to such activities. Inadequate training of teachers and a shortage of study materials are often referred to as factors hampering the activity of peace education. There are genuine differences in the general concept on which peace education is based. For example, in Western countries peace education is conceived primarily as educational work to develop international understanding and cooperation; in socialist countries it is felt that peace education is already carried out in the system of formal education with its goal of educating for humanism, peace, and equality; and in developing countries it is regarded as education to recognize the reality of prevailing social injustices and as work to reduce or remove them (UNESCO 1981).

Regardless of difficulties and differences, peace education for adults is an activity that is on the increase and based on a number of shared values: respect for human dignity, an acceptance of equality between people, solidarity with the less privileged, courage to act in a nonviolent way against injustices in one's own community and internationally, and acceptance of responsibility by each individual for the maintenance of peace.

The definition of peace is the point of departure for peace education. It is not enough to say that peace is the absence of war and armed violence. The goal should be positive peace. This term derived from peace research, implies that structural, that is, "hidden" violence should be excluded from society as well. In order to reach this state of peace, it is argued, humankind will have to eliminate the great injustices still prevalent both within countries and between them. Peace should be conceived as something common to all; a global state of peace must be the goal pursued (Galtung 1974).

From this definition it follows that the goals of peace education have to be universally acceptable. The UNESCO "Recommendation Concerning Education for International Understanding, Co-operation and Peace and Education Relating to Human Rights and Fundamental Freedoms" (1974) can be considered the starting point. What promotes understanding and cooperation across international borders serves peace education and, in this respect, international education corresponds to peace education.

The UNESCO "Recommendation on the Development of Adult Education" (1976), built upon the above principles, has, as one of its basic aims, "To contribute to promoting work for peace, international understanding and co-operation . . ."

It should be noted that promoting peace and education for peace has been placed first. Thus all sectors of adult education are given the task and the contents of education for peace, which is more comprehensive than education for internationalism.

1. *The Objectives of Peace Education*

According to the 1974 UNESCO recommendation,

> Combining learning, training, information and action, international education should further the appropriate intellectual and emotional development of the individual. It should develop a sense of social responsibility and of solidarity with less privileged groups and should lead to observance of the principles of equality in everyday conduct. It should also help develop qualities, aptitudes, and abilities which enable the individual to acquire a critical understanding of problems at the national and the international level; to work in a group; to accept and participate in free discussion; and to base value-judgements and decisions on a rational analysis of relevant facts and factors.

In the UNESCO "Recommendation on the Development of Adult Education" about the objectives and guiding principles of peace education, there is agreement in the spheres of both the school system and adult education. It is affirmed that the task of peace education is to give humankind a solid informational basis for evaluating the world situation, as well as the readiness to find relevant knowledge in the present flow of information and to analyse information and sources of information critically. Peace education should also create the willingness for continuous learning. The goal of peace education is to create an individual capable of critical thinking, feelings of solidarity with the less privileged, and empathy, one who on the basis of his or her own conviction and humanistic orientation towards life is able to act in cooperation with others to create a more just world.

Peace education, as is the case with all education, should take place in three areas: information, attitudes, and action (Haavelsrud 1975). Together these areas constitute an integrated whole. The length and full-time character of the school system make it easier to include peace education in schools than in adult education (Weinberg 1963). Adult education is primarily voluntary; learners themselves make the choices of subjects of study and frequently also participate in selecting the teacher and the learning contents. Peace education is nowhere yet a popular subject of study. It needs to be made available by making it a component of all sectors of adult education. Attention needs to be focused on creating interest in the goals and contents of peace education, the methods of peace education, the quality and contents of information, and on processes of attitude change.

2. *The Quality of Knowledge: The Knowledge Base and Sources of Knowledge*

It has been stated, supported by research, that particularly in Western societies the flow of information is so great that it is difficult for ordinary people to form for themselves a consistent view of the world. Diffusion of knowledge through the mass media is a continuous process, but this process operates on the level of facts in a way that disregards the relationships between them, particularly any cause–effect. People pick up the kind of information that tends to support their previous views and beliefs. Making new knowledge one's own so that it may even bring along changes in one's attitudes and everyday conduct is difficult. Under these circumstances, an important task of peace education is to disseminate integrated, broadly based information. The subject of study could be the conditions of a certain developing country. If so, the first question people usually ask is: "What is its poverty due to?" Answers often received from mass media are nature, population growth, lack of knowledge, and so on. These replies are good starting points for a problem-centred introduction to conditions in the developing countries. One developing country can be used as an example and learning can then proceed to discussing neocolonialism, trade relations, the structure of world trade, and finally the New International Economic Order and the possibilities of achieving it (Jackson and Dubos 1972).

The arms race can be another example in the learning process. People already possess a lot of information about military costs and the rapid obsolescence of arms.

What is needed is more information, a wider knowledge base comprising historical factors of the arms race, related political and economic conflicts and efforts to settle them, the present situation, as well as the background and future prospects of disarmament, and so on. By proceeding in the way described above it has been possible in several countries to carry on peace education under conditions where people originally were not interested in these questions. Understanding problems in their broader context has been a factor increasing the need for information and improving the ability to participate in discussion or even in work to promote disarmament.

An important starting point in peace education is also the selection of information and evaluation of the sources of knowledge (Epstein 1976). Very often there exists the danger of bias and conflict. The New International Information Order adopted by UNESCO could provide a valuable basis for the diffusion of knowledge. Comparing information coming from different sources and evaluating its accuracy is an integral part of peace education. It should also be kept in mind that the results of peace research are important information materials to work with.

3. *The Content and Internalization of Knowledge*

The main subjects for peace education can be found in the UNESCO Recommendation (1974).

> Education should include critical analysis of the historical and contemporary factors of an economic and political nature underlying the contradictions and tensions between countries, together with study of ways of overcoming these contradictions, which are the real impediments to understanding, true international co-operation and the development of world peace.
>
> Education should emphasize the true interests of peoples and their incompatibility with the interests of monopolistic groups holding economic and political power, which practise exploitation and foment war.

Peace education cannot thus ever be passive or neutral; it must be prepared to take up difficult political questions. It should be stressed, however, that one is not always obliged to adopt a position based on doctrines or proposals of political parties or ideologies. One should check and test.

The contents of peace education typically include:

(a) information about the human community;

(b) the causes of war;

(c) the consequences of war;

(d) the work of peace movements;

(e) disarmament possibilities;

(f) nonviolent culture.

These may seem too extensive. Here it is, however, a question of overall discussion of different themes. Both experience and research findings indicate that people can create for themselves an overall picture of the problems of war and peace. Separate parts of the store of knowledge and experiences "find their proper place" and form an overall structure only as a result of organized processing of knowledge based on research (Savard 1981). Furthermore, the six categories above each constitute a separate theme which can be dealt with apart from the others. In practice, the learners usually want to proceed from one category to another including all six.

As the UNESCO Recommendation (1974) indicates, a process of conscientization should take place: diffusion of knowledge should lead to profound understanding, internalization of information received, which, in turn, leads to action. Even where people have obtained adequate information this does not necessarily cause attitude changes and a commitment to action since many people tend to feel they are outsiders and powerless to act. Moreover, it is argued, the continual dissemination of entertainment featuring forms of violence fills the consciousness of many individuals, resulting in confusion and also in intellectual poverty. One task of peace education is, therefore, to help people internalize critically the information they receive and develop their willingness to act in the spirit of the objectives of peace education.

4. *Empathetic Learning*

For an individual to grow in international understanding, and to learn to cooperate, the overall personality, specifically intelligence, feeling, and will, needs to be developed. In peace education the growth of a person's overall personality has to be taken into consideration: knowledge has significance only if it is internalized, that is, understood profoundly, even emotionally. Paying attention to existing injustices is not enough. Individuals should be capable of placing themselves in the position of those starving in the developing countries, as well as identifying themselves with the victims of racism and those who have experienced the sufferings of war, and so on. At the same time, an individual should, in one way or another, begin to work to remove injustices.

It has been found that the arts are a potent instrument promoting the internalization of knowledge. In peace education "empathetic learning" means, among other things, an acquaintance with all kinds of arts promoting peace: watching and analysing theatre and films opposing war; looking for and becoming familiar with peace literature; getting acquainted with cultural products of different peoples. An integral part of peace education is to listen carefully to the voice of even the most distant nations and people (Galtung 1974).

5. *Searching for Problem Solutions*

The authors of *No Limits to Learning* (Bolkin et al. 1979) argue that school systems and educators are, in part, to blame for the present world situation: throughout the world children and youth have been trained to conform to society rather than to foresee its future, discern the problems, and solve them. The authors represent the view that all schools should teach an individual from childhood to look critically at the present world situation, not forgetting its violence, to realize much more profoundly than before the interdependence of different peoples, and to practise a new kind of search for peaceful solutions for the problems of the world. It may be argued that a corresponding educational process should be launched among adults as well. Peace education should both train people to discern problems and give exercise in problem solutions from everyday life and the community level on to the level of international grievances. Learning can start from a "generative theme" in the sense that Paolo Freire uses this term; and from this problem-centred learning, the process spirals toward society, nation, and the world. Adequate planning enables progress to be made from individual problems to those of social structures, political and economic power relations among and between peoples and so on. This problem-centred way of working activates the learners considerably more than attending lectures or other forms of mere dissemination of information. This method also enables the training of learners to work individually and in groups, both on the intellectual level and in concrete action from the beginning of the learning process (IPRA 1974).

Practising and active work are a part of the learning process. Series of lectures, seminars, and courses can also contain activities that enhance peace education: arranging peace evenings, organizing campaigns, and so on. Even small achievements help stimulate adult learners to acquire more theoretical knowledge which, in turn, can be utilized in subsequent action. The circle of indifference, passivity, and apathy can be broken when people are given chances to participate. Concrete work inherent in peace education should be started, for example, with activities promoting peace culture on a level close to an individual: in family life, work, or in his or her neighbourhood or municipality an individual can participate in practising how to solve problems and conflicts in a nonviolent way, that is, through negotiations, concessions, attempts to understand the other party, as well as through protests, appeals, and other forms of nonviolent resistance. Experience in work on a small scale will teach an individual to utilize the same methods in wider contexts, on the national and international level, as well.

Because adult education often takes place in the form of lectures, seminars, or courses these forms of work are used in peace education as well. Current international developments and crisis situations of the world are often the starting point and the learning occasions are arranged either in order to broaden the picture given by mass media or, especially when it is a question of the developing countries, to create interest in and understanding of foreign cultures and the life of far-away peoples. Too often this kind of learning suffers from its temporary character; learning is often discontinued before a stage of permanent study activities corresponding to peace goals is reached and more sustained study will be needed.

6. *Action Days and Weeks, Development of Cooperation, Cultural Activities*

Residential institutions for adults, for example Nordic folk high schools, organize so-called theme days and weeks, even activities of several months' duration intending not only to disseminate peace information but also to acquaint the learners with concrete work, for example, participation in general development cooperation or helping a certain developing country. Both lectures, experiments, interviews, and writing of papers and practical work belong to this kind of learning. In many countries people have launched or have participated in campaigns for the collection of food and money, have activated local inhabitants to work for peace, disseminated information through different channels, or produced cultural programmes of their own for a more extensive use. In a few countries there are folk high schools working specifically and exclusively to promote work for peace. The lack of regularity and continuity has so far kept these activities from becoming known and more generally practised.

Taking part in activities organized by peace movements belongs in some countries to the sphere of peace education. The most common forms of work are collecting signatures to various statements, arranging peace marches and demonstrations and participating in them, as well as making appeals to decision makers (Myrdal 1976).

7. *Education for Peace as an Overall Principle in Adult Education*

Implementation of the UNESCO Recommendations concerning peace education requires a recognition of education for peace as an overall principle in all adult education. This means that in teaching the approach should be a global one, irrespective of the subject of learning, and that the contents of peace education should be included in all teaching activities. Introduction of this peace education approach in adult education on a large scale requires a new kind of training of adult educators. Adult educators should primarily be guided into a deep, personal conscientization of the contents of peace education. Organizing training for adult educators should in each country be an urgent task as part of the implementation of the principles of the UNESCO Recommendations.

The growth to responsibility, the primary goal of peace education, requires deeply humanistic moral education aiming at reaching the full maturity of humankind's overall personality, developed over a lifetime (Paterson 1979). Peace education is, thus, lifelong education and growth. Peace education cannot be neutral or value free: it is essential to have the courage to work on the basis of moral humanistic values. These values are to be found both in the Declaration of Human Rights of the United Nations and the UNESCO Recommendations and should undergird educational activities for men and women in all countries.

Bibliography

Botkin J W, Elmandjra M, Malitza M 1979 *No Limits to Learning: Bridging the Human Gap: A Report to the Club of Rome*. Pergamon, Oxford

Epstein W 1976 *The Last Chance: Nuclear Proliferation and Arms Control*. Free Press, Glencoe, Illinois

Galtung J 1974 *Schooling and Future Society*. University of Oslo, Oslo

Haavelsrud M (ed.) 1975 *Education for Peace: Reflection and Action*. Proc. of the 1st World Conf. of the World Council for Curriculum and Instruction, University of Keele, UK, Sept. 1974. IPC Science and Technology Press, Guildford

Hiroshima Institute for Peace Education (HIPE) 1975 *The Study of Peace Education*. HIPE, Hiroshima

International Peace Research Associates (IPRA) 1974 *Handbook of Peace Education*. IPRA, Oslo

Jackson B W, Dubos R J 1972 *Only One Earth: The Care and Maintenance of a Small Planet*. Norton, New York

Myrdal A R 1976 *The Game of Disarmament: How the United States and Russia Run the Arms Race*. Pantheon, New York

Paterson R W K 1979 *Values, Education, and the Adult*. Routledge and Kegan Paul, London

Savard R 1981 *World Military and Social Expenditures*. World Press, Leesburg, Virginia

UNESCO 1981 *Domination or Sharing*. UNESCO, Paris

Weinberg A M (ed.) 1963 *Instead of Violence: Writings by the Great Advocates of Peace and Nonviolence Throughout History*. Grossman, New York

Section 3

Participation and Recruitment

Section 3

Participation and Recruitment

Introduction

The idea that every individual needs to undertake purposive, systematic learning at some stages during his or her adult life was not born out of the concept of lifelong education. The latter has, however, played a large part in recent years in ensuring that it has received increasingly wide acceptance. This belief is taken further. If one has a need for such learning, runs the argument, then one should have the right and also the duty, to oneself and to society, to undertake it.

Against the idea of obligation runs the principle that adults are mature persons and thus that they must be free to choose themselves whether to participate in purposive learning or not. They are responsible for deciding what their needs are and how to satisfy them. The apparent conflict of principle that this creates is overcome by making the obligation a moral, rather than a legal one. There are, however, certain exceptions to this rule which are detailed in the article *Mandatory Continuing Education* in Section 1.

If adults ought to participate, but are not compelled to do so, how is it possible to ensure that they do take part? Since no country, having once introduced compulsory childhood schooling, has yet risked making school attendance voluntary, it would be naive to suppose that all adults, given what is known about their recollections of schooling and other opportunities for using their time, will do so, if left entirely to their own devices. It is also worth noting that in no country could all adults participate in education at one time, even if they wished to; the facilities available are simply insufficient.

In fact it is not desired that all adults, or even those of a particular age cohort, should take part at any one time. In principle the needs of individuals for structured learning experiences vary in their nature, duration, and timing. Who should decide these variables in each case is a matter of contention. Many educators would say it is for the adult learner to choose, others would argue for negotiation between the adult and the educator/counsellor, yet others believe that there should be an accommodation between the adult and society, though there are differences over who should speak for the latter. In practice there is some sort of accommodation, in that adults may decide not to study and they may also decide what and when to study, but only within limits which are set by the work, social, and family circumstances in which they live and the educational opportunities which are made available.

Some writers on adult education, basing their arguments on the contention that humans are learning animals, have maintained that if some adults do not undertake purposive, systematic learning projects, it is experience and circumstances that prevent them. If, in particular, initial education and family upbringing had exercised a positive influence, if the opportunities were there and their own family, social, and work situations did not discourage them, the majority would do so. This may be the case, but the hypothesis is untested and currently untestable, since, for many, the conditions cannot be met. The fact that many people who do not participate in official adult education programmes perform their own self-directed learning projects gives some support to the hypothesis. On the other hand a very large number appear to do no purposive learning in adult life. It is generally agreed that some of these could be brought to undertake a certain amount of education by measures of facilitation and incentive which are quite within the compass of the existing adult education system. Increasingly efforts are being made to devise and apply such measures, as well as to convince society as a whole to take action to the same end.

Although all adults are held to need continuing education, not all are believed to have an equally great need, or, perhaps more precisely, it is not considered necessary that society should make an equally great effort in every case in order to ensure that the need is both recognized and satisfied. For one reason or another the traditional thrust of adult education has been directed towards those who are educationally and—which is too frequently a corollary of the first—socially and economically disadvantaged. In spite of this, it is they who participate least. It is therefore they who are the particular target of actions taken to encourage participation in adult education.

In order to attract adults to education it is helpful to understand what factors determine their participation or nonparticipation. Against are to be set costs that must be borne in time, money, inconvenience, and effort, in its favour are the benefits to be derived, both as perceived by the learner. The first two articles in this section lay the foundation for subsequent ones by setting out these factors. *Factors in Participation* concentrates on the social and economic factors and those associated with the education system. *Participant Motivation* tackles the question of determinants from the point of view of the motives which impel adults to study or not. It reviews the theoretical and empirical work on the subject and includes some consideration of the problem of dropout from study programmes.

In order to engage those who might not otherwise take part in educational activity many agencies take initiatives outside the traditional institutional framework. *Outreach Work* examines this provision, with particular reference to efforts made to reach specific target groups.

Educationally disadvantaged adults frequently require advice and counselling to enable them to begin purposive study and, during the process, to help them to keep going. *Adult Education Counseling* considers different approaches to the task, some requiring psychologically trained personnel, others open to a wide range of advisers. Older adults present specific tasks and difficulties to the counsellor. *Counseling Older Adults* discusses them and describes the practices of one-to-one counselling, peer counselling, and small-group counselling in this context.

The last two articles in this section are not principally aimed at the educationally disadvantaged. Even when needs are assessed and appropriate advice given, many adults are prevented by other claims on their time from undertaking education. The subject of *Paid Educational Leave* is the granting of time off from work without loss of earnings to employees, in order to permit them to follow a course of study. It examines the arguments at international level which have surrounded the proposed introduction of paid educational leave as a right and assesses what progress has been made in establishing it.

It is almost a truism of adult education that adults have, simply through life experience, acquired a fund of knowledge and skills which can provide a basis for further learning. It is widely believed that many would be encouraged to follow courses of study if they were able to use this experiential learning. *Prior Life Experience and Higher Education* examines practices in the United States and Sweden which give credit for it and so make it easier for adults to take up places in universities and colleges. It also discusses the kind of programmes which make best use of experiential learning.

Factors in Participation

A. J. Cropley

The majority of adults engage regularly in "learning projects". In the United States, for instance, they spend on average about 500 hours a year on such activities, while in Europe, to take the example of Norway, it has been estimated that far less than half of all learning occurs in schools, and that this figure is falling. By "learning" is meant, of course, not "general learning which any intelligent being undergoes in adapting to circumstances", but "planned intentional preparation" (Lawson 1982 p. 103).

Adult education may be conceived of as a set of organized activities aimed at supporting such learning. Typically, it is regarded as being part of the system of education, and is thus distinguishable from work, recreation, or hobby activities, but is at the same time not part of the subsystem comprised by schools, universities, colleges, and the like. According to Knowles (1977), it covers 15 kinds of activity: (a) academic education; (b) education for the elderly; (c) community development; (d) creative arts; (e) economic education; (f) literacy education; (g) health education; (h) family-life education; (i) leadership training; (j) human relations training; (k) liberal education; (l) public affairs education; (m) recreational education; (n) science education; and (o) occupational education.

Impressive as this may sound, however, it is important to bear in mind that: (a) only about 20 percent of adult learning occurs within the framework of organized adult education; (b) only a relatively small proportion of all adults actually participate in such activities. Cross (1981) has likened the structure of participation to a pyramid—the tip consists of the small group of people who have definite and specific educational goals and participate regularly; the centre embraces a larger group (perhaps one-third of the population) who participate intermittently, and the base comprises nonparticipants. The relative size of these groups is indicated by figures such as those cited by Stock (1979) or Eccleston and Schmidt (1979). In Western Europe a little over 40 percent of all adults participate at some time in adult education. It is thus apparent that, even applying a generous definition of participation, at least one-half of the adult population in European–North American-type societies never participates in formal adult education.

The research on adult learning indicates, however, on the one hand that adults are in principle perfectly capable of learning (e.g., Horn 1982), and on the other that they actually do a great deal of learning in their private lives (Cross 1981, Tough 1978). The question thus arises of why so little of this learning occurs within the adult education system, that is, why participation rates are relatively low.

Boshier has looked at this question mainly from the point of view of psychological factors within the adults in question, pointing out, among other things, that it is generally easier to retain adults as students once they have commenced a formal learning activity than it is to coax them into embarking on an activity. He attributes this to the effects of skilful teaching. It is also apparent from research findings that the feeling on the part of learners that the course in question matches their needs, their expectations, or their idea of how they should be treated is a further important determinant of whether they persevere or drop out. On the other hand the question of what factors lead people to enrol at all is also of considerable importance. Houle (1980) has shown that the stock reasons given by adults when they are asked why they do not make use of adult education facilities—lack of time and/or of the funds necessary to cover fees and other expenses—are largely socially acceptable excuses. The problem lies elsewhere, especially in social, economic, and system factors.

1. Motivation as an Explanatory Concept

Many studies of motivation for participation in adult education view it as defined by the goals people hope to reach by means of participation, such as job advancement, acquisition of a new skill, or development of new friendships. It is, however, also possible to treat motivation as a general state of readiness to expend energy on a particular activity. The question of participation in adult education then becomes a matter not of ascertaining what it is that people want to learn or what teaching and learning strategies are most suitable in view of the special characteristics of adult learners, but rather of establishing which factors dispose some people to regard adult education as a good thing, others to see it as irrelevant to their lives, or boring, or snobbish.

As Welford (1980) pointed out, a particular "motive" may be satisfied by a variety of actions, while a particular action may be the result of many motives. The behavioural strategy actually adopted by an individual person is thus dependent upon a combination of factors going well beyond simply the presence or absence of a particular goal (such as getting ahead at work) and the availability or otherwise of a suitable adult education course. These factors include attitudes to learning and to oneself, priorities for the use of time, beliefs about the importance of schooling, and the like. Furthermore, readiness to adopt a certain course of action is influenced by the perceived "costs" involved and the expected benefits to be obtained—in the present context a benefit might be the learning of a new skill, a cost might involve loss of television viewing time, to take two concrete examples.

Thus, although adults' participation in adult education is obviously affected by factors within the individual (such as interests, attitudes, ambitions, and the like), it is also influenced by "framework conditions" which help to determine whether adult education in general or particular activities are regarded as desirable or undesirable, pleasant or unpleasant, suitable or unsuitable. These conditions are largely a function of the circumstances in which people live, especially of factors such as the values, attitudes, habits, priorities and the like of the social groups to which they belong, the economic structure of their society, even features of the education system itself.

2. *Education and the "Relations of Production"*

Marxist writers in particular draw attention to the interrelationship between the system of education and the system of production: according to this approach, education serves to prepare people for certain functions in a society's system of production. It is thus, in a sense, an instrument for assigning roles, status, expectations, aspirations, and the like in such a way that the economic order continues to function smoothly. Adult education must be seen as part of this system, and participation in conventional adult education as a function of the role assigned a particular person by the needs of the system of production. Adult education thus has the potential to increase the social division of labour. On the other hand, it is also possible to envisage forms of adult education which tend to break down this division—emancipatory adult education. This approach is strongly represented in analyses of adult education in Europe, especially since about 1970.

3. *Adult Education and Social Class*

Despite its emancipatory potential, studies of participation consistently show the effects of a "second creaming" (Bengtsson 1975): participation is disproportionately high on the part of people who already have the highest levels of initial education. Although workers often constitute the largest single group taking part in adult education activities, they are still underrepresented. Even in countries which have adopted a conscious emancipatory stance, this remains true—for instance, although demand for adult education rose sharply in France after the passage of the Law of 1971, it had stabilized by about 1975, and was both strongly oriented towards vocational education and also disproportionately high among white-collar workers.

Cropley and Kahl have outlined the mechanisms through which learning behaviour is related to social class: this is partly a matter of the degree to which learning in the formal system is seen as useful, as well as of the extent to which people regard themselves as able to meet the demands of this system. However, it is also related to the acceptance of certain roles, values, and norms. There is a systematic overlap between the norms, roles, and processes accepted by authority figures in the educational system (such as teachers) and those of certain groups of people, namely those of middle-class background. People from other backgrounds tend to find the system difficult to understand, or frequently find that there is a conflict between its norms and those which prevail in the informal system represented by work mates, peers, family, and the like. One common result is that they turn to the informal system for learning experiences, finding in the formal one mainly uncertainty or conflicts, and thus developing little faith in it or even an aversion to it.

Participation in adult education is thus affected by the role people play in the groups to which they belong, by the tactics they prefer for dealing with the external world, by their degree of willingness to accept certain kinds of external authority, their preference for particular learning strategies, and so on. Furthermore, these characteristics are shared with other people, are acquired in group settings, and are reinforced by the groups to which people belong, social classes being among the most important groups.

4. *System Factors*

As has already been mentioned, the educational system itself has features which either encourage or inhibit participation in adult education. An obvious example is to be found in the area of provision: in poor, large, or sparsely populated countries, for instance, geographical isolation of learners may mean that the "costs" associated with participation (not only financial, but also loss of time, separation from the family, and the like) may be very high. If these are not compensated by high "benefits" (once again either material or spiritual), there may be little incentive for participation. A related problem is the relatively straightforward one of absence of information about what is available or of what benefits may be expected. Among possible measures which can be adopted are counselling services, provision of travel or other costs, offering of compact, residential courses, or use of teaching and learning procedures which make it possible to learn at home, especially in the light of increases both in knowledge about processes such as self-directed learning and also in the availability of appropriate educational technology.

To a considerable degree there is an interaction between this area and the two previously mentioned. For instance, there is a strong tendency for formal, school-like learning to be regarded as the only really worthwhile form of learning. Adult education is thus affected by social norms which stereotype it as encompassing either recreational activities for the bored and lonely or else remedial education for those who missed out the first time round. In other words, it has low social status when compared with other segments of the educational system. A further example of this interaction is to be seen in the attitude of many adult educators themselves. They are often content to regard themselves as "handmaidens" or "poor cousins" of *real* education—the kind occurring in schools, colleges, and universities.

The result is an "identity crisis" which can lead to an unwillingness to regard adult education as having any serious theoretical basis and an absence of any special training for teaching personnel, a trivialization of ideas such as self-directed learning or participatory decision making, and general unwillingness to press the case for adult education with any special vigour.

Adult education also suffers from the effects on learning behaviour of adults of another powerful and prestigious element in the formal educational system—the school. It has already been pointed out that many people acquire during their school days attitudes, habits, values, self-image, and the like which predispose them to avoid organized learning situations once they become adults. Since these characteristics are acquired in school, but do not become apparent until adulthood, they may be referred to as "sleeper effects" (Birren 1979). Unfortunately, there is little that adult educators acting alone can do to prevent development of the preconditions for such effects. They can, of course, attempt to develop teaching and learning methods which avoid reactivating them, something which is already widely understood. One problem, however, is that the tendency for the society to regard school-like learning as the only worthwhile kind of learning is often also accepted by learners in adult education. The result is that they tend to regard teaching and learning activities which depart markedly from the norms of school as frivolous.

5. Conclusions

The whole area of adult education is thus beset by a series of factors which inhibit participation—of course these are only to be regarded as problems if it is assumed that higher rates of participation are desirable. At present, many adult educators would be among the first to point out that their budgetary resources could not accommodate a substantial rise in participation rates. Thus, convincing arguments need to be found which indicate that rates should be raised (i.e., there should be a quantitative change in participation) or else that the "right" people need to be encouraged to make use of available resources (i.e., a qualitative change). Such arguments would be most convincing if they were based on a clear statement of the role of adult education in the modern world. Especially useful would be statements which specified the relationship of adult education to other elements of the organized education system, not only those which are concerned with nonformal learning, but also the traditional formal elements (schools, universities, etc.). Such a conceptualization could have important implications for teaching and learning strategies, and would help to rationalize the use in adult education of educational media and other aids. It would also make a contribution to solving the identity crisis of adult education which has already been referred to.

Bibliography

Bengtsson J 1975 Recurrent education and manpower training. *Adult Training* 2: 7–9

Birren J E 1979 Issues in adult development. Paper presented at the Biennial Meeting of the Society for Research in Child Development, San Francisco, California

Cross K P 1981 *Adults as Learners: Increasing Participation and Facilitating Learning*. Jossey-Bass, San Francisco, California

Eccleston J, Schmidt F 1979 *School and Lifelong Learning*. Landesinstitut für Curriculumentwicklung, Lehrerausbildung und Weiterbildung, Neuss

Horn J L 1982 The aging of human abilities. In: Wolman B J (ed.) 1982 *Handbook of Developmental Psychology*. Prentice-Hall, Englewood Cliffs, New Jersey, pp. 847–70

Houle C 1980 *Continuing Learning in the Professions*. Jossey-Bass, San Francisco, California

Knowles M S 1977 *A History of the Adult Education Movement in the United States: Includes Adult Education Institutions Through 1976*, rev. edn. Krieger, Huntington, New York

Lawson K 1982 Lifelong education: Concept or policy. *Inter. J. Lifelong Educ.* 1: 97–108

Stock A K 1979 Developing lifelong education: Post-school perspectives. In: Cropley A J (ed.) 1979 *Lifelong Education: A Stocktaking*. UNESCO Institute for Education, Hamburg, pp. 78–87

Titmus C J 1983 *A Model of the Individual's Relationship with Adult Study*. Open University Press, Milton Keynes

Tough A 1978 Major learning efforts: Recent research and future directions. *The Adult Learner: Current Issues in Higher Education*. American Association for Higher Education, Washington, DC

Welford A T 1980 Where do we go from here? In: Poon L W (ed.) 1980 *Aging in the 1980s*. American Psychological Association, Washington, DC, pp. 615–21

Participant Motivation

R. Boshier

Adult education is usually voluntary so participants choose from among an array of offerings. Thus it is important for adult educators to know what "motivates" people to attend and why some persist and others drop out. However, there is considerable disagreement over the extent to which the focus of research and practice should be the learner or the educational environment. Adult educators seem to be more enamoured with humanistic than with behaviourist psychologies although both perspectives contribute to an understanding of motivation.

When viewed from a behaviourist frame of reference, "motivation" is redundant since adults respond to optimal conditions and reinforcing consequences in the same way as children. It is unduly pessimistic and scientifically dubious to label adults as "unmotivated" or "lazy". A more optimistic and scientifically provocative analysis would hold that many adults have to suffer the effects of adverse conditions and inappropriately managed reinforcement or punishment. Behaviourists criticize humanistic concepts of motivation because they perpetuate the notion that the "problem" resides in the learner, rather than in the environment. Despite this, behaviourism has had little impact on adult education which, despite changes wrought by the development of lifelong education, is still firmly rooted in Third Force (humanistic) and developmental psychology.

Fundamental to the distinction between adult and other forms of education is the widely accepted notion that adults are motivated in different ways than children. Adults are purported to be more "independent" and to occupy a greater variety of social roles than children. They have had more and a greater variety of experience than children. Finally, and most important in this context, they are presumed to be "problem oriented"; their readiness to learn is presumed to spring from "developmental tasks", "dominant concerns", and other needs that arise as adults pass through different stages of the life cycle.

The primary social role occupied by a child is that of learner. In contrast, adults must function as a spouse, family member, and worker. They also have civic, political, social, and other responsibilities. Few adults can stop work to become a full-time adult education participant. Because of competing responsibilities most adults have a diminished "margin" (the "load" they carry divided by the "power" they have to discharge it); thus adult educators are preoccupied with planning programmes congruent with the needs, motives, and expectations of potential participants. Adult educators place a high priority on diagnosing and satisfying individual, community, and societal needs. Thus, adult education is supposed to be more democratic and participatory than higher or pre-adult education and more preoccupied with understanding what "motivates" people to attend and persist with adult education activities.

1. Motivation for Participation

The modern era of adult education began after the First World War, and since that time there has been a persistent interest in motives or reasons that impel people to participate. Conventional wisdom asserts that programme planners should use data concerning participation motivation to design courses that meet learners' needs. But the interest in motives for participation is not all altruistic; the adult educators' salaries and survival are sometimes dependent upon their ability to use motivation data to attract people into their courses. There are two branches to the motives for participation research tradition. The first concerns the structure of motives (or motivational orientations); the second concerns functional relationships between motives and their antecedents.

1.1 Structure of Motivational Orientations

Most adults are volunteers for learning and impelled by a variety of reasons not necessarily connected to the course content or announced purposes of the activity. Some adult educators have used types in an attempt to impose order. Typologies assume that general patterns of behaviour exist and provide a shorthand way of discussing them. In adult education, as in psychology, there are theoretical and empirical typologies.

One theoretical typology was created by Houle (1961) on the basis of interviews with 22 learners. Houle proposed that participants were goal, activity, or learning oriented. The goal oriented were purported to use education as a means of accomplishing fairly clear-cut objectives; the activity oriented were those who took part because they found a meaning in the circumstances of the learning which had no necessary connection, and often no connection at all, with the content or announced purposes of the activity. The third, the learning oriented, sought knowledge for its own sake. For this last group education is a constant activity. Learning was so interwoven with the fabric of their being that they rarely partialled it out for separate attention.

Typologies provide a framework within which individuals can be classified. If a person is not a "pure" type he or she can be described in terms of the extent to which they resemble the types. For Houle, the central emphasis of each orientation was clear; they could however be portrayed as three circles overlapping at the centre. Houle's study spawned a number of quantitative investigations designed to test the veracity of the typology and correlate orientation scores with a variety of sociodemographic and life-cycle variables. As part of an attempt to test Houle's typology, Boshier (1971, 1982) produced successive versions of an "Education Participation Scale" (EPS) which contains 40 items (cast on a four-point Likert scale) based on the typology and interviews with adult education participants. Between 1971 and 1983 this instrument was completed by thousands of participants in North America, Southeast Asia, Africa, Australasia, and Europe. It is estimated that the EPS has been used in more than 60 studies in North America. Boshier and Collins (1983, 1984) factor and cluster analysed data from more than 12,000 learners in different parts of the world and concluded that, while Houle's typology had heuristic value, a six-factor model was the most theoretically and psychometrically defensible. Participants were deemed to enrol because of a need for:

(a) Social contact: these participants want to make and consolidate friendships, to be accepted by others, to gain insight into personal problems, to improve relationships and their social position. They participate because of their need for group activities and congenial friendships.

(b) Social stimulation: participants enrolled for this factor want to get relief from boredom, overcome the frustration of day-to-day living, to escape intellectual narrowness, to have a few hours away from other responsibilities. The essence of the factor is the use of adult education as an escape from boredom or frustration.

(c) Professional advancement: participants enrolled for this factor want to secure professional advancement, higher status in their job, or knowledge that will help in other courses. They are primarily job oriented.

(d) Community service: participants enrolled for this factor want to become more effective as citizens, to prepare for community service, to gain insight into human relationships, and to improve their ability to participate in community work.

(e) External expectations: participants enrolled for this factor are complying with the instructions of someone else. They are enrolled on the recommendation of some authority who is usually an employer, social worker, friend, priest, or counsellor. In North America where mandatory continuing education is widespread, the authority is sometimes a court, professional association, or licensing authority.

(f) Cognitive interest: participants enrolled for this factor enjoy learning for its own sake. Like the archetypal participant in Workers' Educational Association (WEA) classes, they merely want to "satisfy an enquiring mind" or "seek knowledge for its own sake".

The large-scale data analysis reported by Boshier and Collins (1983, 1984) protects the field from conclusions concerning the structure of participant motivation that are locally true but artifactual in the general sense. Houle did not claim his typology had external validity; it was never suggested that the 22 Chicago adults in his study resembled those living elsewhere. Yet both his typology and Boshier's (1971) initial factoring of the EPS were among the most frequently cited work in the American *Adult Education* journal (between 1968 and 1977). But typologies, whether theoretically or empirically derived, are of greatest significance when the various orientations are related to other variables presumed to shape needs that, in turn, motivate each person to participate. It is this second branch of the motives for participation tradition that has been the primary preoccupation of motivational orientation researchers.

1.2 Antecedents of Motivational Orientations

If programme planners know the characteristics of people primarily motivated by, say, the need for social contact, they will be able to target their publicity more precisely and tailor programme methods and formats to the characteristics of specific groups. Until the early 1970s it appeared that stage theory (as exemplified by developmental psychology) provided a sound conceptual foundation for programme planning. Although participation was known to occur as a function of a complex interaction of psychological, social, and institutional variables it was widely thought that motives varied as a function of life-cycle and socioeconomic variables. Thus, women were presumed to be motivated by different reasons than men; old people were purported to enrol for different reasons than young participants; wealthy people for different reasons than the poor. Clientele surveys in the United States, Canada, New Zealand, and the United Kingdom showed that institutional forms of adult education largely catered to a socioeconomic elite and that socioeconomic and life-cycle variables did explain part of the variance in motivation.

In their benchmark study of a national sample of 24,000 adults in the United States, Johnstone and Rivera (1965) showed that while job-centred reasons impel younger people into adult education, the enrolment goals of older participants "are much less pragmatic and utilitarian". Leisure-centred goals also "varied dramatically" among persons of different ages. Only 10 percent of men in their 20s took courses with "sparetime interests" in mind, as compared with 16 percent of those in their 30s, 19 percent in their 40s, and 28 percent of those aged 50 or over. They found that at all ages, men were more concerned with vocational goals while women enrolled "relatively more often in response to home and family life and leisure time interests" (1965 p. 11).

Johnstone and Rivera's 614 page book contained 216 tables. Between 1968 and 1977 this was the work cited most frequently by authors of articles in *Adult Education* (USA). Johnstone and Rivera made extensive use of nonparametric statistics and largely tested single variable relationships between the independent variables, motivation, and other dependent variables. Even though the data were gathered before the 1960s it would be revealing to subject them to multivariate analyses capable of revealing the amount of motivation variance that can be explained by various configurations of independent variables.

Boshier (1977) argued that motives for participation are associated with the extent to which participants have satisfied the lower order needs in Maslow's need hierarchy. It was contended that people moved from life-chance (deficiency) to life-space (growth) motivation as they got older or increased their socioeconomic status. Data gathered in the course of this and similar motivational orientation studies were mildly reassuring for programmers who wanted specific targets for their programmes and could not afford to direct their publicity over a wide front. But rapid social change has now threatened the validity of models that portray life as an orderly series of cycles that give rise to specific learning needs. Havighurst's (1953) life-cycle model, in particular, now seems old fashioned and raises the hackles of feminists who resent the submissive and homemaking roles ascribed to women. Erikson (1950) was more cautious than Havighurst and did not attach ages to the eight stages in his model. But identity crises are no longer the preserve of youth and "generativity versus stagnation" is too general to describe the various stages of old age.

Thus, although adult education participants are motivated by reasons that bear some relationship to socioeconomic and life-cycle variables, their "motives" are largely unexplained. Although correlations between motivational orientation scores and "antecedent" variables usually attain statistical significance, the amount of unexplained variance usually exceeds the amount of explained variance. In a typical motivational orientation study the author administers the EPS and then "explains" orientation scores through multivariate (usually regression) analyses. Most combinations of socioeconomic or life-cycle variables explain 25 to 35 percent of the variance in social contact, social stimulation, or other orientation scores.

Almost without exception, earlier studies of participant motivation (e.g., Johnstone and Rivera 1965) involved bivariate analyses. Although many of the results of these statistical tests employed in these ex post facto studies were significant, most of the variance in the motivational variables remained unexplained. A contemporary echo of this situation was heard from Boshier and Collins (1982) who correlated each of the six Education Participation Scale scores with socioeconomic variables. People of lower socioeconomic status obtained higher scores than high status participants on all the EPS factors except cognitive interest, where the relationship was nonsignificant. Thus participants with "low" education, occupational status, and income were significantly more inclined to be enrolled for social contact, social stimulation, community service, and external expectations reasons than people with "high" education, occupational status, and income. Persons with "low" education were also more inclined to be enrolled for professional advancement. Participants with "high" occupational status were more inclined to be enrolled for cognitive interest than "low" status persons. These authors also examined relationships between motivational orientation scores and sex, age, marital status, number of children, income, previous participation in adult education, and enrollment for credit (or noncredit). Because they had data from 12,191 participants, nearly all their correlations and F-ratios were statistically significant. But none of the socioeconomic or life-cycle variables accounted for more than 7 percent of the variance in social contact, social stimulation, professional advancement, or any other orientation score. As in previous, more localized studies, occupation was the most powerful predictor of motivation for participation.

It thus appears that although the structure of participant motives is reasonably clear, people enrol for reasons that are only marginally related to socioeconomic and life-cycle variables. However, once participants have been attracted to adult education programmes the situation is clearer because inspired instructors can reinforce and strengthen even the most fragile motivation. In general, more is known about what motivates adults to continue learning than what impels them to enrol.

2. The Role of Motivation in Dropout and Persistence

As long ago as 1814, instructors in the adult schools of Bristol in England, were urged to visit the homes of wayward participants who missed classes. Today dropout is described as the "old story" in adult education and is a universal problem. As volunteers for learning, participants vote with their feet when they find the programme content, instructional processes, or learning environment not to their liking. The earliest dropout research focused on the influence of internal participant variables. It was easy to ascribe the blame for dropout to the participant who was not motivated, or who was lazy or lacking in intelligence. Although this type of study produced statistically significant results there was little of theoretical or practical significance. The next wave of studies concerned environmental variables. If dropout variance does not reside in the learner it must stem from environmental influences. Once again, there were significant results. People were more inclined to dropout if classes were large, facilities wanting, or the instructors incompetent. But dropout rates were not dramatically decreased by lowering class sizes or remedying other environmental defects. These variables accounted for some but not a lot of dropout.

One conceptually satisfying way of dealing with motivational problems associated with dropout is to borrow concepts from perceptual psychology and portray dropout as stemming from a lack of "good fit" between persons and environments. For every person there is an optimal environment and for every environment an optimal person. It was this formulation that provided the foundation for Boshier's (1973) person/environment congruence model that satisfactorily distinguished dropouts from persisters. Rubenson (1975) adapted expectancy–valence theory to account for motivational problems manifested in dropout. This Swedish researcher maintained that learners persist if a course or learning activity satisfies an important need (positive valence) and if they expect to be able to cope with and complete the course (positive expectancy). Although placing an appropriate emphasis on the importance of expectations, the model does not specify factors that can be manipulated to enhance valence and expectancy. In another formulation, Irish (1978) developed a model based on assumptions borrowed from operant psychology. She identified three sets of reinforcers that build on positive motivation and thus attendance. In her instrument, 10 items concerned classroom reinforcers, 10 concerned outside-the-classroom reinforcers, and nine concerned the participant's job. Irish's model was conceptually parsimonious and emphasized the optimal arrangement of the external conditions for learning. Instead of blaming the victim it alerted adult education programmers and instructors to the need for inspired practice.

It thus appears that one way adult education instructors can diminish dropout rates is to treat motivation as a hypothetical construct and concentrate on the creation of optimal conditions and consequences that motivate learners. Teachers should create an adult-oriented learning climate which is relaxed, informal, and responsive to participants' needs.

They should use instructional techniques appropriate to the type of outcome sought by the learner. Lectures should only be used when the instructor wants to impart information. If participants are expected to acquire intellectual skills, cognitive strategies, attitudes, or motor skills the instructors should use experiential techniques such as role playing, group discussion, simulation, structured exercises, and case studies. Instructors should use formative evaluation and be willing to modify the course content and processes when motivational problems appear to be developing.

3. *Outstanding Issues*

Despite the longstanding interest in motivation, adult education researchers and practitioners confront many unanswered questions. There is a need for research concerning relationships between motives that impel people into adult education and forces that foster persistence in adult education. There is a need to study (a) motivational changes that occur as a result of participation in adult education; (b) interactions between participant motivation and instructor variables; and (c) the motivation of people who make (and fail to make) use of the broadening array of opportunities for learning in the natural societal setting.

At a more practical level there is a profound need for adult education authorities to ensure that educators recognize the value and utility of the participants' experience and arrange the learning environment accordingly. By definition, adults who volunteer to undertake adult education are already motivated. But when asked to endure boring lecturers and other adverse circumstances, their motivation is easily crushed. When adults return to education they often bring negative memories of schools and teachers. Many have heard and believe the unfounded adage concerning the inability of the old dog to learn new tricks. Thus, although a scientific problem in its own right, learner motivation is bound up with broader issues concerning the purposes of adult education, programme planning, the design and management of instruction, and the training of teachers.

Bibliography

Boshier R W 1971 Motivational orientations of adult education participants: A factor analytic exploration of Houle's typology. *Adult Educ.* 21(2): 3–26

Boshier R W 1973 Educational participation and dropout: A theoretical model. *Adult Educ.* 23(4): 255–82

Boshier R W 1977 Motivational orientations revisited: Life-space motives and the Education Participation Scale. *Adult Educ.* 27: 89–115

Boshier R W 1982 *Education Participation Scale*. Learningpress, Vancouver

Boshier R W, Collins J B 1983 Education Participation Scale factor structure and correlates for twelve thousand learners. *Int. J. Lifelong Educ.* 2(2):163–77

Boshier R W, Collins J B 1984 The Houle typology after 22 years: A large scale empirical test. *Adult Educ.* 35(3): 113-130

Erikson E H 1950 *Childhood and Society*. Norton, New York

Havighurst R J 1953 *Developmental Tasks and Education*, 2nd edn. MacKay, New York

Houle C O 1961 *The Inquiring Mind*. University of Wisconsin Press, Madison, Wisconsin

Irish G H 1978 Persistence and dropout in adult education: Their relation to differential reinforcement of attendance (Unpublished doctoral dissertation, Columbia University) *Dissertation Abstracts International* 1978 39: 1993A–1994A (University Microfilms No. 7819355)

Johnstone J W C, Rivera R J 1965 *Volunteers for Learning: A Study of the Educational Pursuits of American Adults*. Aldine, Chicago, Illinois

Rubenson K 1975 *Participation in Recurrent Education*. Organisation for Economic Co-operation and Development, Paris

Outreach Work

M. Osborn

The term "outreach" describes the provision of education outside the traditional institutional framework aimed at those who might not otherwise participate in educational activity. It is a strategy which is intended to compensate for the limitations of an institution- or centre-based educational service. The motivating philosophy derives from Illich (1971) and Freire (1972), both of whom believe that new strategies are required to tune the educational system to the needs of working-class groups. The term became popular in the 1960s and 1970s when research findings indicated that, far from providing a second chance for adults who had received little formal education initially, adult education frequently reinforced the advantage gained by those who had already succeeded in education. Research in a number of different countries has demonstrated that those who participate in education as adults are likely to have had more formal education in the past and to be of a higher socioeconomic status than those who do not. The problem, then, for adult educators is to devise programmes and methods which will attract those who do not participate in existing schemes and, in particular, to involve the most disadvantaged sections of the population, and to make available educational resources to them.

1. Target Population and Methods

Outreach programmes may be aimed not only at the working class and those who may be termed educationally disadvantaged, but also at other groups who may have particular problems and needs, and who do not participate in centre-based activities for a variety of reasons. These include elderly people, the unemployed, those from ethnic minorities, gypsies, and the mentally and physically handicapped. Another potential target group is housebound women with young children. Outreach activities tend to take one of two main forms, (a) activity at the level of the local community, often involving personal recruitment either individually or through contact with existing local groups and networks, for example the Swedish outreach experiments which recruited participants at their place of work and in their local housing areas; and (b) activity at a national level in the form of "distance education" involving the use of the media and printed materials supplemented by locally based teaching groups, for example the Open University of the United Kingdom community education programme.

Various combinations of the two forms may occur. For example, at a national level the media may be used to arouse initial interest which is then built upon at a local level as in the United Kingdom adult literacy programme.

2. Programmes for Working-class and Educationally Disadvantaged Groups

Attempts to reach working-class adults in a disadvantaged area in Liverpool have been described by Lovett (1975). The tutors, acting as resource agents, educational guides, and teachers, made themselves aware of the activities of informal groups, the problems and needs in the community, and encouraged them to evolve into educational activities. Methods used included a house-to-house survey of a street, involvement of the leadership of various local groups, and the use of local radio.

Another "outreach" project in the United Kingdom began with a community study of Leigh Park, a large overspill housing estate, and then set out to widen the take-up of educational activities (Fordham et al. 1979). Through its community involvement, the project became the facilitator and often the initiator of a wide variety of socially based learning groups which formed a network. The principle on which the network operated was one in which learning was no longer confined to specific subject areas presided over by experts, but an activity which related expertise and knowledge closely to the social experience and particular needs of participants.

In the Swedish outreach experiments, participants were contacted individually, either in their work-place by trade union organizers, or in their local housing areas and were encouraged to join study circles (Rubenson 1979). Participants chose between different enrolment conditions (studies divided between working hours and spare time, spare-time studies with an incentive allowance, or spare-time studies without financial incentive). No charge was made for the courses or the materials used. In addition, financial assistance was available for extra travel, meals, and childminding expense incurred by participants. Interviews with those involved demonstrated that many would not have participated if they had not been contacted in the way they were.

There was considerable variation in the results of the outreach work between different target groups and communities. Interest in participation generally declined with increasing age, and in some areas with increased family income. In mixed sex target groups, more men became involved than women. Interest in participation was often reduced among contacts with three or more children at home. The greatest successes were achieved by recruitment in the work place rather than in housing areas. Several factors contributed to this. Those in housing areas were harder to contact and were often the most disadvantaged and hard to recruit groups. Moreover, contact within housing areas was directed at individuals while contact at the work place was collective and built on the potential participant's most significant member and reference group—his/her work group. A significant distinguishing feature of the Swedish experiments was that the outreaching activity was given a more established form and organization on the basis of earmarked state funds to act as a recruitment model. Selectivity concerning who was approached and the advantageous enrolment conditions contributed to its success.

3. Outreach, Distance Education, and the Media

Distance learning methods are a major form of outreach activity. Learning methods normally combine the use of printed materials with the use of television and radio for publicity and motivational purposes as well as direct teaching. At a local level, animateurs and volunteers provide guidance and help with individual problems. Case studies of the use of distance teaching methods for adult basic education in Europe are described by Kaye and Harry (1982). Some are regional projects—Just the Job in southwest England; Tele-promotion Rurale, Rhone Alpes, and Auvergne in France; and Radio

ECCA in the Canary Islands. The others provide coverage at a national level and include the Open University community education programme, the Danish Radio "Danish for Adults", and the Open School in the Netherlands. In all these projects the most important elements are personal contact (e.g., study groups, meetings, personal tuition, or counselling), the use of specially prepared printed materials, and to varying degrees, the use of the media.

At the level of higher education, the United Kingdom Open University uses such methods not only to reach the mass of its students, but also to reach those who are disadvantaged by physical handicap, by being in prison, or by living in remote areas. An extension of distance methods, telephone teaching, has been a successful means of helping the geographically isolated not only used by the Open University for students in remote parts of Scotland, but also by the Universities of Lund, and of Linkoping in Sweden, and by the University of Wisconsin, in the United States. Educational projects involving distance education and the media have been carried out in Australia, Brazil, Malawi, Mauritius, Korea, Kenya, and Israel, among many other countries. In general, research suggests that television and radio provide the essential spark, or a central role in recruiting but there is little evidence that broadcasts unaccompanied by other teaching methods have a lasting effect after the series has finished.

4. *Outreach and the Elderly*

Most educational work which reaches out to the elderly concentrates on the easily identifiable "captive audience" of those in residential hospitals, homes, and day centres. As yet there is little provision for the housebound elderly and other similarly disadvantaged.

However, methods employed to reach older housebound people include (a) using existing contact networks, for example, social services, community health workers, and so on; (b) distributing leaflets throughout a geographical area; and (c) door-to-door visiting. As in outreach work with other groups, personal contact has been found to be the best method of recruitment (Glendinning 1980).

5. *Outreach and the Unemployed*

Many providers of programmes for the unemployed in Europe, the United States, and the United Kingdom report difficulties in reaching the unemployed and encouraging them to participate, in particular in recruiting the very groups which need assistance most—those with the poorest education as well as older people and the very young. Two schemes in Belgium have made particular efforts to reach those nonparticipants. At Canal-Emploi, cable television and face-to-face workshops are used to help participants to understand their social and economic situation and to give them the necessary confidence and basic skills to go on subsequently to professional training courses organized by other bodies.

Another project, FUNOC (Formation pour l'Université Ouverte de Charleroi) aims particularly at the underqualified aged below 35, and centres learning activities on groups of 12 to 15 people, using local people as tutors–animateurs with the aid of initial training and monthly evaluation training sessions. In 1980 at least 70 percent of participants had no educational qualifications: there had been little drop out after three months, and participants gained confidence, many expressing a wish to carry on further with their studies.

There are numerous examples in the United Kingdom—among them the Sharrow Unemployed Self-help Scheme with its related programme of educational activity, and the community project at Easterhouse, a housing estate near Glasgow which aims, through the setting up of a community company, to generate employment opportunities throughout the area, to provide facilities, services, and amenities not presently available, and to initiate and sustain voluntary initiatives in the area.

6. *Outreach and Women*

The West of Scotland Workers' Educational Association (WEA) describes an outreach attempt to meet the educational needs of women at home. Contact was made with various local women's groups and their members became involved in the production of video tapes dealing with aspects of women's role in society. The process of working towards the production of the video tapes provided all the educational elements of discussion, research, and exchange of ideas characteristic of a WEA class, yet there was no formal structure and very few participants had ever been previously involved in adult education. The tapes were used to stimulate debate in many groups and organizations including other WEA branches.

In general, research suggests that child-care facilities alongside daytime courses remove a major barrier to women's participation and that these should form an essential part of outreach activities aimed at women.

7. *Outreach in Educational Guidance and Counselling*

There are numerous examples of outreach work in the provision of educational information, guidance, and counselling services in the United Kingdom, the United States, and Australia (Osborn et al. 1981). This involves two separate issues: firstly, bringing to the attention of the general public the facilities available in ways which are not conventional; and secondly, reassessing the forms and types of provision in response to the expressed wishes of a public hitherto not using the adult education service.

In the first type, various institutions offer "open days" which are extensively advertised locally and which provide information that enables people to discuss various options, to receive advice, and perhaps make further arrangements for educational guidance. In Sheffield, in the United Kingdom, successful work of this type was done from a mobile caravan on housing estates, and in a factory. A number of community colleges in Ontario have established store-front centres on a main downtown street. In the United Kingdom, "shop-front" premises have been used in a similar way to provide information. In Australia, the Learning Exchange in Melbourne provides an enquiry service, information on local community resources, a newspaper which enables people to initiate discussion and activity groups, a place to meet, a library, and research projects on alternative ways of using community resources. Other local learning exchanges in the United States, Canada, and Australia provide information by mail, telephone, and personal visits about many study opportunities.

In summary, the aim of outreach programmes is to eliminate the obstacles which prevent adults with brief and inadequate formal schooling, and others with particular disadvantages, from participating in learning activities and using the educational resources provided by society. Rubenson, in considering future developments in outreach, suggests that, in order to bring about changes (in provision and organization), the outreaching activity must act as a two-way communication (Rubenson 1979). Thus the information obtained by outreach workers and organizers should be fed back systematically into the organization and should build a foundation on which to evaluate the activity and consequent changes.

See also: Distance Education; Nonformal Education

Bibliography

Advisory Council on Adult and Continuing Education 1983 *Continuing Education: Local Learning Centres*. ACACE, Leicester

Fordham P, Poulton G, Randle L 1979 *Learning Networks in Adult Education: Non-formal Education on a Housing Estate*. Routledge and Kegan Paul, London

Freire P 1972 *Pedagogy of the Oppressed*. Penguin, Harmondsworth

Fuller T, Waldron M 1984 What is university–community outreach? Some types, prospects and problems in a technological age. *Canadian J. of Univ. Cont. Educ.* 10: (2)

Glendinning F (ed.) 1980 *Outreach Education and the Elders: Theory and Practice*. Seminar papers. Beth Johnson Foundation, Stoke-on-Trent

Illich I D 1971 *Deschooling Society*. Calder and Boyars, London

Johnson S E 1985 Faculty perspectives on outreach teaching. *Lifelong Learning* 9(3): 11-13, 27

Kaye A, Harry K (eds.) 1982 *Using the Media for Adult Basic Education*. Croom Helm, London

Lovett T 1975 *Adult Education, Community Development and the Working Class*. Ward Lock, London

McKerrell S 1983 Outreach Work with Women: Education with a Human Face. In: Bruce A (ed.) 1983 *What is Women's Education*? Scottish Adult Basic Education Unit, Edinburgh

Osborn M, Withnall A, Charnley A 1981 *Educational Information, Advice, Guidance, and Counselling for Adults*. National Institute of Adult Education, Leicester

Rubenson K 1979 *Recruitment to Adult Education in the Nordic Countries: Research and Outreaching Activities*. Stockholm Institute of Education Department of Educational Research, Stockholm

Adult Education Counseling

J. A. Farmer

In the past, there has been some confusion about the definition of the term "counseling" when used in relation to adult education. Moreover, a relatively low priority has typically been placed, administratively and financially, on providing counseling in adult education no matter how it has been defined. Nevertheless, this activity has emerged as a reality in various forms in most parts of the world. By the mid-1970s, a growing, worldwide network of persons involved in or knowledgeable about it could be identified and could describe the "state of the art" in their regions or nations in some detail (Farmer et al. 1977 p. 385). International conferences on the topic have been held at least annually, sponsored by such organizations as UNESCO and the European Bureau of Adult Education. Complaints about the scarcity of literature on the topic have been superseded by the observation that the literature on the topic is "bewildering" (DiSilvestro 1981). Fortunately, bibliographic reviews (Ironside and Jacobs 1977, Farmer et al. 1977, Goldberg 1980) on the topic have been published.

Counseling in adult education can be viewed from three, increasingly broad, perspectives. First, viewed most narrowly, counseling is an activity carried out professionally by persons with the title counselor who are employed by institutions, organizations, or agencies that provide adult education. Second, viewed more broadly, it consists of "counseling services or functions" provided to adults in some way relative to their current or prospective efforts to learn. Such functions or services may or may not be offered by professionally trained, institution-based counselors. Third, viewed even more broadly, it is situation-based and focuses first and foremost on difficult or anomalous situations in which adults find themselves and which require adaptation.

1. The Professional, Institution-based Perspective

By the late 1950s, the importance of making available professional counseling to adult learners in organizations, agencies, and institutions providing adult and continuing education was being stressed in the literature (Brunner et al. 1959 pp. 129, 136). Definitions of counseling at this time typically conformed quite closely to the standard dictionary definition of the term. According to the *Webster's Dictionary*, counseling is professional guidance of the individual by utilizing psychological methods, especially in collecting case history data, using various techniques of personal interview, and testing interests and aptitudes. Moreover, a counselor is an adviser, who makes recommendations regarding decisions and provides information.

A decade later, Langdon (1969 pp. 236–62), in describing counseling and guidance services provided by educational institutions for adult learners, stressed the importance of the professional preparation of such counselors. According to Langdon, professional counselors in adult education programs should have a master's degree in counseling and guidance from an accredited college or university. Their academic background should include work in such areas as individual inventory techniques, information services, counseling theory, practicum in counseling, personality theory, group guidance, and adult education. Such professionally trained counselors typically are expected to provide counseling, testing, information, placement, referral, follow-up, and/or record-keeping services for adult learners in the institutions in which they are employed.

Langdon also observed that few programs were preparing counselors specifically to provide counseling and guidance services in adult education programs and anticipated that the time was fast approaching when many such programs would be offered. A shift in emphasis during the 1970s away from a professional, institution-based perspective to a more open-counseling function perspective may well have curtailed the development of graduate programs to prepare professional, institution-based counselors of adult learners and the widespread emergence of professionally staffed, institution-based counseling programs for adult learners. Persons familiar with counseling in adult education in such countries as India, Yugoslavia, Czechoslovakia, Kenya, Egypt, and Barbados indicated (Farmer et al. 1977) that little or no professional, institution-based counseling was available for adult learners. Some indicated that there was a need to develop such services. Others indicated that needed counseling and information services tended to be provided informally or through other means.

2. The Open-counseling Functions Perspective

During the 1970s, increased attention was paid to open forms of adult and continuing education, to self-directed learning, and lifelong learning. Concurrently, attention was focused on more open forms of adult education counseling not necessarily offered by professional, institution-based counselors or in traditional counseling forms. At least in part, the shift away from the professional, institution-based model resulted from expressed concerns that such counseling can be more institution- than client-serving and that professional counseling may be incompatible with the needs of many adult learners to be self-directed. Moreover, traditional forms of counseling seemed incompatible with the needs of adults, particularly those wanting to engage in non-traditional forms of learning.

There has been a shift in the titles of the literature describing counseling of adult learners. Before the 1970s, authors typically used the terms "professional," "counseling," and "adult education programs" in titles of articles and books on the topic. During the 1970s, titles such as "counseling and information services for adult learners" or merely "counseling and information services for adults" were in vogue.

These counseling and information services were usually described (Farmer et al. 1977) as consisting of one or more of the following functions.

(a) Information giving—providing to adults information about specific educational or occupational opportunities or related services, along with assistance to enable them to use such information to plan further education.

(b) Assessment—using assessment instruments, such as inventories, tests, and questionnaires, to assist individual adult learners to relate their interests and values to occupational choices and further education.

(c) Planning—providing assistance with educational and career planning for adult learners.

(d) Assisting adult learners to cope more effectively with personal problems—such as marital conflict, family planning, parenting, nutrition, or occupational adjustment.

(e) Advocacy—of the needs and rights of adult clients to representatives of educational institutions.

(f) Referral—of adult clients to other agencies for other types of assistance.

When viewed in terms of these six functions, counseling for adult learners, at least in part, could be performed not only by professionally trained counselors but also, and perhaps more efficiently and effectively, by a wide variety of others including: teachers, program developers, administrators, service-agency personnel, factory managers, librarians, paraprofessionals, volunteers, and peers. Sometimes those without professional training in counseling provided one or more of the counseling and information service functions described above in their everyday roles as relatives, friends, colleagues, or supervisors. At other times, such persons were trained to perform one or more of those functions and did so as part of the staffs of adult education programs or community-based counseling and information service centers.

Provision of the counseling and information services functions, moreover, was offered not only in educational institutions but also (according to some authors, more effectively and efficiently) in a wide variety of other settings such as libraries, community-based counseling and information centers, factories, rented storefronts, and homes. According to Knox (DiSilvestro 1981), the community-based education guidance center is one of the most significant innovations in counseling adult learners. Ironside (DiSilvestro 1981) has described and illustrated the nature of such centers. Some of the centers make extensive use of or are sponsored by representative community councils; some are sponsored by consortia of the providers of adult education in the community; some are independent educational brokering agencies; some make extensive use of networks of support services in the community or referral networks; some are centers in which centralized services are provided; and some are government sponsored.

The professional, institution-based approach to counseling in adult education was typically provided in the institution providing the service for which the adult student happened to be enrolled. In contrast, differentiated versions of the open-counseling, functions approach were developed and implemented to meet the needs of specific clientele such as women returning to education and work, the disadvantaged, and alien (foreign) employees.

Many innovative programs came into existence during the 1970s based on the open approach and were designed to serve one or more of the six functions specified above. For example, the role of libraries was revised in Yugoslavia and elsewhere. They became counseling and information service centers. Locally based, part-time tutor–counselors were used as part of a regional infrastructure to counsel adult learners through the Open University in the United Kingdom. The Women's Resources Center in Vancouver developed an extensive training program for volunteer counselors of adult learners. Human and computerized networks were developed (Watts and Ballantine 1983) to aid counseling and information-service transactions, and many media and technologies were harnessed in the service of adult learners.

In 1977, Ironside and Jacobs (1977) observed that the professional model was still the most common one but less so than it had been. At the same time, evidence of the need for a third perspective, a situation-based approach, began to appear.

3. The Situation-based Approach

By the late 1970s and early 1980s, questions were raised in the adult education literature about the two perspectives described above. Similar questions were being raised elsewhere about approaches used in education generally (Petrie 1982), counseling generally (Ivey and Simek-Downing 1980), and counseling adults generally (Schlossberg and Entine 1977). Moreover, these authors and others began presenting the elements of a third perspective which reframes the topic and synthesizes aspects of the first two perspectives.

From the third perspective, counseling in adult education is viewed neither in terms of the services (adult education and counseling) provided nor in terms of the styles of service preferred by prospective recipients. In contrast, this third perspective focuses first and foremost on difficult and anomalous situations in which adults find themselves and which require adaptation. According to Petrie (1982), human adaptation comes in two forms: assimilation (changing experience to fit conceptual and representational schemes) and accommodation (changing conceptual and representational schemes to fit experience). Accommodation is generally more difficult and requires quite different forms of assistance than assimilation. Situations requiring adaptation may involve difficulties or anomalies in the adults' personal lives or careers (Brammer 1984, Danish 1983, Schlossberg 1981). They may also involve difficulties or anomalies incurred by the families, organizations, communities, or society of which the individuals are a part. According to Gelpi (Farmer et al. 1977), it is important to relate adult education counseling not only to the needs of individuals but also to associative living. From the third perspective, counseling and adult education are provided to the extent that they help adults with their needed or desired adaptation.

In the provision of adult education counseling from the third perspective:

(a) Counseling and information are viewed more as developed experience than as developed systems.

(b) Care is taken to let the theory of counseling guide the informational and advisory services provided.

(c) How comprehensive a mix of counseling and information services is appropriately provided for any specific location varies with the clientele, programs being offered, and the availability of other counseling and information services.

(d) Persons who are not professionally trained in counseling are used in helping adults with assimilation. Persons with professional training in counseling and/or relevant scholarly, scientific, or technical areas of expertise are used in helping adults with accommodation.

It is quite possible that some, or even many, of the programs providing "adult education counseling" are actually functioning, at least in part, in keeping with the third perspective, even though they may have been initially conceptualized or subsequently described in terms of one of the other perspectives.

See also: Adulthood

Bibliography

Brammer L M 1984 Counseling theory and the older adult *Couns. Psychol.* 12(2): 29–37

Brunner E de S, Wilder D, Kirchner C, Newberry J 1959 *An Overview of Adult Education Research.* Adult Education Association of the United States, Chicago, Illinois

Danish S J 1983 *Helping Skills II: Life Development Interventions.* Human Sciences Press, New York

DiSilvestro F R (ed.) 1981 *Advising and Counseling Adult Learners.* Jossey-Bass, San Francisco, California

Farmer J A, Knox A B, Farmer H S (eds.) 1977 Counseling and information services for adult learners. *Int. Rev. Educ.* 23(4)

Goldberg J C 1980 Counseling the adult learner: A selective review of the literature. *Adult Educ.* 30: 67–81

Ironside D J 1979 Innovations in counseling of and information-giving to adult learners in North America. *Int. J. Adv. Couns.* 2: 199–211

Ironside D J, Jacobs D E 1977 *Trends in Counselling and Information Services for the Adult Learner.* Ontario Institute for Studies in Education, Toronto, Ontario

Ivey A E, Simek-Downing L 1980 *Counseling and Psychotherapy: Skills, Theories, and Practice.* Prentice-Hall, Englewood Cliffs, New Jersey

Langdon G 1969 Counseling and guidance services. In: Shaw N C (ed.) 1969 *Administration of Continuing Education: A Guide for Administrators.* National Association for Public School Adult Education, Washington, DC

Petrie H G 1982 *The Dilemma of Enquiry and Learning.* University of Chicago Press, Chicago, Illinois

Schlossberg N K 1981 A model for analyzing human adaptation to transition. *Couns. Psychol.* 9(2): 2–18

Schlossberg N K, Entine A D (eds.) 1977 *Counseling Adults.* Brooks/Cole, Monterey, California

Watts A G, Ballantine M 1983 Computers in careers guidance: The British experience. *Couns. Psychol.* 11(4) 49–54

Counselling Older Adults

F. Vernon

If elderly persons are looked at from an historical viewpoint, the following vignette sums up their social position over many years. Throughout most of recorded history, the elderly have been few in number. Those elderly who were in an elite position in society controlled the means of production and monopolized wealth and power, and those who were members of the proletariat and working classes were a vital part of the economic well-being of the family and helped maintain it until death. The old in all social classes were repositories of wealth and experience upon which the younger generation could draw in times of trouble.

The Industrial Revolution, which, beginning towards the end of the seventeenth century, swept over the Western world, changed that vignette beyond recognition. One of its benefits, scientific medicine, vanquished most of the childhood diseases which once took such a heavy toll. Formerly only a small percentage of people lived to old age; today, a much higher percentage survive. Growing affluence makes it possible for younger members of society to achieve early economic independence, weakening the traditional controls exercised by the elders. Ever-advancing technology continues to make obsolete the need for skills and knowledge that previously took a lifetime to acquire. To make matters worse, increasingly automated production requires less and less human input. Finally, the breakdown of the extended family and its replacement by the two-generation nuclear family has left the elderly without support and with no sense of usefulness in their declining years.

1. Purpose for Counselling the Elderly

A common attitude toward counselling for older people is one of surprise and disbelief. Counsellors without experience in working with older adults often wonder why they would need counselling assistance when they already have a lifetime of experience in coping and adapting.

In the technologically advanced Western world, retirement from a lifetime job has been accepted as a normal and necessary transition. For many, this late-life event is the most dramatic and often traumatic transition experienced since moving from youth to adulthood.

Some of the problems faced by older adults include: being regarded as "over the hill" and, at best, as someone to be tolerated or, at worst, as nonproductive parasites burdening the productive members of society; not knowing how to shift gears to make effective use of the remaining years of life; seeing old age as a period of life in which nothing can be done to avoid losses and little help is available to alleviate such losses; experiencing mental stress largely as a result of acute loneliness and depression resulting in high rates of suicide; and experiencing difficulty in finding someone to talk to about living, dying, and death.

Lifelong learning, that is, the acceptance of new ideas and new behaviours, is absolutely essential for full physical and mental functioning in late life. The Ulyssean concept expounded by McLeish (1976) gives older adults a goal and structure within which they can "...richly maintain the power to produce, to learn, and to create until the very end of the life journey". To achieve this goal, older persons need help to dispel the myths of aging and to regain a high level of self-worth. Research findings show that counselling, individually or in small-group settings, can benefit the older adult just as much as younger adults. Counselling may be needed by many older adults, at various times and for various reasons, and not just by those with acute problems. Many elderly people are hesitant to seek counselling, the following being some of the reasons why.

(a) To seek counselling is seen by some older adults as implying instability or incompetence, conditions toward which society holds negative attitudes.

(b) Those involved in health and social care services may imply attitudes which are unlikely to encourage the use of counselling services or which devalue the potential benefits of such services for older adults.

(c) Older adults may react with anger to the suggestion that their troubles may, in part, stem from an unwillingness or inability to review the values, knowledge, or skills which they learned in their youth and to change those which are no longer helpful or effective.

(d) Those older adults who experience low self-esteem may feel they have not been very successful in their lives, especially if they measure success against standards related to power and wealth. They may hesitate to try new activities which may yield uncertain results, cause pain, or never reach completion or resolution.

(e) Some older persons may lack essential information for making decisions. They may be engaged in caring for a sick spouse or other dependents. They may feel unable to express themselves clearly, and lack assertiveness.

2. *Counselling in Practice*

In its traditional form, counselling denotes a one-to-one relationship between an individual with a concern and a professional trained to help the individual deal with that concern. More recently, counselling has broadened to include less traditional approaches. This article will consider two such approaches: peer counselling and small-group counselling.

2.1 One-to-one Counselling

This technique assumes that the counsellor is trained in therapeutic counselling and/or problem solving. To be an effective counsellor of older adults, professionals should be knowledgeable about the physiological and psychological aspects of normal aging, as well as about the interaction of disease, disability, malnutrition, social and emotional stress with normal aging. Counsellors would then be able to recognize and deal with the emotional, physical, and social problems which are typical of all adults, as well as those which may be more specifically related to increasing chronological age.

There is a place for what Herr and Weakland (1979) refer to as "applied gerontology". This term includes a wide range of community professionals such as doctors, nurses, ministers, lawyers, and social workers, who have frequent contact with the elderly. Older adults often bring their problems to these professionals even though the identified problem may be only an excuse for making contact and the real problem only peripherally related to the identified problem. For example, a lawyer may be asked to change a will in order to disinherit a son. Through careful questioning, the lawyer may determine that the father feels his son has been neglecting him. The move to disinherit, therefore, may be one way to strike back. The lawyer may be able to assist the father to view the proposed action as an inappropriate solution and to redefine the problem in a manner which will allow for family involvement in the eventual solution.

2.2 Peer Counselling

Peer counselling has grown as a result of necessity. There can never be enough professionally trained counsellors to meet all needs. Peer counselling is an effective approach in which the individual with the problem or concern receives help from a lay person in the same community or of the same age who has a reputation for empathic understanding. In more formal versions of peer counselling, lay persons are identified by trained professionals and given basic training to improve their effectiveness. Training lay counsellors is one means for making more efficient use of the skills of the trained professional. The training programme usually consists of a balance between communicating skills and knowledge of community resources, and is designed to enhance the natural skills of those who demonstrate a natural ability for helping and counselling.

2.3 Small-group Counselling

Group counselling can utilize trained professionals who draw on interactions among the individuals in small groups, all of whom share similar concerns. For example, groups have been formed to assist widows or retired persons. Alternatively, self-help groups may form consisting of untrained or informally trained peers who share a common concern. Alcoholics Anonymous (UK) is one such group.

The small-group process is also viewed as a means for helping several individuals at the same time, even though individual concerns may differ. Older adults, who have no identifiable problem but who suffer from a sense of anomie, isolation, alienation, or general lack of fulfilment, can be encouraged to join a group associated with a day-care or drop-in centre. Such groups often have a trained facilitator who leads the group but the process of group interaction among individual group members is an essential component of the technique. Factual, useful, timely information can be introduced for discussion, or visiting resource persons can attend to give specialized assistance. The group approach is an effective means to change attitudes and to improve self-esteem so that life can be viewed as more personally rewarding.

While specific objectives of the small-group technique vary, the basic goals, common to all such groups, appear to include: helping participants discover themselves and the reality of their own concerns; and helping them to define new goals for themselves (self-renewal) and to develop action plans which help make these goals attainable (self-actualization).

The learning techniques used in small-group counselling include helping participants to improve listening and speaking skills, to express feelings, to improve self-image by emphasizing competencies and accomplishments while acknowledging weaknesses, to be more assertive, and to deal with stress through physical and mental relaxation.

3. Conclusion

Because there is little research on the subject, the question of the benefits to be derived from counselling older adults must be answered subjectively. Those who have been involved in peer counselling, especially using the small-group approach, are unanimous in their praise of its effectiveness. Purists may protest that discussion among peers in small groups is not counselling, but simply a version of teaching and learning. The dictionary defines counselling as "giving advice". In this sense, those professionals who are nondirective are not counsellors either, but must be viewed as facilitators who help clients solve their own concerns.

Perhaps the acceptance and practice of lifelong, self-directed learning in which individuals control self-renewal and self-actualization, will make the distinction appear academic. The important issue is helping older individuals deal with their own problems using whatever techniques appear to work most effectively whatever the label.

See also: Old Age

Bibliography

Herr J J, Weakland J H 1979 *Counseling Elders and Their Families: Practical Techniques in Applied Gerontology*. Springer, New York

Luce G G 1979 *Your Second Life: Vitality and Growth in Maturity and Later Years From the Experiences of the Sage Program*. Delacorte, New York

McLeish J A B 1976 *The Ulyssean Adult: Creativity in the Middle and Later Years*. McGraw-Hill Ryerson, Toronto, Ontario

Sargent S S (ed.) 1980 *Non-traditional Therapy with the Aging*. Springer, New York

Paid Educational Leave

J. Bengtsson

This article presents an overview of the way paid educational leave (PEL) was discussed and introduced as a noneducational right for people at work. It also gives a brief account concerning some of the main features and problems related to the implementation of PEL.

The expansion of initial education experienced by most countries since the early 1950s has not prevented the increase of measures and institutions aimed at improving adult education. This increase was a response to two areas of concern: on the one hand it offered those who wanted it the possibility of acquiring an education they had been unable to obtain at school; on the other it aimed, within the framework of industrial policy, at the adaptation of the skills of the labour force to rapidly changing processes of production.

In reality, however, these opportunities for training and education were restricted to outside work hours and only those most motivated were likely to take advantage of them, sometimes at the expense of their social and family life. In these conditions, the aim of greater social equality through adult education was to some extent frustrated in that it was precisely those who had received an insufficient education in their youth who were least inclined to re-enter the system, as they associated it inevitably with school.

Based on initiatives by progressive employers and under pressure from trade unions, combined with some government action, educational leave of absence during working hours has now been accepted as a matter of private initiative and public policy in many countries, particularly in Europe. During its 1974 conference, the International Labour Organization (ILO) adopted a Convention and a Recommendation in favour of the formal establishment and general availability of the right to such educational leave. Broadly speaking, PEL refers to time spent on formally organized educational activities during normal working hours in which some or all of the worker's wages are maintained by the employer or by the employers in combination with another source, usually the government. The leave may be brief or extended and the content may be vocational or general education. It may be provided in-house by the employer or from outside sources and the study may be full time or part time.

It is unnecessary to go into the detailed reasons here for the increasing concern for PEL. However, it should be recalled that the subject arose at a time when the concepts of lifelong learning and recurrent education were beginning to be developed and to take a hold on the public. It was increasingly realized that general education at whatever level, and vocational and professional training at a certain age, could not provide the once-and-for-all knowledge and experience needed on the one hand to cope with scientific and technological progress and on the other to participate in an active way in economic and social life at the workplace and in the community.

In order to enable people in employment to face these new challenges by using PEL, it was argued that certain basic conditions would have to be fulfilled. For instance:

(a) people needed to be given time off from their work;

(b) they needed to be paid either wages or other types of remuneration;

(c) they would have to be given the opportunity to follow different types of courses, which according to the ILO convention of 1974 were divided into roughly three categories: vocational training; general, social, and civic education; and trade union education.

As obvious as these conditions may have seemed to many people, it was not at all the case with others. Consequently, the debate on PEL was launched. It was not—and is not—free of controversy.

The major divergences of opinion between states and between employers and workers' representatives at ILO deliberations in 1974 focused on four main points.

(a) *Form of instrument*. The first question was the form the instrument should take, that is to say, should it be an ILO convention or an ILO recommendation to governments. The workers' representatives favoured the adoption of a convention, supplemented by a recommendation, that is to say, the convention should lay down basic principles and the recommendation should facilitate their implementation by detailing a wide range of methods of application.

The employers' representatives were on the whole in favour of the adoption of a recommendation alone which should be sufficiently flexible, that is to say, be adaptable to the great diversity of national situations, traditions, and practices, and it should be sufficiently realistic to fall within the range of member states' possibilities.

Governments were divided on the question. Some, who advocated the adoption of a recommendation alone, argued that developing countries were unable to cope with the extra financial burden that a convention would impose on them, that these countries had more pressing problems to solve, and that the idea of paid educational leave was new and far from being generally accepted. Others favoured the adoption of a convention, complemented by a recommendation. They criticized the argument that the adoption of a convention would lead to a reduced number of ratifications. They considered that, on the contrary, it would have a stimulating influence, and finally a convention was adopted.

(b) *New labour right*. The second major controversy was with regard to the use of the term "new labour right" in the preamble which was in the proposed text. The use of the term "right" had given rise to divergencies during earlier discussion of paid educational leave. For many experts, a right to paid educational leave flowed naturally from the right to education. Education was a basic human right proclaimed by the United Nations and was generally accepted. However, it was not effectively available to everyone. Paid educational leave, several experts argued, was an essential right for adults who had not had the benefit of a sound initial education. The right to education could no longer be interpreted in the traditional sense of primary education; lifelong education was increasingly being recognized as a human right and paid educational leave was essential to the exercise of that right. Therefore recognition of that right must be the first step.

Other experts argued that the right to education did not imply a right to paid educational leave. Education was a right of all members of society, not just employed ones; it should be guaranteed by society and not necessarily within the framework of employment. Some experts also felt that while the question of paid educational leave could be examined primarily in terms of the right to education it was also linked with a second right—the right to security of existence and therefore to security of employment. The discussion at the ILO Conference in 1974 led finally to the deletion of the notion of a "right" and it does not appear in the adopted version of the convention.

(c) *Financial entitlements*. The third major divergence was over financing. The definition of paid educational leave which read in the proposed text that leave should be granted "without loss of earnings or other benefits" was finally changed to "adequate financial entitlements". The main question here was whether full or partial compensation should be offered. The discussion on this question showed the need to define paid educational leave in more flexible terms, which would take into account the diversity in national practice. This would permit widest ratification and encourage member states to introduce such leave. Thus the phrase "financial entitlements" left the door open for total or partial compensation for loss of earnings. On the other hand, the concept of full compensation was retained in the recommendation by stating that the financial entitlements of workers during paid educational leave should maintain their standard of living by continued payment of their wages and other benefits or by adequate compensation thereof.

(d) *Education and training*. Finally, the three types of education and training gave rise to some controversy. There were those, mainly employers, who felt that the definition was too ambitious and insisted that priority should be given to training linked with employment in view of its greater importance. But also a number of governments questioned an unconditional right of workers to be released from their employment for every type of training in which they might be interested but which might have no bearing on their employment. The three types of leave were finally kept and adopted, although no priority was mentioned, and so was another important element, namely the obligation for members to have a "policy" on paid educational leave.

What is then happening in those countries where implementation of paid educational leave is taking place? Paid educational leave is relatively recent and that makes it difficult to evaluate. However, OECD has undertaken two studies on PEL. The first one, *Developments in Educational Leave of Absence* (OECD 1976), was an attempt to get an overview of what was happening in the way PEL was introduced, the trend of participation, types of courses offered, ways of financing, the role of the formal educational system, and the relationship between PEL and labour market policy. The countries which participated in this study were Italy, Yugoslavia, France, Belgium, the Netherlands, Denmark, Sweden, the Federal Republic of Germany, the United Kingdom, and the United States.

The second study, *Alternation Between Work and Education: A Study of Educational Leave of Absence at Enterprise Level* (OECD 1978), focused on what was happening at enterprise level where a PEL scheme did exist. This study was carried out in seven countries, namely Italy, Yugoslavia, the Federal Republic of Germany, the United Kingdom, France, Sweden, and the United States. In each country, three-quarters of the enterprises, both in the public and private sectors, were analysed.

It is not possible to go into the detailed findings of these two studies but an assessment of the main findings would briefly look like the following.

(a) First there are a variety of approaches to implementing PEL, through legislation or collective bargaining, and no clear picture is yet emerging as to which of the two approaches will be the dominant one.

(b) Secondly, the participation rate is still rather low. The maximum participation is in the order of 1–2 percent of the labour force in any country. As to the question of who benefits, the results show that so far it has not been the very unskilled but rather the better-off in terms of earlier education and good jobs who have taken advantage of this new opportunity.

(c) Thirdly, the dominant types of courses being taken have been vocation oriented and very rarely has PEL been used for purposes of general and civic education. The main reasons for this are partly a greater interest from workers for vocation and career-oriented courses and partly because the financing system tends to favour such.

(d) Fourthly, in most countries a combination of employer and state subsidies exists, and on the whole it can be said that the employers are ready to pay as long as they have a guarantee that the courses are relevant to the company, but with regard to more general education their position is usually that they should not pay for the deficiencies in the formal education system.

(e) Fifth, the role of the formal education system in responding to this new clientele has been very weak, and it is only very recently, in the perspective of dropping enrolments, that there has been a more positive attitude from the educational system towards PEL.

(f) Sixth, there has so far been hardly any serious attempt to link PEL to the present unemployment situation; that is to say, the possibility of PEL as an alternative to unemployment subsidies.

(g) Finally, it is clearly indicated that the future development of PEL will be largely dependent on the dynamic power relations which exist between labour and management. For instance, in those cases where traditional management is the stronger partner, a vocation-oriented PEL is the most likely outcome while in those cases where labour is strong and management has a broader perspective on the role of training and education, the chances for more general education under PEL regulations are very good.

It is possible then to be at least agnostic about the beneficial effects of an extension of educational leave per se. But in any case, how likely is a major expansion? After all, it seems to be a fact that educational leave is in many cases more or less an outgrowth of vocational training—so is it really plausible to conceive of it as developing very far towards an instrument of individual and collective fulfilment? In reply, the hazardous but often illuminating game of historical parallels may be played, the analogy in this case being very close. The parallel is this: the suggestion of universal paid holidays was greeted with disbelief when it was first mooted—not only impossible, but also unnecessary. Few would now question the right of the worker to a measure of fully paid vacation, or the fact that it is necessary for his or her health and hence, in the last analysis, for the community's economic and social well-being. In the same way, the opportunity for each member of the population to maintain and improve his or her intellectual development and social awareness may come to be recognized as an essential, not a luxury.

See also: Employment Policy and Adult Education; Lifelong Education: Interaction with Adult Education; Recurrent Education; Workers' Education

Bibliography

Organisation for Economic Co-operation and Development (OECD) 1976 *Developments in Educational Leave of Absence.* OECD, Paris

Organisation for Economic Co-operation and Development (OECD) 1978 *Alternation Between Work and Education: A Study of Educational Leave of Absence at Enterprise Level.* OECD, Paris

Von Moltke K, Schneevoigt N 1977 *Educational Leave for Employees: European Experience for American Consideration.* Jossey-Bass, San Francisco, California

Prior Life Experience and Higher Education

K. Abrahamsson

The traditional route to higher education has for the majority of students been through the secondary-school system. Though admission systems and entrance qualifications have varied from country to country, it is inevitable that traditional subject knowledge and study skill have played an important role. This is true whether qualification for admission has been assessed through marks from secondary schools or through various forms of entrance tests or examinations. The transition from elite higher education to mass higher education has challenged the traditional notion of universities and colleges by the introduction of various open-access systems supported by so called "open door" policies for higher education. The broadening of various systems of higher education has also called for new ways of ascribing and assessing formal and, to an increasing extent, nonformal qualifications for higher studies. The notion of experiential learning and the up-grading of life and work experiences became an important part of the educational policies and ideas during the 1970s in many countries, particularly in the United States and Sweden.

Cerych (1978) has carried out a survey of the way work experience is used in a number of European countries on the basis of national reports. He classifies practice according to four factors:

(a) the type of tertiary education (full- or part-time) for which work experience is taken into consideration;

(b) whether such experience is compulsory, and if so, for what subjects;

(c) whether such experience must have been in a related field;

(d) the length of experience taken into consideration.

The countries in Cerych's material which state that they recognise work experience are, first, a number of East European countries (Bulgaria, the German Democratic Republic, Poland, Romania, Ukraine, and Yugoslavia), and, second, two Scandinavian countries (Sweden and Denmark).

Cerych's analysis also demonstrates that there is a relation between the content of work experience and its formal function in relation to higher education. Thus, where work experience is compulsory, it is most often work experience related to the education applied for. When work experience is used as a general additional qualification, a broad sense of the concept is generally meant, for both ideological and practical reasons. When work experience constitutes an alternative route to higher education, general life experience is usually meant (Abrahamsson et al. 1980).

1. Prior Experience in Sweden and the United States: A Comparison

It is not the purpose of this article to map the deep roots of experiential learning (Houle 1977) or to present a current survey of the use of prior experience in different systems of higher education. Rather, the article aims at a comparison of two quite different methods of recognizing prior experience, that is, the Swedish model and some North American perspectives on experiential learning.

1.1 The Swedish Model

It is typical of Swedish development that the up-grading of the emphasis placed on work and life experience in higher education is a result of formal decisions in the Swedish Riksdag (the parliament). The introduction of work experience as an additional admission qualification for young students and an alternative way to higher education for working people played a crucial role in the reforming of Swedish higher education in the mid-1970s. The policy arguments differed for young and old students. For the young group, the idea of counteracting some of the negative effects of theoretical schooling and thereby facilitating educational and vocational choice, was a primary motive. For adult students, educational equality and an adequate use of nonformal qualifications were main policy arguments. In both cases, however, the policy attention focused on the role of prior experiences as a qualification for admission to higher education.

Work experience has two functions in the Swedish admission system. First, it gives general eligibility for higher studies for adult students with insufficient formal schooling. This is not a total open door policy. Adult students and young students have to meet the specific and subject-based entrance requirements. Second, work experience functions, beside formal marks, as an additional selection criterion for young and adult students where work experience is weighted together with upper-secondary marks. It seems reasonable that these two functions have different consequences where the utilization of work experience is concerned. In the admission system, the students are divided into four different quota groups:

(a) applicants with three years upper-secondary schooling;

(b) applicants with two years upper-secondary schooling;

(c) applicants from folk high schools;

(d) applicants with qualifications based on age (at least 25 years) and four years of work experience.

In Swedish higher education, the adult student's prior work experience constitutes an important factor in admission to almost all educational programmes, and especially those with intake restrictions. The 1977 reform of higher education conferred general eligibility for higher studies on all adults over 25 with at least four years job experience. The rules of admission for higher education thus applied more widely the experience gained from the scheme of wider admissions to higher studies which was launched on a minor scale in 1969 (Kim 1981). The application may have been too wide, for in 1980 the Swedish Riksdag decided to lower the relative importance placed on work experience in the admission process. The argument was that students entering higher education direct from school should be given better opportunities for admission. In 1983, a governmental commission was set up aiming at an overall analysis of the admission system, including entrance tests and the role of work experience (Abrahamsson 1986). The final report, which was published at the end of 1985, recommended an increased utilization of entrance tests for students from alternative routes. Further, it gave less value to work experience (SOU 1985).

1.2 Recognition of Prior Experience in the United States

The recognition of prior experience in the United States is not a consequence of any formal decision by the president or decisions taken on state or federal level. Rather it is growing out of changing admission practices at different universities and colleges. Stadtman (1980) shows that a large number of universities and community colleges in the United States take into account experiential learning acquired outside a school or college. Between 1969/70 and 1977/78, the number of universities and colleges applying such principles of admission trebled (rising from 14 percent to 41 percent). The proportion of students admitted on these grounds may be small, however, particularly at minor community colleges. On the other hand, Valentine (1980) tells us that over 1,500 universities and colleges in the United States offer prospective students the chance to have prior learning recognized by using two of the major series of examinations for credit, that is, CLEP (College-level Examination Program) and APP (Advanced Placement Program).

In the United States model, however, which has been developed and described in publications and manuals of the Council for the Advancement of Experiential Learning (CAEL) and the College Entrance Examination Board, special importance is attached to different methods of describing or measuring the individual experiential profile from a learning viewpoint. Descriptions or documentary evidence would seem to be more common than measurements or tests going into greater depth. The autobiographical information is often put together in an individual portfolio of life and work experience.

An important difference between Swedish higher education and the efforts in the United States to give credits for life experience lies in the delineation of the experiential concept itself. The Swedish definition of job experience is extremely broad and, in principle, includes duration and type of employment. Credits are also given for unpaid work and experience as a parent. No attempt is made to evaluate the qualitative content of experience. The computerized procedure of central admission cannot be used to consider whether the student has learned anything during his or her prior life experience.

The difference between the use made in Sweden of prior experience assessment or of the recognition of prior experience (RPL) and that made in the United States is striking. In Sweden's centralized and integrated system of higher education, work experience is mainly used in the admission and selection of students. In the United States it may be used as a measure of the learner's qualifications to enter a programme, to earn the learner an appropriate placement in a programme, such as advanced standing; to help learner and teacher fit the programme to the learner's readiness and needs; to exempt the learner altogether from the programme and possibly award a license or some other credential; or to guide educational planning to serve a whole class of students of whom the learner is an example (Keeton 1981 pp. 632–33).

2. Prior Experience and the Idea of a Shortened Degree

The idea of crediting appropriate life and work experience, thereby exempting the student from certain courses, has a strong face validity. How far it is acceptable should depend logically on whether the value of a programme is measured in terms of its learning outcome, or whether it is seen as a total integrated learning experience. This is largely determined by the traditions of national higher education systems and the level and form of integration of higher education with working life.

In the United States there is a strong tendency to stress outcomes and to adapt programmes to meet individual needs. In Sweden the trend in curriculum reform, particularly in administratively or economically oriented education, or training for nurses and health professionals, has been towards integrated programmes. That is to say, all students must take a common course, followed by different lines of specialization. Exemptions are rare.

The idea of crediting prior learning and exempting academic courses has, however, been applied within the Swedish extramural tradition of higher education. Especially during the 1960s, it was very common in Sweden to join university study circles administered by independent educational associations and get credits within the formal system of higher education (Abrahamsson 1982c). The traditional notion of extramural studies meant that "higher knowledge" was brought from the university to the people. The RPL movement is turning this idea upside down by bringing knowledge from the people to the Academy. This perspective shift challenges or even confronts traditional notions of quality in universities and colleges. Thus, it is not surprising that one of the most difficult problems in the CAEL validation report was to define what constitutes college-level knowledge or the concept of higher education as such (Willingham 1976).

There is a lack of research-based knowledge on the effects of recognizing prior learning. According to Wagner (1981), "after more than a decade of extensive experience with RPL programs, we still know very little about how these programs affect decisions and the magnitude of the financial costs and benefits from the programs". Most studies done at the department level are often designed as case studies with a narrow focus. Comprehensive studies with possibilities of comparing RPL programmes with other forms of academic education are still very unusual. In reviewing the current literature, Wagner found that a majority of students enrolled in RPL programmes could have enrolled without the RPL option. Further, Wagner states that the evidence of a time-shortening effect of the RPL programmes is "sketchy" and he concludes, "In summary, the evidence regarding time-shortening of degree programs appears to suggest that about 10 per cent of RPL participants (the share with a year's worth of credit) do graduate earlier than their peers."

The possibilities of recognizing prior learning by designing adaptive individualized programmes is not always easy to realize in practice. The research done by Wagner and others points out organizational and administrative difficulties in creating flexible and inexpensive programmes.

3. *Experiential Learning as a Criterion for Educational Design*

The functions of life and work experience in higher education are not restricted to the admission process or exemption from courses or study programmes. Prior experience can also be viewed as a motivational, a social and sometimes also a cognitive resource for both students and faculty. As a part of the follow-up programme of the Swedish reform of higher education, a special project has been undertaken on these issues (Abrahamsson et al. 1980, Abrahamsson and Rubenson 1981, Abrahamsson 1982a, Abrahamsson 1982b, Linne 1982). The results of these studies show that the use of life and work experience is to a large extent dependent on programme characteristics such as educational objectives and programme length, kind of knowledge and textbooks, and the balance between theoretical and practical components in the programme. Thus, it was shown to be much easier to utilize students' work experience in teacher training than in a programme of advanced technology. Further, it has been easier to take experiential ideas into consideration in designing shorter separate courses or vocationally oriented programmes for skilled technicians than in programmes in medicine or science. Thus, curriculum code and knowledge scheme set limits to the use of life and work experience in different study programmes.

In a Swedish study by Larsson (1981) on teachers in upper-secondary adult education, different forms of experience were found to serve different functions. There were experiences which one or a few students had had and which could be shared with the rest of the class. There were experiences which most students in the class had had and which could be used to direct the students' attention to the relevant context when a subject was being taught. Job experience could develop practical knowledge which the students might use in the educational context. The student brought into the classroom an outlook on the world that was in conflict with the view of the subject taught. Experiences from life gave a certain capacity for empathy that made it possible for the adult student to understand different perspectives as serious alternatives.

The functions listed above show that life and work experience do not merely confer a specific cognitive skill, subject knowledge, or professional competence. The studies in the project on work experience as a resource in higher education (Abrahamsson 1982b, Linne 1982) stress its social and motivational contributions like, for instance, broader life perspectives, capacities to relate the studies to social identity and possibilities of testing theoretical ideas in the light of personal experiences. Nor can it be neglected that experience makes an important contribution to knowledge of the individual personality, social identity, and the dreams, hopes, and disappointments that define the life span and its development.

4. *In Search of Good Experiential Programmes*

Good examples of experiential programmes are to be found in cooperative education. Programmes of cooperative education are designed with the specific purpose of integrating academic learning and work experience. As a consequence of selective federal support from the beginning of the 1970s, such programmes are available at more than 1,000 universities and colleges in the United States. According to Heinemann (1981) "Cooperative education is a form of experiential learning

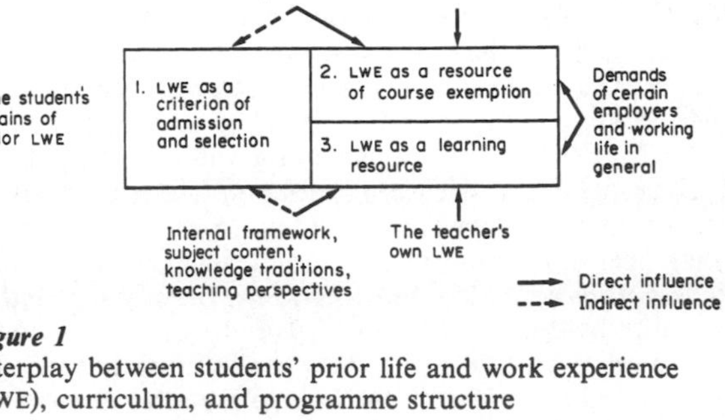

Figure 1
Interplay between students' prior life and work experience (LWE), curriculum, and programme structure

which extends the learning process into the workplace. Students alternate between specific periods of attendance at the college and specific periods of employment." Indeed, this use of prior life and work experience in higher education can be viewed as a special case of the broader policy concept of recurrent education (Abrahamsson and Rubenson 1981).

To construct good experiential programmes in higher education it is necessary to specify certain learning determinants. Analysis shows that the use of prior life and work experience can be related to admission and selection, course exemption, and shortened degrees and it can be a learning resource within certain programmes and courses. Figure 1 also lists a number of factors influencing the experiential process within certain study programmes, for example, knowledge traditions and curricular content, professional backgrounds of faculty and teachers, the balance between practical and theoretical components of a programme, and expectations of the labour market or working life.

Further research in this field calls for some theoretical distinctions. Firstly, it is necessary to distinguish between prior life and work experience and college-sponsored work experience. Secondly, a clarification must be made concerning what relevant experience is. Thirdly, it is important to decide whether prior experience of a certain kind should be a compulsory admission qualification for all applicants, or whether the

Table 1
A conceptual framework for the analysis of educational functions of life and work experience (LWE)

Educational function	Before studies	During studies
Educational qualification	Is LWE exchangeable with theoretical knowledge?	Can LWE confer exemption from certain programmes and courses?
	Is LWE an additional admission qualification or an alternative route to higher education?	Is LWE a study skill or an additional knowledge perspective?
	How much formal learning can be identified in LWE?	Are the programmes especially designed for LWE students, or do they form a marginal group?
Vocational qualification	Does LWE confer broader experience of working life or specific professional competence?	Can LWE confer exemption from practical training or field work?
Socialization	Will LWE imply increasing maturity and personal development?	Does LWE facilitate experiential sharing and active group work in class?
	Will LWE influence the definition of life roles, social understanding, and societal perspectives?	Does LWE provide alternative ways of understanding and processing curricular content?
Selection	Does LWE help the students to define and clarify educational choice?	Can the use of LWE lead to a selection in process (or perhaps by failure) instead of selection at entrance?
	Can LWE be seen as an instrument of informal selection (selection by interest rather than formal admission)?	Is LWE a destructive competence in certain higher education programmes?

experiential route can be considered as an alternative way to higher education. Fourthly, increases have to be made in knowledge of the educational functions of the use of life and work experience in higher education. Without going into details, four such functions could be mentioned, that is, educational qualification, vocational qualification, socialization, and selection (Abrahamsson 1982b). Educational qualification or study preparation involves study skill and necessary theoretical knowledge and understanding, while vocational qualification is a broader concept including certain professional skills and competence. The concept of socialization stands for personal and moral development, social understanding, and societal perspectives, while selection primarily involves the influence of life and work experiences on the individual's educational and vocational choice. Table 1 is an attempt to summarize these aspects.

Given this conceptual framework, it becomes necessary to analyse the idea of recognizing prior life and work experience as a matter of public policy. From this perspective it is evident that the Swedish reform of higher education has a broader policy background than that of the RPL movement, the experientialists, or the supporters of cooperative education in the United States. The Swedish reform has used the upgrading of life and work experience as one tool (among others) to achieve many different objectives; a better interplay between education and working life, as in recurrent education; a better use of information competencies of adults; greater educational equality; and also the use of new learning resources. The introduction of RPL measures, experiential programmes, or cooperative education in the United States, on the other hand, is more a reform from below, affecting only parts of higher education. It also tends to be guided more by principles of good educational design and individualization than by educational equality and ideas of programme integration.

Whether one is facing top-down reforms or bottom-up changes, the increasing recognition of prior life and work experience in universities and colleges calls for a new analysis of the concepts of higher education and higher learning. What roles do such traditional academic ideals as intellectual reflection and critical thinking play in experiential programmes? How are these aspects assessed in different procedures for recognizing prior learning? Further, Sweden has faced a new interest in the humanities and liberal education in the mid-eighties (Abrahamsson 1984, 1985). It is too early to judge how the changed knowledge ideals will influence the use of life and work experience in higher education. The current changes raise the need for a more comprehensive analysis of the boundaries of higher education and its interplay with other forms of education in society. Finally it brings one back to classical problems in the sociology of higher education, for example, the dilemma of quality and equality and the complex interaction between theory and practice.

See also: Experiential Learning for Adults

Bibliography

Abrahamsson K (ed.) 1982a Cooperative education, experiential learning and personal knowledge. Universitäts och Högskole Ämbetet-Rapport 1982: 1. National Board of Universities and Colleges, Stockholm

Abrahamsson K (ed.) 1982b Vad är den goda erfarenheten värd? Om relevant arbetslivser farenhet i den nya högskolan [What is good experience worth? On relevant work experience in the new system of higher education]. Universitäts och Högskole Ämbetet-Rapport 1982: 12. Utbildningsförlaget, Liber, Stockholm

Abrahamsson K 1982c *From Extramural Studies to an Integrated System of Higher Education: The Adult Student in Retrospect.* Conference paper, National Board of Universities and Colleges, Stockholm

Abrahamsson K (ed.) 1984 *Bildningsyn och utbildningsreformer* [Educational perspectives and educational reforms]. National Board of Universities and Colleges, Utbildningsförlaget, Liber, Stockholm

Abrahamsson K (ed.) 1985 *Högskolans bildningsprogram—finns det*? [The learning programme in higher education—Does it exist?] Universitäts och Högskole Ämbetet Skriftserie 1985:2

Abrahamsson K 1986 Adult participation in Swedish higher education. A study of organizational structure, educational design and current policies. *Studies in Higher Education in Sweden.* National Board of Universities and Colleges, Stockholm

Abrahamsson K, Rubenson K 1981 *Higher Education and the "Lost Generation": Some Comments on Adult Students, Knowledge Ideals and Educational Design in Swedish Post-secondary Education.* Conference paper, National Board of Universities and Colleges, Stockholm

Abrahamsson K, Kim L, Rubenson K 1980 The value of work experience in higher education. *Reports on Education and Psychology 2.* Stockholm Institute of Education, Department of Educational Research, Stockholm

Cerych L 1978 *Access to Tertiary Education in the European Member States of UNESCO: A Feasibility Study.* Working document, UNESCO, Paris

Heinemann H 1981 Cooperative education: Integrating work and learning. In: Abrahamsson K (ed.) 1982a

Houle C 1977 Deep traditions of experiential learning. In: Keeton M T (ed.) 1977 *Experiential Learning.* Jossey-Bass, San Francisco, California

Keeton M T 1981 Assessing the credentialing prior experience. In: Chickering A W et al. (eds.) 1981 *The Modern American College.* Jossey-Bass, San Francisco, California

Kim L 1981 Widened admission to higher education in Sweden (the 25/5 scheme): A study of the implementation process. *Studies in Higher Education in Sweden.* National Board of Universities and Colleges, Stockholm

Larsson S 1981 Teachers' interpretation of the concept experience. In: Abrahamsson K (ed.) 1982a

Linne A 1982 *Content Curriculum and Work Experience: Aspects of Educational Integration in Higher Education Programmes.* Conference paper, Stockholm Institute of Education, Stockholm

SOU 1985:57 *Tillträde till Högskolen* [Admission to higher education]

Stadtman V A 1980 *Academic Adaptations: Higher Education Prepares for the 1980s and 1990s.* Carnegie Council on Policy

Studies. Jossey-Bass, San Francisco, California
Valentine J 1980 Credit for learning assessed by examination. *New Directions for Experiential Learning*, No. 7. Jossey-Bass, San Francisco, California
Wagner A 1981 A research agenda for RPL programs. In: Abrahamsson K (ed.) 1982a
Willingham W W 1976 *The CAEL Validation Report*. Council for the Advancement of Experiential Learning, Columbia

Section 4

Teaching and Learning

Section 4

Teaching and Learning

Introduction

The core purpose of all education, ultimately the only justification for it, is that learning shall take place. If there is no learning, then there is no education. This does not imply that there is education whenever learning takes place. If that were accepted, it would make education almost synonymous with life. Much of the continuing process of learning from experience throughout life is unconscious, even more of it unintended and incidental to other activities. A process is normally classified as education only if it is undertaken with the intention of producing learning and only if the outcomes include the learning intended. Things are frequently learnt as a by-product of the educational process, for example, in following a course on child rearing one may acquire knowledge of group dynamics, but if the intended learning outcomes are not achieved, namely one does not learn something about bringing up children, it is doubtful whether in the strictest sense, the process should be called education.

Not all learning, even if purposive, is to be classified as educational. For a number of years, in the southwest of Scotland, there flourished, it seems, a school for safebreakers. Police action forced it to close on a number of occasions, but repeatedly it reopened in the same town. It apparently enjoyed a high reputation for the effective learning which took place, but outside the criminal fraternity few people would consider that what it offered should be called education. To merit that name, the content and/or purpose of learning must conform to certain socially or morally approved criteria. This is an issue which definitions of adult education, even the UNESCO one which is the most comprehensive so far devised, fail to cover. The reason perhaps is that it is difficult to produce a formulation of these criteria in such terms that they are universally applicable, without limiting the traditional function of adult education to stimulate criticism, change, and even subversion of the social status quo.

However, it seems to be generally accepted that, in themselves, the processes which constitute learning do not change according to the acceptability or otherwise of the content of learning or of the purpose for which it is learnt. They are mental and/or physical and as processes they are neither moral nor immoral, social nor antisocial. They operate within the apprentice safebreaker as in the trainee accountant.

Beyond that point of agreement there is a wide area of controversy both about what happens when learning takes place, and how it may be stimulated so that the process is carried through, the learning is retained, and is capable of application to the situations encountered by the learner outside the learning experience. Much work has been done on learning theory. It is significant, however, that the field is still called "theory": one remains in the realm of hypotheses, supported by or derived from experimental observation, it is true, but none of them sufficiently convincing in their scope or explanatory power to gain universal acceptance. Valuable insights have been contributed by behaviourist, cognitive, and humanistic approaches, for example, but they are frequently conflicting and partial. They appear to explain some phenomena but not others.

It may be, indeed, that there is not one process of learning, but a number, which vary from individual to individual, or within individuals according to the situation and the nature of the learning that is being undertaken, whether one is undertaking, for example, simple rote learning, or acquiring knowledge which can apply to a variety of situations, and whether one is engaged in psychomotor, cognitive, or affective learning. It may be that different learning processes produce different outcomes and that the processes will be adapted, either consciously or unconsciously, to suit the intended outcomes. Indeed the efficiency of learning in a given context may depend on the activation of the correct process to achieve the desired outcome.

It is a further complicating factor that, to a significant degree, understanding of the phenomenon of learning appears to be influenced by broader beliefs about the nature and purpose of human life, which in turn are based on value judgements rather than empirical evidence. In all education, including that of adults, it is significant that the theories which have received widest acceptance are those which appear to be most compatible with educators' beliefs about the nature and purpose of education. The idea that learning fundamentally consists of developing conditioned responses to stimuli, as behaviourists maintain, is objectionable to many adult educators. It seems to conflict with their principle that adults can and should make conscious choices in their learning as part of their right and duty as responsible persons.

Education for employment is less concerned with this and more with ensuring that adults do the correct things in a given occupational situation, and behaviourist theories are more applied to occupational training than to general adult education. Humanistic theories of learning, which currently attract wide support, are those most compatible with the view, strongly held by many educators, that the primary goal of adult education is the self-realization of the learner.

Because our knowledge of the process is uncertain, adult learners, and particularly educators, are free to apply learning theories, or parts of them, when they seem to work without violence to their principles. There is evidence that this approach has had some success. On the other hand the uncertainty and the slim possibility that the conflicts of ideas about the learning process will be satisfactorily resolved in the foreseeable future may well have helped to turn many educators from the nature of the process itself to the environment of learning in their search for the means to make it more effective. If it is not possible to be sure of what goes on in the learner, the argument appears to run, consideration should be given to what goes on around him or her which may affect the process and which is more easily observed and, perhaps, modified. A sizeable literature has been produced as a result.

Factors which affect participation in, and the initiatives taken to attract people to, intentional learning experiences have been discussed in Section 3. In Section 4 attention is focused on the experiences themselves. It is divided into four subsections which, in keeping with the centrality of the theme of learning to adult education, constitute the largest section of this *Handbook*.

Learning and Life sets learning in the context of adult life, its stages, its roles and problems, and specific issues raised for the adult educator. Teaching and Evaluation examines the roles and methods of teachers of adults in different contexts, considering also the growth of initiatives to evaluate the effectiveness of adult education provision. Learning: Organization and Support describes research done and measures taken to improve learning by creating educational settings favourable to it, and also reviews the support offered by educational technology. Finally, Self-directed and Distance Learning moves beyond the confines of face-to-face learning and institutional programmes to the theory and practice of self-directed learning and distance education.

Learning and Life

Introduction

There may be uncertainty about the process of learning, but it is clear that it does not take place in a vacuum, nor is it an absolute. It is a process undertaken or undergone by each individual who, even from the moment of birth, has inherited characteristics which differentiate him or her from all others. Learning is change in the individual (although not all change may be learning). Lifelong learning, therefore, is a process of change beginning from and relative to a different base in each individual. Not only is the starting point for learning affected by inherited characteristics, but they continue to influence the nature and extent of learning over the lifespan.

Each individual lives in his or her own experiential and social context, which also affects learning. Prior life experience, present family, work, school, and recreational roles and environments, future prospects and aspirations help to determine whether a person will embark on a purposive learning experience, what it will be, and what will be the outcomes.

There has, for a long time, been dispute as to which plays the larger part, nature or nurture, in making a person what he or she is at any given time in life and, therefore, which exerts more influence on success or failure in learning. In educational research and thinking, however, particularly in that related to adults, more attention has been paid to experience and environment than genetics. In part this may be because little has been known about genetics, and what there was, was not easily accessible to educators. There was probably also an element of reluctance in principle to face up to some of the implications, should genetic inheritance appear to exert too great an influence on individual learning. It has been a matter of faith, as well as of evidence, that all adults, with the exception of a very few suffering from severe mental disabilities, are of themselves capable of learning. Against this it is clear that many do not undertake purposive learning. If inherited characteristics are the principal determinants of their nonparticipation, then there is little that can be done—in practice those people are ineducable. (Whatever prospects appear to be promised by recent developments in genetic engineering, they lie in an uncertain future and would be abhorent to most adult educators anyway.)

On the other hand, although prior experience cannot be modified, current environment and role expectations, future aspirations and possibilities are variables which there is some prospect of changing to make purposive learning possible. The experience of today's children may be so fashioned that they are able to learn in adult life. There is a body of evidence to suggest both that changes in the environment and what is expected of the roles adults fulfil can bring about improvements in participation and achievement in adult education; and that educational experiences may by adaptation to the learner's environment be more successful. For example, by changing the expectations of what is appropriate to a working-class mother, family shock and resistance to such women's participation in higher education, frequently documented in the United Kingdom and elsewhere, would be decreased. Through the Open University and other distance learning programmes they are able to study with less risk of failing in their family role.

Unfortunately only in fairly recent years has adult life been subjected to the same degree of study as childhood, so that what is known about cognitive styles, life roles, and societal requirements of competent adult functions has not yet fully penetrated into adult education thinking. The article *Adulthood* takes the prevailing view of adult life as a process of development, dividing it into three stages, young adulthood (the focus of a later article, *Education for Young Adults*), middle adult years, and maturity, describing the consensus of research about the predominant characteristics of each, and about intellectual development, moral development, social norms, and role transitions. The fourth stage of adulthood is discussed in *Old Age*, which covers the development processes of that stage, the biology of old age, intellectual development, environmental influence, with special reference to retirement and widowhood, family life, and leisure and education.

The educational implications of adulthood are specifically treated in *Lifespan Learning Development*. This article examines and compares two different approaches, one which sees learning in relation to a series of age-specific phases which have normative events and psychosocial tasks, the other which views it in terms of development involving a series of hierarchical, sequential, and qualitative changes in the individual. *Lifespan Learning: Implications for Educators* discusses the organizing structures, processes, and values within an individual, the feedback mechanisms, and the processes of arousal and motivation, which recent research suggests come into play in learning at any of these stages or at any point in development (see also *Participant Motivation*).

In adult education increasing attention is being given both to relating formal study to life experience and to applying learning acquired in life to educational situations. *Experiential Learning for Adults* surveys research in this field under two headings, the pragmatic–institutional, which focuses on the acquisition of skills by practice and its place in institutional programmes; and the individual–existential, which covers self-directed learning, learning from everyday experience and experiential social group processes, such as T-groups and role play exercises.

As human beings grow older they acquire mental sets, they adopt unthinkingly views and standards from their own experience, from the people around them, and from society at large. It is a major task of adult education, often a precondition of further learning and successful development as a person, that these be reconsidered and changed on the basis of knowledge. *Personal Perspective Change through Adult Learning* considers the acquisition of mental sets, and describes the learning processes required for change and the social and educational implications of the problem.

Organized adult education takes place within, and is provided by, institutions. In many cases it is only one, and a minor one, of their functions. As a result education takes place in an environment which is uncongenial and unconducive to success. The last article of this subsection on the context of adult education, *Organizational Change and Adult Education*, examines the problem of changing the environment and suggests ways in which this may be tackled.

Adulthood

C. E. Kennedy

Adulthood comprises life from 18 years of age to death. The period from mid-60s to death, identified as old age, is discussed elsewhere and will largely be omitted here. It is only in recent research that specific work on adulthood will be found. Although adults have managed the affairs of all societies through the generations, it is in the last quarter of a century that the changes an individual experiences after adolescence have been delineated as a major area of scientific study. There is an increasing awareness in education and human service disciplines of an acute need for an adult development perspective in their program development (Levinson 1986). Poets, novelists, and artists down through time have, of course, been faithful chroniclers of the patterns and portents of change in adulthood.

1. Stages of Adult Development

Changes during adulthood are often viewed in terms of life stages. Neugarten suggested that life stages reflect a social clock set by society. The changes an adult moves through are prompted in some measure by biological processes, but also, in a proportionately much larger measure than during childhood, they are prompted by psychological and social influences.

The term development refers to any change in the adult and does not indicate a predetermined direction such as toward greater complexity, as it does in child development. Conceptualization in the study of stages of adulthood reflects constructs from Erikson's developmental stages, Havighurst's developmental tasks, and Kohlberg's stages of moral development. Much of the popular awareness of adult life stages comes from four studies of different groups of persons as they moved through stages of adulthood. Each of these has been published in books appearing since 1975, along with Sheehy's *Passages* (1976), a widely read popularizing synthesis of these and data from other sources. Vaillant (1977) followed a group of college men until they neared 50 years of age; Gould (1978) studied a cross section of men and women between ages 16 and 52; Levinson (1978) interviewed four groups of men: industrial workers, business executives, novelists, and biologists to which he recently compared data from corresponding interviews with women (Levinson 1987). Lowenthal (1975) initiated her study with adults in four life transition stages: graduating from high school; getting married; having their last child leave home; and preparing for retirement. The classifications in each of these studies differ somewhat, but the general patterns of normative transitions are reflected in the outline that follows. Neugarten (1977) indicates that there are normal expectable events that serve as markers along the life cycle calling forth changes in self-concept and in sense of identity.

1.1 Young Adulthood

Young adulthood spans approximately the ages between 18 and 35. The beginning years of this period are occupied with separating, searching, and preparation. The later years are involved with tentative commitments and testing. It usually takes an individual five years or so to move out from his or her family of origin into a somewhat independent status, to choose a career direction, and to begin preparation for that career. Simultaneously with career concerns, young adults are learning more about themselves in relation to others and they are also considering future styles of family living. Erikson has described the searching going on during these years as gaining a sense of identity versus confusion and gaining a sense of intimacy versus isolation.

During the next 10 years of this period the young adult is verifying and becoming established in career and interpersonal identities that will serve as the foundation for succeeding stages of adult life. The decisions made at this time regarding jobs, values, and family relationships are not permanent but formative. This is not the last time the individual will choose directions or consider the meaning of intimacy, but the place arrived at during these years will establish the basis from which he or she moves forward in succeeding stages of life.

A pattern prevails through each of the periods of adulthood. Young adulthood begins with testing and searching and tentative commitment, leading to a more intense involvement. This is followed by a transition period of review. Often this is a time of values clarification or an affirming of a particular aspect of career identity. In the Catch–30 transition, as Sheehy terms it, some young adults decide that their career or marital choice was not the right one and take action to move toward another alternative before becoming too deeply immersed. For others who may have been briefly trying out a number of different roles, the review at around the age of 30 affords the occasion for more lasting commitments. Questions raised around 30 begin to be resolved or put aside as 35 approaches and the individual moves into a new, busy, and usually one of the most productive periods of life—the middle adult years.

1.2 Middle Adult Years

This is a time of complete absorption in career, family, and community affairs. Middle adults are aware of having set aside, for a time, their vacillation and doubts and are now committed to proving to themselves the full abilities and potential they have. These years, from the mid-30s to the mid-40s, are the most pressured of adult life. The pressures involve gaining advancement in a career, time demands for care of family, and for community responsibilities.

Erikson's developmental stage, generativity versus stagnation, characterizes the growth potential of this period. Generativity involves developing a capacity for caring about others: children, adults, culture, and the continuation of society. It means a growth in personal maturity so that people no longer feel themselves children to be nurtured or young people seeking approval from their mentors. Levinson suggests that having a mentor (role model and guide) during young adulthood is important in laying the affective foundation in the self for the later maturing of generativity. While growth in generativity versus stagnation is the prevailing task of middle adulthood, earlier developmental accomplishments, such as intimacy, will require reworking in the light of new growth and circumstances. In some instances, such as with single, divorced, or widowed persons, intimacy becomes a major developmental task. During the mid-40s individuals stop counting age in terms of years they have lived; instead they think in terms of time left to live. It is a transition time that some refer to as middlescence. Middlescence has been compared to adolescence because of its bewildering blend of physiological changes (e.g., menopause) and new responsibilities for determining one's own future. The variety of commitments which have held the adult's world together are no longer so fixed. With the children about ready to leave home and his position in his job nearing its peak, the husband of age 45 is faced with an opportunity to make new, or to reaffirm, previous life commitments concerning who he is and where he is going. This is true also for women, but in a somewhat more complex fashion. Much of the research to date has been with women whose primary identity has been that of homemaker, even though they may also have been working outside the home. As children leave home, the prospect of an "empty nest" holds mixed messages for women. Some may view it as a threat to their identity and reason for being; others may view it as an opportunity for new identity. Research is just beginning on the meaning of this period for the woman who has more explicitly thus far in life pursued a career outside the home, either as a single woman or in a dual career marriage. Educational implications of this period are that it is important for men and women in late middle adult years (45 to 50) to have opportunity to think about family communication, alternatives for second careers, and matters of health regarding themselves and their aging parents. Strength groups, self-discovery workshops, supportive and educational groups for adjustment to widowhood and divorce are illustrative of the developmental resources needed during this period.

1.3 Maturity

Until recently adults went directly from the struggles of work to the status of old age, at 50 plus. Lengthened life coupled with social changes enables adults to experience new social and psychological dynamics. It is possible to think of the range from mid-30s to mid-60s as one period and call it middle age. However, there are sufficient differences in the preoccupation of the 40s and the 50s, so that a designation of a distinct period, maturity, is justified. Maturity begins at around age 50 and continues to retirement or about 65. In this period adults exercise a greater freedom and a greater degree of power than at any other period of their lives.

The soul searching of middlescence has resulted in a new clarification in identity, new approaches to career and life-style. In maturity, men begin to relax in their jobs, where they may have achieved managerial or other senior status. Women, with reduced family responsibility, have begun to move into second careers, either in paid employment or in community work. There is a greater percentage of women of this age in the labor force than of any group except young adult women just out of school. Adults usually have greater income during this time than at any other period; they also have fewer financial obligations. The adult is also more free to accept or reject community and family tasks.

Somewhat different things happen during this period. Men become somewhat more relaxed, more introspective and mellow, more oriented to personal interests and to socializing with others. Women become somewhat more oriented toward productivity in new careers and inclined toward more assertive roles. Developmentally the interests of generativity occupy most people. As the period ends the adult is beginning to be oriented toward the last of Erikson's stages, integrity versus despair, which is the developmental stage of old age. Neugarten has described this blending of the two psychodynamic stages in her observations that individuals in their 50s and 60s develop an increased "interiority" while at the same time maintaining an active, effective instrumental dealing with life.

The years of maturity are much more comfortable years for both men and women than the preceding middle adult years. Where men in their 40s expressed considerable boredom and frustration with their work, even as they pressed hard to get on, men of maturity are much less preoccupied with financial concerns or advancement. Women, though experiencing some of the tensions of emerging aggressive and achievement orientations, are much less hostile and depressed than in their frustrating years of middle adulthood. The woman's uncertainty immediately preceding the empty nest is replaced with self-affirmation as she experiences new opportunities with new freedom.

New relationships are being formed by the adults with their grown children even as they are developing new relationships also with their own increasingly elderly parents. The expression "woman in the middle" is sometimes used to describe the superwoman role that employed women in their 50s take on as they care for an elderly parent, are active grandparents, and still manage their own home. Many women freed from family responsibilities, and some perhaps from a husband's domination, formulate new life goals. New forms of expression emerge for women of maturity which carry them forward to positions of increasing power. This power manifests itself in their marital relationships and/or in more active social roles. Shortly after 60 the consideration of retirement occupies considerable time as the adults plan the details of the transition that moves them toward the fastest growing group in adult life, the period of old age.

2. Intellectual Development

Research by Schaie (1977/78) indicates that intellectual competence continues to increase through most of adulthood. Different kinds of intellectual processes are needed to accomplish the goals of different age groups. The intellectual style of young adulthood is characterized as "achieving"; it is a task-related, competitive, cognitive style. Middle adulthood intellectual style is described as "executive" and "responsible"; in these years the intellectual task is to integrate long-range goals with the solution of current real-life problems which call for organizational, integrative, and interpretive intellectual skills. Later adulthood calls for a "reintegrative" style characterized by the need to attain a sense of meaning in experience; this requires the ability to retrieve and attend selectively to information from the abundance of information that has been accumulated over the life span.

The three phases of intellectual development relate to the different areas of problem solving associated with different stages of adulthood. The first phase emphasizes the attainment of intellectual skills and application to personal and societal goals needed in establishing family units and entering the world of work. The second period is one of relative stability and integration. It is accompanied by some reduction in response speed. The security of the middle adults' social position and their wealth of experience provide adequate compensation for the loss of speed. Theirs is a style appropriate to the solution of practical problems that occur for persons performing the generative tasks of caring, and of being responsible for others. In the final cognitive style of older years there is more selectivity; the focus of intellectual activity shifts from content to context.

Continuing research in educational measurement involves the differentiation between intelligence and competence. Schaie describes intelligence as an inference of underlying traits coming from many observations; competence is a more situation-specific combination of intellectual traits, which, with adequate motivation, will permit adaptive behavior. Schaie's position is that traditional measures of intelligence are not likely to be very useful for predicting many of the more situation-specific skills of the older learner.

3. Moral Development

The study of adult moral development is extending the conceptual frameworks of Kohlberg and Piaget to include stages influenced by "contextual relativism" (Murphy and Gilligan 1980). This reflects a step that accompanies the adult's change from concern about identity to a concern about intimacy. In adulthood the formal categories of moral development are transcended and the adult gains a new awareness of the interdependence of self and others. The ethic of justice gives way to the ethic of responsibility in the maturing development that Erikson labeled sense of generativity.

In the study of moral and cognitive development during adult years, a Piagetian-type stage is being recognized as problem finding, to distinguish it from the problem-solving orientation of formal thought. It is employed in the "contextual relativism" that results in moral development beyond Kohlberg's principled moral judgment. Education and life processes that lead adults to question that which was taken for granted are the catalysts for continued moral and cognitive development during adult years (Murphy and Gilligan 1980). It is through the understanding of other persons' lives, both past and present, that the adult's concern moves from identity to intimacy and then to generativity as manifest in continuing moral development.

4. Social Norms and Role Transitions

In simple societies life may be divided into two periods—childhood and adulthood. Other societies may include three: childhood, adulthood, and old age. Neugarten (1977) has pointed out that where the division of labor is simple and the rate of societal change is slow, a single age-grade system functions well. There, as individuals move from childhood to adulthood, they simultaneously take on new roles. There is a close match between social age grades and chronological periods in the life course. In more complex societies there are multiple systems of age grading. In the United States people are adults in the political system when they are 18 and allowed to vote. They are adults in the family system when they marry and become parents. They are adults in the economic system when they become full-time workers.

There are in each culture and period of history generally recognized age norms. In her study of middle-class American men and women, Neugarten found they expressed a general consensus about the best age for men to marry; when they should be settled in a career; when they should hold their top jobs; when they should be ready to retire, and so on. Adults experience two types of transition—normative and idiosyncratic. Normative transitions are changes expected by social norms such as graduations, marriages, births, and retirement. Idiosyncratic transitions are changes that do not happen in everyone's life or at expected times. Social timetables serve to create a normal, predictable adult-life course. Although role transitions require adjustments, they are not traumatic if they occur "on time," because they have been expected and prepared for. Distress occurs with idiosyncratic transitions, role changes that are unexpected and without preparation. Death of a loved one is accompanied by grief at the loss, but if the death is of an elderly person and in a normal fashion it is "on time" and not devastating. The death of a child or an accidental death is "off time" and creates much more difficult adjustment.

5. Educational Applications

Adults perceive events and are motivated differently at different life stages. Effective development requires that they consider the characteristics of their life stage and have access to information needed for decision making. In addition to adult development courses, other areas for program planning include: family communication, career alternatives, health information for self and aging parents, and adjustment groups for widowhood and divorce. Education needs to plan and develop criterion variables relevant to the cognitive styles, life roles, and societal requirements of competent adult functions (Schaie 1977/78).

See also: Concepts and Definitions

Bibliography

Chickering A W, Havighurst R W 1981 The life cycle. In: Chickering A W (ed.) 1981 *The Modern American College*. Jossey-Bass, San Francisco, California

Erikson E H 1968 *Identity: Youth and Crisis*. Norton, New York

Gould R L 1978 *Transformations: Growth and Change in Adult Life*. Simon and Schuster, New York

Levinson D J 1978 *The Seasons of a Man's Life*. Knopf, New York

Levinson D 1986 A conception of adult development. *Am. Psychol.* 41: 3-13

Levinson D 1987 *The Season of a Woman's Life*. Knopf, New York

Lowenthal M F et al. 1975 *Four Stages of Life: A Comparative Study of Women and Men Facing Transitions*. Jossey-Bass, San Francisco, California

Murphy J M, Gilligan C 1980 Moral development in adolescence and adulthood: A critique and reconstruction of Kohlberg's theory. *Hum. Dev.* 23: 77–104

Neugarten B L 1977 Personality and aging. In: Birren J E, Schaie K W(eds.) 1977 *Handbook of the Psychology of Aging*. Van Nostrand Reinhold, New York

Schaie K W 1977/78 Toward a stage theory of adult cognitive development. *J. Aging Hum. Dev.* 8: 129–38

Sheehy G 1976 *Passages: Predictable Crises of Adult Life*. Dutton, New York

Vaillant G E 1977 *Adaptation to Life*. Little, Brown, Boston, Massachusetts

Old Age

C. E. Kennedy

Old age is a period of adulthood of indeterminate length for two reasons. One is that its ending varies with the length of life of the person. The second reason is that there are differences among researchers' definitions as to when old age begins. Its beginning is most generally identified as age 65, reflecting the legislated age for retirement. Neugarten has conceptualized two groups of persons, the young-old and the old-old. She sees the young-old (perhaps beginning in the 50s with early retirement) as representing a rapidly expanding sector of our society with tremendous energies and resources for social influence and contribution. Entry into the old-old phase is usually in the 70s, depending on health considerations.

There has been a prevailing impression in popular thought that all old people are alike and that old age is synonymous with weakness and lack of creativity. However, research contradicts this stereotype. There is greater diversity among the elderly than among any group of persons. This period poses important developmental tasks, the solution of which comes from the combination of resources from earlier life-styles, from the availability of social, psychological, and economic resources in the community, and from the individual's health and physical energies. Many of the negative values associated in the public mind with old age come from a tendency to confuse the effects of illness and poverty with the effects of the aging process. Illness and poverty bring with them significant limitations, whether the individual is young or old. For much of the period of old age, the majority of people experience relatively good health and satisfactory incomes.

1. Demographic Information

In the 15-year period, 1963–1978, the number of people in the United States who were 65 or older increased by 40 percent, from approximately 17 million to 24 million. About 11 percent of the American population is over 65. Every day more than 1,000 Americans celebrate their 65th birthday. The average lifetime a century ago was less than 50 years; today it is over 70 years. The increased life span has come because there are fewer deaths among children, and also because of better health and lower death rates of young and middle adults. The smallest decline in death rate has been in the group where the population growth rate is most rapidly increasing, those in old age. It is the fact that more people are living to reach the period of old age that accounts for the noteworthy population growth of the old age group. However, improved health care in earlier life and during old age also increases the possibilities for satisfying life during old age.

2. Developmental Processes in Old Age

At the turn of the century, the family life cycle was quite different from today. Then, the last child did not leave home until about the time that one or both of the parents were nearing death. Today, the last child leaves home at about midpoint in the parents' marriage. There are usually as many years ahead for the couple alone as there are behind them with children in the home.

The fact that some people choose to withdraw from active life and some strive to maintain the activity level of earlier years as long as possible has led to two theories of aging: disengagement theory and activity/compensation theory. Current research indicates a more general perspective that accommodates both processes. In old age the individual continues the mode of behavior begun in early life. Except where financial or health factors intervene, the person continues to choose alternatives in accord with the individual's established lifelong pattern of needs. There is usually no abrupt personality shift in old age, but rather the principle of integration promotes increasing consistency within the individual's life. This means, also, that individual differences continue to increase among older persons as they continue to add to their individual collections of unique life histories (Maas and Kuypers 1974).

For both sexes, with increasing age there appears to be an increased interiority, that is, preoccupation with inner life. They are more introspective; they tend to respond to inner stimuli rather than to what the social environment would dictate. They are less likely to respond to new challenges or to be self-assertive. While increased interiority is characteristic of both sexes, there are differences in the patterns that develop for men and women. Men in old age are more responsive to their affiliative, nurturant, sensual promptings and women move toward more expression of their aggressive, egocentric impulses (Neugarten 1977). Since this difference is found in many different cultures, one explanation is that social assignments in most cultures require men to be the breadwinners and women to nurture the family. With old age the assignments are relaxed and the complementary aspects of their personalities are allowed to emerge (Guttman 1977).

Erikson (1978) described two developmental stages of old age—generativity and integrity. Generativity versus stagnation is the stage initiated in middle years in which the individual strives to provide for the coming generation. This continues with the young-old, as they establish family and community resources and train the young to take over in their place. The last of Erikson's eight stages, that of integrity versus despair has increasing prominence with increasing age. Gaining a sense of integrity is the developmental process in which individuals begin to recognize the patterns of their life and affirm the meaning of one's total existence. Older people looking back upon the years accept their strengths and their limitations and in this process express hope and gain wisdom. The individual who does not achieve this sense of integrity experiences despair, tending to reject one's past life and to fear death.

3. Biology of Old Age

Very few people die of old age. Death usually comes from disease. Heart disease is the primary cause of death of people over 65. Aging is associated with gradual decline in the performances of most organs of the body. The amount of blood pumped by the heart falls from 6.5 liters per minute at age 20 to 3.5 liters at age 85. This means that less blood flows through the kidneys and through other organs and muscles, causing them to be increasingly vulnerable to disease. However, there is great individual variability and many old people have circulatory performances of young persons. With the exception of sexual hormones, the endocrine glands retain their ability to produce hormones into advanced ages. In the elderly, tissues that respond to the hormones may require a greater supply of hormones than they do in the young. As a result, responses in the elderly are often slower than in the young. Exercise and life-style influence the effective functioning of the biological system.

4. *Intellectual Development*

Aging causes some degree of physical and psychological change in everyone. In the intellectual area there are changes in visual and auditory acuity and in perceptual speed that cause older persons to be at a disadvantage in intelligence testing. Some age-related decline in ability may be attributable to an increase in cautiousness in older persons. Substantial associations have been found between hearing loss and intellectual functioning, as measured by subtests of the Wechsler Adult Intelligence Scale. Also, old people process information received from the senses more slowly (Schaie and Parr 1981).

People growing up at different periods of history learn different kinds of information and use different approaches to learning. An examination of generational differences in level of function shows that much of what has been thought to be intellectual deficit in older people is not deficit, but rather the effect of older people using skills that are inappropriate in the current educational environment. Improved functioning for older adults can be assisted through helping them develop new learning skills and techniques. Old adults are also limited at times by the conventional values assigned to them by our age-graded society. While there is some decline in the perceptual functions with age, there is much compensation. Often the perceived deficit is the result of a lack of self-confidence or lack of intellectual exercise, resulting from stereotypes that limit opportunities for the elderly to be intellectually active. Effective academic endeavors can be carried on by most adults well into their 70s. Motivation is different for older learners, however. Novelty is of less value to older learners; new skills and information are interesting insofar as they enable learners to cope with present life situations.

5. *Environmental Influence*

Life-style and personality patterns of earlier years set the stage for the functioning of old persons. Individuals with a life-style of conflict or perceived vulnerability often find retirement debilitating. Individuals experienced in a life-style of adaptation and effectiveness in problem solving, and who have some choice in planning their later years, usually find retirement a satisfying experience. Sudden or severe loss of environmental support—through death of a spouse, being moved from a familiar community and friends, or lack of income—may have major negative effects on the individual, resulting in lowered morale and increased susceptibility to physical illness. Environmental conditions that have been found associated with longer lives include a history of satisfactory work experience, high intelligence, sound financial status, intact marriages, lower food intake, and abstinence from smoking (Botwinick 1973). In earlier stages of life, role exits lead to valued new roles, for example, from school to job. With increasing age, role exits are less likely to lead to socially valued roles. Retirement and widowhood are role exits in which morale and physical health are significantly influenced by how the individual deals with these exits, whether the individual is able to experience these as transitions into new roles (Rosow 1976).

5.1 *Retirement*

In earlier periods of history, only the wealthy could afford to retire. In 1900, two-thirds of the men over 65 were working; in 1960 it had dropped to one-third. The manner in which retirement comes about influences its effect on the individual. If the individual can choose his or her own time and pace of retirement, adjustment is usually a smooth transition. Finances may be a cause of concern; retirees often move from a period of highest earnings to positions where their income is the least it has ever been during adult life.

Health tends to improve rather than decline following retirement. The individual's earlier life pattern offers the best predictor of how that person will experience such later life transitions as retirement. For some the interruption caused by retirement brings frustration and a pressured searching to find new ways of self-expression. For others, the decreasing importance of economic achievement frees them to focus on long-desired interpersonal experiences. Many retired persons spend parts of their time in travel and other leisure pursuits. For some, social isolation may be a problem in life.

5.2 *Widowhood*

Although the majority of people in the beginning years of old age are living with their spouses, widowhood increases during this period. It is rare that both spouses die simultaneously. With increasing length of life, widowhood can be expected to last for a longer time. Because women tend to live longer than men, it is unlikely that the rate of remarriage will increase. Nearly five out of six widowed persons in the United States are female. About 60 percent of widowed persons over 65 live alone; 30 percent live with family; 10 percent live with nonrelatives or in institutions (US Bureau of Census 1979). When widowed people live with relatives, it is more likely to be with a daughter than with a son.

In widowhood, old statuses and roles are lost and new relationships must be substituted in order to effect a satisfactory adjustment. Transition to widowhood is made difficult by the lack of clearly defined cultural expectations and by the loss of supportive relationships (Lopota 1973). The loss of a spouse puts a strain on other relationships the individual has with family, neighbors, and community groups (Morgan 1984, Stoller 1985). Women tend to maintain family ties somewhat better than men. Suicide is more prevalent among widowers than among widows.

6. Family Life and Leisure

It is an erroneous notion that people in old age have little contact with family. Although the extended family with several generations living under the same roof is not the norm in Western nations, modern communications and transportation make possible frequent contact among family members. There is an increase in families of three and four generations. A young-old person is quite likely to have at least one surviving parent and one married child and one or more grandchildren. Grandparenting is identified as one of the primary satisfactions of old age (Barranti 1985).

There are often various combinations of intergenerational exchanges of psychological support and other kinds of assistance. Some elderly are involved in assisting grown children and caring for grandchildren; other old people have responsibilities for their even older, and often frail, parents. Many older women are part of the labor force and also have family responsibilities that involve both their children's families and their own parents' needs.

While there is generally a high level of assistance from parents to children, older persons—at least in industrialized Western nations—often prefer to live separately from the younger generations. This is manifest by the growing number of retirement communities. The majority of old people, however, live in two kinds of settings: the inner city and rural/farm areas.

In the years to come, the educational level of elderly people will continue to increase, as persons who grew up after compulsory education laws were in place reach retirement years. Education is likely to be a major leisure-time activity, since those with advanced education are inclined to seek more education.

People in old age continue to eat out and attend concerts, sports events, and church services, following interests characteristic of their earlier life-style. Factors such as education, finances, and transportation figure predominantly in their choice of activities. Those who belonged to country clubs, participated in music guilds, or were frequent users of the library continue this pattern in old age. Senior centers provide a resource for many older persons, particularly those from low-income groups. About one-fourth of those over 65 indicate that they provide active volunteer service. Many older persons state that if a job is worth doing, it is worth having a salary. Political activism, such as Grey Panthers, and involvement with church and social group projects, are also a part of the self-expression of people in old age. In attitude studies older people express more interest in religion than young adults do. However, this is more in the personal domain. They participate in church activities at about the same level as other adults.

7. Educational Implications

The fact that people, as they grow older, process incoming stimuli more slowly suggests that they need to be given the opportunity to absorb information at their own pace. Schaie and Parr (1981) recommend that educators distinguish between those aspects of the older learner's intellectual competence that are related to perceptual speed and those that are related to sensory activity. Prosthetic devices and appropriate classroom sound and lighting can greatly improve the learning experience for the elderly. Also important is the recognition that older learners strive to integrate new information within the pattern of meaning from their lifelong experience. They focus selectively, emphasizing context over content (Schaie and Parr 1981). The fact that individual differences increase among the elderly underscores the importance of individualized counseling in planning educational programs for them. Effective education for people in old age requires programs and teachers that are prepared with their uniqueness in mind.

The following are some of the reasons for having education programs for, and about, old age:

(a) Intelligence is a developmental factor requiring continuing exercise; however, in the average community there is little stimulation or opportunity for older persons to be involved in intellectual activity.

(b) The prejudice of agism expresses itself in misinformation and lack of information about old age. Even the elderly themselves agree with the negative stereotypes associated with old age, although they exclude themselves (Harris et al. 1975).

(c) While many persons enjoy their most satisfying sexual experiences in old age, others are deterred by misinformation and fear that sexual capacities will fail them.

(d) Guidance in reminiscence and life review can assist the elderly to gain a sense of well-being associated with Erikson's last developmental stage, integrity.

(e) Information and encouragement can help the elderly to have better exercise, improved nutrition, and a healthy life-style.

(f) Education and social support assist individuals to prepare for role changes such as retirement and widowhood.

The elderly in the 1980s will be of a cohort that is more inclined to seek education and other support services than were previous groups (Gatz et al. 1980). They will also be more inclined to provide services to peers through paraprofessional services, self-help groups, and peer counseling. Therefore, there will be a demand for training programs focusing on the skills of the helping relationship and built on a foundational understanding of the developmental processes of old age.

While only about 5 percent of the elderly are in nursing homes at any one time, in certain Western countries there is an increasing expectation that families of the future will care for their older members in their own homes, as has been the practice in most societies in the past. With the increasing frequency of four-generation families, many young-old will assume special responsibilities as their parents become frail. These new family constellations underscore the family's need not only for education about the characteristics of old age but also for family-life education that helps the family clarify and develop skills in new role relationships in the family.

See also: Education for Older Adults

Bibliography

Barranti C 1985 The grandparent/grandchild relationship: family resource in an era of voluntary bonds. *Fam. Relations* 34: 343-52

Botwinick J 1973 *Aging and Behavior*. Springer, New York

Chickering A W, Havighurst R W 1981 The life cycle. In: Chickering A W (ed.) 1981 *The Modern American College*. Jossey-Bass, San Francisco, California

Erikson E H 1978 Reflections on Dr. Borg's life cycle. In: Erikson E H (ed.) 1978 *Adulthood*. Norton, New York

Gatz M, Smyer M, Lawton M P 1980 The mental health system and the older adult. In: Poon L W (ed.) 1980 *Aging in the 1980s: Psychological Issues*. American Psychological Association, Washington, DC

Guttman D 1977 The cross-cultural perspective toward a comparative psychology of aging. In: Birren J W, Schaie K W (eds.) 1977 *Handbook on the Psychology of Aging*. Van Nostrand Reinhold, New York

Harris L et al. 1975 *The Myth and Reality of Aging in America*. National Council on the Aging, Washington, DC

Lopota H Z 1973 *Widowhood in America*. Schenkman, Cambridge, Massachusetts

Maas H S, Kuypers J 1974 *From Thirty to Seventy*. Jossey-Bass, San Francisco, California

Morgan L 1984 Changes in family interaction following widowhood. *J. Marriage Fam.* 46: 323-31

Neugarten B L 1977 Personality and aging. In: Birren J W, Schaie K W (eds.) 1977 *Handbook of the Psychology of Aging*. Van Nostrand Reinhold, New York

Palmore E B 1975 *The Honorable Elders: A Cross-cultural Analysis of Aging in Japan*. Duke University Press, Durham, North Carolina

Rosow I 1976 Status and role change. In: Bainstock R, Shanas E (eds.) 1976 *Handbook of Aging and the Social Sciences*. Van Nostrand Reinhold, New York

Schaie K W, Parr J 1981 Intelligence. In: Chickering A W (ed.) 1981 *The Modern American College*. Jossey-Bass, San Francisco, California

Stoller E 1985 Exchange patterns in the informal support networks of the elderly: The impact of reciprocity on morale. *J. Marriage Fam.* 47: 335-48

United States Bureau of the Census 1979 Marital status and living arrangements: March 1978. *Current Population Reports*, Series P-20, No. 338. US Government Printing Office, Washington, DC

Lifespan Learning Development

A. W. Fales

Two major approaches have been used to characterize learning over the life span. Life phase approaches divide the life span into age-specific phases characterized by particular normative life events (such as marriage, occupational identification, retirement) and psychosocial tasks (such as developing intimacy, letting children go, mentoring) which are believed to have substantial effects on the individual's learning needs, motives, and behavior. Various theories of psychological development over the life span (Loevinger 1977, Kohlberg 1973, Perry 1970) propose a series of hierarchical, sequential, qualitative changes in the psychological structures within the individual. These structural changes are age-related only in that each more advanced stage depends on the prior stage having been completed. The major implication of developmental approaches for learning over the life span is that learning processes, goals, and strategies are qualitatively different in the various developmental stages. In general, the literature and practice relating adult learning to life phases or developmental stages have used the two approaches synonymously or interchangeably rather than interactively, or have reflected a lack of awareness of the developmental stage viewpoint altogether. Recent work (Cross 1981, Chickering et al. 1981, Weathersby 1978) has begun, however, to provide a basis for a more comprehensive understanding of the effects of the interaction of life phase events and developmental stage characteristics on adult learning processes and thereby to identify instructional strategies appropriate to different phase–stage life positions.

1. Life Phase Approaches

The idea of life phase has intuitive merit and has been used throughout history to describe the human journey from birth to death. Shakespeare's seven ages of man and the ancient tarot represent diverse examples. Research on phases of adult life and learning has, however, a rather brief history beginning in the 1930s. Early research focused on the patterns of life goals, psychosocial tasks, mastery styles, and intrapsychic changes (Havighurst 1973).

Many of the early researchers related the life phases they identified to changes in learning needs, goals, and processes. More recently a number of researchers have presented life phase models in which common

Table 1
Implications for adult education of ego-development levels for three selected life phases

Levels of ego development	Implications	Three selected life phases		
		1. Separation from family	2. Early middle age	3. Preparation for retirement
Conformist Conformity to external rules; belonging; social acceptance; conceptual simplicity	Facilitation	Reward through approval. Provide structured resources and content. Guidance re. choosing from established work and life-style options	Reward through recognition/status. Provide structured resources and content. Guidance re. assessment of self in relation to progress of peers, status	Attention to aging effects, e.g., lighting, speed of concept presentation, building self-esteem as learner. Permission to change. Emphasis on association of new material to existing concepts. Concrete and directed method. Provide structure. Reward through approval/recognition. Provide emotional support
	Content/interest	Competence in expected adult roles: work, skills, parenting, childbirth, nutrition, literacy	Appropriate role-related progression, e.g., children's sport leadership, financial management, "normal" occupational progression. Current leisure or social fads, e.g., fitness, conservation. Intergenerational activities	Maintenance of self-esteem. Expansion of peer-accepted leisure interests, hobbies, volunteer activities. Relationships with adult children. New vocational skills for post retirement use. Financial and life planning. Understanding social change. Health and fitness
Conscientious Self-evaluated standards; mutual relationships; differential feelings; conceptual complexity	Facilitation	Incorporate interpersonal interaction. Guidance in selection of learning goals (long-term) consistent with self-expectation. Include opportunity for self-evaluation	Incorporate interpersonal and group interaction, and intentional affective learning. Structured, self-directed learning modes appropriate. Guidance in use of self-assessment and evaluation within established contexts. Reward through social interaction and self-approval	Emphasize communication skills. Cross-generational groupings. Use of reflection and introspection for self-assessment and future goal identification. Conscious attention to philosophical issues relative to content. Encourage independence in females and affectivity in males

	Content/interest	Achievement of personally valued competence in work and interpersonal relations. Alternative life-style options. Role and social relationships. Concern with social issues	Exploration and testing of alternative life-styles to own. Perceptions of how to link early choices with possible changes in occupation and life-style. Conscious assessment of self in relation to parents' values. Stress management. Coping with divorce	Alternative post-retirement roles and relationships. Maintenance of physical, mental, and economic well-being. Skills in interpersonal relating intergenerationally
Autonomous Conformist level and conscientious level plus: coping with conflicting inner needs; respect for autonomy and interpersonal interdependence; vivid expression of feelings; integration of physiological, psychological, and social aspects of self; self-fulfilment; increased conceptual complexity; complex patterning and tolerance for ambiguity	Facilitation	Autonomous stage probably not attained by this life phase	Autonomous stage still rare by this life phase. Largely self-directed learning modes and self-planned activity. Opportunity for individual work with group sharing. Life experience assessment for educational credit. Self-based rewards. Reflection as integrative learning tool. Use of imagery, physical activity, creative integrative techniques. Presentation of multiple perspectives	Use of reflection for integrative learning, identification of complex patterns, linking of new understandings with old. Largely self-directed learning modes, and self-planned activity. Provide opportunity for sharing cross-generationally as well as with own life phase cohort. Provide opportunities for expression of complexity of patterns and recognition of value of multiple perspectives. Use in guidance roles with other group members
	Content/interest		Self-discovery. Facilitating others' growth. Freedom and responsibility. Solving social and moral problems. Leadership in areas of ethical and moral concern. Applying coping skills to life planning. Creative stress management. Non-traditional life-style choices	New avocational roles through which self can be expressed. Existential philosophical approaches to knowledge, human problems, and spiritual understanding. Maintenance of physical, mental, and social capacity in integrated form. Expression of own complexity of understanding—wisdom. Welfare of humanity. Biography, mythology, history, spiritual growth

LEFA—H

psychosocial tasks are specified for relatively specific chronological periods.

The various studies of life phases use different research methods and are based on small, nonrepresentative samples of, for the most part, white, middle class, American males. Each presents a slightly different breakdown of chronological periods and key issues in each period. In general, however, the phases identified can be described as follows:

(a) Separating from family of orientation (late teens to early 20s). Tasks include becoming self-supporting, forming attachment with peers, separating emotionally from parents, and forming an identity.

(b) Provisional adulthood (early to late 20s). Tasks include selection of a mate and intimacy, forming a family, deciding on life-style, forming an occupational identity, mastering what one is "supposed" to be in life.

(c) Thirties transition (late 20s and early 30s). Tasks include evaluating and exploring alternatives to choices in phase (b), and establishing an adult relationship with parents.

(d) Thirties stabilization (early to late 30s). Tasks include succeeding at phase (c) choices, solidifying a sense of self, increasing the attachment to the family of procreation, and giving up mentors.

(e) Forties (mid-life) transition (late 30s and early 40s). Tasks include re-evaluating the "dream" of the first half of life, restructuring the time perspective, establishing a sense of meaning, establishing generativity, and expanding emotional repertoire.

(f) Restabilization (middle 40s to middle 50s). Tasks include succeeding at phase (e) choices, developing self-acceptance, maintaining growth and flexibility emotionally and intellectually, and grandparenthood.

(g) Preparation for retirement (late 50s to middle 60s). Tasks include developing adult relationships with children, preparing for the end of an occupational role, and developing alternative sources of self-esteem.

(h) Young old period (middle 60s to late 70s). Tasks include exploring uses of leisure, consolidating a sense of self as continuous, maintaining health, income, social relations, and emotional attachments, re-evaluating meaning, and developing spirituality.

(i) Old old period (late 70s to death). Tasks include establishing self-acceptance, a life review, maintaining emotional attachments, adjusting to declines in health, relationships, and mental functions, facing death, and providing for generational continuity.

While the notion of life stages has been eagerly adopted by some as a basis for adult education program development (see, for example, McCoy 1977, Knox 1979), others caution that research has shown that the stage characteristics may not be valid for even a majority within a specified chronological range, and certainly may not apply to any given individual (Kummerow 1977).

2. *Psychological Development Approaches*

Developmental theories have been central to an understanding of children's learning [development being the acquisition of new psychological structures or the change from an old structure to a new one (Loevinger 1976 p. 32)]. It is only recently, however, that theories of cognitive (Perry 1970), moral (Kohlberg 1973), and ego (Loevinger 1977) development have been seen as having relevance to understanding adult learning (Cross 1981). Developmental theories are presented in terms of stages, which are hierarchical, proceed by gradual step-wise integrations, and are irreversible. These stages may be maturationally related but in adulthood are more likely to be related to the acquisition and integration of experience. Loevinger's theory of ego development incorporates the domains of cognitive, moral, interpersonal, and conscious preoccupation development within an integrated framework and postulates six major stages with three transitional stages. The stages are only minimally age-related and, with the exceptions of the first two, all can be found in "normal," functioning adults. Progression through the stages and the events or experiences which result in transition from one stage to the next are not well-understood. However, the structural transition from one ego stage to another must, theoretically, result in changed perceptions of self, other, knowledge, relationship, feeling, justice, and sources of meaning.

3. *Implications for Adult Learning*

Life phase and developmental stage theories each have distinct implications for the design and facilitation of adult learning. Table 1 presents examples of some implications for facilitation and the content/interest aspects of adult learners in three life phases for three ego development levels. The three life phases are (a) the phase of separation from the family, (b) the phase of early middle age (the 30s), and (c) the phase of preparation for retirement. From the standpoint of such a theory as Loevinger's, it is possible to identify the three levels or phases of ego development as the conformist, the conscientious, and the autonomous. At the conformist level, the individual's self concentrates on adhering to the rules and tenets of the immediate social environment. In the conscientious phase, the emphasis is on doing a good job and personally assessing one's own achievement. In the autonomous phase the emphasis is on respect for autonomy and independence, yet concern for interactions with others. As Table 1 shows, each ego-development level can be related to each of the three selected life stages in terms of implications drawn about the ways adult education can be facilitated and about the typical content that is of interest to persons at that particular developmental life stage.

Many more specific implications could be gleaned from a close examination of the literature. The examples in the table may suffice to illustrate the kinds of approaches an educator of adults might use for adults in different life phase/developmental stage categories. In actual program design and facilitation, the educator often applies an implicit understanding of these interactions in how he or she individualizes instruction, develops materials, and plans program format. In some cases program evaluation research has confirmed the value of use of techniques relevant to the developmental stage/life phase of the learners. For example, a study of the use of demonstration plots in conjunction with literacy training in Iran found that older autonomous farmers benefited significantly from the use of both methods while younger farmers without access to their own land did not (UNFAO 1975). Although such findings do not directly test the relevance of life phase approaches to design and facilitation, they do imply that attention to these factors would produce significant gains in learning.

The practical reality of adult education is usually that the teacher/facilitator does not know the developmental level of his/her students, although the life phase may be easier to estimate. Nevertheless, a little thought can increase provision of alternative learning modes appropriate to different developmental levels. For example, behavioral learning techniques can be used in a teacher-directed or a self-directed manner; skill learning (such as typing or memorization of the alphabet) can be rote learning or can be taught with an emphasis on understanding underlying principles (appropriate to a higher level of cognitive development). Learners in the same classroom can be allowed to choose whether they prefer to learn from the teacher (conformist ego stage), through small group interaction (conscientious ego stage), or independently with group sharing (autonomous ego stage). Thus these concepts can be applied even when the planner or facilitator does not have complete knowledge of the phases/stages of the learners.

If the facilitator perceives his/her role as one of assisting the learner to attain his/her fullest potential, the facilitative techniques used may be intentionally chosen to create a situation where the learner must go beyond his/her usual developmental stage response and will be more likely to produce behaviors appropriate to a level above his/her actual level. The life-phase transitions appear to provide natural "teachable moments" for this type of developmental stage transition, and the experience of a new learning mode which helps resolve or restructure a critical life event during a transitional phase can be a powerful catalyst for progression to the next developmental stage.

See also: Lifelong Education: Research Strategies

Bibliography

Chickering A W 1981 *The Modern American College: Responding to the New Realities of Diverse Students and a Changing Society*. Jossey-Bass, San Francisco, California

Cross K P 1981 *Adults as Learners: Increasing Participation and Facilitating Learning*. Jossey-Bass, San Francisco, California

Havighurst R J 1973 History of developmental psychology: Socialization and personality development through the life span. In: Baltes P B, Schaie K W (eds.) 1973 *Life-span Developmental Psychology: Personality and Socialization*. Academic Press, New York

Knox A B (ed.) 1979 *Programming for Adults Facing Mid-life Change*. Jossey-Bass, San Francisco, California

Kohlberg L 1973 Continuities in childhood and adult moral development revisited. In: Baltes P B, Schaie K W (eds.) 1973 *Life-span Developmental Psychology: Personality and Socialization*. Academic Press, New York

Kummerow J M 1977 Developmental theory and its application in guidance programs. *Pupil Person. Serv. J.* 6 (1)

Loevinger J 1977 *Ego Development: Conceptions and Theories*. Jossey-Bass, San Francisco, California

McCoy V R 1977 Adult life cycle change: How does growth affect our education needs? *Lifelong Learning* 1: 14–18, 31

Perry W G Jr 1970 *Forms of Intellectual and Ethical Development in the College Years: A Scheme*. Holt, Rinehart and Winston, New York

United Nations Food and Agriculture Organization (UNFAO) 1975 The bramble bush of literacy. *Ideas and Action* 105: 5–6

Weathersby R 1978 Life stages and learning interests. *The Adult Learner: Current Issues in Higher Education*. American Association for Higher Education, Washington, DC

Lifespan Learning: Implications for Educators

D. MacKeracher

Available research on learning processes describes a cyclical sequence of activities (Taylor 1981, Kolb et al. 1979, Argyris 1976). Various writers disagree on the nature and order of these activities, on the activity which precipitates learning, and on the relative importance of each activity in the overall process. This article assumes that the importance of each activity varies with the context and goals of learning; that the nature and order of activities vary between situations and learners; and that the nature of the precipitating activity is less important to the learner since the sequence is repetitive, but may be important to the educator in developing strategies for instruction or facilitation. While the description of learning here tends to draw heavily on cognitive and information-processing terms, the learning process is viewed as involving a complex interaction among cognitive, affective, psychomotor, and social behaviors and processes.

Various writers do agree that two conditions are essential for facilitating the learning process. First, the individual must have access to sufficient information from direct experience or secondary sources, with enough variations on themes, presented through a variety of media, to allow similarities and differences to be perceived and patterns of meaning to emerge (Hart 1975). Second, the learner must have enough time and freedom from threat to allow learning to proceed naturally, without anxiety or undue stress (Kidd 1973). A third condition is assumed to be of importance for adult learners: that sufficient and effective patterns of meaning and strategies for learning must have already developed if the individual is to be a competent learner. While children are usually given the time and assistance needed to develop these basic patterns and strategies, adult learners are often assumed to have developed them in earlier years, an assumption which is sometimes false and can create obstacles in the learning process. Learning how to learn is increasingly being viewed as an essential component and precondition for competent adult learning (Smith 1982).

The basic activities in the learning process include some which are internal to the individual—taking in information, searching for and assigning meaning and value to information, utilizing information, making decisions, acting, and receiving feedback from internal sources on the consequences of actions; and some which involve the external environment—receiving feedback from external sources about the consequences of actions, interacting with objects and other persons, and having access to additional sources of new information (Brundage and MacKeracher 1980).

The learner takes in information through sensory receptors from both internal and external sources (Hebb 1972). The richness and accuracy of this information are directly limited by the acuity of the learner's sensory receptors, focus of attention, and personal expectations; and indirectly affected by physical and emotional well-being, cognitive style, and previous experience. The information taken in can be selectively controlled by the learner in spite of the quality and quantity of information actually available. What is learned is not necessarily the same as that presented by the educator.

The learning process continues as the individual searches for and assigns meaning and value to information (Torbert 1972). Personal meanings and values are often idiosyncratic and emerge from the ways in which an individual makes sense of direct personal experience. Social meanings and values are acquired through socialization and make it possible for members of the same social group to communicate with each other. When created through shared interpersonal activity, meanings and values are both social and personal and make sense to all individuals who participated in the creation process.

Information is used in various cognitive activities such as analyzing, comparing, inventing, and organizing (Norman 1973). The outcome of these activities is the development of a personal system for making sense of reality and for determining action strategies. The system is flexible, dynamic, and open to change. Cognitive activities are constantly modified by the emotions. As the level of potency and negativity increases, emotions can turn reflecting into repetitive thinking, curiosity into anxiety, effective coping into irrelevant or ineffective defending, arousal and selective attention into distress and distorted perception (Brown 1980). Conscious cognitive activities involve the use of words, images, sounds, and felt sensations as representational markers for meanings and values. Unconscious activities usually involve nonverbal representational markers and may be raised to consciousness through such processes as dreaming, reflecting, and meditating. Emotional activities modify both conscious and unconscious cognitive activities. Most learning activities occur at unconscious levels, while educational activities tend to occur at conscious levels (Hart 1975).

When an individual is learning in interaction with other persons, there are general social expectations that internal cognitive and emotional activities and representational markers will be made public, usually through the use of words. In this way, the individual's learning activities can be shared with, or assessed by, others.

Information manipulation results in the individual making decisions to act, which may be as unconscious and fleeting as shifting the focus of the eyes or as conscious and extensive as emigrating to a new country. The individual acts in ways which are intended, at least at the conscious level, to be congruent with decisions. Transactions, particularly those intended to change internal conditions, may not be apparent to others, but always provide the individual with new information about the action and its consequences through internal sensory feedback. Actions which involve the external environment provoke a response from persons or objects which, through feedback, also provides the learner with information about the consequences of actions. Responses can vary from silence and immobility to complex dialogues. By this means, an interactive system is established between the learner and both internal and external environments. The educator may be an important component in this interactive system.

Educators, those who facilitate the learning process, can do so directly through presenting information of varying quality and quantity, providing feedback on actions taken by the learner, and interacting with the learner through an exchange of meaning; and indirectly by monitoring internal activities as these are made public by the learner. Facilitation of internal activities is always limited by the learner's willingness to make these public and ability to describe them accurately.

The learning process can begin with any activity in the general sequence. For example, if the individual is presented with wholly new information (as would be the case, for instance, in a new occupation), learning may begin with attempts to make sense of information on the basis of existing personal or social meanings or skills. If the individual becomes aware (perhaps through insight or dreaming) of new ways in which meanings and values are being redefined or transformed at previously unconscious levels, learning may begin with changes in information utilization. If the learner receives feedback which is contrary to expectations (in acquiring bifocals, for instance, or discovering valued meanings are no longer appropriate), learning may begin with attempts to develop new strategies for coping and for reducing any anxiety or disruptive feelings associated with the experience.

Factors which influence the learning process include, among others: whether learning occurs when the individual is acting alone, interacting with objects, or engaged in social interactions (Cross 1976); whether learning is based on information from direct personal experience or from secondary sources such as opinions of others or factual data (Torbert 1972); whether learning focuses on new meanings, values, skills, or strategies (Brim and Wheeler 1966), or on the expansion or transformation of those which already exist (Taylor 1981); whether the learner's learning strategies and communicating skills work, and whether the educator's strategies and skills are effective (Argyris 1976). Several additional factors are critical to the overall process of learning and will be considered in greater detail.

1. System of Personal Structures and Processes

Within each individual, direct personal experiences accumulate over time and are accompanied by the emergence of: (a) a set of meanings and values (structures) by which the individual makes sense of past experiences, imputes sense to current experiences, and predicts future experiences; and (b) a set of skills and strategies (processes) by which the individual reflects on, reconstructs, and reorganizes the past, acts, reacts, and interacts in the present, and anticipates the future. This collective set of meanings, values, skills, and strategies is variously referred to as a set of personal constructs, a representational map, a model of reality, and an evolving self-organizing system. In this article, the term "system" is used and denotes structures and processes which are dynamic rather than static, and open to constant revision, expansion, and potential transformation as the result of experience and learning. Whatever term is used, an individual's system of personal structures and processes has several fundamental characteristics which are critical in the learning process.

1.1 Organizing Structures

Propositions about the schematic organization and generalizable aspects of individual systems are determined by the manner in which writers in this field conceptualize their own experience and their observations of others. One approach which may be useful for educators is to view each learner's system as including organizing structures which provide a framework within which experience can be given meaning and value (Marshall 1980). These organizing structures include: a personal biography for making sense of past experiences; a unique perception of reality for making sense of collective experiences; a self-identity for making sense of how a person acts within biography and reality; and a central or inner purpose in pursuing personal destiny as derived from an idealized version of biography, reality, and self-identity. These organizing structures are not mutually exclusive and, in fact, usually offer different perspectives for any single experience. Each can be viewed as having a cognitive and an affective component (e.g., self-identity includes both self-concept and self-esteem).

These organizing structures determine what information is attended to and taken in, and how selected information is interpreted. That is, while new experiences have the potential for expanding the system, existing structures have a tendency to limit the information taken in to that which already makes sense (Norman 1973). The overall system is characterized by a tendency to maintain internal or personal integrity in spite of change. Personal integrity can be defined as the cohesive, continuous, interactive, and global nature of the total human system.

1.2 Organizing Processes

Processes are activities which occur in the immediate present. In order to examine their nature or to discuss them, processes must be described as if they were structured concepts. For example, some process-related concepts are identified by various writers as cognitive and learning styles (Cross 1976), decision-making and problem-solving strategies (Kolb et al. 1979), action tendencies (Jones 1968), and feedback mechanisms (Torbert 1972). Cognitive style describes the consistent ways in which an individual selects and organizes information into meanings and values, while learning style describes the consistent ways in which an individual changes various parts of the system through experiencing, reflecting, conceptualizing, and experimenting (Kolb et al. 1979).

In general, changing the structures of the system is easier than changing the processes. With the passage of time, individual learners appear to maintain consistency and continuity in their cognitive and learning styles (Cross 1976), but do change meanings and values. The major organizing structures of the system (i.e., biography, perceived reality, self-identity, central purpose) may be changed through such processes as life review, perspective transformation (Taylor 1981), life transitions, life crises, developmental transitions, religious conversions, and so on. An individual may find it easier to expand the useable range of cognitive and learning styles, than to transform basic and preferred styles. In fact, it is apparent that changing the skills and strategies themselves is extremely difficult and requires a higher order of learning skills and strategies, sometimes referred to as meta-learning or double-loop learning (Argyris 1976). In this type of learning, changes in the processes are invariably associated with changes in the major organizing structures (Jantsch 1979).

1.3 Personal Value

As structures and processes emerge over time, they become increasingly valued as an essential reflection and expression of self (Kidd 1973). Each learner enters a learning activity with established preconceptions of experience which provide some predefined meanings and values even for wholly new experiences. The educator must be prepared to accept and acknowledge each learner's personal system as viable for that individual and as a valued and unique resource which affects further learning. A learner responds more willingly to change if individual biography, perception of reality, self-identity, and inner purpose are acknowledged and affirmed by others. To reject any of these personally structured aspects of experience is to impute, however unintentionally, rejection of the individual who lived that biography, holds that perception of reality to be accurate, presents and values that self-identity, or pursues that inner purpose.

It follows that, as individuals age, personal systems increasingly become well-established and accumulate elevated and strengthened potency and value. Older learners may need to be acknowledged and affirmed even more than younger learners.

1.4 Establishing Connections Between Structures and Experiences

Each individual's system of structures varies in relation to the basic means by which experiences and their related meanings and values can be represented or described using combinations of words, images, sounds, and felt sensations. Words are frequently dissociated from both experiences and other representational markers (Bandler and Grinder 1975). An essential facilitating function, therefore, is to assist the learner to re-establish connections among direct personal experiences, representational images, sounds, and felt sensations, and the words which describe or name them.

In addition, personal experiences often remain unnamed unless the learner receives help and encouragement to publicly disclose such experiences. Social meanings and values, as derived from collective experiences, are often acquired first as words and may not be connected to personal experiences. Another facilitating function, therefore, is to assist the learner to understand and establish connections among collective and individual experiences, social and personal meanings and values, in ways which continue to make sense to the individual learner, yet permit sharing with others. These various facilitating functions assist the learner to legitimize biography (Marshall 1980) and to adjust any omitted or distorted aspects of perceived reality (Bandler and Grinder 1975).

2. Feedback Mechanisms

Feedback mechanisms are those processes which provide information to the learner on the actual consequences of personal activity in relation to intended consequences or goals. Feedback comes from three basic sources. First, internal sensory receptors throughout the body provide immediate reflexive feedback about activity as it occurs, thereby giving the individual an immediate and subjective experience of the acting self. For example, the muscular sensations of a bicycle rider provide immediate information about the balance while riding.

Second, the eyes and ears provide slightly delayed feedback about activity, thereby giving the individual observations about the acting self as an object of one's own perception. The length of the delay in the feedback is determined by the individual's capacity for sensory response and self-awareness. For example, the writer's eyes receive slightly delayed information about the quality and accuracy of writing and the speaker's ears receive slightly delayed information about the quality and accuracy of speaking. Such feedback is subjective in the sense that it is about self; objective in the sense that the actions must be viewed as if from the perspective of an observing or listening other; and delayed in the sense that it takes a significant, albeit extremely short, period of time for the feedback to return as information about actions.

Third, other persons and objects in the external environment provide delayed and objective feedback by responding to the activity of the learner. The length of the delay is determined by the degree of responsiveness of the objects or other persons. The response of a car to the driver's actions or the response of another person to the learner's ideas are examples of such feedback. Nonresponsive brakes and a silent listener are providing as much feedback as the car which stops when the driver steps on the brake pedal or the listener who enters into a dialogue with the learner about the ideas expressed.

As feedback is increasingly delayed, its impact on the learner and potential effect on learning is correspondingly diminished. An individual learner is free to selectively ignore or attend to any source or type of feedback.

3. Arousal

Being human means having both body and mind, each of which has continuous needs for being activated through an exchange of energy and for being nurtured through periods of relaxation and restoration. Body and mind interact through arousal and relaxation mechanisms which in turn are affected by biochemical energy, sensory stimulation, and the emotions. Biochemical energy is necessary to initiate minimal levels of arousal, to sustain optimal levels for prolonged activity, and to respond at maximum levels for short bursts of intensive activity. At regular intervals, or whenever exhausted, biochemical energy must be restored through relaxation, sleep, and nourishment.

Sensory stimulation comes from sensory receptors and has two general functions. It activates the general arousal mechanism of the body through the midbrain and reports information to the sensory centers of the cerebral cortex. The informative function has no effect unless accompanied by general arousal. At regular intervals, sensory stimulation must be reduced and mental energy restored through relaxation, reflection, and dreaming.

Once both functions are operative, they interact with each other: more information leads to higher arousal levels and more arousal leads to increasingly organized mental and physical activity and to enhanced attention and perception. The direct correlation between stimulation, arousal, and activity operates only until optimal levels are reached. Beyond these levels, further increases in arousal (through stress or anxiety) or information (through information overload or ambiguity) lead on to increasingly disorganized mental and physical activity, selectively limited attention, and distorted perceptions (Hebb 1972, Brown 1980).

Under conditions of sensory deprivation, the internal arousal mechanisms of the body, in an attempt to avoid boredom and inactivity, will activate the sensory centers of the cerebral cortex from within. The result is that the individual will begin to experience sensory information as being received even when such sensations are clearly impossible. While the individual perceives such sensations as real, external observers, who cannot share these perceptions, tend to label them negatively as hallucinations or positively as revelations. Sensory deprivation can be induced through monotonous activities, repetitive sensory stimulation, bland unvarying environments, reductions in the individual's capacity of sensory intake, reduced interpersonal interactions, and so on (Hebb 1972).

These facts suggest several facilitating concerns. Too little information, repetitive and unproductive learning activities, or any condition which reduces energy levels can result in boredom, inactivity, and sensory deprivation. Too much information, arousal, or anxiety can result in disorganized learning responses, selective inattention, or distorted perceptions. Optimal levels of arousal and information are individually determined and fluctuate over time and in idiosyncratic ways. Educators must be prepared to respond to individual needs for arousal and information and to be attuned to changes in these needs over time. Further, the body and mind must be seen as interactive and the learner as needing and actively seeking both arousal and relaxation, information, and reflection.

The third factor which enters into arousal mechanisms is the emotions, which can be defined as special arousal states in which both internal and external conditions are given special meaning and value based on the current situation, past experiences, and future expectations. The interpretation will determine the type of emotion experienced. That is, emotions are arousal states accompanied by specific meanings, values, and action tendencies which are learned through experience. Stress, an arousal state which is nonspecific, is a response to a real or perceived, but identifiable, threat to personal survival or security. Anxiety is a stress-like response in which the threat remains unlabelled or unidentified (Hebb 1972). Educators should attempt to maintain a learning environment which is free from threat and assist learners to identify unlabelled fears and anxieties.

Arousal is essential to learning and is increased by uncertainty and novelty. As arousal levels increase, learning becomes more efficient and effective until optimal conditions are achieved. Beyond this point, emotional definitions, stress, or anxiety may intervene in ways which sometimes enhance, but more often block further learning. The heightened arousal associated with learning often feels child-like to the adult learner. If aroused learning behavior is defined positively by the educator, the learner may be seen as interested, enthusiastic, and motivated; if it is defined negatively, the learner may be seen as childish, restless, or immature.

4. *Action Tendencies or Motivation*

Motivation is defined by Hebb (1972) as a tendency to produce organized activity. Action tendencies which relate to learning can be described in a wide variety of terms: approach/avoidance tendencies, internal/external locus of control, achievement/affiliation needs, active/passive orientations to information use, coping/irrelevant defenses, and so on. For an educator the relevant issues are to be able to make sense of the action tendencies used by specific learners and to develop strategies for enhancing or blocking specific tendencies (Cross 1976).

One useful way to understand action tendencies is to view most learning-associated behaviors as being expressions of two general trends: the trend to master and the trend to belong (Jones 1968). These two tendencies are not mutually exclusive and most human activity includes varying degrees of both tendencies. A third general tendency toward affection operates between two persons, such as a learner and an educator. Affection tendencies can enhance or block learning but do not operate in all learning situations.

4.1 Mastery

The tendency to master moves the individual to struggle for centrality within personally perceived reality; to organize events, objects and, whenever possible, other persons; to control actions, reactions, and interactions in order to enhance survival and self-esteem. Successful mastery lies in being informed and skilled, in being able to make sense of new experiences in order to reduce uncertainty, and in maintaining self-identity and personal integrity. Failure is related to being ignorant (uninformed or misinformed) or incompetent (unskilled) and to feeling helpless in dealing with disconfirming, novel, or ambiguous situations (Jones 1968).

An educator can demotivate tendencies toward mastery by threatening the survival of the individual. Survival is based on immediate needs and, therefore, can be threatened by rejecting the individual's self-identity (experienced by the learner as loss of self), discounting perceived reality (experienced as bewilderment), or by taking control of the situation away from the individual through such techniques as withholding information, providing excessive information, or beginning skill learning sequences at extremely complex levels (experienced as helplessness and anxiety). An educator can enhance tendencies toward mastery by heightening self-esteem and ensuring personal survival through accepting and confirming the viability of the learner's self-identity and perceived reality, and through making the learning situation controllable by the individual learner.

4.2 Belonging

The tendency to belong moves the individual to strive to become part of something, usually a group or social unit, perceived as larger and more important than themselves, in order to enhance security and sense of connectedness with significant others. Successful belonging lies in feeling connected to both past and future, as well as to other persons, in being able to carry out satisfying interpersonal relationships, and in feeling included in activities and membership of self-selected groups. Failure is related to feeling isolated, discontinuous with the past, mistrusting of the future, and alienated from preferred groups (Jones 1968).

An educator can demotivate tendencies toward belonging by threatening the learner's security. Security is based on a sense of personal connectedness and can be threatened, therefore, through rejecting the individual's biography or connection to the past (experienced by the learner as self-estrangement); through making the learning situation totally unpredictable (experienced as self-doubt or mistrust of the future); and through discouraging group interactions and reducing opportunities to establish connections to others (experienced as isolation). An educator can enhance tendencies toward belonging by reducing potentially threatening situations, by utilizing personal biographies and the past experiences of learners as resources for learning activities, and by promoting group interactions. Educators might wish to hesitate before making the learning situation totally predictable since many adults may draw on their past experiences in elementary or secondary schools to make predictions. However, the educator can use discrepancies between past and current learning experiences as a topic to encourage group interaction.

While some theorists argue as to which trend—mastery or belonging—is more important to learning, it is clear that both trends are important for a fully-functioning human being and that, when things go wrong, the trend to belonging may be more crucial and may give some learners more trouble than the trend toward mastery. Therefore, it is important for an educator to avoid demotivating either tendency and to develop strategies and skills for facilitating both.

See also: Lifelong Education: Research Strategies

Bibliography

Adams J, Hayes J, Hopson B 1976 *Transition: Understanding and Managing Personal Change*. Martin Robertson, London

Argyris C 1976 Theories of action that inhibit individual learning. *Am. Psychol.* 31(9): 638–54

Bandler R, Grinder J 1975 *The Structure of Magic: A Book About Language and Therapy*. Science and Behavior Books, Palo Alto, California

Brim O G, Wheeler S 1966 *Socialization After Childhood: Two Essays*. Wiley, New York

Brown B 1980 *Supermind: The Ultimate Energy*. Harper and Row, New York

Brundage D, MacKeracher D 1980 *Adult Learning Principles and Their Application to Program Planning*. ERIC Document No. ED 181 292

Cross K P 1976 *Accent on Learning*. Jossey-Bass, San Francisco, California

Hart L 1975 *How the Brain Works: A New Understanding of Human Learning, Emotion and Thinking*. Basic Books, New York

Hebb D 1972 *Textbook of Psychology*, 3rd edn. Saunders, Philadelphia, Pennsylvania

Howe M (ed.) 1977 *Adult Learning: Psychological Research and Applications*. Wiley, Chichester

Jantsch E 1979 *The Self-organizing Universe: Scientific and Human Implications of the Emerging Paradigm of Evolution*. Pergamon, Oxford

Jones R 1968 *Fantasy and Feeling in Education*. New York University Press, New York

Kidd J R 1973 *How Adults Learn*. Association Press, New York

Kolb D, Rukin I, McIntyre J 1979 *Organizational Psychology: A Book of Readings*, 3rd edn. Prentice-Hall, Englewood Cliffs, New Jersey

Marshall V 1980 *Last Chapters: A Sociology of Aging and Dying*. Brooks/Cole, Monterey, California

Mezirow J 1978 *Education for Perspective Transformation*. Teachers College, Columbia University, New York

Norman D 1973 *Cognitive Organization and Learning*. ERIC Document No. ED 083 543

Riegel K 1976 The dialectics of human development. *Am. Psychol.* 31(10): 689–700

Smith R M 1982 *Learning How to Learn*. Follett, Chicago, Illinois

Taylor M 1981 The social dimension of the learning process where learning constitutes perspective change. In: Salter L (ed.) 1981 *Communication Studies in Canada.* Butterworth, Toronto, Ontario, pp. 133–46

Torbert W 1972 *Learning from Experience: Toward Consciousness.* Columbia University, New York

Experiential Learning for Adults

L. Melamed

While all learning is an experience, the concept of experiential learning as a subject for educational research began only in the early 1930s in the United States. In its simplest form the term "experiential learning" connotes learning from experience or learning by doing. Interest in this form of learning has expanded in recent years, largely as a reaction to the more passive, traditional methods of education. These latter methods are primarily concerned with transferring already assimilated knowledge from the teacher to the student through books and specialized language.

1. Historical Background

In noncomplex societies living and learning are naturally combined, typically in a family setting and with different adults assuming the role of teachers for succeeding generations. With increasing industrialization, educational systems for providing more specialized knowledge and skills are required. Practical education tends to be supervised by craft guilds, industry, and the workplace while universities assume responsibility for research, technical and professional training, and classical studies. This pattern was particularly evident in Western Europe, with a gradual replacement of older more experience-based systems by formal educational institutions.

The experiential learning "movement" began in the mid-nineteenth century as a means of redressing the balance between formal abstract learning and practical experience. "Laboratory sciences," "applied studies," and "clinical experiences" were introduced into academe at this time. Early in the twentieth century "cooperative education" (various forms of off-campus experiences) were initiated as radically innovative complements to classroom learning. In 1939 John Dewey made an incisive contribution to the developing movement in *Experience and Education.* In this short work Dewey urged that all sources of experience be added to traditional forms of education and suggested an "intellectual" method for affirming such learning.

2. The Experiential Learning Model

Our lives consist of thousands of trivial and significant experiences daily. For these experiences to become learning, or for change to occur in awareness and behavior, selected experiences are singled out, reflected and acted upon. "Experiential learning means the learning that occurs when changes in judgments, feelings, knowledge or skills result for a particular person from living through an event or events" (Chickering 1977). While the subject of experiential learning may have once implied an either/or dichotomy with traditional methods, researchers are beginning to view them as parts of a whole.

A model which illustrates this process (Kolb and Fry 1975) depicts learning as a four-stage cycle with each stage requiring different abilities and skills on the part of the learner. As illustrated in Fig. 1, stage (a) is a concrete personal experience which is followed by (b) observation and reflection of that experience. These reflections are connected to and reworked into (c) abstract concepts and generalizations which are (d) then tested in new situations. In turn these lead to new experiences for a repetition of the cycle. In order for learning or change to take place, the four stages of the cycle must be integrated; for example, an experience which is not reflected upon or is not tested in actual practice, is lost as potential learning.

The process may take place over a span of time, within formal and informal learning environments, intra- or inter-personally, and/or through actual or vicarious experience. One of Kolb's findings suggests that individuals have preferred styles of learning which affect their choices and patterns of learning; for example, some people learn best through experiences while others prefer a more conceptual mode. The traditional (conceptual) method in teaching and learning is described by the model as beginning at stage three. The selection of one predominant mode over another depends on what is being learned, the context in which the learning takes place, and the skills and abilities of the teacher and learner. Whichever mode is selected as a starting point, successful learning depends on realizing each of the stages.

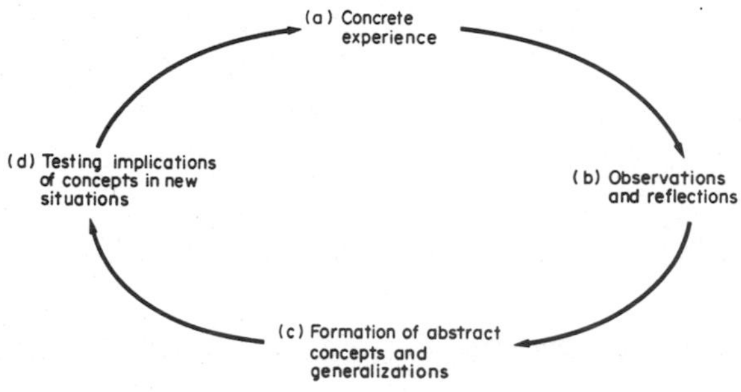

Figure 1

The experiential learning model

3. Approaches to the Study of Experiential Learning

Two main themes can be identified in current research in the field of experiential learning, based on the definition of experience and the context in which it is being examined; pragmatic–institutional and individual–existential. Several approaches are distinguishable within each theme, each with distinct implications for the design, facilitation, and evaluation of learning.

3.1 Theme One: Pragmatic–Institutional

This theme focuses on the participation of the learner in acquiring or mastering concrete skills based on a sequence of learning events specified in advance. While this kind of learning takes place naturally in everyday life, the literature appears to be limited to that which occurs within credit-granting institutions. The following approaches are elaborations of this theme.

(a) *Learning by doing*—learning as a result of direct experience is the commonly accepted definition of experiential learning. In developing countries this term is interchangeable with experience-based education or training. Examples are most forms of apprenticeship, agricultural and industrial training programs, modular instructional programs, athletic and wilderness training.

(b) *Sponsored or cooperative education*—the primary focus in the area of "guided," "sponsored," or "cooperative education" is learning which is undertaken within the structure of a college or university program in an off-campus setting. Close liaison between faculty and field supervisor is considered important for the purpose of designing and measuring learning goals. Programs of this type include preprofessional training practicums and internships, career exploration, service–learning internships, field research, cross-cultural and overseas experiences. Problematic for the institution is the articulation of appropriate learning objectives and the establishment of procedures for measuring skills and competencies gained (Chickering 1977).

(c) *Credit for life experience*—many of the new students enrolling in academic programs have acquired learning through a range of life activities, jobs, and/or community involvement. A large number of these learners tend to be female, from minority groups, and/or working class, who are disadvantaged by seeking work in a society which requires academic qualifications for better paying jobs. One way to help these learners is to validate their prior experience and offer commensurate credit. Traditional intelligence tests and standard assessment procedures have not been found adequate for these learners. The Council for the Advancement of Experiential Learning was formed in the United States in 1973 to conduct research in this area.

3.2 Theme Two: Individual–Existential

This field of inquiry values personal experience as an important source of knowledge and places the learner at the center of the learning process. "Truth" is relative to each learner in his or her particular social context and "teachers" perform supportive or facilitative roles. The whole person (mind, body, and emotions) is involved in the process of discovery on a variety of dimensions. Several different approaches (overlapping in some respects) have developed from this value base.

(a) *Learning how to learn*—living in a society undergoing rapid social change requires continued education and re-education. According to Tough (1971) 80 percent of the population is continually engaged in a series of learning projects of which only 20 percent are occurring in formal classes. Kidd (1973) helped our understanding of how this majority learns and undertook ground-breaking work in revaluing experiential learning on an international institutional level. Knowles (1975) has directly addressed the issue of facilitating self-directed learning for diverse types of learners. Elaboration of the concept of lifelong learning has been an important aspect of research in this area.

(b) *Personal learning from everyday experience*—another focus views experiential learning as moving from concerns with outer-directed world experiences to inner-directed personal ones. "Experiential learning involves becoming aware of the qualities, patterns and consequences of one's own experiences as one experiences it" (Torbert 1972). This author posits four levels of experiences as a basis for learning: (i) the world outside; (ii) a person's behavior; (iii) a person's internal cognitive–emotional–sensory structure; (iv) a person's consciousness or intentional life aims. Compatible with Kolb's experiential learning cycle, each of these levels requires reflection, conceptualization, and testing in new situations for learning to occur. Examples of this type of learning are experiential therapies, for example, Jungian and Gestalt, meditation, dream analysis, and journal writing (Torbert 1972, More 1974).

(c) *Experiential social group processes*—a natural extension of learning from personal experience has been the development of a wide range of social skill training activities frequently referred to as laboratory or human relations training. In T-groups (T for training), the experience of the members in a relatively unstructured environment becomes data for personal and social learning. Experiential learning groups ranging from management training to personal growth have spawned numerous educational innovations. Well-known centers for training leadership in this area have been the National Training Laboratories (US) and Tavistock (England) (Cooper and Alderfer 1978, Torbert 1972).

(d) *Experiential learning in the classroom*—the group process movement has enriched classroom learning with a host of new activities. Role plays, games and simulations, value exercises, and socio- and psychodrama engage learners in concrete experiences which, when processed, lead to cognitive as well as attitudinal and behavioral change. Other activities include the use of audio-visual methods, art, drama, music, dance, and play. Critical in using these methods is the provision of adequate time for reflection and conceptualization (Coleman 1976).

(e) *Experiential learning for social and political action*—the national and international implications of helping individuals and groups learn from their own experience ("name their world") has been explored by Freire (1970) in his work in Africa and South America. In a postcolonial era, survival for poor countries depends on valuing the knowledge, skills, and experiences of their indigenous people, as contrasted with education imposed by the dominant culture. Popular education programs develop skills based on collective experience in the hope that people will act upon and change oppressive social structures.

(f) *Re-visioning the world from women's experience*—in the late 1960s, women in Western societies came together to describe the world from their own perspective. Starting with and validating their personal experiences they began to build a body of knowledge to counteract women's exclusion from centuries of male-dominated scholarship. Extensive research evolving from this collective process is beginning to modify pedagogical methods (Spender 1981), and to produce new paradigms for research and analysis (Gilligan 1983, Reinharz 1984). The emergence of educational theory based on women's experience has major implications for both men and women.

4. Areas for Future Research

Research opportunities will accelerate as learning programs in the 1980s move from academic institutions into living and work places. Interest in learning will progress beyond the concerns of individual students to those of communities and organizations who want to develop their capacities to change and grow. Research into age, stage, and gender differences of the developing adult is already having important implications for the design of learning programs. Attention will likely be focused on understanding more about the reflective process and the social nature of learning. Literacy education will increasingly be based on the life experiences of learners. The problem of assessment will demand further research as institutions and learners face the continuing challenge of awarding credentials to the endless variety of experiences which constitute learning.

The study and application of experiential learning will command increasing attention in formal and informal educational settings as women and men throughout the world demand greater access to learning which is relevant, effective, and engaging.

See also: Prior Life Experience and Higher Education

Bibliography

Chickering A W 1977 *Experience and Learning: An Introduction to Experiential Learning*. Change Magazine Press, New Rochelle, New York

Coleman J S 1976 Differences between experiential and classroom learning. In: Keeton M T (ed.) 1976 *Experiential Learning: Rationale, Characteristics, and Assessment*. Jossey-Bass, San Francisco, California

Cooper C L, Alderfer C P (eds.) 1978 *Advances in Experiential Social Processes*. Wiley, New York

Dewey J 1963 *Experience and Education*. Collier, New York

Freire P 1970 *Pedagogy of the Oppressed*. Seabury, New York

Gilligan C 1983 *In a different Voice: Psychological Theory and Women's Development*. Harvard University Press, Cambridge, Massachusetts

Kidd J R 1973 *How Adults Learn*. Association Press, New York

Knowles M S 1975 *Self-directed Learning: A Guide for Learners and Teachers*. Association Press, New York

Kolb D A 1984 *Experiential Learning: Experience as the Source of Learning and Development*. Prentice-Hall, Englewood Cliffs, New Jersey

More W S 1974 *Emotions and Adult Learning*. Saxon House, Farnborough

Reinharz S 1984 *On Becoming a Social Scientist*. Transaction Books, New Brunswick, New Jersey

Spender D 1981 *Men's Studies Modified*. Pergamon, Oxford

Torbert W R 1972 *Learning from Experience: Toward Consciousness*. Columbia University Press, New York

Tough A M 1971 *The Adult's Learning Projects: A Fresh Approach to Theory and Practice in Adult Learning*. Ontario Institute for Studies in Education (OISE), Toronto, Ontario

Personal Perspective Change through Adult Learning

J. Mezirow

Educational research has long been directed to change and to impediments to change. Attention has been given to slow, step-by-step increments. More recently, attention has focused on large, qualitatively different transformations, and what may cause and inhibit them. Terms and concepts such as paradigm shifts, critical consciousness, perspective transformations, and their equivalents in other languages, are being observed and accounted for in both educational theory and practice, in addition to the more familiar examinations of slow, incremental shifts.

What, when, where, why, and how we learn is largely determined by taken-for-granted meaning schemes and perspectives which may be unreliable and distorting. A crucial function of adult learning involves the process by which cultural and psychological assumptions uncritically assimilated in childhood are brought into consciousness and critically examined for their validity in adult life. These meaning structures may be perpetuated by social norms, institutionalized ideologies, and long established social practices. As learners become more critically reflective, they may discover that distorted meaning structures are shared: private problems become seen as public issues. This often leads to a desire to take collective action to change institutions which support old distorted ways of seeing. In childhood, people are socialized into ways of perceiving reality through meaning schemes and perspectives uncritically assimilated from parents, teachers, role models, and peers. Those who influence others are inevitably the products of the societies and the times in which they live. Every culture and epoch has its conservative mainstream outlook, orthodoxies, taboos, oppressions, parochialisms, prescriptions, ideologies, and distortions. Restrictive language codes and dialogic styles contribute to the problem of understanding in subtle and significant ways. These influences become reinforced and legitimatized by established social practices and institutions—the political, economic, religious, educational, aesthetic, and legal systems—which often prescribe, perpetuate, and enforce the values and arrangements derived from them.

Moreover, every parent and role model has his or her idiosyncratic hang-ups, fears, repressions, compensating mechanisms, dependencies, biases, prejudices, styles of learning and role taking, and self-deceptions. These psychological influences contribute to the way people learn to learn.

Ideologies are belief systems which often are institutionalized and are seen as immutable or God-given and beyond human control. As such, they are falsely perceived and foster dependency relationships which frequently constrain adult development. Ideologies serve as guides for action and legitimation. They may be sexual, racial, religious, educational, occupational, political, economic, psychological, or technological. They become manifest in a set of rules, roles, and social expectations—in meaning schemes—which govern the way people see, feel, think, and act.

Paulo Freire (1970) has demonstrated how adult education may be used to bring dependency-producing cultural assumptions into critical consciousness. Consciousness raising in the women's movement and elsewhere is another example of adult education for perspective transformation. Such transformation involves active negation of an old structure of assumptions and its reorganization through a new definition of oneself and one's relationships which includes a new set of criteria for understanding, judging, and acting.

1. Meaning Schemes and Perspectives

Acquired meaning schemes appear to operate unconsciously, outside awareness, to determine what an individual sees and how they see it. People use their repertoire of meaning schemes to classify objects and events so that what comes into awareness is, in reality, only a selectively interpreted version of what is perceived. Meaning schemes not only arbitrarily and selectively determine the scope of a person's attention, but more generalized meaning perspectives are equally arbitrary and selective in the way they typify objects, make associations, and attribute causality. They provide the basis for reducing complex inferential tasks to simple judgments. They "set us up" with a set of anticipations—pertaining to cause–effect relationships, scenarios of sequences of events, and what others will be like, which tend to become self-fulfilling prophecies. Meaning perspectives provide criteria for judging right and wrong, bad and good, beautiful and ugly, true and false, and appropriate and inappropriate.

They also determine the way people feel about themselves. One of the most important meaning perspectives influencing a person's life is their idealized self-image—the core concept of how they want to be as adults. Meaning schemes and perspectives are structures of psychocultural assumptions within which past experience is assimilated and new experience transformed. These meaning structures are not simply "cognitive structures"; they have strong conative and affective dimensions as well. They indicate appropriate action. As people approach new experiences, meaning structures become their learning structures.

2. Adult Development

Because meaning structures are assimilated uncritically in the process of childhood socialization, they may be untrustworthy, distorted, limited, and dependence-producing; they often reflect biases, reified attitudes, errors in inference, self-deception, distorting ideologies, and prohibitions repressed in childhood which are dysfunctional influences in adult life. In adulthood, a new dimension of development makes it possible for people to extend their understanding and sense of agency by bringing into awareness the meaning schemes and perspectives uncritically acquired in childhood in order to analyze and validate them critically. This is of central significance for adult education.

Contextual awareness and critical reflectivity are adult capacities which appear to emerge as the most significant developmental consequence of the advent of hypothetical–deductive thought processes in adolescence. The emergence of formal operations enables a person to understand how rules governing their thought and action have been deduced by authority figures from abstract principles—and to challenge the validity of the process. Adults can become critically aware of assumptions upon which the principles themselves are predicated. They can bring into critical awareness the ideologies, paradigms, mind sets, orientations, psychological hang-ups, and frames of reference that have been internalized. They can more fully understand how and why they have acquired their meaning perspectives, the functions that the latter fulfill, and the manner in which they have shaped people's lives.

Most significant learning in adulthood takes place during transitions which often involve dilemmas not amenable to problem solving in the usual way (Aslanian and Bricknell 1980). Trying harder just does not work. Graduating from school, moving into a new job, getting married, getting promoted or passed over, making a mid-career change, death of a loved one, divorce, going back to school or work, entering retirement—these and other transitions afford unusual opportunity for perspective transformation. A redefinition of the problem and oneself in relationship to it often becomes essential for forward movement. In such cases, there is a natural tendency to move toward new perspectives which appear more inclusive, discriminating, and integrative of experience.

3. Validity Testing

An important part of adult learning is concerned with values, moral decision making, ideals, feelings, and such abstract ideas as love, freedom, justice, compassion, equality, human rights, and democracy. How can someone know when an assertion made in these areas is valid (or, in the case of feelings, authentic)? Here Jurgen Habermas (1984) persuasively argues that validation is only possible through a consensus—ideally, openly arrived at through free, full participation of informed, objective, and rational persons in a continuing dialogue.

It may be argued that dialogic learning is so indispensable to understanding adult experience that its ideal conditions provide the criteria for structuring a value system with which to judge both adult education and the broader society in which it functions.

In daily life people take propositions or assertions made by others more or less for granted. When a serious question is raised about the comprehensibility, truth, or appropriateness of an assertion or about the truthfulness or sincerity of one making the assertion, dialogue gets stalled. At such key junctures, when validity must be explicitly established, people engage in a special discourse addressing the question. Ideally, like members of a jury, they suspend prior judgments and let the weight of evidence and the better argument determine validity. Ideally, they would arrive at a consensus with which any rational, informed, and objective judge would agree. This is the kind of learning discourse which adult education strives to achieve. The ideal conditions for full, free participation in discourse are also the ideal ones of an adult educational experience, as they are of a learning society committed to lifelong learning.

Participants in an ideal discourse would have a mutual goal of arriving at a consensus based upon evidence and the cogency of argument alone. They would have accurate and complete information on the topic discussed, and participants would have role reciprocity—equal opportunity to interpret, explain, challenge, refute, express themselves, and speak with confidence. Participation would be free from coercion. Participants would bring to the discourse certain essential adult abilities—to reason argumentatively about competing validity claims and argue logically from the evidence, to be critically reflective about cultural assumptions and premises, and to be sufficiently self-reflective to assure participation free from distortion resulting from inhibitions, compensatory mechanisms, or other forms of self-deception.

Educational experiences which in some measure fail to recognize and foster these conditions would be widely judged to be inadequate. When social institutions and practices impede the full participation of every adult learner in construing the meaning of his or her experience through discourse, they are thwarting the most basic human need and should be modified to make them more responsive to this need.

4. Learning Processes

Three learning processes appear to operate not only in the domain of discursive learning but in instrumental and self-reflective learning domains as well (Mezirow 1985). The first process is learning within meaning schemes, that is, differentiating and elaborating the meaning schemes that are usually taken for granted. This process includes learning habitual and stereotypic responses to information received through existing meaning schemes—"recipe learning" and rote learning in which one behavior is stimulus to another behavior. It is possible to become aware of meaning schemes but they do not change. The only thing that changes by correction of errors within a meaning scheme is the specificity of response.

A second process involves learning new meaning schemes which are sufficiently consistent and compatible with existing meaning schemes to complement them within a prevailing or emerging meaning perspective. In this process of learning neither existing meaning schemes nor perspectives change. The prevailing perspective is the product of a course of socialization. Identification plays a large role in this kind of learning.

The third process is learning through meaning transformation—becoming aware of specific assumptions (schemata, criteria, rules, or repressions) upon which a distorted or incomplete meaning scheme is based and, through a reorganization of meaning, transforming it. People encounter an experience which appears meaningless, an anomaly that cannot be given coherence within a prevailing meaning perspective. Illumination comes only through a redefinition of the problem. Reframing the problem is achieved by critically reassessing the assumptions that support the meaning scheme or perspective within which the experience is being interpreted. The affective and conative dimensions of learning become especially important within this transformation process. This is especially true when old ways of seeing oneself and one's values become negated or reinterpreted into a new synthesis as in consciousness raising—a threatening process when social norms and relationships reinforce the old frame of reference.

5. *Social Implications*

The constraints to the ideal of discourse—and hence to freedom and truth—are often political or economic: institutionalized ideologies, arrangements, practices, and systems which result in oppression, coercion, alienation, abrogation of human and civil rights, injustice, and unequal opportunity for security, health, education, shelter, and employment. Acute deprivation and insecurity, desperation, alienation, fear, illness, and ignorance can make a mockery of the ideal of discursive learning. These are the results of common problems that can often best be addressed through collective social action.

Adult educators are concerned with facilitating adult learning. When learning is being constrained and dependency in learning is being fostered by social institutions, practices, or systems, an adult educator becomes inextricably involved. In helping learners through the difficult process of transforming dysfunctional meaning structures, part of an educator's function is to help them come to realize that their problems are often shared and perpetuated by institutions which legitimate and propagate dependence-producing meaning perspectives. Learners will often want to take collective action to change them and need to learn how to do so.

6. *Educational Implications*

Adult educators in every institutional setting have a fundamental obligation to foster the closest approximation possible of the ideal conditions of discourse in creating learning opportunities and relationships. A cardinal function is to help learners move toward meaning perspectives which facilitate their participation in discourse. This involves transcending the obvious necessity of responding to a learner's initially expressed learning interests. The educator must understand that helping a learner move beyond expressed needs is essential. This is how educators can help adults become critically conscious of the reasons for their needs and help them understand how their reality has been shaped and influenced and its impact on their lives and on others. Learners need to know how larger cultural forces and early patterns of reaction to experience have had an impact upon them to shape their ways of understanding. Educators should be concerned with the whole learning process, including critical reflectivity. This commitment has broad implications for adult education—anticipated learning outcomes have no place in fostering critical reflectivity, nor have criteria-referenced systems of evaluation or other practices which falsely assume that all significant learning can be equated with measurable behavior change or with neat linear developmental progressions amenable to formula programming.

Bibliography

Aslanian C B, Brickell H M 1980 *Americans in Transition: Life Changes as Reasons for Adult Learning*. Education Testing Service, Princeton, New Jersey

Freire P 1970 *Pedagogy of the Oppressed*. Herder and Herder, New York

Goleman D 1985 Insights into self-deception. *New York Times Magazine* May 12, p. 42

Gould R L 1978 *Transformations: Growth and Change in Adult Life*. Simon and Schuster, New York

Habermas J 1984 *The Theory of Communicative Action*, Vol. 1: *Reason and the Rationalization of Society*. Beacon Press, Boston, Massachusetts

Mezirow J 1981 A critical theory of adult learning and education. *Adult Education* 32: 3–24

Mezirow J 1985 A critical theory of self-directed learning. In: Brookfield S (ed.) 1985 *Self-directed Learning: From Theory to Practice*, New Directions for Continuing Education, No. 25. Jossey-Bass, San Francisco, California

Nisbett R, Ross L 1980 *Human Inference: Strategies and Shortcomings of Social Judgment*. Prentice-Hall, Englewood Cliffs, New Jersey

Schon D A 1983 *The Reflective Practitioner: How Professionals Think in Action*. Basic Books, New York

Organizational Change and Adult Education

J. C. Votruba

In most countries, adult education may be carried out within governmental institutions but it is often located within a parent organization that does not view the education of adults as its primary purpose. Examples include universities, school systems, corporations, labor unions, libraries, churches, and hospitals. Adult educators working within such organizations are often in a marginal position, dependent upon decision makers who do not have much understanding of or commitment to adult education.

In order for adult education to flourish in such organizations, strategies are needed for strengthening understanding and support. This is a worldwide phenomenon that has not received much attention in adult education literature. Most of the research on this problem has been conducted in the United States and much of it concerns universities, but there are broad international implications, particularly for developing countries.

The process of strengthening organizational support for adult education involves changing the attitudes and behaviors of individuals, groups, or the organization itself. There are several conceptual approaches to planned organizational change and a number of important factors to consider when designing a change strategy (Tichy 1983).

1. Conceptual Approaches to Change

Probably the most comprehensive research and theory building on organizational innovation and change has been conducted at the University of Michigan by Ronald G. Havelock and his associates. Building on Havelock's work, Lindquist suggests that there are essentially four different conceptual approaches to planned organizational change (Lindquist 1978). Each approach emphasizes a different aspect of the basic communication act which involves creating, transmitting, and receiving a message.

The rational planning approach assumes that humans are essentially rational and that organizational change is based on reason and evidence. From this perspective, the best way to accomplish a change in organizations is to marshal as much evidence as possible on behalf of the change, to present it to decision makers, and to let the logic speak for itself. When universities create task forces and commissions to study and recommend ways to strengthen the institution's adult education mission, they are essentially employing the rational planning approach. The problem with this approach is that organizations, like the individuals and groups within them, do not function simply as rational systems. In large complex organizations, there is seldom universal agreement concerning organizational priorities and direction. Rationality is often based on perspective rather than on reason and evidence.

The social interaction approach assumes that humans are essentially social creatures and that *how* the change message is communicated is as important as the message itself. From this perspective, change is dependent upon the organization's opinion leaders and reference groups who can help influence adoption. For example, adult educators working in large ministries of education may try to gain increased support for their programs by identifying and involving persons and groups whom they know to be influential in the formal as well as the informal decision-making process.

The human problem-solving approach emphasizes that there are underlying psychological factors such as fears, habits, anxieties, and prejudices that will influence how the change message is received. For example, a major obstacle in recruiting new teachers of adults is often the teachers' fear that adults are difficult to teach and that the process can lead to embarrassment and rejection. The human problem-solving approach suggests that the task is to identify these often hidden feelings of resistance and incorporate them into the change strategy.

Finally, in the political approach to planned change, political advantage should be utilized to impose change. Because humans essentially seek to protect their vested interests, organizational change can best be accomplished through building coalitions of interests, influencing "gatekeepers" to get the change considered, and negotiating on a basis of compromise. While this approach is often attractive to adult educators, it can be risky. Because it relies on an adversary approach, it can often lead to alienation of the parent organization and a subsequent loss of support. Lindquist emphasizes that it is not enough to rely on only one conceptual approach when trying to change an organization. The most powerful planned change strategies combine the strengths of all four approaches.

2. Designing Change Strategies

There appears to be substantial agreement concerning those factors that most influence the success of planned change efforts. In one of the few attempts to relate planned change theory and research to the process of strengthening organizational support for adult education, Votruba summarizes these factors and recommends their consideration when designing change strategies (Votruba 1981).

Successful change strategies usually begin with a set of realistic, well-defined, and limited goals that describe precisely what is to be accomplished and the measure of accomplishment. To evaluate whether the goals are realistic, they should be assessed in terms of their compatability with the organization's values, traditions, and priorities. They should also be measured in terms of the human and financial resources needed to achieve them. Goals that lack compatibility or are not supported by sufficient resources may not be realistic.

Another useful approach to the assessment of realistic goals is to identify the number, variety, strength, and frequency of forces both internal and external to the organization that will enhance or inhibit the planned change effort. For adult educators who hope to strengthen support for education within their parent organization, these forces may take a variety of forms. For example, they may include influential individuals or groups, they may also include demographic, social, political, or economic trends. The early identification and assessment of sources of support and opposition will not only help in evaluating the likelihood of goal achievement but will also aid in designing an effective planned change strategy. Indeed, by creating an open atmosphere and soliciting the views of both supporters and opponents, adult educators will frequently discover that they need to adjust their initial goals or redefine their strategy for achieving them.

Another important factor in successful planned change is the concept of linkage (Havelock 1973, Havelock et al. 1971). Planned change usually starts with some sort of felt need on the part of a person, group, or organization. Something is wrong. The need is diagnosed, alternative solutions are identified, and a choice of action is made. This problem-solving process is aided when those engaged in the process are linked to helpful external resources. For adult educators, examples of such resources include: others who have dealt with the same problem in similar organizations; process consultants who can assist in strategy development; and sources of research and development that can aid in evaluating alternative solutions. Successful planned change efforts identify and build upon this external resource system. Adult educators may utilize professional associations like the International Council for Adult Education (ICAE) and the various national and regional adult education associations to build networks among people who are addressing similar problems so that they can learn from each other.

The support and involvement of influential people in the organization are important to successful planned change. Particularly when trying to initiate change from below, those who can influence the outcome need to be identified and involved at an early stage in the planned change process. These influential people will have a chance to develop a sense of ownership in the process and are then more likely to contribute their leadership and support. Influentials may come from either inside or outside the organization and may or may not be part of the organization's formal hierarchy. For example, a university continuing education agency that hopes to increase its university budget allocation may find valuable support among influential alumni, professional associations, community and civic groups, and public policy makers, as well as among faculty members and administrators who are opinion leaders on their own campus.

An important element in the development of support for planned change is the extent to which people understand the full range of benefits if the change is adopted. For example, a new university degree program for adults may involve creative new opportunities for faculty, greater productivity for colleges and departments, increased public support for the university, as well as expanded educational opportunity for adults. Chances of success are enhanced to the extent that the intended change is perceived to address the needs of those who may influence the outcome.

Finally, successful planned change strategies are characterized by persistence, patience, and good organization. Failure often occurs because the strategy has been designed or implemented too quickly or haphazardly. Consequently, problems are often ill-defined, alternative solutions are not thoroughly analyzed, available resources are not utilized, sources of organizational support and resistance are not clearly identified, or ideas are introduced at the wrong time.

The utilization of a team of individuals to help design and coordinate the entire change process offers the opportunity for a breadth of perspective and a division of labor that is not available to change agents working alone. Teams will vary in size but are usually no more than 10 people and often are much smaller. For example, a six-person team of faculty members and adult educators at the University of Illinois at Urbana-Champaign recently developed and successfully implemented criteria for evaluating the quality of faculty continuing education and public service activity for purposes of salary, promotion, and tenure consideration. Teams have also been successfully employed by regional adult educators in Arusha, Tanzania to help design and implement education projects for women in several rural villages. Havelock offers many useful suggestions for organizing and managing the team approach (Havelock et al. 1971, Havelock 1973).

3. Need for Further Study

The problem of strengthening organizational support for adult education is an international phenomenon that urgently needs more research and study. With the exception of Havelock and Huberman (1977) who utilized open systems theory to study the process of educational change in developing countries, very little work has been done outside of North America. Planned change theory needs to be tested cross-culturally, particularly in developing countries. International networks of scholars and practitioners interested in the process of adult education innovation and change should be established. National and international conferences are needed to exchange information and ideas. Publications need to be established to provide broad dissemination of planned change theory, research, and practice related to adult education. In summary, much more needs to be learned and shared concerning the process of adapting complex organizations to better meet the educational needs of adults.

Bibliography

Bennis W G, Benne K, Chin R, Cory K 1976 *The Planning of Change*, 3rd edn. Holt, Rinehart and Winston, New York

Havelock R 1973 *The Change Agent's Guide to Innovation in Education*. Educational Technology Publications, Englewood Cliffs, New Jersey

Havelock R G, Huberman A M 1977 *Solving Educational Problems: The Theory and Reality of Innovation in Developing Countries*. UNESCO, Paris

Havelock R G, Guskin A et al. 1971 *Planning for Innovation Through Dissemination and Utilization of Knowledge*. Institute for Social Research, Ann Arbor, Michigan

Katz D, Kahn R L 1978 *The Social Psychology of Organizations*, 2nd edn. Wiley, New York

Lindquist J 1978 *Strategies for Change*. Council for the Advancement of Small Colleges, Washington, DC

Tichy N 1983 *Managing Strategic Change*. John Wiley, New York

Votruba J 1981 *New Directions for Continuing Education: Strengthening Internal Support for Continuing Education*. Jossey-Bass, San Francisco, California

Teaching and Evaluation

Introduction

Just as the fundamental purpose of education is learning, so its central relationship is that between the teacher and the taught, which is intended to produce learning. Traditionally, in the transaction between the two, it has been the teacher who has played the dominant role. It is the teacher who has been the master: master of the body of knowledge and skills which he or she has imparted to the learner; and master of discipline, imposing sanctions upon the learner if it has been infringed. It has been the teacher who has decided the place, time and organization of the learning situation and prescribed the content and methods of the experience.

Both status and function have no doubt derived from the fact that education was traditionally a process in which teachers were adults and learners children, operating face to face. It is to be noted that the status of the teacher was earned through his or her mastery of knowledge and skills that it was valuable for the learner to acquire, rather than through his or her ability to transmit them. Systematic training of teachers in pedagogics only became widespread in the nineteenth century and is not universal for secondary teachers even today. There was a strong body of opinion which held that good teachers were born, not made, that teaching could not be taught and that, in so far as it could be learned, it was through practical experience, rather than study.

Although the circumstances of grown-up learners were different, the teacher–taught relationship in schools strongly affected adult education. Educators' ideas of their role were derived for the most part from their experience as teachers of children, or from their childhood experience as pupils. Adult learners' expectations too were founded on what they remembered of their initial education, if they had had any. Teachers of adults enjoyed respect too, because they were generally of higher social or professional standing than the people they taught. It is still the case that a large number, if not the majority, of teachers of adults have had no training in teaching.

In the field of childhood education, views of the teacher and the teacher's role have changed, although old attitudes and practices show a strong capacity for survival. Adult education has departed even further from tradition, although here too old ways cling on tenaciously. The authority of the teacher has been reduced. With adults the power to apply disciplinary sanctions has disappeared, except in the minority of situations in which it is bolstered by law or economic power. In these egalitarian days the deference shown by one human being to another has decreased at all levels, as parents and school teachers have discovered. That other prop of authority, the masters' command of their mystery, is no longer so impressive. The mastery has become provisional, dependent on constant updating to incorporate advances in knowledge. Furthermore, many adult students have their own mysteries, different from but equal in status to those of the teacher. As many people are aware, knowledge itself is to be seen as only provisional and no longer represents certainty.

The wide availability of print, audio, and video materials has made the face-to-face teacher less important as the repository from whom knowledge is to be acquired and increased the significance of his or her role as a facilitator of access to knowledge from other sources and as a trainer in learning skills.

The development of distinctive philosophies of adult education and of lifelong education have modified ideas of the teacher's function. Many adult educators now believe that ideally their goal should be to work themselves out of a job, by bringing adults to the point at which they take entire responsibility for their own learning and have no need for a teacher. At most, educators would produce materials which adults would be capable of using effectively for learning as, and how, they wished.

The understanding that grown-ups are not merely tall children and that adulthood is not a monolithic state, but may be divided into developmental periods, each with differences for the individual in terms of status, family, and social and economic needs and responsibility, has influenced our ideas of adult learning and consequently of how teachers of adults should operate. In particular teachers have had to come to terms with the freedom of adults, on the whole, to participate or not in intentional learning, of whatever kind it may be. This has affected not only methods, but the environment in which education is offered and the organization of the learning experience, most notably through distance learning and open learning.

Because the education of adults takes place in a varied market, having to respond to a clientele composed not only of very diverse learners, but of many sponsors, with divergent and sometimes conflicting requirements, it covers a vast range at widely different levels and in a multitude of circumstances. Educational practices mirror that diversity. In those contexts where educators exercise disciplinary authority, as they do in the armed forces, penal institutions or, to some degree, in education for employment, traditional instructional modes are still common. At the other extreme, in some of the most loosely structured contexts of outreach work, it is not only difficult to recognize adult educators as teachers in any conventional sense, but it is a title that many would renounce.

Whatever their title may be, teacher, trainer, instructor, or more neutral terms such as educator or educationist, and whatever the evidence of self-directed learning, there is an increasing need for people able and willing to help other adults to learn, either in a face-to-face relationship, as organizers of programmes, or as producers of learning materials. Rather later and to a lesser degree than in the school sector it is becoming recognized that educating adults requires skills and knowledge which can and should be learned. Although the majority of adult educators throughout the world still have no andragogic training, an increasing number have been undergoing education as educators (see *Training of Adult Educators*).

The article *Teaching Methods for Adults* lists the most popular methods of teaching to which adult educators are likely to be introduced, relates them to current theories of learning, and suggests some guidelines for good practice and needs for research. *Teacher Roles and Teaching Styles* adopts a different approach, concentrating on roles the teachers fulfil, as artist, as facilitator, as critical analyst, for example, and relates personal styles of teachers to the learning styles of adults (see *Learning Styles*).

The next two articles in this subsection concentrate mainly on situations in developing countries. The first, *Nonformal Education: Instruction*, considers divergent perceptions of instructional needs and a typology of educational approaches under four headings: the content-centred approach, the problem-focused approach, the conscientization approach, and the human development and creative planning approach. *Integrated Rural Development: Specialized Training Programs* highlights the importance of educational programmes in integrated rural development, their nature, function, and methods.

In the early days of adult education no effort was made to evaluate systematically the operation and outcomes of initiatives. If the educator and educated felt satisfied, that was sufficient. But as more public money has been spent, in large part on attaining objectives measurable in terms of behaviour; as also the options in methods and organization have grown more numerous and it has become important to acquire evidence of their comparative effectiveness; as people have tried to assign priorities to different contents and objectives, so the principle that no educational exercise is complete until it has been subjected to systematic evaluation has grown. As the article *Evaluation in Adult Education* indicates, this is still an underdeveloped field. The author reviews distinctive features of evaluation as applied to adult education, lists some of the most comprehensive studies undertaken, and the methods used, and points to recent trends in the field. *Adult Education Evaluation in Developing Countries* concentrates on studies of the work of major programmes sponsored by such institutions as UNESCO, the World Bank and agencies of advanced countries specializing in aid to developing countries.

Teaching Methods for Adults

M. D. Stephens

Millard (1981) has written, "At present, there exists a largely unbridged gap between the theory and research of adult learning and the actual teaching of mature students." This fact provides a backdrop for any description of teaching methods for adults. The major theories of adult learning discussed in this article in practice are often employed as arguments to justify existing teaching techniques. Scientific knowledge of humankind has not yet reached a degree of sophistication where a tutor's decision on which teaching method to use is determined more by information on adult learning than that tutor's rule-of-thumb experience. The following themes reflect that state of the art. Besides short descriptions of child and adult differences, learning theories, and various teaching methods, the article will touch on trends and issues in the field and areas of research.

1. *Teaching the Child and Teaching the Adult*

When approaching education, Knowles (1978) sees four major areas of difference between teaching adults and children. The first is in self-concept, with adults needing to be self-directing whilst children depend on others. Secondly, adults have much more experience of life and tend to define themselves by that experience rather than by external sources. Thirdly, there is the issue of readiness to learn. Knowles sees this in adults as a role or current projects "need" as compared to the child's "ought". Lastly, adults' learning tends to be problem or project centred and with immediate application whilst the child's is subject centred and of longer term relevance. Of course such tidy differentiation has all the problems of generalization within it. Are most children

Table 1
Teaching techniques and associated learning theories[a]

Method of instruction	Associated learning theorists	Type of theory
Exploratory learning emphasizing freedom and self-expression; evaluation retrospective and subjective		
Leaderless discussion groups	Rogers (1977)	Humanist
Cooperative projects	Maslow (1970)	
Free background reading		
Individual project work	Bruner	Cognitive
Tutor-led discussions	Perry	Developmental
Tutor-led seminars	Marton	
Learning cells	Ausubel	Cognitive
Lectures	Broadbent	
Hand-outs and guided reading	Lindsay and Norman	Information processing
Computer-managed learning	Pask	
Keller plan courses	Gagné (1975)	Task analysis
Programmed learning	Skinner (1953)	Behaviourist
Computer-assisted instruction		
Tight control of content and method; outcomes measured psychometrically and related to predetermined specific objectives		

a Source: Entwistle and Hounsell 1975

subject centred in their learning? When does adulthood begin? After some experience of life, say 25 years, or at the legal age of adulthood (18–21 years), or as some Piagetians suggest at 12–15 years? Despite such criticism, Knowles's four areas provide a useful set of assumptions against which one can look briefly at a number of learning theories at present found in the education of adults.

2. *Learning Theories*

Entwistle and Hounsell (1975) put together a table of instructional methods and learning theories which they thought could be associated with one another (see Table 1). This provides a useful summary of the variety of teaching techniques and some of the major writings in psychology that have appeared since the early 1940s.

The learning theories chosen range from Carl Rogers' (1977) person-centred focus to B. F. Skinner's work on operant conditioning (Skinner 1953). During the 1970s the writings of the humanistic psychologists, perhaps more than such behaviourists as R. M. Gagné (1965), have been gaining ground in the education of adults. Abraham Maslow's term "self-actualization" (the apex of his hierarchy of human needs theory) (Maslow 1970) caught the key flavour. The belief which dominates such writings is that self-awareness is a key factor in the student's learning.

Some of the emerging directions of learning theories in the 1980s can be seen in the work of the Nottingham Andragogy Group (1983) with its review of a number of assumptions (see Table 2).

The group see three categories of learning method:

(a) Expository methods—wherein a source, be it teacher, lecturer, writer, or film maker, organizes a body of content and presents the content to the learner.

(b) Direction methods—wherein leaders, be they discussion leaders, simulation managers, T-group facilitators, or programme instruction writers, organize and structure a process and the content so that those engaged in learning will arrive at some predetermined objective(s).

(c) Discovery methods—wherein learners engage in learning but the exact nature of what will be learned is not known at the outset because part of the process entails the posing of problems, questions, and/or issues. Content, information, and experience are then selected and organized by the learners in order to explore the problems, issues, and/or questions. New questions, problems, and issues arise as a result of this exploration. The primary objective behind this type of method is to engage in thinking. Though the reception of content or information is likely to occur, it will do so as a by-product of the thinking/problem exploration/discovery process.

All categories are acceptable, but the difference is in whether they are used pedagogically or andragogically.

Table 2
Pedagogy with adults versus andragogy: Some assumptions[a]

Concepts	A Continuum of pedagogy with adults		Andragogy
	Traditional	Progressive	
Adults	The adult's nature is determined by internal and/or external factors	Adults are the sole agents of their development—they are active/freely choosing agents	The adult is a social being whose nature results from his/her interactions of transactions with their social/historical context
Adult development	By the age of entry into adulthood, adults should have fully developed cognitive structures. Therefore. . . .		Adults have the potential to undergo further qualitative changes in their thinking throughout their entire lifespans. In so doing they move towards increasing control over their thinking
	Development has to do with further accumulations of knowledge or skills	Development has to do with self-fulfilment or personal growth	
Learning	Is about acquiring knowledge and skill	Is also about gaining further knowledge about self and others and is best facilitated by experiential methods	Is synonymous with thinking and at the level of the group or individual, involves the creation of knowledge, questions, ideas, and skill
Knowledge	Is something which can be acquired through learning and is transmitted from an authoritative source to a learner	Is something which can be discovered by learners	Is something which can be used or created
Teaching	Is the systematic organization of		Is a process which enables learners to be in control of their thinking. It involves learning and thinking with others who are learning and thinking
	Knowledge	or Procedures and processes	
	which cause learning to take place. It involves		
	Transmission	or Facilitation, direction, and leading, i.e., control	
Education	Is about transmitting knowledge and skills	Is about leading people to knowledge and skills	Is about critical thinking, questioning, problem posing, synthesis, and discovery in a cycle so that from each end emerges a new beginning

a Source: Nottingham Andragogy Group 1983

If the latter is the case, then the learning group, which includes the tutor, negotiates objectives, procedures, methods, and other matters relating to the learning experience. This is in contrast to the late Coolie Verner's statement, "Adult education is a relationship between an educational agent and a learner in which the agent selects, arranges, and continually directs a sequence of progressive tasks that provide systematic experiences to achieve learning" (Verner 1964).

J. R. Taylor makes the most important point when he writes, "No one theory is better than another; they simply are different perspectives of the same process. However, they provide an important matrix within which adult educators can practise their art" (Council of Europe 1983).

3. *Guidelines for Good and Bad Practice*

It is possible to put together from various learning theories a list of those things likely to inhibit the effective teaching of adults and guidelines for good practice.

Gibbs et al. (1982) have explored five common explanations for ineffectual learning in adults:

(a) students lack the necessary study skills;

(b) students are of different types, and some students have limited approaches to studying;

(c) students choose their approaches to studying and some students choose ineffective or inappropriate approaches;

(d) students develop in their sophistication as learners and some students are less developed than others;

(e) some aspects of course design constrain students in their learning.

From their research they make the point that people's behaviour is not determined so much by personality, but by the social situations they find themselves in, which suggests that the learning environment will tend to determine the learning style. If this is true, the above five explanations may well be largely teacher induced.

Mackie (1981) has summarized a number of writers in enumerating good practice from learning theory:

(a) The learner must be motivated to learn.

(b) The learning situation should take account of individual differences in learning capacities and learning style.

(c) New learning should take into account the learner's present knowledge and attitudes.

(d) What is to be learned should be reinforced.

(e) The learning situation should give opportunities for practice.

(f) The learner should be an active participant trying out new responses rather than just listening.

(g) The material to be learned should be divided into learnable units and given an appropriately paced sequence.

(h) Coaching or guidance should be given in the development of new responses.

(i) What is learned should be capable of being successfully generalized from the learning situation.

(j) The material to be learned should be presented in a way that will emphasize the characteristics to be learned and do so in a way which is as meaningful as possible to the learner.

Although adults will have much experience of learning, both formally at school and informally, many will feel hostility towards education because of fear of failure or defensiveness over assumed abilities. The choice of teaching method and the creation of a supportive learning group then becomes of great importance.

The range of experience in an adult group (e.g., how recent are their experiences of education?), and the variety of outlook has to be taken into account. Age may mean students with poorer sight or hearing have to be accommodated. They may be slower in speed activity. Adults often find self-pacing learning activities appealing. Allen Tough's research has taught much about self-directed learning (Tough1967, 1980).

The adult has a liking for the familiar so that where new learning is in conflict with established knowledge it may be rejected. The effective teacher will need, if possible, to link the new with the current values and skills.

All learning can be helped by positive reinforcement and careful feedback. Praise and knowledge of progress are important in sustaining interest and enthusiasm.

Practising new learning will help long-term memory retention and can be part of the "learner as an activist" approach. The latter permits the use of an adult's experience, satisfies the student's desire for self-direction, and helps to test the validity of that to which the adult has listened.

What are learnable units for one student may not be for another with different characteristics. The adult will need to understand the relevance of what is being taught and, with pacing, this suggests much greater student control over the individual learning than with children. However, the role of the teacher can be critical in saving time in difficult learning areas and in general encouragement. As a number of texts have stated,

> Most students will expect the teacher first and foremost to provide and interpret information relevant to their particular field of study. In this the teacher's role is that of encouraging the student to greater independence of thought and work, allied to higher standards of performance. The teacher must ensure that the student makes consistent progress in mastering the skill or subject under study. (Stephens and Roderick 1971)

4. Teaching Methods

A variety of teaching methods have already been alluded to. There is a huge literature on a number of individual techniques such as the lecture (Bligh 1972, Squires 1982). These texts are often more substantial than the tutor of adults seeks. A more general book is what most teachers favour, such as, to quote a text in French, Antoine Léon's succinct *Psychopédagogie des adultes* (Léon 1971).

The most favoured teaching techniques in the education of adults are dealt with in a number of books. One which was of great value in the 1960s had a seminal chapter on adult education by Edward Hutchinson (1965).

Hutchinson begins his description of teaching methods with lectures, opening with a quotation from the late J. R. Kidd's classic, "Despite the present popularity of the discussion group more use is still made of the talk, lecture, speech, address, and similar forms than of anything else. By similar forms we refer to the symposium, the forum, the panel, and, to some extent, the debate. We also would include most classes and most large meetings although both are mixed forms" (Kidd 1959). The lecture permits a speaker with special expertise to present it to an audience of small or vast numbers (for example, television will enable a lecturer to address millions). Unfortunately the stimulus to learning can be very limited, and particularly if members of the audience have no opportunity to question the speaker or enter into discussion. Hutchinson refers to some of the research done on the length of a student's attention span, and notably the pioneering work of J. M. Trenaman (1967). However, a talented lecturer can provide the initial stimulus to adult learning, sending away members of the audience determined to study further the subject of the lecture.

Hutchinson's second category was that of tutorial classes. Such groups have been small in membership, the fashion today is for a maximum of 15 students. The class is subject centred with varying degrees of student involvement in designing the syllabus, the style of tutoring, and such like. The most common form of teaching is the seminar with the tutor presenting a paper for discussion by the students. Outside of the class the members have directed reading and writing. A supply of books for the exclusive use of the students is a further tradition, with "works of original scholarship" stressed. Of the tutorial class Hutchinson states, "The organized and self-disciplined study group of interacting individuals guided by a tutor of special academic competence, as exemplified by the tutorial class, has probably been the most important British contribution to techniques of teaching in adult education."

Thirdly, Hutchinson deals with study circles and discussion groups. The study circle is particularly associated with Sweden. The group meets to study, with material provided by a member or some national organization. It is content and process oriented.

In Australia the difficulty of providing tutors for adult discussion groups in some localities has led to similar developments with universities and other institutions providing written guidance and materials.

The historic roots of such "tutorless" discussion groups are well-established, for example the various forms of early nineteenth-century American lyceums favoured the model. Variations under new names, in the ever fashion-conscious field of education, keep reappearing.

The use of "discussion" has been given high status in modern times. Hutchinson gives sensible guidelines to ensure discussion groups are educationally effective by

> defining the purposes of the groups; providing factual material or indicating accessible sources from which it can be obtained—books, pamphlets, study plans, recordings, etc; offering guidance on physical arrangements for seating, lighting, etc; advising leaders about their role—avoiding over-dominance, encouraging the less articulate, curbing loquacity, etc; acting as a centre for "feed-back" if group findings resulting from discussion are intended to result in action.

Since the 1950s much development has gone into exploring discussion as a way of releasing and understanding feelings (Cross 1980, Gagné 1975, Knox 1977).

In dealing with broadcasting, Hutchinson makes the important point that "it may be hazarded that optimistic assumptions about the possibilities of broadcast education are rooted in the traditional overemphasis on *teaching* as opposed to *learning*". The use of broadcasting seems most successful in adult education when it is part of a mix of techniques and materials (Hall 1981). The Open University in the United Kingdom, is a good example of this with its distance education base, "the method being correspondence courses supported by linked television and radio broadcasts and face-to-face tutorials at local centres" (Legge 1982).

Hutchinson suggests group projects as an alternative way of acquiring information and providing learning variety for students and tutors. Here the tutor is guide, but most of the work is done by the students, such as surveying an urban area to evaluate its community resources or studying through various forms of historical record the development of the students' neighbourhood.

Finally, Hutchinson has a category entitled educational visits, study tours, and so on. He writes "whether the occasion is a visit to a local art gallery or council meeting or an extended tour of another country, the tutor has to concern himself with its relevance to the course as a whole, with guidance in advance, conduct of the visit, and subsequent evaluation".

Although there are numerous variations on the teaching methods listed by Hutchinson (panels, brainstorming, gaming, forums, buzz groups, role play, diary) the basic techniques remain the same.

Perhaps the least practised part of teaching adults is the evaluation of the methods used. As in everything to do with teaching methods for adults, the tutor and students need to assess the needs of their unique educational situation before deciding how and what to evaluate. There are useful sources for guidance, but the key element, as in all human relationships, is sensitivity.

5. Some Research Needs

Whilst much progress in teaching methods has been made since it had been realized that adults are not merely tall children, the field is one in need of greater research input. To return to a theme mentioned earlier: whilst there is, as has been seen, much writing on learning theory, there is a need to explore how such research can be applied to more effective teaching. How can students' learning best be guided and what are the most appropriate teaching techniques?

More research is needed on the characteristics of adult students and whether these are the outcome of social or economic factors or cognitive and personality characteristics. There is a generalizing about adult students, whereas tools are required to enable a particular student to be assessed and helped.

Fast growing teaching methods like distance learning are underresearched. As Stephen Brookfield points out, "It is assumed that engaging in correspondence study will result in the learner acquiring the capacity to think critically, to set his own learning goals, to locate appropriate resources, and to assess progress. This assumption remains, for the most part, untested by empirical investigation" (Brookfield 1982).

Many, if not most tutors of adults, will now receive some training in teaching methods, but there is no precise evidence of the benefits accruing to the student from such teacher training.

Of course, in the last analysis there will always be some tutors of genius facing adult students with highly developed learning skills and unparalleled motivation.

The numbers in these categories do not, however, appear to increase as a percentage of the population, so the pressing priority is to train all tutors to be effective in their choice and use of teaching methods and to back up their work with more information resulting from greater research activity.

See also: Andragogy; Training of Adult Educators

Bibliography

Bligh D A 1972 *What's the Use of Lectures?*, 3rd edn. Penguin, Harmondsworth

Brookfield S 1982 *Independent Adult Learning*. Adults: Psychological and Educational Perspectives Series, No. 7. University of Nottingham Department of Adult Education, Nottingham, p. 31

Council of Europe 1983 European materials for the training of adult educators. Reader. *Learning About the Learners*. Open University Press, Milton Keynes, p. 52

Cross P K 1980 *Adults as Learners: Increasing Participation and Facilitating Learning*. Jossey-Bass, San Francisco, California

Entwistle N, Hounsell D (eds.) 1975 *How Students Learn: Implications for Teaching in Higher Education*. University of Lancaster, Lancaster, p. 177

Gagné R M 1965 *The Conditions of Learning*. Holt, Rinehart and Winston, New York

Gagné R M 1975 *Essentials of Learning for Instruction*. Dryden Press, Hinsdale, Illinois

Gibbs G, Morgan A, Taylor E 1982 Why students don't learn. *Institutional Res. Rev.* 1: 10

Hall B L 1981 Mass communication and adult education. In: Bown L, Okedara J T (eds.) 1981 *An Introduction to the Study of Adult Education*. University Press, Ibadan, pp. 215–31

Hutchinson E M 1965 Adult education. In: Peterson A D C (ed.) 1965 *Techniques of Teaching*, Vol. 3: *Tertiary Education*. Pergamon, Oxford, pp. 112–34

Kidd J R 1959 *How Adults Learn*. Association Press, New York, p. 243

Knowles M S 1978 *The Adult Learner: A Neglected Species*, 2nd edn. Gulf, Houston, Texas

Knox A B 1977 *Adult Development and Learning*. Jossey-Bass, San Francisco, California

Legge D 1982 *The Education of Adults in Britain*. Open University Press, Milton Keynes, p. 32

Léon A 1971 *Psychopédagogie des adultes*. Presses Universitaires de France, Paris

Mackie K 1981 *The Application of Learning Theory to Adult Teaching*. Adults: Psychological and Educational Perspectives Series, No. 2. University of Nottingham, Department of Adult Education, Nottingham, pp. 2–3

Maslow A H 1970 *Motivation and Personality*. Harper and Row, New York

Millard L 1981 *Adult Learners: Study Skills and Teaching Methods*. Adults: Psychological and Educational Perspectives Series, No. 4. University of Nottingham, Department of Adult Education, Nottingham, p. 8

Nottingham Andragogy Group 1983 *Towards a Development Theory of Andragogy*. Adults: Psychological and Educational Perspectives Series, No. 9. University of Nottingham, Department of Adult Education, Nottingham, p. 1

Rogers C R 1969 *Freedom to Learn: A View of What Education Might Become*. Merrill, Columbus, Ohio

Rogers C R 1977 *Carl Rogers on Personal Power*. Constable, London

Rogers J (ed.) 1985 *Adults in Education*. BBC, London

Skinner B F 1953 *Science and Human Behavior*. Macmillan, New York

Squires G T C 1982 *The Analysis of Teaching*. University of Hull Department of Adult Education, Hull (Newland Paper No. 8)

Stephens M D, Roderick G W 1971 The teaching of adults. In: Stephens M D, Roderick G W (eds.) 1971 *Teaching Techniques in Adult Education*. David and Charles, Newton Abbot, p. 13

Tough A M 1967 *Learning Without a Teacher: A Study of Tasks and Assistance during Adult Self-teaching Projects*. Ontario Institute for Studies in Education, Toronto, Ontario

Tough A M 1980 *Expand Your Life: A Pocketbook for Personal Change: Future Directions for a Learning Society*. College Entrance Examination Board, New York

Trenaman J M 1967 *Communication and Comprehension: The*

Report of an Investigation, by Statistical Methods, of the Effective Communication of Educative Material and an Assessment of the Factors Making for such Communication. Longman, London

Verner C 1964 Definition of terms. In: Jensen G, Liveright A A, Hallenbeck W C (eds.) 1964 *Adult Education: Outlines of an Emerging Field of University Study*. Adult Education Association of America, Washington, DC

Teacher Roles and Teaching Styles

S. Brookfield

It is often useful to view adult education as a transactional encounter in which learners and educators are engaged in a continual process of negotiating curricular priorities, appropriate methods, and evaluative criteria. If the transactions between teacher and learners exhibit this truly interactive dimension they avoid the danger of allowing the sole responsibility for determining curricula, methods, or evaluative criteria to rest with the teacher or with some factional group of especially articulate learners.

1. Teacher–Learner Transaction

Where such responsibilities do lie solely with the teacher, there may be an authoritarian, one-way transmission of skills and knowledge, exemplifying all the worst aspects of the "banking" system of education in which knowledge is deposited into the empty vaults of learners' minds. On the other hand, if curricula, methods, and evaluation are determined solely by what learners say they want, there is the risk of adult education being governed solely by a service rationale whereby market-economy forces impel the educator to sponsor only programmes which attract large numbers of participants. Acceptance of this "felt-needs" rationale, in which the educator simply meets those "needs" most frequently articulated by groups well-skilled in making themselves heard, can mean that the educator functions as little more than an administrator, publicist, and budget specialist. It can also mean that educators abdicate any responsibility to contribute to the debate about the appropriate purposes or methods in adult education. To say one is meeting the "felt needs" of learners sounds humanistic, learner centred, and admirably democratic; yet to do this and to refuse to allow one's ideas, experience, insights, and knowledge as a teacher to contribute to the educational process makes the educator a service manager, not a full participant in learning. This makes it easier for learners to remain within their own comfortable paradigms of thinking, feeling, and behaving. Since it is difficult without guidance to generate alternative ways of thinking about, and behaving in, the world an important task of the educator is to present learners with a range of alternative interpretations as to how they might think, feel, and act.

One of the greatest myths which has sprung from a denial of the transactional nature of adult education, and from an uncritical acceptance of the "felt-needs" rationale, is the belief that learning is always joyful, a bountiful release of latent potential in which learners are stimulated, exhilarated and fulfilled. This can often happen. But it is also often the case that the most significant learning results from some external event or stimulus which prompts an anxious and uncomfortable reassessment of aspects of the learner's personal, professional, and recreational life. Examples of these events might be the death of a parent, promotion into an unfamiliar occupational position, being fired, being conscripted into war, or coping with divorce.

The learning from such circumstantial events may be unsought and may have many painful aspects. What is significant is that it may cause one to question aspects of ways of thinking and behaving in personal relationships, professional activities, or recreational pursuits. Such questioning is uncomfortable and may be initially resisted, but often leads to a decision to change some aspect(s) of the subject's life. As those who have renegotiated intimate relationships, confronted parents, or attempted to change the patterns of activities and relationships in the workplace know, a critical examination of the validity of the assumptions under which they and others have been living, alterations in one's behaviour or attempts to change the habitual activities and responses of others are not always joyous, releasing, and exhilarating activities. The conclusion may be reached that the anxiety was worthwhile, when it results in a richer, more fulfilling life. Nevertheless this re-examination of values, beliefs, behaviours, and assumptions can be an unsettling process, in which glimpses of insight alternate with confusion, uncertainty, and ambiguity.

The contribution of the educator to the adult education transaction is somewhat analogous to the calamitous events mentioned earlier. It is not enough for teachers of adults to say to learners "do what you want, learn what you want, in whatever manner you wish, because you are the sole determiners of your educational destinies." This resembles a conversation where one partner agrees with whatever the other says. Such conversations may seem initially very agreeable, but eventually one begins to suspect that the listener who reacts to one's every comment and suggestion with enthusiastic agreement is not really listening at all. A conversation, after all, is a transactional dialogue, where the comments and contributions of the participants build organically on each other's views, and where alternative viewpoints, differing interpretations, and criticisms are elements essential to the encounter. Adult education may likewise be thought of as a transactional dialogue between teachers and learners who bring to the encounter experiences, attitudes, alternative ways of viewing their personal, professional, and political worlds, and a multitude of differing purposes, orientations, and expectations. Within this transactional context the particular function of the teacher, where this is not already being performed by other members of the learning group, is to challenge learners with alternative ways of interpreting their experiences and to present them with ideas and behaviours which cause them critically to examine their values, their ways of acting, and the assumptions by which they live. In this way the teacher of adults fulfils the same function as those calamities identified earlier in offering stimuli which cause people to re-examine the ways in which they think and behave.

2. Teacher Roles

Teachers new to adult education will find no shortage of practical handbooks designed to introduce the reader to collections of helpful hints for working with adults. As the article on teaching methods for adults makes clear, there is a body of literature relating to effective techniques for use in different settings and with different groups. Underlying this literature are three broad, and frequently contrasting, conceptions of the appropriate roles for teachers as educators of adults—the teacher as artist, as facilitator, and as critical analyst. Apps (1979) has distinguished six possible teacher roles for individual, group, or community settings—trainer, conditioner, counsellor, model, resource, and guide. Ruddock (1980) recognizes eight major roles for adult educators—resource, expositor, demonstrator, promulgator of values, taskmaster, assessor, helper and group manager. The roles of helper and group manager are in turn divided into several subcategories.

(a) *The teacher as artist*. This is a common metaphor used to refer to a conception of the teaching role in which qualities of creativity, innovation, improvisation, and sensitivity are paramount. For Hostler (1982) teaching can never be reduced to a set of rules routinely applied in a number of situations. The complexity of classroom interactions and the unconscious collusion which may take place between teacher and taught mean that teachers need to be "acutely observant, wisely sympathetic, and constantly attentive" (Hostler 1982 p. 48). Both Hostler (1982) and Lenz (1982) warn that textbook models of exemplary practices are of limited value, since teachers as artists need to improvise in response to the demands of clients and the immediate situation. In this sense the role of the teacher as artist is strikingly similar to the concept of the reflective practitioner developed by Schön (1983). Reflective practitioners engage in an essentially artistic process of reflection-in-action in which they make daily judgements concerning improvizations of technique, and adaptations of accepted patterns of practice, and manifest a readiness to disregard standardized models of exemplary behaviours in favour of "theories-in-use" (Argyris and Schön 1974). Such theories-in-use are context-specific ideas concerning behaviours, techniques and practices which are effective with certain groups in specific situations, but which are inappropriate as an idealized model of good practice.

(b) *The teacher as facilitator*. This is a role conception which has gained considerable academic credibility in recent years, particularly as the concepts of self-directed learning and "andragogy" have become accepted by adult educators. Facilitators of learning see themselves as enablers of, and resources for, learning, rather than as didactic directors. They stress that they are engaged in a democratic, learner-centred enhancement of individual learning, and that control for setting the direction and methods of learning rests as much with the learner as with the educator. Facilitators describe themselves as being in a helping relationship with learners. Such relationships are oriented towards the nurturing of self-directedness in learners, and should be characterized by trust, unconditional acceptance, and mutual exchange between facilitator and learner. The humanistic and democratic associations called to mind by the concept of facilitation has meant that teachers of adults now frequently reject the description "teacher", preferring instead to call themselves facilitators.

A number of writers have specified the characteristics they consider essential in effective facilitators. Tough (1979) described ideal helpers as being (a) warm, loving, caring and accepting towards learners, (b) having a high regard for learners' self-planning abilities, (c) viewing themselves as engaged in a dialogue of equals with their learners, and (d) open to change and new experiences so that their helping activities become learning experiences. In an extensive summary of adult learning principles undertaken by Brundage and MacKeracher (1980), a number of "facilitating" implications derived from these principles are offered. Chief among these are that facilitators should be sensitive to learners' self-concepts, that learners' past experiences should be recognized as providing fruitful curricular material, that facilitators should be willing to share their experiences with learners, and that facilitators should be open to learners' suggestions. Brundage and MacKeracher urge that a balance be struck between encouraging learners' self-directedness and participation in group interaction, and they stress the importance of flexibility on the part of facilitators, responsiveness to learners' needs, readiness to use learners' experiences, and respect for and valuing of learners' dignity. These conclusions concerning exemplary facilitator roles are similar to those of Brockett (1983) who acknowledges explicitly the connection between the concept of educational facilitation and the literature on helping behaviour in the field of counselling. Brockett identifies three broad skill domains—attending, responding and understanding—all of which are important to educators wishing to develop collaborative, interactive patterns of teaching and learning. The exercise of such skills is felt to be especially important to the facilitator's fostering of self-directedness among adult learners.

(c) *The teacher as critical analyst*. This is a conception which is sceptical of the notion of nondirective facilitators who assist learners to achieve self-actualization. Proponents of the critical analysis school consider it the teacher's task to suggest alternatives to current ways of thinking, perceiving, and behaving, to point up contradictions, to draw attention to relationships of dependence, and to prompt a critical scrutiny of values and uncritically assimilated assumptions. Bryson (1936), a supporter of this school of thought, urged teachers of adults to nurture a "rational scepticism" in learners towards their already accepted and verbalised beliefs and "to stand firm against the winds of doctrine" (p. 64). He warned, however, that teachers must expect public criticism, dislike and ridicule from political and opinion leaders because such "rational criticism" would serve as a corrective against adults falling prey to the simplistic solutions and propaganda such leaders may offer. Paulo Freire also rejected the concept of facilitator, stating at a recent conference on "educating the educator" in New York, that he felt the term was "created not to unveil but to obscure". To Freire, using the term facilitator was "as if I were ashamed to be an educator, pretending not to be what I am" (Noble 1983 p. 4).

For critical teachers, the problem with concentrating one's efforts solely on assisting adults to pursue learning projects which they have themselves defined, is that it assumes too great a degree of self-knowledge and awareness on the part of the adult. To act as a facilitator and resource person to adults who are unaware of belief systems, bodies of knowledge, or behavioural possibilities other than those which they have uncritically assimilated since childhood, is to condemn such adults to remaining within existing paradigms of thought and action. Such learners can indeed express felt needs to educators, but these needs will be perceived and articulated from a narrow viewpoint. Adults caught within constrained relationships, unsatisfactory jobs, and closed political systems may feel a sense of alienation and unease, but they often cannot imagine other ways of conducting relationships, earning a living, or taking political action. The critical analyst, therefore, feels impelled to prompt adults to consider alternatives to their present ways of thinking and living. Teachers subscribing to this conception of their role will encourage adults to realize that bodies of knowledge, accepted truths, commonly held values and customary forms of behaviour which comprise their worlds are culturally constructed. In coming to realize that the world is not made up of unalterable propositions, unchallengeable beliefs, and fixed forms of behaviour, and by being prompted to consider alternatives to their fixed ideas, values, and behaviour, adults can develop an awareness of the essential contingencies in the world. Such an awareness is the necessary prelude to their taking action to alter their personal and collective circumstances.

3. Teaching Behaviour and Adult Learning Styles

In any one classroom, the three role conceptions discussed above will at different times probably be apparent in a teacher's behaviour. Additionally, teachers will frequently be called upon to act as counsellors to learners, in terms of assisting adults to recognize and resolve particular learning difficulties, in helping them adjust to the emotional trauma of reassuming the role of learner, or in exploring the range of opportunities for further study open to them.

Discussions of the chief findings of adult learning theorists regarding learning styles and the implications of these for teachers' behaviour have been undertaken by Dubin and Okun (1973), Mackie (1981), and Even (1982). Dubin and Okun offer no definitive conclusions as to the appropriate teacher roles and behaviours to be adopted with adults, since they can find no single theory of learning which can sufficiently explain adults' learning styles. Mackie (1981) is more optimistic about a possible synthesis of research and he outlines 10 pedagogic principles derived from a review of behaviourist, cognitive, and personality theorists' writings. These principles are used by Williams (1980) in training adult educators for the variety of teaching roles they are required to play. The principles are that:

(a) learners must be motivated to learn;

(b) learning formats should allow for individual differences in ability and style;

(c) new learning should build upon existing knowledge and attitudes;

(d) learning should be reinforced;

(e) opportunities for practice should be available;

(f) learners should be active participants;

(g) material to be learned should be organized into manageable units;

(h) guidance should be given in developing new responses;

(i) new skills and knowledge should be generalizable; and

(j) material to be learned should be meaningful to the learner (Mackie 1981 pp. 2–3).

The implications of the "field-independent" and "field-dependent" construct of learning styles for teacher roles and behaviours have been discussed by Even (1982). Field-independent learners (those who are prone to set their own objectives and devise strategies for attaining these independently) do not require a well-organized classroom procedure, structured exercises, or a friendly caring attitude on the part of teachers. If the teacher exhibits a field-independent style, the lack of group process in the class or the lack of clear, externally imposed structure will not concern these learners. However, for those learners who are field-dependent, who value the social setting for learning, take cues from their peers, and prefer to be involved in collaborative learning activities, being under the direction of a field-independent teacher will be a disturbing experience since this teacher will most likely emphasize independent study activities as against participatory exercises. If the validity of the field-independent/dependent construct is accepted, there is good reason to consider matching learners and teachers with similar styles, or at least conducting prior independence/dependence assessment of all participants in a class, so that teachers and learners can adjust to differing styles whenever possible.

Another important construct to consider in any analysis of the disjunctions or congruences which are likely to affect the interactions within a learning group is the learning style inventory of Kolb (1976). In a review of its relevance to the roles and behaviour of adult teachers, Moore (1982) matched the inventory with Brostrom's Training Style Inventory (Brostrom 1979) and concluded that certain learning styles as identified by Kolb were best matched with certain teaching styles as outlined by Brostrom. Hence, "diverger" learners were suited to humanistic teaching styles, "accommodators" were best served by functionalist teachers, "converger" learners responded to a structuralist teaching style, and "assimilators" benefited most from a behaviourist teacher.

It is clear that a great deal more thought needs to be devoted to the question of appropriate teaching behaviours which occur within groups containing adults with widely varying styles of learning. The literature does contain analyses of learning styles of adult students, but the learning styles of teachers, and the significant effect these have on teaching behaviour and on subsequent learner responses, remains under-researched. As the studies above indicate, however, such research is essential if we are to begin to understand some of the highly complex interactions observed within learning groups.

Universal prescriptions concerning a simple method of instruction, concept of the teaching role, or the appropriately "adult" teaching style to be applied in all or most adult education settings are neither empirically based nor practically helpful. Such prescriptions contradict the reality of multi-ability, multi-ethnic groups of adults exhibiting a broad diversity of learning styles which is faced daily by teachers of adults. It is important to acknowledge that teachers of adults are also themselves adult learners. Hence, the learning styles which teachers have used and continue to use in their own learning activities, are likely to be the ones which they assume participants in their classes will also exhibit. Left unchecked, such an assumption can result in sufficiently serious discrepancies between the learners' expectations and the teachers' beliefs concerning appropriate teaching behaviour, such that the continued existence of the learning group is threatened.

It is also clearly desirable that teachers recognize in themselves, and make explicit to learners, their own conception of their role as teachers. Adults who anticipate that adult education classes will resemble the classrooms of their schooldays, and who are then confronted with teachers who see the teacher as facilitator, for example, are likely to be unnerved by the discrepancy between their expectations of authoritative instructors and the nondirective reality they encounter. The belief of these learners that facilitators are not "real" teachers because they do not exhibit direction and authority, may be in total contradiction to the teachers' belief that adult learners both desire, and are best suited to, the facilitator style. The result of such unarticulated assumptions concerning these conceptions of appropriate teacher roles and teaching styles is likely to be a period of confusion, ambiguity, frustration, and possibly withdrawal by learners from the learning group.

The teacher as critical analyst is another role liable to cause anxiety and resentment in learners unless it is performed with great sensitivity. Adults, particularly those who have paid a class fee and see themselves, therefore, as participating in an exchange of services (appropriate instruction) for money, are likely to resist a teacher who suggests that their time is spent most profitably in critically examining their dearly held values, behaviour, and belief systems. Additionally, as Aslanian and Brickell's (1980) study of the motivations of adult learners indicates, such individuals frequently join classes because they feel themselves to be in some kind of transition in their personal or professional lives. To some, the opportunity to examine critically their previously unscrutinized assumptions may be a welcome cathartic or revelatory experience. To others, such an anxiety-provoking activity in the midst of an already traumatic change in, or reassessment of, their personal lives is liable to be too threatening.

It may be more useful, therefore, to regard learning groups not only as transactional encounters, but also as psychosocial dramas in which learners and teachers act out their interpretations of the appropriate student and pedagogic roles. Given the complexity of learning styles and teacher roles already discussed, it is evident that adult teachers should be wary of accepting uncritically a construct such as Malcolm Knowles' theory of "andragogy", in which four prescriptive propositions concerning teaching styles deemed appropriate to adults are accepted as being empirically based (Knowles 1980). Such reductionist conceptions of the teaching role neglect the complexities of actual learning groups. In the search for professional self-esteem and identity, adult educators may embrace such concepts as helping to present to the rest of the educational world an appearance of the uniqueness of the methods of adult education. This may reinforce the sense of professional identity and esteem of adult educators, but it will also mean that the intricate complexity of learning and teaching styles within any learning group is ignored.

See also: Andragogy; Training of Adult Educators

Bibliography

Apps J W 1979 *Problems in Continuing Education*. McGraw-Hill, New York

Argyris C, Schön D A 1974 *Theory in Practice: Increasing Professional Effectiveness*. Jossey-Bass, San Francisco, California

Aslanian C B, Brickell H M 1980 *Americans in Transition*. College Entrance Examination Board, New York

Brockett R 1983 Facilitator roles and skills. *Lifelong Learning* 6(5): 7–9

Brostrom R 1979 Training style inventory. In: *The 1979 Annual Handbook for Group Facilitators*. University Associates, La Jolla, California

Brundage D H, MacKeracher D 1980 *Adult Learning Principles and their Application to Program Planning*. Ontario Ministry of Education, Toronto, Ontario

Bryson L 1936 *Adult Education*. American Book Company, New York

Dubin S S, Okun M 1973 Implications of learning theories for adult instruction. *Adult Educ. (USA)* 24(1): 3–19

Even M J 1982 Adapting cognitive style theory in practice. *Lifelong Learning* 5(5): 14–16

Hostler J 1982 The art of teaching adults. *Studies in Adult Education* 14: 42–49

Knowles M S 1980 *The Modern Practice of Adult Education: From Pedagogy to Andragogy*, 2nd edn. Follett, Chicago, Illinois

Kolb D A 1976 *Learning Style Inventory Technical Manual*. McBer, Boston, Massachusetts

Lenz E 1982 *The Art of Teaching Adults*. Holt, Rinehart and Winston, New York

Mackie K 1981 The Application of Learning Theory to Adult Teaching, *Adults: Psychological and Educational Perspectives series*, Monograph No. 2. University of Nottingham, Nottingham

Moore A B 1982 Learning and teaching styles of adult education teachers. In: *Proc. Adult Education Research Conf.*, Vol. 23. University of Nebraska–Lincoln, Lincoln, Nebraska

Noble P 1983 *Formation of Freirian Facilitators*. Latino Institute, Chicago, Illinois

Ruddock R 1980 Tension and consciousness: An existential approach. In: *Perspectives on Adult Education*, Manchester Monographs 2nd edn. University of Manchester, Manchester

Schön D A 1983 *The Reflective Practitioner*. Basic Books, New York

Tough A M 1979 *The Adult's Learning Projects*, 2nd edn. Ontario Institute for Studies in Education (OISE), Toronto, Ontario

Williams G L 1980 Adults learning about adult learning. *Adult Educ. (UK)* 52(6): 386–91

Nonformal Education: Instruction

L. Srinivasan

Nonformal education as a new and evolving field is not confined to any one single instructional design; rather it uses a wide range of styles, content, and media, and is continuously open to innovation.

The reasons for this flexibility and diversity are many: in order to be relevant to the felt needs of learners themselves and to national priorities as well, the content of the curriculum may often need to be as variable as life itself. Content can significantly influence the choice of instructional style. Similarly, teaching modes have to adapt to the setting in which learning takes place and to the distance separating teachers and learners: the techniques used in small study circles where direct interpersonal communication is possible may have little applicability in distance teaching which uses radio broadcasts, for instance.

Major differences in instructional strategy and techniques arise, however, from differences in diagnosis of the learners' problems and of the growth needs to be addressed. These conceptual differences are clearly linked to a number of philosophical and pedagogical influences, both from the East and the West.

1. Divergent Perceptions of Instructional Needs

Current influences on nonformal education methodology often seem diametrically opposed. Some programs, strongly influenced by humanistic psychologists such as Abraham Maslow and Carl Rogers, emphasize inner growth and learner self-direction as central aims of instruction. Others lean more towards B. F. Skinner's behaviorist theory, using programmed instruction, external rewards and controls, and environmental conditioning as a means to behavior modification.

Similarly the curricula of some programs, influenced by revolutionary social reformers such as Ivan Illich, Paulo Freire, and Saul Alinsky, may place a high value on critical reflection and power confrontation. Others, such as the "Khit-pen" program of Thailand and Sri Lanka's Sarvodaya Movement, though equally concerned with social justice, may take a different route in the search for solutions, guided by principles of harmony derived from Eastern philosophies.

To add to the complexity of the field, several other influences from contemporary applied psychology and the business world are also evident in current nonformal education practice. These include studies of achievement motivation and entrepreneurial behavior, lateral thinking, brainstorming, the use of analogy in creative problem solving, and a variety of other innovations in human relations training, managerial development group dynamics, simulation, and psychodrama.

There is moreover an increasing trend to incorporate local traditional forms of communication into instructional design, including puppetry, folk theatre, parables, proverbs, songs, fairs, and games. The manner in which these are used varies, however, with each program's concept of the roles of teachers and learners in the learning transaction.

A common aim of most innovations in nonformal education is to involve learners more actively in the design and development of the learning program. This is a reaction against traditional didactic teaching styles where decisions regarding content, method, sequence and setting, were the prerogative of the teacher, often resulting in programs of low relevance to learners.

However, not all programs apply the principle of nondirectiveness to the same degree or in the same way. By clustering different nonformal education initiatives according to their basic aims and emphasis, they can be located along a continuum ranging from a directive subject-centered approach at one end, to a nondirective learner-centered approach at the other. Four such different learning designs are described, although in actual practice their distinctions tend to blur through cross-fertilization among programs.

2. Typology of Nonformal Education Approaches

2.1 Content-centered Approach

This approach is commonly used by programs in which a specific body of knowledge, identified by specialists, is to be transferred to learners to facilitate adoption of new practices. Family planning, nutrition, and agriculture programs are typical examples.

Specialists define the basic knowledge, attitudes, and skills required by learners in order to become adopters. These constitute the minimum competency level to be achieved. A baseline survey of the learners' prior knowledge, attitudes, and practices (KAP), helps to define the gap or discrepancy to be overcome between actual and desired competency levels, that is, the KAP-gap.

A curriculum aimed at closing the KAP-gap is then prepared. To help learners assimilate concepts more easily, content is broken down into small units or "messages" to be transmitted to the learners through various means, such as lectures, discussion, personal counseling (e.g. on child spacing), demonstrations (e.g. of improved diets or new agricultural practices), and persuasion tools such as flip charts, posters, comic books, didactic dramatizations (live or on cassette), and documentary films.

Techniques of a more participatory type are sometimes used to reinforce learning. Mothers attending a nutrition class may, for example, join a cooking demonstration, or community members may learn how to build a compost pit or install an improved water system by actually building them. However, the accepted way of doing things has usually been predetermined by outside specialists, and success tends to be measured in terms of learners' abilities to comply with instructions or to recall messages.

This competency-based approach takes on a totally different connotation when decisions regarding content, sequence, and method are made by the learners themselves, rather than by curriculum specialists. The teacher acts as a technical resource and enables the learning group itself to assess its level of competency, identify KAP-gaps, select content, plan the sequence of activities, and accept responsibility for directing their own learning. Thus by a simple shift of decision-making responsiblity from the teacher to the learners, the competency-based curriculum can be changed to an essentially learner-directed one.

2.2 Problem-focused Approach

This approach combines two aims: to help learners develop generalizable skills in the scientific method of problem solving and to generate information useful for the solution of everyday problems. One example of this approach is the "Khit-pen" program of the Ministry of Education in Thailand. "Khit-pen"—literally "to think analytically"—is based on the Buddhist principle of choosing the "right path" or solution after identifying the root causes of suffering.

Since practice in problem solving needs to relate to the learners' reality, the curriculum is planned as a sequence of small units each focused on a real and immediate problem faced by adult learners, and as determined by field surveys. Visual materials are used to help learners recognize the problem as relevant to their lives, but also allow scope for interpretation of causes and analysis of solutions.

The development of problem-solving skills may be treated as a purely cognitive, rational process. However, some programs (e.g. in Turkey and Bangladesh) have found that affective constraints including cultural and personal biases, taboos, and customs, also have to be considered. For this purpose, open-ended problem drama and other projective techniques are found useful.

2.3 The Conscientization Approach

It is only in recent years that nonformal education, particularly in Latin America, has taken on the issue of power imbalance and the exploitation of the poor by vested interests. Paulo Freire brought the term *conscientizacao* or conscientization into popular usage connoting the process by which the poor can become aware of their own humanity and their innate power to reshape an oppressive society. Freire sees the authoritarian teacher as part of an unjust system which diminishes the learners and perpetuates their subservient role as objects (passive recipients) instead of subjects (active agents) of the educational process.

Conscientization methods and materials are accordingly planned and sequenced in ways that promote critical analysis of reality, egalitarian dialogue between teachers and learners, mutual humanization, and praxis, that is, reflection followed by action and further reflection. Materials used to stimulate this dialogue contain visual representations of generative themes drawn from the learners' own perceptions of their reality. Associated with these themes, meaning-loaded words drawn from the learners' everyday vocabulary are used in the discussion and in literacy instruction.

2.4 *Human Development and Creative Planning Approach*

The main thrust in this approach is not the mastery of specific content per se, or the acquisition of generalizable problem-solving skills, or insights into power imbalance, although all of these may enter into the process at their appropriate time. Rather, the focus is on developing the learners' creative and planning capacities so as to enable them to function more dynamically and effectively as decision makers, planners, and change agents. This approach emphasizes the deliberate nurturing of creativity in order to encourage openness to innovation, improve the quality of people's interventions in development, and release new energies through a heightened perception of self. Information gathering, critical analysis, and the use of practical planning techniques are then used by local groups to translate their ideas into action.

Materials such as "flexiflans," "unserialized posters," and simulation games are used in promoting learner participation and self-direction. Initially known as the self-actualizing method and more recently as SARAR, this approach is being utilized at the project level in several countries particularly the Philippines, Kenya, Mexico, Haiti, and Guatemala.

Seen from the point of view of the learner, these various approaches to instruction in nonformal education would seem to be complementary, each responding to a particular developmental need. Their effectiveness depends of course on good training of staff and on meticulous monitoring and evaluation. These preparatory and evaluative activities are gaining more attention as nonformal education develops.

See also: Economics of Nonformal Education; Formal and Nonformal Education: Future Strategies; Nonformal Education

Bibliography

Clark N M, Gakuru O, Acierto P 1979 *Evaluation of Tototo-Kilemba Midpoint*. World Education, New York

Coombs P H (ed.) 1980 *Meeting the Basic Needs of the Rural Poor: The Integrated Community-based Approach*. Pergamon, New York

Crone C D, Srinivasan L 1975 *A Report on the First Two Stages of Phase I of the Women's Project*. World Education, New York

Freire P 1978 *Pedagogy in Process: The Letters to Guinea–Bissau*. Seabury Press, New York

Hoxeng J 1973 *Let Jorge Do It: An Approach to Rural Nonformal Education*. Center for International Education, University of Massachusetts, Amherst, Massachusetts

Knowles M S 1975 *Self Directed Learning: A Guide for Learners and Teachers*. Association Press, New York

McClelland D C, Winter D G 1969 *Motivating Economic Achievements: Accelerative Economic Development Through Psychological Training*. Free Press, New York

Snarey J R (ed.) 1981 *Conflict and Continuity: A History of Ideas on Social Equality and Human Development* (Harvard Educational Review Reprint Series No. 15). Harvard Educational Review, Cambridge, Massachusetts

Srinivasan L 1977 *Perspective on Nonformal Adult Learning: Functional Education for Individual, Community and National Development*. World Education, New York

Integrated Rural Development: Specialized Training Programs

H. W. Roberts

The term "integrated rural development" began to gain currency in the late 1960s. The term itself, and the practices it covered, reflected a disillusionment on the part of development planners with economic measures of development, and an awareness of the need to attack all the causes of rural poverty—social, cultural, medical, educational, as well as economic. This change in perspective is illustrated in the shift in the investment priorities of the World Bank since the 1950s. Whereas in its early years the Bank's policy was to restrict its lending in developing countries to economic infrastructure projects—electricity, transportation, dams, and so on—by the 1960s it recognized education, communication, and social development as proper fields for investment. Such a broad approach to development was endorsed at the 1980 UNESCO General Conference, in a resolution providing for the extension of UNESCO's contribution to integrated rural development, with particular emphasis on educational and training aspects of rural development programs.

The integrated approach was exemplified by the activities in the Intensive Agricultural District Program in India in the early 1960s, as follows: the creation of farm credit through credit cooperatives; improvement of supplies through service cooperatives; use of price incentives and better marketing arrangements; assistance at the local level through intensive educational, technical, and farm management; local participation in farm planning; village organization and planning for leadership; use of local labor in public works; program analysis and evaluation from the outset; and resource coordination.

The invention of the practice of integrated rural development preceded the adoption of the term. The practice had been pursued in China since the establishment of the People's Republic in 1949 (Kidd 1979), and some of its features had been adopted in the Gezira cotton scheme in the Sudan even before the Second World War. There are many other examples.

Education and training are seen typically as crucial to the process. Integrated rural development and nonformal education are thus used almost synonymously, nonformal education being "any organized, systematic, educational activity carried on outside the formal (educational) system to provide selected types of learning to particular subgroups in the population"—children and adults (Coombs and Ahmed 1974). The educational activities proposed in the planning of the Chilalo Agricultural Development Unit in Ethiopia when it was launched in 1968 exemplify this dimension. The activities included: training key Ethiopian staff for research, extension, and management; training local extension assistants, including girls from local secondary schools; training local cooperative leaders; training selected model farmers in improved production; developing extension services in all aspects of farming. In the 1970s training was extended beyond an economic orientation, to include youth club training, education for women in home economics, and more diversified adult education, for example, literacy programs.

The Ethiopian example illustrates an important component of this approach to development: the need to train local extension and management staff as well as farmers and their families. The lack of such training, or its failure to provide lasting skills and competencies to local workers, has been identified as a factor in the failure of such programs.

A Food and Agricultural Organization study in 1971 reinforces this point by suggesting that a leading role in programs must be played by local people, that external assistance is more likely to work if it is in response to initiatives by the local people, that external assistance should aim at strengthening institutions within the community (Higgs and Mbithi 1977). The process must start at the preschool level, and a central element of the school curriculum must become the needs of the local people. In other words, the resources of the whole education system have to be applied, not only to primary and secondary education, but also to adult education. Schools and school teachers, often crucial and singular resources in a rural community, have to become involved in education outside the classroom through programs in community health, family life, nutrition education, and so on (Higgs and Mbithi 1977).

The methods used in education and training programs have become more diverse as the purposes of such education have been extended beyond economic ones (Coombs and Ahmed 1974). Radio has been used widely, for example in Honduras for education in literacy, health, leadership, and community organization. The performing arts, particularly theater, have been used in agricultural, health, and community development education in Botswana and other African countries. In Ecuador, a nonformal education project used games to teach people literacy and to help them analyze their local conditions. In Indonesia this has been extended to the use of simulation games. Of particular importance is the development of participatory research methods as tools not only for learning but for community animation and decision making (Hall 1975).

A study by Moulton (1977) of projects in a number of West African countries suggests some preconditions necessary for a comprehensive rural development program: it must be an integral part of national policy; government administration must be decentralized enough to give local education programs appropriate controls; there must be enough government funding to permit long-term programming; and the national government must be politically and ideologically stable enough to afford opposition. These preconditions emphasize the political element of the process and reinforce the proposition that integrated rural development requires a fundamental transformation across social, political, and economic lines. Training, funding, and the introduction of new technologies are not therefore guarantees of comprehensive development. India's so-called "Green Revolution" has been given as an example of a well-funded and technologically sophisticated program in which the results are problematical because the program did not take into account the sociopolitical context (e.g., the landholding power of local elites, Das Gupta 1977).

Such problems point to the need for the application of national commitment, not simply to the immediate objectives of a particular project, but to a broader program of social and economic restructuring. Probably the best example of this more fundamental approach to development has been postliberation China, where the process of nonformal education was integrated into cadre training, political education (mass media, study groups, propaganda teams), and the social and economic reorganization of rural life through land reallocation, then agricultural cooperatives, and then communes.

The socialist approach to development often leads to criticism of some integrated rural development programs. Thus, even the Ujamaa scheme in Tanzania, which incorporated nonformal education into a program of the collectivization of production in planned villages and 10-family cells, has been questioned regarding its ability to restructure rural institutions and transform production. Forms of nonformal education aimed at simply remedying the disadvantages of rural adults by giving them functional skills, are criticized by some observers as providing a second-class chance and not leading to social reconstruction (Mbilinyi 1979).

This criticism, as well as the establishment of projects aimed at consciousness raising, owe something to the work and writing of Freire, whose educational process of "conscientization" has direct political aims (Freire 1972, 1973). Freire's methods of literacy training have been adopted in a number of development programs (e.g., Thailand and Ecuador). However, a charge levied against such programs is that, in effect, they sometimes coopt Freire's radicalizing methods for the more conservative purpose of adapting the learner to existing conditions.

So the concept and practice of integrated rural development finds itself part of a larger debate about philosophies of political and social change.

See also: Economics of Nonformal Education; Nonformal Education; Participatory Research

Bibliography

Coombs P H, Ahmed M 1974 *Attacking Rural Poverty: How Nonformal Education Can Help.* John Hopkins University Press, Baltimore, Maryland

Das Gupta B 1977 *Village Society and Labour Use.* Oxford University Press, New Delhi

Freire P 1972 *Pedagogy of the Oppressed.* Herder and Herder, New York

Freire P 1973 *Education for Critical Consciousness.* Seabury Press, New York

Hall B L 1975 Participatory research: An approach for change. *Convergence* 8: 24–32

Higgs J, Mbithi P (eds.) 1977 *Learning and Living: Education for Rural Families in Developing Countries.* Food and Agricultural Organization, Rome

Kidd J R 1979 A China plant and an Indian cane: Adult learning programs in India and China. *Indian J. Adult Educ.* 40 (1)

Mbilinyi M 1979 Lifelong basic education for the absolutely poor in Africa. In: Schuller T, Megarry J (eds.) 1979 *Recurrent Education and Lifelong Learning.* Kogan Page, London

Moulton J M 1977 *Animation Rurale: Education for Rural Development.* Massachusetts University Center for International Education, Amherst, Massachusetts

Evaluation in Adult Education

R. Ruddock

The heterogeneity of adult education provision and of its student population renders measurement difficult, but the maturity of its participants facilitates investigation in depth and the use of qualitative methodologies. The planning of an evaluation gives rise to significant questions of value and purpose; the interests of groups involved may conflict. In this article the need for evaluation in adult education, the principal agents, work done, and methods used since the early 1960s are briefly reviewed, with some indications of possible further development.

1. Distinctive Features of Evaluation in Adult Education

It must be stressed that "evaluation" is a term of historically recent currency in adult education, although the need to investigate its effectiveness has long been felt. Many analyses, records of experience, and enquiries carried out in the recent past and recognized as research may now be categorized as evaluation, although that claim is not made by their authors. Systematic evaluations undertaken so far in the field of adult education have not been numerous, nor large in scale. Several reasons can be identified for this and will illuminate the peculiarities of adult education.

Firstly, until recently adult education has not received large allocations of public funds, and has therefore been under less pressure to demonstrate results. Secondly, it has been provided by a wide range of statutory, vocational, and voluntary bodies, many of which will not have had the motive or the resources for evaluation. Thirdly, it is and has always been an activity widely dispersed into local centres, for the most part using premises built for other uses. It has therefore lacked visibility, and not been seen as an obvious target for critical review. Fourthly, the majority of participants were not seeking credit or qualification; the providers did not therefore need to establish their efficiency in this regard.

Beyond these structural considerations, however, there is a historical–ethical one which is perhaps more fundamental. From its early origins, the providers and practitioners of adult education have considered their activities to be worthwhile beyond question. This belief rested on the assumption that education was a primary "good" in itself, and on the liberal principle that all individuals should have access to it. Furthermore, the day-to-day and face-to-face experience of adult educators convinced them of the validity of their ethos. From this perspective, evaluation would be seen as superfluous, and also as unrealistic because of the intangible mysteries of human development.

The increasing significance attached to adult education marks a qualitative shift from the assumptions on which institutional education for young people has been based, assumptions relating to needs, motivation, maturity, and experience. Correspondingly, the areas of provision, the organizational structures, and the objectives are distinct from those of youth education. In working with adults, the opportunities for evaluation in depth are greatly enhanced, while simple models developed for use in schools cannot be applied. In the school situation, groups or classes homogeneous in respect of age, sex, educational background, and even "intelligence" are available, a situation ready-made for controlled experiment. In adult education few classes are so homogeneous. The enhanced possibilities arise from the capacity of the adult to reflect and report on his/her own experience. In the process of evaluation, adult learners will be subjects rather than objects.

It may be relatively easy to measure the extent to which simple objectives have been realized: but those formulated for adult education courses are likely to employ such phrases as "the enrichment of experience", "facilitation of personal development", "growth of insight and empathy", or "interpersonal skills". The problems of ascertaining whether such objectives have been met are considerable. The literatures of academic and clinical psychology, especially the American literatures, are replete with rigorous tests of subjective changes gained by observing the behavioural correlates. Such tests however have not usually convinced teachers of literature, history, or religious studies. Where such tests are used for evaluation, their claims to validity and generalizability are commonly contested.

2. The Felt Needs

Beyond the need recognized by all providers and sponsors of adult education to ensure that money spent is yielding a proportionate return, that objectives are being realized to some degree, and that target populations are being reached, there are the needs felt by administrators and practitioners. The former may wish to know whether local citizens are sufficiently informed of what is on offer; whether programmes are appropriate for towns and districts of differing social composition; whether preset curricula are well-chosen for ostensible purposes. Practitioners may feel the need to discover whether the assembled students have the attainments, motivation, and social characteristics envisaged; whether the teaching methods adopted are effective; whether there is evidence of personal development transcending the aims of cognitive learning; whether location, family, and vocational circumstance, or personal history favour or inhibit the class members' participation in study. It is characteristic of adult education that the desire for knowledge of results is manifested across the range, from the microlevel of the classroom to the directors of international programmes.

3. The Agents of Evaluation: Some Examples

Some of the largest and most sophisticated programme evaluations have been undertaken by the international agencies, notably the World Bank and the World Health Organization, who work under the pressing need to justify their expenditures to the contributing member states. The relative failure of much financial and technical aid has led to an awareness of the centrality of adult education as an instrument for social development (Cuca and Pierce 1977).

At the national level, an example of a multifaceted evaluation of a large programme of education for system and behaviour change is to be found in Nordlie (1981). All of the educational research institutes of the Scandinavian countries have published valuable investigations of the outcomes of legislation directed towards equalization of access to adult education and increased take-up by disadvantaged groups (Höghielm and Rubenson 1980). Because there are so few captive audiences in adult education—it is a sector where participants vote with their feet—providers have always needed to discover the social characteristics, motivation, and responses of the participants. Early researchers of great value in this regard were Johnstone and Rivera (1965) in the United States, and Trenaman (1967) in the United Kingdom. A much cited investigation at the microlevel, identifying goal-oriented, activity-oriented, and learning-oriented students, was that of Houle (1963).

In the United Kingdom, examples of state-sponsored evaluations of publicly financed programmes have been Charnley and Jones (1979) on adult literacy teaching and the report of a joint team from Nottingham University and the National Institute of Adult Education on the training of part-time teachers of adults (Graham et al. 1982). These were in one sense typical in that accurate quantification was known to be impossible from the outset in both cases; each of the researches assembled and analysed a large sample of qualitative material making it possible for convincing conclusions to be reached.

Local authorities and municipalities have similarly sought to inform themselves about citizen participation in education, usually for administrative purposes. The associated reports, where for instance an authority is reorienting its provision towards community education, may be of considerable interest. Although not published, they may be available on request.

In the United Kingdom, much pioneering work has been initiated and evaluated by university adult educators. This has generally been on a small scale, the findings having doubtful significance beyond the local circumstance. In the United States where larger resources have been available, larger enquiries have been possible. These have mainly focused upon existing provision and clientele. It should be remembered however that in the United States alone many hundreds of doctoral and master's theses and dissertations in the field of adult education have been completed, and that similar work is rapidly aggregating in the United Kingdom, Australia, and elsewhere. These individual researches exhibit a wide diversity of sophisticated methodologies.

4. Methods

For reasons mentioned above, the methods used in the evaluation of adult education programmes have tended towards qualitative, anthropological, phenomenological, or illuminative models rather than positive ones (but see Skager 1978). Some researches have involved extensive in-depth semistructured or nondirective interviewing. Survey methods are essential for quantifying and analysing the response of populations to programme provision, and have generally been adopted for large-scale enquiries.

Because all participants in adult education are mature citizens, often sharply aware of civil rights, ethical issues in evaluation are likely to be more salient and more complex than in the investigation of school education. Challenges may be formulated as open questions such as: In whose interest is this evaluation being undertaken? What prior consultation has there been with subjects/students/teachers? Will the policies and the practice of administrators be excluded from investigation? Will all the data be made public? Who will edit the report? To whom will the research be credited? For example, research in hand indicates that industrial training is evaluated almost entirely in terms of its effect on productivity. It hardly needs saying that it might be judged by the learner on a quite different basis. Programme planning and the choice of methods need to be undertaken with such questions in mind.

5. *The Main Areas of Evaluation*

For the purposes of this article the main topics of some 400 books and other items reporting evaluations in adult education, or considered by their authors to be significant for evaluation, have been categorized. They were mainly English language texts, with American, British, and Canadian work predominating, but a smaller number of items from Scandinavia, the Netherlands, France, and the Federal Republic of Germany were also listed. The following conclusions emerged.

In order of frequency, the main areas of concern subjected to evaluation between 1960 and 1980 have been: distance teaching; medical, nursing, and health education; programmes and policy making; basic education and literacy; teaching method; and counselling.

Notable trends during the period appear to have been: a sharp increase in the evaluation of counselling; increases in the evaluation of vocationally oriented courses, those for the disadvantaged and for industrial workers; and a fall in the evaluation of basic adult education.

Liberal adult education, political education, provision for trades unions and cooperatives—all areas of traditional concern—have been little subject to evaluation throughout.

In respect of the above list of subject areas, the following explanatory hypotheses may be offered. There has been an emphasis on distance teaching because: (a) its methods are of historically recent development, not resting on traditional sanctions; (b) large investments have been made in the necessary capital and operational provision; and (c) the learning process is not visible to the providers.

In respect of medical and health education, (a) its vital import calls for a constant review of its effectiveness; (b) health-related behaviour, for example, smoking, drinking, sexual activity, has proved to be resistant to change.

Educational counselling is an expensive provision requiring special justification, which in principle may be obtained from (a) a systematic consideration of evidence of its life-determining function; and (b) the wastage involved in the dropping out of students in whose prior education large sums have been invested.

There has been a low level of activity in the evaluation of liberal adult education, despite the high regard in which it is generally held by adult educators, because (a) its practitioners have felt that its outcomes, for example, the response to poems or pictures, will always elude rational attempts to register and measure them; (b) its courses are rarely linked to marketable qualifications; and (c) its values are felt to be intrinsic and self-validating for teacher and learner.

It should be recognized that 400 evaluation-related publications represent no more than the visible manifestations of a large, almost universal, process. Enquiry has shown that the prevalence of systematic self-determined individual learning is greater than had been supposed. This is a situation that calls for self-evaluation of the chosen learning systems and methods. The work of Allen Tough (1971) has greatly extended knowledge in this field and has related the research findings to practice and policy.

6. *Recent Trends*

Adult education is increasingly called upon to contribute to the resolution of social problems. Examples are (a) programmes of vocational preparation to help unemployed persons to compete more effectively for notified vacancies; and (b) programmes for, or concerned with, ethnic minorities. Both of these disadvantaged groups are increasing in Western societies. Educational measures cannot alone resolve the associated problems; it is predictable that apparent failures will call for an evaluation of programmes.

More positively, a further increase in the provision of part-time, modular, and inservice courses for adults can be foreseen. Researches into this field have revealed a student population exhibiting every variety of circumstance, motivation, social character, and personal history. The need for ongoing evaluation programmes designed to illuminate the complex interrelations of institutional requirements, personal needs, technological change, and vocational choice will become increasingly evident.

The surest prediction is that programme sponsors will continue to be concerned with the difficulty of securing a proportionate response from those sections of the community whose educational attainments are low, and may be presumed to be in greatest need. No general solution to this seemingly intractable problem has been found. Every innovatory problem in this field of action calls for systematic evaluation.

It is less well-recognized that there are extensive unresearched educational programmes for those at the higher end of the scale of privilege, the elites who occupy the seats of power and influence. Examples are to be found in staff college programmes for top civil servants, senior officers of the forces and police services, and the executives of international companies. It is in the public interest to know what teaching in law and economics, for instance, is provided for the generals who so often find themselves called upon to reinforce the civil authority, or even to take over the government of a country; or what training in social studies is available for justices of the high courts. It is to be hoped that the need for formal evaluation in this area will be recognized in the near future.

Adult educators are rapidly made aware of the extent to which the learner's thinking is influenced, or even determined, by the mass media and their content, including all that is communicated by visual images. Attempts to characterize these and to determine their effects on informal learning are in progress in most Western countries.

By way of conclusion, a cautionary word may be in order. Evaluation in other fields of provision has refuted some large claims and disappointed expectations. In Europe overall, the reorganization of secondary education has not succeeded in redistributing life chances to the hoped-for extent. There are as yet few indications that adult education can respond to the challenging requirements of lifelong education, now accepted in principle by most countries around the world. It may be hoped that evaluation *will* highlight the central importance of the organizational flexibility, the community links, and the humane values that have always characterized the best practice of adult education.

Bibliography

Charnley A H, Jones H A 1979 *The Concept of Success in Adult Literacy*. Huntington, Cambridge

Cuca R, Pierce C S 1977 *Experiments in Family Planning: Lessons from the Developing World*. Johns Hopkins University Press for the World Bank, Baltimore, Maryland

Gelpi E 1979 Suggestions for an evaluation of experiences. In: Gelpi E 1979 *A Future for Lifelong Education*. Department of Adult and Higher Education, University of Manchester, Manchester, pp. 97–109

Graham T B, Daines J M, Sullivan T, Harris P, Baum F E 1982 *The Training of Part-time Teachers of Adults*. University of Nottingham and National Institute of Adult Education, Nottingham

Hall B, Tandon R, Grossi F V, Conchelos G, Kassam Y, MacCall B 1981 Participatory research: Developments and issues. *Convergence* 14(3)

Höghielm R, Rubenson K (eds.) 1980 *Adult Education for Social Change: Research on the Swedish Allocation Policy*. Stockholm Institute of Education, Stockholm, Sweden

Houle C 1963 *The Inquiring Mind*. University of Wisconsin Press, Madison, Wisconsin

House E R 1986 (ed.) *New Directions in Educational Evaluation*. Falmer, London

Jenkins D R 1976 *Curriculum Evaluation*. Open University Press, Milton Keynes

Johnstone J W C, Rivera R J 1965 *Volunteers for Learning: A Study of the Educational Pursuits of American Adults*. Aldine, Chicago, Illinois

Nordlie P G 1981 *Monitoring and Evaluating Equal Opportunity Progress in the Army*. United States Commission on Civil Rights, Washington, DC

Parlett M R, Hamilton D 1972 *Evaluation as Illumination: A New Approach to the Study of Innovatory Programs*. Centre for Research in Educational Sciences, University of Edinburgh, Edinburgh

Ruddock R 1981 *Evaluation: A Consideration of Principles and Methods*. Department of Adult and Higher Education, University of Manchester, Manchester

Skager R W 1978 *Lifelong Education and Evaluation Practice: A Study on the Development of a Framework for Designing Evaluation Systems at the School Stage in the Perspective of Lifelong Education*. UNESCO Institute for Education and Pergamon Press, Oxford

Tough A M 1971 *The Adult's Learning Projects: A Fresh Approach to Theory and Practice in Adult Learning*. Ontario Institute for Studies in Education, Toronto, Ontario

Trenaman J M 1967 *Communication and Comprehension: The Report of an Investigation, by Statistical Methods, of the Effective Communication of Educative Material and an Assessment of the Factors Making for such Communication, with Special Reference to Broadcasting*. Longman, London

Adult Education Evaluation in Developing Countries

S. Spaulding

This article will trace the involvement of multinational and bilateral funding and assistance organizations in evaluation activities in adult and nonformal education. It will concentrate on activities in developing countries. No attempt will be made to catalog all evaluation efforts, but rather to identify trends and suggest selected references. Evaluation activities in industrialized countries, such as those funded in the United States by the National Institute of Education, are not included as these are well covered in other standard references.

1. Early Evaluation Efforts in Adult Education

A case can be made that the adult education field, broadly defined, has pioneered many of the approaches now advocated by specialists in program and project evaluation.

In the 1920s and 1930s, agricultural extension specialists in the United States carried out a wide range of studies on the effect of various extension practices. Such studies indicated that farmers were most likely to change practices when they saw a demonstration of a technique on a farm similar to their own. Publications, radio programs, and face-to-face visits of extension workers reinforced efforts to change farming practice. These various techniques in themselves often missed the mark because the change agent lacked an understanding of what the farmer already knew, thought, felt, and did. Agricultural education specialists early practiced what would now be called formative evaluation when they tested extension publications in order to see which words farmers knew, used, could read with ease, and which words were used only by agricultural specialists.

In the 1950s and 1960s, a number of international projects began to build on some of the earlier agricultural extension concepts. UNESCO's Regional Center for Fundamental Education in Latin America (CREFAL), established in Patzcuaro, Mexico, built into its training program various experiences involving the collection of information on the rural population to be served by adult education activities. Such approaches later would be called needs assessment and would be considered as important contributions to formative evaluation.

Also in the 1950s, the Organization of American States (OAS) established the Latin American Fundamental Education Press, a program involving the preparation and testing of a series of adult education booklets designed for adults of limited reading ability in Latin America. This series included booklets in health, agriculture, civics, recreation, and other topics considered at the time important in Latin American development. The series was pretested in a number of Latin American countries by surveying reading interests in rural and urban areas; working with a sample of adults in various socioeconomic settings to see what they could read, understand, and remember of the booklets being prepared; and evaluating the effect of various formats (e.g., illustrations and captions with text) on interest and comprehension (Spaulding and Nannetti in Richards 1959).

During the same period, the Inter-American Institute for Agricultural Sciences, with its headquarters in Costa Rica, embarked on a series of activities, in cooperation with the OAS, involving research and training in agricultural communications. Again, the emphasis was on needs assessment, and formative and summative evaluation. These early efforts led to the establishment of a formal department of agricultural communications at La Molina Agricultural University in Peru, which has taken regional leadership in training and research in this area.

UNESCO's work in adult education, literacy, and reading materials for the new literate during the 1950s and 1960s stressed various kinds of evaluative approaches, described as topic testing, pretesting, posttesting, study of the environment, and so on. In 1957, UNESCO held a regional seminar on reading materials for new literates in Rangoon, Burma, which entailed the collection of information on village needs, writing and pretesting of reading materials, and evaluation of the impact of such materials. A regional meeting was held in Pakistan, which outlined evaluation and research needs in the area of reading materials and literacy programs (Richards 1959). During the 1950s, UNESCO, the Ford Foundation, and other international agencies assisted a number of national programs involved in the creation and evaluation of adult education literature. Among these were the East African Literature Bureau, the Burma Translation Society, the Bureau of Ghanaian Languages, and the Marbial Valley Project in Haiti. In 1962, the East African Literature Bureau, with headquarters in Nairobi, was the host of a UNESCO-sponsored regional workshop on the preparation of reading materials for new literates which included authors, editors, publishers, and artists from both English- and French-speaking African countries. Participants formed teams and worked in village areas to identify needs as felt by villagers and community development experts. They then designed reading materials which were tried out in villages, revised, and duplicated.

2. The UNESCO Experimental World Literacy Program

In the mid-1960s, UNESCO proposed massive support for an experimental world literacy program, designed to combine social and economic skills training with traditional communication skills training. The United Nations Development Program (UNDP) was the usual source of support for such projects within the United Nations system. The UNDP was approached to help finance the effort, but was distinctly cool to the idea. Although economists had begun to treat formal education as investment rather than consumption, there was not yet much acceptance of the case for investment in literacy and adult education. The UNDP finally agreed, however, to finance several experimental projects, on the condition that UNESCO would bring into each project an evaluative system designed to show how each project affected the behavior of individuals and communities involved in the functional literacy programs (Spaulding 1966).

Ultimately, 11 experimental projects were funded under the experimental effort, most of them becoming operational in the late 1960s and terminating in the 1970s. Despite the efforts to design comparable evaluative procedures in each project beforehand, the local context of each project was such that few comparable data were collected. Most governments wanted a national literacy effort rather than a pilot experimental project. Some projects separated evaluation from program development, and the evaluator (usually a social scientist) maintained a distance from the operational staff. Other projects considered evaluation to be a formative activity, with the evaluator collecting data to be shared with program developers in order to help improve the project as it progressed.

In the 1970s, UNESCO established an evaluation unit in Paris which labored without success for some months in an attempt to integrate diverse data from the 11 literacy projects into some kind of comparable reporting design. Finally an international committee of evaluation was established. Two educators were invited to examine and summarize the findings of each project and to report on trends that were evident between and among projects. The result was a joint UNDP/UNESCO report which was generally well-received by the scholarly community, but was considered controversial within UNESCO (Spaulding and Gillette 1976).

The report looked at the political problems that plagued the various projects; the administrative and organizational problems; the staffing problems; the cost of the projects; the nature and effectiveness of the teaching materials and methods used; and the apparent effect on people and communities. Essentially, the report highlighted the complexity of any attempt to make major changes in an adult population through any one adult education or literacy effort; the need to adjust any such program to local conditions; the need to get high-level policy support to ensure success of any program; and the need to integrate such efforts into broader development plans.

3. *Current Evaluation Activities*

During the 1970s and early 1980s, the governing bodies of most international organizations called for more evaluative efforts. Both UNDP and UNESCO established offices of evaluation which, in turn, undertook to jointly evaluate a number of educational projects. UNESCO published guidelines on project evaluation to help short-term consultant teams brought in to do mid-term project evaluations (UNESCO 1979) and a manual on how to do structured evaluations of literacy programs (Couvert 1979). The United States Agency for International Development (USAID) established, in October 1979, a major division for project evaluation which has produced a remarkable series of reports on various USAID-assisted projects in rural education, rural development, and related fields, most with adult education components (i.e., Giovanni et al. 1981).

The United States Agency for International Development (USAID) has also supported a variety of evaluation efforts through contracts with universities and consulting agencies, including the Stanford University Institute for Communications Research and Academy for Educational Development, the Center for International Education at the University of Massachusetts, Michigan State University, World Education, and the Institute for Development Anthropology.

Major studies financed by USAID and others include a three-year effort by Florida State University to evaluate the extensive work of *Acción Popular Cultural* (ACPO) in Colombia. The ACPO, over the years, has evolved a radiophonic education effort which includes publications, volunteer monitors in many villages, and a variety of adult education activities which are supported by the communications infrastructure. The complexity of developing and managing such a program and attracting continuing interest of participants has been highlighted in this study (Bernal et al. 1978, Morgan et al. 1980).

The USAID also initiated in the early 1980s a major demonstration of the uses of satellites to improve communication in rural and community development. This effort will have a major evaluation component. Liberia is the location of the first of several country projects, each of which emphasizes the role of communication in adult education. This effort is consistent with an increasing concern of a number of funding agencies for the integration of adult education services into comprehensive community development efforts (Coombs 1980).

The World Bank has an office which undertakes evaluations of projects funded by the various regional bureaus of the Bank, but most of these "audits" are for internal use only and are not made public. At the end of the 1970s, however, the Bank began to encourage borrowing nations to build into each project it funds a continuous evaluation system, which will provide information useful for improving project performance as it progresses, as well as cumulative information to help in the ultimate summative evaluation of the effort. One of the more elaborate of such built-in feedback evaluation mechanisms, to cost several million dollars over a seven-year period, was developed in Papua New Guinea in 1980 as part of a primary education reform loan (which also included a small adult education component). The Bank also undertakes a variety of efficiency, dropout, rate of return, labor market, and other studies which all contribute to educational decision making and thus fit within the context of evaluation efforts. The Bank, in the mid-1970s, assisted the Saudi Arabian government in a major evaluation of their adult education and literacy efforts, with the help of faculty from the International and Development Education Program of the University of Pittsburgh, the University of Linköping in Sweden, Ain Shaims University in Cairo, World Education, and other groups.

The Canadian International Development Agency (CIDA) has participated in a variety of evaluation efforts, often in cooperation with the International Council for Adult Education in Toronto and the International Development Research Center in Ottawa. The Swedish International Development Authority has similarly funded a variety of adult education projects with an evaluative component, including one to train adult educators in Portugal undertaken by the University of Linköping (Erasmie and Norbeck 1978). The Overseas Development Authority in the United Kingdom has funded a number of such overseas projects, especially through the University of Reading, which has a long-standing interest in agricultural and rural development (Bowers 1977).

Finally, a joint UNESCO–UNICEF program of studies has issued an extensive series of reports which includes evaluative material on a variety of nonformal projects and programs for children, youth, and women. And the

UNESCO Regional Office in Asia is host to the Asian Program for Educational Innovation and Development (APEID) which has supported a number of institutions involved in evaluative studies of educational innovation in the region.

4. Institutional Evaluation Policies

Most international evaluation efforts in nonformal and adult education have been initiated by multinational and bilateral funding and assistance organizations. There is, however, little agreement among and between agencies and governments as to what evaluation is about.

Some in the agencies see evaluation as an exercise whereby experts are sent for a few days or weeks to look at a project in progress to decide whether or not it is meeting its objectives and whether or not any changes are needed in the project plan. Governing boards of international and funding organizations see evaluation as a means of providing data to help them set priorities on what should be funded in the future. National governments, project administrators, and groups involved in projects, however, are more attracted to the idea of evaluation as an information system which can help provide data for ongoing improvement in project management and design.

The picture is further complicated by the internal structures of international and funding organizations. If the evaluation unit of the organization is not placed at a high enough level in the organization and given sufficient resources, autonomy, and authority to do its work, its work will be limited and its information will be little used in policy making and operational decision making.

Perhaps more importantly, evaluation efforts, to be effective in improving performance, must be built into program and project activities with the idea of helping answer participants' questions. External evaluations done by evaluation specialists may serve a function, but until evaluation is a state of mind shared by all participants in a program, evaluation will not be fully effective. For this reason, a major function of any in-house evaluation unit should be to help operational units within the organization in the design of their own self-evaluation efforts.

5. The Future

Since the early 1960s project and program personnel have been sensitized both in international agencies and in national governments to the need for evaluative data on project and program activities. Increasing worldwide interest in nonformal and adult education will be accompanied by increasing interest in assessment and evaluation efforts designed to provide information for the constant improvement of projects and programs (Elsdon 1984). Evaluation models will increasingly stress participation of the target audiences of nonformal and adult education efforts. Such participatory evaluation in itself will be a powerful adult education medium, consistent with current priorities on the development of community-based nonformal education efforts reflecting the needs and interests of local communities.

There will also be increasing awareness of the need to include qualitative data in assessments and evaluations of adult education programmes (Lincoln and Guba 1985, Miles and Huberman 1984). Considering the complex nature of both the goals and the structure of many adult education projects in developing countries, purely quantitative data are rarely sufficient to illuminate the problems and prospects of such efforts. The questions that policy- and decision-makers are asking will require eclectic models of evaluation that creatively combine ethnographic, case study and quantitative assessment approaches.

Bibliography

Bernal H, Masoner P, Masoner L 1978 *Acción Cultural Popular: Pioneer Radiophonic Education Program of Latin America, 1947–1977.* International Division, Acción Cultural Popular, Bogotá, Columbia

Bhola H S 1979 *Evaluating Functional Literacy.* Hulton, Amersham

Bowers J 1977 Functional adult education for rural people: Communications action research and feedback. *Convergence* 10(3): 34–43

Clark N, McCaffery J 1979 *Demystifying Evaluation.* World Education, New York

Coombs P H 1980 *Meeting the Basic Needs of the Rural Poor: The Integrated Community-based Approach.* Pergamon, New York

Couvert R 1979 *The Evaluation of Literacy Programmes: A Practical Guide.* UNESCO, Paris

Erasmie T, Norbeck N 1978 *Annual Report 1977/78: The Portugal Project.* School of Education, Linköping University, Linköping

Elsdon K T 1984 Adult education *Bulletin of the International Bureau of Education* 58(4)

Farmer J A, Papagiannis G 1975 *Program Evaluation.* World Education, New York

Giovanni R S, Armstrong L T, Jansen W H 1981 *Thailand: Rural Non-formal Education: The Mobile Trade Training Schools.* United States Agency for International Development, Washington, DC

Guba E, Lincoln Y S 1981 *Effective Evaluation.* Jossey-Bass, San Francisco, California

Institute for Development Anthropology 1981 *Development Anthropology Network* 1(1): 8

Kinsey D C 1981 Participatory evaluation in adult and nonformal education. *Adult Education* 31(3): 155–68

Lincoln Y S, Guba E G 1985 *Naturalistic Inquiry.* Sage, Beverly Hills, California

Miles M B, Huberman A M 1984 *Qualitative Data Analysis.* Sage, Beverly Hills, California

Morgan R M, Muhlmann L, Masoner P 1980 *Evaluación de sistemas de comunicación educativa.* Acción Cultural Popular, Bogotá, Colombia

Nonformal Education Information Center 1981 NFE *Core Bibliographies.* Institute for International Studies in Education, Michigan State University, East Lansing, Michigan

Richards C G 1959 *The Provision of Popular Reading Materials*. UNESCO, Paris
Spaulding S 1966 The UNESCO world literacy program: A new strategy that may work. *Adult Education* 16(2): 70–84
Spaulding S 1974 Life-long education: A modest model for planning and research. *Comp. Educ.* 10: 101–13
Spaulding S, Gillette A 1976 *The Experimental World Literacy Programme: A Critical Assessment*. UNESCO, Paris
UNESCO 1979 *Evaluation of Technical Cooperation Projects in Education*. Document ED-79/23/159, Paris
Werdelin I 1977 *Evaluation*. Manual of Educational Planning 9, School of Education, Linköping University, Linköping

Learning: Organization and Support

Introduction

This subsection of the *Handbook* will inevitably overlap with subsection 4b, Teaching and Evaluation. After all, some teachers would say that organization and support of learning is an accurate description of their principal functions. Whatever the place of these activities in their hierarchy of tasks, teachers are widely engaged in both, but they are not nowadays the only ones who are. The programme planning and administration operations of providing bodies, indeed the work of all adult education, is directed towards the organization and support of learning. In this subsection, however, consideration will be limited to those measures directly related to the learning situation itself and its immediate context.

It takes very little reflection to recognize that, even in its most simple forms, intentional learning requires some organization. The one-to-one situation in which a mother teaches a child to knit, or a person demonstrates to another how to prune a fruit tree, has to be arranged so that the appropriate materials are accessible to both and the student is placed so that the actions being taught may be observed. The individual, self-directed learner has to acquire the tools of learning and arrange to be in a position in which it will be possible to undertake it. It is difficult to practise fishing techniques in the home, or to learn a foreign language without a textbook, audiovisual materials, or direct contact with people who already speak it.

Between such basic examples and the most complex ones to be found in adult education there stretches a whole range of situations organized so that learning may take place. Ideally, each one should be structured so that learning is maximized and this would involve selecting objectives, content, resources, time, place, and its arrangement (for example, heating, lighting, and seating), to suit the methods most appropriate to the learner, or learners, engaged. In practice the inability to manipulate one or more of these variables as desired always enforces a degree of compromise, so that the objectives must be adapted to the time available, or the methods to the resources. In an extreme, but not uncommon, case drawn from the related sector of higher education, the teacher, confronted by several hundred students and limited teaching room space, is hard put to devise an alternative to the lecture method and may be obliged to repeat the same lecture several times to different audiences, if audiovisual transmission to other rooms is not available.

In adult education one has rarely to teach so many people at a time face to face, but it is necessary to adjust to other constraints on choice of organization. For example, unsuitable accommodation may prevent one from accepting as many students or undertaking the range of activities one would wish. One may not be able to employ the discussion method of teaching/learning, although appropriate to the content, either because the learners lack the basic knowledge, or because there are too many of them for it to be employed usefully.

Even if one had a free hand to set up the externals of the learning situation as one wished, the organization of it might still present difficult problems. Given that the aim of education is to further, as far as possible, the learning development of individuals, it might seem logical, if one could, to offer each person individual tuition. Much store is, indeed, set in certain contexts upon this, for instance in some literacy teaching and in educational counselling. It continues too in the learning process that used to be known in the United Kingdom as "sitting next to Nellie" and in the United States as the "buddy system", and is still much used in education for employment, where a person acquires a competence by observing the practice and following the advice of a skilled worker.

However, there are advantages to be derived from participating in a group which are not open to the individual learner—mutual support, exposure to a range of other views and concerns, the stimulation of competition, to mention only three. This is particularly true when the methods employed are specifically designed to make use of what is known about the characteristics of groups to maximize learning. It also applies, though, to some degree when the chosen method is the lecture or the demonstration, particularly if student questions are allowed and there is time for student discussion. Group learning does, however, reduce the extent to which the learning experience may be tailored to suit each individual and to which attention may be given to each one. If the choice is open, the educator's problem is: where does the balance of advantage lie?

In practice, for reasons of cost, labour resources, and space, among others, most organized adult education takes place in groups and it greatly contributes to the success of learning if the correct choices of their size and composition are made. Organization of learning does not, of course, stop there, or in fitting the best method of teaching to the group, or vice versa. Once the learning situation is created, around a group or an individual, other issues have to be resolved. One may need to plan the time period of each learning meeting to take into account what is known about adult attention spans, varying methods and activities. For such methods as discovery learning, places other than conventional classrooms or workshops may be required. It will be necessary or desirable to arrange for tools of learning to be made available. At the simplest level the educator may need to ensure there is blackboard and chalk, or their equivalent. At a more sophisticated level the tools may run from tape recorders and film projectors to video equipment, elaborate simulators, and computer terminals. The learners' contribution to the organization may be to see that they have writing materials, or the appropriate reading material. It will be part of the educators' role to judge how far learners can and may be expected to take responsibility for the organization of their own learning in a given situation and to give support when and if required.

It is interesting to observe that the growth of means of support for learning, from libraries and museums to the advanced educational technology already mentioned, may have freed some adults in some situations from the need for a teacher, but it has increased the need for the educator in other contexts and made the skills required more complex. It is a truism that new technology may make learning easier, but it makes teaching harder. The educator may even be called upon to help the self-directed or independent learner (a form of learning looked at in closer detail in subsection 4d, Self-directed and Distance Learning).

It is appropriate to consider here not only the externals of learning organization, but also the self-organization that learners must make, consciously or unconsciously, when they set out to study. Much attention has been directed in recent years to explaining differential learning performances by the way individuals organize their approach to a learning task, rather than by variations in intelligence. The article *Learning Styles* provides a critical account of the best-known attempts to do this.

Much of adult education is conducted in small, participatory learning groups, applying the theories of group dynamics. The article *Group Learning* examines the advantages claimed for discussion groups and sensitivity or T-groups, their strengths and weaknesses in practice, and the conditions that have to be met if they are to achieve their potential. The T-group's aim of furthering learning by increasing self-awareness and sensitivity to others may, it is claimed, also be achieved by meditation, biofeedback, imaging and visualizing, fantasy, and dreams, all of which are presented, together with accelerated learning and learning how to learn, in *New Therapies: Adult Education Applications.*

In developing countries special measures of organization and support of learning have been devised. *Integrated Rural Development: Community Organization* describes, with examples, means of mobilizing whole communities to further both educational and development goals. *"Campaign": A Technique in Adult Education* outlines the combination of broadcasting with study groups to promote awareness and help people understand major public issues and policies.

Perhaps the best-known small group organization for learning is the study circle. *Study Circles in Sweden* outlines their nature, history and achievements in the country where they have for a long time been the privileged form of learning environment in adult education.

The penultimate article, *Media Support in Adult Education*, deals with the media of mass communication and information technology—probably the most important of the new technologies in the organization and support of adult learning. The article identifies the principal contributions made by periodicals, radio, television broadcasting and video recording. A more critical line is taken in the final article, *Computers*, which asks whether technology is dehumanizing and examines the problem of who controls the learning environment and process when computers are used, an issue relevant also to the mass media.

Learning Styles

M. Toye

Research in the field of human learning is diffuse and varied, since the roots from which it has grown are themselves very different. In some cases the primary interest has been in laboratory research and the development of psychological theories. In others the main consideration has been more pragmatic: to make sense of classroom events, or to forward the understanding of practical issues of instructional practice. The concept of learning style is an attempt to find a middle way to understanding, through concepts that are close enough to ordinary human activities to be realistic, while at the same time being sufficiently general to permit useful classifications of the way in which human learners set about their tasks. It attempts to explain learning variation between individuals by differences in the way they approach learning tasks, rather than by differences in level of ability.

Research into learning styles is of particular relevance to adult education, which has long worked on the principle that the adult should be responsible for his or her own learning, including the ways he or she goes about it. Awareness of the number of self-directed adult learners, largely inspired by the work of Alan Tough (see *Self-directed Learning: Concepts and Practice*), and the growth of distance education and other forms of independent learning have stimulated attempts to understand how those adults who study for the most part in isolation organize their learning. The idea that approach rather than ability may explain differences in performance between adult learners is an added attraction to many adult educators, because it seems, at first sight at least, to be easier to change the former than the latter.

The interest in the idea of learning styles is to some extent negative, arising as it does from a sense of dissatisfaction with other types of explanation. Formal learning theories seem to maintain their scientific nature—or their pretentions to it—at the cost of remoteness from practical educational action. Attempts at a more direct technology of education through research into the properties of methods have accumulated data which are too indefinite to make actual decisions with. Taxonomies of learning too, often seem to give rise to more doubts than decisions. This article reviews major theories of learning styles and the critiques to which they have given rise. It concludes by noting common elements and difficulties.

1. The Learning Styles Inventory and Associated Theory

Learning styles are described by Fry and Kolb (1979) as emphases on some learning abilities rather than others which arise for reasons of heredity, past experience or the present situation. The Learning Styles Inventory (LSI) is intended to assess learners' preferences on two axes: concrete versus abstract, and active versus reflective. The inventory yields four primary scores: concrete experience (CE); reflective observation (RO); abstract conceptualization (AC); and active experimentation (AE). The two axes are defined as AC–CE and AE–RO.

From combinations of scores on these, four commonly occurring learning types are identified.

(a) *Convergers*. These are high scorers on AC and AE. Their strength is said to be in the application of ideas. The justification for the label "converger" is that application leads in the direction of one, or a few, right answers which are of lesser generality than the ideas being applied. Following Hudson (1966) these learners are characterized as having narrow, technical/scientific interests and as being unemotional.

(b) *Divergers*. These are the high scorers on CE and RO. They are considered to be imaginative, good at forming a "gestalt", emotional, and interested in people. Their interests are broad, tending towards the arts.

(c) *Assimilators*. People in this category lean towards AC and RO. Their inclination is towards inductive reasoning, integration of knowledge and the creation of theoretical models. Their social interest is not strong.

(d) *Accommodators*. Being best at CE and AE, their strength is in doing things, trying out new experiences and taking risks. The title "accommodator" denotes the tendency to adapt to existing circumstances. They are more likely to discard existing plans or ideas than to struggle against the facts. Their approach to problems is often of an intuitive or trial-and-error kind and is likely to depend on drawing in other people. Socially at ease, they may be seen as "pushy".

Any characterization of learner types implies a concomitant theory of the process of learning. In the case of the LSI it is experiential learning theory. This theory sets out the relationship between experience and concepts in a descriptive, molar form, and posits a cyclic process in which experiences prompt reflection, leading to elaborated concepts which then guide exploratory behaviour.

Kolb relates the experiential model to the work of various other scholars. Its pairing of opposite qualities is compared in a general way with Jung's dialectical conception of personality, while the abstract–concrete dimension is related to the ideas of Piaget, of Bruner, and of Harvey, Hunt, and Schroeder. Similarly, the active–reflective dimension is related to the work by Kagan and Kogan on reflectivity–impulsivity.

As with other work on cognitive style, the various kinds of cognitive performance are not rated as good or bad but are seen as alternatives, one of which may predominate in an individual's performance. Ideally, all kinds of performance should be readily available since they are conceived of as necessary parts in the full cycle of learning. However, certain criticisms of the LSI as an instrument have been made, notably by Freedman and Stumpf (1980). Their basic case is that: the LSI has poor reliability; its factors account for little of the observed test score variance; the inventory design and scoring method are biased so as to lend spurious support to the underlying conception of experiential learning.

In defence of the rationale of the instrument, Kolb argues that the critics mistake the nature of its categories, which are not meant to be independent and fixed psychological traits but interdependent and variable (1981a). That is, all four learning modes play an interacting part in determining any particular response, as does the immediate situation itself. Under these circumstances the conventional types of reliability assessment, such as test–retest, are inappropriate.

This type of problem is not peculiar to the LSI, having become a source of controversy in other cases where sensitivity to change is considered important. Kolb goes on to argue that split-half measures of reliability are much more appropriate and that these do in fact meet conventional levels of adequacy for the combination scores AC–CE (abstract–concrete) and AE–RO (active–

reflective), although they are not so good for the four basic scales by themselves. Further, the bias alleged to exist in the LSI, attributed to its forced choice format, is defended as acceptable for reasons of "ecological validity"—the fact that people do have to make choices about learning activities—and as being perfectly acceptable technically. Kolb's point is that a calculated estimation of inbuilt negative correlation as performed by some of his critics, or validation of the scales against external criteria both ensure that such bias is a mere technical feature of the instrument.

External criteria according to Kolb have in fact featured in much of the research based on the LSI. Fry and Kolb (1979) provide an example of such external validity in their application of experiential learning theory and learning styles to the process and outcomes of liberal arts education. Kolb (1981a) also lists 12 other authors who have tested operationalized versions of the theory.

2. Cognitive Preferences

The provenance of this research area is quite distinct from that of the LSI. The idea of cognitive preferences arose in connection with the educational objectives of new curricula in schools. Most of the research has therefore had to do with school-age learners, albeit most often the older ones, but some studies have been made of university students. Furthermore, the curricula of interest were in the physical sciences and this has given the research focus a particular flavour, often thought of as "instructional" by adult educators at large.

The basic idea behind cognitive preferences (Heath 1964) is that learners' interests can be usefully described as being in:

(a) *M*emorizing (particular items of information);

(b) *A*pplication (of knowledge to "real-world" problems);

(c) critical *Q*uestioning (of information); and

(d) formulation of *P*rinciples (underlying the apparent phenomena).

(with the emphasized letter in each element being used to denote the whole).

The standard form of an instrument for assessing cognitive preferences is made up of items which consist of a stem statement followed by four alternative "questions". These represent different kinds of interest which a person might have in following up the information in the stem.

A number of researchers have implied or stated a connection between cognitive preferences and "thinking styles" or "cognitive styles". Tamir (1981) for instance, writes that "cognitive preferences constitute a kind of cognitive style". Brown, in her review of research, notes several workers, who all make such a connection (Brown 1975).

In one of the few studies dealing with people beyond the normal age of formal education, Tamir (1977) produced evidence of the pervasiveness of cognitive preferences across different content areas and concluded that the construct had thus been shown to be valid. The people taking part in this study were teachers in a medical school, the content areas sampled being various disciplines within medicine. In particular terms the sample was "as expected" generally high with respect to *P* and *A*, although the Israeli-born were lower on this factor. Additionally, women scored higher than average on *Q*.

Another study, in this case of medical students, concerned the impact of curriculum design on expressed cognitive preferences. Boreham et al. (1985) compared a lecture which started with theory and then covered its medical applications with one in which that sequence was reversed. The outcome was in one respect clear, in that those who attended the application-to-theory lecture showed a greater subsequent preference for theoretical facts. A complication of the results was that the greater preference for theory was accompanied by poorer recall of that kind of content in the lecture.

These two studies together illustrate the idea behind the use of cognitive preference measures: that such preferences are to some degree generalized styles of cognition, not just specific choices in particular situations and that they can be materially affected by planned educational activities.

However, the validity of cognitive preferences has been sharply attacked, particularly by Brown (1975). She suggests that the evidence for the particular preferences presented by Heath in his original article is unconvincing. Certainly it might seem odd that Heath's categories have persisted with only infrequent alteration when it appears that they were derived from intuitive judgment. Apart from criticism of the statistical evidence for the validity of cognitive preferences, Brown has also pointed to the inventory items themselves and suggests that people might well respond to them on the basis of specific content and type of symbolism.

Looking at a different inventory, the Biology Cognitive Preference Inventory (BCPI) (Tamir 1981), her criticisms seem to be quite applicable. Tamir gives the following sample item:

Sugars reach the body by various foods:

1. The blood sugar level in healthy humans is constant and must not exceed 0.1%. (*P*)
2. Foods rich in carbohydrates are a good source of energy supply for animals. (*A*)
3. Since fats and proteins can also supply energy, it would be interesting to know if the body can exist without a supply of carbohydrates. (*Q*)
4. Carbohydrates are represented by the general formula $C_n(H_20)_n$. (*R*)

The justification for classifying option 1 as *P*rinciples and option 4 as *R*ecall seems to be purely to do with the form of the statements, and is not very convincing even in those terms. It seems quite plausible that someone might choose option 4 because of a wish to explore the matter of chemical structure in a general way. Equally, option 1 might easily be read as a simple statement of fact. Options 2 and 3 could also be read differently, though it is perhaps not so tempting to quarrel with these.

Tamir himself used the BCPI in a study designed to assess the relationship between a preference inventory and other kinds of measures of cognitive preference. These included teacher assessments, students' statements of their own preferences for various learning activities, their assessments of each others' suitability for different types of enquiry, and a measure of their scientific curiosity (Campbell's Scientific Curiosity Inventory). The results showed that, while these other measures generally did intercorrelate well, they did not correlate well with the cognitive preference categories of the BCPI. Tamir concludes that the existence of cognitive preference *R* is well-supported by different measures, and that it is shown to relate inversely to *Q* and *A*. However, *Q* and *A* are themselves not distinguished from each other clearly, and *P* correlates erratically with the other preferences. The relative isolation of the BCPI is not clearly explicable and is tentatively attributed to causes ranging from the possible multidimensionality of the universe of cognitive preferences, to the ipsative nature of the scoring system or to the low reliability of some of the other instruments used.

The validity of this particular inventory, and of preference categories generally, is thus somewhat doubtful so far as these results go, and Tamir suggests that some of the "classic" inventories might usefully be studied in conjunction with the other kinds of assessments.

3. *Field Dependence–Independence (FD–FI)*

Derived from laboratory studies of perception, field independence (FI) referred to the ability to disembed elements from the total perceptual field. Thus, people showing a high degree of FI were defined as those more able, for instance, to make accurate judgments about the verticality of a rod despite misleading background cues, or to locate given shapes which were hidden within larger figures. The distinction has subsequently been generalized to apply to mental style as a whole, including "understanding" rather than just literal "seeing". This more generalized meaning is now usually denoted by the terms "global" versus "analytic" or "articulated".

Those with such a generalized, articulated style are more likely to break away from seeing a hammer as an implement for striking and to use it instead as a weight or a support. Similarly, an articulated style goes with an ability to initiate new structure where none is given, as in the Rorschach inkblot test. As Witkin et al. (1977) point out, such academic disciplines as the social studies are very open to interpretation and leave the learner to find structure independently.

Table 1
Global and articulated learning styles

Global	Articulated
Draws fewer distinctions between concepts: "culture", "society", "civilization"	Draws more distinctions
Relatively poor at learning from a large-step programme. Comes up to par with a small-step version giving frequent subtests	Successful with either programme
Tends to use a "spectator" approach in concept-attainment tasks	Tends to use active hypothesis-testing. Shows sudden improvements
Learns less well when motivation is intrinsic. Does better when goals are socially set	Learns well under intrinsic motivation
Vulnerable to criticism	Copes more easily
Finds it harder to recall concepts when presented in the subordinate → superordinate order	Much less affected by order. Less need of advance organizers
As therapist or teacher, prefers to involve the clients/students. Values a "good" climate	More directive to clients/students. Does more of the talking. Less concerned about climate
As student teacher, learns better from video-modelling than from verbal instruction	Learns equally well by either method

The global style is associated with a greater tendency to stay within existing mental organizations and to be less ready to impose a structure on ambiguous or open material. What this style is positively associated with is greater attention and sensitivity to social cues.

Witkin et al. (1977) have drawn together a large number of studies comparing the global/articulated styles with particular reference to their bearing on education. A brief digest of some of that research is give in Table 1.

A frequent objection to the global/articulated distinction is that the characteristics ascribed to the global style are those of intellectual woolliness and that the distinction being made is not bipolar but one of better and worse. In other words, global/articulated measures are ability tests and not assessments of style. Witkin et al. (1977) acknowledge this as a problem and accept that most commonly used tests require an articulated (FI) approach for successful completion. They argue that it is perfectly possible for these to be acknowledged as tests of ability without compromising the idea of a bipolar style measure. What is missing is a corresponding range of tests that require a global approach, which would seem to concern primarily social attentiveness.

If these characteristics are related to success in significant tasks, then they too can be seen as abilities—which are complementary to the articulated ones. As an example Witkin et al. (1977) point to the case of nursing: in the surgical field, the "good" nurse is likely to score highly on tests of FI, but in psychiatric work he or she is likely to score higher on tests of FD.

Widiger et al. (1980) however are among those who remain sceptical. Their own correlational study puts emphasis on the suspicious tendency of style measures to correlate with standard tests of ability, and the lack of a clear negative correlation between articulated and global measures. On this last point it might be noted that global "measures" are nothing like so well-defined as articulated ones, so that a clear correlation of any kind would be less likely. This adds weight, in a sense to the point that there is no convincing "other end" to the supposedly bipolar concept of style.

This negative definition of the global type (that is, what people are like when they lack analytic ability) does seem to receive support from some of the research reported by Witkin et al. In this case army officers who were categorized as global were better at recognizing photographs of faces, but the analytic group could do as well when consciously intending to. This ability to behave, if necessary, in the "global" manner could also well account for the lack of negative correlation between global and analytic measures. Kogan (1973) reduces the ability/style dichotomy by suggesting a threefold classification of styles: those in which assessment is based on accuracy; those in which there is an implied value judgment—though not accuracy; those in which there is no sense at all of "better" or "worse".

4. *Holism and Serialism*

Both holist and serialist learning result in a structure of knowledge and, in Pask's system, neither is preferred. Using an ingenious and now well-known technique for making the detail of a learner's activity manifest, Pask and Scott (1972) define two distinct strategies. One, the serialist approach, consists of building up string-like sequences in which the elements are related at a low level of generality. The holist strategy, larger and looser in nature, is based on a higher level of generalization under which the details are subsumed. Serialism is a cautious strategy in that the step-by-step procedure reduces complexity. But its characteristic weakness ("pathology" is Pask's term) stems from its relative dependence on memorizing. If the memory load becomes excessive, learning is impaired. Holism also has the vice of its virtue: adventurous generalizing may become incautious and lead quickly to pervasive misunderstanding.

The pervasiveness of the preferred strategy is clear from Pask's (1976) experiment in which teaching programmes designed in holist and serialist styles were given "against the grain" to some learners and "with the grain" to others. Those who were confronted with incompatible materials strenuously remade them to their own liking.

These concepts have remained influential since their appearance, but have been less used by other researchers than some other learner typologies, probably due to the lack of a convenient, standard assessment instrument.

5. *Deep/Surface Processing*

In some ways akin to holism/serialism, the deep/surface distinction arose from a concern as much with how tests perform on learners as with how learners perform on tests. Marton and Säljö (1976a) distinguish two approaches amongst students to the reading of texts: a deep approach in which meaning is sought after and a surface approach which is confined to memorizing facts. In a subsequent report (1976b), they show how the choice between these approaches can depend on the kind of test which learners anticipate. Even tests designed to measure comprehension are likely to be approached in a rote, question-spotting manner—a process Marton and Säljö refer to as "technification".

6. *Concluding Remarks*

Mental styles, whether called learning styles or cognitive styles, constitute a diverse collection of instruments and labels. However, similar principles underly the different approaches, so that it is possible to conclude that a number of pervasive mental qualities are being glimpsed in the light of many different torches.

Part of the problem concerns to what extent style is a characteristic of the individual or a product of the situation. Obviously it must be both, as is shown in the work of Marton and Säljö. Pask holds to a useful distinction: that between "strategies" (holist/serialist) which are circumstantial manifestations, and two underlying "styles"—comprehension learning and operation learning. Once this interactional (or transactional) nature of styles is recognized, their proliferation is more understandable.

Much of the research on learning styles moves in the outwards direction, seeking more characteristics of performance in a variety of tasks so as to enhance the operational definition for a specific concept of style.

The question of the self and how we understand it is not much referred to in the attempts to classify learning activities. An exception to this is the work of Witkin et al. (1974, 1977). They suggest that field-independent (articulated) people are "...more likely to be aware of needs, feelings, attributes, which they experience as their own and as distinct from those of others". These may "provide internal frames of reference to which the person may adhere in dealing with external social referents". Such people may be said to have a self which is "segregated" and "structured". In constrast, global people show "...greater continuity between self and non-self" having "...a more globally experienced self".

At the root of the global/articulated dimension, Witkin et al. (1974) see the crucial difference as lying in the degree of "sense of separate identity". This line of

Table 2
Summary of the interrelationships between self and style

Kind of self-image	Some direct consequences	Consequent attitude to learning	Particular characteristics of learning performance noted from research studies	Corresponding cognitive or learning style labels
Articulated self-image. Self is differentiated clearly from non-self.	'Personalization' is facilitated. The environment is more differentiated. Action and feedback are more differentiated. Clarity and control are enhanced and the self made more secure.	Complexity, ambiguity, and uncertainty can be entertained without serious threat to the self. (Safe socio-economic conditions may reinforce such attitudes.)	Tolerant of criticism. Tolerant of social climate, therefore less socially attentive. Can sustain structure by idiosyncratic means. Less need for feedback or for supplied structure and sequencing. Better able to risk leaving the concrete and to deal in the abstract. More able to raise and test hypotheses. More able to question critically.	Abstract, 'comprehension'/'transformational' learning, deep-level processing, holist strategy, articulated style.
Global self-image. Self-image is relatively undifferentiated from non-self.	'Personalization' is hindered. The environment is less differentiated. Action and feedback are less distinct. Cognition is obscured and control made less certain. The self is left relatively insecure.	Complexity, ambiguity, and uncertainty need to be reduced in order to maintain security and clarity of self. (Unsafe socio-economic conditions may reinforce such attitudes.)	Less tolerant of criticism. Concerned about support from social climate, therefore more socially attentive. Needs more support supplied via feedback, structure and sequence. Less inclined to risk the uncertainties of the abstract. Keeps closer to the concrete. Less able to raise and test hypotheses. Less able to question critically.	Concrete, 'operations' learning, memorizing, surface-level processing, serialist strategy, and global style.

thinking has received some support from the concept developed in the 1980s "personalization" in learning. Schmeck and Meier (1984) show how deliberate involvement of the self-concept in the learning of information improves recall. They conclude that this practice has a self-reinforcing effect in that it helps elaborate the self-concept which thus becomes even more readily available for involvement in subsequent learning. Thomas and Bain (1984) also conclude from their questionnaire study that deep processing in general (that is, reflecting and relating) co-varies with personalizing.

The picture that emerges from this evidence of the articulated type as a learner is of a person with a clear, securely established image of the self which can facilitate learning and thus permit more adventurous strategies to be used. Thus, it is possible for the learner to tolerate longer delays of reinforcement or confirmation and, therefore, to gamble a little with hypotheses, to raise critical questions, to take bigger bites at unknown material, and to pursue less tangible objectives concerning principles, abstractions, and implicit meanings. This would correspond to Pask's use of the term "comprehension style".

By contrast the "operations style" arises from a less developed self-concept. Its primary aims are safety and the reduction of uncertainty. This is achieved by a kind of intellectual work-study of a traditional sort. Short-cycle activities yielding tangible results with a high degree of reliability, are preferred. This necessarily entails staying closer to the concrete as well as a working assumption that the acquisition of knowledge is a matter of bit-by-bit assembly. Table 2 is an attempt to summarize the interrelationships between self and style.

These considerations may now be linked with the "style or ability" question via a consideration of cross-cultural evidence. Gamble and Ginsberg (1981) argue that cross-cultural research gives little support to any trait-based idea of cognitive style, and suggest that social evolutionary adaptation is a more promising explanation of differences. When societies face conditions of difficulty and high risk they tend to play safe by relying on what is known to work and to seek knowledge in a limited, pragmatic way. Specifically, Gamble and Ginsberg describe the conditions which promote such an approach as high complexity of input–output relations, delayed feedback, and importance of outcome. This "knowing that" kind of knowledge corresponds to the global, unanalytic style and is possessed by all cultures. "Knowing how" corresponds to analytic knowledge, and will emerge only when the conditions of life are relatively favourable. The notion that cognitive style is an aspect of culture is reinforced by the finding that, while women are normally found to be more FD than men in Western societies, they appear to equal men in societies where they are assigned more active roles (Witkin et al. 1977).

While it is necessary to recognize that there is a conceptual distinction between abilities and styles, the evidence seems to warn us that, in practice, such a distinction may not be easy to make. Since what we customarily do is constrained by what we are able to do—or think we are able to do—and what we are able to do is constrained by what we have been accustomed to do, it is clear that ability and style cannot be simply disentangled. And still less simply when we realize that the entanglement is cultural and not merely a matter of individual circumstance. If ability is taken to refer to inborn, constitutional limits to performance, the distinction appears to be simpler. But then the uncertainties and conflicts about heredity versus environment are hardly an improvement on our original problem.

As Thomas and Bain (1984) point out, the customary method of intergroup comparison tends to oversimplify the question of style by confounding it with strategy. They suggest that within-learner studies are needed in order to distinguish what is consistent and what is variable. If this advice is taken it is possible reasonably to hope that the criticisms of the reliability and validity of style categories can at least be partway met.

Nonetheless for all of the problems, the excursion away from intellectual performance as something mainly to be scored, and towards the description of its varieties and habits does seem to have taken researchers closer to real life and learning.

Bibliography

Boreham N C, Ellis M R, Morgan C H 1985 The effect of sequence of instruction on students' cognitive preferences and recall in the context of a problem-oriented method of teaching. *Instr. Sci.* 13: 329–45

Brown S A 1975 Cognitive preferences in science: Their nature and analysis. *Stud. Sci. Educ.* 2: 43–65

Freedman R D, Stumpf S A 1980 Learning style theory: Less than meets the eye. *Acad. Manage. Rev.* 5

Fry R, Kolb D 1979 *New Directions for Experiential Learning*, Vol. 6: *Experiential Learning Theory and Learning Experiences in Liberal Arts Education*. Jossey-Bass, San Francisco, California

Gamble T J, Ginsberg P E 1981 Differentiation, cognition and social evolution. *J. Cross Cult. Psychol.* 12: 445–59

Heath R W 1964 Curriculum, cognition and educational measurements. *Educ. Psychol. Meas.* 24(2): 239–53

Hudson L 1966 *Contrary Imaginations*. Methuen, London

Kogan N 1973 Creativity and cognitive style: A life-span perspective. In: Baltes P B, Schaie K W (eds.) 1973 *Life-span Developmental Psychology: Personality and Socialization*. Academic Press, London

Kolb D 1981a Experiential learning theory and the Learning Style Inventory: A reply to Freedman and Stumpf. *Acad. Manage. Rev.*

Kolb D 1981b Future directions for learning style research. Paper prepared for Dalhousie University Conference on Learning Styles in Medical Education, June, Halifax, Nova Scotia

Marton F, Säljö R 1976a On qualitative differences in learning, Pt. I: Outcome and process. *Br. J. Educ. Psychol.* 46: 4–11

Marton F, Säljö R 1976b On qualitative differences in learning, Pt. II: Outcome as a function of the learner's conception of the task. *Br. J. Educ. Psychol.* 46: 115–27

Pask G 1976 Styles and strategies of learning. *Br. J. Educ. Psychol.* 46: 128–48

Pask G, Scott B C E 1972 Learning strategies and individual competence. *Int. J. Man–Machine Stud.* 4: 217–39
Schmeck R R, Meier S T 1984 Self-reference as a learning strategy and a learning style. *Appl. Cog. Psychol. [Human Learning]* 3: 9–17
Tamir P 1977 The relationship between cognitive preferences of students and their teachers. *J. Curric. Stud.* 9(1): 67–74
Tamir P 1981 Validation of cognitive preferences. *Br. Educ. Res. J.* 7(1): 37–49
Thomas P R, Bain J D 1984 Contextual dependence of learning approaches: The effects of assessments. *Hum. Learn.* 3: 227-40
Widiger T A, Knutdson R M, Rorer L G 1980 Convergent and discriminant validity of measures of cognitive style and abilities. *J. Pers. Soc. Psychol.* 39: 116–29
Witkin H A, Dyk R B, Taterson H F, Goodenough D R, Karp S A 1974 *Psychological Differentiation*. Erlbaum, Potomac, Maryland
Witkin H A, Moor C A, Goodenough D R, Cox P W 1977 Field-dependent and field-independent cognitive styles and their educational implications. *Rev. Educ. Res.* 47(1): 1–64

Group Learning

G. G. Darkenwald

This article is principally concerned with the discussion group as a means of facilitating individual learning. Task-oriented groups concerned, for example, with problem solving or with decision making will not be discussed.

1. Theories of Group Behavior

The goal of a general theory of group behavior has yet to be attained. As noted by Cartwright and Zander (1968 p. 24), many classificatory schemes have been proposed, typically by selecting a few properties (for example, size, level of intimacy) "to define 'types' of groups on the basis of whether these properties are present or absent. . . . Usually only dichotomies have resulted: formal–informal, primary–secondary, . . . temporary–permanent, consensual–symbiotic." Such dichotomies seem of little value for furthering our understanding of adult learning in groups.

Theoretical orientations or approaches to the study of group dynamics may have greater utility for contributing to our understanding of adult learning in groups than classification schemes. Among the orientations described by Cartwright and Zander (1968 pp. 26–27), field theory, interaction theory, and systems theory are particularly germane to a basic understanding of the structure and process dimensions of learning groups. Nonetheless, it must be concluded that neither general theoretical typologies nor orientations offer much in the way of direct implications for scholars and practitioners concerned with adult learning groups.

2. Learning in Groups

Nearly all organized adult learning occurs in some kind of group format—classes, workshops, conferences, symposia, and so on. Each of these forms of group learning is appropriate and effective for achieving certain educational purposes, such as information transmission, problem solving, and clarifying issues or problems. The concern here, however, is with the small, participatory learning group, namely the discussion group and, to a lesser extent, the sensitivity training or T-group. A defining characteristic of such groups is mutual education through the free and open sharing of ideas, feelings, and attitudes with respect to a specific issue, topic, or, in the case of T-groups, situation. Small groups of an instrumental, rather than strictly educational nature, do not fall within the scope of this article's concerns. They include problem-solving groups, planning groups, and decision-making groups, among others. Admittedly, adults can and do learn through participation in instrumental groups, but learning is incidental to the principal purposes of such groups.

2.1 Affective and Cognitive Learning

Adult learning groups provide opportunities for both affective and cognitive learning. Typically, these two dimensions of learning are intertwined. This is particularly so in discussion groups, where cognitive learning, such as clarification of concepts or issues, is primary but often accompanied by changes in members' attitudes.

One variant of the discussion group is primarily geared to attitude and behavior change. Of course, cognitive learning occurs in such groups, but is merely instrumental, not an end in itself. Brookfield (1985 p. 58) makes the trenchant observation that "discussions of this nature seem to contradict the essential condition of discussion in that they are undertaken in order to achieve previously specified objectives. To this extent, they are not free or open discussions but exercises in attitudinal manipulation."

Sensitivity training or T-groups are defined by Houle (1972 p. 235) as efforts to "deepen the awareness of individuals concerning their own natures and their relationships with other people, usually by the use of a group process in which the members simultaneously interact with one another and analyze that interaction." Clearly, the learning that occurs in sensitivity training groups is primarily affective. Even so, the affective changes brought about through participation in T-groups necessarily involve cognitive learning, especially in the analysis component of the group process.

3. Discussion Groups

Rogers (1971 p. 174) defines discussion as a "situation where students and teacher can and do make an open, equal, and personal response to a book,. . . social trend, or anything else which needs interpretation to take it beyond a factual statement." Zander (1982 p. 30) further observes that "in a group discussion it is assumed that one does not learn from personal experiences simply by having them; one learns from hearing about the lives or ideas of others. . . . Each member integrates others' thoughts with his own views in whatever way he finds sensible for him."

The specific aims or purposes of group discussion have been conceived in a variety of ways, but in general such formulations are similar. The following list, proposed by Zander, (1982 p. 31) is offered here as illustrative. According to Zander, five purposes are served by group discussion:

(a) It helps members recognize what they do not know but should;

(b) It is an occasion for members to get answers to questions;

(c) It lets members get advice on matters that bother them;

(d) It lets persons share ideas and derive a common wisdom;

(e) It is a way for members to learn about one another as persons.

Other purposes commonly noted in the literature are to clarify complex concepts, issues, or problems and gain a deeper understanding of them.

The degree to which the teacher or leader exerts control over the group is perhaps the most salient factor in determining the nature and outcomes of group activities. Leader control is best conceived as a continuum ranging from virtually complete control—"teaching in which students may raise questions or comment, but the general direction is under the strict control of the teacher" (Bligh 1972 p. 150)—to total abandonment of control, resulting in a self-directed learning group. The definition of group discussion set forth above seems incompatible with strict teacher control. The self-directed learning group, on the other hand, comes closest to the ideal. Although somewhat doctrinaire, the following observation (Brookfield 1985 p. 57) bears directly on this issue:

> A necessary condition of discussion is that there be no preconceived agenda, no cognitive path to be charted, no previously specified objectives. . . . Hence guided discussion is conceptual nonsense in that discussion is free and open by definition.

The position taken in this article is that strict leader control is the equivalent of didactic teaching and thus incompatible with the fundamental nature of group discussion. Guided discussion that is not strictly leader controlled does, however, qualify as a variant of the discussion method. Furthermore, as noted below, the discussion leader plays a key role in any discussion group, including those that eventually become totally self-directed.

4. Discussion Leadership

In any kind of group, the leader, if only in the initial stages designed to lead to total group self-direction, must be able to balance initiating behaviors (task orientation) with supportive behaviors (group maintenance or strengthening). The task function involves coordinating and facilitating group activities to enhance goal achievement. The maintenance function is concerned with strengthening relationships among members by "providing warmth, friendliness; conciliating, resolving conflict, relieving tension, providing personal help, counsel, encouragement; showing understanding, tolerance of different points of view. . ." (Newcomb et al. 1965 p. 481).

Thibaut and Kelley (1959) raise the question of whether task and maintenance functions can or should be performed by the same person. They conclude, based on the research evidence, that for most groups, performance of these functions by different individuals enhances group functioning. Pankowski (1984 p. 21) points out that self-directed groups are almost always characterized by a member who presses for task accomplishment and another who performs the maintenance role, pressing for the satisfaction of the emotional/affective needs of group members.

Space precludes a discussion of the literature concerning the specific responsibilities and roles of discussion group leaders. Zander (1982 p. 31) stresses the leader's role in handling three procedural problems: "reluctance of members to take part; members' lack of ideas during discussion; and conditions in the group that restrain ready give and take." With respect to the first procedural problem, Zander (1982 p. 21) points out that "a leader need not try to get everyone talking; generally only 30 percent of those present do most of the commenting in a comfortable and efficient group." One would expect a higher participation rate than 30 percent in leaderless or self-directed discussion groups, unless broader participation is precluded by group size.

Many experts in group discussion methods stress a different perspective on the leader's principal responsibility, which, in short, is gradually to abandon the leadership role and become just another member of a self-directed discussion group. Haiman (1955 p. 9) succinctly summarizes this viewpoint: "The ultimate aim of a discussion leader in a learning situation should be to gain full status as a *member* of the group by working himself out of the leader's role."

The functioning and effectiveness of discussion groups are influenced significantly by factors other than leadership. These factors have to do with variations in the characteristics of attributes of discussion groups as described below.

5. Salient Attributes of Discussion Groups

All groups possess certain general properties or attributes that have profound effects on the manner in which they function and on the quality of group interaction and outcomes. The following attributes are discussed briefly below: proximity, composition, size, and cohesion.

5.1 Proximity

Physical proximity of group members enhances a sense of group as well as group unity, provided that group size is not too large. "People more readily see themselves as members of a group if there are not too many. . .; less than twenty-five or, better, close to seven" (Zander 1982 p. 2).

5.2 Composition

Homogeneous groups, those whose members share similar characteristics, tend to foster member satisfaction and a group sense. Zander (1982 p. 3) asserts that persons whose values and beliefs "do not fit together will have a hard time forming a strong group." Common sense suggests, however, that too much homogeneity can have the undesirable effect of minimizing the divergent experiences and viewpoints so central to effective group discussion.

5.3 Size

Pankowski (1984 pp. 12–13) notes that research findings reveal that because "larger groups require more control and are generally less friendly, they tend to be less productive." Zander (1982 p. 34) observes that "the size of a group greatly affects how often a member can talk and how much he expects others will contribute. . . . It is hard to develop a full discussion in a meeting of more than twenty-five members; discussion proceeds better in a group of closer to seven or so." Practical experience suggests that groups of fewer than six or seven are too small to sustain a productive group discussion. Seven to twelve seems to be the optimal group size.

5.4 Cohesion

Research has found "group effectiveness to be related to cohesiveness, which is reflected in such things as mutual liking among group members, member satisfaction, and other positive reactions to the group" (Pankowski 1984 p. 18). Zander (1982 pp. 4–5) defines group cohesiveness as "the strength of members' desire to remain members," adding that "as cohesiveness becomes stronger in a group, members talk more readily, listen more carefully, influence one another more often, volunteer more frequently, and adhere to group standards more closely."

Proximity, composition, size, and cohesion are interrelated attributes of discussion groups. They reinforce one another in a synergistic way to promote or hinder group functioning and outcomes.

6. Problems and Issues

Only one source (Brookfield 1985) could be located that provided a thoughtful critique of the assumptions and practices central to group discussion.

According to Brookfield, three cognitive outcomes are generally assumed to result from the use of the discussion method. They are: development of powers of analytic clarity; increased appreciation of the complexity of a topic gained by listening to differing viewpoints; and increased identification with the subject matter in question through stimulation of interest. Brookfield asserts that these outcomes are seldom realized in actual practice. He argues, for example, that clarification of thought is contingent on discussion occurring under emotionally stable circumstances, but for many adults discussion is extremely threatening. Appreciation of the complexities of a topic or issue is often precluded by the rapid pace of many discussion groups, which can lead to confusion rather than enlightenment. Brookfield's thesis is that many of the claims made with respect to the cognitive outcomes of discussion are unsubstantiated.

Other concerns raised by Brookfield (1985) include the often low quality of participants' contributions with respect to their relevance to the topic or issue under consideration and their lack of cumulative development/coherence over time, and the many dysfunctional aspects of the psychodynamics of discussion groups.

Brookfield (1985 p. 65) proposes four conditions that, if met, are likely to foster meaningful and productive discussions:

> First, group members need to devise and to subscribe to an appropriate moral culture for group discussion. . . . This means that the group must spend some time agreeing upon a set of procedural rules concerning the manner in which equity of participation is to be realized. Second, discussion leaders can exercise a degree of forethought regarding the selection of materials that are to form the substantive focus of group discussions. . . . Third, the leader should be well versed both in the subject matter to be covered and in the principles of group dynamics. . . . Fourth, discussion participants can be prepared for discussion. . . through the development of reasoning skills (so that inconsistencies and ambiguities in argument can be detected) and through the improvement of communication abilities (so that ideas can be articulated accurately).

Despite the problems and shortcomings identified by Brookfield, group discussion, properly conducted, can be a powerful tool for promoting adult learning. In best practice, as he himself asserts, it may well be the adult education method par excellence.

Bibliography

Bligh D A 1972 *What's the Use of Lectures?* Penguin Books, Harmondsworth

Brookfield S D 1985 Discussion as an effective educational

method. In: Rosenblum S H (ed.) 1985 *Involving Adults in the Educational Process*. Jossey-Bass, San Francisco, California
Cartwright D, Zander A 1968 *Group Dynamics: Research and Theory*. Harper and Row, New York
Haiman F S 1955 The leader's role. In: Adult Education Association of the USA (eds.) 1955 *How to Lead Discussions*. Adult Eduction Association of the USA, Washington, DC pp. 9–12
Hill W F 1969 *Learning thru Discussion*. Sage, Beverly Hills, California
Houle C O 1972 *The Design of Education*. Jossey-Bass, San Francisco, California
Knowles M, Knowles H 1972 *Introduction to Group Dynamics*. Association Press, New York
Legge D 1971 Discussion methods. In: Stephens M D, Roderick G W (eds.) 1971 *Teaching Techniques in Adult Education*. David and Charles, Newton Abbot, pp. 75–89
Newcomb T M, Turner R H, Converse P E 1965 *Social Psychology: The Study of Human Interaction*. Holt, Rinehart and Winston, New York
Pankowski M L 1984 Creating participatory, task-oriented learning environments. In: Sork T J (ed.) 1984 *Designing and Implementing Effective Workshops*. Jossey-Bass, San Francisco, California
Rogers J 1971 *Adults Learning*. Penguin Books, Harmondsworth
Thibaut J W, Kelley H H 1959 *The Social Psychology of Groups*. Wiley, New York
Zander A 1982 *Making Groups Effective*. Jossey-Bass, San Francisco, California

New Therapies: Adult Education Applications

R. Smith

The new therapies include a wide variety of procedures for expanding consciousness, increasing self-awareness, tapping unused potential, coping with personal problems, and discovering how to learn more effectively. To the extent that these procedures derive from a coherent theoretical framework, they appear to be grounded in both humanistic and transpersonal psychology, although links to the behavioral and Freudian schools as well as to parapsychology can also be found (Roberts 1975). Some of the procedures that educators employ are meditation, hypnosis, relaxation, concentration, biofeedback, human relations training, guided fantasy, dream interpretation, centering, physical exercise, the martial arts, psychodelic drugs, and "whole brain knowing."

During the first and second decades after the Second World War, education involving the concerns mentioned above tended to be concentrated in face-to-face groups and to be called laboratory or sensitivity training. Much theory and practice emanated from such centers as the Tavistock Institution (UK), Esalen (US), and the National Training Laboratories (US). The following desired outcomes were identified: increased sensitivity to emotional reactions and expressions in self and others, increased ability to perceive and learn through attention to feelings, clarification of values, and the making of action more congruent with professed values, increased skills in team building, and problem solving and action. From about 1965, laboratory training tended to move towards "therapy for normals," with increased emphasis on fostering intrapersonal insight and growth; the sensitivity or encounter group supplanted the renowned T-Group as the training vehicle (Benne et al. 1975). More recently those kinds of training for the release of human potential and for personal and group growth have been supplemented by the new therapies, using a wider range of concepts and procedures.

1. Selected Areas of Application

1.1 Meditation

Meditation refers to methods which involve a conscious attempt to focus attention in a nonanalytical manner. Some 16 million persons in the United States were believed to practice either meditation or yoga in 1976. The rigorous meditation discipline associated with Eastern traditions can lead to powerful subjective experiences and altered states of consciousness. Less rigorous applications aim at self-actualization, improved interpersonal relations, and increasing congruence between one's real and ideal self. In addition to such clinical applications as treatment of neurosis, anxiety, and addiction, meditation is used to help people gain increased self-control and ability to follow through on decisions (Shapiro 1980). People are taught to use meditation for inducing a relatively calm, receptive state of mind when engaged in learning or demonstrating what they have learned. Various other relaxation techniques have been shown to have some beneficial effects—for example deep or rhythmic breathing, stretching, and the "letting go" of tense muscles (Roberts and Clark 1975).

1.2 Biofeedback

Biofeedback enables persons to discern and voluntarily control certain physiological functions. It is a concept, a process, and a training method. Heart rate, blood pressure, muscle tension, and brain waves are among the physiological functions that people can learn to control. The early work in biofeedback owed much to operant conditioning theory (rewarding innate biological activities for appropriate performance). Clinical applications aim at preventing illness and enabling individuals to cope with stress, hyperactivity, insomnia, headache, or drug abuse. Neuromuscular re-education is another application, with successful results being reported for spastic conditions and for stroke victims. Training involves providing the learner with information about internal physiological processes and states (by means of instruments or self-monitoring techniques) and help in learning to gain control over those processes (Brown 1977).

1.3 Imaging and Visualizing

The link between mind and body can be utilized to produce behavioral change for enhancing performance. By picturing or imaging a perfect or successful swing of a bat or racquet, for instance, the individual can learn to swing more effectively. Visualizing oneself delivering a lecture with confidence can help overcome stage fright.

These techniques may also be used to control pain and increase stamina and endurance. Individuals are taught to concentrate and to employ the mind to "command" the body. In addition to the world of sport, experimentation in several European nations is aimed at improving health, decreasing the length of treatment time, and aiding in interpersonal relations. Educational efforts may be referred to as autogenics training or sophrology (Ostrander and Schroeder 1979).

1.4 Fantasy and Dreams

Dreams can be said to represent a metaphor of compressed information. They constitute an altered state of consciousness that many regard as a pathway to understanding of self and to problem solving. Some people use dreams systematically as a basis for making major personal decisions. Dream interpretation is at the heart of the Senoi (Malaysia) people's way of life and is seen by British anthropologist Kilton Stewart as critical to their relatively sound mental health and viable social system, in which conflict and crime are reportedly nonexistent (Roberts 1975). Fantasy is assumed to reveal repressed aspects of personality and to constitute a comparable avenue to self-knowledge and to creative expression.

Educators can provide help in recalling dreams and can encourage that they be shared with others. People can learn to link dreams to fantasy and imagination by "finishing" interrupted dreams in short essays or verbal narratives. Recording and analyzing dreams are ways of externalizing recurring personal themes. Training concerning fantasies also includes learning to analyze them in a search for meaning. Also employed are guided exercises in imagining oneself as something else, say a plant or an infant, and seeking to be sensitive to everything in the imagined environment.

2. Additional Implications for Educators

As these procedures become increasingly legitimized by research and institutional adaptations, adult educators can be expected to increase the use of the new therapies. Yoga, meditation, martial arts, and rhythmic exercise courses are already staples of many public programming agencies and private schools. Increasing uses for organizational and human resource development also seem likely.

The new therapies may be increasingly incorporated into higher education, graduate school curricula, and postprofessional education. There is already evidence of medical schools teaching the future physician to teach biofeedback techniques to the patient and of future counselors and school teachers learning to employ guided fantasy and dream interpretation to foster students' self-understanding and self-expression. Practicing elementary and secondary teachers will require inservice education if new understandings of intuitive learning, "whole brain knowing," and mind–body relationships are to be incorporated into classroom instruction (Ferguson 1980). Proponents of transpersonal psychology envision school systems with less emphasis on content and more on processes for discovering and fostering creative potential, with more flexible structures, greater emphasis on inner experience as a focus for learning, and evaluation based on the individual's potential as well as on norms.

2.1 Accelerated Learning

The most startling and publicized effects of the new therapies on education have to do with accelerated learning. The Bulgarian psychologist, Georgi Lozanov, provided the leadership with techniques which enable large quantities of information to be learned and satisfactorily retained in relatively short periods of time. The techniques include concentration and relaxation training, rhythmic breathing exercises, and music to obtain such exceptional results as a sevenfold increase in the rate of foreign language learning by college students and the learning of up to 100 new scientific terms by secondary-school students (Ostrander and Schroeder 1979).

The experiments of Lozanov and others have led to considerable research and development in Europe and North America. Since the dissemination of new methods takes place more rapidly in nonformal education, the techniques for accelerated learning will be widely employed and further evaluated in the setting of adult education.

2.2 Learning How to Learn

The new therapies have potential for the individual seeking to direct personal learning projects and to learn how to learn (Smith 1982, 1983). From the point of view of content, the therapies represent skills and disciplines to be learned as avenues to better physical and mental health and to self-realization. From the process point of view, the adult with awareness of and control over physical and mental processes possesses tools for learning with power, stamina, and confidence for a variety of purposes and in a variety of settings. Such persons are potentially open to new experience and capable of coping with the accelerating rate of social change that confronts contemporary men and women.

Bibliography

Benne K D (ed.) et al. 1975 *The Laboratory Method of Changing and Learning: Theory and Application*. Science and Behavior Books, Palo Alto, California

Brown B B 1977 *Stress and the Art of Biofeedback*. Harper and Row, New York

Ferguson M 1980 *The Aquarian Conspiracy: Personal and Social Transformation in the 1980s*. Tarcher, Los Angeles, California

Lozanov G 1978 *Suggestology and Outlines of Suggestopedy*. Gordon and Breach, New York

Ostrander S, Schroeder L 1979 *Superlearning*. Delacorte, New York

Roberts T B (ed.) 1975 *Four Psychologies Applied to Education: Freudian, Behavioral, Humanistic, Transpersonal*. Wiley, New York

Roberts T B, Clark F V 1975 *Transpersonal Psychology in Education*. Phi Delta Kappa Educational Foundation, Bloomington, Indiana

Shapiro D H 1980 *Meditation, Self-regulation Strategy and Altered States of Consciousness: A Scientific/Personal Exploration*. Aldine, New York

Smith R M 1982 *Learning How to Learn: Applied Theory for Adults*. Cambridge University Press, New York

Smith R M 1983 *Helping Adults Learn How to Learn*. Jossey-Bass, San Francisco, California

Integrated Rural Development: Community Organization

C. Amaratunga

The term "integrated rural development" first became popular in the early 1970s when it became fashionable and financially practical for development agencies and institutions to work in a cooperative way. The term "community organization" has many meanings and many different methodologies. The most striking characteristic of the community organization process is its orientation and commitment to various dependency and liberation ideologies. In this respect, community organization goes beyond traditional community development methods in that it attempts to liberate the peasant classes from the sources of social and economic oppression.

1. The World Conference on Agrarian Reform and Rural Development (WCARRD)

In 1979, the United Nation's world conference on Agrarian Reform and Rural Development proclaimed that rural citizens the world over are entitled to certain fundamental rights: poverty relief, growth with equity, people's participation, national self-reliance, and ecological harmony (FAO 1979). The WCARRD proposals for development provided a new perspective on the strategy of integrated rural development and community organization.

The United Nations WCARRD Program of Action set the stage for community organization projects in the 1980s. The WCARRD asserted that rural adults, in particular those marginal groups such as women, illiterates, the elderly, the unemployed, and so on, be incorporated as the focal groups in development planning, instead of mere recipients of services as in the past. The outcome has been the conceptualization of rural development programs which consider both the social and economic context of the rural adult. The WCARRD contribution to development philosophy has encouraged the analysis of the etiology of rural poverty within the context of land reform and tenure systems, market and exchange systems, agrotechnology, and other socioeconomic factors.

In Asia, for example, concern for the integration of women into the development process has led to recognition of the woman's economic role and contribution to the rural household. A follow-up country workshop in 1980 on the WCARRD Plan of Action in India recommended that the delivery of resources for rural development should be channeled through women's community organizations as opposed to the more conventional extension education routes which tend to provide service to male farmers.

The promotion of agro-based and income-generating activities for the rural poor has been recognized as an important strategy for community organization projects, particularly for the redistribution of wealth and resources to marginal groups. Recognition of the need for growth with equity is a critical step in the planning of integrated rural development programs. The United Nations, through the consultation process, has articulated a progressive strategy for development which recognizes the causes of rural poverty, the need to relieve the rural poor of their domestic and agricultural burdens, and the importance of giving adequate consideration to providing sources of credit, raw materials, markets, and training resources. These resources are considered to be the prerequisite conditions for achieving the goal of fair and equitable integrated rural development. Lastly, the importance of ecological harmony is recognized as a central tenet of the integrated development process.

2. Integrated Rural Development

The integrated rural development process can be described as both an organizational and a political activity which reflects the social policy of funding and executing agencies as well as government philosophy. The integrated rural development approach, which encourages interagency cooperation and goal setting, utilizes a comprehensive and holistic strategy in dealing with the problems of the rural poor. In any given rural community, the cycle of poverty is a complex phenomenon with many interlocking facets. In the integrated rural development approach, development agencies pool expertise and resources in order to tackle the roots of a problem which may be manifest in many different areas. For example, agricultural extension services may be employed to raise the income and productivity of the rural farm family. At the same time, a health education and nutrition program may be started to assist the rural family to improve and maintain an adequate standard of health, nutrition, and sanitation. Together, these two approaches result in an increase in agricultural production which has been assisted by the improved health status of the family agricultural workers. The overall effect should be an improved quality of life for the rural farm family. It is important to note that the unit of development in the integrated rural development approach is the family—and not just the head of the household.

In 1975, development experts from Southeast Asia met in Makati, Philippines, to review and assess the impact of the integrated approach on local rural development. After assessing integrated development projects in Bangladesh, Indonesia, Malaysia, Korea, and the Philippines, the participants shared experiences of projects which utilized an integrated approach to nutrition, family planning, agricultural cooperatives, and so on. Research, training, and information exchange were identified as three important areas for future collaboration. In keeping with the concept of integration, they also recommended that governments recognize the need to incorporate nutrition as an important socioeconomic priority in the rural development process (Campbell 1975).

Integrated rural development programs share the problems of other development programs. The fact that several development organizations may cooperate on a community program demands extra efforts in coordinating communications, needs assessment, and the setting of common development goals. The integrated development approach also reflects the inherent problems of other institutional-based program areas; namely the need to balance concern with program accountability, advocacy for increased resources, and program evaluation aimed at improving existing services.

3. Community Organization

The process of community organization serves to strengthen and complement the integral rural development strategy. Like that of community development, it is essentially a process of human development, that is, the ability of citizens to design and redesign their environment (Biddle and Biddle 1965). The ability of community members to control their social, economic, and physical environment is an important aspect of the community organization activity. One of the first steps in the community organization process therefore is the raising of awareness or consciousness of the rural poor with respect to the social and economic realities of their environment. Their act of mental liberation and communication has become recognized as the process of conscientization, one of the principal proponents of which is Paolo Freire.

Different methods have been used with varying degrees of success in raising the awareness levels of the rural adult, particularly the "Freire Brazilian literacy" approach, in which photographs are used to portray the environment, and the "rural animation" method of Senegal in which dialogue, role playing, and sociodrama are used to depict social reality. These methods and others have been used successfully in mobilizing and organizing rural adult groups in developing as well as developed nations.

The rural animation and dialogue methods are essential steps in establishing a communication base with the rural adult. As the perception and awareness level of the rural adult develops, a process of politicizing takes place in which the oppressed individual becomes more assertive in stating needs and desired social and economic states. The identification of environmental reality is a prerequisite stage in this process. Gradually, the rural adult learns to take more control of the family, work, and community environments. The community organization method provides an assertive strategy for change in which the dignity and intellect of the rural resident are respected and valued as important contributions to the change process.

4. Common Elements of the Self-help Process

The community organization process is essentially the development of a creative partnership between the community and government. During the early phases of development, the responsibility for socioeconomic and environmental improvements is transferred gradually from the agencies of change to the rural residents themselves. The aim of the self-help process according to WCARRD, is improved social welfare through economic "growth with equity." In order to promote and build the partnership between the community and government, several preparatory phases can be identified.

One of the most important steps in the self-help process has been the creation of cooperative groups, specifically the creation of village committees or similar community decision-making bodies. The World Health Organization for example has advocated the formation of rural health committees to assist the community to become responsible for environmental factors such as clean water supplies, sewage and sanitation, and so on. In the United States, community voluntary groups have long played an important and active role in the prevention and treatment of mental illness, life-style diseases such as alcoholism and drug dependency, and the promotion of physical fitness. These voluntary community committees have an important advocacy role and influence on social policy and program services.

In the self-help process, community members are brought together for the purpose of discussing and identifying common problems. Usually a change agent, sometimes referred to as an animateur, a catalyst, or a facilitator, coordinates the dialogue process. As community members begin to take control of the problem the animateur gradually withdraws from the problem-solving process. Ultimately, the community membership assumes responsibility for managing and controlling the local program.

The basic elements of the self-help process are common to most decision-making activities. Once the community members are mobilized and have identified the cause or source of the problem, they are helped to set realistic objectives for cooperative action. This involves assessing the present situation in relation to the ideal or desired goal. Various solutions are tried and evaluated until a satisfactory result is achieved. The self-help philosophy works best in an environment in which the opinion, intelligence, and experience of the community members are respected.

One of the most interesting examples of the self-help process in action can be found in Sri Lanka in the Sarvodaya Shramadana Movement. This program has achieved exceptional success in agro-industry integrated projects, health education, agriculture production, vocational training, and other integrated rural development activities in over 5,000 villages in Sri Lanka (Hewage and Radcliffe 1977).

As rural communities such as those in Sri Lanka begin to develop and take greater responsibility for social, economic, and environmental programs, the need for training and human resources development will continue to grow. Similarly, the stages of the self-help process which form the basis of community organization activity, that is, the consultation process, needs assessment, trial, adoption, and evaluation of new ideas and practices, will continue to require support from the voluntary, national, and international sector. The need for organizational integration will become more important as more and more rural development projects are undertaken in developing countries by community organizations and institutions.

In the 1980s, the emphasis on integrated rural development will continue to be of a socioeconomic nature. Although many rural development programs have achieved the desired goals of income generation, economic growth, population control, improved sanitation, and so on, planners should not lose sight of the overall goal of development which is the improved quality of life. The community organization process and integrated rural development planning provide a practical formula for identifying the causes of rural poverty and for achieving consensus at the community level as to which approaches for development are most compatible with local values and ways of life.

See also: Integrated Rural Development: Specialized Training Programs

Bibliography

Bang S 1975 Integrated approaches for development programs. *Integrated Approach to Local Rural Development*. International Development Research Centre, Ottawa, Ontario

Biddle W W, Biddle L J 1965 *The Community Development Process: The Rediscovery of Local Initiative*. Holt, Rinehart and Winston, New York

Campbell M (ed.) 1975 *Integrated Approach to Local Rural Development*. Report of an interdisciplinary seminar, Makati, Philippines, 31 March–3 April, 1975. International Developmental Research Centre, Ottawa, Ontario

Food and Agriculture Organization (FAO) 1979 *World Conference on Agrarian Reform and Rural Development*. Food and Agriculture Organization of the United Nations, Rome

Freire P 1973 *Education for Critical Consciousness*. Seabury, New York

Hewage L G, Radcliffe D J 1977 The relevance of culture in adult education and development. *Convergence* 10(2): 63–74

LaBelle T J 1977 Liberation, development, and rural nonformal education. *Non-formal Education and Rural Poor*. Michigan State University Press, East Lansing, Michigan

"Campaign": A Technique in Adult Education

R. Kidd and B. L. Hall

A technique in adult education first used in the 1940s (the radio forum) has been given a new significance and a new name: the radio learning group campaign. It is a nonformal education strategy allowing citizen participation and consultation on various national issues. It is a systematic means for communicating information on major national issues to large numbers of people. It brings together people who would not normally participate in organized educational activity for a short-term programme of group study, often in people's homes. In some cases it serves to mobilize mass participation in community action.

The programme lasts from five to ten weeks and deals with a topic of major importance for very large numbers of people. The participants are organized into groups of between 5 and 20 by a network of field workers who recruit, train, and support the people in these groups.

Each learning group meets once or twice a week over the campaign period under the leadership of a trained group leader. Meetings involve listening to a specially prepared radio programme, studying the supporting printed materials, discussing this information and the issues involved, agreeing on an appropriate action (to be taken by group members), making comments, and raising questions on the issues (feedback). These are sent to the campaign organizers for use in the formulation of policy (consultation).

Each radio learning group operates without a subject expert. The radio learning group leader is a group organizer and discussion facilitator, rather than a "teacher" in the usual sense. The source of learning comes from the study materials and the experience and insights of members who share in the discussion. The group leader's job is to organize the meeting and lead the group through the various learning steps (e.g. radio listening, study guide reading, and discussion).

The primary aim of a radio learning group campaign is to promote awareness and to help people understand major issues, policies, or programmes. The underlying rationale is that participation in development requires that people understand what is going on around them. Another common aim is often to get people's views on a new public policy, and in this case, participation requires that people not only be told about new programmes and policies, but requires that they are consulted and involved in shaping them. Some campaigns mobilize local collective action.

In conception, the radio learning group combines the study circle idea (i.e. locally controlled discussion groups) with the possibilities of mass media as a focus and support for study and discussion. It is different from a radio listening group in which information is passively assimilated. The radio learning group starts with information from a central authority, then discusses and debates these ideas and decides on its own response to it.

This combination of mass media and "self-help" group study is of particular value in the Third World. It enables an essentially uneducated populace to have access to expert knowledge. They begin to understand the issues, without a network of suitably qualified teachers. The radio provides the information which would normally be provided by a teacher. The group study helps people analyse this information and relate it to their own lives.

Radio learning group campaigns depend upon a number of preconditions. There must be active political support from the national leaders and the study topic must be of significant interest to engage the attention of large numbers of people. There must be sufficient financial resources (e.g. the 1976 campaign in Botswana cost US $500,000) and the high-priority attention of all who are involved. Organization requires the collaborative effort of several groups (e.g. broadcasters, adult educators, extension networks, and party networks). The recruitment of group members and group-leader training can be organized by existing networks of field workers (e.g. agricultural extension workers and trained health educators). Sufficient time has to be allowed for all of the preparatory tasks before the campaign begins.

A radio learning group campaign is a modification of an educational method which was first developed and used in Canada. Farm Forum (1942–1962) and Citizens' Forum (1944–1962) were radio programmes which were organized for farmers and urban groups respectively. This method was so successful that several Third World nations took up the idea, among them Tanzania and Botswana. However, the latter decided to use the radio learning group idea in a campaign format, focusing on one major national issue over a 5 to 10 week period.

They argued that a year-round, continuous programme was not suitable for their adult population. They also maintained that a short-term campaign would be easier to organize and would attract a much larger audience. Many people who would not take part in an ongoing programme covering a wide range of themes would, and did, participate in short-term campaigns on topics of major national importance. For example, the 1976 "Consultation" campaign in Botswana (on the government's land reform proposals) involved one in six adults in the country (55,000 participants) in over 3,500 radio learning groups which produced 25,000 feedback reports giving their reactions to the proposals. This grass-roots feedback resulted in significant changes to the government's programme (Kidd and Etherington 1978).

In Tanzania the 1973 "Action" campaign on health mobilized over two million participants in over 100,000 radio learning groups which carried out over one million community health projects: destroying mosquito-breeding areas, constructing toilets, digging wells, and boiling/filtering water (Hall 1978).

Radio learning group campaigns have been organized in the Third World in China, Tanzania, Botswana, Somalia, and Nicaragua. Campaign topics have included: sanitation and preventative health (China, Tanzania), civic education (Botswana, Tanzania), land tenure reform proposals (Botswana), and reafforestation (Tanzania). Study group campaigns have also been organized in Europe and North America. Two recent examples are a Swedish consultation in 1980 on the nuclear power issue and a Canadian study campaign in 1979 on economic and political issues.

Bibliography

Byram M 1981 Popular participation in the mass media: An appraisal of a participatory approach to educational radio. *Can. Int. Educ.* 10(2): 48–64

Crowley D, Etherington A, Kidd R 1978 *Radio Learning Group Manual.* Friedrich-Ebert-Stiftung, Bonn

Grenholm L H 1975 *Radio Study Group Campaigns in the United Republic of Tanzania.* International Bureau of Education, Paris

Hall B 1978 *Mtu ni Afya: Tanzania's Health Campaign.* Clearinghouse for Development Communication, Washington, DC

Hall B L, Dodds T 1974 *Voices for Development: The Tanzanian National Radio Study Campaigns.* International Extension College, Cambridge

Jamison D T, McAnany E G 1978 *Radio for Education and Development.* Sage, New York

Kidd R, Etherington A 1978 Radio learning campaigns: The

Botswana experience. *Convergence* 11(3–4): 83–92
Spain P L, Jamison D T, McAnany E G (eds.) 1977 *Radio for Education and Development: Case Studies.* World Bank Staff Working Paper No. 266. World Bank, Washington, DC

Study Circles in Sweden

R. Uddman

The Swedish study circle must be considered in two distinct ways: firstly as an important instrument in the education of Swedish people, and secondly as a method that has stimulated emulation in other countries. Unfortunately, there have not been rigorous comparative studies of the impact of the study circle outside of Sweden. However, it is known that this effect has been so considerable that it might be compared to the "folk high school" and the "farm forum" as an activity which was not always adopted in a precise institutional form but which markedly influenced the thinking about adult education in many countries.

Study circles are found in Norway, Denmark, and Finland and to some extent in Tanzania and other African countries, usually in developing countries associated with the cooperative movement. But influences can also be traced to other European countries, for example to Russia in the early part of the century, and to North America.

The relationship of the study circle to the total endeavour of popular movements such as churches and trade unions, and its impact on educating citizens about social and political issues, are matters that several countries are currently examining.

This article deals primarily with Sweden, but the issues raised have implications for most countries.

1. *Definition*

A study circle is a circle of friends or associates assembled for common and planned studies of a predetermined subject or problem area.

In Sweden, state grants are payable if the study circle has an approved leader and follows an approved plan of study. Studies must total at least 20 hours for the entire course; typically there are not more than two meetings per week and each meeting lasts for up to three hours. The number of participants per meeting must be at least five and not more than 20, including the leader.

Grants are payable to adult education associations responsible for approving the work of study circles. There are 10 such associations affiliated to the popular movements.

2. *Historical Background*

During the second half of the nineteenth century, popular movements grew up in Sweden under the inspiration of an international exchange of ideas, particularly with the United Kingdom and the United States. First came the free church movement, followed by the temperance movement and the labour movement. It soon became clear than an encouragement of popular education would help to waken and animate the people and make members better equipped to serve in their organizations, and that it would raise what is now called the "quality of life".

The real impetus came in 1902, when Oscar Olsson, a secondary-school teacher belonging to the Good Templar Order, established the first study circle in Lund, inspired by a visit to the United States and observation of the successful Chautauqua movement. The study circle as envisaged by Olsson would elect a leader from among its own members, take literature as its starting point, and acquire knowledge in the course of free conversation. Meetings could be held in the participants' homes if necessary, and there were to be as few as five participants. Furthermore, the participants were to choose their own study material and plan their own studies. An economically viable form was thus established; all the members of the circle were friends and associates, one of them would be the leader, and overhead costs were confined to the purchase of materials, which at that time consisted of books. As early as 1905, the Riksdag (Swedish parliament) voted to give grants for the purchase of books, on condition that the books were kept by the study circle which received the grant and were also made available to the general public. Thus were laid the foundations of Sweden's public library system.

The study circle as a method of training members and leaders and as a means of informing and activating the general public soon came to be employed by all popular movements in Sweden. At a very early stage each of the popular movements developed special organizational arrangements for educational activities—usually in the form of an adult education association.

A state committee appointed in 1944 made recommendations which resulted in a scheme of national grants for study circle activities. This scheme, which came into operation in 1947, covered salaries of the circle leaders, the cost of study materials, and administration. For decades, study circles have played a prominent part in political education and the formation of public opinion in Sweden.

From the 1960s onwards, public institutions have chosen to distribute information on vital social issues through the medium of these organized adult education associations. Large-scale campaigns of this kind have, for example, included information about the new school system, preparations for the change from left-hand to right-hand road traffic, and preparations for the energy referendum, which involved very widespread distribution of information concerning the various aspects of nuclear power.

The adult education associations were also involved in the reform of adult education which took place in Sweden during the 1960s. This was partly in recognition of the fact that the study circle constituted free and voluntary work in contrast to the curricular activities, usually salaried, of the school system. Moreover, in a study circle the participants' experience is utilized as a resource in addition to books and study material. Autonomous planning ensures that activities are closely adapted to the interests and personal aptitudes of the learners. Special grants have made it possible from 1970 onwards for study circles in Swedish, English, mathematics, and civics (corresponding to studies in grade 9) to be undertaken at virtually no cost to the participants. The adult education associations also became involved in the education of immigrants, and were made eligible for state subsidies enabling immigrants to be taught Swedish and civics free of charge. Debates in parliament during the 1960s heavily underlined the needs of disadvantaged groups and resulted in a growth of activities among the disabled, pensioners, immigrants, and the undereducated. During the 1970s the number of study hours qualifying for state grants rose from 5.5 million to 12 million. The early 1970s were characterized by a growth of public grants, partly towards measures of social action, and increased financial support for educational activities for all people who wished to learn.

3. Focus and Design

Oscar Olsson, who had been convinced from the very outset that study circles were for the masses and not for an elite of potential leaders, vigorously emphasized their absolute self-determination regarding both the choice of subjects and study methods, and also the unlimited autonomy of each individual study circle. Above all, however, he stressed that the book was the real, central instrument of education. He was, of course, referring to great literature, not just to textbooks. It should be noted that the literature concerned was to a very great extent of the kind whereby the authors' social involvement was conveyed via the study circles. The focus of study circle activities was also profoundly influenced by the well-known writer and popular educator Ellen Key, whose books, articles, and lectures at the turn of the century underlined the necessity of training in aesthetic awareness and augmenting aesthetic knowledge as part of the struggle for the liberation of the masses. She firmly believed that the arts would enrich people's lives, and in this way contributed towards the legal and financial support of culture as an important ingredient in the programmes of the popular movements and, therefore, of all popular education.

The system of state grants introduced in 1947 had brought about a substantial qualitative improvement to the arts. For example, amateur theatricals, which had previously been a very chaotic sector, began in 1952 a more systematic approach adapted to the study circle.

The next major development in the aesthetic sphere concerned arts and crafts and came in the late 1950s and early 1960s when intensive work resulted in a new response to creative activity, with good practice being regarded as something on a level with theoretical studies. It was agreed that studies should convey knowledge, enhance understanding of materials, techniques, colour, and form, acquaint the participants with various means of expression, and increase their ability to express themselves and understand expression within the aesthetic sphere. In addition, an introduction was provided to the historical background of each subject and its relation to other arts and to society, techniques were taught and, not least, the participants' vocabularies were augmented so that they would be better able to communicate about or concretize the problems with which the various subjects were concerned.

4. Period of Innovation

The decade of the 1950s was in many ways a period of innovation and development. This was much facilitated by the 1953 Adult Education Seminar under the leadership of Torsten Husén, whose international contacts brought the participants, representing all the adult education associations, a wealth of information concerning current development work all over the world. The main emphasis of this work was on problems of method, and following the 1958 Seminar a book was published entitled *Adult Learning*, with a very practical emphasis which came to play an important part in the training of leaders in all the adult education associations and in the design of new study material.

There is no uniform code of pedagogical practices for the study circles. Activities in recent years, involving more than 3 million participants and sponsored by 10 adult education associations with almost 1,500 local branches throughout the country present a highly variegated picture. The concept of free and voluntary activities characterizing Swedish popular education has been taken by participants and sponsors to mean that the necessary state grants must be available for activities designed by the participants to suit the essential needs of each circle. Some didactic debate was inspired for a short time by Freire's methodology, in which many people found an exciting development of the methodology of the study circle.

There has always existed a well-supported interest in international studies. An expansion of these activities was made possible in the 1970s by a special grant for information concerning the developing countries. Development work in the first half of the 1970s attained its peak in the so-called Caribou Project, a multimedia project involving cooperation between broadcasting media and the adult education associations, concerning the problems of the Third World, with particular reference to Tanzania. Among other things this project yielded a new experience of ways of integrating international aspects with study material in other subject fields as well, for example, languages, arts and crafts, and social affairs.

5. The Present and Future

In recent years, the Swedish adult education associations have organized over 300,000 study circles with more than three million participants, 61 percent of whom were women. Study hours have totalled as much as 11 million. Of the study circles, 39 percent were "priority" circles, that is, courses at compulsory school level in Swedish, English, mathematics, civics, and trade union education. There were almost 4,000 circles at university level, including a small number following the syllabi of various universities and colleges.

Study circles are reported in the following subject groups: behaviour sciences/humanities; aesthetic subjects; business economics/commerce/office skills; mathematics/natural science; medicine/health care/nursing; social sciences/information; languages; technology. The aesthetic groups bulk largest, about one-third of the total. In addition to the circles mentioned above, the adult education associations organized at least 14,000 study circles in Swedish for immigrants which attracted nearly 150,000 participants.

Clearly, the study circle enterprise is well-established. Observers from abroad are examining its potential for educating citizens respecting social and public issues, and most international questions, as well as providing basic education and aesthetic experience.

See also: Adult Education Legislation in Western Europe; Workers' Education

Bibliography

Adult Education Associations 1980 *Statistical Reports*. Statistiska Centralbyrån, Stockholm

1980 Alla Studiecirklar blir inte studiecirklar [All Study Circles Do Not Become Study Circles]. Raben Sjogren Forlag, Stockholm

Gatenheim E W 1979 *Studiecirkeln 75*. Sober Forlags AB, Stockholm

Kurland N D 1979–80 The Scandinavian study circle: An idea for the US? *College Board Rev.* 114: 20–25

Strawn W 1977 *Sweden's Study Associations*. Swedish Institute, Stockholm

Titmus C J 1981 *Strategies for Adult Education: Practices in Western Europe*. Open University, Milton Keynes

Media Support in Adult Education

J. Robinson and B. Groombridge

In this article the media refer to those means of communication that reach large numbers of people, namely national and regional newspapers, popular magazines, national and local radio, and television (by open transmission, cable system, or video recording). The material conveyed by these means of communication is described as the content or the programmes.

The most remarkable feature of the support these media give to adult learning is the multiplicity of ways in which it works. Any idea that it is always a didactic function is far from the truth. Occasionally the media do work didactically; but that function is generally far down the list of priorities.

The following sections illustrate some of the ways in which the media support adult learning.

1. By Broadening Understanding and Enlarging Interests Among the Adult Community as a Whole

This is a feature of the total content of the media: from topical news to long-term research reports; from ancient history to world geography; from immediate actuality to timeless imagination; from scientific discovery to aesthetic exploration; from intellectual challenges to feats of physical skill; from lighthearted satire to serious discussion; and so on. The content is continually variable—much of it will be unreliable and some may well be deliberately distorted. The degree of reliability of content will depend largely on who controls the various media and for what direct and indirect purposes. Certainly there needs to be an informed critical response to the media, and much of the content will then be seen to be not mindstretching, but rather mindcramping. But overall and in most countries, whatever the political, social, and cultural control of the media, the total effect of news coverage, of articles, documentaries, and discussions, of stories, plays, and drama serials, of cartoons, sketches, and competitions, is to broaden the experience of the whole community, to stimulate a wealth of new interests, and to prepare the way for more systematic study.

Various aspects of this total effect have been examined by Hoggart (1958), Williams (1958), McLuhan (1964), Scupham (1967), Groombridge (1972), and other writers on the media.

2. By Providing a Wider Acceptance of the Total Concept of Learning Continuing Throughout Life

By openly encouraging the development of new interests and the exploration of new areas of experience, the media constantly work either overtly or implicitly against the narrow but deeply ingrained view that learning is a matter only for children and for an elite group of young people. This is an immense aid to the agencies of adult education, which have a huge uphill task changing this narrow view, to which popular opinion has been conditioned by centuries of associating education solely with child development. How quickly that popular opinion may change, so that resources for adult continuing education will be seen to be as necessary to a flourishing community, as are resources for schools and higher education—particularly during a period of galloping technology—will depend a great deal on the success of the media in encouraging this dynamic view of society and breaking down the old static model. This is perhaps the most vital of all the services that the media can perform for education as a whole (while not neglecting their services to children and young people). It is a service that is needed in every country, whatever the present level of educational provision, and a service that has not been sufficiently highlighted in most writing about the media and education.

3. By Encouraging Individuals into more Systematic Learning

For many years it has been recognized that magazine articles and radio and television programmes have stimulated interests in many readers, listeners, and viewers who have then pursued them in more systematic ways, by further reading and by joining classes, study circles, clubs, or societies. This happened at a more academic level when the British Broadcasting Corporation (BBC) in the United Kingdom and Sveriges Radio in Sweden developed their language courses and there was a boom in enrolment in language classes and study circles throughout the United Kingdom and Scandinavia; it happened when a number of universities and colleges in the United States offered credit courses carried partly by radio and television, and partly in newspapers; and it happened in Japan through broadcast and correspondence courses; in Kenya and Malaysia through teacher-updating programmes; and in many countries through the development of Open University-type projects. But it has also been shown to work at the basic levels of adult literacy and numeracy, in the learning of a host country language by immigrant groups, and in basic parental education, in countries with as varied educational provision as the United Kingdom and Italy, India and Brazil. In most cases the media have performed this sensitive task by raising hopes and building confidence, and sometimes by providing confidential referral schemes, rather than by providing direct instruction. A similar service has happened at more practical levels, for example in the radio farm forums in Tanzania and in the SITE Experiment projects in village development in India.

Examples of several of these effects in Europe have been described in studies for the Commission of the European Communities (Kaye and Harry 1982).

4. By Publicizing Local Opportunities for Learning

This is a purpose related to the previous one, but distinguishable from it. It is a purpose particularly suitable for local journalism and local broadcasting and has been amply demonstrated in all parts of the world—especially where the local media are imbued with a strong sense of public service and community involvement, and not just with local commercial interests. The various forms that this publicity can take, including straightforward newspaper display and broadcast announcements, interviews with adult learners who are enjoying their courses, letters in the correspondence columns, phone-in enquiries on radio, telephone and postal enquiry services following such publicity, and many other imaginative ways, can now be illustrated in most countries that have local media. And the service is not limited to local media. It can be found in national and regional broadcasting, in articles and enquiry services in women's magazines and journals devoted to special fields of interest, and in national newspapers from time to time.

5. By Providing Direct Learning Materials for Individual Learning

This introduces a directly didactic purpose for the first time in this summary; and it is not one to be ignored. Especially when the learning materials are offered through several media, for example radio, television, and printed coursebooks, it is clear that the media can provide a direct learning experience of a very satisfactory kind. Perhaps the earliest clear evidence for this came from the broadcasting-and-correspondence courses for adults developed by NHK, the Japanese Broadcasting Corporation, in the early 1960s. This was achieved through the foundation of the NHK Gakuen Correspondence High School in association with the education departments of the broadcasting corporation. It was discovered through surveys among adult students that those who were studying by broadcasts and correspondence showed a success rate in the high school examinations twice as high as that of the correspondence students alone. And that differential has continued over subsequent years. At about the same time the Chicago Television College recorded similar results for its television-based students. The same impression would have been conveyed by many broadcasting organizations in Europe from the modern language courses they had developed in a similar way—without the opportunity to assess them on examination results. Since then there is plenty of impressionistic evidence of such direct learning services in practical skills like cooking, dressmaking, home maintenance, and gardening: at least if continued demand and response is a fair indication of success. Inevitably it is more difficult to evaluate the success of such direct teaching services in basic education and community development in Third World countries; but some projects have been evaluated and have shown encouraging results.

6. *By Providing the Media Components in More Complex Multimedia Learning Schemes*

The Open University in the United Kingdom is probably the clearest example of this mode of support, for, from the inception it was agreed that radio and television should be integral components of each course. While opinions vary among Open University students about the essential value of the broadcast contribution—and this, of course, varies from one course to another—there is no doubt at all that the university has been able to include many courses that would not have been possible without the use of radio and television. In addition to their use in individual courses, the contribution that they make to general communication between staff and students and to enhancing the corporate life of the University can hardly be exaggerated. And now there are many Open University-type systems, in all parts of the world. Some of them manage without the involvement of the public media; but about half of them involve broadcasting to some degree, and some quite extensively.

The Allama Iqbal Open University in Pakistan, for example, already uses radio extensively, for practical instruction in vegetable growing and poultry farming, for updating teachers in curricula and methods, and for general education in mathematics, science, social science, English, and Urdu; and it is beginning to make use of television. The Universidad Nacional de Educacion a Distancia in Spain also uses radio extensively for university and professional courses for adults, and is planning to use television. The Universidad Nacional Abierta in Venezuela, the Free University of Iran, and the University of Mid-America, based in Nebraska, all use both media very widely. The Open Learning Institute in British Columbia has planned to make considerable use of cable television.

In addition to these single-institution systems, consortia schemes have developed in many countries and several of these have made use of the public media. Some examples of these are the California Educational Television Consortium, which links public television series with the state universities, the BBC's collaboration with the Trades Union Congress Education Department and the National Extension College, and the *Zeitungskolleg* in the Federal Republic of Germany, which collaborates with regional newspapers in the publication of academic articles and supports these with individual tuition.

Many detailed case studies of the use of broadcasting in open learning systems were collected for UNESCO during the 1960s and the 1970s. Schramm et al. (1967), Mackenzie et al. (1975), and Hawkridge and Robinson (1982) are a few examples of these.

7. *By Providing Channels and Opportunities for Student Feedback and Learner Exchange*

One of the great drawbacks of the public media in the learning process is the basically one-way nature of their communication. But, by arranging phone-in programmes on radio and television, extensive correspondence columns in newspapers and magazines, and programmes and articles prepared by students, it is possible to make the media available for the expression of direct feedback from the students and to allow the learners to discuss the content and the method of their courses among themselves. Most of the Open University type systems make provision for this as do many of the consortia systems. Inevitably it is a small minority of the learners who take advantage of this opportunity, and that fact has to be noted carefully in any interpretation of the views expressed. But the fact that it can happen at all is an important encouragement to learner involvement. It is probable that the development of lightweight technology in recording systems, word processing, and fibre-optics will make the electronic exchange of learners' views much more extensive and available in the near future.

8. *By Providing Learning Materials for Use by the Group Tutor or Class Teacher in Organized Adult Education*

Both general content and specifically educational content may be useful for the group tutor and there is widespread use of both. They can be a rich source of discussion material and provide a welcome variation in class activity, whether in academic, social, or practical subjects. Broadcast programmes are normally used in recorded form, since they are unlikely to be broadcast at precisely the right time and the tutor will probably wish to see the programmes first. That is by no means strictly necessary and some of the most creative results have developed when tutor and students have responded to a programme together, following their respective preparation. Newspaper and magazine articles are likely to involve photocopying. Broadcast recording and photocopying both raise copyright issues in most countries. Some countries in Europe and Africa have virtually dismissed copyright where educational use is concerned; but in most countries it is still illegal to copy for group tuition use, unless prior permission has been given. In a number of European countries, copyright is previously cleared by the producing organization for educational use of educational content, but not for the use of general content. Copyright is a problem that will have to be resolved more universally in the future.

There is also the question of experience and training in the use of media material. Most tutors have had some direct training in the use of books; but few have been trained in the use of television, radio, and newspapers for direct learning purposes. Again some tutors take to it more readily than others, but in most countries there is a real need for more effective training in the use of the popular media.

9. By Encouraging Individuals to Offer their Services as Voluntary or Part-time Tutors in Adult Education

This is a purpose that has developed particularly strongly since the media became more widely used to serve educationally deprived groups such as nonreaders, the disabled, and immigrants with no working knowledge of the host country language. In all these situations the use of volunteer tutors working on a one-to-one basis in the learner's home or some other informal setting has proved to be of immense value. A basic training for such volunteers has usually been possible, but enough volunteers have not always come forward in the right places. The public media have been used very effectively to encourage the right kind of people to come forward for this work. So in the United Kingdom the referral service for adult nonreaders was also used as a confidential recruiting service for volunteer tutors. Similar methods have been used in other countries, and altogether it has been a surprising new bonus in media support.

10. By Providing Training Material for Voluntary and Part-time Tutors

Basic training has generally been available for these part-time tutors, but more often than not it is both uneven and largely improvised. And in any specialized area there are likely to be very specialized skills involved, such as teaching reading, teaching a second language, teaching the skills of birth control and parenthood, and so on. It has been shown that the public media can help this training process considerably, by providing specialized, topical, nonpersonal training material that makes the work of the trainer much less arduous and the training process more successful.

In all these ways the media have shown that they can and do give valuable support to the whole range of adult learning, group learning, and individual learning, formal and nonformal. Every country can learn from others how these services can be extended, and there is immense scope for development in the future.

Bibliography

Groombridge B 1972 *Television and the People: A Programme for Democratic Participation*. Penguin, Harmondsworth

Hawkridge D, Robinson J 1982 *Organizing Educational Broadcasting*. Croom Helm, London

Hoggart R 1958 *The Uses of Literacy*. Chatto and Windus, London

Kaye A, Harry K (eds.) 1982 *Using the Media for Adult Basic Education*. Croom Helm, London

Mackenzie N I, Postgate R S, Scupham J 1975 *Open Learning: Systems and Problems in Post-secondary Education*. UNESCO, Paris

McLuhan H M 1964 *Understanding Media: The Extensions of Man*. Routledge and Kegan Paul, London

Schramm W L, Coombs P, Kahnert F, Lyle J 1967 *The New Media: Memo to Educational Planners*. UNESCO, Paris

Scupham J 1967 *Broadcasting and the Community*. Watts, London

Williams R 1958 *Culture and Society, 1780–1950*. Chatto and Windus, London

Computers

P. G. Buttedahl

Computers have already been substantially used in the education of adults. Now the microcomputer opens the possibility for the individual adult learner to control his or her own learning. Its use raises, however, important social and ethical questions, as well as technical ones. Little research has so far been done into its function in adult education, but it will clearly play an important role and cause certain basic assumptions about adult education to be re-examined.

Due to the microcomputer's recent massive availability, little time has been devoted to research about its implications and its effectiveness. Thus, any discussion of the use of microcomputers and their impact on adult education is speculative in nature and based on practical observations from the few examples that have been implemented recently.

Initial attempts to introduce the computer in education were influenced by Skinnerian techniques of linear programming. The first computer-assisted instruction (CAI) program, using linear programming, was developed by Rath, Anderson, and Brainerd in 1958. In the initial stages, the role of computers was limited to that of a sophisticated teaching machine which replicated the existing models of programmed instruction. The introduction of time-sharing modes of computer technology in the late 1960s, however, permitted direct and immediate interaction with the computer.

In 1960 the University of Illinois and Control Data Corporation initiated one of the most widely used CAI projects—PLATO (Programmed Logic for Automatic Teacher Operations), which has developed a network of learning centers in more than 50 cities throughout the United States. PLATO has had a number of adult education applications. For example, it is presently being used by the Reading Pennsylvania Area Community College to teach basic reading skills to inadequately educated adults. It is also being used by American Airlines for pilot training and retraining as new aircraft and instruments are introduced. Utility companies make use of PLATO simulations to train plant operators and employees to handle normal and emergency procedures with regard to mechanical, electrical, and nuclear systems. Furthermore, first-line plant supervisors in the health care industry have interacted with simulations to learn how better to solve quality-control problems present in a pharmaceutical company.

Computer-assisted instruction has also been used by NASA for quite a few years. It makes use of the capacity of the computer to provide simulations of possible outcomes of real-life decisions. Consequently, shuttle astronauts train extensively on computer-controlled simulators. Many air forces make use of simulations by staging battles which are meticulously monitored by computers. The aerospace industry also utilizes computer-based instruction where the computer serves as the delivery mode for all the information required as well as testing student achievement.

In 1972, Brigham Young University and the MITRE Corporation began developing the Time-shared, Interactive Computer-controlled Information Television system—TICCIT. The system can deliver individualized instruction for up to 128 students simultaneously, due to its time-sharing capacity. The TICCIT system allows the student to exercise much of the control over his or her own learning experience. Students are also encouraged to interact at their own pace and are presented with opportunities to assess their advancement through practice and testing. TICCIT has been widely used by universities, community colleges, business, and industry as well as by the military.

1. The Microcomputer

Since 1975 a large number of schools and universities have adopted microcomputers for use in the classroom setting. The educational use is to provide learners with programming skills as well as to provide a variety of educational content ranging from accounting and bookkeeping to music composition. In continuing medical education a series of in-depth, computer-based seminars have been developed which keep doctors informed of new developments and help them meet special continuing education requirements. Some computer programs simulate dialogue between the physician and the expert in a particular area of specialization.

One of the most successful applications of computer and microcomputer technology in adult education has been the use of the technology in adult basic education. A report presented at the National Adult Education Association's national conference held at Anaheim, California, in October 1981 articulated the success encountered. The study revealed that:

> There was overall a 90 percent efficiency level in learners gaining an average of one grade level for each 20 hours of computer-assisted instruction. The average gains in reading (using the TABE test) were 0.73 for the first 20 hours of instruction. This result translates into a gain of almost three quarters of a grade level on the average for every 20 hours of computer-assisted instruction. (Judd 1982 p. 54)

Learners in this reading and writing skill development program used the PLATO system, which is now being made available in a microcomputer format.

When it comes to the management of activities the microcomputer has a number of advantages and possibilities because it can often eliminate redundant tasks. It can assist in organizing and cataloging information by making it easily accessible in very little time. It has enormous potential as a delivery mode of instructional content. For example, the capacity of the microcomputer to simulate real-life events has proven to be one of its great assets. Adult learners can thereby practice tasks, relatively inexpensively, by the use of simulations.

Furthermore, microcomputers can facilitate personalized and individualized instruction. Since research has shown that adults often learn more effectively when educational content meets specific needs at a particular place and time the potential of the computer to destandardize educational delivery is one of its most exciting aspects. At the same time, instruction is self-paced, allows for a nonthreatening environment, and provides the opportunity for immediate feedback. In addition, use of the microcomputer for educational purposes spreads computer literacy.

The microcomputer can be particularly helpful to students with special needs. It is anticipated that "computer literacy will soon be a basic requirement of anyone involved in rehabilitation, particularly of individuals with severe or multiple disabilities" (Hortin 1982 p. 98).

The microcomputer's capacity to deliver instruction in an appropriate setting and gear instruction to a pace chosen by the learner in an individualized manner could have much to do with improving the quality of life of many adult learners.

There are, however, a number of problems related to the use of microcomputers for educational purposes. In spite of the microcomputer's widespread availability, high overall costs coupled with frequent equipment malfunctions are issues of concern to educators, particularly those who are in charge of administering adult education programs.

In addition to problems associated with cost and servicing, a significant concern, particularly for adult educators, is the availability and the appropriateness of software or what is referred to by educationists as "courseware." There is presently a considerable amount of it available to the consumer. However, many programs lack quality. Instructors need to utilize the same critical judgment in choosing courseware as they utilize in choosing appropriate textbooks or other teaching materials. The best way to exercise control over the learning content is to be involved in its production. If this is not feasible the educator may try to determine who has been involved in software production. Often it is necessary to scrutinize a diversity of resources utilized in the development of courseware, due to the highly specialized nature of software production.

2. Is the Technology Dehumanizing?

Meierhenry (1982) points out that the field of adult education is resistant to the use of microcomputer technology, and he suggests that this may be related to the impact of sociological theories upon the field. Sociology emphasizes the impact of social relationships on behavior. Hence, it is natural that great emphasis is placed on human interactions, small group involvement and participation. The utilization of computer technology for instructional purposes appears to be inconsistent with sociological theory since "individualized instruction" is one of the key features of computer-assisted learning.

Although individualized instruction is one of the selling features of the technology, many people are concerned that individuals will become isolated and inept at dealing with interpersonal interactions. Most of the research to date has been related to the workplace; however it does provide some food for thought for educators. Recent study illustrates that the blue collar workers and those least involved in decision making will be those most affected by technological innovations (Goleman 1983). For example, it has been pointed out that millworkers who were accustomed to operating heavy equipment in order to perform their trade are now pushing buttons to control robots to do the work. The workers are satisfied with being relieved of much of their heavy labor. They complain, however, about being isolated from their associates. Their interactions are limited because their work has taken on more of a "cerebral," rather than a physical, demand. This supports the idea that human beings are generally social beings with an instinctual desire and need for human stimulation. On the other hand, is it possible that the technology could actually bring together individuals who are isolated? The promise of burgeoning computer "networks" which would facilitate interaction among individuals who have microcomputer interlinkages, much like the telephone system, is an exciting, and yet to many, a frightening aspect of the potential of the technology.

Since microcomputers are invading homes as radio and television did previously and since business, industry, the military, and various professions are making considerable use of microcomputers to develop and deliver adult education, they cannot be rejected. It will therefore be necessary to develop ways of using them which will overcome the problems of isolation.

3. Control of the Learning Environment and Process

There are other social and ethical questions raised by computer use which are particularly relevant to adult education.

The field and practice of adult education stresses making educational content relevant to specific learner needs. Consequently, there is an emphasis on placing control of the learning environment into the hands of the adult learner. The growth of the home computer market, as the price drops, is seen by some as making this possible on a hitherto unknown scale. However, they overlook the question of who controls the information flow. Historically, the priority of education has been to transmit information, or educational content, from source to learner. As Emerson (1978) writes:

> In American society, most of the information flow follows the broadcast, noninteractive model; for example, radio, television, and newspapers. Accordingly, information is distributed from its central source, and there is little opportunity for people to reply or to influence the content, what they read and hear and see.

This may happen with the programs available for home computers and the ethical question is therefore posed, who is or who should be responsible for making decisions regarding the kinds of educational content made available to the learner and is the content relevant to learner needs? (Collins 1982). Some believe that they should be community based because of the potential for such projects to provide a variety of meaningful, contextually relevant adult learning experiences and for encouraging learner control of how, what, where, and when he or she embarks upon educational activities.

In the field of enquiry known as "technological psychology" the control issue is being studied from the perspective of the locus of control in the decision-making process. There is interest in the implicitness of decision rules that are the framework utilized for developing computer programs. The decision rules are the implicit assumptions and biases that are the unalterable facets of the program. All of the information input into the programmed computer must be congruent with the rules. Computerized decision making must be continually assessed in order to ensure that the decision rules that are inherent in the program are relevant to the situation that they are to be applied to. Likewise, the decisions that guide the development of instructional content must be continually evaluated and the instructional content updated.

Ideally, microcomputer availability will encourage a freedom of access whereby most people in industrialized countries will be able to acquire and utilize a microcomputer for their own purposes. At present few of those who have them are aware of their full potential.

Another problem has been posed:

> What will happen to those vast numbers of adults who do not have enough money to buy a microcomputer and thus do not have ready access to the information sources? Will we develop a society that is even more widely split between the haves and have nots? (Apps 1982 p. 5)

It has become evident that countries in the developing world such as Argentina, Brazil, Kenya, and India, to name a few, are interested in keeping pace with these innovations by desperately attempting to produce microcomputers and introduce them not only into business and industry, but into their educational systems as well.

4. Research Trends

Much of the research that has been done emanates from social psychology, computer science, communications, and education in general. The field of adult education has been relatively slow at assuming a role that could influence it. Work related to the use of computers in schools, however, also has implications for adult educators.

A number of studies have concentrated upon the need to develop computer literacy in educators. The Stanford studies examined this issue and in 1968 Donald Michael looked at the computer literacy issue along with the social ramifications of computer interactions. Michael anticipated that there would be a growing separation between people working with computers and the rest of society. Michael's concern at that time was that ignorance of computers would render people as functionally illiterate in the same way as ignorance of reading, writing, and arithmetic. The above contention is supported by the more recent belief that children who are not exposed to computers or do not learn to use them will be considered "illiterate" in coming decades.

Stevens (1980) surveyed Nebraska educators on their knowledge and attitudes towards computers. Some 90 percent agreed that people need to be aware of the societal role of computers. More than 70 percent thought that their students should be able to demonstrate an understanding of computers. These educators recognized the need; however 90 percent of them did not believe that they were qualified to teach computer literacy. Only 30 percent of the teachers surveyed indicated that they felt at ease with computers.

Dickerson and Pritchard (1981) have confirmed the findings that it is difficult to produce trained educators at a rate that can keep up with the production and utilization of computers. Dennis also supports the theme that teacher training is lagging far behind advancing technology (Dennis et al. 1977).

Generally speaking, the above studies indicate that there is great concern that educators are not adequately trained to prepare their students for life in a computer-dependent society. Much of the research being done at the present can be classified as being for the most part speculative, in that it focuses on articulating future scenarios for educational applications, but there also is "human factor" research occurring, combining behavioral and applied research. Behavioral research has made an attempt to simulate "real" life settings by transferring the workplace to the laboratory. Applied research is involved in studying individuals in their social, cultural, and/or work settings. There remains, however, much to be done. The adult educator has a responsibility to the learner to be aware of research being done in other fields as well as a responsibility to stimulate research more applicable to the field and practice of adult education.

5. Implications

Undoubtedly, the growing speed in which technological developments have taken hold of society poses a tremendous burden for the field of adult education. Adult educators as well as adult learners are affected by the changes and transformations caused by these technological developments. The sophistication of the existing information and communication technology impacts directly with the traditional view that adult education should involve group interactions such as courses, workshops, and seminars. The rapid growth of distance education, and the exploration of alternative ways to deliver instruction are a demonstration that the basic assumptions of the field are being challenged and are in need of revision.

Research is incomplete, but the existing evidence suggests that microcomputers as a delivery mode for educational content may fulfill the needs of the adult learner by providing relevant learning experiences which are nonthreatening in nature. The adult learner can be encouraged to pursue learning experiences at his or her own pace, obtaining instant feedback about performance as well as convenient access to remedial instruction as it becomes needed. Moreover, although microcomputers are not yet readily available due to cost factors, a large number of learners spread throughout remote areas could be provided with access to learning experiences in spite of distance and isolation.

As microcomputer technology becomes widely available, extensive work will need to be done in the field of adult education in reorienting interest of the field towards the production of knowledge and the provision of services in adult education. Clearly, the adult educator must facilitate and help the adult learner to cope with advances and appropriate uses of modern technology. Therefore, effort should be invested by the adult educator in

(a) the acquisition of a comprehensive understanding of technological innovations and the development of computer literacy;

(b) the identification of relevant research questions;

(c) the identification of relevant skills required to interact with technological innovations in a meaningful way, and

(d) the promotion and facilitation of learning experiences that will enable the adult learner to achieve a critical understanding of microcomputer technology and its impact upon society.

Finally, lifelong learning will become a reality inasmuch as the provision of educational services can now be rendered continuously through a global system that can accommodate individual differences, individual needs, and anticipate the needs of the future with the technology of today—a task greatly enhanced by the use of the microcomputer.

Bibliography

Apps J 1982 Foreword. In: Guelette D G (ed.) 1982 *Microcomputers for Adult Learning: Potentials and Perils*. Follett, Chicago, Illinois

Collins M 1982 Multiple realities, media and adult learning. *Media Adult Learn*. 4 (1): 30–35

Dennis J, Dillhung C, Muiznieck J 1977 *Computer Activities in Secondary Schools in Illinois*, Illinois Series on Educational Application of Computers, No. 24. University of Illinois, Urbana, Illinois

Dickerson L, Pritchard W H 1981 Microcomputers and educational planning for the coming revolution in the classroom. *Educ. Technol*. 21: 7–12

Emerson S 1978 The community memory project: Description and current status. *J. Community Commun*. 3: 6–9

Goleman D 1983 The electronic Rorschach. *Psychol. Today* 17(2): 36–43

Hannum W H, Briggs L J 1982 How does instructional systems design differ from traditional instruction? *Educ. Technol*. 12 (1): 9–15

Hilts P 1983 The dean of artificial intelligence. *Psychol. Today*. 17(1): 28–33

Hortin J A 1982 Information resources for computer-assisted instruction. In: Guelette D G (ed.) 1982 *Microcomputers for Adult Learning: Potentials and Perils*. Follet, Chicago, Illinois

Huberman A M 1973 *Understanding Change in Education: An Introduction*. UNESCO, Paris; International Bureau of Education, Geneva

Judd D 1982 A microcomputer role in adult reading and writing skill development. In: Guelette D G (ed.) 1982 *Microcomputers for Adult Learning: Potentials and Perils*. Follet, Chicago, Illinois

Kasworm C E, Anderson C A 1982 Perceptions of decision makers concerning microcomputers for adult learning. In: Guelette D G (ed.) 1982 *Microcomputers for Adult Learning: Potentials and Perils*. Follett, Chicago, Illinois

Kniefel D R, Just S B 1979 Impact of microcomputers on educational computer networks. *AEDS J*. 13: 41–52

Kurland N D 1973 *The Impact of Technology on Education*, Educational Technology Review Series. Educational Technology Publications, Englewood Cliffs, New Jersey

Lee C 1982 Adding the new technology to your training repertoire. *Training* 19(4): 18–26

Martin L 1982 Innovative educational technologies: Assets to adult educators. *Lifelong Learn.: Adult Years* 5(8): 18–21

Meierhenry W C 1982 Microcomputers and adult education. In: Guelette D G (ed.) 1982 *Microcomputers for Adult Learning: Potentials and Perils*. Follett, Chicago, Illinois

Patton F D 1980 A third dimension: The future of educational technology in industry. *J. Instr. Dev*. 3(3): 25–29

Spuck D W 1981 An analysis of the cost effectiveness of CAI and factors associated with its successful implementation. *AEDS J*. 15: 10–23

Stevens D J 1980 How educators perceive computers in the classroom, *AEDS J*. 13: 221–23

Wall S M, Wall N 1982 Using interactive computer programs in teaching higher conceptual skills: An approach to instruction in writing. *Educ. Technol*. 12(2): 13–18

West P 1982 Microcomputer software for educational use. In: Guelette D G (ed.) 1982 *Microcomputers for Adult Learning: Potentials and Perils*. Follett, Chicago, Illinois

White M A 1981 Into the electronic era: Implications for education and psychological research. *Educ. Technol*. 12(9): 9–14

Self-directed and Distance Learning

Introduction

It is probable that the greatly increased interest and confidence in self-directed learning over recent years have been stimulated by three principal factors. The first, one of principle, was the belief of many educators that their ultimate goal was to bring adults to the point where they could take charge of their own learning activities. The second, one of resources, was the expansion of distance learning facilities through technological innovations which enabled people to be reached who otherwise would not have been open to adult education. The third, a case of empirical observation, was the evidence that the majority of adults carry out systematic, intentional learning projects and that around 80 percent of those who do, organize and conduct them for themselves, outside the adult education system.

Very considerable advantages, organizational, educational, political, and even moral, have been claimed for self-directed learning. It is clear from the articles in this subsection that self-directed learning is important in principle and practice, and that it should be fostered and will expand. It may be that the goal of lifelong learning for all will only be achieved through adults developing the ability and willingness to practise it.

It is unfortunate that apparently exaggerated claims are made about self-directed learning. It is not proved, for instance, that most adults who realize they may, and know how to, take upon themselves the responsibility for deciding what and how they will learn, will generally wish to do so, as Malcolm Knowles asserts (see *Andragogy*), nor is it necessarily a sign of immaturity if they do not. Some of the claims are ideologically rather than educationally based. To stigmatize learning experiences which are not learner-directed as undemocratic may be correct, but it may be irrelevant to their educational effectiveness. A case can still be made, in certain situations, for arguing that the best person to decide methods and content of learning should be the educator and that a true sign of maturity lies in the learner recognizing this and having the self-confidence to renounce his or her right to self-direction. As will be suggested later, learner direction may, in some situations, impose narrower limits than teacher direction on the learning which may be achieved.

There are misunderstandings about the meaning of self-directed learning. It applies to groups as well as to individuals (see *Study Circles in Sweden*). All adults who decide to take a course, choose which one, how they will take part in class activities, and what work they will do in connection with the course, are to that extent self-directed. The degree of self-direction falls somewhere along a continuum which runs from the soldier who is entirely under the drill-sergeant's orders to the self-taught, who decides and undertakes everything for him- or herself, and not only has recourse to no teacher, adviser or informant, but uses no book, or audiovisual aid.

What is generally called self-directed learning is to some extent arbitrary. Although distance learning courses, like those of the Open University of the United Kingdom, allow the student some choice of subject, they permit no choice of the syllabus within the subject, or of the work prescribed for the course. However, the learner has wide freedom of when and where to do the work. A learning group in an educational institution may have little or no choice of where, what day, and how often it shall meet, but may be entirely free to study what and how it desires. Both would normally be classified as examples of self-directed learning.

Many adults do not have the ability to direct their own learning—it is a skill which may be, and increasingly is, taught in adult educational institutions. No matter how able a learner may be, however, the fields in which self-directed learning is possible, and the degree to which this is so, depend to a large extent on the existence of learning supports, such as libraries, museums, audiovisual and other resources, including educators. A learner may still be considered self-directed and have recourse to these last, as long as he or she is responsible for the major decisions on what to learn, how to learn, and to what end learning is undertaken.

Complete self-direction imposes narrow limits on the learning that is possible. Even if one has recourse to the knowledge and advice of family, friends, and fellow learners, as many people do, one is restricted by their competence. In any situation it may be that the optimum learning experience, which will vary with the learners and the learning to be undertaken, lies at some point on the continuum already mentioned, in which decision making by the learners is combined with recourse to an appropriate range of learning supports, including perhaps a teacher. As the following articles will make clear, there is a large place in self-directed learning for the adult educator.

The first article, *Self-directed Learning: Theories*, concentrates on self-directed groups and the elements to be taken into account if an adequate theory of self-directed learning in groups is to be devised. *Self-directed Learning: Concepts and Practice* describes research which revealed the extent of individual self-planned learning projects, the reasons for undertaking them, and how they are conducted. It discusses the issue of the optimum amount of teacher control and self-directed learning in noncredit and credit courses. The extent of learner freedom and self-management in distance courses is treated in *Self-directed Learning in Distance Learning*.

Distance learning was not primarily developed with the aim of furthering self-direction. From the time its primitive form, correspondence education, was introduced, its main intention was to offer educational opportunities to people who, for any reason, could not attend conventional classes. It has also been attractive because it offers economies of scale and has proved popular with learners because it gives freedom to choose when and where to study. The article *Distance Education* identifies its characteristics, in addition to the physical distancing of teacher from taught, and the advantages it offers, the materials used in it, its institutional structures, and the extent of its development. *Correspondence Study* outlines the history, the operation of correspondence study systems, the needs this kind of study serves and who provides it, and the problems of recognition and validation of correspondence courses.

Self-directed Learning: Theories

V. R. Griffin

Although it may seem a contradiction in terms, self-directed learning in adult learning groups is being actively encouraged in numerous settings—professional schools, community colleges, undergraduate and graduate programs, inservice training programs, and community-based noncredit programs for adults. Most writers acknowledge that adults are capable of achieving more responsibility for their own learning, but do not do so in learning groups without the struggle of replacing self-concepts, expectations of authority sources and of colearners, and habits and skills of learning acquired in their earlier, more traditional schooling.

Although many adult and higher education institutions have included aspects of learner initiative throughout this century, adult educators and university faculties became more intentional about enlarging the scope of learner responsibility in classrooms and other learning groups in the 1960s as a result of work by innovators such as Knowles and Tough, and of increased awareness and acceptance of humanistic theories such as those of Carl Rogers and Abraham Maslow.

There is yet no solid, coherent theory to explain self-directed learning in adult groups; there are however a number of concepts receiving attention and elaboration, namely, assumptions, decision making, structure, teacher style, learner readiness and style, learning processes, and perspective transformation. These concepts are discussed in the following sections, with illustrative, but not exhaustive citations. These concepts could be considered as the skeletal elements on which to "flesh out" the needed theory.

1. Elements for Theory Building

Undergirding all attempts to engage adults in self-directed learning are the beliefs that (a) self-directed adults will learn more, learn better, retain, and make better use of learnings than do reactive learners (Knowles 1975 p. 14); (b) effective adult living requires lifelong, continuous, effective, and creative self-guided learning; and (c) the motivations, attitudes, inner resources, and skills needed to engage in this lifelong learning can be developed and enhanced by participating in well-designed learning situations that give the opportunity to practice them in a conscious way. Also underlying these programs is the hope that self-directing abilities developed in learning environments will help adults to gain greater control over their own destinies, both in their personal lives and in society (Herman 1982 p. 2).

Knowles compares the assumptions on which self-directed learning is based with those of teacher-directed learning in the areas of concept of the learner, role of the learner's experience, readiness to learn, orientation to learning, and motivation. He makes similar comparisons on "process elements" of climate, planning, diagnosing needs, setting goals, designing a learning plan, learning activities, and evaluation (Knowles 1975 p. 60).

A clear statement of working assumptions is provided by Boud as a composite from his own work and his study of a number of programs in several countries. His list of assumptions is divided into three groups: the nature of autonomous learning, characteristics of students, and role of teachers (Boud 1981 pp. 24–29).

Missing in the literature of self-directed learning are discussions of meta-assumptions or philosophical choices relevant to both teachers and learners. One of these is the stance to take concerning existential dilemmas present in all of education, but made more vivid in self-directed learning groups, such as freedom versus control, self versus group, internal experiences versus external knowledge sources. Podeschi and Ruehle (1975) clarify this choice by focusing on the authority–freedom issue. The stance taken toward such issues will greatly affect the nature of the theory that will be developed about self-directed learning in adult groups.

Learners making decisions or choices are at the heart of self-directed learning, therefore an obvious and early concern in self-directed learning in adult groups was the question of who should make which decisions in the classrooms. Some practitioners initially took the position that the learners would be required to make all decisions, including how and when they would use the resources represented by the teacher. Most soon realized that this expectation is too stressful for most learners, unaccustomed to making all their own learning decisions, and began to specify which decisions would be the learners' and which the teacher's. Various typologies of possible decision-making systems were developed (Smith 1976 pp. 44–48, Boud 1981 p. 33). Such typologies have not been used extensively in research, and are now seen as too simplistic. Complex patterns of decision making are emerging which show responsiveness to factors such as readiness of learners, assistance needed by learners to prepare for making their own decisions, and development of learners over the time of a course or program.

Structure in a self-directed learning group is essential, and is usually provided first by the teacher or facilitator, and later by the learners. Five elements of the structure have been identified: clearly defined goals; availability of resources; an understanding of roles and responsibilities of both learners and teacher; preparation for involved persons for meeting the demands of the learning situation in a "fail-safe" way; and having a means for monitoring and altering the course as it proceeds (Boud 1981 pp. 192–93). Knowles suggests a similar list, but adds setting the climate, relationship-building exercises, and means by which to help learners arrive at their own learning goals (Knowles 1975).

A framework provided by Torbert in his "theory of liberating structure" is more reflective of the complex subtleties of providing learning activities to encourage self-direction. He proposes eight qualities of this liberating structure (Torbert 1978 pp. 113–16).

Guiding a self-directed learning group of adults makes different demands on a teacher than does a traditional classroom. Different teachers exhibit different styles in self-directed learning groups (Herman 1982), but common to all are an enormous trust in learners, and an equivalent capacity to relinquish large amounts of control. The teacher's style and value system dictate the skills required. For example, some teachers believe strongly in interdependent learning between learners and therefore require different interpersonal skills than do those who give more emphasis to independent, individual efforts. Another common element suggested by several writers is that facilitators are more effective if they themselves are engaged in learning and are open to having their beliefs, practice, and congruence confronted by learners. Far too little is known about the effects of various teacher styles on adult learning in these groups.

Guglielmino (1977) has developed a self-directed learning readiness scale, reflecting eight factors: openness to learning opportunities, self-concept in an effective learner, initiative and independence in learning, informed acceptance of responsibility for one's own learning, love of learning, creativity, future orientation, and ability to use basic study skills and problem-solving skills. Her scale is being tested in several doctoral studies.

"Nonreadiness" to engage in self-directed learning should not be seen as a deficiency; it may be a reflection of a definite predisposition or preference for another mode of learning. Various means have been devised to help adults identify not only their preferences for general mode of learning, but also the more specific characteristics of their individual learning styles—several are reported by Smith (1976 pp. 43–51). Another instrument for aiding learning-preference identification is based on the phases of experiential learning and was developed by Kolb and his colleagues (Kolb and Fry 1975). Experience indicates that although learners find these instruments very useful, none of them is all-encompassing enough to take account of all the relevant factors.

How programs and teachers attend to the "process elements" identified by Knowles is the subject of many case studies appearing in the literature. Of these, assessment and evaluation are receiving the most attention in literature from degree-granting or certifying institutions, because of the perceived threat to academic or professional standards. Learning contracts (Knowles 1975) and collaborative assessment between learner, peers, and teacher (Boud 1981 pp. 67–68) are two of the solutions developed for these institutions.

Considerably less attention has been given to the internal learning processes experienced by the learner. In one study which has been published, Taylor reports her findings that adult learners in a self-directed learning course experienced four phases in their learning: detachment, divergence, engagement, and convergence; these four phases contain 10 critical points in the learning process [e.g., "state of disorientation and confusion accompanied by loss of confidence, anxiety, and withdrawal from others perceived to be associated with the source of confusion" (Taylor 1981 p. 139)]. Although there have been other studies done at the Ontario Institute for Studies in Education, much work still needs to be done to understand how adults experience self-directed learning in group situations.

Because self-directed learning in groups is based on different values and perspectives than is learning in traditional classrooms, adults encountering it for the first time experience it as a disorienting dilemma. If they deal with the disequilibrium in a satisfying way, they often find they have experienced a major perspective transformation, and develop for themselves new perspectives about themselves, other learners, teachers, the nature of learning, and the nature of knowledge. Studies of this phenomenon are underway at the Ontario Institute for Studies in Education, but have not yet been published. The few studies there have been, have not explored the long-term effect of this transformation or its impact on other areas of life.

2. Work Yet to be Done

Even though there is a growing body of literature about self-directed learning in adult learning groups, indicating that it is a phenomenon increasing in incidence, impact on learners, thoughtfulness, and substance, it is still not a secure, nor a thoroughly developed educational idea. Only the beginnings of underlying theory are evident. There is a lack of conceptual clarity in defining just what is meant by self-directed learning, and in characterizing the various ways it is being made operational in learning groups. Far too little is known about the elements identified in the preceding paragraphs, or about the relationships among them. The information that has been developed through research or systematic study has not yet been submitted to an integrative analysis and synthesis.

See also: Self-directed Learning in Distance Learning; Self-directed Learning: Concepts and Practice

Bibliography

Boud D 1981 *Developing Student Autonomy in Learning*. Kogan Page, London

Brookfield S (ed.) 1985 *Self-directed Learning: From Theory to Practice*. Jossey–Bass, San Francisco

Guglielmino L M 1977 Development of the self-directed learning readiness scale (Doctoral dissertation, University of Georgia) *Dissertation Abstracts International* 1978 38: 6467A (University Microfilms No. 7806004)

Herman R (ed.) 1982 *The Design of Self-directed Learning: A Handbook for Teachers and Administrators*, rev. edn. Department of Adult Education, Ontario Institute for Studies in Education, Toronto, Ontario

Knowles M S 1975 *Self-directed Learning: A Guide for Learners and Teachers*. Association Press, New York

Kolb D, Fry R 1975 Towards an applied theory of experiential learning. In: Cooper C L (ed.) 1975 *Theories of Group Processes*. Wiley, New York, pp. 33–57

Podeschi R L, Ruehle C 1975 The dilemma of teaching: Maslow's "helpful let-be". *New Directions in Teaching* 4(4): 17–21

Smith R M 1976 *Learning How to Learn in Adult Education*. Educational Resources Information Center (ERIC) Clearinghouse in Career Education, Northern Illinois University, DeKalb, Illinois. ERIC Document No. ED 132 245

Taylor M 1981 The social dimension of adult learning. In: Salter L (ed.) 1981 *Communication Studies in Canada*. Butterworth, Toronto, Ontario, pp. 133–46

Torbert W R 1978 Educating toward shared purpose, self-direction and quality work: The theory and practice of liberating structure. *J. Higher Educ.* 49: 109–35

Self-directed Learning: Concepts and Practice

A. M. Tough

Adults spend about 500 hours a year each at major learning efforts, according to research in nine countries. About 73 percent of these highly deliberate learning projects are planned by the learner himself or herself, and another 7 percent are planned by a friend, relative, or other nonprofessional. The other 20 percent are planned by a professional educator or guided by a set of materials.

Interest in self-directed learning has recently been developing rapidly around the world. Various approaches to facilitating self-directed learning are being provided in noncredit settings and in programs for academic credit. These approaches include self-direction in a group, continued individual learning after a course finishes, sets of materials and resources from which the individual chooses, learning networks, learning contracts, self-help books and groups, competency-based programs, and individually chosen paths within an academic course.

1. Self-planned Learning Projects

Men and women are largely responsible for planning their own learning and change, according to studies in several countries. These studies will be summarized here. Details are available in the epilogue section of Tough (1979), in the updated bibliography of research that was added when Tough (1967) was reissued in 1981, and in Tough (1982).

Nearly 60 surveys of highly intentional learning projects have been conducted in Australia, the United Kingdom, Canada, Ghana, Israel, Jamaica, New Zealand, the United States, and Zaire. The basic picture is remarkably consistent from one nation or population to another. The numbers change a little, but the general pattern remains constant. In fact, the really large differences are within any given population, not between populations. About 90 percent of all interviewees have conducted at least one major learning effort during the year before the interview. Highly intentional learning is clearly a common natural human activity.

The typical or average adult learner conducts five distinct learning projects in one year: he or she learns five distinct areas of knowledge and skill. The person spends an average of 100 hours per learning effort. This is a total of 500 hours per year, or almost 10 hours a week.

Every study of adults finds a similar pattern of responsibility for planning what is learned, although the exact figures vary a little. About 73 percent of all adult learning projects are planned largely by the person himself or herself. Self-planned learning is clearly the most common form of highly intentional adult learning. In self-planned learning, the individual assumes the primary responsibility for planning, guiding, and conducting the learning project. Various terms have been used to describe such learning, including self-directed learning, self-teaching, self-instruction, self-education, self-culture, independent study, and individual study. People engaged in such learning have been called autodidacts, autonomous learners, and self-propelled learners.

About 14 percent of all adult learning revolves around a group: 10 percent in groups led by a person who is paid or is designated as the instructor and 4 percent in peer groups. In 10 percent of their learning efforts, people turn the responsibility for planning over to one other person, either a professional such as a sports instructor or music teacher (7 percent) or a friend or relative (3 percent). In only 3 percent of their learning projects do people primarily follow the sequence and instructions provided by nonhuman materials such as programmed instruction, a series of television programs, or a set of tapes or phonograph records.

In summary, about 20 percent of all learning projects are planned by a professional (someone trained, paid, or institutionally designated to facilitate the learning). The professional operates in a group (10 percent), in a one-to-one situation (7 percent), or indirectly through completely preprogrammed nonhuman resources such as programmed instruction or a television series (3 percent). In the other 80 percent of learning projects, the detailed day-to-day planning is handled by an amateur. This is usually the learner himself or herself (73 percent), but occasionally it is a friend (3 percent) or a democratic group of peers (4 percent).

If the entire range of the adult's learning efforts are represented by an iceberg, the extent of self-directed learning can be more easily seen. For many years adult educators paid attention mostly to the highly visible portion of the iceberg showing above the surface of the water. They focused their attention on professionally guided learning. They provided courses, classes, workshops, other learning groups, apprenticeships, tutorials, correspondence study, educational television, programmed instruction, and so on. Virtually everyone still agrees that all of this professionally guided learning is an important phenomenon in the world today. At the same time, though, it turns out to be only 20 percent of the total picture, only the highly visible tip of the iceberg. The massive bulk of the iceberg that is less visible, hidden below the surface, turns out to be 80 percent of the adult's learning efforts. It consists largely of self-planned or self-directed learning, though some is planned by other amateurs such as friends or peers.

During their self-directed learning, men and women perform several of the major teaching tasks that might otherwise be performed by a professional teacher. They perform an average of nine tasks, such as choosing their goal, planning the learning activities, obtaining appropriate resources, and estimating their level of knowledge and skill (Tough 1967). In the typical learning project the person experiences difficulty with about three of these tasks. As a result, he or she seeks suggestions, information, encouragement, resources, or other assistance from an average of 10 people. About three-quarters of these people are friends, acquaintances, family members, and fellow learners; only one-quarter are approached on a business or professional basis (Tough 1967).

The most common motivation (about 70 percent) for learning projects is some anticipated use or application of the knowledge and skill. The person has a task—raising a child, growing vegetables, mending or sewing something, teaching a class, fixing or improving something around the home—and learns certain knowledge and skill in order to perform the task successfully. Less common (about 20 percent) is curiosity or puzzlement, or wanting to possess the knowledge for its own sake. Learning for credit toward a degree, diploma, driver's license, or other certificate is comparatively rare: about 5 percent of all learning projects.

In a national survey in the United States, Penland (1977) was interested in the reasons people have when they choose to learn on their own instead of taking a course. Their responses were surprising, and the traditionally cited factors of money and transportation were ranked last. Penland's rank order, beginning with the reasons most often selected as particularly important (p. 32): (a) desire to set own learning pace; (b) desire to use own style of learning; (c) keeping the learning style flexible and easy to change; (d) desire to put own structure on the project; (e) didn't know of any class that taught what was wanted; (f) wanted to learn this right away and couldn't wait until a class might start; (g) lack of time to engage in a group learning program; (h) didn't like formal classroom situation with a teacher; (i) didn't have enough money for a course or a class; (j) transportation to a class was too hard or expensive. In the four most common reasons, people wanted to retain control or retain their own natural process, not have a professional instructor intervene.

Penland did not find any large differences between the participation of different statistical groups such as different age groups, income, social class, race, or completed education. Differences did exist, but their magnitude was usually small. In participation in learning efforts during adulthood, at least in the United States, there does not seem to be any large imbalance, any grossly underrepresented group, nor any particular unfairness nor injustice.

2. Optimum Amount of Teacher Control

Power or control is a significant recurring theme in various fields and professions. Many examples are provided by Rogers (1977), Gartner and Riessman (1977), Fischer and Brodsky (1978), and Tough (1982).

At one extreme the instructor or other professional helper can have 100 percent of the control and authority; he/she has total responsibility for choosing the learning objectives and planning the strategy for learning. The opposite end of the continuum might be called 100 percent freedom and autonomy, at which point the learner retains full control, turning none of it over to the teacher.

For a given teacher, learner, and content, there will be an optimum or ideal range on the continuum. If the teacher and learner stay within this range, the learning will be facilitated more effectively than if they move higher or lower on the continuum. In many learning situations the extreme ends of the continuum are ineffective: the most effective range is somewhere in the middle of the continuum. Teachers and other professional helpers commonly overcontrol, but occasionally they err in the other direction. The research cited in the previous section has shown that most men and women have a remarkably rich and successful natural process for choosing, planning, and conducting their learning. They largely handle the various tasks on their own, with some help from acquaintances and family. Some teachers ignore, distort, or interfere with the person's natural ongoing process. Instead of treasuring and fostering their natural process, they sometimes take over complete control and force the learner to fit into their teaching process. Many teachers, on the contrary, have recently been decreasing their amount of control. They have been shifting to a shared responsibility for planning the learning, and have been fitting into the learner's natural process in a light-handed manner. They are moving into the optimum range on the control continuum, maximizing their usefulness by avoiding overcontrol and undercontrol.

In both noncredit and credit programs for adults, some educational agencies and teachers are shifting from high control to shared responsibility. Although the approaches are somewhat diverse, they all have in common the shift away from traditional high control by the teacher. The approaches are sometimes referred to by the general term "self-directed learning." Less commonly they are called "open learning" or "independent learning." The next two sections present examples of various approaches to self-directed learning and teaching.

3. *Self-directed Learning in Noncredit Adult Learning*

Various approaches to self-direction have recently been noted where adult learning is not being pursued for a degree, certificate, or other academic credit.

In workshops for managers or supervisors, some instructors have encouraged each participant to diagnose appropriate needs and objectives, and to choose individual learning methods as the workshop progresses. Such approaches have been used by Roger Harrison in the United States and Joffre Ducharme in Canada.

Any workshop or course, regardless of its format, can encourage the participant to continue the learning after the course is finished. Some organizations, in educational programs for their managers, provide a self-assessment instrument and form for listing learning to be continued after the course has finished.

Some approaches rely heavily on tape recordings, programmed instruction materials, and other nonhuman resources. Most of these preprogrammed materials shift at least two sorts of responsibility to the learner: when to learn and at what pace. Distance education is a well-known example of this approach, and is used also for credit programs. In Nancy, France, a person who wants to learn any aspect of English for any purpose is given an excellent range of options at the *Centre de Recherches et d'Application Pédagogiques en Langues*. (Centre for Pedagogical Research and Application in Languages). The person chooses his or her own combination of helper, outside help, simulation, task matching, peer matching, personal reading materials, cassettes, written texts, and a sound library.

Learning networks, such as The Learning Exchange serving Evanston and the greater Chicago area, are very close to the learner-control end of the continuum. They do not try to control either the goals or the methods of learning. Instead, they simply provide the names and telephone numbers of persons who can serve as helpers or teachers with whatever sort of learning the caller wishes. Thousands of learners and teachers have been matched by the successful learning networks.

Individual learning contracts are being used more and more for continuing professional development. A learning contract spells out the person's goals and strategies, and perhaps the methods for evaluating achievement, for one major learning project. In some professions, members of the profession must undertake continuing education in order to retain their professional license or certificate: sometimes recognition is given to individual self-directed learning (as well as courses and workshops) through approving learning contracts.

A few institutions are experimenting with group support and stimulation for self-planned learning projects. Ronald Gross in the United States is establishing several centers for advanced scholars who are not working at a university or similar institution.

Several methods of psychotherapy encourage the relevant material or content to arise spontaneously: the therapist does not choose the content for a particular session. Examples of such approaches include free association, LSD therapy sessions, dream work, primal therapy, and the Diabasis approach of John W. Perry.

In many countries, peer self-help groups are rapidly becoming widespread for those with addictions, mental health problems, emotional crises, and various specific health problems. In these groups, peers are the source of information and advice, and each member not only receives help but also helps others. Professional helpers are involved at times with some of these groups, but are rarely permitted to control them. Professionals in several fields of practice are struggling to work out appropriate forms of interaction with self-help groups (Gartner and Riessman 1977).

Many self-help books provide suggestions, exercises, and techniques for use when appropriate. Most of these books leave the person free to incorporate these suggestions into the ongoing process of learning and change. Several self-help books help people to learn for themselves the various principles of behavioral self-control.

4. *Self-directed Learning in Credit Programs*

Various approaches to self-direction are evident in programs pursued for credit toward a degree, certificate, or other academic credentials. In recent years, various efforts to reduce instructor control have been implemented. Although somewhat diverse at first glance, these efforts have one thing in common: an attempt to shift from a high degree of control by the instructor, from an attitude of the instructor always knows best, to greater choice and control in the hands of the student. The responsibility for choosing what and how to learn is partially shifted away from the instructor. It may be shifted to a set of materials, to the individual learner, to small groups of learners, or to the whole class.

Several examples have a long history. Over the decades, some instructors have given their students a free choice of topic or focus for essays, projects, and other assignments. Many theses and dissertations have been examples of shared responsibility. On many campuses, students have had an option of taking one or two individual reading courses or independent study courses.

Competency-based degree programs have become common in recent years. The competencies required for the degree are spelled out, along with assessment procedures for judging when the student has gained each competency. Basing credentials and hiring on demonstrated competencies (rather than on the method used to gain them) is one step toward greater freedom in educational institutions. Some writers have urged that students be encouraged to write their own competence statements, which may differ from those of other students.

In a few colleges and universities, students are helped to learn how to set goals and plan their strategies, and generally "learn how to learn." This approach has been used by Laurie Thomas and Sheila Harri-Augstein at Brunel University in England, for example, and by Robert Smith at Northern Illinois University in the United States.

In Canada, Virginia Griffin has developed a highly effective self-directed approach to teaching in her graduate courses at the Ontario Institute for Studies in Education. Early in the course she brings differences in learning styles and philosophy to the surface through questionnaires and discussion. Throughout the course she increasingly leaves the decision making with the students. Her approach has been described in periodical articles, theses, and videotape recordings.

Malcolm Knowles (1975 pp. 44–58) has described his approach to a 15-session graduate course. Before and during the third session each student develops a learning contract, which can subsequently be revised or renegotiated as the student's interests change or become clearer. Certain knowledge and skill that most students have included in their contracts are handled by small groups ("enquiry teams"), who make class presentations during the eighth meeting through the thirteenth meeting. At the end of the course, each student is allotted up to 45 minutes to present evidence, to two peers, of having accomplished his or her objective.

Allen Tough (1982 Chap. 6) has described in detail his approach to teaching Canadian and American graduate students. He retains some control over what and how the students learn, but tries to keep the structure and requirements to a minimum. As a result of his research on self-directed learning and change, he has increasingly encouraged his students to have a large degree of freedom in what and how they learn. Each student in his courses is largely free to plan and modify an individual learning path. At the same time, his approach tries to ensure that students have adequate access to help and resources.

Scott Armstrong has experimented with time contracts in five marketing courses at the Wharton School of the University of Pennsylvania. The students who selected this option kept a daily diary on course activities, time spent, and knowledge and skill learned. Students who satisfied the instructor that they had spent between 100 and 124 hours on the course received a pass, those with 125-140 hours were graded as high pass, and those with over 140 hours were "distinguished." Armstrong's evaluations indicated that students using time contracts spent more time at learning, felt more responsible for their learning, and were more successful at changing attitudes and behavior, compared to their experiences under traditional teaching approaches.

In some colleges and universities, students take almost no courses in which a group of students begins on a certain date to learn within one subject matter area. Instead, each student (in consultation with a faculty adviser or mentor) develops individual objectives and learning activities for each course. If groups of students meet at all, they do so to help and encourage and perhaps evaluate one another, not to learn and discuss content. In Canada, examples are provided by the McMaster University program for health professionals (Boud 1981) and by Holland College (Prince Edward Island). In the United States, examples are provided by Empire State College, and by the Community College of Vermont.

Since the early 1940s, several schools and teachers have experimented with a shift from high teacher control to shared responsibility. In 1977 the Association for Supervision and Curriculum Development established a project on self-directed learning in the United States, and in 1979 published a book focusing specifically on that approach.

Bibliography

Boud D (ed.) 1981 *Developing Student Autonomy in Learning.* Kogan Page, London

Brookfield S (ed.) 1985 *Self-directed Learning: From Theory to Practice.* Jossey–Bass, San Francisco

Fischer C T, Brodsky S L (eds.) 1978 *Client Participation in Human Services: The Prometheus Principle.* Transaction, New Brunswick, New Jersey

Gartner A, Riessman F 1977 *Self-help in the Human Services.* Jossey-Bass, San Francisco, California

Knowles M S 1975 *Self-directed Learning: A Guide for Learners and Teachers.* Cambridge Book Co., New York

Penland P R 1977 *Self-planned Learning in America.* University of Pittsburgh Book Store, Pittsburgh, Pennsylvania

Rogers C R 1977 *Carl Rogers on Personal Power.* Delacorte, New York

Tough A M 1967 *Learning Without a Teacher: A Study of Tasks and Assistance during Adult Self-teaching Projects.* Ontario Institute for Studies in Education, Toronto, Ontario

Tough A M 1979 *The Adult's Learning Projects: A Fresh Approach to Theory and Practice in Adult Learning,* 2nd edn. University Associates (Learning Concepts), San Diego, and Ontario Institute for Studies in Education, Toronto, Ontario

Tough A M 1982 *Intentional Changes: A Fresh Approach to Helping People Change.* Cambridge Book Co., New York

Self-directed Learning in Distance Learning

E. J. Burge and C. C. Frewin

The 1970s and early 1980s have seen some major developments in the design, delivery, and administration of distance learning programs. Distance learning is defined here as learning activities designed by an educational institution and undertaken by a learner who chooses not to, or cannot, attend regular classroom instruction. The learning activities can be a mix of methods related to resources, settings, delivery systems, and program design. Types of resources include print, audiovisual, and computer-based materials and the learner might use these materials individually or in groups in home or work settings. Delivery systems have been enhanced by the use of various technologies. Administration has grown, especially in developing countries, through the establishment of distance education institutions (Daniel et al. 1982). Developments in the design of learning programs are not as consistently researched and documented as the aforementioned fields, especially as these developments relate to the learning processes undertaken by adult learners.

This article summarizes work in the design of learning processes in distance learning and indicates scope for developing self-directedness in distance learner behavior. An increasing number of adult educators are paying attention to the concept of self-directedness in learning because they recognize its contribution to critical awareness and constructive, creative thinking which in turn contribute to the further general development of the adult (see, for example, Nottingham Andragogy Group 1983).

The principles and procedures around which distance learning courses are designed (e.g., Jenkins 1981, Lewis 1981) have been developed from studies on learners and their interactions with course materials. Learners have been described from various perspectives, including their educational backgrounds, attitudes to study, perceptions of personal gain from courses, and methods for dealing with tutors and materials. Their interactions with course materials have been assessed in terms of levels of learning skills, use of information-processing styles and learning, selection of appropriate teaching models, kinds of interactions with resources and course learning guides, local personal and institutional support systems counselling strategies, and the impact of various audiovisual technologies on learning.

The principles and procedures derived from these studies enable a greater degree of quality control of course materials—an advantage which is not inherent in teacher changes in classroom situations. High-quality distance learning courses are characterized by academic rigour, high levels of learner interaction with materials, and sophisticated graphic design. Well-known examples of high quality learning materials are those from the Open University in the United Kingdom, but there are many other examples. Such materials are designed to lead students through a series of preplanned activities, often based on specific learning objectives and student assignments. This approach does not specifically encourage learners to develop self-directed approaches to learning.

However, this application of specific principles and systematic procedures has been accompanied by some questioning of the consistent use of an objectives-based, educational technology approach to learning design (Farnes 1976). Such an approach, it has been argued, can lead to unnecessary or inappropriate institutional controls over the learner's activity, which the learner can reject. Experience has shown that when distance learners are given options and some leeway to develop their own learning goals, they will take those opportunities, and under skilled guidance, show evidence of creative, relevant, and sound learning. Experience has also shown that many learners do not follow instructions strictly or sequentially. They tend, for example, to read and use printed materials selectively. Research has indicated that the use of highly specific learning objectives can inhibit incidental learning as well as initial intentional learning (Marland and Store 1982). This practical experience with what and how learners learn has been supported at a more theoretical level by the recognition of the general autonomy of the distance learner (Moore 1972).

Early responses to this problem of dealing with and even taking advantage of the autonomy inherent in distance learning have concentrated on increasing learner involvement and control in various ways. The self-pacing of distance learning is a traditional way. Pacing is usually controlled by the learner anyway, unless courses demand completion within a certain time period. The inclusion of experiential learning activities in courses has sometimes allowed choices for learners based on their own experience (Baume and Hipwell 1977, Fales and Burge 1984). Individual project work (Morgan 1983) can, with tutor guidance, allow learners considerable freedom and guided self-directedness. The design of different routes through a course (Melton 1982) can upgrade the levels of participation by learners in choosing how they will learn.

These design responses indicate new trends in distance learning, and recognize several important factors. First, adult distance learners can demonstrate high levels of initiative and responsibility while accomplishing learning. Second, the learners will respond to learning activities in accord with the demands of their individual situations—their relative isolation from the classroom allows them to do this. This response reduces the effective control of the tutor. Third, adult distance learners can become frustrated with a lock-step course process that is based on highly specific objectives. Adult learners will not easily tolerate learning activities which they see as tedious, repetitive, and irrelevant.

These factors contribute to the growing recognition for distance learning course design that adult learners can use more meaningful choices in what and how they learn (Taylor and Kaye 1986). A key issue in providing these choices is determining course structures and activities that will provide appropriate support and direction, and encourage freedom to choose the content and methods for their learning. Traditional distance learning courses have always allowed choices to be made concerning enrollment and self-pacing through a course. New developments and adult education practices suggest that further choices can be designed around learning objectives, methods, and styles of learning, and evaluation of learning.

The development of procedures to encourage learners to make these choices for increased self-responsibility and direction creates further concerns for course designers and tutors. These include the development of learners' skills and styles of learning, the identification of their attitudes to learning and teaching, and the provision of human and material resources needed for learning and psychological support (Morgan et al. 1982). Relating these factors to course design can directly affect the development of self-directedness, notwithstanding course structure and regular interactions with tutors and peers. If implemented, these factors will enhance the facilitative and guidance roles of the tutor, and develop collaborative rather than dependent relationships between tutor and learner. The factors can also be used to increase the degrees of peer learning and support among distance learners.

Another factor which will claim further attention will be that of the autonomy inherent in the distance learning situation. Adult learners can be encouraged to use time on their own for decision making and reflection about their learning, but their ability to do this will depend on their level of learning skill and on legitimate opportunities for this that are built into their courses.

These issues in developing self-directedness in distance learners are more directly discussed in literature relevant to classroom-based learning (Boud 1982). However, the next significant increment in the quality of distance learning course design will depend on their increased application to nonclassroom distance learning. The continuing development of a design perspective which centers on the learner, and on the application of adult learning principles to nonclassroom learning will help in the reduction of unnecessary levels of didactic teaching prevalent in many traditional distance learning courses.

Bibliography

Baume D, Hipwell J 1977 Adaptable correspondence courses for offshore engineers: A course that learns. *Teaching at a Distance* 9: 27–35

Boud C (ed.) 1982 *Developing Student Autonomy in Learning*. Kogan Page, London

Daniel J S, Stroud M A, Thompson J R (eds.) 1982 *Learning at a Distance: A World Perspective*. Athabasca University/ International Council for Correspondence Education, Edmonton

Fales A W, Burge E J 1984. Self-direction by design: Self-directed learning in distance course design. *Can. J. Univ. Cont. Educ.* 10: 68–78

Farnes N 1976 An educational technologist looks at student-centred learning. *Br. J. Educ. Technol.* 7: 61–65

Jenkins J 1981 *Materials for Learning: How to Teach Adults at a Distance*. Routledge and Kegan Paul, London

Lewis R 1981 *How to Write Self-study Materials*. Council for Educational Technology, London

Marland P W, Store R E 1982 Some instructional strategies for improved learning from distance teaching materials. *Distance Educ.* 3: 72–106

Melton R F 1982 *Instructional Models for Course Design and*

Development. Educational Technology Publications, Englewood Cliffs, New Jersey
Moore M G 1972 Learner autonomy: The second dimension of independent learning. *Convergence* 5(2): 76–87
Morgan A 1983 Theoretical aspects of project-based learning in higher education. *Br. J. Educ. Technol.* 14(1)
Morgan A, Taylor E, Gibbs C 1982 Variations in students' approaches to studying. *Br. J. Educ. Technol.* 13(2): 107–13
Nottingham Andragogy Group 1983 *Towards a Developmental Theory of Andragogy*. University of Nottingham, Nottingham
Taylor E, Kaye T 1986 Andragogy by design? Control and self-direction in the design of an Open University course. *Program. Learn. Educ. Technol.* 23: 62–69

Distance Education

A. R. Kaye

Distance education, simply and somewhat broadly defined, is "education which either does not imply the physical presence of the teacher appointed to dispense it in the place where it is received, or in which the teacher is present only on occasions or for selected tasks". This French Government definition of the term *télé-enseignement* (Loi 71.556 du 12 juillet 1971) contains two basic elements: the physical separation of teacher and learner and the changed role of the teacher, who may meet students only for "selected tasks" such as counselling, giving tutorials or seminars, or solving study problems.

Distance education methods can be successfully used for catering to groups who, for geographical, economic, or social reasons, are unable or unwilling to make use of traditional (e.g., classroom-based) provision. In so doing, they can liberate the student from constraints of space, time, and age.

1. Principal Defining Features

In addition to the key element of physical separation of teacher and learner cited above, Holmberg identifies six main categories of description for the term (Holmberg 1981 pp. 11–13):

(a) the use of preproduced courses as the main basis for study;

(b) the existence of organized two-way communication between the student and a supporting organization, that is, the university, college, or school with its tutors and counsellors;

(c) the planned and explicit catering for individual study;

(d) the cost effectiveness of the educational use of mass communication methods when large numbers of students follow the same preproduced courses;

(e) the application of industrial work methods to the production of learning materials and to the administration of a distance education scheme (Peters 1973);

(f) the notion of distance study as a mediated form of guided didactic conversation.

The same characteristics will be found embedded in other definitions. For example, in discussing the planning and design of distance learning systems, Kaye and Rumble identify a number of key features, which, although not all found in every instance, contribute to the overall notion of a generalized distance learning system. Concerning students these are:

(a) an enlargement or "opening" of educational opportunity to new target populations, previously deprived either through geographical isolation, lack of formal academic requirements, or employment conditions;

(b) the identification of particular target groups and their key characteristics (needs, age, distribution, time available for study, local facilities, etc.) to enable appropriate courses, learning methods, and delivery systems to be designed on a systematic basis.

Concerning the learning materials and teaching methods which characterize the courses, notable features are:

(a) flexibility in the curriculum and content of the learning materials through, for example, modular structures or credit systems;

(b) the conscious and systematic design of learning material for independent study, incorporating, for example, clearly formulated learning objectives, self-assessment devices, student activities, and the provision of feedback from students to learning system staff and vice versa;

(c) the planned use of a wide range of media and other resources, selected from those available in the context of the system, and suited to the needs of the students; these media may include specially prepared correspondence texts, books, newspaper supplements, posters, radio and television broadcasts, audio-and video-cassettes, films, computer-assisted learning, kits, local tuition and counselling, student self-help groups, lending-library facilities, and so on.

Finally, the following logistical and economic features are characteristic of distance learning systems:

(a) great potential flexibility compared to conventional provision in implementation, in teaching methods, and in student groups covered;

(b) centralized, mass production of standardized learning materials (such as texts, broadcasts, kits, and so on) in an almost industrialized manner, implying clear division of labour in the creation and production procedures;

(c) a systematic search for, and use of, existing infrastructure and facilities as part of the system (e.g., libraries, postal and other distribution services, printers, publishers, broadcasting organizations, manufacturers, etc.);

(d) potentially a significantly lower recurrent unit cost per student than that obtainable through conventional (classroom or equivalent) teaching arrangements and also potentially a considerably lower capital cost per student (Kaye and Rumble 1981 pp. 18–19).

The development of distance education methods in the recent past owes a great deal to the pioneering work carried out in the field of correspondence education. The print-based materials have remained but have been supplemented by modern communication media and personal contact. Thus distance education is often distinguished from correspondence study (Keegan 1980) by the notion of three-way teaching, combining "...the permanence of print, the reach of radio, and the intimacy of face-to-face study" (Young et al. 1980 p. 21). Slightly extending this definition, distance education can be equated with the combined, systematic, and flexible use of at least three major elements: print-based communication, broadcasting and/or other technologies, and face-to-face contact, in support of an independent learner.

Distance education methods imply major differences to intramural or classroom-based provision on three main dimensions: the learning experiences of the students, the nature of the teaching/learning materials, and the administrative and organizational structure of the providing institution. These three facets are briefly discussed below and are broadly relevant to the whole range of distance education provision, be it small, flexible, and localized, or large scale and highly centralized.

2. *Learning at a Distance*

Distance education methods cater *par excellence* for the individual learner studying independently. This entails, in most instances, high levels of motivation amongst the learners, and is a key reason for the fact that the great majority of distance education projects are aimed primarily at adults. Nevertheless, distance education provision does exist in some countries for school-age children unable (e.g., for geographical or health reasons) to attend classes. Examples, dating back for many years, can be found in Australia (radio plus correspondence tuition and personal contact), and in France, where the *Centre National d'Enseignement par Correspondance* was originally established during the Second World War to provide teaching, at a distance, to children unable to go to school. Most of its provision nowadays, however, is aimed at adults.

In general, then, distance students are adults. They also tend to form very heterogeneous groups, compared to those following more traditional educational channels, so it is difficult to characterize the "typical" distance student. In a review of student characteristics at distance teaching universities in 10 different countries, the following features were highlighted (Kaye and Rumble 1981 pp. 35–38):

(a) an age range of 20–40 years;

(b) majority studying on a part-time basis;

(c) men generally outnumber women;

(d) study is primarily carried out at home;

(e) high levels of motivation;

(f) the majority of students are from less privileged social groups;

(g) students studying voluntarily (as opposed to those in compulsory inservice courses) tend to be from urban areas.

Concerning reasons for study, it is evident that the obtaining of examinations, diplomas, and degrees, and the acquisition and/or updating of professional and career-related skills rank very highly amongst a large proportion of students enrolled on distance courses (see, for example, Holmberg 1981 pp. 21–24).

The skills needed for study at a distance have some features in common with those required in any learning environment. However, certain skills are of particular importance in the distance learning situation. These include:

(a) setting of personal study objectives;

(b) development of personal confidence in the ability to study primarily on one's own;

(c) planning and organizing study time and study strategies;

(d) developing study skills in learning from the reading and analysis of self-instructional and other print materials, and, where appropriate, from listening to and viewing broadcasts, using audio- and videotape material, participating in group discussions, and undertaking practical work alone and/or in a group situation;

(e) making use of, and communicating with, a tutor—in writing, by telephone, or at face-to-face meetings. Tutors may play a range of different roles: counsellor, problem solver, provider of feedback, resource person, assessor.

The skills listed above are of particular importance because the distance learner does not benefit from the same levels and amounts of pacing, structure, and formal and informal contact with peers and teachers as a student in an intramural educational institution. However, distance students do have the advantage of being able to plan their study activities around a personal timetable in a relatively flexible manner, and this is one of the overwhelming reasons cited for enrolling on distance education courses, especially when employment and family obligations make other options impractical or inconvenient. Furthermore, it is evident that in well-planned and adequately financed distance education systems, the distance learner need not feel disadvantaged and may, in fact, be better served than many studying through more traditional channels.

The range of distance education situations and courses is now so diverse that it is impossible to make generalizations about study patterns and strategies adopted by learners. Even different students following the same course in the same institution will adopt and develop different approaches, according to their own tastes and interests. However, it is fair to say that in a large proportion of cases, the majority of the learner's time is taken up by individual study of specially prepared printed materials (which as the main "information channel" can be considered as analogous to a classroom presentation or lecture in a traditional context). Students may be provided with sets of learning objectives and related self-assessment questions and exercises, with model answers, against which they can check their understanding and progress. A much smaller proportion of time may be spent in viewing or listening to broadcasts or recorded audiovisual and audio material, often ideal for presenting real-life situations, or case-study or experimental material which cannot be clearly communicated in printed form. From time to time, either at the student's discretion, or by certain predetermined dates, the student will submit written work to a correspondence tutor in response to preset assignments. Assignment modes may consist of multiple-choice tests, short answer questions, essays on set topics, or more extensive self-chosen projects or dissertations. The correspondence tutor may grade and comment on this work, and may also be able to meet the student to discuss it at a regular tutorial. In many instances, tutorial sessions at local study centres also exist to enable students to discuss general study problems and clear up difficulties in understanding. For example, the Lesotho Distance Teaching Centre, because of difficulties experienced by students in studying at home, set up a network of local study centres where "...students could come once or twice a week, work in adequate comfort and good light by themselves at their courses and seek help from an 'elbow tutor' as they needed it" (Young et al. 1980 p. 71). Other opportunities for interpersonal contact also exist in many systems—ranging from informally organized "self-help" groups established by students living in the same neighbourhood, to week-long residential contact programmes (such as the British Open University's "summer schools") which can provide an opportunity for extended personal and group tuition and, for example, laboratory practicals and field work.

3. Distance Teaching Materials

Teaching materials designed for use in a classroom or other intramural learning environment are generally not suitable, and certainly not sufficient, for the distance learning situation. A standard school or college textbook, for example, is often designed to be used either as a source of reference, and/or as a basis for discussion and exposition by a teacher in a classroom situation. And it is assumed that the student will be able to refer to peers, teachers, or other information sources (e.g., a library) when experiencing difficulties in following the material in the textbook. Audiovisual material for classroom use is also generally designed for a group situation with a teacher's presence assumed. Some of these materials may be suitable for use in group tutorials in a distance education programme, but would probably not fit the situation of a distance learner viewing or listening to a broadcast in isolation, at home.

A number of criteria are of key importance in the design of materials for distance learning. Firstly, it is necessary to take a global approach to the range of media and materials that will be available within a given system, and decide on clear pedagogical functions and roles for each of them. For example, if radio is to be used only in a group situation at a local centre, say in the presence of an *animateur*, then the structure and objectives of the programme will be quite different from one made for individual listening in the home. And an audiotape for individual use will again have different functions to a radio programme for individual listening: a tape can be stopped, and replayed, or used in association with diagrams or experimental equipment.

Secondly, the organization of the materials needs to take into account the resources, capacities, and abilities, of both students and tutors. Prerequisite requirements for starting a course (i.e., knowledge and skills assumed by the course planners) need to be made explicit. Likely areas of difficulty need to be "signposted" to the tutors and perhaps covered by special guidance notes for tutorial and group work. And scheduling of course work should take into account realistic estimates of how much time a typical student is liable to be able to devote to study each week or month.

Materials designed for individual study—and in most cases these will be predominantly print materials—are prepared in a "self-instructional" format, namely: written and presented in a stimulating style (maybe a colloquial style in some cultures); easily "accessible" to the student through the use of aids such as lists of learning objectives, concept maps, indices, glossaries, self-tests, and reviews; attractively designed, making good use of illustrations and of different typographical styles; "student active", containing opportunities for the student to test and monitor progress through activities, questions, and self-assessment exercises embedded in the text; flexible, with some provision for alternative routes and bypasses through the material, (without necessarily resorting to the complexity of a traditional branching programmed text).

A final important criterion of good quality distance-teaching materials concerns the care with which the different media components are integrated with each other. Integration can be considered at two levels. Firstly, materials for tutors, *animateurs*, and other intermediaries in the system must complement and relate clearly to the materials provided for the students; this implies that items such as notes for tutors need to be developed in parallel with the students' course materials. Secondly, when the individual student may be required to use material in several different media (say print, radio, and television), then clear decisions need to be made as to how closely the different media are integrated within the segments of the course. Levels of integration may vary from occasional cross-references, to a very tight structure which obliges the student, for example, to view a specific television programme before being able to proceed with the next section of text.

An example of an extreme form of integration of broadcast and print material is that developed by Radio ECCA, in the Canary Islands, and subsequently adapted for use on the Spanish mainland and in distance education projects in several Latin American countries. In the ECCA system

> . . . every lesson is centred upon a "lesson master sheet". The teacher has a copy of the lesson master sheet in front of him while he broadcasts over the radio, and the student follows his own copy simultaneously in his own home. . . . The student is required to respond to the radio teacher by writing on the lesson master sheet during the course of the broadcast. . . . a full set of master sheets comprises a student's text book. Exercises are included on the back of each master sheet. . . to be completed after the student has listened to the radio broadcast. (Cepeda 1982 pp. 213–14)

This degree of integration of print and broadcast materials is perhaps unusual in the field of distance education, but experience shows that it can be successful in a range of contexts.

4. *Institutional Structures*

A great variety of institutional structures can be found amongst distance education organizations. In many cases, structures are derived from those of conventional teaching institutions such as universities or schools, which in themselves vary from country to country. In other cases, broadcasting organizations, commercial correspondence colleges, or voluntary organizations, may have provided the original structure on which a distance institution has been built. And more recently, there has been a growth in the number of projects which have involved collaboration between a number of institutions of different sorts, either on a long-term basis or for short-term campaigns.

However, regardless of the underlying institutional structure, a number of specific services to students need to be provided, organized, and administered:

(a) provision (acquisition, development, production), storage, and distribution of course materials;

(b) provision of educational support services (correspondence tuition, possibly telephone or other electronic communication, tutorial classes, study centres, counselling, etc.);

(c) maintenance of administrative and academic records and provision of administrative communication channels (e.g., for enrolment, fee payment, assignment data, etc.);

(d) in some instances, accreditation and the delivery of diplomas, certificates, and degrees.

The question of provision of course materials deserves particular attention in this context, because it is here that differences are perhaps greatest as compared to traditional educational methods, and where economies of scale are most noticeable (when large numbers of students use the same preproduced course materials). Some distance education projects use materials acquired elsewhere, that is, not produced in-house. However, even in this simplest model, the acquired materials may need adapting, translating, and reprinting or reproducing. The majority of projects develop their own teaching materials, both printed and audiovisual, either using their own full-time subject matter specialists and/or academic staff, and/or through the use of part-time consultants. Physical production of materials (printing, audiovisual production) may either be in-house, subcontracted, or carried out in collaboration with a production agency such as a publishing house, broadcasting organization, or a commercial audiovisual producer. Whatever the origin of the materials, they will require storage and distribution facilities, and the greater the variety or range of courses or materials on offer, the greater and more complex will these facilities need to be.

The overriding importance of these aspects of procurement, production, storage, and distribution calls for two comments which illustrate a clear-cut difference between distance and conventional educational provision. Firstly, it implies that distance education is ". . . an industrialized form of teaching and learning" (Peters 1973 p. 206). Rumble has pointed out that, in institutions such as distance-teaching universities which ". . . have to undertake directly a number of quasi-industrial processes. . . there is a need for a clear definition of the interrelationships between two broad areas, one of which is more in the nature of a business enterprise. . . while the other is more in the nature of traditionally conceived academic areas" (Kaye and Rumble

1981 p. 179). The industrial, or quasi-industrial, nature of the materials development and production aspects of distance teaching is certainly a reality in many of the large-scale centralized systems. Course development planning may start five or six years before the finished product is "launched"; orders need to be placed with suppliers and subcontractors; deadlines and production schedules drawn up and adhered to; personnel needs estimated; and contracts prepared. The constraints imposed by the production and distribution needs can lead to a situation of potential conflict between production demands and the working methods and values of the originators of the course materials—be they full-time academic staff employed by the institution, or outside consultants and lesson writers. This is related to a second main difference between traditional and distance education institutions: namely the changed role of the teacher in a mediated or distance learning system. A number of aspects contribute to this changed role:

(a) the need to develop skills in preparing mediated materials (print, audiovisual, etc.) both for individual use, and for use by tutors and learners in group situations; these are not necessarily the same skills as those required of a good face-to-face or classroom teacher;

(b) the loss of direct personal control of the teaching/learning process and the lack of direct feedback from students characteristic of the classroom situation;

(c) the need to work with other professionals (designers, producers, editors) in the preparation and production of materials, and the resultant requirement to submit one's work to scrutiny and comment.

These aspects are present regardless of the course creation models adopted in any particular institution—which may vary from that of an author and editor working together, to that of a large-scale course team of academics, editors, educational technologists, producers, and designers.

When, in addition to course provision, the other three service areas (educational support, records, and accreditation) are provided by the same institution, and the number of students is large, then the need to adopt industrial working methods already referred to becomes even more imperative. For example, computerized systems for organizing despatch of course materials, and for maintenance of tutor and student records may become a necessity; industrial-style management and control methods may need to be introduced to ensure efficient integration of the work in a range of different specialized areas.

However, many distance learning projects and schemes are decentralized and even localized, with different organizations being responsible for each of the categories of services listed above. Such projects can maintain a flexibility of operation which is often more difficult to achieve in large-scale and centrally controlled institutions such as the British Open University.

Neil has presented an institutional analysis of distance learning systems on the basis of the locus and nature of the control of four key areas: finance, examination and accreditation, curriculum and materials, and delivery and student support systems (Neil 1981 pp. 140–41). He quotes five models or types of institution based on this analysis:

(a) the classic centre–periphery model, such as the British Open University, with high levels of control in all four areas;

(b) the associated centre model such as Spain's Universidad Nacional de Educación a Distancia which works with over 50 associated centres each responsible for their own delivery and student support services;

(c) the dispersed centre model (e.g., Coastline Community College, California) which cooperates with a whole range of organizations and bodies in the community but retains a fair measure of central control over accreditation for many courses;

(d) the switchboard organization model, exemplified by Norway's recently created distance education institute (Norskfjernundervisning) which has essentially enabling, coordinating, initiating, and approving roles in the further development of the country's existing educational resources for distance students;

(e) the service institution model, for example the Deutsches Institut für Fernstudien (DIFF) at Tübingen which provides services to a range of distance teaching organizations (e.g., materials development, consultancy, evaluation), and has little control over any areas except in the creation and production of course materials.

5. The Extent of Distance Education

With Perraton, the main early developments of distance education (as defined in this entry) would be traced to the mid-1960s when "...a series of projects began in which attempts were made to link the three components of broadcasting, correspondence, and face-to-face tuition" (Perraton 1979 p. 14). There were a few isolated earlier examples of broadcasts linked to correspondence tuition (e.g., using radio in New Zealand in 1937, and the programmes of the Chicago Television College, which started in 1956) but since the 1960s there has been a very significant quantitative and qualitative increase in the number and range of distance programmes throughout the world. Much of this development has built on earlier experiences of correspondence tuition (e.g., the United Kingdom, Scandinavia, and the United States), correspondence plus face-to-face tuition (e.g., the very extensive programmes in existence in the Soviet Union since the 1920s), and the combined use of broadcasting

Table 1
Examples of distance education provision

Programmes not equivalent to formal education levels:	
(a) Basic education	ACPO, Colombia
	Adult Literacy Project, United Kingdom
(b) Community education	Radio Learning Campaigns, Tanzania
(c) Agricultural extension	Radio Educative, Senegal
	Radio Farm Forums, Thailand
(d) Vocational	UNED, Costa Rica
Programmes equivalent to formal education levels:	
(a) Primary	Radio ECCA, Canary Islands
(b) General secondary	Air Correspondence High School, Korea
(c) Technical secondary	Open University of Sri Lanka
(d) Higher	Everyman's University, Israel
	Open University, United Kingdom
	Polytechnic Institutes, Soviet Union
(e) Teacher training	Allama Iqbal Open University, Pakistan
	Correspondence Course Unit, Kenya

and study groups (e.g., farm radio forums in Canada, India, and a number of African countries).

It is not possible within the scope of this article to provide a complete coverage of distance education projects worldwide. Firstly, the number and range of projects is so large: in a small country like the United Kingdom alone, over 70 distance education projects have started since 1970—ranging from the national highly centralized Open University, to decentralized and community-based projects and campaigns. Secondly, developments in communications technology are likely to bring about qualitative and structural changes in the design of distance education systems in the near future in a number of countries. These developments include applications of satellite communications (e.g., the University of the South Pacific, or the Open Learning Institute in British Columbia), of computers (e.g., the PLATOsystem in the United States), and of course the increasingly widespread availability of audio- and video-cassette/videodisc equipment. These developments are likely to bring about major changes in the roles of both broadcasting and print-based communication in distance education, at least in the industrially advanced countries.

At the present time, distance education projects exist in the majority of countries in the world at one level or another (see, for example, Daniel et al. 1982). The major part of this provision is concerned with adult education, which the Organisation for Economic Co-operation and Development defines as "organized programmes of education provided for the benefit of, and adapted to the needs of, persons not in the regular school or university system and generally older than 15". There appears to be no internationally recognized system for classifying adult education, but it is generally agreed that it covers both formal and nonformal curricula. Table 1 lists, purely for illustrative purposes, examples of the use of distance methods for a variety of adult education programmes. A number of the projects listed in the table emanate from institutions which also provide courses in other areas.

The examples listed form only a tiny fraction of existing provision, but detailed accounts of a wide range of projects can be found in a number of recent publications. Young et al. (1980) list over 120 projects in developing countries, excluding those only operating at degree level. Rumble and Harry (1982) describe 9 institutions (from both developed and developing countries) which have been established in the 1970s to provide primarily degree-level programmes. MacKenzie et al. (1975) include case studies of postsecondary-level distance and open education projects drawn from 13 countries. And detailed accounts of eight basic education projects in Europe can be found in Kaye and Harry (1982). Finally, interesting samples of print materials taken from 30 or so distance education courses (from 10 different countries) can be found in the manual on writing for distance education prepared by the International Extension College (1979).

Bibliography

Cepeda L E 1982 Radio ECCA, Canary Islands. In: Kaye A R, Harry K (eds.) 1982

Daniel J F, Stroud M F, Thompson J (eds.) 1982 *Learning at a Distance: A World Perspective.* Athabasca University/ICDE, Edmonton

Holmberg B 1981 *Status and Trends of Distance Education.* Kogan Page, London

International Extension College (IEC) 1979 *Writing for Distance Education: A Manual for Writers of Distance Teaching Texts and Independent Study Materials.* IEC, Cambridge

Jenkins J 1981 *Materials for Learning: How to Teach Adults at a Distance.* Routledge and Kegan Paul, London

Kaye A R, Harry K (eds.) 1982 *Using the Media for Adult Basic Education.* Croom Helm, London

Kaye A R, Rumble G (eds.) 1981 *Distance Teaching for Higher and Adult Education.* Croom Helm, London

Keegan D J 1980 Defining distance education. *Distance Educ.* 1: 13–36

MacKenzie N I, Postgate R S, Scupham J, Bartram B (eds.) 1975 *Open Learning: Systems and Problems in Post-secondary Education. UNESCO, Paris (also in French and Spanish versions)*

Neil M W (ed.) 1981 *Education of Adults at a Distance.* Kogan Page, London

Perraton H D (ed.) 1979 *Alternative Routes to Formal Education: Distance Teaching for School Equivalency.* World Bank, Washington, DC

Perraton H D 1981 A theory for distance education. *Prospects* 11 (1)

Peters O 1973 *Die Didaktische Struktur des Fernunterrichts: Untersuchungen zu einer Industrialisierten Form des Lehrens und Lernens.* Tübingen Beiträge zum Fernstudium, 7. Weinheim, Beltz

Rumble G, Harry K (eds.) 1982 *The Distance Teaching*

Universities. Croom Helm, London
Young M, Perraton H D, Jenkins J, Dodds T 1980 *Distance Teaching for the Third World: The Lion and the Clockwork Mouse*. Routledge and Kegan Paul, London

Correspondence Study

C. A. Wedemeyer

Correspondence study makes use of correspondence (the writing and sending of materials through the mail) as the medium of communication between teacher and student (Mackenzie et al. 1968 p. 4).

Other aspects of correspondence study include the use of specially prepared materials, written in a self-explanatory fashion, and arranged in a series of lessons; supplementary printed and other materials; a series of exercises to be worked out by the student; the evaluation of these exercises by a competent instructor with the student being informed of the evaluation; and a final examination covering the whole course (Houle 1965 pp. 544–45).

Since 1856, correspondence study has been almost the only institutionalized system of teaching and learning available to people who lack access to regular schooling. Its accessibility, effectiveness, and economy accounted for its spread throughout the world as the primary alternative to classroom instruction. Today the term itself (correspondence study) is falling into disuse not because of any inherent failure in the method, but because of technological change. As correspondence changed from being the only means of communication with distant learners, to only one of several communications media employed, efforts to classify such programs emphasized the distance across which education had to be made effective, and led to such terms as distance study, distance learning, and distance education (Holmberg 1981 p. 11) in place of correspondence study. The earlier reliance on nineteenth-century communications technology (print and a reliable postal service) began to give way to the use of electronic technologies (radio, television, telephone, cassettes, satellite, discs). But correspondence study is still a basic element, although identified now by different terms (Sewart et al. 1983 p. 1, Rumble and Harry 1982 p. 11).

Historically, the providers and proponents of correspondence study felt that the use of correspondence as a medium of communications did not entirely compensate for the lack of face-to-face instruction. Today however, programs of distance study, independent study, external study, and open learning are provided from the viewpoint that physical distance between learner and teacher is a situation to be exploited for its benefits to the learner, rather than as a disadvantage. Correspondence study combined with a variety of electronic communications enables learners anywhere to have improved access to instruction, and enables them to exercise an important degree of autonomy, self-direction, and evaluation over the education they obtain for themselves.

1. The System of Correspondence Study

Correspondence study is a two-phased educational process. In the first phase the course of instruction (often called a syllabus or study guide) is prepared by academic specialists. The syllabus sets forth the objectives of the course, provides for overall organization, directs the student to sources of information, indicates the reading to be done and activities to be carried out to achieve course objectives, provides supplementary information, explains concepts, and assigns reports and other evidences of achievement that the student will submit to his or her correspondence teacher.

The second phase occurs as the student submits evidence of progress. The teacher who receives the lessons from a student must evaluate them, and return to the students the results of the evaluation, along with an individualized assessment of the progress the student is making, corrections of errors, and suggestions for further study or remedial work if necessary (Wedemeyer and Childs 1961 pp. 7–8). Periodic supervised examinations, and the successful completion of a final examination are required if academic credit is sought by the learner.

Correspondence study employs a methodology in which a student is taught by at least two teachers—the writer of the course, study guide, or syllabus, and the teacher of the course. In practice, more teachers may work with the student because the modern production of a study guide usually involves a team of academic specialists, and lesson instruction and evaluation may be carried out by a team of teachers assigned to instruct students in the course (Erdos 1967 p. 11). The generally acknowledged success of correspondence study with learners at a distance was undoubtedly the result of the intensive two-way flow of communication between teacher(s) and learner, as a result of which the learner effectively learned how to learn, take responsibility, and exercise some degree of autonomy and responsibility in learning.

The complexity of the correspondence study process (instructing individuals scattered perhaps over half the earth's surface, residing in different countries, responsive to different languages, cultures, and life styles, and facing different needs and problems) led to highly specialized patterns of institutional organization and administration, logistical plans, budgets, and structures of faculty resources. The basic system of correspondence study was carried over, with only slight variation, into the new nontraditional programs and institutions that employ other media besides correspondence in providing distance, open, external, and independent learning access and opportunity in many countries.

2. Different Needs and Different Providers

Learners who select correspondence study have a broad range of needs, and accordingly turn to different providers for the kind of instruction they seek. Those who seek academic instruction turn to universities, university extension, university external studies programs, correspondence programs provided by various units of government, and private correspondence schools. Literacy, elementary, and high-school instruction by correspondence are often available from the same institutions that provide collegiate level instruction. The special needs of blind and deaf learners for academic and general education are usually met by specialized private correspondence schools.

Technical, vocational, and professional level correspondence courses are available from private schools, vocational–technical schools, government departments, and professional associations.

Workers seeking advancement in government, labor, business, and industry may find special correspondence programs provided by government departments (state, education, post office, military, agriculture, commerce), and by separate industries and businesses (insurance, marketing, finance, administration, personnel) or by associations (city management, for example) and labor unions (stewardship, labor union history and principles, contract negotiation, etc.). Some of the correspondence courses provided are intended for group as well as individual study, and are combined with other kinds of learning activities. Workers in government, business, and industry are usually encouraged to improve themselves by some form of subsidy or fee remission. Trade associations in some countries provide correspondence courses for workers seeking improvement and advancement. Numerous religious institutions make correspondence courses available for the preparation of preachers and the spread of religious doctrine.

Literacy, agriculture, and citizenship courses are available in many countries from government departments, university extension programs, private schools, and public service organizations.

While educational opportunity throughout the world is uneven in scope and quality, the correspondence learner has one significant advantage over the school-bound learner: if local or regional schools do not provide the access to opportunity needed, he or she can obtain access by enrolling in correspondence courses offered in other areas or countries, using the mail to communicate with a teacher at a distance. Language barriers, quality of postal service, monetary exchange, and political policies may restrict access to educational opportunity across national boundaries, but resourceful learners have long used correspondence study to supplement, extend, or replace the educational opportunity available or lacking in their local communities. The wide range of learning needs in any human society are rarely matched evenly and consistently by either the traditional local schools or the nontraditional learning systems that cross regional and national boundaries. But the two used together improve access and opportunity, as illustrated by the history of correspondence study.

3. Origins and Growth

The use of writing for the preservation and transmission of information and knowledge has ancient origins. Even "talking drums" in Africa are an example of the basic concept of linking persons at a distance for the exchange of information and instruction (Kabwasa and Kaunda 1973 p. 3). However, correspondence study appears to have originated after the concept of regular schooling was established but when its unavailability, inaccessibility, or inflexibility was seen to exclude people in need of education. Idealistic teachers, preachers, printers, and (later) librarians saw the need for a system of teaching and learning that was not confined by the rigidities of regular schooling, and learners in search of opportunity found in the invention of correspondence study not only a means of learning, but a mechanism of social mobility (Wedemeyer 1981 p. 202–03).

The motive for profit from the sale of instruction has also been significant. Private schools for profit, good and bad, have been a characteristic of correspondence study since its origins. But on the whole, the originators and developers of correspondence study were persons whose idealism and motives for public service matched well with the motives and needs of learners seeking opportunity.

One of the earliest expressions of the idealism and public service that led eventually to university extension and correspondence study, was made in 1850 by William Sewell, fellow and senior tutor at Exeter College, Oxford. In 1850, the individual and social consequences of the industrial revolution were plainly evident, especially the need for education for all. Sewell said, "Though it may be impossible to bring the masses requiring education to the university, may it not be possible to carry the university to them?" (Hall-Quest 1926 p. 8).

In Berlin six years later (1856), Charles Toussaint, a teacher of French, and Gustav Langenscheidt, a member of the Modern Language Society, began a school for teaching foreign languages by correspondence because they were unable to meet the widespread need for language courses in Europe through regular class instruction. The Toussaint–Langenscheidt school, which survived until 1936, is generally regarded as the first formally organized correspondence school.

From then on, correspondence study grew steadily. A sampling of dates—only partially representative of the hundreds of correspondence schools established—gives a panorama of the variety of schools founded as correspondence study spread throughout the world:

1873 Anne Ticknor's Society to Encourage Studies at Home, Boston, Massachusetts
1881 Baptist Theological Seminary, Illinois (W. R. Harper)
1883 Correspondence University, Ithaca, New York
1886 Thomas J. Foster founded miner's publication which became International Correspondence Schools in 1891
1891 Hermods, Sweden
1891 The University of Chicago (W. R. Harper)
1891 The Regents of the University of Wisconsin approved correspondence study, but the program was not successfully implemented until 1906
1894 J. W. Knipe began courses for teachers in England, and Wolsey Hall, Oxford, emerged
1895 The American School, Chicago, secondary, general, and vocational courses
1901 The American Institute of Banking, USA, courses for bank personnel
1902 Westinghouse Electric, industrial courses for workers, USA
1905 The Calvert School, elementary courses for children, USA
1907 Oregon State Department of Education, USA
1908 International Typographical Union, USA, courses for typesetters union
1910 W. A. Grundy, New South Wales, Australia, courses for health inspectors; led to Australian technical institutes
1914 Victoria, Australia, courses for children in the outback
1919 University of South Africa, full academic curricula
1921 Workers Education Bureau, USA, courses for labor
1923 Benton Harbor (Michigan) Plan of supervised correspondence study; spread to over 100 American high schools
1928 US Coast Guard courses for personnel
1930 Insurance Institute, USA, courses for personnel in insurance business
1935 City Manager's Association, USA, courses for personnel in city administration
1938 International Council for Correspondence Education founded, Canada
1940 American Academy of Ophthalmology and Otolaryngology, courses for physician specialists
1941 United States Armed Forces Institute, civil courses for US military personnel and dependants worldwide
1945 Federal Aviation Agency, USA
1948 US Post Office Department
1959 American Dietetic Association
1960 The USSR reported $1^{1/4}$ million students enrolled in correspondence courses as part of state education system
1962 American Society of Abdominal Surgeons, courses for physician specialists
1962 The University of Delhi, India
1962 First African Correspondence School, Brazzaville, Congo
1964 64 American universities offering accredited instruction by correspondence, collegiate and secondary levels
1964 *Instituto Nacional Cooperativa Educación*, Venezuela, began instruction by correspondence, technical, vocational, citizenship
1969 Open University of United Kingdom, correspondence courses with radio, television
1972 36 African correspondence schools in operation in 18 countries, with proposals for programs in 9 additional countries

The list does not begin to enumerate the many institutions in Canada, Australia, Japan, the United Kingdom, the Scandinavian Countries, Poland, Czechoslovakia, Israel, Spain, France, Italy, Africa, Asia, the Federal Republic of Germany, the Netherlands, South America, Malaysia, the South Pacific, the Caribbean, the Mediterranean—in fact, correspondence study covers the globe.

It is not known how many correspondence schools there are in the world, nor how many students learn by this method. It is estimated that there are hundreds of correspondence schools and programs, offering thousands of courses, to millions of learners at all levels of development and employment.

4. Acceptance and Other Problems

Despite the steady growth of correspondence study throughout more than a century, the way has frequently been hard for both institutions and students. Growth has not always meant acceptance.

Standards are always presumed to be inferior in any new educational venture, and, even if there are students who take advantage of the new endeavor, ways can be found to deny accreditation both to the correspondence institutions and to the students who learn by the method. Recently however the situation has improved with the creation of new nontraditional institutions which control the granting of their own diplomas and degrees; for these are less dependent upon established accrediting mechanisms and traditional educational policy.

Internal to correspondence study are other problems: finding and keeping talented academics and specialists who will not be lured away by more conventional and usually more rewarding careers in academia; managing the complex development and production processes for the maintenance of quality and timely courses; combining correspondence study with modern media of communication; learning how to survive the struggle for subsidy in a period of tight money; modifying correspondence study in accordance with new learning theory and a broadened understanding of the needs and characteristics of learning lifelong; and finally, avoiding the tendency of all successful institutions to become rigid and unresponsive to change brought on by an evolving society.

5. Changing Significance

Correspondence study has survived in part because it worked well as a learning system for learners who were to some extent foreclosed from other more conventional systems. As more options become accessible to serve the lifespan needs of learners, correspondence study will have to compete with new as well as old institutions for survival. If it can continue to place meeting learner needs above all else, it is likely that correspondence study will continue to adapt and survive throughout the world.

Bibliography

Erdos R F 1967 *Teaching by Correspondence*. Longman, London

Hall-Quest A L 1926 *The University Afield*. Macmillan, New York

Holmberg B 1981 *Status and Trends of Distance Education*. Kogan Page, London

Houle C O 1965 Correspondence instruction. *Encyclopedia Britannica*, Vol. 6, 14th edn.

Kabwasa A, Kaunda M M (eds.) 1973 *Correspondence Education in Africa*. Routledge and Kegan Paul, London

MacKenzie O, Christensen E L, Rigley P H 1968 *Correspondence Instruction in the United States: A Study of What it is, How it Functions, and What its Potential may be*. McGraw-Hill, New York

Rumble G, Harry K 1982 *The Distance Teaching Universities*. Croom Helm, London

Sewart D, Keegan D, Holmberg B 1983 *Distance Education: International Perspectives*. Croom Helm, London

Wedemeyer C A 1977 Independent study. In: Knowles A S (ed.) 1977 *International Encyclopedia of Higher Education*, Vol. 5. Jossey-Bass, San Francisco, California

Wedemeyer C A 1981 *Learning at the Back Door: Reflections on Nontraditional Learning in the Lifespan*. University of Wisconsin Press, Madison, Wisconsin

Wedemeyer C A, Childs G B 1961 *New Perspectives in University Correspondence Study*. Center for the Study of Liberal Education for Adults, Chicago, Illinois

Section 5

Providers

Section 5

Providers

Introduction

The essential function of adult education is to promote learning. One would therefore expect that accounts of adult education and its history would concentrate on the learning that takes place. Not a bit of it. Almost without exception they are built round those people and organizations which provide opportunities to learn or teaching for adults. Nor is it difficult to see why.

In the first place, accounts of adult education are written for the providers, not the consumers. Secondly, records of learning are sparse, particularly as the adult education movement throughout the world has been reluctant to engage in systematic evaluation of its work and is still imperfectly skilled in it. Such data as do exist are to be found for the most part in the archives of the providers.

Moreover, education has been, and to a significant degree still is, perceived as the transmission of knowledge from the teacher to the learner, so that the former has equal importance in the process to the latter. It could be argued that, unless there has been learning, there has been no transmission, therefore no teaching, and conversely, in so far as there has been teaching, there has been transmission and therefore learning. Taking an over-literal view: to the extent that there has been teaching, there has been learning. Unfortunately, of course, included within the concepts of education and teaching is imperfect transmission of knowledge, so that an accurate assessment of the amount of teaching done does not help us to assess the amount of learning achieved. Nevertheless, it is not difficult to understand why so much emphasis is placed on provision and teaching.

A superficial reading of subsection 4d of this Handbook, Self-directed and Distance Learning, may suggest that the role of providers has not been so central to adult learning as has hitherto been believed. It is not clear, however, how important basic education in general, and literacy in particular, are to the ability, confidence, and will to undertake self-directed, intentional learning projects, nor is it clear how much the spread of such projects owes to the development of mass media and other knowledge resources. Therefore it cannot be assumed that the same amount of adult individual learning existed before quasiuniversal schooling. Furthermore a closer reading of subsection 4d would seem to suggest that rather than declining, the role of providers has been changing, perhaps, more towards fulfilling the role of resource centres rather than instructional agencies. The growth of distance learning would appear to indicate an increasing need for organizations to offer both teaching and resources.

Not that providers (both state and private) have ever operated in a purely instructional role. The circumstances of adult education have almost precluded it. They have had to establish or procure the settings and the climate in which teaching could take place. The private ones have been propagandists, not only recruiting participants, but drumming up support from influential and wealthy private patronage and politicking to obtain, if not government backing, at least acquiescence in their efforts. The recruitment role has been general, even in the case of state providers. It has been necessary not only to make known that learning opportunities existed, but also to offer persuasion or inducements to participation. Comparatively little provision, aimed, as most of it has been historically, at the socially and educationally disadvantaged, has been a response to active student demand. Adult education has not, in that sense been a popular movement, although some providers have striven mightily to make it so. Structured opportunities for organized adult learning have predominantly been created by people who believed that others needed them, and were thus designed to meet the purposes of the providers or what the providers perceived the needs of the intended clientele to be, rather than in response to needs that such a clientele had actually expressed.

Even nowadays, when providing organizations exert themselves much more to engage learners in programme planning, and negotiated curricula are commonplace, the adult newly come to education—even one who knows exactly what he or she wants—will in most cases be obliged to choose what is nearest to his or her tastes from an existing programme. Providers do not prescribe the choice—adults can reject the offering altogether—but because programmes may contain courses which students would quite like to take, although not the ones they most wish to, they exert a significant determining influence on what people study. It is to escape from this that educational brokering and learning exchanges have been set up. It is also one reason for the popularity of independent learning.

So many and various are the organizations offering or promoting adult education that it would be impossible to present adequately all the different kinds. Section 5 gives only an indicative selection. *Providers of Adult Education*, the first article, besides offering a historical perspective upon these organizations, identifies and classifies them into governmental and nongovernmental agencies and into those which were expressly created for adult education and those for which it is a secondary, albeit perhaps a major, purpose. It also outlines the support services providers give to adult learning.

Almost everywhere adult education developed out of private, voluntary initiative. However, as the state takes a growing interest in adult education, so its role as a direct provider increases. *Adult Education in Public Schools* reviews the role played by the public school system, predominant in the United Kingdom, strong in the United States, and increasing elsewhere. *Community Colleges in Adult Education* describes the part played by these institutions—a comparatively recent creation of the United States for college-age people, with many important equivalents in other countries—in providing lifelong education for adults. *Universities and Adult Education: Policies and Programs* recounts the history of university provision for adults and concentrates on extension, the study and teaching of adult education as a discipline, and the development of university studies for adults in developing countries.

The question of access for adults to educational activities leading to qualifications has much exercised educators and policy planners in the 1980s. Distance learning has opened access by not restricting study to a particular time and place, and the relaxing of formal educational requirements for entry has further helped. *Open Access Institutions for Adults* considers what open access means and the kinds of institution that have been set up to provide it, concentrating on open universities in several countries.

In the private sector it is traditionally assumed that adult education has been dependent on altruistic, voluntary initiative. The long-existing contribution of commercial organizations making a living out of adult education tends to be ignored or belittled. *Adult Education for Profit* recounts and evaluates the work done by such agencies. It discusses the question of their regulation and the public supervision of their standards.

Religious bodies have played a crucial role in the history of adult education. Their principle aim has been to educate people to greater faith and better living. Some, however, have taken a wide view of how this should be done and religiously inspired agencies have been active in many areas of adult education. *Christian Churches and Adult Education* recounts both their history and, particularly, their current practice.

As attention shifts from the formal class provision by adult education organizations to other roles, the educational functions of libraries, museums, and galleries assume increasing importance. They have always been essential resource centres for learners, but increasingly, as *Libraries and Adult Education* and *Museums and Galleries in Adult Education* point out, they are taking their active teaching, guidance, and outreach role seriously and with a high degree of sophistication.

Providers of Adult Education

E. M. Hutchinson and E. K. Townsend Coles

This article gives a brief historical review of the providers of adult education to the present day. It offers three ways in which contemporary providers can be classified. These are by distinguishing between governmental and nongovernmental organizations, by their degrees of involvement in adult education, and whether or not they are in the work for profit. National organizations are considered and the article concludes with comment on future trends.

1. Historical Background

The providers of adult education, however that term is defined, have always constituted a motley array, at any rate since the time when religious organizations ceased to be the sole or main purveyors of education. Indeed a contemporary commentator referring to the number of providers described the field of adult education as either a rich profusion or as a muddle.

From earliest times there have been associated with temples, mosques, churches, and later chapels a diversity of organizations and activities which could be regarded as being adult education. Indeed, spiritual proselytization played a major role in most countries by being the dynamics which encouraged the development of avenues for adult learning.

It was in the eighteenth century in Europe, and later in North America, that secular as well as religious interests emerged, though the latter were still predominant. It was voluntary religious organizations such as the Society for Promoting Christian Knowledge in England which first became involved in literacy as a means of spreading religious enlightenment. At the same time the salons of Paris and the commercial coffee houses and clubs of London and elsewhere were becoming important centres of learning for the aristocracy.

The nineteenth saw the great proliferation in the providers of adult education. Much of this also stemmed from religious concern for the working populations of the sprawling cities. The mechanics' institutes in the United Kingdom were a means of stimulating thought on the scientific issues of the day, described as being "an educational reflection of the new political and economic aspirations of the working classes". In the middle of the century, two international organizations were founded in Switzerland, the Young Men's Christian Association and later the sister organization for women. To care for the whole person, in mind, body, and spirit, was the essential emphasis in both. They thus provided adult education of many forms—second-chance schooling, religious and other instruction, physical education, and in many cases even the provision of technical education before governments entered this field. Their willingness to respond to changing needs, relinquishing activities when other better equipped agencies emerged, has been a hallmark of these and other international voluntary organizations.

The Industrial Revolution had been a stimulus for much adult education. Of a wholly different genesis were the folk high schools, which were rooted in agrarian Denmark and which quickly spread throughout Scandinavia, Germany, and as far as Poland. Across the Atlantic, egalitarian societies in Massachusetts were holding town meetings and the Chautauqua summer meetings, originally established in 1874 for systematic Bible study, were broadening their scope to include a wide range of secular subjects. Towards the end of the century the universities in the anglophone world were entering the field of extension education, and there was also the establishment of organizations specifically for workers such as the Workers' Educational Association in the United Kingdom.

Voluntary organizations continued to be the main providers of adult education until well into the first third of the present century. Statutory authorities were concerned with the increasing demands for formal schooling for children and had little energy for what they regarded as being a peripheral interest, the education of adults. This attitude was exported by the metropolitan powers of Europe to their dependent colonial countries in Asia, Africa, and South and Central America.

Most cultures have had their own indigenous forms of adult education. The many activities which emanated from mosques and temples were potent means of bringing education to those in Asia who were untouched by formal education. In Africa, most societies had well-developed procedures for educating youths through puberty to adolescence and finally to their emergence as adult members of society. These indigenous forms of adult education continue in many countries today. However, the advent of colonialism brought a new wave of providers, of which Christian Missions initially were predominant, together with their associated voluntary organizations. Government interest in adult education started with the establishment of extension departments in agriculture and health as a means of spreading education in the two aspects of life most urgently needed, namely curbing disease and providing food.

The Second World War became a watershed in the provision of adult education throughout the world. Up until then, the main providers had been nongovernmental; after the war, governments increasingly emerged as the principal providers of adult education. Local education authorities took over many of the less formal aspects of adult education initially the preserve of voluntary organizations. The demands for training and retraining were beyond the capacity of private institutions and governments everywhere had to shoulder this responsibility.

2. The Contemporary Scene

There are various ways in which the providers of adult education can be classified. From the preceding paragraphs it will be understood that one way is to draw the distinction between governmental, both central and local, on the one hand and nongovernmental on the other. The borderline is not always sharp since there are several institutions which lie between the two. Providers divided in this manner can be illustrated as follows (Townsend Coles 1977):

(a) Governmental: central government, local authorities.

(b) Quasigovernmental: universities, parastatal organizations, information services.

(c) Nongovernmental: voluntary organizations, churches, temples, mosques, workers organizations, employing bodies, political organizations.

This classification is useful in that it indicates the role and significance which nongovernmental organizations play in adult education. It fails, however, to differentiate within that large group, the degree of involvement of each in the work. It also makes no distinction between the various agencies of government.

It is possible to classify according to the degree of involvement an agency has in adult education. Two broad categories may be established, as follows:

(a) *Organizations created expressly for adult education, or in which adult education is their primary function.* They are not very numerous. Examples are to be found in the adult schools and mechanics' institutes founded in England in the early nineteenth century and in the Workers' Educational Association (WEA) of the twentieth. The latter body is notable for the links developed with universities.

Institutions catering specially for the individual and social development of young adults were created from the middle of the nineteenth century in Denmark. Offering residential courses of some months' duration, they were designated (in English translation) folk high schools. They were in part a reaction against formalized higher education and in part a response to external pressures expressed in the claim "What is lost without must be won within". This organizational form was influential in other Scandinavian countries.

The German language version—*Volkshochschulen*—describes a sharply different institutional form designed to offer facilities for part-time nonresidential study. They have developed into a large-scale national movement since the Second World War.

The Danish folk high schools also influenced the establishment of residential centres for adult education in the United Kingdom and North America. These necessarily differed from their exemplars because they reflected fundamentally different historical, economic, and social circumstances. This illustrates the important fact that, although imitation has made a considerable contribution to the emergence of organizations for adult education, exact replication is virtually unknown. Even in the Scandinavian countries with their apparently close ethnic and historical similarities, folk high schools differ materially in concept, clientele, and curriculum in Denmark, Finland, Norway, and Sweden. Today virtually all types of provider maintain at least some residential centres for adults.

National coordinating bodies, specifically designed to advance adult education, exist, but usually there would be only one such organization in a country. Sometimes there are voluntary organizations which were established entirely for adult education such as the People's Educational Association of Ghana. Some national and international organizations for women and youths may be included, though most are better classified in the next category. In the Third World, there has been a tendency to set up distinct organizations to marshall resources for the eradication of illiteracy. In general, however, this grouping tends to be small.

(b) *Organizations in which adult education is an important element of their work.* This category is generally quite numerous. Central and local government agencies dealing with education, agriculture, health, social services, and industry, usually have significant departments dealing with adult education. It cannot be described as their primary purpose, but it is nevertheless a significant one. Many, though not all, universities would come into this category. Religious and workers' organizations would do likewise, as would those voluntary organizations in which the education of their members is regarded as being of importance. There would thus be seen to be a distinction between, for example, many youth and women's organizations in which adult education features as a normal part of the programme, and organizations which are more concerned with social work and the provision of community services. Many industrial undertakings regard continuing education of their employees as being important.

The Scandinavian countries again offer classical examples of educational agencies constituted and supported by, for example, churches, political parties, trade unions, and temperance movements. The actual instrument of education most commonly (although not uniquely) associated with those agencies is the "study circle"—a voluntary coming together of people, for mutually supportive learning, without necessarily involving a specialist teacher or instructor but often using materials supplied by the agency. Such flexibly structured learning opportunities are not unknown elsewhere: the National Adult School Union in the United Kingdom, largely sponsored by the Society of Friends, involved large numbers of people in similar groups at the beginning of the century: in the 1960s there were some 450 "livingroom learning" groups in British Columbia. But only in Scandinavia—and the outside world associates them particularly with Sweden—do study circles constitute what a museum curator might describe as the "type specimen" of adult education organizations.

The range of bodies that regard themselves as contributing to adult education without necessarily creating special service elements for the purpose is illustrated by some of those associated with the National Institute of Adult Education (England and Wales). They include the Cooperative Movement (some societies do have separate education committees); the Trades Union Congress; the British Association for Commercial and Industrial Education. Religious interests are represented by the British Council of Churches and the Christian Association for Adult and Continuing Education. There are three affiliated women's organizations—the National Federation of Women's Institutes (women in rural and smaller communities); the National Union of Townswomen's Guilds; the National Association of Women's Clubs. Other associated organizations are concerned, for example, with older people, health promotion, and community relations. So are voluntary organizations such as Rotary and Lions.

3. *Commercial Agencies*

Most of the organizations mentioned so far are nongovernmental. They are usually nonprofit making and commonly enjoy some form of legal or customary status that gives them exemption from some or all forms of national and local taxation, this itself being, effectively, a form of public subsidy.

A great deal of adult education is, however, on offer for sale by commercial providers. This applies to a great deal of distance teaching by correspondence, the greater part of which is directed to acquiring certificates of academic or vocational competence.

There are also many commercial organizations offering face-to-face tuition notably in languages and elementary office and other skills but often extending well beyond this into areas of new technology such as radio, television, and computer programming.

4. *Governmental and Nongovernmental Organizations*

With the increasing role played by the state in adult education there is a growing number of governmental organizations and of ones which are neither strictly governmental, nor unequivocally private. These quasigovernmental organizations are normally constitutionally protected from direct government control and their governing body will include a number of independent members or representatives of private associations. On the other hand the governing body will also include state nominees, or have its relation and responsibility to the state specifically defined, and be principally or entirely dependent on state funding.

How organizations are to be categorized varies in large part with the political and social systems in which they operate. Socialist countries and authoritarian regimes tend to place greater reliance on agencies of government, liberal democracies take a more laissez faire approach, although even there the involvement of government in adult education is on the increase.

The mass media, important instruments of education, are state agencies under socialism and they may be state, quasigovernmental, or private in Western countries. Universities are in a similar position. Adult education in socialist states and, unusually, in the United Kingdom, is predominantly provided by the public education system. In most countries, whatever their political complexion, the armed forces are recipients of funds earmarked for the education of their members. Similar arrangements are frequently made for the police and for the inmates of prisons.

5. *Relations with Governments*

An important part of the work of nongovernmental organizations is stimulating public education authorities either to provide facilities themselves or to offer support and subsidy for voluntary efforts to do so. Whatever may be done outside the statutory framework it is unlikely to be on a substantial, let alone adequate scale unless it is recognized and under written by central or local government. Only a few governments have accepted wholeheartedly that nongovernmental organizations are particularly appropriate as agencies for the provision of adult education because they are more immediately responsive to the needs and demands of their members. This view is formalized, for example, in the Danish law on leisure-time instruction. The scale of action by study circle promoters in Norway and Sweden and by folk high schools in all the Scandinavian countries is only possible because of official recognition of their significance by national governments that is detailed in primary and subordinate legislation. This may not prevent those involved from complaining about inadequacies and imperfections of such public support but their status and scale of action is undoubtedly superior to that of their equivalents in many other countries. Many organizations in the United Kingdom in recent years have had reason to regret that the education acts as now interpreted give them no assurance of adequate support and subsidy.

6. *Cooperative and Support Services*

Apart from direct recruitment of people into classes and study groups, nongovernmental organizations perform vital roles as pressure groups to secure adequate and appropriate governmental action and in the promotion of liaison, research, and communication. This was spelled out in the report of a conference organized by the International Council for Adult Education in conjunction with the (English) National Institute of Adult

Education in 1974 (ICAE 1980). "The initial hypothesis", states the report, "was that some national mechanism or some combination of means are required in every region and country:

(a) to foster recognition and attention for the special needs and services of adult education;

(b) to help link up adult education within the entire educational system and learning community—adult education seen within the perspective of lifelong learning;

(c) to persuade governments, inter-governmental agencies, and non-governmental organizations to provide more adequate resources;

(d) to help establish and maintain high standards of performance;

(e) to develop improved means of communication and to encourage training and research;

(f) to found adult education as a response to the needs of the nation and human family."

If these objectives are to be achieved, the responsible organizations will be faced with a need to perform as many as possible of the following tasks:

(a) maintaining a documentation centre and library;

(b) taking responsibility for the issue of recurrent and occasional publications;

(c) organizing regular meetings between representatives of public and private organizations that give direct service to the public at large;

(d) arranging congresses, conferences, seminars, and other group meetings accessible to substantial numbers of functionaries, teachers, and other people employed professionally or voluntarily in giving such service;

(e) initiating and/or undertaking enquiries at various levels of detail to a point that may justify the term "research";

(f) fostering and, in some circumstances, undertaking the training of practitioners of adult education at various levels;

(g) serving as a point of first reference whether for people from home or overseas seeking information about national or local aspects of adult education provision;

(h) serving as a centre of advocacy and appraisal in relation to the policies of central and local government.

In some countries a major organization constituted to give direct service to the public at large may also undertake some or all of the tasks indicated above. It is also true that some of the functions described are sometimes performed by national departments of education or by bodies created by and responsible to them. Examples exist in New Zealand and in some Australian states, as well as in some excolonial territories and in Eastern bloc countries.

With this reservation it can fairly be said that the most effective national organizations promoting cooperation and some or all of the other work outlined, are nonstatutory creations. This does not, however, preclude them from seeking and receiving recognition and financial support from national and local governments.

The earliest example was the British Institute of Adult Education (1919) now the National Institute of Adult Continuing Education (England and Wales). The American Association of Adult Education was set up in 1926 and re-established as the Adult Education Association of the USA in 1951.

A more detailed analysis (Charters et al. 1981) suggests that, just as most legislation directly concerned with adult education is of a comparatively recent date, so there has been an accompanying growth of national organizations of the kind indicated but with more of them reflecting governmental intervention. An undoubted impetus was given to these developments by the UNESCO-convened international conference in Tokyo in 1972. The same source notes that "Underlying all differences of structure purposes common to all national organisations are those of collecting and disseminating information—the maintenance of libraries and documentation centres and the publication of regular and occasional publications. . . ." Three outstanding centres are those maintained by the Swiss Federation, the Netherlands Centre, and the New Zealand Council. The first two are nongovernmental organizations and the third is the statutory successor to another.

7. *Trends*

In the developed countries, four factors are likely to determine the form which adult education will take and consequently the roles which the various providers will be expected to play. The first factor concerns primarily young people entering what is conventionally called the labour market. The need to be rethinking the whole concept of work in the light of increasing unemployment is bound to direct attention to new forms of training. There will also be greater emphasis on what traditionally were regarded as spare-time activities and which now will occupy a greater proportion of a person's life. To meet these needs there will have to be cooperation between governments, employers, and voluntary organizations in the provision of programmes, as well as radical changes in their content. The second factor is the increasing need for constant employee training and retraining to keep pace with changing technologies. This is particularly obvious in the industries involved in electronics, but it is also profoundly changing the nature of others, for example clerical and secretarial staffs.

Even the nature of heavy industry is being altered, calling for different forms of employee training. In industry at first the educational function was merely a secondary aspect of the line operation—an extra duty of the master craftsmen. Then as personnel management became differentiated as a function, responsibility for training tended to become subsumed under it. Later there was a tendency for departments of training, personal development, or employee's education to become separated out as independent units responsible to top management. Undoubtedly, this move will quicken pace in the years ahead. Thirdly is the whole question of leisure and how to make the most enjoyable use of it. This aspect of adult education will increasingly make demands on both government, and especially local government services and on the voluntary organizations. The fourth factor is that of ageing and the need to concentrate more on activities for the retired. This is likely also to require governments and voluntary organizations to expand their offerings, and to be working cooperatively together.

The developed world seems to call for improved working relationships between governmental and nongovernmental agencies. Third World demands are increasingly having to be met either through governments or through government-sponsored parastatal institutions. This is not to deny the place of voluntary enterprises but where they exist they are likely to become the agents of government-backed interests. Throughout most of the Third World is the need for massive literacy and basic education programmes. These can only be effectively supplied by governments. It is not surprising therefore that Third World countries are actively instituting special arms of government to control this work. India, Nigeria, Tanzania, Afghanistan, and Botswana may be cited in this respect. The Mobral organization of Brazil is an example of a quasigovernmental arrangement for the provision of literacy programmes. At the same time governments are having to accelerate their provision of vocational training, calling for increasing cooperation between state and commercial undertakings. Third World countries are in the forefront of efforts to explore the relationship between education and the world of work, a growing interest which inevitably will be reflected in the educational programmes available for adults.

Bibliography

Charters A N et al. 1981 *Comparing Adult Education Worldwide*. Jossey-Bass, San Francisco, California

European Bureau of Adult Education (EBAE) 1978 *Directory of Adult Education Organisations in Europe*. EBAE, Amersfoort

Hutchinson E M 1974 Adult education. *Encyclopaedia Britannica*, 15th edn., Macropaedia Vol. 1, pp. 97–101

International Council for Adult Education (ICAE) 1980 *National Organisations for Cooperation in Adult Education 1974*. ICAE, Toronto, Ontario

Kelly T 1970 *A History of Adult Education in Great Britain*, 2nd edn. Liverpool University Press, Liverpool

Knowles M S 1970 *The Modern Practice of Adult Education: Andragogy Versus Pedagogy*. Association Press, Chicago, Illinois

Peterson R E et al. 1980 *Adult Education Opportunities in Nine Industrialised Countries*. Educational Testing Service, Princeton, New Jersey

Smith R M, Allen G F, Kidd J R (eds.) 1970 *Handbook of Adult Education*. Macmillan, New York

Titmus C 1981 *Strategies for Adult Education: Practices in Western Europe*. Open University Press, Milton Keynes

Townsend Coles E K 1977 *Adult Education in Developing Countries*, 2nd edn. Pergamon, Oxford

Townsend Coles E K 1982 *Maverick of the Education Family: Two Essays in Non-formal Education*. Pergamon, Oxford

Adult Education in Public Schools

S. Brookfield

Such is the emphasis in the adult education literature on voluntary and informal initiatives such as the cooperative extension service in the United States, the folk high school in Northern Europe, and the Workers' Educational Association in the United Kingdom, that the chief providers of state-sponsored education in modern societies—the public schools—have tended to be ignored. Histories of the field tend to regard public school provision as adult education somehow of a lower intellectual order. The following article discusses adult education programmes and classes which are provided by public schools; that is, schools which are financed by public authorities, regional or national. In the United Kingdom the misnomer "public" school is applied to privately funded institutions. This article deals only with publicly maintained and supervised schools and examines the adult education dimension to their activities.

1. The United States

The extent of adult participation in public school adult education in the United States is notoriously hard to determine. However, the National Association for Public Continuing and Adult Education (NAPCAE) estimated in the mid-1970s that over $8\frac{1}{2}$ million Americans were engaged in public school adult education. The majority of these (over 5 million) were enrolled in general education programmes. The other main categories of participation were high-school diploma courses (1,109,212), adult basic education programmes

(1,087,344), and business and commercial programmes (666,600). High-school equivalency and Americanization and citizenship programmes accounted for most of the rest of public school adult education.

In a 1970 analysis of public school continuing education Finch declared that greater change had occurred in the 1960s than in over a century. As well as increased enrolments he cited favourable teacher wages and conditions of service and a dramatic increase in the number of states with full-time directors of adult education. A major overview of lifelong learning in the United States (Peterson et al. 1979) identified five important adult education functions performed by public schools—allowing elementary or secondary school dropouts to return and earn the equivalent of their high-school diploma, campaigning against adult illiteracy, arranging English as a Second Language and socialization programmes for non-English-speaking immigrants, offering a variety of occupational skills courses, and providing academic and avocational courses for community members. Optimistically, he declared that "From a lifelong learning perspective, public school adult education, in both content and spirit, seems exemplary indeed as a school-based source of education."

It is important to recognize, however, that the curricula of schools reflect the interests and concerns of their local communities. In inner-city or depressed rural areas, vocational training programmes or remedial education will predominate. It is in middle-class suburbs and affluent small towns that avocational and general interest courses will be most successful. Despite the optimism noted earlier, public school adult education has not as yet flourished to the extent that might be expected in an era of declining school-age student enrolments. One reason for this may be the increased competition for the adult student clientele offered by the community college sector.

2. The United Kingdom

Section 41 of the 1944 Education Act (England and Wales) requires local education authorities (l.e.a.s) to secure the provision of adequate facilities for further education in their area. This provision comprises full- and part-time education for persons over compulsory school age including cultural and recreational activities. Because adult education is deemed to be part of further education provision, it is, by implication, a statutory duty. However, as an acceptable level of adult education provision has never been quantified each l.e.a. is free to determine what constitutes appropriate provision. Nonetheless, those adults participating in l.e.a. courses represent over four-fifths of all adult education enrolments. Stock has identified three major categories of local authority provision—area adult education centres (mostly based on schools), community and village colleges, and adult studies departments in colleges of further education. Schools run very few adult education programmes during the day and area adult education centres use the classrooms, laboratories, and gymnasia of primary and secondary schools for evening classes. These classes and courses are usually known either as evening institutes or adult education centres (Stock 1980).

In 1979–80 approximately $3\frac{1}{2}$ million adults attended l.e.a. courses and 2,000 staff were employed full-time by l.e.a.s as adult educators (Legge 1982). Evening institutes, based on local schools, are the most common models of provision, though their unsuitability for adult education purposes has received frequent documentation. There are difficulties over room and chair sizes, poor storage facilities, unhelpful ancillary staff, and a lack of assistance from daytime schoolteachers. The range of provision is wide, with courses related to the home and family being the most popular. A major research report into the curricula of adult education (Mee and Wiltshire 1978) analysed 34,368 courses offered in 36 authorities across England and Wales. Craft and aesthetic skills courses related to the household economy and leisure accounted for an overall majority (approximately 53.8 percent) of courses offered. These were followed by physical skills courses (approximately 23.6 percent), cognitive and intellectual skills courses (approximately 17.3 percent), and courses for disadvantaged groups (approximately 5.4 percent). In an overview of adult education in the United Kingdom the director of the National Institute of Adult Education similarly ranked the popularity of adult fields of study (Stock 1980).

The adult education literature generally paints a depressing picture of much public school adult education provision in the United Kingdom characterized by grossly inadequate staffing, little student participation, and poor physical facilities. The lowering effect on morale was identified in Mee and Wiltshire's research where adult educators forced to "borrow" school accommodation complained of unhelpful school caretakers, indifferent day schoolteachers, and a lack of political weight accorded to the adult education work within schools.

3. Sweden

The major role played by public school adult education in the United States and the United Kingdom is exceptional among capitalist countries of the developed world. Adult education has usually been provided by private initiative, sometimes, as in France, in reaction against the rigidities of public education. However, as governments have appreciated the potential of adult education as an instrument of social and economic policy, they have increasingly used the public education system, which they control, to carry out adult education initiatives.

Sweden provides an unusually clear example of this trend. Concerned to achieve intergenerational equality of educational opportunity, in 1967 the state established municipal adult schools by law. Their purpose was to open to adults the opportunities of secondary education which were available to children and to that end they would offer to adults free tuition in the secondary-school curriculum (which is uniform throughout the country). Adults would be taught by schoolteachers in existing school premises and some 25 percent of teaching time was allocated for individual counselling and tuition. In 1975 the "Act Concerning an Employee's Right to Educational Leave" was passed to provide grants to adults who now possess the right to claim (unpaid) leave for study. By 1975, 392,000 students were enrolled in municipal adult education with 43 percent on general courses, 30 percent on vocational courses, and 27 percent in compulsory school courses. The functions of municipal adult schools were extended in 1977 to include providing basic education for adults with deficient or nonexistent educational experience. Titmus (1981) has declared that the creation of public school adult education paralleling that offered by the school curriculum exemplifies a European tradition in which adult education is seen as an integral and major element in a policy of lifelong education.

4. *Eastern Europe*

Savićević (1981) indicates a number of determinants of adult education which are common to all European socialist countries. Adults have a right in law to education and receive inducements to take up this opportunity. Economic priorities determine much of the adult education curriculum and which elements receive greater financial support. The State, which controls all education, has linked youth and adult education in a unified system and schools are regarded as institutions of lifelong learning. It is therefore to be expected that they will play an important part in adult education.

In Albania, a significant sector of adult education is organized into schools of elementary adult education, lower technical schools, secondary schools of general education for adults, and secondary vocational schools for adults. The sector of the Czechoslovakian adult education system sited in schools is known as the "second educational path" and is organized through the general educational primary school, the general education secondary school, and the secondary vocational school.

In 1965, the German Democratic Republic passed a law in which adult education was seen as an integral element in a unified, lifelong education system. A similar pattern of school adult education provision exists in Hungary including special adult classes sited within schools for young people. Since the Second World War, one million Hungarian adults have completed primary school education and half a million have finished secondary school. The Polish network of schools for adults includes schools for primary adult education, secondary general educational schools, and technical schools, with many school classes sited in factories.

5. *Trends and Issues*

Although adult educators' objections to siting their activities in school premises are legion, it is likely that such an arrangement will remain in the forseeable future. This being the case, it may be that the course for adult education is to make a virtue of necessity and insist that the schools beome true centres of lifelong education in which adults, youths, and children receive instruction at all times. The community school movement is one such initiative and a world review of the education of adults proposed such a model as the most satisfactory mode of adult education provision (Lowe 1975). It is certainly true that the scope for radical practice and curriculum development in adult education is limited in public school provision (other than that occurring in community schools) and that adult educators working within higher education or further education settings have demonstrated a much greater capacity for experiment and innovation.

One innovation of particular importance to the field would be the inclusion of an adult education component in school teacher-training courses. At present very few institutions of teacher training pay any more than lip service to the notion of lifelong learning. If schools are to become centres of lifelong learning then their staff will need a greater understanding of adult psychology and practice in teaching adult students. Teacher-training courses could widen their curriculum to include such a component. It has also been suggested that school governing bodies and management boards should include an adult education representation. Given that crucial decisions concerning school operations and priorities rest in the hands of such bodies, adult educators will continue to experience a sense of marginality and vulnerability if their interests remain unrepresented. Without such fundamental changes in the training of schoolteachers and composition of school management bodies, adult education will continue to represent a peripheral element in the schools' operations. There is little that individual adult educators can do to change the importance attached to their operations without these larger structural and attitudinal changes. Sweden is an example of a society in which public school adult education has been enhanced by a firm expression of political will.

The most pressing research topic in this field which requires exploration is the effect on teacher and learner behaviours of including adult classes as a central component of the schools' operation, or even of introducing adult students into school classes. Mee and Wiltshire, however, noted a strong resistance to such a mixing among adult educators. In addition, the much invoked concept of andragogy is predicated on the assumption that adults' life experience requires teachers to adopt a set of behaviours contrasting markedly with those of schoolteachers. There seems to have been a recent acceptance, however, that andragogy and pedagogy are overlapping parts of a continuum rather than mutually exclusive categories. Certainly, given the numerical significance of the numbers of adults attending classes in public schools, it is surprising that virtually no attempt has been made to study the consequences of their presence on the rest of the school's operations.

If adult and continuing education is to become one element in a unified system of truly lifelong education, then the public schools will have to occupy a central place in any such system.

Schools are, after all, the agencies of educational provision into which is poured the greater part of governmental educational expenditure. They are accessible sites of educational activity located in many villages, all towns, and urban neighbourhoods. For most adults their only involvement with organized education is through their children's school experience. In addition, if the adults of tomorrow are to be lifelong learners possessing self-directed learning skills and the ability to adapt to periods of retraining at various times during their working lives, then it is the schools which will be responsible for developing the required cognitive skills and affective dispositions.

Bibliography

Finch R E 1970 Public schools. In: Aker G, Smith R M, Kidd J R(eds.) 1970 *Handbook of Adult Education.* Macmillan, New York

Legge D 1982 *The Education of Adults in Britain.* Open University Press, Milton Keynes

Lowe J 1975 *The Education of Adults: A World Perspective.* UNESCO, Paris

Mee G, Wiltshire H 1978 *Structure and Performance in Adult Education.* Longman, London

National Association for Public Continuing and Adult Education (NAPCAE) 1976 *Public Continuing and Adult Education 1976 Almanac.* NAPCAE, Washington, DC

Peterson R E et al. 1979 *Lifelong Learning in America: An Overview of Current Practices, Available Resources, and Future Prospects.* Jossey-Bass, San Francisco, California

Savićević D M 1981 Adult education systems in European socialist countries. In: Charters A N et al. (eds.) 1981 *Comparing Adult Education Worldwide.* Jossey-Bass, San Francisco, California

Stock A 1980 *Adult Education in the United Kingdom.* National Institute of Adult Education, Leicester

Titmus C 1981 *Strategies for Adult Education: Practices in Western Europe.* Open University Press, Milton Keynes

Community Colleges in Adult Education

R. Yarrington

Postsecondary institutions called community colleges were created in great numbers in the 1960s, primarily to serve a growing population of college-age youth. But, once these institutions were in place, persons of all ages began to use them. In the early 1980s, the college-age population began to decline. However, enrollments in community colleges continued to grow. This growth is attributed to a number of causes, for example the continuing need for more technicians and the attraction of low tuition fees. But, the chief factor is clearly the trend toward lifelong education for all adults.

The average age of the students in many United States community colleges in the 1980s is 28 to 30 years. The fastest growing segment of the student population in community colleges is women older than the traditional college age. It is not uncommon for colleges to report that 10 to 15 percent of their students already have baccalaureate and graduate degrees. Community colleges, which began as local institutions to assure access to higher education for all young people, have retained that function but have also become community-based institutions for adult education.

One of the reasons this development has taken place in community colleges is that adult education services were needed because of trends in the economy and in society: the need for workers with more training; the desire for more education because of the attached earning power and social prestige; and the increased complexity of all phases of life. The main reason, however, is that the colleges were created in large numbers at just the right time and with a policy framework that allowed them to be sufficiently flexible and responsive to community needs. As the need for continuing education of adults was identified by the colleges, they adapted and created new programs.

In the mid-1960s, for example, community service was identified as an additional function. The term meant different things in different places but, in general, it was applied to a wide range of services that community colleges were developing in response to local needs. Often, but not exclusively, the services were noncredit programs. Short courses, seminars, lecture series, cultural events, were used to respond to community interests. Sometimes community service involved taking educational programs to new locations and offering them at new times so that more persons could participate.

By the mid-1970s an additional strategy became apparent. Cooperative efforts were arranged with other community education agencies, such as secondary schools (often called community schools), and with local park and recreation departments. The community college served as a cooperating institution (often the coordinating agency) in a community-wide program of adult education. Surveys by the American Association of Community and Junior Colleges at the turn of the decade indicated that the typical community college had nearly 100 working partnerships in its community. Mostly these were with other schools and adult education agencies, and, not surprisingly, with local businesses.

1. Connections with Businesses

Local business people were usually key citizens working for the establishment of local community colleges. Boards of trustees tend to be made up of local business people. Each occupational education program in a community college will have an advisory committee made up of local employers and practitioners. It has been a logical development, therefore, for community colleges to have close working relationships with local business and industry. The majority of the students are already employed locally; graduates go to work for local employers; the colleges are supported primarily by local taxes.

During the 1960s and 1970s occupational education programs developed dramatically in community colleges. These are programs to prepare graduates for job entry, rather than university transfer. In 1965, 14 percent of the community college credit enrollments were in occupational education programs. By 1980 this had grown to 63 percent of the credit enrollment. Community colleges prepare students for work in more than 1,400 occupations. A typical community college has approximately 30 to 50 different occupational programs.

While these programs, like most others, were developed to prepare traditional college youth, they have become increasingly used by persons of all ages. An observer visiting community colleges in the 1970s to examine programs set up in cooperation with local labor unions reported more retraining than training. They were providing apprenticeship training, the retraining of journeymen, labor education for union leaders, and preretirement education for older workers preparing for new careers (often self-employment). It is now standard practice for community colleges to survey local businesses for employee training needs and to set up employer-specific training programs.

In some of the states the community colleges are well-integrated into the economic development program with state funds set aside to pay for the training of employees for new industries that are attracted into the state and for businesses that expand existing operations. The expansion of industry into automated production techniques, the use of computers, high technology, and the need for improved management and supervisory skills indicate that close cooperation arrangements between community colleges and local businesses will continue. As they do, the institutions will be used increasingly for adult education.

2. Developments in Other Countries

Japan opened its first temporary junior college in 1950. In the next two decades more than 400 were established. They served one sex; were mostly private; predominantly terminal, rather than transfer; and often single purpose, such as the Tokyo Junior College of Photography. In 1964 a law was passed making the "short-term" colleges a permanent part of the nation's higher education system. The effort to achieve permanent recognition was led by the Association of Private Junior Colleges in Japan.

Canada has the national Association of Canadian Community Colleges for two-year colleges. Canadian colleges trace their beginnings, primarily, to activities that took place in several provinces in the mid-1960s. Some of these institutions, especially in western provinces (British Columbia, Alberta, and Saskatchewan), are similar to their American neighbors.

Other countries have established community colleges. Australia for example has many urban and regional colleges offering postsecondary education and vocational training. There is no formal transfer arrangement between the tripartite system of higher education. Many colleges of technical and further education offer community-based educational programs, trade training, and technician-level vocational courses. Colleges of advanced education cater for students at three-year diploma and four-year baccalaureate levels. Taiwan has more than 70 technical junior colleges. Institutions with some university parallel, occupational, or adult education missions may be found in other countries. They may or may not be called community colleges. Most are not comprehensive, but provide one or more of the typical community college services. Countries as disparate as Ireland, Jordan, Denmark, Sri Lanka, and Venezuela have forms of community colleges.

In 1981 UNESCO published a *World-wide Inventory of Non-traditional, Post-secondary Educational Institutions* which includes entries from nearly two dozen countries with institutions that have two-year programs. The majority are on the African continent. Most are institutions for technical education and teacher training.

In Europe, expressions of interest in community college programs have come from regional colleges in Norway, colleges of further education in the United Kingdom, and technical colleges in other countries, such as the Netherlands. Most often international interest has focused not on the community college as an institutional form so much as on the programs they offer. Adult education, especially adult basic education, is the chief example of such program interest, along with vocational–technical education and community-based education.

With the exception of Japan, where the junior college idea was implanted during the United States occupation, American educators have generally not advocated the exportation of the community college as an institution. Rather they have encouraged international dialogue with educators who have similar programmatic interests, representing whatever institutional forms such programs may take in other countries. Feeling has been that the community college, as it has taken shape in the United States, is a response to a specific culture and has evolved from a particular educational tradition. Other institutional forms may well perform similar program functions in other countries. The value of international dialogue is for each country to learn from the others.

Nevertheless, interest in adapting the community college idea to other cultures has persisted. In such cases, American educators have urged an application of the same process followed by individual states in the United States. This requires a study of postsecondary educational needs and the establishment of an institution responsive to identified local needs, rather than importation of a model established in response to needs in another country at another time.

There have been international meetings of educators interested in community college programs held annually since 1970. That year, the American Association, as part of its 50th anniversary, sponsored an international assembly at the East–West Center at the University of Hawaii for educators around the Pacific rim. The Association has since served as host for international meetings at each of its annual conventions. There have been other international meetings in countries such as Canada, India, and England. In recent years there has been a TransAtlantic Institute meeting held each summer for community college educators in the United States and England, the location alternating from one side of the Atlantic to the other.

Because of the tremendous range of different institutional forms and missions represented in such international meetings, a new term came into use in the 1970s: "short-cycle" education. The term illustrates the most common uniting factor that has brought the participants together—postsecondary education that is less than baccalaureate in level and less than four years in length. As in the United States, "postsecondary" is often used in these discussions to mean an age level rather than a grade level. One of the continuing topics of universal concern among educators in "short-cycle" institutions is adult education. The International Council for Adult Education has been one of the forums with consistent interest in such institutions.

Bibliography

Breneman D W 1981 *Financing Community Colleges: An Economic Perspective.* Brookings, Washington, DC

Campbell G 1971 *Community Colleges in Canada.* McGraw-Hill, Scarborough

Fersh S 1979 *International Developments in Post-secondary Short-cycle Education.* American Association of Community and Junior Colleges, Washington, DC

Gleazer E J 1980 *The Community College: Values, Vision and Vitality.* American Association of Community and Junior Colleges, Washington, DC

Jennings B (ed.) 1980 *Community Colleges in England and Wales.* National Institute of Adult Education, Leicester

Kintzer F C 1979 World adaptation of the community college concept. In: King M C, Breuder R L (eds.) 1979 *Advancing International Education: New Directions for Community Colleges,* No. 26. Jossey-Bass, San Francisco, California, pp. 65–78

UNESCO 1981 *World-wide Inventory of Non-traditional Post-secondary Educational Institutions.* UNESCO, Paris

Yarrington R 1970 *International Development of the Junior College Idea.* American Association of Junior Colleges, Washington, DC

Universities and Adult Education: Policies and Programmes

P. Fordham

This article examines university involvement in adult education as a worldwide phenomenon, but it recognizes two major difficulties. Firstly, university interest in adult education is far from universal. For example, in countries like Sweden or the Federal Republic of Germany, the large adult education programmes are usually provided by other kinds of institution. Secondly, adult education in any society is inevitably dominated by local culture in a more marked way than might be true, say, of the science curriculum of the secondary school. A high level of public participation in adult education implies a high level of voluntary commitment. It is therefore inevitable that effective programmes, at whatever level, must spring directly from the needs of a particular society with its own culture and history and contemporary frame of reference. Of course this must to some extent be true of universities as a whole. Nevertheless, where universities are involved in the direct provision of education for adults there is likely to be much less in common between work done in one country and another than would be true, say, for the training of engineers or the study of urban geography (Wiltshire 1971).

A further problem is that involvement in the practice of adult education does not come easily to most universities. Universities are primarily concerned with two quite different functions: (a) extending the frontiers of knowledge through research at the highest level, and (b) passing on that knowledge to succeeding generations through teaching. And this major teaching function puts them at the apex of a formal system of education which depends for its viability on the existence of an appropriate grading and selection system at each successive stage. It is inevitable that a very high proportion of any university's collective energy should be concentrated on undergraduate/postgraduate teaching and its accompanying research. Direct provision of adult education for the surrounding community usually arises only in exceptional circumstances.

This article concentrates on the most significant of these exceptional circumstances using a historical perspective. It also notes the effects of one important attempt at cultural and institutional transfer (from the United Kingdom to Anglophone Africa). It includes an analysis of the different types of university involvement and concludes that future developments are likely to be seen most clearly within a framework which assumes a growing acceptance of the concept of recurrent education.

1. Types of Involvement

In looking at policies and programmes in this field, it is helpful for the purposes of analysis to make a distinction between four different activities:

(a) Part-time higher education for adults, leading to university or professional qualifications.

(b) Short, professional, or other refresher courses at undergraduate, or postgraduate levels, often referred to as "university continuing education".

(c) A contribution to the general education of adults in the surrounding area. For example, participation in literacy schemes in India (see Sect. 4) or "extramural studies" in the United Kingdom (Russell 1973).

(d) The development of adult education as a field of study and the training of adult educators.

The first two of these activities (part-time study for qualifications and advanced short courses) are phenomena of particular importance in developed countries. Higher education for school leavers is already widespread and there is increasing concern about the rapid obsolescence of knowledge acquired in full-time education. Moreover, pressures for the renewal and updating of previously acquired knowledge coincide both with pressures for increasing access for previously neglected social groups and with the expected decline in the 18+ age groups in advanced industrial societies. More mature students, more part-time study, and more open access seem to be in the interests of all.

Part-time higher education and advanced short courses have long been established in North America, the Soviet Union, Eastern Europe, and in developed countries (e.g., Australia) elsewhere. Both are now spreading rapidly to Western Europe, sometimes through "open" universities using distance teaching methods. Indeed, the latter phenomenon has attracted universal interest (Lowe 1975).

The first two of the four activities mentioned above are also the most specialized sectors of university adult education in the academic sense. They are thus the ones which come most easily to existing institutions and which, though far from universal in the early 1980s, are the ones most likely to become so.

As has already been noted, some responses to community needs are likely to be highly culture bound. Indeed, as a fully developed phenomenon of more than a few years standing, university adult education which embraces all the four strands listed above is confined to the English-speaking world. Even here one should not assume universality. For example, Indian universities have only recently begun to take on an adult education function. Adult education as a field of study, on the other hand, is clearly a branch of educational studies and thus a "proper" university activity. Although of more recent development than the other three, it has already spread to universities which have very little in the way of other adult educational activities.

2. Contributions to General Adult Education

A commitment to make a contribution to the general education of adults in the local region of each university can be traced directly to the liberal social conscience of some university professors in nineteenth-century England. It was the direct result of "the moral indignation of dons at Cambridge and Oxford at the cumulative social injustice they saw in the denial to so many citizens of the knowledge to which only a small elite in the universities had access" (Houle 1952). The first manifestation of this moral indignation was the establishment in the 1870s of university extension courses (Jepson 1973).

The mode of provision—still influential to this day—was a series of 12 or so evening lectures, each followed by a class or discussion for those members of the audience who wished to stay. Some of the early audiences consisted of women's associations and cooperative societies but, increasingly, a new organizational pattern emerged with the creation of autonomous voluntary associations called university extension societies; and voluntary effort remains to this day an important feature of adult education in the United Kingdom. The subjects of study were many and varied but were essentially directed towards the wider spread of an existing elite culture and in the interests of individual self-improvement; the core subjects were history and English literature.

2.1 Developments and Programmes in the United States

University extension in the United Kingdom was one of the influences which helped give rise to a parallel development in the United States, particularly the early efforts of long established eastern universities like Johns Hopkins and Columbia (Knowles 1962). But the American variant of university extension did not continue to follow the United Kingdom model for long. Inevitably, a different setting and a different culture produced quite different responses. What remained for many practitioners was a similar underlying ideology: the conviction of Anglo–Saxon liberal scholarship that universities ought to be involved in the education of wider adult publics. The ideology was perhaps best expressed in the famous 1919 Report (Wiltshire 1980), where adult education, including a university commitment, is seen as a necessary support for the maintenance of a politically democratic society.

Besides the commitment to a liberal political ideology, there were other local influences at work in the

United States during the nineteenth century which helped to determine the present distinctive pattern of university adult education in that country. Of these the two most important were, firstly, the Chautauqua Institution and secondly, the environmental circumstances of an expanding frontier economy.

Chautauqua grew out of a summer school for Sunday-school teachers which from 1878 onwards rapidly expanded into a broadly based cultural programme of adult education. It was a pioneer of many new forms of instruction, including correspondence study, summer schools, book clubs, and reading circles, all of which were adopted and adapted by American university extension. Its curriculum was very broadly based, and included not only the liberal arts but practical and vocational subjects like domestic science and library training.

By 1883 the Chautauqua University (later incorporated into the State University of New York) was granting liberal arts degrees to its part-time students. Two essential features of modern university extension in the United States thus emerged from Chautauqua: a concern for access to part-time higher education and a recognition that student needs were both cultural and vocational.

These features were also emphasized by environmental circumstances, particularly in the more recently settled areas away from the eastern seabord. As a result, a revived pattern of university extension—less academic, more suited to new social and vocational needs—began to emerge, first with the 1907 reorganization of the extension division of the University of Wisconsin and later elsewhere. What came to be known as the "Wisconsin idea" saw extension not only as covering the whole field of knowledge from agriculture (including farm institutes) to the fine arts, but also the geographical extension of that knowledge; in the words of Wisconsin President, Robert Foss (1932), "the boundaries of the campus are the boundaries of the state" (Schoenfeld 1977).

Today, university extension in the United States provides a vast array of courses and programmes for credit (i.e., part-time higher education) or without credit, vocational and nonvocational. The most comprehensive programmes are found in the various land grant universities, where more general extension work is associated with the government-sponsored agricultural extension service (more properly called "cooperative extension service") (Smith et al. 1970). Universities in North America (including Canada) are uniquely placed among the universities of the world. That is to say, many of them provide extensive programmes in all the four main activities listed in Sect. 1 above.

2.2 Patterns of Provision in the United Kingdom

The early divergence between patterns of provision in the United States and the United Kingdom has already been noted. The influential voluntary body was the Workers' Educational Association, founded in 1903 as a means of bringing a university-type education within reach of an emerging working-class leadership, especially in the trades' unions, the cooperative movement, and the infant Labour Party. It aimed to create a "partnership between enlightened scholarship and working class aspirations" (Stocks 1953). The university extramural idea which emerged from that partnership was essentially a meeting of the liberal university tradition with the leaders and potential leaders of a group of relatively new aspirants, to social, political, and economic power (Fordham 1970).

The ideological and practical issues arising from this partnership were examined with great thoroughness by a committee established by the British Ministry of Reconstruction whose findings were published in the 1919 Report. Among other things, this influential document—written in time of war—examined the social and economic ills of the country and the changes which would have to be made if political democracy were to be preserved and extended; in this "design for democracy", adult education, and particularly the university variant, was to play a great part. Note the positive political role proposed; adult education was not neutral: it was for social/economic improvement and the advance of political democracy. It was this report which recommended the establishment of university extramural departments "responsible for the whole field of nonvocational . . . education" (Wiltshire 1980 p. 159). And it is this which remains the essential organizational pattern right into the 1980s.

As a result of these origins and the needs then identified, there are essential differences between "extramural studies" in the United Kingdom and university extension in the United States. The former is much smaller in scale, more heavily subsidized by state funds, more protected by regulations and funding arrangements, and therefore less obliged to respond to evident market demands. But it is also constrained by the regulations which protect it. Provision must be "nonvocational". There has been little development in the American sense of courses "for credit" and it has been difficult for extramural departments to break into the rapidly expanding field of professional training. The most famous contribution in the United Kingdom to part-time higher education, the Open University, could not have emerged from traditional extramural work, while professional "continuing" education has grown more vigorously in other sections of universities in the United Kingdom (e.g., faculties of engineering, law, or medicine) which are already involved in the professional education of young undergraduates.

Extramural teaching programmes in the United Kingdom are thus still heavily concentrated on liberal arts and social sciences. The emphasis on political emancipation has almost disappeared while that of individual self-fulfilment has markedly increased. But the ideological emphasis is still that of 1919 with its emphasis on university standards as an approach to controversial issues of public policy or personal growth, and its insistence that the "essence of the best academic spirit is a willingness to face facts, to discard cherished theories when fuller evidence no longer makes them tenable, to suspend judgment upon matters upon which certainty is unobtainable, to welcome criticisms and to hear differences of opinion with tolerance" (Wiltshire 1980 p. 64). Subjects like history, literature, politics, or philosophy—often studied for "their own sake"—remain the core provision.

As modern extramural departments have tried to respond to new and pressing demands they have, in part, been able to provide more avowedly vocational courses like the professional training of mature-age social workers or inservice work for the adult education staff of other agencies. But they remain constrained by their original nonvocational brief. Coming to terms with vocational motivation and the ever-increasing demands both for part-time higher education and for professional retraining may well be the crucial test for the continuance of the distinctive "extramural" tradition in universities in the United Kingdom.

3. *The Transformation of a Cultural Transplant*

The international significance of the university extramural idea lies in its export to those countries where British-type universities were established, firstly in Australia, New Zealand, and parts of Canada, and more recently (post-1945) in Anglophone Africa, the University of the West Indies, and in a few Commonwealth countries in Asia (but *not* the Indian subcontinent). In the developed Commonwealth, the original idea remains more or less intact, though much influenced by models from the United States. In Anglophone Africa it is now almost totally transformed.

Before the transformation, extramural departments were established in a mould which sought to replicate the tradition of the United Kingdom on African soil. Nonvocational liberal studies (especially in economics, political science, and English), a concern for objective thinking and intellectual freedom, the creation of "resident tutor" posts to serve areas remote from the university, teaching methods which placed great emphasis on regular evening classes, discussion-based learning, and widened access to university scholarship were all copied. Governments were anxious to ensure "responsible leadership", while expatriate adult educators saw themselves helping in the emancipation of Africans in the same way that an earlier generation of liberal professors had tried to help in the emancipation of the working class of the United Kingdom. In all these Anglophone countries before independence, the extramural departments performed very well their traditional function of the education of a political elite and its supporters.

Very rapidly after independence, however, the first stage in the transformation occurred. The elite which had supported the young extramural departments now became preoccupied with the exercise of power. In politics, the civil service and later in business enterprise, members of the educated elite were either moving into positions of power or busily engaged in training to do so. Simultaneously, new pressures were emerging from English-speaking primary-school leavers denied entry to full-time secondary and higher education. Without any conscious policy decisions, what actually happened was an ambiguous response by university "extramural studies" to a mass of students demanding courses for secondary-school-level examinations from institutions officially unwilling to provide them. The extramural departments were in danger of becoming substitute secondary schools, but with neither the structure nor the resources to provide either an effective service or to meet an insistent and growing demand. Some of this work still remains, but has largely been replaced by the fourth function mentioned in Sect. 1 above, namely, the training of adult educators from other institutions and the development of adult education as a field of study.

It is a remarkable fact that, whereas in developed English-speaking countries the actual provision of university adult education is far greater in quantity than the time and resources devoted to research and training, in many developing countries (e.g., Nigeria or Kenya) the reverse applies. English-type "extramural studies" have, since the early 1960s, been transformed into the university discipline of adult education. There is still some direct provision, especially of an experimental kind: there is a residue of secondary-school-level work and the beginnings of professional continuing education (e.g., at the University of Lagos). But in most cases the extramural work of African universities has been transformed into adult education training and research. The universities are seeking to meet the needs of other providing agencies while themselves withdrawing from direct provision.

4. *Nonformal Education*

Before looking at training and research it is necessary to take note of one kind of adult education which has not yet been discussed in this article. In the jargon of the 1980s, it would probably be called "nonformal" education, but writers using an earlier terminology would probably have been content with "community development", or think simply of a university contribution to functional literacy or to agricultural extension. The distinguishing features are that the activity stems directly from a concern with the needs of the poor, that it is directed as much towards economic and social action as to learning, and that the learning is not necessarily closely related to the internal teaching of the university.

One of the most famous (and earliest) examples is that of St. Francis Xavier University in Nova Scotia, Canada. The starting point was the need, first expressed in the 1920s by Father Tompkins (Laidlaw 1961) to do something which would help to bring economic and social change to the area: the major tool for the change was adult education. In the years which followed, the university became intimately involved in economic and social development. And its adult education work helped promote credit unions, cooperative societies, and other economic or social enterprises as well as specifically educational ventures like study clubs. In its outreach work for the rural poor it was both successful and years before its time.

In the 1970s and 1980s concepts of development are becoming familiar which involve a determined attack on poverty, progress towards social transformation, and an increase in mass participation; these require a contribution from all levels of society, including the universities. Increasingly, societies expect universities to do more than their traditional research and the training of young school leavers, more even than extension or extramural teaching: they have to be centrally concerned with development, with questions of employment, of social equity, and with the alleviation of poverty.

The recent example of India is instructive. Universities which had been content with a role which isolated them from the majority of the people and with no adult education tradition were in 1978 urged by the Indian University Grants Commission's (UGC) Guidelines, "to accept service to the community as one of their important responsibilities". It was, moreover, "important to establish an organic link between adult education/extension and university curricula". The former, it was argued, should not be looked upon merely as a welfare activity for the deprived social groups, but as a process of interaction with the society leading to valuable learning experience and as a means for making higher education relevant to the needs of the society and oriented towards a solution of existing problems. Without such interaction on a continuing basis, the UGC asserted that "the universities will remain isolated from the society and their programmes out of tune with the reality around them". As a first result of this initiative there was major student participation in India's national adult education (literacy) programme. Similar university involvement in nonformal programmes can now be found in a number of developing countries.

5. Adult Education as a Field of Study

Unlike the study of school education, adult education training and research began from the field practice with which universities were already associated. This remains an important strength, especially as the idea of graduate or undergraduate study in adult education is relatively new. The first adult education doctorate awarded in the United States came only in 1935; most, even in that country, have come since the 1940s (Jensen et al. 1964). In the United Kingdom the study of adult education in universities became firmly established only in the 1960s.

Because the knowledge base for adult education is weak when compared with that of school education, it could be argued that direct provision of field programmes in adult education—whether of a nonformal or a more traditional kind—are not merely a strength but an essential precondition of university involvement in adult education as a field of study, including the training and research for which there is a growing demand. Universities which have field programmes can not only provide an adult service to their communities but also an essential laboratory for their own adult education research. An extension programme which offers a wide range of activities at different levels and for a broad band of socioeconomic groups provides the firmest base. If within this programme there is a high proportion of experimental work, the university is more likely to help other agencies in new programme activities through, for example, needs-based curricula, new teaching materials and approaches, and the adaptation of subject disciplines for a broad spectrum of adult students.

In many countries, reporting of this experimental work and the development of adult education research is very recent. As a result, most of the established general texts are North American in origin. For such a culture-bound discipline they must therefore be used with some caution in other settings (Houle 1972).

6. Future Developments

It has already been suggested that future developments are likely to be seen most clearly in terms of recurrent education. Knowledge gained in youth is increasingly in need of reassessment. New tasks and new professions will require access to a growing range of part-and full-time higher or continuing education courses throughout the adult life span. The education of adults is likely to become a major part of total educational provision. The future of a university contribution to part-time higher education, to continuing education, and to the new adult education discipline seems assured. But what of the contribution to general adult education? It has been shown that this is far from universal. Its future will depend on broad political judgments about the nature of particular societies and the sense of social responsibility of universities within them.

Bibliography

Blyth J A 1983 *English University Adult Education 1908-1958: The Unique Tradition.* Manchester University Press, Manchester

Fordham P E 1970 Adapting a tradition: Extramural policy in Africa. *Universities Q.* 25: 59–70

Houle C O 1952 *Introduction to Universities in Adult Education.* UNESCO, Paris, p. 10

Houle C O 1972 *The Design of Education.* Jossey-Bass, San Francisco, California

Jensen G E, Liveright A A, Hallenbeck W 1964 *Adult Education: Outlines of an Emerging Field of University Study.* Adult Education Association of the USA, Washington, DC

Jepson N A 1973 *The Beginnings of English University Adult Education: Policy and Problems: A Critical Study of the Early Cambridge and Oxford University Extension Lecture Movements between 1873 and 1907, with Special Reference to Yorkshire.* Michael Joseph, London

Knowles M S 1962 *The Adult Education Movement in the United States*. Holt, Rinehart and Winston, New York
Laidlaw A F 1961 *The Campus and the Community: The Global Impact of the Antigonish Movement*. Harvest House, Montreal, Quebec
Lowe J 1975 *The Education of Adults: A World Perspective*. UNESCO, Paris
Marriot S 1984 *Extramural Empires: Service and Self-Interest in English University Adult Education 1873-1983*. Department of Adult Education, University of Nottingham, Nottingham
Russell L 1973 *Adult Education: A Plan for Development*. Her Majesty's Stationery Office, London
Schoenfeld C A 1977 *The Outreach University: A Case History in the Public Relationships of Higher Education, University of Wisconsin Extension 1881–1975*. University of Wisconsin, Madison, Wisconsin
Smith R M, Aker G F, Kidd J R (eds.) 1970 *Handbook of Adult Education*. Macmillan, New York
Stocks M D 1953 *The Workers' Educational Association: The First Fifty Years*. Allen and Unwin, London
Wiltshire H C 1971 The international contribution of British adult education. In: Rogers A (ed.) 1976 *The Spirit and the Form: Essays in Adult Education*. Department of Adult Education, University of Nottingham, Nottingham, pp. 77–81
Wiltshire H C (ed.) 1980 *The 1919 Report: The Final and Interim Reports of the Adult Education Committee of the Ministry of Reconstruction, 1918–1919*. Department of Adult Education, University of Nottingham, Nottingham

Open Access Institutions for Adults: Some Higher Education Cases

M. E. Richardson

This article will examine the need for open access to education for adults in order to achieve the goals of learning which is both universal and lifelong. It will consider the nature of open access and the issues relating to it, with particular reference to higher education. It will describe examples of open access universities in four different countries.

1. History of the Development of Open Learning Systems

Since the late 1960s there has been a rapid growth of learning systems for adults, which are open, both in the sense of physical accessibility (time, place, distance) and in the sense that conventional academic requirements for entrance are reduced or nonexistent. The Faure Report, produced for the International Commission on the Development of Education under the aegis of UNESCO, particularly saw them as meeting "...the need...felt throughout the world for institutions aimed at special categories of adults, workers wanting qualifications, professional men, executives and technicians on whom political or social changes suddenly impose responsibilities for which they were not trained or which technological changes have superseded" (Faure et al. 1972). They would offer access to a central stock of resources which could be individualized: computer-stored or taped data and subscriptions to distribution networks such as radio, television, and correspondence courses.

The development of such learning was given a strong boost by the foundation of the British Open University in 1969. Five years later the National Association of Educational Broadcasters (NAEB) (the professional association which links all educational broadcasting practitioners in the United States) published a report on open learning systems. The report defined the following "essential characteristics" of open learning systems:

> The system must guide a student by eliciting, interpreting and analysing goals at the beginning point and throughout the student's contact with the programme of instruction.
>
> The system must formulate learning objectives in such a way that they serve as the basis for making decisions in instructional design, including evaluation, and in such a way that they will be fully known to, accepted by or capable of modification by students.
>
> The system must facilitate the participation of learners without imposing traditional academic entry requirements, without the pursuit of an academic degree or other certification as the exclusive reward.
>
> To provide the flexibility required to satisfy a variety of individual needs, the system should make it operationally possible to employ sound, television, film and print as options for mediating learning experiences.
>
> The system should use testing and evaluation principally to diagnose and analyse the extent to which specified learning objectives have been accomplished. In other words, the system should be competence-based.
>
> The system must be able to accommodate distance between the instructional staff resources and the learner, employing the distance as a positive element in the development of independence in learning. (MacKenzie et al. 1975)

The same report suggests that open learning should be regarded as a fundamentally new institutional concept of education: "open education is not a variant form of traditional education but the opposite of it".

The "essential characteristics" defined by the NAEB report remain a sound guide to both principle and practice in open learning. Inevitably the potential extension of opportunity and awareness have roused fears both of dilution of standards (where the host society has an established, selective system of adult education) and of social dislocation—both in established and developing societies. Perry (1974) in his Rede Lecture "Where More means Better" addressed the standards debate in the

United Kingdom where he argued convincingly, backed up by employers and academics, on the quality of the graduates of the British Open University. Ten years later, Horlock (1984), looking back on the experience of the British Open University, identified the following as grounds which may attract a society to establish such an open learning institution:

(a) the philanthropic (the opportunity to provide a widening university education through a second chance);

(b) the internationalist (the export of a successful system to benefit the underprivileged, the developing countries);

(c) the practical (the development of a cost-effective contribution to education and training which makes a major contribution to national wealth production); and

(d) the elitist (the provision of a high standard, for both first and higher degree courses, which enables the entrant to go through to the highest academic achievement).

By 1984 44 countries, both developed and developing, had established their own variety of "open" university—and numerous other experiments in openness (whether physical or academic) were under way at secondary and further education levels and in the areas of professional development and updating within industry itself. Within the compass of this article it is not possible to detail them. Basic resource and reference material across a range of institutions and levels can, however, be found in MacKenzie et al. (1975) and Holmberg (1985).

2. Open Learning Systems—Examples

This section will concentrate on four institutional profiles, drawn from Kaye and Rumble (1981), which illustrate a range of models of "openness", showing instances and absences of both physical and academic accessibility at university level.

2.1 Everyman's University, Tel Aviv, Israel

Israel's Everyman's University was established in 1974, to provide all strata of the population that are unable for a variety of reasons to study within the existing educational framework, with the opportunity of obtaining higher education in their homes without interrupting their normal occupations; to assist teachers in the elementary and junior-high schools to study towards an academic degree; to provide a second and equal chance to those who, for one reason or another, had to discontinue their studies at an early age; and to contribute to raising the general educational standards of Israel's population. There are no formal entry qualifications.

The main programmes of courses consist of a first (bachelor's) degree programme; special pre-academic preparatory courses; vocational courses, planned in conjunction with the Centre for Educational Technology and the Ministry of Labour; and general education and continuing education courses. A degree is obtained on completion of 18 courses. Academic courses usually run for an 18-week semester and are comprised of 12 study units, each of which requires 12–18 hours study time. Most students study one course per semester, but, following successful completion of one course, they may take two courses simultaneously. The bulk of the teaching is through correspondence materials, but radio, television and audio cassettes are also employed. There are home experiment kits for some courses, study centre tutorials and telephone tutoring.

Courses are advertised in the national press. Sample packages of course materials are available at a small fee, or can be viewed at study centres. Tuition fees are payable. There is support for student learning in 25 hired study centres, resources of which include a library containing set books, laboratory facilities, and facilities for meeting tutors. Assessment is by self-assessment questions throughout the correspondence texts, tutor- or computer-marked assignments, and supervised end of course examinations.

2.2 Fernuniversität, Hagen, Federal Republic of Germany

The Fernuniversität was founded in 1974 by the government of North Rhine–Westphalia with the aim of increasing higher-education capacity, engaging actively in the reform of university teaching, and developing a system of academic continuing education. The largest student group is composed of part-time students in employment (about 40 percent), followed by "guest students" enrolled for a single course of study (30–35 percent), students of other universities, and full-time students (less than 10 percent). With the exception of "guest students", access is restricted to those with university entrance qualifications.

Courses are offered at first and master's degree levels. One course comprises 14 units, each of which represents 20 hours study time. Full-time students take four courses per year, part-time students take fewer. The principal teaching medium is correspondence text, but audio cassettes, films, and video cassettes are also employed. Tutoring and counselling is given in study centres.

There is no large-scale advertisement of courses and there are no tuition fees. Twenty-eight study centres are maintained in North Rhine–Westphalia and eight other states of the Republic. Study centres contain books and audio visual equipment, and facilities for tutorials by Fernuniversität staff and individual tutoring and counselling by staff members of other universities. Assessment is by self-assessment questions, tutor- and computer-marked assignments, and by conventional examinations.

2.3 *Open University, Milton Keynes, United Kingdom*

Intended to provide a second chance to adults who have not received higher education, and to provide post-experience and refresher courses, the Open University in the United Kingdom began teaching in 1971. From its earliest years the largest proportion of applicants have been teachers and professional people, but now nearly one-third are manual and routine non-manual workers. No formal qualifications are required, but for degree courses students must be at least 21 years of age.

First and post graduate degree courses are offered as well as self-contained non-degree programmes for associate students. Six credits are required for a bachelor's degree, eight for a bachelor's degree with honours. A full credit is awarded on completion of a one-year course comprising 32 units of work, each requiring 10–14 hours of study. A half-credit course requires 16 units. A student may take a maximum of 2 credits per year. Teaching is principally through printed correspondence texts. There is some back-up by television and radio broadcasts, and some use of audio tapes, audio discs and slides. Home experimental kits are issued, tutorial assistance and counselling are given in study centres, and summer schools are held.

Courses are advertised nationally. Regional and course quotas operate for applications. Tuition fees are payable. Two hundred and sixty study centres, each catering for between 50 and 1,000 students, provide facilities for tutoring and counselling, viewing and listening to Open University programmes, and sometimes access to libraries and computer terminals. Each student is allocated a tutor counsellor for the duration of his or her Open University career and a course tutor for each course. Assessment is by self-assessed questions, tutor- and computer-marked assignments, and an end of course examination.

2.4 *Universidad Nacional Abierta (UNA), Caracas, Venezuela*

Formally founded in 1977, the UNA was established to supplement inadequate higher-education provision and to provide adult and continuing education. Students are secondary-school leavers unable or unwilling to attend conventional universities or other higher-education institutions. Admission is limited to those with a secondary-school leaving certificate. Undergraduate courses are structured into three levels: introductory course, general studies, and professional or specialist studies. One hundred and fifty credits are required for a first degree. Each credit represents 36 hours of study and the average student work-load is around 20 hours per week.

Courses are made up of modules, each of which is comprised of printed texts, a guide to self-assessment, a study guide, and experimental equipment where necessary. There are television and radio broadcasts and counselling and tutoring is given in local centres.

Applications for enrolment may be made direct to UNA. Tuition is free, but students buy instructional materials at low cost. Assessment is by self-assessment questions and regular formal examinations.

3. *The Range and Flexibility of Open Learning Systems*

The list of institutions such as the four detailed above is now extensive, showing different degrees of openness. It includes, to exemplify the range, Radio ECCA in Spain, and the Radio and Television University of China (RTVU), arguably the world's biggest learning system (78,000 people graduated in 1982).

At levels other than that of the university sector, open learning for adults, taking the United Kingdom as an example, can occur in areas as diverse as computer literacy, zoo animal management, the training of youth and community workers, and concrete technology (Lewis 1984). The National Extension College (NEC) (Cambridge, UK) and the International Extension College, its sister organization, have pioneered a wide range of flexible open learning schemes across the educational spectrum, including "Flexistudy" (NEC 1979) in the further education sector. An "Open Tech" development in the United Kingdom, initiated by the government, has also carried open learning into industry in a major thrust which reflects industry's constant and increasing need for updating in specific skills in order to remain competitive. By the end of the first phase of the Open Tech activity (1986/87) some 140 projects had been commissioned, both in "creation" and delivery modes. It is worth noting that the Open Tech does not operate as a separate institution: a small central Open Tech Unit stimulates a programme of activity through other institutions and a database has been established (NEC 1985).

Industry itself, both in the United Kingdom and the United States, has begun to appreciate directly the potential of open and independent learning methods. The establishment of open learning programmes and/or resource centres in the Austin Rover automobile company and within the General Electric Company, alongside the development of programmes of Tutored Video Instruction (TVI) within companies on both sides of the Atlantic, exemplifies the application of open learning principles by overtly "noneducational" institutions. This in itself may be seen as an important step in removing the arguably over-rigid and dysfunctional divide between what constitutes "education" and what is seen to be "training".

4. *Requirements of Open Learning Systems*

In summary, to provide systems within institutions capable of offering the "essential characteristics" of open learning as defined by NAEB above, the following essential components are required.

(a) *A learning package.* This rather clumsy phrase acknowledges the need to remove the human agent (the teacher/lecturer)—necessarily constrained by space and time—from the dominant centre of the stage. The shift of emphasis throws the weight onto structured learning materials which may include print, video, audio, broadcast transmission, and computer software. The teacher/lecturer becomes a facilitator, a manager of the learning situation, and intervenes only selectively. Within the United Kingdom, the Open University and the National Extension College present the most extensive range of such packages.

(b) *Support system.* The high drop-out from *unsupported* open learning courses at a range of levels highlights the need for adequate support systems. These will usually provide: access to tutors, counselling and support staff; local centres for study; special library arrangements; access to other students; telephone conferencing; residential or weekend facilities; and dedicated computer networks. There is also a significant role for non-course based institutional materials and systems such as student associations and institutional newspapers.

(c) *Access and credit systems.* To give an end value to the experience of open learning, the "currency" must be transferable. The demonstrability of new skills and their portability between institutions is essential. This argues for national and even international credit transfer and recognition systems at a range of educational levels and a scheme of recognized vocational qualifications which itself has currency across academic boundaries.

5. The Future

As open learning systems continue to develop—and the climate for development is encouraged by mobility, aspirations, development of new work–nonwork patterns, together with the onward march of new information technologies—some profound changes may be witnessed. Arguably they will be related to changing roles—of teacher and taught—to the role of the home and the educational institution as loci for learning, and to the staffing boundaries between work-related learning (which tends to be known as training) and self-related learning (which tends to be known as education).

Research, both in terms of the educational and cost effectiveness of open learning systems, is necessary to the developmental trajectory of individual institutions and systems. Hence the Open University of the United Kingdom is the most exhaustively researched of the existing systems. However, the rapidly widening research base is well-reflected in the journals listed below, and the extensive systematic bibliography in Holmberg (1985) is a valuable point of entry into the available data. The select bibliography of Kaye and Rumble (1985), while more sharply focused, provides a useful alternative access route.

Bibliography

Barnet College of Further Education 1980 *Flexistudy—A Manual for Local Colleges*, 2nd edn. National Extension College, Cambridge

Faure E, Herrera F, Kaddoura A-R, Lopes H, Petrovsky A V, Rahnema M, Ward F C 1972 *Learning to Be—The World of Education Today and Tomorrow.* UNESCO, Paris

Holmberg B 1985 *Status and Trends of Distance Education*, 2nd edn. Lectur, Lund

Horlock J H 1984 *The Open University after 15 years.* Manchester Statistical Society, Manchester

Kaye A, Rumble G 1985 *Distance Teaching for Higher and Adult Education.* Croom Helm, London

Lewis R (ed.) 1984 *Open Learning in Action: Case Studies*, Open Learning Guide No. 1. Council for Educational Technology, London

MacKenzie N, Postgate R, Scupham J 1975 *Open Learning—Systems and Problems of Post-secondary Education.* UNESCO, Paris

National Extension College 1985 *The Open Tech Directory.* National Extension College, Cambridge

Perry W 1974 *Higher Education for Adults—Where More Means Better*, Rede Lecture. Cambridge University Press, London

Adult Education for Profit

L. March and I. Wilson

In most countries adult education is sponsored by the government, or by nonprofit organizations such as churches and trade unions, or by colleges and universities. However, in some countries, programmes of education for adults are planned and administered by private agencies to return a profit. Many are vocational or career education programmes, but included are general and recreational courses, and degree programmes of private or profit-making colleges and universities, which are permitted in some countries. In a number of countries, educational courses are offered for sale by commercial enterprises and in the United States the term "proprietary schools" is used to denote these businesses.

Where there has been a shortage of higher education, particularly in some Asian countries, one solution at least has been to offer higher education, not just for a fee, but in order to return a profit. The colleges operating for profit have, of course, been obliged to fulfil legal and educational requirements for licensure. As the state exercises more control, however, the private enterprise aspect of higher education tends to dwindle. Nevertheless, in the United States and some countries of Western Europe, corporations have offered courses at a level and with facilities which equal any university and their research programmes may outpace much of the research of universities. Private enterprise also continues in the teaching of various skills (languages, operating office equipment, mathematics, computer programs) and through correspondence courses, again mainly vocational. There are few statistics kept of these enrolments, but in some urban areas the total number is very large, and in equipment, teaching staff, and enrolments, such programmes may equal those run under the auspices of public authorities.

1. Problems of Data Collection

Research into proprietary schools is difficult. This is partly because they are closely affected by economic conditions and by public educational policy, so that numbers of pupils, of schools, and of fields of study fluctuate. Moreover, information about the situation at any one time is hard to obtain. Official statistics cover only those parts in which public authorities have some interest, for governments have been less concerned to regulate private adult education than in the case of primary and secondary education. Associations to which private institutions belong and which could provide data are not normally all-inclusive, nor always willing to cooperate, and the institutions themselves may not wish to reveal business secrets. Studies have, however, been made in the United States, England and Wales, Canada, and the Federal Republic of Germany.

It has therefore been possible to estimate that three million American adults are enrolled in proprietary face-to-face schools in any given year, which means that such institutions cater for about 21 percent of students in vocational education (Carnegie Commission 1973 p.2). In Western Europe and in spite of an increase in government-sponsored programmes, enrolments seem to have continued to rise. In 1975 there were 106,500 people enrolled in private vocational education courses in England and Wales (that is, between 16 and 20 percent of total vocational enrolments) (Williams et al. 1979 pp.24–96). For the Federal Republic of Germany an estimate of 22,000 has been made (Woodall 1977 p.159). Obviously for many people these private schools have an appeal, often on the grounds that, since they are offered by commercially motivated enterprises, they will offer a good preparation for employment.

2. Kinds of Proprietary Adult Education

The range of subjects which may be studied through organizations operating for profit is very wide. In the United States, where proprietary education is very highly developed, subjects include accounting, advertising, airline personnel training, commercial and fine art, barbering, beauty, charm, dancing, dramatic art, design, dental technology, driving, electronics, estimating, flight, foremanship, hairdressing, homemaking, insurance, modelling, music, nursing, real estate, sewing, voice, and the whole range of crafts and trades. In most countries where companies are established, the main strength of profit-making organizations is in business and technical education and in the study of languages.

Independent schools of business cover the minor and major office skills, bookkeeping and accounting, and business administration. They offer the most advanced automated and computerized techniques. They vary greatly in size, some in the United States having more than 2,000 students and offering courses ranging from a few weeks to four years. Proprietary technical schools operate in the development of engineering technical aides and assistants. In the United States they are very numerous. Approximately 30 percent of the institutions affiliated to the National Council of Technical Schools (among the members of which are many collegiate institutions) are private establishments. Some proprietary organizations are international, for example the Berlitz School of Languages, which has branches worldwide. The increase in foreign travel, for both business and tourist purposes, has given a considerable boost to commercial language schools. The south coast of England, for instance, is scattered with firms of varying size and quality, to which people, mainly young, come to learn English.

Until recent years, with the foundation of the Open University and other similar institutions, the field of home or correspondence study was almost a monopoly of the proprietary sector. The size of this market may be judged by the fact that at the end of the 1960s there were 2,000,000 students enrolled in private correspondence courses in the United States; 360,000 in England and Wales; 320,000 in the Netherlands; 300,000 in France; and 250,000 in the Federal Republic of Germany (Glatter and Wedell 1971). In 1971 in the Netherlands, 27 percent of those taking vocational training were doing so through correspondence courses.

3. Regulation and Control

Quality in the proprietary sector is very variable. Some of the private business schools, for example, are among the best in the world, but the provision by some organizations is highly suspect. This fact and the size of educational provision for profit has drawn the attention of governments. In a number of countries, such as the Federal Republic of Germany, the Netherlands, and Sweden, profit-making schools and colleges are subject to state regulation to ensure quality and fair treatment for the customer. In Norway the earnings of correspondence schools are restricted to the level necessary for the secure operation and development of the school. On the other hand there is no regulation in the United Kingdom or the United States. In the latter country, systems of accreditation, with fixed standards of quality, have been set up by associations of proprietary schools themselves, although there is some doubt about the quality of the accreditation. Nevertheless, public authorities make student loans available to people studying in proprietary schools, in itself a gesture of public recognition.

The United States policy, to allow purely market forces to regulate the private sector, was carried further in France, when a national adult vocational education system was established in the late 1960s and early 1970s. For ideological reasons and because existing educational institutions were considered incapable of catering for the expansion of provision that would be required, organizations of all kinds, public and private, profit and nonprofit making, were invited to offer courses, which would be funded either directly by the state, or by employers through payments made in lieu of training tax. The result was the rise of many firms offering adult courses for profit, highly favoured by both employers and the then French Government, and subject to hardly any control.

4. The Attractions of the Proprietary Sector

The growth of public sector and non-profit-making adult education provides increasing competition for the proprietary providers, but they continue to flourish. They have qualities which appeal both to adult students and, an important factor in vocational courses, to employers. The proprietary sector has shown itself quick to perceive a market, for example during the 1970s in computer programming and diving. It claims to be more aware of the demands of the occupation for which it trains and is unhampered in its response to them by educational principles of its own, which may conflict with those of the customer. It claims to give students the genuine atmosphere of industry. It provides, on the whole, shorter, more intensive courses. Commercial forces also tend to prompt more flexibility. Proprietary schools are readier to allow students to start at different times of the year, to stay only as long as they feel they need, to vary the number of hours they attend, and to go at their own pace.

They claim to give more personal attention to students and to help those with special needs or handicaps. There is some evidence that their students do in fact have special needs and that they are more likely to be either less able or more able than the average (Wilms 1974 p.182, Williams et al. 1979 p.99). In the United States they tend to be poorer and less well-educated than those in public vocational education.

5. Prospects

Since advanced countries have become increasingly aware that not all educational needs can be met out of the public purse, there may be increasing scope for private initiative in adult education. Profit-making educational organizations are not likely therefore to disappear in capitalist states. Their greatest danger may well be in closer government regulation and control brought upon them by their own success. If the proprietary sector is to play a significant role in the future, much more needs to be known about it: its size, what it does, how it is organized, who its students are, why they choose private rather than public provision, among other things. Opportunities to explore these questions may arise as the state takes more interest in this important part of adult education.

Bibliography

Carnegie Commission on Higher Education 1973 *Toward a Learning Society: Alternative Channels to Life, Work and Service: A Report and Recommendations by the Carnegie Commission on Higher Education*. McGraw-Hill, New York

Glatter R, Wedell E G 1971 *Study by Correspondence*. Longman, London

Williams G, Woodhall M, March L 1979 *Independent Further Education*. Policy Studies Institute, London

Wilms W W 1974 *Public and Proprietary Vocational Training: A Study of Effectiveness*. Center for Research and Development in Higher Education, Berkeley, California

Woodhall M 1977 *Learning Opportunities for Adults*. Organisation for Economic Co-operation and Development (OECD), Paris

Christian Churches and Adult Education

V. Strudwick

From the beginning of the Christian church, adult education has played a significant role in its existence. Through a study of the forms that it takes, a fourfold purpose can be detected:

(a) to encourage its adult members to contribute to an understanding of the world in which they live through research and educational activity in all fields of human knowledge;

(b) to provide education for its members in matters of belief, history, tradition and custom, ethics, spiritual disciplines, and the management of their common life;

(c) to provide education in beliefs and goals for those who are outside its membership;

(d) to provide a theological contribution to the development of thought in other disciplines by taking account of the insights of Christian belief and practice.

1. Medieval Learning

In medieval Europe there was no carefully drawn line between sacred and secular and the content and form of medieval adult education was as much shaped by the conditions of feudal society as by religious ideas. Early adult education programmes were centred around cathedral and monastic houses and their libraries. Popular provision was made through miracle and morality plays, the visual impact of stained glass and wall paintings, and the liturgy. In the mass (as in liturgy today) participants were invited to join in a drama which recalled for them the biblical basis for their beliefs and provided them with an arena for renewal of their membership in the community founded on the basis of their beliefs.

The turmoil of the Reformation brought little change though it did stimulate certain forms of adult education, not only in restating and teaching articles of belief, but in applying some of those articles to the economic and social needs of the day and formulating new ethical norms. The Protestant work ethic is widely regarded as being an instance where the thought and teaching of theologians in books, sermons, and personal influence had a large effect in reshaping the economic and social life of Western Europe.

2. The Beginnings of Voluntary Provision

From 1789, however, there was a growing attack on the power and influence of the Christian churches and organized blocks of believers and unbelievers formed. Religion was no longer a focus of unity but rather the basis for group identity. This self-consciousness produced societies in all the churches, of which an example is provided by the Church of England's "Society for the Promotion of Christian Knowledge". This society attempted to promote night schools for adults, although it was not until towards the end of the eighteenth century that these began to flourish in large numbers.

In the first half of the nineteenth century adult members of the middle and working classes became aware of their educational needs in a new way. Side by side with the adult educational work of the trades unions, the cooperative movement, and the Workers' Educational Association, church-based institutes evolved as part of the same movements and with similar objectives. In 1844 the Young Men's Christian Association (YMCA) was formed and only seven years later there were eight London branches and 16 provincial ones. This period too saw the extensive growth of adult schools meeting customarily on Sundays. It was in these schools that many illiterate or semi-illiterate people were provided with the basic tools of learning. In 1854, F. D. Morris, with some of his Christian Socialist colleagues, founded the London Working Men's College.

3. Christian Influence in Adult Education in the United Kingdom

Churchmen were active in early university extension work which began in 1873 under the auspices of the University of Cambridge and also with the development of university settlements in deprived areas, most of which did some form of educational work. The Workers' Educational Association (WEA) itself was strongly influenced by Christian people and ideas. Its founder, Dr. Albert Mansbridge, was an employee of the Cooperative Wholesale Society and a lay preacher of the Church of England. He gained the support of William Temple (later Archbishop of Canterbury), who was president of the WEA from 1908 until 1924.

During the prewar years of the twentieth century this early impetus in adult education waned and in 1944 the Church of England set up a commission to make recommendations about adult education. The report speaks of the neglect of adult education, which is not confined to the church, but "is a weakness of the nation". It speaks of the way in which the systematic education of the citizen has been regarded as something to be completed at a specific age as though he or she was then equipped with the educational luggage necessary for the journey of life, whereas it should be seen as a lifelong process. The Lutheran churches in Scandinavia and the Federal Republic of Germany created residential colleges to which people could withdraw for specialist courses of study, and the lifelong education of adults became a perceived task.

4. Roman Catholic Developments

The Roman Catholic Church came rather later to adult education. Nineteenth-century ventures included the Catholic Social Guild and the Catholic Workers' College. This was a sort of Catholic WEA with a largely working-class following. What it taught was ideology based on adherence to the social encyclicals of Popes Leo XIII and Pius XII. It was adult education in which experience and changed conditions of the real world were related to traditional theology and a *modus vivendi* was offered to the faithful. This of course helped to increase the tribal or group identity of Catholics, giving them a strong sense of belonging—an identity within a church that had something to say about economic and social conditions as well as personal piety.

Following the second Vatican Council a change took place. First there was an increase in the provision of lectures, courses, and conferences to help the adult Catholic take a fresh look at his or her beliefs. In some dioceses this has been done in cooperation with local authority adult education institutes. Secondly, there was a growth of pastoral centres, catering for adult groups on a residential and nonresidential basis, and adult education centres such as the Upholland Northern Institute which serves the eight northern dioceses of the United Kingdom and their one million Roman Catholics. The staff of the centres not only run courses and conferences there but go out into the parishes, with their skills, as a kind of mobile resource unit.

5. United States Contribution

The American Episcopal Church was instrumental in interesting the Christian churches in the influence and working methods of small interactive groups, and the way in which a group has power over its individual members which can control, change, or influence their behaviour as learners. The encounter group, T-group, process study, and interaction analysis were increasingly used by the American churches to enable learning. An American team came to the United Kingdom, and representatives from England trained in institutes at Bossey in Switzerland and Bethel in the United States. This in turn led to liaison between the churches and the Tavistock Clinic in London and by 1967 training institutes in this type of work had been set up in eight English cities. This work is now done on an ecumenical (interchurch) basis by regional training groups offering a variety of courses in personal growth, and the development of skills in human relationships, as well as leadership and task training of different kinds.

6. The Work of Paulo Freire

Contemporary insights into the purpose and functions of adult education in the churches are closely associated with the work of Paulo Freire (b. 1921). In 1970 he became a consultant on the Education staff of the World Council of Churches, which was formed in 1948 to include most of the major Christian churches among its membership. The Education Office has a specialist staff who travel the world encouraging the churches to think about their educational systems and devise new ones when appropriate. Through international conferences, newsletters, and research projects, the office brings educational issues before the attention of its member churches. The way in which Freire's thinking has influenced the World Council is illustrated in the report of its fifth assembly held in 1975:

> Education in too many societies is a consciously used instrument of power; designed to produce those who accept and serve the system; designed to prevent the growth of a critical consciousness which would lead people to want alternatives.... The Christian community is placed in the human community to present the total message of Christ and to be a sign of God's liberating power....

These insights into purpose and function have sprung from the encouragement that the church gives to its adult members to contribute to research in, among other things, educational theory and practice. They have had profound effects on the other forms of the church's involvement in adult education.

7. Faith Education

Traditionally, the education of church members in matters of belief and practice has been thought of as the transmission of a deposit of knowledge. Encapsulated in stories, decisions, and judgments from the past, reinforced by liturgical repetition, this knowledge has been transmitted from generation to generation by the sermon or lecture and the corporate assumptions of the group. While this view is still held by Christians with fundamentalist views about the Bible or the church, new insights are gaining ground and in March 1981 the Bishop of Bristol, Chairman of the Church of England's Board of Education, wrote, "There has been much debating in recent years as to whether Christian theology is best thought of as a deposit for transmission or whether it is primarily a quest for exploration. To speak of the Christ as pedagogue means that his deposit is of such a kind as to necessitate a quest."

In the United Kingdom the way in which this process has been developed is via small learning groups in people's homes. The skills of group dynamics brought into the churches during the 1960s have flowered in the profusion of networks of locally based learning groups consisting of between 8 and 12 people who work in "teams" with specific open-ended programmes which are largely self-chosen. Speakers, tapes, and booklets may form resource materials for these learning groups but the main resource of the group is the experience of the members themselves and the skill of the group is shown by the way in which this experience is elicited, reflected on, shared, and used by the group. While this method has been widely used in the Church of England and Protestant churches, it is now becoming part of the life of the Roman Catholic Church as well. In *The Easter People* (1980) the Roman Catholic bishops of England and Wales wrote, "The continuing Christian education and formation of adult members of the church must become a priority in our Church's educational labours." The Westminster Adult Religious Education Centre has established a new programme entitled "Theology for Parishioners" which is a set of 12 related but independent programmes of adult religious education based on group learning and learning by extension. Similar programmes can be found in most of the European churches, Catholic and Protestant, on the lines of the Dutch *Theologie Voor U* (1982).

Similarly, the process of educating the uninitiated by preaching and attracting them into a "religious world" of the church life, and teaching with well-defined boundaries, is being replaced by conception of dialogue with the secular world, and other religious cultures helping some Christians to venture out from their communities of faith into the world even though they are regarded there as to some degree eccentric. The thrust of mission has changed from a process of Christianization to a sharing of Christian insights in a common search for what it means to be truly human.

8. Putting Theology to Work

The impetus towards using Christian insights and experience in evolving new ways of looking at domestic, social, and political issues is increasing. At an international conference of adult educators working in the churches, held in 1980, under the title of "Education for Change", the following commissions were at work: Change in Rural Society; Change in Work and Employment through New Technology; Change in a Multiracial Society; Change in the Roles of Men and Women.

In 1981, members of the Protestant Association for Adult Education in Europe were invited to join the Roman Catholic Association for Adult Education in Europe in four commissions: Faith in the World; Social Questions; Managing the Family; and Training Programmes for Adult Educators in the Churches.

Certainly in the Protestant churches the purpose and function of such education is strongly influenced by the educational theory of Paulo Freire. For example, in the Federal Republic of Germany, family education has traditionally been given in "Schools for Future Mothers", which at the same time dealt with domestic science and pedagogics. The churches are challenging the idea that family education should be orientated on the ideas of the nineteenth century and are attempting to recognize new needs and experience in the conviction that the communication of the gospel does not equal first providing Christian answers but rather providing evidence that all the questions have been sensitively and personally felt. In the Federal Republic of Germany, the work of family education is distributed in 54 parish centres of education by over 200 paid or honorary workers. In England and Wales, the ecumenical Family Life Education Group is providing a network of resources and stimulation to help churches work with adults more effectively at all points of growth and need.

In the Roman Catholic Church, organizations like the Catholic Marriage Advisory Council and Marriage Encounter enter into partnership with parish priests in an effort to achieve a pastoral rather than cognitive approach to education.

Another example of the way in which certain areas of study have been affected by a new impetus from the churches is that of peace studies. The pioneers have been the Dutch churches and in 1979 the Interchurch Peace Council began a campaign under the title "Rid the World of Nuclear Weapons beginning with the Netherlands". A great deal of money and energy from the church's adult education departments went into this campaign which produced programmes for local groups, regional institutes, and nationwide television. Not only did this programme significantly change the church's traditional view but radically affected the perceptions of many outside the churches, becoming a significant factor in the creating and strengthening of political opposition to the siting of Cruise and Pershing missiles on Dutch soil.

9. *Development Education*

It is clear that in recent years the churches have accepted a particular responsibility for the needs of the disadvantaged. They are strategically placed at the bridgehead between adult education and social work and have strengthened their contribution by drawing attention to areas of social need and motivating those who have the resources to equip people with the ability to meet those needs. They have also been involved in education to help create special conditions which will make the most of human potentialities within the community.

Much of the effort of the national missionary societies is now spent in enabling programmes which help the understanding of different cultures and religions, and organizations like Christian Aid have an adult education function as well as a fund-raising role. Most local churches have bookstalls and societies which represent the concerns of the Third World.

10. *Ministerial Education*

During the decade 1970–1980 there has been a movement among churches to mobilize and train people to perform ministerial tasks which have traditionally been performed by a professional stipendiary clerical caste. This need has been brought about by inflation and the fall in recruitment. The new "ministerial" training for volunteers is taking place in two ways. Firstly, through adult education structures, church-based but often linked with university extramural departments and, secondly, on an individual basis through extension courses in which individual students are enabled to work through a programme by means of books, tapes, and postal communication with a tutor, meeting only occasionally for tutorial or group work. Such programmes are popular in the United States and parts of Africa where long distances would otherwise have to be travelled, but are now being used increasingly in the United Kingdom as a means of providing ministerial education for very busy people.

11. *Structures of Adult Education in the Churches*

The Roman Catholic Association for Adult Education in Europe and the Protestant Association for Adult Education in Europe began to work seriously together in 1981. Within the Protestant Association, member churches in different countries have their own national organization and since 1978, when the Christian Association for Adult and Continuing Education (CAACE) was formed in England, the impetus towards cooperation has increased. Most national associations are of fairly recent origin and in the case of countries where they are a minority church (e.g. France), the adult education network is based on national and regional centres. However, the Protestant Association for Adult Education in Western Germany, which was founded in 1961, and represents the interest of its members on a federal level, is a much larger organization including a membership of over 40 smaller organizations and working groups. Here, as in England, the main support for the churches' adult education work is to be found in the parishes whose various activities are supplemented by the work of regional education centres, residential colleges, family conference centres, and academies. The Protestant academies were founded after 1945 in almost all the territorial Lutheran churches and their aim was to reach areas of life beyond the local congregation, and people who remained distant from the structures of the church. In the Federal Republic of Germany the 12 pioneering centres of dialogue at the interface between church and society have become particularly important as centres of research and education for social issues which affect public life within that country.

12. Cooperation between the Churches and the Secular Provision

In the early part of the twentieth century when the structures of the present secular provision of adult education were being formulated, the churches were effective in influencing and shaping the provision. Again, after the Second World War, the churches were similarly active in university departments and pioneering learning and listening groups with the British Broadcasting Corporation (BBC). However, by 1949 it was possible for E. M. Bellchambers to write, "At a time when education is increasingly news, it seems paradoxical that the churches have narrowed their frontiers and withdrawn largely from adult education with its amazing potential for the church to exert her profound and creative influence" (Bellchambers and Appleton 1965).

This withdrawal reflected the interest in "congregation building" which from the late 1950s until the early 1970s was the churches' reaction to falling numbers, a changed role for the clergy, and a new economic and social scene.

However, the publication of the Russell Report on Adult Education in 1973 produced a vigorous response from the working party of the British Council of Churches. This body represents all the major churches in the United Kingdom, except the Roman Catholics. Among its recommendations were that there should be more courses available which related religion to contemporary life through art, music, and social action, and that the churches should participate and cooperate in the development work of the short-term residential colleges as well as local institutes. It recommended that the churches should seek to be represented on and participate in the work of any local development councils and area organizations which would be set up as a result of the Russell Report's recommendations, and local initiatives followed in many areas.

The churches failed to appoint a national officer to develop working relationships at national and local levels between the churches and other providing bodies in the adult education service, but the creation of a national association (CAACE) and increased participation at national level (through the National Institute of Adult Education) and in many areas on local development councils, has helped to make expertise from the churches more widely available again and also brought a theological critique of their work to bear upon the secular provision. For example, it has been said that much of the work of the short-term residential conferences is for a very small clientele on a fairly narrow range of courses and the churches' concern for the poor and disadvantaged is not realistically reflected in the opportunities given by the secular provision.

13. Adult Education and the Churches' Task

A joint study commission on education presented a report on the Uppsala Assembly of the World Council of Churches in 1968, and in it stated: "It is a Christian's concern for the wholeness of the human being, for the quality of human life, for the direction in which man goes, that turns him towards education, now sets him inside it and will not let him disengage." Members of the churches see themselves as engaged in adult education, not as a peripheral interest but because it is integral to the purpose for which Christians join together.

Bibliography

Bellchambers E F, Appleton L G 1965 The voluntary associations. In: Jessup F W (ed.) 1969 *Lifelong Learning: A Symposium on Continuing Education*. Pergamon, Oxford, pp. 122–37

Elias J 1982 *A Foundation and Practice of Adult Religious Education*. Krieger, Melbourne, Florida

Freire P 1976 *Education: The Practice of Freedom*. Writers and Readers Publishing Cooperative, London

Hull J 1985 *What Prevents Christian Adults from Learning*. SCM, London

Kane M 1975 *Theology in an Industrial Society*. SCM, London

Lovell G 1972 *The Church and Community Development: An Introduction*. Grail, London

Rodger P 1985 *All are Called: Towards a Theology of the Laity. Essays from a Working Party*. CIO, London

Libraries and Adult Education

J. Allred

This article covers the role libraries play in the support of adult learners whether or not the learner attends a formal education programme and whether or not the library is part of an educational institution. By adult education is meant the learning activities adults follow, after completing their full-time education, for recreation, personal development, or improvement in job skills. These learning activities occur in formal and informal education programmes but are distinguished by their emphasis on self-direction and independent learning strategies. These strategies are present, too, in conventional education with project work, reading, and research.

1. History

Libraries have long had connections with adult learners. As far back as the Middle Ages in Europe monks pursued their studies with the help of monastic libraries which maintained proficient systems for book production and location. The Reformation and the subsequent establishment of Protestant states and cities relied partly on libraries to implement educational programmes. The town libraries of Europe (Ipswich and Norwich in England, Hamburg in Germany) and in the United States (Boston and New Haven), and parish libraries, notably in Scotland under James Kirkwood's ideas in the eighteenth century, were resources of variable quality for adult independent learners.

In more modern times, industrial societies have faced the problem of an undereducated workforce. More schooling was an obvious solution. For adults this was impracticable and in some cases libraries had to be relied upon to fill the gap. Mechanics' institutes in the United Kingdom were forerunners of public libraries providing, alongside class programmes, libraries for the self-education of the artisan. The rate- (local tax)-supported public library was established in the United Kingdom in 1850 as an educational agency in the vacuum created by parliamentary dispute over the provision of state schooling. The government's Select Committee of Inquiry was told, at that time, that reading would "add a softening and expanding influence to the great practical education the Englishman received from incessant intercourse between man and man in trade".

Public libraries were promoted as an educational force in both the United Kingdom and the United States, not by popular demand, but by the efforts of a few enlightened and philanthropic individuals who believed in the virtues of "self-help" and in the value of access to carefully chosen bookstocks. In practice, their impact upon adult education was limited by the conservatism of their stocks and by the librarian's preoccupation with the mechanics of collection and conservation (Lee 1966, Johnson 1938).

Adult education through libraries was not always in the interests of the government of the time. In Russia, the adult education movement of the Kul'turniki after the Crimean War relied upon educational centres, societies, and public libraries and was linked to the post revolutionary educational programmes of the Communist governments working through the same agencies (Raymond 1981). Adult education in the Eastern Bloc is seen as a cooperative effort, which includes all libraries, working in the direct interests of the state's own philosophy.

Western Europe and the United States did not take such a directive approach. Adult education in these countries was served by libraries working with, for example, the university extramural movement in the United Kingdom. University lecturers travelled to give courses of a high standard to people who had little chance of going to a university. Some universities built up large extramural libraries of their own (London, Birmingham) with specialist staff to supply students of these courses with reading matter. These libraries now provide a wide range of teaching materials for university extramural programmes. The Central Circulating Library for Students was founded in 1916 from the Workers' Educational Association's Central Library for Tutorial Classes with help from the Carnegie United Kingdom Trust to provide books for students either directly or through public libraries. It became the National Central Library and is now part of the British Library Document Supply Centre.

After the First World War, both the United Kingdom and the United States included adult education in their programmes of reconstruction. The Ministry of Reconstruction's Adult Education Committee report in the United Kingdom provided the impetus for the 1919 Public Library Act, which put public libraries under local education authorities and presented them as places for "self-development in an atmosphere of freedom" contrasted with schooling as "training in an atmosphere of restraint or discipline". In 1924 the American Library Association's Commission on Libraries and Adult Education reinforced the role of the reader's advisor in public libraries whose job it was to plan personalized reading programmes. This meant close involvement between the librarian and the library user. Historians have remarked upon the disappearance of this role after the 1930s when help for adult learners became much more an assumed role of the general library service. This continued until the 1960s and 1970s when a renewed concern for people, underprivileged by lack of education and information, caused librarians to develop community information services and services for adult independent learners.

2. Role of the Library

A distinction might be made between the library's support for other providers of adult education (for example book box supplies to evening classes) and "library learning" itself where the librarian might provide a course of directed reading. Librarians are not usually trained as teachers and therefore more easily see themselves as supporting other educational providers. There have been moves in several countries to ensure that public libraries are placed under government departments responsible for education. Though many library laws recognize the educational role of libraries, education laws commonly do not. The Norwegian Libraries Act 1971 stressed the importance of public libraries in adult education but the 1976 Adult Education Act did not.

A study of United Kingdom public libraries (Allred and Hay 1979) attempted to discover the extent to which they offered special services to adult learners. Their findings were as follows.

(a) *The general library service.* Access to general library stocks with special borrowing privileges in a few cases. Problems arose when materials were not available at the time required or for the length of time required. Sometimes materials would be delivered to adult education classes. Material includes books, audio and video tapes, film and specially prepared teaching packs, for example on local history. Adult classes were held in the library as a convenient and relaxed setting. In Sweden grant-aided "study circles" often met in public libraries and, as in the United Kingdom and other countries, the libraries showed films, and held concerts and exhibitions, all of which might be considered as part of adult learning (Griffiths 1971).

(b) *The provision of educational information and advice (educational brokering).* In the late 1970s this was a rapidly growing activity. The expansion of educational opportunities and retraining needs increased the demands for such services. In the United Kingdom these were established in colleges and as independent services [Hatfield's Educational Guidance Service for Adults (EGSA), Northern Ireland's EGSA, Wigan's Contact for Learning and Educational Opportunities (CLEO)]. Libraries provided educational information themselves, but the staff were not trained to advise and counsel. Some public libraries assisted these services by sharing premises (Birmingham), by acting as a referral link (Newcastle-upon-Tyne had a direct telephone line), and by compiling indexes and information sheets (Bradford Public Library created a computerized information service). The need for an information service to support the planned Open Tech in the United Kingdom may start a new chapter in such services.

Many educational providers placed their publicity in libraries and some libraries collaborated in educational "fairs" or information weeks (Leicestershire County Council, Guildford in Surrey).

Learning exchanges (an idea of Illich and others in the United States) are an extension of educational information services where prospective learners and "tutors" (who do not need to be trained teachers) are matched to facilitate less formal, but not independent, learning. In New Zealand such an exchange became part of the services of Wellington City Library. In the United Kingdom an experimental service was started in Orton, at the Cambridgeshire County Library.

(c) *Instruction in library use.* A most useful service provided by librarians was that of the instruction of adult learners in the use of the library. Competent library use is a major part of study skill and such instruction is commonplace in colleges and universities. East Sussex County Library and Norfolk County Library staff taught evening classes in public library use in connection with local history and genealogy and were surprised by their popularity.

Guides to library services in some regions were published by the Open University and other educational providers. Many public libraries had adult education liaison staff to maintain contacts with tutors. A well-developed service was provided by Derbyshire County Library with a current awareness bulletin on the subject of adult education and with participation in tutor training programmes. A similar information service based on nine educational libraries but on a larger scale and computerized is operated in Austria called *Das Dokumentationssystem Erwachsenenbildung* (DOKEB) or Documentation System for Adults.

Specialist library services for professionals and others working in adult education exist in most countries. For example Syracuse University in the United States operates a Clearing House of Resources for Educators of Adults. In the United Kingdom the National Institute of Adult Education in Leicester maintains a library and a register of research.

3. *Library Programmes*

3.1 Developing Countries

The important Malmö Seminar (Houle 1951) had one of its three groups devoted to this subject. In countries where resources are scarce and educational systems limited, libraries provide a valuable extension of educational provision. In the 1970s, the Indian government's National Education Programme was urged to recognize the need of adults for access to books and to realize the help that public libraries can provide through discussion groups and reading aloud groups, with visual aids and drama activities. In Tanzania it is the job of the Tanzania Library Service to help people to participate in national development. Where the government has failed to emphasize the role of the library as in Zambia, the library profession has drawn attention to this.

3.2 Adult Basic Education

In 1955 in Brooklyn in the United States, the public library started a reading improvement programme in collaboration with Brooklyn College, which continues to this day. Librarians are trained to teach adults at all levels. The American Library Association Adult Services Division published its *Service to Adult Illiterates* in 1964 and libraries such as Kalamazoo, the Free Library of Philadelphia, Enoch Pratt Free Library, and many others were soon providing adult reading centres and discussion groups, as well as materials. Libraries had to cooperate with other agencies and this was not always easy. A common problem was a lack of appropriate reading materials for adults.

A major project in the United States was that promoted by the Appalachian Adult Education Center of Morehead (Kentucky) State University in 1972, which involved 77 libraries in 10 states by 1976. The library profession in the United States more readily accepted responsibility for adult illiterates than that in the United Kingdom (Lyman 1977), but the concern for illiteracy did spread to the United Kingdom where libraries, public and academic, cooperated in the Adult Literacy Campaign.

3.3 Distance Learning: Broadcasting

The United Kingdom literacy programme of the 1970s was considerably reinforced by the participation of the British Broadcasting Corporation (BBC), and public libraries played a part, though a variable one. The activity brought about a much closer relationship between broadcasting and libraries. Programmes such as Yorkshire Television's *Disraeli*, the BBC's *Roadshow*, and *Speak for Yourself* drew the public library into the systematic provision of back-up materials for the audiences of these programmes.

Broadcast educational programmes have been initiated by libraries. In the 1940s, Louisville Public Library in the United States ran a radio station and later used television in its "neighbourhood college", run in conjunction with the university. The Open University of the United Kingdom is an important example of a worldwide movement. Its own librarians are members of the course production teams and its course materials are stocked by many libraries. Prince George's County Library in Maryland provides Open University and other material for its university's independent students. Public libraries in Quebec supported their local tele-university. In practice, students have little time to use anything other than the learning materials supplied direct to them but the adoption of project-based work by the Open University has resulted in fresh demands being made on libraries. Dependence upon libraries by adult learners may be more a function of the learning style than of the distance from the educational provider.

Some major developments in distance education fail to include libraries. The Norwegian Distance Education Institution set up in 1978 to coordinate television, the National Film Centre, and the University Press made no mention of the place of libraries, but the National Library Office now takes part in all planning discussions.

3.4 Open Entry to Education

Adults should not be debarred from education because of a lack of formal entry qualifications, and provision should be easily accessible. These principles have provided another reason for "library learning". Between 1972 and 1976 a major project was undertaken by the United States College Entrance Examination Board's (CEEB's) Office of Independent Study and Guidance Projects. Nine library systems across the States were involved in providing library-based guidance and tutorial support for learners wishing to gain credits for university courses or to learn for any other reason. The work was based on the researches of Allen Tough, which demonstrated that adults undertake a great number of learning projects but often with unsatisfactory guidance and resources. The public library staff were trained, not to teach, but to make available suitable resources, to support and encourage, and to refer when necessary. Great emphasis was placed on evaluation of the outcomes for the library and for the learners (Mavor et al. 1976, Boles and Smith 1979). The idea has been paralleled and copied in other libraries and in other countries. Philadelphia Free Library created a "Lifelong Learning Center" in 1976. The Netherlands has an Open School, in which libraries cooperate in adult education by providing tours of the library, instruction in library use, and reading lists. Islington Public Library and the Inner London Education Authority in the United Kingdom have embarked on a research project to provide educational guidance and support services in collaboration with educational providers.

4. The Future

The high costs of formal education, the need for adults to retrain and adapt to change, and the emphasis on lifelong learning have resulted in alternative and more flexible learning systems. New teaching methods in secondary schools have trained people in independent study skills. All learning resource centres, often integrated with libraries, are under great pressure (de la Court 1974). College libraries are asked to allow adult independent learners access to their collections. Public libraries are expected to support broadcast learning. Professional training for librarians incorporates "user needs" in general and sometimes the needs of adult learners in particular. Their needs are for more than information; they need encouragement, clarification, motivation, and review. Special groups of learners claim the librarian's attention. In Oud-Gastel, in the Netherlands, the public library provided a course in social awareness for women, which resulted in greater use of the library's information services. The CEEB project referred to above attracted many older adults.

Research shows that it is important for librarians to concern themselves with the intentions of those who use their libraries and not simply with delivery of material. New technologies are likely to replace librarians for many of the mechanical tasks of collection and delivery. The future will tell how far libraries as resource centres for adult learners will be replaced by electronic resources delivered direct, and how far librarians will supply the need adult learners have for experienced and sympathetic guidance to the multiplicity of resources and systems available to them.

Bibliography

Allred J, Hay W 1979 *A Preliminary Study of the Involvement of Public Libraries with Adult Learners*. Leeds Polytechnic Public Libraries Management Research Unit, Leeds

Birge L E 1981 *Serving Adult Learners: A Public Library Tradition*. American Library Association, Chicago, Illinois

Boles S, Smith B D 1979 The learner's advisory service. *Library Trends* 28: 165–78

de la Court W 1974 *Openbare Bibliotheck en Permanente Educatie* [Public libraries and permanent education]. Tjeenk Willink, Groningen

Griffiths T E 1971 Adult education and libraries in Sweden. *Library Association Record* 73(6): 105–07
Houle C O 1951 *Libraries in Adult and Fundamental Education.* The Report of the Malmö Seminar. UNESCO, Paris
Johnson A S 1938 *The Public Library: A People's University.* American Association for Adult Education, New York
Lee R E 1966 *Continuing Education for Adults Through the American Public Library, 1833–1964.* American Library Association, Chicago, Illinois
Lyman H H 1977 *Literacy and the Nation's Libraries.* American Library Association, Chicago, Illinois
Mavor A S, Toro J O, De Prospo E R 1976 *The Role of the Public Libraries in Adult Independent Learning.* College Entrance Examination Board, New York
Raymond B 1981 Libraries and adult education: The Russian experience. *J. Libr. Hist.* 16(2): 394–403

Museums and Galleries in Adult Education

D. S. Abbey

For those who control museums and galleries, be they public corporations or private individuals, professionals, or amateurs, there exists a continual tension between the two functions of a collection—as the material for scholarship and as something to be made available for public enjoyment. The design of contemporary museums reflects a variety of solutions to this problem.

During the twentieth century, the educational role and functions of museums and galleries have brought the public into increasing contact with objects which were formerly seen only by their owners, or by the privileged scholar who gained limited access to the collections. Thus, in the early part of the nineteenth century, one had to apply weeks in advance and give evidence of serious scholarly purpose in order to gain access to a collection in the British Museum. Today, by contrast, not only is the Viking Museum at Roskilde, outside Copenhagen, open to any member of the public, but the chance visitor may chat with marine archaeologists as they preserve and reconstruct the remains of Viking ships. Even today the British Museum and Roskilde represent two very different types of collections, of course.

The former is one of the great museums of the world, which has, for the most part, presented works from all ages, from all parts of the world, and from many academic disciplines, as major galleries have presented wide spectra of artists, styles, periods, and subject matter. The latter belongs to a smaller kind, which on the whole show a more limited range of artifacts having a connection with the locality or country in which they are situated. The two types, however, are alike in their acceptance of an educational role, not only towards the scholar, but towards the general adult public. Museums and galleries operate increasingly as presenters of a people's heritage and are activators of community or natural development.

1. The Publics Served

The question of who visits museums and galleries has been studied more or less rigorously since the 1930s. Hudson (1977) concludes: "We have incontrovertible evidence that the typical museum visitor, whether in a socialist or a capitalist country, is extremely unlikely to be someone who left school at the earliest possible moment, who does unskilled, or semi-skilled manual work, and who is over forty years of age. We know, too, that women of all ages visit museums less than men." While this appears to be true in the case of local visitors to the normal permanent galleries of most museums, there are seasonal variations. The influx of tourists and widely advertised shows such as the Treasures of Tutankhamen nearly always broaden the socioeconomic characteristics of the visitor. To widen the public further, the concept of a "mass market" to be reached and served has been replaced in many centers by a view of the adult public as being highly differentiated with specialized needs and interests.

Galleries attached to museums have been specifically designed to serve the needs of particular adult groups. There now exist galleries and exhibits for the blind; for those confined to wheelchairs; for the deaf; for the illiterate; and for the emotionally disturbed. Many urban museums have designed specific exhibits to serve the needs of ghetto residents (from their immediate neighborhood, in some cases), and attention to the needs of the elderly has increased since the early 1970s.

In general, there has been little interaction between the labor movement and museums for purposes of education or for the enrichment of the worker, although some attempts to remedy this are noted in Austria, Mexico, and the Soviet Union. In the Soviet Union, the Society of Inventors and Rationalizers and the Polytechnical Museum in Moscow work to pass on the latest scientific developments to members of trade unions, as well as to the larger public audiences which they attract. In the Netherlands, a major manufacturer has taken art works into its factories, and occasional lectures in neighboring galleries have been held to supplement this activity.

2. The Educational Activities

For adults, formal educational activities in museums and galleries have, for many years, been very similar to those provided for juveniles and children. Typically the visitor encounters the object or the display in a small group under the direction of a lecturer or guide. More recently, technology has increased the variety of these activities.

Small portable cassette recorders provide what is called individualized instruction, but what is, in reality, a tour identical for all, varying only in the time the individual chooses to devote to it. Some exhibits have been animated with audio and visual systems that permit visitors to respond to preset questions, and to receive immediate feedback to their response via pushbuttons. In Milwaukee, a sustained program of exhibit design and research has used teaching machines which embody learning theory principles. This work has shown that adults are highly motivated to acquire information and capable of making aesthetic judgments.

Many museums and galleries offer regular courses in crafts and arts, and some provide opportunities for hands-on experiential learning in such technical fields as experimental physics (National Museum of Science and Technology, Milan), and engineering (National Museum, Niger). The willing volunteer on archaeological digs provides labor, often bearing all personal costs, in exchange for involvement and learning.

The mass media, notably television, have brought the museum artifact, and curators, archaeologists, and education specialists, into the home through a wide variety of programming. Examples of this museum extension range from the panel of experts attempting to identify objects drawn from the museum's collection, or provided by studio audiences, to formal lecture series offered in conjunction with the programs of degree-granting institutions.

Noon-hour talks by specialists are a favorite in many centers, as are the slide-tape travel and exploration presentations of museum scholars and museum members. Weekend programs at planetaria offer experiences which provide entertainment, as well as formal and informal learning opportunities.

Shopping centers, civic airports, municipal buildings, and subway platforms have become sites for the display of objects and explanatory panels. Other forms of "outreach" by museums include the use of large mobile vans; travelling exhibits within cases; and whole trains (the "Heritage Train" in Canada). Few of these activities appear, however, to have been specifically planned or designed with the adult learner in mind, rather than visitors/participants of high-school age (or younger).

3. *Learning in the Museum Environment*

3.1 Goals for Learning

The adult visitor to the museum or gallery may have an educational objective. In the past, the vast majority of visits have been motivated by social or recreational considerations, but increases in self-directed inquiry, adult learning projects, and contract learning are leading to new demands on all cultural institutions as resources for learning. The development in the United States of educational brokering will undoubtedly increase demands on museums and galleries as a community resource to be used by adults pursuing a wide variety of educational goals. Another development, the granting of academic credit for work done outside the formal education system, may encourage many adults who have pursued their own interests in museum settings, and who subsequently wish to move into degree or certificate programs. The Council for the Advancement of Experiential Learning, Columbia, Maryland, is one organization studying this problem.

In the professions, the need for continuous upgrading and refresher courses is increasing at an alarming rate. The science and technology museums with active programs and facilities for research, and with expertise in display, may become vital centers for the dissemination of new technical information.

3.2 Programming

There are a growing number of museum educators in North America, Latin America, and Europe who appear to have moved in the direction of systematic programming for adult learners. Knowles (1981) has presented a five-stage planning model which appears to coincide with the development of some of the newer and better learning opportunities for adults. His steps, needs assessment, context analysis, statement of objectives, design of learning activities, and evaluation are familiar to most adult educators. Recently, major museums, some with new staff positions in exhibit planning, design, and evaluation, have followed these steps in a more systematic manner than in the past.

The question of needs assessment has proved the most vexing for museum educators. Attempts to design educational programs and activities to meet the learning needs of visitors have frequently been initiated by conducting a survey of visitors or of the general public as part of a needs assessment. However, such activities have rarely affected exhibit design, and there is little evidence of survey results having had any effect on educational programs which consist of formal, guided tours. In general, the nature of the collection and the curator have dictated what will be made available to the public, and the form in which it will be presented. Current literature in the field argues for increased use of community groups, more attention to the actual demands of individual visitors, greater access to collections, and increased attention to the development and use of data retrieval systems to assist with independent learning projects.

3.3 Evaluation

Since the early 1960s, the evaluation of museum and gallery programming has moved from mere "head counting" to more sophisticated measures of educational impact. While attendance figures continue to be an important indicator of the drawing power of an institution, or a specific gallery, or even a specific object or display, it is now widely recognized that number of visits is not equivalent to numbers of visitors. In some major museums, it has been shown that the adult visitor comes to the museum on average about twice a year:

some come once; some come as many as six times or more.

In place of attendance statistics, more detailed analysis of visiting behavior has been undertaken. Conversations within families and groups have been unobtrusively sampled and analyzed to determine the impact of specific exhibits, the reaction of the visitor to lighting, and the reaction to signs. The duration of the visits has been recorded. Other studies have examined the comments in visitor's books for evidence of reaction to the exhibits.

Many museums have tried using questionnaires with visitors (either after, or both before and after, a visit) to determine changes in knowledge or attitudes about an exhibit's subject matter. In some early work in this area, eye movements and length of time spent reading labels, or looking at individual paintings or objects, were recorded in an attempt to understand what attracted the visitor's attention. Other institutions have used more subtle "projective" tests which asked for impressionistic data about the exhibits, or about the museum itself.

The International Council of Museums (ICOM) has obtained evidence which indicates a small but sustained interest in exhibit evaluation. However, there are relatively few studies examining the relevance of the museum, its collections, its staff, or its overall programming to the specific learning needs or learning styles of adult visitors. It was noted above that not all the latter feel a need to learn, but given the increasing numbers of adults who are engaged in learning, whether of a formal or informal nature, little attention appears to be paid to making the current museum a more obvious source of support for the individual's learning.

Bibliography

Abbey D S, Cameron D F 1959–61 *The Museum Visitor*. Royal Ontario Museum, Toronto, Ontario

Brawne M 1966 *The New Museum: Architecture and Display*. Praeger, New York

Center for Museum Education 1978 *Lifelong Learning/Adult Audiences*. George Washington University, Washington, DC

Collins Z W (ed.) 1981 *Museums, Adults and the Humanities: A Guide for Educational Programming*. American Association of Museums, Washington, DC

Hudson K 1977 *Museums for the 1980's: A Survey of World Trends*. Holmes and Meir, New York

International Council of Museums (ICOM) 1981a *Museums, Education, Cultural Action: Selective Bibliography Prepared by the* UNESCO—ICOM *Documentation Center*. ICOM, Paris

International Council of Museums (ICOM) 1981b *Museum Interpretation and Education in a Cross-cultural Context: Selective Bibliography Prepared by the* UNESCO–ICOM *Documentation Center*. ICOM, Paris

Knowles A B 1981 Basic components of adult programming. In: Collins Z W (ed.) 1981

Royal Ontario Museum (ROM) 1976 *Communicating with the Museum Visitor: Guidelines for Planning*. ROM, Toronto, Ontario

Screven C G 1967 *The Application of Programmed Learning and Teaching Systems Procedures for Instruction in a Museum Environment*. University of Wisconsin, Milwaukee, Wisconsin. ERIC Document No. ED 048 745

Zetterberg H L 1968 *Museums and Adult Education*. Evelyn, Adams and Mackay, London

Section 6

Target Groups

Section 6

Target Groups

Introduction

Although separate provision is made, at least in some societies, for handicapped and other categories of children with special needs, the great majority are subjected by design to the same process of schooling until the upper secondary stage. Then, and in subsequent higher and other tertiary education, studies are increasingly diversified to meet diverging needs. It is therefore unsurprising that, as that divergence of experience extends in adulthood and as that period of life covers a much longer time than any previous one, so the variations of educational provision will become greater. What requires rather more consideration, perhaps, is the common phenomenon of highly specific targeting, often on social rather than educational grounds, which in many cases goes so far as to exclude the majority of the adult population from a particular programme.

It was not always thus. In the nineteenth century and before it was possible to detect a broad division between adult education aimed at the labouring classes and the kind of cultural activities, such as literary and scientific societies, engaged in by people of better education and higher social standing. There were wide variations in the content and manner of education offered to labourers, but this mostly derived not from perceived differences of target population, but from disagreements between providers about what was appropriate to that population—a decision that was made by the providers, not the learners. The groups aimed at were on the whole defined in broad and vague terms, although one should not forget that trade union and adult vocational education had more specific targets.

In the twentieth century increasing adherence to democratization of society and to the principle that all adults needed the chance to continue their education throughout life encouraged the development in a number of countries of programmes, particularly of general or liberal education, which were open and intended to be open to any adult who cared to join. Targeting was only to begin after a class or learning group had formed, when the curriculum and working methods were to be adapted to meet the needs and desires of the participants. Outside the vocational field this type of provision became dominant in many countries.

Although this policy offered theoretical advantages, some of which were borne out in practice, it had a number of weaknesses. There were obvious groups, such as shift workers, the physically and mentally handicapped, and those in prisons, which could not take part unless special arrangements could be made for them, and others, such as ethnic minorities, who would not, even when they could. In most countries a major priority of adult education's democratizing role remained to close educational gaps by giving those who were educationally disadvantaged, principally the urban and rural working class, the opportunity of a second chance. In reality, however, it was the well-educated middle class who participated most in programmes and whose interests, it was increasingly believed, came to dominate planners' thinking, so that the educational gap widened.

In spite of sincere attempts in many general programmes to identify and respond to the needs of the individual learner, it was unusual to see provision directed at specific social or economic groups. There was and is a strong similarity of subject matter in general adult education throughout the advanced countries, indicating perhaps that the people who take part in them have very similar interests, or that the providers intend some process of acculturation to a common socioeducational norm. The first alternative may be true and the second appropriate in such homogeneous societies as those of the Nordic countries, or of Japan. Other states, however, such as the United Kingdom, the United States and France, have recognized that they are not homogeneous, that they contain a diverse range of cultural, social, and interest groups which have a right to preserve their distinctive identity. They have abandoned, or are in the process of abandoning, a policy of integration into a common culture and in differing degrees are coming to terms with their own pluralism. In such countries the adequacy of a single, general provision open to all has increasingly been brought into question.

Studies in adult learning and development suggest that adulthood is not a uniform state, but a succession of developmental stages, each with its own needs. The fragmentation of roles in modern life and widening acceptance that adults require educating for these roles calls for specialized provision of varying kinds. A growing understanding of the needs of marginalized groups indicates that these too should receive more specialized education than used to be thought.

All these and, no doubt, other factors have contributed to the development over recent years of specific targeting in adult education to a degree that had previously only been seen in vocational programmes. Sometimes this has taken place on social or political, rather than educational, grounds. It has brought several gains, not least in that it has recruited from groups previously barely touched. It may also create problems. Even in the most pluralistic of societies, or particularly in these it may be argued, adult education should play a socializing role. It should be educating people, not merely as members of a specific group within that society, or as players of a specific role, or as persons having reached a certain developmental stage, but as citizens of society as a whole, containing many diverse groups, where other people play many roles and are at other stages of development than one's own. This may happen, of course, within specialized groups, but there is little evidence that it does; few of the reports of work with target groups indicate that they are engaged with concerns other than those specific to the group.

This fragmentation of educational opportunities may hit the individual, who may be a target of multiple provision, in that he or she belongs to more than one group, as woman, disabled, parent, employee, for example. Little attention appears so far to have been paid to integrating such diverse experiences into a coherent whole. Moreover fragmentation, occurring as a result of a greater sensitivity to the needs of the parts of society, seems to have developed without adequate consideration for its effect on the whole. Like most of adult education it has grown in an ad hoc fashion and it may be that serious investigation of the phenomenon and its consequences is called for.

So numerous are the target groups of adult education that it would be impossible to examine them all. Some, such as adult illiterates, families, and vocational educators, are treated in other sections of the *Handbook* (see for instance Section 2). This section contains articles on major groupings which are, or will be, long-term or permanent objects of provision. They fall into three categories distinguished by (a) age and sex; (b) social isolation; and (c) occupation. As has already been noted, an individual may identify with more than one of these target groups.

Age and Sex Groups

Introduction

One of the advantages of bringing adults of all ages together in one class or programme, it has been argued, is that the learning experience is thereby enriched by a wide range of experience, to the benefit of all the participants. The medical profession is generally agreed that, for health reasons, the elderly should be encouraged to integrate as long as possible with the population as a whole, that they should not be ghettoized. A strong movement is arising against "ageism", that is, discrimination against people in any situation on grounds of advancing age. Similar opinions are held about young adults too, although it may seem perhaps less necessary to do anything about them. The young grow out of youth, but only death puts an end to old age.

On the other hand, studies into adult learning and the adult condition, which suggest that adult life may be divided into a number of developmental stages, each with its own specific needs, would indicate that each stage should be separately targeted. It is this view which currently attracts most attention in adult education, and it affects the extremes of adulthood, the young and the old, in particular.

Education for Young Adults examines the growth of a young adult subculture, distinct from the adolescent one, the participation of its members in higher education and other forms of postsecondary study, their impact on the labour market, and the combination of work and study. *Education for Older Adults* may profitably be read together with the article on *Old Age* in subsection 4a. It touches on the relationship between ageing and ability to learn, covers specific educational needs of the elderly, including preparation for retirement, and describes initiatives, notably the University of the Third Age and elderhostel, designed to meet those needs.

It has been accepted for centuries that women have different needs and expectations from those of men, usually to the detriment of women. Serious consideration of their disadvantage has only been given in the second half of the twentieth century, usually by women, and steps have been taken to eradicate it. *Adult Education for Women* takes a broad view. It examines their educational position globally and then treats in turn women in developed and developing countries. In the former it considers vocational education, the problems and constraints to which women are subject, and projects designed to counteract these. In discussing developing countries it devotes sections to agricultural education, other vocational education, and literacy. The article also outlines the growth of women's studies—the systematic study of the situation of women in society—that is a product of the women's movement.

Education for Young Adults

D. B. P. Kallen

In Western societies the term *young adult* is now widely used to denote persons in a specific period of life immediately following adolescence. The limits of this period are differently perceived in different countries, but young adulthood is seen as developing its own subculture and having its own problems. This article describes and analyzes the participation of young adults in education. Largely under the influence of labour market requirements the number undergoing education is increasing. Many follow full-time courses, but many more study part-time and combine education with work. Although a significant number are in higher education, the majority are in other kinds of post-secondary institutions.

1. Adolescent Subculture

In the nineteenth century there emerged an adolescent subculture, restricted to a social and intellectual elite and under the strong influence of Romanticism on the philosophy of the upper and middle classes. On a much larger scale, adolescent subcultures have made their appearance in the 20th century. Their emergence and their characteristics are well documented in sociological literature. The Romantic vein has been explored in depth in the German literature during the Weimar Republic. Eduard Spranger's writings are in this context still fascinating reading. In the United States adolescent subcultures have found their most poignant manifestation in and around the high school. In Europe, the sociological literature about adolescents has been more concerned with the world outside the school and eventually with the young people of adolescent age who had left school and were engaged in gainful employment. The "young worker" is a much explored theme, whereas in the United States it draws very little specific attention. In the literature of the United States youth gangs and juvenile delinquency are closely connected with high schools in urban centres. In Europe they are associated with young people in suburban slum areas who have left school and are floating between school and adult (working) life.

There is a ready explanation for this difference in focus and locus of adolescent subculture: the full-time schooling of the adolescent in the United States goes back to the early twentieth century, whereas in Europe it has only been achieved in the last few decades. The typical adolescent in the United States has for many decades spent his or her adolescence in school, whereas the typical European adolescent has been in the work place.

But there is a second, more interesting, explanation: whereas the US high school is more a "way of life" than a mere place of learning, the European school is not at the centre of the European adolescent's life. It organizes and provides for little, if any, opportunities for social learning. Hence in Europe adolescent subcultures could not, on the whole, develop in the school. They had to develop in and around the family, the neighbourhood, and the workplace. In Europe too, however, the school has now replaced the factory as the place where most adolescents exercise their main activity. That is perhaps one of the main reasons for the retreat of adolescent subcultures, at least their earlier manifestations, from the European scene. Or, perhaps, contemporary youth subcultures manifest themselves in new forms of expression in other domains of life, such as in consumption patterns, in fashion, and in leisure time behaviour.

The term "young adults" in the title of this article refers to newcomers on the social scene of the developed countries. It suggests that between adolescence and adulthood lies another anteroom to full participation in adult life and adult responsibilities. Or, at least, there lie ways of participation and forms of responsibility that are different from those of the "mature" adult.

2. Young Adult Subculture

The age for the beginning of the period of "young adulthood" is defined rather clearly, that is, age 18, but the end is fixed rather arbitrarily. A usable upper limit may be age 25, the age at which first year students in the United Kingdom are considered as "mature" students, and also the age limit for some of the youth training schemes in the European Community. Admittedly, however, there is no consensus and hitherto little discussion as to the precise upper limit.

Belated entry into full adult roles and responsibilities was until quite recently the privilege of a very small elite of university students, representing at the most a few percent of the population. They considered themselves rather more as prolonged "youth" than as oncoming adults and often behaved accordingly. Undeniably theirs was a subculture of its own, aggressively distinct from that of their less fortunate peers. The self-imposed social isolation of the university students, particularly marked in the German-speaking countries, sustained this "young adult" subculture.

The factors that engender and sustain the emergence of a "young adult" subculture in present society are more complex. The continued involvement in education and training of a very substantial part of the age group under consideration is certainly a very important element. But labour market factors also play a role. During the early years of the segmentation of the labour market, young school leavers aged 16 to 18 were progressively excluded from immediate entry to the central labour market, with its guaranteed employment and its potential for further qualification and hence social promotion. The 16- to18-year-olds are, in the mid-1980s, either being retained in school, or are "parked" in special training schemes. In this period the over 18-year-olds face the same difficulties in acceding to employment that the 16- to 18-year-olds faced in the 1970s. For a while it was the 18- to 21-year-olds that were most directly concerned. There are several indications, however, that more and more of the young adults in their early twenties (i.e., up to age 25) find themselves in a suspended situation vis-à-vis employment.

A third factor, the cultural one, must be briefly mentioned. Manifestations of youth subcultures that occupied the front scene in the 1960s—at least their most conspicuous forms—have only seemingly disappeared. New variants of youth subcultures cause less concern, partly because they are less aggressively distinctive, but partly because they are much more widespread and much less restricted to a specific age group. Young adults display in their dress codes, use of language, consumption patterns, political preferences, and in their personal life—in particular in the domains of sex and marriage—a nonconformist behaviour pattern that in many ways is a continuation of those of the younger age group, that is, of the adolescent. Many of them feel closer to the world of the adolescent than to that of the "mature" adult.

3. Participation in Education

In most highly developed European countries, in the 1980s, a majority of the 16- to 17-year-olds are in full-time education. In France, Sweden, and the Netherlands the percentage is well above 70 and, if one adds part-time enrolments, almost the whole of the age group is engaged in education. Those that are not registered as full- or part-time students are nearly all taking part in youth training schemes. The United Kingdom is a noticeable exception: in 1980 less than two in three of the 16- to 17-year-old population were in either full- or part-time education and only one in three engaged in full-time education. In the United States, by comparison, over 90 percent were in full-time education.

Enrolment ratios for the youngest of the "young adults", that is, the 18- to 19-year-olds, were everywhere much lower, due in particular to the fact that most students have completed secondary education. In France they were (in 1980) roughly 35 percent, in Sweden (in 1978) just over 20 percent, and in the Netherlands just over 40 percent. In the United Kingdom full-time enrolments at this level were as low as 14 percent, mainly due to the low participation rate in higher education in comparison with most other Western European countries.

Adding part-time enrolments, however, changes the picture considerably. In France they are almost insignificant and hence do not change the general picture. In the Netherlands they are somewhat more important and bring total enrolments close to 50 percent. In the United Kingdom they exceed full-time participation and bring the total to almost 40 percent—higher than in France and almost as high as in the Netherlands. In comparison, enrolment ratios for the 18- to 19-year-olds in the United States average only 45 percent, but no reliable data for part-time enrolments are available (Organisation for Economic Co-operation and Development 1984).

After age 20, full-time enrolments in the above-mentioned European countries decrease very rapidly as they are virtually restricted to higher education, but large differences between the countries exist. France, the Federal Republic of Germany, Sweden, and the Netherlands have high participation rates in higher education, the United Kingdom a very low one. Contrary to expectations only a few years ago, participation in higher education is slowly but steadily increasing. Already in several European countries—in particular in France, the Federal Republic of Germany, the Netherlands, and Sweden—the percentage of young adults enrolling in full-time higher education is close to or even exceeds the 25 percent mark. Whereas higher education policies in the 1970s tended to restrict access, at the national policy level the present attitude can best be described as laissez faire. At the level of the higher education institutions, more or less open and active recruitment and competition policies are becoming increasingly common. Greater institutional autonomy—and in particular a greater responsibility for their own resource management—is one of the factors that encourages this shift in admissions policies. The other factor is that of actual or expected effects of the lower birth rates in the late 1960s and in the 1970s on the number of potential candidates.

4. *Impact of the Labour Market*

A third factor that explains the change in climate as to enrolment in full-time studies after secondary school relates to the labour market. Unemployment notoriously hits school leavers most of all, as by definition, they are newcomers on the labour market. In the early 1970s this still concerned very great numbers of 16- to 17-year-olds, that is, adolescents; in the 1980s, however, the average age of school leavers and hence that of novices on the labour market has moved up. The "problem group" in this period consists primarily of young adults. With a higher school-leaving age, their educational and professional qualifications have increased, but as a result of fiercer competition for new jobs (as well as rapid technological progress) employers in both the secondary and the tertiary sector demand higher levels of educational and vocational attainment from job candidates than in the recent past. Furthermore, work experience has become an indispensable complement to education and training.

The impact of the above development on enrolments in full-time postsecondary education is not well-established. There is some—admittedly scarce—evidence to show that there is no correlation between regional unemployment rates and enrolment in full-time education. A complicating factor is, however, that often no reliable data is available as to the regional origin of students in postsecondary education. It seems likely that the impact of unemployment and of an overall precarious job market for young adults on part-time education and training is much greater. Young adults engaging in part-time education simultaneously pursue two objectives that are of great importance for their chances on the labour market: they improve their educational and professional proficiency and they acquire work experience.

5. *Combining Work and Study*

In all likelihood combined work–study schemes will in the near future become the dominant education model for young adults. Schematically, this model has two main variants: a study–work variant in which study is the main activity and work experience is complementary and, secondly, a work–study variant in which work is the main activity and education or training is complementary.

Data, derived from unpublished reports on the participation of adults in higher education in member countries of the Organisation for Economic Co-operation and Development (OECD), show an increase of part-time as compared with full-time students. These studies were commissioned in 1984 by the OECD's Centre for Educational Research Innovation (CERI). In the Australian universities, 39.5 percent of all students in 1983 were part-time, compared with 37.0 percent in 1970. In "technical and further education", over 90 percent of students were part-time. Swedish data indicate that part-time studies are closely related to students' age. Whereas one in two of students in arts and sciences under the age of 25 were part-time in the first half of the 1970s, 78 percent of those between ages 25 and 44 were part-time. The same OECD report for Sweden mentions that 27 percent of all arts and science students in the sample were gainfully employed, but as many as 74 percent of the 25- to 44-year-olds. In Canada the part-timers numbered 38.5 percent of all university students in 1981–82, but the percentage was much higher for 20- to 24-year-olds than for those under 20. The highest percentages of part-timers, however, were found among the age-groups 25 to 29 and 30 to 39. After age 40 the percentage of part-time students decreases.

Data on employment of students in higher education corroborate the hypothesis that combined study–work schemes are on the increase among young adults and in particular among those in their 20s and 30s. In Canada only 6 percent of full-time students held full-time jobs in 1978, but not less than 78.4 percent of part-time students. On the other hand, 27.1 percent of full-time students and 10.7 percent of part-time students held part-time jobs. It appears thus that the work–study scheme refers in most cases to a full-time job combined with part-time studies. It may safely be assumed that most of these (young) adults took up part-time study when they had already been engaged in full-time employment for some time and, furthermore, that their study was in most cases related in one way or another to their employment, that is, aimed at either securing or improving their position and their competitiveness in the labour market.

Many of the full-time students engaging in part-time employment have in all likelihood taken up work in the first place for economic reasons, that is, in order to secure their income. More often than not their work is probably unrelated to their studies.

In several other countries the proportion of students working full- or part-time is higher than in Canada. In England and Wales in 1980–81 one in four university students over age 25 was in paid employment. In the polytechnics, however, the percentage was close to 70, and of the Open University students over 25, three out of four students were in employment. In France, well over half of all students in higher education are in full- or part-time employment. In 1982–83 in the University of Milan half of all first-year students were full- or part-time employed. The highest percentages were found among the students in political sciences, humanities, and law (De Francesco 1984).

The same Italian study reveals that nonworking full-time students spent only 26.3 hours in a typical week on study and course attendance, as compared to 22.5 hours for full-time students with a part-time job. In the light of these data it may well be worth exploring the hypothesis that the full-time student is becoming a rarity. Young adults engaging in study, even if they do not exercise paid employment, have many family, social, cultural, and political responsibilities that take a considerable part of their time. This would be at variance with the model of the full-time student that prevails in the organization of postsecondary studies.

6. Other Postsecondary Education

The numbers of young adults enrolled in universities and assimilated institutions such as polytechnics and the French Institut Universitaires de Technologie is, however, much smaller than those in other types of further education. Thus in Australia more than twice as many students are enrolled in "technical and further" than in universities and colleges of advanced education; almost all of them are part-time and very many of them "young adults". Data for Canada for 1979 indicate that of over 3.2 million adults engaged in all forms of continuing education, over 2.2 million studied in other than university or community college programmes. In Sweden in 1980 one in three adults took part in education and training programmes, but only one in 40 in higher education. Everywhere, participation rates under age 24 or 25 are higher than those above this age, even if one takes only nonuniversity programmes into account, as the OECD reports show.

The increased initial education level of young adults, the need to present the best possible education and training credentials on the labour market, and the rapid pace of technological development, all will, in the future, represent strong incentives for young adults to engage in further education and training. A small percentage will be enrolled in full-time programmes. But even these full-time students will in increasing numbers take up full- or part-time work. The majority will be in part-time programmes, some of which will be in universities and other institutions of higher education. Their share in the part-time enrolments will largely depend on their willingness and ability to accommodate young adults whose family and work conditions require great organizational flexibility by higher education. In particular in the highly developed European countries—in contrast, for example, to the United States—institutions often lack the incentives and the imagination to provide adequate study conditions for these part-time students. Hence many young adults will continue to be offered programmes in the rapidly expanding education and training market outside the formal higher education system.

Bibliography

Coleman J S, Husén T 1985 Becoming Adult in a Changing Society. Organisation for Economic Co-operation and Development (OECD), Paris

De Francesco 1984 Italy: A part-time higher education system? *Europ. J. Educ.* 19(2): 173–82

Organisation for Economic Co-operation and Development (OECD) 1984 *Educational Trends in the 1970's: A Quantitative Analysis.* OECD, Paris

Education for Older Adults

A. M. E. Withnall and N. O. Kabwasa

It is well-documented that the populations in most countries are ageing: in the United States, for example, 33 percent of the population is expected to be older than 45 years in the year 2000 compared to 28 percent in 1950. Whereas 8 percent of the population was over 65 years of age in 1950, by 2000 the percentage is expected to be 12 percent—that is about 30 million people out of a total of 262 million (Bureau of the Census 1977). However, the population of older people is heterogeneous. There is a marked individuality about ageing and chronological age is not always a sure measure of performance. There are also variations in previous education, health, housing, income, and family circumstances and it is likely that the population of people nearing the older age groups is similarly varied. With early retirement becoming increasingly common in industrialized countries both as a means of combating unemployment and hastening technological change, the proportion of people who need to cope with problems posed by retirement, expanding leisure time, and advancing age is likely to grow. Thus there has been increased recognition in recent years, particularly in the United States, that this section of the population, although difficult to define in precise terms, will have educational needs and interests for which existing educational provision may be inadequate.

1. *Ageing and the Ability to Learn*

There is a considerable body of research on ageing relevant to adult education and such topics as intelligence, short-term memory, disengagement (retirement), personality, and motivation have been dealt with at length in the literature of developmental psychology and social gerontology. Adult learning activity has attracted similar attention from researchers. In general, it is felt that physically active adults decline substantially less than sedentary adults and whilst vision, hearing, smell, touch, and the related ability of speech tend to be reduced, any observed decline in intellectual functioning is usually attributed to poor health, social isolation, economic plight, limited education, lowered motivation, and other variables not related to the ageing process. Recent research suggests that adults over 65 years of age can learn, given good health, if material is clearly presented and appeals to all learners, if each learner is given sufficient opportunity and time for practice, if material is organized to assist memorizing, and if different contexts for learning are provided such as lectures, seminars, tutorials, practical work, and so on (Osborn et al. 1982). Although much depends on an older person's willingness to learn and attitude to life, all indications are that mental exercise will lead to the recovery of functional loss caused by disuse and to the prolongation of capacity (Bromley 1980). Older people are capable of learning and evidence suggests that the elderly should be regarded as one of the community's resources and that they should have a continuing role as both givers and receivers in the adult education system (Withnall et al. 1983).

2. *Educational Needs Specific to the Elderly*

There is a marked division of opinion amongst providers of education for older people as to whether courses should be specially organized, for example, for people over 60, or whether over-60s should join in normal "all age" classes. What little research there is on this subject suggests that older people dislike segregation, but there are certain situations where age-segregated classes may be preferable (Withnall et al. 1980), as illustrated by the three categories that follow.

2.1 Subject Areas Referring to Role Needs

Apart from the widely observed need to prepare people for retirement, it has been shown that older people may have special educational needs which may often be forgotten. In the United Kingdom, for example, the Geriatric Nutrition Unit at Queen Elizabeth College, University of London, has carried out research into nutrition education with the aim of producing findings which will have both implications for other academics and practical relevance for the elderly. American educators have argued that sex is important to old people and that taboos against sex add to the loneliness, depression, and frustration of the elderly; hence there is a need for special sex education for older people. In both the United States and the United Kingdom, a number of institutes have begun courses in "death education" for elderly people which aim to approach the subject of death from both a practical and emotional standpoint.

2.2 Subjects Requiring Special Teaching Methods

Because of the general decline in the physical abilities of some elderly people, those concerned with providing education for the elderly stress the need to adapt to circumstances. It has been found possible to provide art education for the elderly blind by nonvisual means; low-stress exercise programmes have been designed for the elderly in several countries; and reading programmes which were found to generate not only discussion of reading and books but also of life reminiscences and social problems have been successful with the elderly in the United States.

2.3 The Elderly in Isolated Units

Isolated units may include geriatric hospitals, where activities which seem popular are painting, modelling, music, cooking, local history, and games; or residential homes where reading programmes, described above, have been occasionally used in the United States with reasonable success. The needs of the housebound or those living in sheltered accommodation obviously merit special attention as participation in education is as much a matter of the supply of services as student inclination. At present, this is an area of disadvantage which many adult educators feel deserves priority in attention and resources.

Finally, it has been suggested that controversy over age-integrated and age-segregated models of provision is unnecessary and that both can profitably coexist in view of the great need for educational opportunities for older adults and their diversity (Marcus 1978).

3. Preparation for Retirement

Preretirement education can be defined as the acquisition of information, understanding, and appreciation which will assist in facilitating personal adjustment and self-fulfilment after retirement from the labour force at whatever age this occurs. There are a variety of forms which it may take including individual and group counselling, lectures and discussion groups, books and magazines dealing with retirement planning, and radio and television programmes. Many large companies conduct courses for their own employees and there are examples of organizations which include spouses of retirees in their programme schedules. In Europe, the involvement of pension insurance companies in preretirement activities is noteworthy as is the practice of using private institutions for educational purposes. One problem facing adult educators in this sphere is the timing and presentation of preretirement programmes; current thinking suggests that preretirement education is too important to be left until later working life and that it should begin perhaps in the mid-40s when changes in family patterns occur and when there is a need for personal reappraisal and reorientation. Although it is obviously difficult to assess the effect that preretirement education will have on the quality of life in retirement, it can be expected that in different countries and communities, various community organizations, voluntary and statutory agencies, and industrial concerns will eventually recognize local need by expanding the provision of this special form of education.

4. University of the Third Age

The University of the Third Age was planned in France on the initiative of Pierre Vellas in 1972, accepted by the board of the University of Toulouse in 1973, and became operational that year. Broadly, its aims are to contribute to raising the standard of living of elderly people by health-promoting and sociocultural activities and by research; to improve the living conditions of elderly people through multidisciplinary research in law, economics, and related subjects, and by conferences, seminars, and the dissemination of information; to help private and public services and business through cooperative activities in training, information, and applied research. There is a monthly programme for about eight or nine months per year which anyone over retiring age can join for a modest fee. Classes include physical education, swimming, yoga, language classes, social and cultural topics, films and expeditions, all of which were initially based on the campus of the University of Social Sciences at Toulouse, although home study courses are available on radio and television. However, the University's prime task is to bring the elderly out of isolation into the stimulating atmosphere of a university campus where teachers and students are of different ages. Whilst the University undoubtedly provides a focal point for continuing education for the local elderly population, it has been criticized in that the present clientele are mainly drawn from the well-educated middle class. Nevertheless, the paradigm of the University has led to the development of similar projects elsewhere in France, Belgium, Canada, Switzerland, Poland, and the United Kingdom and has provided a focus for further consideration of a range of philosophical and pedagogical issues among leading European gerontologists (Midwinter 1984).

5. Elderhostel

There have been some initiatives to provide ease of access to higher education for the elderly, in the United States particularly, by legal provision for either free or reduced tuition. However, admitting older adults to the traditional university may pose problems of managing the campus environment and possibly reconsidering the potential role of faculty and support services. Thus an innovative attempt to use campus resources has been made through the elderhostel programme, originally organized at the University of New Hampshire in 1975.

The original concept of the elderhostel combined higher education opportunities on campus during the summer months with travel at low cost. It was inspired, indirectly, by the youth hostels and folk high schools, but was guided by the needs of older citizens for intellectual stimulation and physical adventure.

An original feature of the elderhostel is the network approach. Several colleges and universities participate in the programme. The participants move from campus to campus residing an average of one week on each campus. In 1975, only five institutions were involved. By 1981, 406 colleges and universities sponsored various courses for nearly 40,000 older adults. The 1983 programme projection estimated an enrolment of more than 60,000. Elderhostel is now a network embracing universities, folk high schools, and other institutions in the United States, Canada, the United Kingdom, Denmark, Sweden, Finland, and Norway. In terms of levels of previous education, a 1978 survey of elderhostellers showed the following breakdown: elementary school only, 2 percent; high school, 15 percent; some college, 29 percent; college degree, 24 percent; and graduate school,

30 percent (Gurewitsch 1980). This finding contradicts to some extent the original idea of elderhostel which was "to attract older people who had never had an opportunity to go to college and to create a meeting ground for perennial students and seniors who wouldn't or couldn't go to college in their youth".

Courses offered by each institution may vary. However, a typical programme includes liberal-arts courses, cultural offerings, and physical fitness programmes. The participants live on campus in regular students' dormitories and take their meals in the student cafeteria. They use all the campus facilities such as libraries and tennis courts, and participate in concerts and picnics. Elderhostels are only open to people who are at least 60 years of age or married to someone who is.

6. *Other Educational Initiatives*

6.1 Statutory and Voluntary Provision

Although elderly people can join general adult education classes, much educational activity takes place within day centres, senior centres, and clubs whose aim is essentially to enable older people to live in their own homes but also to get out into the community as far as health will allow. They are mainly recreational centres for caring and sharing; they aim also to provide mental stimulus and act as pressure groups to remind the community of its responsibility towards the elderly. Although considerable variation exists with regard to the perception of these organizations as meeting places and community focal points among various agencies concerned with the elderly, they have been found to serve a broad cross section of older persons and they can provide an important structure for continuing self-realization through classes and lectures, creative, sedentary, or active recreational activities.

In the United States, a number of community colleges have mounted projects aimed to improve the quality of life of the elderly through innovative educational activities—those concerned with arts and crafts seem to prove the most popular. However, success depends on involving older people and their organizations in planning and operating activities, particularly with regard to transportation and the timing of classes.

6.2 The Mass Media

A notable development has been the provision of regular series or features for and about the elderly by the media, especially television. In many countries, the role of the elderly in society has become a major topic of discussion and some television networks have launched programmes aimed at retired people and those planning retirement, featuring a number of aspects including regular political items of relevance to viewers, features on health, finance, leisure activities, safety, and so on. However, it can be argued that the priority need is to educate everyone on these matters and correct the broad image of ageing established through caricatures of the elderly on television.

Education for the retired is also provided through a growing number of retirement magazines and journals; obviously it is difficult to assess the actual impact of these, but they mostly aim to offer help in retirement with practical problems and with suggestions for new leisure activities.

6.3 Self-help

Many people who are retired live outside an institutional framework and for these people self-help groups form a means of avoiding social isolation. Examples include self-help keep-fit courses organized by and for senior citizens; self-managed educational courses including those of an intellectual nature; self-help groups with a specific type of membership such as the Institute for Retired Professionals at the School of Social Research in New York City which offers members, usually highly trained professionals from a variety of occupations, an opportunity to renew their education at university level. In practice, self-help may have its limitations; most self-help groups require professional assistance before becoming self-sufficient (Midwinter 1982).

6.4 Assisting in the Educational Process

Information from the United States suggests that older people are increasingly being regarded as a useful resource in the educational system (Harris 1975), perhaps serving as volunteer teaching aides or resource persons in educational institutions or teaching in recreation, nutrition, and cultural programmes, thereby furthering their own educational experiences. In most countries, however, attitudes toward using people in the educational service appear generally restrictive.

7. *Conclusion*

To summarize, elderly people are able to learn and gain from learning even though some specific skills may wither. Their educational needs are as varied as is the population of the elderly, so that a range of provision is necessary together with a flexible approach to their problems on the part of educational gerontologists. Work in the area is only beginning and a great deal more needs to be done (Peterson 1983, Glendenning 1985). In spite of the increasing efforts to respond to their needs only about 5 percent of elderly people participate in organized learning experiences (MacKeracher 1980). This limited take-up is due, as one writer indicates "... less to monolithic, biologically mediated decline than to a complex matrix of environmental and situation-specific variables" (Rebok 1981).

See also: Lifespan Learning Development; Lifespan Learning: Implications for Educators

Bibliography

Agruso Jr. V M 1978 *Learning in the Later Years: Principles of Educational Gerontology*. Academic Press, New York

Bromley D B 1980 Age and adult education. *Studies in Adult Educ.* 2(2)

Bureau of the Census 1977 *Statistical Abstract of the United States*, 98th edn. United States Government Printing Office, Washington, DC. Government Publication No. C3.134: 977

Glendinning F (ed.) 1985 *Educational Gerontology: International Perspectives*. Croom Helm, London

Gurewitsch E 1980 Elderhostel: A good idea is growing and growing. *Ageing*

Harris L 1975 *The Myth and Reality of Aging in America*. National Council on Aging, Washington, DC

Jones S (ed.) 1976 *Liberation of the Elders*. Speeches and papers from a seminar held at the University of Keele, 26–28 Mar 1976. Beth Johnson Foundation, Stoke-on-Trent

Kaplan M 1979 *Leisure, Lifestyle and Lifespan: Perspectives for Gerontology*, Saunders, Philadelphia, Pennsylvania

MacKeracher D 1980 Learning opportunities for older people. *Learning* 3(2)

Marcus L 1978 Ageing and education. In: Hobman D (ed.) 1978 *The Social Challenge of Ageing*. Croom Helm, London, pp. 117-48

Midwinter E 1982 *Age is Opportunity: Education and Older People*, Policy Studies in Ageing No. 2. Centre for Policy on Ageing, London

Midwinter E 1984 *Mutual Aid Universities*. Croom Helm, London

Osborn M, Charnley A, Withnall A 1982 The psychology of adult learning and development. *Review of Existing Research in Adult and Continuing Education*, Vol. 11. National Institute of Adult Education, Leicester

Peterson D A 1983 *Facilitating Education for Older Learners*. Jossey-Bass, San Francisco, California

Rebok W G 1981 Ageing and higher education: Prospects for intervention. *Educ. Gerontology* 6(2)

Tiberi D M, Boyack V L, Kerschner P A 1978 A comparative analysis of four pre-retirement models. *Educ. Gerontology* 3(4)

UNESCO 1982 *Education and Aging: Report to the World Assembly on Aging*. UNESCO, Paris

Weinstock R 1978 *The Graying of the Campus: A Report from EFL*. Educational Facilities Laboratories, New York

Withnall A, Charnley A, Osborn M 1983 The elderly. *Review of Existing Research in Adult and Continuing Education*, Vol. 2, rev. edn. National Institute of Adult Education, Leicester

Adult Education for Women[1]

K. L. Oglesby, A. Krajnc, and M. Mbilinyi

Although, overall, more women than men participate in adult education activities, their presence and their views appear to have had little impact on education organization and policy until the 1970s. The United Nations (UN) International Women's Year of 1975 prompted more adult education planners, organizers, administrators, and tutors to bring women's educational needs to the forefront and specifically design programmes, promote courses, or institute references to women's role in society in their policy statements.

The UN's 1975 World Plan of Action for the Decade for Women listed minimum objectives which governments were urged to adopt. They fall into four major areas of concern: education; employment; health and welfare; and the social, political, and economic sphere.

Various international organizations responded to the UN's call in different ways but almost all emphasized the need for education and training for women. The Food and Agricultural Organization's (FAO) World Conference on Agrarian Reform and Rural Development, 1979, adopted a programme of action which included a section on educational and employment opportunities. Their recommendations echoed the United Nations' objectives but also emphasized the need for special incentives, such as reduced fees to encourage increased enrolment of girls and women in schools and training programmes; equal wage rates for men and women for work of equal value; the further provision of nonformal educational opportunities for rural women, including leadership training and instruction in agricultural activities; and steps to be taken to evaluate and minimize the possible negative effects on women's employment and income arising from changes in traditional economic patterns and the introduction of new technology. The International Council for Adult Education (ICAE) 1979 Annual General Meeting proposed a five-year plan to increase women's participation in adult and nonformal education programmes. The International Labour Organization (ILO) Medium Term Plan 1982–87 gave prominence to the problems of working women, and was concerned with the impact on their work, incomes, and roles in society of the changes occurring in the economy and labour market at the national and international level. The ILO envisaged that in the developed countries a process of economic reconstruction would involve a reduction of those industries in which women are predominantly employed, and that in the developing countries modernization and technological change would seriously threaten the already low incomes of rural women.

International Women's Year, and the United Nations' designation of 1976–85 as the Decade for Women, prompted the production of statistics summarizing the position of women globally. These indicate that women make up over 30 percent of the "official" labour force, perform 60–89 percent of all agricultural work, and produce at least 50 percent of all food, receive 10 percent of the world's income, and possess

1 This article was written by Leni Oglesby and includes material provided by Ana Krajnc and Marjorie Mbilinyi.

less than 1 percent of the world's wealth. Women and girls constitute 50 percent of the world's population and 75 percent of the world's undernourished (Gayfer 1980). Given that women use adult education programmes more extensively than men, such statistics have implications for the education they receive and the educational needs they have.

There are very few large-scale projects cataloguing evidence of the extent and nature of women's participation in adult education. Before the early 1970s, evidence of women's participation had to be searched for amongst the general material published on adult education developments. However, more recently, articles have been published particularly on women and their participation in education both formal and nonformal. In both the developed and developing countries there are a number of studies which plot the position of women in specific areas of adult education development, but, as yet, no comprehensive international review of the position of women in adult education has been published.

The case study reports of women's programmes fall into two categories: those few that are analytical and contain useful theoretical and practical insights for practitioners and the majority which contain interesting descriptions of what is being provided but little evidence of analytical thought, or impetus for further development. In the survey which follows of adult education for women in the developed and developing countries some indications will be given of the programmes in which women currently participate with emphasis on particular developments such as vocationally oriented courses, literacy, and women's studies. Explanations of women's participation in varying types of programme are many and vary in both their nature and conceptual level, and in the degree to which they are governed by the prevailing social, cultural, economic, and political climates of particular societies.

1. Adult Education for Women in the Developed Countries

The present provision of educational programmes for adults in the developed countries tends to fall into three categories:

(a) the liberal education courses, including subjects concerned with the arts, language, literature, and recreational topics;

(b) re-entry programmes and vocational training courses;

(c) basic education courses of a remedial kind for literacy and numeracy subjects.

Women participate in all three types of course but in varying proportions in different countries according to their immediate and long-term needs.

The reasons for which they participate fall into four classes: social, that is, meeting and mixing with people; remedial, that is, completing their education or taking "second chance" opportunities to recover lost educational ground; compensatory, that is, to counterbalance felt deficiencies in their life-style; and occupational mobility, that is, education for promotion in their present work or for entering a different occupational field.

Empirical studies have shown that the main motives for women are social security, independence, a wish to be of help to others, to be generally better educated, and to further their personal development (which includes the possibility of furthering their professional or occupational interests). In a recent study in the United Kingdom (ACACE 1982) women showed a wider range of motives for studying than men, but there was no fundamental difference from men in their attitudes towards education and work, with approximately 70 percent of both sexes being favourably disposed towards education on both personal and vocational grounds. Whatever the particular motivation, the underlying fear of inadequacy, whether socially or educationally based, is usually common to both. After a period of child rearing, women view their former levels of education as woefully inadequate or outdated given the rapid technological and economic changes which have occurred since their last spell in the official labour market.

The attraction and choice of particular adult education activity accords with one or more of these motives, but it is also part of the education process that the motivation for achievement is inculcated in the participants. One important feature of adult education programmes for women is that they usually help to enhance women's self-confidence and self-esteem, as well as developing their intellectual and personal skills.

1.1 Vocational Adult Education Programmes

Since 1960, the participation rate of women in the labour market in developed countries, that is, Western and Southern Europe, Japan, Canada, the United States, Australia, and New Zealand, has increased, despite the recession, and the projections for the future indicate that the rate will continue to rise (OECD 1976, OECD 1980, Paukert 1984). Analysis of the female labour force indicates that more women of child-bearing years are remaining in the labour market with fewer and shorter interruptions for childbirth; more middle-aged women with grown-up children are returning to the job market; and there is a rapid increase in the number of single-parent families supported by women.

An unpublished survey by Emily S. Andrews (OECD 1979) reviewed the factors which influence women's participation rates in the labour market in seven OECD countries—Belgium, France, the Federal Republic of Germany, Italy, Japan, the United Kingdom, and the United States. These countries provided a range of stages of economic development and showed differences in female labour force participation rates due to educational and cultural factors. However, the factors which affected their entry into the official labour market appeared to be: economic, with women entering the labour market to increase the family income to cover both their present and possible future needs; their marital status, and the number, age, and spacing of their children; the availability and cost of child-care provision; contraction or expansion of those sectors of the economy in which women are most often employed; conditions of employment, such as the availability of flexi-time or part-time work. Women also wished to establish their rights to employment at a level and occupation of their choice, to economic independence, and to a social status independent of familial connections.

Continuing education provision in Western European countries has, in recent years, reflected the growing concern about equal access to employment and education fields for men and women, and in addition to the adult education programmes which women have traditionally followed, various types of entry and re-entry courses have been provided for those with low levels of initial education or too few or unsuitable educational qualifications for the kind of career they wish to follow, or in need of updating their knowledge and qualifications. Entry and re-entry programmes can be loosely divided into two categories: the general education programmes and the vocationally oriented entry or retraining programmes.

The general education programmes may be entered by women on the basis of straightforward subject interest or they may have a vocational aim in mind and be seeking to improve their initial educational qualifications prior to entering vocational courses or re-entering the labour market. These tend to be of two kinds: courses leading to recognized qualifications and courses offering re-entry to study programmes.

Courses leading to recognized qualifications follow prescribed syllabi required for examinations and are taken at different stages of education, for example, completion of compulsory secondary education, or after a few more years of study at school or college, or at university degree or diploma level. Examples of this include the Netherlands Open School Programme, for those wishing to reach the level of education usually expected after eight years of formal schooling, or who wish to improve their manual and/or their social skills. The Moeder MAVO programme was initiated in 1975 in the Netherlands and allows for the acquisition of cumulative certificates, undertaken by day-time study, leading to the MAVO which is the lowest level of general secondary-school diploma. The large number of young housewives who take this particular route to the qualification prompted its nickname (Hootsmans 1980). The Open University of the United Kingdom founded in 1971, allows students who do not possess university entrance qualifications to obtain a sufficient number of cumulative course credits by part-time study to qualify for a first-level degree. None of these programmes were expressly designed for women but they have proved to be a significant section of the student population on these courses.

Courses offering re-entry to study programmes tend to provide a broadly based programme for those students who wish to reappraise their general education levels, improve them, and consider new avenues of personal development, and/or careers. They enable students either to obtain the necessary entry qualifications for university or college or provide those institutions with evidence that these students can be admitted to degree courses under alternative entry schemes. Examples of this in the United Kingdom are the "Fresh Horizons" course at London's City Literary Institute; general education courses offered by some long-term residential colleges; and preparatory courses for higher education provided by some universities such as Hull and Sheffield.

The vocationally oriented programmes are those which include prevocational and specific vocational elements.

Prevocational courses tend to be short courses of not more than three months which aim to show women the range of job opportunities available to them, discuss the realities of the labour market, and inculcate confidence and necessary basic skills for them to enter the labour force. A number of these courses include work placement opportunities. Examples of these can be found in the United Kingdom, the Federal Republic of Germany, France, Ireland, and the United States, which all offer general orientation courses for re-entry to work. In the United Kingdom the Manpower Services Commission (MSC) Training Division, under the aegis of the Department of Employment, organizes a Wider Opportunities for Women (WOW) programme, which provides opportunities for women to sample different kinds of work and helps them to find appropriate training courses. Some *Volkshochshulen* in the Federal Republic of Germany provide programmes such as the Professional Orientation for Women Course and Women Back to Work Course in Berlin. ANCO, the Industrial Training Authority in Ireland, set up a Return to Work Course for Women in 1977. In France the *Retravailler Centre* in Paris provides help for women to evaluate and upgrade their labour market skills, and has been sufficiently successful for its courses to be copied both in the rest of the country and in Switzerland. The French UFCS (Women's Civic and Social Union) course is similar to the Paris one but provides for women with fewer educational attainments (Hootsmans 1980). In the United States, courses are run by a variety of organizations including women's centres, community colleges, women's organizations, and universities extension units to help women bridge the transition between home and work or further education. The aims of these courses are to promote self-awareness, to reduce any guilt feelings women may experience in resuming work, and to help women plan their career development (Hartnett 1980).

Vocational training courses are provided by all countries, but a majority of course places are taken by men. It has been observed that many more occupations which are undertaken by men provide training schemes for their members than do those occupations traditionally undertaken by women; in those occupations which are mainly undertaken by women, but include some men, the take-up rate of training course places by the men in those fields is disproportionately higher than that of the women; at a time of economic recession and rising unemployment, priority for training and education tends to be given to categories of workers other than women re-entrants to the labour market; and there is a need for specific guidance and counselling on available training provisions open to women, such as the career development guide for women published by the MSC in the United Kingdom. Women's difficulties are also compounded by the problem that in a number of countries the adult education sector is divorced from the vocational and technical education sector both in the structure and the administration of the education system, which usually means that neither sector has a clear idea or understanding of the other's provisions.

In most developed countries, the majority of vocational courses are in principle open to women. However, in practice, a large majority of those women who undertake vocational training are to be found in the traditional occupational fields such as the commercial and service industries; for example, in the United Kingdom in 1981–82, 70 percent of women under the MSC's Training Opportunities Scheme (TOPS) were receiving clerical and office skills training.

Given the shortage of labour in certain skilled trades, a number of countries are encouraging moves to draw women into the nontraditional occupational areas.

In the United Kingdom in 1981–82, women on the MSC's TOPS scheme made up 13 percent of the trainees on management courses and 16 percent of the trainees on computer skills courses. A small but increasing number of women were training for nontraditional fields such as motor vehicle repair, carpentry, and basic engineering, and an experimental programme has been introduced of single sex courses in manual trades in skill centres to overcome the problem of female isolation on those courses which traditionally recruit men.

Sweden and Norway have similar labour market training programmes whose objectives are to qualify workers for new occupations and industries. Sweden also has a Working Life and Training course which aims to ease the entry of women into male-dominated occupations. This was set up at the time of a high labour shortage in certain fields of the manufacturing sector, such as the metal and woodworking industries. The advantages accruing to the women who entered were that no objections were raised from the trade unions concerned and that they entered as a collective group and not as isolated individuals (Hootsmans 1980).

Only a few countries, notably the United States, provide programmes to enable women to enter management fields. Women who already hold managerial positions do usually have access to training seminars provided by their companies, but it tends to be a case of finding and holding the position and then undertaking inservice training. There are job-linked re-entry academic programmes in the United States leading to managerial level professional posts which encourage the recruitment of women applicants. Two business schools in the United Kingdom are also encouraging the admission of women to their academic programmes for prospective managers.

1.2 Problems and Constraints for Women in Relation to Vocational Courses

Sex discrimination and sex stereotyping of the labour market are seen as being of major concern to a number of women's organizations and equal opportunities commissions because of their correlation with unequal access to education and training, unequal pay, and low remuneration. The problems experienced by women workers and trainees are reflections of their countries' socioeconomic and cultural climates, including the views not only of the men but of their female relatives and themselves. The main reasons for the low representation of women in adult vocational training courses are: their previous education experience and achievements; a strong feeling that it may not be worth their while to do so in occupational terms—completion of a training course does not necessarily ensure a suitable job at the level for which the trainees are qualified; problems of finance; insufficient child-care facilities; and a course organization which is insufficiently flexible to allow for both their educational and domestic commitments. There are a number of problems connected with the new vocational education courses specifically designed for women. There is often inadequate evaluation on the nature and rate of employment which follows training. The majority of programmes are not government administered or part of labour union activity, with consequent problems for recognition of their standing. The programmes are usually not integrated into further vocational or technical education training programmes. Only a few courses match the criteria required of the qualification courses recognized by the state and industries and which provide access to all levels of the trades or professions in question. The probability is that women following these courses will still find themselves confined to the lower levels of their new occupations.

All programmes have been affected by the economic crisis stemming from the mid-1970s, and the falling demand for workers in all sectors of industry. In some countries programmes and initiatives for both traditional and nontraditional occupations have been cut back. Adult education budgets have been cut in nearly all countries. In the United Kingdom in 1977–78 the MSC trained 43,204 females under the TOPS scheme, but by 1981–82 this figure had fallen to 19,000 (MSC Annual Reports 1978, 1982).

1.3 Projects to Counteract These Problems

Programmes which offer equal access, in theory, without making provision for women to overcome the barriers listed above, are unlikely to achieve any practical improvement in the participation rates. Two strands of action are involved in improving women's participation rates in education and employment.

The first includes matters concerned with intrinsic structural changes to the education system. These include adjusting the balance between female and male teachers who tend to be found, respectively, in the lower and higher range of the career ladder, and provide implicit role models, including status, for their pupils; promoting the same expectations of boys and girls in respect of that part of the curriculum which influences the occupational and educational aspirations of pupils; reviewing admissions policies for institutions of higher and vocational education to allow for employment or family experience to be accepted in lieu of examination qualifications; the provision of guidance and counselling services; the extension of any grant or loan system to mature students; improving access to courses, for example, part-time study, distance education teaching methods, paid educational leave; the provision of study skills courses, and precourse general education study (Darling 1975).

Changes at one level of education are of limited value without corresponding changes at the other levels. Improved access to higher education will not result in a significant change in female participation rates unless the preparatory grounding at secondary level is provided for women, and it is the adult education field which appears to offer women the most chances of remedying the gaps or shortfall in their educational experience, or of updating their knowledge and skills in particular fields.

The second includes matters concerned with changes extrinsic to the education system but whose effects impinge strongly upon it. These include: attempts to combat sex role stereotyping, for example, in the media; improvement in child-care provision, for example, nurseries, creche facilities; changes in labour market policy to encourage women to train for occupations usually reserved for men, and vice versa.

Some countries have adopted affirmative action programmes to counteract sex differentiation and segregation in training. Sweden's national plan of action for equality (National Committee on Equality 1979) encourages vocational guidance to be geared towards the promotion of occupational choices and training which cross sex lines. Since 1974 the regional development policy has provided financial inducements to counteract sex segregation. The government subsidizes regions for plant location, training, and induction on condition that at least 40 percent of all additional jobs which are created are reserved for each sex. Employers receive special equality grants to hire and train workers for nontraditional occupations. Special programmes also exist in labour market training for those who want occupations usually categorized as appropriate for the opposite sex. The United Kingdom and the United States both have legislation prohibiting discrimination on the basis of sex in access to education and training programmes and most employment fields.

Attempts are also being made to involve women more actively in the work of their respective trade unions. The Educational Association of Salaried Workers in Sweden has one officer in each branch responsible for promoting equal opportunities for women, mainly through the provision of material for training purposes and for promoting discussion on how women can participate in union activities (EBAE 1980). An adult education programme for women trade union members is undertaken by the Manchester Workers' Educational Association in the United Kingdom.

2. Adult Education and Women in Developing Countries

"Socio-economic conditions in less developed countries and the inadequacy of welfare services have made it imperative that non-formal programmes focus on the satisfaction of basic needs" (Jayaweera 1979). The immediate problems for the rural and poor urban women include poor environmental sanitation and health standards, maternal and infant mortality, and malnutrition and short life expectancy. The adult education provision in the developing countries reflects these needs, and the majority of adult education programmes tend to fall into three categories: family health education, for example health, sanitation, nutrition, maternity and child care, family planning; agricultural extension programmes; and literacy programmes. Some efforts have also been made to promote programmes in vocational education.

2.1 Health Education

Maternal and child-care clinics have been established in many countries to serve rural areas, but often without adequate resources and staff, and not within easy access for many villages. Preventative health measures and family planning are seen as an integral part of most clinic programmes, although the latter depends considerably for acceptance on cultural practices and religious beliefs. Where possible, and particularly through paraprofessional and/or village health workers, the maternal and child-care clinics provide education in disease prevention and hygiene, food and nutrition, safe drinking water, methods of processing foods, the reasons for inoculations, improved sanitation practices, and the benefits to mothers and children of spaced childbirth. Health and nutrition are also covered in nutrition rehabilitation units which may be attached to maternal and child-care clinics, or set up as a separate hospital ward.

These forms of education are only for women, but usually only reach a small proportion of rural women because of the urban bias in the allocation of health services. Evaluations of these programmes have drawn the following conclusions. Mothers exposed to health education at the clinic or nutrition rehabilitation units while nursing a sick child lack the time or frame of mind to participate. Women only come to maternal and child-care clinics when a child is sick or when they are bringing infants for inoculation. Women do not have time to make weaning foods on an individual household basis and mass production of weaning foods by private or state industry is usually priced out of reach of the poor. Health education alone cannot solve the health crisis in underdeveloped countries (Loutfi 1980, Mascarenhas and Mbilinyi 1983, Rogers 1980).

2.2 Agricultural Extension Programmes

There is extensive participation by women in agriculture, but preference is usually given to men in any agricultural education and extension programmes on modern techniques and technological innovations. Where provision is made for women they tend to be offered domestic science programmes, and handicraft and cottage crafts programmes rather than agriculture. Domestic science is taught to women in many different kinds of adult education programmes, including functional literacy and settlement schemes, and vocational training programmes. According to the Economic Commission for Africa, 50 percent of all adult education provided for African women is on domestic science, compared with 15 percent on agriculture and zero percent on trade and commerce (Rogers 1980). These vocational programmes and courses appear to be unpopular with the women, since they have high drop-out rates, but they are constantly promoted by international agencies and state institutions.

A report on an evaluation of a programme of nonformal education, provided by the Botswana Ministry of Agriculture for women farmers at rural training centres, showed that a large part of the male population of Botswana tends to migrate to South Africa to work in the cities, leaving the women responsible for agricultural development in the area. Despite these responsibilities the courses offered to women at the rural training centres by male extension staff concentrated on topics associated with domestic interests, for example, sewing, knitting, and cookery. With the encouragement of a women's extension officer the women requested that the course programme included the topics of poultry care and management and cattle and small-stock management.

On review of the work of the rural training centres it was proposed that the curriculum for programmes include the four content areas of home management education; agricultural extension; education for income-generating activities; and social and civic education (Higgins 1982).

Examples of programmes offered to Asian women indicate similar problems. In Sri Lanka a farm workers' agricultural extension programme, introduced in 1974, attempted to integrate rural women in the development process and improve the standard of living of farm families. However, problems relating to marketing facilities, the quality of the local crafts produced, and the dearth of trained personnel affected the income generation aspect of the programme and it also had a high drop-out rate.

Women's development centres were initiated in the 1970s, also in Sri Lanka, to improve the standards of living of rural families. Courses were offered to village trainees in home gardening, food production and preparation, appropriate technology, crafts, needlework, nutrition, and health. The problems with these have been a lack of capital resources and skilled personnel; poor facilities in terms of buildings and equipment; a training programme mainly concerned with needlework as opposed to instruction in modern agricultural methods, food processing, economically viable crafts, nutrition, and health. The income generation was low because the output was of low marketable standards, and the future employment prospects of trainees proved to be low: 90 percent were unemployed and 85 percent of the self-employed had no income (Jayaweera 1979).

In China, the transformation of agriculture became a central priority by the end of the 1950s. A complete change in the position of women was found necessary in production and the family to release male labourers and to carry through the transformation of social relations. Special training programmes were developed for women production brigades, as well as the establishment of communal crèches, canteens, laundries, and other facilities which would dramatically reduce female labour in domestic activities. However, by the end of the 1960s, a sexual division of labour in communal production had clearly emerged, with women allocated to less skilled, lighter work which earned lower work points than men. This division of labour still exists (Croll 1979).

2.3 Vocational Education

Entry or re-entry training programmes for women in developing countries have not been promoted in any significant fashion, because the demand for unskilled labour is adequately satisfied by the available pool of inexpensive labour. The rate of unemployment is usually high in developing countries and is much higher for women than men. The limited jobs available are unskilled, low paying, and seasonal. There appear also to have been few efforts to train women for nontraditional occupations.

It is difficult to generalize about employment and training patterns for women in underdeveloped countries because of the extremely diverse economies. Uneven development is found within each country, as well as within a given region. Certain common tendencies do emerge however as developing countries are increasingly absorbed into the worldwide economy. Islands of industrial enterprises employing a relatively small number of people are surrounded by large numbers of landless rural labourers, peasants, and artisans.

Similar patterns of sex differentiation in education and vocational training are found in developing countries as compared to developed countries. For example, in Ghana, Zambia, and Tanzania, the majority of women with any vocational or technical training are registered in domestic science, secretarial, commercial, and catering subjects (Akerele 1979, Mascarenhas and Mbilinyi 1983). Few women are enrolled in basic craft training courses which recruit directly into apprenticeship training programmes and wage employment. Small-scale industrial training programmes, set up to train self-employed producers, place most of their women trainees on skills courses such as spinning, tailoring, pottery, and knitting. These tendencies exist in other African countries and in Asia, Latin America, and the Caribbean (Fordham 1980, Rogers 1980, Ellis 1984).

Of the trainees on the training programmes offered by the Department of Small Industries in Sri Lanka, in 1971, 72.8 percent were women. However, they were to be found on the training programmes associated with the traditional female crafts, for example hand-woven textiles, pottery, and cane industries (Jayaweera 1979).

However, one notable example of a vocational programme for a nontraditional field was a special training programme in welding and carpentry for 48 women in Jamaica (Antrobus and Rogers 1982). The content of the training scheme covered, on the vocational side, production skills, cooperative management and accounting, and on the social–cultural side, family-life education, and consciousness raising. The women mastered the woodworking and welding skills, but the course suffered from a high drop-out rate and the women tended not to become self-reliant after finishing the programme.

A significant contrast to the Jamaican scheme is the Self-employed Women's Association (SEWA) in Ahmedabad, in India (Jain 1980). It arose out of the political struggle of women headloaders who sought assistance from the Textile Labour Association. They were later joined by over one-third of the self-employed women of the area. The association provides seven basic services to its members: bargaining and representation with clients as well as police and other state officials; legal aid; credit and savings services; supply of raw materials, tools, and equipment and technical assistance; social security and welfare inputs; productive skills training, which now includes functional literacy; and the development of economic organizations leading to higher and more steady incomes. The functional literacy component of the skills training programme was initially rejected by the women as irrelevant, but it is now demanded as a result of progress already made in the economic and political sphere. Crucial to the success of SEWA is the high degree of political consciousness among the women participants, the mode of self-management developed, and the political nature of the organization itself. Its organizers have consistently lobbied through demonstrations, use of the press and public meetings, and through careful involvement of local women's leadership in each expansion drive.

Many of the vocational programmes are oriented to self-employment and as a matter of policy they provide no formal links to wage employment and no grade tests to increase the employability of the participants. The form and level of technology demonstrated in the teaching resources of these courses has usually been displaced by modern technology in factory production, which makes it increasingly difficult for such skills to lead to viable self-employment. Special skills training programmes of this nature, for women, experience a very high drop-out rate. One explanation offered for this is that women seek short training programmes which lead to immediate income possibilities with very little capital investment required (Fordham 1980).

2.4 Constraints and Problems Associated with Courses

Despite the great diversity of economic, political, and cultural systems, the factor affecting motivation to attend courses which is common for women in the developing countries of Asia and Africa is the overriding need for education which is designed to generate more income. However, the impact of the programmes on living standards and income generation seems to have been limited and they appear not to have reached the poorest and most educationally disadvantaged women for a number of reasons. On the organizational front the agencies mounting the programmes do not centrally plan or coordinate their provision in order to maximize use of the available resources. Economic constraints affect the material and staffing resources which can be allocated to courses, and restrict their number. Trainees are reluctant or unable to become self-employed following course completion because of the lack of credit and marketing facilities. The educational background of women also raises barriers for them. The curriculum and courses considered suitable for women in schools, universities, and vocational institutions limits the range of vocational skills and choices available to them. Training and employment opportunities can be seen as of marginal importance in view of the massive unemployment situation in many countries. It is suggested that the socialization process has conditioned many women to accept their cultural roles and match their career aspirations accordingly. A survey of vocational aspirations of secondary-school girls in Sri Lanka indicated that nearly 90 percent wished to be employed after marriage but 50–60 percent accepted the view that there were women's jobs and men's jobs (Jayaweera 1979).

In common with women in the developed countries they have to balance the demands of their working day between their agricultural or industrial work and the care of the family. As in the developed countries, poor transport facilities in the rural areas have restricted access to courses. The living conditions of women from rural low-income families are particularly hard with heavy demands being made on their time in the collection of water, fuel, and food, which has meant that they have little time available to undertake courses. Most of these reasons are broadly similar to those behind the low participation rates of women in developed countries but with one major difference: very few women, or men, have completed a full primary education and the highest illiteracy rates in the world are for women in the developing countries.

3. *Literacy Programmes for Women*

Female illiteracy is deemed to have adverse effects not only on the well-being of the family and their children's level of education but also on their prospects of labour force productivity. Different countries have adopted differing approaches to the problem but on the whole programmes tend to fall within five general categories: the political, economic, population, cultural, or religious approaches.

With the political approach, programme objectives are closely tied in with a country's political aims. Portugal's literacy work was regarded as a fundamental plank in the construction of a new society. In 1970 it was estimated that 32.5 percent of the total population aged 20 and over was illiterate, and of these 64.6 percent were women. It was further estimated that 92.1 percent of the appropriate age female population had only basic elementary schooling, and more than 70 percent of the working women had inadequate vocational training (Neves 1982). Similarly it was estimated that by the mid-1970s, 2.2 million adults in Iraq between the ages of 15 and 44 could not read or write, and 70 percent of these were women (Lucas 1982). As with the Cuban scheme in the early 1960s, Iraq chose to mount an almost military-style national and nationalistic campaign, using the existing educational system and the mass media. In addition to basic literacy and numeracy skills, classes were provided on familial responsibilities, child care, nutrition, community welfare, and appreciation of the cultural heritage. Classes were arranged to suit the working arrangement of the participants with housewives attending early in the day or during the evening. By 1979 the campaign had entered a postliteracy stage with the provision of education to higher levels.

Although functional literacy programmes are promoted normally in connection with specific occupations, little attention has been given to the kind and conditions of work that illiterates have been engaged in, or whether the acquisition of literacy will materially affect their income. King (1979) has pointed out that illiterates are usually to be found in the employment categories of households and family labour, particularly women and subsistence level workers in urban and rural areas who are often self-employed. The problem is to motivate the illiterates to acquire new skills, and approaches generally used to do this are set in the context of the local environment and aim to indicate the possibilities of improved income revenue, and to inform illiterates of the structure of their world and use literacy as a vehicle for heightened political awareness.

One programme for women which exemplifies some of these points was an adult literacy scheme which UNESCO promoted in 1968 in the Upper Volta as part of its experimental programme for equality of access of girls and women to education. The aims were to enable adult women to improve the standard of living of their families and schoolgirls to be better prepared for future developmental needs in the agrarian economy. The project also undertook to train teachers, instructors, and female leaders in the village in order to have staff to carry out the programme. When the programme came to be implemented, a number of points were highlighted. Following a survey of the position of women in this region the literacy project had to be postponed until improvements could be effected in their health, hygiene, and nutrition. Improvement in the standard of living through informal education was a precondition for even a basic literacy programme. The period of 5 months in the year in which classes were held was insufficient to achieve literacy within the designed two year span. If programmes were not provided also for the men they tended to discourage their wives and daughters from attending classes. The programme appears to have been effective enough for members of a village literacy class to note the concrete results of their education in the improved health of their children and the improved conditions of living (UNESCO 1975).

Although the low rate of female literacy is generally known, and current figures are available from UNESCO statistical yearbooks, there appears to be a dearth of detailed accounts of literacy programmes and support systems used by women in particular. As a result, the justification for programmes tends to be given on the grounds of humanitarian principle rather than specific purpose. The objectives of many international associations, including women's organizations, call for literacy training for women usually on the grounds that Bhola (1981) cites: that illiteracy endangers the principle of equality of humankind because it not only violates the individual's right to education but is one of the major obstacles to the effective enjoyment of other human rights. The Udaipur Literacy Declaration (Report 1981) called for priority to be given in the literacy field to the needs of disadvantaged groups, and especially women. It would be interesting to know of the ways and manner in which more of the international organizations apart from UNESCO put their policies into practice.

4. *Women's Studies and Adult Education*

One effect of the consciousness-raising promoted by women's movements and organizations has been the introduction into educational programmes since the early 1970s of studies concerned with the position of women. The content of these courses usually covers examinations of the role and status of women in society, and women in relation to specific topics such as trade unions, health, legal, and welfare rights. A number of national and international journals have been launched and publishing houses established with primary interests in this new field. The manner in which the courses are structured and taught differs from the usual formal education course but echoes the ethos of adult education in that they are democratically organized with an emphasis on cooperation, mutual support, and the equal participation of all members.

The growth of women's studies is acknowledged to stem from a recognition that

> mere formal equal rights in education would have little effect on women's lives in terms of guaranteeing them equal opportunities, as long as they were accompanied by educational contents which continued to display the stereotypes. . . . women would not and could not come into their own as long as knowledge about themselves, especially in the humanities and social sciences, was either totally absent or distorted by prejudices and as long as teaching and research served to maintain a situation that in today's world must be recognised not only as dysfunctional but also as anti-female, and—in the rigid assignment to roles for both sexes—as antihuman. (Schöpp-Schilling 1979)

Women's studies form part of the adult education provision of the developing countries through the nonformal education programmes on topics such as women and health, and women and society. In China, during the first half of the 1960s, study groups were created to raise women's consciousness of their position and role. Both separate and mixed groups involved peasants, workers, and students in an analysis of women's history, problems of equal pay, traditional marriage customs, and the sexual division of labour in the household. These educational programmes were stopped with the disbanding of the Women's Movement during the Chinese Cultural Revolution in the mid-1960s but commenced again during the later 1960s and early 1970s (Croll 1979).

Similar nonformal and nonqualification discussion courses were provided in the developed countries, with themes concerning the changing role of women in society and women's relationship to current issues in society. Examples of these courses are the Women Orienting in Society programme, started in North Holland in 1974 but now spread throughout the Netherlands, for women with only one or two years of secondary-school education. This kind of programme is also offered to women with higher levels of education such as the Dutch Housewives' Association programme Women of Today; the Frauen-forum courses in the Federal Republic of Germany; and the Women's Studies courses offered by the Workers' Educational Association in the United Kingdom (Hootsmans 1980). Some courses are more specific in their objectives such as the United Kingdom and the United States special leadership training courses for women who wish to take an active role in public life (Harnett 1980).

There has also been a distinct move in the developed countries to promote women's studies courses within the formal education system. In 1979 there were women's studies programmes at over 260 American colleges and universities, varying in length and style according to the philosophy and structures of their host institutions. These programmes could be multidisciplinary or concentrate on specific subjects in relation to women, for example, psychology, sociology, history, science, literature, education, and could be studied mainly at undergraduate level but occasionally up to doctoral level (Harnett 1980).

In the Federal Republic of Germany, women's studies have been introduced into university courses, but are not always accepted as credit courses. Research centres have also been established and some within higher education institutions. The aim of the Free University of Berlin Centre is to promote feminist research in all relevant disciplines at the university through research projects geared to the improvement of the position of women. It also aims to provide scholarships for women, promote continuing education programmes for women, and provide a resources centre. In the United Kingdom both the voluntary and formal education organizations mount short courses in women's studies, and Kent University has inaugurated a degree programme in the field. Most Australian universities offer women's studies courses on an interdisciplinary basis, mainly to students undertaking arts or social science degrees (Walker and Smith 1979).

Women's groups have been formed in response to the revival of interest in and education on women's rights. Some groups concentrate on specific issues, such as reform of the tax laws or aid for women who have been subjected to domestic or sexual violence, but whatever the specific objectives are of the particular groups, the overall directive of the movement is to campaign for social change and the main thrust of this is seen to be through education. A further development along the same lines is the establishment of women's centres in urban areas which provide educational, social, and personal facilities for women to use if and when these are needed.

Women have also formed international research networks to exchange information, results of projects, and to chart new areas for investigation. The Association of African Women for Research and Development, for example, was founded at the end of 1977 to meet the special needs of African women. Among the adult education organizations, the women's programmes of the International Council for Adult Education serve to link those involved in research and women's education at regional and international levels.

5. *Conclusion*

One of the principal historical reasons given for the submergence of women's interests and needs in the adult education field, and for the lack of concern in its literature, is that education and its systems reflect male thinking and have been designed primarily for the needs of the dominant socioeconomic groups in society. In an attempt to prove equivalence of worth and educability, education for females adopted the existing patterns. However, this conformity carried implications for the curriculum, with women being offered either a complete imitation of the male curriculum, or, given cultural assumptions about the role and position of women in society and their place in the occupational structure, a very much watered-down version. The majority of the female population who have access to any kind of education opportunity are offered education with an emphasis on low-level skills to prepare them for work in the domestic and service fields or basic levels of industry and agriculture. Where women do have opportunities to train for occupations where they will work alongside men it is commonly assumed that the men's training programme will suit them equally. The problems for women in relation to such training programmes stem from the fact that it is not organizationally acknowledged that although women share equally with the men the problems associated with modernization and technological change, and the dependency and exploitation resulting from poverty, in addition they are subjected to the cultural, social, and domestic pressures of being women.

Much of the literature on adult education and women is concerned with an exposure of the inequalities suffered by women and calls for changes in the various political, cultural, and social systems which maintain and support these inequalities. This would seem to be a necessary stage in the raising of general awareness about the problems but it would be useful if more was to be offered in the way of practical action to overcome them. There is a need for research and action to effect improvements in women's situations, even if these are only on a small scale; it is the small steps which usually produce a climate in which larger changes appear more manageable and acceptable.

The gap between the rhetoric calling for rectification of the inequalities and the actual implementation of programmes for action can be attributed to a number of theoretical, organizational, and economic factors. There is a widely held, but mistaken, view that benefits gained for society will eventually reach the women: the "trickle-down" theory. This clearly does not appear to be happening, except perhaps in the field of welfare benefits associated with children. A report from a five-year review of the United Nations 1975 World Action Plan to improve the situation of women concluded that progress had been minimal and the conditions of daily life had deteriorated for most women of the world, especially those in the rural and poorer urban sectors. It is a common practice in those countries where governments are concerned about the problems to put "women's affairs" into a category of activity separate from everything else, apart from possibly social welfare. The width of a "women's affairs" brief coupled with a small administrative secretariat can mean that action programmes fail to achieve their aims either because their scope is too wide and/or because these are obstructed by interdepartmental barriers which have to be negotiated. The lack of women members of national policy and planning teams means that the women's point of view is either absent from crucial initial stages of planning development, or is represented through men. The economic problem relates to the fact that in a world economic recession women's programmes are usually the first to be cut back.

In order to try to bridge the gap between rhetoric and action, the United Nations has supported, through the Voluntary Fund for the UN Decade for Women, three categories of projects. The first is to increase the numbers of women adult educators with the idea of establishing support networks of women working in the adult education field. It is hoped that these networks would encourage the recruitment of other female workers, would identify areas of action, and would serve as role models for young women. An example of such a project is the recruitment of Egyptian and Sudanese women for community development programmes in Oman, who then train Omani women. The second is to promote research on the participation of women in adult education, for example, the assessment of the UNESCO literacy programme in Upper Volta which demonstrated the programme's value to women. The third type of project is aimed at increasing the number of women learners, for example, projects to aid the acquisition of small business and marketing skills and the conservation of energy resources. UNESCO, from its research findings, considered that there were three prerequisites for success in broadening educational opportunities for women, which were "comprehensiveness, flexibility, and adaptability to an existing situation" (UNESCO 1975). Comprehensiveness was essential because, given the inevitable complexities of women's situations, there was a need to implement a programme on several levels and to include the collaboration of all the public and private agencies with a remit and interests in the field. Flexibility was needed to allow for possible changes of direction or focus in a programme according to changing circumstances. Adaptability to the prevailing social, cultural, and political climate and realities of the programme's context was needed both for the programme's objectives, staffing, and resources.

One notable attempt to marry the theoretical and descriptive approaches to research on women and adult education is being promoted by the International Council for Adult Education (ICAE), with the aid of funding from the International Development Research Centre. This project aims to review the extent and nature of women's participation in adult and nonformal education in the seven Third World regions of Africa, the Arab countries, the Caribbean, North America, South Asia, Southeast Asia and the South Pacific. A workshop and study tour in 1982 discussed the regional report findings, identified issues which were seen as generally common as well as those specific to particular regions, and developed recommendations and proposals for the next stage of action.

The similarity is striking between the findings of this project, concerned with developing countries, and the case studies which are available for the developed countries. Clearly there are differences in emphasis between the developing and developed countries relating to their economic, social, and political situation and historical and cultural biases, but the common issues and problems for women and adult education include the following. Men must be partners in the women's development process, as men's image of women and women's image of themselves can prove a major barrier to equality of access to educational opportunity. Greater continuity and coordination of education and training programmes and research projects is necessary, between the providing agencies, to avoid duplication of effort and to provide an integrated provision which women can use to aid their educational progress. Guidance and counselling systems are essential for this purpose. There is a need for governments to formulate more precise, consistent, and integrated policies in support of women's educational development and to provide the resources, training, and monitoring that will ensure the implementation of such policies.

Research is an important and neglected factor in women's adult education, but research is one stage in a process of education, training, and action, and can often be undertaken at the expense of action. It is quite often the case that useful research results are neither disseminated nor applied. Part of the problem with the conduct of research into this field may lie with the premises on which it is built.

Two of the major premises which seem to underlie adult education literature and programmes for women's development are that economic growth and development are a sufficient condition for the advancement of women; and that improvements made in women's standing in educational and employment terms will have a spin-off in political and social terms which will enable women to effect permanent improvements to their lives and standing in society. In the light of the report reviewing the United Nations' World Action Plan, African agricultural case studies, and other evidence that women continue in their existing roles and occupational levels, these premises would appear to be in need of questioning and re-evaluation. In order to gauge the problems and assess the impact and effect of adult education programmes more accurately it might be useful for more microcase research studies to be undertaken on the lives and situations of different groups and classes, looking at the range of activities performed, the time needed, the skills used and needed, and the social constraints faced by women. Much of the justification for spending resources on such research is not that it is simply concerned with women's education but that to ignore the problems and constraints facing half of the population is to misunderstand the educational needs and issues of the whole.

Bibliography

Advisory Council for Adult and Continuing Education (ACACE) 1982 *Adults: Their Educational Experiences and Needs: The Report of a National Survey.* ACACE, Leicester

1979 *Women Workers in Ghana, Kenya, Zambia.* Economic Commission for Africa, African Training and Research Centre for Women, Addis Ababa

Antrobus P, Rogers B 1982 Hanover Street: Jamaican women in welding and woodworking. Supplement to the *Women's Stud. Int. Q.* 5: 10–14

Bernard A K, Gayfer M 1981 Women hold up more than half the sky: The ICAE women's project. *Convergence* 14(4): 59–71

Bernard A K, Gayfer M 1983 *Women Hold Up More Than Half the Sky: A Third World Perspective on Women and Nonformal Education for Development.* International Council for Adult Education, Ontario

Bhola H S 1981 Why literacy can't wait: Issues for the 1980s. *Convergence* 14(1): 6–23

Blaug M 1966 Literacy and economic development. *Sch. Rev.* 74: 393–415

Croll E 1979 *Women in Rural Development: The People's Republic of China.* International Labour Organization (ILO), Geneva

Darling M 1975 *The Role of Women in the Economy: A Summary Based on Ten National Reports.* Organisation for Economic Co-operation and Development, Manpower and Social Affairs Committee, Paris

Ellis P 1984 Women, adult education and literacy: a Caribbean perspective. *Convergence* 17(4): 44–53

European Bureau of Adult Education (EBAE) 1980 *Women and Adult Education: Learning New Roles for a Changing World.* EBAE, Amersfoort

Fordham P 1980 *Participation, Learning and Change: Commonwealth Approaches to Nonformal Education.* Commonwealth Secretariat, London

Gayfer M 1979 Issues, programs and priorities for the 1980s. *Convergence* 12(3): 55–64

Gayfer M 1980 Women speaking and learning for ourselves. *Convergence* 13 (1–2): 1–13

Harnett O 1980 Transition from home to work: Some training efforts in the USA. *Convergence* 13(1–2): 118–23

Higgins K M 1982 What kind of training for women farmers? *Convergence* 15(4): 7–18

Hootsmans H M 1980 Educational and employment opportunities for women: Main issues in adult education in Europe. *Convergence* 13(1–2): 79–90

Jain D 1980 *Women's Quest for Power: Five Indian Case Studies.* Vikas, Sahibabad

Jayaweera S 1979 Programmes of non-formal education for women. *Convergence* 12(3): 21–31

King K 1979 Research on literacy and work among the rural poor. *Convergence* 12(3): 32–41

Loutfi M F 1980 *Rural Women: Unequal Partners in Development.* International Labour Organization (ILO), Geneva

Lucas C J 1982 Mass mobilization for illiteracy eradication in Iraq. *Convergence* 15(3): 19–27

Manpower Services Commission (MSC) 1978 *Annual Report 1977–78.* MSC, Sheffield

Manpower Services Commission (MSC) 1982 *Annual Report 1981–2.* MSC, Sheffield

Mascarenhas O, Mbilinyi M 1983 *Women and Development in Tanzania: An Analytical Bibliography.* Scandinavian Institute of African Studies, Uppsala

Mirie N W 1980 Literacy for and by the people: Kenya's Kamirithu Project. *Convergence* 13(4): 55–61

National Committee on Equality between Men and Women 1979 *Step by Step: National Plan of Action for Equality.* The Committee, Stockholm

Neves H 1982 Role of the women's movement in literacy campaigns: The Portuguese experience. *Convergence* 15(3): 73–76
Organisation for Economic Co-operation and Development (OECD) 1976 *The 1974–75 Recession and the Employment of Women.* OECD, Paris
Organisation for Economic Co-operation and Development (OECD) 1979 *Equal Opportunities for Women.* OECD, Paris
Organisation for Economic Co-operation and Development (OECD) 1980 *Women and Employment, Policies for Equal Opportunities.* OECD, Paris
Paukert L 1984 *The Employment and Unemployment of Women in OECD Countries.* Organisation for Economic Co-operation and Development (OECD), Paris
Report 1980 Five year review shows little progress on critical issues for women. *Convergence* 13(4): 35–40
Report 1981 Literacy for all by the year 2000: Udaipur literacy declaration. *Convergence* 14(4): 7–9
Rogers B 1980 *The Domestication of Women: Discrimination in Developing Societies.* Tavistock, London
Schöpp-Schilling H-B 1979 Women's studies, women's research and research centres: Recent developments in the USA and in the FRG. *Women's Stud. Int. Q.* 2(1): 103–16
UNESCO 1975 *Women, Education, Equality: A Decade of Experiment.* UNESCO, Paris
UNESCO 1980 *Literacy 1972–76: Progress Achieved in Literacy Throughout the World.* UNESCO, Paris
Walker B, Smith M 1979 Women's studies courses in Australian universities. *Women's Stud. Int. Q.* 2: 375–83

Socially Isolated Groups

Introduction

The desirability discussed in the previous subsection of keeping younger and older people integrated in the general population applies more forcibly to the socially isolated. They have long been treated as special target groups, but with the clear aim of bringing them out of isolation and into participation in society. Technical developments in educational delivery systems such as distance education, and improvements in the design of buildings to make it practicable for physically disabled persons to attend courses, have made the task easier. Legislative action by several countries has sought to ensure that resources are devoted to their needs. Positive action in favour of at least some of the socially isolated has been less controversial than the targeting of most groups with special needs, for example ethnic minorities.

This is certainly true of the group which is the subject of the article *Disabled Adults: Educational Provision.* After briefly distinguishing between impairment, disability, and handicap, it reviews the major barriers in the way of disabled adults' participation in society. It outlines different measures taken to provide adult education for the physically disabled, the learning disabled, and the developmentally disabled. *Educating the Isolated* touches briefly on these, but is mainly about a different group, those who "are precluded from participating in a system which provides for continuing, direct, personal contact between the teacher and the learner, and, usually, between learners", for other reasons, particularly those of geographical isolation. It surveys the evolution of demand and response from this population, and illustrations are given of current programmes and approaches.

Perhaps the most socially isolated group addressed by adult education (the psychologically disturbed are subjects for therapy rather than education) consists of the inmates of correctional institutions. The nature and extent of adult education's role depends in large degree on whether the institutions are correctional or penal, on the mixture of seclusion, punishment, or rehabilitation in their purpose. The article *Adult Education in Prisons* briefly surveys the criminological objectives of which education is an extension, considers the problems it presents, the function it fulfils in the management of penal institutions, the curriculum, and trends and developments. It notes both the dearth of research on the subject and the difficulties of conducting investigations in such a context.

Disabled Adults: Educational Provision

J. A. Niemi, H. Dahlgren, and R. B. Brooks

The World Health Organization (WHO) gives definitions of impairment, disability, and handicap. An impairment is any loss or abnormality of psychological, physiological, or anatomical structure or function. A disability is any restriction or lack (resulting from an impairment) of ability to perform an activity in the manner or within the range considered normal for a human being. A handicap is a disadvantage for a given individual, resulting from an impairment or a disability, that limits or prevents the fulfillment of a role that is normal (depending on age, sex, and social and cultural factors) for that individual. This article examines the educational needs, and the provision made for them, of disabled adults, that is, those who have physical or mental impairments which substantially limit their life functions. These include caring for themselves and others, fulfilling work and social roles, engaging in physical activities, and learning.

The definition and its implications suggest significant guidelines for public policy and the development of programs for disabled adults. The importance of such guidelines was acknowledged by the General Assembly of the United Nations when it proclaimed 1981 as the International Year of Disabled Persons (IYDP). The United Nations also specified objectives aimed at assisting disabled persons to overcome barriers, to adjust to society, and to obtain needed training and education; encouraging research designed to improve the physical environment for disabled persons; educating the public concerning the rights of disabled persons; and preventing disability and rehabilitating disabled persons.

Like everyone else, the disabled need social contacts. They also need to acquire new knowledge and new skills, and opportunities to use them, and to advance their personal development. They are, however, more frequently and more sharply aware of the obstacles in their environment than are other people.

Even with normally functioning adults, it is necessary to consider their specific characteristics and needs as learners. Planning for disabled adults must be based as well on an understanding of the difficulties they experience in society at large as a result of their condition.

1. Barriers in the Way of Disabled Adults

The following interrelated barriers in the way of disabled adults have been noted: architectural, attitudinal, occupational, legal, personal, and educational (Bowe 1978).

1.1 Architectural

These barriers refer to such obstacles as curbs, stairs, and narrow doorways. In recent years, in the United States, federal laws have been passed requiring removal of such barriers, or special provisions for the disabled, in present buildings and new buildings.

1.2 Attitudinal

Historically, attitudes toward the disabled have been shaped by a wide spectrum of beliefs. These include the Greek view that the physically disabled are inferior, the Hebraic view that the sick are being punished by God, the Christian view that moral virtue is served in helping the disabled, the Calvinistic assumption that failure in life attributable to a disability is visible evidence of lack of grace, Darwin's theory of the survival of the fittest, and faith in humankind's progress through science and technology (Gellman 1973 p. 6). In many countries, ignorant or negative attitudes toward disabled adults have changed for the better. The change is partly due to passage of legislation forbidding the exclusion of qualified handicapped persons from employment by reason of their handicap; and partly due to strides toward their rehabilitation made by the medical profession.

1.3 Occupational

In many countries the occupational problems of the disabled relate to difficulties in obtaining employment, to underemployment, seasonal employment, part-time employment, and minimum wage jobs with little security and high turnover (Bowe 1978 pp. 27–30). Such job discrimination often occurs in countries that give the highest priority to maximum production. The reason is that organizations hiring disabled adults must make certain modifications to accommodate their needs, and these modifications increase costs and may slow production.

1.4 Legal

Although legislation has greatly helped the legal position of disabled adults with respect to access to buildings, transportation, civil rights, housing, and education, many laws are symbolic or not adequately enforced. Also, disabled adults are often poorly informed about the legal protection available to them, because of dissemination problems. For example, public service announcements frequently convey insufficient information, or the information is not specific enough. Moreover, disabled adults can be difficult to reach. Sometimes they resist being "found," because of their sensitivity about their condition.

1.5 Personal

Inferior education or training and low incomes pose restrictions for some disabled adults. Often these restrictions, combined with the disability, induce a low self-concept which further hinders them in their search for satisfying activity. Others compensate for disabilities by overachieving. Still others try to hide disabilities and suffer anxiety in the process, or they withdraw from society. Disabled adults are vulnerable to attacks by thieves, rapists, and the like (Bowe 1978).

1.6 Educational

A major educational problem with disabled adults arises from the fact that their early education was restricted or interrupted because of their disabilities. This circumstance has limited their ability to take advantage of later opportunities to continue learning.

2. Adult Education

Adult education for the disabled embraces rehabilitation, training, vocational education, and general education. Its clientele include the physically disabled, the learning disabled, and the developmentally disabled. A fourth group, the socially disabled, is considered elsewhere (see *Adult Literacy in Developed Countries*). A fifth population, the psychologically disabled, is not included in this article because programs for the emotionally disturbed, for instance, require therapeutic assistance that does not come within the scope of adult education.

2.1 Physically Disabled

Many countries have legislation and regulations related to the education of the handicapped, much of it covering all the kinds of impairment treated in this article. In terms of implementation, however, it is the physically disabled who benefit most from the laws, partly because of the numbers requiring assistance. In the United

States the number of physically disabled of all ages has been estimated as 11.4 million with visual impairment, 16.2 million having hearing disabilities, 1.2 million speech impaired, 1.5 million suffering partial paralysis, 358,000 with missing extremities, and 19.5 million with orthopedic disabilities (Feller 1981). Other countries have comparable populations.

The genesis of most educational programs for physically disabled adults can be traced to advances made during the First World War in orthopedic surgery and the advent of physical and occupational therapy. Initially rehabilitation was medically oriented, aimed at physical recovery, but later the concept embraced the social and work roles of the disabled and led to vocational rehabilitation programs that prepared them for the competitive labor market. For the severely disabled, however, competitive employment is an unrealistic goal, and so emphasis is placed on interpersonal and intrapsychic aspects of work through vocational rehabilitation programs offered in sheltered workshops or in homes.

In the United States, the initial success of vocational rehabilitation was achieved with First World War veterans, and led to the passage of a 1920 act designed to develop a similar program for civilians. The program for Second World War veterans was the most significant for the development of rehabilitation. It included education and rehabilitation counseling and job placement. The passage of the 1954 Vocational Rehabilitation Act Amendments extended the services to disabled civilians. Between 1954 and 1972, the composition of this group expanded from the physically disabled to persons separated from work for physical or psychosocial reasons (Gellman 1973 pp. 7–9).

The passage of the 1973 Rehabilitation Act extended affirmative action and antidiscrimination provisions to the disabled. These provisions applied to schools, colleges, and social service agencies in receipt of federal funds. In addition, the act recommended nondiscriminatory practices for colleges and other postsecondary institutions in the recruitment, admission, and treatment of the disabled. These practices relate to testing, accessibility of programs by elimination of architectural barriers, and policies that support flexible programs for disabled adults. Finally, the act not only clarified their rights and responsibilities; it came closer to making rehabilitation programs an entitlement, rather than discretionary actions by agencies or counselors.

Other countries have legislation with similar aims. In the Federal Republic of Germany, for example, special provisions to facilitate the training of disabled persons for employment were introduced for the first time in the Vocational Education Act of 1969. The 1974 Law on the Integration of the Severely Handicapped in the World of Work and Society authorizes the establishment of sheltered workshops in which those too severely disabled to find work in the open labor market may obtain work training and occupational therapy. The 1974 Law on Social Assistance contains further provisions to enable disabled persons to undertake occupational training (Sutter and Schulte 1981).

In the United Kingdom, the 1970 Chronically Sick and Disabled Persons Act lays upon local authorities a statutory duty to ascertain the number of disabled and chronically sick people living in their areas and to provide them with any help they need. Information is to be given concerning assistance in obtaining recreation and education services, and educational establishments are required to furnish physical facilities to meet the needs of the disabled (Groombridge 1981).

In Denmark the Act on Leisure-time Instruction, 1968, lays down that special education must be availble for both the physically and mentally handicapped. Other legislation decrees that rehabilitation centers must establish courses for retraining and vocational education. In Norway, responsibility for the education of physically and otherwise handicapped persons is laid upon the education and social welfare authorities (Nordic Council 1976).

There is a considerable gap, however, between the passage of legislation and its implementation. Of the 1970 law in the United Kingdom it has been written, "This Act has not been consistently interpreted or vigorously enforced" (Groombridge 1981). Provision has grown, but unevenly and uncertainly.

In most countries the emphasis has been on rendering disabled persons capable of earning a living as far as possible. The Federal Republic of Germany has a network of vocational rehabilitation centers in which vocational training for the handicapped goes with intensive medical, social, and psychological care (Sutter and Schulte 1981). At vocational promotion institutions handicapped persons between the ages of 18 and 59 are trained for qualifications up to higher education level. In the United Kingdom the Manpower Services Commission also runs Employment Rehabilitation Centres, where both rehabilitation and assessment are carried out, after which disabled adults may proceed to sheltered work or to further training in Skill Centres or colleges of further education.

General education for the disabled tends to be more unevenly distributed. In the United Kingdom local authorities, which have considerable autonomy in educational provision, vary greatly in their attitude. Only a few have a coherent policy of education for disabled adults backed by the allocation of financial resources. On the whole, policy is directed towards making it possible for the disabled to be integrated into ordinary adult education programs. Also, a number of day centers for the physically handicapped exist throughout the country. Most offer occupational therapy, discussions, and lectures, and they are extending their formal adult education work. Local authorities also employ teachers to give courses in hospitals and residential homes.

Distance education has particular attractions for disabled adults. Such institutions as the Federal German *Telekolleg* and *Téléenseignement* in France offer multimedia educational programs based on television which enable the housebound to participate. Concern for the disabled has perhaps been carried furthest by the United Kingdom Open University which has been very successful in attracting and retaining disabled students. It has a special department for them and its counseling service is geared to identifying special needs and giving practical assistance.

Those whose sight or hearing is impaired have particular problems in participating in education. In the Federal Republic of Germany the German Educational Institution for the Blind is engaged in the preparation of distance learning courses leading to state examinations in the general and vocational sectors. The Open University has taped most of its material for the visually handicapped, in many cases with tactual diagrams. For those with hearing difficulties, transcripts of radio and television programs are available on request.

2.2 Learning Disabled

The learning disabled are a more restricted and neglected group. The following is a comprehensive definition of the term "learning disabilities":

> ...a disorder in one or more of the basic psychological processes involved in understanding or in using language, spoken or written, which may manifest itself in an imperfect ability to listen, think, speak, read, write, spell, or do mathematical computations. The term includes such conditions as perceptual handicaps, brain injury, minimal brain dysfunction, dyslexia, and developmental aphasia. (United States Office of Education 1977 p. 65083)

In North America where a number of programs began in 1963, the study of learning disabilities has focused primarily on children. Today it is difficult to locate those learning disabled adults who left school before 1963 or who have not been diagnosed as learning disabled. One reason why their problems continue to be ignored is that by the time people reach adulthood, they have acquired certain minimal coping behaviors which assist them in their jobs and their personal lives, but which do not allow adults to learn to their fullest potential. Many such persons enroll in adult basic education classes, but failure to fulfill their learning needs contributes to their high attrition rate.

Work on adult illiteracy in developed countries has drawn attention to the plight of other disabled adults. Yet while in the United States the 1968 amendments to the Vocational Education Act and the 1973 Vocational Rehabilitation Act attempted to equip the learning disabled with marketable skills through specific job training, here, as in other countries, learning disabled adults continue to attract little help. In both Canada and the United States, educators still need to recognize that the learning disabled constitute a special population and that their problems demand concerned joint efforts by adult educators and learning disability specialists.

2.3 Developmentally Disabled

The "developmentally disabled," more commonly known as the "mentally retarded," are those whose intellect functions at less than average efficiency. The condition, which may begin before birth, originates in genetic disorders, effects of disease and injury, or environmental factors. Three percent of the world's population is developmentally disabled. An estimated 6 million Americans, over half of them adults, are developmentally disabled. In the past, people in this group were usually institutionalized, in response to society's view of their condition. That view included the convictions that the developmentally disabled constituted a menace to society; that society had an obligation to provide care for them in an institutional setting; that the developmentally disabled are "eternal children" dependent on institutional care; and that they are unwell and need treatment or rehabilitation (Roos 1976).

Another problem relates to the schooling of the noninstitutionalized developmentally disabled. The child who left public school in the early grades usually failed to achieve social maturity or to obtain the training needed to cope with life.

In North America, in the late 1960s, a process of developmental growth was seen as attainable for the developmentally disabled; that is, the individual was considered capable of acquiring and maintaining acceptable personal behavior. Using a variety of delivery systems, programs have been designed around the learning capacities of adults whose degree of retardation has been classified from "profoundly retarded" to "mildly retarded." Facilities include sheltered workshops, which embrace a variety of services, including training, counseling, work experience, job placement, and follow up; community-supported centers offering purposeful activities for the developmentally disabled; and vocational rehabilitation programs that combine work study with counseling to train and place their clients. The curricula range from motor skill development and occupational training for individuals preparing for employment to recreational and socialization skills for those less able to achieve social relationships. Although the worth of these programs has been demonstrated in various countries, funding for them is still very limited.

It has been estimated that one person in every 100 in the United Kingdom is mentally retarded, therefore it is reasonable to assume that the total of mentally retarded/handicapped people is about half a million. Although some live with their families, the majority live in hospitals, hostels, or group homes. Consequently, the bulk of adult education provision for the mentally retarded over the years has taken the form of classes organized in the hospitals where they live. It is likely that most of those courses were in the category of arts and crafts. Some courses have been financed by local authorities and others by social services departments, but most have been organized by the hospitals and their management committees. The disadvantage of this "internal" system was that the students did not experience a change of environment when they attended a class, nor did they meet other people engaged in adult education activities. To overcome these disadvantages, experiments have been conducted whereby hospitalized mentally handicapped adults have attended courses in a local education center. Although initially they attended segregated classes, some were able later to attend general public classes and to benefit greatly from them.

3. Research

Most research into the education of the disabled has concentrated on children. There has been little study of disabled adults. In the United Kingdom the majority of studies have been local and lack a comparative or national dimension. They are concerned with the scale of provision, the nature of demand, and the problems of meeting it. For example, in 1970, it was found that 11 percent of local authorities made specific provision for blind students, 28 percent for the mentally handicapped, and there was no information available on the hard of hearing for lack of a national pattern of provision (Clyne 1972). A more recent study showed that in English and Welsh county boroughs there were 242 courses for the physically handicapped other than the blind and partially sighted (207) and the hearing handicapped (190) (Osborn et al. 1980). Disabled prefer to attend ordinary classes rather than ones specifically designed for them. Researchers agree that the disabled have special problems of access, transport, special equipment, counseling, support, and financial assistance (Osborn et al. 1980).

In Sweden the long-term outreach program *Fövux* was aimed at adults with defective vision, hearing defects, and orthopedic handicaps among other categories. Experimental folk high school courses have been provided for similar groups. There has been evidence of substantial response to these offers of study opportunities.

A review of the literature in the United States shows that work on mentally handicapped adults was sparse and of recent origin (Long 1973). Provision was inadequate, but retarded adults could achieve fair levels of independence through vocational rehabilitation. This is confirmed by other work (Howard 1975). Evidence also shows that better results are achieved in open rather than segregated learning situations. Almost all aspects of education for disabled adults require further study—the numbers within different handicapped groups, the impact of courses on students' lives, organization of provision, the training of tutors, counseling, normalization programs. In particular, there is very little literature on instructional techniques for the disabled, yet there are grounds for believing that some disabled adults, at least, require teaching methods tailored to their situation and teachers trained in their use.

See also: Adult Literacy in Developed Countries

Bibliography

Anderson D, Niemi J A 1969 *Adult Education and the Disadvantaged Adult.* Syracuse University, Syracuse, New York

Bowe F 1978 *Handicapping America: Barriers to Disabled People.* Harper and Row, New York

Brooks R B 1978 Adult education and the mentally handicapped student. *Adult Educ.* 51(4)

Brooks R B 1980 Adult education and the mentally handicapped. *Newsletter of the European Bureau of Adult Education* December

Carnes G D 1979 *European Rehabilitation Service Providers and Programs.* Michigan State University, East Lansing, Michigan

Clyne P 1972 *The Disadvantaged Adult: Educational and Social Needs of Minority Groups.* Longmans, London

Feller B A 1981 Prevalence of selected impairments. *Prevalence of Selected Impairments, United States 1977.* United States Department of Health and Human Services, Public Health Service, Office of Health Research, Statistics, and Technology, National Center for Health Statistics, Hyattsville, Maryland

Gellman W 1973 Fundamentals of rehabilitation. In: Garrett J F, Levine E S (eds.) 1973 *Rehabilitation Practices with the Physically Disabled.* Columbia University Press, New York

Groombridge B 1981 Education and disadvantaged adults in the United Kingdom 1970–1979. *Learning Opportunities for Adults,* Vol. 5: *Widening Access for the Disadvantaged.* Organisation for Economic Co-operation and Development, Paris

Howard M 1975 Adult training centres: The trainees and their instructors. *Adult Educ.* 48: 88–94

Long H B 1973 *The Education of the Mentally Retarded Adult: A Selective Review of Recent Literature.* ERIC Clearinghouse on Adult Education, Adult Education Association of the United States, Washington, DC

Nordic Council 1976 *Adult Education in the Nordic Countries: Nordic Co-operation in the Field of Education.* Nordic Council, Stockholm

Northcutt N 1975 *Adult Functional Competency: A Summary.* University of Texas, Austin, Texas

Osborn M, Withnall A W, Charnley A H 1980 *Review of Existing Research in Adult and Continuing Education,* Vol. 3: *The Disadvantaged.* National Institute of Adult Education (England and Wales), Leicester

Roos P 1976 *Trends in Residential Institutions for the Mentally Retarded.* Trends in Education Series. United Council for Educational Administration, Columbus, Ohio

Sutter H, Schulte E 1981 A German case study. *Learning Opportunities for Adults,* Vol. 5: *Widening Access for the Disadvantaged.* Organisation for Economic Co-operation and Development, Paris

United Nations General Assembly, December 20, 1971 *Declaration on the Rights of Mentally Retarded Persons.* A/RES/2856 (XXVI), New York

United States Office of Education 1977 *Assistance to States: Procedures for Evaluating Learning Disabilities.* Washington Federal Registrar, Washington, DC

Educating the Isolated

J. H. Eedle

The "isolated" in the context of this article is taken to mean all those who are precluded from participating in a system of education which provides for continuing, direct, personal contact between the teacher and the learner, and, usually, between learners. The nature of isolation is reviewed, the evolution of demand and response surveyed briefly, and some illustrations are given of current programmes and approaches.

The nature and degree of isolation vary; the most apparent form of isolation is that of physical distance, but others are equally inhibiting. This article is about, but includes more than, "distance education". At least six forms of isolation can be identified in addition to distance. They are the isolation caused by linguistic, cultural, cognitive, socioeconomic, psychological, and hierarchical factors (Broadbent 1981). All of these are further influenced by the perceptions of the potential learner about isolation (in which manner and to what degree the person appears to be isolated); and about self-image (to what extent the person appears to be excluded from, or inappropriate to, available educational facilities).

While some notice has been taken of all the factors that lead to isolation, there has been a preoccupation by educationists with geographical distance. Most of the writing and research, and the conferences, have consisted of demonstrations of how distance has been physically overcome. It would have been equally true to consider the entire international year of the handicapped and the disabled as a large exercise to understand and cope with isolation, although many such people live in crowded cities. Some excellent papers began to appear about these forms of isolation but they have not yet reached the mainstream of educational practice. This article reflects a disparity that must be changed.

It is equally true that most educationists lag far behind anthropologists, and indeed the people that anthropologists study, in their appreciation of isolation within certain cultural enclaves. Many tribal peoples in Australia or India or Canada have much to teach educationists about support for human growth and expression within cultural islands (Commonwealth Secretariat 1974).

Many isolating factors, impeding access to and benefit from educational services, are poorly recognized. Because participation in adult education is most frequently voluntary, it is easily assumed that nonparticipation results from unwillingness rather than inability (Hall and Kidd 1978). For example, linguistic isolation may be obvious in the case of the individual who does not speak the language used for education; it is less obvious where the problem is linguistic deprivation, that is, a lack of familiarity with the vocabulary and "codes" necessary to benefit from educational programmes. This form of isolation relates closely to cognitive inadequacies, where a lack of basic knowledge inhibits the prospective learner. It is a frequent handicap in rural areas, and among those who are disadvantaged socially and economically.

Time and cost exclude some potential learners. Somewhat related to socioeconomic isolation is cultural isolation. Where individuals do not share concepts, perhaps, number systems, or values with the mainstream providers of education, they can profit only marginally from participation. Psychological isolation may be related to cultural factors in terms of self-image, motivation, and aspiration. Finally, hierarchical isolation may convince prospective learners that educational services are not intended for them.

All of these factors, often interwoven and interdependent, exist as inhibitions precluding individual adults from taking advantage of educational services. More study of the causes, manifestations, and remedies is required.

Physical distance is the form of isolation which is most easily overcome (although services to those without a fixed base, such as nomadic peoples or peripatetic workers, present special complications). Itinerant teachers have a long tradition, as wandering scholars, holy people, or entertainers, of making themselves accessible to people otherwise isolated. Frontier College's labourer–teachers in the mines, rail gangs, and construction camps of Canada, the teachers of the Flying Art School travelling through Queensland to bring art education to the outback of Australia, or the People's University of Norway, have followed in a similar fashion (Young et al. 1978). So, too, have those academic staff of the University of the West Indies and the University of the South Pacific who are located at a series of education centres throughout their regions, shortening the lines of communication to isolated learners. The San Juan Center for Higher Education, Utah, in the United States, provides visiting teachers in another fashion. The centre has no academic staff but negotiates on behalf of isolated students for the supply of educational services from a number of universities and colleges, ensuring a matching of visiting teachers and programmes to the precise needs, from degrees in arts and sciences to vocational training.

For more than a century, universities have been reaching out to isolated adults long before such concepts as "distance education" were developed (Kelly 1962). The service began with the organization of lectures and lecture tours by university teachers. This led to a demand for courses rather than single presentations, and the universities moved progressively into the provision of extramural and extension programmes.

University extension centres (Cambridge had 100 throughout England by 1875–76) and university settlements in poor areas of cities (the first, Toynbee Hall, London, opened in 1885) were soon supplemented by self-help organizations such as the Workers' Educational Association (founded in 1904), and the agricultural extension work of the Land Grant Colleges in the United States (which helped substantially to transform farming in that country). These institutions established the feasibility and acceptability of programmes reaching out to isolated individuals in both urban and rural areas, providing services for improving specific skills and broadening cultural experience.

Education provision for isolated adults, other than through visiting teachers, depended for its inauguration upon the spread of literacy. Literate students and a cheap, reliable mail service made possible the introduction of correspondence education.

The first external study programme, using the postal system for communicating with students who could not attend classes in person, was that established in Europe in 1856 by Charles Toussaint and Gustav Langenscheidt. (Correspondence education has been "invented" again and again in human history.) In the nineteenth century it had developed largely through private enterprise outside the universities or state education systems. As late as 1962, a standard *History of Adult Education in Great Britain*, by Thomas Kelly, made no mention of correspondence schools. However, a number of reputable private correspondence institutions had been in existence since the turn of the century, serving needs ranging from individuals seeking professional qualifications in fields such as banking, accountancy, and law, to seamen working through the College of the Sea to improve their skills and broaden their cultural experience. At that time dropout rates from all correspondence schools were high.

In an attempt to improve conventional learning methods, techniques to adapt printed materials for individual learning were developed in the armed services during the Second World War. Closely structured sequential texts for training in military and technical skills led to the production in the 1950s of programmed texts and teaching machines. While facilities of this nature have value, in the period since the early 1950s, the visiting teacher, the correspondence course, and the printed word have been progressively complemented by increasingly sophisticated media, from films, broadcasting, and television to computers and satellites. New methods of communication and cheaper means of copying teaching material have made it possible for a greater range of effective educational facilities to be extended, with a minimum of time delay, to more people, in a greater variety of isolating circumstances (Erdos 1975).

The Open University (Perry 1980) in the United Kingdom, upon which many other countries are now modelling their own adaptations, is the inheritor of the experience of the period since the late nineteenth century and of adaptations in Nordic countries (people's universities) and Yugoslavia, as well as at home. Other universities previously had agreed to register external students (London University, for example, registered individual students worldwide and since 1951, the University of South Africa catered exclusively for external students). Queen's University had been providing academic education for teachers all over Canada from about 1850, but the chief service to these students was to provide course outlines and reading lists, sometimes correspondence texts, and to allow admission for examinations. External students still resorted to private correspondence schools or tutors.

With the chartering of the Open University in 1969, a fully recognized, publicly funded university began to teach students exclusively by external techniques, based on the correspondence method. These techniques were supplemented by aids, such as photographic slides and film, recorded tapes, radio, television, telephone-linked home computers, summer schools, and vacation courses. This university education for individual adults now stands as a genuine alternative to conventional education. The Open University is "open" in two respects: it minimizes the preconditions for any adult to register for its courses and it teaches them entirely off-campus. In so doing, it offers "access, equality, and excellence".

Such provision transcends the barrier of physical distance, and facilitates participation by those isolated by handicap, language, psychology, home duties, or other restraints. For example, at Deakin University in Australia (which operates substantially with open access and off-campus teaching) one of the first graduates (in 1981) was an inmate of a maximum security prison.

Less comprehensive uses of modern media are common, and contribute effectively to the needs of the isolated adult learner.

Radio has the advantage of being available to the casual listener; it can reach the isolated individual who may, by chance, become aware of the value of such educational programmes. Radio forums for farmers are well-established in countries such as Canada, Guyana, India, and Zambia, and throughout Francophone Africa. They serve the individual, but they also provide the opportunity for otherwise isolated individuals to gather periodically in a listening and discussion group. Foreign language teaching by radio has been promoted extensively by organizations such as the British Broadcasting Corporation (BBC) and the International Extension College in Mauritius. Radio can help to overcome isolation resulting from physical distance, linguistic, and occupational factors.

Television has amplified the range of services which can be provided for isolated learners. For example, it forms an important aid to the programmes of the Open University and is essential for the Italian *telescuola* and the BBC series designed to meet the needs of adult illiterates.

The increasing availability of both audio and video recordings eliminates disruption caused to broadcasts by climatic conditions, technical malfunction, or the inability of the learner to tune in at a specific time. While some immediacy and sense of direct participation may be lost, these advantages are outweighed by isolated students being able to play recorded material at their convenience and repeat the film or tape an indefinite number of times.

The development whereby domestic television receivers may be linked to data banks (systems such as Teletext in the United Kingdom or Telidon in Canada) make possible an almost unlimited supply of information to isolated learners. Increasingly, the individual will need the ability to select and discriminate among the vast quantity of material available. The role of the teacher of the isolated adult is likely to develop in the direction of assisting with techniques of self-learning and evaluation as much as with the direct imparting of information.

The need to moderate the sense of isolation on the part of the learner has long been recognized by the providers of educational services. Correspondence schools usually allocate students to specific tutors and offer question-answering and counselling services (Erdos 1975). Some provide students with recorded tapes containing the comments of their tutors. Tutoring by telephone has been provided. Such devices give a one-to-one relationship but do not permit isolated students to participate in a group with other individuals studying at the same level. Short-term residential schools or vacation courses can serve some students, but not all. Two-way radio can be extended to include a conference facility. Where students are spread over large areas, satellites now offer a new possibility.

Provided that there are no major linguistic or cultural differences in the region to be served, satellite broadcasts can reach large numbers of isolated learners and can include two-way transmissions, with all participants able to hear all the exchanges. In a country such as India, with 17 official languages and local dialects, centrally produced and transmitted programmes have limited value. On the other hand, the University of the South Pacific Satellite Communication Project (USPNET) has been operating since 1972 using a satellite made available by the United States National Aeronautical and Space Administration (Apted 1980).

There are 10 terminals in nine South Pacific countries that provide two-way radio communications which are currently used for extension studies and "outreach" programmes in continuing education, agriculture, rural development, and health education. Isolated tutors are able to confer with each other and community development groups can share information. Virtually the whole of the Pacific area is thus linked by satellite, making possible services previously not feasible for small and widely scattered populations.

Many unmet needs remain (Hall and Kidd 1978). In most countries, adult education, particularly the education of the isolated adult, has not yet succeeded in gaining a high priority in public funding. Individual learners, private agencies, and universities still bear a substantial part of the burden, especially in Western industrialized countries.

Unofficial endeavours continue. International organizations facilitate co-operation among those engaged in correspondence education, external studies and other forms of distance education, through meetings and publications (Blokland 1979, Commonwealth Secretariat 1974b, Daniel et al. 1982). Many professional organizations support their isolated members by journals, supplemented by book and film library services; an increasing number are extending this support to recorded tapes and films. The College of General Practitioners in England, for example, provides a recorded tape service by which its members, working alone or in small group practices, keep abreast of new developments.

Most isolated adults acquire new skills and improved knowledge informally. Instructional manuals supporting the massive trend to "do it yourself" in Western industrialized countries, as well as the continuous presentation of information and instruction through newspapers, journals, books, radio, and television, have increased the awareness and competencies of vast numbers of individuals throughout the world without their having recourse to public or private education programmes.

Future research and development and major improvements can be expected from two main sources: first, those groups trying to understand and cope more effectively with various forms of emotional and psychological isolation, and second, those who are helping improve practice generally in self-education.

The availability of opportunities for learning, and the increasing propensity for self-directed learning in adulthood rather than full-time education immediately after schooling, suggest several matters of importance to educators and planners preparing for the decades ahead. A prime need of the isolated adult learner is assistance in the techniques of learning. The training of tutors for isolated adults is grossly inadequate.

Isolation is not always an unmitigated disadvantage. Among isolated adults there is a great volume of knowledge and experience. It can be a reservoir of self-reliance, forming the basis of self-directed learning and mutual assistance among individuals and small groups. The best teachers of isolated adults may be their own peers; only a few "learning exchanges" have been attempted. Mutual self-help remains a potentially significant development.

See also: Distance Education; Self-directed Learning in Distance Learning

Bibliography

Apted M 1980 *Pacific Outreach: An Outline of the University of the South Pacific's Satellite Communications Project—Action for Development*. University of the South Pacific, Suva

Blokland G G van 1979 *Distance Education: Selected Titles.* Bernard van Leer Foundation, The Hague
Broadbent R F (ed.) 1981 *Education of the Isolated: Geographic and Cultural Aspects.* The Australian College of Education, Melbourne
Commonwealth Secretariat 1974a *Interfaces: Universities, Societies and Governments.* Commonwealth Secretariat, London
Commonwealth Secretariat 1974b *New Media in Education in Education in the Commonwealth.* Commonwealth Secretariat, London
Convergence. International Council for Adult Education, Toronto, Ontario
Daniel J S, Stroud M A, Thompson J R 1982 *Learning at a Distance: A World Perspective.* International Council for Correspondence Education, Edmonton, Alberta
Erdos R F 1975 *Establishing an Institution Teaching by Correspondence.* UNESCO, Paris
Hall B L, Kidd J 1978 *Adult Learning, A Design for Action: A Comprehensive International Survey.* Int. Conf. on Adult Education and Development, Dar Es Salaam, Tanzania, June 1976. Pergamon, Oxford
Kaye A, Rumble G 1981 *Distance Teaching for Higher and Adult Education.* Croom Helm, London
Kelly T 1962 *A History of Adult Education in Great Britain.* Liverpool University Press, Liverpool
Perry W 1980 The Open University: The first decade. *Royal Soc. Arts J.* 128: 396–408
Teaching at a Distance. Open University, Milton Keynes
Wedemeyer C A 1981 *Learning at the Back Door: Reflections on Non-traditional Learning in the Lifespan.* University of Wisconsin, Madison, Wisconsin
Young M, Perraton H, Jenkins J, Dodds T 1978 *Distance Teaching for the Third World: The Lion and the Clockwork Mouse: Incorporating a Directory of Distance Teaching Projects.* Routledge and Kegan Paul, London

Adult Education in Prisons

W. Forster

Most Western societies provide education for their prison inmates. In many cases, the prison education service is an extension of the public service but in some it is administered, provided, and funded separately. Whichever of these applies, the special circumstances of prison life means that various special factors have to be taken into consideration and that criminological and penological thinking dominates a great deal of practice. Before the prison curriculum is approached, account has to be taken of the contexts of criminological theory and the management problems of prisons.

1. The Context

The theory and practice of prison education throughout the world vary as much as does each culture's view of imprisonment. A society which uses prisons as a simple means of keeping offenders out of sight will not provide educational services, any more than it will provide any services above a level aimed at the bare sustenance of physical survival; a society viewing certain political and intellectual ideologies as socially deviant may use its penal service as part of a "brain-washing" process—an "educational" extreme. And between these two extremes, of neglect and coercion, there is a wide range of differing attitudes.

The starting point, then, for the study of adult education in prisons in any given society must be contextual. Account must be taken of that society's definition of deviance, and its use of containment, as well as the expression of those views in penological theory. A second contextual factor is the system used to maintain a prison service; such systems bear heavily upon, for example, the priority given to educational provision and the relationship between educational provision for those imprisoned and the free citizen. The management of prisons is concerned with a wide range of responsibilities, from security to clothing, food, and drink; education may be one of those responsibilities but, inevitably, it has to take its place in the complex. Thirdly, whilst recognizing the "special" nature of education in prisons, account has to be taken of attitudes towards education held by society at large, for these will inevitably permeate the prison system; whatever society provides by way of educational services within its prison system must depend, in the end, upon what that society perceives "education" as being.

2. Criminological Theory

Educational objectives within prisons are plainly an extension of criminological and penological objectives. A useful account of five major schools of penological theory is to be found in *The Growth of Crime* (Radzinowicz and King 1977). They identify the following.

2.1 The Classical School

Here, the concentration is upon the crime, and the appropriateness of the punishment to the crime already committed rather than either the idiosyncrasies of the individual criminal or as a tool to prevent future crimes; the emphasis is very much upon the concept of justice.

2.2 The Positivist School

The positivists would place more emphasis upon the personality of the criminal and would be much more concerned with activities related to the criminal's future behaviour than with the cold appraisal of the severity of sentence and its relationship to the magnitude of the crime already committed.

2.3 The Sociological School

This school moves the emphasis away from both the crime and the criminal into the study of those social factors which cause crime, perceiving crime as a phenomenon arising from society rather than as evidence of individual deviance.

2.4 The Socialist School

The ideas of this school may be seen as very close to those of the sociological school, with the extension that the laws of a hierarchical society do not necessarily reflect the consensus in that society and are more often class and power based.

2.5 The Radical School

Radzinowicz and King use this as a portmanteau term to describe many working, individually, in the field in recent years. What they all have in common is an interest in the matrix of relationships concerned with crime and the criminal—the police, the prison officer, the victim, the criminal, and so on—and the manner in which a definition of a criminal is arrived at.

This oversimple summary is intended only to give some guide to the range of policies and, perhaps more importantly, attitudes within which education in prison is provided. Jepson's paper, The Relevance of Criminological Theory? (Forster 1981 pp. 17–26) discusses how they might bear upon such provision. He points out, for example, that the "classical school" educationalist may have little concern for individual reform, that the "positivist school" educationalist will be much concerned with personal provision leading to future conformity, and the "sociological school" educationalist might wish to concentrate more upon the prison society. Most importantly, Jepson observes that individuals with widely varied views might be working within a system built upon a philosophy different again. In the end, the practice of adult education in prisons most likely owes more to the tensions arising from these complex interrelationships than any carefully declared policy.

3. Management and Education in Prisons

Each country has its own management system for its prison service; some carefully separate the penal system from the judiciary, others see the two as complementary; some are heavily centralized, with the governor of the penal establishment acting simply as an extension of the central bureaucracy, others attempt to invest the governor with a degree of autonomy. It is, therefore, impossible to generalize on an international basis about the system for managing prisons. On the other hand, as the penal education service can do no more than the penal service allows it to, it is impossible to ignore this aspect. An attempt can be made to identify some management problems which both bear upon educational provision within prisons and apply, to a greater or lesser degree, in all countries with a reasonably sophisticated penal system.

Each prison governor has three basic tasks; containment, control, and treatment. The first—containment—is certainly the one which is at the forefront of the public mind and, indirectly, bears heavily upon the services provided within the walls. For containment is expensive and, in the eyes of public opinion, it is generally easier to claim resources for this purpose than it is to claim resources for the provision of services to inmates. Paradoxically, increasingly efficient containment can give a boost to the provision of services within prison; the build-up of pressure within an "escape-proof" prison is such that alternative activities become essential to the maintenance of control. At its very lowest form, in the context of control, education in prison can be seen as "keeping the inmates happy"—at its best, but still in the context of control, it can be seen as assisting the prisoner to maintain a lively and critical mind and thus to "survive" the total institution of prison. This area, perhaps more than any other, creates debate between prison educators; is it ever possible to see prison education in a "pure" form and divorced from control? Is it ever possible to reconcile notions of "pure" education with the fact that resources for education nearly always stem from concerns about control?

Thirdly, there is the most ambivalent charge of all; that of "treatment". Semantically, the term is difficult, and can range in meaning from "treating them as they deserve" (i.e., punishment) to "treatment" in the radical sense (i.e., intervention intended to improve); in the centre of this sliding scale is a cluster of meanings loosely related to the notion of "welfare" which in turn may be related to a general humanitarian feeling about the immediate welfare of one's fellow beings, always balanced with the general good of the institution, or to a more positive intention not to return physical, intellectual, or spiritual cripples to society. Plainly, the provision of educational services is profoundly affected by this complex.

These formal tasks, and the interpretation of them, are only the starting point in the management of the prison. Three prevalent attitudes may be adopted towards prison education by the senior administrators or governor. First, that prison is a place of correction/punishment and education is a "frill" which may be deserved or not; secondly, that prison is a place of improvement and education and training should be at the forefront of the service; thirdly, that as in the outside world, education is a part of an extremely complex society and, whilst not to be decried, has to take its place amongst all sorts of other pressures.

Starting from one of these points, there then has to be taken into account the following.

3.1 Public Opinion

It is only in the most repressive of societies that the prison system can ignore public opinion in the long run. Most democratic societies abhor inhumane incarceration; on the other hand, public outcry and anxiety caused by riots and escapes can effectively turn the clock back a whole generation.

3.2 The Central Bureaucracy

In some societies—the United Kingdom for example—the prison governor has a high degree of autonomy. But he or she can do no more than the central allocation of resources can allow him or her to (although it is interesting to note that a recent experiment in the United Kingdom encourages prisons to establish their own priorities within budget allocations, thus allowing a certain shift of resources), and he or she has to be sensitive to central policy statements. The adoptions, for example, of the Mountbatten and May Reports in the United Kingdom, have both had an effect, first upon the general administration of prisons and indirectly, but profoundly, upon the education service. The first, arising from concern over escapes and long sentences, was concerned with security and the classification and disposition of prisoners; this affected the availability of different types of education in prisons throughout the country. The second, a more general report, has given a thrust to the importance of education in prisons (though at a time of dwindling resources).

3.3 The Power Base of the Institution

The power of a prison governor rests mainly in his or her ability to establish priorities whilst balancing the institutional power of others; the inmates themselves, the central bureaucracy, the "services" (psychologists, doctors, teachers, chaplains, and others), and the security officers. The balance changes constantly and can profoundly affect the provision of education. In the United Kingdom, for example, the uniformed officer, historically of lower status in the service, has, by the use of industrial action, assumed a great deal of power. Education for prisoners is not highly regarded by this group and their noncooperation has, in some prisons, affected the service severely. In other countries, the power of the central bureaucracy can allow politicians, for example, to have a similar or opposite effect.

3.4 Local Conditions

It must not be forgotten that even within national systems, individual prisons vary enormously. A few only of the local conditions which affect educational provision in any prison would include: overcrowding and the availability of space; a heavy concentration of one social or ethnic group in the system or in an individual prison; the location of the prison and the availability of services and teachers; the average length of stay in the prison; the sex and age of prisoners.

4. The Curriculum

Within this complex of attitudes towards crimes and punishment, management techniques, and institutional pressures, certain areas of educational activity have become generally established.

4.1 Vocational Training

Here, the intention is clear; the proclivity towards criminal behaviour is increased by the inability to maintain a job and status and income in society. Many prison systems run vocational training programmes (which can be compulsory) in a wide range of skilled and semiskilled trades. This often (as in the UK) involves negotiations with external examining and validating bodies, and with trade unions. Only recently in the United Kingdom has vocational training come to be seen as part of "education". A little-charted but interesting area of vocational training is that provided in the professions; this is often designed to help the prisoner whose offence precludes him or her from return to his or her own profession to retrain for another.

Although often expensive to provide it has usually managed to attract resources. The employment situation outside is now beginning to bear upon these programmes.

4.2 Remedial Education

There is a close link between certain types of crime and illiteracy; in the early 1970s, a survey of 18 percent of the United Kingdom prison population showed that 30 percent of the sample had a reading age of under 12 years of age. Basic literacy and numeracy were taught in most prison systems long before similar public programmes were launched and contributed a great deal to those programmes. Ethnic deviancy rates are often linked to this; and, at least in British prisons, the problem is critical, not least because many such prisoners are involved in petty crime and are serving short sentences. Both the prison service and voluntary organizations are attempting to link prison programmes with outside programmes for the benefit of released offenders.

4.3 Life Skills

This is a development of the remedial programme and is designed to help the prisoner "cope" better with a whole range of situations, from the highly bureaucratized society in which we all live to his or her own family situation and the dynamics of his or her work-place. At one extreme, this can take the form of simple instruction—coping with tax forms, car licences, and so on—and at the other, involve the prisoner in various forms of group dynamics, aiming at an enhanced "self-knowledge". This technique has been developed particularly in the Netherlands, and there is a great deal of interest in Canada in the role of various forms of discussion in self-discovery.

4.4 Arts and Crafts

At least in the British system, the pursuit of arts and crafts as recreation, with instruction provided as part of the educational service, is widespread. A catalogue of the activities pursued would be endless; national prizes are awarded and motifs occur with a regularity which suggests the development of a folk art in its own right.

Undoubtedly, creativity is enhancing; only too often are such activities repetitive rather than incremental and developmental. Generally, they are viewed as harmless activities which enable a sentence to be lived more easily.

4.5 Academic Programmes

This category of provision is astonishingly varied and widespread. At one end there is the attempt—often successful— to lead the "remedial" student into his or her first public examinations; at the other, there is the provision of university courses up to degree and postgraduate level. The long-sentence prisoner can, of course, progress from one to the other. The system is supported in a variety of ways; the full-time prison teacher; the part-time teacher; those employed in public institutions whose contract requires them to teach in the local prison; or where the prison service will (as at Simon Frazer University, British Columbia) maintain university staff to teach in prisons. The contact afforded with the outside world—via examining bodies and teachers—in this area of work is of great importance.

4.6 Community Education

Many educational programmes—including many of those above—are designed to bring the hitherto isolated prisoner closer to the community he or she will ultimately rejoin. There is the increasing frequency of the use of "outsiders" to conduct teaching programmes, and the development of the concept of "openness" often allows prisoners to visit outside educational establishments. Classes of adults can be encouraged to meet inside a prison, thus allowing prisoners to enrol and to be educated in a context of "normality".

5. Trends and Developments

Significant developments have taken place in recent years in the reconsideration of the place of prison education in relation both to other areas of the prison service and to the external adult education service. Many prisons are now seen as "total" educational institutions, and the formal education service as part of that. Similarly, with both the professional expertise of the practitioner in mind and the need to link the prisoner to the outside world, organizational links outside the prison have been established.

Reinforcing this is the growing notion, at least in the Western world, that education is a "right", as much as food and drink and that incarceration should not deprive an offender of access to general, public educational services. On the other hand, uncertainty about what a prison—and hence its educational service—is "for", increases and the tension between those who regard education as strictly noninterventionist in the complex world of social deviancy, and the movement via psychology, and therapeutic relationships towards reformative work, develops.

Noneducational, social pressures are making their mark. The absence of work to go to diminishes the significance of vocational programmes, and in times of recession prison workshops close, and both time and space available for education are reduced. But, overall, prisons are but mirrors of the societies which build them, and any major shift within that society has its effect. The increased provision of higher education, for example, both leads to increased provision of the same in prison and produces a prison population with a greater previous exposure to education and a different range of expectation. Similarly, it can be argued that if prisons are to reflect the state of their society, it is right that they should share the hardships. It is, nevertheless, an irony that when ideas are carrying penal education forward, resources are drying up.

6. Research

Very little research has been conducted in this field. This is partly because of the "closed" nature of many penal systems and partly because of the dominance of the disciplines of criminology and penology. Descriptive work is available (and needs to be extended), often of a very local nature; most countries have issued major reports on their prison services, and many prison departments issue annual reports.

Several areas beg investigation. Enquiries into the longer term effects of prison educational experience are hampered both by the necessary privacy of the exprisoner and by the difficulty of isolating education, per se, from all the other effects of imprisonment. There is, however, much valuable debate, especially in Canada, on the immediate impact of different curriculum areas. Meanwhile, useful work remains to be done in applying the findings of research conducted outside prison to the prison setting, especially where the prison provides unusual opportunities of working with concentrations of minority groups, the socially inadequate, and special categories such as women prisoners.

The backgrounds, motivation, and career structure of those who elect to follow the profession of education within the prison system make an interesting field of investigation, as do the institutional relationships between education, other prison services, and the central penal system.

Bibliography

Ayers J D 1974 *Evaluation of Academic Education Programs in Canadian Correctional Institutions*. Report to Canadian Corrections Service, Ottawa

Forster W 1976 *The Higher Education of Prisoners*. University of Leicester, Leicester

Forster W (ed.) 1981 *Prison Education in England and Wales*. National Institute of Adult Education (NIAE), Leicester

Levine M, Kravitz M (eds.) 1979 *Jail-based Inmate Programs: A Selected Bibliography*. Superintendent of Documents, United States Government Printing Office, Washington, DC

May J D 1979 *Report of the Committee of Inquiry into the United Kingdom Prison Services* (The May Report). Her Majesty's Stationery Office (HMSO), London

Morin L 1981 *On Prison Education*. Minister of Supply and Services, Ottawa.

Mountbatten, Earl of Burma 1966 *Report of the Inquiry into Prison Escapes and Security* (The Mountbatten Report). Cmnd. 3175. Her Majesty's Stationery Office, London

Radzinowicz L, King J 1977 *The Growth of Crime: The International Experience*. Basic Books, New York

Seashire B 1976 *Prison Education: Project Newgate and Other College Programs*. Praeger, New York

Willis M J et al. 1978 *Resources for Educators of Adults. Annotated Bibliography for the Education of Public Offenders: By Descriptive Subject Headings*. ERIC Clearinghouse, Washington, DC

Occupational Groups

Introduction

Education for employment has long been the most specifically targeted area of adult education. Essentially this springs from the specialization and fragmentation of tasks so characteristic of modern production methods. As has already been mentioned in Section 2b of this *Handbook*, which should be read with this subsection, both the targeting and curriculum have in some ways been too specific. There is continuing debate on whether personnel should be trained for particular jobs, or educated in skills and knowledge which may be adapted to a range of tasks as circumstances require. However, all of the occupational groups discussed in the immediately following articles, which are only a few among many, undergo, with one exception, a comparatively broad occupational education.

Workers' Education is directed at employees as a body, organized through their trade unions. It thus engages skilled and unskilled labour, mainly below executive level. Unskilled workers are those most frequently given purely job-specific training. This article is not, however, concerned with education for work performance, but with education for service in the labour movement. It examines the content of such education to meet the manifold purposes of unions, the needs of rural workers, women, and other special target groups throughout the world. It considers the structures, systems, and institutions of workers' education, including labour colleges, higher education, the Workers' Educational Association and government agencies. It discusses how workers' education is financed, by unions, public revenues, employers and, in developing countries, through international organizations.

Education in the Armed Forces includes education both for military competence and for nonmilitary ends. Under the first heading it covers training for enlisted personnel, officer training and education, professional development education, command and staff colleges, and other higher education for senior officers. Under the second heading come education for personal interest or development, political education, and education for return to civilian life.

In its own interest adult education has become increasingly concerned with one target group, the educators of adults. There are, as the article *Training of Adult Educators* states, differing views about the desirability of professional education for work in this field, but the majority opinion is in favour of it. The article defines the nature and scope of such education, surveys published views of the educator's training needs, the modes of provision and providing bodies, the skill and subject areas, and the methods used. It examines trends and issues, including adequacy of training provision, priorities for training, professionalization, mandatory training, and the differences between general teacher training and education for work with adults.

Those groups which have already received the highest level of initial occupational education are also the ones who are most likely to undergo continuing education during their professional career. In this subsection there are two articles treating such groups. *Continuing Education of the Business Executive* describes the scope, proliferation, and expansion of provision of such education, the many forms it takes, its content, methods, and techniques. It also reviews research into the subject. *Continuing Education of the Professional* has as its subject those groups which constitute professions, such as lawyers, doctors, engineers, architects, and clergy. It discusses the characteristics of professionalization, issues of career development, and its relationship to continuing education. The providers, methods, and programmes of the latter are described, and its purposes and development analysed. The article also raises a number of policy issues affecting continuing education in the professions.

Workers' Education

J. R. W. Whitehouse

Inadequate attention has been paid to the emergence of urban and rural workers' organizations as institutions with a significant educational role. A unique and identifiable form of workers' education has evolved which, in terms of objectives, structure, and often content differentiates it from activities having to do with adult education in general.

The development, form, and content of labour education have evolved with the need for workers' organizations to confront more complex and exacting challenges within industrial relations systems; changing conditions of work in response to the introduction of sophisticated technology, and growing acceptance of the increasing rights and responsibilities of both urban and rural workers' organizations in the social and economic life and development of the nation.

While the concept of "workers' education" varies from country to country, central to the concept of "labour education" is the role of the trade union organization. Labour education, therefore, for the purpose of this article, is taken to be any planned educational activity undertaken by a trade union itself, or by an external educational institute or agency in partnership with the trade union. Labour education, therefore, is distinguished by its ties with the organized labour movement, and is specifically designed to involve trade union members in educative and training programmes directly through their organization, or in cooperation with institutions sympathetic to, and having the support of, the trade union. Its basic goals are the development of skills, understanding, and knowledge for service within and through the workers' organization, for the achievement of the union's broadest institutional social and economic objectives. It incorporates motivational aspects designed to relate the learner to the trade union and this further distinguishes labour education from general adult educational activities.

1. Subject Matter of Labour Education

The content of labour education is as broad and diverse as the educational needs that emerge from the increasing role and responsibilities of trade unions. Education is needed, for example, to cope with the evolving services and structures of the organization itself, traditionally identified as trade union training. Changing structures of industry and conditions of work, the increasing complexities of labour legislation and labour management relations, and the extension of trade union services to wider categories of workers such as nonwage-earning and professional groups, have extended the content of labour education over the years. The growing participation of trade union representatives in bodies external to the trade union itself, at the level of the enterprise, industry, or national economy, has stimulated programme development in the field of workers' participation.

The role of trade unions in the promotion of economic and social development, in employment policies, and the imperatives of unemployment and underemployment have stimulated programmes on economic issues, international trade relationships, and the impact of transnational enterprises on employment and employment policies.

The evolution of the basic needs strategy for development has stimulated trade union organizations in a significant number of developing countries to establish self-help social and economic enterprises as extended services to their members. This more recent development is placing heavy demands on trade union educational facilities, and is stimulating the search for appropriate training programmes that will respond to the planning, administrative, and operational needs of self-help enterprises.

1.1 Trade Union Education and Training

The foundation of labour education can be traced to the need to educate members to participate in their trade union and to make effective use of its services. The cross-fertilization of education and organization has long been recognized. Potential members are more likely to associate themselves with a trade union organization when they understand the principles, objectives, and available services of the union.

Subject matter priorities differ with national circumstances, not the least of which are the varying economic, political, and cultural circumstances within which workers' organizations evolve, and the varying degrees of development of the organization. Nevertheless, courses at the general membership level might be expected to include the historical development of the union; the role and functions of the organization in society; the union constitution and by-laws; union structure and services; labour and social legislation; grievance and dispute settlement procedures, as well as the principles and procedures of collective bargaining. Education and training are required to equip those workers elected or appointed to union office, or to special committees, to carry out their duties.

Education is needed to enable unions to cope with problems created by the growth of transnational enterprises, changes in industrial structures, mergers of companies, and the creation of conglomerates. The introduction of new technology at the work place, and the growing application of computer technology have created the need for courses related to technological change, its impact on working conditions and employment, union involvement in decision making, and the protection of the rights of workers affected by technological change.

Accelerated change has made it necessary for trade unions to develop and strengthen services, particularly in the educational and research fields. Education of labour educators concentrates on how workers learn, on advances in adult training techniques and methodology, and on the production and use of learning aids. It is recognized, however, that skill development is not enough—that an understanding of, and empathy with, workers as trade unionists, are essential ingredients in labour education. The research functions of trade unions call for courses to be given which equip representatives with skills in the analysis of complex facts and figures; in the collection and interpretation of statistical data; and in the preparation of union briefs and positions.

1.2 Workers' Participation within Undertakings

Increased worker participation in the management of enterprises has given rise to three major categories of training course. First, there are courses related to trade union organization, including functions and policies and the role and responsibilities of workers' representatives. The second type meets the need to understand and analyse balance sheets, financial statements, marketing and investment plans, and to acquire knowledge of the enterprise, management, and structures determined by law and practice. The third treats the socioeconomic system within which the enterprise functions.

1.3 Participation for Social and Economic Development

During the Second Development Decade, development strategies have changed, particularly since the International Labour Organization's (ILO's) 1976 World Employment Conference. The "basic needs" approach to resolving the problems of abject poverty has replaced the "trickle down" theory of development. One of the most important characteristics of the former is the emphasis it places on the effective participation of people in the formulation and implementation of policies, plans, and programmes of development. For trade unions, participation implies their spontaneous and democratic involvement in contributing to the development effort, with workers sharing equitably in the benefits derived therefrom.

Where this is happening, courses have been required to establish a basic understanding of relevant macroeconomic tools such as national accounting and employment policies, elements of industrial economics, family life and population, employment and human resource planning and assessments, as well as economic and social policies relating to prices, income, money, credit, and fiscal systems.

1.4 Trade Union Self-help Ventures

Trade unions in developing countries have perceived the need to begin social and economic ventures to help generate employment opportunities. Though stimulated primarily by the unemployment problem, and the realization that workers could not entirely depend upon public and private investment to create employment, such ventures are often also motivated by the perception that extension of trade union services into direct economic development will encourage self-reliance and membership commitment to the organization. Trade union development of credit unions, consumer cooperatives, health and welfare schemes for members and their families, low cost housing, insurance schemes and workers' banks, and in some developing countries new industries and enterprises, has created needs and expectations for relevant education and training.

Illustrative of trade union involvement in economic ventures are the commercial, industrial, and cooperative enterprises in Malaysia and Singapore; rural cooperative developments in India; the development of cooperative-type societies and housing schemes in Kenya, Nigeria, and Mali; the workers' investment corporation in Tanzania; and the development of workers' banks, health facilities, workers' housing, and agro-industrial undertakings in Venezuela, Honduras, and in other countries in Latin America and the Caribbean.

Though global in dimension, the rationale for union-centred socioeconomic ventures, and the labour education responses required, have been consistently articulated by trade union leadership in Asian countries, where diverse enterprise development has become established. Trade union programme objectives in Asia have been defined as "the formulation and implementation of a project oriented socioeconomic and education programme for trade unions in the developing countries of Asia" (Nair 1977 p. 1). Advocates are suggesting that the development of union economic enterprises and social services is directly linked to that of educational activities designed both to promote and to facilitate such ventures.

Unlike the more traditional labour education courses, activities related to the planning, development, and operation of a union enterprise cannot rely on established knowledge and experience. Hence the suggestion that initially "a productive series of national educational programmes would, of course, be to bring trade union leaders together to discuss and study means of identifying viable socioeconomic projects in their countries, as well as obtain knowledge with regard to sound management structures for such projects" (Nair 1977 p. 25). Dialogue is required to identify appropriate content, form, and methodology of relevant education and training programmes.

1.5 Educational Needs of Specific Groups

1.5.1 Rural Workers

In most developing countries the largest concentration of both wage-earning and nonwage-earning workers, is in the rural sector, and it is there that basic needs development strategies present the greatest challenge. Significant extension of labour education activities in the rural field, by national and international trade union organizations, with supportive assistance of the ILO, particularly through the Workers' Education Programme, followed the adoption of the Declaration of Principles and Programme of Action by the 1976 World Employment Conference.

The primary objective of educational activities in this sector is to strengthen the capacity of rural workers to develop and administer strong and representative organizations of their own choice and making. It was, however, recognized that different categories, for example wage-earning rural workers and self-employed peasants, had diverse needs and that programmes should be adapted to the cultural, social, and economic environments of different localities and nations.

At the international level therefore, in the rural development field, there has been considerable stress on information gathering and exchange through national, regional, and international seminars, advisory missions, and studies of rural workers' organizations at the country level. Expertise and technical assistance is being provided in the training of rural worker educators, leadership development, and the education and training required for the promotion and development of self-help services and enterprises in the rural sector.

In a significant number of countries, organizations of rural workers, including small farmers, tenants, and share croppers, have embarked on the development of comprehensive cooperative ventures, in which there is priority need for education and training relevant to administration and management; agro-industrial skills, finance, and marketing. The Organization of the Rural Poor in Ghazipur, India is one such union socioeconomic development.

1.5.2 Trade Union Women's Studies

The principle of equal treatment for women workers, including equal pay, has been embodied in the constitution of the International Labour Organization since its creation in 1919. International Women's Year, with a resultant series of international conferences in 1975, stimulated renewed emphasis on education activities for women workers.

Particular attention was paid to the need to increase employment opportunities for women in both developed and developing countries; to practical measures for the implementation of the equal pay principle; to the elimination of discrimination against women in systems of social security; to the need for improvement of education, training, and retraining for women workers; and international labour standards of special interest to women workers.

In the period since 1975 education has been used to stimulate and increase the participation of women in trade unions, cooperatives, and related social institutions. Labour education has been recognized as an appropriate vehicle to foster awareness of the contribution of women workers to economic and social development. In many countries where women form a growing proportion of the labour movement, efforts have been made through studies, symposia, and other educational activities to identify and help women overcome the various barriers impeding their participation in union leadership. Given the family and home responsibilities of many women trade unionists, special part-time and short courses have been developed on public speaking, the handling of grievances centred on women's issues, women and the law. Instructor training programmes, to supplement teaching skills developed by women trade unionists in the fulfilment of union duties, have substantially increased the number of women engaged in trade union educational activities.

1.5.3 Other Special Target Groups

There is growing interest in identifying, and responding to, the specific interests and needs of young trade unionists who have recently entered the work force.

Basic trade union education and training designed to stimulate the organization of young workers, and to facilitate active participation in trade union activities, is usually followed by leadership training programmes and instruction in social roles and responsibilities.

National, regional, and international workshops and seminars focus attention on major youth issues, such as unemployment and employment opportunities; and to help to identify action-oriented responses. Included are literacy programmes, appropriate vocational and technical training, vocational guidance, the establishment of union youth employment services, and assistance in the development of cooperative projects and self-employment schemes for young workers.

The Workers' Institute of Technology in Port Kelang, Malaysia, founded by the Transport Workers' Union in 1971, provides an example of union efforts to train people skilled in crafts and technicians from among the children of workers in Malaysia. The Malaysian Trades Union Congress, with the assistance of the International Labour Organization, plans to set up an Institute of Labour Studies within the Institute to conduct courses, seminars, and workshops on trade unionism as well as personnel and industrial relations.

The special educational needs of seafarers who spend long periods at sea, and dockers who often face irregular work shifts, have attracted attention in several national, regional, and international symposia and seminars. There is a need to include labour education in existing shipboard training programmes, in which distance learning systems can play a part. Seafarers' unions in several countries have accepted responsibility for education and training related to professional advancement with a broad range of courses including marine and labour legislation, safety and health aboard ship, and transportation economics.

The unique problems of migrant workers in many countries have been identified and considered in forums at country and international levels. Unions in the home country have recognized the need to develop short sessions on the social and cultural environment, as well as the conditions of work, in the country of future employment. More extensive programmes are devoted to relevant vocational training and language study. Trade unions in the receiving country have the tasks of basic trade union training and the advanced training of immigrant workers as union officials and counsellors.

2. Labour Education Structures and Systems

Trade union education has evolved from ad hoc offerings in response to particular needs and problems to its present institutional form in many countries, because of pressures on unions, their extended responsibilities, and the realization that to be effective, education and training must be undertaken on a systematic and continuing basis. The need for such training within the trade union itself, at membership, officer, and cadre levels has stimulated the establishment of national education departments, as well as education officers and committees at enterprise and village levels. Recognition that not all trade unions have the facilities to respond to the full range of specialized education and training requirements has resulted in collaborative agreements with educational institutions and agencies external to the trade union.

Clearly the activities of the several types of institution engaged in labour education activities need to be rationalized and coordinated. Within the trade-union centred concept of labour education, it is possible to envisage a comprehensive national system capable of providing the worker–learner with the opportunity to proceed systematically to more advanced levels of education and skill development.

Creation of forums at the international level, such as the meeting of ILO consultants on workers' education, held in Geneva, Switzerland in 1979, help union decision makers, workers' education administrators, and practitioners share experiences, knowledge, and ideas. They produce cross-fertilization that nurtures structural developments at the national level.

2.1 Educational Services Within the Trade Union

The development of a basic organizational framework for labour education, through organizations of workers, continues to be a priority need in a significant number of developing countries. The initial step involves a commitment by the trade union body to appoint or establish an individual, group, or department responsible for education and training activities, supported by a financial allocation from membership contributions specifically for education activities.

Educational structures at national, branch, or local levels can then evolve in response to learning needs. These vary according to the trade union target group, for example, potential or beginning members, renewal education for continuing members, and specialized training for officers and national representatives. They may lead to the identification of problems of structure both in quantitative and qualitative terms.

National trade union organizations in a number of countries have developed a system of labour education services and institutions designed to respond to the need for continuity and progressive learning experience in the educational process. The German Confederation of Trade Unions (DGB), for example, has established three basic tiers of education and training. There are local schemes consisting of evening seminars and weekend courses, a second stage involving DGB residential federal schools and an apex consisting of three specialized advanced colleges, that is, the Labour College, the Social Science College, and the Institute for Economic and Political Studies.

The trade union movement in Sweden has a system that involves "study circles", local and regional courses of short duration, centrally arranged weekend seminars and courses, and longer residential programmes through labour colleges and the People's High Schools. Labour education structures in Norway and Denmark follow a similar pattern.

The Canadian Labour Congress has responded to geographic imperatives with the establishment of a regional structure with full-time education representatives stationed in five different regions. Weekend and longer residential schools are held in each region with the collaboration of local labour councils and provincial federations of labour. At the apex of the system is the eight-week residential programme at the Labour College of Canada. The need for a national developmental and support agency was recognized when, in 1977, the Canadian Labour Congress Labour Education and Studies Centre was established with substantial public financial assistance. The system of training and renewal for trade union cadres and functionaries in the Soviet Union consists of a number of training echelons at local and regional levels, with the central place in the system held by two institutions, the N. M. Shvernik Higher School of the Trade Union Movement (AUCCTU) and the Higher Trade Union School of Culture.

These structural developments in some countries are complicated by the fact that, parallel to the educational thrust of the central labour body, major national affiliated unions have established comprehensive educational and training structures, often including residential labour colleges. This creates the need for a national advisory or coordinating committee to minimize duplication of effort and maximize the proportion of union members and officials served by the combined educational facilities.

2.2 Labour Colleges and Institutions

The number of residential labour colleges and institutions established in industrial and developing countries is high and rapidly increasing. The global dimension of this development is illustrated by reference to the contribution of Ruskin College in Oxford, England; the George Meany Center for Labor Studies, United States; the Labour College of Canada; the Barbados Workers' Union Labour College; Critchlow Labour College, Guyana; Ghana Labour College; the Metalworkers' Trade Union College in India; the Arab Petroleum Institute for Labour Studies, and the Workers' Education Institute in Iraq.

The development of such central institutions is seen as a priority need by an increasing number of national and regional labour organizations in developing countries.

This is reflected by more recent initiatives by the labour movement in Columbia, the Central Organization of Trade Unions in Kenya, the Egyptian Trade Unions Federation, and the Organization for African Trade Union Unity, related to the development of labour colleges.

The challenge for international trade union bodies and international aid agencies is threefold: (a) to respond adequately to increasing requests for technical advice on the planning and development of labour colleges, for assistance in the development and training of instructors and administrators, and for instructional aids; (b) to act as clearing houses of information on existing trade union educational institutions—a task undertaken by the ILO with publication of a *Directory of Workers' Education Institutions and Programmes in Developing Countries*; and finally (c) to act as a catalyst for the creation of forums where administrative and teaching staff of labour colleges can disseminate information and exchange views about problems of development, administration, financing, and programmes.

Labour colleges were developed in response to needs for advanced studies, higher level technical skills, and union leadership development. They may, however, have a role in developing and extending labour education structures and services at the national level, for example in the development and training of worker educators in the theory and practice of adult learning and teaching; in the development of community outreach programmes by colleges which would extend their services throughout regions they serve; and in the use of college research and developmental capacities to assist trade unions to solve basic educational problems and to provide guidance and counselling, when requested, on appropriate structures.

2.3 The Role of Universities and Colleges

In industrial countries, the involvement of universities in the education of workers has a long tradition. Generally these activities have resulted from pioneer initiatives taken by university staff, and consisted mostly of activities subsidiary to trade union educational initiatives.

In those market economy countries where there was union confidence in the value of cooperation with universities, patterns of partnerships and collaboration were established. Where there was acceptance of basic labour education criteria, with focus on promoting the collective advancement of labour, joint organizational and administrative structures were adopted. These facilitated the provision of university-centred education to selected trade unionists at all levels, and enabled them to better carry out their work in the trade unions, and, through them, in society in general.

By 1969, the global significance of this development justified the undertaking of a research project through the Workers' Education Programme of the ILO on the role of universities in workers' education, followed by an international symposium in 1973. Publication of the research project findings and the symposium papers materially advanced knowledge, identified the needs which university collaboration can help satisfy in the field of trade union education, and analysed the forms and structures of collaboration adopted by unions and universities (ILO 1974).

In Canada, the labour movement has generally considered colleges and universities as educational mechanisms through which trade union goals could be achieved. Special relationships, including the formation of advisory committees and labour education centres, were developed with specific institutions. Thus programme-oriented labour studies committees were established at St. Francis Xavier, Dalhousie, the University of Manitoba, and later at the University of British Columbia and McMaster University in Hamilton, Ontario. In 1969, through a joint college–trade union advisory committee, a School of Labour Studies and Industrial Relations was founded by Niagara College of Applied Arts and Technology in Ontario. Identical in status, it is financed in the same way as the other schools, and offers the first labour education credit programme for trade unionists through a community college.

Union–university collaboration in the United States has stood the test of time and, generally, has worked to the mutual benefit of the academic and labour institutions. University and college labour education programmes continue to multiply as do their curriculum offerings, the numbers of trade union students served, while the quality of their programmes improve. Again the primary vehicle for union–university collaboration is the labour advisory or consulting committee. A unique feature of growth in the United States has been interuniversity collaboration at the national level, first attempted in the early 1950s through the Inter University Labour Education Committee of eight universities. By 1979 some 43 universities and colleges were affiliated to the University and College Labour Education Association, which was established to promote cooperation, assist with the expansion of labour education, serve as the national representative of university and college labour education, and develop professional standards in the field of labour education.

In France, the first initiative, taken in Strasbourg, did not lead to the creation of an independent labour institute of advanced studies but to the integration of the new body within the university. Over a period of 20 years similar institutes were established at the universities of Aix-en-Provence, Bordeaux, Grenoble, Lyon, Nancy, and Paris, and their programmes were determined by a board of an equal number of trade union representatives and university faculty.

In the United Kingdom, participation of universities in workers' education can be traced to the latter part of the nineteenth century, with the creation of Ruskin College, in close cooperation with Oxford University and the Trades Union Congress. Since the mid-1950s universities have recognized the specific needs of trade unionists by providing day release courses for students recruited directly from the work place, and labour education programmes developed in association with polytechnics and colleges of further education.

The involvement of universities in labour education is still incipient in many developing countries, though in some, particularly in Latin America, action to promote that participation is evident with the establishment of bodies for university and trade union cooperation within the framework of the extension departments. Courses for workers, such as those held at the University of Nicaragua applied the principles of joint administration and planning, representation in terms of trade union pluralism, selection of participants through trade union centres linked with universities, and respect for the mutual independence of both university and trade union.

In the Caribbean, where the extramural system had taken root, there was clear awareness of the role of the university in labour education. Training and research work constituted the main joint venture. Structures providing for collaboration in the planning and implementation of labour-oriented projects have been established, notably through the Trade Union Education Institute of the University of the West Indies.

In Asia and the South Pacific, university interest in labour education has been increasing. Indeed, the University of the Philippines has been engaged since the 1950s in trade union education of regional scope. A labour advisory council composed of representatives of major labour federations provided assistance in the setting up and adaptation of study programmes.

In a number of African countries, such as Kenya, Ghana, Senegal, and Sierra Leone, initiatives in the 1970s increased collaboration between universities and trade union organizations. More recently, the concern of the University of Zaire with labour education has resulted in courses and study programmes for trade union members.

2.4 Workers' Education Association

Trade unions in several countries have traditionally carried out labour education activities in partnership with nongovernmental agencies in the field of adult education, and have used the facilities of existing adult residential colleges. In the United Kingdom, for example, the Trades Union Congress and affiliated unions, conduct education activities in partnership with the Workers' Education Association (WEA). Trade unions have also long-supported the activities of Ruskin College and, to a lesser extent, six other longer term residential colleges offering social and labour studies programmes of at least a year's duration.

In Sweden, as in other Scandinavian countries, trade unions carry out a high proportion of courses, in the form of "study circles" through the workers' education association (ABF) of which the central labour bodies and affiliated unions are members. Additionally, trade union residential courses of up to 30 weeks are conducted through the People's High Schools.

Illustrative of similar activities in the Third World was the establishment of the Workers' Education Association of Egypt in 1960 which, from its inception, included trade union representatives on the Board of Directors. Through 50 provincial training centres, and six advanced-level institutes for leadership development, the WEA, in collaboration with the Egyptian Trade Unions Federation and affiliated national unions, has been the main vehicle for trade union education in that country. Recent structural changes, including the establishment of the Workers' University in Nasr City, have brought the WEA under the direction of the Egyptian Trade Unions Federation.

2.5 Government Agencies

In the consideration of national labour education structures, the increasing involvement of governments and parastatal agencies, often in collaboration with workers' organizations, raises questions related to the role of trade unions in the planning, administration, and implementation of programmes offered through governmental agencies.

Trade unions in India, for example, have collaborated in the work of the Central Board of Workers' Education since it was established in 1958 as a semiautonomous, tripartite organization for the implementation of workers' education activities at national, regional, and enterprise levels. Objectives include the development of strong, united, and responsible trade unions through education and training, the strengthening of democratic processes in the trade union movement, and the ultimate transfer of educational functions to trade unions.

The Singapore National Trade Union Congress, as an effective social institution, advocates active participation in the decision-making process in national development. Accordingly its representatives act on the Adult Education Board, Industrial Training Board, the Extramural Studies Department of the University of Singapore, and the Tripartite Advisory Council of the Ministry of Education.

With the support of the General Federation of Trade Unions in the Sudan, a Public Corporation for Workers' Education carries out trade union training, while in Pakistan, labour education and training programmes for trade unionists are conducted by government agencies such as the National Institute of Labour Administration Training.

3. Financing Labour Education

Under the impetus of extended education and training needs, many trade union centres have developed educational structures and programmes to a point where the financial resources required are greater than unions can provide from their own limited resources. As a consequence, in countries where traditionally trade union autonomy and independence have been valued, a number of significant national trade union bodies have accepted financial support from both private and public sources under mutually acceptable criteria. Another spur to financing labour education by agencies external to the trade union is the recognition in many countries, particularly those in the Third World, that high priority must be placed on trade union education and training if workers' organizations are to participate effectively in the planning, development, and achievement of social and economic objectives.

Labour education is financed through four categories of agencies, including the trade union itself: (a) financial resources allocated by the workers' organization from union dues paid by members; (b) resources provided from public revenues by the state, local authorities, or through agencies established by public authorities; (c) resources from employers by means of a negotiated per capita payment to the unions' education fund, negotiated paid educational leave, and tuition refund provisions, or through legislated paid educational leave provisions; and (d) financial assistance from international trade union bodies and international aid agencies.

3.1 Trade Union Financial Resources

Given that the primary responsibility for trade union education and training lies with the labour organization, that body needs to allocate financial resources for the purpose. This fact has been acknowledged, and the principle accepted, in several international and regional activities in which the ILO has been involved.

The way such financial resources are mobilized, and the form the education fund takes, varies according to trade union structures and circumstances at the national level. Trade union centres can establish an education fund in several ways, for example: by allocating a proportion of union dues received from members or affiliated organizations, by special levies on, or voluntary contributions from, affiliates, or by an annual educational allocation, related to programme requirements, from the union's general treasury.

3.2 Support from Public Revenues

Trade unions in many market economy countries have traditionally held the view, often embedded in constitutional provisions and by-laws, that their operations should be financed from their own resources. Trade union organizations functioning in countries with planned economies, or in countries where the notion of social partnership has evolved, often rely heavily on public revenues to finance educational activities.

In industrialized countries, where hitherto trade unions have been self-sufficient in financing educational activities, they rely increasingly on public funds to finance labour education. Arrangements are made between central trade union bodies and governments which provide access to public revenues for educational purposes, but which at the same time maintain trade union control of purposes, programmes, and priorities. Because of past traditions and the innovative nature of bilateral agreements made between the central labour bodies and respective governments, recent developments in the United Kingdom, Canada, and Australia are noteworthy.

In the United Kingdom, for the year 1976–77, the Government, through the Department of Education and Science, approved a direct education grant of up to £400,000 sterling to the Trades Union Congress (TUC), and this grant aid was steadily increased in subsequent years. The educational criteria and administrative procedures to be followed were set out in a memorandum mutually agreed upon by the TUC and the appropriate government departments, and a joint liaison committee was established. This grant aid was made available for four purposes, namely to reimburse course fees paid by the TUC to public educational bodies providing day release courses in cooperation with the TUC; to help cover the cost of course development and teaching materials production by the TUC training college; to train tutors; and to defray the cost of union residential courses of more than four days' duration.

In Canada, the 1975 National Conference on Labour Education recommended that both federal and provincial governments increase financial support to labour unions for education and training programmes carried out directly or in cooperation with public institutions. As a result, an agreement was concluded between the Department of Labour, on behalf of the Government, and the Canadian Labour Congress (CLC), providing a direct grant of two million dollars to the CLC for each programme year, over an initial period of five years. The purpose of the grant was to enable the Congress to establish a national labour education and studies centre and five regional centres, together with specific programmes and projects necessary for the conduct of a labour education programme. Government financial assistance was extended to other unions submitting acceptable projects in the educational field, and modest allocations were made available to postsecondary institutions carrying out trade union programmes.

In Australia, the federal parliament was called upon to establish a statutory authority for trade union education which would receive public funds, but which would include leaders of the trade union movement in its governing body. After consultations with central trade union bodies, legislation establishing the Australian Trade Union Training Authority (TUTA) was enacted in 1975. TUTA's work includes the provision of a training and education programme for trade unionists, the promotion of trade union education and training programmes, and the coordination of ongoing activities in these fields. This work is carried out through six major nonresidential centres at state levels, and advanced leadership development programmes at the residential Clyde Cameron College in Wodonga.

In other industrial countries, the Nordic countries and Belgium for example, trade unions have long accepted public financial assistance for educational activities. In Sweden, state subsidies are available, through application to the Board of Education, for teachers' salaries, materials, travel expenses, and board and lodging at residential colleges. In Belgium, trade union organizations receive certain grants from the Office of Productivity and other public agencies for labour education programmes.

3.3 Financial Resources Through Employers

Traditionally trade unions have engaged in collective bargaining in order to improve wages, working conditions, health and safety provisions, pension rights, and so on. Now trade unions in a growing number of countries, particularly in Europe and North America, are giving high priority to trade union education and training provisions in the collective agreements sought with employers.

There are several forms of financial resources secured through collective bargaining to support labour education activities. A sum equivalent to an agreed percentage of the company payroll may be allocated for educational and cultural programmes carried out by the trade union. This amount is deposited by the employers, on a regular basis, into a separate fund or trust controlled and administered by the trade union. A fixed sum may be negotiated to be expended on labour education. Some trade unions, notably the United Automobile Workers in Canada, have given high priority to reaching agreements whereby employers refund the tuition costs incurred on paid educational leave programmes for trade union training. Educational funds and plans to be financed by employers' resources and administered by the trade union bodies, are negotiated in Scandinavia, Belgium, France, Italy, the Federal Republic of Germany, Canada, the United States, and elsewhere.

3.4 Financial Assistance—International Agencies

The increased support for trade unions in developing countries by a wide range of international aid agencies is a significant development. These agencies include international trade union organizations, such as sectorial International Trade Secretariats, specialized agencies within the United Nations family, and international development agencies of such countries as Norway, Sweden, Denmark, the Federal Republic of Germany, Canada, and the United States. Those from the United States respond to trade union requests from developing countries either on a bilateral basis, or through multilateral arrangements with the United Nations or its agencies.

International assistance in the field of labour education can be illustrated by the form, and means of action, applied by the Workers' Education Programme of the International Labour Organization which, as a tripartite body representative of governments, employers, and workers, is particularly suited to the task. Assistance, in response to identified needs at the country and regional levels, takes the form of provision of technical and material assistance; professional help in the planning of trade union education services; the training of instructors in methodology and techniques, in which the ILO's International Centre for Advanced Technical and Vocational Training in Turin, Italy, plays an important role; encouraging the development of trade union education departments, labour colleges, and training centres; developing study materials and teaching aids; organizing seminars and meetings on special subjects; offering grants and fellowships to trade union educators, and undertaking research and dissemination of information on specific labour education problems and developments.

Pressure from developing countries to increase assistance in the field of trade union education is insistent and increasing. Beyond the limitation of financial resources and expertise, it can be anticipated that dialogue between the donor and recipient agencies, concerning criteria for the acceptance of assistance in the building of trade union education services, and the apparent need for rationalization and coordination of international cooperation, will be increasingly important in the years ahead.

See also: Recurrent Education

Bibliography

International Labour Organization (ILO) 1972 *New Dimensions for Development*. ILO, Geneva

International Labour Organization (ILO) 1974 *The Role of Universities in Workers' Education*. ILO, Geneva

International Labour Organization (ILO) 1979 *Report of a Meeting of Consultants on Workers' Education*. ILO, Geneva

Nair C V D 1977 *Asian Labour and the Dynamics of Change*. Eurasia Press, Singapore

Whitehouse J R W 1978 Organizing labour education in the college. In: Kidd J R, Selman G R (eds.) 1978 *Coming of Age: Canadian Adult Education in the 1960s*. Canadian Association for Adult Education, Toronto, Ontario, pp. 175–81

Whitehouse J R W 1979 Labour education: Developing concepts and dimensions. *Labour Educ.* 39: 2–7

Education in the Armed Forces

G. Tilson and G. Kauvar

Adult education in any systematic form has always had some association with military needs. Perhaps the first examples of career teachers in adult education were those in the British Navy and Prussian Army. Formal university work for military personnel was organized in the Khaki College of Canada during the First World War and this practice was soon adopted by many other countries. When the armies of Iran and Israel drafted army recruits as teachers in a national literacy program, this practice underlined a relationship that has often been close. One of the attractions of military life that is used in publicity is the fact that potential recruits have an opportunity to obtain vocational training and higher education after service.

Studies have been conducted on education programs associated with personnel leaving active service, and also with personnel retiring from service. The total size of this educational effort, measured either in expenditures or in numbers of "students" or "teachers" involved, is very large.

Accounts of military education and research about practice are prepared quite frequently in India, in the Soviet Union, in the People's Republic of China, and in many other countries, but it is uncommon for these reports to be published or given public distribution. A military education program that has often been described is that in the United States, but while much of what follows refers to the American program, many of the features seem to be typical also of other countries.

Because soldiering is a profession with no lateral entry into upper echelons, recurrent education and retraining is a hallmark of military life. The military authorities provide extensive training from their own resources, primarily to develop specialized skills—only 10 percent of which are unique to military service. The United States Department of Defense spends about US$13 billion annually on training and education; at any time, about one-sixth of all military personnel have training as their primary duty.

1. Training for Enlisted Personnel

The development of enlisted service members through formal training and education and practical experience in the United States follows a pattern common to most countries. The new service member first receives training designed to develop the basic attributes of all members of his or her service. In most cases, these graduates are then taught the skills required for a military job at the lowest skill level. Those who remain for extended service, the career members, will further develop their military knowledge and skills through experience in military jobs, interspersed, as required, with training or education needed to prepare them for more responsible positions. A combination of job experience, training, and education is essential to the development of a military force capable of carrying out the national security mission.

In many armed services, particularly those which have a conscript element, it is found necessary to give some recruits a substantial program of literacy and other basic education as a prerequisite of training in military skills. This is not only true of developing countries, but also of ones such as Hungary, France, and the United States as well. The British Army, which is a volunteer, not a conscript force, has a School of Preliminary Education, where recruits of low attainment undergo courses in English and arithmetic (Legge 1982 p. 54).

It is customary, if not universal, that career rather than conscript personnel be required to demonstrate an appropriate level of educational achievement before being considered for promotion. In the British Army, for instance, potential senior noncommissioned officers take Education Promotion Certificates in communication skills, military calculations, military management, and "The army in the contemporary world" among subjects. For the Officers' Qualification Scheme subjects include leadership, personnel management, international relations, and "The soldier in society" (Legge 1982 p. 54).

2. Officer Training and Education

Officer training and education can be divided generally into four categories. First, there is training leading to a commission. In the United States the majority of new officers are commissioned through the Reserve Officers Training Corps—military training conducted while a student is at a college or university. Other countries, including the United Kingdom, have similar schemes. Another route runs through army, navy, and air force academies, which most countries have, and in which, through courses of several years duration, candidates for commissions receive a general higher education as well as extensive military training.

The second category of education and training includes the many specific skill-producing courses which are conducted to enable the officer to perform immediately upon assignment to a specialized or functional area, such as duty as an aircraft pilot or an artillery officer. These courses vary in length from a few days to several months. They present, for the most part, strictly job-oriented training.

Third, each service maintains a system of professional military education related more to the increasing responsibilities associated with career progression to more senior grades than to the individual's current assignment or speciality.

Finally, the services also provide selected officers with advanced academic education, either at civilian institutions or at schools operated by the services, to meet specific requirements for officers educated in technical, scientific, engineering, and managerial fields.

3. Professional Development Education

Education in the armed forces school system is considered fundamental to the development of service officers who are fully qualified to perform duties of high responsibility in both war and peace. In most nonmilitary professions, growth in ability and knowledge is gained through experience. In the military, opportunities for full practice of the profession are limited to wartime, and even those officers with combat experience have not had the opportunity for thorough exercise of the decision skills they might require to meet all contingencies. The military school system serves partially to fill this shortfall by educating the military officer in the skills and knowledge needed to perform his or her duties in a variety of locales and situations, both in peacetime and wartime. The American system described below has parallels in most advanced countries, including socialist ones.

3.1 Command and Staff Colleges

In the United States, each of the services maintains a Command and Staff College. While there are differences in approach and curriculum based on the requirements of the parent service, each course prepares officers for command and staff duties in all echelons of their parent service and in joint or allied commands. A relatively small number of officers from each service attends one of the Command and Staff Colleges of the other services; a few attend Allied Schools at the same level.

Another school at about the same professional level is the Defense Systems Management College. This is a joint school that conducts a primary 20-week course in management concepts and methods. The major purpose is to prepare selected military officers and civilian personnel for assignments as program or project managers to oversee development and procurement of major weapon systems.

3.2 Senior Service Colleges

Each of the military departments in the United States maintains a Senior Service College, or "War College." In addition, the National Defense University, consisting of two joint Senior Service Colleges, the National War College and the Industrial College of the Armed Forces, is attended by students from all four services.

The common purpose of the Senior Service Colleges is to prepare students for senior command and staff positions at the highest levels in the national security establishment and the allied command structure. The unifying focus is the study of national goals and national security policy.

Each of the colleges integrates the study of economic, scientific, political, sociological, and other factors into the consideration of national security problems. The Industrial College, in its approach to national security problems, emphasizes the use and management of national resources.

3.3 Full-time, Fully Funded Graduate Education

The United States Department of Defense needs military officers with specialized advanced knowledge, at a graduate level, to perform effectively in certain military jobs. The graduate education program in each of the services provides graduate-level education in required disciplines to the officers required to maintain an inventory of qualified officers. Under the program, military officers undertake graduate education on a full-time, fully funded basis.

4. Nonmilitary Education

This article has concentrated its attention so far on education and training needed for the efficient exercise of military functions. It is also a widespread practice of armed forces to encourage personnel to pursue studies for their personal interest or development, in fields which may be, but do not need to be, related to service duties. Much of this study is carried out in off-duty hours, but leave is also given in duty hours, provided the exigencies of the service permit. In the American and British forces, for example, personnel may work towards a university degree, either by distance study, as through the University of Maryland or Open University courses, or, in selected cases, personnel may follow full-time courses on a university campus. The majority of voluntary adult students, however, follow cultural or hobby interests, or take civilian vocational training courses.

The provision of these study opportunities is largely subsidized by the state and is undertaken as part of a general policy of increasing the technical qualifications and educational level of the armed forces; also as part of the range of leisure activities offered to service men and women for morale reasons and as an incentive to recruitment and to continuing service.

Increasingly, armed forces have acknowledged a responsibility to prepare personnel approaching the end of their engagement for return to civilian life. In the British and American forces, advice and counseling are available on resettlement and growing programs of vocational training exist in many countries.

In the Federal Republic of Germany, for example, the Office of the Armed Forces for Job Promotion came into being in 1960. "Its task is to facilitate the soldiers' (re-) entry into civilian life, regardless of whether they resume their former professions or whether they change jobs. Enrollment in the various facilities of further education is in principle voluntary. The costs are met by the Office for Job Promotion. Essentially, the measures concerning vocational training consist of co-ordinating bodies of specialists, specialized courses and correspondence courses" (Knoll 1980).

5. Political Education

All countries consider it important that their armed forces are not only technically trained to preserve the country's security, but that they understand what they are defending and why they are doing it. To a greater or lesser degree, therefore, in all countries members of the armed services are subjected to political education. In the socialist states of Eastern Europe education in Marxism–Leninism is a formal and integrated part of military training. In some developing countries, national consciousness is promoted within and through the armed services. In Western Europe and North America this political education role may be less explicit and less prominent, but it is there, as some of the examples quoted above of subjects taught for promotion examinations in the British Army demonstrate.

6. Providers of Education for Armed Services Personnel

Nearly all the teaching of specifically military skills is carried out by the armed services themselves, or, in the case of developing countries, by instructors from friendly states. The pattern of training in other skills used in military service is, however, more complex. In some developed countries the services themselves have corps of educators, as in the United Kingdom, where there are the Royal Army Educational Corps, the Royal Navy Education Service, and the Royal Air Force Education Branch. They also run their own schools and colleges. The Federal Republic of Germany, for instance, runs the Military Academy of the Armed Forces, the Armed Forces School for Internal Administration, and the Federal Academy for Military Administration and Military Technology.

A considerable amount of training, particularly at the higher levels, of technological and managerial personnel is, however, carried out in civilian institutions. Engineers, doctors, accountants, and many other specialists study in universities and other institutions of higher education, not only at the expense of the armed services, but often in courses specifically commissioned by them.

The civilian role in leisure-time and self-development education and in prerelease courses is even greater. It would probably be correct to say that most of the teaching in these fields is done by civilian organizations, either the public education system, or private agencies, by arrangement with the armed forces. Members of the services are, because of their job mobility, important customers of the distance teaching organizations. For example, free correspondence education is widely provided to members of the armed forces with the approval of the Civilian Education Board of the Norwegian Armed Forces (Titmus 1981 p. 169).

Some armed forces do retain a direct role for themselves. The British and Americans maintain educational centers in nearly all large army, naval, and air force bases, where personnel may study and/or be taught at a variety of levels, from basic education to postgraduate. To provide training for civilian occupations the Federal German armed forces have established over 100 educational institutions (Knoll 1980 pp. 44–45).

7. Research and Development

Armed services in every country offer the largest captive body of adult research subjects. They are vitally concerned with problems of training and associated questions of adult learning. It is thus not surprising that they have undertaken much study in these fields. Their experience goes back a long way and some of the basic work on the measurement of adult intelligence was undertaken by or for military authorities.

The prime purpose of educational research within the armed forces is to improve learning efficiency, so the stress is on work which will lead to better learning materials and instructional techniques. The United States Department of Defense maintains human research laboratories, which sponsor extensive research to that end. The British Army's Institute of Adult Education and the Army School of Instructional Technology also undertake research, the latter particularly into subjects such as job analysis, learning systems, audiovisual aids, and interview techniques. In both countries the results are shared with civilian educators, as are some of the instructional materials applying them. Training aids and kits produced by the American and British armed services are highly valued and widely used in civilian vocational education.

Bibliography

Bradsky N 1970 The armed forces. In: Smith R M (ed.) 1970 *Handbook of Adult Education*. Macmillan, New York

Clark H F, Sloan H S 1964 *Classrooms in the Military: An Account of Education in the Armed Forces of the United States*. Teachers College, New York

Knoll J H 1980 *Adult Education in the Federal Republic of Germany*. European Centre for Leisure and Education, Prague

Legge D 1982 *The Education of Adults in Britain*. Open University Press, Milton Keynes

Office of the Assistant Secretary of Defense *Military Manpower Training Report (Annual)*. Office of the Assistant Secretary of Defense, Manpower, Installations and Logistics, Washington, DC

Titmus C 1981 *Strategies for Adult Education*. Open University Press, Milton Keynes

Training of Adult Educators

C. Duke

Teacher education for adult education means courses for adult education personnel, including industrial, commercial, and governmental training staff and other adult, continuing, and nonformal education functionaries, to perform their duties better. Personnel may be full-time, part-time, or voluntary. Teacher education may be preservice and accredited, but academic education in adult education typically follows work experience. The larger part of teacher education takes in-service short-course forms.

Different views are held about the desirability of formal professional training and accreditation, which are thought to contradict adult education traditions and values, including voluntarism, and equality between teacher and taught. Universities play a central role in teaching leading adult educators. In some countries teachers' colleges and special centres are important. Most teacher education for adult education is provided by employer organizations and adult education agencies in the form of short courses. Courses vary in content and skill areas but there is emerging a consensus which finds expression in the content of graduate programmes in a number of countries.

Congruence between methods of teacher education and good adult education practice is stressed. Provision is inadequate to meet demand, and there are different views about where priorities lie. Despite close links between adult and school-oriented teacher education and educational provision in some countries, it is likely that a degree of separation, with distinct philosophy and methodology, will generally be sustained.

1. Definition and Scope

Any teaching intended to enhance the capacity of others to teach, or assist the learning of adults, is considered teacher education for adult education. The term adult education has various connotations: at one extreme it embraces all forms of education of those considered adult by their society by any means and for any purposes; in some countries it has more specific connotations, such as basic, remedial education or literacy teaching for adults; and in several Western societies it refers to a particular tradition of liberal education for adults not related to their employment. Other terms often used inaccurately as alternatives, without precise meaning, include continuing education, nonformal education and, in certain contexts, extramural or extension studies and community education; the term recurrent education is sometimes used as if to mean adult education but is properly restricted to a policy or strategy for educational provision. Industrial, commercial, and other training is included.

The term teacher education is seldom used in relation to adult education, the practice being to speak of the training of adult educators or staff, or professional development. Teachers of adults and others working in the field of adult education such as policy makers and administrators tend to prefer other terms over teacher, among them tutor, facilitator, or animator (*animateur*). Trainer is commonly used in the vocational training sector and other terms are used in different settings, such as lecturer, counsellor, and catalyst or change agent. All come within the scope of teacher education for adult education.

Other facets of the management and practice of adult education impinge upon teacher training and staff development, especially selection and recruitment of personnel and the status and reward systems of adult educators, but are beyond the scope of teacher education as such. Although training carries different connotations from education, and the difference is a subject of academic analysis by adult educators, there is no agreed and practised distinction; teacher education and teacher training are at present interchangeable as terms in adult education. However, universities tend to use education to refer to academic graduate programmes and they and other agencies tend to prefer training for professionally oriented and especially short-course teaching of adult educators and training personnel.

2. The Adult Educator's Training Needs

There is a widely acknowledged, pressing need to improve the teaching of adult educators, but there are difficulties and uncertainties concerning the way of defining and meeting this need. The systematization, regulation and control found in regular, school-oriented teacher education is lacking, and is unlikely to come into being. The 1972 UNESCO International Conference on Adult Education described mobilizing and training sufficient professional personnel as the biggest challenge facing adult education in the 1970s. The UNESCO Recommendation on the Development of Adult Education (1976) was very general and unspecific: "training for adult education should, as far as practicable, include all those aspects of skill, knowledge, understanding, and personal attitude which are relevant to the various functions undertaken, taking into account the general background against which adult education takes place. By integrating these aspects with each other, training should itself be a demonstration of sound adult education practice." Countries strong in the liberal (nonvocational) tradition, such as the United Kingdom and others sharing that tradition, and the Scandinavian countries, produce many statements to the effect that adult education training is a crucial but neglected area. The need is also recognized as a matter of urgency by countries attempting massive social or economic development through adult education: India in its National Adult Education Programme; China in its quest for the "four modernizations".

The "great tradition" of liberal adult education, as it is called in the United Kingdom, Australia, and elsewhere, emphasizes the importance of certain values, purposes, and personal qualities, as well as the part-time and voluntaristic traditions, all of which present problems for the training of adult educators. It is disputable whether many of the personal qualities extolled among teachers of adults can be systematically taught, rather than being either inherited or acquired through experience and maturation. The emphasis upon values, and on congruence between what is taught and what is practised in teacher education, also has implications for methods of teacher education. A 1979 British conference working document on new directions for adult education illustrates this: it prefers the term staff to professional development as being wider and less status seeking, and insists that staff development should axiomatically be an example of good adult education practice. Among principles enunciated, adult education training should be: a transaction between equals;

entirely free from compulsion; unrelated to career advancement; unencumbered by examination, grading, and accreditation; open; and a "self-transforming learning system" inspired by "disciplined ad hocery" (as well as being vertically and horizontally integrated and communicating an awareness of politics and of socio-economic milieu). Belief in participation, and the approach to teaching for social change expounded by Paulo Freire, similarly provide directions and suggest prohibitions for methods of teaching adult educators. The value system shared by many adult educators is suspicious of or inimical to any professionalization of adult education which suggests exclusiveness, elitism, and a widening gap between teachers and taught. Resistance to professionalization, together with the difficulty of professionalizing the field, complicate the case for the provision of professional education.

The field (or profession) of adult education is not unitary but confused, diverse, and fragmented. Its relationship to the formal education system is described as marginal, although the same phenomenon, like the diversity, is also ascribed the positive character of flexibility. There have been many analyses and typologies of adult educators, and of their training needs. Houle (1970) in a frequently cited paper noted that not all adult educators perceive themselves as such, that the claim to be professional is sometimes made with an uneasy air, and that it can be asserted only in a loose and analogical fashion. Four main categories of adult educators are: (a) those who provide direct guidance to learners; (b) those who design and promote programmes; (c) those who administer programmes; and (d) those, such as research scholars and association leaders, who advance adult education as a field. Most of the first category are part-time and/or voluntary workers, as are an undesirably large proportion of the second and third categories.

In another often cited paper Houle (1956) wrote of the "pyramid of leadership", distinguishing the large group at the base who are volunteers from the intermediate level who combine adult education with other parts of their paid duties as educational, museum and library, governmental, media, and other personnel; and from the full-time adult education specialists at the apex of the pyramid. Other authors have attempted other categorizations for scholarly or practical purposes. An Asian seminar on training of adult educators distinguished field workers, supervisors, and administrators or leaders for purposes of training needs (Dutta and Fischer 1972), and a subsequent Asian regional seminar distinguished five categories according to their duties and training needs: (a) teaching personnel (the great majority, including voluntary and part-time workers); (b) policy makers and others mainly in administration; (c) facilitators or *animateurs*, such as supervisors and course designers; (d) the teachers of adult educators (trainers of trainers); and (e) research and evaluation personnel (UNESCO 1981). An Indian handbook for the training of adult education functionaries for the National Adult Education Programme (Directorate of Adult Education 1978) identified five categories: (a) key functionaries at national and state levels; (b) professionals and experts in such areas as curriculum and materials design, training, and evaluation; (c) functionaries at district and local levels; (d) field level supervisors; and (e) instructors in adult education centres. Instructional responsibility would be assigned to: school teachers; students; village youth; exservicemen and other retired personnel; field level government and other functionaries; and voluntary social workers. Some mass literacy campaigns, and some definitions of adult education and the adult educator for the "lifelong education" or "learning" society, treat every adult person as an adult educator as well as a learner.

Campbell (1977) draws two conclusions about adult education as a field of study and practice: "that there are many facets of adult education practice; and that all draw on a branch of education which is distinct in its character". Campbell considers adult education "a particular and unique element of the education system", and notes that its fragmentation is at once its greatest strength and its greatest weakness. He distinguishes four levels of leadership, all of which would benefit from access to training, and notes the extremely wide range of organizations providing education and training to adults, the dependence upon a host of largely untrained part-time and voluntary workers, the significance of training for adult education demonstrated by the recent spate of reports on the subject, and the increasing emphasis, in British and European settings, upon systems of provision rather than ad hoc arrangements. There may also be discerned, notably in symposia and unpublished working papers, a more sophisticated approach to defining the educational needs of adult educators and attempting to specify the functions, roles, and tasks which indicate required competencies with more precision than the broad and general categories such as administrator. Apart from hesitancy deriving from lack of specificity of role and required competencies, and hesitancy deriving from concerns about professionalization and elitism, the training of adult educators is obviously hampered by the high proportion of voluntary and part-time personnel not easily available for or amenable to training, and some uncertainty as to where the priority belongs: for instance in China the emphasis is upon updating the subject matter being taught, while elsewhere higher priority is given to teaching and learning processes; some emphasize the development of a leading cadre of professional adult educators while others consider that the larger numbers of "grass-roots" part-time teachers should attract the main attention. Some stress conceptual understanding of the field, others practical skills of instruction, others again the largely intangible personal qualities of empathy and rapport which are held to distinguish the best adult educators.

3. *Modes of Provision and Providing Bodies*

Training of adult educators, like adult education itself, takes many forms and modes. Houle (1970) emphasizes that "most leadership training, like most adult education, is self-directed and therefore is undertaken with varying degrees of thoroughness and continuity". He also emphasizes that those studying adult education at universities have in the main substantial prior experience; the typical doctorate in North America is taken in the late thirties and represents a second career. On the other hand more adult educators are now receiving formal, accredited training directly upon graduation. This runs counter to a strong tradition and view among adult educators that good teachers of adults should have substantial work experience before becoming teachers of adults, but raises less difficulty if the young graduate moves into an administrative rather than a teaching role in the field of adult education.

The majority of adult education training is for those who have work experience already, and usually experience as adult educators. It may take the form of full-time or part-time accredited training, or the form of short nonaccredited inservice courses. Much of this short-course provision is unsystematic and ad hoc, but there are now attempts to make it more regular and systematic in many countries. Part of the planning for the Indian National Adult Education Programme was a systematic scheme of training of personnel for different teaching and organizing roles. Some short courses are publicly advertised and available to all who are interested and able to attend, but very many are conducted within employing organizations or by the providers of adult education and training programmes for their own full- or part-time, paid or voluntary personnel. They are therefore not widely known and it is not possible to state the total scale of such training of trainers and educators of adults.

International conferences on adult education periodically call for more opportunities for adult educators to be trained, stressing the need for different modes. Recommendation 28 of the UNESCO International Conference (1972) sought both short inservice and longer accredited courses in universities; recommendation 30 called for regional seminars open to nongovernmental as well as government personnel. A survey of training opportunities in British universities in 1970 noted the recent growth of accredited training courses (as distinct from short orientation and refresher courses), identifying part-time and full-time certificate and diploma courses in adult education and community development, as well as a sandwich (or cooperative) form of provision for industrial education and training. These courses were apart from opportunities to study for research degrees. An Australian survey a decade later (Knights and Peace 1981) found a preference in New South Wales for accredited training to be "one to three years part-time", with over half of respondents also considering one year's full-time course useful. For short-term noncredit training, weekend workshops were the most popular, followed by occasional evening meetings, series of evening meetings, meetings during the week, and correspondence courses—an indication of the availability of part-time adult educators for their own professional development. A common form of noncredit training especially for full-time adult educators in both industrialized and nonindustrialized countries (reflecting a common format for work-related adult education) is the short intensive residential course of one or two weeks' duration up to perhaps three months, which may be in-house for adult educators in one organization or system, or open to people from different agencies. Recruitment may be local, national, or international. Participants in these and other training courses may be those whose work is exclusively adult education, or others whose professional role includes an adult education component, such as health, agricultural extension, or media workers; they are unlikely to be people who are employed in some quite other field and teach on a part-time basis, since these are not easily available in working hours for training related to their spare-time activity.

Although there is debate in some countries about whether adult education is a distinct discipline or part of the study of (school-oriented) education, there has recently been an increase in opportunities to study for a graduate qualification in adult education in many countries. Verner (1980), who strongly argues a case for adult education as a distinct social science discipline as well as field of social practice, identifies Canada and the United States, the United Kingdom, Belgium, and Yugoslavia as countries where it is particularly accepted and valued as a subject of study at universities; by 1980, 2,239 doctorates had been awarded in adult education in the United States, where by that year over 175 universities taught adult education. Japan is another country where many universities study and teach adult education, and more universities are opening departments or programmes in this field; for example India, the Philippines, the Republic of Korea, and Thailand.

In North America, in particular, and in other countries to differing degrees, formal study opportunities are available, full-time and sometimes part-time, to take adult education as a subject at the level of Ph.D., Ed.D., M.A. or M.Ed., Dip.Ed., or Cert.Ed., as well as to attend noncredit courses of a few hours up to a few months in length. Some noncredit courses provide a certificate of attendance or participation and satisfactory completion which, while not a formal qualification, may still have modest utility for career purposes. Accredited university study therefore takes both mainly academic (Ph.D., M.A.) and more clearly professional forms. Houle (1970) suggested that adult education had a similar status to that of sociology prior to the emergence of social work, or botany prior to agriculture and forestry; the fundamentals were still being explored and were only gradually being crystallized into programmes of the Ed.D. type. He judged that the result would be an open rather than closed cluster of professions, more like business studies than medicine. In Australia, a country where the profession and its training is poorly recognized and differentiated, of 183 students attending postgraduate courses in New South Wales in 1979 only 7 were categorized as adult educators; others were staff trainers, health educators, extension officers, tertiary teachers, librarians, and in other roles (Knights and Peace 1981).

Universities are widely recognized as the main institutions for formal training of full-time adult educators; the importance of their role, and the desirability of strengthening and extending such teaching, are frequently reiterated in studies of adult educator training and in the deliberations of international seminars of adult educators. Such a meeting convened by UNESCO in Bangkok in 1980 noted the recent involvement of universities in the professional training of adult educators often deriving from their concern for professional development of their own teaching staff, and called for a broadening of this interest to provide training for adult educators in such areas as liberal education and second language teaching. Adult education departments are most commonly located in faculties of education in some countries, but in others they may be separate, or linked instead with an extension or continuing education service of the university. Different organizational arrangements reflect different views as to whether adult education is a distinct field or discipline or, rather, a subsystem of general education. Likewise some universities offer one or two adult education options in an M.A. or M.Ed. programme, but not a complete distinct degree in adult education.

There are different views and practices in relation to the inclusion of adult education as a subject or option in normal schools or colleges of teacher education. Some maintain that since it is a distinct field with values and methods different from general education, its professional education also should be kept distinct. On the other hand it is held, especially in rural Third World situations, that much of the teaching of adults will be done by primary- and secondary-school teachers, so that their professional preparation in the distinctive learning needs of adults is essential. The UNESCO International Conference in 1972, recommending that high priority be given to the training of adult education personnel, made reference to "the study of adult education to be included in the curricula of teacher education, and in the training of librarians and other educational personnel" and called for programmes to train teachers to specialize in adult education coordinated with the normal teacher-training system. It also recommended seminars and courses for adult educators as an integral part of the education system (including industrial training officers, other training personnel, and administrators), and the use of mass media and other distance forms of adult teacher education.

On the one hand, training of adult educators is provided in some universities and teachers' colleges in some countries; on the other, the argument is advanced that because it is a distinct and under-regarded field, it is better to build distinct special-purpose centres to train adult educators. Several countries such as Kenya and Tanzania have developed separate adult education institutes. Some aid agencies active in adult education encourage Third World countries either to establish such a national centre or to identify and strengthen a particular university department as the key to professional development in adult education in their country. A working party on the training of adult educators recommended in 1977 that the National Council of Adult Education in New Zealand should assume primary responsibility for the training of adult educators, a recommendation which Verner (1980) considers "unfortunate" since it does not encourage universities to accept responsibility in this area.

Regional and international meetings often call attention to the need for regional training centres so that adult education personnel can widen their understanding and competence on a comparative basis, in a setting exclusively oriented to training adult educators. The UNESCO International Conference in 1972 called for feasibility studies for regional training centres for key personnel working in collaboration with national institutions, and the Asian and South Pacific Bureau of Adult Education (ASPBAE) reached similar conclusions in a regional seminar on the training of adult educators earlier that year. The strengthening of regional and international cooperation has seen an increase in the number of noncredit or certificated training programmes provided by regional organizations, for example in the Caribbean (general adult education) and Southeast Asia (urban-oriented training). Some universities, mostly in industrialized countries, also play a regional or international training role, either through regular graduate programmes (such as the University of British Columbia and the Ontario Institute for Studies in Education (OISE) in Canada, Manchester University in the United Kingdom, and Massachusetts and Michigan State Universities in the United States) or through regular or occasional short courses (such as the annual three-month programme for Asian and Pacific adult educators at the Australian National University supported by the W.K. Kellogg Foundation). Educational foundations and aid agencies play a prominent role in fostering national, regional, and other forms of adult education training for Third World adult educators, whether through regular educational institutions, national or regional associations, or special training centres. Although it has been suggested periodically that adult education associations should take the initiative and provide accreditation for the adult education profession, there has been a reluctance to appear to usurp the role of universities; consequently the staff development and training work of professional associations of adult education is generally restricted to providing short training courses and other noncredit study opportunities, and to arranging seminars, conferences, publications, and other aids to adult education training. A recent development in China has been the creation of a national adult education association and an increasing number of provincial and city associations, a main purpose of which is to provide staff development services and opportunities.

The 1976 conference of the International Council for Adult Education (ICAE) in Tanzania called for the creation of regional training centres to serve countries not yet able to mount the kinds of training required at the country level. Cooperative programmes were recommended wherever there were regional bonds of culture, ideology or language, or geographical or economic factors which favoured this. At least one such centre was sought, under indigenous leadership, in each of four main Third World regions, within three years. The tendency has been for regional training programmes to be established rather than distinct centres, using the existing facilities and infrastructures of different countries for regional purposes.

Apart from universities and colleges, and associations supported by intergovernmental and other aid agencies, a large part of all training of adult educators is provided by their employing organizations and agencies, and takes the form of short intensive sessions and courses. According to Houle (1970) the largest volume of organized, as distinct from self-directed, training of adult education leaders takes place within providing institutions such as the public schools, industrial and commercial establishments, government departments, and voluntary associations. Some of these have systematic provision with required steps for advancement by means of short courses. An account of adult education training in Denmark in the mid-1970s noted that there were four main types: basic, leader training, training for remedial teaching, and training to teach in study groups; and that the training was decentralized, principally to private sponsors of leisure-time instruction, county councils, teacher associations, the Royal Danish College of Education, and the Directorate for Primary Schools, Adult and Youth Education, Teacher Training Colleges, etc.

4. Skill and Subject Areas

Content of educational and training programmes for adult educators varies greatly according to the situation, circumstances, and presumed needs of those being trained as well as the length of time available for training. University programmes may incline more towards academic and theoretical study or, rather, towards practical and technical skills and knowledge thought to equip the practitioner–teacher, and the resulting qualification may lean more to the academic or the professional side. Short courses tend to be concerned more with practical skills and insights than sequential academic study, although they may also provide opportunity for conceptual learning in a specified area. The emphasis in adult education circles upon integrating theory with practice, and upon relevance, however tends to give such work an applied character and focus. Some short programmes enrol groups or teams of adult educators from one agency, especially in the form of in-house training, and there may be an organizational change purpose as well as an objective of individual learning and enhanced competence. Because of the importance accorded to personality, attitudes, and values in much adult education, some of the training is mainly experiential and intended to foster personal growth and change.

The importance of values, qualities, and attitudes poses a problem for the training of adult educators, especially in the liberal tradition where there is more emphasis upon personal dialogue and interaction through discussion than in some technical skill training areas. It is acknowledged that the somewhat intangible qualities held to mark a good adult educator are difficult or impossible to teach. There is thus the dilemma that aspects of the professional role and identity most highly valued in this tradition are also thought to be little if at all amenable to teaching. A further difficulty is the acknowledged situation and context specificity of most adult educators' work, which means that short-course training, in particular, needs to be adapted to each unique or partly unique situation. This makes generalization and routinized teaching of adult educators unsatisfactory.

A third difficulty is that the learning needs of adult educators are often not clearly defined: general definitions in terms of role, such as administrator or teacher, encompass a wide range of the possible skills needed. Knox (1979) notes repeated efforts over the past two decades to identify important areas of proficiency which graduate programmes should seek to develop, and suggests that broader conceptualizations of "important practitioner proficiencies" could improve such programmes. "Although proficiencies are hard to specify, an understanding of their major areas can be used to select effective staff members, to focus self-directed study efforts, and to plan in-service educational activities for practitioners." Apps (1972) suggests four basic qualifications required of the future adult educator, whether a specialist in administration, method, subject matter, or professional teaching or research: have an understanding of his or her personal philosophy of education; be oriented to people; be oriented to problems; and be oriented to change.

Many other prescriptions and descriptions of learning needs and subject areas may be found. The UNESCO 1972 International Conference held that part-time adult educators must at least know something about adult learning and be able to identify with the people they serve, and that training should generally take place in the milieu in which they are to work. The International Council for Adult Education conference in 1976 in Tanzania indicated that training, especially at middle and higher levels, should include a sound knowledge of and experience in communication techniques, and should increase sensitivity to the problems of the less privileged. Literacy instructors should learn techniques of animation and participation, as well as evaluation, administration, and reporting skills. An account of the needs of Kenyan extension workers to the 1979 Commonwealth Conference on Nonformal Education referred to: understanding governmental policies and problems; understanding the local community; knowledge of the subject matter of agriculture; knowledge of other related and some rather distant subjects; and skills in communication, organization, needs analysis, leadership, and self-evaluation.

Other accounts and analyses refer more to subject areas than to required skills. Knox (1979) is among those who discern core proficiencies of all practitioners through analysis of previous studies; frequently mentioned are proficiencies related to educational goals for adults, adult development and learning, programme development procedures, and general agency functioning. "Specific procedures and terminology related to a specific type of agency or role... tend to vary greatly from situation to situation." Knox suggests that all categories of practitioner would benefit from three broad areas of proficiency: understanding the field of adult education, understanding adults as learners, and, in the affective domain, having "personal qualities such as positive attitudes to lifelong learning, effective interpersonal relations, and innovativeness". Administrators require additional competence in administration, programme development, and planning and using research; teachers and counsellors need knowledge about subject matter and adult development, and capability with programme development procedures, while policy makers must understand desirable directions for the agency's development.

Verner (1980) cites from Brunner eight categories of core knowledge of the discipline of adult education: adult learning; psychology of adults; instructional design; instructional management; instructional materials and equipment; the client system; the organizational system; and the social setting of adult education. Houle (1956) sets out six general objectives of most university programmes reflecting what are seen as the basic attributes of a good adult educator: "(a) a sound philosophic conception of adult education based on a consideration of its major aims and issues and embodying convictions concerning the basic values which it should seek to achieve; (b) an understanding of the psychological and social foundations on which all education (and particularly adult education) rests; (c) an understanding of the development, scope, and complexity of the specific agency or programme in which he works and the broad field of adult education...; (d) an ability to undertake and direct the basic processes of education: the refinement of objectives; the selection and use of methods and content; the training of leaders; the provision of guidance and counselling; the promotion of programmes; the coordination and supervision of activities, and the evaluation of results; (e) personal effectiveness and leadership in working with other individuals, with groups, and with the general public; and (f) a constant concern with the continuance of his own education throughout life."

Campbell (1977) frames the content of adult education as a field of study in a model comprising six elements: "the adult learner—the psychological context; the adult learner—the sociological context; adult education—the philosophical–historical context; adult education—methods and resources; adult education systems—organization and administration; adult education—provision to a particular clientele/environment." A somewhat different six-way classification was attempted by the participants in the 1980 UNESCO Asian regional seminar on adult education and development: methodology (i.e., concepts, principles, problem solving, skills, attitudes, and values); psychology of the adult learner; teaching skills and techniques; evaluation; sociology relevant to adult education; and development studies. These areas are seen as essential to any training programme, long- or short-term for full- or part-time teachers of adults, although the depth of study will vary. The Asian and South Pacific Bureau of Adult Education seminar in the same region in 1972 indicated seven areas as a course outline for regional training: history and philosophy, nature, scope and need; sociology of adult education; psychology of adult learning; principles of adult education administration; techniques, methods, processes, and practices, including evaluation; economics of developing countries; curriculum development and material preparation. The report also identified six specialist areas, and listed the knowledge, skills, and attitudes which training should develop in adult educators.

Different analyses of adult educators' professional learning needs, and of the programmes developed to meet them, show much commonality among both industrialized and developing countries, and lay much stress upon the process of teaching, even sometimes somewhat to the exclusion of the subject matter which the educator is to teach his or her adult students. Campbell (1977) states that "capability in the application of adult education methodology is no less important to the adult education teacher than is his expertise in his subject field". In the People's Republic of China the present emphasis, in circumstances of great demand for worker–peasant education and absence of formal teacher education of adult educators, is upon up-to-date knowledge of the subject matter to be taught; at the same time there is felt to be a need for the study of adult learning processes and appropriate methods of adult teaching.

5. Methods of Teaching the Educators of Adults

It is usual to stress the adult status of learners in adult teacher education, and the importance of congruity between how they are taught and what they are taught is the appropriate teaching methodology with other adults. "The principle of the sovereignty of the learner must be given priority" (UNESCO 1981). The International Council for Adult Education 1976 conference emphasized "the mutual exchange of experiences between the teacher and the 'taught' (in training) and the development of participatory methods and activities that teach learners how to participate in decision-making" (Hall and Kidd 1978). "Training for adult education must itself be consistent with adult education principles. Indeed, it ought to epitomize adult education at its best" (Campbell 1977). "Everything which is done in the name of adult education by the government training offices or by the non-government training institutes, should be a good example of adult education, and this applies to the training of adult educators . . ." (UNESCO 1981). The report adds that good results have been obtained through nonformal workshops where adult educators meet together, set their agendas, and rely on group interaction and discovery learning; "the facilitator or group leader in such a workshop" has a demanding role "but the knowledge of group dynamics and interpersonal communication which is needed for such work is a valuable field of study for anyone who sets out to train the trainers". A wide variety of methods is used to teach adult educators, including lectures, handbooks and manuals, correspondence or mass media courses, simulation, microlaboratory work, attachments and internships, and teaching practice, but discussion and other group work tends to play an especially prominent part.

Belief in the importance of participation in adult education also produces forms of training of personnel which emphasize participation. The Freedom from Hunger Campaign/Action for Development of the Food and Agricultural Organisation of the United Nations has sponsored regional change agents' training programmes in South and Southeast Asia led by Kamla Bhasin. Bhasin (1979) provides a nontechnical guide in the form of a report for field-based and applied training for development. She lists barriers which have been broken, fully or in part, by an approach which emphasizes direct learning and exchange of an in situ and experiential kind, with heavy reliance on dialogue, confrontation, and mutual teaching and learning. Barriers identified in more conventional training which are at least partly breached include: classroom–field; trainer–trainee; the barrier between desk-bound knowledge and one's own experience; barriers between theory and practice of concepts like shared authority, and participation; men–women; government–nongovernment; and barriers to exchange of experience between neighbouring countries.

The methodology for training personnel for the National Adult Education Programme in India derived directly from the objectives of the programme "which is radically different from all earlier attempts at mass adult education in India" (Directorate of Adult Education 1978). "The training programme itself is fundamentally a process of adult education and has to reflect the main characteristics of the methodology that the functionaries would have to follow while working with the learning groups at the grass-roots level." The first step is helping trainees towards self-knowledge or "value clarification", then to develop a "social eye" to understand the dynamics of the group or "small society" in which they themselves are learning. Nonauthoritarian values are to be understood and acquired through experience of the training programme, along with necessary knowledge and skills to teach within the National Adult Education Programme. The following features are identified for the training: it should be participatory; an opportunity for mutual learning; emphasize group discussion; allow learning to emerge out of experience; closely approximate the field and the realities; and be an experiment in community living. Typical methods of training are: activity-based methods including problem solving, project methods, and discussion; lecture, lecture–demonstration, and their links with discussion; individual learning; and combined methods, including residential (or camp) training, field operational seminars, and other forms of combining training with field work. Training is a continuous process starting with initial training to provide a "first-aid kit" and followed by inservice training. The handbook suggests several questions to help trainers teach the instructors, who are front-line workers in the National Adult Education Programme: What is the learning situation in which the instructor has to function? What is the background of the instructor? What is the instructor expected to do in this programme (followed by encouragement to explore eight components of the role)? What competencies (knowledge, skills, attitudes, and values) should the instructor develop for doing his work? What kind of training programme is necessary and how can it develop the skills and qualities desired?

6. *Trends and Issues*

6.1 *Adequacy of Provision*

Teaching of adult educators reflects many characteristics of adult education itself. The total amount of adult education activity is very large in many societies, and estimated to exceed the quantity of formal education, but it is not conceived and organized as a system. Much of it takes place in a dispersed manner and much is informal and ad hoc. A large amount of in-organization vocationally oriented training is excluded from many accounts of adult education and there is little knowledge of its scale and procedures in many countries. Preparation and inservice education of teachers for this diversity of adult education is similarly diverse, dispersed, and incompletely known and understood. There is wide agreement among adult education leaders in most countries that the preparation of adult educators, both the full-time teachers, administrators and other specialists, and the much larger number of voluntary and part-time workers, is inadequate.

Reviews of adult education and its teacher education, both scholarly studies and international conferences, largely agree in calling for much more massive and systematic training, including cooperation and rationalization between kinds of institutions and programmes. Despite severe reservations about the ability of universities to adapt their resources to the needs of adult educators' professional preparation, leading to some preference for distinct training and research centres, the commonest view is that universities have an essential part to play in teaching the leading members of the profession. North American studies of adult educator teaching plot the increase in number of university graduate programmes and doctoral graduates from the 1960s to the present time. A similar, somewhat later, expansion has occurred in the United Kingdom where, in 1970, only seven universities offered any kind of credit (certificate, diploma, or degree) programme. The fortunes of particular university adult education programmes in these and other countries have waxed and waned with the reputation and size of faculty, and there has been some contraction reflecting political and economic changes in the societies generally; overall the impression is one of "a growing stability" (Houle 1970) as consensus has increased about the core components and requirements of the field and (as it is claimed to be) discipline.

In planned economies and in many developing countries where priority is given to literacy and adult/nonformal education for development, more deliberate and systematic provision for teaching adult education is made both through universities and teachers' colleges and, in some countries, through special adult education institutes. In these countries there are generally fewer reservations about providing adult education as a strand or option in preservice education, especially of teachers, reflecting a tendency to treat adult or nonformal education more as part of the total national education system.

6.2 Priorities for Training

There is more agreement about the general inadequacy of teacher education for adult education than about where the priorities lie. This reflects the complex and dispersed nature of the profession and its work, as well as a reservation about professionalization. The Commonwealth conference on nonformal education in 1979 noted the importance of training for securing good training of senior personnel and teachers. However, "whereas 'training' in formal education is largely a matter for teachers or superiors, in nonformal education the scope has to be widened to include many more groups and individuals. Indeed it could be argued that the whole society needs to receive some kind of training to be aware of the contributions nonformal education can make to economic and social development" (Commonwealth Secretariat 1980). The conference listed as priority groups for training: "senior policy makers; specialists, such as doctors, nurses and other health workers, agriculturalists, veterinarians, and others working with community groups; all those working in a nonformal education capacity with community groups and organizations (e.g. agricultural extension workers and village-level workers); those who train the trainers of non-formal educators; curriculum developers and researchers engaged in non-formal education activities".

The difficulty in setting operational priorities is demonstrated by this list, which acknowledges the systemic character of adult/nonformal education when conceived as a means to development. The UNESCO International Conference in 1972 stressed the importance of part-time and voluntary teachers as "a democratically desirable practice", in considering the training of personnel, but also stressed the need for a much stronger full-time cadre. The word cadre has recently been used in a somewhat different sense in discussions in India about the key personnel for training; here the emphasis is upon local or village-level workers dedicated to adult education for development who are in touch with local communities rather than detached through academic education, yet equipped to play a vital leadership role. Australia is another country where there is now concern about the absence of adequate training for adult educators mingled with reservation about the utility of long academic accredited programmes thought likely to foster professional exclusiveness; consequently discussions tend to suggest that priority should be given to short courses, or part-time certificate programmes, for the army of part-time workers at the base of the pyramid. On the other hand scholars like Verner (1980) lay emphasis both upon developing the intellectual leadership of adult education and more firmly delineating its academic field and standing; Campbell (1977), noting that few in adult education agencies have qualifications appropriate to the training task, holds that "the principal initial thrust of training for adult education in Canada, as elsewhere, ought to be the development of a core of trained personnel within the ranks of full-time leadership".

The main question of priorities concerns who most urgently needs training: those at the base or the apex of the pyramid, or some other specialist groups or mix calculated to advance the teaching of adult education systemically. Other issues include the case for at least some preservice as well as postservice experience and inservice education, the respective contributions of local, national, and regional or international training opportunities, and the priority to be given to training compared with, for instance, research.

6.3 Professionalization and Mandatory Training

The drawback of professionalization of services generally, as analysed in the writing of Ivan Illich and others, is a major concern of many adult education teachers and policy makers who value a relationship of reciprocity and relative equality between teacher and adult learner. This produces a tension, since there is also concern about the low status and marginality of much adult education, one source of which is recognized to be the fragmentary, diffuse, and voluntaristic character of much of the work, and the lack of formal training and qualifications of adult education practitioners. Resistance to mandatory training and certification is widespread. It is frequently asserted that good adult educators are born (or matured by experience) rather than produced by formal training, and that many of the essential qualities and even skills are difficult or impossible to teach. Even at senior levels there is resistance to requiring formal qualifications in candidates for positions. On the other hand the increasing numbers of graduate programmes available especially in North America, and the access to these programmes of adult educators from Third World and other countries, is producing a widespread expectation approaching a requirement, for certain professional and administrative as well as academic positions, of having a higher degree in adult education.

Another trend is towards requiring all adult educators, part-time as well as full-time, to undertake training by means of periodic short courses, perhaps preservice as well as inservice. An Asian regional seminar on training adult educators (Dutta and Fischer 1972) called for at least two weeks of full-time preparatory training of part-time adult educators lacking basic teachers' training, and three months full-time in a teachers' college or special-purpose adult education institute for full-time workers, together with inservice training and guidance. A government proposal in Denmark in 1969 for a basic course for adult education teachers of 180 hours has been generally followed; the Workers' Educational Association has established its own 100 hour course instead. Although the Scandinavian countries generally provide orientation and inservice training for adult educators in different areas, from labour force training to leading study circles, mandatory training is not general. In the United Kingdom an advisory committee report proposing a three-stage plan for the training of part-time teachers of adults had the general support of the Advisory Council on Adult and Continuing Education (ACACE 1981). The first two stages would be taken by all newly appointed part-time teachers in further and adult education not already qualified as school teachers; "consideration was given to whether a shorter period of training might be suitable for those teaching only 2 or 3 hours a week, but it was agreed that the requirements of this group were basically the same as those with heavier teaching loads". These stages together require at least 36 plus 60 hours of course attendance and 30 hours of supervised teaching practice. "On the completion of stages I and II, part-time teachers should have the opportunity to undertake further inservice training leading to full certification, by means of stage III courses of some 300 hours and appropriate teaching practice."

6.4 General Teacher Education and Andragogy

There is ambivalence and controversy among adult educators about the extent to which teacher education for adult education should be integrated with or separated from general teacher education. Those who favour an integrated and lifelong system of educational provision, with formal and nonformal options at all stages, tend to favour integration of training also, and see a major role for teachers' colleges and faculties of education. Others argue that adult education, or andragogy, is a distinct field and discipline which needs to be kept somewhat apart from school-oriented teacher education and academic study. "Adult education is involved with learning in a wide social milieu; it represents a broader conception of education than that of schooling. It deals with education in diverse forms scarcely recognizable to those whose perceptions are limited to institutionalized patterns and structures; consequently, traditional teacher education programmes now conducted by teachers' colleges cannot prepare professional leaders for adult education. Teachers' colleges are geared to training teachers of children. . ." (Verner 1980). In New Zealand, Verner considered, "enthusiasm for lifelong education is in danger of masking crucial differences between pre-adult and adult education which have critical implications for the training of adult educators". Knox (1979) is among many authors who note that the preparatory education experienced by school teachers may be inappropriate to working with adults. In the People's Republic of China, by contrast, worker–peasant education is conceived as part of the "formal" system of education, and as providing alternative modes for the acquisition of knowledge, skills, and qualifications: the different circumstances and learning needs of adults with family and working responsibilities are acknowledged, but there is not a separate methodology and andragogy requiring separate teacher training; the emphasis is mainly upon keeping up to date in the subject matter to be taught.

While many adult educators are resistant to merging training with general teacher education and fear loss of distinctive identity and methodology, analyses of the whole education system from a perspective of lifelong education suggest that the values and approaches distinctive of adult education may be carried across in part to influence formal teacher education. This was suggested in the report of the UNESCO Faure Commission, *Learning to Be* in 1972, and in a more recent consideration of the implications of lifelong education for the training of teachers by Cropley and Dave (1978). Although teacher education for adult education is not addressed directly, analysis of cumulative changes in the system of teacher education in several countries suggests that much of the philosophy and methodology of adult education is being adapted and assimilated piecemeal. This may indicate more transaction between school-oriented and adult teacher education in the future, a tendency likely to be encouraged by demographic changes in many countries which may release regular educational resources for adult education. It is likely however that the study and teaching of adult education will continue to sustain a separate identity and some separate institutional bases for training.

Bibliography

Advisory Committee for Adult and Continuing Education 1981 *Specialist Training for Part-time Teachers of Adults.* Advisory Council for Adult and Continuing Education, Leicester

Apps J W 1972 Tomorrow's adult educator—some thoughts and questions. *Adult Educ.* (U.S.A.) 22: 218–26

Asian and South Pacific Bureau of Adult Education (ASPBAE) 1979 *Training Symposium. Courier 15.* ASPBAE, Canberra

Asian and South Pacific Bureau of Adult Education (ASPBAE) 1985 *Report of the International Workshop on the Training and Accreditation of Adult Educators (Macao).* ASPBAE. Canberra

Bhasin K 1979 *Breaking Barriers: A South Asian Experience of Training for Participatory Development.* FFHC/AD, Food and Agricultural Organisation of the United Nations, Bangkok

Campbell D D 1977 *Adult Education as a Field of Study and Practice.* University of British Columbia/ICAE, Vancouver

Cropley A J, Dave R H 1978 *Lifelong Education and the Training of Teachers.* Advances in Lifelong Education, Vol. 5. Pergamon Press, Oxford

Commonwealth Secretariat 1980 *Participation, Learning and Change: Commonwealth Approaches to Nonformal Education.* Commonwealth Secretariat, London

Directorate of Adult Education 1978 *Training of Adult Education Functionaries: A Handbook.* Directorate of Adult Education, New Delhi

Dutta S C, Fischer H J (eds.) 1972 *Training of Adult Educators.* Shakuntala, Bombay

Elsdon K T 1975 *Training for Adult Education.* Nottingham Studies in the Theory and Practice of Education of Adults, Vol. 1. University of Nottingham, Nottingham

European Bureau of Adult Education 1980 *Training for Part-time Adult Educators and Volunteers: Newsletter.* European Bureau of Adult Education, Amersfoort

Hall B L, Kidd J R (eds.) 1978 *Adult Learning: A Design for Action.* Pergamon Press, Oxford

Houle C O 1956 Professional education for educators of adults. In: Houle C O (ed.) 1956 *Professional Preparation of Adult Educators: A Symposium.* Center for the Study of Liberal Education for Adults, Chicago, Illinois

Houle C O 1970 The educators of adults. In: Smith R M, Aker G F, Kidd J R (eds.) 1970 *Handbook of Adult Education.* Macmillan, New York

Knights S M, Peace B W 1981 Training adult educators. *Aust. J. Adult Educ.* 21 (1): 19–25

Knowles M S 1970 *The Modern Practice of Adult Education: Andragogy versus Pedagogy.* Association Press, New York

Knox A B (ed.) 1979 *Enhancing Proficiencies of Continuing Educators.* Jossey-Bass, San Francisco, California

UNESCO 1972 *Final Report: Third International Conference on Adult Education.* UNESCO, Paris

UNESCO 1976 *Recommendation on the Development of Adult Education.* UNESCO, Paris

UNESCO 1981 *Prospects for Adult Education and Development in Asia and the Pacific.* UNESCO, Bangkok

Verner C 1980 Academic education about adult education. In: Boshier R (ed.) 1980 *Towards a Learning Society.* Learning Press, Vancouver

Continuing Education of the Business Executive

G. F. Aker

The continuing education of business executives refers to the participation of managerial personnel in adult or recurrent education designed to enhance their professional proficiencies. The term business executive includes persons in private, public, and voluntary organizations. They have responsibility for developing and implementing policy and managing organizational resources, such as environmental, human, and fiscal. Their responsibilities range from those of department heads of small agencies to those of chief executive officers of large multinational organizations. Access to the rapidly expanding literature on this topic is most readily achieved by using the descriptors of management training and organizational development.

1. Scope, Proliferation, and Expansion

The number of programs and participants in this area has increased rapidly on a worldwide scale since the early 1970s. In 1981, approximately 160,000 business executives in the United States participated in the continuing education programs of the American Management Association alone. Many more were involved in the executive development programs of a host of other agencies.

Programs relating to the development of executives are a post-Second World War phenomenon in both North America and Europe. Since 1955 they have spread throughout the industrial world. Since the early 1970s the developing nations have experienced a significant growth in the number and types of educational programs for business executives. No longer do the more highly developed, technological societies have a monopoly on innovations in this expanding area.

An examination of the international literature reveals differences in program emphasis and methodology depending upon the stage of technological development, urbanization, political system, and sociocultural background. However, the similarities between countries and regions of the world (in terms of program content, instructional methods and techniques, and the procedures followed in planning and designing) are much greater than are any of the differences. Innovations in one country quickly spread to the others as was the case in sensitivity training and quality circles.

Several interdependent forces help explain the rapid expansion and proliferation of continuing education for executives. First, there are those factors which make continuing education increasingly important in all professions and technologies. Firstly, the accelerating rate of economic, social, technological, scientific, and ecological change gives rise to professional and technological obsolescence. Second is the fact that most executives were not prepared in the field of management during their formal and preservice education. More likely than not, today's business executives prepared for careers in engineering, marketing, production, research, accounting, sales, or legal services and were promoted into management and executive roles. It is through continuing education that such people learn the theory, practice, and skills of their new craft.

The third factor is the accelerating development of the theory and knowledge of management itself. This base draws heavily upon a wide array of old and new disciplines in the social sciences and new interdisciplinary fields of theory and research. Fourth, continuing education itself has become professionalized through national and international associations, university preparation programs, and a multitude of private training organizations. And fifth, as organizations of many kinds increase in number, so do the numbers of executives who service them. Little wonder, then, that the continuing education of executives is one of the fastest growing areas in the educational spectrum.

To help meet the increasing demand for executive development, there has evolved a worldwide cooperative network of management associations, international development organizations, institutions of higher education, and numerous other providers of continuing education. Information is shared at national and international conferences and by computers through international data banks.

2. Modes of Continuing Education

The most frequently observed modes of continuing education take the form of workshops, seminars, short courses, and clinics. Such programs can be in-house, where the employing agency makes continuing education available through its own staff or by importing outside consultants or trainers; or they can be arranged through programs conducted outside the agency. The leading providers of this type of continuing education include professional associations, colleges and universities, national development centers, and an increasing number of private training firms. Within this framework, the education can be formal or nonformal, residential or nonresidential, and range in time from less than a day to several years of part-time study. Typically, such programs use the format of a conference, make extensive use of participation techniques, and provide limited pre- and post-conference learning activities.

A second and less obvious mode of continuing education for business executives is that of planned, self-directed learning. There is some evidence that nearly all executives employ this activity as a major part of their lifelong learning program. It is also believed, though not documented by research, that the higher up a business executive is in the organizational hierarchy, the more likely it is that self-directed learning (alone or in small autonomous groups) becomes their dominant and preferred method of continuing education. Houle (1980) has made an elaborate study of such learning in several professions. Obviously, there are some forms of continuing education which fall between that of pursuing self-education and that of participating in education designed and conducted by an agency. A frequent example is the use of a mentor or tutor: a highly experienced officer in the organization assumes responsibility for facilitating the development of a junior member. This is sometimes accomplished by the careful assignment of job opportunities, each leading to a progressively higher level of complexity and responsibility. The tutor serves as a role model and, through a continuing dialog provides a critical analysis of experience.

3. The Content of Continuing Education for Executives

The content of executive training falls within two broad categories: content related to the needs of the organization, and content related to the needs of the individual. In the former, programs focus on problems and needs within the organization, such as the need to increase sales, reduce employee turnover, raise morale, develop new products, or improve quality control. In the latter, programs are of two general kinds: those which are designed to improve the function of the individual in the organization, and those which are designed to improve specific abilities within the individual.

Some educational programs aim to improve both the organization and the individual. Examples are those which emphasize general managerial theory or organizational renewal, matrix management, team building, and management by objectives.

Frequently programs are designed for special groups such as women in management, junior executives, or executives approaching retirement. Some programs focus on the special problems of an entire industrial sector; others are aimed at the achievement of national or international goals.

A particular area of content which is gaining attention in the literature relates to the role of the executive as trainer or facilitator of learning. In this field the executive is viewed as one who has a major responsibility in seeing that others have access to needed information and that they have or acquire the skills needed to effectively analyze, assimilate, and take appropriate actions. In the final analysis the executive becomes a trainer of trainers, making certain that the individuals within the organization develop and maintain the knowledge, skills, and sensitivities required to achieve the purposes and goals of the organization (Luke 1981).

4. Methods and Techniques of Continuing Education

Group processes which encourage participatory learning, sharing of experience, attitudinal change, and problem solving dominate in the continuing education of business executives. These include the techniques of role play, buzz sessions, gaming, brainstorming, panels, video feedback, simulation, and case studies. Such techniques are frequently supported and enriched with a wide variety of audio-visual materials. Printed handouts, illustrated talks, and minilectures are also common features in many executive development programs. Trainers and consultants are often leaders in their own areas of expertise and many are exceptionally well-qualified in the dynamics of adult learning.

5. Research on Continuing Education of Executives

Since the early 1970s there has been an acceleration in research activity into the psychological, sociological, and cultural forces which facilitate or interfere with adult life-cycle development and learning. The theoretical and research-based knowledge generated by this flurry of activity is analyzed and synthesized in the recent works of Knox (1977), Cross (1981), and Kidd (1973). Similarly, considerable research has been undertaken to improve the processes of program development and instructional design in adult/continuing education. The highlights of this research have been incorporated into the writings of Knowles (1980), Peters et al. (1980), and Apps (1979). While much of this research has implications for the continuing education of executives, it should be noted that the focus has not been on executive development per se.

A relatively sparse, yet identifiable, body of knowledge about executive development via continuing education is beginning to appear. Much of this research is descriptive, using data obtained from surveys and observations. Such studies provide the basis for estimates of the numbers and demographic characteristics of executives involved in continuing education, educational formats most frequently employed, costs of training, numbers and types of agencies providing training, and on occasion, the extent that desired educational outcomes are achieved. There is also an expansion in efforts to identify competencies most needed for proficient executive performance and in research to determine the relative advantages of different models of educational needs assessment. Unfortunately, studies of the more sophisticated programs of executive development are frequently not reported in the literature because of the competitive positions of many industrial and training organizations. The essence of the knowledge that has been made public is summarized in the writing of Nadler (1980) and Stern (1983).

While much of the research underway lacks a theoretical base and rigorous design or controls, investigators have recently turned their attention to the impact of innovative training approaches developed at university centers for executive development such as those at Harvard, Stanford, and the University of Michigan. Frequently such innovations are grounded in the theoretical development and research into the phenomena of motivation as conceptualized by David McClelland, Abraham Maslow, and Fredrick Herzberg.

Numerous contemporary continuing education programs for executives are designed to overcome specific problems which have been identified by social science researchers, that is "burnout," alienation, need for change, depression, and similar manifestations of psycho or social dysfunctioning. Trainers and continuing educators are quick to offer programs designed to remedy such conditions—through clinics or workshops on value clarification, sensitivity training, career enhancement, and so on, yet the processes used in such programs are rarely researched as to their efficacy in achieving desired change.

Curiously, research into fundamental problems and issues in the continuing education of executives is conspicuous by its absence in the literature of management, human resource development, and continuing education. This is not because the problems of executive development are purposefully ignored by researchers in adult/continuing education, rather, it is that to date researchers have not focused their attention on this rapidly expanding area of continuing education.

6. Suggestions for Future Research

Much remains to be done through research to improve the effectiveness of needs assessment, instructional resources, learning techniques, and evaluation procedures in the continuing education of executives. Descriptive research is needed to determine the quantitative dimensions of executive development. Most of what goes on is not systematically recorded or reported. Qualitative research is needed to assess the benefits of such education to the individual participants, to their organizations, and to society. Precise answers to the questions of who participates, where, when, why, how often, and with what effect are still be to found. Basic research into the relationships which may exist between characteristics of the participant and the format of continuing education has yet, in the main, to be undertaken.

Although still dominated by the ideology of the industrial society, innovative programs in executive development are emerging to facilitate effective transitions into the post-industrial society (Golembiewski et al. 1975).

Bibliography

Apps J W 1979 *Problems in Continuing Education.* McGraw-Hill, New York

Cross K P 1981 *Adults as Learners.* Jossey-Bass, San Francisco, California
Golembiewski R T, Gibson F, Miller G (eds.) 1975 *Managerial Behavior and Organization Demands: Management as a Linking of Levels of Interaction.* Peacock, Itasca, Illinois
Houle C O 1980 *Continuing Learning in the Professions.* Jossey-Bass, San Francisco, California
Kidd J R 1973 *How Adults Learn,* rev. edn. Follett, Chicago, Illinois
Knowles M S 1980 *The Modern Practice of Adult Education: From Pedagogy to Andragogy.* Follett, Chicago, Illinois
Knox A B 1977 *Adult Development and Learning.* Jossey-Bass, San Francisco, California
Luke R A 1981 Managers as learners. *Training Dev. J.* 35(8):24–30
Nadler L 1979 *Developing Human Resources: Learning Concepts.* Gulf, Austin, Texas
Nadler L 1980 Human resource development for managers. In: Boone E J, Shearon R W, White E E et al. (eds.) 1980 *Serving Personal and Community Needs Through Adult Education.* Jossey-Bass, San Francisco, California
Peters J M et al. 1980 *Building an Effective Adult Education Enterprise.* Jossey-Bass, San Francisco, California
Stern M R 1983 *Power and Conflict in Continuing Professional Education.* Wadsworth, Belmont, California
Taylor B, Lippitt G L (eds.) 1975 *Management Development and Training Handbook.* McGraw-Hill, London

Continuing Education of the Professional

A. B. Knox and J. A. B. McLeish

Freedom and responsibility are major issues that confront members of professional occupations. Professionals enjoy substantial freedom to practice their skills based on complex knowledge, within guidelines established by their profession and without undue interference by the general public. They should also accept responsibility for standards of professional performance throughout their careers.

People outside each profession also have a stake in the quality of professional performance, because they are greatly affected by the decisions made by professionals. Such decisions reflect, among other things, traditions, state-of-the-art, guidelines for practice within each nation, and the interest some people have in influencing the quality and distribution of professional practice. Mostly such decisions reflect the individual and collective outlook of members of the profession regarding professional roles, standards of achievable best practice, and career-long learning which comes under the heading of continuing professional education. This phrase refers to all types of self directed and externally provided activities which professionals use to enhance their proficiencies and enrich their careers.

"Continuing professional education" is a recent phrase. Earlier, such concern as existed in the professions for the education of graduate practitioners took the form usually of providing "refresher" or informative lectures at one- or two-day annual meetings of professional societies, regional and national. An advantage of these professional meetings was the opportunity they provided for practitioners to exchange experiences and possibly learn of new professional approaches or resources for problem solving from distant colleagues more advantageously placed.

Often, however, the topics taken up might have been of little relevance or interest to many of those attending, and even when they were, no provision existed for ongoing inquiry and study of the subject.

These difficulties were partly met by the development of the practice within many professional faculties of providing short-term courses on campus for practitioners, usually at times such as summer term when the professional person might be, or could arrange to be, free for at least a week of "professional improvement." Teaching was done either by faculty staff or by professional colleagues especially equipped and distinguished in a speciality area.

This arrangement was often reached through cooperation between the university and the professional society, and had a number of advantages over the professional meeting as a resource for further education of the professional. Although also a brief and usually annual experience, it was wholly devoted to the study and discussion of certain professional topics; the leaders of the seminar or workshop were usually continuously available for the period; ample library and laboratory resources were immediately at hand; and the practitioner often coming in from a demanding practice or professional responsibility was able, even though briefly, to re-establish contact with research, creative theory, and developing techniques in his or her own field.

In certain professions, for example teaching and social work, an attempt was made to extend this method by requiring practitioners to attend full summer or evening and Saturday winter courses at university or professional college if they wished to maintain or advance professional accreditation. Although this arrangement undoubtedly has helped stimulate professional improvement, it has done nothing to ensure that the field practitioner would continue his or her professional and personal upgrading once this goal had been attained.

There have also been drawbacks to the short on-campus seminar or workshop experience described earlier. Although enrollment has been voluntary, great numbers of practitioners particularly in entrepreneurial professions like medicine, dentistry, veterinary medicine, and law, have felt unwilling or unable to take extended time out from busy practices. This has often been true of those who stood in greatest need of the experience: practitioners in small, sometimes isolated communities and rural areas. Again, even if excellent in themselves, the on-campus seminar curricula were usually chosen by faculty people who, in their zeal to present some of the newest developments in their speciality, might overlook the actual needs of the practitioners temporarily enrolled as their students. Even when the practitioner returned to his or her professional arena with fresh insights and enthusiasm, he or she might well look upon the campus experience as an annual period of renewal, and become wholly engulfed again in daily routines, rather than acquire the philosophy and the skills of continuing professional education.

1. Characteristics of Professionalization

Since its beginnings, however, continuing professional education has made significant strides. Most of the work to identify needs, purposes, scope, and issues in this field has been done in the United States, a situation which is reflected in this article. Despite national differences in the context and practices of a profession, the basic questions to be answered appear, however, to be similar in most technologically advanced countries. In the developing world the problems may be different in both kind and degree.

Occupations vary in the extent of their potential professionalization. Houle (1980) studied 17 occupations which in the United States, and probably in many industrialized nations, have been most concerned with professionalization. The workers in these occupations were: accountants, architects, clergy, dentists, engineers, foresters, health care administrators, lawyers, librarians, military officers, nurses, pharmacists, physicians and surgeons, school administrators, school teachers, social workers, and veterinarians. Although each occupation has distinctive features to which continuing professional education should be adapted, Houle found some widespread characteristics of professionalization which constitute common goals, some typical providers of continuing learning opportunities, and some generally accepted ways of addressing program-development practices and policy issues.

Houle (1980) identified 14 characteristics of the professionalization process, all of which support goals for continuing learning. They are: clarification of the defining functions of the occupation, mastery of theoretical knowledge, capacity to solve problems, use of practical knowledge, self-enhancement beyond the speciality to maintain perspective, formal education in the essential knowledge and techniques, credentialing or other designation of those qualified to practice, creation of a professional subculture, legal reinforcement of professional privileges, public acceptance of a distinctive role, ethical practices and procedures for dealing with ethical issues, penalties for substandard performance, relations to other occupations, and relations to users of service.

These characteristics of professionalization in each occupation constitute goals for the continuum of preparatory and continuing professional education, and even relate to other aspects of lifelong learning. Continuing professional education includes all ways in which professionals enhance their proficiencies related to these characteristics, as well as to their individual and collective efforts to specify standards of practice related to these characteristics. It thus includes both mastery of procedures important to professional practice, and consideration of the goals and standards toward which to strive.

2. Career Development

The purpose of continuing professional education is improvement of occupational proficiencies and enhancement of career development. Although education is only one of many influences it can be a major influence, especially if relationships between knowledge and action are addressed. This may begin in general education and preservice preparatory professional education, if lifelong learning is emphasized, and if students have early associations with members of their profession to gain a sense of what actually happens in practice (Houle 1980). Examples include clinical practice in the health professions, lawyering for attorneys, and working with recipients of service in the helping professions generally.

For continuing education to benefit career development it is desirable for its providers to understand the dynamics of the process generally, and especially in their own professional field. In addition to the trends and issues that influence current career development in each field, there are widespread dynamics of career development that affect the occupational life cycle of most professionals (Knox 1977).

The essence of professional practice in most fields is decision making and problem solving. Professional practitioners encounter people to help or problems to solve, many of which are unique or distinctive. To take effective action entails attention both to specifics in each instance and to the application of general concepts and knowledge to the specific situation. A major contribution of continuing education is to help individual practitioners strengthen their strategies for alternating between action problems in professional practice and knowledge resources that can enrich practice. This process is influenced by the setting in which a practitioner works. Houle (1980) makes distinctions among entrepreneurial, collective, hierarchical, adjunct, and facilitative settings. Five elements are reflected in the most comprehensive rationales for relating continuing education to career development (Houle 1980, Suter et al. 1981). The elements are individual practitioner, occupational role and task, occupational setting, educational activities, and continuing education providers.

During a professional career there are many aspects of stability and change. Stability and continuity reflect personal values and other enduring personality characteristics, habit and inertia, enduring features of the professional role, and societal expectations and stereotypes.

Change and growth reflect general developmental trends during adulthood, obsolescence reflecting both new knowledge and new expectations, major change events, and shifting aspirations (Knox 1977).

The primary responsibility for the quality of professional performance rests with the individual practitioner, but others can help. The same point applies to continuing education. Self-directed learning is the core of continuing professional education, and is supplemented by more formal and public learning activities provided by associations, higher education institutions, employers, and other providers.

The heavy emphasis of some continuing professional education activities on keeping up to date, remedying deficiencies, and combating obsolescence seems unnecessarily negative and remedial. In addition to restricting offerings, this remedial emphasis may brand participants as substandard. In contrast, and more desirable, is the developmental emphasis with its attention to personal excellence and self-renewal, as well as to addressing issues important to the entire profession and its relation to the larger society. Included in this more positive, developmental approach is attention to reasoning, problem solving, aspirations (Argyris 1982), and to career changes (Aslanian and Brickell 1980, Hill et al. 1981).

Although a central concern of continuing professional education is improvement of performance of individual practitioners, the connection between education and performance has not been well established. Even if practitioners act on what they learn, other people can influence the ultimate results. For example, in the helping professions, recipients of service may not take professional advice. In organizational settings, supervisors and others may nullify practitioners' efforts to change. Also, some continuing professional education is for practitioners preparing for a career advancement or change, so that what they learn cannot be applied to practice at that time.

Thus, the concept of proficiency (the capability to perform effectively if given the opportunity) provides a useful bridge between knowledge and action. Most professional proficiencies depend on some combination of knowledge, attitudes, and skills. Concepts related to proficiency have many uses for practitioners (regarding self-directed learning) and for those who help them learn (Knowles 1980). A person with a strong sense of proficiency or competence is more willing to take risks and accept change. A practitioner's awareness of discrepancies between current and desired proficiencies contributes to his or her motivation to learn, the specification of educational needs, the selection of relevant learning activities, and the evaluation of progress. Providers of continuing professional education programs can use information about proficiencies to guide program development decisions so that educational activities emerge from and have an impact on performance (Knox et al. 1980). Also, for mastering a procedure that can be hazardous (such as for a surgeon, pilot, or power plant operator), specification of crucial proficiencies facilitates use of simulation activities to learn without the high risks that can be associated with actual performance settings.

The limited connection between education and performance is a major reason why it is so unproductive to require all members to devote at least a minimum number of hours each year to continuing education participation, in order to protect the public against substandard performance by some members. Some professions have recognized that it is more defensible to monitor the quality of actual performance.

3. Continuing Education Providers

In most professional fields, continuing education activities are conducted by three major types of providers: higher education institutions, professional associations, and employers. Each type of provider can make a distinctive contribution: higher education institutions for multidisciplinary perspectives, associations for standards, employers for application. There are some noteworthy instances of collaboration, especially by two types of providers (such as a medical school and a community hospital, or a social work school and an association) in which complementary contributions combined with shared purposes and benefits encourage continued cooperation.

Distinctive traditions and issues in each field influence not only relations among providers, but also attention to standards and program development. As a result, effective providers of continuing education in each field benefit from widespread concepts and practices in continuing education generally but they also select and adapt to specific circumstances related to the field and provider agency (Le Breton et al. 1979).

For example, providers of continuing medical education have available more professional literature on procedures for planning and conducting continuing education for physicians and surgeons than do providers in other professional fields (Houle 1980). Inexperienced providers have available overviews of continuing education trends, issues, and widespread practices as part of their orientation. Related attention to professional problem solving, practice profiles, and practice-oriented records enables practitioners to relate educational activities to their professional practice. Standards of clinical practice are assumed to be widely accepted.

By contrast, some other professional fields (such as pharmacy) have conducted studies to specify major areas of proficiency. In some fields (such as the religious ministry), there has been much consideration for multiple roles and tasks, but the implications for continuing education tend to be overwhelming. In some fields (such as law), what is taught in professional school contrasts so much with actual occupational tasks performed by practitioners that there is little continuity of methods, content, or instructors between preparatory and continuing professional education.

In most fields, the extent and type of continuing education available depends in part on organizational arrangements for the person or office that coordinates it on behalf of the association, employer, or higher education institution. In professional associations, paid staff members and members of a continuing education committee or program committee decide on and help plan continuing education activities for interested members, which are conducted by members and by outside specialists. Many organizations with more than a few hundred employees have employee education and development departments that coordinate inservice education activities for staff members in professional occupations (Craig 1976). Higher education institutions, and especially professional schools, have offices for continuing education that help faculty members and outside experts conduct continuing education activities.

University continuing professional education offices vary greatly in size and vitality (Knox 1980b, 1982b). The greatest source of vitality for such offices is the educational leadership of the director and perhaps a few associates, as reflected in the attention given to relations with both the school and the clientele, in a sense of direction regarding the types of continuing education activities especially responsive to concerns of members and to issues in the field, in obtaining support for new ventures, and in active involvement by practitioners.

4. Program Development

The core of continuing professional education is the program development procedures used to plan and conduct educational activities for practitioners. Many people who conduct or coordinate continuing professional education activities are unfamiliar with concepts and practices from other providers, and therefore evolve their own strategies. Thus, there are many useful but little used ideas that could enrich decision making by providers.

Most program development decisions can be grouped into one of five interrelated categories of program development. They are (a) analysis of purposes, resources, and barriers in the agency and work setting that have implications for each continuing education program; (b) assessment of educational needs of potential participants, to increase relevance and participation; (c) selection of educational objectives that have high priority for both participants and resource persons; (d) selection and organization of learning activities that fit both objectives and participants; and (e) databased evaluative judgments of the worth and effectiveness of program aspects, conducted so as to encourage use of findings for program planning, improvement, and justification.

These categories can guide self-directed learning activities by individual practitioners as well as programs conducted in individual (coaching, distance learning), temporary group (workshop, study group), or organizational (team building) settings (Houle 1972, Houle 1980, Knowles 1980, Knox et al. 1980).

When application to professional problem solving is important, activities such as simulation or analysis of a videotaped record of performance can be usefully included when developing a program. In addition to achievement of established objectives, it is sometimes desirable to include attention to assumptions, values, and implications associated with the educational objectives (Argyris 1982).

5. Methods and Programs

New methods and programs have developed especially since the 1960s, some of which are listed below.

In the United States in continuing medical education a specific regional area is defined, and hospitals and practitioners within that area are asked to identify significant local problems. Following this, in a two-way action, faculty of the involved educational institution and other experts visit the region for study, returning to use the rich resources of the campus in organizing seminars and workshops, to be held at convenient times, to discuss the identified problems. Much of the value of this model, also used successfully in theological education, lies in the organization of strong local radial centers, enrichment of local resources, and some organization by local practitioners on a rotated basis to aid the needed careful coordination with the participating university or college and professional society. Evaluation of the various components of such a campus–field continuing professional education arena is continual, with adjustments being made as needed.

It is important for professional education to take into account the special needs of field practitioners. But how are those needs to be identified when professional people, busy in active practice, do not themselves always recognize them?

One interesting strategy, again from a medical science, is to make available to practitioners in the discipline, test centers where they may check their current knowledge annually against the many recent and valuable developments useful to field professionals. The results of the test are made available only to the individual practitioner who, it is hoped, will be motivated to upgrade his or her knowledge and skills in deficient areas. This strategy also helps to minimize the exhausting and professionally dangerous assumption of many practitioners that they are expected to be omniscient.

Although such methods and programs help provide important feedback to organizers of continuing education projects, and also to the practitioners themselves, the need to foster self-directed learning for professional field people still remains. Here the advantages of audio and video technology in contemporary society have been usefully harnessed. Thus, in legal continuing education, an important American institute makes available to several thousand subscribing lawyers across the country audiotapes and videotapes of seminars and workshops. These can be used either in groups or individually at distant points.

An important development in medical education is the setting up of diagnosis and treatment support centers for reference by field practitioners. Through the use of a telephone network and ultimately by computer, physicians and other medical science professionals can use these centers for more efficient practice, and also for their continual professional learning. This resource will be enormously amplified as the television medium delivers to communities and homes many channels for individual or "solo" learning.

6. *Provider Assistance*

Most practitioners have available many continuing professional education opportunities from various providers such as professional associations, higher education institutions, employers, and private consulting firms. Some providers have greater vitality than others, as evidenced by innovative and effective learning activities and usually expanding enrollments. The most vital offices that provide continuing professional education typically have one or several people who provide effective educational leadership (Knox 1980b, 1982b). But many continuing professional education offices are directed by people who are unaware of many of the concepts and procedures on which those who direct these innovative offices depend. Thus, one way to raise the effectiveness and impact of continuing education is through the continuing education of the providers.

In recent years, guidelines have been prepared to help those who plan, conduct, and coordinate continuing professional education programs to enhance their proficiencies. In most professional fields, informal associations have been formed of people who coordinate continuing professional education programs. In the United States, some national associations of continuing education administrators (such as the National University Continuing Education Association, and the American Association for Adult and Continuing Education) have had divisions concerned with continuing professional education. Many university graduate programs that prepare continuing education practitioners offer courses and workshops on continuing professional education. These organizations can use such guidelines to help continuing professional education providers strengthen their efforts.

Some broad areas of proficiency are important for most continuing education providers. Included are an understanding of adult development and learning, program development (setting, needs, objectives, activities, evaluation), and program administration (participation, marketing, staffing, resources, leadership). Understanding the concepts and procedures that other providers have found useful can enable inexperienced providers to enhance their proficiencies and strengthen the educational programs they provide to members of the profession (Knox 1979, Knox 1980a, Knox et al. 1980, Strother and Klus 1982).

The 14 characteristics of professionalization already mentioned provide a comprehensive set of goals for professional development. A major task of providers is to work with the experts and resource persons who conduct courses and workshops, to assist them to increase their effectiveness in achieving those goals (Knox 1980a). In their administrative roles, coordinators of continuing professional education can strengthen their leadership strategies generally (Knox 1982a) and especially increase organizational support for their efforts (Lindquist 1978, Votruba 1981).

Within many professional fields, standards have been prepared to judge the quality of continuing education programs and providers, with special attention being paid to distinctive features and issues. For example, guidelines have been prepared for the health professions—nursing, medicine, pharmacy, and the helping professions—social work, librarianship, and school teaching (Suter et al. 1981, Ferver 1981).

7. *Policy Issues*

Various issues for practice, policy, and research in continuing professional education recur across fields. Six issues are likely to be important for continuing education in most professions. The first is the relation between continuing education and professional practice. Specification of essential proficiencies and problem solving in each profession can be used to increase the relevance of continuing education (Argyris 1982). Effective needs assessment procedures can identify discrepancies between current and desired proficiencies on which to focus continuing education activities (Pennington 1980). Assessing the impact of continuing professional education can indicate the extent to which it results in improved performance.

The second is the connection between continuing education and recredentialing. Well-designed education activities can have a substantial impact on professional practice. However, requiring that all members of a profession devote at least a minimum number of hours each year to continuing education activities is no guarantee against substandard performance by a small minority of the profession. Mandatory continuing education as a requirement for periodic recredentialing therefore seems to occur because it is less objectionable than challenge exams or peer review. It seems preferable for each profession to monitor substandard performance directly, and to use continuing education to help all members enhance their proficiencies regardless of level of speciality.

The third issue is the use of continuing education to optimize practitioner productivity and satisfaction at each stage of the career cycle. Practitioners' performance, satisfactions, and aspirations evolve as they enter a profession, shift assignments or specialities, and deal with major career changes especially related to mid-career and retirement. The contribution of continuing education, considering practitioners, their work settings, and the people they serve, has to be assessed (Craig 1976, Schein 1978).

Fourth is attention to serving hard-to-reach members of the profession. Continuing professional education programs in each field serve only a portion of the membership, and the least able are under-represented. However, the innovators and early adopters in each field tend to look to different sources of new ideas more often than the majority of members, and certainly the laggards. Providers of continuing education in each field can decide on the portion of their effort they will devote to serving hard-to-reach members, and there are concepts and procedures from program development and marketing that can be useful (Darkenwald and Larson 1980).

Fifth is collaborative relationships among continuing education providers in various fields. There are notable examples of continuing education activities that serve practitioners from several fields, such as hospital inservice programs for nurses and allied health practitioners, tax law conferences for attorneys and accountants, and workshops on helping relationships for social workers and clergy. It would be very desirable for more extensive multiprofessional continuing education activities to address relations among professional fields as well as topics of joint interest.

The sixth issue is the strengthening of offices that provide continuing professional education on behalf of educational institutions, employers, and associations. Fluctuations in enrollments, financial support, contributions by resource persons, and relations with practitioners and the parent organization contribute to instability of such offices. Leadership by the director is a major source of stability and continuity. Statements on major proficiencies of and guidelines for continuing education providers are helpful.

Continuing professional education is of great and growing importance to members of professions and to the larger society. Leadership by those who coordinate continuing education offices of higher education institutions, professional associations, and employers of professionals, is important to the vitality of such efforts. The foregoing concepts and procedures can contribute to the vitality of such efforts. It is also important that such leaders have a sense of direction so that the effort serves both the profession and the larger society.

See also: Mandatory Continuing Education

Bibliography

Argyris C 1982 *Reasoning, Learning and Action: Individual and Organizational*. Jossey-Bass, San Francisco, California

Aslanian C B, Brickell H M 1980 *Americans in Transition: Life Changes as Reasons for Adult Learning*. College Entrance Examination Board, New York

Cervero R M, Scanlan C L (eds.) 1985 Problems and prospects in continuing professional education, *New Directions For Continuing Education* No. 27. Jossey-Bass, San Francisco, California

Craig R L (ed.) 1976 *Training and Development Handbook: A Guide to Human Resource Development*, 2nd edn. McGraw-Hill, New York

Darkenwald G G, Larson G A (eds.) 1980 *Reaching Hard-to-reach Adults*. Jossey-Bass, San Francisco, California

Ferver J C (ed.) 1981 Coordinating inservice programs of colleges of education. *J. Res. Dev. Educ.* 15(3): 2–72

Hill R E, Miller E L, Lowther M A (eds.) 1981 *Adult Career Transitions: Current Research Perspectives*. Graduate School of Business Administration, University of Michigan, Ann Arbor, Michigan

Houle C O 1972 *The Design of Education*. Jossey-Bass, San Francisco, California

Houle C O 1980 *Continuing Learning in the Professions*. Jossey-Bass, San Francisco, California

Knowles M S 1980 *The Modern Practice of Adult Education: From Pedagogy to Andragogy*, rev. edn. Follett, Chicago, Illinois

Knox A B 1977 *Adult Development and Learning*. Jossey-Bass, San Francisco, California

Knox A B (ed.) 1979 *Enhancing Proficiencies of Continuing Educators*. Jossey-Bass, San Francisco, California

Knox A B (ed.) 1980a *Teaching Adults Effectively*. Jossey-Bass, San Francisco, California

Knox A B 1980b *University Continuing Professional Education*. Office for the Study of Continuing Professional Education, University of Illinois, Urbana, Illinois

Knox A B 1982a *Leadership Strategies for Meeting New Challenges*. Jossey-Bass, San Francisco, California

Knox A B 1982b Organizational dynamics in university continuing education. *Adult Educ.* 32: 117–29

Knox A B et al. 1980 *Developing, Administering and Evaluating Adult Education*. Jossey-Bass, San Francisco, California

Le Breton P P et al. (eds.) 1979 *The Evaluation of Continuing Education for Professionals: A Systems View*. Continuing Education, University of Washington, Seattle, Washington

Lindquist J 1978 *Strategies for Change*. Council for the Advancement of Small Colleges, Washington, DC

Merrian S B, Simpson E L 1984 *A Guide to Research for Educators and Trainers of Adults*. Krieger, Melbourne, Florida

Pennington F C (ed.) 1980 *Assessing Educational Needs of Adults*. Jossey-Bass, San Francisco, California

Schein E H 1978 *Career Dynamics: Matching Individual and Organizational Needs*. Addison-Wesley, Reading, Massachusetts

Strother G B, Klus J P 1982 *Administration of Continuing Education*. Wadsworth, Belmont, California

Suter E, Green J S, Lawrence K, Walthall D B 1981 Continuing education of health professionals: Proposal for a definition of quality. *J. Medical Educ.* 56: 687–707

Votruba J C (ed.) 1981 *Strengthening Internal Support for Continuing Education*. Jossey-Bass, San Francisco, California

Section 7

National Programs and Organization

Section 7

National Programs and Organization

Introduction

In no country is the history of formal structures in adult education a lengthy one. The record in some countries is more than half a century, while for other countries it is only a year or two. The observations that follow are based more on countries with a somewhat more extensive history where there has been a longer span of time for certain principles and practices to be exhibited.

No country with the exception, perhaps, of China has a national system of adult education, that is, a coherent whole of interconnecting parts. At best it can be said that countries are moving at different rates from conglomeration to organic entity. The position each has reached is determined by its history, its economic and social development, its political and administrative system, its concept of adult education, and its drive to advancement. The power of this last has been demonstrated by Eastern European countries and China.

1. Historical Influences on National Structure

The contemporary concept of adult education derives in effect from a rationalization, after the event, of a variety of initiatives which have grown in a piecemeal fashion to meet specific perceived needs, rather than as the systematic realization of a priori principles. The untidy structures which prevail in many countries are, in large part, a consequence of this diversity of initiatives and providers, mostly private until the second half of the twentieth century. Central governments might have brought coherence to this diversity of agencies and aims, but, except in socialist countries, they intervened little in adult education before the Second World War. Broadly, governments saw education in terms of initial schooling and higher education. To these, adult education might make a useful supplement, which could be left in private hands, supported perhaps by a modest contribution from public funds. This division of roles in adult education was elevated to a principle in some countries and has been strongly defended by voluntary bodies.

After 1945, adult education came increasingly to be recognized as sufficiently important in national policy to call for more active attention by the state. This was a consequence of the same forces which led to general adoption of the principle of lifelong education. The latter, with its concepts of horizontal and vertical integration, has not only turned educators and governments towards the idea of adult education as a coherent whole, but has directed their attention to the necessity of integrating it with other sectors of education to form a total lifelong education process.

2. State Systems and Pluralist Systems of Adult Education

In socialist countries and in other countries where governments exercise direction of economic, social, and cultural life, either for ideological reasons, or pragmatically to meet the demands of security or development, the solution has been, explicitly or implicitly, a takeover of adult education by the state. Existing private organizations of provision have been turned into public agencies, abolished, or entirely subordinated to national policy aims. In these countries, however, adult education has been comparatively underdeveloped until recent years, although most of the spectacular campaigns for literacy have occurred in socialist countries (e.g. the Soviet Union, Cuba, Vietnam).

The problem of bringing order and facilitating growth has been more complex in those liberal democratic states where educational and economic development has been most advanced. There already existed a rich provision of learning opportunities offered by private associations, which often had competing ideologies and also were politically influential. They had reservations about increased government involvement in adult education, except as a provider of subsidy. Experience in many lands made them suspicious lest it become an instrument of indoctrination and control. The state was associated with centralization of decision making, rigidity, and bureaucratization of administration. Their principle was that learners, as volunteers and responsible adults, should have a part in deciding what and how they should study, and that organization should be locally based in order to respond flexibly to adult needs. They feared also to lose their own independence and influence.

To some degree, governments have respected or shared these views, although to give the impression that any government has spoken with one voice on adult education is likely to be misleading. Many departments of the state have been and still are operating in their own corners of the field, among them not only education, but ministries responsible for interior, manpower and economic policy, agriculture, social services, and cultural affairs. The multiplicity of public agencies has been as important an obstacle to a coherent policy of adult education as the number of private ones. Broadly, government intervention, as control or provider, has been greatest in vocational and second-chance education, which are the most formally organized parts of adult education and the closest to the initial education system. The area of sociocultural activities, informal and loosely structured, has been mostly left to voluntary bodies. Even in socialist countries, such as the Soviet Union, there are major nongovernmental organizations (NGOs) for these activities.

3. Influence of National Administrative Structures

The actual role of a central government and, indeed, of public authorities of any kind, is much influenced by whether a state is a unitary or a federal one, and by whether its administration is centralized or decentralized. In federations there is a certain devolution of power from the centre, in that each member state or province, not the federal government, tends to control its own education, but this is significantly offset by a central government's retention in all states of authority over vocational education. In adult education as a whole there is a decentralization of decision making down to local level, but less so in the vocational sector, where central government plays a more directive role.

Where the school system is centrally controlled, as in France, devolution of authority in adult education is sometimes to be seen as a reaction against it. Outside of socialist countries there are signs that the more centrally controlled a school system is, the more probably it will have left adult education to private initiative. Conversely, in two of the most decentralized states, the United States and the United Kingdom, where municipal and county authorities are responsible for public schools, those bodies have for many years been major providers of courses for adults.

4. *Forces that Shape National Structures*

The balance of forces which shape adult education structures varies from country to country. In liberal democratic states this balance has produced a pluralistic provision, with private and public providers and control which combines direction, facilitation, and permissiveness.

4.1 Function of Legislation

Adult education legislation was sparse before the 1960s; since then there has been a spate of it. Although laws imposing a pattern on the whole field are common in socialist states, in the Western democracies the only single act which seeks to do so is the Norwegian Education Act, 1976. Other laws merely affect certain aspects of it. There are laws relating to vocational education, general education, trade union and adult educator training, for example. Their objectives are varied. They may lay down the strategies and principles which shall govern policy. They may prescribe what functions public agencies shall fulfil, or say what organizations, public or private, shall be responsible for particular types of provision. In this they are directive towards public bodies and they offer only guidance or protection to private ones. They may lay down structures of decision making and consultation. They offer inducements to adults to participate.

4.2 Finance as an Instrument of Control

Above all, legislation is used to prescribe which public funds shall be allocated to adult education, how they shall be raised, to whom they shall be distributed, and for what purposes. This power to grant or withhold money is the major instrument of state control, exercised by central, provincial, and local government. In liberal democracies it is often the only effective means by which influence can be exerted on the private sector. Voluntary bodies are susceptible to it, because they have become largely dependent on public subsidy for the scale of operations they are able to maintain. The degree to which agencies depend on student fees and private benevolence in the United States is exceptional.

Government affects the content of provision, by allocating extra funds to basic education, for example, and not subsidizing other activities. By paying the full cost of some courses, or offering 100 percent subsidy to certain classes of student, such as the elderly, the illiterate, the handicapped, or the unemployed, it offers inducements to adults to participate. In devolved systems of government, even where there is no legal power to enforce policy on provincial or local authorities, the central state's power to determine the nature and amount of financial contribution it will make, exerts a powerful influence on them.

4.3 Market Forces

The market forces which mould adult education are not limited to active demands by learners. They extend to demands exerted by groups, such as employers, political or other sectional interests, which require adults other than themselves to be educated. The state itself, as a consumer of its own and private provision, is part of the market. The predominant manner of organizing adult education into short programmes, subject to annual revision, composed of learning experiences arranged largely for adult leisure time, evenings, weekends, vacations, and taught by personnel principally on short-term contracts, is determined by the need to respond to these market forces. So too are educational leave schemes and other measures to attract adults to study.

5. Framework of National Structures

5.1 Principles

The instruments of direction operate within a set of principles which governments accept more or less universally, although they apply them differently in practice. Every adult is believed not only to have a right to adequate educational opportunities, but to need them, as society needs each individual to continue education in adulthood. Learning opportunities should be organized to meet the wishes of both individual and society. Participation in adult education should be voluntary and an integral part of a lifelong process of education. The principles and practices of adult education should conform to and/or be animated by the fundamental principles on which society is based.

5.2 Purposes

For purposes of description and analysis, it is possible to see a shape in national provisions of adult education, according to certain typologies. The purposes for which provision is made can be classified under four headings:

(a) second-chance education, which offers adults who missed it the kind of education obtainable in the initial education system. This may range from basic literacy to mature entrance to university;

(b) role education, which is education for social function (outside employment) and includes social role education (e.g., as citizen, member of an association) and personal role education (e.g., as parent, spouse, retired person);

(c) vocational education, that is, education in the skills and knowledge required in employment;

(d) personal enrichment education, or education intended to develop the individual without regard to his or her social or economic function which includes, in effect, anything not covered by the other headings.

5.3 Subject Content

The field may be classified according to areas of study content: basic literacy and numeracy; occupation skills; knowledge and skills for personal function and their application;

knowledge and skills for social function and their application; artistic and craft skills; understanding and appreciation of literature and the arts; communication skills; standard academic disciplines unapplied to specific functions; physical education and sporting skills; nonphysical games.

5.4 Providing Organizations

Structure may be seen in terms of the agencies, public or private, which provide educational opportunities. At the national level the principal direct providers are usually the ministries responsible for education and manpower, with more limited provision made by others. In federal states provision is made by provincial ministries, with the notable exception of manpower, which is usually a federal department. At the local level, county and municipal authorities offer their own programmes. Particularly at the national level, a favourite device in order to achieve greater flexibility than would be possible to a state organization, is the creation of semipublic agencies, under joint direction of the state and private bodies, such as employers' associations or trade unions.

There are national, provincial, and local private organizations, which may be classified according to whether they are profit making (e.g., employers) or nonprofit making (e.g., voluntary associations), whether adult education is their primary purpose (e.g., the Workers' Educational Association in a number of states) or whether it is an incidental function (e.g., trade unions).

5.5 Decision Making

Decision making has broadly a two-, or in federal states, a three-tier structure. Except insofar as the legislature plays this role, a national authority covering the whole field is rare. There are commonly several vertical lines of authority, one descending from each department of state involved in adult education. Few detailed programmes are decided at national or provincial level. Instead, general policies are drawn up, to be presented as directives to local agencies of government, and as guidelines to private organizations in receipt of subsidy from the ministry. National private organizations have similar structures. In contrast to school systems, where curricula are commonly determined centrally, the content of adult education programmes is normally decided at the point of provision, that is, most often, locally. At this point students are frequently brought into planning and management.

Public agencies commonly involve private associations interested in their field, either as providers or consumers, to participate in their decision-making process at all levels. Increasingly, coordinating bodies have been set up at all levels. They may bring together public sector agencies, or private associations, or the whole field. Their role is usually advisory, and on the whole they exert influence rather than authority.

5.6 Finance: Source and Distribution

Finance for adult education is derived from five types of source: national general taxation; special government levies; taxes levied by regional and/or local authorities; payments made by private organizations; and tuition fees paid by learners.

6. Complexities of Structure

These typologies of structure—purpose, subject fields, providers, decision making, finance—are simplifications of reality. An action, for example, may not fall neatly into any one type of purpose or subject matter category. The typologies are also imperfectly congruent with each other, even in those countries under central state direction. One cannot say that certain subject content only occurs in actions for a particular purpose, that provision for certain purposes is restricted to certain types of organizations, or that direction and finance of certain sectors of activity come only from a particular ministry. Each national system of adult education must be seen in terms of a complex multidimensional framework of attributes, which constitute vectors. Any action or agency can only be situated within the framework in terms of the intersection of these vectors. Each one is likely to occupy a unique place.

7. Links Between the Adult and Other Parts of Education

The articulation between the adult and other parts of education is imperfect, least so perhaps in socialist countries and some developing countries, which, never having had a national system of education, are effectively building a lifelong one from scratch. It has probably gone furthest in sociocultural activities, where in some countries out-of-school youth work combines with adult provision in a unified all-age popular or community education sector. With formal initial education, it is made more difficult by that sector's rigid structure and predominant organization as a once-and-for-all process providing all education likely to be needed in life. School students are still not taught in a perspective of lifelong learning and the system is still ill adapted to permit adult re-entry to it. Progress has been made in that some countries make second-chance provision, notably at secondary and higher levels, in the initial education sector. An integrated structure of initial and continuing education, even in public school and university organizations which provide both, is still, however, far from realization.

The structures and organization of national systems of adult education have been little studied. The most significant contributions have been made under the aegis of intergovernmental organizations, such as UNESCO, the Organisation for Economic Co-operation and Development (OECD), and the Council of Europe, or international nongovernmental associations, such as the European Bureau of Adult Education. With financial support from UNESCO, the European Centre for Leisure and Education has undertaken a major project, in which the operation of national systems of adult education in both socialist and capitalist states is being investigated. The results so far suggest that under national diversities strong similarities exist.

These are, however, only the first stages of research. Much more requires to be done, throughout the developed and the developing world. There are many imperfections in national structures of adult education. Most could be made more efficient, more coherent. Nevertheless, it must be remembered that they exist to make possible appropriate responses to the needs of all adults. It may be questioned whether simplified and precisely defined structures, such as those of initial education, would be compatible with this purpose.

8. Case Studies

There is not space in a single volume work of the size of this *Handbook* to review the provision of adult education country by country round the world, as has been done for national education systems in the *International Encyclopedia of Education*. Instead regional case studies have been commissioned, which present the salient features of adult education organization and activities in a number of broad geographical areas of the globe.

This approach enables the reader to identify features shared by countries, to perceive that there are many which are similar and produced by pressures which transcend individual frontiers. One may see that adult education is not merely undertaken by educators in response to local and national needs, but constitutes rather a continuing phenomenon called into being by the realities of the human condition worldwide. The community of interest of educators runs beyond national to regional level, and even beyond that.

The regions have been chosen principally on geographical grounds, without reference to other variables, such as political systems or level of economic development. Some therefore appear to have fewer common features than others. Southeast Asia is more obvious for its diversity than its similarities. Western Europe, in spite of the large number of states and languages within it, has clear general features.

In order to facilitate comparison of like with like the articles of this section have been divided into two subsections: (a) Developed Countries, in which are to be found the regions of North America, Western Europe, Eastern Europe, and Australasia, plus a single-nation study of Japan, treated on its own for its importance as a developed country among surrounding developing ones; and (b) Developing Countries, including the Caribbean, Africa, the Indian Subcontinent, Southeast Asia, and the People's Republic of China, which, by its size and population constitutes a region in itself.

Developed Countries

Introduction

All the countries treated in this subsection are significantly more advanced economically than those treated in subsection 7b (except for South Africa). With the exception of Japan, which has been under significant American influence since the Second World War, they all belong to the European cultural tradition. There are marked differences in the degree to which they are developed. Eastern Europe is still some way behind North America and, for example, Greece and Portugal are behind Sweden and the Federal Republic of Germany. Together with a European cultural heritage, which includes a long history of adult education for most of them, they have a strong sense of nationhood, as has Japan, although the more recently established societies of Australia, New Zealand and, particularly, Canada feel a continuing need to assert and reinforce this.

The article *Provision in the United States* outlines the history of adult education in that country, the fragmented nature of its decision making linked to the country's size and diversity, and the field's lack of a sense of identity. The forces influencing adult education are seen to be immigration, democratization, the effect of knowledge creation on the world of work, and changes in work patterns. Provision is perceived as having broadened from educational institutions to a variety of agencies. Finance, by public and private institutions and participants, is seen as an investment, which individuals and organizations are encouraged to make, because it is widely tax deductible. The development and nature of professional education for adult educators is described.

In the review of Canada emphasis is laid on the patterns of participation in adult education, its laissez-faire pattern of administration, the sources and methods of finance, and the function of continuing education in national policies.

Provision in Western Europe includes in its scope 15 countries, ranging from the Scandinavian states to Portugal and from the United Kingdom to Greece. The article draws attention to the long history of adult education and the variety of providing organizations and purposes. It treats the question of administration, noting the tendency to decentralization, the function of legislation, particularly that relating to paid educational leave. Fields of special activity, including adult basic education, education for the unemployed, for older people, women, and cultural minorities are discussed. The function and training of adult educators, the offer of information, guidance and counselling, and the activities of international organizations in Western Europe are also described.

Albania, Bulgaria, Czechoslovakia, the German Democratic Republic, Hungary, Poland, Romania, the Soviet Union and Yugoslavia are all socialist states, although Albania, and Yugoslavia differ in taking an independent line from that of the others, which follow the lead of the Soviet Union. The article *Provision in Eastern Europe and the Soviet Union* marks out the long tradition of adult education as an instrument of national self-assertion and of the continuing need to use it as a tool of advancement from quite backwards economic status. It discusses the Eastern European concepts of adult education and considers provision under three systems common in these countries: the formal or school system; place-of-work training; and nonformal or out-of-school education. It also outlines measures taken to train adult educators.

The article *Provision in Australasia* deals with adult education in Australia and New Zealand. It explains the scope and terminology of adult education in those countries. Organization and funding are described, notably the devolution of authority to the states under Australia's federal constitution and the lack of coordination that results. Areas of special activity in the two countries are discussed, particularly work with indigenous minorities and ethnic immigrants. The ongoing debate over adult education as a movement or a profession is mentioned and reference is made to the growing tendency for closer cooperation with countries of Asia and the Pacific.

Provision in Japan locates the beginning of the Japanese school system in the nineteenth century, but shows that the great variety and comprehensiveness of adult education, which goes under the term social education, belongs almost entirely to the second half of the twentieth century. It has formal and nonformal sides. Legislation to encourage the latter has led to the creation of community centres and the growth of libraries and public museums. Features of formal education include extension courses; part-time and correspondence courses offered by institutions of higher education; the establishment of special training schools to provide second-chance opportunities up to higher education level; and correspondence and other forms of education by profit-making and other private agencies. In addition to educational transmissions by public and private broadcasting corporations, Japan is creating a university of the air with open access. Education for employment is undertaken by public bodies and by employers and private profit-making companies.

Provision in the United States

A. N. Charters

The United States of America constitutes a federal state with limited central direction. Its extreme diversity is reflected in its adult education provision. This article can offer only an outline of the principal general features of that provision. It examines what is meant by adult education against the background of its historic development. It underlines the lack of national policy and diversity of policy makers, offset by the consensus-creating influence of national associations. It considers the identity and number of adult participants in study, the parameters of the field recognized as adult education, and main forces influencing its nature. There is discussion of the needs of adult learners, the factors affecting the programs offered to them, the kinds of agencies which provide them, and the sources of finance. It concludes by considering the roles, training, and associations of adult educators, and the provision of resources for research.

1. The Field

The adult education enterprise in the United States is built upon three generally accepted premises:

(a) that the mission of adult education is to assist adults to obtain further control of their current circumstances and their future destinies;

(b) that adults have the lifelong right to learning opportunities; and

(c) that adults can, should, and must continue to learn.

Although there is not yet consensus among educators of adults about the use of the terms "adult education" and "continuing education," sufficient consistency and enough mutual understanding have emerged out of practice for them to communicate effectively in order to gain information and experience from each other. In this article adult education is defined as:

> the identification, selection, provision, arrangement, and evaluation of learning activities for adults who are: physically developed; consciously learning in order to achieve their selected goals; learning on a part-time basis or on a full-time basis for only short periods of time as part of their life pattern; and learning in order to better assume responsibility as a citizen, worker, family person, and social being living in a particular physical environment.

Despite the lack of conceptual clarity, adult education in the United States may be characterized as a phenomenon of diverse parts that has developed from a series of individual programs for adults into a broad movement. Yet there is no overall policy stated for state or federal government or for nongovernmental agencies. Perhaps the unwritten understanding and commitment by individuals, sponsors, and government may in itself be a kind of national policy. At least these considered decisions become general consensus and are followed with commitment. This consensus pervades all aspects of adult education including sponsoring agencies, program development, and financing.

2. Historical Background

A multitude of educational programs for adults has developed since the colonial days of the United States. Perhaps the only common factor in this development was the preoccupation of adult Americans with education, first for their children and then for themselves. This somewhat vague desire for education became reflected in the commitment to education as a means to advance upward socioeconomic mobility, improve the quality of life, and solve national problems. For these reasons, diverse individuals and agencies developed programs for adults which formed the fabric of American adult education. It should be noted that many programs were developed on the initiative of one or two individuals who had a cause which they felt compelled to develop and spread with missionary zeal.

The education of adults in the United States is traditionally traced back to the Town Meetings of colonial times. They were decision-making bodies but had an educational component. The first such agency of adult education was the Junto founded by Benjamin Franklin in 1727, which had among its purposes the support of public schools and the organization of libraries and museums. The first public library supported by tax funds was established in Peterborough, New Hampshire in 1833. The Mechanics Institutes were formed after 1820 to prepare people for the workforce in the technology of the time. In 1826 Josiah Holbrook initiated the Lyceum movement which offered lectures and discussion sessions. Cooper Union was set up in 1859 to provide free courses relating science and art to practical affairs. The Chautauqua Institution was founded by

John Vincent and Lewis Miller as a tent encampment to train Sunday School teachers. It soon spread to an array of cultural, liberal arts, and religious programs. The same concept was followed by the traveling Chautauquas which spread all over the states of the United States and the provinces of Canada. The Chautauqua Institution in New York State remains to this day a viable adult education experience.

As for postsecondary education institutions, university extension emerged about 1887, and was given impetus when the President of the then-new University of Chicago declared that the extension of resources to adult learners was a legitimate part of the University. Charles Van Hise, President of the University of Wisconsin, proclaimed in 1906 that the boundaries of the University of Wisconsin were the boundaries of the entire state.

The idea of general extension was soon supplemented by the Cooperative Agricultural Extension Service authorized under the Smith–Lever Act of 1914. It was based on cooperatives among the United States Department of Agriculture, the State Land Grant Colleges, and counties. Cooperative extension in conjunction with state land grant universities developed a vast system of extending the new research knowledge developed in schools of agriculture and home economics to America's farmers, principally through county agents.

During the First World War, the Americanization Program was launched to teach English and to inform the influx of millions of immigrants about American citizenship. Then, in 1917, the Smith Hughes Act was passed by Congress to fund vocational education.

After the boom following the First World War, the United States fell into the worldwide economic depression of the 1930s. The response of the federal government was to establish the Public Works Administration, which among its many facets, had a strong educational component for the adults in the program. One such program was the Civilian Conservation Corps.

As Europe became embroiled in the Second World War, the development of the United States as the "arsenal of democracy" required the training or retooling of workers, some of whom had not previously been in work. This national effort clearly demonstrated that adults could learn if properly motivated and trained. In the readaptation to peace the government, through the GI Bill for veterans and other plans, launched massive adult education programs. The creation of the Fund for Adult Education of the Ford Foundation, with its emphasis on the arts and humanities, gave balance to the programs in science, technology, and the professions. In 1967 the Corporation for Public Broadcasting was established and gave television a role in the education of adults. Concurrently government, the private sector, nonprofit organizations, and proprietary organizations were developing a wide range of programs which resulted in a comprehensive program with the character of a national movement.

3. Decision Making

A response to the basic question of who decides which programs are to be offered to adults may give some understanding of the nature of adult education in the United States. The decision makers are really the composite of all individuals, agencies, and other sponsors who develop, support, or participate in the programs or learning programs. Even the programs of the federal government are not organized under one policy or administrative unit. The term "policy" is used here as a statement of ideas which is presumably to be put into effect by its adherents. There is the Federal Interagency Committee on Education but this is an information-sharing body, not a sponsoring or coordinating committee. It should also be noted that in the United States, education is a function of each of the 51 states and is not mentioned in the Constitution. Although there is much sharing of information, there is little coordination in adult education among the states. Within the states, there is usually no coordinating body for government programs in adult education at the state or county level. In practice, therefore, at the national, state, or local level of government, decisions about adult education are made by whatever government agency authorizes expenditures or otherwise sponsors the programs.

In the private sector each agency sponsors its own programs for adults for whatever reasons it considers appropriate. In some cases national organizations such as the League of Women Voters or the American Red Cross may set national guidelines for branches or affiliates. The same applies to large national businesses and industries, such as the Xerox Corporation, which may set firm guidelines and policy on training for its divisions or subsidiaries within or outside the United States. Although there are some federal regulations governing nonprofit organizations and some for business, particularly in respect of tax allowance for educational programs, in general each agency in the private sector is independent.

Some proprietary business organizations have been set up to develop educational programs and to sell the programs as products or services for profit. Examples are so-called "business schools" which train secretarial/clerical personnel in return for tuition or fees. These organizations are quite distinct from a business such as International Business Machines (IBM) which provides internal, self-developed educational programs for its employees or dealers as support services for the production or sale of its products. In addition, International Business Machines pays for degrees and noncredit programs by other providers, including higher education institutions. Proprietary organizations in the business of adult education sell all types of print and nonprint materials as well as seminars primarily to business and industry. Their programs, like the products of other businesses, are competitive with each other and often with programs sponsored by nonprofit providers.

4. National Associations

Many of the types of nongovernmental agencies have national associations. For example, the National University Continuing Education Association (NUCEA) is composed of members from universities and colleges, while the American Society for Training and Development (ASTD) has members primarily from business concerned with their employees' education and training. There is also an umbrella organization called the Coalition of Adult Education Organizations (CAEO) which was created in 1964 to serve as an information-sharing body for its 25 member organizations such as those mentioned above. It should be noted, however, that some well-known organizations such as Cooperative Extension (agriculture and home economics) do not belong to CAEO.

At the local level, an example of an information-sharing body is the Metropolitan Syracuse Committee on Adult and Continuing Education, in Syracuse, New York. It has members from the government, as well as the private and proprietary sector.

5. Adult Participants

The decision makers in the public, private, and proprietary sectors who offer learning opportunities are always subject to the decision makers, the adult participants themselves, who select the programs in which they wish to participate. After all, learning is an individual process and accordingly, learning by adults is what may be termed "the bottom line." They are not legally required to attend but they may, of course, be pressured to do so by employers, peers, family, professional licensing bodies, and by their personal commitment to an idea, organization, or interest. For example, some professions such as pharmacy or accounting require mandatory continuing education. Again there is no overall policy for most adult participants, although there may be professional interest groups and organizations that foster adult education. This dearth of policy among the various decision makers of adult education is balanced, however, by substantial sharing of knowledge and information through such means as publications, seminars/workshops, associations, promotional materials, networks, and partnerships.

While adult education is extensive, participants and the agencies providing the learning experiences do not always identify with the field of adult education. The identification issue is illustrated by the fact that of the 25 member organizations of CAEO only three have the word "adult" in their title, while "continuing"—although in this context often used synonymously for "adult"—is used in the title of five organizations, and the word "training" appears in only one title. CAEO estimates that its members alone number over 30 million participants. In 1980, the number of people in the United States 17 years old and older was 166,000,000. In the same year the number of adults (unduplicated) over postsecondary-school age who participated in organized sessions of instruction (excluding self-directed and on-the-job training) was 65,000,000 (Wagner 1982). The number of adults learning independently through newspaper, radio, television, library, and computers, while surely vast, is not available.

6. Forces Influencing Adult Education

Of course political, social, economic, and technological forces in the United States have changed over the years and have had an impact on education including the public, private, and proprietary agencies engaged in adult education. The corollary is that education, including adult education, has in turn had some impact on the development of these forces and their influence on individuals and the nation. Four forces have had a particular relationship to adult education.

First, immigration has been a key force in the United States since the Pilgrims settled in 1620. The English and other Europeans, Asians, Africans, and other people have arrived in shiploads. In the last few decades Puerto Ricans, Hispanics, East Asians, and others have arrived by the hundreds of thousands as well as undocumented numbers of illegal migrant workers and refugees. Most of these adult immigrants require programs in literacy, English as a second language, career and vocational education, and Americanization or preparation for citizenship. Educated immigrants participate in adult education programs at the appropriate level.

Second, democratization has been an issue since colonial times. Independence, the abolition of slavery, and the franchise for women in 1919 have been major steps in its progress. More recently the Supreme Court Decision 347 US 483 (1954) *Brown versus Board of Education of Topeka, Kansas* established equal rights for Blacks and the Women's Education Equity Act Program was authorized by the Elementary and Secondary Education Act (ESEA) of 1965 amendment concerning equal rights for women. Both of these measures created the need to provide education for adults so that they could occupy their equal place in all aspects of life, but particularly in the labor market. The latter also helped to wipe out cheap labor. As women entered the paid workforce there was a fall in the numbers of volunteers for teaching and other roles in education and for other human services activities.

Third, the creation of knowledge and the development of technology have had a considerable impact on the world of work. The significant fact is not that technology and knowledge are new, but that during the past few decades they have developed at an accelerating rate. It has meant the continuing obsolescence of some categories of jobs and the creation of new ones. This may necessitate adult education for career changes one or more times during the course of a lifetime. It often makes inroads into employment policies related to tenure and seniority. It has also meant a continual updating of the knowledge of those adults, particularly those professionals whose jobs have not changed. It has resulted in sponsors such as professional organizations, businesses, labor groups, and governmental bodies designing and offering large-scale continuing professional education programs for their employees and members. One recent estimate suggests that nearly US$60 billion a year is spent on corporate-run education, a cost similar to that of the nation's four-year colleges and universities (Eurich 1985). The explosion of new technology has created the need for literacy progress beyond reading, writing, and arithmetic to the new literacy programs in media and computers. It has spurred the development of programs such as those authorized under the Manpower Development and Training Act of 1962 and of educational programs on higher technology for preentry into the workforce.

The increase in knowledge and technology has resulted in new ways of processing and distributing knowledge to masses of potential users. Devices for searching for information have also improved the effectiveness and efficiency of the transmission of appropriate information to users. Some publications are now in a format to facilitate scanning and thus a new term or process has emerged. These developments reflect concern that unless the quality of information is evaluated before processing, the reader may waste time in reading, reviewing, or listening to unnecessary material.

Fourth, there have been changes in workforce patterns. For example, the working week has shortened since the first half of the twentieth century and the workforce is getting older. The desire to earn more money and to avoid boredom has resulted in a considerable amount of "moonlighting," that is, taking on second jobs. Women entering the paid workforce often find that their home responsibilities have not lessened. In a sense they are moonlighting away from home to a paid job. In any case, the shorter working week means that adults are not so tired and hence that they have more time and energy to engage in adult education if they are motivated to do so. Moreover, as shown in the number of adults participating in educational activities, agencies do offer appropriate learning activities.

It is interesting to note that the percentage of persons 65 years and older in the United States increased from 9.5 percent in 1965 to 12 percent in 1985 and is projected to increase at a greater rate in the future (United Way 1983). The federal government has passed a law giving people the opportunity to work to the age of 70 and beyond, if they so wish. Social security and pension plans are generally designed for retirement at the age of 65.

It appears that some senior adults are finding their work and shifts in careers to be sufficiently interesting for them to want to continue in the labor force beyond what has hitherto been considered "normal" retirement age. People may need the additional income but many seek the challenge of making a further contribution. In any case, there are many preretirement programs available that are designed to help people to make the transition from life with a major full-time employment to retirement. Hobbies, travel, and the pursuit of interests previously not developed because of lack of funds are some of the reasons for participation in these adult education activities.

A pervading issue that arises from these forces is the sense of, and need for, immediacy in making decisions. Communications systems and broadcasting networks operate instantaneously. Within a few hours news reaches virtually all leaders and citizens. These people in turn often have to make immediate decisions which require access to up-to-date information. The result is that priorities keep shifting and little time is left for depth of study and consideration. While this can be a disturbing circumstance for many adults it also provides motivation for education.

7. *Programming for Adult Education*

The adult education movement includes different types of adults. Those who are served range on continua from illiterates to intellectuals; from unskilled workers to professionals; artists to scientists; citizens to leaders; and labor to management. The above ranges are cited without any sense of elitism; rather they indicate that all adults require continuing education throughout life. Whether or not there is a class structure in the United States may be a debatable issue. What is clear, however, is that if there are classes, the purpose of adult education is not to help adults to move from one class to another but rather to raise the level of the whole class.

Programs for adults are offered in a wide range of delivery systems that give adults alternative learning opportunities. The delivery system must be convenient and accessible to adults interested in learning. For example, it can be as simple as in the case of a program conducted by one individual. This person may put up notices in supermarkets, community centers, churches, and other places. Persons interested in teaching something or learning something telephone this person, who then simply matches up the information and notifies the individuals. More often, however, the delivery process is more complicated, even though the goal is the same.

The subject matter or content of programs for adults is boundless, for it depends on the interests of the learner and sponsor. It includes knowledge in all life activities such as careers, family life, citizenship, art, music, and recreation.

The methods selected for a given program in adult education depend on the ability of adults to cope with a given method; the nature of the subject matter; and the accessibility of equipment and facilities. From time to time, however, one method may be more popular than other methods, for example, radio in the 1930s, discussion groups in the 1950s, television in the 1960s and 1970s, and computers in the 1980s.

The setting or location of one adult education activity

is in general without limits. An adult education center has been defined as the terminus of a journey. The location or setting is wherever adults are or are willing to go. Activities may, for example, be in houses, agencies, residential centers, hotels and motels, parks, on board ships, or on tours. Adult education is an organized activity but it may take place in a variety of informal settings besides classrooms. It is, however, important to recognize practical requirements such as proximity to transportation—for example airplane, bus, subway, or parking—at times convenient to fit the schedules of participants and at costs within their budget range.

The United States is sometimes referred to as a credential-oriented society. Certainly in the work or career sector of life, credentials are important in obtaining a job or gaining promotion. Documents to prove educational accomplishment as well as successful work experience are required. Yet perhaps more basic than the securing of a credential is the receipt of personal recognition. Such informal recognition seems to be a desirable custom in all segments of work, life, and volunteerism, as well as for paid activity. Formal recognition includes continuing education units (CEUs), certificates, letters, diplomas, and plaques. Recognition at a "graduation" dinner or ceremonial group gathering is another form. Some form of recognition is usually provided after successful completion of adult education programs.

8. *Agencies of Adult Education*

Agencies in the field of adult education are the sponsors or providers of learning opportunities for adults and are the base for the development and arrangement of programs. Adults can engage in these programs in order to achieve goals which they have personally selected. Yet the sponsors or providers also have reasons for providing the programs. Indeed, different sponsors may be promoting opposing points of view. A built-in factor is what motivates adults to work toward their own goals which may coincide with the goals of the sponsors. In some ways adults select or "vote with their feet." It is the diversity of agencies with their commitment to a cause that gives the vigor, enthusiasm, and comprehensiveness to learning opportunities for adults.

In addition to governmental bodies and proprietary organizations, there are many agencies offering educational programs. The types of agencies include colleges and universities, public secondary tax-supported schools, libraries, museums, art galleries, labor organizations, hospitals, gerontology centers, service clubs, theaters, religious institutions, correspondence and distance education organizations, health centers and organizations, business and industry, radio, television, newspapers, and other media, publishing houses, and men's and women's clubs and organizations.

The broadening of this agency base reflects the fact that adult education has moved from a strong educational institution base (secondary schools, colleges, and universities) to a much broader provider base. In a sense, there has been a deschooling of adult education by adding a comprehensive array of agencies to the stability of the more traditional educational institutions.

9. *Financing of Adult Eduction*

Financing, like other aspects of adult education, is characterized by diversity. There is no one financial source and among the sources there is no evident pattern. The following, however, are some of the characteristics of the financing of adult education. First, since adult education is not compulsory, funds invested are considered as an investment in a cause or in adults to work for that cause. Sponsors provide funds for programs promoting missions that range from the altruistic to the pragmatic. This characteristic is especially evident in programs sponsored by agencies such as government, churches, and business. It should be noted in this connection that the Internal Revenue Service has ruled that funds spent for adult education are tax deductible.

Second, since sponsors give money to promote causes, funds are earmarked for the programs themselves and not much is allowed for administrative staff, buildings, or core expenditures. The W.K. Kellogg Foundation gave funds to assist in building conference centers in order that the conference-type programs that they were intending to promote would have existing facilities on university campuses. Even when sponsors give money they may stipulate that there be matching funds or in-kind contributions by the recipient agency. Government grants may give funds to institutions and may also provide some overhead allowances. In general, funds are designated for line items in specified programs.

Third, there is usually a fee or charge of some kind, assessed by sponsors, which the individual participant must pay. Exceptions include Adult Basic Education Programs and the Job Training Partnership Act of 1982. In general, however, the adult participant makes a financial commitment as well as one of time and energy. In some cases, for example, the fees for university and proprietary institutions may be very substantial. They can range from a minimum cost for a meal or beverage breaks, duplicated materials, or bus fare to several hundred dollars. In some cases a business will reimburse the employee for full or partial costs of a program offered by another party. Whatever the rationale, if any, there is general consensus that adults should pay something, or at least put money up-front, toward their own education.

The sources of funds may be grouped into several categories. First, government at all levels provides funding for adult education in a number of ways: funds to other agencies they contract for education; paying tuition and/or grants or loans to students directly; paying as a recruiting device for persons to enter, for example, the military at the end of the program. Second, in the private sector, business and industry pay for inservice training for employees within the organization or expenses at another agency's program. Another aspect of the private sector is that of nonprofit organizations that sponsor programs for adults. Third are foundations which have provided substantial grants to adult education agencies. For example, the Carnegie Corporation in the 1920s gave funds to create the American Association of Adult Education (AAAE) and to begin a graduate program at Columbia University. Later, among other grants, they funded original special degree programs for adults and early programs for mature women designed for entry or reentry into a professional field. The Fund for Adult Education of the Ford Foundation put millions into programs in liberal education, funding programs such as the Center for the Study of Liberal Education of Adults (CSLEA), the American Foundation for Continuing Education (AFCE), and Great Books programs. The W.K. Kellogg Foundation funded the early conference programs and, as previously indicated, provided for the planning and development of conference facilities. Kellogg funds are also provided directly in fellowships to individuals for tuition fees and expenses. The Mott Foundation has provided significant grants to launch the community education concept.

The lack of overall policy and plan leaves the priorities to be set by the sponsors. Some people argue that this arrangement may not give balance to adult education in art, music, and the humanities and that it emphasizes economic development at the expense of quality of life. Others suggest that some of the money spent on art galleries, art collections, and symphonies might better be spent on adult education to help the poor get jobs. Likewise, some propose that cuts in expenditure in defense and transportation subsidies would release funds for adult education. Educators of adults do, in general, seem to agree that the lack of funds prevents the full development of appropriate programs. And, as massive as expenditures are and as little as the cost may be to the adult participant, cost does seem to be a barrier, particularly for the less educated and low income groups. This may simply be a reflection of a lack of understanding of the economic and upward-mobility use of education—or at least that it has a lower priority than other luxuries.

10. Professional Development of Educators of Adults

Educators of adults have the major role in the development of the adult education movement and they need continuing professional development for the same reasons as all other professional and other career adults.

Educators of adults have many titles in the area of adult education. Many educators of adults are not identified as such by others or even by themselves, but they include all who have a concern for persons who are in adult education agencies and/or have functions, such as the following, who are involved with organized learning by adults: organizers, principals, program and other administrators, supervisors, deans, directors, advisors and counselors, members of clergy, librarians, media specialists, and other support personnel, tutors, facilitators and teachers, faculty and students of adult education as a field, community developers and community educators, research workers, consultants, policy makers, elected officials, and board members of adult education agencies. Their importance should be considered in the light of the individual roles and competencies they fulfill in an adult education agency. They may be paid employees or volunteers.

Many adult educators enter the field from other diverse disciplines and vocations. Accordingly they may add to the field of adult education an expanded knowledge base and research expertise which help to place adult education in a more global perspective. Other educators of adults enter the field with varying degrees of professional training in adult education and/or related experience. Because they have key roles in the development, provision, and evaluation of learning opportunities, they have need to plan for their own professional development. Sometimes such planning is considered a part of what is called human resource development. A plan may consist of four stages: preentry education (training), orientation, inservice or continuing inservice, and exit or retirement stages.

An important part of programs that are offered for professional development of adults are those sponsored by universities and colleges. In the late 1920s at Columbia University a graduate program in the field of adult education was begun. Now there are representatives of some 200 college and university graduate programs holding membership in the Commission of Professors of Adult Education. Many of these students have had some experience and are studying either part-time or full-time. There are other freestanding institutions, for example Nova University, that award degrees for successful completion of what are often referred to as independent studies programs. These nonprofit institutions and proprietary organizations offer seminars, workshops, and other programs for fees. In addition, the continuing professional development of educators of adults by all employing agencies is a thriving enterprise. By using professional promotion, opportunities, funding, and time-off, they have motivated their personnel to engage in continuing education. Government also provides grants and contracts. Professional organizations such as the members of the Coalition of Adult Education Organizations (CAEO), National University Continuing Education Association (NUCEA), Association of Continuing Higher Education (ACHE), American Association for Adult Continuing Education (AAACE), and American Society for Training and Development (ASTD) sponsor national conferences, regional meetings, and local programs. In addition, newsletters and journals are increasing in number. Media and computerized programs for professional development are becoming more common. Many commercial publishers are, of course, increasing the number and sales of books and other materials. Overall the literature on adult education in the United States is substantial and is growing to include many current special interests such as community development, self-directed learning, community education, and distance education.

Closely related to these programs for professional development of educators of adults are the resources necessary to support or complement them. Many colleges and universities have substantial libraries in adult education literature and many agencies at all levels of operation are developing staff, libraries, or resource centers. Networks in informal settings are seeking ways to improve communication, often in a subjective way. Collections for research such as those being developed by Syracuse University Resources for Educators of Adults (SUREA) are beginning or being planned.

Complementing the professional development programs and resources is a growing body of research in adult education, adult learning, and related fields such as psychology, sociology, biology, and gerontology. The adult education movement was given great impetus by the research and subsequent publication of *Adult Learning* by Thorndike in 1928. Since then, the concern for research and for developing a theoretical base has been substantial. The expanding body of research is clearly indicated, for example, in the number of items produced by an Education Resources Information Center (ERIC) search. Much of the research relates to practice. Factors of evaluation and feedback are also becoming increasingly recognized as significant data for accounting to sponsors who paid for programs.

In summary, adult education in the United States is characterized by extreme diversity in the type of educational programs, their purposes and delivery systems, and a great variety of providers and funding mechanisms. Although they clearly serve some national purposes in economic development, there is no clearly defined overall policy and, indeed, individuals and separate organizations make the basic decisions about adult education. The expansion of the field and the growing interest in offering appropriate and high-quality programs are the products of the system, balanced by the deep conviction and commitment of individuals and other sponsors to the value of adult education.

Bibliography

Eurich N P 1985 *Corporate Classrooms: The Learning Business*. Carnegie Foundation, Princeton, New Jersey

Knowles M S 1980 *The Modern Practice of Adult Education: From Pedagogy to Andragogy*, 2nd edn. Follett, Chicago, Illinois

Peterson R E, Cross K P, Hartle T W, Hirabayashi J B, Kutner M A, Powell S A, Valley J R 1979 *Lifelong Learning in America: An Overview of Current Practices, Available Resources, and Future Prospects*. Jossey-Bass, San Francisco, California

Peterson R E, Gaff S S, Helmick J S, Feldmesser R A, Valley J R, Nielsen H D 1982 *Adult Education and Training in Industrialized Countries*. Praeger, New York

Smith R M, Aker G F, Kidd J R 1970 *Handbook of Adult Education*. Macmillan, New York

Thorndike E L 1928 *Adult Learning*. Macmillan, New York

United Way 1983 *What Lies Ahead: A New Look*. United Way of America, Alexandria, Virginia

Wagner A P 1982 *Education and Urban Society* 14(3): 271–300

Provision in Canada

I. Morrison

Canada is a federal state and continuing education, like education in general, is primarily a responsibility of the Canadian provinces. Each of these 10 jurisdictions has developed systems of continuing education which display distinct characteristics. Yet there are elements of continuity in the Canadian experience introduced by such factors as occupational training policies and expenditures of the Canadian federal government, patterns of communication which increase the flow of ideas and people between regions, and the influence of nongovernmental organization in the voluntary, enterprise, and labour sectors. Among important features of Canadian continuing education are growth in the overall participation of adults, diversity in the means of provision, and substantial variations in participation based upon demographic and social class characteristics.

This article will summarize the evidence concerning patterns of participation, distinguish the roles of the various providers of continuing education (both structural and administrative), outline financial arrangements, and identify the role of continuing education in national policies and priorities. It will conclude with a brief comment upon critical issues awaiting research and policy consideration.

1. Patterns of Participation

In January 1984 the statistical agency of the Canadian government administered an adult education survey to a random sample of almost 100,000 Canadians of 17 years of age and over (0.6 percent of the adult population). In all, some 30 questions regarding adult learning behaviour were added as a supplement to the regular monthly labour force survey, which is the basis of Canada's employment statistics. As a result, for the first time, detailed information on participation factors in Canadian adult education are available. The adult education survey covers the year 1983 and includes all adult education other than full-time courses (Secretary of State 1984).

Overall, women participate more in adult education (at 21 percent) than do men (17 percent), but the nature of their participation is different in such respects as the type of course chosen and the reason for taking the course. Men are twice as likely as women to take job-related types of courses, and almost twice as often they cite job-related reasons for taking courses. While male and female participation rates are similar in publicly-funded institutions like community colleges and universities, men predominate in employer-sponsored courses and those offered by unions and professional organizations. Women constitute the great majority in courses offered by private schools and voluntary organizations. Although women constitute more than 40 percent of the Canadian labour force, employers are three times as likely to pay for a course taken by a male than a female employee.

Wide variations occur in adult education participation among different educational attainment groups. University graduates are (at 41 percent) more than eight times as likely to participate in adult education as are persons with 0–8 years of education (5 percent). Participation rises steadily with increased educational attainment: 16 percent for persons with high school education, 28 percent for those with some postsecondary education, and 33 percent for persons with postsecondary diplomas.

Table 1
Participation in adult education by age group

Age group	Percentage
17 – 24	21
25 – 34	29
35 – 44	25
45 – 54	15
55 – 64	10
65 +	4

Participation also varies widely between the various provinces, ranging from a low of 9 percent in Newfoundland to a high of 25 percent in Alberta. On average in Canada one in every five adults (19 percent) participated in adult education courses in 1983. Substantial differences are evident in the participation rates of various age groups, as shown in Table 1. The data reveal that persons in middle age groups are more likely than are younger or older people to choose job-related courses.

Employed Canadians take courses offered by their employers more frequently (23 percent of the total) than they do from any other provider of adult education. Unemployed people (defined as "actively seeking work") prefer community colleges (24 percent) to other providers of adult education. Adults not in the labour force prefer voluntary organizations (33 percent).

Table 2 shows how Canadian providers of adult education rank in descending order by size. When these provider groups are compared by the educational attainment of the adult participants they attract to courses, wide variations emerge. Employers, unions and professional associations, and private schools offer substantially the same proportion of courses to each educational attainment group. Voluntary organizations and school boards offer proportionately greater learning opportunities to people with lower levels of educational attainment. Community colleges offer less to both lower and higher educational attainment groups than to those with some postsecondary education, while universities cater for the educationally advantaged.

Table 2
Providers of adult education in Canada

Provider	Percentage
Employers	18
Community colleges	18
Voluntary organizations	17
School boards	14
Private schools	13
Universities	12
Unions and professional associations	8

Voluntary organizations are the most important providers of adult education courses to those with 0–8 years of education and to those with high school education; colleges to those with some postsecondary education; employers to those with postsecondary diplomas; and universities to those with university degrees. In Canada, with the exception of school boards, it is the private sector providers which offer the most learning opportunities to the educationally disadvantaged.

When participants are asked their "most important reason" for taking a course, and the responses are divided into two broad categories, job-related and personal interest, the pattern of course provision shown in Table 3 emerges (expressed in descending order of importance by provider).

2. Structure and Administration of Continuing Education

In general, continuing education operates in a laissez-faire environment in Canada. Governments typically

Table 3
Providers of adult education ranked according to participant interest

Job-related	Personal interest
Employers	Voluntary organizations
Colleges	Private schools
Universities	School boards
Unions and professional associations	Colleges
School boards	Universities
Private schools	Unions and professional associations
Voluntary organizations	Employer

provide incentive structures, and occasionally suggest means to effect coordination. By far the majority of educational offerings organized by employers, unions, and professional associations operate without any form of supervision or control from public authorities. Voluntary organizations operate independently of governments but, in some jurisdictions, enjoy grants according to the number of student hours in support of some of their work. Private schools operating for profit operate under only loose supervision of public authorities.

In both universities and colleges, an important distinction is whether the course of instruction leads to credit for a degree or diploma. If it does, the part-time student's fees are often proportionately on a par with those of full-time students. Usually noncredit learning is more flexible in its curriculum content and students are expected to meet the full cost. In most Canadian jurisdictions, school boards are important adult education providers. They are active in literacy and second language instruction, and demonstrate accessibility (as noted in the participation data above).

Governmental influence and control is strongest in the area of occupational education. Canada's federal government operates extensive employment training programmes under the authority of its National Training Act (1982). Each year approximately $1 billion (Canadian) is spent through conditional transfers to provincial governments to pay the infrastructure costs of occupational education and also to offer training allowances to adults who qualify. Most of this funding supports full-time training, usually offered by community colleges. In this area, the federal government controls detailed decisions regarding eligibility, duration, and subject matter.

In 1983 the federal government amended the Canada Student Loan Act to provide part-time students in recognized educational institutions with loans to assist in the financing of their educational costs.

Three innovations by provincial governments in the field of continuing education deserve special mention. The Quebec government has developed a policy of financing "popular education" (i.e. nonformal, noncredit education) by voluntary organizations that is unequalled in Canada. In Saskatchewan, a unique community college system operates on a noninstitutional basis whereby the colleges serve as brokers for the provision of noncredit programming, utilizing existing facilities and enabling the delivery of programmes locally by the two universities and the three technological institutions in that province. Alberta has developed a Further Education Policy which mandates the creation of approximately 80 Local Further Education Councils in all population centres in the province. These Councils assemble all the providers in the local area, seek to enhance communication between them, offer a liaison service through the employment of a Council Coordinator, and provide grants on the basis of student "contact" hours to voluntary groups who are involved in the delivery of adult education services locally.

3. *Financing*

In addition to the funds flowing from the federal government to support occupational education, public funds reach continuing education through tax deductibility of tuition, student loans, and general subsidies to publicly-funded organizations—universities, colleges, and school boards—as well as grants to voluntary groups. Employers obtain reimbursement of some of their training costs through taxation benefits and subsidies for on-the-job training schemes. The cost to the student varies from full-cost recovery (through tuition) to complete subsidy.

4. *Continuing Education in National Policies*

After Canada's 1984 general election, a new federal government took office with a mandate to review policies across the board. Its first published policy discussion paper was on the subject of "Training" and contained the following introductory statement:

> The Government of Canada has placed a high priority on its support of effective training. A strong flexible base of skills is an essential ingredient to our competitive position and our economic health. It is equally a necessary ingredient in building an exciting, rewarding, equitable society. There can be no better investment than an intelligent investment in people's skills. (Minister of Employment 1985)

Whether this statement is or is not fulfilled, several issues arise for research and critical scrutiny:

(a) How can the return on investment in skill development be measured?

(b) How much emphasis should be placed on the development of specific occupational skills as opposed to a base of generic skills?

(c) How can entrepreneurial skills be taught effectively?

(d) Can an appropriate balance be drawn between investments in occupational and other skills, such as skills of parenting, citizenship, and culture?

(e) How can public policy work to improve the access of educationally disadvantaged adults to continuing education?

Bibliography

Canada, Minister of Employment and Immigration 1985 *Training: A Discussion Paper*. Ministry of Supply and Services, Ottawa, Ontario

Canadian Association for Adult Education (CAAE) 1985 *An Analysis of the Statistics*. Canada Adult Education Survey. CAAE, Toronto, Ontario

Devereaux M S 1984 *One in Every Five: A Survey of Adult Education in Canada*. Ministry of Supply and Services, Ottawa, Ontario

Provision in Western Europe

W. Bax

The purpose of this article is to undertake an overview of national adult education organization and practices in Western Europe. It will examine the kinds of providing agencies and the forms of provision, with particular attention paid to new activities designed for target groups with special needs, for whom guidance and counselling services are increasingly offered. The main features of administration are considered, including the trend towards decentralization, the roles played by the state and voluntary associations, and the increasing tendency to introduce legislation to control and support adult education, the latter notably by measures to encourage paid educational leave. Attention is also paid to the provision of training for adult educators in Western Europe, to the work of international organizations and finally to the subject of international cooperation in adult education.

Adult education in Western Europe has its origins in private initiatives, and voluntary organizations still continue to play an important role. In the different countries, various types of system have developed, and continue to develop, in response to specific needs and aims. An analysis of the Directory of Adult Education Organizations in Europe (EBAE 1983) reveals a wide range of organizations and institutions.

1. Organizations with a Broad Educational Aim

The oldest adult education facilities date from the period of the Enlightenment. They were typically set up with the aim "to bring light and citizenship to fellow citizens who earn their living with their hands", as was the stated purpose for an adult education organization established in the Netherlands in 1784. These early general educational organizations were followed in the nineteenth and twentieth centuries by many initiatives to spread knowledge about a wide range of subjects. The British initiatives in the field of university extension in the nineteenth century, for example, which started by extending the number of universities and later moved on to providing part-time courses for adults, stimulated similar initiatives in many European countries. Where it was not possible to succeed in opening up the universities to adults, these initiatives were taken over by voluntary organizations.

2. Religious and Social Organizations

There were a large number of initiatives taken by religious groups, which started with the aim of enabling people to read and understand the Bible, and later developed towards providing very diversified programmes. Organizations were established in some countries with the aim of promoting and revitalizing their own national or regional culture (this being one of the aims of the Folk High Schools in Scandinavia, of associations in Flanders in 1855 and in Ireland in 1893, to mention a few examples).

Educational activities have been mounted by specific groups in the population, often with a strong emancipatory background, for example, the workers' movement, farmers, women and the elderly. Citizens' education is provided by a wide range of organizations; in many countries political parties have also undertaken educational activities for their members as well as for the public at large. There are movements concerned with specific problems, such as the temperance movement in Sweden and more recently environmental issues, relations with developing countries and the peace movement.

To this range of nonformal education activities can be added the provision made by local authorities in a number of countries, and educational programmes in neighbourhood centres and similar institutions having adult education as their secondary aim.

3. Second-chance Education

In most countries the regular school system provides school programmes for adults, or provision is made for alternative avenues for adults to obtain regular school qualifications. In Austria for example, since 1962 courses for adults leading to formal secondary school qualifications are recognized as a component of the education system. In Denmark such courses are provided by the "Amter" (counties), free of charge. In Sweden since 1968 the municipalities have been obliged to establish schools to provide equivalents of formal education at different levels for adults; in the Netherlands there are over 80 day and evening schools for adults which are fully subsidized by the state.

In these courses attempts are made to develop special working and teaching methods adapted to adults. In many cases, to make it possible for adults to combine their learning activities with other obligations, a unit credit system has been introduced which makes it possible to gradually acquire the certificates leading to regular diplomas. The university system is also opening up for adults, with a strong impetus being given by the establishment of special "open universities" (e.g. in the United Kingdom, the Federal Republic of Germany, the Netherlands, and Spain).

4. Adult Vocational Training

In the field of vocational education for adults wide provision is made by formal educational establishments, employers' organizations, private firms and the workers' movements. In the various countries of Europe public authorities have accepted a responsibility for the training of young people and their transition to working life. For employed youngsters and adults a great deal of the needs for training (apprenticeship) and further training are covered by their firms or employers' organizations.

Apart from this provision, however, the need for extra training facilities which are wider than the interests of the firm itself and/or the industry has been felt. In a number of countries provision for this need has traditionally been met by organizations established by trade unions, or by tripartite arrangements between the state, industry and the unions. Public provision is increasing in this field, however, for example for those wishing to change jobs, for people wishing to improve their qualifications and for persons wishing to reenter the labour market (housewives, and so on). These forms of vocational training had an important role in periods of rapid economic expansion, not only in the field of refresher training but also in the retraining of the limited excess labour in the labour market.

The need for the further extension of vocational training has also made itself felt in times of economic and employment difficulties and technological change, when unskilled and semiskilled labour in manufacturing and office occupations face particular threats.

When we add to this extensive list the residential colleges (long- and short-term in Scandinavia, the Federal Republic of Germany and the United Kingdom; short-term in other countries of central Europe), correspondence education and educational broadcasts (national, regional, and now also local) we get a picture of a wide range of studies and a great pluriformity of activities. This variety of institutions is to be found in most countries of Europe. Their relative importance, however, is strongly influenced by national policies, for example the types of organizations similar to those that flourished in Sweden were repressed until the mid-1970s in Portugal and Spain.

5. Cooperation Among Adult Education Organizations

In most countries of north and middle Europe, national organizations have been established to facilitate communication between the various adult education organizations and to undertake joint action. As nongovernmetal organizations these bodies represent the common interest of adult education organization vis à vis their respective governments. The services offered by these bodies usually include the publication of a journal on adult education, documentation services, the setting up of joint projects, training facilities and the promotion of international relations. In a number of cases these bodies also have a function in the field of research and development; more often, however, these tasks are undertaken by institutes established especially for this purpose, or by universities.

6. Administration

In most countries of Europe the field of adult education is the concern of national governments. In federal states, such as Switzerland and the Federal Republic of Germany, the responsibility, as far as general education is concerned, rests with the provinces (cantons and Länder respectively). An attempt made by plebiscite in Switzerland in 1973 failed to change this situation. Austria has a mixed system, with legislation at national level and responsibility for provision lying with the provinces. Vocational training in these countries, however, is a national responsibility.

In Belgium, where three cultural communities were established in 1970, sociocultural education is now the responsibility of the communities for the Dutch language, for the French language and for the German language; formal and vocational education still come under the national government.

Vocational education is usually catered for by the ministries of labour, with various provisions being dealt with by other ministries (in France, for example, this includes the ministries of agriculture, health, culture, welfare and women's rights). As far as administration is concerned, adult education is thus a very scattered field, due to this compartmentalization.

In recent years there have been attempts to establish better coordination between the various sectors. The Netherlands government, for example, has appointed the Minister of Education as the coordinating minister for the entire field of adult education, and in France the Ministry of Vocational Training is nominated as the coordinating ministry for the important field of continuing training. Another means of coordination tried out in various countries is the establishment of advisory committees, with a membership covering various sectors.

Apart from the attempts at coordination within the adult education sector itself, a number of countries have also pursued a policy aimed at better communication with the other sectors of education. Based on the principle of "*éducation permanente*" attempts have been made to give adult education an equal place in the total system of education, alongside the sectors of primary, secondary and university education. This policy has been most consistently pursued in the Federal Republic of Germany, with its comprehensive plan for education (*Bildungsgesamtplan* 1970), and in the Scandinavian countries. By 1965 the Norwegian Parliament had already adopted Proposition Nr. 92, which emphasized the two principles that adult education should be on an equal footing with school education, and that the definition of adult education should include liberal, general education, as well as vocational education.

7. *Decentralization*

The organizational problems of fragmentation and compartmentalization mentioned in the previous section led to a strong movement in the 1970s towards decentralization of power.

There was a general idea that governments' tasks would have to be restricted to setting down general requirements, but not working out details of educational plans and programmes. These more detailed tasks were considered to be best performed as close as possible to the level where the work is to be done in order to relate to the needs of the people for whom the provisions were being made, and to allow them to participate in the decision-making process. In France decentralization was advocated as a means of simplifying the organization and diminishing bureaucratic procedures, of increasing the participation of the population and of taking into account the cultural identity of regions. In the southern European countries with their traditionally very centralized administrations, however, this new policy meant a total change of concept, a "silent revolution".

In middle and northern Europe local and regional governments already had a number of responsibilities. In the United Kingdom local education authorities were traditionally free to respond to demands for provision, either through their own institutions or through local voluntary bodies. As the 1944 Act (England and Wales) by which this system was promoted is permissive legislation, there remain wide variations in provision between the various local authorities, in line with local needs and interests and the means of those authorities. The United Kingdom is the only country where at present this local power is restricted by central government. In a number of Länder of the Federal Republic of Germany the local authorities are obliged to make provision for nonformal adult education by establishing special institutions (*Volkshochschulen*) which are financed partly by the Länder and partly by local government. Finnish municipalities are also providing similar institutes. Since 1968 municipalities in Sweden have had to make provision for formal adult education following the school curriculum.

Elsewhere the responsibilities of local and/or regional authorities were extended. In France, for example, a law on decentralization was passed in 1982 which affected the system of vocational training in 1983, when the regions were made responsible for important fields such as apprenticeship training, courses leading to qualifications (social advancement courses) and the remuneration of adults undertaking or resuming studies on a voluntary basis.

In Italy in 1977 a wide range of central administrative functions was transferred from the central state to the regional councils. The central ministry is responsible only for literacy education and educational leave for the completion of compulsory education. Regional councils have since made provision to meet specific needs of local communities in cooperation with local authorities, district school councils and labour organizations, in an attempt to overcome the split between formal and nonformal education.

In the Netherlands as well a move towards decentralization was made by national government, and informal adult education was one of the first sectors to follow this new pattern. The planning of adult education was consequently undertaken by local government, with the development of local centres in which various adult education organizations coordinate their efforts and cooperate in providing educational advice and undertaking "outreach" work.

8. *Adult Education Legislation*

The first provisions for adult education made in legislation were concerned with providing school education for adults. In all countries measures have been taken to provide "second chance" education for adults. Many of these activities take place in regular schools or in institutions especially established for this purpose, such as the municipal adult education centres established in Sweden after 1968. The Norwegian Law on Adult Education of 1976 also expressly mentioned the alternative provision of formal education, that is, programmes which make use of combined teaching methods and adapt their content, methods and examination regulations to the interests and needs of adults in view of their experience at work and in their social life. Similar programmes have also been set up in other countries, but very often examination regulations are badly adapted to this approach.

Legislation in the field of nonformal adult education has gradually developed in parallel with the increase of support for this section. Legislation has thus tended to reflect the diversified structure of this type of adult education as various ministries undertook to support different fields of work. Consequently, there were and still are in every country a number of regulations and decrees dealing with limited aspects. Provisions about certain programmes may be inserted in legislation on other items (for example, safety at work, works' councils). With the growing support given to adult education the need was felt for provision of a more comprehensive legal framework to serve as a basis for further development. Since the end of the 1960s new legislation has been enacted in most countries of middle and northern Europe.

Because of the private character of much of adult education provision there is a strong apprehension concerning centralization and uniformity. In much of the present legislation an endeavour has been made to combine the necessary flexibility with the need for some form of coordination and overall structures. The Danish Act on Leisure Education (1968) is an example of legislation which gives maximum scope to private initiatives. A basic principle of this Act is that every group of adults, comprising at least 12 members at any time, should be eligible for public support for almost any kind of education. Any voluntary organization can, with very few formal requirements, receive public support. There are of course a number of larger national organizations making use of the regulations, but in principle this is a very open system. Following the introduction of the Act the number of participants has greatly increased. The decree of 1976 (Wallonia, Belgium) also promotes a very open system covering national, regional and local organizations.

In other countries the system of subsidizing adult education organizations is more formalized; subsidies for study work tend to pass through a limited number of national study organizations which are acknowledged by the central government. Austria, for example, passed a national law on adult education in 1973 which allowed financial support to be granted to non-profit-making providers in the field of cultural, vocational and citizenship education, which in practice meant a number of large national organizations.

The most comprehensive legislation is the Norwegian Adult Education Act of 1976 which deals with education provided by voluntary organizations—formal education for adults as well as vocational training—as a means of labour market policy and training in industrial firms. Aimed at promoting more equal status between individuals as well as between groups in the population, and between the poorer and richer regions, the legislation provides for special grants for courses for the disabled, persons having had little primary education and persons with special family obligations, and courses for union stewards. Even so, this legislation does not cover all sectors of work concerned.

In general it can be stated that the consequences of the economic difficulties have tempered the full execution of the legislation as enacted in the various countries. Instead of working towards a comprehensive provision of adult education, governments now tend to choose programmes dealing with the effects of the economic crisis, and priority is given to specific projects.

9. Paid Educational Leave

At the 59th Session of the General Conference of the International Labour Organisation, held in 1974, Convention No. 140 concerning paid educational leave was adopted. This convention asked the member countries to formulate and apply a policy designed to promote the granting of paid educational leave for the provision of training at any level and for general, social, or civic education, and trade union education. In a number of countries action has been taken following this convention; several countries, however, have been reluctant to formulate a national policy because of the expected financial implications.

In countries which have not taken any official action, the lack of formal guarantees for paid educational leave does not mean, of course, that there are no arrangements of this sort. In practice, there are many schemes run by enterprises which require training to ensure their continuity. Most often such courses are short vocational courses for supervisory and professional groups. The formal regulations adopted in a number of countries only set out the formal right to study leave, leaving it to the work contracts to define the financial compensation.

This is, for example, the case in Finland where a formal right to study leave was stated for a maximum of three months during three years, after one year of employment. Also in Italy the law adopted in 1970 only formally stated the possibility of making use of study leave. The practical implementation of the law began in 1973 when the first contract negotiated was in the metal and mechanical industry, setting out the right to "150 hours" of paid educational leave and the same number of unpaid free hours for study. The right can be used for courses of vocational training, as well as for general education.

Since the end of the 1950s France has legislated in the field of educational leave for economic or trades unions training (1957: 12 days per year unpaid leave), for programmes of social advancement (1959) and leadership in popular education (1961). In the 1960s the facilities for leave for training programmes were gradually extended: the 1971 law made educational leave a right for all paid and nonpaid workers, allowing them to follow a training course during working hours, with pay under certain conditions. The law has made it compulsory for all firms employing more than nine people to spend a certain percentage of the total wages (at present 1.1 percent) on training for employees.

In the amendments to the more recent Law of 1978, an endeavour was made to increase the rights of the Works' Council in the field of training, and to distinguish between individual educational leave and the training programme established by the employer. In 1980, 34,000 employees out of 1,700,000 trainees employed in firms benefited from an individual educational leave taken on their own initiative in training programmes which made it possible for workers "to reach a higher level of qualification, to change their jobs or their careers, and to open themselves more fully to culture and social life". At the same time, provision was made to facilitate the access to training activities for special groups in the population, such as the self-employed, women wishing to take up work again and youngsters between 16 and 26 years of age.

In six of the German "Länder", legislation on paid educational leave was enacted, stating the right of every employee to take five days paid educational leave per year, preferably in the field of vocational or civic education.

In Belgium in 1973 a part-time release system was established by law to make it possible to follow general education programmes. This law was amended in 1985 with the effect that employees would be entitled to paid leave for general education (160 hours per year) as well as vocational training (240 hours per year). Here the state contributes 50 percent of the earnings of employees in vocational training programmes, and 100 percent of the leave for general education.

In Sweden a system of educational leave was established by a series of measures. The law regarding the right to educational leave applies to all employees. With regard to the financing of studies, the individual is referred to the various forms of support for adult education, such as an education bursary within labour market training, compensation for basic education for adults, hourly study support for participation in study circles with priority (e.g. Swedish, social science, and trades union education), compensation for lost income and boarding costs for short courses in Folk High Schools and support for full-time studies of at least two weeks' duration in a Folk High School, municipal adult education association or Technical High School. Moreover, adults taking part in long-term studies can benefit from the same study support regulations as university students.

Experience demonstrates that a great number of those eligible for educational leave are not very well informed about their right to claim it, and have only a vague knowledge of the provision of programmes. This is especially the case with older workers, foreign workers and workers in small firms. There is apparently a great need for good information and advisory services in connection with paid educational leave.

10. Adult Educators: Function and Training

In line with its voluntary background, adult education traditionally was not thought of as a career but as voluntary work. Since the Second World War, however, adult education has been seen more as a profession, but it is only since the beginning of the 1960s and especially during the 1970s that an increasing number of people have become professionally engaged in this field. Between 1965 and 1976 the number of full-time adult educators in the German *Volkschochschule*, for example, increased from 300 to 1,120; in England the number of full-time staff in nonvocational adult education in 1950 was nearly nonexistent, but had increased to over 2,000 in 1980.

Most full-time staff members work as tutors/organizers, with an accent on the organizing function. Moreover they have an important role to play in the training and guidance of (part-time) staff. They are drawn from a wide range of fields and academic disciplines. Although there are specialized preservice training programmes for executive functions, preference is usually given to inservice training which provides an opportunity to combine training with practice, following a short preservice induction course. The provision of this type of training has always been one of the most important tasks of the various adult education organizations, but other institutions (universities) may be involved as well. To meet the need for practical experience, preservice training tends also to give a stronger emphasis to this aspect.

Over the past few years a number of initiatives have been taken to bring training facilities as close as possible to the field of work through the establishment of local or regional centres as a basis for training, the dissemination of information and centres of research. In Denmark such institutions have existed since the late 1970s; similar institutions exist in the Netherlands and Sweden. In the United Kingdom local education authorities, voluntary organizations and universities cooperate to make this sort of flexible provision in the field of training at the regional level, responsive to the training needs of their members.

Also in the United Kingdom a scheme has been elaborated for regional provision of courses for part-time adult education tutors, consisting of a minimum of 35 hours in courses combined with home study, visits of observation and teaching practice in their own class. Following this stage a second stage may be taken of at least 60—but more usually 100—content hours which is followed by a substantial proportion of part-timers. For those willing to proceed to full professional certification a much more demanding third stage is optional. Another recent development in the field of training is the provision of self-study materials.

The number of full-time staff members is far exceeded by the number of part-time staff which has also greatly increased with the growth of adult education provision. The figures given for part-time staff at the German *Volkschochschule* increased from 50,000 in 1965 to 81,279 in 1976. The involvement of part timers, who very often teach in their own time in adult education and have full-time functions in other sectors of society, makes it possible for adult education to keep close to new developments and interests. Very often, however, part-timers do not have enough background in educational work and there is a strong need for training in this field. An impediment in this respect is that many part-timers do not anticipate a career in adult education because of their full-time occupations elsewhere, and it is not always certain whether enough participants will continue to attend their courses. Moreover, organizations very often have little time to guide them in their work and they may feel a sense of isolation.

In countries where the state has taken more responsibility for adult education, voluntary organizations very often have grown into semiofficial bodies working with full-time staff. In southern Europe this is less the case, and in northern Europe there is a notable revival of the voluntary spirit of adult education organizations: the value of educational activities undertaken by volunteers with the same social and educational background as the learner is emphasized, and an increasing part of the organizational work is again undertaken by volunteers. Moreover, there are a number of new organizations, concerned with problems of, for example, the environment, peace and relations with developing countries, which have an educational component, and which totally rely on volunteers.

11. Adult Education Information and Activities: Guidance and Counselling

Since the beginning of the 1970s much attention has been paid to improving the participation in adult education of educationally/socially disadvantaged groups in society, which are underrepresented in adult education. It was clear that conventional methods of information dissemination such as leaflets and posters were not sufficient to reach these groups, and various ways have been tried out to provide relevant information and to activate people:

(a) Direct contacts on the work floor as well as in private homes, and so on ("outreach work" as tried out in the Scandinavian countries).

(b) Education shops or mobile information services making use of community centres, job centres, libraries and so on.

(c) Cooperation with existing organizations, associations for the disabled, the unemployed, or women's groups.

(d) Using (local) radio or television as a medium for publicity.

(e) Setting up telephone referral services.

(f) Using advanced technology to supply centrally collected information to people in their own environment by "user-friendly" systems.

(g) Schemes in which information suppliers cooperate with existing organizations, such as women's groups, associations for the disabled, and organizations for the unemployed.

More attention is also being paid to guidance and counselling in the framework of adult education programmes. A number of courses are themselves directed to finding "new horizons" in life and helping people find new educational opportunities.

An example of this opportunity is the collective training campaigns in France, started in 1964, following the recession in the Lorraine industrial basin. Such campaigns are closely related to the local situation; efforts are made not to turn away any applicant coming from the area but to adjust the educational responses to the demands as they are defined and developed. Collective training thus appears as an educational situation where adults may express their requests for education, whatever these may be, and map out for themselves training routes consistent with the objectives they pursue or may discover.

In more formal theme-oriented courses more attention is given to the needs for advice and counselling for students. Usually these tasks are undertaken by members of staff who also have a teaching function. This work needs a back-up service which embraces training opportunities—a referral service within the individual organization as well as a general service for problems/needs which are best dealt with outside the limits of one specific organization. In a number of countries such independent counselling and advisory centres have been established, which, apart from their information and counselling services, also have an important function in making adult education organizations aware of unmet needs.

12. Adult Basic Education

For a long time the official standpoint of governments in the industrially developed countries of Europe was that there was no problem of adult illiteracy, as a result of the introduction of compulsory elementary schooling in their respective countries.

The work of voluntary organizations in the United Kingdom at the beginning of the 1970s made it clear, however, that a considerable percentage of the adult population was unable to adequately read, write, or spell, and that there was a need for a wider provision in this field. The campaign "A Right to Read" led to the establishment of the Adult Literacy Campaign, where the use of broadcasting as an important medium was used to activate people, to teach, and to bring people into contact with a national referral service. At the same time a wide provision of courses was made by local education authorities, making use of the help of a great number of volunteers. In 1976 49,522 students received tuition in this way; in that year in total 41,618 volunteers were involved, mostly after a short preparatory training, and very often on a one-to-one basis.

The experiences in the United Kingdom and also in Sweden made other countries aware of the problem of adult illiteracy and the provision in this field has been greatly extended during the past few years. In general it was estimated that approximately 4 percent of the population was in need of literacy training. In Portugal, however, where after the 1974 revolution more attention was given to adult education, the number of illiterates was assessed as 23 percent of the population above 14 years old. At the same time it became evident, however, that participants in literacy courses were in need of a far wider range of abilities and skills, which led to a widening of the provision following the concept of adult basic education.

Adult basic education, following a much-used definition, includes the imparting of communication skills (literacy, numeracy, general civic, scientific and cultural knowledge, values and attitudes); living skills (knowledge of health, sanitation, nutrition, family planning, the environment, etc); and production skills. Adult basic education is provided in a wide range of contexts to adapt to the varied situations of potential students: in community groups, in programmes related with and to the employment situation, in special settings (like prisons, mental hospitals), with organizations of ethnic minority groups, in second-chance education, in introductory programmes to vocational training in more formal second-chance education. In the Netherlands, the

Open School, a special multimedia programme in social and general education, was set up for underprivileged groups in Dutch society. In general, adult basic education has developed following a student-centred model, and endeavours are made in the training of tutors and in the preparation of learning materials to strengthen this approach.

13. Adult Education and Unemployment

As a consequence of the economic crisis and technological development, high unemployment has become a characteristic of most countries of Europe. The total figures for the 10 countries of the European Community increased from 5.1 percent of the professional population in 1978 to 10.6 percent in 1984.

New programmes and didactic methods have been tried out and many educational activities have been started in relation to projects for the unemployed. The view is increasingly being taken that it is not sufficient for such programmes to offer a short-term adjustment to new circumstances, technologies, and jobs. The value of education which is broader than that required for the direct performance of a function is increasingly realized and more attention is being given to the integration of general and vocational education in these programmes: the acquisition of occupational skills is becoming increasingly inseparable from the acquisition of general and social competence.

Moreover, guidance and counselling have become focal points in these programmes. In the Federal Republic of Germany special information and guidance courses are organized for 4–6 weeks, giving information about the labour market, occupational needs, training opportunities, and financial assistance that can be obtained. This scheme has contributed to an increased self-confidence of participants and willingness to attend further training courses. Educational activities are also undertaken to help the unemployed to improve their quality of life, and position in society (courses helping people to spend their time in a meaningful way, teaching them how to defend their own interests and how to improve the effectiveness of their organizations).

In general the programmes are related to the local or regional unemployment situation. In a number of courses these activities are also connected with local community development and work creation. Many of these programmes are supported by the European Social Fund.

14. Adult Education and Older People

In view of the rising proportion in the population of people aged 65 years and over, education for older people is an emerging field of work. In many countries preretirement courses are now organized, sometimes by private firms or by residential adult education or local adult education colleges. This provision is becoming more important as early retirement schemes are increasingly put into effect as a means of combating unemployment and the swiftly approaching technological changes. The courses help people to explore new activities and adapt to the new situation.

Programmes for older people cover a large range of activities such as health education, life management skills, social and cultural topics, creative activities, language classes and so on. An important aspect of all these activities is to bring older people out of their isolation and to help them undertake mutual activities. The initiative taken in 1973 of establishing a "University of the Third Age", in Toulouse, is now being followed in many more countries. In addition to a programme of courses such as those mentioned above, this provision also stimulates the undertaking of research as a way of experiential learning.

In view of the dislike the active elderly feel for being segregated from the rest of society, special attention should be paid to the accessibility of the general provision of adult education to older people. In various countries groups of elderly people have endeavoured to reach out to younger generations by special activities such as drama, and information about their personal and/or local history.

15. Women's Education

At the General Conference of UNESCO held in 1976 in Nairobi, an instrument for the development of adult education was ratified which was adopted by all member countries. This instrument required that each country work towards ensuring the equality of access of girls and women to the entire range of adult education activities, including those which provide training for qualifications leading to activities or responsibilities which have hitherto been reserved for boys and men. When evaluating the progress made by the women's movement in the past years, it appears, however, that the biggest gains are in the area of consciousness, becoming confident, fighting the effects of oppression in women themselves, and developing a great many structures through which to spread this consciousness.

In the 1970s a type of course was initiated which aimed at giving housewives an opportunity to "discover" society and to make a new start. These courses are widely spread and are intended for women working in the household who have only received an elementary education. In discussions among themselves they are given an opportunity to break through the isolation of their homes, to deal with issues of common interest and to work out options for further development. Very often, attendance at these courses leads to further study; the final aim however is to acquire economic independence, and the hope for social contacts in a working situation with interesting and satisfying work.

To help women to get a place in the labour market there are the general facilities for vocational training, but apart from that, the need is felt to make special initiatives to gear courses more to the needs of women. In the training for office jobs, for example, it is felt necessary to go more deeply into the life situation of participants and their future situation as women engaged in office work; attention, therefore, is paid to personal and group counselling during these courses and raising the consciousness of participants. Similarly, courses for working women have to deal with special items, such as the double load of work of women undertaking paid work and working in the household, and to discuss how to bring forward their interests and change their situation. A special item in this context is the preparation of women for the introduction of new technologies in the working situation.

As far as the second point—women and power—is concerned, activities are increasingly being undertaken to increase the participation of women in politics, and to achieve more equality in the decision-making process. Courses for women and management, and the establishment of women's leadership support groups, are seen as ways in which to achieve this aim.

16. Adult Education and Cultural Minority Groups

The immigration of foreign workers and their families, as well as of those originating from former colonies, has greatly influenced the social scene in many countries of Europe. The percentage of foreign nationals in the Federal Republic of Germany, for example, is estimated to be 8.08 percent; in France and Belgium the percentages are assessed as 7.27 percent and 9.79 percent respectively. Until the 1980s governments in general took for granted that the employment of foreign workers was only a temporary phenomenon. Since then, however, it has now been acknowledged that this was not to be the case, and that it has become necessary to pursue an active policy in view of the growing tensions in the population of the "host" countries. This has led to wider possibilities for educational programmes organized by adult education institutions, as well as by minority groups themselves.

The main types of programmes deal with:

(a) language courses in the language of the "host" country of residence, but also in the native language;

(b) literacy and basic education programmes;

(c) programmes aimed at strengthening the immigrants' own identity by cultural manifestations presenting their own culture to the population at large (dance, music, food and so on);

(d) programmes for groups with special difficulties, that is, the second generation of immigrants (who often lack the background to participate in training leading to employment) and immigrant women who are living in isolation; and

(e) programmes in the field of vocational training in which there is an increasing interest.

Apart from these activities there is a great need for educational measures directed towards the population at large, aimed at understanding minority groups and combating racism.

17. Activities of International Organizations in the Field of Adult Education

With the growing importance of adult education in policy making there is an increasing interest in international governmental organizations in this field. UNESCO has been instrumental in defining the lines of development of the total field and has undertaken special action in literacy work and basic education. The UNESCO European Centre for Leisure and Education (ECLE) publishes adult education materials from Eastern and Western Europe.

Since the beginning of the 1960s the *Council of Europe* has been active in the field of adult education. At the end of the 1960s the Council was involved in studies on the implementation of *éducation permanente*. During the past few years projects have been undertaken in the field of "adult education and community development". Other activities of the Council are related to the teaching of modern languages and the promotion of womens' studies in postacademic education.

Following the Resolution of 9 February 1976, the cooperation in the field of education within the European Community has been greatly extended. In view of the high unemployment rates among the youth, priority is given in these programmes to vocational education, and the transition for young adults from school to the labour market. A second focus for the activities in the field of education and research is technological innovation, and it is planned to work towards a closer cooperation between higher education and industry, in the light of the social and technological developments in the countries of the Community.

The European Bureau of Adult Education (EBAE) is a nongovernmental organization comprising 160 organizations in 18 countries of Europe. The Bureau regularly organizes study conferences on topical issues in adult education (adult basic education, use of media, educational leave, unemployment, cooperation of residential and nonresidential adult education, women and adult education, development of information, guidance, and counselling services in adult education, training and further training of adult educators, policy and legislation in adult education, local/regional authorities and adult education, adult education and local/regional development, changing concepts of work, adult education and cultural minorities, information and documentation in adult education). The Bureau also publishes basic documentation on adult education (Directory of Adult Education Organizations, Survey of Adult Education Legislation, Terminologies of Adult Education in English, French, German, Dutch, and Italian) as well as a regular periodical *Newsletter* twice a year.

Adult education organizations in Europe of a Roman Catholic background also cooperate in a separate body, the FEECA, the Federation for Catholic Adult Education. A similar body exists for Protestant organizations.

See also: Adult Education Legislation in Western Europe

Bibliography

European Bureau of Adult Education (EBAE) 1983 *Directory of Adult Education Organizations in Europe*, 4th edn. EBAE, Amersfoort

European Bureau of Adult Education (EBAE) 1985 *Survey of Adult Education Legislation.* EBAE, Amersfoort

European Centre for Leisure and Education (ECLE) 1974–84 *Adult Education in Europe, Studies and Documents*, No. 2 France; No. 7 Austria; No. 8 Federal Republic of Germany; No. 9 United Kingdom; No. 10–11 Italy; No. 16 Portugal; No. 18 France II; No. 21–22 Ireland. ECLE, Prague

Titmus C 1981 *Strategies for Adult Education, Practices in Western Europe*. Open University Press, Milton Keynes

Provision in Eastern Europe and the Soviet Union

J. Kulich

The roots of contemporary adult education in the Eastern European countries reach into the widespread ethnic and national revival which swept this region during the nineteenth century. Since its origins, adult education in Russia and Eastern Europe has been viewed very broadly. Thus today it typically encompasses not only the usual school-type provision at the elementary, secondary, and postsecondary levels, as well as considerable training in government, business, and industry, but also a widespread provision of nonformal adult education through libraries, houses and palaces of culture, trade union and village clubs, people's and workers' universities, societies for the popularization of science, political party organizations, amateur art, music, theatre, and folklore groups, mass organizations for culture, education and physical culture, and many others. Consequently, adult education in Eastern Europe is often referred to as "enlightenment work" or "cultural–educational work", and adult educators are called cultural or cultural–educational workers. Consistent with the ideological, political, and economic system established in the Soviet Union after 1917 and in Eastern Europe since 1945, all forms of adult education have to fit into the prevailing social system and planned economy. Adult education is considered an important ideological tool and throughout the region it is subject to Communist Party and state control.

1. Socioeconomic Background and Historical Development

Eastern Europe is often dealt with as if it were one country or a monolithic block. The countries of this region (Albania, Bulgaria, Czechoslovakia, the German Democratic Republic (GDR), Hungary, Poland, Romania, the Soviet Union and Yugoslavia) do share some historical similarities, and since the end of the 1940s all have become part of the "socialist camp". However, differences in their origin, historical development, ethnic composition, and stages of economic development must not be disregarded.

Prior to 1918 many of the current Eastern European states were occupied or governed by foreign powers. Bulgaria and Romania gained independence from Turkish suzerainty in 1878, while Albania remained under Turkish rule until 1912. Hungary was part of the Austrian Hapsburg Empire, gaining home rule in 1867. Several Yugoslav provinces, as well as all of what is now Czechoslovakia, were also under Austrian rule. Poland was partitioned between Austria, Prussia, and Russia.

In ethnic composition Slavs predominate throughout the region, but there are major non-Slavonic areas. The Hungarians are part of the Finno-Ugric branch, the Albanians are Illyrian-Thracians, and the Romanians are Latins. The population of the German Democractic Republic is German. The languages of these four ethnic groups are non-Slavic, as are their cultural roots. There are also significant ethnic minority groups living in most of the countries of Eastern Europe.

In the wake of the First World War and the breaking up of the Hapsburg Empire, new states emerged in Eastern Europe. Czechoslovakia was formed from Bohemia and Slovakia, Hungary gained full independence, Yugoslavia was formed as a new state out of several South Slavic territories, and Poland was unified again. Albania gained full independence in 1920. After the 1917 revolution and the subsequent civil war, Russia became the Union of Soviet Socialist Republics (USSR) in 1922. Between the two world wars, Czechoslovakia, Germany, Hungary, Poland, and the Soviet Union were republics, while Albania, Bulgaria, Romania, and Yugoslavia were kingdoms.

There were significant differences and disparities among the Eastern European countries, up to the Second World War, in terms of their economic development: Albania remained a peasant feudal fiefdom; Germany and Czechoslovakia were highly developed industrial countries; the Soviet Union was developing rapidly in the 1930s; Bulgaria, Hungary, Poland, Romania, and Yugoslavia were predominantly agricultural countries.

The level of literacy also varied significantly. Between the two world wars Albania had 83 percent illiteracy, Bulgaria 27.8 percent (1934), Czechoslovakia 4.1 percent (1930), Germany 0.05 percent (1901), Hungary 6.9 percent (1941), Poland 23 percent (1931), Romania 38.9 percent (1930), the USSR 18.8 percent (1939), and Yugoslavia 44.6 percent (1931).

At the end of the Second World War Eastern Europe had been ravaged by war and was in ruins economically, politically, and spiritually. In the early postwar years of reconstruction there were far-reaching social, economic, and political changes and by 1950 all the countries in Eastern Europe had governments in which the Communist Party played a dominant role. These developments had also a significant impact on adult education throughout the region.

2. The Beginnings and Development of Adult Education in Eastern Europe and the Soviet Union

The historical roots of adult education in this area go back to the mid-nineteenth century, the great period of national linguistic and cultural awakening throughout the region. A number of literary, reading, and educational societies and circles appeared in the cities, and later spread to the villages. The national awakening movements, led by the growing indigenous intelligentsia, and the struggle for ethnic survival in the face of foreign cultural domination, were significant motivating forces for adult education throughout Eastern Europe during the second half of the nineteenth century.

Among the societies established to foster national cultural revival were in Poland the Polish Foundation (established 1822); in Yugoslavia the Serbian Foundation (established 1826), the Croatian Foundation (established 1847), and the Slovenian Foundation (established 1864); in Czechoslovakia the Bohemian Foundation (established 1831) and the Slovak Foundation (established 1863); in Romania the Association for Romanian Literature and Popular Education (established 1861); and in Bulgaria the Bulgarian Scholars' Society (established 1869).

As elsewhere, Sunday schools were the first formal adult education institutions in Eastern and Central Europe. In Germany such schools were established as early as the eighteenth century, while in the rest of the region Sunday schools did not come into being until the mid-nineteenth century. In Russia these schools, set up by the progressive intelligentsia and funded by local government, were the most characteristic form of adult education before the First World War. In Bulgaria Sunday schools were used in the struggle against Turkish influence, but were not very successful until they became attached to the network of popular reading centres after 1869. At the turn of the century, Sunday schools were replaced by adult evening schools. These schools at first provided elementary education, but later on branched out into the provision of secondary education to adults. Private and public correspondence schools also appeared throughout the region around the turn of the century.

A number of national institutions were established in the late nineteenth century to foster adult education. In Germany, the Society for the Promotion of Popular Education was popularizing science from 1871, while the Hungarian Association for the Investigation of Nature was offering lectures to the general public from 1873. Bohemia (part of what is now Czechoslovakia) had a Labour Academy, established in 1896 and a Central Labour School, founded in 1897. In Romania, the Education Home was established in 1897 with the task of setting up public libraries, publishing books suitable for adults, and organizing cultural circles for village teachers.

The role played by the village-school teachers in Eastern Europe in the national awakening in the nineteenth century and the popular enlightenment in the early twentieth century was significant. It would be hard to conceive of the progress achieved in adult elementary education, agricultural innovation, public health education, cultural development, and civic education of the rural population, without the major contribution of the village teachers.

The increasing number of reading rooms and private and public libraries spreading throughout the region in the mid-nineteenth century was another significant contribution to the people's enlightenment. Many of these institutions worked in close cooperation with or were established by the great variety of voluntary educational associations.

University extension is the British contribution to adult education successfully established in many other countries. This idea was also transplanted to several Eastern and Central European countries around the turn of the century. The Charles University in Prague established public university lectures which survived for several decades. In Romania, similar activities were set up at the University of Cluj and soon spread to other Romanian universities. The University of Lvov and the University of Cracow in Poland offered public lectures from the late 1800s, and at the University of Belgrade in what is now Yugoslavia such public lectures were in existence from 1888. Similar developments occurred in other areas of the region. From the 1920s, extramural study and correspondence courses leading to degrees were added to the noncredit public university lectures. Nevertheless, with the notable exception of the Soviet Union, where separate workers' universities paralleling the old established universities were set up in the 1920s, university extension in Eastern and Central Europe never attained the same magnitude and significance as in the English-speaking countries of the world.

One of the reasons why general university extension did not take root in Eastern and Central Europe, in spite of some promising beginnings around the turn of the century, was the institution of the very successful People's Universities. These popular institutions paralleled university extension and were engaged in very much the same work, but without any formal organizational link to the universities. However, most of their lecturers came from the universities and from university educated professionals.

The first of these institutions in Eastern Europe were established in Moscow in the 1890s; by 1906 societies of People's Universities were operating in Moscow, St Petersburg, and elsewhere. The University for All was established in Poland in 1905. The establishment of People's Universities, organized by the Polish School Foundation, followed in 1906. The first People's University in Yugoslavia was the Citizens' University of Zagreb, founded in 1907. During the period between the two world wars, People's Universities were the major adult education institution throughout Eastern Europe. In Germany, Hungary, and Poland, in addition to People's Universities (which were primarily city and town evening institutions), there developed local adaptations of the Danish residential folk high schools, serving the rural population.

The physical education associations which developed on a major scale throughout Eastern and Central Europe in the late nineteenth century played a significant role and are possibly the first example of the implementation of lifelong education provision. Having originated in Germany, these associations which organized activities for children, youth, and adults soon spread throughout the region. The most influential of them was the *Sokol*, established in Bohemia in 1862 and which soon thereafter branched out to other Slavic provinces and countries. These physical education associations did not limit their activities to physical education, but also played a significant role in civic education.

For countries created or re-established largely as a result of the First World War and struggling, with a varying degree of success, with the democratization of their society, civic education in schools as well as for adults was seen as of prime importance. In some of these countries civic education was anchored in legislation, as in Czechoslovakia (1919) and Yugoslavia (1929). Civic education for children and adults as carried out by schools, voluntary associations, popular movements, and the armed forces in Eastern Europe was unequalled anywhere in Western Europe. Unfortunately, this promising process was interrupted by authoritarian regimes instituted in most of the East European countries in the 1930s, and by the Second World War.

Given the low level of literacy which prevailed in most areas of the region well into the twentieth century, attempts were made during the 1920s and 1930s to eliminate or reduce illiteracy. However, the only country showing any significant results was the Soviet Union, where a major military-style campaign reduced illiteracy from 48.8 percent in 1926 to 18.8 percent in 1939. In most of the other Eastern European countries, the gains in literacy between the two world wars were only short-lived, and widespread relapses into illiteracy occurred, primarily among the peasant population.

Any historical background to adult education in Eastern Europe would be incomplete without mention of the numerous amateur circles, clubs, and ensembles devoted to the preservation and enjoyment of the rich heritage of folk art, folk music, and folk dancing. This activity has its roots in the national awakening movements of the nineteenth century and continues to be a vital element of national life and pride throughout Eastern Europe. This activity is unequalled anywhere in Western Europe.

Systems of and developments in adult education in Eastern Europe and in the Soviet Union can be understood only against their historical background.

3. Concepts and Definitions of Adult Education in Eastern Europe and the Soviet Union

It has been mentioned that the concept of adult education in Eastern Europe, its early beginnings in the nineteenth century, was different and much broader than in other regions. Undoubtedly this has its cause in the varying societal needs of the time when organized modern adult education was beginning to take shape, but primarily in the national awakening which was so important a force throughout Eastern Europe.

The terminology used in all parts of the region until the early 1950s, "enlightenment work", "cultural enlightenment work", "cultural–educational work", "popular education", illustrate well the breadth of institutions and activities seen as part of adult education.

Unlike almost anywhere else, the concept of self-education, of self-development, has deep roots and is seen as an important factor in Eastern Europe. The institution of the external examination at university level, which enabled adults to advance by challenging examinations, is one of the manifestations of this belief in self-education.

The development of adult education in the Soviet Union and the Eastern European countries in the period between the two world wars differed significantly. The Soviet Union established a system of elementary, secondary, higher, and vocational education of adults which had as an overarching goal the building up of the new socialist citizen and society, under the guidance and control of the state and the Communist Party. Mass ideological work and political indoctrination increasingly became part of daily life and permeated all educational and cultural activities. However, in most of the Eastern European countries during this period a variety of primarily voluntary associations, aimed at general enlightenment of the population, and enjoying only a small measure of state support or involvement, formed the backbone of adult education.

Most of the indigenous adult education institutions and voluntary associations in Eastern Europe, except for Yugoslavia, were dismantled during the 1950s as a result of the far-reaching political–ideological, social, and economic changes which occurred in the late 1940s and which made the countries in the region part of the socialist camp led by the Soviet Union. At the same time Soviet concepts and methods of mass political work were introduced all over the region.

As a result of the political changes which followed the end of the Stalinist era in 1956, many of the old indigenous institutions and associations began to reappear and were soon flourishing again. At the same time, some of the significant positive changes brought about by the new social order, such as increased access to secondary and postsecondary education, continued.

In the 1980s adult education in Eastern Europe and the Soviet Union is most often thought of as a process for the development of the new socialist citizen in all social and individual aspects. The linking and intertwining of work and education is seen as an important method in the ongoing development of personality. Adult education is considered as an integral part of a lifelong process of Communist education.

The system of adult education which developed in the Soviet Union and Eastern Europe from the 1960s consists of three subsystems: (a) the formal school subsystem, (b) the subsystem of training on-the-job, and (c) the nonformal, out-of-school subsystem. Due to a unique system of worker self-management, instituted in Yugoslavia, this country alone in Eastern Europe does not have a clear distinction between the three subsystems of adult education. Although there are some differences among the East European countries, especially in the nonformal subsystem, the similarities seem in the 1980s to outweigh the differences.

4. The Formal or School Subsystem of Adult Education

The Soviet Union has the longest and broadest experience with the provision of adult education at the elementary, secondary, vocational–technical, and higher education levels. Between the two world wars these schools were full-time secondary and university level schools for workers, charged with the task of creating a new intelligentsia coming entirely from the working class. Since the 1950s these institutions have changed to part-time evening, and later distance education programmes. "At present, the night (shift) school mainly comprises the senior grades. . . in which 95 percent of the total number of students are enrolled. Distance education classes have become very popular: more than 60 percent of all the night school students now choose this form". (Onushkin and Tonkonogaya 1984 p. 23). In 1980–81 more than 8 percent of all secondary general education students were attending part-time adult schools; there were 12,500 of such schools with 4.7 million students (Onushkin and Tonkonogaya 1984 p. 19).

The establishment of the widespread network of separate evening and distance education schools and university faculties was the result of postwar reconstruction and the rapid technological and scientific development, with its demand for a highly trained and skilled work force. Part-time study for adults in the Soviet Union is considered as an important economic development tool, as it raises the qualifications of a significant percentage of the work force without interruption of work. The adult programmes usually take only a year longer to complete than full-time day programmes.

Part-time study is fostered and supported by the state and the Communist Party through public recognition as well as through tangible rewards for adults who participate in it. Since 1945 workers studying part-time alongside full employment have been given paid leave for examination preparation (15–20 work days); since the early 1960s additional work release has been legislated, including 36 days per academic year with 50 percent of regular wages paid (Onushkin and Tonkonogaya 1984 pp. 18–19). The constitutional and political support of adult part-time study is anchored in Article 26 of the Fundamentals of Legislation of the Soviet Union and its constituent republics: "Enterprises, institutions, and organizations must assist the involvement of the working youth in night schools, create the necessary conditions for combining work and study, and provide for the normal operation of these schools and studies of their students" (quoted by Onushkin and Tonkonogaya 1984 p. 19).

The Soviet Union adult part-time schooling prototype was adopted by the East European countries (particularly by Albania, Bulgaria, and Romania) during the 1950s in order to eliminate high levels of illiteracy, to increase the number of skilled workers, and to increase access to postsecondary education and so change the social composition of the student body. Except for Czechoslovakia and the German Democractic Republic, where there was no need for schooling at that level, elementary schools for adults were established throughout the region. Separate full-time day schools for adults as well as part-time evening and correspondence schools, offering general secondary education, followed.

In Czechoslovakia, where there was not such a pressing need for separate day schools for adults, the adult schools are almost exclusively of the evening and distance education type. General secondary education evening schools were established in 1953; this form of study reached its climax in 1959–60. Secondary residential schools for working people were established in 1972 to provide prerequisites for entry to university-level institutions.

In East Germany, the folk high schools which were re-established in 1945 to provide general noncredit adult education programmes were reorganized in 1956 into secondary adult schools, preparing for the final examination of the secondary or advanced secondary school. The programme of study in the folk high schools parallels that of the general polytechnical secondary schools.

The schools are attended by some 20,000 adults per year to attain the grade 10 school-leaving certificate (Schmelzer et al. 1978).

In addition to special adult schools, regular youth schools in many East European countries are engaged in the education of adults. There is also close cooperation between factories and other employers and adult schools. Thus in Poland, for example, school classes for adults are often scheduled on the employer's premises. In Yugoslavia, since the introduction of self-management in all aspects of social and economic organization, and the educational reforms which followed, industrial and business enterprises and educational institutions work very closely together on the provision of education to adults in their jurisdiction.

Vocational–technical secondary schools for adults expanded rapidly to provide the work force needed for planned or ongoing industrialization. There is rather more differentiation in this area among the countries of the region than there was in elementary and secondary general education adult schools. Thus the German Democratic Republic established enterprise academies (of which there are in the mid-1980s some 1,000 in operation) and enterprise schools (some 420) for vocational training and the further education of workers, foremen, and supervisors. Bulgaria set up school centres for vocational education as well as rural agricultural schools. Poland has 10 rural residential folk high schools, in addition to the standard type of evening and day-release vocational schools, prevalent in most countries in the region.

All the countries in Eastern Europe operate postsecondary evening, correspondence, and distance education programmes for adults. As is the case in the Soviet Union, study towards a degree in these part-time programmes usually takes only one year longer than in full-time programmes. The fact that in Poland some 40 percent of all students in higher education are part-time students, and that the figure in Bulgaria, Czechoslovakia, Romania, and Yugoslavia is approximately 30 percent, illustrates well the magnitude of the part-time study provision in postsecondary education in the region.

Although evening courses are provided throughout Eastern Europe, distance education or correspondence study is by far the most prevalent form of part-time study. In postsecondary education, less than 5 percent of part-time students in Bulgaria and Romania attend evening courses; in the German Democratic Republic it is only 1 percent. In the Soviet Union and in Hungary on the other hand, evening course enrolment accounts for one quarter and one third of all part-time students respectively. In Czechoslovakia, practically all part-time students are in distance education with only a handful in evening courses; correspondence courses are not available in Czechoslovakia.

As in the Soviet Union, adult part-time students at all levels of the school subsystem are accorded public social support as well as a variety of benefits, ranging from payment of full or partial wages while studying, to work release for examination preparation, and visits to consultation centres. The specific regulations vary somewhat from country to country, but the principle of paid educational leave for increasing educational and vocational qualification is uniformly accepted.

However, it is interesting to note that part-time credit study, which in the 1950s was uniformly and unquestioningly promoted and supported, has in the 1980s fared somewhat differently in the countries of the region. This type of study has begun to be questioned most in Czechoslovakia, especially in its distance education form, primarily on the basis of efficiency (low completion rate); at the same time there also seems to be a decreasing interest among potential students in part-time study. To some extent a similar situation can be observed in Hungary and Poland. Yet this form of study still seems to enjoy widespread support and popularity in the Soviet Union and in the German Democratic Republic.

It is important nevertheless to stress that throughout the Soviet Union and all East European countries the school subsystem of adult education in all its manifestations is considered as a significant and integral part of the comprehensive educational provision. It is supported by manifestations of the Communist Party, government decrees and legislation, and controlled by government and Party organs at all levels. The formal school adult education subsystem is funded on an equal basis with the rest of the school system.

5. *The Subsystem of Training On-the-job*

Involvement of business, industry, and government agencies in vocational and technical training on-the-job is widespread both in East and West European countries. However, unlike in Western Europe and North America, such training in Eastern Europe is seen as a part of the comprehensive education system, and often encompasses not only vocational training but also elementary and secondary education as well as political–ideological indoctrination. There is a close link between work and education throughout the region, although its manifestations may vary somewhat from country to country. Albania, Romania, and Yugoslavia have achieved, each for its own reasons and in their own way, the highest degree of integration between work and education.

The authorities and the trade unions in the Soviet Union attach great importance to the direct provision of training, retraining, and the upgrading of workers at their place of work. This training plays an important role in the supply of a skilled workforce to the planned national economy. Enterprises are responsible for three types of on-the-job training: initial qualification training for new workers, retraining of workers transferred to other jobs or enterprises, and the upgrading of workers' qualifications. This subsystem in the Soviet Union yearly prepares 6 million workers for new trades and upgrades over 20 million workers (Yazykova 1983, p. 57). Both training leading to certification and noncredit training is provided.

Bulgaria, similar to the past practice of the Soviet Union, has relied for a long period after 1945 on training through the so-called brigade method. This method relies on a skilled and politically highly motivated worker, whose skills and behaviour provide a model to emulate, leading a group of workers in on-the-job settings. A systematic institutionalized approach to vocational–technical training was not introduced in Bulgaria until the early 1970s.

A decree of the Council of Ministers of 22 January 1972, established a new system of training and upgrading for workers, including the setting up of vocational study centres in the enterprises. "At present there are 628 vocational study centres in the country with 192 branches comprising, through various forms of education and training, more than 400,000 workers" (Micheva et al. 1982 p. 43). These centres provide an extensive variety of training and education through short-term courses.

In Hungary a government decree of 28 April 1971 set out the objectives of workers' continuing education, which included upgrading specialized knowledge, mastering new skills and knowledge, and acquiring or improving political and general education (Fukász 1978). While vocational schools assist with the organization and implementation of this training, the enterprise is the responsible body and has to provide for the training costs as well as for wages during the training period. In cases where the enterprise cannot provide the required training, arrangements can be made for selected workers to attend training at other enterprises. Prior to 1971 there was only very minimal provision of training and upgrading of workers in the enterprises.

In Poland the situation was reversed. Until the late 1970s the training provided by enterprises was one of the main forms of vocational training and some 70 percent of the workforce were trained for their job by the enterprise; the prognosis for 1990 is that only slightly more than 20 percent of the workforce will be trained in this way while the remaining 80 percent will attend vocational schools. It is estimated that "the larger industrial and other establishments spend about 2 percent of their income on vocational courses" (Pachociński and Półturzycki 1979 p. 33). Since there are no official statistics for this subsystem, it is impossible to measure the real financial cost or the participation; estimates of participation vary from 3.5 to 7 million participants.

The forced process of rapid industrialization in Romania in the early 1970s brought with it the need and demand for intensive vocational–technical training. All ministries and other state organs have been charged, since 1970, with direct responsibility for such training in the areas under their jurisdiction. Since 1970 legislation, directives, and Communist Party declarations stress the need for the upgrading of the workforce and for continuing professional development. Integration of research, higher education, and production in industry and agriculture was legislated for in 1976; this has had a significant impact in the 1980s and will continue to have far-reaching consequences for all three sectors.

The most developed subsystem of on-the-job training in Eastern Europe can be found in Czechoslovakia and the German Democractic Republic. The components of this system provide vocational–technical upgrading, qualification training, and specialization training.

In Czechoslovakia there are three main forms of on-the-job training: group instruction (still the prevalent form of training), self-education, and training through the work process. Since the mid-1970s there has been a trend in Czechoslovakia to shift the emphasis from group instruction to self-education; at the same time the current theory and practice of on-the-job training places emphasis on study integrated with the work process (Skalka and Livečka 1977). The training is carried out by a widespread network of factory schools, technical schools, and enterprise institutes.

In the German Democractic Republic there is a system of well-staffed and well-equipped industrial enterprise academies, and of village academies for the agricultural sector. All workers who lack vocational training are provided with the opportunity to acquire skills through training organized by the enterprise. This takes the form of classes held during working hours, supplemented by extensive guided independent study; practical training takes place as part of regular work. This is funded by the enterprise, as is further training of skilled workers and the training of supervisors and managers. It is interesting that in the German Democratic Republic the "managers of nationally owned enterprises and of cooperatives are responsible not only for the training of working people as skilled workers but also for their employment in accordance with the degree of qualification they have attained" (Schmelzer et al. 1978 p. 39).

Yugoslavia, as has been mentioned, is in the process of implementing the concept of decentralized self-management of all social and economic aspects of society. As part of this process, the three subsystems of adult education are beginning to mesh and merge in the increasing provision for close links between work and education, and between production collectives and educational institutions and social services. The constitutional changes introduced in 1974, through their provisions for a move away from full-time education after initial schooling and towards alternation between work and education, have accelerated this process. Unfortunately, very little data are available as yet to measure adequately the degree of success of the new social measures and their impact on education and training.

6. *The Nonformal or Out-of-school Subsystem of Adult Education*

In examining adult education in Eastern Europe it is important to keep in mind that the state and the Communist Party have the ultimate control of all types of education at all levels. This is also true of the nonformal subsystem of adult education. In the 1920s the state and its organs in the Soviet Union took over full responsibility for and control over adult education, which previously had been carried out by a number of voluntary associations. The same shift in power and control occurred in the East European countries during the late 1940s. This control is wielded by the Party and state organs at the national (or federal) level, at the provincial or state level, and at the district and local level. Yugoslavia with its self-management concept is the one significant exception to the centralist state pattern of Eastern Europe.

The role of the mass organizations, among these trade unions, youth organizations, defence leagues, and peace movements, in the ideological–political education of the citizens is considered of crucial importance in Eastern Europe. This is even more intensified for members of the ruling Communist Party. All of the countries in the region have a widespread network of Party schools and evening universities of Marxism–Leninism, with compulsory attendance by Party members, an activity which is unmatched anywhere in Western Europe.

The houses of culture were among the typical Soviet institutions transplanted to East European countries in the 1950s. In the Soviet Union, the houses of culture were prominent in providing for the cultural and general educational needs of the population as a whole, as well as in serving the socialization needs of the state. These comprehensive institutions, which usually contain a library, house amateur groups, special interest and hobby groups, and a variety of courses. They often have cinemas, theatre halls, and exhibition halls, and have grown in the major cities of the Soviet Union from houses into palaces of culture.

Universities in Eastern Europe have not been directly involved in the postwar period in the provision of popular public lectures. This activity was taken over by societies for the dissemination of scientific knowledge, formed after the model of the Znanie (Knowledge) Society established in the Soviet Union in 1947. The only East European country which does not have such a society is Yugoslavia. The societies are formed by scientists and other members of the intelligentsia who are expected by the state and the Communist Party to volunteer to give popular lectures in their special fields. Some of the societies have an extensive lecturing programme of their own, while others mainly provide lecturers to other bodies. In addition, each of the societies owns a publishing house with a considerable output of popular books and periodicals. Lately some of the societies have started to experiment with televised educational programmes.

The Znanie Society was established in 1947 as the Society for the Dissemination of Political and Scientific Knowledge; it has in the mid-1980s some 3.5 million members. It is a national voluntary organization with some 130,000 local branches. The society is responsible for some 25 million lectures attended by more than 1,300 million participants per year.

The Society for the Dissemination of Scientific Knowledge Georgi Kirkov was established in Bulgaria in 1971. "The objective of the association is to assist the Communist Party of Bulgaria in the education of the future active builders of the socialist society—persons who will be highly conscious from the ideological point of view, with a solid morality and good physical health, and a keen awareness of their duties and responsibilities" (Micheva et al. 1982 p. 57). The society has a national as well as district and local councils. The society organizes some 300,000 lectures and lecture cycles annually, attended by over one million adults.

The Czechoslovak Society for the Dissemination of Political and Scientific Knowledge was established in 1952. Later it was reorganized into the Socialist Academy with state, district, and local organizations. The Socialist Academy provides lecturers primarily for the various people's universities and people's academies of science, technology, and the arts.

The Society for the Dissemination of Scientific Knowledge in the German Democratic Republic, Urania, has long historical roots, but was re-established in 1971. At that time the Urania organized 233,372 lectures and other events, attended by 7.9 million participants; in 1978 the society organized 355,111 events, attended by 11.7 million adults. Like most of the lecture societies in Eastern Europe, Urania is organized by subject matter into sections.

The Hungarian Society, TIT, also has roots in the mid-nineteenth century. It has existed in its present form since 1953. Membership is in excess of 24,000 and in 1983 the society organized 159,729 lectures and other events which attracted 7.3 million participants. A Free University, established by the TIT in 1954, accounts for approximately 10 percent of its activities. The society also organizes a series of summer universities which attract annually some 2,400 to 2,900 participants from Hungary and abroad.

The Polish society, TWP, dates from 1950, but it too has historical antecedents. By 1980, TWP had 43,999 members who gave 142,657 lectures to an audience of several million participants. The society also provides lecturers to the people's universities which serve some 200,000 adults per year. In the 1980s there was a reduction in these activities due to the political situation in Poland.

Among the main providers of general adult education are the people's universities which often work closely with or are a part of the lecture societies described above. Except for the German Democratic Republic and Yugoslavia, the people's universities were abolished on government orders in the late 1940s and were re-established in the late 1950s. Although these institutions can now again be found throughout the region, there are more or less marked differences among them from country to country.

These institutions were re-established in East Germany, with Soviet encouragement, in 1945 to carry out primarily political re-education. In 1956 they were incorporated into the educational system as general and vocational education schools for adults, and thus are no longer part of the nonformal subsystem. This trend is also evident to some extent in Romania, where the People's Universities were re-established in 1954 as centres of humanistic culture and political education and where, in the 1970s, vocational subjects were added to their programme. The People's Universities in Czechoslovakia, Poland, and the Soviet Union developed into a considerable differentiated network of separate specialized People's Universities for special groups in society such as parents, the elderly, and the military. The Yugoslav People's and Workers' Universities, having enjoyed uninterrupted and orderly development since 1944, are the best developed and functioning institutions for general adult education in Eastern Europe.

The widespread and popular amateur groups for folk art, folk music, and folk dancing, which have deep historical roots in Eastern Europe have already been mentioned. Their popularity can be illustrated by the case of Hungary, where there are over 10,000 folk music and dancing ensembles, with some 20,000 members. These activities which keep the rich cultural heritage of the Eastern European peoples alive are seen as an integral part of cultural–educational work.

Finally, the residential folk high schools of Poland need to be mentioned. The first of these schools, inspired by the model of the Danish folk high schools, were established at the turn of the century in the Russian-governed part of the then divided Poland. During the period between the two world wars these Polish folk high schools combined very successfully the Danish model and Polish needs and ideas, and served well the peasant population. Destroyed by the Second World War, the schools re-emerged in 1946, only to be closed down again in the 1950s. Ten of these schools have reopened since the 1960s and through a transformation process have become training schools for village cultural workers and thus part of the formal subsystem. Although residential folk high schools existed in East Germany between the two wars, and in Hungary from 1935 to 1948, no country in Eastern Europe other than Poland has residential folk high schools in the 1980s.

7. *Training of Adult Educators*

The rapid postwar development of the provision of adult education required considerable cadres of adult educators to staff this expanding system. A great many volunteers and employees who had very little or no experience in or training for adult education had to be called upon, and short-term intensive training programmes had to be established.

The School for Adult Educators, established in 1958 in Yugoslavia, is among the best examples of this compensatory training. Other such programmes were the one-year special programme for adult educators already working in the field, established in 1953 in Czechoslovakia, and the distance education programme established in Poland by the TWP Society in 1958 and later taken over by the Ministry of Culture.

More adequate training programmes for adult educators followed, with the establishment of a number of such programmes in the secondary technical schools. Typically these programmes are less than four years long, are available for full- or part-time study, and often combine within one institution a training for adult education, cultural work, and librarianship. Most of the students participating in these programmes are relatively young.

Training at this level was introduced in Czechoslovakia in 1953 with the establishment of three schools of adult education. These schools were reorganized several times, and in 1962 became schools of librarianship.

A 3-year training programme for librarians and adult educators was established at the teacher training colleges in Hungary. This programme included considerable practical training in addition to theoretical courses. The programme was eliminated in the mid-1970s.

In Poland, training at this level is provided through the State Cultural, Educational, and Library Studies, situated in five regions, and the State Extramural Study in the Education and Culture of Adults in Warsaw, with branches in 22 towns. More recently, the residential folk high schools have been transformed into training schools for cultural–educational workers.

The 3-year technical schools preparing vocational teachers in the German Democratic Republic offer elective courses on adult psychology and instruction.

Since the mid-1960s, training programmes for adult educators offered by a variety of higher education institutions were introduced in Eastern Europe and developed well in most of the countries except Albania.

After a short-lived beginning from 1947 to 1950, a university programme for adult educators was established in Czechoslovakia in 1960. In the mid-1980s a full training programme was available at four universities. Study of adult education can be completed in a 5-year full-time or in a 6-year part-time (distance education) programme. A master's degree programme as well as Ph.D. research degree programmes are available.

In Hungary a university programme was introduced in 1956 at the University of Debrecen, but a full adult education department was not established until 1971. A programme was also established in 1961 at the University of Budapest. Minor subject diploma programmes exist in other higher education institutions, as well as in the six teacher-training colleges. The adult education programme can be completed by 5 years of full-time or 6 years of part-time study.

In Poland, university training for adult educators has been provided since the 1960s by five universities and six higher schools of pedagogy. A 4-year M.A. programme in education, with specialization in adult education, is offered by all nine Polish universities and 11 teacher-training colleges. There are also two post-M.A. programmes, introduced in 1977, and a doctoral programme.

Yugoslavia has extensive provision for adult education training in many higher education institutions. Full programmes are available at three levels: undergraduate (diploma), master's (introduced in 1963), and doctoral (introduced in the 1970s).

In the Soviet Union there is provision for the training of cultural workers in the institutes of culture, and for Communist Party propagandists in the Higher Party School. However, teachers for the widespread adult evening and correspondence schools are still trained only as school teachers, with just one compulsory course in adult pedagogy. There is no comprehensive higher education training programme for the broad field of adult education.

University training in adult education in the German Democratic Republic is offered as a major subject in the study of pedagogy at two universities. In Romania such training is relatively new, with the University of Bucharest being the main centre. In Bulgaria this study is in its formative stages at the University of Sofia. There is no such programme available in Albania.

The provision of inservice training and continuing education for professional adult educators is relatively well-developed in Eastern Europe.

In the German Democratic Republic this centres on continuing education for vocational teachers. In 1970 the German Democratic Republic established a system of lifelong further training for adult education teachers, compulsory for all vocational teachers. The Universities of Budapest and Debrecen offer fortnightly continuing education meetings for their graduates. The School for Adult Educators in Yugoslavia is one of the models of inservice training and continuing education.

All the societies for the dissemination of science in the region provide more or less extensive basic training and methodological assistance to the great numbers of volunteer lecturers who form their membership and who are the mainstay of much general adult education. The same applies to the many volunteer instructors and leaders of the widespread amateur art and folk art groups.

This general outline reveals that the training of adult educators of all types and at all levels is, with some notable exceptions, well-developed in Eastern Europe.

Bibliography

Charters A N et al. 1981 *Comparing Adult Education Worldwide*. Jossey-Bass, San Francisco

Fukász G 1978 *Adult Education in the Hungarian People's Republic (HPR)*. European Centre for Leisure and Education, Prague

Int. J. University Adult Educ. 1985 24(3) (issue devoted to Eastern Europe)

Knoll J H (ed.) 1985 *Motivation for Adult Education*. German Commission for UNESCO, Bonn Saur, Munich

Krajnc A, Mrmak I 1978 *Adult Education in Yugoslavia*. European Centre for Leisure and Education, Prague

Micheva P, Bizhkov G, Petkov I 1982 *Adult Education in the People's Republic of Bulgaria*. European Centre for Leisure and Education, Prague

Onushkin V G, Tonkonogaya E P 1984 *Adult Education in the USSR*. European Centre for Leisure and Education, Prague

Pachociński R, Półturzycki J 1979 *Adult Education in the People's Republic of Poland*. European Centre for Leisure and Education, Prague

Schmelzer G, Fleischauer K-H, Pogodda G 1978 *Adult Education in the German Democratic Republic*. European Centre for Leisure and Education, Prague

Skalka J, Livečka E 1977 *Adult Education in the Czechoslovak Socialist Republic (ČSSR)*. European Centre for Leisure and Education, Prague

Yazykova V S 1983 *The Role of Soviet Trade Unions in the Lifelong Education of Workers*. European Centre for Leisure and Education, Prague

Provision in Australasia

C. Duke

This article describes the scope of and arrangements for providing education for adults in different parts of Australia and, more briefly, in New Zealand. These systems reflect both British antecedents and the special circumstances and needs of the two countries. Despite some efforts to enhance federal government involvement, the Australian systems in particular display great diversity, lack of central state commitment, and relative marginality, accompanied by spontaneity and a capacity for innovation. There is more central direction and purpose in Victoria, and perhaps in New Zealand in the mid-1980s, than in the other Australian states and territories. Special provision is made for significant minority groups: Aborigines, Maoris, and ethnic groups of recent immigrant origin.

1. Scope and Terminology

Several different terms are used to refer to educational provision for adults in Australia and New Zealand. "Adult education" is a term still in wide use, to refer mainly to education for personal development and leisure. In Australia this is known administratively as "Stream 6" provision, referring to the last of six classifications of work in the technical and further education

(TAFE) system; this, like most traditional adult education, is non-award-bearing. "Continuing education" has become established as the common and official term to embrace the whole field and has partly displaced "adult education" (earlier in New Zealand than in Australia); but it is also used to refer more narrowly to professional updating or continuing professional education (CPE). The term "community education" has become well-established in Australia. It embraces the community use of the school as well as education in and of the community. Consequently it is arguably both a broader and a narrower term than "continuing education". More recently, partly reflecting the proximity to and closer association with developing countries in Asia and the Pacific, "nonformal education" has come into use, both as an alternative all-encompassing term and as a prescriptive term which implies a need for less institutionalized forms of education for adults.

One source of confusion is that whereas "continuing education" is used at times to encompass all forms of postexperience education for adults, it is normally used within colleges and universities to refer only to non-award-bearing provision. Such courses normally require payment of fees, whereas most award-bearing courses are free to home students. Secondly, the term may be used to distinguish professionally and vocationally oriented courses from general adult education, or it may encompass the latter. The trend in Australian educational institutions is to include all such work as continuing education but to reduce the proportion and significance of the liberal or general component.

Other terms have special meanings and refer to special categories of work. "External studies" refers to award-bearing courses taught at a distance (usually with an occasional on-campus component). It is normally administered quite separately from continuing education. Training tends to be loosely separated from continuing education in practice, in terms of the funding and providing agencies, rather than necessarily by the nature of instruction or even the learners' objectives. Special purpose funds for youth and adult training and retraining are provided by departments of employment rather than education. Literacy is seen as a branch of adult or continuing education but tends to be treated as a distinct category with its own subcategories according to target group, method, and level. In Australia it has come to attract special purpose funds distinct from those for general adult education.

There is no Open University in Australia or New Zealand. A Committee on Open University to the Universities Commission in Australia recommended in 1974 that a national institute be created to foster greater openness in existing higher education rather than create a new institution. More recently there have been informal discussions about stimulating open access and open learning in postsecondary education. Deakin University in Victoria concentrates on the external mode of education and four other universities have significant external degree programmes, as do many colleges of advanced education and technical and further education colleges. Australian further and higher education is also quite readily accessible to adults for full- and part-time study; in this respect, and because more young undergraduates study at a local university or college than is the case in Britain, such institutions tend to have a closer relationship with their local community and to serve as continuing education centres in the broad sense. This article, however, follows local convention in excluding award-bearing educational opportunities for adults from "continuing education". The existence of these opportunities on a relatively generous basis and scale may influence attitudes to and the provision of (non-award-bearing) continuing education. The distinction is sharpened so long as fees are charged only for non-award-bearing courses.

2. *Organization and Funding*

In New Zealand a National Council of Adult Education provides advice to the Government and produces the *New Zealand Journal of Adult Learning* (successor to *Continuing Education in New Zealand* in 1983). There is a unit for continuing education in the Department of Education. The National Council was heavily emasculated by the Muldoon administration, which also terminated support to the Workers' Educational Association (WEA). In the mid-1980s the Lange administration restored support to continuing education generally, as well as to the WEA specifically, but the position of the National Council remained ambiguous, since in its greatly reduced form and with staff appointed under the previous administration, it was unacceptable to the adult education movement. Nevertheless, New Zealand does have a system for making policy and providing resources to continuing education throughout the country. A common view would be that continuing education is strong in some special areas and respects but has been generally underresourced.

Education in Australia is a state responsibility although the federal government, which has a department of education and various other advisory bodies in Canberra, has acquired increasing influence, through funding, over the past 30 years. The Northern Territory, which is approaching statehood, and the Australian Capital Territory, where some form of local self-government appears imminent, as well as the six states of the Commonwealth, each have their own education systems, and the organization and provision of continuing education also varies. There have been attempts during the 1970s and 1980s to persuade the federal government to create some kind of advisory body for continuing education, such as a national council, or more modestly a subcommittee of the Commonwealth Tertiary Education Commission (CTEC). In 1984 Johnson, a CTEC Special Commissioner and former Secretary for Education in the Department of Education, and Hinton prepared a draft report to the Commission on adult and continuing education in Australia. This concluded that adult and continuing education was an idea "whose time, if it has not come, is fast approaching", that the concepts of lifelong learning and de-institutionalized education were now widely accepted and that the Commission might at least create a Standing Committee on continuing education "to set national goals and policies, to ensure that gaps in provision are filled and that the provision should be systematic, that outreach to the disadvantaged should be guaranteed, that information and experience should be exchanged more readily between providers, between states and between this country and others" (Johnson and Hinton 1984 pp. 38–39).

At present, although continuing and also recurrent education have frequently featured in reports of the CTEC and of its component and predecessor councils and commissions, it is a specific responsibility of the Technical and Further Education (TAFE) Council only in which it comprises only a minor part (Stream 6) of its field, as Stream 6 TAFE, and is limited by the small amount of money available annually to allocate within each state for noninstitutionalized adult education. There is no officer in the Commonwealth Department of Education who is charged with continuing education throughout the Commonwealth.

Within Australia, systems of provision and coordination vary. Nowhere is there overall planning and direction. Universities, colleges of advanced education, TAFE colleges, some schools, and various voluntary and private community as well as profit-making organizations arrange programmes of continuing education ranging from vocational updating and national conferences to localized, community-based courses with a community development intent. The most widely recognized and long-established adult education association, the Workers' Educational Association (WEA), has survived only in New South Wales and South Australia. On the other hand, neighbourhood learning centres and other community-based continuing education groups have proliferated, especially in the eastern and southern parts of the country, and attract some measure of support from state adult education bodies. Boards of adult education in Queensland and Tasmania disappeared in the early 1970s and the function of supporting adult education was subsumed into the mainstream TAFE administration. This generated some resentment, mainly from a view that non-award-bearing and community-based work would be subordinated to the training priorities of TAFE. In Queensland this is said to have assisted in the burgeoning of local school-based adult education programmes on a self-supporting basis, somewhat as the recent political and financial crisis of the WEA in New Zealand forced the Association back into a stronger voluntary mode with a more active and independent political profile. In Western Australia, the Northern Territory, and the Australian Capital Territory adult education (as it is still more commonly known) is the responsibility of the TAFE administration. The same is true in South Australia. Here, however, a strong and separate department of further education under a forceful administrator, Max Bone, created a stronger official base for adult education at state level.

In Victoria Colin Badger moved from the University of Melbourne in the late 1940s to create the Council of Adult Education, which has led and dominated the development of adult education in that State subsequently (Badger 1984). The Council of Adult Education (CAE) is a provider of adult education as well as an advisory body and an agency for the development of adult education by other organizations throughout the state. It runs a large metropolitan programme and an imaginative range of special provision for the country regions of the state as well as for special groups such as the illiterate, Aborigines, prisoners, and others. It has generally succeeded in publicizing and promoting adult education with successive state governments, as well as sustaining good relations with other providers in Victoria. The present director came from a TAFE background and has strengthened the political and administrative standing of the Council with state TAFE administration. On the other hand, despite some criticism from both metropolitan neighbourhood groups, often radical and feminist, and from country centres fearful of metropolitan absorption and domination, the Council has generally succeeded in reassuring and supporting diverse groups in the process of developing a more coordinated system of provision throughout the state. In the most populous state, New South Wales, a more recent development, from the early 1970s, has been a coordinating Board of Adult Education which administers grants in support of adult education to different formal and community education agencies. The Board represents different adult education interests to the Minister for Education and advises on policy and funding, as well as providing guidance and support for the training of adult educators, undertaking enquiries into need, and so on. In the absence of a federal responsibility for continuing education the Victoria Council and the New South Wales Board also tend to represent and promote Australian continuing education overseas and at international events.

Public funding of continuing education appears to be modest in scale. It is highly dispersed and hard to measure, as is the scale of participation in continuing education itself. The Australian Association of Adult Education attempted a survey of provision and an analysis of need in 1978 (Davies and Duke 1978). Johnson and Hinton commented on the absence of quantitative data in 1984, and suggested that a thorough survey be undertaken by federal government. Generally liberal adult education is supported partly by subvention to the providing body (overtly or through meeting infrastructure costs such that adult education operates on marginal costs) and partly by fees paid by the student. Vocationally oriented continuing education is normally expected to recover all direct costs from the student through fees, but frequently the employer meets this cost. There has been a tendency since the 1970s for different agencies to meet the costs of continuing education for special needs groups, such as ethnic minorities and the unemployed. As a result such continuing education tends to be separated off within existing or through new providing bodies, with some concern, in consequence, about "ghettoization". The level of public support for continuing education, and the mix of beneficiaries, probably varies considerably between different parts of the country. Support for general-purpose and liberal adult education appears to have declined. The substantial provision for ethnic minorities is concentrated on English-language courses and an increasing proportion of all public expenditure appears to be concentrated on retraining courses intended to assist economic recovery. It is not possible to estimate the value of voluntary effort but the level of such effort has probably been raised significantly since the early 1970s.

3. *Areas of Special Activity*

Both Australia and New Zealand are large-scale immigrant societies with indigenous minorities. Australian Aborigines have acquired higher political salience since 1972, and official policy has altered from integration to self-management, coinciding with a similar change of official policy towards immigrant groups from assimilation to multiculturalism. New Zealand's Maori population has been more seriously regarded for a longer time, and this probably reflects in better developed continuing education provision for Maoris within New Zealand's unitary system of government, than for Aborigines within federal Australia. The Maori presence is also much more evident in New Zealand's general provision of continuing education and in the manifestations of its continuing education overseas, a factor possibly influenced also by New Zealand's Pacific location, its sense of Pacific destiny, and the large population of Pacific islanders found in New Zealand. Respect for Aboriginal cultures is reflected in the use and teaching of Aboriginal languages within some adult education programmes, and in a measure of devolution to more local regions and to Aboriginal communities in some instances. The confused state of control and provision reflects the ambivalence in Australia about the identity and future of Aboriginal peoples.

Continuing education for other ethnic minorities, most of them immigrants since the Second World War and their descendants, is sometimes associated with Aboriginal education, although the indigenous minority has tended to distinguish itself sharply from immigrant groups. There is large-scale provision of English instruction for non-English-speaking immigrants, some of it more closely related to preparation for employment, including upgrading and conversion of qualifications from overseas to meet Australian circumstances and requirements. Both voluntary providers and public educational institutions are involved. There is a plethora of federal and state level instrumentalities and advisory bodies involved, notably the Department of Immigration and the Australian Institute of Multicultural Affairs. A criticism of continuing education for immigrants is that it is too narrowly limited to English-language instruction, and too little concerned with either social and economic equity or the attitudes to ethnic diversity on the part of the dominant society.

The Workers' Educational Association (WEA) is a general-purpose provider of adult education without a distinctive working class clientele. However, the Trade Union Training Authority, established in the early 1970s with its headquarters as the national Clyde Cameron College on the New South Wales–Victoria border, has developed a substantial programme of trade union education through a system of state organizers and centres. Its main focus is on short courses to equip unionists for their union roles, rather than on the general education of working class men and women of the kind traditionally provided by WEAs. The Australian Council for Adult Literacy reflects and has contributed to developing concern for the newly recognized problem of adult illiteracy in the English-speaking population. Thus adult literacy schemes grew between 1970 and 1980 from five to 172 in number (Dymock 1982 p. 56). The need has recently been recognized by the Commonwealth Tertiary Education Commission (CTEC) in allocating increased funding specifically for work to reduce adult illiteracy. Another special need which is distinctively Australasian is that of the geographically isolated. A strong external studies tradition developed in response to this need, making further and higher education more accessible to different categories of learners than has British further and higher education, from which the Australasian systems derived. Both countries have developed informal adult education—through radio and also through various forms of correspondence and discussion group tuition, which provide a study kit but not a paid visiting tutor. In Australia the network of community radio stations, drawn together as the Public Broadcasting Association of Australia, constitutes a significant interactive community learning resource, and a form of continuing education in the wider sense in which that term is now used.

4. *Some Trends and Issues*

Australia and New Zealand are geographically remote from the region whence their dominant settler populations were drawn, and the influence of Britain has also substantially declined internationally. Self-reliance, in which New Zealand has long taken pride, and innovation to meet distinctive national and local needs, have acquired higher salience among continuing educators in both countries. There is greater awareness and influence of continuing education practices in developing countries of the neighbouring Asian and Pacific regions, and a desire for closer involvement and partnership. This is reflected in a much greater exchange of adult educators with neighbouring countries, and in participation in regional programmes of adult and nonformal education through the UNESCO Regional Office and the Asian and South Pacific Bureau of Adult Education. It is also reflected in a tendency to employ new concepts, such as "nonformal education for development", and to look at continuing provision in a more systematic and critical way.

The tension between adult education as a movement and as a profession takes the form of hostility among community-level and voluntary workers towards institutionalized provision, and specifically towards the technical and further education system (TAFE) as the largest institutional provider. Training of continuing educators takes place mainly through a small number of colleges of advanced education, at diploma level, through the graduate level programmes of the University of New England, offered externally and so widely accessible to senior practitioners, and through local, largely ad hoc, short courses. There is ambivalence about professional training and especially accreditation, from a view that the strong adult education movement working through neighbourhood centres will be weakened by institutional developments. The sense of movement is strong among rank-and-file voluntary workers, and expressed through the national bodies for both adult education and community education, which it is suggested should merge. Although relations are informal, resting in networks rather than structures, there is a strong sense of an adult education movement allied to women's peace, and ecological movements and committed to social change and equity, in both Australia and New Zealand. While the large part of public expenditure on the education of adults will probably continue to go towards continuing education conceived as having an economic and social function approved by federal or state government, it is likely that the leadership and direction of what is known as continuing or adult education will manifest strong commitment to quality of life, equity, and work with the disadvantaged.

Bibliography

Australian Government Committee on Open University 1975 *Open Tertiary Education in Australia.* Australian Government Publishing Service, Canberra

Badger C R 1984 *Who Was Badger?* Council of Adult Education, Victoria

Boshier R 1980 *Towards a Learning Society: New Zealand Adult Education in Transition.* Learning Press, Vancouver

Davies A, Duke C 1978 *Need and Provision in Australian Adult Education.* Australian Association of Adult Education, Canberra

Duke C, Davis D, Rudnik H 1985 *Immigration, Adult Education and Multiculturalism in Australia.* Council for Continuing Education, Australian National University, Canberra

Dymock D 1982 *Adult Literacy Provision in Australia: Trends and Needs.* Australian Council for Adult Literacy, Armidale

Hall D O W 1970 *New Zealand Adult Education.* Michael Joseph, London

Johnson R, Hinton F 1984 *Adult and Continuing Education in Australia.* Draft report to the Commonwealth Tertiary Education Commission, Commonwealth Tertiary Education Commission, Canberra

Whitelock D (ed.) 1970 *Adult Education in Australia.* Pergamon, Sydney

Provision in Japan

K. Moro'oka

The modern Japanese education system was founded in 1872 and has developed, particularly in the second half of the twentieth century, so that currently over 90 percent of young people undertake upper secondary schooling and more than 35 percent enter higher education. This growth has been significantly affected by changes in the national economy towards the service industries, which require highly educated manpower. Increases in family income, the availability of modern labour saving devices, declining numbers of children and higher life expectancy have increased the time available to all adults, especially women, for educational and cultural pursuits. There is considerable enthusiasm for learning of some kind, on which the average Japanese adult is prepared, according to a recent survey, to spend between 1 and 3 percent of their income. Since the Second World War a large provision of adult or continuing education, backed by legislation, has developed. It is provided by the state and private agencies, offers a wide range of opportunities, and uses many different modes of delivery.

1. Features of Continuing Education

Continuing education (CE) consists of formal education (FE) such as special training schools and miscellaneous schools and nonformal education (NFE) which comes into being when learners act spontaneously. In the latter case, availability of the educational environments is vital, since meaningful encounters between learners and their milieux cannot occur without such an environment. Therefore, the Social Education Law of 1949 states that national and local public bodies are obligated to promote an environment congenial to cultural enhancement for all citizens so that each citizen can make the most of himself or herself. This law encouraged the public bodies of all levels to build "Kominkan" (citizens' public halls) as a main organ for the promotion of CE. The Kominkan played the most important role in rebuilding the communities after the war, and has later developed its original aims and functions as a multipurpose community center into a more educational institution for adult people. The Standard regarding Establishment and Operation of Kominkan which was issued in 1959 helped further to improve the provisions and activities of Kominkan. In 1983, the total number of Kominkan was 17,520 and the number of staff was 46,528.

To provide the libraries and museums as NFE institutions, the Library Law was enacted in 1950, the Museum Law in 1951, and the Standard regarding Establishment and Operation of Public Museums was issued in 1973 and the Standard regarding Establishment and Operation of Public Libraries in 1977, all of which greatly promoted the establishment and improvement of these institutions. As of 1983, the total number of public libraries was 1,644 with 13,145 staff, while that of the public museums was 676 with 10,368 staff.

Soon after the war, when the enrollment level of students in upper secondary schools was not very high, the Youth Classes Promotion Act was issued in 1953 in order to promote learning activities among working youth who started work directly after their nine-year compulsory education. With the increase in number of those advancing to upper secondary schools and also to colleges and universities, however, these youth classes have gradually lost popularity.

As a guideline for the promotion of CE, the *Report on Social Education in a Rapidly Changing Society*, which was published by the Social Education Council in 1971, has been playing a leading part in the actual enforcement of the policy since the 1970s. The main recommendations of this report were: (a) broadening of the concept of social education; (b) systematization of social education from the viewpoint of lifelong education; (c) improvement of educational content and methods for meeting the variety of demands; (d) promotion of organized activities and voluntary activities; and (e) emphasis on social education administration.

1.1 Part-time and Correspondence Education

Part-time and correspondence courses of upper secondary schools, and evening and correspondence courses of universities and junior colleges are available to those young workers who find it difficult to advance to day courses and who still wish to receive formal schooling. Some courses are designed mainly to provide general education, while others primarily aim at offering technical and professional knowledge and skills. As of 1983, 253 upper secondary schools provided part-time courses for 138,000 students and another 85 schools provided correspondence courses in which 72,000 students were enrolled. Sixty-six universities and 140 junior colleges provided evening courses for 117,263 and 26,591 students respectively, while 13 universities and 9 junior colleges gave correspondence courses to 100,540 and 78,038 students respectively.

1.2 Social Correspondence Education

There are two large categories in what is called correspondence education: school correspondence education, which is mentioned above, and social correspondence education, which is provided mainly by corporate bodies, nonprofit private bodies, and enterprises. To encourage worthwhile correspondence courses, the Ministry of Education, Science, and Culture authorizes some of the correspondence courses offered by voluntary organizations as "recognized correspondence courses." In 1983 there were 180 recognized courses organized by 42 organizations. There is a great variety of such courses including business courses in such areas as business administration and computer science, technical and technological courses in such areas as electrical engineering, mechanical engineering, and architecture, and other courses in such areas as dressmaking, cooking, and foreign languages. As of 1983, there were 68 clerical courses, 80 technical, and 32 cultural courses. The total number of students was some 280,000 and the ratio of male to female was 5:2.

1.3 University Extension Courses

In complying with the present-day demands for higher education among adults, an increasing number of extension courses are offered by universities and junior colleges. Some courses are provided by the universities themselves with the financial support of the Ministry of Education, Science, and Culture, and others at the request of firms and organizations. The themes of studies range widely, including technical subjects, contemporary social problems, topics concerned with family life and its techniques, and cultural subjects in general. In 1983, 1895 of these courses were offered by 291 public junior colleges and universities, and 216,000 people attended.

1.4 Special Training Schools (Senshu-gakko)

Special training schools are a new type of educational institution initiated in 1976, which originate in the educational establishments known as Kakushu-gakko or "miscellaneous schools." They are designed to offer systematic programs of education aimed at developing each individual's ability to bring out the best in their working and daily life and raising their level of general education. Courses at special training schools last one year or more, the schools are required to give instruction for 800 class hours per year, and schools must have an enrollment of at least 40 students.

The courses offered at special training schools are of three types: "upper secondary courses" admitting lower secondary-school graduates; "advanced or college courses" admitting upper secondary graduates; and "general courses" specifying no particular requirement. In May 1982, there were 2,804 special training schools with about 480,000 students, offering numerous courses in a great variety of areas, for example, civil engineering and architecture, electricity, electronics, electronic computer science, training of hospital nurses, dental technician training, cooking, beauty art, training of nursery governesses and teachers, accounting and book-keeping, typing, dressmaking, knitting, handicrafts, designing, and foreign languages. And there were also 4,867 miscellaneous schools with about 630,000 students, providing mainly young people with vocational and practical training in such fields as dressmaking, cooking, bookkeeping, typing, automobile driving and repairing, computer techniques, and so on.

1.5 Provision by Education Businesses

A growing number of continuing courses are organized by so-called "Kyouiku Sangyou" or education businesses, in larger cities with a view to helping improve general culture and vocational knowledge and skills of adults. Many of these courses and lectures are offered at special centers called, for example, "culture centers." These programs have great variety in their course contents and use university teachers and other eminent experts as lecturers. According to a recent survey, 38 newspaper publishers, 22 broadcasting companies, and 41 department stores run some 400 centers for about 400,000 people. The tuition fee of classes and courses offered by Kominkan is nominal in most cases, while for the programs of these culture centers, people are expected to spend much more money on a variety of courses.

1.6 Educational Broadcasting

There are two types of radio and television broadcasting companies in Japan. One is the Nippon Hoso Kyokai (NHK or Japan Broadcasting Corporation) which is a public corporation financed by license fees, and the other consists of commercial broadcasting companies. It is 60 years since radio broadcasting began in 1925, when NHK was established. The corporation transmitted black-and-white television broadcasts for the first time in 1953 and regular color television broadcasts in 1960. NHK has put continuous effort into the educational use of broadcasting, and produces many types of educational as well as cultural programs.

Commercial broadcasting companies also transmit numerous educational and cultural programs which together account for more than 30 percent of total broadcasting hours. The Commercial Broadcasters' Educational Association (CBEA), set up in 1959, now has 41 affiliated member companies, and has been attempting to improve these programs with special concern for their educational potential. In order to secure a high rate of audience participation, NHK distributes a broadsheet titled "NHK Channel Eye," while CBEA publishes a guidebook on "Through the Eyes of Parents and Children" to the general public. As of September 1983, more than 3 million out of 33 million households had registered television sets. Thus broadcast and television programs are accessible to many families and individuals learning by these means across the country. Along with the availability of good broadcasting programs, the number of classes making use of those programs has been increasing remarkably. A survey done by NHK indicates the classes numbered 206 in 1971; 1,445 in 1975; 2,962 in 1980, and 2,984 in 1984; with a total of 156,000 participants. The most popular programs are "Mothers' Study Room," "The Diary of Lower Secondary School Pupils," "NHK Special Edition," "Today's Health," "Good Morning Journal," "NHK Citizens' University," "Today's Cuisine," "Hobby Courses," "Bright Countryside," and "Lady's Encyclopedia."

1.7 The University of the Air

The University of the Air is a formal education institution under the School Education Law. Its structure and curriculum organization should therefore comply with the standards for universities, and the standards for university correspondence education determined by the Ministry of Education, Science, and Culture. The aim of the university is to provide a new educational institution as a nucleus of the lifelong education system, by making effective use of radio and TV for university-level education. The four major purposes of the university are: (a) to provide university-level education for workers, including women working in the home; (b) to ensure a flexible opportunity for university education for those who complete upper secondary education as a new method of higher education; (c) to provide the education of a new era, sharing the fruits of the latest researches and educational techniques as an education institute which can mobilize the cooperation of as many people concerned with university education as possible; and (d) to help the improvement of university education in Japan by promoting the exchange of teaching staff and the interchangeable credit system between existing universities, and by extending the use of the materials developed for the University of the Air. There are three major courses provided on "Life Science," "Industry and Society," and "Humanities and Nature," consisting of more than 230 subjects. The standard hours of study per week necessary for a fully-fledged student to graduate from the university in the minimum four-year period are: listening to five 45-minute programs; approximately five hours study with textbooks and so on; and schooling of one instruction course of three hours. The study centers for the university are to be built in each prefecture to offer schooling and counselling. So far the service area of the university has been limited to Kanto region, around metropolitan Tokyo area.

1.8 Vocational Training

There are two major types of vocational training in Japan: one is "public vocational training" which is given in public facilities set up by the national, prefectural, or municipal government or by the Employment Promotion Projects Corporation (EPPC), and the other is that which is provided by nongovernmental bodies including individual employers, associations of employers, and other nonprofit voluntary organizations. Among the latter that are considered to be of equal level to those offered in public vocational training facilities are those designated by the prefectural governor as "authorized" vocational training. Vocational training is broadly classified into basic training, upgrading training, updating training, and instructor training, with programs for new graduates from schools, for in-service workers, and for the unemployed. There are currently 267 public General Vocational Training Centers (GVTC), with an enrollment of 110,000 trainees, and 140 public Advanced Vocational Training Centers (AVTC), of which 90 are established by EPPC, with an enrollment of 70,000 trainees. "Authorized" establishments number 513 independent and 788 cooperative with about 40,000 and 50,000 trainees respectively.

2. *Perspectives and Problems*

With the Meiji Restoration, the modern Japanese Government hoisted high the ideal of education for every member of the nation, saying "There shall be no villagers but pursue learning and no family members but are given an education." And the modern education system was introduced with the Government setting up elementary and secondary schools throughout the country. This educational system of an open type was made possible with the background of various educational establishments which had developed to serve the needs of the different social classes; for example, special schools for the children of the warrior class, schools for the wealthier members of the merchant and farming classes, private schools called "terakoya" where reading, writing, and arithmetic were taught to the children of the common people. Therefore, the crusade against illiteracy which has been a major problem in most of the developing countries has not been the main issue in this country.

From the ethnic standpoint, the Japanese are a unitary race with 120 million people speaking only one language, Japanese, which has created an unusually homogeneous people with a strong sense of national identity and common purpose. The high standard of education and the strength and stability derived from these features of national life were the very bases of development in this country. The development is not necessarily limited to the scientific and technological field but is also extended to the artistic and cultural areas where the delicate senses of the Japanese are highly valued.

The rapid social changes after the Second World War, however, have given rise to a great number of serious problems such as too rapid urbanization, environmental pollution, and the social problems of nuclear families and the aged. The diffusion of democracy after the war has certainly made people recognize the importance of the individual, but at the same time it has produced many people who are inclined to be egoistic or self-centered. Community education in the 1980s therefore aims at the further development of social welfare, raising of the consciousness of citizenship, and the creation of community culture. In the past, Japan sought a model for an educational system in the advanced Western nations. In the 1980s, Japan, facing what is called the third educational reform, can no longer depend on a foreign model. For the nation is confronted not merely, as a highly industrialized society, with common problems facing Western countries, but also with unique problems of its own brought about by rapid industrialization. The essential aim of CE in Japan is to produce youths and adults who do not seek for their own interest but search for the ways to live and let live peacefully with other people on the earth from a more global standpoint.

Bibliography

Ministry of Education, Science and Culture 1980 *Japan's Modern Educational System: A History of the First Hundred Years*. Maruzen, Tokyo

Ministry of Foreign Affairs, Japan 1985 *The Japan of Today*. International Society for Educational Information, Tokyo

Moro'oka K 1976 *Recurrent Education: Japan*. Organisation for Economic Co-operation and Development (OECD), Paris

Developing Countries

Introduction

Since the advanced countries, most of which have a long history of organized adult education, lack common structures, or even national structures directed to clear and coherent goals, it is not surprising that they are missing in developing nations. In the regions discussed in this subsection provision is extremely patchy and, as some of the articles indicate, adult education, or nonformal education, which is frequently the preferred term, is often given low priority by governments which have grave needs and few resources. Not, however, in all societies, as the amount and nature of provision described in these articles demonstrates. Indeed China is not only an exception among developing countries, but appears to have created a systematic provision which is only approached, and probably not matched, by the socialist countries of Eastern Europe.

The over-riding purposes of adult education in these regions are to overcome illiteracy and help create a pool of skilled and aware labour for national development. There is little room for fostering the enrichment of the individual personality, except as it may advance the progress of society. One may detect both the legacy of former colonial powers in national thinking and practice and the struggle for hegemony between socialist and capitalist ideologies, but the first is declining and ideologies are being adapted to meet the requirements of conditions in countries which have their own cultural traditions, with established national sentiments, or are striving to establish national consciousness.

The article, *Provision in the Caribbean*, covers Cuba, Haiti, Santo Domingo, the French Antilles and French Guyana, the old British colonies of Jamaica, Trinidad, Barbados, Guyana, the Bahamas and other lesser islands, and the Netherlands Antilles. It points out the cultural and linguistic diversity and the common concern with literacy, except in the French Antilles and French Guyana, which are still territories of France. Because of this they mirror adult education provision in France, as the Commonwealth states, although independent, continue to display British influence. The article reports the creation of national adult education associations and the creation of a Caribbean Regional Council for Adult Education (CARCAE).

Africa is one of the areas where nonformal education is the preferred term, as the articles on Africa indicate. There are two articles covering this region, the first dealing with Black Africa and the second, South Africa. It may seem inappropriate to include the latter in this subsection, but it is justified by the level of development of its Black population, whose adult education the article examines. The main part of the article, although it confines itself to sub-Saharan Africa, still mentions Angola, Botswana, The Central African Republic, Ethiopia, Ghana, Kenya, Liberia, Malawi, Mali, Mozambique, Niger, Nigeria, Somalia, and Zambia. Adult education is presented as a tool for development, but operating as a reaction to emergencies rather than as a product of long-term policy. Nevertheless the article identifies legally established government organizations in some states, as well as agencies of business, commerce, and voluntary associations. It sketches administrative structures, methods of finance, and names the characteristics of programmes.

India, Pakistan, Bangladesh, Nepal, and Sri Lanka are the countries treated in the article *Provision in the Indian Subcontinent*. Most emphasis is laid on India, where provision goes back to the 1870s. A description is given of the work and goals of the adult education undertaken by Indian universities; the activities in workers' education under the aegis of the Ministry of Labour; the use of mass media for continuing education; the network of polyvalent education centres for workers; continuing education for administrators and professional groups; and of the creation of open universities and schools. The Allama Iqbal Open University in Pakistan is also described. The article reports rural development and distance learning in Bangladesh, teacher education and occupational education in Nepal, and open distance education and the continuing education of teachers in Sri Lanka.

Provision in Southeast Asia also covers a number of countries, Burma, Laos, Kampuchea, Korea, Hong Kong, Macao, Malaysia, Singapore, Indonesia, Philippines, and Thailand. This area is a particular battleground for hegemony between world powers, being comprised of socialist states such as the first three in the list, strongly capitalist ones such as the Philippines and Singapore, and capitalist ones under Chinese influence in Hong Kong and Macao. The article notes varying degrees of sympathy between adult education organizations and the prevailing political regime, and different degrees of commitment by governments to adult education. The main purposes are, as elsewhere, literacy and basic education, rural development, and training in vocational skills.

Provision in the People's Republic of China draws attention to the size of the country and the fact that its basically centralized administration goes with a diversity of sponsorship and forms of delivery of adult education. It presents the provision as highly formal, with stress on regulations, certificates, and equivalence to the school system. There is cooperation between different government ministries and departments, offering education at all levels from basic literacy to higher education. There is separate structured provision for workers, farmers, and party cadres, there are university-based correspondence and evening colleges, radio and television university and college courses, and higher education examinations for those undertaking self-instruction. The article indicates the main administrative features: supervision by government, reliance on mass organizations, and cooperation between various sectors. Sources and channels of funding are outlined and the research and problems discussed.

Provision in the Caribbean

E. D. Ramesar

The Caribbean area consists of the archipelago of islands stretching from the Bahamas in the north to Trinidad and Tobago in the south; the mainland countries of Guyana, Suriname, and Guyane (Cayenne) on the South American continent; Belize in Central America; and Curaçao and Aruba off the northern coast of South America.

The area is made up of territories with a relatively long history of independence (Haiti became independent in 1804) to territories which have only recently achieved nationhood (Antigua and Barbuda became independent in 1981). Their populations vary from as many as 10 million in Cuba to 10,000 in the British Virgin Islands. Their language, culture, and education reflect their colonial past. For example, the language, culture, and education in Cuba, Santo Domingo, and Puerto Rico reflect a Spanish past; in the Commonwealth Caribbean an English past is reflected; in Haiti, Martinique, Guadeloupe, and Guyane a French past is reflected; and in Netherlands Antilles and Suriname it is a Dutch past that is reflected. There are also pockets of original, native people in Guyana and in Belize.

The ethnic composition of the area is equally varied—from the descendants of Dutch settlers in the Netherlands Windwards to descendants of African slaves in Haiti; mulattos in Santo Domingo; large proportions of descendants of immigrants from India in Suriname (60 percent), Guyana (55 percent), and Trinidad and Tobago (45 percent); Indonesians in Suriname, and Chinese and Arabs in most countries. Ideologically, there is also variety—from the Marxist Socialist Left of Cuba to the Liberal Democratic Right of Barbados. In economic terms, there is a disparity of wealth from the relatively high per capita income of US$4,000 (Trinidad and Tobago) to the relatively low per capita income of US$150 (Haiti).

The keynote is diversity, and adult education in the Caribbean reflects all these many and varied backgrounds.

1. Cuba

The 1959 Revolution put the emphasis on mass education. The National Literacy Commission made an all-out drive on the eradication of illiteracy, which was 25 percent at the time. This "battle for literacy" was accomplished and completed in 1962. Then the thrust was to bring adults into the national mainstream of education. Over the 15-year period 1962–76, adult education programmes played a leading role in giving about 1,500,000 persons a sixth-grade education through the systematic efforts of the Ministry of Education, the Central Organization of Cuba Trade Unions, and other mass organizations. This "battle of the sixth grade" has been followed by the "battle of the ninth grade" to help adults upgrade their education. During the five-year period 1976–80, graduates within the national education system included 755,000 adults achieving the sixth grade, 115,000 adults graduating at the junior-high school level, and 45,000 adults from worker–farmer university extension programmes. In addition to providing adults with the opportunity to improve and complete their technical training at night classes and in other special programmes of technical and professional education, the aims and efforts of adult education are also directed to the development of the general culture of people with low-level education, in keeping with the Marxist–Socialist ideals of the Revolution.

2. Haiti

In 1947, Haiti was the first country to seek United Nations assistance in solving its illiteracy problem which was 90 percent at the time. The "Office National d'Alphabétisation et d'Action Communautaire" (ONAAC) was an organization formed in 1961 as a result of the fusion between urban adult education services and rural community development services of the Department of Agriculture.

During the period 1977–80, ONAAC organized a number of projects in the field of adult education including a literacy programme which made literate some 182,204 adults in 1977/78 and 188,460 in 1979/80. ONAAC's field officers number 8,367 divided as follows: 40 coordinators, 140 polyvalent and auxiliary animateurs, 209 agents in home economics, 798 subinspectors, and 7,180 monitors in eight regions, in addition to office staff.

Since 1980, the new thrust in literacy has been to link it with general development, which draws on the motivation of the population through community participation. Promotion of the rural artisan class in community workshops has been functioning with support from L'Association Française de Volontaires du Progress (AFVP).

3. *Santo Domingo*

Adult education projects are undertaken by the Secretary of State for Education, Fine Arts, and Culture on a regional basis. During 1980 about 350,000 persons benefited from (a) community participation in the literacy and adult education programmes; (b) the production of free reading pamphlets for new adult readers and the provision of teaching materials at adult education centres. Following this, the illiteracy rate decreased from 41 percent in 1970 to 32 percent in 1980.

Adult education efforts aim at upgrading the skills of agricultural workers and at preserving the cultural heritage of the nation.

4. *The French Antilles and Guyane (Cayenne)*

Most of the official adult education programmes in Martinique, Guadeloupe, and Guyane are part of larger programmes instituted for France and its overseas departments/territories. Illiteracy is considered to be nonexistent; there is therefore no formal programme.

The Ministry of Education which is responsible for government programmes of adult education in France extends to Martinique, Guadeloupe, and Cayenne through the Centre de Formation Continue des Universités which began in 1959. Thus in 1977 there were 135,587 adult students in 78 centres throughout all the departments of France including the Antilles/Guyane.

One innovation was the law of 1971 which made it obligatory for employers to finance the training of their employees within the continuing education centres mentioned above. The law also stressed education for particular neglected groups such as women, immigrants, the young unemployed, and the undereducated. Another innovation was the setting up of the Université du Troisième Age in 1973 by the University of Bordeaux with which the Centre Universitaire des Antilles et de la Guyane (CUAG) is affiliated. Its aim is to find occupation for retired men and women. The wide difference in social, economic, and educational levels of participants is reflected in the range of the classes offered—yoga, gymnastics, regional travel, history, languages, politics, and so on.

In 1981 in Guyane, a Centre Professionelle des Jeunes de Suzini was established in two rural locations under the French Ministry of Agriculture and the Director-General of Teaching and Research. The intention is to assist young agriculturists.

The Federation des Oeuvres Laiques in Martinique, Guadeloupe, and Cayenne is affiliated to la Lique Française de L'Enseignement et de l'Education Permanente of France and conducts programmes of mass education.

5. *The Commonwealth Caribbean*

As in the case of most of the non-English-speaking Caribbean, in the Commonwealth Caribbean adult education is offered formally and informally through governmental and voluntary agencies, and the extramural arm of the University of the West Indies. Formal adult education is pursued by participants preparing for a career or by those interested in upgrading their occupational skills. Informal adult education is pursued through cultural classes and lectures in the creative arts offered by the extramural arm of the university and through craft classes of the appropriate ministry of government and through voluntary agencies.

Adult literacy is a significant problem in most of the territories except Barbados. The Jamaica Movement for the Advancement of Learning (JAMAL) Foundation has been doing pioneering work in literacy in Jamaica. Initiatives are now being undertaken in other territories to deal with illiteracy.

Throughout the English-speaking Caribbean there is a heavy concentration on remedial classes. This is related to a desire to improve occupational/promotional opportunity or to meet university admission requirements. General enrichment programmes are also offered, but these have fewer clients because of their low income-generating possibilities. It is therefore not surprising that in a region where there is such high unemployment, young adults are attracted to technical and vocational courses offered by employers or church bodies. Trade union organizations also offer classes and operate several workers' colleges.

The extramural arm of the University is perhaps the most widespread regional agency of adult education in the Commonwealth Caribbean. The extramural department of the University consists of a director responsible to the vice-chancellor located on the Mona (Jamaica) campus with resident tutors (Belize, Bahamas, Jamaica, Antigua, St. Kitts/Nevis/Anguilla, Montserrat, Dominica, St. Lucia, St. Vincent, and Grenada); one staff (specialist) tutor each for drama, labour education, social work, radio education, creative writing, and preschool child training. An extramural tutor on the Cave Hill (Barbados) campus and a tutor for extramural studies on the St. Augustine (Trinidad) campus, report separately to respective campus pro-vice-chancellors.

Each resident tutor is responsible for developing a full adult education programme for the territory and works in close relationship with government and other agencies within the territory. Each programme includes general courses in English language and literature, modern languages, social studies, mathematics, natural sciences, and business studies; and special courses in public administration, industrial relations, drama, and business management.

6. *The Netherlands Antilles and Suriname*

Adult education outside the school system is offered through vocational training by large industrial firms in Curaçao and through the Labour College in Suriname. In Curaçao, the Department of Labour carries out a vocational training programme for adults including courses for bricklayers and carpenters. In Bonaire, the International Labour Organization has been operating a training programme in woodcarving, silver and leather work—craft courses related to the tourist trade.

The Suriname Labour College provides courses in industrial relations, labour economics, cooperatives, occupational safety and health, and so on, and mounts a public education programme through radio, television, public lectures, and films. The national adult education programme is coordinated by the college.

7. *The Caribbean Regional Council for Adult Education (CARCAE)*

CARCAE was established in 1978 as a separate region within the realm of the International Council for Adult Education (ICAE). The regional council seeks (a) to promote and facilitate cooperation among national continuing education organizations and agencies in the non-Spanish-speaking territories of the region; (b) to advance activities of member associations and institutions and to encourage cooperation amongst them; (c) to promote awareness and recognition of the importance of continuing education and to seek and encourage adequate funding for this purpose from governments; (d) to serve as an advisory body to governments on regional matters relating to continuing education; (e) to initiate and/or to support the mounting of conferences, seminars, training courses, workshops, and so on, as well as undertaking research in the field of continuing education, and the operation of a documentation centre and a publications programme.

The following national associations have already been formed:

(a) The Adult Education Association of Guyana (AEAG) 1952;

(b) The Congress of Adult Education of Trinidad and Tobago (CAETT) 1980;

(c) The Barbados Adult Education Association (BAEA) 1981;

(d) The St. Lucia Association of Continuing Education (SLACE) 1981;

(e) The Adult Education Organization of Jamaica (AEOJ) 1982.

Bibliography

Caribbean Community Secretariat 1976 *Report on Survey of Adult Education Activities in the Caribbean.* Castries, St. Lucia, Georgetown

Caribbean Community Secretariat 1977 *Report on Seminar Workshop on Adult Education.* Castries, St. Lucia, Georgetown

Dominican Republic Secretariado Tecnico de la Presidente 1979 *Oficina Nacional de Planification Plan Regional de Desarrollo de Cibao Oriental.* Dominican Republic Secretario Tecnico de la Presidente, Santo Domingo

Final report on a meeting of experts from adult education institutions in the Caribbean 1980 Sponsored by St. Lucia and UNESCO Regional Office of Latin America and the Caribbean. Castries, St. Lucia, Georgetown

UNESCO Netherlands Antilles 1976 *Education: Issues and Priorities for Development.* UNESCO, Paris

UNESCO 1980 *International Yearbook of Education*, Vol. 32. UNESCO, Paris

Provision in Africa

E. A. Ulzen

Continuing education in Africa can be loosely defined as the training of adults in specific skills and knowledge which fit them into the employment market, or improve their efficiency in the jobs they hold, or enable them to undertake a trade for themselves. This article will look at the role of continuing education in Africa, its varied forms and structures and the major problems it faces.

1. *Types of Continuing Education*

The provision of continuing education which various agencies in Africa are making for the increase of a skilled workforce of all types, ranges from highly prescriptive and structured adult education programmes, through moderately structured or loosely structured educational activities associated with nonformal education, to those services offered by a broad range of information and education media, from which people select according to their interests. Most noneducational agencies and organizations prefer, however, the use of the term "nonformal education" to either "adult" or "continuing" education to describe their educational activities, because "nonformal education generally refers to a wide assortment of organized and systematic learning activities with specified target groups and specified learning objectives, taking place outside the formal system of education. Nonformal education is sponsored by a variety of agencies and institutions, governmental and nongovernmental" (Coombs and Ahmed 1974).

In Africa the term "continuing education" is not commonly used outside educational academic institutions, where it is loosely understood to be "the forms of education for learners who have had some contact with the school system and are building on to knowledge, skills or ideas already acquired" (Bown and Olu Tomori 1979). "Nonformal education" or "adult education" will therefore be the preferred expressions in this article.

2. *The Importance of Adult Education*

During the period of independence in the early 1960s, many African governments lacked the human resources with which to develop their politically young and economically fragile countries. To remedy this deficiency, most governments, firstly, made heavy financial investments for the expansion and renovation of the formal education system inherited from the colonial administration. Secondly, at the same time, they embarked upon literacy campaigns and programmes in order to provide educational opportunities for the majority of the adult population which had missed out on formal education.

After nearly 20 years of independence, African governments have realized that the heavy financial investments they have made, and continue to make, in providing facilities for primary and secondary education, are being outstripped by rapid population growth; that the renovation of the formal education system has failed to equip its outputs with appropriate knowledge, relevant skills and the right attitudes for productive work or self-employment; and finally, that the high rates of illiteracy and low rate of skills available for socioeconomic development ought to be countered by forms of education and training other than the formal system. They have now accepted, therefore, not only in principle but in fact, that nonformal education may offer a parallel system of education for children and adolescents who are not catered for by the formal education system, as well as a means for providing remedial teaching or upgrading of skills to its teeming unemployed and unemployable youth and adults.

To this end, at the governmental level, periodic national policies on education as well as national development plans take due cognizance of and give due weight to the development of adult education programmes. One example of this is apparent in Clause 52 of the National Policy on Education of the government of Nigeria, which has five objectives, covering functional literacy education; functional and remedial education; further education for those who have completed their formal education; inservice on-the-job professional training; and aesthetic cultural and civic education for public enlightenment. In all the national development plans of Kenya, the government has recognized and expressed the significant role adult education is expected to play in national development. In its Decadal Report 1960–1970, the government of Kenya has also recognized the key aims of adult education during the 1970s, among which was the need for synchronizing formal education for children and education for adults and integrating them as a continuous lifelong education.

At the Pan-African level, the role of adult continuing education has steadily gained a paramount importance in the 1980s, as reflected by the number of regional meetings held on the subject. The meeting of the heads of state and government of the Organization of African Unity in Lagos, Nigeria, 1980, issued a statement on the crucial importance of training and skills development in the areas of continuing education. A conference on higher education, organized jointly by the Organization of African Unity and the United Nations Economic Commission for Africa, which was held in Addis Ababa in January 1983, discussed the importance of adult and continuing education in the study programmes of universities in the context of preparing graduates for meaningful employment.

In July 1982 a UNESCO conference of African ministers of education and those responsible for economic planning, held in Harare, Zimbabwe, considered the democratization and renovation of education and emphasized the contribution which literacy and adult/continuing education can make to its achievement. The United Nations Economic Commission for Africa had one session of its Fifth Biennial Training Development Conference of the African Association for Training and Development in Addis Ababa in November 1984 to discuss papers on the basic and major issues in the theory and practice of nonformal education.

3. *Structures of Adult Education*

No uniform and well-defined systems of nonformal education obtain in any one African country, primarily due to the diverse sources from which programmes and activities originate. Further, unlike the formal system of education where one single ministry is invariably in charge of all its segments (i.e. primary, secondary, technical, and higher education), nonformal education programmes have in the past appeared and presently appear spontaneously, often without prior long-term planning, from different ministries, departments, and nongovernmental organizations in order to meet emergency situations. For this reason, the process of developing regulated and coordinated systems of nonformal education has been made difficult, notwithstanding the efforts which governments have been making towards that end.

African governments have set up various bodies with responsibilities for advising them on the development of adult education; on the establishment of appropriate institutions and training programmes; and to coordinate activities by governmental and nongovernmental agencies. For instance, in Kenya and Zambia, the governments established, by Acts of Parliament, boards of adult education (Kenya in 1966) charged with advising on all matters pertaining to adult education, including the formulation of curricula; the establishment of appropriate institutions as well as the use of existing ones; the assessment and identification of needs for new developments; and the coordination of activities by the government and nongovernmental agencies, and so forth. In Ghana, Liberia, Nigeria, and Malawi, national committees/boards have been established by governments, on which are represented all the main agencies—ministries, parastatal and nongovernmental—engaged in adult education, with objectives and functions similar to the Boards of Kenya and Zambia. Yet in other countries, such as Zimbabwe, the ministries of education and of community development and womens' affairs have been jointly charged with these responsibilities in conjunction with nongovernmental organizations.

Notwithstanding these attempts to establish systems for cooperation and collaboration, especially at the deliberative level, there is little effective liaison, consultation, and coordination among various agencies in the designing of the varied and numerous training programmes undertaken as well as in their delivery systems. In brief, nonformal education "systems" in sub-Saharan Africa are very fragile and may be considered nonexistent at present.

Continuing education, as with adult education structures in Africa, has emerged from the need to cope with developmental programmes, in which nearly all institutions and organizations of each country are deeply involved. They fall into the following categories: government organizations; semigovernmental or parastatal bodies; museums, libraries, and so on; business, commercial, financial, and industrial concerns; and nongovernmental organizations.

3.1 Government Organizations

African governments are the direct and major providers of all forms of nonformal education but especially of adult education, functional and work-oriented literacy education, including both initial education for work and vocational education of all types and, lastly, continuing education in higher education. Therefore, they provide the institutions, facilities, and the facilitators and teachers for these programmes, whose curricula are developed by relevant ministries and departments. All governments are, for instance, undertaking some form of literacy education: national literacy campaigns in Ethiopia, Zimbabwe, Mozambique, and Angola; large national literacy and adult programmes in Somalia, Kenya, Nigeria, Niger, Mali, Botswana; and preparation for undertaking national campaigns or programmes, in Liberia, the Gambia, and Central African Republic.

Most of the "academic" work in continuing education is directed from ministries of education and those responsible for adult education, such as the Ministry of Culture and Social Services in Kenya or the Ministry of Rural Development in Ghana, through evening classes for illiterate adults, organized by government employees and volunteers under the supervision of professional staff. In addition, ministries of education, of community development and local government, and of health and of agriculture undertake both refresher and upgrading courses for their staff as well as general courses for the benefit of public enlightenment. In Kenya, there is at least one farmers' training centre in each of 40 districts catering for small-scale farmers; low-cost polytechnics for the training of youth in trades: carpentry, shoe making and repair, tailoring, masonry, and so on; the National Youth Service for secretarial and middle-level technical subjects; vocational rehabilitation centres and industrial training centres. In Zimbabwe, the Ministry of Labour, Social Welfare and Manpower Planning conducts evening classes in polytechnic colleges which provide technical, vocational, and commercial courses. In Liberia, the Ministry of Youth and Sports and the Ministry of Education's Women's Vocational Training Programme conduct short-term training courses under the youth-on-the-job training scheme. In Ghana, there are the trade schools providing courses in the trades, and the polytechnic colleges, which provide medium- to high-level training in various commercial, technical and accountancy programmes. All ministries of information and broadcasting provide ample space in their print media and time on both the radio and television for continuing education information in a variety of subjects for adults in general.

3.2 Semigovernmental and Parastatal Bodies

Governments have established and financed quasi-governmental or parastatal bodies and institutions to undertake continuing education programmes: for instance in Ghana, the National Council on Women and Development, the national mobilization programme; in Nigeria, the Industrial Training Fund, responsible for the National Apprenticeship Scheme with a number of vocational training centres; in Botswana, the Bridges; and in Malawi, the Young Pioneers, with training programmes similar to Nigeria's Industrial Training Fund. In Zambia, the President Citizenship College, and in Liberia, the Ministry of Internal Affairs conducts courses in leadership training for chiefs, party officers, civic counsellors, project officers, and so on.

In most African countries, governments have established institutes of management and public administration, which offer certificates and diploma courses as well as upgrading professional and refresher courses for senior administrators and managers in financial administration, project designing and management, evaluation of programmes, and personnel management. Colleges of adult and distance education, institutes or departments of adult education, and centres for continuing education of universities in Africa, almost wholly financed by their governments, play an important role by providing courses in curriculum development, methodology and pedagogy to personnel of ministries, industrial and commercial concerns, and voluntary organizations for the development of their programmes in continuing education.

At the same time, through their extramural divisions, these institutions provide leadership in initiating and providing a wide range of nonformal education courses for those who want it, either directly through their own extramural sections, or through voluntary national associations, such as the People's Educational Association of Ghana and Sierra Leone and the national adult education associations in a number of countries. Further, they are continually requested by other organizations to design and conduct short-term training courses, seminars and conferences in specific aspects and areas of rural and urban development, in which specific aspects of adult education form essential components.

But by far the greatest service these colleges/departments/institutes/centres render to adult education programmes has been, and continues to be, the preparation and training of students for academic and professional qualifications, starting from the certificate to the postgraduate levels, in order to provide the expertise for the development and direction of the variety of programmes in adult education in their countries. Together with other university institutions and departments, such as the Open University of Nigeria, the correspondence departments and similar institutions within universities, they have provided opportunities, for those adults who wish to learn while they work, to attain academic and professional qualifications normally available only to residential students of universities.

3.3 Media Agencies, Arts Councils, Museums, and Libraries

Radio and television, mainly owned and financed by governments, bring to their listeners and viewers programmes on current issues and problems, and news on development activities. For women there are, for example, programmes on housecraft and nutrition. For farmers in rural areas and fishermen, programmes are geared to their needs, which introduce new technology to them for their industries. By Acts of Parliament or statutory regulations, governments have established museums which show citizens the history and works of arts of their past; national arts councils, which portray through the performing arts of drama, music and dance, the cultural heritage of their countries; and national library services, with mobile units, which provide journals, periodicals, books on history, biography, travel, fiction, and so on, for the education and leisure of their clients. Newspapers, mostly owned by governments, provide another means of general and special educational information. All these institutions and organs support the continuing education programme in the area generally termed "informational and educational services" and cover a wide spectrum of interests to the general public.

3.4 Business, Commercial, Financial, and Industrial Organizations

Business, commercial, financial, and industrial organizations carry out a wide range of continuing programmes in the field of inservice training, in-plant and on-the-job training, upgrading and promotion courses, for which they give their employees full sponsorship and release from work. In many countries there is legislation, for instance the Industrial Levy Act in Kenya and the Industrial Training Fund Act in Nigeria, which stipulates and prescribes the manner in which employees should be given periodic training in order to improve their efficiency, as well as for promotional purposes. Apart from the organizations undertaking these training and education courses for their employees primarily from their own success motive, ministries of labour and trade unions ensure that the courses conducted are appropriate and meaningful. Some of these organizations have their own training schools, while others use the facilities of other institutions for their training courses.

3.5 Nongovernmental and Private Organizations

Numerous voluntary and nongovernmental organizations, mostly indigenous, but a few branches of international nongovernmental organizations, have specialized interests with development issues as their prime concern and carry out programmes in adult continuing education. In Ghana, there are welfare associations; recreational groups; churches and their related executing and service organizations; voluntary education and development associations; specialized associations, such as the Young Men's Christian Association (YMCA) and Young Women's Christian Association (YWCA), Scouts and Guides; health associations; the Trade Union Congress—all of which have educational and training programmes spanning the wide continuum of adult education. Similar and comparable associations, organizations, and agencies exist in nearly all African countries.

There are, further, numerous indigenous organizations which cater for specific categories of the population. For instance, in Kenya, the Undugu Society caters for unemployed boys and adolescents and for young unmarried mothers, and provides them with educational programmes from basic literacy to vocational training leading to the acquisition of skills for a trade, such as masonry, or tailoring. In Zimbabwe, the Adult Literacy Organization of Zimbabwe, in addition to its programmes in literacy, is deeply involved in home economics, nutrition, and credit and savings for its members. In Kenya, the Maendeleo ya Wanawake, a national voluntary organization of women, carries programmes in adult basic literacy, integrating it with self-reliant and income-generating projects, such as poultry and other cottage industries, as well as in management, civics, simple economics and marketing, cooperative principles, health education and social development. Some commercial and industrial concerns undertake free training programmes for young people; examples are the Vocational Training Centre and the Opportunities Industrialization Centre in Liberia.

4. Administration of Adult Education Programmes

The administration of adult education is incoherent and uneven in all the countries, because of the numerous agencies involved and the different clientele catered for. The natures and styles of administration, therefore, are as diverse as the programmes offered. Even in one institution offering adult education programmes, the administration would depend upon the type and nature of the particular programme being offered at a specific point in time and for the specific clientele.

Generally, however, courses or aspects of continuing education such as part-time degree courses or those leading to recognizable and public certification require a fairly rigid administration, while those meant to give social education through the media are usually put out without a specific audience, and scarcely administered at all.

5. Characteristics of Programmes

The urgent pace with which nonformal education programmes are currently being undertaken in African countries, coupled with the diversity of programme offerings and the variety of providers, all reflect the paramount attention which African governments and communities are giving to the development of a skilled workforce for development, which Lewis defines as the "process aimed at transforming people so that they can contribute more effectively to the social and economic development of their society" (Lewis 1978). The relationship between nonformal education programmes and the development of skilled workforce gives the former characteristics which are different from those of the formal education system.

The first characteristic of nonformal education programmes is that, unlike the formal education system, they do not have a central authority, say of ministry of education for the planning, designing, dispensing and monitoring of the programmes. These tasks are carried out by the various types of provider already described.

The second characteristic relates to the flexible and amorphous nature of most nonformal education programmes. The majority are best handled by people—facilitators and clients—working as a team and in cooperation, formulating objectives and constantly reviewing courses for various and differing target groups.

The third characteristic arises from the employment of (a) various methodologies; (b) differing venues; and (c) the directions within a programme. Depending upon the target group and their needs, except for programmes for the acquisition of certificates or qualifications, the facilitators in conjunction with the target groups can choose a combination of teaching methodologies—face-to-face, discussion, "talk and chalk", demonstration study groups, discussions, broadcast sessions; various venues—classroom, market, farm, under a tree, on-the-job; and time, duration and/or frequency of sessions for the programmes: afternoons, evenings, weekends, three-day, one week, residential or nonresidential. Because the target groups are adults, their participation in planning the framework of each course is a necessary ingredient for its success and accomplishment.

The fourth characteristic is the availability of approaches from which different types of programmes can be designed for different sections of communities and working people.

In short, the field of nonformal education in the context of the current stage of economic and social development of African countries is so wide and the traditional structures of adult education so diverse and rich that innovative ideas and creative and imaginative resourcefulness are being combined to develop meaningful programmes and to avoid the rigid typologies which govern the formal education systems.

6. How Nonformal Education is Financed

6.1 Governments

It is difficult to quantify the money spent on nonformal education in the different countries, as is borne out by a study done in 1971 by Dorothy Thomas. The problems which confronted her in determining the funds allocated by the government within various ministries and departments in Kenya are not dissimilar to those encountered in other countries in respect of adult education. Many organizations undertaking programmes for adults, especially in the extension services, do not consider their work as falling within continuing education. It is difficult to identify estimates for adult education expenditure in printed estimates of recurrent expenditure. Costs for training are often included under a general title of "miscellaneous other charges" and cannot be isolated readily. Very often adult education is just one of a number of functions performed by some workers. For those institutions providing indirect adult education, such as libraries and museums, it is necessary to obtain estimates of the percentage of adults who use their facilities in relation to the total number of users. In the case of radio and television it is not possible to determine the number of adult listeners (Thomas 1971).

Most of these problems have been resolved in Kenya and other countries since 1971 and figures for adult education may be less painfully extracted should similar studies be undertaken. The point which must be emphasized, however, is that governments have been allocating greater and greater funds towards the various types of adult education programmes and activities for which their ministries and departments are directly responsible. For instance, in Kenya a fully fledged department of adult education has been established since 1979 in place of the previous Division of Literacy, and this not only indicates the importance which the government now attaches to nonformal education, especially to adult basic education, but has also meant more than a tenfold increase of the funds provided for the Department, which received in 1979 K£1,000,000 compared with the division's 1970/71 allocation of K£87,375.

As in Kenya, this pattern exists in all African countries. Governments provide physical development, facilities, equipment, and personnel for the continuing education for all the training and extension programmes and activities in their ministries. They further provide all the funds to cover the expenditure in most departments/institutes/centres of adult/continuing/distance education either through direct allocations to them or through their universities as special and earmarked grants and, therefore, not subject to virement or diminution by the universities. The same level of financial provision is made for quasi-governmental or parastatal organizations, such as the Institute of Management and Administration, institutes of technology, polytechnics, trade schools, vocational/farmers and cooperative training centres, village polytechnics, libraries, museums, and radio and television for the wide and varied range of programmes in the continuum of adult education.

A number of governments have, as stated earlier, legislated the imposition of training levy on commercial and industrial firms (e.g. in Nigeria and Kenya), and have established interagency committees (e.g. in Nigeria), which in turn have instituted training schemes (e.g. the Industrial Training Fund National Apprenticeship Scheme in Nigeria) to ensure that funds are made available to provide inservice and day release training for upgrading and retraining for change of jobs of the technical staff of these concerns.

Several governments also make annual grants to a number of nongovernmental organizations, whether they are branches of international organizations or are totally indigenous, because their adult education programmes and activities appertain to areas of concern to these governments. The Kenya government makes grants to the Green Belt Movement and the Family Planning Association of Kenya because the first mobilizes the population and motivates them to be interested in programmes for afforestation/environment and the second promotes population education. Subsidies are given to Maendeleo ya Wanawake in Kenya and the National Council for Women and Development in Ghana, both of which have the primary objective of training ordinary women to become self-reliant, self-employed and generally to reduce their inferior status in African society.

6.2 External Donor/Aid and Collaborating Agencies

External donor/aid and collaborating agencies have made and continue to make great financial and material contributions to indigenous voluntary and nongovernmental organizations, especially at the national and local levels. Figures are not readily available but taking as an example the African Adult Education Association, one of the two predecessors of the African Association for Literacy and Adult Education which is a regional nonprofit, voluntary and nongovernmental organization, intergovernmental agencies of the United Nations, governmental and nongovernmental donor/aid agencies contributed a total of Kenya Shillings 12,749,517 (exchange rates ranging from KSh 7:US$1.00 in 1977 to KSh 16.40:US$1.00 in 1985) from 1976 to 1984 towards its training workshops, conferences, seminars and other activities.

6.3 Nongovernmental and Private Organizations

Local and national organizations generate funds from within their countries from all sources—commercial and industrial concerns, national trusts and so on—and through raffles, sponsored walks and membership subscriptions to embark upon their programmes.

6.4 Fees and Sponsorship for Courses

The nonpayment or otherwise of fees by participants in the various adult education programmes depends upon the funding, objectives and purposes of the particular programme. Generally, where the training programme is the direct responsibility of the government, or any of its parastatal organizations, the entire financial resources are provided by the government and participants are released on their full salaries or at a minimal contributory fee for the programme, irrespective of its duration and of whether it is inductive, refresher, upgrading, vocational, technical or leading to higher academic and professional qualifications.

Governments make annual subventions to a number of nongovernmental organizations to enable these to conduct, free of charge to participants, training and educational programmes in subjects of paramount national importance to the government, such as leadership training for women, population education, or environmental education.

Nongovernmental and voluntary organzations often conduct programmes financed from their own resources for their members and/or specific interest or target groups. These resources may consist of funds generated locally by themselves and supplemented by grants from external governmental and nongovernmental aid agencies.

The training programmes conducted by business, commercial, finance, and industrial organizations of their own volition for their employees are free to the latter. Those provided under legislation, such as the Industrial Levy Act, are generally free to all unionized employees. The trade unions also provide free education programmes for their officers and their members free of charge.

Commercial, secretarial, and correspondence colleges charge economic fees for the courses they provide. Governments are now regulating these courses to ensure that they meet the curricula of the specific public qualifications for which they prepare adults, to maintain teaching standards and to protect students' interests. In Zimbabwe, adults qualify not only for subsidized fees, but can also request the government to pay the salary of a member to supervise, guide, and administer their studies, should they form a study group of at least 20 persons.

Generally all government, church or nongovernmental-organization-sponsored programmes in adult basic education, functional, work-oriented and postliteracy education, are provided free to participants, who buy the reading and other materials at greatly reduced cost. In some cases, the facilitators are paid a token honorarium by the sponors, but in the main most facilitators are volunteers.

7. Issues and Problems

Governments are attracted to adult or nonformal education by a number of qualities which are not to be found in the formal education system: the low costs involved in the development of continuing education programmes; the limited time-duration of its courses, with frequent termination points for students; the clear and definite base its courses have in immediate human needs—be they economic, political, social, health, nutritional, or educational; the capacity its programmes have for the provision and accommodation of aspirations of clients and participant; the direct linkage between its courses and real employment opportunities, especially in agriculture, industry, and rural development; the opportunity its programmes give for decentralized planning and freedom from the rigidity of the time- and place-bound process of the formal education system; the high potential for the distribution of whatever commodities are associated with its programmes; and the opportunity its programmes provide for people to learn while they work.

However, while in theory the link between adult education and national development has been accepted by governments since the early 1960s, and several conferences and seminars have been held to discuss the theme and its implications, no serious scholarly work has been attempted to develop educationally effective and integrated programmes to reflect the linkage. Such work would greatly assist adult education in gaining both recognition and appropriate funding from governments, which currently, in spite of their declarations on its vital importance, fund it marginally, compared with the formal education system.

Adult education faces a number of problems. The majority of current programmes are designed for meeting short-term objectives and are provided by so many diverse agencies and organizations, that it is almost impossible for them to have the supervision which would ensure that the training and education carried out are relevant to their clientele. In the fields for technical and vocational education and training, the quantity, variety, and diversity of programmes have made it difficult for the curricula used to be standardized and made commensurate with the government trade test examinations, undertaken by students for appointments or promotion in employment. In the same fields, there is acute shortage of equipment, machinery, tools, consumable materials, and properly qualified instructors for the training programmes to be relevant to industries.

As for adult education, there is an acute shortage of qualified personnel for nonformal education; training for facilitators is scanty and not properly structured and standardized. The salary and conditions of service for professional and fieldworkers in nonformal education are generally inferior to their counterparts in the formal education system, making the staff frustrated and therefore transient. Internally there is a scarcity of funds for programmes and therefore too much dependence on external sources, whose continuity cannot be assured for the sustenance and continuation of programmes undertaken.

Personnel and volunteers of nongovernmental organizations engaged in developmental and humanitarian programmes do not have adequate training in the essential aspects of adult education disciplines, such as methodology, or psychology, to enable them to engage and teach adults, with whom they are in direct and constant contact.

Funds for undertaking studies and research into nonformal education, as in adult education generally, are scarce because governments and donor agencies consider research an academic exercise, which should be confined to universities. They do not appreciate that fieldworkers need to be trained to undertake simple investigations and to apply their result to new programmes in order to make them relevant to the environment and milieu in which they work.

By far the biggest problem besetting adult education is the absence of high-level coordinating national bodies, which, while not making programmes as rigid as formal education programmes, would coordinate and supervise the conduct of programmes, in order to ensure their durability and validity as well as facilitate the exchange of innovative ideas, method, and theories among the numerous providers. This would enhance, standardize, and ensure that the programmes really do contribute to the attainment of those skills required to maintain and advance economic and social development in African countries.

Bibliography

Bown L, Olu Tomori S H 1979 *A Handbook of Adult Education in West Africa.* Hutchinson University Library for Africa, London

Coombs P H, Ahmed M 1974 *Attacking Rural Poverty: How Nonformal Education can Help—A Research Report for the*

World Bank. Johns Hopkins University Press, Baltimore, Maryland
Lewis J 1978 *In-plant Training and Apprenticeship Training in Nigeria*. ITF/International Labour Organization, Geneva
Omolewa M 1981 *Adult Education Practice in Nigeria*. Evans Brothers, Ibadan
Organization of African Unity 1981 *Lagos Plan of Action for the Economic Development of Africa 1980-2000*. International Institute of Labour Studies, Geneva
Thomas D 1971 *Who Pays for Adult Education in Kenya?*. Board of Education, Nairobi, Kenya
United Nations Economic Commission for Africa (UNECA) 1984 Monograph No. 2, United Nations Economic Commission for Africa, Addis Ababa

Provision in South Africa

C. Millar

It is misleading to talk of a "system" of nonformal continuing education in South Africa. In the first place the provision of nonformal education is rudimentary and underdeveloped in contrast to the formal system of initial education. In the second, such provision is characterized by fragmentation of control and policy. However, 1981 marked a striking shift in official thinking. Following two Government reports, which stressed the need for the development of various forms of job-related and industrial relations training (Riekert 1979, Wiehahn 1979, 1980), for the first time nonformal adult education was identified by a state-appointed education commission as an area for development (De Lange 1981). The explanation for this changed perspective is to be found in the period of political and economic crisis, the explosive moments of which were 1976 and 1980, that brought the Black schooling system to a halt, established the formal system of Black education as a chronically vulnerable site of conflict and resistance, and propelled a period of active political reform on a wide front. What characterized this reform initiative was the active partnership of state and private sector, with the twin agendas of social stability and economic growth.

A major factor in this reformative response was public government commitment, for the first time, to equality in educational provision as a social goal. This goal was addressed predominantly in terms of improved school systems, with finance, structure, and control as major issues. However, the issue of a possible alternative or nonformal "system" was introduced both as a corrective device and as one containing the possibility of a substantial reconstruction of the core system itself. In pursuit of this latter possibility a government-sponsored research team was established with active support of private sector reform theorists to provide the conceptual foundation for the possible national provision of nonformal education in South Africa, and to research such matters as coordination, structure, finance, accreditation, and the linkages between formal and nonformal systems.

In the mid-1980s continuing education as a system remained at the blueprint stage, to be contrasted with the untidy reality of continuing education provision of various forms and under various auspices. It is helpful in overviewing such practice to use three broad classifications of nonformal education, seeing it as serving "compensatory", "upgrading", and "cultural/political" functions. All official publications use the apartheid classification of "Black", "Coloured", "Asian", and "White", and these terms have been used in this article to illuminate various aspects of inequality. However, for "Black" I have substituted "African", preferring to use "Black" as the term to describe all people in South Africa not classified "White" and thus subject to legislated discrimination.

1. Compensatory Education

Compensatory education for adults, seen as the replacement in some form of incomplete or missing initial education, finds its justification in the huge disparities in educational provision and experience across class and racial lines that persist in South Africa today. The following figures are crude indices of this disparity. Over half the African pupils who left school in 1982 did so after four or fewer years of schooling. They were illiterate or semiliterate (Verwey et al. 1983). The percentage of pupils who started school in 1963 and completed a full 12 years of schooling was as follows: White pupils 58.4 percent; Asian pupils 22.3 percent; Coloured pupils 4.4 percent; African pupils 1.96 percent (De Lange 1981).

A longstanding small-scale response to this situation has been networks of privately established literacy classes and night schools, started in the 1920s and 1930s mainly by radical and liberal political groupings, developing in urban centres and catering mainly for workers engaged in the broad processes of urbanization and industrialization. By 1955 there were about 10,000 African night-school students in the cities of Johannesburg, Cape Town, Durban, and Pietermaritzburg (Bird 1984).

The forced closure of such night schools took place during the 1960s when the apartheid policies of the Afrikaner government that had achieved power in 1948 finally took effect. This policy called for total government control of Black education, an end to any assimilative or integrative tradition, whatever its scale, and a prevention of any educational enterprise by church, cultural, or political organizations that could be seen as "subversive".

It has taken nearly 20 years for a night-school system to be reconstructed, this time under strict state control within the separate state departments concerned with

African, Coloured, and Asian education and within the industrial sector itself. The expansion of the African night-school system has been particularly rapid. The Department of Education and Training, the state department that controls African education outside of the "national states", has 386 registered adult education centres throughout the country (including those within industrial companies) at which 35,467 adult students are engaged in part-time school-level study (Republic of South Africa 1985).

The late 1970s and early 1980s also saw a thaw in state restrictions on private initiatives in Black education and a number of community organizations initiated compensatory programmes for adults, particularly at the levels of literacy and postliteracy training. There was an expansion too of the scope of adult basic education within industrial contexts.

2. *Education for Upgrading*

Upgrading refers to continuing education that has as its function the development of knowledge and competence that leads to increased effectiveness in specific contexts, usually the workplace. Whereas compensatory education is school related and general, upgrading is work related and specific.

In all sectors of commerce and industry there remains a gross imbalance in Black as opposed to White penetration into skilled and managerial occupational categories, with the formal system of technical education doing little to alter this situation. In 1979, for example, 99 percent of the engineers, 78 percent of the natural scientists, 91 percent of the technicians and 72 percent of the artisans and apprentices were White (De Lange 1981). It is this untenable situation that propels current attempts to upgrade worker skills. The industrial training effort has as a major goal the incorporation of Black workers at rising levels in the industrial sector.

By South African standards, investment in upgrading in the form of private sector industrial training is substantial, with annual operating and capital expenditures estimated at 840 million Rand and 2,810 million Rand respectively (Republic of South Africa 1984). Such training programmes are a form of government–private enterprise partnership, funded by tax concession and subsidy, and controlled by a National Training Board within the Department of Manpower. During 1980/81 an estimated 1.25 to 1.75 million workers were engaged in this form of continuing education. More advanced forms of technical education include courses in technical tertiary institutions. Current expansion in this upgrading programme is at the operative level, though traditionally a major investment in workplace upgrading has been in the area of management itself.

Professional continuing education, in contrast to industrial training, is the responsibility of professional associations, universities, and *technikons*. The correspondence University of South Africa, with a total enrolment in 1985 of 76,000, plays a major role in providing opportunities across the spectrum of the population for advanced professional and general education that has major implications for career mobility.

Massive disparities in the quality of schooling are paralleled by sharp contrasts in teacher supply and qualification. Eighty-five percent of African teachers are underqualified for the posts they hold (De Lange 1981). For equality in educational provision by 2020 at a pupil–teacher ratio of 30:1 it has been estimated that 300,000 teachers will need to be trained. This situation has prompted the development of intensive upgrading programmes for Black teachers. These are administered by the employing education departments, sometimes with the assistance of tertiary institutions and private sector funding. The number of teachers thus engaged is large and increasing. In the Department of Education and Training the number of underqualified teachers in upgrading programmes rose from 300 in 1974 to 7,000 in 1984 (Republic of South Africa 1985).

A final form of upgrading—not strictly speaking a form of continuing education—is that taking place within those open universities opposed to racial admission criteria. Here again, the impulse is acceleration of progress in institutional terms, Black school systems being unsuccessful in preparing Black matriculants for academic competition with White students. Academic upgrading is thus interventionist—a selective form of positive discrimination. Such programmes within, and to a more limited extent outside, the open universities are new and experimental and their effectiveness has yet to be determined.

3. *Cultural/Political Nonformal Education*

The present moves towards constructing a national system of continuing education, the general provision of adult equivalents of schooling and the administration of various forms of work-related upgrading programmes—described above—have lodged firmly in the hands of state departments or the private sector in cooperation with state departments. This is by no means the case in the broad field of cultural and political education in South Africa. What characterizes this field is the very wide range of participants, the extent to which a segment of these opposes state hegemony in education and the contest in cultural production manifested in this sector of nonformal education.

At one extreme of this ideological contest are two powerful nonformal educational apparatuses of the state—military service and media control. The first is a compulsory two-year period of military training for White males following schooling or tertiary education—a coercive programme of continuing education on a vast scale aimed at securing the internal and external stability of the state. The second is a programme of media control and censorship designed to shape and safeguard the formation of national culture. At the other extreme are networks of community, worker, and student organizations, with goals of social reconstruction and conscientizing agendas. These associations maintain and develop the traditions of opposition among exploited groups, both populist and sectarian. At times of overt political crisis they face the severest of sanctions.

Between the above positions lies a great range of continuing education provision, for the most part small-scale, loosely structured and uncoordinated local initiative. This includes the educational programmes of various religious denominations, sporting associations, cultural associations, and the extramural programmes of certain South African universities.

4. *Nonformal Continuing Education as a Reform Agenda*

There are two levels at which current moves towards state-sponsored development of a system of nonformal continuing education can be analysed as a reform agenda. The first sees nonformal education as an effective solution to problems implicit in formal education: nonformal education as a cooperative enterprise in education provision represents the recruitment of the private sector in financial partnership and thus addresses the scale of needed educational reform; nonformal education meets instrumental criteria of educational relevance, especially in relation to labour force development and employability; nonformal education is "efficient" in being organized in response to specific needs or objectives in specific contexts; nonformal education represents a second chance or educational rescue capacity: it offers immediate educational intervention into adult lives where formal education has failed to deliver its promise. Furthermore, nonformal education offers a space for social development free from the restrictions of bureaucratized and possibly ritualistic educational practice: it is a territory for pragmatic, project-like social and educational development.

However, the development of a system of nonformal education entails more than this. Beyond effective management lies a response to crisis of a more substantial kind and a recognition that in South Africa Black education has failed in its structural tasks. It can be seen as a structuring of new forms of cooperation and consent.

The consent of Black students to meet the normative claims of schooling is of the greatest fragility. Their school system is an isolated target of hostility. It lacks both the ideological support of its community and the utilitarian rewards of a developing economy. Soaring enrolments, massive unemployment and heritage of barriers to Black advancement in industry and commerce increase the contradiction between educational achievement and economic participation. By contrast, nonformal education is a form of educational engagement embedded in and subservient to the logic and institutionalized forms of major social processes, in the case of Black workers, urbanization, social mobility, or simply survival in the labour market; and this very embeddedness gives it a degree of protection denied the formal system.

Furthermore, the development of a national system of nonformal education holds the possibility of drawing into strategic cooperation—through sponsorship, accreditation, and coordinating structures—a wide range of community agencies with development goals, some of whose agendas would run counter to those of the present state/capital reform alliance. Given the state and status of Black formal education, such a development would represent for the state a recruitment of community support for educational reform as well as a diffusion of responsibility and accountability for education provision. But it would also mean a significant weakening of the state's hegemonic hold on its own untidily expanding system and therefore on the process of the reform agenda itself.

5. *The "State of Emergency"*

The above account of nonformal education in South Africa represents the situation up to 1985, when in response to widespread and sustained popular revolt the government declared a "state of emergency" that has been in force ever since. The reform impulse of the early 80s yielded to a stage of repression that included the banning or restriction of anti-government initiatives in both formal and nonformal education, in particular that of a community-based movement aimed at changing both the system of control and the curriculum of Black schooling, known as "People's Education". While the possibility of any state system of nonformal education has receded, nonformal education remains the site for a multiplicity of small-scale, innovative, educational programmes and projects, working under great difficulty, that are concerned with developing the educational resources for a post-apartheid South Africa.

See also: Nonformal Education

Bibliography

Bird A 1984 The adult night school movement for blacks on the Witwatersrand 1920–1980. In: Kallaway P (ed.) 1984 *Apartheid and Education.* Ravan Press, Johannesburg, pp. 192–221

De Lange J P 1981 *Report of the Main Committee of the Human Sciences Research Council Investigation.* Human Sciences Research Council (HSRC), Pretoria

Republic of South Africa 1984 *Report of the National Manpower Commission on Inservice Training in the Republic of South Africa, 1980–91.* RP 24, Government Printers, Republic of South Africa, Pretoria

Republic of South Africa 1985 *Annual Report for 1984.* Department of Education and Training, Pretoria

Riekert P J 1979 *Report of the Commission of Inquiry into Legislation Affecting the Utilisation of Manpower (Excluding the Legislation Administered by the Department of Labour and Mines).* RP 32, Republic of South Africa, Pretoria

Verwey C T, Carstens P D, Plessis A du 1983 *Education and*

Manpower Production (Blacks), No. 3, 1982. Research Institute for Education Planning, University of the Orange Free State, Bloomfontein

Wiehahn N E 1979, 1980, 1981 *Report of the Commission of Inquiry into Labour Legislation*, RP 47, RP 48. Department of Manpower Utilisation, Pretoria

Provision in the Indian Subcontinent

C. Naik

The history of continuing education for adults in India and West Asia stretches over a span of well over 100 years. By 1947, it covered the entire Indian subcontinent consisting of India, Pakistan, and Bangladesh. Night classes for industrial workers and social education for jute workers began in Calcutta as far back as 1872. Part-time courses were initiated in 1877 by the Victoria Jubilee Technical Institute, Bombay, for the provision of skilled labour to the local textile industry. By the dawn of the twentieth century, most of the larger cities of India had begun to offer facilities for part-time primary and secondary education to working youth. Part-time secretarial and commercial diploma courses then instituted by the provincial governments have continued to the present day. In the 1930s part-time degree courses in legal education were initiated. Private organizations also began to offer correspondence courses in several occupational fields and contributed substantially to the continuing education programmes. Between 1955 and 1965, "condensed" primary and secondary courses were instituted for women in the Indian countryside. Adult literacy programmes and workers' education gathered momentum during this period.

1. Recent Developments in Continuing Education

The idea and programmes of lifelong, continuing education in various areas of knowledge and occupations secured considerable government support and popular approval in the decade 1975-85. In the region as a whole, the 1960s and 1970s witnessed the rise of correspondence courses in higher education and teacher education. In addition, the traditional external degree courses widened their subject scope and also permitted the use of regional languages for written examinations, thus making it possible for women tied to the home and working youths to continue participation in higher education. Part-time and short-term courses grew in number and variety for the education and training of preschool teachers, village artisans, village-level extension workers, personnel of cooperative societies, unofficial office-bearers of local self-government agencies, officials in charge of development schemes, schoolteachers, school inspectors, and other officials. The funding and organization of such courses became integrated with India's 5-year plans of development through various ministries of the Union government, departments of state governments, and voluntary agencies, supported by an elaborate grant-in-aid system.

In 1977, the idea of an Open University caught the public imagination. At the same time staff colleges were established to prepare administrators for a shift from traditional "maintenance administration" to "development administration". Literacy movements gathered strength.

In India in the late 1980s, out of 153 universities, 82 have established adult and continuing education departments. In Pakistan, the Allama Iqbal Open University in Islamabad, and in India, the Open University at Hyderabad and the Indira Gandhi Open University in New Delhi, are setting up innovative programmes of initial and continuing education at various educational stages.

As an aspect of open and continuing adult education, distance education has recently begun to make rapid strides in India, Pakistan, Bangladesh, and Nepal. However, the public still sees it as somewhat inferior to conventional, campus-bound education. The problems associated with distance education are many: a lack of personnel for developing materials, the recruitment of teachers who can adjust to distance-learning techniques; the allotment of broadcast and telecast time; the communication problems faced by learners in remote, hilly, and sparsely populated areas, and so on. In spite of such difficulties, distance education holds much promise of enlarging the horizons of diverse types of continuing education programmes in the Asian region. India has made rapid strides in installing distance education capacity in a planned manner, while Bangladesh and Pakistan are in a state of readiness to develop their distance education programmes further.

The concept of lifelong, need-based education for the cultural and occupational growth of individuals and communities is now stabilizing in most of the Asian region. India, with its large population and territory, naturally has the largest coverage and variety of continuing education programmes.

2. India

2.1 Growth of Adult and Continuing Education (ACE) Programmes

The first Extension and Communication department in India was established by the Mysore University in 1932. It organized extension lectures in English as well as in Kannada, the local language. The clients were, to begin with, English-speaking university-educated people from Bangalore and Mysore. In late 1932, rural lecture series were organized in Kannada; literature, social sciences, natural sciences, and technology proved popular subjects. These lectures were published as small books and the University invested its own funds in the activity. The second university to undertake extramural work was the University of Poona, established in 1948. Its Board of Extramural Studies was given a full-time secretary with the status of a reader, who, assisted by several small committees, organized summer and winter schools, extramural camps, and lectures. Lecture synopses were published and supplied to participants. In 1963, the University of Rajasthan set up a department of adult education with a full-time director. Along with continuing education for the community, it promoted research into the problems of adult education. The outstanding contribution of the late Dr Mohan Sinh Mehta, then Vice-Chancellor of Rajasthan University, stimulated a systematic development of departments of adult and continuing education in Indian universities.

The adult and continuing education (ACE) departments are expected to establish an organic link between their work and the teaching and research conducted in other departments. The new guidelines of the University Grants Commission (UGC) have brought under the umbrella of the ACE departments several of the older and smaller programmes such as planning forums for students, population education, extramural lectures, and teacher development programmes. Since the inception of the National Adult Education Programme in 1978, ACE departments have also become involved in guiding and conducting adult literacy programmes, particularly through the agency of affiliated colleges. In all, 705 colleges are assisted by the UGC and guided by ACE departments in their adult literacy activities.

2.2 Objectives of ACE Departments

The programme objectives of ACE departments have recently been reformulated by a working group of the UGC, as follows.

(a) To enable the universities to establish links with the community with a view to promoting social change.

(b) To provide opportunities for teachers and students to disseminate knowledge to various segments of the population in order to stimulate their interest in contemporary issues and in professional and technical growth.

(c) To cater for the felt needs of society, with particular emphasis on underprivileged groups so as to motivate them to participate in development.

(d) To enrich higher education by integrating continuing and adult education programmes and extension work with various branches of studies so as to build up links between the universities and the community.

(e) To provide field experience to teachers and students in order to sensitize them towards the realities of the socioeconomic situation and those problems which require academic investigation.

(f) To enable colleges and university departments to organize action research in relation to the problems of development.

2.3 Organization of ACE Departments

The staff of an ACE department enjoy a status similar to that of the staff in other university departments. But, unlike other departments, the ACE department does not have a board of studies. Instead, an advisory board with the vice-chancellor as chairperson, plans and oversees its programmes. The department is staffed by a director, one or two assistant directors, and one or two project officers. The advisory board prepares the budget for submission to the executive council of the university. One of the important tasks of the ACE department is to guide colleges affiliated to the university, to set up continuing education cells and organize programmes.

The UGC gives 100 percent financial support for the core and administrative staff and 75 percent for programmes. Colleges are also given some funds for administrative purposes. The universities monitor and evaluate their own programmes. Along with emphasis on adult education including literacy work, the university system is expected to provide extension services to schools, colleges, and the community.

Courses offered in continuing education include the humanities, social sciences, and natural sciences. Professional courses in medicine, engineering, agriculture, domestic science, pharmacy, nursing, and so on, are organized under the auspices of the ACE department, in collaboration with the professional organizations concerned. Courses in public relations, leadership, and management techniques are also being considered. Short-term and part-time courses for workers in the organized and unorganized employment sectors are also to come within the purview of ACE departments, to be conducted in collaboration with business, industry, and social work institutions.

The introduction of diploma and degree courses in adult and continuing education has been mooted in order to strengthen and professionalize ACE departments. Initiatives in this direction have already been taken by the University of Rajasthan, the Shreemati N D Thackersey (SNDT) Women's University, Shivaji University, and a few others. For establishing links between universities and the rural community, interdisciplinary investigations into rural problems and collaborative research on the process of social change are expected to flourish under the new objectives and programmes of the ACE departments of Indian universities.

2.4 Continuing Education for Workers

The Central Board of Workers' Education (CBWE), established in 1958 as an autonomous body sponsored by the Ministry of Labour, is the chief agency organizing educational programmes for workers at the national, regional, and enterprise levels. Various programmes have been developed under its auspices, for the preparatory training as well as the continuing education of worker–teachers, workers, and organizational personnel like education officers, zonal officers, and trade union workers. When the scope of the Board's activities increased, it established the Indian Institute of Workers' Education in Bombay (1970). The Institute conducts national and zonal courses for various types of higher personnel engaged in worker education programmes or trade union activities. The national programme includes pre-employment training and refresher courses for education officers, courses for trade union officials, and seminars for officials and others concerned with industrial relations and the trade union movement. The Institute maintains close contacts with the International Labour Organization (ILO), international programmes for workers' education, and trade union movements.

Education officers are the main target group for the Institute's training programmes. The present training syllabus, formulated in 1983, reflects the new dimensions of worker education which visualize an all-round development of workers for their personal benefit, along with that of the industry in which they are employed. Preparatory training for education officers consists of five months of theory and one month of practical training for which they are attached to trade union organizations, employers, and the labour department. Education officers have also to undergo two-week refresher courses several times during their tenure. These short courses are need-based and emphasize new developments in the field of labour, industry, and communication. For trade union officials, the Institute organizes full-time one-week residential courses. These emphasize the role of trade unions, labour legislation, industrial relations, and the problems of workers generally and particularly those of female workers. Matters like wage policy, family welfare, population education, and worker participation in industry are also discussed in these courses. In addition, courses have been instituted for trade union journalists, covering such topics as the freedom of the press, communications media, techniques of news coverage, editing, and feature writing. Organization of national and zonal seminars and conferences is another responsibility of the Institute. These are used as devices for continuing education and reorientation of personnel in leadership positions in labour administration, workers' education, and trade unions.

The establishment of the Institute in 1970 was a landmark in the field of continuing education programmes for workers in India. The Board of Governors of the Central Board of Workers' Education is the final authority for granting approval to the Institute's programmes. The Board has also established a Standing Advisory Committee for the Institute. It consists of representatives of trade unions and employers. The Director of the Board is an ex-officio member. A specialized library on labour has been developed at the Institute for the purposes of research and reference. It is the main centre of information for regional directors, education officers, trade union officials, and researchers interested in the problems of labour and industry. The Institute has a full-time faculty consisting of a deputy director (training) and three lecturers. The faculty is normally supported by zonal and regional directors, and officials from the headquarters of the Board.

The country has been divided into four zones for conducting the activities of the Central Board of Workers' Education. The zonal officers in Delhi, Bombay, Calcutta, and Madras carry out short-duration programmes for reorientation of regional directors and education officers. The training programmes organized under the auspices of the Central Board of Workers' Education and the Institute for Workers' Education are reviewed periodically and reformulated.

The most impressive contribution of the CBWE has been in the training and education of worker–teachers and workers, with a coverage of 72,208 worker–teachers and 3,414,408 workers among whom 86,465 are women. The Board has also developed special education courses for handicapped workers, women in the unorganized sectors, landless labourers, and other casual or self-employed workers in the informal sector who had been neglected in the past. Continuing education programmes are now offered to landless labourers, marginal farmers, agricultural and fishing workers, rural artisans, tribal people, forest labourers, and the educated unemployed in the rural areas. The Ministry of Labour has formulated a scheme for training organizers for rural workers at the regional centres of the Board. Since 1979, continuing training programmes have been devised for workers employed in such unorganized sectors as handloom, powerloom, and rural industries, small-scale industries, handicrafts, sericulture, coir industries, and so forth. Courses are preceded by surveys to find out the extent and type of clientele and the nature of courses to be formulated. Organization of courses for the informal and unorganized sector is an extremely difficult operation since identifying willing learners and getting them together for training programmes involves many constraints and confrontations which are beyond the scope of labour legislation. Along with innovative nonformal courses directed towards workers in the unorganized sector, the Board conducts adult literacy programmes for workers under the National Adult Education Programme.

The Board has produced a large quantity of teaching and learning materials for all its programmes. Most of the materials are profusely illustrated since the content to be communicated has to be adjusted to the low level of literacy of most industrial workers.

2.5 Use of Mass Media for Continuing Education

Regular broadcasts and telecasts have been specially designed for the general reorientation and continuing education of farmers and industrial workers. A "Radio School for Farmers" has been operating from several stations of All India Radio for many years and has received an excellent response from the clientele. With increases in the number of radio stations and relay outlets for television, the coverage of these programmes is expected to increase severalfold by the early 1990s.

2.6 Polyvalent Education for Workers (Shramik Vidyapeeth)

In 1967, the Government of India initiated the scheme of Shramik Vidyapeeth (polyvalent education centres for workers). Financial assistance is given under this scheme either to the state governments, or universities, or voluntary agencies, for conducting multifaceted continuing nonformal education of urban workers employed in industry, business establishments, servicing units, mines, plantations, and similar workplaces in organized and unorganized sectors. The scheme also covers the continuing nonformal education of the families of workers. Its main aim is the enrichment of the personal life of workers. Further education, talent development, physical culture, and recreation are some of its components. An allied aim is to promote the vertical mobility of workers in their occupations and to supplement their incomes by helping them acquire skills in craftwork for home-based production of additional earnings through established enterprise.

The Shramik Vidyapeeths work under the aegis of the Ministry of Human Resource Development (Department of Education) and are supervised by state education departments. However, representatives of the Ministry of Labour are included in the managing board of every Shramik Vidyapeeth in order to coordinate its work with that of the Central Board of Workers' Education. Close contact with industry is achieved by placing industrialists on the managing board of the Vidyapeeth. Between 1967 and 1986, 50 Shramik Vidyapeeths were established. There is a plan to open one Shramik Vidyapeeth in each district, ultimately raising their number to about 450. A recent decision to cover workers in the unorganized sector will expand the activities of the Shramik Vidyapeeths to cover new facets of continuing education for workers.

2.7 Continuing Education for Administrators and Professional Groups

The Indian Institute of Public Administration (IIPA) was established in New Delhi in the mid-1950s with a view to enabling administrators from all ministries and departments of government at the central and state levels to participate in programmes of self-development. The Institute has a membership of nearly 6,000. Regional conferences and an annual conference are held to discuss important contemporary issues in development planning and administration. Frequent seminars and training courses are organized for all categories of government officials, and branches of the IIPA are found in every state. Some of these work in collaboration with university departments of social sciences, particularly political science. The Lal Bahadur Shastri National Academy of Administration at Mussoorie is the premier staff college for Indian administrators. During the 1970s institutes of development administration were independently established in several states of India, for organizing the recurrent training and orientation of officials functioning from the block to the state level. (A district is divided into several development blocks which are the basic units of administration.)

Apart from institutional arrangements for the training of general administrators, a system of offering continuing education to particular sectors is also emerging. For instance, the National Institute of Educational Planning and Administration (NIEPA) covers a wide range of education officials working at the state and central levels.

Other professional groups which conduct recurrent orientation courses are the Institute of Engineers, the Indian Medical Council, and the Indian Law Society, which collaborate with counterpart departments of universities. The National Institute of Bank Management, the colleges of banking, and institutes of cooperative education and management are further examples of some of the varied avenues for continuing professional education.

District-level recurrent education for rural functionaries is conducted in all states to cover members of Grampanchayats (village councils), Gramsevaks (village-level workers), workers in health, nutrition, primary education, agriculture, agro-based industries, and so on. Most of these programmes are organized and financed by appropriate government departments.

For the teaching profession at the school level, the National Council of Educational Research and Training, regional colleges of education, and state councils and institutes of educational research and training offer a variety of reorientation courses. (There is a general rule that all education personnel should undergo about three months of reorientation for every five years of service.) Subject teachers' associations are another agency for continued orientation and training of teachers, operating in some states. These cater for the developmental needs of their members and publish journals which keep up information flows.

For teachers of higher education, some universities have developed an inservice diploma in higher education, emphasizing collegiate teaching techniques. These are intended for newly appointed junior staff. For the rest, faculty seminars, summer institutes, and annual conferences are the usual avenues of continuing education.

2.8 Open Education

The idea of open, spare-time, and own-time education came into prominence when the possibility of establishing open universities was first discussed in a conference held in New Delhi under the auspices of the Ministry of Education in 1977. The model of the Open University in the United Kingdom was considered for adaptation in India. The experiment began with the establishment of an Open University in Hyderabad, Andhra Pradesh

(1982), with courses leading to B.A., B.Com., and B.Sc. degrees. No formal enrolment qualifications are laid down but an entrance test is administered by the University. Lessons by correspondence are supported by audio cassettes, radio, and video. Study centres provide opportunities for interaction with counsellors and other students, and summer schools are held in April and May. Being a multilingual country, India has planned open universities for different regions. The Indira Gandhi National Open University (IGNOU) has already been inaugurated by the Prime Minister, and plans to establish an open university in Maharashtra state are being finalized. Open courses in social sciences have been launched by the Tilak Maharashtra Vidyapeeth, Poona, using Marathi as the medium of instruction.

Along with the open university idea, the open school idea is also being propagated. The programme has already begun in Delhi, at the secondary stage. Evening classes and night schools have prospered in India since the early twentieth century at the secondary stage and, in a few instances, at the primary stage as well. But these have catered mostly for the educational needs of employed men. The recent open school arrangement may lead to much greater participation of women in secondary education. At the primary stage, part-time education for illiterate working children and youth who have missed the opportunity of schooling is becoming an acceptable arrangement. A scheme of nonformal primary education is being implemented in the rural areas for working children in the 9–14 age-group. In this ungraded system, self-learning materials are the mainstay of the instructional process. This programme should help increase access for deprived groups, and particularly girls, to primary education. The new education policy recently formulated by the Government of India visualizes the provision of open and continuing education of all types at all stages. A variety of skill-training and vocational programmes are expected to be organized on a part-time basis for primary- and secondary-school dropouts as well as for those who have matriculated, in a practical "on-the-job" arrangement.

3. *Pakistan: The Allama Iqbal Open University*

Recognizing that the formal education system would be unable to cope with the heavy task of functional mass education, Pakistan has turned towards the alternative of open education. This option also provides scope for innovation and experimentation for linking education to raising the people's quality of life.

Pakistan's Allama Iqbal Open University (AIOU) was established in the early 1970s to provide a variety of educational opportunities to adults. It offers programmes ranging from tertiary education to adult literacy and promotion of functional education in remote rural areas. The multimedia system adopted by AIOU consists of correspondence, radio, television, tutorial sessions, flip-charts, audio-cassettes, and other techniques of communication and learning. The open education programmes are assisted by institutions of formal education. The reported enrolment of AIOU is about 65,000 which includes teachers, adults in other occupations, and housewives. The programme is disseminated through 10 regional study centres and 150 local study centres. Library facilities, workshops, and technical services which cannot be provided in the local centres are provided in the regional centres from where the work of local tutors is supervised and assisted. The local study centres use the services of about 1,000 part-time tutors during a semester. As many as 65 courses are offered by the university, including training courses for teachers, and formal courses leading to a B.A. in Education and M.A. in Educational Planning and Management. The tutors are normally drawn from the institution which serves as a local study centre.

The University develops and produces course materials including 300 radio programmes and 75 television programmes during a semester. The programme for training personnel in distance education consists of internship with senior tutors and use of tutors' guides. Some of the staff for tertiary open education have been trained in the United Kingdom. A comprehensive programme has been drawn up for training personnel in distance education and will be launched in the near future.

The objectives of the AIOU are as follows:

(a) to provide educational facilities to people who cannot leave their homes and jobs to attend institutional courses;

(b) to provide facilities for continuing education;

(c) to organize initial and further training of teachers;

(d) to provide instruction in technologies and different types of occupations; and

(e) to undertake research and experimentation in the interest of advancement and dissemination of knowledge.

Apart from its tertiary programmes, the other most significant programme developed by AIOU offers functional courses primarily aimed at increasing the literacy levels and productivity of the rural population. The total range of programmes covers four sectors: general education, functional education, teacher education, and research and development. Several of these are carried out by the university in collaboration with other training agencies such as the National Literacy and Mass Education Commission, Provincial Councils for Literacy, the All Pakistan Women's Association, Pakistan Television Corporation (PTC), and the Ministry of Local Government and Rural Development.

The work plan of AIOU consists of:

(a) an assessment of needs and priorities within each programme in order to determine the courses to be offered;

(b) the setting up of course teams and preparation of course outline, specifying the aims and objectives and teaching/learning methodologies to be used;

(c) drafting of individual units of a course by full-time academic staff assisted by external experts;

(d) preparation of illustrations and diagrams for each written unit and its editing before printing;

(e) printing of the units;

(f) preparation of radio and television programmes where necessary in order to supplement the written text;

(g) distribution of printed units to the clients by post;

(h) transmission of radio and television programmes;

(i) continuous assessment and examination of learners by part-time tutors supervised by full-time faculty; and

(j) student meetings at study centres, with or without tutors.

In the rural programmes of literacy and functional education, the nation-building departments (NBD) have begun to offer AIOU considerable collaboration and facilities. The AIOU has grown into an impressive model of a well-structured system, building educational links between the University, government, and community, with a view to promoting continuing and adult education from the grass-roots to higher education levels.

4. Bangladesh

4.1 Continuing Education for Rural Development

The Bangladesh Academy for Rural Development (BARD) has developed various nonformal education programmes especially for women and rural youth. These consist of adult literacy programmes; development of cooperatives; training in youth leadership; training of skills in agriculture, poultry, and animal husbandry, and so on. Programmes of health education and health care are also organized with focus on women and children. Schoolteachers are trained to participate in these nonformal continuing education programmes as leaders and instructors. The development departments of government collaborate with academic personnel in order to provide continuing training in growing vegetables, developing livestock, and undertaking marketable craftwork like clay modelling, needlework, and other traditional handicrafts. This system of need-based education and training provides rural youth and women with continued access to new opportunities for development.

Several voluntary agencies in Bangladesh provide similar continuing education programmes, including adult literacy. The most extensive programme of education and training for rural development is conducted by the Bangladesh Rural Advancement Committee (BRAC). Many of these education and development projects receive external funding from sources like the Danish International Development Agencies, the Canadian International Development Agency, the Ford Foundation, the Lutheran World Service, and some West German, Dutch, and Norwegian foundations.

4.2 Distance Education

The National Institute of Educational Media and Technology, Bangladesh, has been working on a multimedia distance education scheme for improving the quality of schoolteaching. Eventually, distance education will be linked up with an open university system to provide greater access to high school and collegiate education. Education of the general public will also be attempted, especially regarding health and family planning. At present, programmes of open education in Bangladesh are organized and controlled by government. Substantial assistance was received for them from Japan in 1978, mainly in the form of equipment.

5. Nepal

5.1 Teacher Education

Nepal is a mountainous country with one third of its districts classified as remote areas. Since the training of teachers for such areas presents a special problem, a project called Radio Education Teacher Training Programme (RETTP) was started in 1978 for imparting basic and continuing education to rural teachers. The project is conducted collaboratively by the Ministry of Education and Culture, the Ministry of Communication, and the Institute of Education. With financial assistance from United States Agency for International Development (USAID), and technical assistance from the Southern Illinois University, a radio set and instructional materials are supplied to each teacher covered by the project. This has set a new trend in recurrent education for rural teachers.

5.2 Occupational Education

The Tribhuvan University in Nepal is active in organizing basic, as well as continuing, vocational and technical education. The programme is conducted through rural and urban technical schools and a scheme of modules for "on-the-job" skill training at the local level, and is designed to meet changing labour needs for various sectors of rural development. Nepal also conducts a comprehensive programme of continuing education for rural adults. It is planned and implemented collaboratively by government departments of education, agriculture, health, forestry, and construction.

6. Sri Lanka: Distance and Open Education

The school system in Sri Lanka has reached almost total coverage. Large-scale extension of secondary schooling has increased the demand for places in higher education. There has also been an enhancement of expectation to pursue vocational and technical careers of an advanced nature. As a consequence, in 1976 the technical education extension service unit at Sri Lankan Technical College, Maradana, Colombo, began to organize correspondence education for those who were unable to gain admission to the university. Later, this came to be called Sri Lanka Institute of Distance Education. It offers courses of studies in management, mathematics, science, electrical technology, electronics, and telecommunications.

Sri Lanka started its open university in 1980. To begin with, it concentrated on diploma and certificate courses and continued the emphasis on mathematics, science, management studies, electronics, and telecommunications technology. However, a number of new courses for food science and technology, entrepreneurship, and foreign languages have now been formulated. Foundation courses have been devised for students whose basic preparation to enter the tertiary level is insufficient. The usual open education system of instruction, based on printed material supported by weekend and vacation sessions, is followed. The course duration varies from six months to three years depending on the level of achievement desired. Radio and television support is provided. In general, Sri Lanka has planned its open university on the model developed by the United Kingdom.

For the continuing education of teachers, Sri Lanka has developed distance education programmes which follow the approved techniques of open education: supply of material supported by district teacher centres, numerous study groups and contact sessions, and radio and television support. Courses for teachers are organized by the Ministry of Education. The personnel required for distance education and open university programmes has been trained with assistance from Swedish International Development Aid.

See also: Nonformal Education Policy: Developing Countries

Bibliography

Central Board of Workers' Education 1983a *Indian Institute of Workers' Education.*

Central Board of Workers' Education 1983b *Workers' Education Programmes* (Brochure - 1983)

Central Board of Workers' Education 1984 *Report of Silver Jubilee Conference, 1984.*

Jayasuria J E 1981 *Education in the Third World: Some Reflections.* Indian Institute of Education, Poona, Somaiya, Bombay

Kakkar N K 1973 *Workers' Education in India.* Sterling, New Delhi

Mathur M V, Naik C 1970 *Lifelong Education.* Asian Institute of Educational Planning, New Delhi

UNESCO 1978 *Open Education: Experiments and Experiences in Asia and Oceania*, Bulletin No. 19. UNESCO, Bangkok

UNESCO 1984 *Literacy Situation in Asia and the Pacific: Country Studies: Bangladesh, India, Pakistan, Nepal, Sri Lanka.* UNESCO, Bangkok

UNESCO 1985 *Distance Education in Asia and the Pacific*, Bulletin No. 26. UNESCO, Regional Office for Education in Asia and the Pacific (ROEAP), Bangkok

UNESCO 1986 *Building Multidisciplinary Training Networks for Rural Development.* UNESCO, Bangkok

University Grants Commission 1985 *Report 1984-85 (section 10).* University Grants Commission, New Delhi

Workers' Education June 1958 (Quarterly Journal of the Central Board of Workers' Education)

Provision in Southeast Asia

C. Duke

This article refers to and briefly compares some characteristics of the systems of continuing education in Southeast Asia, including some smaller systems of East Asia which tend to be associated with Southeast Asia. The countries display great diversity in their priorities and provisions. Systems are generally development oriented, and literacy, rural development, and national integration are important in many instances. The main provision tends to be governmental, though there is also vigorous nongovernmental activity. Political, economic, and cultural diversity is reflected in the diversity of systems. Despite this, and despite language differences, regional cooperation and exchange have tended to increase.

1. Diversity of Terminology and Priority

"Continuing education" is not yet a term widely in use in Southeast Asia, although it is gaining in popularity in some countries in the region. It tends to be used to refer to professionally oriented courses in the more industrialized countries, notably Singapore, though here, as in Hong Kong and Macao, it is also used as a term broadly encompassing the education of adults. "Adult education" is still quite commonly used, but has tended to be displaced by the term "nonformal education", for example in Indonesia and Thailand. Sometimes the term "adult nonformal education" is preferred. In Laos, Burma, and perhaps Kampuchea the main effort is in literacy and consequently the term "literacy" has sometimes become virtually an equivalent for "adult education". Vietnam uses the term "complementary education" to refer to its production-oriented provision. "Community education" is commonly used in Indonesia and also in the Philippines, which uses a plethora of terms freely and almost interchangeably. The term "lifelong education" has been adopted in Korea in official quarters and in legislation. This diversity of terminology reflects the great diversity in the region with regard to economic development, political systems, cultural backgrounds, and the educational attainment of its peoples.

In some countries adult illiteracy is still a major problem. While Vietnam achieved 90 percent adult literacy some years ago and has since concentrated on education aimed at enhancing industrial and agricultural productivity, Singapore has committed itself to a very ambitious system of continuously upgrading the nation's skills to be able to exploit high technology and advanced information systems. In Singapore as in the predominantly Chinese cities of Hong Kong and Macao, English language is recognised as a major adult education need for modern development, although the future of the latter cities is clearly with China, and this has begun to reflect in the orientation of continuing education there. In the larger and predominantly rural countries, continuing education is conceived and provided for within the context of national development planning and through a department or division of the ministry of education. Apart from literacy, programmes tend to concentrate on rural development, basic and second chance education (with examinations and certificates as for the school system), and to some extent on national integration and self-reliance for local small-scale economic development. The major thrust of large government programmes tends to be towards vocational and related skills for modernization. In the more industrialized and urban societies there is a growing awareness of and provision for the special needs of women and the elderly.

2. Continuing Education in Different Countries

2.1 Burma, Laos, Kampuchea

Little is known about adult education in the early 1980s in Kampuchea because of the disruption of war and the destruction which followed. It is assumed that such work as is done combines literacy with complementary education but predominantly reflects the political and strategic priorities of the different warring parties.

In the Lao People's Democratic Republic the first stage of a literacy drive was completed in 1980. Mass organization, flexibility of provision, and paid leave from government service are said to have been features. Literacy education is followed by complementary education in day and boarding schools from central to local level. As in Thailand, ethnic minorities in mountainous areas are a particular concern, probably especially for reasons of national security (UNESCO 1982 pp. 57–59).

Burma has chosen a path of socialist isolation from the main political groupings, although there is regular participation and exchange of information through UNESCO, particularly the UNESCO Regional Office for Education in Asia and the Pacific in Bangkok. Burma is widely known for its literacy work, starting with the first literacy campaign launched in 1965. It was claimed in 1981 that illiteracy had been effectively eliminated in 196 of the country's 314 administrative areas. Community voluntary effort and pride are mobilized through township literacy committees, and ceremonies and awards are employed to foster a competitive spirit whereby townships aspire to full literacy. As with other countries in this region, special approaches have been adopted for non-Burmese-speaking indigenous minorities (UNESCO 1982 pp. 21–32).

2.2 Vietnam

Vietnam attached importance to the elimination of illiteracy in the early days of independence in the North, and presumably also following unification in the South. It seems likely that, as with Cuba and other postrevolutionary societies, mass campaigning and mobilization led quickly to a very high level of literacy. Statements of objectives tend to encompass both ideological and economic objectives, such as the transformation of the old society and the construction of a new, just, and prosperous society. Economic development features prominently as an objective. Ethnic minorities especially in the mountainous areas are a special target group and, as in neighbouring countries, there is a mix of national economic development and national security objectives. Adult education is seen as a tool of government policy for economic and cultural development, probably modelled on the system of complementary education in the USSR, with which the Socialist Republic of Vietnam is politically aligned. As in the other socialist countries of the region, the system of continuing education is a government matter within an overall policy of national economic and political development. Although in Burma the role of voluntary effort is stressed and resources are thus mobilized which are essential to the literacy campaigns, the system is still planned and directed from the governing party through an administrative system reaching out from the centre to the local level.

2.3 The Republic of Korea, Hong Kong and Macao

South Korea, Hong Kong, and more recently Macao have been associated with the countries of Southeast Asia in terms of regional exchange in continuing education, although Korea also has some links with Japan, and the two Chinese cities under British and Portuguese administration look increasingly to China in terms of their future. They differ markedly from the socialist systems referred to above, and have more in common with the nonsocialist countries which constitute the Association of Southeast Asian Nations (ASEAN). There are also links with Taiwan, which, however, has tended to be isolated from regional exchanges for political reasons.

In Hong Kong and Macao there is very little government commitment to continuing education as a development strategy, although there is a substantial programme of courses provided by the Adult Education Department in Hong Kong. In all three places, though only very recently in Macao, national associations of continuing education (adult and youth education in the case of South Korea) have come to play a lobbying role with respective governments and, especially in the case of South Korea, to serve also as a forum for the professional development of continuing educators. Continuing education in Hong Kong tends to have a strongly instrumental orientation, whether offered by the government, the two university extramural departments, or the various voluntary and private bodies. Literacy and vocational courses tend to dominate, although there are also courses of a liberal and cultural nature. Much of the instruction is in Chinese, and this trend is likely to accelerate as exchange with China increases. The Hong Kong and Macao associations of continuing education are developing relationships and exchanges with neighbouring cities in China, as well as with the central administration in Beijing. Hong Kong was the channel for a major international symposium on adult education in Shanghai in 1984. Thus the two city states currently have a confused patchwork of provision more typical of Western societies, but may move towards a more integrated system as relations with China strengthen.

The Saemaul Movement in the Republic of Korea is the most distinctive adult education programme in that country. The movement (Saemaul Undong) is "a national campaign for community development aimed at improving the spiritual quality and economic progress of the nation" (Hwang 1985 p. 9). It was preceded by the National Reconstruction Movement in the 1960s and has national integration and security objectives as well as economic and moral ones. It is a large-scale and well-organized national system of courses and training, centred on the Saemaul Leaders' Training Institute and involving many government departments including the Department of Education. It has attracted criticism from within the country and beyond as having authoritarian characteristics and as placing national security ahead of people's development. It is, however, credited with contributing significantly to South Korean development and prosperity, especially of rural areas (Cheong 1985).

2.4 Malaysia and Singapore

Continuing education is barely recognized by the Malaysian government. There are various government programmes for rural development, including a literacy programme, focusing especially on the needs of the Malay population, and priority is given to the vocational training of youth for employment which could contribute to national development. There is, however, little recognition of continuing education as a tool for development, for example by the Economic Development Unit, and there is no national government-led or supported system of continuing education. Malaysia thus resembles Western nations more than its neighbours in the absence of an officially sanctioned system of continuing education. Malaysia does have a recently formed association for continuing education, but it is very weak and has been unable either to win the support of government departments at federal or state level, or to attract support from more vigorous community-based and radical workers.

In contrast, Singapore has a much stronger national association for continuing education which attracts support from public and private sector organizations, including training agencies, and also the National University. The country has tended to provide a lead within the region in arranging short training courses for continuing educators, on a national and regional basis. The provision of adult education somewhat resembles that in Hong Kong, with strong emphasis on the functional and on acquiring knowledge and skills for employment.

2.5 Indonesia, the Philippines, Thailand

These three larger countries of ASEAN tend to be grouped for some purposes. Each has a system of continuing education provided by the government, but there is great diversity between the systems, reflecting the difference in context and circumstance between the three countries. They have in common large rural populations and a continuing problem of adult illiteracy, although this is now at quite a low level in the Philippines, and Thailand is part-way through a major national literacy programme which it is expected will leave adult illiteracy at a low level. In all three countries literacy work is undertaken in a development context, whether for modernization or, rather, for local self-reliance. Indonesia and Thailand, with World Bank support and the involvement of small nongovernmental international organizations, have sought to combine literacy learning and the acquisition of useful skills with the setting up of local economic activities, so that what is learned can be directly applied and built into local rural development. In these two countries there has been some linkage of government and nongovernmental efforts to pioneer new forms of association between educational and economic activity. In Thailand linkage between formal and nonformal education and cooperation and coordination of effort between different government departments at central through to local village level have also been priorities of the Department of Nonformal Education.

Government support for continuing education in the Philippines is concentrated through the regular administrative system and schools of the Ministry of Education and Culture, with a small Continuing Education Bureau seeking to bring resources and programmes to adults in a context of government-led and controlled, mainly rural but also urban, development. The national association for continuing education in the Philippines appears to be virtually an agency of the government; there is also an association of private schools and colleges for nonformal education. On the fringe of government and outside it, and critical of it, there are other adult education and development agencies. The more radical of these were, in the mid-1980s, highly critical of their present system of government, and shade into resistance and guerrilla movements. The political polarization and regression of the Philippines mean that provision of continuing education is itself polarized and fragmented. One consequence of this may be that the attempt to use the formal education system of government for continuing as well as initial education has been little recognized and undervalued outside the country.

Community education in Indonesia (formerly Penmas, now Dikmas) is a large-scale and complex system of government provision which concentrates on the integration of basic literacy education with the acquisition of vocational skills at village level. The learning fund is a device intended to enable communities to put what they have learned into immediate productive use by means of learning groups. The government system in Indonesia has enjoyed imaginative professional leadership and contact with nongovernmental workers within the country and beyond, which have provided an innovative edge to the large-scale system of provision. Similar characteristics are found in Thailand, where a large and highly professionalized system of government provision has also been open to new ideas and experimentation from within the country and beyond.

Thailand is known in particular for the Khit-Pen philosophy of adult education, anchored in Buddhism and inadequately translated as "to know how to think" (or rather, to know how to solve problems and live in harmony). Khit-Pen has attracted much interest from beyond Thailand, most of it favourable, but it has also been charged with being too passive and accepting. Although the bulk of provision of adult education in Thailand is by the state through the Department of Nonformal Education, members of this service have in many cases studied abroad and combined traditional values with other, sometimes radical, perspectives. There are also various small nongovernmental agencies working in different parts of the country which have formal or informal links with the government system and provide some opportunity for experimentation and innovation outside the system itself yet with a capacity for changing the formal system of continuing education. As with other countries in the region, the education of ethnic minorities assumes special importance. Thai is not the first language for over half the population, and programmes for hill tribes in the North, Malays in the South, and other minorities, have strategic as well as educational significance.

3. General Observations

Southeast Asia displays great ethnic, cultural, linguistic, and economic diversity. There is no single dominating political and economic influence over the whole region, although different major nations have great influence over different parts of the region, and its continuing education systems naturally reflect these different influences. Despite the competition of major world forces for hegemony in Southeast Asia, the different countries manifest great diversity reflecting different religious and other cultural factors. The diversity of language and tradition has not, however, prevented the development of a substantial amount of regional cooperation in the 1970s and 1980s, with the exchange of ideas, personnel, and materials. There is, however, very little exchange between the socialist and nonsocialist systems.

The UNESCO Regional Office has succeeded in bringing together those involved in continuing education through a regular system of conferences, workshops, seminars, etc., and has probably contributed materially to the exchange of best practices between the countries of Southeast Asia and in other Asian countries to the enhancement of the respective systems. Different countries tend to send senior adult educators and potential leaders overseas for graduate training, but in the main local traditions and forces have resisted international homogenization.

The Asian and South Pacific Bureau of Adult Education (ASPBAE) has particularly fostered and placed value on "South–South" exchanges, and several countries in the region now enjoy reciprocal arrangements for the exchange of experience on a basis of relative equality with countries of the industrialized North. Among recent common developments in several countries, for example Malaysia, South Korea, and Thailand, there are open university developments which may draw on but have substantially adapted the experience of the British and other such systems.

Most countries in the region now have some kind of national association, but this particular form of voluntary organization is not well anchored in local traditions, and the nature and strength of these organizations vary greatly. Some are independent and critical of government, yet supportive for instance of legislation for lifelong education as in South Korea, or of establishing a policy for continuing education as in Hong Kong. Others are apolitical and professionally active, as in Singapore. Some are largely nominal and do not attract the more committed and radical adult educators, as in Malaysia and the Philippines, while in Thailand a new national association will probably include both government and nongovernmental elements and provide a channel for nonrevolutionary innovation to the continuing education system of that country.

Bibliography

Armstrong G 1981 *Some Aspects of Policy Formulation, Implementation and Decentralization in the Thai Nonformal Education.* Ann Arbor, Michigan

ASPBAE Courier 1978. Asian and South Pacific Bureau of Adult Education (ASPBAE), Canberra
ASPBAE Courier 1980. Asian and South Pacific Bureau of Adult Education (ASPBAE), Canberra
Bernard A 1981 *System Evaluation: A Case Study of the Thai Department of Nonformal Education.* Ann Arbor, Michigan
Cheong J W 1985 Saemaul education and the reduction of poverty. In: Duke C (ed.) 1985 *Combatting Poverty through Adult Education: National Development Strategies.* Croom Helm, London pp. 155–85
Duke C, Vorapipatana K 1982 *Nonformal Education in Asia and the Pacific.* APEID, UNESCO, Bangkok
Hwang Jong-Gon 1985 *Trends in Korean Adult Education.* KAAYE, Seoul
Kindervatter S 1979 *Nonformal Education as an Empowering Process with Case Studies from Indonesia and Thailand.* University of Massachusetts, Amherst, Massachusetts
Nopakun Oonta 1985 *Thai Concept of Khit-Pen for Adult and Nonformal Education.* Chulalongkorn University, Bangkok
Otner A N 1983 University outreach in Southeast Asia. *Int. J. Univ. Adult Educ.* 22 (2)
UNESCO 1982 *Adult Education in Asia and the Pacific,* Bulletin of the UNESCO Regional Office for Education in Asia and the Pacific (Special Issue). UNESCO, Bangkok

Provision in the People's Republic of China

Zhou Nan-zhao

This article is intended to present an overview of continuing education in China from a broad perspective, dealing with its role, structure, sponsoring organizations, administration, finance, research, and issues to be resolved. Emphasis is laid on the situation in the 1980s rather than on historical development. Though in China it does not encompass so much as in many other countries, "continuing education" is used in this article to include all education for adults which replaces or repeats what is normally available in youth education, from basic literacy to higher education.

1. Aim and Roles

Continuing education in China is a mass undertaking involving hundreds of millions of adults. Its major aims are (a) to raise the general cultural level of the whole people for better citizenship and personal development, (b) to improve technical skills and professional qualifications of working adults for higher production efficiency, and (c) to enhance political consciousness and inculcate ethical values for more active participation in national life.

The political and social significance of continuing education has long been emphasized by the Chinese Communist Party and government. Workers' and farmers' education has been regarded as a necessary condition for the strengthening of political power and economic reconstruction. Along with the national shift of the focus of work in the late 1970s to the modernization of industry, agriculture, national defense, and science and technology, continuing education has been playing a more significant role in national policies. The State Council and relevant ministries under it have sponsored national conferences on workers' and farmers' education; continuing education has become an integrated part of the Chinese education system; its development programs have been incorporated into national, social, and economic development plans; professional organizations like the National Association of Adult Education and the National Society of Continuing Engineering Education have been formed; and practical measures have been taken to further enhance the role of continuing education and its infrastructure.

2. Characteristics of the System

Major characteristics of continuing education in China include the following.

(a) *The largeness of the target population.* The continuing education system in China has to cater for the various educational needs of the following sectors of the 1,032 million people: 4,415,000 with college education; 245 million with secondary education (junior and senior high-school levels); over 350 million with only elementary education; and 235 million illiterates and semiliterates.

(b) *A basically centralized administration.* Major policies, planning, curriculum, teaching standards, and financing format are all centrally administered, while programs, instructional organization, and teaching materials are decentralized.

(c) *Diversity.* In terms of instructional forms, there are formal classes and schools, correspondence courses, radio and television education, and self-study programs; in terms of learning time, there are spare-time (including evening) schools, schools operating on a 6–2 (6 hours for work and 2 hours for study) or 4–4 basis, and schools for between 2 and 3 years full-time on-leave study. In terms of sponsorship, there are various continuing education institutions run by government organizations, industrial enterprises, rural administrative units, schools, private business, and individuals; in terms of learners' ages, there are colleges for the old and retired as well as colleges which set age limits.

(d) *Formal nature.* Continuing education in China is more formal in nature than in many other countries. The state recognizes, through regulations and certification, the equivalence of adult education to that of formal education.

(e) *Cooperation and coordination*. The efforts of different sectors including ministries and commissions, education departments, trade unions, and women's unions, the Communist Youth League, and science associations achieve coordination through the Party and central government.

(f) *A national network*. A systematic national network has been formed for implementation of continuing education, which is organized at elementary (including literacy), secondary, and higher levels and composed of general education, vocational education, and upgrading, refresher training.

At the higher level, there were in 1985 1,216 adult higher education institutions of different kinds, among which were (a) 29 radio and television universities, with an enrollment of 673,634; (b) 4 farmers' colleges, with an enrollment of 895; (c) 102 institutes for administrators and managers, with 40,297 enrolled; (d) two independent correspondence colleges, with 40,297 enrolled; (e) 216 colleges of education for inservice teachers and school administrators, with 247,122 enrolled; and (f) 591 universities and colleges run correspondence higher education and evening colleges, with a total enrollment of 492,976. The percentages for those enrolled in different fields by 1984 were as follows: 37.8 percent in engineering and technology; 0.7 percent in agriculture; 0.1 percent in forestry; 1.5 percent in medicine; 23.8 percent in teacher education; 15.8 percent in humanities and social sciences; 2.2 percent in natural sciences; 16.4 percent in finance and accounting; 1.5 percent in law; 0.1 percent in physical education; and 0.1 percent in arts.

3. Structure and Organization

For convenience of description, continuing education of adults in the Chinese context will be dealt with respectively in terms of workers', farmers', and cadres' education.

3.1 Workers' Education

By "workers" it is meant to include workers in both state and collective industrial, commercial, and mining enterprises, technical personnel, and staff members in government organizations at all levels.

In accordance with the variety of occupations and differences in workers' initial education, training, and interests, workers' education covers a wide range of areas of study and is of different levels, standards, and forms.

For systematic general and specialized education, workers' education is undertaken at higher, secondary, elementary, and literacy levels. Workers' higher education usually enrolls workers who have had senior high-school education and two years' working experience. It is aimed at turning out engineers, technicians, and managing personnel through 2–3 years' full-time study or 4–5 years' spare-time study for an education equivalent to that offered in higher technical colleges. Workers' education usually takes the form of workers' colleges and workers' spare-time colleges. There are also refresher courses/classes and upgrading institutes for technicians, engineers, and science-related professionals for them to keep abreast of the latest developments in their fields. Organizations providing workers' higher education include industrial, mining, and trade enterprises, state organizations, educational administrations, trade unions, and science associations at different levels. Programs offered in workers' (spare-time) colleges are closely related to production and professional work and are therefore of an applied nature. Those enrolled study either full- or part-time, depending on specific programs.

Workers' secondary education is intended to provide education equivalent to junior and senior high-school education or secondary specialized education, aiming at turning out a qualified intermediate-level technical force badly needed by enterprises. It is effected mainly by means of workers' spare-time high schools, or workers' secondary specialized schools, which offer programs in engineering, agronomy, forestry, medicine, finance and economics, political study and law, and physical education, and usually run for 3 years full time, or longer if on a work-study or spare-time basis. Since the majority of the workers did not actually complete junior high-school education, a high priority of workers' education in recent years has been the provision to young and middle-aged workers of political education and cultural and technical education at junior high-school level, with the aim of enabling 60–80 percent of those below that level to complete required fill-in courses by 1985. To assure the qualifications of new workers, most big and medium-sized enterprises have programs for initial vocational training.

Workers' elementary education caters for the needs of those who have had little previous schooling and is provided through spare-time schools and classes, run either in or independent of regular full-time elementary schools. Literacy education caters for the needs of illiterate or semiliterate workers to read and write Chinese characters.

Workers' technical education can be classified into intermediate and junior levels, and is done in accordance with standards set for different ranks in the scale for skilled workers. Technical education is provided through full- or spare-time training classes or on-the-spot sessions, with varying lengths, sponsored by enterprises or supervising agencies.

3.2 Farmers' Education

While continuing efforts in literacy programs, and further developing spare-time elementary and junior high-school education, there are literacy classes or groups, winter classes, folk schools, spare-time elementary and secondary schools/classes, usually based in formal full-time rural schools; technical training classes/groups for specialized households; elementary technical schools usually run by townships (administrative units under the county and equivalent to the former "commune"); and farmers' secondary technical schools run at the county level. There are also various short-term courses, lecture series, and correspondence and broadcasting programs. For example, the Chinese Farmers' Broadcasting School, sponsored by the Ministry of Agriculture and Forestry, had in 1984 an enrollment of 400,000 taking courses in agricultural technical education through radio and correspondence materials. In organizing farmers' education, the following principles are observed:

(a) production units function concurrently as teaching units for the benefit of a unified administration;

(b) classroom teaching is supplemented by flexible group or individual learning during harvest time;

(c) learning classes/groups operate on a spare-time basis, with more time spent in learning during the slack season, less time during the busy season, and vacation during harvest time;

(d) farmers' technical schools operate on a full- or part-time basis, depending on needs and conditions.

3.3 Cadres' Education

The term "cadres" refers to administrative and managing personnel holding various leading positions in the Party and state organizations. Cadres' education has always been an important part of the continuing education system in China since they are perceived as a decisive factor in both revolution and economic reconstruction. Along with the shift of emphasis in national work from "class struggle" to modernization, cadres are required to be revolutionalized, knowledgeable, and professionally qualified, and more younger cadres are promoted. In this context the central government is making great efforts to further strengthen cadres' education and make it more formal and systematic. All staff members in central Party and government offices are required to participate in training in rotation, generally six months' full-time study every 3 years. Their employment is closely related to their education and training and their grades in examinations are used as references which are as important as their working experience and practical achievements.

Cadres' education is provided in the following forms: (a) cadres' training classes, 1–2 years for secondary specialized level, and 2–3 years for higher education level attended on a non-boarding basis; (b) training or upgrading classes in Party schools or cadres' schools; (c) 2–3 year special training courses sponsored by higher or secondary specialized education institutions under the State Commission for Education and other ministries, (d) short-term refresher courses during sabbatical leave in higher education institutions or research centers; (e) inservice training through independent study, correspondence courses, or radio and television programs; (f) 2–3 years in institutes for administrative cadres, (g) institutes of educational administration, for the inservice training of college and school administrators.

4. University-based Correspondence Education and Evening Colleges

These are an important part of spare-time continuing higher education as well as an integral part of the formal higher education system.

University-based correspondence education and evening colleges enroll inservice teachers, technicians, and office workers or educated youth, who have completed senior high school or secondary specialized school. The programs and courses offered are closely oriented towards the specific needs of jobs the participants are doing. In view of conditions of spare-time study, there is much flexibility as regards curriculum, teaching content, and length of study. It is offered at either undergraduate level or just on a single-subject basis for inservice updating in scientific and technological advances.

The Ministry of Education sets general guidelines for goals, teaching programs, length of study, curriculum format, textbooks, and number of teaching hours, while the universities and colleges concerned operate according to these guidelines. Those who complete required courses and pass examinations are recognized by the state as full equivalents of graduates from formal universities and colleges. Those who have completed a single course will be granted a certificate of learning. Degree-granting institutions can also award degrees to selected graduates from correspondence programs or evening colleges.

5. Radio and Television Universities and Colleges

Television colleges came into operation in some provinces and municipalities in China in the early 1960s. In 1979 the Central Radio and Television University was set up, jointly sponsored by the Ministry of Education and the Central Broadcasting Administration. With 28 other television universities at provincial or municipal level, a national network of televised higher education has been formed. These television colleges mainly enroll inservice workers, cadres, scientific and technical personnel, school teachers, army men, and also a certain number of senior high-school graduates who have neither been admitted to formal universities nor employed. Students are selected through entrance examinations in different courses. They can be classified into two categories: (a) those who pass the exam, who are formally admitted and registered, and who study either full-time, part-time or for on-the-spot learning in a single subject; and (b) those who have not taken the entrance examination and who view the programs on a voluntary basis and take part in classroom tests.

6. *A System of Examination for Higher Education through Self-learning*

This is a state-regulated examination system developed in recent years to encourage young people to pursue higher learning through independent study and to train larger numbers of qualified professionals by diversified means. It was made an integrated part of the Chinese higher education system in 1981 upon the approval of the State Council.

All Chinese citizens, regardless of schooling, can apply for the examination.

The syllabus, number, and kinds of required courses, standards and unified tests are regulated by national, provincial, and municipal committees of examination for higher education through self-learning, and are implemented by relevant accredited universities. Learners can take exams in one or more subjects after completing a certain number of courses, and if they pass the exams they will be awarded certificates either in single subjects or as the equivalent of college graduation.

7. *Administration*

A major principle guiding the administration of continuing education in China is "supervision by the government, reliance on mass organizations, and cooperation of various sectors."

For workers' education there are (a) the National Commission for the Administration of Workers' Education, which formulates major policies and unified planning, supervises their implementation, and coordinates efforts of relevant sectors in the field; (b) the Adult Education Department in the State Commission for Education, responsible for comprehensive studies and guidance of administrative and instructional work of all workers's schools, for the formulation of relevant policies, for the compiling and approving of textbooks, and for teacher training. In the State Commission for Education there is also a third higher education department supervising most adult higher education; (c) education departments in all ministries and commissions under the State Council responsible for planning and implementing workers' education in their respective systems; (d) trade unions and the Communist Youth League which also participate in the administration of workers' continuing education; (e) at the provincial and municipal level, committees for workers' education administration; and (f) at the grass-roots level, education units for large and medium sized enterprises and a full-time staff member for small ones.

Farmers' education is administered by Party committees and government agencies at different levels. The Adult Education Department in the State Commission for Education and the Education Department in the Ministry of Agriculture and Forestry play a major role in organizing and supervising farmers' education, in full cooperation with farmers' education administration at provincial, autonomous, regional, municipal, prefectural, and county levels and with the agricultural production organizations, the Youth League, women's unions, and scientific associations.

Correspondence higher education and evening colleges are mainly administered by the State Commission for Education and through sponsoring formal universities. Television universities are jointly supervised by the State Commission for Education and the Central Broadcasting Administration and their corresponding departments or bureaux at the provincial and municipal levels.

For the administration of examinations in higher education through self-learning, there is the National Committee on Examination of Higher Education through Self-learning, located in the State Commission for Education, and corresponding committees in nearly all provinces and municipalities directly under the central government.

8. *Finance*

To assure the steady development of continuing education the state has formulated various regulations and policies concerning financial support to workers', farmers', cadres', and other forms of adult education.

For the education of workers in industrial and mining enterprises, the state provides an expenditure equivalent to 1.5 percent of the total of workers' wages, which is taken into account in production costs. For the education of workers and staff members in administrative organs and the state organizations, an amount equivalent to 1.5 percent of the workers' and staff's wages can be spent and it is included in administrative and operating expenses. In addition to the above, enterprises can allocate to workers' education part of their funds and profits. Workers' education may also absorb 25–37.5 percent of the fund of trade unions which is allocated by enterprise administrations. Workers' education sponsored by educational institutions is financed by the state through educational operating expenses. Those grass-root units which have difficulties in running workers' education can apply to finance administrative agencies for additional funds.

Finance of farmers' continuing education is mainly provided by farmers and collective units on a voluntary basis and within their financial capacity, while the state provides for expenditure on teachers' training, meetings, teaching materials, merit pay, and some other items.

Cadres' education is financed by the state, which provides for full-time teachers' salaries and major instructional expenses, by trade unions, which provide for part-time teachers' stipends and students' textbook fees, and by the sponsoring institutions.

Correspondence higher education and evening colleges and television universities are mainly financed by the state through its budget for spare-time higher education.

9. Research and Problems to be Solved

Research and studies on continuing education lag behind the enriched practice. In the early 1980s, however, administrators became increasingly aware of the significance of theoretical as well as applied research, and efforts have been made to encourage and organize research projects. In the Central Institute of Educational Research, the national research institution directly affiliated to the State Commission for Education, there is the Division of Studies on Adult Education. There are similar research institutions at provincial and municipal levels, which are staffed with full-time researchers. Many practitioners are doing part-time research. Administrative authorities also conduct studies of an applied nature. There are societies for adult education studies in general and continuing engineering education in particular in many regions; special journals and books on adult education have been published, and theories and methods of continuing education in developed and other developing countries have been made known to the research community. Among topics of priority for research are: implications of continuing education to national development and modernization; its economic returns and their calculation; legislation for continuing education; theoretical foundations of continuing and lifelong education; accreditation of adult higher education institutions; vocational/technical education in rural areas under new economic conditions; adult learning theories and their application in curriculum development and teaching methodology; and evaluation of educational performance of adults.

Despite the great progress made over a period of more than three decades after the founding of the Republic, there are still many problems remaining to be solved, which include: (a) the status of adult education, which is still lower than that of formal schooling and universities because of the pervasive influence of traditional conceptions of education; (b) flaws in the division of administrative responsibilities and coordination of various administration agencies; (c) some kind of over-expansion of adult higher education institutions without appropriate accreditation procedures and the lack of assurance of their quality; (d) shortage of trained and qualified teachers for adult education, especially for continuing vocational/technical education; and (e) insufficient financial support in some enterprises and in some regions.

Overall, however, with correct policies guiding the practices and millions of people enthusiastically pursuing further learning, continuing education in China promises brighter prospects in the context of the national modernization drive.

Bibliography

China, Ministry of Education, Adult Education Department 1984 *A General Survey of Worker–Staff Education in China*. Ministry of Education, Beijing, pp. 1–2, 19

China, Ministry of Education, Adult Education Department 1985 *Glossary of Chinese Adult Education*. Ministry of Education, Beijing

China, State Bureau of Statistics 1984 *Bulletin of Major Statistical Figures of the 2nd National Census in 1982*. State Bureau of Statistics, Beijing

Hunter C St J, Keehn M M (ed.) 1985 *Adult Education in China*. Croom Helm, London

Pu Tong-xiu 1984 Priorities of workers' education. *Adult Educ.* 1: 3–4

Yao Zhong-da et al. 1984 Adult education. In: *China Education Yearbook 1949–1981*. China Encyclopedia Press, Beijing, pp. 575–6, 585–8, 595–6

Section 8

Regional and International Organizations

Section 8

Regional and International Organizations

Introduction

At a time when national organization of adult education is still weak in most countries, it is interesting to note the development of international organizations at worldwide and regional level devoted to its advance. The nature and functions of these bodies are diverse, they are unevenly distributed, but they have become an important part of the adult education landscape.

Regional organizations are of two basic kinds, the intergovernmental ones and the nongovernmental ones. Of the former, most, like the Organization of American States and the Council of Europe, include adult education as a marginal activity among the many in which they are involved. The socialist countries of Eastern Europe have their own networks, all intergovernmental, in all fields of national activity. There appears to be nothing distinctive for adult education. The Arab Literacy and Adult Education Organization (ARLO) is unusual in having adult education as a prime reason for its existence. The Regional Centre for Adult Education and Functional Literacy in Latin America (CREFAL) and ARLO are examples of collaboration between regional governments and the worldwide work of UNESCO.

The nongovernmental organizations mirror the importance of private initiative in adult education in many parts of the world. Some regional associations have no government representation, others combine private and governmental membership. The European Bureau of Adult Education (EBAE) is an example of the first, the Asian–South Pacific Bureau of Adult Education (ASPBAE), the African Adult Education Association, and the Caribbean Regional Council for Adult Education (CARCAE) of the second.

Regional groupings, such as Latin America, North America, the Caribbean, Western Europe, Africa, and the Arab countries, seem to conform to conventional geographical or cultural boundaries, but combining Asia and the South Pacific in one region, running from Turkey to the People's Republic of China and down to Australia and New Zealand, appears to have little logic, other than the historical circumstances attending its creation.

It would be impossible to identify a set of characteristics common to all the regions. Although no other can match the diversity of Asia and the South Pacific, some are very varied in their component parts. The Arab countries are united by one language, a common culture, a powerful if vague Arab nationalism and an overriding concern with literacy and basic education. In Latin America Spanish is spoken in all the countries, with the exception of Brazil, which is Portuguese in language and culture, and there too literacy is the principal concern. They do not, however, share a Latin American nationalism. In North America regional organization has been undermined, in spite of a common language and similar cultures and stage of development, by the need felt by Canadians to maintain their separate identity from the United States.

The Caribbean is a scattering of small states, mostly poor, in which there are a variety of ethnic groups, whose cultures are strongly overlaid by the European ones of their former colonial masters, British, French, Spanish and Dutch, whose languages are still predominant. Western Europe is a comparatively small region geographically, but it contains many states, which have strong national traditions, and more than a dozen languages are spoken in the region. There is, on the other hand, the unifying sense of a recognizable European culture, together with a high level of economic development and a long, rich provision of adult education in most of the countries. Africa is diverse, ethnically, linguistically, culturally, and most of its states are artificially imposed relics of colonialism trying to establish themselves on a more firmly rooted tribal structure. Apart from South Africa, all its countries are united by a low level of economic development.

All regional bodies function as networks for consultation, production, and dissemination of data on adult education. Their most obvious work lies in publications and the holding of conferences and seminars. They also seek to influence government policy in favour of adult education and to improve the performance of adult educators. Intergovernmental ones exercise a greater influence on decision making than private or mixed ones, particularly, it appears, in developing countries, where CREFAL and ARLO, for instance, help to coordinate and strengthen action in areas where individual governments lack the resources to take effective measures on their own. In advanced countries supranational organizations are an expression of the richness of their adult education, and spring from the recognition by a strong pool of professional or quasiprofessional educators that they have common needs and a common desire to make their expertise felt. It is significant that in the United States and Canada, where regional organization lacks formal structure, the pools of educators seem strong enough to stand on their own. Elsewhere associations are being created, as in the Caribbean and the Arab countries, to help build such a body, often with outside assistance.

Such outside assistance comes principally from UNESCO, but also from other organizations active worldwide, which are named in the article *International Adult Education.* By its examination of the kinds of activity these agencies have engaged in and their achievements, this article demonstrates how much adult education owes to them. The particular contribution since 1973 of the International Council for Adult Education, the worldwide private organization of associations for the education of adults, which has probably done more than any body except UNESCO to foster regional groupings, is described in the article which bears its name.

North America

J. C. Ferver and A. M. Thomas

A regional perspective for adult education organization in North America must be discarded at a first glance. Except for a few continental-based specialized organizations such as the Society for the Advancement of Continuing Education for the Ministry (SACEM) and some subregional organizations such as the Pacific Northwest Adult Education Association, the field is pretty barren.

In most cases, because the American organizations were founded earlier, many individual Canadians took part in them by taking out memberships and participating in annual meetings and conferences. They included the National Association for Public School Adult Education, the National University Extension Association, and a number of others, usually based on institutional interests. This pattern has continued, in part due to the prevailing "over-the-shoulder" nature of Canadian life, played out in the vicinity of a giant neighbor, and the unfailing generosity and hospitality of American colleagues, who have always welcomed Canadians to their meetings.

One major United States organization, the American Association for Adult and Continuing Education (AAACE), includes parts of Canada in three of its eight regions and a number of Canadian adult educators are active participants in the program and administrative affairs of the organization as regular members. But the 1983 Board of Directors were all United States citizens; the annual conferences are held within one of the states; and legislative activity is invariably directed at the United States Congress from the Association's Washington, DC headquarters.

Other major adult education organizations in the United States have pursued cooperative relationships and exchanges with their Canadian counterparts. For instance, the National University Continuing Education Association (NUCEA) has for several years had an exchange of presidents with its Canadian counterparts, and five Canadian universities are affiliated with NUCEA through regions of their choice. Also, the American Association of Community and Junior Colleges (AACJC) has had an active exchange program with the Association of Canadian Community Colleges.

One area organization, the Pacific Northwest International/Intercultural Consortium, has effectively brought together Canadian and United States higher education institutions at the community college level for work in such areas as community outreach, technical training, and management training.

Canadian and United States adult educators and their organizations and institutions are coming together and working together through various international organizations, particularly the International Council for Adult Education. Adult educators from both Canada and the United States also have opportunities for interaction on an international basis through organizations of a broader higher education interest such as the Consortium for International Cooperation in Higher Education (CICHE) and the Postsecondary International Network (PIN).

Table 1
Number of people participating in adult education programs in the United States

Adult education program source	People participating (millions)
Agricultural (cooperative) extension	12.0
Community organization	7.4
Private industry	5.8
Professional associations	5.5
College and part time	5.3
City recreation	5.0
Churches and synagogues	3.3
College and university extension and community education	3.3
Government services	3.0
Public school adult education	1.8
Federal manpower program	1.7
Military services	1.5
Graduate and professional education	1.5
Trade unions	0.6
Community education	0.5
Free universities	0.2
Total	58.4

One area that seems to foster regional cooperation in North America is adult education research. A number of research meetings have brought together Canadian and United States adult education researchers, and the 1983 meeting of the American Adult Education Research Association (AERA) was held in Canada. However, the formation in 1981 of the Canadian Association for the Study of Adult Education has meant that although some Canadians will participate in both organizations, increasing numbers will concentrate on the latter.

1. United States

Within the United States, adult education is a large and diverse enterprise as may be noted from Table 1, pulled together through the "Future Directions for a Learning Society" project of the College Board.

Participation data compiled by the United States Department of Education's National Center for Education Statistics in 1980 includes only adults engaged in "organized" adult education activities, and a more modest participation of 18 million people is indicated. A much greater participation is indicated using the individual "learning projects" approach established through the research of Allen Tough. In any event, all predictions into the future see increased participation as the "baby boom" of the post-Second World War period clears the traditional college ages and there is a "greying of America." Already the numbers of part-time adults in United States institutions of higher education surpass the numbers in the traditional college ages.

Because of its diversity, the field of adult education in the United States cannot readily be classified for descriptive purposes. In analyzing the data of the college board above, a simple "in school organizations" and "in nonschool organizations" differentiation was used to show that of the 58.4 million participants, 12.4 million were "in school organizations" and 46.0 million were "in nonschool organizations."

In their book, *Adult Education: Foundations of Practice*, Darkenwald and Merriam use a classification scheme suggested by Cyril Houle and Malcolm Knowles which is based upon the relationship of adult education to other purposes of the agencies in which it takes place. A few examples within this classification system might include the following.

(a) In the nineteenth century, independent institutions devoted primarily to adult education, such as the lyceums or Chatauqua, played a larger role than in recent years, but once again these types of organizations seem to be growing. Newer forms include community-based agencies, proprietary (private for profit schools of which there are over 9,000), and external degree agencies.

(b) According to the National Center for Educational Statistics, nearly one-half of participants in organized adult education activities are enrolled in public school, college, and university programs. Also included in this category is the Cooperative or Agricultural Extension Service that is believed to be the world's largest publicly supported informal adult education and development organization.

(c) In quasi-educational organizations, adult education is an allied function employed to fulfill only some of the needs which these agencies recognize as their responsibility. Examples include cultural organizations such as libraries and museums; community organizations such as churches and senior citizen centers; and occupational associations.

(d) In some noneducational organizations adult education is more of a means than an end. Education in business, government, military, hospitals, unions, and correctional institutions may be offered to help enhance the achievement of such goals as making money, curing the sick, rehabilitating prisoners, or advancing the economic interests of workers.

Just as agencies range from central to marginal in their emphasis on adult education, so do the professional organizations in which adult educators participate. An adult educator practicing in a library, for instance, might belong to the American Library Association (ALA), in which adult education is but one of many interests, and also to the American Association for Adult and Continuing Education, in which adult education is the central focus. In this case the ALA might be regarded as the primary professional organization of the librarian, and the AAACE the secondary professional organization. Thus it is with thousands of adult education practitioners in the United States.

AAACE, the major membership association for adult education in the United States, was formed in November 1982, as a result of the merger of the Adult Education Association of America (AEA/USA) and the National Association for Public Continuing and Adult Education (NAPCAE). AAACE provides leadership in advancing the adult stage of the lifelong learning process by unifying the profession; advocating broad public awareness and understanding of adult education; developing human resources; encouraging and using research; communicating with the public and the association membership; and encouraging political action to further the field.

2. Canada

Despite the similarity of constituents, and of the two societies in general, patterns of evolution of adult education organizations have been different. The size of the Canadian population in contrast to its geography, the official and actual bilingual character of Canadian society, and a rather distinct difference in the relationship between individuals and the state, account in part for the differences to be found between Canada and the United States.

In Canada, among organizations with an exclusive concern for education there are two dominant ones: the English-speaking Canadian Association for Adult Education (CAAE) (1935), and the French-speaking *Institut Canadien de l'Education des Adultes* (ICEA) (1956). The CAAE has its headquarters in Toronto, and is aided in its activities by eight provincial associations, each one of which is represented on the CAAE Board of Directors. The ICEA is located in Montreal and functions mostly in the province of Quebec, though it does provide assistance to French-speaking Canadians in other parts of Canada. For the first 15 years of its existence, the CAAE tried to include the interests of French-speaking Canadians in its activities, but by the early 1950s Francophones decided to establish their own "national" organization. In many respects, the relationships between the two organizations have symbolized the difficulties and the achievements of the partnership of the two language groups on which Canada is based.

Each organization has members who are committed to adult education, as well as those professionally engaged in it. Each acts as an advocate for adult learners and for organizations engaged in adult education by means of presentations to various levels of government, coordinating activities of other groups through workshops and conferences, and by publishing. Inevitably they have from time to time become involved in issues of substance such as cultural policy, broadcasting, co-operative movements, and the like, and also become directly engaged in programs. The CAAE in particular is known for its experimentation with broadcasting and discussion groups on a national basis through such programs as the National Farm Radio Forum (1939–1965), Citizen's Forum (1943–1963), and more recently People Talking Back (1979). Both organizations are voluntary and depend heavily upon government financial assistance for their survival, a combination characteristic of Canadian life.

In addition to the two national inclusive organizations, there have appeared more recently numbers of specialized adult education organizations, such as those devoted to women's education (the Canadian Congress for Learning Opportunities for Women), to literacy (World Literacy Canada), and others devoted to adult basic education.

The second category is composed of organizations primarily interested in the education of the young, but which in recent years, for a great variety of reasons, have increasingly extended their concerns to adult education. The Association of Universities and Colleges in Canada, founded in the last century, has maintained a minimal interest in adult education, largely because of a mixed commitment to university extension. Since the 1960s, its interests have been more systematically focused by the former Canadian Association of Directors of Extension and Summer School, an organization that began as a committee of the CAAE, and which is now the Canadian Association of University Continuing Education (CAUCE). CAUCE has flourished in recent years and now maintains provincial organizations and a national journal. A second outgrowth of the CAAE is the Association of Canadian Community Colleges (ACCC), founded in 1971, and representing the interests of the approximately 100 nonuniversity postsecondary colleges founded in Canada in the decade of the 1960s. This organization has some provincial affiliates, and while it does not maintain a distinct interest in adult education, there has been tacit recognition since its foundation that the students of the colleges are adults. The ACCC publishes a national journal for colleges, and provides a program of workshops, training, and other "professional" activities for its members. Finally, there is a growing network of provincial organizations of adult educators who are employed by school boards (local education authorities) and who have been attracting increasing numbers of adult students wishing to complete secondary education.

In the last category are literally countless organizations of individuals who engage in adult education in the pursuit of other objectives. Included among these are organizations of the professions whose members are devoted to continuing education among the professions. Another example is the Ontario Society for Training and Development, now linked to a national body as well as to its American parent, which is made up of individuals who engage in adult education in large industries and government departments. Activities of this organization are devoted to the improvement of their members by means of workshops, conferences, research projects, and a journal.

It does seem as though the development of organizations for cooperation and coordination in North America will continue mainly on a national and internal regional basis, though with the advent of the less formal idea of "networking" it is possible that some growth will be seen of continental networks devoted to special interest in adult education.

Bibliography

Darkenwald G G, Merriam S B 1982 *Adult Education: Foundations of Practice.* Harper and Row, New York

Faris R 1975 *The Passionate Educators: Voluntary Associations and the Struggle for Control of Adult Educational Broadcasting in Canada, 1919–1952.* Martin, Toronto, Ontario

Kidd J R 1979 *Some Preliminary Notes Concerning an Enquiry into the Heritage of Canadian Adult Education.* Centre for Continuing Education, University of British Columbia, Vancouver, British Columbia

Selman G R 1981 *The Canadian Association for Adult Education in the Corbett Years: A Re-evaluation.* Centre for Continuing Education, University of British Columbia, Vancouver, British Columbia

Smith R M, Aker G F, Kidd J R (ed.) 1970 *Handbook of Adult Education.* MacMillan, New York

Latin America

P. G. Buttedahl

It was not until the early 1960s that the pressure to provide educational opportunities for adults was acknowledged by governments in Latin America. At the Conference of Punta del Este (1967), the Presidents of Latin American countries agreed on a plan for modernization and development for the entire region. As a result, government structures were modernized, countries actively pursued educational reforms, agrarian reforms, changes in the revenue systems, expansion of housing services, reduction in mortality rates, and improvements in health and sanitary conditions in each country. These reforms were a precondition to receiving massive injections of international aid aimed at accelerating the modernization process of the entire region.

Under these circumstances, adult and nonformal education entered an expansionary period characterized by an accelerated growth. The use of night schools, of extension departments in universities, and of public ministries, libraries, government agencies, voluntary organizations, cooperatives, church groups, military forces, neighborhood associations, trade unions, political parties, and others multiplied tenfold, providing access and educational services to a large sector of the adult population previously untouched by the limited educational services available through the formal system of education.

As adult education activities became institutionalized in Latin America in the 1970s, so did understanding of the characteristics of this particular target group within society. This led to the development of training and research programs that largely contributed to institutionalization.

1. Structures of Adult Education in the Region

Education in Latin America is largely centralized and considered to be the responsibility of governments, who must ensure accessibility and the provision of universal primary education. Education is largely perceived as an integral part of the development process, thus it can only be explained in relation to the social, cultural, and economic development of each country. For most governments at least in principle, adult education unquestionably is a prerequisite to the development of Latin American society. On the one hand it signifies implementation of the principles of justice, through which society meets its responsibilities to those whom it earlier failed to provide with educational opportunities. On the other hand, it is a factor linked with progress. The adult members of a population that can become incorporated into a nation's productive life become a more valuable work force resource for economic development. Some of the efforts of Latin American countries to develop adult education have been scattered, as institutions, plans, programs, and methods have multiplied, and as problems have been approached without prior experience in this field. However, most governments have agreed in principle that comprehensive adult education should at least include the following major components in the various stages of its institutionalization and development: community education, vocational training, literacy programs, and general education.

Since the late 1960s, the institutionalization of adult education has taken place in Latin America through the efforts of governmental, intergovernmental, and nongovernmental organizations.

1.1 Governmental

Since the early 1970s, most governments in Latin America have undertaken educational reforms which have been implemented through the reformulation of legislation. Included in this legislation has been the provision for the establishment of adult education services and the allocation of resources to provide for literacy training, general education, vocational training, and other services. Concurrently, provisions have been made to provide for inservice training opportunities for adult educators and for the development of educational materials that better serve the needs of the adult population. Countries such as Argentina, Chile, Bolivia, Brazil, Peru, Ecuador, Colombia, Venezuela, Guatemala, Honduras, El Salvador, Costa Rica, Panama, Mexico, and Cuba have incorporated in recent years a national bureau of adult education within the structure of their ministries of education. In each of these cases the bureau is under the responsibility of a professional educator holding the rank of director general, reporting directly to the deputy minister of education. The main responsibilities of the national bureaux of adult education are to: assess adult education needs; project budgetary requirements on a yearly basis; produce curriculum guides and instructional materials; allocate staff; provide inservice training for ministry personnel moving into adult education; collect and disseminate statistical information; and liaise with intergovernmental and nongovernmental organizations inside and outside the respective country.

In the process of implementing adult education facilities through the school system, teachers in the primary sector were rewarded with assignments to teach the new adult education courses. Seniority was the main criteria for reassignment. Adult education courses, usually offered through night school, were either perceived as an extra reward in addition to the regular pay for the school teacher, or as an alternative for a senior teacher to teach in the evening thus freeing the daytime for alternative work. Soon teachers saw the need to organize themselves into professional organizations that functioned primarily as trade unions rather than as professional organizations. In the early 1970s the following countries had created a national association of adult education: Costa Rica, Honduras, El Salvador, Nicaragua, Panama, Colombia, Venezuela, and Peru. Usually the president was the national director of adult education in each of these countries, and the entire membership comprised the teachers employed by the government in literacy programs and in adult basic education courses.

In 1971, prior to the Tokyo Conference on Adult Education, a Federation of Adult Education Associations (FIDEA) was created in the Latin American countries, drawing its membership from the adult education associations in the region. Its founder and first president was Dr. Felix Adam from Venezuela, where the secretariat was established. Associate members met periodically and exchanged information about the activities in their own countries. Since its inception, FIDEA has played a very active role in promoting an understanding of adult education within the region. Dr. Adam wrote the first book ever to be published in this field in Latin America, expanding on the concept of "andragogy." However, the organization never moved towards recruiting members from the voluntary sector. It served mainly as a forum for teachers and members of the ministries of education to discuss and share their experiences in the field. By 1975, FIDEA had lost most of its membership and become dormant until December of 1980.

1.2 Intergovernmental

Two major intergovernmental bodies have had a significant impact on adult education in the region: the Organization of American States (OAS) and the United Nations Educational, Scientific and Cultural Organization (UNESCO) have both played a role.

UNESCO facilitated the creation of a regional training organization to provide for inservice training and research in the areas of literacy training and adult basic education. The *Centro Regional de Educacion de Adultos y Alfabetizacion Funcional para America Latina* or CREFAL (Regional Center for Adult Education and Functional Literacy in Latin America) was created in May of 1951 under the joint auspices of the Mexican Government, UNESCO, and OAS.

The services of CREFAL were extended to all the countries in the Latin American region. In recent years these have also been made available to adult educators from Europe, Africa, and Asia. In the beginning, CREFAL was the only organization within the region that could provide systematic training for teachers responsible for literacy programs and adult basic education. Over the years more than 6,000 adult educators within the region have received some form of training from CREFAL. Most of this training was provided on residential courses lasting from two weeks to two years. Attempts were made to provide a masters program in adult education, but problems related to accreditation finally prevented the continuation of this program.

The influence CREFAL had on the institutionalization and conceptualization of adult education in the Latin American context is undeniable. The major contributions were made in the field of literacy training, contributing both to the development of instructional materials and adequate methodologies and to the formulation of adult education policy acceptable to the governments of the region.

The most significant contribution of CREFAL, however, lies in the fact that it created and supported a network of adult educators in the Latin American region which served as the "critical mass" for the expansion and institutionalization of this field of study.

The other major intergovernmental body is the OAS. In February of 1968 in Maracay, Venezuela, at the fifth meeting of the Inter-American Cultural Council (CIC) of the OAS, the Regional Program for Educational Development (PREDE) was created.

The objectives for PREDE were:

(a) To encourage and complement national efforts to improve the quality of education and to accelerate the expansion of educational systems at all levels; improve the administration and planning of education; and suitably adjust the educational systems to the demands of economic, social, and cultural development.

(b) To encourage research and the incorporation of modern methods into education and related fields.

(c) To encourage Latin American cooperation in educational affairs, according to the principles of the Charter of the Organization of American States and the mandates regarding education included in the Declaration of the Presidents of America.

(d) To promote the integration of Latin America through education, with a view to raising the economic and social levels of the region and as an important step towards the creation of a Latin American community in education, with due regard to the educational and cultural identity of the various nations.

The implementation of PREDE was conceived in terms of five multinational projects prepared by the General Secretariat of the OAS.

Within the context of PREDE, adult education activities have been implemented through four major project phases: the Experimental Multinational Adult Education Project (1968–71); the Multinational Adult Education Project (1971–77); the Alberto Masferrer Multinational Integrated Adult Education Project; and the Regional Project of Literacy Training and Adult Education, PREDAL.

The overall purpose of these projects over the years has been to incorporate and improve the delivery of adult education services in all the countries affiliated to the OAS.

Activities include the provision of fellowships to various institutions for further training, meetings and conferences sponsored to facilitate exchanges of information, research in adult education, preparation of instructional materials for literacy training and adult basic education, technical assistance provided on request, establishment of multinational centers throughout the region, a series of publications, and the formulation of policy and legislation related to adult education for member countries.

Countries involved in the various stages of implementation of these projects have been: Chile, Argentina, Brazil, Peru, Ecuador, Colombia, Venezuela, Costa Rica, Guatemala, Honduras, El Salvador, Nicaragua, Panama, and the Dominican Republic.

Over the years the contributions of the OAS and of UNESCO to the development of adult education in the region have been crucial in terms of facilitating and promoting action in this field at the government level. As indicated earlier, most activities in the field of education in Latin America are government oriented and adult education is no exception to this. A review of the documentation available points to the fact that most of the adult education activities currently implemented in the region are either sponsored by, or the spin-off from, some government supported initiative, which in turn has received funding and technical assistance from the OAS or from UNESCO.

1.3 Nongovernmental

The Catholic Church in Latin America traditionally has accepted responsibility for provision of adult education services in most of the countries. Perhaps the most sustained contribution has been the establishment of radio schools which operate in many countries. These radio schools provided alternative "delivery modes" for literacy training, adult basic education, community development, agricultural extension, and family education. There are 23 radio schools in the entire region, with Radio Sutatenza in Colombia being the best known. The Latin American Association for Radio School Education (ALER), based in Ecuador, is the regional body to which these schools are affiliated.

In 1975 the International Council for Adult Education (ICAE) established its Latin American Program. The purpose of the program was to identify the existing infrastructure of adult education in the region, to facilitate the mobilization and organization of national adult education bodies that could include both the governmental and nongovernmental sector, and to facilitate the dissemination of adult education information both within and outside the region.

Over a period of five years, the program was able to identify and establish a data bank of institutions and agencies providing adult education services, an inventory of qualified human resources available within the region, an inventory of specialized publications in the field, and the publication of a monthly newsletter reaching a network of 3,000 adult educators.

During that period, the ICAE program provided technical assistance to several adult education projects ranging from two-day seminars on educational technology to the formulation of funding proposals for the creation of university programs to train adult educators. In 1980, the ICAE program was terminated and was later replaced by the creation of CEAL (Latin American Council for Adult Education) affiliated to the ICAE.

Finally, there is one other extensive network of adult educators devoted primarily to literacy training in Latin America—ALFALIT. There are various ALFALIT offices in the region. The most important one is based in San José, Costa Rica.

2. Conclusion

In summary, adult education in Latin America has grown in a spectacular fashion since the late 1960s. Most of it continues to be remedial in nature, but a significant attempt to institutionalize it and deliver it through alternative modes has been made to the extent that every country in the region has recognized it as a special field within education in general. There are special resources allocated to it on a yearly basis, national legislation has been written to regulate its activities, significant efforts have been made to improve and expand its services, and a number of professional training programs at the masters level have been created.

At present there are national bureaux of adult education within the ministry of education of every Latin American country. National Associations of Adult Education, functioning as professional organizations, are found in Mexico, Argentina, Chile, Peru, Colombia, Venezuela, and Costa Rica. In addition, multinational centers for inservice training and materials production are located in Costa Rica, Chile, and Brazil. Currently there are three regional coordinating bodies: FIDEA, CEAL, and ALER.

Finally, research and development activities have multiplied in the region within the nongovernmental sector, particularly in the areas of community development and popular education.

The most remarkable advance of recent years has been the increased effectiveness and acceptance of a dialogue between the governmental and the nongovernmental sectors, thus contributing to the qualitative growth and fertilization of adult education in the region as a whole.

Bibliography

Buttedahl P C, Buttedahl K 1976 Participation: The transformation of society and the Peruvian experience. *Convergence* 9(3): 16–26

Centro Regional de Educacion de Adultos y Alfabetizacion Funcional Para America Latina 1976 *Descripcion de actividades 1976* [Report on activities]. Patzcuaro, Michoacan

Centro Regional de Educacion de Adultos y Alfabetizacion Funcional Para America Latina (CREFAL) 1976 *Que es el CREFAL*. CREFAL, Mexico

Consejo de Educacion de Adultos de America Latina (CEAAL) 1983 *Carta mensual*. CEAAL, Santiago

International Council for Adult Education (ICAE) 1979a *Educacion de adultos en America Latina*. ICAE, Toronto, Ontario

International Council for Adult Education (ICAE) 1979b *Educacion de adultos en America Latina: Edicion suplementaria 1979*. ICAE, Toronto, Ontario

International Council for Adult Education (ICAE) 1979c *Independent Minds in a Dependent World*. ICAE Latin American Programs 1975–79, ICAE, Toronto, Ontario

Organization of American States (OAS) 1971 *Education and Science Development: Three Years of Inter-American Cooperation*. OAS, Washington, DC

UNESCO 1978 *Inventario de alfabetizacion y educacion de adultos en America Latina y El Caribe: Chile, Bolivia, Costa Rica, Colombia, Guatemala, Nicaragua, Panama, Peru, Venezuela* (Directory of literacy and adult education in Latin America and the Caribbean). Patzcuaro, Michocacan

UNESCO 1979 *Education in the Context of Development in Latin America and the Caribbean*. UNESCO, Mexico City

Western Europe

W. Bax

Adult education in Western Europe is provided by a wide variety of institutions and organizations. They are coordinated by the European Bureau for Adult Education (EBAE), an organization that provides a comprehensive network of information for the providers of adult education aimed at resourcing individual organizations and facilitating an exchange of ideas and cooperation between them on a European scale, rather than acting as a force for streamlining adult education in the region.

1. Establishment and Purpose of the EBAE

After the Second World War, various organizations took the initiative to re-establish international contacts between adult educators. Usually these relations were restricted to their own sector of work.

In 1952, the European Cultural Centre in Geneva undertook to bring together representatives from a wide range of organizations to investigate the possibility of establishing coordination in the field of cultural work and adult education. This initiative resulted in the establishment in 1953 of the European Bureau for Adult Education, although the various organizations involved chose a somewhat different approach from that originally foreseen. The founders of the new organization decided that there was no point in setting up an international federation of adult education organizations because it was felt that nothing could be a greater waste of time than levelling up and schematizing something which was conceived as flexible and adaptable to local traditions.

The founders' conception was that of creating an instrument, which would be at the service of the different associations, a kind of information centre which would employ all means at its disposal to facilitate the exchange of persons and ideas, to encourage discussions and debates to enable adult educators to gain a better understanding of current problems, and to examine how these could be alleviated through closer cooperation between European countries.

The revision of the constitution at the beginning of the 1970s introduced as a new field of activities, the advocacy function: to stimulate public action and pressure for the further development of adult education.

In framing the Bureau's first constitution there had been a very basic discussion on the European character of the organization, as there was a concern lest the political and strategical concept of European unity become a handicap for the relations with other parts of the world. However, since the establishment of the International Council for Adult Education, the Bureau has been associated with this body as a regional associate and tries to collaborate in the wider international context.

2. Organization of the EBAE

The composition of the Bureau's membership greatly facilitates direct contacts with all levels of adult education.

The backbone of the organization is formed by the charter members, namely the national institutes of adult education or similar coordinating bodies from those countries where such organizations exist. For countries where there are no such organizations, the coordinating role is assumed by large national bodies embracing different approaches and practices in adult education.

In addition to these organizations, about 50 national providing agencies and 90 regional and local institutions are associated directly with the Bureau.

The Bureau is served by a small secretariat since the scale of its work can only be maintained by the goodwill and effort of its associates. The expenses are met out of membership fees, subsidies from national governments, and earmarked subsidies granted by international organizations or raised by associates for activities in their respective countries.

3. Activities of the EBAE

As a forum for exchange and cooperation the Bureau has organized numerous meetings and conferences. In the first decade of its existence, themes dealt mainly with problems of European cooperation and work in residential adult education and rural development.

In the 1960s, a section for nonresidential adult education was established and met regularly. In this period a number of meetings were organized in cooperation with the Council of Europe and the European Communities, dealing with matters of mutual concern such as policies in the training of adult educators and the relationships between adult education and industrial training.

In the 1970s meetings focused on new developments which were of importance for policy making in various countries. These policies related to the implementation of educational leave and of legislation in the field of adult education (Oslo 1972, Marly-le-Roi 1975, Berlin 1979), the development of adult education on the local level (Munster 1977, Berne 1978), the setting up of multimedia systems (Brussels 1976), and educational provision geared towards specific target groups such as illiterates (Farnham 1976), unemployed (Chatenay-Malabry 1979), and women (Wansfell College 1980).

In the early 1980s, plans were established to follow up these activities, as well as to cover new ground by planning meetings on information and counselling services in adult education, on the training of adult educators, and on establishing closer contacts between Northern and Southern Europe.

4. *Publications of the EBAE*

Like the programme of meetings, the Bureau's publications aim at providing reports of experiences which can be of use for the development of adult education in various countries.

Since the inception of the Bureau, a small periodical, *Notes and Studies*, has been published. In 1981 it was amalgamated with *Newsletter*, a larger publication. Two editions are distributed each year on topical issues in adult education, preferably connected with the themes of conferences so as to provide basic documentation for these meetings. Much of the collection and distribution of basic facts, national experiences, and information about research is accomplished in this informal way. The publication was first started with a subsidy from the International Council for Adult Education and is being continued with the support of associates who provide financial backing or who undertake the editorial work for specific issues.

Apart from this regular publication, the Bureau issues basic materials to facilitate contacts between adult education organizations in Europe such as: a directory of adult education organizations giving information on the kinds of agencies and the structures of adult education in various European countries; a list of adult education terms in different languages; and a survey of adult education legislation.

In the years of its existence the Bureau's work has been based on the fact that its associates in various countries found themselves confronted with similar educational problems, and were willing to find cooperative solutions. This has been true not only in periods of economic growth, but also—and is perhaps even more the case—in periods of economic difficulty when the need to find creative answers to common problems has increased.

Bibliography

Schouten G H L 1978 *The European Bureau for Adult Education, 1953–1978*. The European Bureau for Adult Education (EBAE), Amersfoort

Africa

E. A. Ulzen

The foundation of the African Adult Education Association took place in 1968. There had been a number of previous attempts at the national and international levels to bring together professionals in adult education for the promotion of adult education programmes and the creation of a Pan-African Association. The founder members were Ethiopia, Ghana, Kenya, Tanzania, Sudan, Uganda, and Zambia.

The main objectives of the Association are: to arrange study and research into the problems of adult education in contemporary Africa; to encourage affiliated national associations to arrange educational activities for adult citizens; to cooperate with any organization, private or public, in furthering adult education; to act as a clearing house for information, and to produce publications on adult education; to plan programmes for educators; and to promote the creation of networks of communication between adult education agencies and adult educators and the general public.

The Association believes the creation of national associations to be very important since, as professional organizations, they can exert an influence on the direction of education and attain consultative status with their economic planners and policy makers. There are now 18 such affiliated national associations including ones from French-, Portuguese-, and Arabic-speaking countries. The Association seeks the affiliation of national and university institutes of adult education, which have the responsibility for backing up fieldwork in adult education with research publications and the training of personnel. It welcomes non-African organizations as associate members and individual persons may join the Association.

So that national associations and institutional members may address themselves primarily to the problems of adult education in their own countries, each member association has its own constitution, registered in its own country. It is accepted for membership to the Association, provided its statutes and objectives subscribe generally to the main objectives of the Association. All are allowed freedom to plan and carry out their national programmes, with advice from the Association when needed and requested. Since 1978, all have been involved in the programmes organized by the Association's Secretariat, which are decided upon at the biennial conferences of the Association, during which the executive committee is elected.

Prior to the establishment of the Secretariat in 1976, the Association's main activity was the holding of the biennial conference, which still continues. Their subjects have included training for adult education and national development; the relationship between formal and nonformal education in Africa; environmental education; and integrated community education.

Since its establishment, the Secretariat has organized regional and subregional training workshops mainly for adult education practitioners. The countries in which they have been held are Kenya, Tanzania, Mauritius, Sierra Leone, Togo, Nigeria, and Ghana. Among the topics examined have been evaluation research, environmental education, leadership of voluntary associations, part-time agencies, and leadership training for women.

The Association has carried out research and development projects on the following subjects:

(a) The relevance of the education system to employment in the rural areas and for rural development in Kenya.

(b) The production of samples of a basic and practical approach to the preparation of readings in environmental education by adult educators for neoliterate adult learners in the areas of culture, religion, and economics.

(c) A case study in environmental education and training in two rural communities in Kenya.

(d) Collaboration and links between formal and nonformal education organizations in a number of West African countries.

The Association publishes a newsletter, its *Journal*, proceedings of conferences, reports of workshops, and produces handbooks and guides for workers in adult education.

Up to 1976, the members of the Association met the expenses of its biennial conferences from their own resources, with substantial help from the German Adult Education Association and the Joseph Rowntree Trust (UK). Since 1976, the Canadian International Development Agency has provided funds to meet the administrative costs of the Secretariat. Further financial support has been given by several international agencies and by organizations, public or private, from the United Kingdom, the Federal Republic of Germany, and the United States.

Substantial in-kind contributions have been provided by African governments, which have promised direct cash subventions, and are now supporting national associations, as well as from Pan-African and national institutions and organizations.

Bibliography

African Adult Education Association (AAEA) *Journal*. AAEA, Nairobi

Bown L, Tomori S H (eds.) 1979 *A Handbook of Adult Education for West Africa*. Hutchinson, London

Kabwassa A Kaunda M M (eds.) 1973 *Correspondence Education in Africa*. Routledge and Kegan Paul, London

Prosser R 1967 *Adult Education for Developing Countries*. East African Publishing House, Nairobi

The Arab Countries

A. W. A. Yousif

The overriding concern in the field of adult education in the Arab countries today is the eradication of illiteracy. The region has the second highest illiteracy rate in the world. It is estimated that in 1980 there were in the region of 55 million illiterates aged 10 years and over, and the absolute number may continue to rise over the next 20 years, because of the high wastage rate and the low enrolment rate in the primary stage of education in many countries. Other objectives in adult education can be broadly stated as:

(a) providing youths and adults with the opportunity to acquire technical and vocational skills;

(b) offering youths and adults an opportunity for intellectual and aesthetic development;

(c) providing youths and adults with education for cultural and recreative activities.

1. Size and Scope of Adult Education Activities

Official responsibility for planning and executing adult education activities rests with the ministries of education. Other ministries, like agriculture, labour, culture, health, and manpower, conduct vast training programmes for youths and adults as well, but such programmes are not listed under adult education. In the Arab countries the contribution of nongovernmental organizations to adult education is rather limited.

The content of the programmes ranges from basic courses in reading, writing, and arithmetic through traditional subjects, to computer refresher courses and management training for business and government.

2. Problems of Implementation

The diversity of sponsorship has led to a diversity of provision. An inevitable consequence has been wasteful fragmentation but this problem is not unique to the Arab region. The major problem in many countries in the region is the lack of adequate resources, material and financial, but particularly in personnel. This is a consequence of the hitherto low priority given to adult education, compared to the high priority given to schools and other social projects. In most countries in the region there is a shortage of professionally trained personnel, suitable study materials, and a lack of effective service organizations such as libraries, museums, community centres, art galleries, and so on.

Because of the homogeneous character of the cultural heritage of these countries, and as a demonstration of their desire to work together in all fields of education, science, and culture, the Arab countries perceive the problems facing adult education and are planning to cope with them in a regional perspective.

3. Regional Cooperation

The Arab countries have in recent years adopted a policy of close consultation and cooperation in the fields of education, science, and culture. The organizing body for such activities is the Arab League Educational, Cultural and Scientific Organization (ALECSO), which enjoys the support of all 21 member states. One of its major areas of activity is literacy and adult education, for which a specialized agency was created as evidence of the importance the region attaches to this field. The organization is the Arab Literacy and Adult Education Organization (ARLO) which is designed to be the "think tank" of the programme. ARLO offers advice and technical support to member states; analyses common problems, develops plans, and helps member states find suitable solutions to them. It has a board of governors representing all states, a technical secretariat, and two subregional training centres in Bahrain and Tripoli. It produces a professional journal of adult education, in Arabic with a résumé in English, and publishes specialized works and papers.

ARLO maintains contacts with all national bodies and institutions in the field of literacy and adult education in the region and also supports international cooperation with specialized agencies. Its closest ties have so far been with UNESCO through the Regional Office for Education in Arab States (UNEDBAS), which is charged, among other things, with the responsibility of implementing UNESCO literacy and adult education programmes in these countries. UNEDBAS also publishes a quarterly review of education—*L'Education Nouvelle*—which appears in Arabic with a résumé in English or French. It frequently reviews developments in literacy and adult education in the region. ARLO maintains close links with the International Council for Adult Education (ICAE) of which it is a member, as does ALECSO, and the Director of ALECSO in 1986 was one of the vice-presidents of ICAE.

ARLO has succeeded in giving literacy and adult education a focus within the entire region. That in itself is a major achievement. One of the most significant contributions of ARLO was the launching in 1976 of the Arab Literacy Strategy which was formulated in collaboration with the then UNESCO Regional Centre for Functional Literacy in Rural Areas in the Arab States (ASFEC). The strategy envisages the eradication of illiteracy from the Arab homeland by 1990—given the necessary conditions. It ties the eradication of illiteracy among adults to the universalization of primary education among children. At least six Arab states, Iraq, Syria, the Yemen Arab Republic, the Democratic Republic of Yemen, Kuwait and Sudan have carried out mass literacy campaigns that were largely based on the Arab Literacy Strategy. Many countries are now planning their literacy campaigns in accordance with the strategy.

4. New Trends

Recent trends in the region indicate a commitment to the development of adult education programmes, starting with literacy, within the context of lifelong learning. The conference of the Arab ministers of education and ministers of economic planning, which was held in Abu-Dhabi in 1977, endorsed the notion of the "open educational system" based on the principle of educational democratization and relevance, which, according to the Conference Report, implies:

> measures to remove obstacles to universal access to education of one kind or another; the barriers between education, work, and production, and artificial walls between formal and nonformal education.

Many encouraging developments have taken place since 1977. More countries in the region have introduced special legislation for literacy and adult education; many have increased their material and financial support to literacy and adult education programmes. There is an increase in the number of programmes for women, in the use of broadcasting for adult education and oral and video recordings, in the availability of computers for education, in the direct involvement of organizations such as trade unions in literacy activities, in the planning of more "infrastructure" (libraries, museums, etc.) and in the training of competent people. Plans are underway (1986) for the use of satellites (Arabsat) for literacy and adult education. Pilot programmes have already been prepared.

More individuals are taking interest in adult education as a career, the universities are taking a more active role in the training of personnel, and discussions are underway proposing the development of a Regional Adult Education Association. All professional exchanges in the Arab countries have continuously emphasized the need for regional cooperation.

Bibliography

Arab League Educational, Cultural and Scientific Organization (ALECSO) 1981 *Education of the Masses*. Arab Literacy and Adult Education Organization (ARLO), Baghdad

Arab Literacy and Adult Education Organization 1981 *Education of the Masses*. Arab Literacy and Adult Education Organization (ARLO), Baghdad

Arab Literacy and Adult Education Organization 1984 *Education of the Masses*. Arab Literacy and Adult Education Organization (ARLO), Baghdad

Arab League Educational, Cultural and Scientific Organization (ALECSO)/UNESCO 1977 Report of the 4th conference of ministers of education and those responsible for economic planning in the Arab States, Abu-Dhabi, 7–14 Nov, 1977. UNESCO, Paris

Azab S A 1985 The national adult literacy campaign in Iraq.

Prospects, UNESCO quarterly review of education, 15(3)
Hayani I 1980 The changing role of Arab women. *Convergence* 13: 1–20
International Institute for Adult Literacy Methods 1977 Literacy and adult education: The Arab experience. *Literacy Discussion Teheran* 8(3)
Muller J 1975 *Adult Education and Development: Arab States.* German Foundation for International Development, Bonn
Saber M el-D 1977 *Development and Adult Education in the Arab States: An Analysis of Some Issues.* Arab League Educational, Cultural and Scientific Organization (ALECSO)
UNESCO Regional Centre for Functional Literacy in Rural Areas in the Arab States (ASFEC) 1981 *Proposed Literacy Strategy for the Arab States.* ASFEC, Sirs-El-Layyan

Asia

C. Duke

The large size and population, and the diversity of the Asian region, make regional organization of adult education difficult. The main intergovernmental agency which fosters regional cooperation and exchange, UNESCO, is not directly concerned with regional organization for adult education. The Asian and South Pacific Bureau of Adult Education (ASPBAE) is a professional organization dedicated to adult education for development, membership of which is mainly through national associations and secondly through government departments. It fosters the exchange of information and experience between countries within the region and cooperation with other regional and subregional organizations relevant to adult education, as well as professional exchanges with adult educators in other regions of the world. Activities of ASPBAE are mainly on a national or subregional basis; they include the publication, promotion, and dissemination of adult education, training, and exchange of experience through individual visits, conferences, and seminars.

1. The Asian Region

The region of Asia includes the two largest countries, by population, in the world—the People's Republic of China and India. On its Western boundary, it is normally taken to exclude the Arab countries but to include Iran and sometimes Turkey. The Soviet Union is frequently included in Asian regional activities though it also has a European identity. To the east and southeast, Australasia and the small countries of the Pacific region are often included with Asia but are sometimes treated as separate. Large size and great distances affect regional organization of adult education.

The historical, cultural, political, and economic diversity of the region also affects regional organization of adult education, which reflects and expresses the different circumstances and traditions. Different terms are used to refer to the same or similar work: adult education, social education, community education, nonformal education, and continuing education, in particular. The main emphasis in the work varies from country to country, and includes combinations of pure literacy, functional literacy, skills-oriented training, education for rural development or self-reliance, alternative and complementary means of gaining formal educational qualifications, postexperience professional updating, and education for civic, national, ideological, or personal development purposes. Much education of adults takes place outside government and nongovernment agencies the primary purpose of which is adult education, for example in agriculture, health, and industry ministries, churches, and political and cultural organizations.

There are two further complications. Much of the Asian region is undergoing rapid and sometimes violent political, social, and economic changes, which drastically affect arrangements for regional organization and cooperation. Secondly, boundary definitions for the whole region and for subregions within it vary and complicate matters of organization and cooperation. For instance, the Pacific area, also identified at times as the South Pacific or as Oceania, is distinct in culture and identity but sometimes included inappropriately for administrative convenience. Organization of adult education is indeed essentially a matter for countries at the national or subnational level. Regional cooperation relates to cooperation and exchange of experience for mutual benefit, but is hampered by linguistic as well as other diversity. The widely shared colonial tradition of most of the Asian region is however a bond, and a factor for regional cooperation of effort in adult education.

2. Intergovernmental Cooperation

UNESCO has a strong office for education, the UNESCO Regional Office for Education in Asia and the Pacific (ROEAP), located in Bangkok, which supports a network of innovatory education centres through the Asian Programme of Educational Innovation for Development (APEID). Both the Regional Office and the activities promoted through APEID give considerable prominence to adult education. Literacy and integrated rural development attract much effort, as do vocational skill training, universalization of education by nonformal as well as formal means, effective use of educational technology and educational personnel in adult education, use of indigenous models and materials, and, generally, education of adults to promote economic and social development. The UNESCO Regional Office organized a major regional seminar on adult education and development in late 1980 (UNESCO 1981).

Some other intergovernmental organizations with regionwide responsibilities also periodically promote organization or cooperation in adult education, for example the International Labour Organization in the area of vocational and union education, and the Food and Agriculture Organization, which has sponsored subregional participatory training of adult educators as change agents (Bhasin 1979). The Asian–Pacific Institute of Broadcasting Development (AIBD) located in Kuala Lumpur includes adult nonformal education among its areas of application (Ahamed et al. 1979). There are also subregional intergovernmental organizations which provide periodic support to adult education and thereby tend to promote its organization. Prominent in the Pacific area is the South Pacific Commission which has an out-of-school youth and adult education specialist. In Southeast Asia the five ASEAN countries are active members of the South-East Asian Ministers of Education Organization (SEAMEO) which also includes in nonactive membership the three countries of Indochina. Some of the SEAMEO centres in different member countries promote adult education from time to time, for instance INNOTECH, now located in the Philippines, but the main SEAMEO contribution to adult education has been through its SEAMEO Nonformal Education Project (SNEP), through which subregional seminars and training courses were arranged. Other international bodies and organizations, such as the Commonwealth, promote regional organization in adult education from time to time through particular activities, but do not include all or most countries of the region.

3. The Asian–South Pacific Bureau of Adult Education (ASPBAE)

Regional organization and cooperation are promoted mainly through the nongovernmental organization, ASPBAE, which was founded in 1964. The Bureau operated tenuously as a unitary organization until 1976. Distances and costs of communication severely restricted regionwide activity to printed information exchange and very occasional meetings. In 1976 a decision was taken to work mainly through subregions, and a revised constitution reflected this arrangement. Three such subregions were initially identified. One of these has remained unaltered, the South Asian region extending from Turkey, which joined a little later, to Nepal and Sri Lanka. A second subregion comprising the countries with communist systems in 1976 has not operated as an active subregion and modes of possible participation remain under review. The third subregion initially comprised the countries of Southeast Asia and the South Pacific together with Hong Kong, Japan, and the Republic of Korea. In 1978, by decision of members of a South Pacific ASPBAE conference on adult education in national development, the South Pacific was identified as a distinct subregion, and has subsequently been identified as ASPBAE Region 4. While the principle of subregional activity areas has remained firm, the work of the Bureau is characterized by a high level of flexibility, and within minimal constitutional requirements forms of membership and participation remain fluid.

Membership is first by country, by means of the national association of adult education where such a body exists, or by means of some other body, normally the leading government department or instrumentality responsible for adult education, in other cases. There are also both institutional and individual members, mainly within the Asian and Pacific region but including a few with professional involvement or interest in other parts of the world. The Bureau itself is the regional arm of the more recently formed (1972) International Council for Adult Education. It seeks through this and other means to foster exchange of experience with other, especially developing, regions of the world. The International Council contributes to organization of adult education in the region, mainly through ASPBAE, but it also conducts international activities, mainly seminars, within the region from time to time, thereby contributing indirectly to regional exchange, organization, and development. Recent Council trends towards decentralization of some programme areas suggest a more direct and continuing regional contribution, for instance in adult education for primary health care and in participatory research in adult education.

3.1 Purposes and Principles

The Asian and South Pacific Bureau of Adult Education as a professional, nongovernmental organization seeks to create and foster networks of adult educators rather than to create formal organizations. Its infrastructure and secretariat are small and enjoy low visibility; the Bureau may be described as a nonorganization which relies largely on professional exchange and rapport and on senior adult educators who serve as members-at-large and mobile resource persons in different parts of the region. There are no regular paid staff, and the Bureau relies substantially on the voluntarily contributed nonmeasurable resources of various adult education institutions in participating countries. In this and other ways it avoids competing with other organizations, governmental, intergovernmental, and nongovernmental, seeking rather to publicize and complement the contribution to adult education of each of these.

The broad purpose of the Bureau is to advance adult education as a means of social and cultural as well as economic development. Adult education is thus promoted in socioeconomic, political, and cultural contexts rather than as an end in itself. The principle of technical cooperation between developing countries is respected, and it is unusual for resource persons to be drawn from industrialized countries beyond the region, or for models and methods of adult education to be drawn deliberately from these countries. Indigenous models are encouraged, along with use of local materials and technologies, and the use and promotion of traditional cultural and communication forms. The cultural diversity of the region leads naturally to awareness of the relation of different models and methods to, and their effectiveness or otherwise in, different cultural milieux. Issues which tend to recur in activities of the Bureau include:

interdisciplinary and interdepartmental cooperation at different levels of government from central to village; the application of adult education to the practical needs of the people; the attempt to reach those in greatest need; cooperation between government and both voluntary and community organizations and resources; the links between formal and nonformal adult education; methods of educational innovation, including involvement of top level official personnel with local level pilot operations; and means of participation and mobilization in adult education. The Bureau seeks to partner larger and more formal adult-education-providing agencies, including governments and those giving aid to governments for purposes which include adult education, in an effort to foster innovation and greater effectiveness in the larger programmes. In these ways the Bureau serves too as a promoter of adult education in the region and as a source of personal and moral, as well as more formal professional, support for adult educators who share similar purposes in different countries.

3.2 Activities

Each subregion functions largely autonomously in terms of programmes of activity. Levels and forms of activity therefore vary between subregions as well as over time. The main regionwide activity of the Bureau is the production and dissemination of a thrice-yearly package *Courier Service* which includes a journal component and news, learning materials, and other forms of learning exchange and special enclosures. This is alternated with a thrice-yearly newsletter of more limited circulation. These information services seek to publicize and disseminate information about the publications, teaching/learning materials, activities, and other resources of adult educators in the region, and any other information and materials which might be of use to adult educators. They thus emphasize publicity and accessibility of existing resources rather than originality, although publication of original material, especially reports of innovations, is also included. In some countries, distribution is by national member centres to a country network; in other cases mailing is direct to readers. Some materials are translated and further reproduced, fully or abstracted, in country journals.

The most substantial and regular programmes of activity have tended to be in East and Southeast Asia, which have enjoyed a regular though modest flow of funds for training courses, conferences, and seminars, and a travelling-fellow scheme, as well as for some specialized publications supplementary to the more widely used Bureau materials. Very recently, as a result of deliberate policy, some resources have been shifted into programmes of work in South Africa, the South Pacific, and China. The majority of training courses, workshops, and seminars are for adult educators of one or another country and may be national, provincial, or local in level. Many are conducted in the national language, but some may have outside resource persons and work wholly or partly in English. At the subregional level there is an annual training course of five or six weeks for adult educators working in urban settings; normally an annual regional conference on a theme particularly significant to, and chosen by, the host country, which is also the occasion for an annual meeting of the Bureau and subregional executives; and one or two other activities, such as training seminars undertaken in cooperation with SEAMEO or AIBD. Each year a few adult educators undertake study tours in one or more other countries in the region; while there is always an element of reciprocity, in some cases the main emphasis is on the visitor as a learner, in others more on him or her serving as a resource person. Publications within the subregion are usually reports and proceedings arising from these workshops and other activities, together with occasional surveys and other reports, and translations of materials into national languages.

One cumulative effect of the various activities has been to develop a progressively widening community or network of adult educators who share a common set of professional purposes and approaches and tend to draw on experience of neighbouring countries to examine, illuminate, and modify their own practices, while retaining the distinctive approaches relevant to their different circumstances. Comparative and shared experience has both strengthened and sharpened some differences and fostered more commonality of practice. Insofar as organization of adult education per se is strengthened this occurs at the national and subnational levels. The regional supporting network plays, rather, a coordinating and complementary role, providing channels and means for adult educators of different persuasions and in different employment or voluntary situations better to organize their efforts. The rapid and often dramatic political, social, cultural, and economic changes occurring in many parts of the region may indicate that a more formal, visible, and at the same time rigid system of organization of adult education would be less well-adapted to the particular circumstances of the region.

Bibliography

Ahamed U et al. 1979 *Broadcasting for Non-formal Education.* Asian–Pacific Institute of Broadcasting Development (AIBD), Kuala Lumpur

Asian Programme of Educational Innovation for Development (APEID) 1981 *Work Plan of APEID 1982–1986.* UNESCO, Bangkok

Asian and South Pacific Bureau of Adult Education (ASPBAE) 1976–82 *Courier Service.* ASPBAE, Canberra

Asian and South Pacific Bureau of Adult Education (ASPBAE) 1981 DVV–ASPBAE partnership: Evaluative review 1977–1980. *Adult Education and Development*, Vol. 17. DVV, Bonn

Bhasin K 1979 *Breaking Barriers: A South Asian Experience of Training for Participatory Development.* Food and Agriculture Organization (FAO), Bangkok

South-East Asian Ministers of Education Organization (SEAMEO) 1980 *Revised Development Plan for SEAMEO Nonformal Education Programme (SNEP) 1980–83.* SEAMEO, Bangkok

South Pacific Commission 1978 *Regional Planning Conference on Adult Education in National Development*. South Pacific Commission, Noumea

UNESCO 1981 *Prospects for Adult Education and Development of Asia and the Pacific*. UNESCO, Bangkok

International Adult Education

C. Duke

International relations and cooperation including but extending beyond comparative studies and aid programmes in wealthy as well as Third World countries are important in adult education. International efforts are frequently intended to inform and change adult education practice, and to enhance government interest in and support for adult education efforts. Much adult education within individual countries is less committed to change and development than internationally oriented efforts and there is consequently some tension between these two fields.

There have been considerable, albeit somewhat intangible, achievements as a result of international relations and activity. More may be expected in the future in terms of effective promotion of important areas of work, aid, training, and research. Several problems and tensions persist, including the inevitable limits to what can be achieved for development by education alone, problems of North–South relations and dependency induced by aid, the balance between international and regional work, and the tension between parochialism, chauvinism, or ethnocentrism and internationalism in the minds and work of adult educators.

1. *Internationalism and Comparative Studies*

International comparative studies in many fields are an obvious form of international cooperation and exchange. Charters et al. (1981), referring to the interdependence of peoples and countries, finds value in comparing adult education worldwide so that adult educators and scholars can learn from one another:

> those who use lifelong education to achieve personal or societal ends can benefit in their planning and execution by some understanding of lifelong education in other countries. The benefits include a better understanding of oneself, of one's own culture, and of others whose ideas and experience may prove useful. . . . Studies in comparative adult education that transcend national boundaries should enable educators of adults to use adult education to facilitate people's control of the quality of their lives. (Charters 1981 pp. xiii–xiv, 16–17)

Duke (1979, 1981) compares aspects of adult education in Australia and very different countries of the Asian region, and suggests that there may be more to be gained by such comparisons than comparisons of very similar situations. Adult education is more commonly and overtly dedicated to social change and development than is the formal education system. Comparative studies are thus if anything more demanding, since awareness of the social, cultural, political, and economic context and texture is implied, and more applied to practice because such scholarship tends to be a means rather than an end in itself.

2. *Adult Education for Development*

The general report of the Third International Conference on Adult Education (UNESCO 1972) stressed adult education as a factor in economic and social development and as a factor in cultural development. The major Commonwealth Conference in New Delhi in 1979 was on "nonformal education for development" and focused its attention on the overall standard of living of the most needy sections of society. The introductory chapter to the "design for action" arising from the International Conference on Adult Education (ICAE) at Dar es Salaam in 1976 was entitled "An urgency: Adult education in and for development". It quotes Nyerere's opening address:

> Adult education is not something which can deal with just "agriculture" or "health" or "literacy" or "mechanical skill", etc. All these separate branches are related to the total life a man is living, and to the man he is and will become. . . . This means that adult education will promote changes in men and society. And it means that adult education *should* promote change, at the same time as it assists men to control both the change which they induce, and that which is forced upon them by the decisions of other men or the cataclysms of nature. (Hall and Kidd 1978 p. 12)

The themes of development and action dominate much international discussion of adult education. Adult education is promoted as a means to development within different programmes concerned with agriculture, industry, health, preservation of the environment, and population control, as well as through literacy and other exclusively educational programmes. Those to be persuaded include international, national, and nongovernmental aid agencies, governments and ministries responsible for formulating and implementing policies and programmes, and adult educators themselves. Recent historical and contemporary political, social, and economic circumstances have given adult education in some countries, both industrialized and developing, a similar strong orientation to economic and cultural development and related social and civic concerns.

In general, however, the majority of adult educators and the courses which comprise their programmes have little ideological purpose, whether the content be vocational and technical skills or skills and knowledge for personal enrichment. Internationalism in the field of adult education thus means promoting development and similar causes with adult educators themselves as well as with those whose policies and finances determine and limit what can be done. The result is a tension which may be discerned in many countries, more especially those in the Western tradition of liberal leisure-time-oriented adult education, between the small number of adult educators involved in international exchanges and other activities and those in national associations and councils whose principal interest and responsibility is with domestic needs. The tension is periodically polarized as a choice between internationalism and nationalism.

On the other hand, international relations and exchanges significantly increased through the 1970s, and play a more significant part in widening the horizons and professional understanding of adult educators within almost every country of the world. They are being made conscious of the development possibilities of adult education, its relation to the work of other ministries and sectors, and its place in development plans of countries which practise national development planning.

3. Intergovernmental and Nongovernmental Organizations

3.1 Intergovernmental Organizations

The main intergovernmental organization to promote international exchange and activity in adult education is UNESCO. Education is the concern of one of its major sectors, within which literacy, adult education, and rural development comprise one division. Its adult education section produces *Adult Education Notes and News* and generally promotes adult education, particularly towards Third World development. UNESCO's work is partly decentralized to regional offices, of which the largest and oldest, for Asia, is located in Bangkok. It stresses education and gives considerable importance to adult education (including literacy, population education, integrated rural development, and skills-oriented training) in its programmes. It includes the Asian Programme of Educational Innovation for Development (APEID), which also emphasizes the role of adult education in many of its priority areas. Associated with UNESCO are several international specialized agencies which promote aspects of adult education theory or practice as part of their work: the UNESCO Institute for Education in Hamburg which concentrates on lifelong education; the International Institute of Educational Planning in Paris; and the International Bureau of Education, a documentation centre, in Geneva. UNESCO is also instrumental in promoting specialized centres and programmes in the different regions, including analogies to the APEID network in Asia, some of which more or less directly promote adult education.

Other intergovernmental organizations, the primary purposes of which are not educational, nonetheless support international exchange and development of adult education as it is relevant to their particular areas of competence, reflecting the applied, development-oriented nature of most international activity in adult education. United Nations agencies thus involved include the International Labour Organization (ILO), the Food and Agriculture Organization (FAO), the World Health Organization (WHO), and the United Nations Children's Fund (UNICEF). The World Bank also promotes adult education. The Organisation for Economic Co-operation and Development (OECD) has had a particular concern for matters of economic relevance, particularly recurrent education and paid educational leave. The Council of Europe has done valuable work in the field of nonformal adult education and sociocultural animation. The Arab Region Literacy Organization (ARLO) promotes literacy in the Arab region, and the South-East Asian Ministers of Education Organization promotes nonformal education.

3.2 Nongovernmental Organizations

The International Council for Adult Education (ICAE) founded in 1972, is the most influential and comprehensive international organization in the field, with approximately 80 countries in membership from most regions of the world. It enjoys 'Category A' NCO status with UNESCO, and appears likely to become still more influential because of the UNESCO crisis occasioned by the withdrawal of USA and Britain. It has formalized relations with existing and new regional nongovernmental organizations such as the European Bureau of Adult Education, the African Association for Literacy and Adult Education Association (AALAE), and the Asian–South Pacific Bureau of Adult Education (ASPBAE).

An older, but less active and influential, nongovernmental association is the International Congress of University Adult Education. Its scope is restricted to adult education within higher education, with emphasis on research, training, and extension. A more recent international association is the International Association of Community Education, the purposes of which embrace school and school-age education, making its scope wider in some respects though narrower in others than that of ICAE. In 1985 a Commonwealth Association for the Education of Adults (CAEA) was formed. Some other international bodies promote particular aspects of adult education as part of their work from time to time, while regional adult education associations play a large role in encouraging internationalism but mainly at a regional level.

3.3 Complementary Roles

Intergovernmental and nongovernmental organizations (IGOs and NGOs) play related but usually distinct roles in fostering internationalism in adult education. The major agencies of both kinds are mostly dedicated to development-oriented adult education and so have a harmony of outlook and purpose among their professional personnel who mainly work in close, informal cooperation. The dominant, usually unspoken, tension is between industrialized and Third World groups and thus reflects the tension referred to as the North–South dialogue. A common purpose of adult educators working for international understanding is to bridge this gap and to find mutually acceptable forms of exchange, cooperation, and aid between wealthy industrialized and developing countries.

The two kinds of organizations have different strengths and limitations, such that partnership can be attractive to both. Intergovernmental organizations have the authority of governments behind them and directly or indirectly can influence the nature and quantity of national and international aid funds which may directly enhance adult education programmes in the Third World. Their formal recommendations and other conclusions of deliberation have some formal authority with member governments. Nongovernmental organizations, by contrast, lack formal authority with governments, although in some countries their voice may be comparably influential and perhaps more greatly heeded and respected. In some countries, the government gives strong and visible support to the work of international and regional NGOs; elsewhere the involvement and interest is at the level of a department or section of government only, or is restricted to the participation of adult educators working in both nongovernment and government sectors within the country. Whereas this restricts NGOs in formal influence, they have an advantage in terms of flexibility and more rapid responsiveness to new situations and needs, compared with IGOs. There is thus a logical complementarity of role and function, and internationally active adult educators seek periodically to refine and enhance this relationship.

4. Kinds of International Activity

4.1 Information Exchange

Much international activity in adult education is restricted to exchange of information and experience, through meetings of various kinds but more substantially, because of travel costs, by means of various publications. Both intergovernmental and nongovernmental organizations as well as some other institutions, notably universities with an international orientation, publish regular and occasional means of disseminating knowledge and experience. Some chiefly promote scholarship through comparative studies but even with these there is frequently an intention to inform and influence policy and practice. UNESCO and OECD produce occasional monographs on aspects of adult education with such intent, as does the UNESCO Institute for Education in Hamburg. UNESCO and IBE Geneva, along with ASPBAE and Michigan State University, for example, have regular means of disseminating information about adult education materials. These and other regional and international agencies also disseminate news about developments, such as new courses, methods and materials, research programmes, and training opportunities. The *International Journal of University Adult Education* concentrates on professional experience and research findings in this sector, though with a more practical orientation than more strictly scholarly national adult education journals. *Convergence*, produced by ICAE, is designed to inform and enhance professional practice internationally, as is for instance the ASPBAE *Courier Service* regionally, in the Asian–Pacific area.

4.2 Lobbying

The international meetings of adult educators organized by ICAE, UNESCO, and other agencies fulfil many functions, including exchange of information leading to enhanced professional morale and competence. A major purpose of many such meetings, however, is to define and clarify the role and contribution of adult education, especially in development, and to produce guidelines, policy statements, and manifestos for action. Such statements are intended for many audiences: for adult educators whose horizons may be too limited by particular national circumstances and constraints; for governments responsible for providing circumstances and often resources to facilitate or hamper work in adult education; and for international aid agencies and others, which may see or fail to see the possible contribution of adult education to development and therefore include it in, or omit it from, aid programmes and funding. Apart from producing statements and lobbying for aid, both UNESCO and ICAE, along with the regional associates of the latter such as ASPBAE, foster the creation of national adult education associations through which national activity and learning can be fostered. In the Asian region, for example, the Republic of Korea, Hong Kong, Singapore, Sri Lanka, Malaysia, Bangladesh and Thailand have established associations with regional and international membership, joining with older bodies like those of India and Australia.

Among prominent international meetings are the periodic meetings of UNESCO at Elsinore (1949), Montreal (1960), Tokyo (1972), and Paris (1985), which have constituted landmarks in the definition of adult education internationally. Through their statements and reports they act as means of leverage and promotion for adult education within member states. The UNESCO Recommendation for the Development of Adult Education, 1976, plays a similar role and has been used to help adult education associations, and even ministries and departments, to advance the case for recognition and funding within their own countries. Also influential are regional meetings of UNESCO such as the seminar on Adult Education and Development at Bangkok in 1980. Other United Nations agencies also include adult education among their deliberations and concluding statements from time to time, and are themselves a target for policy statements emanating from specialized gatherings of adult educators. Another intergovernmental organization, the Commonwealth Secretariat, arranged a major conference on adult education and development in New Delhi, 1979. ICAE has arranged a number of specialized conferences which have produced statements and recommendations, such as that at Persepolis in 1975 and another in Udaipur in 1982, both on the subject of literacy, and the large and broader international conferences in 1976 at Dar es Salaam, 1982 in Paris, and 1985 in Buenos Aires.

4.3 Professional Development

Conferences, seminars, and workshops are important means for professional development of adult education leaders. They provide ways of widening understanding, for example by increasing the connections between adult and formal education, and between adult education and economic development; by practising educational innovation through contact with experimentation elsewhere; and by sustaining and raising morale, which may be low where there is a lack of stimulation and support for adult education leaders, who may be few and isolated in their own society.

Professional development is more overtly fostered by international agencies and exchanges in the form of training courses, workshops, and scholarships enabling formal study overseas. UNESCO and ICAE both allocate modest amounts of money for training courses which may be regional, subregional, or within countries, usually with some comparative perspective and outside professional contribution; and they encourage and advise other bodies to make direct financial allocations for recurring or occasional professional development activities. Examples include a regional training programme for Caribbean adult educators and another for adult educators in urban settings of East and Southeast Asia. Funding agencies for such international work include the Canadian International Development Agency, the W. K. Kellogg Foundation, and the *Deutscher Volkshochschul-Verband* (DVV).

4.4 Research

Theoretical research in most disciplines is substantially international, or universal, in character. Comparative international studies are deliberately promoted also in adult education. There tends to be much emphasis upon applied, action, and participatory research in adult education. ICAE has strongly promoted participatory research in adult education through its international and regional networks. Internationalism in research is however limited by restrictions on funds, although UNESCO periodically makes small grants for data collection and survey research.

4.5 Aid

International organizations, both governmental and nongovernmental, promote different forms of aid for adult education in developing countries. Such funds may be distributed through the IGO or NGO itself, or adult education components may be included in the aid programme of other agencies. Such programmes may be agency-to-country, country-to-country, country-to-region, or on other bases. Although aid can be important in fostering innovation in adult education the total amount of international adult education aid is very small compared with economic development aid and aid in the formal sector of education.

5. Achievements and Prospects

5.1 Achievements

Internationalism has achieved considerable results in the period since the Second World War, dating from the first UNESCO International Conference on Adult Education at Elsinore, Denmark, in 1949. It has gained momentum from the postwar reaction against global warfare and the enhanced globalism and international contact in the succeeding decades. This contact and activity may be described as a movement, which gained further energy and enhancement of ideals with the creation of ICAE in 1972 following the Third UNESCO International Conference on Adult Education. As a result, adult education is now commonly conceived as a means to development. It is increasingly recognized as relevant to health, agricultural, industrial, and other development programmes. Lobbying activities have proved successful in a number of arenas and at different levels, from local to international. The role of international efforts and international education, though substantial, is hard to measure. Policies have been clarified, and adult education budgets in many developing countries significantly increased. There are more, and more varied, training opportunities available for adult educators in most countries.

5.2 Prospects and Tensions

It is probable that needs will be further clarified and resources enhanced through international means for more training and, perhaps, research in adult education. The case for including adult education as a component in all development programmes will be advanced by adult educators, but, because it is difficult to quantify, may not find easy adoption. The persistence of major needs and problems, for instance the increasing absolute number of illiterates (despite massive literacy programmes and proportional reductions in illiteracy), illustrates the fact that there is no easy solution to problems addressed by adult education internationally. Adult education alone cannot resolve problems which have political, social, economic, or cultural roots and require solutions in similar terms.

Organizationally, there are possible tensions between international and regional levels of activity, but there is no evidence of tension or role ambiguity between the intergovernmental and nongovernmental agencies. For the NGOs there is a need to manage the relationship between formal country membership and the sometimes more animated and radical activity of individual members and networks within the countries and regions. Related to this is a tension between the more idealist, sometimes ideological, stance of international adult education oriented to action for development and the more eclectic and sometimes parochial work of adult education within countries. A main challenge is to sustain effective internationalism for reciprocal gain in the context of the inequalities and debates represented by the differences between North and South in world affairs generally.

Bibliography

Bennett C, Kidd J R, Kulich J 1975 *Comparative Studies in Adult Education: An Anthology*. Syracuse University, Syracuse, New York

Charters A N et al. (eds.) 1981 *Comparing Adult Education Worldwide*. Jossey-Bass, San Francisco, California

Commonwealth Secretariat 1980 *Participation, Learning and Change: Commonwealth Approaches to Nonformal Education.* Commonwealth Secretariat, London

Duke C 1979 Asia and the South Pacific: The exchange of ideas with Australia. In: Schuller T, Megarry J (eds.) 1979 *Recurrent Education and Lifelong Learning*. Kogan Page, London

Duke C 1981 Australia in Asia: Comparison as learning. In: Charters A N et al. (eds.) 1981

Hall B L, Kidd J R 1978 *Adult Learning: A Design for Action.* Int. Conf. on Adult Education and Development, Dar es Salaam, 1976. Pergamon, Oxford

UNESCO 1972 *Final Report, Third Int. Conf. Adult Education*, Tokyo, 25 Jul–7 Aug, 1972. UNESCO, Paris

UNESCO 1976 *Recommendation on the Development of Adult Education*. UNESCO, Paris

UNESCO 1981 *Prospects for Adult Education and Development in Asia and the Pacific*. UNESCO, Bangkok

UNESCO 1985 *Adult Education since the Third International Conference*. UNESCO, Paris

UNESCO 1985 *The Development of Adult Education: Aspects and Trends*. UNESCO, Paris

UNESCO 1985 *Final Report, Fourth Int. Conf. Adult Education*. UNESCO, Paris

International Council for Adult Education

J. Sullivan

Voluntary, nonprofit organizations operate worldwide. Unofficially, they number about 8,000 and most have an education component. Their number has been increasing rapidly, especially since the Second World War. The majority of these nongovernmental organizations have been created to serve a particular sector as evidenced by their names: the World Confederation of Organizations of the Teaching Profession (WCOTP), the International Confederation of Free Trade Unions (ICFTU), the International Reading Association (IRA), the International Federation of Library Associations and Institutions (IFLA), and the International Council of Voluntary Agencies (ICVA). The International Association of Community Education is a recent addition to this group.

As nations have confronted such problems as illiteracy, family planning, and health, these international nongovernmental organizations (INGOs) have played an important role in combating them. Many are committed to overcoming the problems of the Third World and carry out their programs with their own resources, through the United Nations or through a variety of aid organizations.

International and regional conferences and seminars held by INGOs have been of major significance to adult education. The World Federation of the Teaching Profession has arranged meetings in many parts of the world. The World Federation of Trade Unions (WFTU) collaborated with UNESCO in 1967 to organize a world conference on functional literacy.

Discussion and controversy about the role of voluntary organizations were part of the UNESCO World Conference on Adult Education in Elsinore in 1949. Some delegates believed only the free voluntary movements could adequately represent the diverse interests in adult education. Others thought it was the responsibility of the state or UNESCO. At the second world conference in Montreal (1960), one of the resolutions adopted stated: "The conference urges governments to encourage the development of voluntary organizations since without the freedom, the creative resources, and the experimental approach that should characterize such bodies, an essential element in the education of adults is lacking." At the third conference in Tokyo (1972) the Director-General of UNESCO concluded his remarks with: "Our work in promoting adult education must be appreciably strengthened."

It was the informal talks at the Tokyo conference and the long-time work of a Canadian professor, J. Roby Kidd, that brought the International Council for Adult Education into reality in 1973.

1. History

From 1919 to the outbreak of the Second World War there had existed a World Association for Adult Education based in London. It launched comparative studies, issued publications, and supported international programs. However, it was not revived after the war. The possibility of a new voluntary international adult education association was discussed at the UNESCO conferences in Elsinore (1949) and Montreal (1960), but on both occasions the notion was considered premature and the delegates agreed to continue working through the United Nations.

By the early 1970s the situation had changed noticeably. More and more developing countries were creating national associations or boards of education and some form of regional cooperation existed. Also, nongovernmental organizations and specialized agencies had developed an interest in adult education. The idea of forming an international association was being discussed in more than 50 countries. The Tokyo conference (1972) provided the opportunity for further meetings and the incentive for action.

Roby Kidd was a Canadian observer at the conference. Convinced of the need for a permanent coordinating council and with strong positive support from a majority of countries with some form of national organization, he advanced the idea of an international council. In spite of arguments that such an organization would weaken existing groups and lead to more intense competition for funds, the idea won support. The view that such an organization would strengthen what existed and ensure world solidarity was accepted by many present. With this support Kidd succeeded in incorporating the International Council for Adult Education in Canada in 1973.

From this beginning it has developed into a positive response to the need for a cooperative network of mutual support for advocacy and promotion of the education of adults. It is made up of over 70 national and regional member associations. It works in cooperation with the United Nations through UNESCO and UNICEF, with nongovernmental organizations that share its aims, with intergovernmental bodies, voluntary groups, universities, and research or training institutions.

2. *Aims and Objectives*

As set out in its constitution, the Council stresses the importance of adult learning, in a variety of forms and for the healthy growth and development of individuals, communities, and societies. The ICAE is one means of helping individuals and groups gain the kinds of knowledge, skills, and competency needed to achieve a just and equitable economic, social, and cultural development.

Equally important is the organization's support for international understanding and world peace. Since it operates in partnership with colleagues around the world, the ICAE provides an international forum for debate and dialogue on how adult education can help to alleviate entrenched poverty and its resulting forms of exploitation and inequity. In carrying out these aims, the ICAE works for the implementation of the UNESCO *Recommendation on the Development of Adult Education*.

3. *Structure and Membership*

The Council operates from a small secretariat in Toronto, Ontario, Canada. There are three major, elected bodies that control the affairs and activities of the Council:

(a) the general assembly, which is the gathering of the entire membership and takes place once within a three-year period;

(b) the executive committee, which is the responsible governing body and is accountable to the general assembly. The committee is elected for a three-year term and is made up of the president, the immediate past president, the treasurer, and representatives named by identified regions. The committee appoints the secretary-general of the ICAE and convenes annually;

(c) the bureau, which comprises the collective group of officers, the secretary-general, and the associate secretary-general.

The basic membership units are national and regional associations. Where a regional association exists, national bodies can first join it and then apply for membership in the ICAE. There is a membership category for international associations that have a major interest in the education of adults, such as the International Congress for University Adult Education. The constitution does not provide an open membership for individuals. It does, however, allow an invitation into membership by the executive committee for individuals who have particular relevant knowledge and experience.

The Council has a cooperative relationship with a number of international nongovernmental organizations. It also has cooperative linkages with agencies of the United Nations and other intergovernmental organizations. With UNESCO, it is placed in the highest category of "consultative and associate relations." Projects and programs of the Council are supported financially by the Canadian International Development Agency and other public aid agencies. The W. K. Kellogg and other foundations, UNESCO, and other international organizations, such as the World Health Organization, have also given financial assistance.

4. *Programs*

The work of the Council is carried out in all regions of the world through member associations, networks, and collaborative projects supervised by individuals in various countries. It includes research, training, information exchange, and advocacy; the organization of international seminars and workshops; comparative studies; and the publication of a quarterly journal (*Convergence*), occasional papers, reports, and a newsletter.

Programs respond directly to issues and needs identified by member associations and active practitioners, particularly to those of Third World countries and of the underprivileged within these. Participatory research is a feature of ICAE's work, which also includes workers' education, primary health care, participation by women, and literacy. It is involved in radio-learning groups, mass literacy campaigns, the welfare of indigenous people, the alleviation of poverty through education, popular culture, and the education of women in Third World regions. International networks have been formed around such issues as peace, the older adult, and new technologies. ICAE has held two major world conferences, in 1976 in Dar es Salaam, and in 1982 in Paris. The standing of the Council is evidenced by the fact that the former was opened by President Nyerere of Tanzania, and the latter, which was attended by over 500 people from 110 countries, by President Mitterrand of France.

Bibliography

Gayfer M 1974 The International Council for Adult Education. *Adult Leadership* 23(5): 130–32, 158–59

International Council for Adult Education (ICAE) 1981 *Policies and Plans*. Background Paper. ICAE, Toronto, Ontario

International Council for Adult Education (ICAE) 1982 *A Partnership in Development*. Background Paper. ICAE, Toronto, Ontario

Kidd J R 1974 *A Tale of Three Cities. Elsinore–Montreal–Tokyo; The Influence of Three UNESCO World Conferences upon the Development of Adult Education*. Syracuse University Publications in Continuing Education, Syracuse, New York

Lowe J 1975 *The Education of Adults: A World Perspective*. UNESCO, Paris

Section 9

Legislation and Finance

Section 9

Legislation and Finance

Introduction

For the greater part of its history adult education did quite well in most countries without specific laws or state regulations applied to it. For all of its history it has, in the opinion of its practitioners, had to do without adequate funds and has suffered in consequence. In recent years the amount of legislation has, for good or ill, significantly increased, much of it related to the continually vexed question of finance, as the amount of state money allocated to adult education has grown. Indeed much the same reasons that have inspired national legislation have also provoked for the first time serious consideration of national policies on the funding of education for adults.

The key concerns have been influence and size, and the interaction between them. In the years since the Second World War the growth of adult education has drawn it to the attention of governments. They have become aware of its potential as an instrument both of social and of economic action. Their interest has further contributed to its growth. As it has become a significant element in educational policy, or its potential to do so has been perceived, so states, of their own accord, or spurred on by other interests, including those of adult education itself, have increasingly felt the need to grasp the nettle of regulation and resource.

Some early encounters between adult educators and the law in the nineteenth century were not happy. Because adult educators frequently set out expressly to change society, or the views they put forward did not conform to those of the regime, they ran the risk of being perceived as subversive and were treated as such. This kind of experience has been repeated in the latter half of the twentieth century, in South Africa and Latin America, for example. The difference now is that the intention has not been to abolish education for adults altogether, but to bring it in line with government thinking.

Not all countries have had that experience, but the majority now find the state taking a regulatory interest in the field. Adult educators are resigned to it or seek it. Even in those countries where provision of learning opportunities for adults has been predominantly left to voluntary organizations, the providers, as in Denmark and Sweden, have welcomed laws, part of the purpose of which has been to protect their status and independence against the state itself.

The extent and nature of legislation relating to adult education varies greatly from country to country. A few general observations may be hazarded. In those countries which have a formal legal code, where there is often uncertainty about the permissibility of anything that is not specifically covered by law, there would seem to be a need to spell out the rights and duties of the state, of private associations, of adult learners. This would appear to be less necessary in countries following the English case law tradition, in which anything tends to be allowed that is not specifically forbidden by law or case precedent.

Much adult education activity has derived its legitimacy from legislation not aimed at it at all. In France, for example, sociocultural animation has been essentially built on a law of 1901 spelling out the right to free association. This is, however, becoming less and less the case. One finds that measures are enacted to cover adult education as a whole, or some aspect of it. In particular, education for employment has been the subject of specific laws or regulations. Some countries, mostly in Western Europe, have enacted legislation intended to give broad, general coverage of the adult education field. The effect of other laws has been to establish adult education as an integral part of the national education system, in some cases under the influence of the concept of lifelong education. The countries of Eastern Europe situate it firmly within a comprehensive framework of education and keep it firmly, as do other socialist countries, under state control. In the People's Republic of China it has been the subject of a string of directives over the years.

In developing countries as a whole, the integration of adult with other education is to a large extent forced upon them by their need to achieve education in any form they can, regardless of age distinctions. They have difficulty in implementing legislation, although it does often exist.

The foregoing observations represent random impressions. There has been very little systematic study of adult education legislation throughout the world—much less than its importance would seem to require. Even in Western Europe, the only region where it has been the subject of systematic study, expertise in adult education has not been enriched, as it needs to be, by an equal knowledge of comparative law. The first article in this section, *Adult Education Legislation in Western Europe*, gives an accurate review of the principal features of laws enacted in different countries. They include statements of rights to education in adulthood, its aims and objectives, the allocation of responsibility between the state and other organizations, and measures relating to finance, staffing, and training. But much more needs to be done, particularly in situating these laws in the general context of each country's legal system, if their significance and potential are to be fully understood.

Laws are often strong, even verbose, on principle, but their main effect is frequently felt in the field of money. Repeatedly they prescribe what funds government shall make available, to whom, for what purposes and how they shall be distributed. They lay down supervisory machinery to ensure the intentions of the state are followed. Ironically they rarely concern themselves with ensuring educational quality. It may well be wondered whether some of the more laissez-faire states, the United States for instance, would enact legislation on adult education at all, were public money not involved.

To say that the extent of financial problems is a function of influence and size is plainly a truism. But the situation is complicated by other factors. Up to a certain dimension of activity adult education could rely on part-time educators and volunteer organizations and borrow premises on a temporary basis from other organizations. Once it grew beyond a certain size it needed full-time staff, both administrative and teaching, and had a growing need of permanent premises. Thus its recurrent costs increased. It not only needed more money, but a guarantee of the continuing supply of it. Almost without exception in the advanced world the only source of funds with the security and on the scale required, even in those countries where the state, as a matter of principle, does not take all education under its control, has been found to lie in government, whether it be central, provincial or local. In the developing countries, where governments often do not have the resources to meet this need, international organizations, such as UNESCO or the World Bank, or national ones, such as the Canadian International Development Agency, provide large-scale assistance, but without the long-term security needed.

The effect of dependence upon permanent state funding has been to place adult education as firmly under the control of the government as any law could do. By its power to give or withhold money the state can and does weigh heavily even upon the decision making of nongovernmental organizations. In some countries legislation tries to protect educational organizations against this, but if the state does refrain from using its power, it is by a self-denying ordinance, which it can easily renounce, as British experience since the late 1970s demonstrates.

Some governments do refrain, however, whether on principle, under public pressure, or because they are unable or unwilling to commit large-scale public expenditure to adult education. Since the 1960s economic stringency and disappointment that education has not realized the high expectations then placed upon it have made states more careful of their educational budgets. Adult education, less protected by statutory obligation than the school system, has suffered most. There is widespread acceptance that adults should have opportunities for education, but less agreement that it should be free, as for children, and considerable controversy over the proportion of the cost that the state should meet. These are among the issues discussed in the articles on finance in this section. As state-of-the-art papers they are strong on problems, but short on solutions.

The first, *Financing Lifelong Education*, addresses the question of how to distribute public funds available for education so as to provide for extension of learning opportunities throughout life. It considers the sources of finance, public or private; which people or which activities should be the beneficiaries of public funds; and the methods by which such monies might be distributed.

Financing Adult Education examines a narrower field. It makes the point that comparatively little knowledge exists of how adult education is funded and records the main points of what is. It considers the issues of an appropriate balance between public and private finance; who should benefit from subsidies and who does; and how funds are allocated.

Financing Adult Education for Employment reveals clearly that this area of adult education has been subject to closer investigation of its funding than others. It discusses the difficulty of estimating expenditure, treats at some length the role of governments, such problems as the cost and benefits of job-specific and general training, of on-the-job and off-the-job training, and the desirable balance between public and private finance, with special reference to apprenticeships, and paid educational leave.

The last article in the section, *Economics of Nonformal Education*, takes a rather different line. It is concerned with the use of economic analysis as a planning and management tool for educational activities which may be categorized as nonformal. It considers the differences between formal and nonformal education which affect analysis of the latter, and examines the resources available, which are classified as financial, physical, and time. It then considers the meanings and behaviour of costs and the identification of benefits, and proposes the best ways of using cost-effectiveness analysis in planning nonformal education.

Adult Education Legislation in Western Europe

A. Stock

This review of adult education legislation in Western Europe uses a certain definition of legislation and presents, against a brief historical background, an analysis and comparison of some key features of that legislation, based on its treatments of basic rights to education, aims and objectives, organization and structure, finance, staffing, staff training, and educational leave.

"Legislation" is here defined as the constitutional pronouncements of legally elected or appointed governing authorities, relating to the education of adults. Certain countries such as the United Kingdom and the Republic of Ireland enact laws which are essentially frameworks indicating the nature of provision and the duties or powers devolving upon the designated agents of that provision. Further administrative, logistical, or financial details appear in specific regulations which can vary as circumstances require within the terms of the same original laws. By contrast, the laws of certain of the autonomous lander of the Federal Republic of Germany encapsulate fine details of the provision in those particular states including catchment areas, staffing ratios, and financial dispensations.

The complexity of the legislation is further compounded by the contrasting nature of the Western European family of nations: some have highly centralized single-state forms of governance (e.g. France, Sweden), some are unified nation–states made up of diverse cultural, linguistic, or ethnic elements (e.g. Belgium and the United Kingdom), and others are federal entities made up of regional elements with considerable local autonomy (e.g. Austria, Federal Republic of Germany, and Switzerland). In these latter instances, the responsibilities for education lie for the most part with the individual lander or cantons; and in the case of the Federal Republic of Germany and Switzerland relevant laws must be promulgated in the 11 lander and 22 cantons respectively. In fact the attempt to implement a single federal adult education law in Austria (1973) has met many difficulties over the demarcation of responsibilities between federal and provincial governments.

1. Historical Background

It was not until the mid-1960s that West European countries began to pass laws concerned specifically with adult education (e.g. the Netherlands 1965 and Denmark 1968). Before that time, provision for the education of adults was more likely to have been subsumed or implied within the sections of more general education acts, as in the case of England and Wales where the Education Act of 1944 spelt out "further education" duties for the defined local education authorities. Specifically designated adult education laws continued to be developed (or revised) in the 1970s with Norway and Belgium producing most recent versions, both in 1976.

Moreover, during the 1970s there occurred various related legal enactments, such as laws about general or limited rights of educational leave for workers, and laws about professional education and industrial training. Also, in the latter part of the decade, as the economic climate cooled markedly, various new regulations or revised interpretations of earlier laws appeared; often relating to forms of finance to support the growing range of educational offers.

In an attempt to further the development of supportive legislation in all Western European countries, the European Association for Catholic Adult Education produced and published in 1976 a "model" draft adult education act (FEECA 1977), based on international consultation and analysis. Other comparative studies have been undertaken by the European Bureau of Adult Education under the auspices of the Council of Europe (EBAE 1974) and UNESCO (EBAE 1985).

In the 1980s the rate of legislation has slowed down. France, the Federal Republic of Germany, Scotland and Sweden have passed measures which modify existing ones without major changes to the overall shape of their legislation. Portugal and Spain have issued decrees which continue their piecemeal build-up of regulations governing adult education, which they began in the late 1970s. In 1982 Greece issued a decree of popular education, which covered nonformal adult education. There have, however, been no laws on the scale of the French Law on Continuing Education of 1971, or the Norwegian Adult Education Act of 1976. Other states are reviewing existing legislation with a view to reform (England and Wales), or are considering quite new ones (Iceland).

2. Analysis and Comparison

2.1 Basic Rights to Education in Adulthood

Although frequently identified as an essential feature of future legislation, specific reference in existing education laws to the "rights" of adults is, in fact, difficult to find. The laws refer to "adequate facilities" (1944 Act—England and Wales) or to levels of "the offer" of services (as in several German laws). Only in the law of North Rhine/Westphalia is the basic right to general adult education conceded. In Sweden the right to basic or school-equivalent education (also higher education under certain conditions) is accepted, and in several countries (e.g. France, Belgium) rights to professional education and training are included in relevant laws. Moreover the paid education leave laws of France, Sweden, and Belgium imply basic legal rights to certain amounts of general as well as vocational education for working people.

Several national commissions and reports have grappled with this "rights" issue [e.g. the Roelfsema Committee in the Netherlands (1974) and the Advisory Council for Adult and Continuing Education in England and Wales (1982)]; but little has resulted in terms of legislation.

2.2 Aims, Objectives, and Tasks

This is an area of law making where legislative draftspersons (and, no doubt, politicians) appear to have been inspired to lengthy utterances. For the purpose of analysis there appear to be three major groupings of objectives: general; professional/vocational; civic/political/community.

The first objective uses descriptive phrases such as "...gain knowledge and capabilities or to increase them. It shall promote the independence of judgment, stimulate discussion and assist in coping with personal and professional problems" (Lower Saxony Act to promote Adult Education 1970); and again "... This Act shall contribute to providing adult persons with equal opportunities to acquire knowledge, understanding and skill, which will improve the individual's sense of value and personal development and strengthen the basis for independence, achievement and cooperation with others in working and social life" (Norwegian Adult Education Act 1976). Clearly these phrases, quite typical of several pieces of legislation, stress the aspect of self-development ultimately contributing to the betterment of society as well as the individual.

In the second group of objectives—that is professional/vocational education and training—there is much legislation, regulation, and also considerable financial support. The Danish Act of 1968 states unequivocally that "...subsidy will be granted for approved courses, that is courses of study offering leisuretime instruction aiming at a definite field of occupation". Again in the Hesse Act of 1970 "...the objective of folk high schools, residential colleges and educational centres is to provide knowledge and qualifications for social, cultural and professional life". And in the 1976 Norwegian Adult Education Act, the scope of the Act is specifically extended to "Vocational training for adults as part of labour market policy" (Chapter 1, Section 2, paragraph 6). An additional important factor reinforcing these vocational/professional elements of the various acts is the very large amount of finance backing the education and training so engendered. Support finance for individual participants at a rate substantially above social security pay for unemployed persons is a common feature of current provision in the majority of West European countries. Similarly, formulas providing for teaching, materials, and other provision costs are frequently more generous than those appertaining to general academic or cultural provision. The importance of professional and vocational education and training is underlined by the volume of legislation specifically devoted to it. Austria, Denmark, Finland, the Federal Republic of Germany, France, Italy, the Netherlands, Portugal, Spain, Sweden, Switzerland, and the United Kingdom all have such laws (EBAE 1985).

In the third group of objectives, that is, civic/political/community, there is often considerable emphasis within the wording of the relevant legislation, but in few cases is this backed by significant financial dispensation. The Belgium (Flanders) Royal Decree of 1971 states that "...the process of adult education...will enable the recipients to gain a better understanding of themselves and their position, to arrive at a critical appreciation of that position and to avail themselves more rationally and effectively of the opportunities open to them in the community in which they live". The Education Act (England and Wales) 1944 has a similar passage. Also, the Belgian Law (1971) and the Norwegian Act (1976) both stress the importance in organizational as well as objective terms of engaging in "democratic" forms of association. Indeed, the official commentary (OECD 1977) on the Norwegian Act identifies "...the achievement of a higher degree of equality and democratization" as being the "...major political objective" of the Bill put before the Storting, and which (with some minor amendment) subsequently became the Act.

The European Bureau of Adult Education in its study conference held in Norway in December 1972 (EBAE 1974) identified a fourth sector of objectives to which adult education legislation should address itself, namely "priority areas of provision". This aspect, that is, the naming of priorities, is hardly ever found in relevant European laws except in the most general terms; although more recently specific regulations, administrative memoranda, or guidelines offered as administrative interpretations of these various acts have identified particular "target groups" or "priority areas" with increasing frequency; thus special services or dispensations are provided for unemployed persons (UK, France, Denmark) and for those requiring "basic" (UK), "fundamental" (Norway), or "literacy" education. Similarly, special provision for ethnic minorities is often provided by specific administrative fiat deriving from the respective acts (Portugal). Several countries have enacted legislative measures offering a second chance to adults to obtain secondary school qualifications (Norway, Sweden, Denmark, Italy, Spain, and Switzerland).

2.3 Organization and Structure

The several studies previously referred to laid great stress on the legal endorsement of adult education as a full and equal partner with other identified sectors—for example, primary, secondary, and higher education—within the total educational systems of the respective countries. Only in the laws of England and Wales, Scotland, Northern Ireland, Hesse, and Saarland is this stated categorically. The implication is certainly there in the Danish and Norwegian laws; but in relevant French legislation, for example, the emphasis on the "private organizations", whilst appearing as an important element elsewhere, leads to the inference that the "out-of-school" education for adults may be considered to be outside the normal public system of education entirely.

There may be discerned in some countries a tension between the status and provenance of the traditional "voluntary" associations on the one hand and more recently promoted "municipal" (e.g. in Sweden and the Netherlands) provision on the other. But in the 1944 Act of England and Wales there was a particular requirement laid upon each local education authority to "...have regard to any facilities for further education provided for their area by universities, educational associations, and other bodies, and shall consult any such bodies as aforesaid and the local education authorities of adjacent areas".

A very large part of all the extant legislation relates to the responsibilities to be exercised at the various levels of governmental and educational organization, that is, national or state, regional or local. Thus a tabulation of levels of responsibility applying in five of the countries of North West Europe exemplifies this division of responsibility (see Table 1). Whereas there is a strong tendency in other forms of adult education to devolve responsibility to provincial or local authorities, control over vocational responsibility tends to be placed by law with central (United Kingdom, France) or federal governments (Austria, Federal Republic of Germany, Switzerland).

In several of the European adult education legislations there is requirement for the establishment of infrastructural cooperating/coordinating bodies to ensure complementarity of provision, avoidance of wasteful duplication, and also to ensure relevance of the educational offers. The Danish Act (1968) requires that an "...evening school committee" shall be formed and "...should consist of seven to eleven members—representing towns and rural districts—nominated by the county council upon joint recommendation by the educational associations, home economics organizations and other organizations within the county council district that, during the last electoral period...have been active within evening school instruction, and one representative for the leaders of the municipal evening schools nominated by the members of the county youth board". The Further Education Regulations 1969 (England and Wales) state that "...Every authority shall in consultation where appropriate with the Regional Advisory Council for Further Education secure that so far as may be reasonable:

(a) the courses provided by the authority do not duplicate the courses provided in the areas of neighbouring authorities; and

(b) the fees charged by them do not differ substantially from the corresponding fees charged in those areas".

The Lower Saxony (1970) Act provides for the appointment of a Land Committee whose duties include promoting "...the development of adult education by preparing experts' records, reports, arranging surveys...and they give advice to the Minister of Education regarding principles of adult education and its financial promotion".

By administrative regulation possible under their respective Acts, Scotland, the Republic of Ireland, and the Netherlands currently have national Advisory Councils for adult and/or continuing education, though these are not permanent organizational features in those

Table 1
Levels of responsibility for the provision of adult education in North West Europe

Country	Level of responsibility	Provider
Austria	State	Adult education associations
Belgium	State/local authorities	Cultural centres
	State	Adult education associations
Denmark	State/local authorities	Adult education associations
	State/local authorities	Individuals
	State/local authorities	Municipal provision
England and Wales	State/local authorities	Local education authority provision
	State	"Responsible bodies" (i.e. designated universities, Workers' Educational Association, etc.)
	State/local authorities	Other voluntary agencies
Federal Republic of Germany		
Hesse	"Land"/local authorities	Folk high schools
	"Land"	Adult education associations
Saarland	"Land"	Adult education associations

countries. Similar tasks, together with research, development, documentation, production of materials, and training are performed by the respective "national institutes" of Norway, the Netherlands, Federal Republic of Germany (*Pedagogische Arbeitsstelle*), England and Wales, and Scotland. All of these are supported in part or in whole by public finance; and legal provision exists to enable their functions to be funded.

2.4 *Finance, Staffing, Training*

The remaining major concerns of adult education legislative enactment tend to be part of the supporting regulatory structure of law. German legislation tends to be highly specific about full-time staffing, for example, the Lower Saxony Law (1970) spells out the ratios of full-time professional adult education organizers to annual "lesson hour" totals.

The distribution and extent of professional staff may be closely associated with financial disbursements from central, regional, or local government as in several instances the grants are based on proportions of total salary costs or fees charged. This principle applies particularly in the cases of the many relevant subsections of the cantonal educational laws in Switzerland and the "land" law in the Federal Republic of Germany.

The respective Danish and Lower Saxony–Saarland laws have much to say about the status of adult education staff, and their conditions of service—including, in the case of the German laws, the implications of their becoming, on appointment, public civil servants.

Austria, Denmark, England and Wales, Hesse, Lower Saxony, Saarland, and France all have sections of law or regulations allowing for the promotion, support, and requirement for either initial or inservice training or full-time or part-time staff.

Finally, the instrumental factor of public legal rights to educational leave needs outlining. Clearly a universal application of educational leave with or without pay (but guaranteeing return to employment without loss of rights or status) could be an enormous factor in the further development of continuing education for adults.

Only France (the Law of July 1971), Belgium (1973), and Sweden (1975) have broad-based liberal laws of educational leave which could allow for general, academic, or cultural study by individuals as well as vocational or professional training.

Educational leave laws for specific categories of workers exist in the United Kingdom, the Federal Republic of Germany (in Hamburg, Bremen, Hesse, and West Berlin), Italy, and the Netherlands. Even in these "limited" cases there has been considerable stimulus to educational promotion and wider involvement in the relevant fields of provision (e.g. in the United Kingdom, trades union education has been significantly enhanced since the Safety at Work Act and the Protection of Employment Act introduced the right to paid educational leave for trades union representatives).

Such a review of adult education legislation may lead to speculation about its real significance in the progress, extension, and effectiveness of adult education. The general view is that specific legislative endorsement for services, dispensations, and priority provision can help considerably those already committed to gain the support of influential persons in furthering the aims and objectives of adult education activities. It cannot, however, of itself make for effective relevant services.

Bibliography

European Association for Catholic Adult Education (FEECA) *Draft Model Adult Education Act*. FEECA, Bonn

Notes and Studies (Nos. 62/63) 1974 European Bureau of Adult Education, Amersfoort

European Bureau of Adult Education 1985 *Survey of Adult Education*. European Bureau of Adult Education (EBAE), Amersfoort

Organisation for Economic Co-operation and Development (OECD) 1977 *Case Study: The Norwegian Adult Education Act*. OECD, Paris

Notes and Studies (Nos. 55/56) 1973 European Bureau of Adult Education, Amersfoort

Financing Lifelong Education

N. D. Kurland

Most studies of educational financing focus on government financing of education for youth. A few scholars in recent years have addressed issues of public support for adult education. Lifelong education encompasses the education of both youth and adults, viewing education as extending from "the cradle to the grave." The issues associated with the financing of education, that is, both lifelong and lifewide are, therefore, necessarily complex.

Since almost all societies now provide some public support for the education of youth and many support some adult education, the first issue is whether lifelong education is to be financed simply by extending existing arrangements downward to start earlier and upward to allow for participation by older persons in existing traditional arrangements. Both of these adaptations have been made, often without any explicit public decision to do so but because the demand for increased services has developed and institutions have been willing to meet it. This adjustment, however, is not likely to be satisfactory if the demand is very large, since it requires greater resources than most societies are able to devote to education.

The basic issue then becomes how to distribute available public funds so as to provide for extension of learning opportunities throughout life. Must resources for youth be reduced to make more available for adults? Advocates of lifelong education try to strike an intergenerational balance. They argue that it is not an "either–or" situation but one of promoting an appropriate mix that benefits all generations. They claim that children learn best in families and communities in which the parents and other adults are also learners. They also argue that the lifelong learning perspective requires a comprehensive reform of all education so that more education can be delivered throughout life without a proportional increase in the public funds used for education.

But the resource problem cannot be so easily dodged: educating more people for longer periods during their lives than at present will cost more than without such increases. The advocates of lifelong education, therefore, have had to try to show that, through appropriate reorganization of the way education is delivered and through the reconceptualization of what is meant by education, some of the problems of financing lifelong education can be met. As long as there is to be some public involvement in the financing of lifelong education, the classic finance issues must be addressed: the sources of finance, the beneficiaries, and the allocation of funds among contending claimants.

1. Sources of Finance

Lifelong education does not inherently require any different form of taxation than traditional education. However, the following should be borne in mind:

(a) Adults may earn their living and pay income taxes under one jurisdiction, shop and pay sales taxes primarily under another, reside and pay property taxes under a third, and pay education taxes under a fourth. Education programs that rely primarily on a local tax base may, therefore, not raise taxes from the people who seek to participate in those programs.

(b) Adults are more mobile than children, particularly over the time span relevant to lifelong education. Thus, adults may pay taxes in one locality for many years and, when they are ready to undertake study, may find themselves in a different locality. They may have paid taxes in the former in the expectation of someday benefiting from its lifelong education program, only to find that in their new location there is no such program.

Another factor that distinguishes adults from children is that many adults or their employers are able and willing to pay a larger share of the cost of education than is the case with youth. In recognition of this factor a number of countries, such as France, the United Kingdom, and Sweden, levy special payroll taxes for the education and training of workers.

There is another circumstance that distinguishes lifelong education from youth education and adult education and that is the relationship between generations. It is generally held that the parental generation pays for the education of the children. Education is thus conceived as an investment in a nation's future. In lifelong education the parental generation must pay both for the education of the children and for its own education. This circumstance raises the issue of the beneficiaries of education.

2. The Beneficiaries

The problem of determining who should be the beneficiaries of the public support of lifelong education is difficult. For all countries, but particularly those where funds for public enterprises of any kind are limited, the issue of whether lifelong education is an investment or consumption expenditure is critical. No discussion of the financing of lifelong education can avoid grappling with this issue and trying to develop criteria for deciding which forms of education for which parts of the populace will produce the greatest benefits for the society. Trade-offs are inevitable, as when a society must decide whether to educate a small number of engineers in the hope that they will help strengthen the total economy or to bring larger numbers of people up to some minimal level of literacy in the hope that they will provide a broad base for economic development and political stability.

These trade-off questions raise the further issue of equity among different groups in society. To put the issue in an extreme form: should society provide most of its support to those adults who went further in their early schooling because their greater earlier effort should be rewarded and because they have the greatest potential for providing a good return to society for further investment in their education? Or, should society provide most of its support to those who got the least education while young on the grounds that the well-being of society requires that all citizens be helped to achieve some minimum level of educational attainment and that equity should be measured not in terms of opportunity but in terms of outcome?

Most advocates of lifelong education have been in favor of using public subsidies to help those adults who are farthest behind in their educational attainment. Thus, there is heavy emphasis on literacy training in public financing schemes, and it is regularly pointed out that the participants in nonsubsidized adult education tend to be better educated, younger, and have higher incomes than nonparticipants.

However, if equity of either access or attainment is an ideal, there is the problem of deciding what time span should be taken into account in determining whether or not an individual has received equitable treatment. So difficult is this question that Levin (1977) has concluded that the only way to achieve equity is to use a financing arrangement that provides a lifelong educational subsidy or entitlement to each individual and then to allow the individuals to distribute that amount over their lifetime for educational purposes that they judge best for themselves.

A variation on the entitlement concept has been proposed by Rehn (1973) who would link unemployment insurance and educational entitlements so that instead of receiving unemployment benefits during times when work is unavailable, workers would be encouraged to take educational benefits to further their education and enhance their skills in preparation for a return to the workforce.

Nolfi (1977) has proposed that a test of educational and economic disadvantagement should be carried out at the time of entry into an educational endeavor to determine whether or not a public subsidy should be granted. Others would use public funds to create open access opportunities at low or no charge to users, much as public library services are provided in some countries. Allocation would essentially be on a first-come first-served basis. This has generally been the approach of community colleges in the United States.

As can be seen from this brief discussion of who benefits, the answer very much depends upon the methods used to allocate subsidies among claimants. Or, to put it the other way round, the choice among methods of allocation very much depends on who the beneficiaries of public subsidy are intended to be: those most in need, those most able to benefit, or anyone who has the inclination to participate.

3. Allocation of Funds

The methods by which public funds can be distributed are numerous. Three have already been noted: general entitlements, needs-based student aid, and general institutional support. These exemplify the four basic alternatives:

(a) Funds can be made available to individuals who will use them to purchase educational services. These may be in the form of grants, loans, loan guarantees, or various forms of tax adjustments.

(b) Funds can be made available to specific categories of individuals or institutions for specific purposes such as literacy education or job training.

(c) Funds can be given to institutions to enable them to offer services at reduced or no cost to individuals.

(d) The tax system can be used as a way to support lifelong education either by giving tax benefits to learners directly or to employers to encourage them to provide educational opportunities, such as on-the-job training and paid educational leave.

The possible variations and combinations of these alternatives are great. In the United States each of the states has its own unique arrangement. This is not to imply that each state has adopted a system of lifelong education. However, as a special project of the Education Commission of the States is showing, most states are moving in this direction. They are impelled by the triple forces of changing demography, movement into the age of information, and heightened public demand for lifelong education. If the United States experience is indicative of worldwide trends, all societies are going to have to grapple with the problems of financing lifelong education.

Bibliography

Holmes B, Ryba R 1973 *Recurrent Education: Concepts and Policies for Lifelong Education*. Proc. of the Comparative Education Society in Europe. Bury Times, Bury

Kurland N D (ed.) 1977 *Entitlement Papers*. United States Department of Health, Education, and Welfare, Washington, DC

Kurland N D 1980 Alternative financing arrangements for lifelong education. In: Cropley A J (ed.) 1980 *Towards a System of Lifelong Education: Some Practical Considerations*. UNESCO, Hamburg

Levin H 1977 Post-secondary entitlements: An exploration. In: Kurland N D (ed.) 1977

Mushkin S J (ed.) 1973 *Recurrent Education*. Georgetown University Conf., 1973. National Institute of Education, Washington, DC

Nolfi G J 1977 A national adult recurrent education entitlement voucher program: Financing open learning and continuing education through selective entitlements. In: Kurland N D (ed.) 1977

Rehn G 1973 Towards flexibility in working life. In: Mushkin S J (ed.) 1973

von Moltke K, Schneevoigt N 1977 *Educational Leaves for Employees: European Experience for American Consideration*. Jossey-Bass, San Francisco, California

Windham D M, Kurland N D, Levinsohn F H 1978 Financing the learning society. *Sch. Rev.* 86(3): whole issue

Financing Adult Education

M. Woodhall

The term "adult education" refers to a wide range of educational activities in which adults take part and includes vocational education and training, nonvocational courses, correspondence education, and full-time and part-time courses. Because of the very wide range of educational activities included in the term "adult education" there are a wide variety of financing methods and mechanisms adopted in different countries. It is frequently very difficult to obtain accurate information about the finance of adult education because so many different agencies or institutions are involved, both public and private funds are used, educational cost statistics do not always distinguish between adult education and the regular provision of education for children and young people, and it is sometimes difficult to distinguish between adult education and sporting activities. For all these reasons it is difficult to give an accurate description of how adult education is financed around the world. This article summarizes the information available and the research carried out on the financing of adult education. However, it must be emphasized that much less information is available about the financing of adult education than about the finance of the regular school and higher education system.

1. Information About the Financing of Adult Education

The Organisation for Economic Co-operation and Development (OECD) carried out a series of studies on adult education which was published in 1977 and attempted to collect statistics and quantitative evidence about the magnitude and characteristics of adult education in a number of OECD member countries. The reason for this study was that OECD felt that "Few countries have as yet formed comprehensive policies for adult education and, in general the field lacks the capital and personnel resources to satisfy adult learning needs in a comprehensive and systematic fashion. One reason for the material weakness of adult education is that public authorities can seldom refer to statistical and other data which would enable them to formulate realistic policies" (OECD 1977 p. 4).

It was to overcome this shortage of information that case studies were commissioned by the OECD on adult education in Austria, Canada, Denmark, the Federal Republic of Germany, Italy, Netherlands, Sweden, the United Kingdom, and the United States. However, the conclusion of the study was that the case studies "confirm that remarkably little information is available about the financing of adult education. . . although crucially important, it is a subject which has escaped the attention of researchers. . . . As the public authorities spend more money on adult education so they become more interested in the economics of adult education. But the dearth of solid information remains and what there is does not easily lend itself to comparative treatment" (OECD 1977 p. 17).

The difficulties of collecting information on financing adult education were summarized, in this OECD study, as follows:

(a) Adult education programmes are often run by agencies for which adult education is a secondary or incidental concern. For example, universities which run extramural courses often do not keep information on costs apart from teachers' salaries.

(b) The proportion of central or local government expenditure that is allocated to adult education may be "so small a percentage of the gross expenditure on education that it is not worthwhile administratively to keep a separate account" (OECD 1977 p. 18).

(c) It is difficult to disentangle central and local government contributions to public programmes of adult education.

(d) The responsibility for administering adult education programmes frequently falls on individuals, such as trade union officials, for whom adult education is only a peripheral part of their work.

(e) There is a danger of double counting when public authorities give grants to nongovernmental education agencies for adult education, and both donors and recipients include these in their total expenditure figures.

(f) Many institutions support adult education indirectly, for example public libraries may supply accommodation for classes and may provide many other services, as well as providing books for participants, yet it is difficult to separate this from other activities.

(g) No information is available on the payments by individuals for books or other direct expenditures, let alone the indirect costs such as earnings forgone or travel expenses.

For all these reasons, the OECD study concludes with a plea for more research: "Before national policies for the promotion of adult education can be formulated with any precision it is obvious that detailed information is required about the present scale of expenditure and the means employed for financing programmes. Decisions about the state's share of costs vis-à-vis private agencies, or about which agencies should receive financial support, or about the extent to which the participants themselves should bear the economic costs hinge upon knowing the facts of the present situation" (OECD 1977 p. 19). The following summary of patterns of financing is thus based on admittedly inadequate data.

2. The Main Sources of Finance

In most countries finance for adult education is provided from both public and private sources. Central and local governments frequently provide funds either out of general taxation or, in a few cases, out of specific, earmarked taxes. General sources of government revenue, which may be used to provide subsidies for adult education, include income and expenditure taxes, customs and excise duties, grants or loans from foreign governments or international agencies which provide foreign aid, other forms of government borrowing and government income from property, and investments or profits from state-owned enterprises. In addition, some countries have specific, earmarked taxes which are used to finance education, for example local property taxes or, in some cases, lotteries which are organized to raise money for education.

In a very few cases there are specific taxes earmarked for adult education. For example, in Sweden, employers pay a special payroll tax which is used to finance vocational training and other forms of adult education, and in France there is a compulsory payroll tax which is used to finance a system of training funds. In the United Kingdom between 1964 and 1973 there was a compulsory levy-grant system under which employers in some industries had to pay a special training levy, and in some cases received a grant towards the costs of industrial training. This system was replaced in 1973 by a levy-exemption scheme under which employers who could demonstrate that they were financing training of adequate quality and quantity could claim exemption from the levy.

Apart from public funds for adult education there are three main sources of private funds. In many countries the main responsibility for financing adult education falls on the churches, religious organizations, cultural or other voluntary organizations, or local community organizations such as chambers of trade or commerce, which provide voluntary contributions or assistance for adult education. In other cases political organizations and trade unions provide funds for adult education on a voluntary basis.

Another important source of finance for adult education is the employer. Employers may provide paid leave for workers to enable them to attend educational courses, and may pay fees for courses which workers attend either during working hours or in their leisure hours. Employers may also pay fees for correspondence courses for their employees. There is a growing trend towards the provision of paid educational leave for employees in some countries, for example Italy, and there have been a number of recent surveys of the extent of paid educational leave, or educational leave of absence as it is called in some countries (OECD 1976a, Killeen and Bird 1981).

The third main source of funds for adult education is the individual participant who may pay tuition fees or purchase books, equipment, or materials, and usually this is the most difficult source of finance to quantify. Fees for adult education vary enormously in different countries and in different institutions. In some cases adult education is provided free or is highly subsidized by central or local government, and fees are low or negligible. In other cases adults are expected to pay fees which cover the full costs.

In the United States a study showed that the majority of the participants in adult education finance their own activities. Of the students questioned, 55 percent gave self or family as their main source of finance while employers provided finance for 25 percent of the students and public funding was the main source of finance for only 18 percent (OECD 1977 p. 402).

3. The Balance Between Public and Private Finance for Adult Education

In some countries the case for public subsidy of adult education rests mainly on grounds of equity. The Swedish government, for example, argues that "It is natural that adult learners should be eligible in principle for the same tuition-free instruction and at least the same study benefits (i.e. financial aid for students) when taking the same types of courses as their younger counterparts". Thus in Sweden there are no tuition fees for adult education courses, which are provided in study circles organized by the local branches of Sweden's educational associations, or in municipal adult schools, folk high schools, or for vocational courses for unemployed adults organized by the National Labour Market Board and the National Board of Education. Adults may also be entitled to receive grants or loans to compensate for loss of earnings while they are studying.

The justification for this is that adults should not be treated less favourably than children and young people, who are entitled to free tuition. However, it is recognized that the policy of offering financial assistance to adults might impose a considerable burden on public funds and the regulations state that: "Resources are limited, and not all those formally entitled to this benefit will be able to receive it in reality. Priority is therefore given to those with the greatest need of education and assistance" (CSN 1981 p. 7).

This makes it clear that the main objective of the policy of subsidizing adult education in Sweden is one of intergenerational equity, as a government publication on adult education explains: "Adult education should provide older people who received little formal education in their youth. . . the opportunity to raise their level of general knowledge to that of today's young people, who have access to at least nine years of schooling and most often eleven or more" (Swedish Institute 1976). However the argument that if young people are entitled to free education then older groups should also be entitled to the same benefit raises the question of the purpose of subsidies for schooling. One of the main arguments for subsidizing education is an economic one. Since education brings financial benefits both to individuals and to society in the form of increased productivity and earnings, there is a case for subsidizing it if the social benefits exceed the private benefits, in order to prevent underinvestment. Economists argue that the social benefits of education do exceed the private benefits because of "spillover effects".

When this argument is applied to the question of subsidies for adult education, however, it raises some awkward issues. For example, should a distinction be made between vocational and nonvocational courses, on the grounds that vocational education for adults may raise their future productivity, whereas nonvocational courses will not? Should charges be levied for courses which are largely recreational?

This is still a matter of controversy in many countries, and the controversy was succinctly summarized in the report of a government committee which reported on adult education in the United Kingdom in 1973 (the Russell Report): "At one extreme it is argued that adult education should be regarded as a social service and provided free. It makes an important contribution to the well-being of the community and is a valuable public investment.... Adult education is regarded as a 'second chance' for those who received the minimum of education in their youth and who later wish to improve themselves for their own benefit and for the benefit of society.... At the other extreme there are those who regard adult education as a luxury and who believe that those who benefit from it should be expected to meet the economic costs" (DES 1973 pp.102–03).

In practice, the majority of countries adopt a middle way, and financing policies reflect the fact that adult education is regarded as a public investment which should be subsidized, but one which must compete for resources with other public services.

It also reflects the fact that while adult education represents a second chance for some participants, it is perhaps a luxury for others, and therefore contributions in the form of tuition fees should be levied in many cases. Thus many governments would agree with the final conclusion of the Russell Report: "Unlike school children the majority of the consumers of adult education have salaries, wages, or other income and can afford to make a contribution towards the cost of their courses. The claims for increased expenditure on public education are pressing and an established source of income like student fees could not easily be foregone". Nevertheless the report recommended that "Adult education should be readily available to all who wish to take advantage of it: therefore, student contributions should be set at such a level as would not discourage any significant number or category of people from making use of the provision and special arrangements should be made for those who might be deprived of the opportunity to attend classes because of their inability to pay" (DES 1973 p. 103).

4. *The Beneficiaries of Subsidies for Adult Education*

Because of this combination of objectives of financing policies there are, in most countries, selective policies which favour a variety of beneficiaries. For example in the United Kingdom, pensioners, handicapped adults, or the unemployed frequently pay reduced fees for courses organized by local education authorities, whereas other adults must pay substantially higher fees. In other countries governments subsidize particular types of adult education more heavily than others, and vocational training for the unemployed is usually more generously subsidized than other forms of adult education. Some countries deliberately favour those who most need a "second chance". For example, the system of grants for adult education in Sweden is intended to discriminate in favour of the most disadvantaged adults: "Competition is stiff and experience shows that the only applicants who are normally granted assistance are those who: (a) have only a basic seven-year or nine-year schooling behind them, (b) have been gainfully employed for at least ten years, (c) are at least thirty years old" (CSN 1981 p. 7).

However, studies of participation in adult education in several countries show that despite these aims it is not those with the lowest levels of formal education who are most likely to benefit from subsidies. Research in France and in the United States confirms this, and the OECD report on adult education concludes "The key determinant of participation is the level of previous education: the higher the level the more likely there will be participation (in adult education). In general, participants come from the higher socio-economic groups, especially from the professional classes".

This same study suggests that participants, on the whole, live in high-income residential areas, women outnumber men in nonvocational courses, whereas the reverse is true for vocational education, and younger people outnumber older people. "The fact that participation in adult education is mainly a middle-class phenomenon is now so well-established that policy makers and educational administrators spend considerable time discussing ways and means of attracting the attention of adults with a low educational attainment, especially those classified as 'the underprivileged'" (OECD 1977 p. 16).

In order to concentrate subsidies on the more disadvantaged, one policy, adopted in some countries, is to subsidize particular institutions or courses which cater for them. For example, in the United Kingdom, the government has made special grants for adult literacy teaching. In 1975 the Adult Literacy Resource Agency (ALRA) was set up to stimulate literacy teaching and the number of adults attending such courses rose from 5,000 in 1973 to 70,000 in 1979. The government regarded the grants to ALRA as a "pump-priming effort". Between 1975 and 1978 specific government grants were provided for adult literacy teaching, but this central funding was withdrawn after 1978, when local education authorities were expected to finance literacy teaching together with other forms of adult education (see *Adult Literacy in Developed Countries*).

5. *The Distribution of Finance for Adult Education*

This policy of providing central government funding for a specific type of adult education for a limited period, in order to stimulate and assist the establishment of new courses or institutions is one way of distributing subsidies that has been used in several countries. Another way is for central government to provide a proportion of the funds to institutions but to leave local or state governments or voluntary agencies to provide the remainder. The OECD study cited earlier found that in the United States "Most of the federal government programmes require some matching funds from the states or other participating institutions. For example, for every federal dollar provided by the Agriculture Department for the Co-operative Extension Service, $1.38 is provided by co-operating state, local and other agencies" (OECD 1977 p. 403).

In the case of vocational training for adults, government funds are distributed either to training schools or colleges to enable them to meet all or some of the costs of tuition, or to individuals, to enable them to pay tuition fees, or to employers, to cover part or all of the costs of training provided for their employees. Some countries, such as Sweden, provide the bulk of vocational training for unemployed adults in public institutions, whereas others, such as Australia, provide public subsidies to employers to encourage them to train more workers. In Canada in some instances the government uses spare capacity in employers' premises for training the unemployed, so that the costs of training are shared between government and employers, although the bulk of training for the unemployed is provided in public institutions, and financed under the Canada Manpower Training Program.

In some cases, institutions are given earmarked funds for adult education. For example, universities may be given special funds for extramural courses. However, in many countries government finance for adult education is provided as part of the general funding of all educational activities, and this sometimes means that the competing claims of other sectors of education result in a very small share of the total going to adult education. A study of adult education in the United Kingdom concluded that "adults taking nonvocational courses, who represent more than 20 percent of the total number of young people in full-time education, receive less than 1 percent of total educational resources" (Woodhall in OECD 1977 p. 355).

Thus, although it is very difficult to obtain a comprehensive picture of the funding of adult education, the general impression that emerges from case studies or international comparisons can be summed up by the conclusion of an OECD study:

> Only a few countries have enunciated an explicit administrative and financial policy on adult education. In most countries, it is not given the resources of a front-rank public service and its provision tends to be fragmentary, underfinanced and understaffed. (OECD 1976b p. 6)

Bibliography

Centrala Studiestöds Nämnden (CSN) 1982 *A Survey of National Benefits for Students*. CSN, Sundsvall

Department of Education and Science (DES) 1973 *Adult Education: A Plan for Development*. Report by a Committee of Inquiry under the chairmanship of Sir Lionel Russell (Russell Report). Her Majesty's Stationery Office, London

Killeen J, Bird M 1981 *Education and Work: A Study of Paid Educational Leave in England and Wales (1976/77)*. National Institute of Adult Education, Leicester

Organisation for Economic Co-operation and Development (OECD) 1976a *Developments in Educational Leave of Absence*. OECD, Paris

Organisation for Economic Co-operation and Development (OECD) 1976b *Comprehensive Policies for Adult Education*. OECD, Paris

Organisation for Economic Co-operation and Development (OECD) 1977 *Learning Opportunities for Adults*, Vol. 4: *Participation in Adult Education*. OECD, Paris

Swedish Institute *Adult Education in Sweden*. (Fact Sheets on Sweden FS64). Swedish Institute, Stockholm

Financing Adult Education for Employment

M. Woodhall

Vocational and industrial education and training takes many forms. In the past, the bulk of all vocational and industrial education was provided on the job by employers for their own workers. The costs of this education and training were shared between the employers, who provided personnel, equipment, and other facilities, and the trainees, who accepted low wages during the period of training. For many workers the period of vocational education and training was long and it consisted largely of observation and imitation of a skilled worker, either as part of a formal apprenticeship, or through an informal period of training. However, as the skill requirements of the jobs became more complex, the need for more formal types of vocational education and training was widely accepted. Vocational schools were established, and new types of combined on-the-job and off-the-job training were created. The questions of the means of finance, the relative contributions of employers, workers, and government funds, the distribution of costs and benefits of vocational education and industrial training, and the policy and institutional implications of alternative financing mechanisms have attracted increasing attention. Throughout the world governments have become increasingly involved in the provision and financing of vocational education and training, both because of its importance for economic and manpower policy and because of increasing concern about the need to share the costs and benefits of education and training equitably.

Studies of the financing of vocational education and training have been concerned with such issues as:

(a) The overall level of resources devoted to vocational education and training; and the adequacy of resources for sufficient quantity and quality of training to meet personnel needs.

(b) The distribution of resources between general and vocational education, between different types and levels of education, between general training and training for specific jobs, between different groups of workers, and between on-the-job and off-the-job training.

(c) The distribution of the costs and benefits of vocational education and training and the profitability of training as an investment for employers, for individual workers, and for the community as a whole.

(d) The role of the government and the reasons for government intervention. Should it take the form of legislative action and regulation of training, or should it take the form of financial intervention, through taxation and payment of subsidies to employers or individual workers, or should the government be involved in the actual provision of vocational education and training?

(e) The effectiveness and implications of different financial mechanisms, for example payroll taxes, training levies, and the payment of selective subsidies for training. What are the economic and educational consequences of different methods of financing vocational education and industrial training?

In some cases, also, there have been extensive studies of particular types or methods of vocational education and training, including apprenticeship and the provision of retraining opportunities for unemployed workers, or paid educational leave for employees.

Economists have also been much concerned with the question of whether the distinction between general and vocational education is valid. Since general education also prepares students or pupils for employment, the distinction between general and vocational education may be misleading, and one writer goes so far as to call the emphasis on vocational education in some developing countries the "vocational school fallacy in development planning" (Foster 1965). Much of this debate is not particularly concerned with the financing of education and training; however, the question of how the financing of education should be shared between the government, employers, and workers is sometimes linked with arguments about the distinction between general and vocational education even though, as Blaug argues, much confusion is created by:

> ...the conventional distinction between academic and vocational education. This distinction, which is actually grounded in the nature of the two curricula, is allowed to carry the implication that some education prepares students for the world of work and some does not. All too frequently, however, those who have taken courses of study generally called "academic"...reap substantial financial returns from their education, thus producing the paradoxical conclusion that academic education has a greater "vocational" value than vocational education. The traditional distinction was developed by educators but the labour market has its own way of appraising qualifications. (Blaug 1972 p. 247)

Controversies about the distinction between general and vocational education, and similarly controversies about the distinction between education and training fall outside the scope of this article, although they may impinge upon debates about how education should be financed.

1. Resources Devoted to Vocational Education and Training

It is difficult to estimate the total costs of vocational education and industrial training, since employers do not necessarily keep accurate records of the time or expenditure devoted to on-the-job training, and it is difficult to estimate the contribution of individual trainees, since this would require estimates of the value of their productive work and the distribution of their time between learning and producing. An early study of the costs of industrial training in the United States by Mincer estimated that the total opportunity cost of vocational training, including informal "learning by doing" as well as formal training programmes was over US$16 billion in 1958; about US$10 billion of this represented the cost of training in private firms or corporate enterprises, and approximately 70 percent of this was the result of informal on-the-job training and only 30 percent was attributable to formal training programmes (Mincer 1962).

However, there are many practical and conceptual difficulties involved in estimating the total costs of vocational education and industrial training. Data from enterprises is often nonexistent or inaccurate, and it is difficult to find estimates of the value of the productive work of trainees; for example, one study of the costs of training in the engineering industry in the United Kingdom produced estimates of the value of the output of trainees which ranged from zero to 60 percent of the output of a skilled worker in a trainee's second year of training, and 25 to 85 percent in the third year. To estimate the opportunity cost of training would require such estimates of the productive value of trainees' work, in order to compare this with the actual earnings of trainees. As a result of the difficulties of such an exercise there have been few attempts to measure the resources devoted to vocational education and training, although very rough estimates suggest that the total costs of industrial training may be as much as a third or a half of total expenditure on education. Estimates of the costs of vocational education and training in the United Kingdom suggest that in 1970 this amounted to roughly half the total expenditure on full-time formal education (Woodhall 1977), and a recent review of training in the United Kingdom concluded: "The cost of education is about £9,000 million per annum (in Great Britain). It is hard to put a boundary around vocational training activities but a rough estimate would put the cost at about £3,000 million a year" (Johnson 1979 p. 1093).

Nevertheless, there is a feeling in many countries that not enough resources have been invested in vocational education and training, particularly during periods of recession. The result of such underinvestment in training may be a shortage of skilled workers when there is an increase in economic activity. It is in order to stimulate investment in vocational education and training, and to avoid such shortages, that governments in many countries have become increasingly involved in the financing or provision of vocational education. In some cases, governments have simply provided a legislative or regulatory framework for the redistribution of the costs of training, for example by means of a levy–grant system. In other cases governments have provided direct subsidies to encourage investment in vocational education and training.

2. The Role of Government in the Financing of Vocational Education and Training

Traditionally, the finance and the provision of vocational education and training has been the responsibility of employers who, in some cases, have passed on to trainees the direct costs of training. It has been assumed that employers will invest in training if it is profitable in terms of increased productivity of workers, or necessary in order to achieve desired levels of output and efficiency. In such cases, there is no obvious need for government activity. Regulations governing safety or standards of training have, in many cases, been the sole form of government involvement. However, in recent decades government involvement has increased, partly in order to link vocational education and training more closely to general economic and employment policies, partly because of a growing concern with questions about the distribution of training opportunities or with underinvestment in training, from the point of view of the economy as a whole.

In many countries, the role of government has widened, in order to increase the supply of training opportunities, either as a part of general economic or manpower policy, or as a countercyclical measure, or as a part of regional policy. In some countries governments have tried to improve the transition from school to working life by developing closer links between formal education and industrial training, or by improving the quality of vocational education and training. In other cases, government involvement has developed because of a concern about the distribution of the costs and benefits of vocational education and training.

For example, in the United Kingdom the Industrial Training Act was passed in 1964 with the threefold aim of increasing the amount of training in industry, improving its quality, and redistributing the costs of training more fairly between firms, by means of a levy–grant system. The Act created 30 industrial-training boards, whose function was to stimulate training activity and reallocate the costs of training by imposing a compulsory levy on firms, in proportion to their total expenditure on wages and salaries, and distributing a series of training grants to firms which provided training. The purpose of the levy–grant system was to redistribute the costs of training by ensuring that all firms contributed towards the costs of training regardless of whether they actually provided training. The levies imposed by the industrial-training boards ranged from under one percent to over three percent of total wages and salaries, and in addition to the operation of the levy–grant system, industrial-training boards provided advice and guidance to firms on industrial training and set quality standards. There is evidence that this system of "sticks and carrots", designed to stimulate and regulate training, did increase the quantity of training provided in the United Kingdom. However, the industrial-training boards and the Industrial Training Act were subject to considerable criticism (Woodhall 1974).

The compulsory levy–grant system of the Industrial Training Act was replaced in 1974 by a selective levy–grant system involving exemptions for small firms, or firms judged by the industrial-training boards to be providing adequate training for their own labour needs. This meant that the levies were no longer compulsory, but were imposed on firms which provided no training for their own employees, or provided only very limited training, or training judged to be of poor quality. In other words, the levies were more in the nature of a "fine" imposed on firms for underinvesting in training, than a "tax" which could be used to help finance training.

Another example of a selective levy–grant system was proposed in the Federal Republic of Germany by the Edding Commission on the costs and financing of vocational training, which reported in 1974. As a result of these proposals, a new law was passed in 1976, the law on the promotion of new training places (*Ausbildungsplatzforderungsgestz*), which allowed a levy–grant system to be created if the supply of training places in industry was insufficient for the future needs of the economy. Thus, the policy was based on the principle that industry should be responsible for recruiting and training sufficient personnel, and that government intervention would be justified only if there was a shortage of training opportunities. However, this scheme has now been withdrawn.

In many countries, however, there has been a debate about whether more permanent government intervention is needed, and in some cases legislation has been introduced to provide a permanent mechanism for redistributing the costs of training or for increasing investment in vocational education and training. In France, for example, there is a compulsory system of training funds and an apprenticeship tax, so that all firms must pay a proportion of their total wages and salaries as a payroll tax, and these funds are used to finance vocational education and training. In Sweden employers must pay a special employment tax which is used to finance vocational education for adults.

In other countries the government provides subsidies to encourage training, and the costs of these are met out of general taxation. For example, in Australia, the Commonwealth Rebate for Apprenticeship Full-time Training (CRAFT) is a subsidy which is intended to reimburse employers for part of the costs of apprenticeship training.

In some other countries, however, the government role is wider and includes the provision of vocational education and training in public institutions, rather than subsidies towards the cost of training provided by employers. In Canada, for example, the bulk of the training financed under the Canada Manpower Training Program is provided in public institutions, such as community colleges or vocational education centres, but in some cases the government may finance training which is provided on employers' premises.

In many countries initial vocational education is provided in schools and other public institutions and this is financed in exactly the same way as general education, by means of national or local taxation. In the Federal Republic of Germany a dual system of vocational education has developed, with vocational education taking place partly in vocational schools, which are financed out of public funds, and partly by means of on-the-job training, provided and financed by employers. The training provided by employers is subject to various government regulations, under the Vocational Education Act of 1969, and all young trainees under the age of 18 are obliged to attend a vocational school on a part-time basis, in addition to receiving on-the-job training. Thus, in the Federal Republic of Germany the responsibility for providing and financing vocational education and training is shared between government and employers. Austria, too, has developed a dual system of vocational education. In other countries it is only a minority of young workers who are enrolled in formal apprenticeship programmes whose training is jointly financed in this way.

In some countries there have been debates about the desirability or need for a permanent system of collective funding for vocational education and training, with the costs being shared between government and employers. In the United Kingdom proposals were put forward in 1976 for a system of collective funding which would be jointly financed by employers and government, and would have as its main objective "the achievement of a high and stable intake into training for skills of vital importance to the economy" (United Kingdom Department of Employment 1976 p. 16). The main argument for a system of collective funding was that training in transferable skills, that is, skills which are needed in more than one specific job, benefits the whole economy, and not just one employer. Therefore the costs of training should be shared between employers and the community as a whole. However, the proposals for a system of collective funding for transferable skills which were put forward in the United Kingdom in 1976 did not gain acceptance at that time, although the government, through the Manpower Services Commission, has become increasingly involved in the financing of training for key skills, that is, skills which are regarded as vitally important for the economy and are likely to be in short supply. Training grants, financed out of public funds, have been provided to encourage employers to take on additional trainees.

In many countries some system of subsidies or grants is provided by the government to stimulate training by employers, and this has been increasing in recent years. Another area of increasing government involvement is the finance and provision of vocational education and training for the unemployed. Partly as a result of the worldwide recession of the 1970s and early 1980s and the growing problem of unemployment particularly among young people, and partly because of a growing awareness of the economic importance of vocational education and training, there has been a general trend towards increased government involvement in both the finance and the provision of training, and a gradual shift in many countries in the balance of resources contributed by government, employers, and trainees.

The question of how the costs of training should be shared between government, employers, and individuals raises the question of who benefits from expenditure on training. Vocational education and training, like other forms of education and training, is an investment in human capital which brings benefits in the form of enhanced productivity, and higher levels of output and earnings. These benefits are enjoyed by the individual, by his or her employer, and by the community at large. However, the way in which the costs and benefits of education and training are distributed between the individual, the employer, and the taxpayer raises many issues and depends, partly, on the nature of the training, and particularly on whether it is general or specific.

3. *General and Specific Training*

One of the earliest attempts to analyse expenditure on education and training as a form of investment in human capital was by the United States economist, Gary Becker, who drew the distinction between general and specific training. Becker (1964) argued that the costs of general training, which increases the potential productivity of a worker in a wide range of jobs, in many different enterprises, will be borne mainly by the worker, in the form of lower wages, that is to say, forgone earnings, during the period of training. Specific training, on the other hand, increases the worker's productivity only in one job or a narrow range of jobs in a single firm or enterprise. Therefore the employer will be willing to bear the costs of specific training, in the expectation of the benefits, in the form of higher levels of future output (Becker 1964). In practice, of course, it is seldom possible to differentiate completely between general and specific training; it will depend not only on the content of the training but on mobility of labour and other conditions in the labour market, and trade-union bargaining will influence the distribution of costs between employers and employees. Moreover, Becker's analysis was concerned with on-the-job training whereas much vocational education and training takes place off the job, as well as on the job, and the question of how this is financed raises even more questions. Nevertheless, the distinction between general and specific training is an important one, and it is likely to determine, at least in part, the extent to which employers are willing to finance vocational training.

The increasing involvement of governments in the finance and provision of training in many countries is on the grounds that much of the vocational education and training provided for new entrants to the labour market, or for unemployed workers, is general training which will benefit the whole community and in this context the term "training for transferable skills" is often used. It is argued that while employers will be willing to finance specific training, or training for their own immediate needs, there is a need for governments to help finance training for wider needs. For example a discussion document produced by the United Kingdom government distinguishes between five different types, or levels, of training:

(a) training arranged by particular employers to meet their own immediate or foreseeable needs;

(b) training going beyond the obvious needs of particular employers but necessary to meet the foreseeable needs of an industry as a whole;

(c) training given to individuals to meet national economic needs, going beyond the obvious needs of particular industries;

(d) training given to individuals to enable them to take new—or better—jobs which they cannot get without first acquiring new skills; and

(e) the contribution of education.

Different methods of finance are appropriate for these five different types of vocational education and training. The first, in most countries, is the responsibility of the employers who finance and provide the training themselves. The second may require a sharing of financial responsibility between different firms or enterprises within an industry, for example, through the levy–grant system operated by the industrial-training boards in the United Kingdom. However, for the other types of training listed, there is likely to be an increasing proportion of the costs of training which are met by central, state, or local government, on the grounds that the training benefits the whole community.

In the case of training given to individuals to enable them to take new jobs, this may be financed directly by the government, which provides free training places in public institutions, or it may be financed indirectly by means of training allowances to individuals, to enable them to meet the costs of vocational training, as part of the general policy on student aid. However, even if individuals are given grants or loans to help them to finance vocational education and training, some part of the opportunity cost will fall on the individual in the form of forgone earnings, although the opportunity cost of training for the unemployed may be very low.

4. The Choice between On-the-job and Off-the-job Training

The precise way in which the costs of different types of vocational education and training should be shared between individuals, employers, and government is still a matter of controversy in many countries, together with the question of how much training is general and how much is specific, and how much should be provided on the job and how much in vocational schools or other institutions.

A study for the World Bank reviewed the literature on these questions, including 54 studies of industrial training in both developed and developing countries and concluded:

> The survey of the literature raised more questions than it answered and uncovered no universally applicable solution to the problem of whether vocational school or on-the-job training is more effective.... It is impossible to determine the cost effectiveness of any method on the basis of these studies, and there is no conclusive evidence that one type of training is superior to others. (Zymelman 1976 pp. 5–6)

The same could be said for the question of the relative superiority of different methods of financing vocational education and training. No universally applicable solution is available to the problem of how the costs of training should be met. Zymelman suggests that the choice between on-the-job and off-the-job training will depend not only on cost, but on general economic and institutional factors, and he lists such factors as the rate of unemployment, level of wages, the entry requirements for jobs, the attitude of firms and trade unions, the quality and availability of instructors, as well as the average and marginal costs of training, labour market conditions (including the degree of competition between firms), and finally the administrative machinery for allocating public resources by means of subsidies or tax incentives. All these factors will also determine the method of financing training.

Zymelman (1976) emphasizes that the choice between on-the-job and off-the-job training is not a simple one: "the array of training methods can be arranged along a continuum, with off-the-job training at one extreme and

Table 1
Activities of young people on leaving compulsory school in selected OECD countries: Percentage of school leavers in each activity[a]

<table>
<tr><th>Country</th><th>Year
1</th><th>Full-time general education
2</th><th>Vocational education
3</th><th>Apprenticeship
4</th><th>Work or unemployment
5</th><th>Others and unknown
6</th><th>Total
7</th></tr>
<tr><td>Austria[c]</td><td>1976</td><td>14.8</td><td>24.3</td><td>53.5</td><td colspan="2">7.4</td><td>100</td></tr>
<tr><td>Federal Republic of Germany[b]</td><td>1976</td><td colspan="2">47.8</td><td>46.2</td><td>2.7</td><td>3.3</td><td>100</td></tr>
<tr><td>Switzerland[c]</td><td>1975</td><td colspan="2">17.0</td><td>55.0</td><td colspan="2">28.0</td><td>100</td></tr>
<tr><td>Australia[c]</td><td>1975</td><td colspan="2">24.0</td><td>15.0</td><td colspan="2">61.0</td><td>100</td></tr>
<tr><td>Finland[c]</td><td>1975</td><td>—</td><td>77.7</td><td>2.1</td><td>—</td><td>—</td><td>100</td></tr>
<tr><td>France[c]</td><td>1975</td><td>33.3</td><td>31.2</td><td>12.5</td><td colspan="2">23.0</td><td>100</td></tr>
<tr><td>Ireland[d]</td><td>1975</td><td colspan="2">26.0</td><td>10.0</td><td>59.0</td><td>5.0</td><td>100</td></tr>
<tr><td>England and Wales[c]</td><td>1974</td><td colspan="2">20.8</td><td>17.8</td><td>51.1</td><td>10.4</td><td>100</td></tr>
<tr><td>Denmark[d]</td><td>1973</td><td>65.0</td><td>3.0</td><td>15.0</td><td>15.0</td><td>2.0</td><td>100</td></tr>
<tr><td>United States[e]</td><td>1972</td><td>51.5</td><td>8.0</td><td>2.4</td><td>28.0[f]</td><td>10.0</td><td>100</td></tr>
<tr><td>Netherlands[c]</td><td>1968/69</td><td colspan="2">75.0</td><td>3.0</td><td>18.0</td><td>4.0</td><td>100</td></tr>
</table>

Notes
a Source: Organisation for Economic Co-operation and Development 1979 p. 27 b Plans of school leavers aged 15–19 (mostly 15–16). Includes *Gymnasia* leavers of which there were 133,314 out of a total of 888,949 leavers c Age 15–16 or completion of compulsory school d Age 16, completion of school beyond compulsory e Plans of seniors in high school, mostly 17–18 years old f Includes other vocational training

on-the-job at the other" (p. 11). He concludes that "the choice of a mode of training will depend not on any pat answers but on the careful assessment of all relevant influences. . .only with an overview of both economic and noneconomic considerations can the decision maker arrive at a judicious selection" (p. 39).

5. The Balance Between Public and Private Financing of Vocational and Industrial Education

Similarly, questions of the balance between public and private finance and provision of vocational education and training depend on both economic, political, and institutional factors. In many countries the proportion of public funds being devoted to vocational training as part of manpower and employment policies or countercyclical measures designed to influence the overall level of demand in the economy, has increased since the early 1970s. At the same time there have been various developments in national policies towards vocational education which are designed to improve the transition from school to work. These include the introduction of work experience for pupils in upper-secondary school; teaching about the world of work, known as *arbeitslehre* in the Federal Republic of Germany, where it plays an important part in the vocational preparation of young people in secondary schools; and various new approaches and innovations in combining practical experience and theoretical instruction, for example preapprenticeship courses in Australia and France, or the introduction of a "basic year" for apprentices in the Federal Republic of Germany and Denmark, or the development of career education in the United States. All these innovations are designed to improve the transition from school to work, to improve the vocational preparation of young people, and to help to minimize unemployment among young people. One effect of all these measures, however, is to shift the balance of financing of vocational and industrial education and training away from employers, including private firms and enterprises, and towards public financing and provision. In some cases this is an unintended result of educational and manpower policies, while in other countries it reflects conscious economic planning decisions.

6. Apprenticeship

One way of combining practical experience with theoretical vocational education which is important in many countries is apprenticeship. This is a formal contract between an employer and a trainee, or apprentice; under the terms of this contract the trainee undertakes to work for the employer for a specified period and the employer undertakes to provide practical experience and instruction which will allow the apprentice to attain the status of a skilled craftsman. In the past it was common practice in some occupations, and in some countries, for the apprentice to pay the employer, or "master" for instruction, but the common practice now is for apprentices to be paid a wage while they are training, which is lower than that of a skilled craftsman, but gradually increases during the period of the apprenticeship, until it reaches the level of a skilled worker's wage. Thus, the traditional way of financing apprenticeship training involved a sharing of the costs between employers and trainees (in the form of reduced wages).

However, in recent years, there have been increasing criticisms of traditional apprenticeship training in many countries, and gradual changes both in the methods of education and training and in the methods of finance. For example a report in Canada in 1973 concluded:

"The available evidence strongly suggests that complete reliance on the traditional wage mechanism to finance on-the-job instruction for apprentices is no longer practical" (quoted in Organisation for Economic Co-operation and Development 1979 p. 56). The changes that have taken place involve a shift towards collective funding of apprenticeship training, with the government playing an increasing role. These changes have been reviewed by the Organisation for Economic Co-operation and Development (OECD) in an analysis of policies for apprenticeship (Organisation for Economic Co-operation and Development 1979). Mechanisms for collective funding of apprenticeship include the pooling of voluntary contributions from employers and trade unions in a training fund, as in the United States; a compulsory apprenticeship tax, as in France; the provision of tax incentives or subsidies for employers providing apprenticeship training, as in Australia; subsidies in the form of additional training allowances for apprentices with very low wages, as in the Federal Republic of Germany where a means-tested training allowance known as *berufsausbildungsbeihilfe* exists; and various subsidies such as family allowances or tax deductions for parents of apprentices, such as exist in Austria, Denmark, and some other European countries.

The proportion of young workers receiving apprenticeship training, compared with other forms of vocational education or general education varies considerably between countries. Table 1, which is derived from the OECD report on apprenticeship policies, shows that the proportion of school pupils aged 15 to 18 entering apprenticeship programmes varied from 55 and 53 percent in Austria and Switzerland in 1975 and 1976 to about 2 percent in Finland and the United States. The OECD report concludes: "All efforts to reform the apprenticeship system have found it extremely difficult to solve the questions of financing and cost sharing.... The pressure on governments to devise collective financing measures such as already exist in several countries is considerable" (OECD 1979 p. 80).

7. Paid Educational Leave

Another recent development which has changed the pattern of financing vocational and industrial education in some countries is the provision of paid educational leave for employees (described as educational leave of absence in some countries), which means that employers continue to pay wages to employees while they receive part-time or full-time vocational or general education. The possibility of paid educational leave or educational leave of absence has existed in some occupations, and in some countries, for many years but it is only in recent years that legislative changes have made the provision of paid educational leave a matter of right for workers in some countries. In 1973 the International Labour Organization (ILO) adopted the recommendation that "the principle of paid educational leave should be regarded as a new labour right". However, the extent to which workers do have the right to paid educational leave varies considerably among countries. Some European countries, for example France and Sweden, have introduced legislation giving workers this right. In some countries trade-union negotiations have won this right for many workers, for example in Italy. In other countries paid educational leave is very rare, or is confined to a few privileged occupations.

Similarly, there are considerable variations in the methods of financing paid educational leave. The conclusions of a study by OECD in 1976 is that "the system that has been adopted, whereby employers are expected to bear the brunt of the financial effort, gives rise to many ambiguous situations which are a source of conflict". But the report also notes "The type of financing adopted, whereby employers are required to make a considerable effort, gives no clue as to who finally bears the financial burden of the system. Virtually all countries have...tended to make the financing of educational leave the responsibility of the community (via taxpayers and/or consumers) or to require a limited contribution from the workers" (OECD 1976 p. 40).

In other words, paid educational leave, like other financial mechanisms described above, is simply one way of distributing the costs of vocational education and training between employers, workers, and taxpayers. The best way of sharing these costs remains a controversial issue in many countries.

Bibliography

Becker G S 1964 *Human Capital: A Theoretical and Empirical Analysis, with Special Reference to Education*. Columbia University Press, New York

Blaug M 1972 *An Introduction to the Economics of Education*. Penguin, Harmondsworth

Foster P J 1965 The vocational school fallacy in development planning. In: Anderson C A, Bowman M J (eds.) 1965 *Education and Economic Development*. Aldine, Chicago, Illinois

Johnson R 1979 Education and training in the '80's. *Department of Employment Gazette* 87 (11): 1093–95

Mincer J 1962 On-the-job training: Costs, returns, and some implications. *J. Polit. Econ.* 70: 50–79

Organisation for Economic Co-operation and Development (OECD) 1976 *Developments in Educational Leave of Absence*. OECD, Paris

Organisation for Economic Co-operation and Development (OECD) 1979 *Policies for Apprenticeship*. OECD, Paris

United Kingdom Department of Employment and Manpower Services Commission 1976 *Training for Vital Skills: A Consultative Document*. Department of Employment, London

Woodhall M 1974 Investment in industrial training: An assessment of the effects of the Industrial Training Act on the volume and costs of training. *Br. J. Ind. Relations* 12(1): 71–90

Woodhall M 1977 Adult education and training: An estimate of the volume and costs. In: Organisation for Economic Co-operation and Development (OECD) 1977 *Learning Opportunities for Adults*, Vol. 4: *Participation in Adult Education*. OECD, Paris, pp. 317–58

Zymelman M 1976 *The Economic Evaluation of Vocational Training Programs*. Johns Hopkins University Press, Baltimore, Maryland

Economics of Nonformal Education

M. Ahmed

This article will be concerned with the use of economic analysis as a planning and management tool for educational activities which may be categorized as nonformal. As an economic activity, defined as the process of using resources to produce something of value, nonformal education is not fundamentally different from formal education. The resources consumed (the time and skills of instructors and learners, physical space and structures, equipment and books) and the yields produced (the increased skills, knowledge, and understanding gained by successful learners) are similar in both modes of education.

There are, however, differences in the ways formal and nonformal educational activities are usually organized and in the specific aims they serve. First, the management of nonformal activities is extremely dispersed. There is no single central agency, such as a ministry of education or a board of education, that controls and directs the activities within a country or a region. Therefore, there is no single budget, source of revenue, norm of expenditure, or financial control arrangement. Second, many nonformal programmes are not discrete, independent activities, but are parts of broader programmes—for example, an extension service within an agricultural project. The costs as well as the products of such an activity are inseparable from those of noneducational elements of the total project. Finally, the clientele served, locations of learning, objectives pursued, durations of courses, teaching methodology used, and kinds of personnel employed are extremely varied in nonformal education. As a result, there is a great flexibility and diversity in the ways the different types of resources are used—unlike the relatively standardized ways of formal education.

The cost and financing models used normally in educational cost estimates, projections, and analyses depend on assumptions regarding the structure of education operations derived from formal education. A particular "production function" of education is implied, into which the inputs and the function itself (personnel costs, teacher–pupil ratios, for example) are relatively stable.

This is not to say that the logic and principles of analysing and calculating costs, finances, and benefits of education that have been developed so far are totally inapplicable to nonformal education. However, the special features and the special problems of nonformal education have to be taken into account if economic analysis is to be used for improving the planning and management of nonformal education.

1. Resources

One important economic question concerns the resources of education: their existing and potential availability, their capacity for growth, and their efficiency of use.

Resources used in education can be divided into three major categories: financial, physical, and time. The first two categories are clear. Time as an educational resource refers to the human factors: the time consumed by instructors, supervisors, administrators, planners, and above all, learners. Obviously, the three categories are not mutually exclusive. Money is not a real resource, but it can be used to purchase the two other kinds of resources. However, not all educational resources are purchased with cash (examples: instructional time contributed voluntarily by someone with special expertise or experience, free use of a physical facility, or the high motivation of the learners). Moreover, money values, especially as expressed in educational budgets, seldom represent the true values or significance of real resources in the educational process. It is, therefore, useful to bear the threefold classification in mind, even though the first category overlaps with the others.

Financial resources can be further classified on the basis of the sources of funds. First, there are public funds; all funds that come from national, regional, and local government sources, allocated expressly for educational purposes. The second category is household funds; all funds derived from households and spent directly as educational expenses for tuition, room and board, transportation, books, and so on, for members of the household. This category should exclude taxes or levies because taxation proceeds are public funds. The third category, private and voluntary contributions, is made up of funds contributed by philanthropic organizations, foundations, trusts, religious organizations, business firms, and individual citizens for the financing of educational programmes and institutions. The last category (funds derived from economic enterprises) includes funds spent for training and skill development activities to meet personnel needs but excludes philanthropic contribution to education by business firms. Funds generated from the sales of services and goods produced by the educational programmes themselves and from the investment of resources of educational institutions may also be included in this category.

The above taxonomy suggests three conclusions. First, educational resources need to be viewed much more broadly than the revenues shown in the budget or even the totality of all financial resources. Without such a view, a rational effort to assess and mobilize educational resources cannot be maintained. Second, many resources, particularly the time of learners and of the voluntary and unpaid instructional and support personnel, are not traded in the market, but the manner of their use and allocation can make crucial differences in educational outcome. Finally, the inherent flexibility of nonformal education offers the opportunity for mobilizing new educational resources and improving the use and allocation of existing resources. (Whether the opportunities are actually seized is another question.)

2. Costs

2.1 Meanings of Cost

When a resource is put to use in an educational programme, it becomes unavailable for alternative use and becomes a cost item. When a money value is imputed to the resource used, the money or financial cost is derived. An important cost question is cost to whom, because there can be private cost, public cost, and social cost for the same educational service. Costs can also be looked at from the point of view of an economic transactor—that is, the owner of a factor of production, a producer, or a consumer. Cost for the same educational services to any of these parties may be quite different.

Who pays what for an educational service and who benefits from it are obviously important policy questions. Similarly, the concept of opportunity costs helps to keep in view the real resource cost and is, therefore, of value in formulating social policies and allocating resources among different social investments. Its appraisal also helps in understanding the real private cost burdens to individuals, households, and groups intended to be the beneficiaries of educational programmes. For instance, a rural youth or a slum resident may be able to attend an evening or spare-time educational activity but cannot afford to go to a full-time day school, even if the school is "free".

Another way of classifying costs is on the basis of expenditure for durable items such as buildings and equipment (capital costs) and items which are used up within the fiscal year (recurrent costs). There is often a possibility of reducing costs in nonformal education when fixed physical installations and equipment are not required. It has been found useful to have a separate category of initial development costs for new experimental educational projects. These may be one-time costs, but may not be for durable items and do not fall neatly in either of the conventional categories.

2.2 Behaviour of Costs

Generalizations about the behaviour of educational costs have been drawn from experiences essentially in formal education (Coombs and Hallak 1972). To what extent are these observations applicable to nonformal education? The answer is not clear or straightforward for two reasons. First, sufficient experience with large-scale systematic operations of nonformal programmes in different countries has not been obtained. The patterns of nonformal programmes that would provide the basis for cost generalizations have not developed, as they have in formal education. Second, by its nature nonformal education is extremely diverse in pedagogical approaches, organization, and objectives. Therefore, inferences about the general behaviour of costs in nonformal education would be much more difficult to arrive at than in formal education.

Available evidence from studies of nonformal education experiences suggests that the possibility of savings in costs in nonformal programmes exist in at least four ways: low capital costs, low personnel costs, self-financing, and marginality of costs (Ahmed 1975).

In many nonformal programmes there is little or no capital cost involved. Programmes such as 4-H Clubs and their variations, rural farm forums, on-the-job training of various kinds, youth and women's clubs, village self-help groups, and correspondence courses do not require special physical facilities at the field level. Opportunities for saving in personnel costs arise from the use of part-time instructors (who are paid a proportionate or less than proportionate wage) and volunteers (who may have special experience and offer their services free of charge). Some nonformal programmes have been able to reduce their net operating cost by generating some income or in-kind contribution from programme activities. As many nonformal programmes are able both to use existing resources and personnel without diverting these from other uses and conduct the activities with only a relatively small marginal addition of resources, the net cost of programmes is reduced. It must, however, be noted that while these possibilities exist, it cannot be said that all nonformal programmes will be invariably characterized by these cost-saving features.

3. Benefits

In the planning and management of education, formal and nonformal, it makes little sense to talk about high or low costs without relating the costs of an educational activity to the results achieved. The economic analysis of an educational programme, therefore, leads invariably to a juxtaposition of the costs incurred and the benefits derived.

The relationship between the former and the latter is referred to as the external productivity of the educational programme. Expressed in numerical terms, external productivity is the same as the benefit–cost ratio. The relationship between cost inputs and the direct learning outputs such as knowledge and skills embodied in the learner is known as the internal efficiency of the educational programme (Coombs and Hallak 1972 pp. 82–84).

High internal efficiency does not guarantee high external productivity although the reverse is not true; that is, a high benefit–cost ratio would require a high measure of internal efficiency. There are obvious problems, with external productivity measures (or cost–benefit analysis) and internal efficiency measures (or cost-effectiveness analysis in the narrow sense) as bases for relating costs and benefits. Cost–benefit analysis is better viewed as a notional concept, because the full range of benefits from a programme can hardly be quantified or even estimated.

What would be extremely useful from a practical educational and management angle is a pragmatic compromise between the narrow internal efficiency approach and the impossible task of a total cost–benefit analysis. Judging a programme's value, deciding whether it is achieving its main objectives at a reasonable cost, and improving its performance—such efforts can be enormously helped by attempts to juxtapose the known cost inputs against the evidences that can be gathered of the achievement of the main stated and predetermined objectives and the intended benefits of the programme. This relatively modest but feasible effort can be a firmer basis for forming a realistic cost-effectiveness judgment (taken to be broader than a synonym for internal efficiency) about a programme than the misleading "precision" of internal efficiency measures, the benefit–cost ratio, or the rate of return calculation.

The concept of the cost–benefit relationship, however, should not be considered useless or redundant. The role of the stated objectives and intended benefits is emphasized in cost-effectiveness analysis, because only what is stated and intended is susceptible to the planning and management process, not the incidental and unsuspected by-products. The hypothetical construct of total benefits provides a framework for cost-effectiveness analysis and a rationale for constantly attempting to improve the cost-effectiveness of programmes. It is possible retrospectively to examine the incidental benefits and their relationship to the cost inputs; this information can then become incorporated in subsequent programme planning and cost-effectiveness analysis.

Cost-effectiveness analysis can be a helpful tool for the planning and management of nonformal educational programmes if it is used to seek the best available evidences regarding questions such as the following:

(a) Does the programme follow the least costly alternative for achieving its educational goals?

(b) Does the programme follow a feasible educational approach in terms of the programme's long-range viability and meet the learning needs of a sizable proportion of the potential clientele?

(c) Do the learning outputs fit the ultimate objectives and benefits intended from the programme?

(d) Does the programme fit into a broader design for meeting the "learning needs" of the population, particularly those needs that are related and complementary to the needs served by the particular programme?

(e) Does the programme meet set criteria, if any, regarding who pays for the programme and who benefits from it?

Bibliography

Ahmed M 1975 *The Economics of Nonformal Education: Resources, Cost, and Benefits.* Praeger, New York

Ahmed M, Coombs P H 1975 *Education for Rural Development: Case Studies for Planners.* Praeger, New York

Blaug M 1972 *An Introduction to the Economics of Education.* Penguin, Harmondsworth

Coombs P H, Hallak J 1972 *Managing Educational Costs.* Oxford University Press, New York

Section 10

Research

Section 10

Research

Introduction

Comparatively little research has been undertaken into adult or lifelong education. Only in the last few decades has the former been recognized as a significant worldwide phenomenon and the widespread acceptance of the latter as a goal for policy is even more recent. Even had there been sufficient incentives to study these subjects, there appeared to be little to investigate.

In those countries where adult education was firmly established, even before the Second World War, it was regarded as peripheral to school and higher education. Educational researchers concentrated almost exclusively on the formal system, appearing to consider, when they thought about it at all, that theories and conclusions that applied to the rest of education could be assumed to apply to adult education as well. It is still largely the case, indeed, that education is taken by theorists and researchers to mean formal schooling and higher education.

Researchers in the social sciences from outside education either appear to have taken the same line, or else they have seen no reputations to be made in adult education, or have not been clear what it was they might be called to investigate under that name. This was not surprising. The concept of adult education as a distinctive sector of education was unknown in many countries and even today has hardly entered into common discourse.

As for those who were engaged in the education of adults, many would not have described what they were doing in those terms, even when it was their full-time occupation. They considered themselves to be occupational trainers, trade union workers, temperance campaigners, political activists, welfare workers. They saw adult education, as many of those who followed them still do today, as a means to an end with which they identified. Those who have called themselves adult educators, seeing adult education as a worthy end in itself, have been slow to accept the desirability of systematic study of their field of action. This attitude was in part a product both of the kind of people they were and of the circumstances in which they worked.

No more than school teachers, who at least have long had the security of an established career structure not enjoyed by adult educators, have they been encouraged by the pressures of the teaching situation to examine or to reflect upon the structures of which they are a part, or the processes to which they contribute, except within a very short-term perspective. They had a body of knowledge that they wanted to share and which they thought adults should have. The strong belief in the selfevident value of what they were doing, which hampered the development of evaluation of adult education provision—itself a form of research—made dispassionate investigation of other aspects of it a luxury which could be ill-afforded and was unlikely to bring results that would justify the effort.

In any case their activities were not easily researched. They lacked structure, system, and continuity, their public was constantly changing, and there appeared to be no overall pattern. Their field of action appeared to be, as has been frequently pointed out, a conglomerate of disparate elements within shifting boundaries. There was shortage of information. It was often nobody's business (and remains so) to record expenditure, numbers of participants or who they were, or even to report what went on in study circles, classes, and other forms of activity and what were the outcomes. Not that it mattered, since the outcomes were the only things of importance, and they, being intangible, were not susceptible to measurement.

That these factors unfavourable to research have to any significant extent been overcome requires explanation. The most plausible answer is that research has increased as a product of, and then as a producer and justifier of, growth in the importance and size of adult education, which has already been discussed in the Introduction to Section 9 in relation to legislation and finance. Above a certain scale of operation, adult educators could not proceed in the traditional ad hoc, reactive manner. Organization and planning, a more certain knowledge of what they were doing, was required and had to be acquired. The recognition of adult education's importance opened up new possibilities, but they could not count on its or their value being selfevident. They had to convince potential sponsors of their understanding of the field. Governments, employers, and other sources of funding, for their part, wanted knowledge of the field in which they intended to spend their money.

The expansion of activity brought in new personnel, so that the balance of influence shifted. Those committed to adult education as a movement lost much of their predominance, as the influence grew of those who were in it as a profession. As one of the characteristics of a profession is mastery of a body of knowledge specific to it, the professionals have had to create one. The need they felt to preserve their identity as distinct from other educators in order to establish their status helped to encourage specifically adult education research. It benefited from interest in lifelong education as a goal, because it was the comparatively unknown element of education throughout the lifespan. The increasing participation of centres of higher education in the professional education of adult education personnel also encouraged interest in adult education as a field of study and research.

These influences cannot be said to have entirely triumphed. Old habits have shown a strong capacity for survival. The quality and nature of some of the research come under justifiable criticism in at least one of the articles in this section. Lack of quantifiable data is presented as a handicap in another. There is little sign of coherent, systematic policies in research. Nevertheless there have been significant achievements, even if there is a long way to go before there is the same information about and understanding of adult education as there is for the formal education system.

Section 10 is divided into two subsections. Regional Overviews contains surveys of research emphases and achievements in different parts of the world. Subjects and Approaches to Research consists of case studies of types of research and areas of investigation within adult education. They are, however, only examples. The breadth of subjects covered and the variety of approaches taken by articles in this *Handbook* give an indication of the full scope of research being undertaken into adult education.

Regional Overviews

Introduction

The first article in this subsection, *Adult Education Research: General*, provides a review of the field. It addresses the assumptions and perceptions of the territory to be covered by such research, it discusses the conflicting views of adult education as a field of practice and a scientific discipline, the question of borrowing insights and techniques from other areas of study, and the conceptualization of research questions. Through the criteria for assessing it as a field of study it examines the research traditions that dominate in adult education, and proposes some alternative ones.

Then follow four area studies, on the United States, Latin America, Western Europe, and Eastern Europe. It can be seen, from a comparison of these, that the range and level of research correlate closely with the stage of development of the field of study and that the subjects match its preoccupations. As the field is uncoordinated, so is research. Even in the centrally controlled countries of Eastern Europe, it seems, it is piecemeal and patchy.

The article *Adult Education Research: United States* covers its scope, the topics and trends, the dissemination of findings, who produces research, what are its priorities, support, and use. *Adult Education Research: Latin America* gives a more homogeneous picture than the other reviews, possibly because of a necessary concentration on problems of literacy and basic education and of the importance of the phenomenon of popular education. It considers the question of interpretative frameworks, programmes, and particularly reports studies in nonformal and popular education and their role.

Adult Education Research: Western Europe covers the most diverse area, containing a number of states, and many different languages and political traditions. Common features are identified in institutions producing research, in the forms it takes, and the fields of study, but it also stresses national differences in research practice. A similar diversity is portrayed in *Adult Education Research: Eastern Europe and the Soviet Union* in spite of their common political system. A major part of the article presents the directions and scope of research in the Soviet Union, but Bulgaria, Czechoslovakia, the German Democratic Republic, Hungary, Poland, Romania, and Yugoslavia are also reviewed.

Adult Education Research: General

K. Rubenson

The continuously growing interest in adult education research in developed as well as in developing countries is a very recent phenomenon. During the rapid expansion of the social sciences, especially of education in the 1950s and 1960s, very little attention was paid to adult education. The lack of interest in conducting research in adult education could be explained by the marginality of the adult education enterprise or, as in the Scandinavian countries, for example, by the independent standing adult education has had in relation to government and the public school system. In addition to considering the fact of marginality and independence, another reason for the lack of research in adult education may have been the strong influence of the need for practicability in programs and training of instructors.

During the 1970s, adult education shed its marginal role and came to the forefront of public interest. It is now increasingly being regarded as an integrated part of the education sector—especially in some of the Third World countries and in the Nordic countries. Another sign of this phenomenon has been the development of concepts such as lifelong education, *education permanente*, and recurrent education. The new role for adult education in society has created an interest for research corresponding to the one which emerged during the period of enormous growth of public expenditures on schools and universities in the 1960s.

The response to the demand for research has varied between countries depending on governmental policy and the institutional context of research. In the Nordic countries, improvement in the status of adult education in the 1970s was followed by a sharp rise in the resources for research and development in this area. Norway has established a special institute for research and development in adult education outside the university structure. In Sweden the adult education share of the National Board of Education's research and development grants increased from 1 percent in 1969 to 20 percent in 1980/81. Further, the Swedish parliament has decided to create a chair in adult education. This is the first time that the authorities have allowed a specialization and differentiation in the discipline of education.

Looking at Continental Europe, it is possible to observe the beginning of an institutionalization of adult education in the universities as indicated by the creation of special chairs. After a decade of exciting developments in adult education research, there is a need to scrutinize the state of this field of study.

Törnebohm (1974) states that any scientific discipline might, on an epistemological level, be described in terms of its territory. He further assumes that research is concerned with a part of the real world and that knowledge produced in a field may then be described as an authorized map of the territory. Departing from Törnebohm's epistemological perspective, this article is intended to analyze what governs the drawing of the map (the knowledge production) in adult education. This will be done by trying to answer the following two questions:

(a) Which assumptions and perceptions of the territory govern the efforts to accumulate knowledge within adult education, that is, which questions are regarded as legitimate within the field?

(b) Which research traditions (scientific ideals and perspectives) govern research in adult education?

The choice of material to be analyzed will, of course, determine the answer to the questions posed.

Up until the late 1960s, with some exceptions, there existed little systematic research in the area of adult education outside the United States. Therefore, it is understandable that it is research done in the United States that has come to set the boundaries of the field. Due to the rapid expansion of research in other parts of the world, this is less true today than it was in the early 1970s, despite the overwhelming number of studies produced in North America. One problem in trying to give a balanced picture is the lack of material describing and analyzing research outside the Anglo–Saxon countries.

1. Assumptions and Perceptions of the Territory

The question of which assumptions and perceptions of the territory have governed the research will be answered by looking at the following three aspects: (a) adult education as a field of practice versus (b) adult education as a field of scholarly inquiry borrowing from various disciplines, and (c) conceptualizations of research questions.

1.1 Field of Practice Versus Scientific Discipline

One of the classic debates is whether adult education is only a field of social practice or if it also should be considered a field of study. With the institutionalization of adult education in the universities and the resultant growing body of research, this question has lost most of its relevance. The task today is rather to look at which direction the research is going with regard to practice.

In order to understand knowledge production in adult education people should be made aware that it grew as a field of study out of the movement toward professionalization and institutionalization marked by an expansion of programs in adult education. Consequently, there has been a stress on practicability and the needs of the field have come to determine which problems have been selected as "legitimate."

With reference to the somewhat hazy concept of research and development, adult education research has mostly been of the "development kind." Practice-oriented research aimed at solving an immediate problem is not intrinsically negative. The heart of the matter is the lack of balance between practice-oriented research and discipline-oriented research, where the purpose is to develop and test theories and lay the necessary foundations for applied research. Due to a lack of intradisciplinary orientation, practice-oriented research has tended to be almost atheoretical. Thus, there are two interrelated problems facing adult education—the balance between practice- and discipline-oriented research, and the atheoretical approach of applied research.

Adult education is often characterized as a normative study in which the purpose of the research is to evolve programs which have the most likelihood of promoting such learning situations in which behavior changes may best be brought about. As a consequence of the "normative" view, research has mostly come to deal with the development of programs and/or instructional methods while critical analysis of the prerequisites for developing adult education in a certain desired way has been neglected.

In the 1970s there has been somewhat more interest in discipline-oriented questions. This is especially true of the Federal Republic of Germany and the Nordic countries. However, this kind of research has met sharp criticism from the field. In fact, one common characteristic among adult educators around the world seems to be a negative attitude towards research. The view is that the research carried out has been of little if any use to those concerned with the practicalities of education. Moreover, this attitude can also be found inside the universities. Many of those occupying positions of leadership in the universities have reached their positions not by doing research in adult education but by serving the field. The stress on practicalities is further nourished by graduate students in adult education. They tend to be older than the general graduate student, come from jobs which they expect to return to, and embark on research which applies directly to their own situation.

1.2 Borrowing from Other Fields of Study

Jensen (1964), discussing the situation in the United States, suggested that adult education could develop a unique body of knowledge suited to its purposes through two methods: (a) experiences from practice could be used to formulate principles or generalizations, and (b) knowledge which has been developed in other fields of study could be borrowed and reformulated for use in adult education.

With reference to the second point, adult education researchers in North America, apart from some common psychological theories, failed to follow the route set by Jensen. Seldom is any serious effort made to build on or integrate findings or theories of a more general nature. In fact, Boshier and Pickard (1979) show that, to an increasing extent, researchers who publish in *Adult Education* rely primarily on adult education literature. Only 20 percent of citations appearing in Volume 19 (1968) of *Adult Education* referred to primary sources. By 1977 (Volume 27), this figure had increased to nearly 60 percent.

Among advocates for a discipline of adult education, there is a strong belief that not only is borrowing of little value for adult education, but it is also damaging. In *Redefining the Discipline of Adult Education*, Boyd and Apps (1980) argue that it would be an error to seek assistance from recognized disciplines before the field of adult education itself is clearly understood. This line of reasoning has been criticized by Rubenson (1980) who argues that it is in the effort to understand the structure, the function, and the problems of adult education that help from a number of disciplines is needed.

The attitude toward borrowing is linked to the institutional setting. In Sweden, adult education research has been carried out in unified departments of education research or in sociology and psychology departments. The research is judged in comparison to scholarly activities in the social sciences in general and not to adult education as a specific field of study. The same is true, but less marked, elsewhere in Europe. In the Federal Republic of Germany, only 9 percent of the research was done in special departments of adult education while 29 percent was carried out in departments of education and 27 percent in departments of social science (Siebert 1979). The situation is different in North America where almost all research in the area occurs within special units of adult education and the scholastic activities are judged within a specific field of study, adult education.

1.3 Conceptualization of Research Questions

There is a difference between North America and Europe with regard to the conceptualization of research questions in adult education. To simplify somewhat, it could be argued that the North American premise appears to be that of "people-over-society" while the European is that of "people-in-society."

A very obvious observation that can be made from reviewing research in adult education in North America is the dominant influence of psychology, whether it be in program planning, instruction, or participation. The problem of instruction simply becomes a question of learning. Departing from one of the learning theories, the researcher tries to arrange, or describe, the external conditions in accordance with the theory in order to study the relationship between instruction (process) variables and student learning (product) variables.

The popularity of the psychologically oriented process–product research is easy to understand in the light of the myth that instruction derives in a linear fashion from research. The appeal of this research tradition then is that it promises results that may be directly translated into prescriptions for practice.

The individualistic perspective is also evident in research on participation, a major area of adult education research in North America. Many scholars seem to assume that motivation is the sole determinant of participation by adults in education. Further, the concept of motivation has often been formulated in terms of psychological constructs that deal with people *in abstracto* (e.g., the general nature of motives and needs) and do not consider specific psychological processes as related to concrete situations.

It is especially in the area of participation research that the difference between North America and Europe becomes apparent. The North Americans have had the individual person in the focus while the Europeans have given relatively more attention to participation from a social perspective. As a consequence the latter have been less interested in motivation orientations and attitudes per se and given more attention to how the objective world influences the perception of reality. Further, Western Europeans have gone from a preoccupation with comparing participants with nonparticipants to analyzing the phenomenon in relation to broad social movements. This development should partly be understood in the political context. In those Western European countries where adult education became an integrated part of the social and economic policy, the governments supported "decision-oriented" research which greatly influenced the direction and conceptualization of participation research.

Reviewing the Western European research it is possible to detect some tendencies to a situation in adult education research in which North American reductionism is replaced by "sociological deductionism" with a concomitant restriction on the development of the field of study. An understanding of problems of the complexity that adult education addresses requires not a single theory but a conjunction of a variety of theories. Thus it is difficult to perceive a single comprehensive theory on participation. Instead it has been argued that in order to understand participation, theoretical models in at least three areas are necessary; adult education as a societal process, the individual's psychological conceptual apparatus, and, in addition, the links between these levels (Rubenson 1980). Recently there have been attempts to take this holistic approach in adult education research, for example, in the long-range research agenda developed by the Norwegian Institute of Adult Education.

In summary, the analysis of the first question: "Which

assumptions and perceptions of the territory govern the efforts to accumulate knowledge," shows that the stress on practicability has limited the map that has been developed. Further, it reveals that the territory has been defined mainly from assumptions about the characteristics of the learner but that there is a reorientation—mainly in Europe—to a more sociological approach.

2. Governing Research Traditions in Adult Education

The question of which research traditions have governed knowledge production will be answered through looking at the criteria that have been used in review of adult education research and by looking at the latest developments in this field of research.

2.1 Criteria for Assessing Adult Education as a Field of Study

Over the years there have been attempts to examine the production of knowledge relating to adult education in North America in order to study the emergence of adult education as a field of study (Dickinson and Rusnell 1971, Long and Agyekum 1974, Boshier and Pickard 1979). There is general agreement in these articles that the research has been of intradisciplinary importance and has contributed to the development of a discipline of adult education.

Dickinson and Rusnell (1971) stated that the gradual emergence of a discipline (between 1959 and 1970) of adult education was indicated by, among other things, an increase in the number of articles classified as empirical research (from 8 to 44 percent), interpretive literature reviews (from 3 to 12 percent), and historical studies (from 1 to 8 percent). Further, they observed a growing sophistication in research methodology. The experimental studies rose from zero to 35 percent and the surveys became less descriptive in character. Long and Agyekum (1974) also pointed to the growing stress on research between 1964 and 1973. While the quantity and proportion of descriptive research articles was constant, the reviewers found that the quality of the descriptive research had increased from rather loose case reports and status surveys to more analytical and multivariate studies. The same observation is made by Copeland and Grabowski (1971), with regard to adult education research in the United States in general. They claim that the quality of descriptive studies has been enhanced by the development of more powerful statistical tools and that more studies have been formulated within a theoretical framework. Boshier and Pickard (1979) stated: "It is ironic and reflective of the state of adult education research that Johnstone and Rivera's monumental survey which produced numerous bivariate contingency tables was cited twenty times, yet Miller's multivariate analysis, which portrayed participation as a function of complex multivariate interactions between psychological, social and institutional variables was cited less than six times in the ten year period" (p. 76).

The conclusion here is that the claim for the growing intradisciplinary importance of adult education research has, to quite a large extent, been made on the basis of a growing empiricism and the use of more advanced statistical methods.

The claim of intradisciplinary advancement can be criticized. If the positivistic research ideal and its set of methodological "do's and don'ts" are accepted, it is true, as the reviewers have pointed out, that there has been an increase in the use of sophisticated statistical methods. Still, adult education researchers are seldom found attempting anything beyond what is available in a standard data package. Despite the improvements pointed out, it is possible to be skeptical as regards the viewer's positive assessment, since the methodological standard of the research seldom has been of such quality that any major development could be talked about. In fact, the technical standard of the research was never really scrutinized in the above-mentioned reviews.

The emphasis on empiricism and research methodology in order to build a field of study of adult education in North America is easy to understand as this is consistent with the prevailing tradition in education research as such.

Unfortunately, research outside North America has not been studied thoroughly. There is no lack of personal statements from different scholars on how research in adult education should be conducted but there have been hardly any attempts to study the developments in a systematic fashion. However, available analysis shows that experimental research is rare in Europe and that surveys play a larger role in North America (Siebert 1979). To the extent that the Europeans have had more interest in historical and philosophical concerns, qualitative models of inquiry are more useful. However, empirical research dominates on both continents. Looking at research done within special departments for adult education it is quite obvious that North American research is more sophisticated than that done in other parts of the world. At the same time it is also true to say that studies in the area of adult education undertaken in departments of psychology, sociology, and education tend to be of a higher quality with regard to design and methodology than research in departments of adult education.

2.2 Alternative Research Traditions

There has been growing support for alternative research traditions among adult educators. This is quite in line with the general developments in the social sciences, where the positivistic research tradition has come under heavy fire. One trend is a revival of Marxist theory coupled with a focus on conflict, power, control, and the effect of structural factors on the educational process. The conflict school with its emphasis on societal factors has so far had little influence on the new directions in adult education research. With few exceptions not even those dealing with questions like social change try to relate to this line of research.

Another approach more popular in the firmament of adult educational research is the "new sociology," sometimes called the "interpretative framework." The focus here is on the structuring of knowledge and symbols in the educational institutions and how this is related to principles and practices of social and cultural control in society. The "interpretativists" are heavily influenced by symbolic interactionism phenomenology and ethnomethodology. These approaches, though undeniably "research," are fundamentally different from traditional positivistic research. The concern is the problem of subjective meaning as basic for an understanding of the social world.

The "interpretative school" is of special interest, as its choice of research tradition is in harmony with some of the alternative views that are put forward in adult education. It is easy to understand the enthusiasm among adult educators for phenomenological-oriented approaches as they seemingly fit well with the general individualistic orientation of adult education.

Finally, the Glaser and Strauss work, *The Discovery of Grounded Theory*, has had great influence on research in adult education both in North America and Europe. Traditionally adult education research follows a logico-deductive procedure, whereby the stress is on theory verification. Grounded theory, on the other hand, deals with the generation of theory from data and is thus inductive in character. It should be noted that it is common to find in the adult education research literature that the grounded theory concept is used as if it were interchangeable with qualitatively oriented research. However, as Glaser and Strauss (1968) point out, there is no fundamental clash between qualitative and quantitative approaches and each form of data is useful for both verification and generation of theory.

The strategy of grounded theory is central to adult education as it is believed that adult education partly can develop a unique body of knowledge suited to its purposes through formulating principles or generalizations from experiences in practice. In reality, however, there has been more lip-service paid than serious attempts made to generate theories from data systematically obtained from adult education research. The inductive phase, whereby the event is "translated" into concepts and the relationships between the concepts are spelled out with the purpose of forming a theory, has received little attention. The criticism is not against the principle of grounded theory as such but against the way it has been used by adult education researchers to legitimate an atheoretical approach.

3. Concluding Remarks

This article has tried to outline the assumptions and perceptions that have governed the development of adult education as a field of study. The largest stumbling block in this process has been and still is the overwhelming preoccupation with practicality, and a negative and sometimes anti-intellectual attitude toward research among adult educators.

One sign of the lack of scholarly development as well as interest to engage in this process is the prevailing isolationism. A good example is *Changing Approaches to Studying Adult Education* (Long and Hiemstra 1980) which is one of nine handbooks published by the Adult Education Association of the United States. Out of the books and articles listed, almost all are North American publications. The omission of research from other parts of the world cannot be explained by language barriers, as research from other English-speaking countries or works translated into English also are neglected. The reason for the lack of interest may be that the fast-growing research in, for example, the European countries originates not from the instructor training perspective but from broader social issues such as the relationship of social structure and social change to adult education.

One barrier to the international exchange of research and thus to the growth of the universal body of knowledge is the lack of an internationally recognized journal on adult education research. The focus of such a journal should be how to integrate the more psychological-oriented research in North America with the more sociological-directed research in Europe and other parts of the world. Such a synthesis is one step on the way to solve the fundamental problem facing adult education research; how to integrate the holistic (structural) and the individualistic approaches.

Bibliography

Boshier R, Pickard L 1979 Citation patterns of articles published in Adult Education 1968–1977. *Adult Educ.* 30: 34–51

Boyd R D, Apps J W 1980 A conceptual model for adult education. In: Boyd R D, Apps J W (eds.) 1980 *Redefining the Discipline of Adult Education.* Jossey-Bass, San Francisco, California

Copeland H G, Grabowski S M 1971 Research and investigation in the United States. *Convergence* 4(4): 23–32

Dickinson G, Rusnell D 1971 A content analysis of Adult Education. *Adult Educ.* 21: 177–85

Glaser B G, Strauss A L 1968 *The Discovery of Grounded Theory: Strategies for Qualitative Research.* Weidenfeld and Nicolson, London

Jensen G E 1964 How adult education borrows and reformulates knowledge of other disciplines. In: Jensen G E, Liveright A A, Hallenbeck W (eds.) 1964 *Adult Education: Outlines of an Emerging Field of University Study.* Adult Education Association of the United States, Washington, DC

Long H B, Agyekum S 1974 Adult education 1964–1973: Reflections of a changing discipline. *Adult Educ.* 24: 99–120

Long H B, Hiemstra R 1980 *Changing Approaches to Studying Adult Education.* Jossey-Bass, San Francisco, California

Rubenson K 1980 Background and theoretical context. In: Hoghielm R, Rubenson K (eds.) 1980 *Adult Education for Social Change: Research on the Swedish Allocation Policy: Studies in Education and Psychology,* Vol. 9. Liberlaromedel, Stockholm

Siebert H (ed.) 1979 *Taschenbuch der Weiterbildungsforschung.* Burgbücherei Schneider, Baltmannsweiler

Törnebohm H 1974 *Scientific Knowledge Formation.* Department of Theory Science, University of Goteborg, Goteborg

Adult Education Research: United States

A. B. Knox

Adult education research in the United States is decentralized, as is the field to which it is related. The amount and quality of research related to adult education has increased since the 1930s. While an increasing proportion has been produced by researchers who identify mainly with the field, more than half is still produced by scholars from related fields. Multiple influences affect priorities for new research topics, and proposals help to obtain external financial support. Publications, meetings, and the use of research and evaluation findings, also help build support for research in the forms of cooperation, funding, collegial networks, facilities, and recognition.

1. Scope of Adult Education Research

Research findings include any data-based outcomes from scholarly inquiry published for the benefit of practitioners or researchers associated with the broad field of adult, continuing, recurrent, and lifelong education. Included are technical reports from major research studies, summaries of research findings related to a given topic, and evaluation reports. Some practitioners conduct and publish research and evaluation studies. In this article they are referred to as researchers.

In the United States, arrangements to produce to use research findings reflect the pluralistic and decentralized nature of adult education. Each segment of the broad field has evolved its own distinctive tradition and terminology. However, there is growing recognition that successful practitioners have similar proficiencies, which may be enriched by adult education research findings (Knox 1979a).

The methods used to conduct these research and evaluation studies have become increasingly specialized since the 1930s. In the early 1930s, adult education research could be characterized as scattered studies from psychological research about adult learning; from sociological research about group behavior and social change; and from historical research about adult education providers. Most of it was conducted by psychologists or sociologists who became interested in adult education. Doctoral programs, with a specialization in adult education, provided a growing source of research findings relevant to the field. However, in the late 1950s most research relevant to adult education was still being produced by related fields (Brunner et al. 1959).

In the 1980s, adult education research is produced by people associated with dozens of specialities in the social and behavioral sciences. Although they vary in rationale, in procedures for collecting and analyzing data, and in applicability to practice, each research speciality constitutes a disciplined area of inquiry. All emphasize objectivity, replicability, and data-based conclusions and generalizations. Many studies combine research with procedures to judge program effectiveness and worth. Practitioners are encouraged to use their conclusions for program planning, improvement, and accountability. Other studies emphasize theory building and testing and are especially useful for understanding or explaining the complex phenomena that practitioners confront. Most adult education research has been relatively descriptive, with the aim of helping to generalize or explain.

As research methodologies have become increasingly specialized and technical, researchers have mastered the method selected and applied it to a topic related to adult education. Typical models of inquiry used for adult education research include: survey, historical, ethnographic, longitudinal, experimental, and systemic. Each of these methodological specialties has distinctive topics, theories, procedures, and insights into adult education practice.

2. Topics and Trends

Most adult education research topics can be grouped in one of four categories. Adult development and learning includes all aspects of adults as learners; program development includes planning, conducting, and evaluating adult learning and teaching activities; organization and administration include the study of adult education agencies as social systems related to parent organizations and to the larger society and the examination of all tasks performed by adult education administrators and supervisors; and contextual trends and issues include the history of the field, relations among providers, and social and philosophical issues that confront adult education.

Both quantity and quality of adult education research in the United States has increased since the early 1930s. By the early 1980s about one-third had been on program development, but the proportion of studies on adult development and learning has increased greatly. This reflects contributions by scholars from the fields of lifespan human development and gerontology. There has been a small but steady amount of research being produced related to organization and administration, and to societal trends and issues.

3. Sources of Findings

Over the decades, associations, institutes, agencies, and publishers interested in adult education have made special contributions to the dissemination of research findings. The American Association for Adult Education (AAAE), the Institute of Adult Education at Teachers College, Columbia University, and more recently, the Adult Education Association of the United States (AEA) have been active in this work. Both AAAE and AEA arrange for publication of handbooks of adult education, which include highlights of research findings related to many aspects of adult education.

The AEA published the first major overview of adult education research (Brunner et al. 1959), along with its Commission of Professors of Adult Education volume on organized knowledge to be taught in adult education courses (Jensen et al. 1964). Most recently in 1980–81, the AEA has been responsible for a series of handbooks reporting studies on a number of topics.

The AEA's quarterly research journal, *Adult Education*, has been a major source of research-based articles, and it also used to carry a listing of research studies. For some years the American Educational Research Association (AERA) *Review of Education Research* devoted special issues to adult education research. This function has been assumed by the National Institute of Education. Its Educational Resources Information Center (ERIC), located variously at Syracuse University, Northern Illinois University, and Ohio State University, is a clearinghouse that covers the field of adult education. Abstracts of adult education research are published in *Resources in Education*.

For more than two decades the Adult Education Research Conference (AERC), formerly the National Seminar on Adult Education Research, has provided a meeting place for researchers from all segments of the field to share findings, establish collegial relationships, and plan collaborative studies. Summaries of scholarly papers presented at the AERCs have been shared with a wider audience; some papers have been available through ERIC. Syntheses of research findings have been prepared on various topics, such as adult development and learning (Knox 1977a), administrative decision making (Knox 1982), trends and issues (Knowles 1977), and program development (Houle 1972). This last contains an excellent bibliographic essay.

4. *Production of Research*

One source of research reports is represented by graduate students specializing in adult education. Master's theses and doctoral dissertations constitute perhaps one-third of adult education research each year. More than half of the research-based publications pertinent to adult education have been produced by researchers and scholars identified with related fields. Examples include a professor of education psychology who conducted several studies on adult learning style; a doctoral student in sociology who conducted a dissertation on public school adult education (see *Adult Education in Public Schools*); and a labor economist who studied adult education as a way to increase human capital. Most of these scholars from other fields conduct only a few studies related to adult education. However, some of those whose interest continued are prolific producers of adult education research findings. As with most professional fields, very few practitioners produce adult education research, mainly because they lack preparation and time to do so.

Most of the scholars from related fields who have produced adult education research, have come from psychology, sociology, economics, or history. Their discipline affects the research topics they select and the procedures they use for data collection, analysis, and reporting. Most of the researchers who have studied in adult education have been associated, either as a student or faculty member, with one of the approximately 80 graduate programs. A disproportionately large amount of research has been produced at relatively few institutions. Favorite topics have been preparation of program administrators; program development; administration; and scope, trends, and issues. In most of these graduate programs, limited attention has been given to research and evaluation procedures.

5. *Research Priorities, Support, and Use*

Choice of research topics is largely influenced by researchers' own interests, previous research, the expressed wishes of adult educators, and the priorities of organizations that encourage and support research. This information may be found in published lists of research needing to be done.

Government agencies are major sources of grants or contracts to support research, evaluation, or demonstration projects on topics relevant to adult education. Examples include the National Institute of Education, National Institutes of Health, the National Science Foundation, and dozens of others.

A second major source of funding is private philanthropic foundations, either at national, regional, or local levels if the topic relates to their priorities.

Support and encouragement for researchers are not confined to money. Universities provide libraries, laboratories, computers, and consultation about research design and procedures. Associations of adult education practitioners encourage research production and use. For example, AEA has a commission on research and makes an annual Okes Award for outstanding research. Associations of educational researchers, such as AERA and AERC provide publications and meetings that bring researchers in contact with those who have similar interests. In addition, almost every association related to the professions and to the social and behavioral sciences has a few researchers interested in some aspect of adult education. In recent years, papers and sessions related to adult education have appeared more frequently in their publications and meetings.

One major reason for adult education research is to produce findings that practitioners can use to improve practice. It is, therefore, frustrating that few research and evaluation reports are read and that many practitioners are unaware of relevant research available to them. Publication in research journals benefits other researchers but reaches few practitioners.

Attempts are made to encourage adult educators to use research findings to strengthen their practice, by research-based presentations at association meetings, articles in association publications, and discussion of research findings at agency staff meetings. These are important because the best guarantee of interest and support for adult education research is a substantial number of practitioners who value and use past contributions of research.

Bibliography

Boone E J, Shearon R W, White E E et al. 1980 *Serving Personal and Community Needs Through Adult Education*. Jossey-Bass, San Francisco, California

Boyd R D, Apps J W et al. 1980 *Redefining the Discipline of Adult Education*. Jossey-Bass, San Francisco, California

Brunner E De S et al. 1959 *An Overview of Adult Education Research*. Adult Education Association of the United States, Chicago, Illinois

Charters A N et al. 1981 *Comparing Adult Education Worldwide*. Jossey-Bass, San Francisco, California

Darkenwald G G, Larson G A 1980 *Reaching Hard to Reach Adults: New Directions for Continuing Education*, No. 8. Jossey-Bass, San Francisco, California

Ely M L (ed.) 1948 *Handbook of Adult Education in the United States*. Institute of Adult Education, Teachers College, Columbia University, New York

Houle C O 1972 *The Design of Education*. Jossey-Bass, San Francisco, California

Jensen G E, Liveright A A, Hallenbeck W (eds.) 1964 *Adult Education: Outlines of an Emerging Field of University Study*. Adult Education Association of the United States, Washington, DC

Knowles M S (ed.) 1960 *Handbook of Adult Education in the United States*. Adult Education Association of the United States, Washington, DC

Knowles M S 1977 *A History of the Adult Education Movement in the United States: Includes Adult Education Institutions through 1976*. Krieger, Huntington, New York

Knox A B 1977a *Adult Development and Learning: A Handbook on Individual Growth and Competence in Adult Years for Education and the Helping Professions*. Jossey-Bass, San Francisco, California

Knox A B 1977b *Current Research Needs Related to Systematic Learning by Adults*. Occasional Paper No. 4. Office for the Study of Continuing Professional Education, University of Illinois, Urbana, Illinois

Knox A B (ed.) 1979a *Programming for Adults Facing Mid-life Change: New Directions for Continuing Education*. Jossey-Bass, San Francisco, California

Knox A B (ed.) 1979b *Assessing the Impact of Continuing Education: New Directions for Continuing Education*, No. 3. Jossey-Bass, San Francisco, California

Knox A B 1982 *Leadership Strategies for Meeting New Challenges: New Directions for Continuing Education*, No. 13. Jossey-Bass, San Francisco, California

Knox A B et al. 1980 *Developing, Administering, and Evaluating Adult Education*. Jossey-Bass, San Francisco, California

Kreitlow B W et al. (eds.) 1981 *Examining Controversies in Adult Education*. Jossey-Bass, San Francisco, California

Long H B, Hiemstra R et al. 1980 *Changing Approaches to Studying Adult Education*. Jossey-Bass, San Francisco, California

Merriam S B, Simpson E L 1984 *A Guide to Research for Educators and Trainers of Adults*. Krieger, Malabar, Florida

Peters J M et al. 1980 *Building an Effective Adult Education Enterprise*. Jossey-Bass, San Francisco, California

Review of Education Research (special issues on adult education) June 1950, June 1953, June 1959, June 1965

Rowden D (ed.) 1934 *Handbook of Adult Education in the United States*. American Association for Adult Education, New York

Smith R M, Aker G F, Kidd J R (eds.) 1970 *Handbook of Adult Education*. Macmillan, New York

Adult Education Research: Latin America

E. L. Ormeño

Two interpretative frameworks for the social function of adult education in Latin America have revealed several changes in the types of adult education programs developed since the 1960s. Research has begun to be incorporated into new programs; however, the results, as a whole, have not yet contributed significantly to the organic development of the field. Uneven theoretical–methodological developments can be observed, due to a greater concentration on scientific activities in some types of programs than in others. Nevertheless, influential research has been generated, particularly on nonformal and popular education programs, which could well determine future orientations for adult education.

1. Interpretative Frameworks, Programs, and Research

The diversification among adult education programs and the initiation of a systematic process for their theoretical–methodological development can be attributed to the appearance of two frameworks for interpreting the role of educational practices among adults in Latin American society.

The first of these reflects the explicit intention to make more coherent and functional the relationship between adult education programs and the dominant model of politicoeconomic structure in Latin America; specifically, the processes of import substitution and developmentalist proposals. "This model, even though it is a project for domination, seeks to incorporate within it the participation of popular sectors" (Garcia Huidobro 1980 p. 15). Research within this perspective has concentrated on evaluation of existing programs of adult education, which has led toward experimentation with new designs, and their dissemination within both formal and nonformal educational systems.

The second interpretative framework has developed from the global analysis of Latin American society, of existing disequilibriums, and the consequences of applying models and policies derived from dominant tendencies within the mass of population, especially the middle and lower sectors, and within both urban and rural areas. Within this focus, the analyses, experiments, and research projects as such have centered upon the search for alternative approaches, on innovative activities, on the planning of change, and on the creation, selection, utilization, or adaptation of methodological instruments which are appropriate for consolidating competing approaches.

Viewed as a whole, the diversification of these educational programs has broadened, without doubt, the scope of attention to the target population which, when added to the enrichment brought by the new theoretical–methodological approaches, has allowed since the early 1960s, variations in the perception of the roles of this type of education in society and its limits as a system. If in fact the predominant idea associated with adult education was actions which were strictly the responsibility of the ministry of education, this perception has been replaced by one which has seen it as a group of programs, developed by different organizations within the state apparatus and by intermediate institutions, or as programs generated by the very communities in which they were based (Picon 1982 p. 336).

Throughout 40 years of adult education, between 1920 and 1960, the process of the accumulation of knowledge and experiences, achieved almost totally by means of trial and error, has had the result of setting in motion the development of five main programs: complementary–supplementary elementary education for adults; local, regional, and national literacy campaigns; training personnel in urban–industrial enterprises; fundamental education for community development; and agricultural extension. Starting from the diversification of programs and the theoretical–methodological rupture begun in the 1960s, eight new approaches have since appeared: nonformal education, fundamental integral education, functional adult education, permanent education, formation and training for work, andragogy, open education, and popular education.

These programs have absorbed, by reinterpretation, the fundamental ideas and methods of the majority of the adult education programs of the previous era.

Examined in its totality, the collection of accumulated knowledge, despite the significance of its concepts, approaches, and methods, is still far from constituting an organic whole, which can serve as a theoretical–methodological support for all those who are engaged in the activities of adult education as educators, administrators, or researchers. The reasons for this may be found, perhaps, in the very nature of the theoretical–operative bases of each separate approach, in the style developed for each program, and the greater or lesser dialectic assumed by each of the various modes with others. Each one of the programs of adult education currently in existence has aimed at conceptual, operative, and theoretical–methodological self-sufficiency, with little interest in mutual compatibility with the others. Each approach defines for itself the purpose of its research, to the degree that it poses the question of what type of knowledge it needs, how it must go about creating that knowledge, and who will benefit from it. Hence not all the adult education programs currently being developed produce the same answers.

There are programs in which investigations are conceived as processes of the social production of knowledge and experiences, directly developed within a social base, with the members of the community participating in all of its stages, thereby unifying educational practice with scientific practice in a continuous process. In others, investigations are directed "toward" specific objects of study which, for the purposes of analysis, frequently need to be extracted from the contexts in which they are found. In general, these investigations are oriented toward the accumulation of information and data to solve problems or to optimize levels of decision making and performance.

Programs of adult education contributed unequally to the theory and practice of this particular mode, primarily because of a greater degree of concentration upon scientific activity in some, and upon ideology in others. The emphasis upon scientific activity in some programs of adult education creates possibilities for the development of influential research, not only because it offers an increase in present knowledge about theory and practice, but also because it offers the prospect of outlining the types of educational practices which may develop in the future.

This is the case in some research which is being developed within two approaches to adult education in Latin America: those educational projects oriented toward marginal rural and urban sectors found within nonformal education, and those projects located within popular education, the specific practices of which are known as action research and participatory research. These constitute examples of the types of scientific practices which are being developed within adult education in Latin America.

2. Some Approaches to Investigations of Adult Education for Popular Sectors in Latin America

2.1 Approaches and Research in Nonformal Education

Nonformal education comprises all types of programs "directed toward marginal and oppressed populations and consisting of a series of activities conducted outside of the school and designed and organized to increase the decision-making power and socioeconomic status of the participant" (La Belle 1982 p. 111). From this perspective, nonformal education should assume an active role in social change, not only by improving the skills of adults, but also by inducing new types of behavior within the social structure. Taking into account these concepts, Thomas La Belle investigated the theoretical–ideological bases of support in different programs of nonformal education, and the way in which these programs reinterpreted their educational outreach. He identified two sources for the theoretical foundations of these programs which interpreted the cause of underdevelopment. One is the thesis of "dependency," which explains the relationship between economic and political domination as stemming from a developed structure (center) toward a dependent one (periphery). This same type of relationship is manifested toward the interior of each underdeveloped country. From this perspective, the role of nonformal education is to achieve active participation in the process of liberation from the imposed system of control by means of re-evaluation by the persons affected. The works of Paulo Freire (1970), Francisco Gutierrez (1974), Ivan Illich (1970), and Everett Reimer (1971) adopt this conceptual framework. The second source of objectives for nonformal education is to be found in the thesis of "privation." In contrast to the previous thesis, this one locates the causes of underdevelopment within the very same Latin American countries, in their traditional values, types of behavior, technology, and social structure. According to this approach, the situation of underdevelopment can be overcome if the criteria of progress and modernization are adopted. Nonformal education is assigned a role to induce participation in broad projects for motivating the population, as well as in programs which improve their material conditions. Programs of literacy, basic adult education, and community development are related to this model.

The research of Thomas La Belle has also analyzed the predominance of psychological criteria in nonformal education, identified with both the thesis of "dependency–liberation" and that of "privation–development." The dominant position of such criteria in these programs generates a biased view of the necessary prerequisites for social change (La Belle 1982 pp. 114–16). Other investigations carried out under the theme of marginality–nonformal education, are based upon similar criteria. One such study was developed by the Peruvian National Institute of Research and Development in Education to investigate the degree of social differentiation within the marginal sectors, and the way in which individual behaviors exercise decisive effects upon the levels of success in programs of adult education (Aliaga 1979). In the same way, the results of educational experiences directed toward groups of people in a situation of extreme poverty in Chile suggested a need to make available processes of personalized learning, since with these, goals of self-affirmation, internal growth, and self-esteem, when achieved along with concrete learning, remove the barriers to new opportunities (Calvo and Lemke 1982 p. 416).

In his research, La Belle identified the existence of nonformal education programs integrated at the microlevel, the objectives of which were elaborated on the basis of sociological criteria. The basic concepts of culture and society are integrated and are related with two particular sociological theories: the theory of equilibrium and the theory of conflict. Linking these theories with the ideological interpretations of "privation–development" and "dependency–liberation" makes up the source of objectives for nonformal education. Programs which are oriented toward the "privation–development" interpretation adopt the criteria of the "equilibrium theory," and those oriented toward the theory of "dependency–liberation" define their objectives in terms of "conflict theory" (La Belle 1982 p. 116).

Some investigations of marginality and adult education adopt the sociological criteria previously mentioned, as, for example, in the works developed by the Regional Center of Adult Education in Venezuela (Melfo 1981).

Nonformal educational programs in Latin America have provided a topic of permanent interest, especially their relationship to the role of institutionalized education. From Latin American perspectives, formal and nonformal education are not mutually exclusive but complementary and may permeate each other in as much as they can be nourished by the contents of the popular cultural "vital fluid" and have a vision of the whole which emerges from informal education (Picon 1982 p. 348). This idea has been converted into an important source for the analysis and development of future research in adult education.

2.2 Popular Education: Approach and Role of Research

Just as it is difficult to find a generalized concept of nonformal education, by the same token, it is also difficult to find one for popular education. The latter brings together a group of action projects whose sources arise from the ideas of Paulo Freire, from the work on action research by Joao Bosco Pinto (1971), from the Latin American Participatory Network of the International Council of Adult Education, and fundamentally, from the multiplicity of experiences of education based in the urban and rural sectors. In general terms, popular education is understood as a process which begins with the historical–concrete situations (reality) of the participants. Its work methods aim toward the growth of individuals in their relationships with others. The relationships between educators and learners are horizontal. It is an education linked to action for the purpose of transforming reality, and as a process, it must integrate the whole of educational actions with social–economic activities (Garcia Huidobro 1980 pp. 28–31).

The term "popular education" comprises a group of connotations which specify that these types of programs are a dialectical process between individuals and their life conditions, with the knowledge generated by this relationship being directed toward the structural change of that reality (Vio et al. 1981 p. 10). Other concepts, such as those of "action research" and "participatory research," are associated with popular education as a generic expression of various types of programs. Both postulate a critical and alternative attitude toward traditional social research as a limited way of understanding and transforming reality, because it reduces such knowledge to a synchronous reality, from the reality defined on the basis of the unilateral perception of a knowing subject apart from the sociocultural reality which is the object of study (Pinto 1969).

The need to look for a method or type of investigation which unifies educational practice with scientific practice leads to action research. Such research does not end upon arriving at pedagogical programming, but is a permanent activity throughout the entire process. Given that reality is understood as a changing process, it has to be continually reflected in a liberating consciousness, which idea posits also a continuing investigative effort (Pinto 1971).

Criticism of traditional social research is also found in the idea of participatory research. A study based upon concrete application of this and action research is the adult education and rural development project undertaken by the Peasant Training Center of the University of San Cristobal of Huamanga in Ayacucho, Peru. The methodology applied is developed according to the principle of "basing all activities in the unique socio-economic and technological reality of the indigenous communities. It is necessary to salvage and to respect native technology, therefore it should be the basis for training courses" (De Wit and Gianotten 1981 p. 212). This principle is rendered more specific by the adoption of the following criteria upon which the actions of the Peasant Training Center are sustained: any peasant group or community has the potential to define its problems and to take charge of its own development; it is necessary to promote the active participation of the population in this same process; the process should generate in the participants consciousness of their own potential and confidence in themselves; the participation of the community in the research process permits a more exact analysis of reality; and research and training should be oriented toward change and creative action.

Considering the principle previously mentioned, the concept of training must be defined in response to the following questions: what kind of knowledge is needed (production of knowledge)? And, who will benefit from this knowledge (socialization of knowledge)? (De Wit and Gianotten 1981 pp. 204–06).

Bibliography

Aliaga E J 1979 *Investigaciónes básicas en apoyâ a la educación de adultos*. Instituto Nacional de Investigación y Desarrollo de la Educación (INIDE), Lima

Calvo G, Lemke D 1982 Una educación de adultos centrada en la persona y su aplicación en programas de extrema pobreza. *Ensayos sobre educación de los adultos en América Latina*. Centro de Estudios Educativos, México

De Wit T, Gianotten V 1981 Teoría y praxis en educación de adultos y desarrollo rural. *Investigación participativa y praxis rural*. Mosca Azul Editores, Lima

Freire P 1970 *Pedagogy of the Oppressed*. Herder and Herder, New York

Freire P 1979 *Education for Critical Consciousness*. Seabury, New York

Garcia Huidobro J E 1980 *Aportes para el análisis y la sistematización de experiencias no formales de educación*. Oficina Regional de la UNESCO para América Latina y el Caribe, Santiago

Gutierrez F 1974 *Pedagogía de la comunicación*. Editorial Costa Rica, San José

Hall B 1981 El conocimiento como mercancía y la investigación participativa. *Investigación participativa y praxis rural*. Mosca Azul Editores, Lima

Illich I D 1970 *Deschooling Society*. Harper and Row, New York

La Belle T J 1976 *Nonformal Education and Social Change in Latin America*. Latin American Center Publications, University of California, Los Angeles, California

La Belle T J 1982 Metas y estrategias de la educación no formal en América Latina. *Ensayos sobre educación de los adultos en América Latina*. Centro de Estudios Educativos, México

McGill M E, Horton M E 1973 *Action Research Designs for Training and Development*. National Training and Development Services Press, Washington, DC

Melfo H D 1981 *Marginalidad: Un enfoque educativo*. Centro Regional de Educación de Adultos, Caracas

Picón C 1982 La educación de adultos en América Latina en la década de los ochenta: Situación y perspectivas. *Ensayos sobre educación de los adultos en América Latina*. Centro de Estudios Educativos, México

Pinto J B 1969 Metodología de la Investigación Temática. *Serie Informes, Conferencias, Cursos no. 101*. IICA-CIRA, Bogotá

Pinto J B 1971 Educación Liberadora: Ubicación teórica y práctica. *Serie Informes, Conferencias, Cursos No. 36*. IICA-CIRA, Bogotá

Reimer E 1971 *School is Dead: An Essay on Alternatives in Education*. Doubleday, New York

Vio F, De Wit T, Gignotten V 1981 Introducción. *Investigación participativa y praxis rural*. Mosca Azul Editores, Lima

Adult Education Research: Western Europe

C. J. Titmus

For the purpose of comparison with other regions of the world it may be helpful to see Western Europe as a homogeneous area, but this leads inevitably to a simplification of reality. In research, as in other aspects of adult education, Western Europe combines common elements with marked national characteristics.

Research and scholarly enquiry into adult education were slow to grow in Western Europe because, among other reasons, practitioners were more concerned with meeting urgent needs for provision than reflecting upon and asking questions about what they were doing. On the other hand, adult education was not sufficiently important, or distinct from school education, to attract investigation by outsiders. Moreover, in countries such as the Federal Republic of Germany, France, Sweden, Denmark, and the Netherlands, universities, from which the impetus for research might have come, both rejected adult education as a field of their concern, with very few exceptions, and, perhaps more importantly, were kept at a distance by the adult education associations, who distrusted both their elitist ethos and their concentration on scholarship rather than effective teaching. The United Kingdom was an exception, but the teaching tradition in British universities, which made them successful with adults, went with a comparative lack of interest in research. Until very recently it had not been expected that professors of adult education in the United Kingdom should engage in research. They are still judged more by the programme of courses they arrange than by their scholarship.

1. Research Institutions

Although some important work was completed earlier, research was sparse and spasmodic until the 1960s. Only in the 1970s did centres of systematic study become established in most countries. This development was a consequence of the growth of adult education activity to a position of social, economic, and cultural importance throughout the region. Universities in France, the Federal Republic of Germany, the Netherlands, Sweden, and other countries set up courses for the professional education of persons who were seeking a career in the field and began to develop graduate programmes, out of which came both staff and student research. Following on the example of the Universities of Nottingham and Manchester, universities in the United Kingdom set up graduate programmes as offshoots of their traditional extramural work.

There is no accurate register of work done, but it is certain that by no means all research came from universities, although their share is increasing. A number of adult education institutes, largely established to encourage coordination, development, and training activities, have made a significant contribution to research and some, indeed, engaged in it earlier than most universities. In the Federal Republic of Germany the *Pädagogische Arbeitsstelle* [educational centre] of the Folk High School Association goes back to 1957. Another creation of the 1950s was the *Institut National d'Education Populaire* (INEP) [National Institute for Popular Education] in France. In England and Wales the roots of the National Institute of Adult Education go back before the Second World War. A more recent foundation, the *Institut National de Formation des Adultes* (INFA) [National Institute of Adult Education], which existed for just a few years, in the late 1960s and early 1970s, produced a substantial volume of work before the French government closed it. Even more recently national institutes of adult education have been founded in the Netherlands and Norway. In the United Kingdom the Advisory Council for Adult and Continuing Education (1977–83) was particularly active. Although these institutes have been, to a greater or lesser extent, subsidized by government departments, only INEP is, and INFA was, a state institution. The Advisory Council for Adult and Continuing Education (ACACE) was state appointed and financed, but functionally independent. The others are close to the field of adult education provision, the *Pädagogische Arbeitsstelle* being a section of a private association, and the institutes in the United Kingdom, the Netherlands, and Norway directly representing the interests of providers of adult education, either state or private.

International organizations have played a useful role in Western European research in the field of adult education, notably the Council of Europe and the European Bureau of Adult Education. They have not done much themselves, but have provided stimulation and foci for research activities. They have had little financial support to give, but their study groups and working parties, largely composed of representatives of university adult education departments and of adult education associations, have to some degree initiated and coordinated studies in a number of countries. They have thereby helped to direct research effort to major topics of common Western European interest, and to give a homogeneous research profile to the region, which may, however, be misleading.

2. Kinds of Research

For the most part research is a response to problems of practice and seeks to illuminate and improve it in the short term. If it does not, it tends to be suspect or disregarded. Behind this approach lies the influence of adult educators and their organizations, whose traditional suspicion of the academic's isolation from the realities of the field partly explains the continuing research work of the institutes already mentioned. Even in universities the emphasis is directed to applied studies by their dependence on research funding by government agencies and private sources, such as employers, trade unions, and private foundations, whose concern is with the practice of adult education.

There is therefore a close link between research and development. For example, a number of substantial experimental projects have been carried out to test new ways of engaging hitherto nonparticipants in adult education; in Liverpool at the end of the 1960s (Lovett 1975); at about the same time in the Briey basin of Lorraine (Lesne et al. 1970); in Sweden (Extended Adult Education 1974); and in southern England (Fordham et al. 1979). Although much of it is not conceived of as research, a lot of innovations on a smaller scale have been monitored and have contributed valuably to knowledge.

The most widely practised form of enquiry has probably been, however, the survey. It is largely through surveys that patterns of participation in adult education

(NIAE 1970), adult attitudes to education, and their learning needs (Strzelewicz et al. 1966, ACACE 1982) have been investigated. Surveys have been used to evaluate government policy (Van Dieman and Kraan 1979), to study the providers, participants, and activities of citizenship education (Neubeck 1968), in fact for any subject susceptible to quantitative investigation and, in the form of extended interviews, for much qualitative work too.

The initiation and organization of adult education research appears to follow no common pattern in Western Europe. Except in the United Kingdom, most of the internationally known projects seem to have originated and been conducted outside the universities. Cooperation between government and adult education interests exerts a strong influence on the choice of topics for study, which, in the case of large investigations, mainly depend on state funding. There is little sign, however, that governments have coherent research policies. The growing number of small individual studies, carried out by graduate students and staff in universities, have made comparatively little impact.

3. *Fields of Study*

Research in Western Europe is sociologically, rather than psychologically oriented. The central concern of adult education is the individual learner, but that is not reflected in a large body of research into the psychology of adult learning. Rather the emphasis is likely to be on the needs and behaviour of social groups in relation to adult education. There have been numerous studies devoted to mapping out the field of educational provision, to examining the history, organization, and function of providing institutions, and to identifying their clientele. Attention has been given, as has already been indicated, to the problem of attracting the undereducated to study, by new ways of organizing the education offer, or by measures to facilitate participation, such as educational leave. There is a growing interest in adult education as an instrument of public policy.

The continuing concern with the methods and techniques of educating adults has been given a considerable stimulus by the importance attached to vocational education. In the United Kingdom substantial work on adult learning and teaching has been done by the Industrial Training Research Unit, of University College, University of London. In France, INFA addressed itself to similar vocationally directed questions.

Largely through the Council of Europe and the European Bureau of Adult Education, the study of adult education has taken on an international dimension. The problem of communication between scholars of different countries and, thus, of terminology, has engaged attention (EBAE 1976). The Council of Europe has sponsored a number of projects, most of which, like the feasibility study of policies for the promotion of cultural democracy (Council of Europe 1978), have involved both research and development. The European Bureau has collated and analysed adult education legislation from European countries (EBAE 1985). Western European scholars have been major participants in the project on organization and structures of adult education in Europe, which is coordinated in Prague and includes the socialist countries of Eastern Europe.

Adult education research in Western Europe is criticized for lacking theoretical underpinning. It is said to be superficial and all too closely tied to immediate application. That is largely true of empirical work, but not of thinking at the broad strategic level. Western Europeans, working in a number of instances, admittedly within international organizations such as UNESCO and the Organisation for Economic Co-operation and Development (OECD), have contributed centrally to the evolution of the concepts of lifelong education, recurrent education, and sociocultural animation. The French have made the last particularly their own.

4. *National Characteristics in Research*

France is a good example of national particularity in Western Europe. Until the 1960s the concept of adult education was foreign to French thinking. It was replaced in theory and in practice by sociocultural animation, all-age, nonformal education. It was the need for postexperience vocational training of workers, of which the government became conscious during the 1960s, which directed research attention to questions of systematic education for adults. The result has been that studies into sociocultural animation may relate to, but are not specific to, adults, and studies specifically concerned with adults respond almost entirely to situations created by vocational training activities. There has also been an awakening of interest in the history of adult education, which had formerly been completely ignored.

In the United Kingdom and the Federal Republic of Germany history has long been a research interest to a degree not matched by any other European countries. More recently in the Federal Republic of Germany, substantial work has been done on the psychology of adult learning and curriculum development, although the largest number of university publications have been in the field of vocational training. In the United Kingdom small pieces of research from graduate students have proliferated, but the most notable feature of the late 1970s was the development of a research policy by the Department of Education and Science, which has seen a move to sizable team projects financed by the ministry. Some of these have been contracted out directly to universities, but much of the work has been done directly by the NIAE and ACACE, or contracted through them to institutions of higher education. They include studies of the nature and extent of paid educational leave (Killean and Bird 1981); adult education and the black community (Little et al. 1982); and the relationship between the structure and performance of adult education institutions (Mee and Wiltshire 1978).

In Sweden there has not been the growth of adult education departments in universities, which can be observed in France, the Federal Republic of Germany, the United Kingdom, or the Netherlands. University research there is in the hands of social scientists and education departments and therefore less directly governed by considerations of practice. The continuing concern to relate research to the needs of practitioners is, however, demonstrated by the action of the National Education Board in offering to local adult education associations money to carry out their own research and development projects (Höghielm 1981). Another example of freedom of university research from field constraints is to be found in the Netherlands, where much theoretical work has been done on andragogy (Ten Have 1971), and that too has been balanced by work of more immediate application outside higher education.

The tension between fundamental research and policy- and practice-oriented work will continue in Western Europe. It may be that increasing effort in universities will redress the balance towards the latter. Certainly countries like the United Kingdom need to develop a better theoretical base, a task which has hitherto been almost completely neglected. The pressure from the funders of research, in most cases the state, makes it unlikely this will happen in the foreseeable future. Adult education is perceived too much as an instrument of urgent social and economic policies for the requirements of its long-term development to be given a higher priority.

Bibliography

Advisory Council for Adult and Continuing Education 1982 *Adults: Their Educational Experience and Needs*. Advisory Council for Adult and Continuing Education, Leicester

Council for Cultural Cooperation 1978 *Sociocultural Animation*. Council for Cultural Cooperation, Strasbourg

European Bureau for Adult Education (EBAE) 1985 *Survey of Adult Education Legislation*. EBAE, Amersfoort

European Bureau for Adult Education (EBAE) 1976 *The Terminology of Adult/Continuing Education*. EBAE, Amersfoort

Extended Adult Education 1974 Liber Tryck, Stockholm

Fordham P et al. 1979 *Learning Networks in Adult Education. Nonformal Education on a Housing Estate*. Routledge and Kegan Paul, London

Höghielm R 1981 The consequences for research of decentralisation. An evaluation of local research in Swedish adult education. In: Harvey B et al. (eds.) 1981 *Policy and Research in Adult Education: The First Nottingham International Colloquium 1981*. University of Nottingham, Nottingham

Killean J, Bird M 1981 *Education and Work*. National Institute of Adult Education, Leicester

Lesne M, Collon C, Oeconomo C 1970 *Changement socio-professionnel et formation: Étude d'une situation de crise dans le bassin de Briey*. Institut National de Formation des Adultes (INFA), Paris

Little A et al. 1982 *Adult Education and the Black Communities*. Advisory Council for Adult and Continuing Education (ACACE), Leicester

Lovett T 1975 *Adult Education, Community Education and the Working Class*. Ward Lock Educational, London

Mee G, Wiltshire H 1978 *Structure and Performance in Adult Education*. Longman, London

Neubeck H 1968 *Ein Beitrag zur Bestandsaufnahme der Einrichtungen politischer Erwachsenenbildung in der Bundesrepublik*. Pädagogische Arbeitsstelle des Deutschen Volkschochschul-Verbandes, Frankfurt/Main

National Institute of Adult Education (NIAE) 1970 *Adequacy of Provision*. NIAE, London

Strzelewicz W, Raapke H D, Schulenberg W 1966 *Bildung und gesellschaftliches Bewusstsein: Eine mehrstufige Soziologische Untersuchung in Westdeutschland*. Enke, Stuttgart

Ten Have T T 1971 Training and research in the field of adult education at the Dutch universities. *Int. Congress of Univ. Adult Educ. J.* 10 (3)

Van Dieman A, Kraan R 1979 *Evaluatie van Educatieve Planning, Verkorte Verslag* [Evaluation of educational planning, summary report]. Studiecentrum NCVO, Amersfoort

Adult Education Research: Eastern Europe and the Soviet Union

E. Livečka

Since the Second World War, the socialist countries of Eastern Europe have devoted a substantial effort to both personnel and money for research into the education of adults. The nature of this effort reflects the emphases of adult education practice and purposes in these countries and these, in their turn, have been determined by the Marxist–Leninist ideology common to all of them and by the strong influence of the Soviet Union, as well as by the individual traditions and social, economic, and cultural situations of each country.

1. Institutional Basis of Adult Education Research in the Soviet Union

Adult education research in the Soviet Union, like the management of adult education itself, is centrally controlled, different areas of work coming under different state agencies. Formal general adult education comes under the Ministry of Education, which is responsible for secondary education and has under its direction the All-Union Academy of Pedagogical Sciences of the Soviet Union. Institutes of this Academy are concerned with questions of general adult education, particularly the Research Institute of General Adult Education in Leningrad, which undertakes both basic and applied research.

The Ministry of Universities and Secondary Vocational Schools has a number of specialized research and methodological centres which also undertake work in adult education, mainly of an applied nature. The Committee for Vocational Training directs the preparation of young people for manual occupations and the postexperience education of skilled workers. Its research centres concentrate on questions associated with these activities.

The Communist Party itself has a network of Party schools, at higher education and lower levels, designed for Party workers. Major research into the political and ideological education of workers is undertaken by the Party's Department of Research into the Effectiveness of Party Propaganda and Political Information.

The central offices of Soviet trade unions direct trade union colleges, which do important adult education research.

The Ministry of Culture of the Soviet Union maintains institutes of culture which train most of the workers employed in nonformal sociocultural education. These centres also engage in research, some of it basic, but most of it applied.

2. Main Directions of Adult Education Research in the Soviet Union

In the 1980s, research into adult education concentrates on historical, sociological, didactic, economic, and organizational–methodological questions. It is largely undertaken in specialized research organizations. Theoretical and methodological problems of adult pedagogy, for example, are studied at the Departments of Pedagogy and Psychology of the Institute of Culture in Moscow and Leningrad, at the V. I. Lenin Pedagogical Institute in Moscow, the Scientific–Methodological Council of University Pedagogy of the Ministry of Universities, and at the Research Institute of General Adult Education, Leningrad.

The study of the sociology of adult education is undertaken at the universities of Moscow and Leningrad as well as in specialized centres. Research into sociology is often linked to psychologically oriented studies. It has mainly concentrated on preferences, sentiments, and educational interests of various groups of the population, for example, workers, farmers, young people, men and women; questions of public opinion and scale of values in relation to education and self-education; and cultural customs and habits. Particular attention has been devoted to the influence of the mass media on adult education, especially at the Institute of Philosophy of the Academy of Sciences of the Soviet Union.

Research into the education of managerial cadres is conducted in institutes whose aim is to raise the qualifications of managerial workers in various republics of the Soviet Union and by the All-Union Scientific–Methodological Centre for the Organization of Labour and Production Management of the Council of Ministers of the Soviet Union.

3. The Scope of Adult Education Research

There have been different classifications of the subjects which should be the concern of adult education research in the Soviet Union. The most authoritative is that drawn up by Professor A. O. Pint, Head of the Department of Pedagogy and Psychology of the Institute of Culture in Moscow (1980):

(a) General problems of adult pedagogy. The content, specificity, and system of adult pedagogy; the methodology and methods of adult pedagogy as a science; the relation of adult pedagogy to other sciences; pedagogical problems of the all-round and harmonious development of the adult personality; the leader of an adult collective as a pedagogue–educator; the stages of adult psychological development and individual psychological characteristics; pedagogical foundations of sociocultural work; pedagogical problems in party work; pedagogical foundations for improving the forms and methods of party, trade union, and Komsomol work with people; problems of vocational pedagogy; and problems of social pedagogy of adults.

(b) Principal stages in the history of adult pedagogy.

(c) Theoretical problems of raising the cultural and educational standards of adults, and pedagogical control of their self-education.

(d) Practical problems of the education, self-education, and re-education of adults. The specificity and content of the educational process and pedagogical conditions for effective educational work with various groups of adults; principles and system of methods and means of educational influence on adults and their psychologico–pedagogical characteristics; interconnections between emotional, rational, and volitional factors and means of influence in adult education; the collective and adult education; self-education and its pedagogical control; pedagogy of labour; pedagogical problems of socialist emulation and the movement for communist work; the arts and adult education.

(e) Pedagogical problems of leisure. Pedagogical conditions and prerequisites for effective use of leisure time as a factor of all-round development of the personality; unity and interconnection between work and rest in all-round development of the personality; the place of social organizations in the rational use of leisure; pedagogical prerequisites for effective work by sociocultural establishments in the rational use of leisure by different groups of the population; pedagogical conditions for effective educational influence by film, radio, television, and the press; the culture of recreation; the promotion and educational importance of tourism; physical culture as a factor and means of all-round development of the adult's personality.

(f) Problems of applied adult pedagogy. Pedagogical prerequisites for effective verbal propaganda; objective propaganda and its pedagogical requirements; pedagogical foundations of comprehensive forms of work with adults; specificity and content of educational work with adults in clubs, libraries, and museums; methods of teaching various kinds of arts, technical creativity, and so on.

Professor Pint at the same time stresses that adult pedagogy has its own, specific methods of research. The traditional methods of pedagogy, such as observation and pedagogical experiments, have a place in adult pedagogy too, but only on condition that they are subjected to specific concrete interpretation.

4. Adult Education Research Institutions in Other European Socialist Countries

As in the Soviet Union, adult education research is carried out largely in research institutions controlled by state or quasistate organizations. A wide range of agencies undertake study in this field. Some institutions derive directly from ministries, notably those responsible for education, labour, and economic affairs. In Poland, for example, the Ministry of Education set up five institutes in 1972, some of which engage in adult educational research. In Hungary, the State Research Institute for the Qualification Development of Workmen and Specialists, was established in 1974 under the Ministry of Labour.

The Communist Parties have a hand in research through scientific academies, which are an element of the party apparatus. The College of Social Management of the Bulgarian Academy of Social Sciences and Management and the Romanian Academy of Social and Political Sciences may be cited as examples.

Trade unions also engage in study and research through their own specialist centres. In Bulgaria the Central Council of Trade Unions maintains the Georgi Dimitrov Institute for Research. Organizations which also contribute to the study of adult education include the cooperative movement, the mass media, sports and physical education bodies, and the health services.

Universities play a significant part in all the socialist states of Europe, through departments or faculties of pedagogy or philosophy as in the University of Sofia, Bulgaria, the Humboldt University in Berlin, and the Universities of Budapest and Debrecen in Hungary. In Poland, 11 universities have adult education departments, or sections within education departments; in Yugoslavia the Philosophical Faculties of the universities in Belgrade, Ljubljana, Sarajevo, Skopje, and Zagreb; in Czechoslovakia the universities of Olomouc, Presŏv, Bratislava, Brno, and the Charles University of Prague, are active in adult education research.

5. Directions of Adult Education Research

The extent to which the national research effort in adult education is coordinated varies from country to country. In the German Democratic Republic the Central Institute for Vocational Education at the State Secretariat for Vocational Training has the responsibility for coordinating all research directed to the development of a national system of education, including that of adults. In Czechoslovakia from 1976 to 1980, there was a set state programme for basic research: "Adult education, its qualities and relation to youth education—the fundamentals of adult pedagogy". That was followed by another, "Adult education in the system of lifelong education". In Poland, on the other hand, research is not nationally coordinated at all.

As a broad generalization, basic research is largely undertaken in universities and scientific academies, applied research in specialized institutes. There are, however, exceptions to this rule. Student theses at the Humboldt and Dresden Universities have significantly contributed to the solution of problems in various branches of the national economy. The State Research Institute for the Qualification Development of Workmen and Specialists, run by the Hungarian Ministry of Labour, engages in theoretical study.

In some socialist states the need to develop principles and practices appropriate to adult education led to the formulation of the concept of andragogy. Research and study in Yugoslavia, Hungary, and Poland has concentrated on the development of its theory and application. In other European socialist states, although andragogy may not be an accepted term, theoretical research has concerned itself with the same problems, notably the place of adult education in a system of lifelong education and the place of adult education in socialist thought and life.

The goal of education in the Eastern European countries is declared to be the development of the individual, but as the work role is held to be essential to full self-realization there is a strong emphasis in initial and adult education on preparation for economic activity. Research effort is strongly directed in all the socialist states to problems of vocational education, particularly training for higher qualifications and training of supervisors and managerial cadres. The study of the education of adult educators is also important, both at independent centres, such as the Andragogical Centre in Zagreb, and universities, including those already mentioned.

The strong participation of the socialist countries in the project, Comparative Research in the Organization and Structures of Adult Education in Europe indicates an interest in both comparative and organizational studies.

Although there are underlying themes common to adult education research in all, or nearly all, of the European socialist countries, each has its own national interests. In Bulgaria, study is undertaken in adult education planning and management. In Czechoslovakia work is carried out into the aesthetic, language, and special education of adults. The overall theme of research in the German Democratic Republic is the development of workers' personalities, to which is related the topic of culture and work, and there has been some study of adult education planning and management. In Hungary there is research oriented to problems of adult teaching and learning—target analyses, determination of optimal course contents, active methods, the forms of adult education, self-directed learning for qualifications. In Yugoslavia all adult education research is accommodated under the umbrella of andragogy and includes history, comparative andragogy, methodology of research, and the application of andragogy to specific educational sectors—industrial, military, social, penological, and gerontological. In Poland, research has been conducted into nonformal education, self-directed learning, the history of adult education, and teaching methods. Romania's concern with the eradication of illiteracy and with second chance education may reflect shortcomings in the initial education system and it is not surprising to find scholars there concerned with teaching and learning—target analyses, optimal course content, methods, and forms of adult education.

Bibliography

Fukász G et al. 1978 *Adult Education in the Hungarian People's Republic: Adult Education in Europe*, Vol. 3. European Centre for Leisure and Education, Prague

Krajnc A, Mrmak I 1978 *Adult Education in Yugoslavia: Adult Education in Europe*, Vol. 4. European Centre for Leisure and Education, Prague

Pacociński R, Połturzycki J 1979 *Adult Education in People's Poland: Adult Education in Europe*, Vol. 6. European Centre for Leisure and Education, Prague

Schmelzer G, Fleischhauer K H, Pogodda G 1978 *Adult Education in the German Democratic Republic: Adult Education in Europe*, Vol. 5. European Centre for Leisure and Education, Prague

Subjects and Approaches to Research

Introduction

The articles in this subsection are of two kinds. The first three address specific fields of investigation, possibly the most important ones in adult education worldwide over the last decades. The last two provide examples of approaches to the investigation of adult education, both of which seem particularly appropriate to the situation and purposes of education, including that of adults.

Lifelong Education: Research Strategies has little to report of work done, but concerns itself with what needs to be done. It points to the necessity of supporting the theory of lifelong education, which has certainly proved seductive, with empirical evidence. It outlines the special difficulties of achieving this, given the range and length of lifelong learning, and suggests, with reference to examples that have already been tried, how it might be done.

The problem of literacy is one of the most intractable ones that confront adult education. *Literacy Research* reviews the investigations that have been conducted. Some of it has already been mentioned. This article reports study of the nature of literacy and particularly of methods of teaching. It also proposes lines for future development.

Adult Education for Employment: Research identifies the dominant topics in this field, and surveys what studies show about policy and participation, programme design and development, and instructional methods and techniques. It draws attention to efforts to develop a theoretical base, points to the need for more work on this, and lists a wide range of other research needs.

Participatory Research discusses a form of research which is particularly attractive to adult educators because, by involving learners in study of their own situation and activities, it constitutes an educational experience as well as an approach to inquiry. The article under this title lists the characteristics of such study, traces the origins of its current popularity, especially in developing countries, and discusses issues raised by this approach, particularly the researcher as learner, the nature of participation, the creation of popular knowledge, the power vested in the professional researcher and the state, and participatory research as an instrument of empowerment for popular groups.

Comparative Studies in Adult and Lifelong Education details a less controversial form of investigation, which finds support in the continuing thread of internationalism which runs through the field. This article outlines the purposes of comparative study, and distinguishes between different kinds of comparative and international research, single nation studies, overviews, cross-cultural views, and descriptive and analytical comparisons. It describes examples of research and discusses the problems and issues which need to be confronted.

Lifelong Education: Research Strategies

A. J. Cropley

The term "lifelong education" appeared in English language writings in the 1920s, and many of the main ideas to be found in contemporary literature were stated immediately after the Second World War (Jacks 1946). Although the basic idea is thus by no means novel, recent years have been marked by a concentrated effort to work out the practical consequences of implementing lifelong education as the guiding principle for future development of educational systems in all countries, as was suggested by Faure in the early 1970s (Faure et al. 1972). Such a sweeping recommendation requires detailed specification of what the concept of lifelong education means in practice, to what outcomes it should lead, what benefits these will bring, how the outcomes are to be achieved, and many more. In other words, if lifelong education is to advance beyond the status of merely a ringing catch phrase, it will have to become the subject of an enormous research effort. The purpose of the present article is to review some of the research strategies which have been adopted to date, and to indicate a little of what still needs to be done.

1. Lifelong Learning

The central characteristic of lifelong education is to be found in its label—learning takes place at all ages and not merely during childhood, and should be systematically supported throughout each person's lifetime. Lifelong education is, therefore, a set of financial, organizational, administrative, and didactic procedures for the fostering of lifelong learning. It is important to make clear that what is meant here by "learning" is not the spontaneous, everyday learning of ordinary life. What is important in the present context is what Tough (1971) called "deliberate" learning. Lifelong education is thus concerned with the purposeful, systematic facilitation throughout the lifespan of deliberate, goal-oriented learning.

It is also important to bear in mind that lifelong learning occurs throughout the entire lifespan, not merely in the adult years. Although it is quite obvious that most lifelong learning takes place in adulthood, simply because most people spend more of their lives as adults than as children, the term "lifelong education" is not a synonym for "adult education", despite a tendency for some writers to use it in this way. Nor is it a new term for nontraditional forms of education, although it emphasizes the importance of educational processes outside the traditional system. On the contrary, many proponents of lifelong education emphasize both that its implementation would have enormous implications for traditional institutions and traditional students, and that schools would be an important element in a system of lifelong education. Schools would, for instance, continue to be the earliest form of contact with formal education, and thus potentially in a position to lay a foundation for later learning.

2. Lifewide Learning

A second major notion has become so well-established in writings about lifelong education that it now forms, in effect, part of the definition. This is the idea that lifelong learning, as the term is used here, could not be carried out exclusively in schools and school-like settings, but would have to take place at work, in recreational settings, in the home, in clubs, in political or religious organizations, and so on. Otherwise, lifelong education could come to mean schooling "as a life sentence"! Thus, lifelong education would encompass not only lifelong learning, but also "lifewide" learning.

3. Other Definitive Characteristics

Current writings about lifelong education take for granted certain goals or guiding principles which, despite the fact that there is no inherent connection between them and the ideas of lifelong and lifewide learning, have come to have the status of definitive characteristics: these include principles such as the need for education to have as a goal eliminating social and economic inequities, the importance of education as an instrument for bettering the quality of life, the role of education as an instrument for the emancipation of disadvantaged groups or peoples, and the like.

It is also frequently emphasized in the literature on lifelong education that participation would have to be voluntary—otherwise lifelong education could become an instrument of oppression. This means that lifelong education would depend for its existence upon possession by adults of "prerequisites" for lifelong learning (Cropley 1979), these include knowledge, skills, attitudes, values, and self-image, which are, to some extent, summed up in the concept of "self-directed learning".

4. Research Problems

The conduct of research in the area of education is beset with many problems, some of which appear in especially difficult forms in the area of lifelong education. Particularly when one is dealing with a concept which aims at functioning as a guiding principle for reform of all levels of education in all countries, goals can only be stated in broad, general terms, which not infrequently have different meanings in practice in different societies—"creative participation in the life of the society" would be an example of such a goal. Empirical studies of the effects of changes in educational practice based on adoption of the principle of lifelong education would require studies stretching over the lifetime of the people being studied. Large-scale educational research, especially on a worldwide basis, is often made difficult by the fact that there are powerful sources of influence which may have a vested interest in seeing to it that research findings come out in a particular way, regardless of the data obtained.

Problems of this kind have led to a situation where, in the area of lifelong education, traditional research studies are extremely difficult to conduct: the scope is simply too vast, and the stakes too high. Despite this, as will be seen, many attempts have been made to develop the necessary research basis.

5. Some Research Strategies

One activity which has been common in this area is the holding of meetings of experts. Typically, a number of people who for one reason or another are thought to be in a position to clarify important issues are called together, and charged with the task of identifying and discussing issues in the area of lifelong education and making recommendations of an appropriate kind. Reports issuing from such meetings are, however, sometimes abstract, vague and general, bland, impractical, and based more on wishful thinking or ideology than on a sober review of available empirical data.

A second research strategy which has been applied in this area involves the conducting of surveys. Typically, questionnaires or similar instruments are sent to persons or agencies directly affected by proposed changes or thought likely to be in a position to cast light on important issues because, for instance, of special experience or expertise. Some surveys of this kind have concerned themselves with experts (see previous comments) or with local or national educational agencies, others with potential learners or teachers. Although empirical in the sense that they seek to collect information and not merely isolated opinions, surveys in this area have suffered from many of the weaknesses already outlined in connection with meetings of experts. In addition, the "findings" are beset with all the well-known difficulties which arise in connection with surveys, such as the tendency for people to give answers conforming to what they think is expected of them.

Another kind of empirical strategy is to be seen in case studies. Sometimes these have concerned themselves with efforts to implement lifelong education in a particular area of the total education system (for instance teacher education), and at other times they have involved study of a particular activity thought to be especially valuable for implementing lifelong education (such as instruction by radio). Although case studies have assembled much valuable information, it is often difficult to draw more general conclusions because of lack of methodological uniformity from study to study, while conclusions may also reflect preconceptions or ideology as much as empirical facts. Thus, all three research strategies mentioned suffer from lack of objectivity, of clarity, and of generalizability.

A small number of attempts have been made to conduct "experimental" studies of the traditional kind, characterized by design of an innovation on the basis of the principles of lifelong education, implementation of the innovation, systematic collection of data with the help of appropriate instruments, comparison of pretest and posttest or experimental group-control group data, objective analysis (for instance, with the aid of statistics), and so on. Such studies may be essentially of the "laboratory" type (such as studies of the ability of adults to learn nonsense syllables under various conditions), or of the "field" type (such as studies of the effects of appropriate teacher training on the subsequent real-life behaviour of student teachers in comparison with students who did not receive the new kind of training). As has been demonstrated by, for instance, Cropley and Dave (1978), large-scale, international studies of this kind are plagued by problems of lack of uniformity of design, and enormous variability in the sophistication of instruments and the thoroughness of statistical analysis, as well as straightforward bureaucratic problems such as obtaining permission to introduce appropriate changes in existing institutions or systems.

6. *Future Research Needs*

Proponents of lifelong education argue that deliberate learning is possible at all ages, that it can be fostered in certain ways, that there are good reasons for wishing to do this, and that desirable outcomes both for individuals and societies will result. It is apparent from the literature that the implementation of lifelong education would have implications for the organization and structure of educational systems, for teaching and learning strategies adopted in those systems, and for the personal properties of learners actually engaging in lifelong learning. Finally, it is clear that the implementation of lifelong education would affect all kinds of educational institutions, teachers and teacher training, materials and media, and the like. However, by the mid-1980s there was only a minimal amount of research capable of showing that the kinds of change envisaged by theorists will indeed have the effects claimed for them, and that these effects will in turn lead to beneficial end results (such as improved quality of life, democracy, and international understanding).

What is needed, then, are research studies which are capable of casting light on these issues, such as the study in Thailand (Thongchua et al. 1982) in which, under the aegis of regional lifelong education centres, women were taught sewing and typing skills. Subsequent evaluation included assessment of the effects of this training on the day-to-day lives of women, as well as an evaluation of the effects of variables such as special training for instructors.

One group of studies would have to be concerned with what might be called "basic" research. These studies would involve questions such as whether or not educational experiences can affect the development of "personal prerequisites" for lifelong learning, whether there are critical ages during which such effects occur, what variables exercise decisive influences and under what circumstances? A second group of studies would need to be concerned with the people who will actually carry on lifelong learning, looking, for example, at what learning needs they have, which variables determine their willingness to learn in adult life, to what extent are they capable of planning their own learning experiences, and so on. A third group of studies will need to be concerned with teaching and learning methods and materials. What kinds of procedures in schools lead to later lifelong learning, how effective are various kinds of media in linking learning in the classroom with learning outside it? Finally, there is a need for a group of research studies concerned with educational institutions and systems. How is learning in real-life settings to be coordinated with learning in formal institutions, how can such learning be evaluated, how can resistance on the part of educational personnel be overcome, what new and special forms of teacher education are necessary, and so on?

7. Future Prospects

A major problem for research in the area of lifelong education, apart from the omnipresent research problems of design, measurement, and analysis, is that the whole concept has been presented at such a general and all-encompassing level that research has tended to be either global and diffuse or else narrow and unconnected to general issues. This tendency has been encouraged by the fact that the concept has received much attention from international agencies, especially UNESCO, which because of its very nature has difficulty avoiding such problems. What is needed is for the concept to be broken down into more discrete areas which can be dealt with using less rhetoric and more empirical rigour. Attempts by some economists, sociologists, psychologists, planners, and the like to outline specific, manageable, empirically testable issues are a step in the right direction. Also needed are practical studies in definite settings, such as a specific school type in a particular national setting, carried out, to be sure, under a number of different conditions, but with sufficient uniformity to yield generalizable, but still practical findings. Whether the necessary studies will take place, or whether lifelong education will remain a catchall elastic concept meaning whatever the person using it wants it to mean, is unclear.

Bibliography

Cropley A J (ed.) 1979 *Lifelong Education: A Stocktaking.* UNESCO, Hamburg

Cropley A J (ed.) 1980 *Towards a System of Lifelong Education.* Pergamon, Oxford

Cropley A J, Dave R H 1978 *Lifelong Education and the Training of Teachers.* Pergamon, Oxford

Faure E, Herrera F, Kaddsoura A-R, Lopes H, Petrovsky A V, Rahnema M, Ward F C 1972 *Learning to Be: The World of Education Today and Tomorrow.* UNESCO, Paris

Jacks M L 1946 *Total Education: A Plea for Synthesis.* Paul, Trench and Trubner, London

Thongchua V, Phaholvech N, Jiratatprasoot K 1982 Adult education project: Thailand. *Eval. Educ.* 6: 53–81

Tough A M 1971 *The Adult's Learning Projects: A Fresh Approach to Theory and Practices in Adult Learning.* Ontario Institute for Studies in Education, Toronto, Ontario

Literacy Research

H. S. Bhola

Literacy as an area of study can be usefully distinguished from the area of reading research which is typically concerned with the teaching of reading and writing to children and youth within formal school settings.

Professional interest in literacy is comparatively recent, and research and development (the process whereby research is converted into curriculum products and educational practices usable by practitioners) in literacy is meager compared to needs.

1. Available Research and Development in Adult Literacy

Important beginnings have, however, been made. Predictably perhaps, the first set of research questions has dealt with the motivations of adult learners and the methodology of literacy teaching to adults.

Adult motivations determine whether adults will come to literacy classes, and once there, whether or not they will drop out without completing the instructional cycle. Identified learner motivations seem to be rooted in the socioeconomic and cultural environments of learners: they differ in men and women, in rural and urban areas, and across occupations and age groups. Understandably, motivational profiles of adult learners in developed countries (Kidd 1969, Rossman 1971) have differed somewhat from those in underdeveloped countries (Hussain 1973, UNESCO 1973).

Motivations expressed by adults in developing countries (where most of the world's illiterates live) have ranged from the desire to write one's own name, to want to read and write letters, to be able to keep accounts and particularly to avoid being cheated in the market, to acquire vocational knowledge, to secure better employment or to advance economically, to participate more fully in the institutions at the community level, to avail oneself of extension and loan services, to earn pride and prestige that comes from being literate, to teach one's children and to help them with their homework, to learn more about the world and its people, to read religious books, and finally to use the available spare time profitably (NFEC 1967, Couvert 1971, Kaufmann and Bazany 1970, UNESCO/FREPD 1979).

The dropout phenomenon, as the inverse of motivation, has also attracted the attention of researchers. Dropout rates have been known to vary from 30 percent to as high as 90 percent or more. Reasons stated for dropping out have included competing occupational obligations and work schedules, family and religious obligations, illness and fatigue, economic hardships, attitude towards learning, unreasonable expectations from the learning process, inconducive learning environment, teacher absences or misbehavior, change of residence, distances from classes and transportation problems, weather conditions, and unsuitable curricula (IALM 1980).

Organizers of literacy programs seem to be greatly preoccupied with economic motivations, even though the economic returns from literacy are not always clear and direct, and are indeed often postponed (Bhola 1981b). On the other hand, poverty is real and immediate and the urgent need to cope with deprivations leads to learners dropping out (UNESCO/FREPD 1979). An understanding is also emerging that motivations are seldom spontaneous but require mobilization, first to generate them and then to sustain them (Bhola 1982).

Considerable research and development effort has been focused on the methodology of teaching literacy. Useful basic research has been done by linguists and cognition scientists on the nature of the reading act (Gorman 1977). Sociolinguists and psycholinguists have pointed out how language and literacy are conditioned by social and psychological factors (Andrews 1981, Baucom 1978, Doob 1966, Gorman 1977). At the other end, vocabulary researchers have provided frequency counts of words that speakers of different languages use; words not always spoken but understood; and words that must be learned to master new economic skills or to participate in social and political organizations.

Literacy has been shown to be a combination of the skills dimension and the knowledge dimension. In turn, the skills dimension has as its constituents visual pattern recognition, ability to parse and pronounce, orthographic to phonological translation, lexical retrieval, ability to retain several words in short-term memory, and ability to resolve ambiguities and to anticipate words by using linguistic and semantic context. The knowledge dimension, again, must include knowledge of orthography and grammar as well as lexical knowledge. Also, the reader must have a basic knowledge of how the world works, knowledge of the subject matter being read and of linguistic redundancies.

If all these are the constituent skills of literacy, what is taught in literacy education and, more importantly, what are better, more effective methods of teaching literacy?

Questions about the choice of the language of literacy seem to have been settled. The use of the vernacular in the teaching of literacy, while generally preferable (UNESCO 1953), is not always feasible and need not become an orthodoxy (Gorman 1977).

In regard to the comparative effectiveness of different methods of teaching reading and writing, Gray (1969) was a model of professional caution as he concluded:

> Unfortunately, the evidence available does not show conclusively which of the methods in current use is the best. Only a few of the many methods have been studied experimentally, and then this was not always done with sufficient care to ensure that differences in results were due solely to variations in teaching methods. Again, very few studies have been concerned with adult subjects. Finally, the studies have not been repeated in sufficient cultural and language areas to show that tentative conclusions reached have universal applications.

Yet variations of the analytical method which begin with words, phrases, or short sentences rather than with the alphabets are considered, by practitioners at least, as a breakthrough in the methodology of teaching literacy to adults or to children. Practitioners seem to prize the fact that the teaching of reading does not have to start with the memorization of the alphabet chart. The teacher can instead start with meaningful sentences or words; break sentences into words, words into syllables and syllables into alphabets; teach recognition of syllables and alphabets generated by this analytical process; and then use these few alphabets and syllables as building blocks to make new words and sentences. This method has indeed come to be *the* method of teaching literacy to adults in literacy programs all over the world (Singh 1977, Bhola 1982).

The ability to start with meaningful words and sentences has had important consequences for the choice of content of literacy materials and programs. The words chosen could be "family," "Jesus," and "child,"—the cultural approach most widely used by the missionaries and other apolitical groups (Gray 1969); the words chosen could be "hoe," "seeds," and "cooperative,"—the work-oriented functional literacy approach (UNESCO 1965, Bhola 1969); or the words chosen could be "hunger," "oppression," and "justice," —the radical humanist approach associated with the work of Paulo Freire (Freire 1970, Brown 1975).

Literacy primers using different variations of the analytical method have typically used pictures to introduce words, phrases, or sentences. The reading of pictures, therefore, has also attracted some research attention. Picture recognition has been found to be a universal phenomenon unless the picture has been unduly conventionalized; and cut-out photos have been found to be the easiest to recognize (Fuglesang 1973). For reasons of cost of reproduction, however, line drawings continue to be the most widely used in adult literacy materials.

To ensure the continuation of gains in literacy programs, researchers have given considerable attention to the study of retention of literacy skills and to reading interests of adults in order to be able to write suitable follow-up materials for new literates.

There are two widely held, though not fully verified, views about retention of literacy. Firstly, that once literacy is acquired beyond a basic threshold, it is unlikely ever to be lost, and secondly, that this basic threshold is the equivalent of the third or fourth grade level of the United States primary school. Retainable literacy skills can be learned, under favorable conditions, in some 350 hours spread over as few as two to three months. For retention of literacy, the favorable conditions are that the new literate should have materials to read and opportunities to practice the new skills (Sheffield 1977).

Reading interests of adults, like expressed motivations for learning to read, have varied according to socioeconomic and cultural environments of learners, and according to the way the researcher formulated the research question. New literates and adults in literacy classes have expressed a desire to read materials dealing with agriculture, business, occupational techniques, citizenship, folk and religious lore, biographies of political leaders, history, philosophy, science, general knowledge, family health, child care, home making, shopping, preparing and serving foods, and games and sports (Bhola 1980).

Vocabulary research has been much more extensive in the European languages than in the indigenous languages of Asia, Africa, and Latin America. Literacy practitioners in developing countries have done useful vocabulary research within the context of their own programs and projects but results have seldom been reported (Bhola 1981a).

More recently, topics such as motivations of literacy teachers and supervisors, approaches to the training of professionals and paraprofessionals, effects of organizational strategies on program implementation, economic and structural effects of literacy, and policy issues of various kinds are beginning to attract researchers' attention. Once again, most of these questions have been dealt with within the context of ongoing programs and projects and have seldom been systematically reported. A flavor of the ferment in this area is provided by UNESCO's assessment of its Experimental World Literacy Program (UNESCO 1976) and the ICAE study on literacy policy, research, and action (ICAE/1979).

Easily the most useful work done in the area of adult literacy in the 1970s and the early 1980s has been developmental, with a clear-cut research-into-practice orientation. The series *Literacy in Development* (a series of training monographs) commissioned by the UNESCO/Iranian International Institute for Adult Literacy Methods provides an impressive example.

Training and curriculum development in the literacy and postliteracy stages have also attracted developmental attention. UNESCO's operational seminars and the German Foundation for International Development's action training model are important contributions to training strategies. The German Foundation for International Development has also organized in East and Central Africa a series of workshops on curriculum development, writing for new readers, postliteracy education, planning and organization, and evaluation, and made experiences more widely available through dissemination of manuals and documentation.

With the characterization by UNESCO of literacy as the priority of priorities, the UNESCO Institute of Education at Hamburg and the UNESCO International Institute for Educational Planning, with leadership from the UNESCO office in Paris, have undertaken important research and development work in the areas of postliteracy, planning and management of literacy programs, and evaluation.

2. *Research and Development Needs*

The catalog of research needs still to be fulfilled is substantial and may be divided into two main categories: (a) literacy design research and (b) literacy policy research.

Some examples of research themes and questions under the category of literacy design research would be the following: research related to typical problems of literacy work, such as the comparative advantage of teaching literacy in the mother tongue, reading motivations of participants, reading interests of adults, selection and training of teachers, mobilization of publics, field organization, coordination and follow-up; research on more basic questions, such as cognitive correlates of becoming literate, literacy and conceptual skills, literacy and new role learning, literacy and social stratification, literacy and political participation, effects of literacy on transformation of institutions; naturalistic studies and explorations of various aspects of "living" literacy programs and intensive versus mass campaigns; and syntheses of literacy research, instructional development research, organizational and communication research with implications for program design (Bhola 1981a).

Literacy policies normally consist of ideologically or normatively derived statements of goals (e.g., literacy for all) and assertions of socioeconomic relationships which are, in fact, hypotheses (e.g., literacy for social equality). The former, as value statements, are not researchable, although a good deal of definition and specification is required before such general assertions can be empirically tested. These relationships should be investigated as policy makers need better answers to the questions, "Why literacy?" and "What for literacy?" Elsewhere, Bhola has discussed a typology of literacy effects (1981b). It is evident that the research required to address an issue as broad and as general as the effects of literacy must itself be broad, drawing upon many fields in education and all the social sciences. Literacy may continue to be justified in terms of ideological values, but science should play a larger part in the debate.

Two perennial problems in formulating and implementing social policies are how resources are to be allocated and how action is to be organized. With respect to the first, the results from a given investment in primary education are known with some (but not a very high degree of) certainty. There is less certainty regarding investments in adult literacy and still less regarding investment in what has been termed "the learning society," that is, the development of press, publishing industries, and so on. Lastly, there is a paucity of information on the interaction effects of such investments, although these are generally regarded as extremely important. In what ways and to what degree, for example, do investments in literacy for adults facilitate the education of their offspring? Information and insights on the set of issues cited above are of fundamental importance for rational policy and efficient allocation of scarce resources. Issues relating to the organization of action are implicit in what has been presented in the preceding sections. There is a good deal of useful work to be done in the vineyards of literacy policy research.

Some significant research themes and questions subsumed under the literacy policy research area would be: historical analyses of the diffusion of literacy in different societies, developed and underdeveloped, and lessons for policy makers; philosophical, political, social, economic, and communicational analyses of justifications for literacy in different societies; policy analyses of the future role of literacy in different countries and regions with discussions of national missions and institutional arrangements necessary for developing regional and national strategies; future scenarios of societies based on the assumptions of universal literacy, literacy and media combinations, of widespread use of media without literacy, and of eradication of illiteracy through the expansion of primary education; and implementation of some projects as "social experiments" to test the results of particular policy issues (Bhola 1981a).

What does research reveal about the effects of literacy? What does literacy do to the newly literate as individuals and to the societies that change from preliteracy to literacy? Answers are just beginning to become available. Research on literacy effects has been more in the theoretical and historical mode than in the empirical. The generalized claim that literacy changes the "technology of intellect" of the new literate (Goody 1968) is now being considered somewhat excessive.

Literacy effects may be language specific, contextual, and rooted in what is read. Some analyses of historical data have talked of the "literacy myth," but these analyses may have confounded history with history making. Data from the field is beginning to show that literacy is certainly a "potential added" to new literates and their communities and that literacy does increase returns on extension services and on overall efforts to social change (Bhola 1981b).

Bibliography

Andrews T E 1981 *Adult Learners: A Research Study*. Association of Teacher Educators, Washington, DC

Baucom K L 1978 *The ABCs of Literacy: Lessons from Linguistics*. Hulton, Amersham

Bhola H S 1969 Functional literacy: The concept and the program. *Indian J. Adult Educ.* 30(12): 3–4, 10–16

Bhola H S 1979 *Evaluating Functional Literacy*. Hulton, Amersham

Bhola H S 1980 Reading materials for the new reading public: A policy brief. *Literacy Rev.* 1: 1–45

Bhola H S 1981a Needed research in adult literacy for policy makers and planners. *Adult Educ.* 31: 169–76

Bhola H S 1981b Why literacy can't wait: Issues for the 1980s. *Convergence* 14: 6–23

Bhola H S 1982 *Campaigning for Literacy (A Critical Analysis of Some Selected Literacy Campaigns of the 20th Century, with a Memorandum to Decision Makers)*. Literacy, Adult Education and Rural Development Division, UNESCO, Paris

Brown C 1975 *Literacy in 30 Hours: Paulo Freire's Process in North East Brazil.* Writers and Readers Publishing Cooperative, London

Couvert R 1971 Motivations of Malagasy peasants. *Literacy Discussion* 2(2): 35–62

Doob L W 1966 *Communication in Africa: A Search for Boundaries.* Yale University Press, New Haven, Connecticut

Freire P 1970 *Pedagogy of the Oppressed.* Herder and Herder, New York

Fuglesang A 1973 *Applied Communication in Developing Countries.* Dag Hammarskjöld Foundation, Uppsala

Goody J (ed.) 1968 *Literacy in Traditional Societies*. Cambridge University Press, Cambridge

Gorman T P (ed.) 1977 *Language and Literacy: Current Issues and Research.* International Institute for Adult Literacy Methods, Tehran

Gray W S 1969 *The Teaching of Reading and Writing: An International Survey,* 2nd edn. UNESCO, Paris

Hussain Ch G 1973 Motivating adults for learning. *Literacy Work* 3(1–2): 71–82

International Council for Adult Education (TCAE/International Development Research Center (IDRC) 1979 *The World of Literacy: Policy, Research and Action.* IDRC, Ottawa, Ontario

International Institute for Adult Literacy Methods (IIALM) 1980 *The Problem of Drop-outs (Interpretative Bibliography).* IIALM, Tehran

Kaufmann H D, Bazany M 1970 *Motives of Participation in Functional Literacy Courses, Dezful, 1970.* Work-oriented Adult Literacy Project, Esfahan

Kidd J R 1969 *How Adults Learn.* Association Press, New York

National Fundamental Education Center (NFEC) 1967 *Evaluation Study of an Adult Literacy Project in the Union Territory of Delhi.* Department of Adult Education, Government of India, New Delhi

Rossman M H 1971 *A Model to Recruit Functionally Illiterate Adults into Adult Basic Education Program in Massachusetts.* School of Education, University of Massachusetts, Amherst, Massachusetts

Sheffield J R 1977 Retention of literacy and basic skills. A review of literature. Prepared for the Education Department of the World Bank, Washington, DC

Singh S 1977 *Learning to Read and Reading to Learn (An Approach to a System of Literacy Instruction).* Hulton, Amersham

UNESCO 1953 *The Use of Vernacular Languages in Education.* UNESCO, Paris

UNESCO 1965 *World Congress of Ministers of Education on the Eradication of Illiteracy, Teheran, 1965: Final Report.* UNESCO, Paris

UNESCO 1973 *Motivations for Rural Development.* UNESCO, Paris

UNESCO 1976 *The Experimental World Literacy Programme: A Critical Assessment.* UNESCO, Paris

UNESCO/Foundation for Research on Educational Planning and Development (FREPD) 1979 *Adult Literacy Motivation (A Survey of Adult Education in Bangladesh).* FREPD, Bangladesh, in cooperation with UNESCO, Paris

Versluys J D N 1977 *Research in Adult Literacy: A Bibliography.* International Institute for Adult Literacy Methods, Tehran

Adult Education for Employment: Research

G. E. Spear

A review of the literature of research related to adult education for employment immediately encounters difficulties beginning with the use of terms. In the United Kingdom the term most frequently used is vocational training. In the United States, the field is most frequently referred to as training or human resource development (HRD). Vocational education is used ordinarily to designate preservice schooling in occupational skills. An official Japanese response to the text of recommendations related to worker education and training at the 45th session of the International Labor Conference in Geneva in 1961 noted a similar differentiation. The Japanese pointed out that vocational education was under the Ministry of Education while technical education was covered by the Vocational Training Law and was a responsibility of the Ministry of Labor.

A second problem arises from the nature of the field itself which does not have a specific academic base of preparation of practice for trainers/adult educators. The vast majority of trainers are selected from the ranks of their respective organizations, without regard to either formal education, experience, or preparation, and assigned responsibility for organizing and conducting adult vocational education programs. If these trainers undergo preparation for their roles it is at the hands of outside consultants who are synthesizers and purveyors of research conducted in related but generic social and behavioral sciences.

Most research may be said to be about the field rather than of it. It is predominantly of survey design and descriptive rather than experimental and evaluative. The literature produced from within the field pertains primarily to recitations of successful practice drawing on experience rather than objective data. It is generally acknowledged that even evaluation is neglected. So it is that the field moves along knowing little about itself that might contribute to improvement in its practices.

1. *Scope of the Field*

The absence of a significant data or knowledge base does not imply at the same time poverty of practice. Estimates of expenditure for training in business and industry in the United States alone place the figure at about US$100 billion annually which is equal to the combined budgets of the nation's higher education institutions. It is the more remarkable that so vast an enterprise should be conducted with so little data or knowledge at its foundation.

In the United States adult education for employment has undergone significant growth since the mid-1960s. In 1962 only 20 percent of businesses surveyed provided training regularly for their employees with a sparse seven percent of their workers enrolled in training. Several descriptive surveys in the past six years (Craig 1979, Goldstein 1980, Editors 1982, Carnevale and Goldstein 1983) combine to present evidence that suggests nearly one-half of workers or 50 million now receive training. Approximately 34 percent of the total education for employment programs are provided by company organizations with 16 percent offered through colleges and universities.

The survey by Craig (1979) revealed that 89 percent of surveyed organizations provided tuition aid to employees for after-hours course work, 74 percent offered outside course work during work hours, 70 percent offered company courses during work hours, and 39 percent offered company courses after work hours. Thirty-seven percent of the courses offered are related to management and supervision, 61 percent are of functional/technical content, and 10 percent are basic remedial. Eighty-nine percent of all expenditures are for company-developed courses.

Topics dominating the training agendas are supervisory skills, orientation to the organization, management skills and development, communications, technical skills and updating, time management, and safety.

2. *National Policies for Worker Education*

Problems with industrial productivity in both industrialized and developing countries have produced greater governmental concern for adult education for employment. The recession of the early 1980s persuaded the United States government to encourage employee training through a liberalizing of vocational education regulations that helped create partnerships between state vocational schools and area industries in skill-related programs. However, for the most part, the United States has been less ready to generate policies that promote worker training. This stands in contrast to Mexico, for example, where laws require that businesses provide training for workers, and failure to do so can be punished by imposing fines. South Africa demonstrates its concern by reimbursing companies 115 percent of the cost of worker training. Mandatory training boards to ensure quality training in various segments of the economy are required by a 1973 United Kingdom law under which employers must provide financial support to maintain the boards according to a formula based on their respective payrolls.

Goldstein (1980) suggests that given the theory of human capital, industrial investments in the development of workers justify the granting of federal tax credits for training expenditures. He also favors government aid to industrial training and encourages the establishing of technical aid agencies in each city in the country to provide direct assistance in developing and improving the quality of adult education for employment.

The effects of organized worker unions in a struggle against what has been called the undemocratic organization of the workplace has had a visible impact upon national policy regarding education for workers in a number of countries. Beginning with the premise that the control of the distribution of knowledge by management solidifies its authority in the organization, Sweden's labor unions, representing 95 percent of the blue-collar workers and 75 percent of the white-collar workers, succeeded in forcing national legislation that brought together the impact of negotiating and education. The result was broadly based education for mobilizing workers for the shaping and installation of reforms as well as educational programs to assist workers in carrying out the intent of the reforms.

The impact of technology and the changes it brings to the workplace have been addressed by labor-supported legislation in Norway. It assures worker rights to full information regarding the nature and potential impact of new technologies on their jobs and what investments management intends to make in that technology. Worker representatives are given time and support to study the effects of technology and are provided with extensive training to prepare themselves to function as knowledgeable investigators.

Workers in France benefit from the Law of 1971, which provides for paid educational leave for employees of many industries. Although imperfect in application, French workers may obtain training and education within certain schemes provided by their employers. Approximately half of such education is conducted within the industry and half by outside public and private providers. There is a countrywide network of well-regarded skill centers and about 1.7 million workers out of the 10 million eligible benefit from these. Employers pay 1.1 percent of their total payrolls to support the provisions of the Law of 1971.

3. *Participants and Participation*

Although training is pervasive in United States business, it varies in character and quantity as it is distributed among different strata in organizations. Craig (1979) found that most blue-collar workers are trained at their work stations while their supervisors get on-the-job training, coaching, tuition assistance, and attend company-sponsored courses. Moving up the hierarchy, middle managers are involved more in programs provided by outside consultants and professional associations. Top executives are more likely to attend university-based development programs.

Least likely to be enrolled in training courses are office clerical staff and production workers. Most likely to be engaged in training are first-line supervisors and customer relations personnel. Middle managers and technical professional workers receive the most hours of training on the average but top executives and senior managers are most likely to attend programs offered outside of the organization.

A growing concern for worker performance at the lower levels of the ogranization has generated increasing activity in remedial education in the work place. One firm estimated that clerical errors due to faulty reading skills among clerical workers cost the firm nearly US$250,000 annually.

Another industry has experimented with career planning for blue-collar workers. This experiment includes a combination of training, education, and career mobility, usually reserved for management personnel. Results from three years of this effort show that 90 percent of the participants reported improved morale, improved communications with supervisors and co-workers, and increased job satisfaction. Tuition reimbursements to workers attending classes at colleges and universities increased by 2,000 percent.

Fraser (1980) noted that 1.6 million workers were covered in union-negotiated education tuition reimbursement plans. However, only 3–5 percent of those entitled to these benefits take advantage of them and the percentage for blue-collar workers is even lower. As productivity concerns increase worldwide, a trend toward greater attention to lower level workers may be evidenced.

In developing countries, such as India and the countries of Latin America, the Middle East, and Africa, there is an increasing vacuum in the pool of available managers for growing industrial organizations, many of which are nationalized. Emphasis in these nations centers on management training and some United States organizations are finding a healthy market for selling training packages.

4. *Program Design and Development*

The dominant theoretical base for the organization of most adult education for employment in the United States is behaviorist, drawing on the work of B.F. Skinner. Behavioral objectives for instruction, planning, and measurable evaluation have incurred the almost blind devotion of the majority of adult vocational educators in the United States. American Telephone and Telegraph (AT&T), which, before its breakup, boasted the largest annual training budget among United States corporations at US$1 billion, standardized all its jobs and insisted there was only one correct way to perform each job. The goal was to provide uniform and efficient service in all areas of the nation and 80 training technologists were engaged continuously in the assessment of needs and the development of training programs (Luxenberg 1980). The AT&T approach characterizes the planning of worker education among United States businesses which lends itself to uniformity in predictable situations.

In management training where job requirements are less precise, there is a strong and growing interest in the humanist approach advocated by a number of research theorists including David Kolb, Frederick Herzberg,

Robert Blake, and Jane Mouton. These theorists advocate greater attention to understanding than to measurable behavior and an emphasis on human needs as equal to organization needs. Program development in the humanist mode provides for greater employee participation in planning both the goals and means of training and more responsibility for outcome and evaluation.

The liberal tradition dominates adult education for employment approaches in most areas of the world. At its base is the delivery, usually by lecture, of information from the trainer to the trainees in a generally passive learning situation. Less recognition of the work of the trainer as a professional career tends to encourage training programs patterned after traditional and familiar school classrooms.

Some evidence of the growing sophistication in the adult vocational training field can be found in efforts to apply the systems development approach to the program design function. Drawing on the wartime military invention of a dynamic input–implementation–output and evaluation process, United States trainers have sought to apply the approach to their planning. The approach is usually termed *instructional systems design* (ISD) and has generated a number of different models, all of which have analysis as their central theme. While the effort moves beyond common wisdom as its base, Montenerlo and Tennyson (1976) surveyed nearly 100 manuals intended to instruct trainers in the art of ISD and discovered 18 topics on which there was consensus. However, he suggested that inherent in the systems approach is an implicit expectation of continuing review and alterations conducted by experts. This, he concluded, was missing from the efforts set forth in the ISD manuals and furthermore, such a continuous review process was not amenable to the simplification necessary to enable it to be carried out by laypersons.

5. *Instructional Methods and Techniques*

The field of adult education for employment suffers no more from uncertainty about the merits of various instructional methods and techniques than do other fields of more traditional study. It does, however, suffer somewhat the imperative of developing knowledge about instructional effectiveness because of accountability in economic terms. A continuing pressure is maintained on training departments by organizations to demonstrate their ability to improve performance and productivity of workers.

While the lecture is probably the most widely used instructional method in vocational training across the world, the field is continually enticed to sample an ongoing parade of instructional fads. The introduction of programmed instruction into training in the 1950s has continued with its extension, computer-assisted instruction (CAI), to the present as the most fascinating of alternatives to traditional instructional methods. Research studies to ascertain the effectiveness of CAI have produced mixed results. Time savings appear to be the most impressive benefit with a United States Navy study showing selected savings of time in training amounting to 69 percent. In most studies, achievement has not been shown to be demonstrably better through use of computers. Hinrich (1983) admits to time saving but suggests the CAI cost is high and may produce the "pinball machine effect." He takes the position that passive display methods using learning materials such as lectures, textbooks, or films provide for little feedback to the learner, an element he views as necessary for effective learning. He further cites some data indicating that discussions, case studies, simulators, and games do provide for feedback and so are more likely to produce a change in learning.

The merging of simulators with computer capabilities has led to the growing use of simulators for training. Most prominent is their use by the military, airlines, and aerospace industries. Studies suggest that these applications are effective and Orlansky and String (1981) found that military trainees performed equally well or better when trained with simulators. In addition, cost savings in acquiring simulators compared with the equipment simulated ranged as high as 60 percent.

Business games for training management personnel enjoy wide usage and are reasonably effective in teaching transferable skills, are nonpunitive which encourages risk taking and experimentation, and have an intrinsic motivation factor. However, critics note that these simulation games at times do not allow or encourage normal approaches; trainees get involved in the playing and neglect analyzing their behaviors; sometimes the urge to win obscures the purpose of the exercise, and some games involve costly software.

The study of instructional technologies has been limited in many areas and has failed to address many of the most important questions regarding use.

6. *In Search of Theory*

Two recent efforts drawn from the 1983 *Handbook of Industrial and Organizational Psychology* demonstrate a measure of the limited attention being given to the development of a theoretical base specifically for training applications. Burris (1983) addresses the area of human learning and, building on research from the learning theorists, provides a frame of reference for developing a planning model for training activities. Such planning should, he suggests, include attention to performance criteria, learning sequencing, learning strategies, instructional modes and media, motivation, and individual differences.

Questions to be answered are: What is included when we say that someone "knows?" What should the structure of the material be? What must one do in order to learn or know the material? What strategies will best facilitate the learning? What are the affective needs of the learners? and What characteristics such as preferences, attitudes, learning styles, and capacity are present with respect to each individual learner? Burris raises the question of whether recent evidence generated by studies of learning styles may be laid at the door of simple "Hawthorne effect," i.e., whether apparent changes in a learner's capacity to learn might simply be the result of the learner's response to being studied.

The second chapter of interest to adult vocational educators is by Hinrich (1983) who proposes a training or skills acquisition model using a systems approach. Hinrich notes that little change in the field of training has taken place in the decades of the 1940s through the 1970s. Without the attention of psychologists to its needs, the field is dominated by practitioners who place emphasis on activity rather than solving organizational problems. Their program designs are influenced by fads and, with little concern for theory, do not seriously evaluate the effectiveness of their work. To achieve a merger of organizational and individual development needs, Hinrich proposes a skill-acquisition model comprised of input–operator–output–feedback components.

Inputs are subclassified as maintenance inputs which include individual and organizational variables, and signal inputs which are cognitive materials and practice activities. The training activity is the operator and outputs are reckoned as formal achievement and group needs satisfaction. Feedback loops tie signal inputs together with formal achievement while maintenance inputs relate to group needs satisfaction. Decisions concerning training needs are made based on job analysis and workforce analysis.

Hinrich insists that evaluations that are not experimental, which have no pre–post tests, and that do not have adequate control groups, are really not evaluations. The training field is supported by a general belief in the value of education and its benefits taken for granted. Only evaluations of the type he proposes will determine the validity of this pervasive faith in education.

7. Needs for Future Research

Research needs for adult education for employment and the broader field of human resource development are frequently suggested by observers from both within and without the field of practice. One significant effort to tap the insights of those who practice in the field was mounted in 1980 at the Annual Invitational Research Seminar (AIRS), sponsored by the ASTD Research Committee. The seminar final report identified 34 research needs and divided these into three categories: issues concerned with HRD organization and process; issues of job requirements and organizational needs; and issues concerned with social trends and factors. A sampling of specific topics includes learning strategies, microcomputer-assisted instruction, on-the-job training, manager behavior, quality work life, career changes, and early retirement. The report suggests specific research questions to study and gives a rationale for the topics' importance.

Research dealing with adult education for employment has been neglected by both practitioners and academics but has continued to grow at spectacular rates in both industrialized and developing nations. The lack of definitive knowledge to underpin training practice gives reason for doubt regarding its value to any nation or organization. At the same time, both nations and organizations are spending substantial resources on adult education for employment. Enlightened policies are needed at both the national and organizational levels to encourage research which will contribute to the knowledge necessary for development and progress.

Bibliography

American Society for Training and Development (ASTD) Research Commitee 1980 *Critical Research Issues in Human Resource Development: A Preliminary List.* American Society for Training and Development, Kansas City, Missouri

Burris R W 1983 Human learning. In: Dunnette M D (ed.) *Handbook of Industrial and Organizational Psychology.* Wiley, New York, pp. 131–46

Carnevale A P, Goldstein H 1983 *Employee Training: Its Changing Role and an Analysis of New Data*, American Society for Training and Development National Issues Series. American Society for Training and Development, Washington, DC

Craig R 1979 *National Report for Training and Development.* American Society for Training and Development, Washington, DC

Editors 1982 Who gets trained and how. *Training Magazine* 19(10): 30–31

Fraser B S 1980 *The Structure of Adult Learning, Education, and Training Opportunity in the United States: Worker Education and Training Policies Project.* National Institute for Work and Learning, Washington, DC (ERIC Document Reproduction Service No. ED 200 723)

Goldstein H 1980 *Training and Education in Industry: Worker Education and Training Policies Project.* National Institute for Work and Learning, Washington, DC (ERIC Document Reproduction Service No. 200 721)

Hinrich J R 1983 Personnel training. In: Dunnette M D (ed.) *Handbook of Industrial and Organizational Psychology.* Wiley, New York, pp. 829–60

Luxenberg S 1980 AT&T and Citicorp: Prototypes in job training among large corporations. *Phi Delta Kappan* 61: 314–17

Montenerlo M D, Tennyson M E 1976 *Instructional Systems Development: Conceptual Analysis and Comprehensive Bibliography*, Interim Report. Naval Training Equipment Center, Orlando, Florida (ERIC Document Reproduction Service No. 121 356)

Orlansky J, String J 1981 *Cost-effectiveness of Maintenance Simulators for Military Training*, Final Report. Institute for Defense Analysis, Arlington, Virginia (ERIC Document Reproduction Service No. ED 212 254)

Participatory Research

B. L. Hall and Y. Kassam

Participatory research is most commonly described as an integral activity that combines social investigation, educational work, and action. The combination of these elements in an interrelated process has provided both stimulation and difficulty for those who have become engaged in participatory research or who have tried to understand it. Some of the characteristics of the process are listed below.

(a) The problem to be studied originates in the community or workplace itself.

(b) The ultimate goal of the research is fundamental structural transformation and the improvement of the lives of those involved. The beneficiaries are the workers or people concerned.

(c) Participatory research involves the people in the workplace or the community who control the entire process of the research.

(d) The focus of participatory research is on work with a wide range of exploited or oppressed groups; immigrants, labour forces, indigenous peoples, women.

(e) Central to participatory research is its role of strengthening the awareness in people of their own abilities and resources and its support for mobilizing or organizing.

(f) The term "researcher" can refer to both the community or workplace persons involved as well as those with specialized training.

(g) Although those with specialized knowledge and training often come from outside the situation, they are committed participants and learners in a process that leads to militancy rather than detachment.

1. The Origins of Participatory Research

It is important to recognize that, while the term "participatory research" may be new, the concerns being expressed have a history and continuity in social science. Many of the ideas that are finding new opportunities for expression can be traced as far back as the early field work of Engels in his alignment with the working classes of Manchester during his early period. Marx's use of the structured interview—*L'Enquête Ouvrière*—with French factory workers is another sometimes forgotten antecedent. More recently, aspects of the work of Dewey, George Herbert Mead, and the Tavistock Institute in London have outlined methods of social investigation that are based on other than a positivistic epistemology.

By the late 1950s and early 1960s, the dominant international research paradigm was a version of the North American and European model based on empiricism and positivism and characterized by an attention to instrument construction and rigour defined by statistical precision and replicability. Through the elaborate mechanisms of international scholarships, cultural exchanges, and training of researchers in Europe and North America, this dominant paradigm was extended to the Third World. Research methods, through an illusion of objectivity and scientific credibility, become one more manifestation of cultural dependency.

The reaction from the Third World—beginning in Latin America—has taken many forms. Dependency theorists, such as Dos Santos, Frank Amin, and Leys, outlined some of the mechanisms of economic and cultural dependency. Hence, in the field of research methods, Third World perspectives have grown out of a reaction to approaches developed in North America and Europe; approaches that have been not only created in different cultural settings but that contribute to already existing class distinctions. The Third World's contribution to social science research methods represents an attempt to find ways of uncovering knowledge that work better in societies where interpretation of reality must take second place to the changing of that reality.

Practical experience in what was becoming known as participatory research occurred in the work of the Tanzanian Bureau of Resource Allocation and Land Use Planning. Here, Marja-Liisa Swantz and teams of students and village workers were involved in the questions of youth and employment in the Coast region and later in studies of socioeconomic causes of malnutrition in Central Kilimanjaro. A visit by Paulo Freire to Tanzania in 1971 was a stimulus to many social scientists who might not otherwise have been as impressed by the existing experience of many adult educators or community development workers.

What happened in Tanzania in a small way, had already begun in Latin America in the early 1960s. Stimulated in part by the success of the Cuban revolution, Latin American social scientists began exploring more committed forms of research. One of the most useful roles of Paulo Freire has been to bring some of the current ideas of Latin American social scientists to the attention of persons in other parts of the world. His work on thematic investigation, first in Brazil and later in Chile, was an expression of this search. Others, such as Beltran and Gerace Larufa, have explored alternatives through concepts of horizontal communication (Beltran 1976, Gerace Larufa 1973). Fals Barda (1980) and others in Colombia have been engaged in *investigación y acción*, while the Darcy de Oliveiras have made people aware of the value of militant observation (Darcy de Oliveira and Darcy de Oliveira 1975).

2. *Not the Third World Alone*

While the specific term "participatory research" developed in the Third World, due to crises caused by dysfunctional concepts of one-way, detached research in a world of immediate and urgent problems, a consciousness was growing in Europe and North America. The Frankfurt School was rediscovered through Habermas and Adorno. Action sociology was placed on the agenda of most academic meetings. In Switzerland, researchers in curriculum development adapted methodologies from political research to their needs. In Canada, Stinson developed methods of evaluation along action research lines for community development (Stinson 1979). In the Netherlands, Jan de Vries has explored alternatives from a firm philosophical base. The National Institute for Adult Education in the United Kingdom pioneered participatory research through its evaluation of the United Kingdom adult literacy campaign (Holmes 1976). In Italy, Paolo Orefice and colleagues at the University of Naples have been applying the methodology to their investigations of community and district awareness of power and control (Orefice 1981). In the United States, the Highlander Center in Tennessee has been using approaches similar to participatory research for many years, most recently to deal with issues of land ownership and use (Horton 1981).

3. *Feminist Research*

Feminist critiques of research have been part of the larger search for a form of working with people in a way that empowers them rather than prolongs the status quo. Both feminist research and participatory research seek to shift the centre from which knowledge is generated. Dale Spender has described the field of women's studies:

> Its multi-disciplinary nature challenges the arrangement of knowledge into academic disciplines; its methodology breaks down many of the traditional distinctions between theoretical and empirical and between objective and subjective. It is in the process of redefining knowledge, knowledge gathering and making. . . . (Spender 1978)

In addition, Callaway has demonstrated that women have been largely excluded from producing the dominant forms of knowledge and that the social sciences have been not only a science of male society but also a male science of society (Callaway 1981). Spender urges women "to learn to create our own knowledge". It is crucially important, she states,

> . . . that women begin to create our own means for producing and validating knowledge which is consistent with our own personal experience. We need to formulate our own yardsticks, for we are doomed to deviancy if we persist in measuring ourselves against the male standard. This is our area of learning, with learning used in a widely encompassing, highly charged, political and revolutionary sense. (Spender 1978)

4. *Debate and Discussion*

Many of the developments at both the theoretical and the practical levels were reviewed at an International Forum on Participatory Research which took place in Yugoslavia in April, 1980. The forum brought together about 60 activists and practitioners from all regions and, rare for international seminars, nearly half of the participants were women. The forum's objectives were: (a) sharing and consolidating experiences in participatory research; (b) development of practical guidelines; (c) strengthening of international linkages among regional networks; and (d) development of future strategies. A number of key issues, or themes, emerged from these deliberations. Whether in working group discussions or theoretical plenaries, participants addressed these issues with a sense of exploration, self-clarification, commitment, and mutual respect.

5. *The Researcher as Learner*

The role of the researcher is an important issue. It has been suggested that the researcher must (a) be committed to seeing the participatory research process through to the end, (b) avoid actions that endanger community members, and (c) see clearly, and support changes improving the situation of the subordinate groups within the community. It was recognized that these commitments were likely to run counter to the interests of the professional researcher, but that the researcher, along with the community, learns and develops through the educative process. The researcher can make significant contributions by building new understandings and realities so that he or she is no longer an outsider, by bringing new information, and by helping to find funds for the development of technical skills. In all cases, the outside researcher is involved particularly in building an indigenous capacity for collective analysis and action and for the generation of new knowledge by the people concerned.

There has been considerable discussion about the role of the organic intellectual in participatory research. The term comes from Antonio Gramsci, the Italian political activist and theoretician who wrote from his prison cell in the 1930s. Although the term sounds awkward when not placed within Gramsci's overall framework, the idea is not very far removed from what many adult educators mean by "the empowerment of people through learning". The adjective organic means that such leadership arises from, and is nourished by, the actual situation of workers and peasants; such a person is not an outsider, although someone outside the situation can facilitate the necessary growth, awareness, and knowledge.

The term organic intellectual is really a collective expression for the new consciousness of the working class through its own social organization, such as the formation of political parties. Although participatory research may support and help such organizations, it should never seek to replace them. Organic intellectuals are also viewed as individual members of the peasant/working class whose consciousness and technical expertise has been raised through active struggle, of which participatory research may be one means. A third position argues that organic intellectuals may be middle-class intellectuals who have been radicalized through action and struggle and who may be located along a continuum from those engaged only in intellectual work—such as participatory research—to those engaged in a considerable amount of manual, as well as intellectual work. The first two positions are generally favoured. However, further examination of the relationship of the organic intellectual to participatory research is of high priority.

6. *Nature of Participation*

Participation has been used to cover microactivities, such as the learning of literacy skills, and macroactivities, such as the popular organization for class struggle at a national level. The particular role of participatory research, it has been argued, lies in the process of mobilization of people for their collective creation of new knowledge about themselves and their own reality. Again, this is part of the educative component of the process.

An important distinction has been advanced between participation and manipulation. Under the guise of participation rhetoric, and strategies to involve the people, outside interests might attempt to manipulate communities or workplace groups for purposes of domestication, integration, and exploitation. In contrast, participatory research is seen as a front line against such manipulation since it advocates and provides training in critical and collective analysis of the kind that establishes and maintains control and learning in the hands of the people, and explicitly rejects manipulation. Participatory forms of social action that lead from such collective analyses have also been advocated. A key methodological issue is the problem of how collective a participatory research process should become in view of the internal power relations within communities and workplace groups and the degree of new learning that individuals within a group must engage in.

7. *Popular Knowledge*

The creation of popular knowledge has emerged as a goal of participatory research. For many, participatory research is a process by which the "raw" and somewhat unformed—or at least, unexpressed—knowledge of ordinary people is brought into the open and incorporated into a connectable whole through discussion, analysis, and the "reflected" knowledge gained with or without allied intellectuals and those who have both broader and deeper insights.

Discussions of these matters have highlighted the dynamic interaction between the kind of practical technology and expertise that people who live in the situation have and the kind known as official technology and expertise. The identification of the various means of controlling this process of interaction that can be made available to local community or workplace groups is central to such discussions.

A further critical question is how the creation and dissemination of new knowledge is linked to social transformation. One position is that participatory research can, through successive movements of popular analysis over time, move people from looking at more peripheral contradictions in the local reality to focusing more clearly on central contradictions that actually influence and control their lives. In the process, they become more aware of how power groups can divert their attention to peripheral and short-term issues so that the inequitable status quo can be maintained. Thus, the linking of action to such analysis moves from action that addresses short-term needs to action based on strategies for bringing about fundamental social change.

8. *Historical Materialism*

The relationship between historical materialism and participatory research is also of interest. A strong position has been taken by some that the historical materialist method, in contrast to a pragmatic approach, is essential to the participatory research process. Here, class analysis and class struggle are fundamental ideas; popularly created knowledge in interaction with historical materialistic methodology can be regarded as yielding rich potential for social change. Another position held is that participatory research must embrace a variety of analytic approaches and that historical materialism has sometimes been an alienating, elitist endeavour. However, there is considerable agreement on two related points. First, the use of the historical materialist method should be nondogmatic, given the fact that participatory research is a generative process. Secondly, the historical materialist method can be used in strategic ways, such as to study the dominant class forces (state, corporate) both globally and locally. An important challenge is to popularize such knowledge, to interpret it, and see it placed in the minds and hands of the people the dominant class seeks to exclude and to dominate.

9. *Local Autonomy and Broader Struggles*

Several tensions exist in the field. For example, there is tension between the requirement of local autonomy for a given participatory research process and the demand for coordinated social action at the national or regional levels. A national struggle must be more than an aggregate of participatory research experiences at the local level; forms of popular organizations developed by social movements are complex and variable and are rooted in local political and economic conditions. It must be noted that, at certain critical moments, a local-level participatory research process may, in fact, hinder the progress of broader social movements by overemphasizing the localized nature of the problems. Consequently there is a need to set ground rules across different levels of struggle. Again, participatory research is not seen as a panacea. However, there is general recognition that, at certain stages, participatory research can enrich broader social organizations.

10. A Question of Power

Emerging from the discussions, debates, and activities of participatory research is the central question of power. Participatory research can only be judged in the long run by whether or not it has the ability to serve the specific and real interests of the working class and other oppressed peoples. For Gaventa of the Highlander Research and Education Center in the Appalachian region of the United States, power can be described as follows: "A exercises power over B when A affects B in a manner contrary to B's interests." In this idea, A may exercise power over B by getting B to do what he does not want to do; A also exercises power by influencing, shaping, or determining B's very wants (Gaventa 1981).

How, then, can participatory research be useful in shifting more power into the hands of popular groups and oppressed peoples? There are at least three possibilities.

10.1 Unmasking the Myths

Vio Grossi (1981) has given considerable thought to the task of participatory research as initiating a process of disindoctrination that allows people to detach themselves from the myths imposed on them by the power structure that have prevented them from seeing their own oppression or from seeing possibilities for breaking free. In Marxian terms, participatory research leads to the analysis of secondary contradictions that exist within society (how does oppression look in our world?) to the location of primary contradictions (what are the hidden structures that shape society?), and then to a process of action.

In this context, structural transformation can be seen as the strategic goal to be reached in the medium or long term. A participatory research process carried out in conjunction with popular groups (and under their control) is designed to facilitate the analysis of stages towards that goal.

10.2 The Creation of Popular Knowledge

The stages of disindoctrination that Vio Grossi (1981) has outlined are discussed in working papers on methods that have been used over the past years by the Toronto-based Participatory Research Group. The papers describe a variety of methods for developing and activating collective analysis. These include drama, drawing, thematic photographs (both still and in photonovel form), videotape, meetings, radio, and interview surveys as a means of helping people to examine the deeper layers of the social structure. Such action can lead to systematization of new knowledge; knowledge not generated by the dominant ideological producers in the superstructure but generated by and consistent with the experiences and world view of ordinary people.

Fals Barda has contributed to the discussion of popular knowledge in his paper on *Science and the Common People* (Fals Barda 1980). He says the creation of knowledge that comes from the people contributes to the realization of a people's science which serves and is understood by the common people, and no longer perpetuates the status quo. The process of this new paradigm involves: (a) returning information to the people in the language and cultural form in which it originated; (b) establishing control of the work by the popular and base movements; (c) popularizing research techniques; (d) integrating the information as the base of the organic intellectual; (e) maintaining a conscious effort in the action/reflection rhythm of work; (f) recognizing science as part of the everyday lives of all people; and (g) learning to listen.

The creation of popular knowledge is a form of antihegemonic activity, an instrument in the struggle to control what the social agenda is. In Gaventa's terms, popular knowledge can be seen as preventing those in power from maintaining the monopoly of determining the wants of others, thus, in effect, transferring power to those groups engaged in the production of popular knowledge (Gaventa 1981).

10.3 Contribution to Organizing

Participatory research is conceived to be an integral process of investigation, education, and action. When one addresses the question of power it is clearer than ever that the first two aspects are empty without the third. But action must be explained still further. From several years of sharing information and results it has become clear that the most common action and the critical necessity is that of organizing, in its various phases. It has meant supporting the efforts of farmers' or womens' groups, or workers' health committees, or neighbourhoods, or campesinos to get together to understand issues and discuss options. It has meant building alliances with other social movements and strengthening the links within various progressive sectors. Action is not, however, a substitute for the organizing of the popular movements themselves. With its stress on collective analysis and on the working out of options and solutions together, the participatory research process reinforces the organizing potential of the base groups which use it.

11. Power for Whom?

It would be an error to assume that naive or uncontrolled use of participatory research results in strengthening the power of the powerless at the base of society. Without control over the participatory research process, experience has shown that power can easily accrue to those already in control. There has been a certain lack of clarity in some earlier writings on participatory research around this issue, and it has resulted in misunderstanding and manipulation.

11.1 Professional Researchers

Participatory research has been used by some researchers to provide them with insights and views that they could not ordinarily have had access to or know about. Some writings, with an emphasis on an increased scientific accuracy, have inadvertently encouraged abuses of participatory research, including the manipulation of groups by researchers. Participatory research has become the key by which these researchers have gained more power for themselves within the academic status quo, even admitting that the academic world allows for a wide range of ideological positions. In these cases, participatory researchers have fed the process of ideological control by giving more power to the institutions of the state for which they work. In fairness, participatory research has also legitimized the work of certain researchers in support of various popular groups, thereby resulting in a shift of skills and resources from the institution to the community or workplace.

11.2 The State

Some activists and social workers have seen participatory research as a way to get people to agree to a position, an action, a policy that social workers, adult educators, or others, feel is important for their purposes. Moreover, participatory research can be debased as a powerful tool for getting the predominant view of the state into the hearts and minds of a particularly meddlesome sector of the population. Many organizations use studies or commissions as excuses for not taking action. They are usually promoted as "taking the pulse of the people". However, hours of debate, scores of witnesses, piles of money can go up in smoke—and the real problems are not dealt with. The question remains as to what happens after people have spoken up on such issues, have made alliances, or have had a taste of countering the dominant forces of the day? Is there a memory of power which will resurface at a later time? Is one role of adult education to not let such memories fade and to build on the momentum, the learning, the collective analysis that inquiries can generate?

11.3 Popular Groups and Links to Social Movements

Under circumstances of control by popular groups, participatory research processes have produced increased power for some groups. The recently completed Appalachian Land Use Study, carried out by a coalition of citizen groups with some support from the Highlander Research and Education Center, has produced dramatic evidence of unequal taxation policies—and is leading to legislation and action in several states.

One often finds that the researcher and the base group are not the only parties involved; usually there is a third: the funder. In some experiences, the funder has presented the most difficulty in maintaining the integrity of the work. Funding policies of governments can, for example, expand into procedures that regulate certain groups in the society, such as immigrants and native peoples. Research with popular groups that is funded by the state will often be subject to such intervention and influence. Also, what happens when independent researchers apply for funds as an intermediary group for popular organizations is not entirely satisfactory. This has led, at times, to an unsavoury situation where the needs and weakness of some parts of the population are presented to funders for grants, with the result that the funds got to the researchers and intermediary group but not always to the actual base groups that the work was to serve.

At present, the most promising results for work might be found through better integration with groups that represent basic progressive interests and which can be characterized as social movements. This means working in conditions where the movement has an ability to control and shape the larger organizational and political process, independent of possible participatory research activities. Working with such social movements gives a natural channel for the mobilizing and creative energies of participatory research to feed the larger struggle. It would mean, for example, working within the framework of the women's movement, labour unions, native peoples' political organizations, public interest research groups, tenant associations, or groups of landless labourers.

Bibliography

Beltran L R 1976 Alien premises, objects, and methods in Latin American communication research. *Commun. Res.* 3: 107–34

Callaway H 1981 Women's perspectives: Research as re-vision. In: Reason P, Rowan J (eds.) 1981 *Human Inquiry: A Sourcebook of New Paradigm Research.* Wiley, London

Darcy de Oliveira R, Darcy de Oliveira M 1975 *The Militant Observer: A Sociological Alternative.* Institut d'Action Culturelle, Geneva

Fals Barda O 1980 *Science and the Common People.* International Forum on Participatory Research, Yugoslavia

Gaventa J 1981 *Power and Powerlessness: Quiescence and Rebellion in an Appalachian Valley.* University of Illinois Press, Urbana, Illinois

Gerace Larufa F 1973 *Communicación Horizontal.* Librería Studium, Lima

Holmes J 1976 Thoughts on research methodology. *Stud. Adult Educ.* 8: 149–63

Horton B D 1981 On the potential of participatory research: An evaluation of a regional experiment. Paper prepared for annual meeting of the Society for the Study of Social Problems, Toronto, Canada, 21–24 August

Orefice P 1981 Cultural self-awareness of local community: An experience in the south of Italy. *Convergence* 14: 56–64

Spender D 1978 Editorial. *Women's Stud. Int. Q.* 1: 1–2

Stinson A (ed.) 1979 *Canadians Participate: Annotated Bibliography of Case Studies.* Centre for Social Welfare Studies, Ottawa, Ontario

Vio Grossi F 1981 The socio-political implications of participatory research. International Forum on Participatory Research, Yugoslavia. *Convergence* 14(3): 43–51

Comparative Studies in Adult and Lifelong Education

C. J. Titmus

Little attention has been devoted in comparative education to the marginal area of adult education. Thus, as educational opportunities for adults became of global significance after the Second World War, comparative studies in this field developed independently, not as a subsection of, but as a supplement to, comparative education. In this article the development, purposes, topics of study, problems, and issues of comparative adult education are considered, together with the added dimensions of lifelong and recurrent education.

1. Development

Quite early in its history adult education acquired an international dimension through such organizations as the Young Men's Christian Association (YMCA) and, in 1925, the World Organization for Adult Education, which attracted into membership most of the countries in which the education of adults was established on any substantial scale. It did not survive the Second World War, but after 1945 its work was taken up by a number of world and regional organizations.

Perhaps because they were created just as adult education began its expansion worldwide, several United Nations agencies, the World Bank, and the Organisation for Economic Co-operation and Development (OECD), among other bodies, became involved in studies of the educational needs and realizations of adults. Several UNESCO regional centres have been particularly active in this field. Also at a regional level the Council of Europe, the European Community, and the Organization of American States have played a similar role.

A number of nongovernmental organizations have been formed. These include the Asian and South Pacific Bureau of Adult Education (ASPBAE), the African Adult Education Association (AAEA), and the European Bureau of Adult Education (EBAE) and, since 1973, a world association, the International Council of Adult Education (ICAE), all a product of interest in international development and all stimulating it through their meetings and publications.

Their work has greatly helped to create a demand for more effective ways of comparing adult education activities in different countries. The First International Conference on the subject was held at Exeter, New Hampshire, in 1966 on the initiative of the International Congress of University Adult Education (Liveright and Haygood 1968). Over the years since then efforts have continued slowly to build it up as a field of systematic study. Mainly in North America and Europe scholars have been feeling their way towards real comparison through rule of thumb studies of practice, while others have been trying to devise a framework of principles, purposes, and methods appropriate to the peculiar circumstances of adult education.

It may be asked whether in all this they have not been re-inventing the wheel, whether they should not have learned their lessons from the work already done in comparative education. This has indeed occurred (Bennett et al. 1975), but just as students of other aspects of adult education have been wary of too slavishly following the ideas of educational science, so have some comparativists, and for similar reasons. Comparative education concerns itself for the most part with a narrower field than its name implies, concentrating its attention on school and higher education systems; comparative adult education, it is therefore argued, does not cast a spotlight on one part *within* comparative education, but it shines it on a new part of the field. This new area has features it does not share with initial education, so that a critical assessment of the applicability of comparative education's experience to comparative adult education is needed.

2. Purposes of Comparative Adult Education

Other things being equal the purposes of comparative adult education ought to be broadly similar to those of comparative education. Since they are not equal, expectations of achievement in the short or medium term are rather more limited. The Exeter Conference suggested areas for further study, for example, data gathering about activities; the development of a taxonomy of adult education structures; the definition of terms and concepts; cultural, political, and economic impacts on the nature and organization of adult education. These would pave the way for comparison rather than be topics of comparison (Liveright and Haygood 1968). Kidd identified a modest set of goals:

> to become better informed about the educational system for adults of other countries; to become better informed about the ways in which people in other cultures have carried out certain social functions by means of education; to become better informed about the historical roots of certain activities and thus to develop criteria for assessing developments and testing possible outcomes; to better understand the educational forms and systems operating in one's own country; to satisfy an interest in how other human beings live and learn; to better understand oneself; to reveal how one's cultural biases and personal attributes affect one's judgments about

possible ways of carrying on learning transactions. (Bennett et al. 1975 p. 10)

It appears that he considered comparative studies principally as illuminating the understanding of practitioners in the field. There is no reference to their application as a direct aid to decision making, which now seems the principal concern of comparative education. In fact most people now engaged in comparative adult education, while they would not repudiate Kidd, would agree with King that all comparative studies today are intended to aid decisions (King 1967). There is, however, considerable awareness that the means are not yet equal to the task, with the consequence that, although realities of funding and the immediacy of policy making call for the application to specific issues of such means as we have, some scholars believe that the emphasis should lie on more long-term and theoretical studies, designed to perfect the tools of enquiry and fundamental understanding of the education of adults which is the context in which these specific issues arise.

3. Subjects of International and Comparative Study

The growth of adult education and the development of identifiable national patterns of provision as worldwide phenomena only belong to the period since the Second World War. Hence, of necessity, there has been a continuing flow of basic single-nation studies. Many are purely factual descriptions of what is done and how it is organized, notably those which are sponsored or published by government agencies. The Scandinavian countries have brought out a number of these accounts, individually or in collaboration. More attempts at analysis and judgment are to be found in the work of private scholars. For the most part they write about their own countries, but foreigners have offered a new perspective and perception to single-nation studies (Titmus 1967).

Since 1977 the European Centre of Leisure and Education (ECLE) in Prague has, with UNESCO financial support, commissioned 12 studies of individual European states. They are intended to provide the basis for comparative investigation of the structures and organization of adult education in Europe (European Centre for Leisure and Education 1977-84). This project, still incomplete, constitutes the most ambitious yet in comparative adult education.

Intergovernmental organizations have called for reports on adult education provision from their member states and have then commissioned general regional or global overviews based on the material supplied. As an example, the Council of Europe published *Today and Tomorrow in European Adult Education*, which covered recent developments, current problems, and possible progress in its member states (Simpson 1972). As part of the preparations for its periodic world conferences on adult education UNESCO has several times commissioned global reviews, which have constituted the best factual and analytical accounts of adult education's worldwide growth (Lowe 1975).

The overview or crossnational study is a standard product of initiatives in specific aspects of adult education. This is in large degree because the initiatives are intended to transcend national boundaries and the concern of the studies has been to identify common features of policy, practice, and their determinants over the whole range of societies covered, rather than to distinguish differences between individual nations, since the common features promise to be more valuable in that they may apply to future contexts.

The efforts to eradicate illiteracy in the world, to which a number of UNESCO agencies, the World Bank, and other international and national agencies have devoted themselves, have been adult education's largest concern and still remain so. They have involved workers indigenous to the countries in which action has been taken as well as outside experts; they have covered almost all the developing world; they have provided examples, otherwise rarely known in adult education, of measurable inputs, of similar kinds, applied simultaneously to a number of different national situations, thus creating cases more than usually favourable to comparative study. Indeed out of all this activity have come many reports, of campaigns in individual countries, in groups of countries, and of world studies (UNESCO 1976).

Nonformal education and the development needs of the Third World have also been the focus of international initiatives and of comparative studies on a large scale (Ahmed and Coombs 1975). Sociocultural animation, closely related to nonformal education, but without the development dimension, was for several years the subject of a Council of Europe project, which produced a number of papers from member countries.

Where topics in adult education have been subjected to extended international or crossnational study, it has usually been because they have captured the attention of some international organization, governmental or nongovernmental, and that they have some immediate policy significance. The OECD sponsored studies of learning opportunities for adults, of adult participation in study, and of recurrent education. In addition to literacy, UNESCO has encouraged work on lifelong education and adult education terminology (Titmus et al. 1979). The European Bureau of Adult Education has made a speciality of collating and reviewing legislation (European Bureau of Adult Education 1985) and terminology (European Bureau of Adult Education 1980).

Some topics have, however, generated their own head of steam and have stimulated a wide range of studies from many different sources. Women's education is a theme to which many articles and several books have been devoted (European Centre for the Development of Vocational Training 1982). The literature of correspondence and distance education overlaps with accounts of the use of mass media in adult education and of open learning systems (Harry et al. 1981). The experience of other countries in the training of adult educators is seen to be of central importance as the professionalization of the field has developed and numerous descriptive accounts have been given (Kulich 1977), some devoted to the training of specialists such as vocational educators (Théry 1984).

As the drive to achieve the right of adults to leave from work for educational purposes without loss of earnings gained momentum, governments, confronted with the prospect of having to make policy decisions on the subject, commissioned, singly or through intergovernmental organizations, a number of studies of paid educational leave practice. For example the British sponsored an enquiry into France, the Federal Republic of Germany, and Sweden (Charnley 1975), the OECD undertook several pieces of work, and a review of European experience was specifically undertaken for American consumption (von Moltke and Schneevoigt 1977).

Paid educational leave is closely related to adult vocational education, to which more international attention has been directed than to any aspect of adult education except, perhaps, literacy. For example UNESCO has published a series of reports on developing countries, including Botswana, Egypt, Argentina, and the Republic of Korea. A number of regional overviews have appeared (Corvalan 1977). The European Centre for the Development of Vocational Training CEDEFOP, set up by the European Communities, has been particularly active in sponsoring single-nation studies and regional syntheses on youth unemployment and vocational training, equal opportunities for women (CEDEFOP 1982), the training of educators (Théry 1984), and migrant workers.

4. *Comparative Studies in Lifelong and Recurrent Education*

Comparative studies, like other studies in adult education, increasingly take a lifelong perspective, without for the most part addressing their topics explicitly within the concept of lifelong education. The distinction between youth and continuing education is rather more blurred in developing countries and studies of literacy campaigns, nonformal education, and integrated rural development are necessarily conducted in a cradle to grave framework. In advanced countries adult or continuing education is still perceived and studied as a distinct sector. On the other hand there is a tendency to include lifelong or recurrent education in titles of publications, with only minimal attention paid to the wider concepts.

However, for a number of years the Council of Europe conducted an enquiry into the extent to which permanent education or lifelong education was being achieved in its member states and followed it up with several experimental projects in permanent education (Schwartz et al. 1977). The UNESCO Institute for Education, Hamburg, has made for itself a corner in lifelong education, but its work is largely conceptual and general and its cases are mainly school oriented. The Organisation for Economic Co-operation and Development (OECD) was principally responsible for launching the concept of recurrent education internationally. The idea, the alternation of periods of education with periods of work or other activity throughout life, has attracted comparative study because it is more concrete than that of lifelong education and is already to some degree realized in adult vocational education and is linked closely to issues of paid educational leave (Schuller and Megarry 1979).

5. *Problems and Issues Confronting Comparative Adult Education*

From this selective account of subjects and publications it is easy to derive an exaggerated impression of comparative adult education's achievements. It is still largely at the stage of descriptive surveys, often incomplete and impressionistic, if not anecdotal. Analysis and explanation of phenomena in contextual terms are frequently weak. Comparison, in the sense of identifying differences and similarities between phenomena, is rare. Many so-called comparative studies consist of juxtapositions rather than comparisons. There are very few examples of explanatory comparison (Titmus 1981).

Students of comparative adult education have been conscious of their imperfections, perhaps excessively so. Kidd exhorted those in comparative adult education to pay more attention to developing systematic methods of enquiry (Kidd 1981) and in recent years his advice has been taken up (Titmus 1985). The ECLE comparative research into the structures and organization of adult education in Europe has been as occupied in devising an appropriate methodology and a framework as in conducting single-nation studies (Maydl et al. 1983).

But the problems do not lie so much in the techniques of enquiry as in the state of adult education itself. To compare phenomena in it is particularly difficult, because of the breadth and diversity of what is comprehended within the term "adult education", of the variations in meaning given to it from country to country, if indeed a concept of it as a distinctive process or system exists at all.

It is rich but not precise in its terminology and the connotations of its terms have been very culturally specific. Some progress is, however, being made towards international understanding by the definition of its vocabulary and the compilation of international glossaries. That of the EBAE, first produced in English, French, and German (EBAE 1980), has now fathered supplements in Italian and Dutch, the UNESCO one has grown from English, French, and Spanish to include Arabic (Titmus et al. 1979) and an offshoot has appeared in Chinese (People's Republic of China 1985).

Whereas initial education has a common framework, to which national systems either conform or aspire, adult education is still very largely unstructured throughout the world, or else the structure is complex and the patterns yet to be identified with confidence—hence the ECLE research already referred to.

It is because of its continuing state of flux and our ignorance of its constituent elements that some comparative scholars believe in the current necessity to undertake macro studies, which help to map the field of adult education, identify the determinant influences upon it and its influence upon the society in which it exists. Specific, limited enquiries into components of it have contributions to make to decisions directly affecting educational practice, but they have little value unless they can be set within their societal context, however broadly this has to be sketched in.

Macro or micro comparative studies in adult education, however, are most handicapped by a dearth of quantitative data. The fragmentation of the field, lack of organization, and a traditional reluctance to attribute much importance to numbers has meant that statistics have either not been compiled or have been presented in unusable forms. Some attempts have been made to encourage their collection internationally according to a uniform pattern (UNESCO 1975), but without significant success. For example, a substantial survey of adult education in nine industrial countries found it impossible to undertake a planned comparative study of participation statistics for lack of comparable data (Peterson et al. 1982).

The conditions do not yet exist therefore within adult education, nor yet do the means, for researchers to undertake complex qualitative and quantitative comparisons of the kind now being attempted in comparative education. At present, and for some time to come, they will be restricted to qualitative ones. Their role will continue to be in great part that of explorers in still largely unexplored territory. Much more work needs to be done on deciding what data is essential, in what form it should be gathered, and exerting influence to see that this is done. The only area where one may hope for success is, unfortunately, that of adult vocational education, where governments can see the desirability of devoting organization and money to the collection of reliable statistics, because they relate to the labour market. Nevertheless the qualitative and conceptual work that may be done may be of the highest value, both to comparative studies and to the field of adult education.

Bibliography

Ahmed M, Coombs P H (eds.) 1975 *Education for Rural Development: Case Studies for Planners.* Praeger, New York

Bennett C, Kidd J R, Kulich J 1975 *Comparative Studies in Adult Education: An Anthology.* Syracuse University Press, Syracuse, New York

Charnley A 1975 *Paid Educational Leave.* Hart-Davis International, St Albans

Corvalan Vasquez O 1977 *Vocational Training in Latin America: A Comparative Perspective.* University of British Columbia, Vancouver

European Bureau of Adult Education (EBAE) 1980 *The Terminology of Adult Education/Continuing Education*, 2nd edn. EBAE, Amersfoort

European Bureau of Adult Education (EBAE) 1985 *Survey of Adult Education Legislation.* EBAE, Amersfoort

European Centre for Leisure and Education (ECLE) 1977-84 *Adult Education in Europe, Studies and Documents*, ECLE, Prague (Vol. 1 Czechoslovakia; 2 France; 3 Hungary; 4 Yugoslavia; 5 German Democratic Republic; 6 Poland; 7 Austria; 8 Federal Republic of Germany; 9 United Kingdom; 10-11 Italy; 12 Bulgaria; 16 Portugal; 19-20 USSR)

European Centre for the Development of Vocational Training (CEDEFOP) 1982 *Equal Opportunities and Vocational Training: A Survey on Vocational Training Initiatives for Women in the European Community.* CEDEFOP, Berlin

Harry K, Kaye T, Wilson K 1982 *The European Experience of the Use of Mass Media and Distance Methods for Adult Basic Education*, Vol. 1: *Main Report.* Open University, Milton Keynes

Kidd J R 1981 Research. In: Charters A N (ed.) 1981 *Comparing Adult Education Worldwide.* Jossey-Bass, San Francisco, California, pp. 218–39

King E 1967 Comparative studies and policy decisions, *Comp. Educ.* 4(1): 51-63

Kulich J (ed.) 1977 *Training of Adult Educators in East Europe.* University of British Columbia, Vancouver, and International Council for Adult Education, Toronto

Liveright A A, Haygood N (eds.) 1968 *The Exeter Papers. Report of the First International Conference on the Comparative Study of Adult Education.* Syracuse University Press, Syracuse, New York

Lowe J 1975 *The Education of Adults: A Worldwide Perspective.* UNESCO, Paris

Maydl P et al. 1983 *Adult Education in Europe: Methodological Framework for Comparative Studies*, Parts 1 and 2. Adult Education in Europe, Studies and Documents No. 14,15, European Centre for Leisure and Education, Prague

People's Republic of China 1985 *The Glossary of Chinese Adult Education.* Ministry of Education, Beijing

Peterson R E, Gaff S S, Helmich J S, Feldmesser R A, Valley J R, Nielsen H D 1982 *Adult Education and Training in Industrialized Countries.* Praeger, New York

Schuller T, Megarry J (eds.) 1979 *World Yearbook of Education 1979: Recurrent Education and Lifelong Learning.* Kogan Page, London

Schwartz B 1977 *Permanent Education: Work of Consolidation of the Evaluation of Pilot Experiments in the Permanent Education Field.* Council of Europe, Strasbourg

Simpson J A 1972 *Today and Tomorrow in European Adult Education.* Council of Europe, Strasbourg

Théry B 1984 *Professional Situation and Training of Trainers in the Member States of the European Communities, Synthesis Report.* CEDEFOP, Berlin

Titmus C J 1967 *Adult Education in France.* Pergamon, Oxford

Titmus C J 1979 *Terminology of Adult Education.* UNESCO Paris

Titmus C J 1981 *Strategies for Adult Education: Practices in Western Europe.* Open University Press, Milton Keynes

Titmus C J 1985 Comparative adult education: Questions of Method. *Stud. Educ. Adults* 17: 83–93

UNESCO 1975 *Manual for the Collection of Adult Education Statistics.* UNESCO, Paris

UNESCO 1976 *The Experimental World Literacy Programme: A Critical Assessment.* UNESCO, Paris

von Moltke K, Schneevoigt N 1977 *Educational Leaves for Employees.* Jossey-Bass, San Francisco, California

Appendix

Glossary of Adult and Lifelong Education

***adult education**[1]
The entire body of organized educational processes, whatever the content, level and method, whether formal or otherwise, whether they prolong or replace initial education in schools, colleges and universities as well as in apprenticeship, whereby persons regarded as adults by the society to which they belong develop their activities, enrich their knowledge, improve their technical and professional qualifications or turn them in a new direction and bring about changes in their attitudes or behaviour in the twofold perspective of full personal development and participation in balanced and independent social, economic and cultural development (Unesco Recommendation on the Development of Adult Education). In the United Kingdom and other countries in the British tradition the term has historically been limited to the non-vocational education of adults.

***adulthood**
1. The period of life following adolescence and extending for the rest of life
2. The state of physical, psychological and social maturity which characterizes the period following adolescence

âge adulte
French term
See: **adulthood** (1)

***agricultural extension**
Education and counselling carried out in the farming community by institutions of agricultural education to improve practices in agriculture

***andragogy**
The art and science of helping adults to learn. The study of adult education theory, processes and technology

animation globale
French term. Animation going beyond educational or social objectives, aiming at total development of the individual as a personality in the belief that social or cultural advancement and economic progress are interdependent and should be considered as an integrated process

animation socio-culturelle
French term. Also animation socio-éducative. Equivalent of sociocultural animation
See: **sociocultural animation**

capacitación
Spanish term. Denotes education and training for skilled labour and technical employment

circulating schools
Eighteenth century Welsh system, whereby an attempt was made to maintain a school in every village by the use of itinerant teachers

***community college**
1. In the United Kingdom a multi-purpose establishment, equipped as a secondary school, as a continuing education centre and having facilities for social and cultural activities for adults and adolescents. The intention is to provide a centre for community activities and to encourage an integrated community life for those living within the catchment area of the college
2. In North America a public post-secondary institution, set up to meet the needs of a particular community and offering two year programmes, either terminal or preparatory, related to professional, technical or liberal arts fields, and leading to Associate Degrees. Most community colleges offer general interest non-credit programmes as well.

***community development**
Activities directed to improving the material and social welfare of the inhabitants of a limited urban or rural

1 Definitions marked with an asterisk* are taken from Colin Titmus et al. 1979 *Terminology of Adult Education*, first edition, © UNESCO, Paris. The permission of the publishers to reproduce these definitions is gratefully acknowledged

locality, sharing a sense of group identity and a body of common interests. The inhabitants should in principle play a major role in decision-making and participate in the activities

***community education**

Body of social, recreational, cultural and educational activities, organized outside the formal school system for people of all ages, intended to improve the life of a community. The members of the community should play a major role in decision-making and in running the activities
See also: **sociocultural animation**

continuing education

Synonym of adult education, but widely used to denote particularly vocationally oriented adult education
See also: **adult education**; **formation continue**; **Weiterbildung**

***co-operative extension**

United States term to denote the co-operation of the government and land grant institutions for the purpose of offering, through demonstrations, publications and other means, useful and practical information and learning experiences on agriculture, home economics and related subjects to meet current problems. The range of subjects is increasingly broadened to enable people in urban as well as rural settings to gain skills in meeting economic and social needs

credit transfer

Recognition by an educational institution of credits or qualifications awarded by another, so that a student may transfer to a new institution at the same level he/she has reached in previous studies

Dikmas

Formerly called Penmas. A large-scale and complex system of government provision in Indonesia, which concentrates on the integration of basic literacy education with acquisition of vocational skills at village level

***discussion method**

A method of group learning in which members of a group contribute their ideas orally to the solution of a problem or to enlarge knowledge and understanding of a topic. For the successful employment of the method participants should have knowledge or experience which is relevant to the subject of the discussion

***distance education**

Education conducted through the postal services, radio, television, telephone or newspaper, without face-to-face contact between teacher and learner. Teaching is done by specially prepared material transmitted to individuals or learning groups. Learners' progress is monitored through written or taped exercises sent to the teacher, who normally corrects them and returns them to learners with criticism and advice

edad adulta

Spanish term
See: **adulthood**

éducation permanente

French term
See: **lifelong education**

éducation populaire

French term
See: **community education**

***educational brokering**

Learner-centred information and counselling linking adults with the broad array of educational resources available. It consists of information giving, counselling, assessment, referral of adults to appropriate agencies and support of their applications to learn

empowerment

The process of becoming, or the condition of being capable of exercising control over the social, economic, cultural and political forces and institutions which primarily influence the nature, material level and quality of one's life

***entrenamiento**

Spanish term. Training for unskilled jobs, military training, sports training
See also: **capacitación**; **formación**

equivalency programme

A programme of adult education offering the equivalent of formal school education, intended for persons who have not received it, or have not successfully completed it in childhood

***experiential learning**

Learning which derives either from the general life-experience or from specific activities of the learner. Learning derived from the feelings and thoughts aroused in the learner while or after undergoing such experiences

***folk high school**

1. An institution offering courses of study for adults, mainly in the evening, but also in the daytime, in Austria, the Federal Republic of Germany, the Netherlands and Switzerland
2. An institution of residential education, at post-secondary, pre-university level, mainly attended by young people in their late teens and early twenties. Folk high schools of this kind were created and are mainly found in Scandinavia
See also: **Volkshochschule**

***formación**

Spanish term. The acquisition of knowledge, attitudes, skills and behaviour associated with a professional field, such as those required by lawyers, medical doctors, educators
See also: **capacitación**; **entrenamiento**

***formal education**
The structured, chronologically ordered education provided in primary and secondary schools, in universities and specialized courses of full-time technical and higher education. Also the body of institutions which provide such education

formation continue
French term
See: **continuing education**

formation permanente
French term
See: **lifelong education**

***functional literacy**
The ability to read, write and calculate so that a person may engage in all those activities in which literacy is required for effective functioning of his/her group and community and also enabling him/her to continue to use reading, writing and calculation for his/her own and the community's development

***generative words**
Within the psychosocial methods of literacy training used in developing countries this is a set of words which is the identified outcome of research on the thematic environment and which is then used as a basis to teach the mechanics of reading and writing

***group dynamics**
The principles underlying the interaction of the behaviour of individuals as members of a group and of the behaviour of groups generally. The study of group dynamics provides theoretical support for group methods of education and training

guest student
Person not registered as a regular student of an institution of higher education, but given access to some of the privileges of studentship, such as attendance at classes, etc. Guest students do not qualify for standard degrees and diplomas, but in some countries foreign guest students may be awarded special certificates of study

horizontal integration
The structuring as a unified educational experience of an individual's learning, intentional or non-intentional, over the whole diversity of activities and roles which make up his/her life at a given time. The idea that it should be so organized forms a central part of the contemporary concept of lifelong education
See also: **lifelong education**; **formal education**; **informal education**; **nonformal education**

human resource development
A strategy for the education and training of the personnel of an organization. They are seen as a resource which the strategy seeks to bind to the activities and purposes of the organization by promoting education to meet both their individual and occupational needs

***informal education**
The lifelong process whereby every individual acquires attitudes, values, skills and knowledge from daily experience, educative influences and resources in his/her environment—from family and neighbours, from work and play, from the market place, the library and mass media
See also: **formal education**; **nonformal education**

integrated rural development
The policy of combining economic, social and educational programmes in a unified strategy designed to solve the problems and advance the standard of living in rural areas, specifically those of developing countries
See also: **community development**

Khit-Pen
Thai philosophy and programme of adult education. Basically a problem solving approach, based on the Buddhist principle of choosing the 'right path' or solution after identifying the root causes of suffering

Kominkan
Japanese term denoting citizens' public halls, originally designed as multi-purpose community centres, which have developed into centres of nonformal education for adults
See also: **nonformal education**

learning exchange
A service intended to extend the possibilities of learning open to adults by putting those who wish to acquire a specific body of knowledge or develop a skill in touch with persons who are competent in the appropriate field or skill and wish to teach it

learning society
A state or other human community, which has as a basic principle of its ethos and practice the need for its members to continue learning over their lifespan. It is structured and its resources allocated so as to encourage them to do this, both through specifically educational organizations and through the social, economic and cultural activities of the society

***liberal adult education**
Education intended to equip the adult with a broad general culture, which will enable him/her to realize himself/herself as an individual and as a citizen. It excludes direct occupational training. Although in principle no subject is excluded, since any subject may be taught in such a way as to achieve the aims of liberal adult education, it favours literary, social, philosophical, historical and artistic studies as the ones through which its aims may most easily be attained

***lifelong education**

The concept that education is not a once-for-all experience confined to the initial cycle of full-time education commenced in childhood, but a process that must continue throughout life. Life itself is a continuous learning process, but each person also needs specific opportunities for further and new education, both vocational and general, throughout life, in order that he/she may keep abreast of technical and social change, may adapt to changes in his/her own circumstances (marriage, parenthood, professional situation, old age, etc.) and may achieve his/her fullest potential for individual development. Lifelong education comprehends both an individual's intentional and incidental learning experiences

***literacy**

The ability to read and write. The concept sometimes includes the ability to calculate
See also: **functional literacy**

***literacy campaign**

Co-ordinated actions of publicity, counselling and teaching designed to increase the number of literate persons in a community

mandatory continuing education

Any education beyond the minimum legal school leaving age which a person is compelled to undertake. It occurs, for example, in military organizations and in penitentiaries, but it is mainly associated with the continuing education of professionals, certain of whom are required to participate in educational activities in order to keep their membership of their professional organization or maintain their certification or licence
See also: **recertification**

mechanics institute

Nineteenth century United Kingdom institution of adult education, intended to offer courses in "useful knowledge" to working men. A number of mechanics institutes developed into universities

multimedia teaching

Teaching which uses a combination of two or more of video, television, radio, audio-tapes, film, slides and other instructional means, with or without face-to-face teaching

nonformal education

Organized educational programmes conducted outside the formal school and higher education system
See also: **formal education**; **informal education**

open access

Term normally used to describe a course or programme which displays some or all of the features of open learning
See also: **open learning**

open learning

The term open learning has a variety of meanings. It normally denotes learning which combines some or all of the following features: the learner may choose when and where to undertake learning; the learner is not obliged to fulfill any educational preconditions before beginning study; the learner may choose what to learn, how to do so and over what period of time

***outreach**

Process designed to increase the availability and utilization of educational and social services, especially through direct intervention in and interaction with a target population. Outreach programmes are usually aimed at educationally and socially deprived groups

***paid educational leave**

Leave from work without loss of earnings in order that the recipient may follow a course of education or training

participatory research

The study of a problem in the community or the workplace, with the active participation of the people involved in the situation to be investigated. They control and take part in the planning and conduct of the study, usually with the help of outside experts. The purpose of the exercise is not only to investigate the problem, but to educate the participants and to instigate action which will solve the problem and improve the lives of those involved

people's university

Terms which translate into English as "people's university" are used in a number of languages to designate a variety of adult education institutions, none of which are of university level so they do not offer degrees. For example, the expression, "folk high school", is a mistranslation of terms in Scandinavian languages and in German which mean "people's university". In current English usage "people's university" is primarily used to designate organizations in European socialist countries engaged in general and vocationally oriented education for adults. In Scandinavian countries and in France some associations for general adult education, other than folk high schools, call themselves "people's universities"

polyvalent education centre

Institution in the Third World offering adult education intended to develop the full human potential of the learner, by integrating economic, social, civic and cultural education
See also: **Shramik Vidyapeeth**

***post-experience education**

Education undertaken by or provided for a person who has already had experience of full-time employment, including employment as a housewife

primary health care
The first contact of individuals, the family and the community with the national health system, bringing health care as close as possible to where people live and work, through their own efforts and those of such persons as health visitors, health educators, etc. Its emphasis is on the maintenance of health rather than cure of illness

***promotion collective**
French term. Denotes the body of activities aimed at improving the conditions of work and advancing the situation and status of an economic group or class. It is used primarily of activities within the urban or rural working class

proprietary school
An independent educational institution operated for profit

recertification
The process of relicensing which members of certain professions are obliged periodically to undergo. A condition of recertification may be that the practitioner is required to undergo some refresher or updating study (also relicensing; requalification)
See also: **mandatory continuing education**

***recurrent education**
Organization of lifelong education into periods of systematic study alternating with extended periods of other activity, e.g. work or leisure
See also: **sandwich course**

Saemaul Movement
In the Republic of Korea a national campaign for community development aimed at improving the spiritual quality and economic progress of the nation
See also: **community development**

***sandwich course**
A course in which periods of full-time instruction alternate with associated full-time industrial, professional or commercial experience
See also: **recurrent education**

SARAR
Method of nonformal education used in a number of Third World countries. It emphasizes the deliberate nurturing of creativity in order to encourage openness to innovation, improve the quality of people's interventions in development and release new energies through a heightened perception of self
See also: **nonformal education**

Sarvodaya Shramadana Movement
Movement of integrated rural development in Sri Lanka. Based on traditional Buddhist values, it defines development as an awakening process which may take place at all levels of the world community, simultaneously in spiritual, moral, cultural, social, political and economic life
See also: **integrated rural development**

scuola popolare
Italian term. Denotes an institution of literacy and basic education for children and adults. Immediately after the Second World War scuola popolare (people's schools) were set up by law all over Italy. They took many forms to meet the conditions of the localities in which they were established

***self-directed learning**
A process by which an individual or group initiates and takes primary responsibility for planning, conducting and evaluating its own learning projects. Unlike independent learning, it usually takes place with the help of persons such as teachers or friends, or of an institution

Senshu-Gakko
Special training schools in Japan, designed to offer systematic programmes of education aimed at developing each individual's ability to bring out the best in his/her working life and raising his/her level of general education. Courses last at least a year and include upper secondary and college level education

***sensitivity training**
An activity carried out to deepen the awareness of individuals concerning their own natures and their relationships with other people, usually in small groups in which members simultaneously or intermittently interact and then analyse that interaction

Shramik Vidyapeeth
Indian term denoting polyvalent education centres for workers
See also: **polyvalent education centre**

social education
English translation of a term used in certain countries, notably Japan and China, to denote education, other than education for employment, carried on outside the formal school and higher education system
See also: **nonformal education**

sociocultural animation
1. The stimulation of people to awareness of their needs as a group, so that they define the nature of the needs, determine the means to satisfy those needs and act to do so. Thus it is neither organization nor teaching, but initiation, catalysis and counselling. This definition is rather a goal to be aimed at than a description of current practice
2. A synonym of community education
See also: **community education**; **éducation populaire**

***study circle**
A group of people meeting regularly for the co-operative study of a subject or problem. A study circle does not, in principle, require a teacher with specialized knowledge of the subject or problem, but may have a leader trained in the techniques of group leadership

technikon

South African institution of tertiary education, offering full-time, part-time and sandwich courses in technological subjects. Technikons do not award degrees, but some of their diplomas and certificates are of degree equivalent level, accepted as a basis for post-graduate work in some universities

T-group

See: **sensitivity training**

***university extension**

Activities by which the teaching and other resources of a university—on or off the campus—are offered to adults living in the region served by the university, other than those belonging to the regular student body. It may include a varied programme of credit or non-credit instruction, counselling, advisory services, etc

university extra-mural education

See: **university extension**

university of the third age

An organization created to serve the specific educational needs of people of retirement age and beyond. Founded in Toulouse, France, universities of the third age now exist in a number of advanced countries. Participants are encouraged to take responsibility for organizing and carrying out the activities, which are not normally of university level. Some gerontological research is also carried out

vertical integration

The organization of all an individual's learning, intentional and non-intentional, over successive periods of life, as a unified, coherent educational experience. The idea that it should be so structured forms a central part of the contemporary concept of lifelong education

vocational education

In North America the term is used to denote instruction given during schooling to prepare students for an occupation. In other English-speaking parts of the world it denotes any education for employment, undertaken before or during working life

Volksbildung

German term, literally meaning "popular education", formerly used to denote adult education, but now replaced by "Erwachsenenbildung" and, more recently, "Weiterbildung"
See also: **Weiterbildung**

Volkshochschule

German term
See: **folk high school**

Weiterbildung

German term
See: **continuing education**

***workers' education**

The systematic development in working class adults of the knowledge, attitudes and skills to enable them to fulfil the social roles they are called upon to play, particularly in trade unions

Znanie

Popular education society in the Soviet Union, run by volunteer workers and engaged in popularizing information relating to social and political issues, culture, science, technology and advanced production methods

Contributors Index

Contributors are listed in alphabetical order together with their affiliations. Titles of articles which they have authored follow in alphabetical order, along with the respective page numbers. Where articles are co-authored, this has been indicated by an asterisk preceding the article title.

COOMBS P. H. (International Council for Educational Development, Essex, Connecticut, USA)
Formal and Nonformal Education: Future Strategies 57-60

CROPLEY A. J. (University of Hamburg, Hamburg, FRG)
Factors in Participation 145-47; *Lifelong Education: Interaction with Adult Education* 9-12; *Lifelong Education: Research Strategies* 525-28

DAHLGREN H. (University of Gothenburg, Mölndal, Sweden)
**Disabled Adults: Educational Provision* 335-39

DARKENWALD G. G. (Rutgers University, New Brunswick, New Jersey, USA)
Group Learning 233-36

DAVIES C. T. (University of Manchester, Manchester, UK)
Population Education 131-33

DUKE C. (University of Warwick, Coventry, UK)
Asia 465-68; *International Adult Education* 468-72; *Provision in Australasia* 415-19; *Provision in Southeast Asia* 442-46; *Training of Adult Educators* 360-70

EEDLE J. H. (University of the Northern Territory, Darwin, Northern Territory, Australia)
Educating the Isolated 340-43

EMMELIN L. (University of Trondheim, Trondheim, Norway)
Environmental Education 133-34

ENTWISTLE H. (Concordia University, Montreal, Quebec, Canada)
Ideologies in Adult Education 35-39

FALES A. W. (Ontario Institute for Studies in Education, Toronto, Ontario, Canada)
Lifespan Learning Development 183-87

FARMER J. A. (University of Illinois, Urbana-Champaign, Illinois, USA)
Adult Education Counseling 154-57

FERVER J. C. (University of Wisconsin, Madison, Wisconsin, USA)
**North America* 455-57

FORDHAM P. (University of Southampton, Southampton, UK)
Universities and Adult Education: Policies and Programs 288-93

FORSTER W. (University of Leicester, Leicester, UK)
Adult Education in Prisons 343-47

FRANK E. (Unversity of Bath, Bath, UK)
The Educators 101-05

FREWIN C. C. (Noranda Mines, Thunder Bay, Ontario, Canada)
**Self-directed Learning in Distance Learning* 260-62

GRIFFIN V. R. (Ontario Institute for Studies in Education, Toronto, Ontario, Canada)
Self-directed Learning: Theories 254-56

GROOMBRIDGE B. (University of London, London, UK)
**Media Support in Adult Education* 244-47

HALL B. L. (International Council for Adult Education, Toronto, Ontario, Canada)
"Campaign": A Technique in Adult Education 240-42;
**Participatory Research* 536-41

HUNTER C. St. J. (World Education, New York, USA)
Adult Literacy in Developed Countries 84-87

HUTCHINSON E. M. (Richmond, Surrey, UK)
**Providers of Adult Education* 279-83

IRONSIDE D. J. (Ontario Institute for Studies in Education, Toronto, Ontario, Canada)
Concepts and Definitions 13-18

JARVIS P. (University of Surrey, Guildford, UK)
Content, Purpose, and Practice 22-28

KABWASA N. O. (UNESCO, Paris, France)
**Education for Older Adults* 319-22

KALLEN D. B. P. (University of Paris VIII, St. Denis, France)
Education for Young Adults 315-18

KASSAM Y. (International Council for Adult Education, Toronto, Ontario, Canada)
**Participatory Research* 536-41

KAUVAR G. (Office of the United States Secretary of Defense, The Pentagon, Washington DC, USA)
**Education in the Armed Forces* 357-60

KAYE A. R. (The Open University, Milton Keynes, UK)
Distance Education 262-68

KEKKONEN H. (Association of Finnish Adult Education Organizations, Helsinki, Finland)
Peace Education 134-38

KENNEDY C. E. (Kansas State University, Manhattan, Kansas, USA)
Adulthood 176-79; *Old Age* 179-83

† deceased

Name Index

The Name Index has been compiled so that the reader can proceed either directly to the page where an author's work is cited, or to the reference itself in the bibliography. For each name, the page numbers for the bibliographic citation are given first, followed by the page number(s) in parentheses where that reference is cited in text. Where a name is referred to only in text, and not in the bibliography, the page number appears only in parentheses.

The accuracy of the spelling of author's names has been affected by the use of different initials by some authors, or a different spelling of their name in different papers or review articles (sometimes this may arise from a transliteration process), and by those journals which give only one initial to each author.

Subject Index

The Subject Index has been compiled as a guide to the reader who is interested in locating all the references to a particular subject area within the Encyclopedia. Entries may have up to three levels of heading. Where the page numbers appear in bold italic type, this indicates a substantive discussion of the topic. Every effort has been made to index as comprehensively as possible and to standardize the terms used in the index. Given the diverse nature of the field and the varied use of terms throughout the international community, synonyms and foreign language terms have been included with appropriate cross-references. As a further aid to the reader, cross-references have also been given to terms of related interest.